JOHN D. HICKS

University of California, Berkeley

GEORGE E. MOWRY

University of North Carolina

ROBERT E. BURKE

University of Washington

THE
AMERICAN
NATION

Fifth Edition

A HISTORY OF THE UNITED STATES
FROM 1865 TO THE PRESENT

Houghton Mifflin Company · Boston

NEW YORK · ATLANTA · GENEVA, ILL. · DALLAS · PALO ALTO

To

J. H., C., and M.; and Libby

ACKNOWLEDGMENT

Eight lines on page 348 from the poem *Theodore Roosevelt* by Stephen Vincent Benet. From *A Book of Americans* by Rosemary and Stephen Vincent Benet. Holt, Rinehart and Winston, Inc. Copyright, 1933, by Rosemary and Stephen Vincent Benet. Reprinted by permission of Brandt & Brandt.

LIBRARY OF CONGRESS CATALOG CARD NUMBER: 72–137794
ISBN: 0-395-04621-1

CONTENTS

Section One

THE AFTERMATH OF CIVIL WAR
1865–1890

Section Two

THE NEW NATION EMERGES
1865–1898

v

Contents

Section Three

EXPANSION AND REFORM

1890–1917

Section Four

WAR AND PEACE

1914–1929

Section Five

DEPRESSION AND WAR

1929–1945

Contents

Section Six

THE POSTWAR WORLD

1945–1970

Appendix

PREFACE

The fifth edition of *The American Nation*, like the fourth, draws heavily upon the new interpretations made available by post-World War II scholarship. Perhaps in no other period have the writers of American history produced so rich a harvest. It also shortens materially the account of the period from the Great Depression to the present, where increasing perspective enables the authors to eliminate detail that no longer seems as important as it once did. Throughout the book, the bibliographies that follow each chapter have been completely reworked by Burke, and seek to embody and evaluate the best of the new literature, even at the expense of omitting many older titles. To facilitate reading beyond the textbook, which we hope that all teachers will encourage, we have marked with asterisks the titles now available at moderate prices in paperbacks.

We call particular attention to the chapters on social and intellectual history, mainly the work of Mowry. Their importance is indicated by their titles: "Society in the Gilded Age," "Science, Social Ideas, and the Arts," "Mass Culture," "Ideas and the Fine Arts in the Machine Age," "The Affluent Society," and "Minority Groups." In the colored plates we have sought also to provide a glimpse into the growth of American art.

Our list of acknowledgments for this edition includes the names of those who helped us with its predecessor, and a number of others. We acknowledge our considerable indebtedness to Charles A. Barker, Johns Hopkins University; Arthur Bestor and Thomas J. Pressley, University of Washington; E. David Cronan, University of Wisconsin; Jasper Cross and Edward J. Maguire, St. Louis University; Gilbert Fite, University of Oklahoma; Emma Beekman Gavras, Los Angeles Trade-Technical College; Dewey Grantham, Vanderbilt University; Edwin Miles, University of Houston; Richard D. Poll, Brigham Young University; Hugh Rankin, Tulane University; Madeleine H. Rice, Hunter College; Charles G. Sellers, Jr., University of California, Berkeley; David A. Shannon, University of Virginia; Wilbert H. Timmons, University of Texas at El Paso; and Frank E. Vandiver, Rice University. In addition, we have received much helpful advice on specific items from numerous unnamed teachers and students, to all of whom we extend our thanks. For editorial assistance and proofreading of the highest competence we have Helen E. Burke and Edith Baras of Seattle to thank. And for research assistance, especially on the bibliographies, we are similarly indebted to Ronald Marsh and Luci Stolzenburg of the University of Washington.

We owe much also to the very cooperative staff of Houghton Mifflin Company. The field representatives of this distinguished publishing house have not only promoted the sale of our books with becoming zeal, but also have reported to us many valuable ideas for their improvement. To Daniel Sortwell, the resourceful history editor, and to the many other company collaborators who have had a part in the making of this book, we are deeply grateful.

JOHN D. HICKS
GEORGE E. MOWRY
ROBERT E. BURKE

List of Maps and Charts

Picture Credits

In the following page-by-page list of credits, page numbers appear in bold face. The following abbreviations have been used for a few sources from which a great many illustrations have been obtained: Bettmann— The Bettmann Archive; Brown — Brown Brothers; Culver— Culver Service; L. of C. — Library of Congress; N.Y.P.L. — New York Public Library; UPI — United Press International; W.W. — Wide World.

5 N.Y.P.L. **6** Brady Collection in the National Archives, U.S. Signal Corps photo No. 111-B-131. **7** Bettmann. **9** Bettmann. **14** above, Bettmann; below, courtesy of Bland Gallery, N.Y.C. **15** through Courtesy of Wildenstein & Co., Inc. N.Y. **21** all from Brady-Handy Collection, L. of C. **25** *Harper's Weekly,* March 21, 1868. **26** above, Culver; below, Brown. **27** L. of C. **28** *Harper's Weekly,* Nov. 3, 1866. **31** *Harper's Weekly,* Nov. 16, 1867. **32** both Culver. **36** Ansco Historical Collection. **38** *Frank Leslie's Ills. Nsprs.* 1872. **40** right, Bettmann. **42** Brown. **54** Culver. **55** Bettmann. **62** Culver. **63** Brown. **64** *Puck,* Sept. 20, 1882. **66** Brown. **67** Bettmann. **72** Brady-Handy Collection, L. of C. **74** upper right, *Puck,* Dec. 20, 1882; lower right, *Puck,* Oct. 1, 1890. **78** Bettmann. **79** Courtesy of The New-York Hist. Soc. **80** Culver. **81** Culver. **83** Utah State Hist. Soc. **86** Photo No. 111-SC-94112 U.S. Signal Corps in the National Archives. **88** U.S. Geological Survey. **91** upper left and right, The Smithsonian Institution; below, Culver. **96** Nebraska State Hist. Soc. **97** Old Print Shop. **101** above, National Archives; middle, The Kansas State Hist. Soc., Topeka; below, courtesy, Swift and Co. **102** Kansas State Hist. Soc. **109** Bethlehem Steel Co. **111** above, Union Pacific Railroad photo; below, Bettmann. **114** both Bettmann. **115** Courtesy of The New-York Hist. Soc. **123** Bettmann. **125** upper left, A. T. & T. Co.; upper right and lower, Con Edison of New York. **128** Bethlehem Steel Co. **129** Brown. **130-31** Standard Oil Co., (N.J.). **131** Brown. **133** Courtesy of The New-York Hist. Soc. **135** Culver. **140** *Harper's Weekly,* 1873. **141** upper right, L. of C. **143** Brown. **144** both Bettmann. **145** N.Y.P.L. **147** Bettmann. **149** N.Y.P.L. **152** L. of C., photo by Stannard Baker. **154** Museum of the City of New York. **156** both Alexander Alland Collection. **157** Alexander Alland Collection. **158** Museum of the City of New York. **159** Alexander Alland Collection, photo by Riis. **162** Corcoran Gallery of Art. **167** both Bettmann. **168** upper left, Bettmann. **169** United States Steel Corporation. **174** Oklahoma Hist. Soc. **183** *Puck,* Aug. 27, 1890. **184** The Kansas State Hist. Soc. **187** Midland Lyceum Bureau. **189** Brown. **192** Vox Populi Co., 1894. **194** Chicago Hist. Soc. **198** left, *Harper's Magazine,* June 25, 1898; right, The Western Reserve Historical Society. **200**

Culver. **202** Chicago Hist. Soc. **203** Chicago Hist. Soc. **208** *Harper's Weekly,* Oct. 1, 1898. **212** Chicago Hist. Soc. **213** left, Bettmann; right, Chicago Hist. Soc. **214** Courtesy of The New-York Hist. Soc. **215** A. T. & T. Co. **216** left, Chicago Hist. Soc.; right, Museum of the City of New York, Jacob A. Riis Collection. **218** Museum of the City of New York, The J. Clarence Davies Collection. **220** upper left, *Harper's Weekly,* Nov. 11, 1871; lower left, *Harper's Weekly,* Nov. 25, 1871. **225** upper, Collection, City Art Museum of St. Louis. **227** Chicago Hist. Soc. **229** left, Culver; middle, N.Y.P.L.; right, Brady-Handy collection, L. of C. **230** both *St. Louis Post-Dispatch.* **231** both the *Daily Examiner.* **232** National Archives. **233** *Frank Leslie's Ills. Nsprs.,* Feb. 21, 1874. **234** Culver. **236** left, National Archives; right, Harvard University News Office. **237** Brady-Handy Collection. **238** The Historical Soc. of Penna. **243** Keystone View Co. **245** both Courtesy Chicago Hist. Soc. **246** Yale University News Bureau. **248** left, Keystone View Co.; right, Columbia University. **249** American Antiquarian Society. **254** upper right, Brown. **257** right, Houghton Mifflin Company. **258** left, N.Y.P.L.; right, Brady-Handy Collection, L. of C. **261** Charmian London, *The Book of Jack London,* Copyright Appleton-Century Crofts. **263** Philips Academy, Andover, Mass. **264** left, George M. Cushing Jr.; right, Courtesy The Museum of Modern Art, New York City. **265** both Bettmann. **268** *The Rocky Mountain News,* Denver, 1900. **269** Culver. **271** *Puck,* 1900. **279** both the Mariner's Museum, Newport News, Va. **288** U.S. Army Photographer. **293** Culver. **296** all Brown. **300** Galloway. **302** upper right, Brown; lower right, *Harper's Weekly,* 1904. **305** Brown. **309** Culver. **310** The Metropolitan Museum of Art. **311** Canal Zone Authority. **315** Courtesy of LCDR R.A. Underwood, U.S.N. **318** both Brown. **319** lower, Brown; upper, U.S. Signal Corps. **325** State Hist. Soc. of Wisconsin. **326** L. of C. **329** National Archives. **333** upper left, The National Archives; lower, Brown. **334** Culver. **337** Culver. **339** upper left and lower, Brown; upper right, Bettmann. **342** *Harper's Weekly,* May 27, 1905. **345** both U.S. Forest Service. **353** Chief of Air Service, Washington, D.C. **358** U.S. Forest Service. **359** Bettmann. **360** Bettmann. **361** Culver. **364** N.Y. World. **368** Culver. **371**

Courtesy of Frank C. Kirk, A.N.A. **372-73** Brown. **375** Bettmann. **378** Dallas News. **379** National Archives. **381** drawing by John Strail. **384** Keystone View Co. **385** Bettmann. **386** U.P.I. **387** all Brown. **389** Culver. **394** above, Electric Boat Division, Gen. Dynamics Corp. Groton, Conn.; below, Chief of Information, Navy Dept. **395** Bettmann. **397** Culver. **398** Brown. **399** National Archives, Navy Dept. **400** Underwood & Underwood. **405** Brown. **410** Bureau of Engraving & Printing. **413** Photo from the American Red Cross. **414** L. of C. **415** Culver. **418** Bettmann. **420** National Archives Record Group III. **421** above, Official U.S. Navy Photo; below, National Archives, Record Group III. **423** National Archives. **424** U.S. Army Photograph. **425** National Archives. **427** Brown. **429-30** Wide World. **432** *Chicago Tribune.* **435** Brown. **436** National Archives. **439** Bettmann. **440** Brown. **441** Brown. **445** Keystone View Co. **447** Brown. **449** *Brooklyn Eagle.* **450** L. of C. **451** Brady-Handy Collection. **453** Culver. **457** H. Armstrong Roberts. **459** lower right, U.P.I.; all others, Brown. **461** Bettmann. **469** Bettmann. **475** Culver. **477** Culver. **481** Culver. **485** above, Brown; below, Bettmann. **490** Culver. **493** bottom, Educational Affairs Dept., Ford Motor Co. **496** Brown. **499** Culver. **501** Wyoming State Archives and Historical Dept. **502** Brown. **503** FBI. **504** W.W. **506-7** Culver. **512** Brown. **513** Clark University. **514** left, Acme. **515** Brown. **517** *Herald Tribune.* **519** Philadelphia Museum of Art. **520** both Brown. **521** Brown. **526** above, Random House, Inc.; below, Brown. **527** above, Random House, Inc.; below, Col. Cofield. **528** W.W. **529** Brown. **530** Historical and Philosophical Soc., Cincinnati, Ohio. **531** photo by Fred Fehl. **537** Culver. **538** Brady-Handy Collection. **542** Culver. **545** Rollin Kirby. **546** Bureau of Reclamation. **549** U.P.I. **550** Brown. **555** National Archives, W.P.A. **556** Franklin D. Roosevelt Library. **557** Brown. **559** Brown. **560** Underwood & Underwood. **561** National Archives, W.P.A. **562** Culver. **567** U.P.I. **569** both Brown. **570** Underwood & Underwood. **572** Brown. **575** both TVA. **584** Keystone View Co. **587** W.W. **593** W.W. **594** David Low, Copyright Low All Countries. **599** Culver. **605** W.W. **606** Underwood & Underwood. **613** W.W. **614** U.S. Office of War Information in the National Archives. **615** W.W. **616** U.S. Army photograph. **618** above, U.S. Army photograph; below, Air Force photograph. **621** W.W. **623** Underwood & Underwood. **629** United Nations. **631** W.W. **632** U.S. Office of War Information in the National Archives. **633** W.W. **634** UNATIONS. **635** W.W. **637** Underwood & Underwood. **640** National Archives. **645** both U.P.I. **647** Air Force Photo. **648** Culver. **653** Brown. **654** U.S. Army Photograph. **658** United Nations. **659** Brown. **660** U.P.I. **663** Underwood & Underwood. **665** above and below, Brown; middle, Underwood & Underwood. **669** U.P.I. **671** W.W. **674** W.W. **675** Underwood & Underwood.

676 Black Star. **681** U.P.I. **683** W.W. **684** W.W. **686** Underwood & Underwood. **687** Fritz Henle, Monkmeyer Press. **689** W.W. **693** Wehner Wolff from Black Star. **694** White House photo. **700** DuPont. **702** San Francisco Chamber of Commerce. **703** Frank J. Fahey, *Wilmington Morning News.* **704** Agriculture Extension Service, Athens, Ga. **707** Underwood & Underwood. **717** photo by Angus Bean, Courtesy *New Directions.* **722** photo by Declan Haun, Black Star. **723** The Byron Collection, Museum of the City of New York. **724** Museum of the City of New York. **726** Bettmann. **727**

Culver. **728** Brown. **730** Bettmann. **731** Culver. **734** photo by Charles Moore, Black Star. **737** photo by Gene Daniels, Black Star. **739** Western Ways. **740** Pacific Citizen. **744** photo by Roger Malloch, Magnum. **745** photo by Ivan Massar, Black Star. **746** photo by Ted Cowell, Black Star. **747** photo by Flip Schulke, Black Star. **749** photo by Stephen Bosch, Black Star. **751** U.S. Army photo. **753** photo by Marc St. Gil, Black Star. **763** photo by Gene Daniels, Black Star. **765** *The Washington Post.*

THE

AMERICAN

NATION

"We Have Come to Stay."

Section One

THE AFTERMATH OF

CIVIL WAR

[1865 - 1890]

A long and bitterly-fought Civil War is about the most difficult experience a nation can be called upon to endure. The scars of battle are bad enough, but they are far more easily erased than the shocking damage done to the minds and spirits of the men and women who have lived through the ordeal. The Civil War in the United States ended as a military struggle soon after Lee's defeat at Appomattox, but it left in its wake a callousness toward suffering and destruction, an acceptance of ruthlessness and deceit, and a legacy of hatred and mistrust that lived on for many years to come. The period of reconstruction was strongly colored by these attitudes, and cannot be understood apart from them. The cessation of hostilities did not mean that the sections were reconciled to living with each other amicably; too many on both sides were determined to prolong the contest by political means. And so the suffering continued.

The South was hurt more by the war than the North. Except for a few engagements, the fighting had taken place on southern soil, and the toll in dead and injured in the South, when compared to the total population of the section, was much larger than in the North. Besides, the South had lost the war, and to a great extent lay at the mercy of the victorious North.

Slavery, the peculiar institution of the South, and state sovereignty, the political principle by which the South had justified its action, both had to go. The South had suffered not only a defeat, but also an enforced revolution.

The reconstruction of the South was badly done. After the death of Lincoln the government of the United States fell into the hands of Republican "Radicals," who were frightened at the thought of losing power to the ex-Confederates and the northern "peace-at-any-price" Democrats. Andrew Johnson, although he was from the South and to some extent understood its needs, was temperamentally unfitted for the Presidency, and was swept first out of power, then out of office, and with General Grant as an ineffective front the Radicals in Congress had their way. Out of this storm and stress emerged the "solid South." The hatreds engendered by the war grew more intense during the initial years of peace; and the "road to reunion" grew harder to find.

That the nation must inevitably travel such a road became apparent, however, as the growth of the West went on. The United States that fought the Civil War was for all practical purposes confined to the eastern half of its borders. A great new West was in the making which had had relatively little to do with the war. Its people were drawn from both North and South. It required national aid for the solving of its problems — transportation, public lands, Indians. Its weight in the balance naturally went toward an increase in national powers. Thus with the new West a part of the nation, the spirit of nationalism was the surer to survive and grow; the South had no choice but to make terms with it.

In politics the nation was slow to emerge from the shadow of Civil War and reconstruction. The Republican Party was the product of the tension over slavery; it thought of itself as the party of the Union that had won the war; it had a record to defend on reconstruction. The Democratic Party had opposed the Republicans on slavery; it had stood out for a fuller recognition of states' rights; it, too, had a record to defend, both on war and reconstruction. Neither party was ready to face up to the new issues; both looked over their shoulders at the past. As a result American political life for a quarter century after the war was bleak indeed.

I

THE PROBLEM OF

THE SOUTH

Postwar problems · Conditions in the South · The Freedmen's Bureau · "Forty Acres and a Mule" · The army of occupation · Private benevolence · Scarcity of capital · The southern tenant system · Lincoln's plan of reconstruction · The Wade-Davis Manifesto · Johnson's plan of reconstruction · Joint Committee on Reconstruction · The "Black Codes" · The mood of the South

Postwar Problems

The generation that has come of age in the United States since the Second World War will not need to be told that the end of hostilities may precipitate problems quite as perplexing as those which mark the progress of a war itself. With the spring of 1865 the American Civil War had worn itself out, but the tardy arrival of peace introduced other difficulties more appalling, perhaps, than the nation had ever faced before. The South, after four years of warfare within its borders, was not only defeated; its whole pattern of social organization lay in hopeless ruins. How were the people of the New South to live? What was to be the status of the freedmen? When and how were the normal processes of government to be resumed? Nor were the problems of the day confined wholly, or even mainly, to the South. The government of the United States, and, indeed, the governments of the northern states also, had become accustomed to the exercise of unusual wartime prerogatives. Were these practices to become permanent, or were they to be trimmed to fit the needs of peace? A million men were under arms. How could their speedy absorption into the ordinary walks of life be best facilitated? A huge national debt, an inflated currency, an overgrown system of taxation were parts of the inevitable legacy of war. What should the new financial picture be like? Manufactures of many sorts and kinds, stimulated by war orders and war profits, had reached a phenomenal development. Could their prosperity be preserved with the nation at peace? Agriculture, too,

THE "STRONG" GOVERNMENT 1869–1877. *Reconstruction was a heavy burden on the South.* Puck, *1880.*

Ruins of Fredericksburg, Virginia, *a photograph from the Brady collection in the National Archives, well illustrates the almost total ruin that the war brought to many southern cities.*

particularly in the Northwest, had expanded abnormally. How were the farmers to find markets for their produce? Less tangible, but no less important, the peoples of North and South for full four years had unbridled their prejudices, each against the other, and had carefully nourished their hatreds. How were the two parts of the restored Union ever to become one again in spirit? How could they learn to forgive and forget?

Reconstruction

"Reconstruction" is the label that historians have generally applied to these postwar years. The word gained currency on the eve of the Civil War, when a "reconstruction of the Union" that would satisfy the South was often suggested as an alternative to secession. It was applied during and immediately after the war to the "reconstruction" of loyal governments in states from which secessionist officials had fled. As a descriptive term it leaves much to be desired. Neither the prewar South nor the prewar Union could ever be rebuilt or restored. Out of the ordeal of war and its aftermath there emerged a new nation,

a nation so different from the old that the term "revolution" would scarcely overstate. But "reconstruction" has the sanction of long usage, and, properly redefined, it may still be permitted to serve. In a narrow sense, "reconstruction" means the process by which state government was revived in the South; broadly speaking, it must include all the drastic transformations of the period, both North and South.

Conditions in the South

Four years of warfare had left their marks upon the South. Armies had marched, camped, foraged, and fought in practically every southern state, and in a few of them, where the fighting was most concentrated, almost continuously. Sherman's exultant report of the desolation wrought by his column on the way from Atlanta to the sea speaks for itself:

We have consumed the corn and fodder in the region of country thirty miles on either side of a line from Atlanta to Savannah as also the sweet potatoes, cattle, hogs, sheep and poultry, and have carried away more than 10,000 horses and mules as well as a countless number of slaves. I estimate the damage done to the State of Georgia and its military resources at $100,000,000; at least $20,000,000 of which has inured to our advantage and the remainder is simple waste and destruction.

The sight of Charleston, once the proudest city of the South, shocked even the war-hardened veteran, Carl Schurz.

There was no shipping in the harbor except a few quartermaster's vessels and two or three small steamers. We made fast to a decaying pier constructed of palmetto-logs. There was not a human being visible on the wharf. The warehouses seemed to be completely deserted. There was no wall and no roof that did not bear eloquent marks of having been under the fire of siege guns.

Many another southern city had been similarly despoiled. Columbia, the thriving prewar capital of South Carolina, was a "mass of blackened chimneys and crumbling walls." The fire that destroyed it had swept eighty-four blocks, and had consumed every building for "three-fourths of a mile on each side of twelve streets." Atlanta was a riot of tangled brick and mortar, charred timbers, and rubbish. "Hell has laid her egg," one Georgian observed, "and right here it hatched." Mobile,

too, had suffered from fire and had fallen into "torpor and decay." Galveston was described as "a city of dogs and desolation."

Transportation

The havoc that the war had wrought on the South's transportation system was one of the worst of the calamities from which it suffered. Columbia, South Carolina, had been a railway center before the war, with five lines converging upon it. By the time Sherman's troops had departed, the tracks had been torn up for thirty miles in every direction. Rolling stock was left standing in the fields to be used by the homeless as dwellings. Rails were heated in the middle and twisted fantastically around trees. Similar thoroughness had characterized railroad destruction in Georgia, Mississippi, and various other parts of the South, while the wear and tear of wartime usage without adequate repairs had made the railroads outside the devastated regions almost as worthless as those within. Before the war river traffic had played a large part in moving the produce of the South. Now river channels were blocked, steamboats were destroyed, and wharves were missing. Seaports, so essential to the trade of the

Richmond Ladies. *Going for government rations: "Don't you think that Yankee must feel like shrinking before such high-toned Southern ladies as we?" Drawing by A. R. Waud, 1865.*

prewar South, were in similar disarray. Country roads were nonexistent or worse; bridges were gone; horses, mules, oxen, carriages, wagons, and carts had all too frequently been commandeered by the troops of North or South.

Southern Losses from War

Property losses suffered in the states of the former Confederacy included numerous other items. The Confederate bonds, both state and national, into which much southern capital had gone, had ceased altogether to be of value. So also had Confederate currency. Banks were closed; factories were idle; land values had toppled to nearly nothing; business in general was shattered. Property in slaves, which before the war accounted for so much of the South's wealth, was completely wiped out. Worse still, confiscation, contrary to a common opinion, took a heavy toll from the scanty resources of the defeated states. It was generally agreed that the property of the Confederate government was now the property of the United States, and that all such property must be located and attached. Agents of the Treasury Department, sent south on a 25 per cent commission basis to locate the 150,000 bales of cotton that the Confederate government was supposed to have had on hand at the close of the war, developed a tendency to take whatever cotton they happened to find, and to turn over to the United States only such of their takings as they saw fit. "I am sure I sent some honest cotton agents South," Secretary of the Treasury McCulloch admitted ruefully, "but it sometimes seems doubtful whether any of them remained honest for long." Not only cotton, but livestock, tobacco, rice, sugar, or anything of value was seized by individuals who represented themselves as agents of the United States. The total sum realized by the Treasury from seizures was $34 million, a considerable part of which was later returned. But this sum represents only a fraction of the damage done. As Secretary McCulloch reported in 1866, "Lawless men, singly and in organized bands, engaged in general plunder; every species of intrigue and peculation and theft were resorted to."

In assessing the losses that the South had sustained from the war, the personal element must not be ignored. Perhaps a quarter of a million soldiers and an untold number of civilians had lost their lives because of the clash of arms. Among those who perished were a large portion of the natural leaders of the South — men who, had they lived, could have helped most during the trials of the reconstruction era. Many of the survivors were themselves immeasurably the worse for their experiences; even when they were not maimed or broken in body, men trained in the school of war could never be quite the same as if trained in the normal pursuits of peace. Moreover, the southern veterans, unlike those of the North, went home to a broken and disorganized society. With so much that they had loved and valued gone, what difference did anything make? It is not surprising, under the circumstances, that a breakdown in moral fiber disqualified some of them from bearing the heavy burdens that the times demanded. An unregenerate few, particularly along the western frontier, continued the brigandage and pillage that had so often accompanied the war. Fortunately, the vast majority undertook, however wearily, the task of rebuilding and remaking their defeated section, while in the place of the leaders lost new, if possibly less able, leaders arose. Even so, the damage that the war had done to the people of the South, both whites and Negroes, is hard to overemphasize.

The Negroes

As for the Negroes, the boon of freedom was not without its unfortunate con-

Distributing Rations. *This contemporary drawing was designed to show that northern supplies were issued freely both to Negroes and to whites.*

sequences. Before the end of the war about 180,000 of them had been enrolled as free soldiers in the United States armies; others were merely camp-followers and refugees. The downfall of the Confederacy plunged all the rest into freedom — a state of society for which they were almost totally unprepared. As slaves, they had looked to their masters for food, shelter, and protection. As free men most of them had little idea how to provide such things for themselves. Freedom meant freedom from work, and the right to leave the plantation at will; that it might carry with it unpleasant responsibilities few of the Negroes were able to understand. Some stayed with the old masters and worked on as if nothing had happened; others wandered away to places they had never seen before. From one point of view the abolition of slavery had cost the South nothing. The Negroes were still there, and they could do as much work as ever before — if only they would. But

the evidence compounded that most of the ex-slaves, temporarily at least, had little will to work. And with the freedmen constituting nearly 40 per cent of the total population, this was a frightfully serious matter.

National Policy

At the present time the people of the United States, or of any other great power, if confronted with such a condition as existed in the South of 1865, would take it for granted that the government must play the principal part in restoring the economic life of the war-stricken section. What the South needed was something comparable to the European Recovery Plan that the United States instituted shortly after the Second World War. In the middle of the nineteenth century, however, there were few who would have thought of such a thing. The "less government the better" was still the dominant philosophy, not only of the Democrats, but also of the great majority of the Republicans. Indeed, the doctrine of rugged individualism, whether derived from the experience of the American frontier, or from the writings of European savants, or from both, was never more universally accepted in theory, even if those same "rugged individualists" were willing to take whatever they could get *from* government, such as subsidies, tariffs, land grants, and the like. In the main, therefore, the economic problems of the South were regarded as the concern of the southern people rather than of government, and in their solution the government gave only incidental assistance.

The Freedmen's Bureau

The necessity of direct aid for the freedmen, however, was something that could not easily be overlooked. The power of the national government had been used to free the slaves; hence the Negroes, now that they were free, had become in a sense the wards of the nation. The freedmen themselves were by no means unaware of this obligation. Just as their masters had cared for them in the past, so now they expected their "deliverers" to look after them. That Congress was ready to accept such a responsibility, at least for a limited time, was shown by the passage in March, 1865, of an act creating the Bureau of Refugees, Freedmen, and Abandoned Lands, or as it was generally called, the Freedmen's Bureau. This organization, which was to last for a year after the close of the war, was to be set up in the War Department under a commissioner appointed by the President, and an assistant commissioner for each of the insurrectionary states. It was authorized to distribute "such issues of provisions, clothing, and fuel" as might be necessary to relieve the "destitute and suffering refugees and freedmen and their wives and children." It had also the right to take over any land within the designated states that had been abandoned by its owners or confiscated by the United States, and to distribute it in tracts of forty acres or less, on a three-year rental basis, to "loyal refugees and freedmen."

Under the leadership of General Oliver O. Howard, an able and conscientious man, the Freedmen's Bureau went promptly to work. Its agents soon penetrated to every portion of the South, and were kept busy, for a time, distributing the bare necessities of life to hundreds of thousands of the needy, regardless of color. Without this assistance there can be no doubt that many of both races would have starved to death; or, one might properly say, many more might have starved than did. The Bureau also made a laudable effort to provide its dependents with medical care and hospitalization, but among the Negroes, who knew so little about how to take care of themselves, illness took a frightful toll. The mortality among Negro children, who in slavery times might even have been nursed through their illnesses by the plantation mistress herself, but now had to depend upon the pitifully inadequate ministrations of their parents, was particularly appalling.

"Forty Acres and a Mule"

The plan to distribute abandoned land to the freedmen led to an unfortunate misunderstanding. It was inferred at first that all land, "abandoned" because its owners had left it for Confederate service, would be available for distribution under the Confiscation Act of 1862, but President Johnson's policy permitted the pardoned owners of such property to recover it. The result was that the Bureau had comparatively little land of value to give away, in the aggregate not more than 800,000 acres. The Negroes, however, got the impression, often deliberately spread by unscrupulous agents, that each freedman would soon be given "forty acres of land and a mule." Some rumors included, for good measure, a white man to do the work. With so rosy a prospect for the future, and an abundance of free rations for the present, many of the Negroes found it difficult to see why they should do more than await the "day of jubilo." For some of them this day was dated. On January 1, 1866, they believed, the redistribution of land would take place:

O don't you know dat
Babylon is fallen,
And we's gwine to occupy de land?

Later that year Congress responded to the freedmen's hunger for land by modifying the Homestead Act of 1862 in a manner to meet southern needs. There were still some 46 million acres of public lands within the boundaries of five southern states — Florida, Alabama, Mississippi, Louisiana, and Arkansas. These lands Congress now made available in eighty-acre homestead tracts (during the first year for Negroes only), while ending also all cash sales and pre-emption entries. A House amendment would have forfeited for the same purpose 5 million additional acres of land previously granted to southern railroads, but the Senate, fearing that such a move might dis-credit the currently popular railroad land grant policy, turned the amendment down. Since the lands open to homesteaders had long been available for purchase at marked-down rates, there were few parcels that earlier settlers and speculators had not for good reason rejected. Nevertheless, during the decade that the "Southern Homestead Act" lasted, from 1866 to 1876, there were no less than 40,000 entries on southern land, by both Negro and white farmers, and no doubt by speculators also. In deference to the latter, particularly those with an eye to the value of southern timber and mineral resources, Congress repealed the act in 1876. The homestead policy no doubt did something, while it lasted, toward meeting the needs of the landless freedmen, although not nearly enough. The federal government might well have purchased land in the South with a view to making it available to the needy, but this somewhat revolutionary idea won little support in a business-minded age.

The Army of Occupation

In noting the governmental assistance given to the South after the war, one should remember the army of occupation. For

The Freedmen's Union Industrial School *of Richmond, Virginia, as seen by an illustrator for* Frank Leslie's Illustrated Newspaper, *September 22, 1866.*

several years detachments of federal troops were not far away in any part of the South, and there were regions in which the hated "blue-bellies," as they were inelegantly termed, were very numerous. The northern army, always abundantly provided with rations, clothing, and other supplies, shared its plenty with the destitute. This was the more natural because some of the federal troops were themselves Negroes, although General Grant, out of deference to the wishes of the southern whites, removed practically all Negro troops from the South by the end of 1866. The soldiers, whether white or Negro, had money to spend, and the government spent still larger sums for their maintenance. Directly or indirectly, the army thus contributed appreciably to the economic rehabilitation of the South.

Southern Railroads

One other item of governmental aid to the South deserves mention, and that, curiously, was given to the southern railroads. While northern troops accounted for an enormous amount of railroad destruction, it is also a fact that wherever the operations of the federal army required the reconditioning of the railroads, that, too, was done. In those portions of the upper South that the North had long held, the railroads were actually left in better condition than they were found. At the end of the war the United States War Department even went so far as to take over and reorganize some of the bankrupt railroad companies, and then, with "loyal" boards of directors assured, to return them to their owners.

Regrettably, the federal government did next to nothing for the badly damaged southern system of water transportation. The Rivers and Harbors Act of 1866, for example, which appropriated $3.5 million for the nation as a whole, awarded only $75,000 to the entire South. Such great southern harbors as Charleston, Savannah, Mobile, and New Orleans remained for years so inadequately repaired as to turn foreign trade, possibly by deliberate intent, to northern ports of entry. Southern rivers were likewise neglected, and the Lower Mississippi, with its dikes broken and its channel choked, annually spread its flood waters over millions of valuable acres. Discrimination against the South in appropriations for public works lasted for many years. Between 1865 and 1873 the total of such expenditures for the entire Union exceeded $100 million, of which the ex-Confederate states (plus Kentucky) received less than $9.5 million.

Private Benevolence

Private benevolence added a little to the aid given by the government. The Negroes, naturally, were the recipients of much such attention. Even before the end of the war the American Missionary Association, for example, had begun a work among them that led to expenditures after the return of peace of about $100,000 annually, mostly on Negro education. Also, the churches of the North sent a sizable army of missionaries, preachers, and teachers into the South, who among other things helped with the creation of separate all-Negro churches. Church contributions were supplemented by occasional gifts from philanthropists. The most notable donation of this kind came from George Peabody, who gave the income from a fund of $2 million, or more, "to the suffering South for the good of the whole country." The Peabody Education Fund was wisely administered, and proved to be an effective aid to the establishment of better common schools in the South. The Negroes themselves were pathetically eager for book-learning, and flocked into whatever schools were provided for them.

Scarcity of Capital

Southerners were at first hopeful that a great outpouring of northern capital would aid in the rehabilitation of the South, but in this they were to be sadly disappointed. Northern investors did, indeed, buy southern railway securities in sufficient amounts to make possible a rapid recovery on the part of the southern railroads, and they also purchased, to their later regret, the new bond issues of the southern states. But their southern investments went little further. The North, with its own fields of endeavor to look after — industrial expansion, agricultural extension, the building of transcontinental railroads, the development of the mining and ranching West[1] — had little left to risk in a region where political conditions were disturbed and a racial conflict was in the making. Thrown back upon its own meager resources, the South made numerous small beginnings in the lumbering industry, in the manufacture of tobacco, in the establishment of cotton mills, in the exploitation of its resources in coal and iron, as well as in the restoration of its agricultural activities, particularly the growing of cotton, which became again, as before the war, its chief concern.

Cotton Culture

Fortunately for the South the world had need of cotton, but to restore production was no easy matter. Seed was lacking, tools and machinery were worn out, horses and mules were scarce, and the labor supply was an unknown quantity. Many southerners, convinced that without slavery the Negroes could never be induced to work, hoped to devise some scheme for sending them back to Africa or to the West Indies; and still more believed that the salvation of the South lay in replacing or supplementing Negro labor with that of immigrants from Europe or elsewhere. But the Negroes could not go and the immigrants would not come. Some of the planters attempted to revive the old plantation system on the basis of free labor. Backed with

[1] See pp. 49–50, and Section Two.

whatever money the promise of cotton enabled them to borrow in Europe or in the North, they offered the Negroes wages to return to their former duties. Such transactions were carefully watched by the Freedmen's Bureau, which usually insisted on a written contract, with the amount of wages and the conditions of labor carefully set down. But the freedmen found it difficult to understand the conditions of free labor, they resented the ordeal of working in gangs under overseers as in slavery times, and they felt betrayed when the government failed to deliver on what they thought it had promised. Moreover, they no longer had adequate protection from the Freedman's Bureau after 1869, although the Bureau was not formally discontinued until 1872.

The Southern Tenant System

In the end the plantation system had to go, and in a sense the promise of "forty acres and a mule" was realized. The planters found by experience that only when they split up their land into small plots, with a Negro, or it might be a white tenant, in charge of each, could they obtain satisfactory results. Each tenant had usually to be supplied with not only his mule, but his seed, his tools, and his living until the crop was harvested; all this the landlord either furnished directly, or by obtaining credit for his tenants at one of the numerous "country stores" that sprang up all over the South. A crop lien secured both the landlord and the storekeeper against loss. As a rule the tenant turned over from a third to a half of his produce to the landlord as rental, and all the rest went to repay his debts; but by working on his own time in his own way he at least produced a part of a crop. His status, bound as he was by his crop lien, lay somewhere between slavery and freedom. The first few crops after the war, with the

POSTWAR COTTON CULTURE.
The Civil War did not alter the basic dependence of the lower South upon cotton culture. Nor did the substitution of free labor for slave labor emancipate the Negroes from the backbreaking duties that cotton culture entailed.

A COTTON PLANTATION. As idealized in a Currier and Ives print.

A COTTON PICKER'S HOME, as portrayed by W. A. Walker, the painter.

Negroes unsettled and the Freedmen's Bureau at hand to back them up in fantastic demands, were miserable failures, but by 1869 a cotton crop worth a quarter of a billion dollars was marketed. From that time forward the acute poverty of the South began to abate.[1]

The White Farmer

So much attention has been focused upon the Negroes, whether slave or free, that the role of the small white farmer of the South has rarely received the prominence it deserves. Even before the Civil War white labor accounted for a considerable part of the South's crop of cotton, and after the war the proportion tended to increase. In general the land worked by the whites in the time of slavery was inferior to that included in the great plantations

[1] See pp. 175–178.

and worked by slaves. But after the war the planters were glad to obtain tenants, white as well as Negro, and they often found it necessary to sell a part, or even all, of their land. Indeed, the old planter aristocracy was as much a casualty of the war and the peace as the plantation system itself; large holdings passed increasingly to men who had never owned slaves, while small farmers tended to achieve a degree of importance in public affairs that they had never known before.

Independent ownership was greatly stimulated by the low prices that landowners were obliged to accept. Land that had been worth from $20 to $30 an acre before the war sold for from $3 to $5 an acre after the war, and sometimes for less. Many of the whites who had owned poor land before, or no land at all, took advantage of this remarkable opportunity to buy. In ten years, according to the census of 1870,

THE COTTON PICKERS. A painting by Winslow Homer, 1876.

the number of farms in South Carolina had increased from 33,000 to 52,000; in Mississippi, from 43,000 to 68,000; in Louisiana, from 17,000 to 28,000. In the other southern states the figures, while not so striking, show the same general trend. Some of the new landowners were Negroes, but their holdings were generally very small, and most of the land that changed hands went to whites. A considerable number of northerners were attracted into the South by the low prices of land, but most of them were unable to adjust themselves satisfactorily to the new environment.

Rice, Sugar, and Tobacco

While cotton was the best money crop of the South, it must not be forgotten that southern agriculture, both before and after the war, produced some of nearly everything that can be grown on farms. Rice culture, which had been an important activity in South Carolina and Georgia before the war, showed in those states few symptoms of revival, but in Louisiana the production of both rice and sugar cane was successfully undertaken. Tobacco-growing in the upper South made rapid headway, particularly in Kentucky, where the crop increased from 54 million pounds in 1865 to 103 million pounds in 1871. In the states where cotton had never been "king," and where in consequence the concentration of slavery had been less marked, the problem of restoring normal production was far more easily solved. After the first two or three hard years, livestock and foodstuffs could be found practically anywhere in abundance.

The Southern States

Unfortunately, the North seemed far more interested in the political than in the economic restoration of the South. Most northerners, while the war lasted, accepted the theory that secession, under the Constitution, was illegal and impossible; a state simply could not leave the Union. Logically, therefore, the pretense of secession had not changed the legal status of the southern states in the slightest; the American nation, as Chief Justice Chase held later, was an "indestructible Union, composed of indestructible States." This kind of reasoning, together with concern over the disorder that might ensue if all government in the conquered states should disappear, underlay the proposed surrender terms that General Sherman had signed with General Johnston a few days after Lincoln's death. The President, according to this agreement, should recognize the existing state governments of the South, on condition that their officers and legislators should take "the oaths prescribed by the Constitution of the United States." In thus attempting to deal with a political rather than a strictly military matter, Sherman may have exceeded his authority,[1] and his agreement with Johnston was promptly repudiated in Washington. Moreover, the bitterness toward the South that followed the assassination of Lincoln made completely impossible, if it had not been so before, the adoption of so generous a program of conciliation. In practice, southern state officials and legislators ceased almost immediately to perform their duties, while detachments of northern troops, widely dispersed throughout the South, provided whatever protection existed against disorder. For a period of from four to six months the states most lately conquered were left virtually without civil government.

Lincoln's Plan of Reconstruction

For those states that the northern armies had occupied earlier, the situation was different. Faced with the alternative of main-

[1] Sherman claimed, however, that Lincoln had authorized him to recognize temporarily the North Carolina "state government then in existence." W. B. Hesseltine, *Lincoln's Plan of Reconstruction* (1960), p. 137.

taining military rule within their borders, or providing some method for the revival of civilian government, Lincoln chose the latter course. For each of the conquered states he appointed a military governor, whose duty it was to re-establish normal civilian government whenever as many as one-tenth of the number of voters who had participated in the election of 1860 should take a prescribed oath of loyalty to the United States. The President promised to pardon all who would take the oath, except for high-ranking Confederate military and civilian personnel, and to recognize any new government they should establish. Operating under this plan, three states, Tennessee, Louisiana, and Arkansas, succeeded during the year 1864 in re-creating state governments, and were accorded presidential recognition. The President also recognized a loyal, although decidedly impotent, government in Virginia that, after the admission of West Virginia in 1863, had maintained a precarious existence at Alexandria. From these acts, and from his various utterances it was evident that he intended to remake the Union with a minimum of friction. Undoubtedly he had in mind no inflexible plan, and was prepared to modify his program as circumstances might require; but he was totally unwilling to compromise on the supremacy of the Union, which in his opinion was what the war was about. He would be charitable toward the people of the South, but adamant in his opposition to states' rights.

Radical Opposition

Lincoln's magnanimous attitude toward the South was not shared by a majority of his party in Congress. Republican critics of the President, generally called the "Radicals," wished to adopt a much sterner policy of reconstruction. The motives of this faction were varied, and changed considerably as the years wore on. Some of Lincoln's opponents were no doubt genuine idealists who believed that the President's plan would leave the freedmen too completely at the mercy of the southern whites; it did not, in fact, insist on the abolition of slavery, much less, Negro suffrage. How could the Negroes hope to defend themselves against white domination without firmer guarantees? Others were strongly influenced by party considerations. States reconstructed under the President's plan might eventually send Democratic senators and representatives to Congress who, with the help of northern Democrats, could even put an end to Republican supremacy. Still others thought beyond party advantage to what the parties stood for. During the war the Republican Party had become pre-eminently a businessman's party. It advocated protective tariffs, hard money and a national banking system, repayment of the national debt in gold, and generous land grants to the builders of western railroads. Would the agrarian South go along with these policies, or would it place obstacles in their way? Could it even be trusted not to seek, with Copperhead support, the repudiation of the national debt? Most Radicals, whatever their other sentiments, also deplored the manner in which the President had ignored Congress in his planning for reconstruction. Had the Executive the right to determine so important a matter on his own? Was it not about time to deal a heavy blow against the practice of "Executive usurpation," so much in evidence during the war? Also, not far from the surface in nearly every Radical mind was the deep-seated conviction that the South had precipitated the war, and was therefore responsible for all it had cost in blood and treasure. How could such a crime be left unpunished? Was it fair to the North to receive the South back into the Union as if nothing had happened?

The Wade-Davis Bill

The Radicals were not slow to record their displeasure with Lincoln's plan of reconstruction. When senators and repre-

sentatives from two states so reanimated, Louisiana and Arkansas, sought to take their seats in Congress, both houses refused to receive them. Congress likewise firmly rebuffed the efforts of Tennessee and Louisiana to cast electoral votes in the election of 1864. Also, well before that election, Congress embodied in the Wade-Davis bill a reconstruction plan of its own, according to which the President should appoint a provisional governor for each of the Confederate states, who should then take a census of white male citizens. If a majority (rather than 10 per cent) of these potential voters should take the oath of allegiance, the provisional governor might then allow them to choose delegates to a constitutional convention, the duty of which would be to accept for themselves, and to include in a new constitution, three provisions: (1) the denial of political rights to all high-ranking civil and military officers of the Confederacy; (2) the abolition of slavery; and (3) the outlawing of state or Confederate debts incurred in the war against the Union. With this document duly approved by the voters at the polls, the President, *after obtaining the consent of Congress*, might recognize the state government established under its provisions.

The Wade-Davis Manifesto

Since the Wade-Davis bill passed Congress during the last ten days of a session, Lincoln was able to give it a pocket veto, but this did not mean that he was necessarily opposed to all its provisions. In fact, he issued a formal proclamation, calling attention to the congressional plan as well as his own, and implying that, while he was as yet uncommitted to any one plan for every state, the ideas set forth in the Wade-Davis bill were well worth considering. The fundamental difference between Lincoln's plan and the congressional plan lay in whether the President or Congress should take charge of the process of reconstruction. If the President could maintain the control he had assumed, the way would be open for a relatively simple means of reviving state government in the South; but if Congress was to have the last word, then the Radicals might substitute (as indeed they did) a far harsher plan than they had proposed in the Wade-Davis bill. Lincoln's unwillingness to go along with them greatly angered the Radicals, who in a document known as the Wade-Davis Manifesto denounced him savagely. The President, declared the Manifesto, "must understand that tne authority of Congress is paramount and must be respected." If he wished congressional support "he must confine himself to his executive duties — to obey and execute, not to make the laws — to suppress by arms armed rebellion, and leave political reorganization to Congress." Lincoln was thus well advised of the views held by the Radicals, and had he lived he might have sought to make terms with them. But he might also have continued to fight them. There is much "wishful thinking" in the idea that, if only Lincoln had lived, he could have prevented all the worst features of reconstruction.

Andrew Johnson

Andrew Johnson (1808–1875), the Vice-President who had succeeded to the Presidency when Lincoln was assassinated, was in no sense of the word a Republican. He had won second place on the Union Party ticket in 1864 precisely because he was a prominent southern Democrat who had remained loyal to the Union during the war. Born in North Carolina, he had lived most of his life in the mountain country of eastern Tennessee, and was about as far removed from the planter aristocracy of the South as any southerner could be. He had grown up in poverty as grinding as that which surrounded Lincoln, and he had received no formal schooling, although learning much from his schoolteacher wife. A tailor by trade, he early discovered an aptitude for politics and for oratory, which he indulged freely. As a firm defender of the workingman and a bitter opponent of the southern aristocrats, he mounted the political ladder step by step. When only twenty-one years old he became an alderman in Greeneville, Tennessee, the city in which he then resided, after which he won elections that made him successively mayor, member of the state legislature, member of Congress, governor, United States Senator, and Vice-President. Thickset and dark-complexioned, he had about him an air of contentiousness and belligerence in marked contrast with the mild-mannered Lincoln. Nor was there anything deceiving about Johnson's appearance; his intransigence was to cost his country dear. The Radicals thought at first that they could use him against the southern leaders, but they were soon disillusioned, for Johnson shared with Lincoln, whatever their external differences, the belief that the best way to heal the nation's wounds was to deal generously with the defeated South. As for the southern aristocrats he had once hated, he soon saw that they had suffered much for their sins and were no longer to be feared.

Johnson's Plan of Reconstruction

To the immense indignation of the Radicals, Johnson soon made it clear that he intended in the main to follow Lincoln's theory of presidential reconstruction, and to ignore the pointed warning of the Wade-Davis Manifesto. Since, in the President's judgment, the states of the now defunct Confederacy had never legally left the Union, all that remained to be done, as he saw it, was for them somehow to regain their normal governments. To guide them in this course he believed that, as Commander-in-Chief of the armed forces, he possessed without any especial authorization by Congress all the power he needed. Drawing upon both Lincoln's plan of reconstruction and the Wade-Davis bill, he therefore elaborated a plan of his own. First, he accepted as fully restored to their place in the Union the states that Lincoln had recognized, Tennessee, Louisiana, Arkansas, and Virginia. For the seven other ex-Confederate states he appointed provisional governors who differed in name only from the military governors of Lincoln's plan, and whose salaries in most instances came from War Department funds. For each governorship he chose a local man who had shown sympathy for the Union during the war; none of them had fought on the Union side, but only one, Judge Benjamin F. Perry of South Carolina, had ever served the Confederacy in any way.

The next step in presidential reconstruction was for each provisional governor to call for elections to a constitutional convention under the same suffrage provisions that had existed before the war, provided that such voters were eligible to take, and had taken, the prescribed oath of allegiance to the United States. There was thus no provision for Negro suffrage, and high Confederate leaders, including those whose property exceeded $20,000 in value, were still denied pardons and political rights. The conventions must invalidate the various ordinances of secession, abolish slavery, and repudiate all debts contracted to help the Confederacy; otherwise they were free to write into their constitutions such provisions as they chose. Johnson let it be known privately that, for the effect such action would have upon the northern Radicals, he hoped that Negroes who could read and write, or who owned a small amount of real estate, would be permitted to vote. But he specifically acknowledged that this was a matter for the conventions to decide.

Johnson foresaw that for several months he could proceed with his plan unhampered by Congress, which, to the distress of the Radicals, could not convene without the President's call until the following Decem-

Andrew Johnson of Tennessee. *Seventeenth President of the United States. Ironically, it was a Southerner who succeeded Lincoln, but Johnson's good intentions toward the South betrayed him into much bad politics. His tempestuous character and his free-wheeling oratory cost him dear.*

ber. By this time he hoped to have state governments restored throughout the South. He knew that the Radical leaders of Congress would resent deeply whatever he did, but he believed that they would find it difficult to undo a series of accomplished facts. Furthermore, he counted upon the approval of a majority of the people both in the South and in the North for what he was doing. In the former section, the easy terms he had prescribed should insure him a strong following, while in the latter he hoped to rally to his standard most of the Democrats as well as the more moderate Republicans. He took seriously the name and implications of the Union Party, on whose ticket he had been elected, and hoped to see it become, with himself at its head, a kind of party of the center, opposed only by the northern Radicals at one extreme and the southern irreconcilables at the other. He had kept on the members of Lincoln's cabinet, most of whom held moderate views, and he counted strongly on their support.

Johnson Misleads the Southern Whites

It was a great mistake for Andrew Johnson, an accidental President, a southerner, and a Democrat, to assume that without so much as consulting Congress he could carry through on his own responsibility the entire process of reconstruction. With the war ended, party politics was bound to reappear, and did. The Republicans promptly turned their backs on the Union coalition they had formed for the election of 1864, and operated strictly as Republicans. Moreover, without Lincoln's restraining hand, the party tended increasingly to fall under the domination of the Radicals, leaving Johnson virtually a man without a party, and dependent mainly upon the Democrats for support. Worse still, Johnson's policy gave the South good reason to believe that it could achieve restoration to the Union on far easier terms than proved to be the case. When the war ended the defeated southerners were prepared for stern measures, even reprisals. They knew that they had lost the war and they expected the consequences to be grim, especially in view of the northern demand for vengeance that followed the death of Lincoln. Many prominent southern leaders, including Jefferson Davis, were imprisoned for a time, although happily there were no executions for treason, and all political prisoners were eventually released.[1] It is reasonable to suppose that the South in the spring of 1865 would have accepted with little protest a program of reconstruction far more satisfactory to the Radicals than the President's. Johnson's plan aroused false hopes. Pondering it,

southerners concluded that they could salvage much of their former way of life. Slavery was gone, but the civil status of the Negroes would remain in southern hands. National sovereignty had won out over state sovereignty, but the South might still become "a nation within a nation," capable of protecting "southern rights," even if the old states' rights argument had lost its potency.

Johnson's Plan in Effect

When Congress met in December, Johnson's work of restoration was far along. The provisional governors had revived the old county and municipal governments sometimes with little change of personnel. They had called constitutional conventions, and in every state but Texas the conventions had met. Unfortunately, perhaps, none of them had accepted the President's advice about allowing exceptional Negroes to vote; nor did they show any disposition to place restrictions upon the political rights of the former enemies of the Union. Furthermore, the first elections that were held showed that, for the most part, the leaders of the Confederacy were still regarded by the voters as the leaders of the South. In Mississippi, for example, an ex-Confederate brigadier-general who had not even been pardoned as yet by the President, was chosen governor; in Alabama three-fourths of the members of the legislature had at one time or another fought for the Confederacy; and in Georgia the legislature chose Alexander H. Stephens, late Vice-President of the Confederate States of America, to be United States Senator. Every legislature, however, except that of Mississippi, had promptly ratified the Thirteenth Amendment, submitted early in 1865, and before the end of the year the President was able to tell Congress that only in Florida and Texas was the work of restoration incomplete, and that in those states it would be finished soon.

---

[1] The execution of Henry Wirz, who had been in command of Andersonville prison, was not for treason, but for atrocities committed within the prison walls while he was in charge. See p. 29.

GENERAL WADE HAMPTON OF SOUTH CAROLINA, a gallant Confederate cavalry officer, supported Johnson's plan of reconstruction, and worked hard to prevent armed conflict within his state while the Radicals were in control. He was elected governor in 1876, and later became United States Senator.

GENERAL WILLIAM MAHONE OF VIRGINIA fought in many of Lee's campaigns, and became active during reconstruction in southern railroad affairs. A quiet but effective opponent of the Radicals, he suffered financial losses after the Panic of 1873, and several years later led a "Readjuster" movement, which favored scaling down the state debt and social reforms. He was elected to the United States Senate in 1880.

GENERAL JOHN B. GORDON OF GEORGIA, one of Lee's officers, was Democratic candidate for governor of Georgia in 1868, but was defeated. He was an indefatigable worker for "home rule," and when it came he represented his state in the United States Senate, 1873–1880.

CONFEDERATE GENERALS AFTER THE WAR. *Of far greater significance than is sometimes realized was the fact that so many high-ranking Confederate officers were able to enjoy successful careers after the war. Perhaps the "vindictiveness" of Radical reconstruction has been overstressed.*

Joint Committee on Reconstruction

Congressional resentment against the President's effort to carry through reconstruction on his own was soon in evidence. The two houses of Congress not only agreed in refusing to seat the newly-elected senators and representatives from the South, but they created also a "Joint Committee on Reconstruction," consisting of six senators and nine representatives, to probe further into this and related problems. Party considerations crowded hard on principle; one reason why the Republicans so greatly resented the return of the southern delegations was that, if seated, they would whittle down Republican majorities to uncomfortably small margins. On the Lincoln-Johnson theory that the states could never die, Congress also had opinions. The most outstanding member of the House, Thaddeus Stevens (1792–1868) of Pennsylvania, a lifelong opponent of slavery whom the war had further filled with anger toward the South, held that the southern states were no longer states at all, but only conquered provinces with which Congress might deal as it chose. In the Senate, the equally powerful Charles Sumner (1811–1874) of Massachusetts, whose body still bore the marks of Preston Brooks' assault, maintained that the traitorous states, by the very act of secession, had committed suicide. Since they had ceased to exist, Congress had now the same power over them that the Constitution had given it over the territories, and could deal with them in any way it chose. Sumner's views were not held by every member of his party in the Senate, nor were Stevens' in the House. But the evidence was overwhelming that Congress, on some pretext, meant to play an important role in reconstruction.

The "Black Codes"

Nevertheless, the states that Johnson had recognized, lulled into a false sense of security by the President's favor, went forward with programs that confirmed the Radicals in their worst fears. Representation in Congress was less important to the South than the effective functioning of the reconstructed state governments, a task to which their newly-elected legislature turned painstaking attention. Of the many pressing problems that confronted them, the most perplexing, no doubt, was how to deal with the Negroes. Probably the South understood better than the North the great distance that lay between freedom and slavery; it would take far more than a presidential proclamation and a constitutional amendment to bridge this gap. Not only did the states that Johnson had reconstructed deny the Negroes the vote, they also enacted "black codes," defining the civil rights of the ex-slaves, and prescribing for them a status definitely inferior to that of the whites. In formulating these discriminatory laws, according to Professor Fleming, southern legislators drew upon "the old laws for free Negroes, the vagrancy laws of North and South for whites, the customs of slavery times, the British West Indies legislation for ex-slaves, and the regulations of the United States War and Treasury Departments and of the Freedmen's Bureau."[1] Of these codes

[1] W. L. Fleming, *The Sequel of Appomattox* (1921), p. 94.

the most severe and the most quoted was that of Mississippi, but they all denied to Negroes the privilege of sitting on juries, and usually rejected Negro testimony in cases involving a white defendant. Among the provisions most criticized in the North (mainly from the Mississippi code) were those requiring labor contracts to be in writing, and if broken the wages not to be payable; those directing that Negroes under eighteen years of age whose parents could not support them be apprenticed to some white "master," preferably their former owner; those prescribing stiff fines for vagrancy, which if not paid might be collected by selling the services of the offender; and those forbidding Negroes "to carry fire arms or other deadly weapons, to make seditious speeches, to treat animals cruelly, to sell liquors, or to preach without a license."

Johnson and Congress

The worst of these codes seemed to the Radicals little less than a direct defiance of the Thirteenth Amendment, and a conscious effort to retain slavery in fact if not in form. In general, however, they never went into effect, principally because of the presence within the South of Union troops who made the welfare of the Negroes an object of especial solicitude, and the work of the Freedmen's Bureau, which as a national agency set up to protect the rights of the ex-slaves paid little respect to the new state laws. But the existence of the Freedmen's Bureau, according to the law creating it, was to terminate a year after the war. In this provision Congressional leaders were quick to see an ideal opportunity for a test of strength with the President. Should the Freedmen's Bureau, with its program of national supervision of the freed slaves, be continued, or should the Negro problem be turned over to the reconstructed states to handle as they chose? Johnson, a states' rights Democrat by training and conviction, favored the latter course, but Congress, with overwhelming majorities, sent up for the President's signature a law continuing the Freedmen's Bureau, with greatly increased powers. Thus challenged, Johnson responded with an anticipated veto, which to his delight the Senate sustained by a slender margin. But his rejoicing was far more public than was wise, and included heated denunciations of the Radical leaders, the net result of which was to lose him the votes he needed to continue his policies.

The Mood of the South

The mood of the South as these events unfolded was no real help to the President. While he carried through his plan of reconstruction without the complete withdrawal of northern troops from the South, he did withdraw enough troops to give some of the southern states a pretext for establishing militia of their own. Such action made it easy for the Radicals to charge that what the southern leaders really had in mind was the complete subjugation of the Negro, and perhaps even preparation for another rebellion. Radicals could also point to the prevalence of racial conflicts, particularly between the lower-class southern whites and the Negroes, groups whose longstanding hatred for one another was greatly aggravated by the fact of emancipation. In these new conflicts the Negroes lacked whatever protection their masters had once given them as property, and needed all the help they could get from the army and the Freedmen's Bureau. Moreover, the South made little effort to conceal its intense dislike for the northern Radicals, and its hope for the success of the President's plan. It was neither broken nor contrite in spirit. Carl Schurz, whom the President himself had sent in the summer of 1865 to study conditions in the South, complained in a much-quoted report that southerners did not recognize the "criminality" of their recent treason, and displayed an "utter absence of national feeling." In this judgment Schurz was no doubt right, but, as General Grant reported after a similar mission, the South also accepted the fact that it had lost the war. What it really wanted was freedom to work out its future with as little national interference as possible; or in short, to be treated as if it had not lost the war.

BIBLIOGRAPHY

The most convenient guide to recent scholarship on Reconstruction is David Donald's revision (1969) of J. G. Randall's *Civil War and Reconstruction;* Donald has also compiled a useful bibliography, *The Nation in Crisis, 1861–1877* (1969). Of great value are the following basic tools: *The Harvard Guide to American History* (1954), edited by Oscar Handlin and others; *Dictionary of American Biography* (22 vols., 1928–1958), edited by Allen Johnson and Dumas Malone; and *Documents of American History* (2 vols., 8th ed., 1968), edited by H. S. Commager. Single-volume surveys of recent southern history are T. D. Clark and A. D. Kirwan, *The South since Appomattox* (1967); and J. S. Ezell, *The South since 1865* (1963). Unique and provocative is W. J. Cash, *The Mind of the South* (1941). Varying historical interpretations are gathered in *The South: A Central Theme?* (1969), edited by M. L. Billington.

Excellent brief surveys of the period by leading scholars are J. H. Franklin, *Reconstruction* (1961); and K. M. Stampp, *The Era of Reconstruction* (1965). R. W. Patrick, *The Reconstruction of the Nation* (1967),

*Items starred throughout are available in paperback.

gives much space to developments outside the South. Avery Craven, *Reconstruction: The Ending of the Civil War* (1969), is a senior scholar's assessment of the three years following the peace. Other works which focus on the immediate postwar period are LaWanda and J. H. Cox, *Politics, Principle, and Prejudice* (1963); and W. R. Brock, *An American Crisis* (1963). Suggestive lectures by a leading authority are in David Donald, *The Politics of Reconstruction* (1965).

The interpretation of Reconstruction is a subject of heated dispute among historians. W. A. Dunning, whose basic work was *Reconstruction, Political and Economic* (1907), set the tone for interpretation of the era for two generations. His followers were political-minded, emphasizing the evils and hypocrisy of Radicalism, taking a dim view of black aspirations and competence, and finding little good to say about carpetbaggers, scalawags, and the Republican Party. A journalistic expression of the Dunning line is Claude Bowers, *The Tragic Era* (1929); traces of the same view are found in a more recent scholarly book by E. M. Coulter, *The South during Reconstruction* (1947). Two articles provide excellent discussions of the historiography: H. K. Beale, "On Rewriting Reconstruction History," *American Historical Review*, XLV (1940), 807–827; and B. A. Weisberger, "The Dark and Bloody Ground of Reconstruction Historiography," *Journal of Southern History*, XXV (1959), 427–449. Among the many useful collections of conflicting interpretations are *Reconstruction in Retrospect* (1969), edited by R. N. Current; *Reconstruction in the South* (1952), edited by E. C. Rozwenc; *Reconstruction: A Tragic Era?* (1968), edited by S. M. Scheiner; and *Reconstruction: An Anthology of Revisionist Writings* (1969), edited by K. M. Stampp and L. F. Litwack.

A Documentary History of Reconstruction (2 vols., 1906), edited by W. L. Fleming, remains a great sourcebook. Recent shorter documentary collections include *Reconstruction* (1965), edited by R. N. Current; *Reconstruction* (1967), edited by Staughton Lynd; and *The Reconstruction* (1963), edited by J. P. Shenton. Rich and much broader than its title indicates is *The Radical Republicans and Reconstruction, 1861–1870* (1967), edited by H. M. Hyman. An interesting reminiscence by a black participant is J. R. Lynch, *The Facts of Reconstruction* (1913).

The history of the blacks has become of very great interest. The standard general history is J. H. Franklin, *From Slavery to Freedom* (3rd ed., 1967); a brief introduction is provided by R. W. Logan, *The Negro in the United States* (1957). W. E. B. DuBois, *Black Reconstruction in America* (1935), has exerted a strong influence. Robert Cruden, *The Negro in Reconstruction* (1969), is a brief survey of a complex subject. There are two convenient biographies of the black leader Frederick Douglass, by Benjamin Quarles (1948) and by P. S. Foner (1964); both are in paperback. State studies of merit include Joel Williamson, *After Slavery* (1965), on South Carolina; J. M. Richardson, *The Negro in the Reconstruction of Florida* (1965); and V. L. Wharton, *The Negro in Mississippi, 1865–1890* (1947). There are two modern studies of General O. O. Howard, head of the Freedmen's Bureau: J. A. Carpenter, *Sword and Olive Branch* (1964); and W. S. McFeely, *Yankee Stepfather* (1968). See also H. H. Donald, *The Negro Freedman* (1952); G. R. Bentley, *A History of the Freedmen's Bureau* (1955); Martin Abbott, *The Freedmen's Bureau in South Carolina* (1967); O. A. Singletary, *Negro Militia and Reconstruction* (1957); and J. E. Sefton, *The United States Army and Reconstruction* (1967). An important book on a hitherto obscure subject is W. L. Rose, *Rehearsal for Reconstruction: The Port Royal Experiment* (1964). Two excellent recent monographs exploring fresh terrain are J. M. McPherson, *The Struggle for Equality: Abolitionists and the Negro in the Civil War and Reconstruction* (1964); and David Montgomery, *Beyond Equality: Labor and the Radical Republicans* (1967).

2

RADICAL

RECONSTRUCTION

Presidential or congressional leadership? · The Fourteenth Amendment · Elections of 1866 · Impeachment of Johnson · The Supreme Court · "Thorough" reconstruction · Election of 1868 · The Grant scandals · The Ku Klux Klan · The Redemption movement · Liberal Republicanism · Elections of 1872 and 1876 · The Compromise of 1877 · Diplomatic reconstruction

Presidential or Congressional Leadership?

The scene was now set for a monumental contest between the President and Congress. Would the President be able, despite the opposition of the Radicals, to carry through his plan of reconstruction, or would Congress bend him to its will? All that the Radicals required in order to overturn Johnson's plan was a two-thirds majority in each house of Congress, an objective that was now in sight. Johnson's indiscreet remarks at the time the Senate sustained his Freedmen's Bureau veto were widely publicized, gave great offense, and changed several important votes. The President had asserted, among other things, that such men as Thaddeus Stevens, Charles Sumner, and Wendell Phillips were as much opposed to the Union as "the Davises, the Toombses, and the Slidells." Congress now passed, then re-passed over the President's veto, a Civil Rights Bill, which declared the Negro to be a citizen and gave him the same civil rights as were enjoyed by the whites. This action it followed with a somewhat different version of the Freedmen's Bureau Bill, which the President again vetoed, but which this time won re-passage by the requisite majorities. Thus the leadership in reconstruction seemed to have passed from the President and the moderates to Congress and the Radicals.

The Fourteenth Amendment

By this time — the summer of 1866 — the Joint Committee on Reconstruction was ready to report a congressional substitute for the President's plan. Its recommendations, after slight modifications, were embodied in the Fourteenth Amendment to the Constitution, and submitted to the states

THADDEUS STEVENS *closing the debate of March 2, 1868, on the impeachment of President Johnson.*

Charles Sumner, *brilliant Senator from Massachusetts, led the forces opposed to President Johnson in the United States Senate.*

Thaddeus Stevens *of Pennsylvania, Republican leader of the House of Representatives, was one of the chief architects of Radical reconstruction.*

for ratification. The first section repeated the provisions of the Civil Rights Bill, about the constitutionality of which some doubts existed, and forbade "any state to deprive any person of life, liberty, or property without due process of law," or to "deny to any person within its jurisdiction the equal protection of the laws." The second dealt with Negro suffrage, but refrained from requiring it outright, providing instead that to the extent that any state should deny eligible males over twenty-one the right to vote, to that same extent the representation of such a state in Congress and in the electoral college should be reduced. The third section was designed to repudiate the free bestowal of presidential pardons upon persons who had broken an oath of allegiance to the United States in order to serve the Confederacy. Only Congress, by a two-thirds vote of each house, could remove such a disability. A fourth section asserted that the debt of the United States, incurred for any cause, including the suppression of rebellion, should never be questioned, and at the same time denied both to the United States and to the several states the right to assume any debts incurred in aid of rebellion, or for losses due to the emancipation of slaves. All this Congress was given full authority to enforce by appropriate legislation.

Despite the Radical contention that the seceded states were no longer in the Union, Congress had submitted the Thirteenth Amendment to them for ratification, and it now submitted to them the Fourteenth, with the implication that they must ratify, or be reconstructed all over again. Of the eleven states concerned, however, only Tennessee complied; all the rest turned the Amendment down, an act of questionable wisdom in view of subsequent events, but understandable enough at the time, especially since President Johnson had counseled such a course. Congress now declared Tennessee, ostensibly for its cooperation,

The Civil Rights Bill *was of intense interest, for its success or failure would determine whether Congress or the President would control reconstruction. The picture shows the lobby of the House of Representatives in Washington during the passage of the bill.*

to be fully restored to the Union, but the state was already in the hands of a Radical government, and it was probably this fact, rather than ratification merely, that won it congressional recognition. Had the other ten states followed Tennessee's example, there is no certainty that Congress would have readmitted them; nevertheless, it would have had less excuse for the stronger program it finally adopted. To add to the generally bad impression made in the North by southern rejection of the Fourteenth Amendment, race riots had occurred during the year in Memphis and New Orleans, proof, according to the Radicals, of what the South meant to do to the Negro if left to its own devices.

Elections of 1866

The contest between the President and Congress came to a head in the elections of 1866. If the President's friends could win one more than one-third of the seats in either house of Congress, they could make his vetoes stand, and thus prevent the Radicals from pushing their program further; on the other hand, if the Radicals could win a two-thirds majority in each house, they could devise their own program, and drive the President before them. Johnson seems at first to have thought that he could make use of the Union coalition that had elected him in 1864, and gave earnest support to a National Union Convention, held during the late summer of 1866, which southern as well as northern delegates attended. But

he was eventually to learn that this was a vain hope. A few of the more moderate Republicans still stood by him, but he could count on more help from the Democrats than from any other quarter.

The Radicals, on the other hand, had not only the advantage of the growing anti-southern sentiment they were building up in the North, but they had also won enormously useful support from financial and business circles. Here the fear was genuine that a revived Democratic Party, composed of the old alliance of northern and southern Democrats, might if it took over the federal government do something to deflate the business boom that had buoyed up the North during and after the war. Business leaders of this period showed none of the fear of national powers that came to characterize them later on, when the specter of national regulation appeared. So far the national government had served only to aid them in their plans. They wanted, and were obtaining from the Radicals, lower internal taxes, a continuation of the high wartime tariffs, a benevolent attitude toward the holders of national bonds, a sound currency, and generous subsidies for the building of western railroads. Why risk all this by making it possible for the Democrats to return to power? The preferable policy, obviously, was to delay the course of reconstruction until the Radicals could build up in the South, on Negro votes if necessary, a Republican wing strong enough to keep the businessman's party in power.

Had Johnson remained in Washington and kept quiet during the campaign, he might have won the one-more-than-one-third minority that he needed in either the House or the Senate. But he essayed instead a "swing around the circle" to Chicago, where he laid the cornerstone for a monument to the late Stephen A. Douglas, and back again to Washington. Johnson was not a drunkard, but he had been ill and had taken too much to drink at the time of his inauguration as Vice-President. Naturally his political opponents made much of the sorry figure he cut on that occasion, and implied, quite contrary to fact, that the intemperance of his utterances as a campaign orator resulted from his addiction to

"**King Andy I**," *a bitter caricature of Johnson by Thomas Nast, well portrayed the hatred with which the President was regarded by the northern Radicals.*

drink. The violence of Johnson's statements, well publicized by a hostile press, lost rather than gained him votes, and as a result of the elections the Radicals obtained far more than the minimum two-thirds majority they required in each house of Congress. Furthermore, a law passed during the preceding session over the President's veto required the new Congress to convene on March 4, 1867, the day after the old Congress adjourned, instead of in December, 1867, as would otherwise have been the case. The new Congress would thus be on hand without delay to carry on the Radical program, which by this time was abundantly clear: (1) to impeach the President and remove him from office, and (2) to inflict on the southern whites a new and far harsher plan of reconstruction than the one outlined for campaign purposes in the Fourteenth Amendment.

Impeachment of Johnson

Two acts which became law just before the adjournment of the old Congress revealed clearly the attitude of the Radicals toward the President. By the Command of the Army Act he was required to issue all military orders through the General of the Army, Ulysses S. Grant, and by the Tenure of Office Act he was forbidden, except with the consent of the Senate, to remove civil officeholders whose original appointment had required Senate confirmation. Perhaps the latter measure was meant as a trap for the President, in whose opinion (and later also the Supreme Court's) it was unconstitutional; the only way he could test it was to violate it. For a long time Edwin M. Stanton, the Secretary of War whom Lincoln had appointed in part to appease the Radicals, had been a thorn in the flesh to Johnson. Finally, in the summer of 1867, Johnson suspended Stanton, and turned his office over to General Grant. But when the Senate, in January, 1868, refused to concur in the suspension, Grant weakly, and probably in disregard of an agreement with the President not to do so, allowed Stanton to resume his duties. Johnson now, in open defiance of the Tenure Act, removed Stanton from office, while Stanton, in his turn, defied the President's order and stayed on. The Radicals, thus presented with the opportunity they craved, acted with alacrity; the House brought the necessary impeachment charges to the Senate, and the Senate, sitting as a trial court with Salmon P. Chase (whom Lincoln had made Chief Justice) presiding, heard the case. Since the Republicans had more than the two-thirds majority necessary for a conviction, the Radicals were confident they would win, but seven Republicans risked their political lives to stand by the President. The case against him, as good lawyers knew, was not sound. There was grave doubt that the law was intended to apply to one of Lincoln's cabinet appointees whom Johnson had merely inherited, and that Congress had the right to limit the President's power of removal so drastically. The test vote, taken May 16, 1868, stood thirty-five to nineteen, to that the President kept his office by a single vote.

The anger of the Radicals at having failed to wreak their vengeance on the President was intense, the more so because some of them apparently had in mind a revolutionary change in the American system of government. What they desired was to challenge the established principle of equality between the three departments — executive, legislative, and judicial — and to promote instead the permanent supremacy of the legislative branch, as in the parliamentary system of England, where a hostile vote of Parliament could bring down a ministry at will. To achieve this goal they proposed to use the weapon of impeachment in a purely partisan way. If Congress by this process could remove a President with whom it disagreed, then the legislative branch could dominate the executive branch, instead of the other

The "Final Act of Republican Wrath" *against Johnson was his impeachment trial, for which spectators were admitted by ticket. The facsimile here presented is from* Harper's Weekly, *April 4, 1868.*

way round, as had happened under Lincoln, and as Johnson also had attempted. The Radical effort failed in this instance because seven Republican Senators chose to vote, not as partisans, but as judges. Their action confirmed the traditional view of impeachment as a judicial process, unsuitable for partisan purposes.

Congress and the Supreme Court

The Radicals also had in mind the disciplining of the Supreme Court, and had already scored heavily against it. An 1866 decision of the Court, *Ex parte Milligan,* condemned as illegal the trial of civilians by military courts in regions where the civil courts were open for business. Although this case came up with reference to the action of a military tribunal in Indiana during the war, the decision seemed to cast serious doubt upon the legality of any such structure of military rule as that which Congress, notwithstanding, soon proceeded to establish in the South. Furthermore, if this decision held, numerous important verdicts of military commissions had been illegal, among them the one that had resulted in the execution of four persons, including the innocent Mrs. Surratt, for conspiring to bring about the death of Abraham Lincoln, and another that had cost Henry Wirz the

Andersonville commandant, his life.

After the Milligan decision Radical denunciation of the Supreme Court went to violent extremes, and leading Republicans in Congress took thought as to how they might most effectively lessen its power. In July, 1866, they pushed through a law reducing the number of justices from nine to seven.[1] By providing that the next two vacancies among the associate justices should not be filled, they not only, in effect, reprimanded the Court, but they also diminished the danger that President Johnson might appoint any moderates to sit upon it. Two years later another measure, providing that, to set aside a law of Congress, a two-thirds majority of the justices should be required, passed the House, but was not brought to a vote in the Senate. Congress did provide, however, that the Supreme Court might not hear appeals from the lower courts in cases involving the right of *habeas corpus*. Reeling under these blows, the Court took pains to avoid as completely as possible all decisions that might offend Congress, although in the case of *Texas* vs. *White* (1869) it went on record as favoring the Johnson theory that the southern states, in spite of their acts of secession, had never legally ceased to exist.

"Thorough" Reconstruction

Meantime Congress had worked out in 1867 a second and more "thorough" plan of reconstruction, which wiped out as nearly as possible everything that Lincoln and Johnson had done, and started all over again. As an intended rebuke to the idea of "state perdurance," Congress divided the ten states involved into five military districts, over each of which it required the President to place a general. These mili-

---

[1] By an Act of March 3, 1863, Congress had raised the number of Supreme Court justices to ten, but Johnson's nominee to fill a vacancy which occurred early in 1865 was not confirmed by the Senate.

tary officers must then call for the election of a constitutional convention in each state, to be chosen by the male citizens "of whatever race, color, or previous condition," except such as were disfranchised by the Fourteenth Amendment. The convention must then frame a constitution granting the suffrage to male citizens "of whatever race, color, or previous condition," which would then be submitted to the same electorate for ratification. If this document should be approved by the people and by Congress, the state should then hold elections, and the newly chosen legislature must ratify the Fourteenth Amendment. With this process completed, the state might confidently expect readmission.

Negro Suffrage

The key to the new system of reconstruction was of course Negro suffrage. Only by possessing the right to vote, the Radicals argued, could the Negroes hope to defend themselves against white oppression. Many observers have questioned the wisdom of conferring so important a privilege upon the ex-slaves until their education was further along and their experience with freedom was greater. But how the freedmen, without the ballot, were ever to achieve an adequate education remains unresolved. What they really needed was economic and educational assistance on a scale that the Radicals were quite unprepared to provide, with the suffrage as the reward of achievement. Undoubtedly the nation would have profited greatly had congressional leaders thought more about the orderly tranformation of the South into a free society, and less about the speedy establishment of Radical governments in the southern states. But from the latter course the Radical leaders in Congress expected a greatly desired end, the indefinite perpetuation of their control over the national government. Perhaps a few of them were swayed by idealistic theories, but their actions revealed in the main the normal desire of politicians to stay in power. With numerous southern whites disfranchised, and with all the Negroes voting, there was every reason to suppose that the new electorates would be overwhelmingly Republican, and would send solidly Republican delegations to Congress.

Negro suffrage, immediately after the war, quite possibly would not have meant Republican rule in the South. At that time the Negroes, totally untutored in politics as they were, might have deferred to the judgment of their former masters, and voted accordingly. But in the two years since Appomattox new leaders, "carpetbaggers," "scalawags," and a few native Negroes, had arisen to teach the ex-slaves the meaning of freedom.

The Carpetbaggers

The "carpetbaggers" were northerners who had come South after the war, sometimes with all their worldly possessions crammed into a single "carpetbag," hence the name. Prominent among these newcomers were many minor officials of the Freedmen's Bureau, who as time went on all too frequently turned their attention from benevolence to politics, and became ardent supporters of Radical policies. Their ranks were reinforced by other governmental agents, army officers, missionaries both religious and educational, adventurers seeking new worlds to conquer in agriculture, business, or politics, and a few northern Negroes. The carpetbaggers were not all bad nor all good, but their very presence made them suspect to a majority of the southern whites. They were very likely to be members of the Union League, a northern order created in 1862 to counter "Copperhead" activities, but devoted after the war mainly to indoctrinating the southern Negroes with Radical propaganda. The Republican Party, Union Leaguers maintained, had freed the slaves, and was entitled to the freedmen's political support; only by

The First Vote. *This drawing by A. R. Waud, 1867, shows Negroes going to the polls in their first state election. They took understandable pride in exercising this right, and were far less to blame for the excesses of carpetbag rule than the whites who influenced them.*

voting Republican could they hope to escape re-enslavement. Armed with an attractive ritual, and often also with army or Freedmen's Bureau supplies, the Union League Clubs were extraordinarily successful in winning the Negroes to the Radical cause.

The Scalawags

The "scalawags" were southerners who cooperated with the Radicals. They were not all drawn from the "scaly scum" of southern society, nor motivated only, as their opponents claimed, by hope of office or of private gain. Some of them, no doubt, answered to this description, but others were ex-Whigs who shared the businessman's point of view so prevalent among the northern Radicals, and were quite as distrustful of Democratic leadership as they had been before the war. Instinctively they

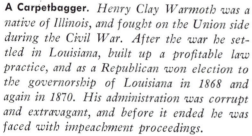

A Carpetbagger. *Henry Clay Warmoth was a native of Illinois, and fought on the Union side during the Civil War. After the war he settled in Louisiana, built up a profitable law practice, and as a Republican won election to the governorship of Louisiana in 1868 and again in 1870. His administration was corrupt and extravagant, and before it ended he was faced with impeachment proceedings.*

A Scalawag. *William W. Holden was a North Carolinian who cooled toward the Confederacy during the war, and became in 1865 one of Johnson's provisional governors. In 1868, as a supporter of the whole radical program, he was elected governor, but the partisan excesses of his administration made him so unpopular that later a Democratic legislature impeached and removed him from office.*

favored a program of political and economic conciliation. Still others acknowledged the futility of offering resistance to any policy the North chose to adopt. As one prominent Mississippian pointed out, "We have nothing to do but submit." For these or similar reasons many "respectable, intelligent, realistic southerners" deemed it wiser to collaborate with the Radicals than to fight them. Scalawags of this type hoped to act as a restraining influence within Radical circles, to help prepare the Negroes for their new civic responsibilities, and to avert further disorder.

Negro Leaders

The native Negro leaders were mostly pre-Civil War freedmen who had long occupied a recognized place in the southern social structure. Some of them owned property, and some had acquired enough education to enable them to understand reasonably well the unfolding political situation. They were more numerous than most northerners supposed, but they were probably less influential with the more recently freed slaves than the carpetbaggers and the scalawags, for Negro deference to white superiority was of long standing and hard to eradicate. Under the intense pressure of this new leadership, the great mass of the Negroes tended to believe as they were taught, that the Republican Party had freed them, and that to keep their freedom they must vote Republican at every opportunity. Thanks to the carefully devised provisions of the second congressional plan and to the protective presence of northern troops in the South, the Negro often found it easier to vote as the Radicals wished him to vote than to abstain from voting.

Carpetbag Rule

Down to the time that the new electorates took over in 1867, reconstruction in the South had proceeded without undue tension. Military government was usually efficient in keeping order, and even when locally elected civilian officials disagreed with their military overlords, and were removed from office, the effect on the ordinary citizen was likely to be insignificant. The Lincoln and Johnson governments had built upon such remnants of the former secessionist governments as they found in existence, and the military authorities who administered the second congressional plan had made similar use of the Johnson governments. But when the new constitutions were drawn and went into effect, the control of state government in the South passed from the hands of the more conservative southern whites into the hands of the carpetbaggers, the scalawags, and such Negroes as were able to participate. White Radicals, regardless of the number of the Negro delegates, dominated every constitutional convention, and wrote their views into every new constitution. These included, besides complete civil and political equality for Negroes with whites, many provisions aimed at social equality, and many provisions, borrowed from northern constitutions, that greatly improved the antiquated systems of taxation and finance, and of local and judicial administration, that had prevailed in the Old South. Also, the new constitutions tended to liberalize the legal status of women, to accept the principle of protecting homesteads up to a certain minimum value against creditors, and to provide for free educational systems such as few Southern states had ever

had. For this latter innovation the Negro delegates were far more than passively responsible.

Radicals vs. Conservatives

The issue of adoption or rejection of the new constitutions drew a political line in the South that had long been on the way. Before the war southern whites had divided on politics between Whigs and Democrats, or when the Whigs faded out, between Know-Nothings, or Americans, or Constitutional Unionists, and Democrats. Immediately after the war, to avoid the memory of past differences, some southerners made use of the designation Conservatives, in opposition to the Radicals, whose views they so greatly feared. But as time went on most of the southern whites tended, whatever their prewar affiliations, to accept the Democratic label. Their best friends in the North were Democrats, and their worst enemies everywhere were the Republicans, now almost completely dominated by the Radicals. Opposed to the Democratic Party in the South was the carpetbagger-scalawag-Negro combination that had not only framed the new constitutions, but now also voted for their ratification, and under their provisions elected governors, legislatures, and other officials to carry on the business of government. While the terms Radical and Conservative long persisted in the South, Radical became virtually synonymous with Republican, and Conservative with Democrat.

The struggle to delay the day of carpetbag rule lasted longer in some of the southern states than in others, and sometimes required the direct intervention of Congress. In Alabama, for example, when the new Radical constitution failed to secure a majority of the registered voters, as the law originally required, Congress reversed its former stand by decreeing that a majority of those voting would be sufficient. Also, to insure the general eligibility to

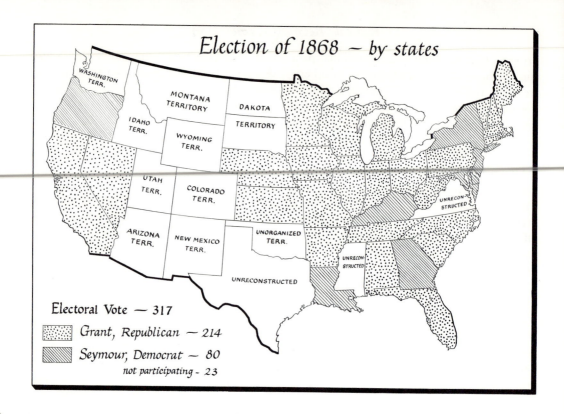

Election of 1868 — by states

WASHINGTON TERR.

MONTANA TERRITORY

DAKOTA TERRITORY

IDAHO TERR.

WYOMING TERR.

UTAH TERR.

COLORADO TERR.

ARIZONA TERR.

NEW MEXICO TERR.

UNORGANIZED TERR.

UNRECONSTRUCTED

UNRECON-STRUCTED

UNRECON-STRUCTED

Electoral Vote — 317

Grant, Republican — 214

Seymour, Democrat — 80

not participating - 23

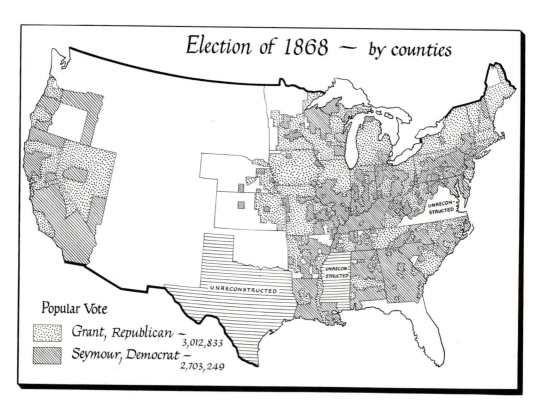

Election of 1868 — by counties

UNRECON-STRUCTED

UNRECONSTRUCTED

UNRECON-STRUCTED

Popular Vote

Grant, Republican ~ 3,012,833

Seymour, Democrat ~ 2,703,249

vote of the Negroes, who had a habit of wandering from place to place, Congress decided that residence anywhere for a period of ten days prior to an election was adequate, and that, if the voter happened to have lost his certification of registration, he might by affadavit, or "other satisfactory evidence," establish his right to cast his ballot. The first state to complete the process of "thorough" reconstruction was Arkansas, which Congress readmitted in June, 1868, and the last was Georgia, readmitted for a second time in July, 1870. (Georgia, after readmission in 1868, had expelled all Negroes from the legislature, and in consequence was again remanded by Congress to military rule.) All but three southern states, Virginia, Mississippi, and Texas, participated in the election of 1868, and all but two of them, Louisiana and Georgia, voted Republican.

Election of 1868

In the election of 1868 the Republicans nominated the apparently popular General Grant for President, and Schuyler Colfax of Indiana, a dependable Radical, for Vice-President. The Democrats might logically have nominated President Johnson as their candidate to succeed himself, for they had made his attitude toward reconstruction their own.[1] But they passed him by for Horatio Seymour of New York, and chose for Vice-President, Francis P. Blair, Jr., of Missouri. Democratic flirtation with the "Ohio idea," a "soft-money" scheme advocated by George H. Pendleton, an Ohio Democrat, for the payment of the national debt in greenbacks, failed to win Seymour's support, but tended to confirm the business world of the North in its adherence to the Republican Party. The Republican campaign involved much "waving of the bloody shirt," as blaming the South for the

[1] Johnson served again as United States Senator from Tennessee, from March, 1875, until the time of his death the following July.

war was usually called, and much denunciation of the Democratic Party as the party of treason and rebellion. With so many southern states legislated into the Republican column, Grant won an easy triumph in the electoral college, 214 to 80, although his margin of victory in many northern states was surprisingly narrow. By this time Grant had gone wholeheartedly over to the Radicals, and his election was expected to end the deadlock between the President and Congress, in both houses of which the Radicals retained control.

The importance of Negro voting in the election came as something of a surprise, even to the Radicals. Grant's popular majority, which was only about 300,000, was made possible by some 450,000 Negro ballots; a majority of the nation's white voters opposed him. In Congress, also, the Republican majority now contained many carpetbaggers and scalawags, and a few Negroes. Local offices in the newly reconstructed states showed a similar composition, with the Radical whites absorbing for themselves most of the important offices, and leaving only the less consequential for the Negroes. But viewed from any angle, Radical reconstruction rested upon the foundation of Negro voting. Fully conscious of this situation, Congress, in February, 1869, submitted to the states for ratification the Fifteenth Amendment, which forbade the states to deny or abridge the right to vote "on account of race, color, or previous condition of servitude." Furthermore, states still undergoing reconstruction must ratify this Amendment as a condition of readmission. Thirteen months later the Amendment was declared in force.

Grant and the Supreme Court

It took Grant some time as President to adjust to the ways of the political world, and during his term of office the Presidency never at any time really offered a threat to the leadership of Congress. On

reconstruction he was a willing tool of the legislative branch, and backed it up in every extreme. As rapidly as possible he replaced Johnson's appointees in the South with uncompromising Radicals; even the federal judges he chose displayed unbecoming zeal in furthering the Radical cause. If the President during these years was no match for Congress, neither was the Supreme Court. When Grant became President Congress raised the number of justices again to nine, with results that the famous Legal Tender Cases soon made apparent. These cases involved the constitutionality of the Civil War legislation making greenback issues legal tender for the payment of debts. Before Grant's appointees took office, the Supreme Court in a split decision, *Hepburn* vs. *Griswold* (1870), had held that the Legal Tender Acts of 1862 and 1863, in so far as they concerned the fulfillment of contracts entered into *before* their passage, were unconstitu-

tional. But the very next year the two new judges that Grant had chosen joined with the minority in the Hepburn case to reverse this decision, and to hold that the Legal Tender Acts were justifiable under the emergency power of the government, and were therefore valid in every respect. The new decision was far more palatable to the Radicals than the one it supplanted, but the Court's quick reversal, seemingly under political pressure, of a stand it had just taken, detracted seriously from its prestige.

Carpetbag Innovations

As for the newly reconstructed governments of the southern states, they rested frankly on federal bayonets; only the presence of Union troops, acting under the President's orders, enabled them to survive against the overwhelming majority of the native whites. Carpetbaggers and scalawags, to a greater or lesser degree, were everywhere in control; it is a complete misnomer to speak of "Negro rule." Only two states, South Carolina and Louisiana, ever had Negro majorities in their legislatures, and here as elsewhere the freedmen were dominated by their new white leaders. What the new governments did was by no means all evil. Following out the provisions of the new constitutions, they made many useful administrative innovations, and they sought to better the lot of the ordinary man, whether Negro or white. They gave generous support to the cause of public education; they redistributed the tax burden with an eye to the welfare of the less well-to-do; they provided perhaps more amply than their resources justified for poor relief; and they replaced as rapidly as possible the public buildings, roads, and bridges that the war had left in ruins.

Corruption in the South

The worst aspect of "alien rule," as the South called the new regimes, lay in the venality of many of the white leaders who had come to power. Reconstruction governments piled up extravagant debts for later generations to deal with, and the money they borrowed far too frequently went in large part to enrich corruptionists. Faithless officials sold state and municipal bonds at a fraction of their value; they backed with public credit dubious or frankly dishonest financial enterprises, railroad and otherwise; they levied upon landowners taxes so burdensome as greatly to depreciate land values; and they often showed as great disdain for personal as for property rights. Some of the states organized Negro militia, which in general served more to promote than to quell violence and disorder. But blame for the excesses of Radical reconstruction rests far less upon the Negroes than upon the white carpetbaggers and scalawags who misled them, and upon the majority in Congress that sponsored the system. Some blame must go also to the irreconcilable attitude of most Southern

whites, and to the "spirit of the times" that gave so little quarter to reason. The freedmen, encouraged by their new leaders to believe

> De bottom rail's on de top,
> An' we's gwine to keep it dar,

eventually found themselves at the bottom again, and obliged to pay a heavy penalty for the misdeeds of others. Negro legislators and officials were sometimes guilty of ridiculous and childlike behavior, but these faults were of little moment in comparison with the very real crimes of those who betrayed them.

In extenuation, if the term is not too generous, it should be said that the reconstruction period was one of gross corruption, North as well as South. There was little that the carpetbaggers and scalawags did wrong that could not be duplicated elsewhere. The Tweed Ring, which operated in New York City during the very years that Radical reconstruction was doing its worst in the South, took from the taxpayers of the nation's greatest city an estimated $100 million in loot.

The Grant Scandals

The scandals of the Grant administration were similarly devastating. The infamous "gold conspiracy," engineered in 1869 by two speculators, Jay Gould and James Fisk, was actually accomplished with the effective, although unintended, assistance of the President himself. While gold coin did not then circulate as money, it was constantly in demand for such needs as the payment of customs duties and the adjustment of international trade balances. The government of the United States, although not on the gold standard, constantly received large quantities of gold into the Treasury, and from time to time the Secretary of the Treasury was accustomed to sell enough gold to satisfy the normal demands of trade.

It occurred to Gould, who already controlled large stores of gold, that if the government would only stop its sales of gold for a while he might "corner" the country's supply, drive the price to a fancy figure, and so make a huge profit. Gould therefore managed, through one of Grant's numerous brood of unsavory relatives, to meet the President from time to time, and even to win his confidence. On one such occasion he set forth at length a fine-spun theory to the effect that it would be a great help for western farm prices if the government should cease its sales of gold. Grant naïvely fell for this talk, and presently, even before the order had been given, Gould learned through his confederate, Grant's relative, that the President was about to stop the Treasury from selling gold. Immediately Gould began his activities, but, finding his own resources inadequate for the undertaking, he invited into the speculation his ally, Fisk, who not only bought heavily, but, in order to induce others to buy, spread the false story that the President himself and all his political friends were in on the deal. Between Monday, September 20, and "Black Friday," September 24, the price of gold rose from 140 to 163½. Then the Secretary of the Treasury, under emergency orders from the President, announced the sale of government gold, and the price came down. In the meantime, however, many legitimate businesses had been disastrously affected, and the stock exchange had experienced a violent panic.

There was a scandal, too, connected with the Union Pacific Railroad, which Congress

Our Modern Belshazzar. *This is an English cartoon by Matt Morgan bitterly censuring the morality of Grant and his aides. Roscoe Conkling is pouring and the President is receiving.*

had chartered in 1862 to build the eastern half of the first great transcontinental line, providing for the purpose a heavy subsidy in government bonds and government lands. The Crédit Mobilier was a construction company, which consisted of the principal Union Pacific officials. As Union Pacific stockholders they voted the Crédit Mobilier, which they also owned, enormously profitable contracts, but to insure that the government subsidies would keep coming they offered Crédit Mobilier stock to members of Congress on bargain terms. Many prominent congressmen, and the Vice-President also, accepted this ill-concealed bribe. A similar company, organized by the Central Pacific Railroad, which was charged with the building of the western half of the same transcontinental, was equally lucrative, but did not involve members of Congress. The new road to the Pacific, completed in 1869, was a great asset to the nation, but the profits taken by its builders were notoriously excessive.[1]

These were only a beginning; there were other "Grant scandals," such as the Sanborn contracts, by which the Treasury Department allowed a 50 per cent commission to a favored contractor for the collection of back taxes; and the Whiskey Ring, which defrauded the government of millions of dollars in excise taxes on liquor; and the Salary Grab Act, by which Congress in March, 1873, voted its members an additional $2,500 a year, with back pay for two years; and wholesale graft in the Indian Service, where, for example, one Indian trader who was making a good thing of his post sought to keep it by paying a stipulated sum each year to the wife of the Secretary of War. And it may safely be assumed that for every fraud exposed many others occurred that were never made public, while for every dishonest act that involved government there were hundreds

[1] See pp. 110–112.

that did not. Thus the crimes committed by the reconstruction governments in the South were quite in keeping with the peculations that so generally disgraced the times. There was this difference, however. The South was being victimized to a large extent by outsiders, and the resentment its people felt was the greater because the misdeeds were associated with "alien rule."

The Ku Klux Klan

Republican hopes of building up in the ex-Confederate states a new and dependable wing of the party were soon doomed to disappointment. The first substantial successes of the southern opponents of congressional reconstruction came with the activities of the Ku Klux Klan, a secret order that grew up in the South after the war, and made its influence felt by vigilante methods. Members of the Klan wore white gowns and hoods which both concealed their identity and struck terror to the hearts of many Negroes. Operating mainly at night, gangs of Klansmen beat up Negro militiamen, terrorized freedmen who had the temerity to vote, broke up Union League meetings, and committeed innumerable other depredations designed to discourage alien rule and Negro equality. The Klan was widely imitated by similar orders, while its methods and disguises were freely utilized by bands of ruffians who belonged to no order, and knew no restraint — whippings, fiendish torture, and outright murder, particularly of Negroes, became all too common. Alarmed at these excesses, the Klan leaders sought as early as 1869 to disband the order, but they had little control over the forces they had unleashed.

Finally Congress felt obliged to take a hand. A series of Enforcement Acts, passed in 1870 and 1871, condemned as crimes the various activities for which the Klan and its imitators were held responsible, and provided drastic punishment for

TERRORISM. Klan members stealing a victim's crop. Woodcut. 1880.

POLITICAL SIGNIFICANCE. Cartoon branding the 1868 Democratic ticket with KKK initials. *Harper's Weekly*, 1868.

KU KLUX KLAN. *This secret organization terrorized many Negro and carpetbag voters, and helped the southern whites regain control of their state and local governments.*

their perpetrators. Grant enforced these laws vigorously, even suspending the writ of *habeas corpus* in certain areas, as Congress had authorized him to do, and using federal troops to see that federal courts were unmolested because of unpopular decisions. As a consequence, vigilante activities diminished greatly, but the Negro votes on which the reconstruction governments depended were thereafter less certain to be cast. Congress also appointed a committee, generally known as the Ku Klux Klan Committee, to investigate what was going on in the South. This Committee through extensive hearings not only succeeded in revealing the iniquities of those who opposed the will of Congress in the South, but also, quite unintentionally, brought to light the complaints of the southerners. Widely publicized in the newspapers, and printed eventually in twelve large volumes, the hearing brought home to northerners, almost for the first time, the true plight of the South under carpetbag-scalawag-Negro rule, and prepared the way for reform.

The Redemption Movement

Gradually, even with federal troops standing guard, the native whites of the South who opposed Radical reconstruction began to take over. This "Redemption movement," as it was sometimes called, found ways short of physical violence to persuade the Negroes not to vote; trickery, bribery, and economic pressure proved in many cases to be quite as effective as physical intimidation, and Negro ballots were not always counted. Radical propaganda among the Negroes, which often involved many unfulfilled promises, also wore thin, and the southern Radicals, sensing that their day was about done, fell to quarreling among themselves. Of great aid to the Redeemers was the growing demand in the North for a more generous treatment of the defeated South. Even Congress felt obliged in 1872 to pass an Amnesty Act, which restored the voting privileges of nearly all ex-Confederates. Thereafter in state after state the Democrats took over the offices from the Republicans, made life so uncomfortable for the carpetbaggers that most of them got out, absorbed great numbers of more-or-less repentant scalawags into the "white man's party," and shattered Negro hopes for social and political equality. Federal troops might hold off this eventuality for a time, but not indefinitely, and their removal invariably meant the doom of "thorough" reconstruction. The "solid South," at which the Radicals had connived, did indeed materialize, but it turned out to be a Democratic, not a Republican, "solid South."

The New Departure

Time was soon to prove that some of the Redeemers had other objectives than merely the restoration of home rule and white supremacy in the South. Among them were many former Henry Clay Whigs who were primarily interested in the pro-

motion of industry and commerce, and looked forward eagerly to cooperation with northern capitalists in such profitable enterprises as the construction of new railroads and the building up of southern manufacture. Once in power they showed as little regard for the less-well-to-do whites as for the now largely disfranchised Negroes; they cheerfully lowered taxes levied by the Radicals to support better school systems and other social services; they allowed the southern school term to fall off in length by 20 per cent; and they showed little concern that illiteracy, which had begun to decline, tended as a result of their policies to increase steadily until the beginning of the twentieth century. They also promoted state constitutional changes that substituted easily-controlled appointive for elective officials, and they gerrymandered election districts in such a way as to reduce materially the representation

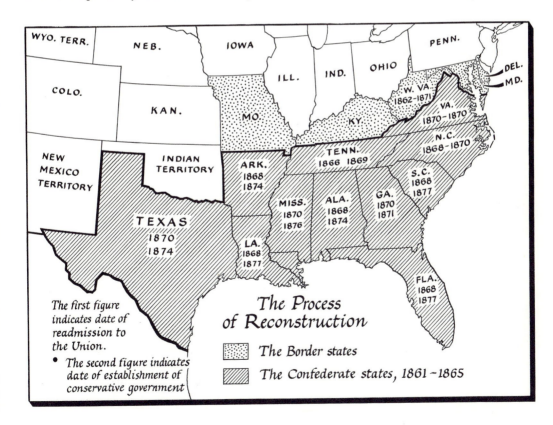

The first figure indicates date of readmission to the Union.

• The second figure indicates date of establishment of conservative government

The Process of Reconstruction

The Border states

The Confederate states, 1861–1865

of the poorer white farming communities. Simultaneously they gave railroads and other business enterprises preferential treatment, including low taxes and freedom from state regulation. For a while this business-minded movement, which was sometimes called "the New Departure," and sometimes, less accurately, "Bourbon rule," carried all before it, but its reactionary character greatly disturbed many southerners, and paved the way for a vigorous protest later. Nevertheless, in deference to the real, or fancied, need for white solidarity, the South presented for many years the appearance of solidarity, and settled its differences within the framework of the Democratic Party.

Liberal Republicanism

When time came for the election of 1872, the opposition to Radical reconstruction that had long permeated the Democratic Party had reached over also into

Horace Greeley, *eccentric editor of the* New York Tribune, *had little chance in 1872 to defeat the still-popular war hero, President Grant. Greeley's unusual appearance and his contradictory record made him an easy prey for Republican cartoonists and journalists.*

Republican ranks. There the reformers, in order to distinguish themselves from the Radicals, adopted the designation "Liberals," and even threatened to leave the Republican Party altogether if they could not convert it to their point of view. The Liberal movement began in Missouri as an attack on the rabidly anti-southern provisions of a state constitution adopted in 1865, and in the elections of 1870 it won substantial victories. Many prominent citizens helped to make Liberal Republicanism national, among them Carl Schurz, who became United States Senator from Missouri, Horace Greeley, editor of the powerful *New York Tribune*, and Charles Francis Adams, Lincoln's minister to Great Britain during the Civil War. With some Liberals, opposition to "Grantism" went much further than mere denunciation of the administration's southern policy. Civil service reformers hoped for the day when appointments would be made on merit, and tariff reformers were determined that through Liberal auspices they should scale down the unreasonably high protective duties that had lasted on after the Civil War. A good many Liberals, moreover, were opposed to the increasing and often corrupt connection between big business and government, and hoped for the end of government subservience to business.

Election of 1872

Unable to dent the hard shell of Radical Republicanism, the Liberals determined in the election of 1872 to go it alone, with such Democratic support as they could muster. But the convention they held in Cincinnati, May 1, 1872, unfortunately chose Horace Greeley as the Liberal Republican candidate for the Presidency, a mistake unrectified by the nomination of the relatively unknown B. Gratz Brown of Missouri for Vice-President. Greeley was a firm believer in high tariffs, and to please him the Liberal tariff plank had to be made

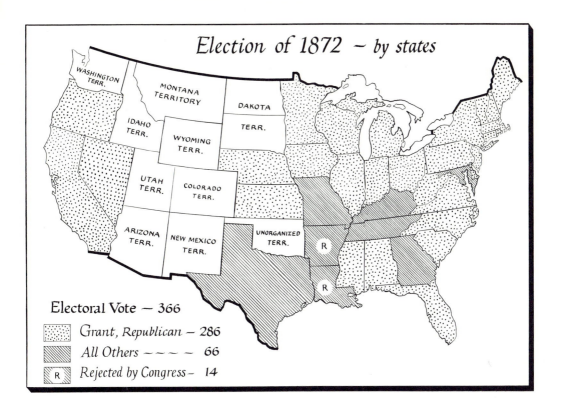

Election of 1872 – by states

Electoral Vote – 366

- Grant, Republican – 286
- All Others ~ ~ ~ ~ 66
- R Rejected by Congress – 14

WASHINGTON TERR.

MONTANA TERRITORY

DAKOTA TERR.

IDAHO TERR.

WYOMING TERR.

UTAH TERR.

COLORADO TERR.

ARIZONA TERR.

NEW MEXICO TERR.

UNORGANIZED TERR.

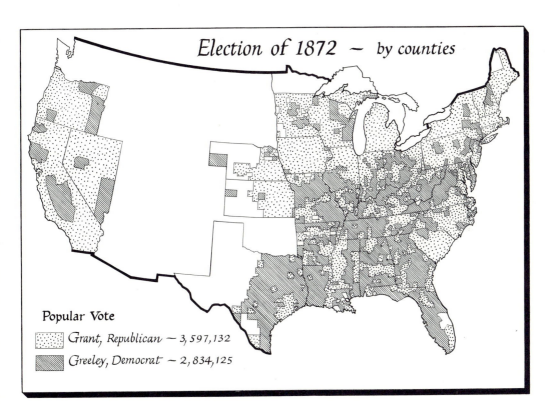

Election of 1872 – by counties

Popular Vote

- Grant, Republican – 3,597,132
- Greeley, Democrat – 2,834,125

thoroughly innocuous; further, he was a life-long enemy of the Democratic Party, for the support of which the Liberals meant to bid. He had, to be sure, signed Jefferson Davis's bail bond, when the former President of the Confederacy was under arrest for treason, and he had been outspoken in his criticism of Radical reconstruction. And so the Democrats, with what grace they could muster, accepted the Liberal Republican candidates, and endorsed the Liberal platform, which on the treatment of the defeated South echoed views they had long expressed.

The Republicans, of course, renominated Grant, but they dropped Colfax for second place on the ticket in favor of Henry Wilson of Massachusetts. At the time of the election most of the scandals that were later associated wtih the Grant regime had not yet come to light, and there were those who believed that "To doubt Grant is to doubt Christ." Moreover, Greeley's many idiosyncrasies made him an easy target for Republican campaigners, and for the Republican cartoonist, Thomas Nast, who heaped every ridicule upon him. In the election Greeley carried only two states from the lower South, Georgia and Texas, and four of the border states, Missouri, Tennessee, Maryland, and Kentucky. Three weeks after the election, and before the electoral votes were counted, Greeley died, thus leaving the electoral count in much confusion, but Congress awarded 286 votes to Grant and Wilson, and 66 to all other combinations. Returns from Arkansas and Louisiana were rejected. The Liberal Republican Party did not long survive its disastrous defeat, although its ideas lived on and ultimately leavened both older parties. What the results of the election of 1872 might have been had the Liberal Republicans and the Democrats agreed on a candidate, one can only guess; as it was, undoubtedly many disappointed adherents of both factions failed to vote.

Election of 1876

Despite the Republican triumph, Radical reconstruction was soon on the rocks. The Grant scandals began to come out, one after another, to the great chagrin of even the most devoted Republicans. Worse still, the Panic of 1873 dried up the abounding prosperity that the North, if not the South, had enjoyed since the war, and for five long years hard times gripped the nation.[1] In the midterm election of 1874 the Democrats scored notable victories, winning the ascendancy in nine northern and five southern states, and taking easy control of the national House of Representatives. Fearful of a complete Democratic triumph in 1876, the agonized Republican leaders sought to draw the Liberals back into the party ranks by nominating for the Presidency that year a moderate of unimpeachable integrity, Rutherford B. Hayes, for three terms governor of Ohio; while the Democrats, equally desirous of attracting Liberal voters, chose as their candidate Samuel J. Tilden of New York, who had achieved political eminence by successfully prosecuting the Tweed Ring in New York City, and in consequence had won election to the governorship of his state in 1874. Disappointed factions in each party took what comfort they could from their respective nominees for Vice-President. For this office the Republicans chose William A. Wheeler of New York, a dependable but obscure Radical, while the Democrats, aware that Tilden was no less conservative on the money question than Hayes, chose Thomas A. Hendricks of Indiana, a soft-money man, and an ex-Copperhead. Extremists on the money question gave their votes to a new Independent, or "Greenback," Party, which favored expansion of the currency by the issue of more paper money, and supported the candidacies of

[1] See pp. 114–117.

Peter Cooper of New York for President and Samuel F. Cary of Ohio for Vice-President. Most voters, however, even if they held soft-money views, were too enthralled by the main contest to take the Greenbackers seriously.

The Disputed Returns

By the time the election was held, the supremacy of the carpetbaggers had been overthrown in all but three of the southern states, South Carolina, Louisiana, and Florida. It was known in advance that every other southern state would vote for Tilden, and on the evening of election day, November 7, it appeared that these states, too, were safely in the Democratic column. Since New York and several other northern states had gone Democratic, the election of Tilden seemed assured. But the Republican leaders, confident that they could correct the conduct of the three carpetbag states, claimed that these states had in reality voted for Hayes and Wheeler, who would thus have 185 electoral votes to their opponents' 184. Eventually, after much dubious activity on both sides, rival Democratic and Republican canvassing boards provided double returns from each of the three states, while to confuse the situation further conflicting returns came also from Oregon, where the Democratic governor had adjudged one of the Republican electors to be ineligible. This was the confused result that came to Congress after the meeting of the electors in their various state capitals on December 6, 1876. Who was now to decide which votes to count? According to the Constitution, the President of the Senate, in the presence of the Senate and the House of Representatives, shall "open all the certificates and the votes shall then be counted." Counted by whom? If by the President of the Senate, then he, being a Republican, could count Hayes in. If by the two houses separately, there would be a tie, for the Senate was Republican and the House was Democratic. If by a majority of the Senators and Representatives voting as individuals, then the Democrats would probably win. If under the "twenty-second joint rule," which had been in force from 1864 to 1874, but had not been re-adopted by the current Congress, then either house might reject a certificate, and pure chaos could result. Partisan anger grew ominously, and on both sides there was talk of resort to force.

The Electoral Commission

The situation called clearly for a compromise, and Congress after weeks of wrangling rose to the occasion. To rule on the returns it created by a law of January 29, 1877, an Electoral Commission of fifteen members, five each to be chosen from the Senate, the House, and the Supreme Court. It was agreed in advance that the congressional members should be equally divided between the two parties, while two Republican and two Democratic justices, named in the bill, would choose the fifth justice, probably David Davis of Illinois, whose party loyalties were somewhat obscure. But a Democratic-Greenbacker combination in the Illinois legislature, by electing Davis to the United States Senate while the Electoral Commission bill was before Congress, lost Tilden whatever chance he had of becoming President. Davis maintained that as Senator-elect he was ineligible to serve on the Commission, and since the remaining members of the Supreme Court were all Republicans, the Commission, as finally constituted, had a dependable eight to seven Republican majority. By counting all disputed returns for Hayes, it insured his election. There was so much fraud and intimidation in the three southern states whose votes were in doubt that it is difficult to determine what their electorates wanted to do, but recent students of the subject

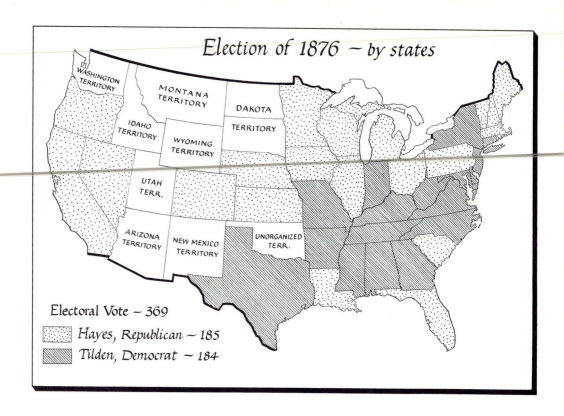

Election of 1876 — by states

WASHINGTON TERRITORY
MONTANA TERRITORY
DAKOTA TERRITORY
IDAHO TERRITORY
WYOMING TERRITORY
UTAH TERR.
ARIZONA TERRITORY
NEW MEXICO TERRITORY
UNORGANIZED TERR.

Electoral Vote — 369

Hayes, Republican — 185

Tilden, Democrat — 184

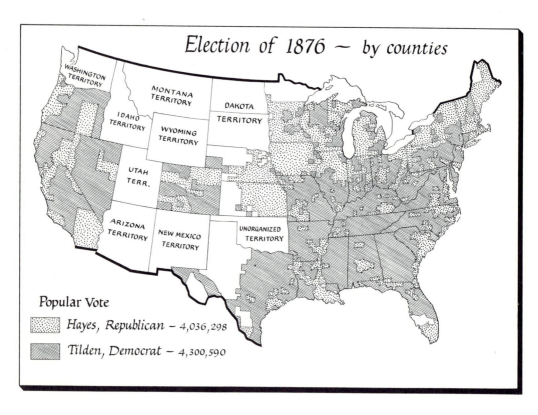

Election of 1876 — by counties

WASHINGTON TERRITORY
MONTANA TERRITORY
DAKOTA TERRITORY
IDAHO TERRITORY
WYOMING TERRITORY
UTAH TERR.
ARIZONA TERRITORY
NEW MEXICO TERRITORY
UNORGANIZED TERRITORY

Popular Vote

Hayes, Republican — 4,036,298

Tilden, Democrat — 4,300,590

tend to agree that the votes of Florida should have gone to Tilden, who, on the basis of the votes cast, was counted out. But this ignores the fraud and violence practised elsewhere in the South by the Redeemers. In the popular vote the Democratic plurality, the nation over, was more than 250,000, even by the Republican count; the new House of Representatives was safely Democratic; and the new Senate was Republican by so slender a margin that the "wavering vote" of David Davis often held the balance of power. The former justice, one wit noted, had transferred his rather considerable bulk "from the bench to the fence."

The final acceptance by Congress of the Commission's verdict did not come until four o'clock on the morning of Friday, March 2, with the formal inauguration of Hayes set for the following Monday, March 5. The reason for this delay was a long-drawn-out filibuster, conducted by southern Democrats in the House, with the object, ostensibly, of forcing certain concessions from the incoming administration. To work out the terms of a deal, so the story goes, Democratic and Republican politicians held a protracted conference at the Wormley Hotel in Washington, and agreed that Hayes might assume the Presidency, on condition that he should end alien rule in the South. This he would assure by withdrawing federal troops from Louisiana and South Carolina, thus permitting the Democrats to take over the state offices in each. (By this time Florida was already in Democratic hands.) The Democrats, in return for these concessions, promised further that the new state governments would take no bloody reprisals against their opponents, and would safeguard the rights of the Negroes.

Compromise of 1877

But in point of fact these terms were an oversimpification of a much broader deal that had been long in the making, and that has sometimes been called the "Compromise of 1877." The country as a whole was weary of the sectional controversy, and ready for a settlement similar in scope to those achieved by the Compromises of 1820 and 1850. Certain elements within both parties and in both sections found the task of reaching such an agreement not too difficult. Among the southerners many ex-Whigs and "New Departure" Democrats shared the business principles of the leading eastern Republicans, and had little in common with other Democrats. These conservatives were far less interested in putting a Democrat into the White House than in obtaining substantial economic favors for their section and class. During the campaign Hayes had expressed his willingness to withdraw federal troops from the South, and everyone knew that any such action would mean the end of thorough reconstruction and the rights of the southern Negroes. As a reminder to the new President on this matter, however, Congress had failed to make the customary appropriations for the army, so that during the early months of the Hayes administration the enlisted officers and men did not receive their pay. Many reputable southerners stood ready to concede Hayes the Presidency if, in addition to the overthrow of the carpetbaggers, he would also guarantee them a reasonable share of patronage appointments, a seat or two in his cabinet, generous support for the public works the South so desperately needed, and aid to the southern railroads, particularly to the projected Texas and Pacific transcontinental. Southern business interests had come to look with especial favor on this railroad, chartered in 1871 but in deep trouble after the Panic of 1873. They supported ardently a bill then before Congress granting additional assistance to the railroad, a measure that Tilden openly opposed, but Hayes seemed to favor. Well before the Wormley conference conservative northern Republicans and conservative southern Democrats had reached a meeting of minds. In exchange for the favors indicated, Hayes could have the Presidency, and perhaps even the support of an intersectional coalition that would enable the Republican minority in the House of Representatives to organize that body with James A. Garfield as speaker. This was the well-understood deal that made Hayes President, and for which the Wormley conference served only as window dressing.

The inauguration of Hayes, in consequence, took place without incident. Fortunately Tilden was opposed to violence, and took his betrayal calmly. Throughout the tense situation the American people held their peace; and they accepted the decision, when it came, whether they liked it or not. The inside terms of the settlement were not made known, but it did not take much perspicacity to see that the Republicans had got the Presidency, and the southern whites had got "home rule," including, for better or for worse, the determination of what rights the Negroes might have.

The Compromise of 1877 was carried out in considerable part. Hayes chose as his Postmaster-General a southern Democrat, David M. Key, an ex-Confederate officer who had succeeded Andrew Johnson as Senator from Tennessee. Key saw to it that about one-third of the appointments to postmasterships in the South went to Democrats, while the President in making other southern appointments also pursued a bipartisan policy. After some hesitation, which tried southern patience, Hayes ordered to their barracks federal troops protecting the carpetbag governments of South Carolina and Louisiana. Thereupon the Democratic "Redeemers" took over in both states, and received official recognition. The Louisiana decision was particularly difficult for Hayes, since the local Republican candidate for governor had actually received a larger majority than the Republican electors whose votes had seated Hayes. The President took his time about calling a special session of Congress to deliver on the public works and railroad commitments. With reference to the former, Congress was less generous than the South had hoped, although, notably, appropriations for Louisiana during the fiscal year 1877–1878 were greater than for any other state, north or south. As for the Texas and Pacific bill, Hayes belatedly began to fear another set of Crédit Mobilier scandals, and Congress did nothing. Nor did Garfield win the speakership.

Negro Rights Ignored

Implicit in this compromise arrangement, as noted, was Republican abandonment of further responsibility for the Negro as the ward of the nation. Congress had, and still has, full authority to enforce the Fourteenth and Fifteenth Amendments "by appropriate legislation," but the majorities necessary to continue the effort were no longer available. The power of the Freedmen's Bureau diminished rapidly after 1869, so that the Negro could not look to that organization for help. The withdrawal of federal troops, upon whose support the carpetbag governments had depended, finished the process of taking the national government completely out of the interracial picture. Thereafter the freedmen and their descendants were at the mercy of the new state governments set up by the Redeemers. Finally, in 1883, the Supreme Court of the United States ruled in the Civil Rights cases that the restrictions of the Fourteenth Amendment applied to states only, and could not be used to restrain individuals or organizations from conduct designed to enforce social discriminations against the Negroes, thus opening the way to every kind of "Jim Crowism." Negro voting was sometimes tolerated,

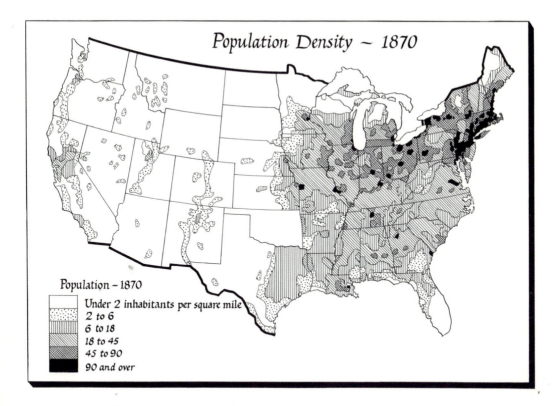

Population Density ~ 1870

Population ~ 1870

	Under 2 inhabitants per square mile
	2 to 6
	6 to 18
	18 to 45
	45 to 90
	90 and over

provided the Negro voters were in a helpless minority, or would vote as the governing authorities desired. With the advent of Populism, however, party competition for Negro support posed a threat to white supremacy, and led to a search for legal means of disfranchisement, such as difficult educational tests or non-payment of poll taxes. As a result, by the turn of the century Negroes no longer voted in most of the lower South.

The Second American Revolution

In dealing with the complicated problems of the South after the Civil War, it is all too easy to overlook the North, where the industrial basis of what Lincoln had called "a new nation" was being laid. The shift from a preponderant interest in agriculture to an ever increasing interest in manufacturing began before the Civil War, grew phenomenally with the needs of the

war, and continued unabated at its close.[1] Naturally, the dominant economic interest tended with time to rule also in politics, and to replace the old alliance between the agricultural South and the agricultural West which had controlled the nation before the war. The historian, Charles A. Beard, perhaps identifying these changes with the war itself more fully than the facts warranted, renamed that struggle the "Second American Revolution." But if the name overstates for the war, it by no means overstates for the transformation that occurred during the Civil War and reconstruction period. Railroads had come into their own, and the nation was united as never before by an effective transportation

[1] Thomas C. Cochran, "Did the Civil War Retard Industrialization?" *Mississippi Valley Historical Review*, XLVIII (September, 1961), pp. 197–210, argues that the role of the Civil War in promoting industrialization has been much exaggerated.

network. New machines had put an end to the old domestic system of manufacturing, and had made the factory system everywhere triumphant. Even agriculture had participated in the revolution, for agricultural machinery and the new means of transportation had changed the pattern from production mainly for use to production mainly for sale; the very farms themselves were on the way to becoming factories.

Northern Prosperity

The contrasts between North and South at the close of the war could hardly have been more marked. All that the South lacked the North had in great abundance. Huge capital gains, piled up during the war, provided the means for further business expansion. Unlike those of the Confederacy, the debts of the United States, although contracted for the most part in depreciated paper currency, were paid in gold; not only did the lender get back in value far more than he had lent, but the interest also was paid in gold. The greenbacks themselves, with the war won, rose steadily in value; thus every dollar one had was worth more, and every debt one collected, private as well as public, carried with it a neat built-in profit. Considerable capital was available from such disappearing industries as fur, whaling, and to some extent shipping; also, the new corporations were able by stock flotations to tap individual savings with even better success. Banks shared generously in the new prosperity. Not until 1864 had the national banking system, created during the war, really begun to function, but by 1865 more than 1500 national banks were scattered throughout the country, with a bank-note circulation that was soon almost equal to that of the greenbacks. The exploitation of gold and silver mines of the Far West, so helpful to the North during the war, continued actively at its close. American credit, except for the South, was good abroad, and bankers found that they could easily float overseas such industrial loans as American investors failed to absorb.

Rich natural resources added to the nation's wealth. The Old and the New Northwest furnished lumber; the Pittsburgh area furnished coal and oil; the surface mines of the Lake Superior region were the world's richest in iron ore; and the mines of the Far West were by no means confined to the production of precious metals. Heavy industries, with a growing emphasis on steel rather than iron, turned without difficulty from manufacturing the matériel of war to supplying the necessities for the expanding western railroads, and for the construction required to keep pace with the rapidly growing cities. Factories that had made boots and shoes, or uniforms, or blankets, or other items needed by soldiers, found an ample civilian market for the same or similar goods. The textile mills of New England, the flour mills of Minnesota, the meat-packing plants of the Middle Border, the makers of agricultural machinery in and about Chicago, these and scores of other industries participated in the northern postwar boom. For a time agriculture also did well; production throughout the North continued at a generally high level, and soon came to include the output of the Great Plains cattle industry. Much of this abundance the burgeoning American economy was itself able to absorb, while the outbreak of the Bismarckian wars in Europe provided another war market to replace the one lost by the ending of the Civil War.

Panic and Depression

And yet, as already indicated, the business cycle was still at work; the Panic of 1873 ended the boom and began the depression.[1] Business confidence remained at low ebb until well toward the end of the decade,

[1] See pp. 113–115.

while agriculture, with production mounting and the world market becoming more competitive was also in serious trouble. Throughout most of the seventies unemployment was rife, labor difficulties were frequent, farmer protests rose loud and long, despair and discouragement were the order of the day. But as usual the prophets of gloom and doom were not to have it all their own way indefinitely. By 1879 the evidence of returning prosperity was overwhelming, both in industry and in agriculture, and the nation soon began to resume its normal economic behavior. By this time, too, the South, with a "new South" devoted to industry, had begun to add to the national economy more than it subtracted from it. The excesses of reconstruction were over, and home rule replaced alien rule. Even so, it would take time, much time, before the once seceded states could see eye to eye with the rest of the Union on the civil and political rights of the Negro, or could feel themselves full partners in the new nation.[1]

Diplomatic Reconstruction

So absorbed were most Americans in their domestic problems that they possibly took less interest in foreign affairs than the facts now seem to justify. There was a significant diplomatic aspect to reconstruction. While the nation was divided, its strength in dealing with foreign countries was seriously curtailed; it could not even prevent the outright challenge to the Monroe Doctrine of French intervention in Mexico. But at the close of the war, with the American army and navy among the strongest in the world, and with 50,000 Union troops under General Sheridan poised ominously on the Mexican border, the protests that the American State Department had merely voiced

[1] Many of the subjects mentioned in the preceding four paragraphs will be developed more fully in Section Two, beginning on p. 106.

before took on a more commanding tone. Also, Napoleon III, the French monarch, could now no longer ignore the progress of Prussian expansion in Europe, and needed all his troops at home. So when Secretary Seward delivered an ultimatum in February, 1866, demanding the withdrawal of French forces from Mexico, the results were as satisfactory as they had been previously unsatisfactory. By the spring of 1867 the French were out of Mexico, leaving their puppet, Maximilian I, to face a Mexican firing squad. Later, had President Grant been allowed to have his way, he might have turned the Monroe Doctrine into an instrument of aggression by absorbing the Dominican Republic, where the Spanish government had sought unsuccessfully during the Civil War to resume its sway. But his efforts were frustrated largely by Charles Sumner, Chairman of the Senate Committee on Foreign Relations, who blocked ratification of the necessary treaty of annexation.

Alaska

The reconstruction era, however, did witness significant additions to the territory of the United States. Secretary Seward, who was as ardent an expansionist as Grant, had in his time sought but failed to acquire the Danish West Indies (now the Virgin Islands). But he was completely successful in obtaining Alaska from Russia by a treaty signed in 1867. The purchase price for "Seward's Folly," as the new territory was sometimes called, $7.2 million, seemed to many Americans excessive, and the House of Representatives was reluctant to pass the necessary appropriation bill. But Russia wanted greatly to be rid of Alaska, which had ceased to be profitable and was too far away to be properly governed, so the Russian Minister to the United States, Baron Edoard de Stoeckl, resorted to bribery, and so influenced enough House members to permit the deal to go through. What the history of the United States and the world might have been in the twentieth century had Alaska remained a part of Russia, one may only surmise. It is also worth noting that the Midway Islands, which an American sea captain had discovered in 1859, were officially occupied in 1867.

The Fenians

Undoubtedly some American expansionists cherished the thought of adding Canada to the United States, and their loose talk, together with plots by the Fenian Brotherhood for the invasion of Canada, tended during the postwar years to unsettle Canadian-American relations. The Fenians drew their membership and support from Irish-Americans who were devoted to the cause of independence for Ireland, and in order to promote this end they actually sent bands of armed raiders across the Canadian border, both in 1866 and in 1870. Canadian militiamen had no difficulty in dispersing the invaders, but their annoying activities tended to confirm Canadians in their determination to resist absorption into the United States, and to regard with favor the independent status they had achieved, under the British North America Act of 1867, as the Dominion of Canada.

The Geneva Awards

The most important diplomatic stroke of the period in the eyes of contemporaries was no doubt the settlement of the claims by the United States against Great Britain, claims arising from admitted British laxness in enforcing the duties of a neutral during the Civil War. By the Treaty of Washington, signed in 1871, the British government agreed to submit to arbitration the so-called *Alabama* claims, which the United States demanded as compensation for the damages done to American shipping by certain Confederate commerce destroyers that had operated during the war from British ports. As a result, an international tribunal of arbitration, meeting at Geneva, Switzerland, in 1872, awarded the United States the sum of $15.5 million damages, which the British government paid. Also, under the terms of the Treaty of Washington, other less important differences between the two nations were settled amicably. The United States had as yet no premonition of the role it was to play later in international affairs, but it had shown the strength it needed to deal with the problems it then faced, and it had reinforced the already significant precedent for the settlement short of war of its diplomatic disputes with Great Britain.

BIBLIOGRAPHY

E. L. McKitrick, *Andrew Johnson and Reconstruction* (1960), contests vigorously the position taken by H. K. Beale, *The Critical Year: A Study of Andrew Johnson and Reconstruction* (1930). While Beale was himself a revisionist, he saw the Radicals as economically motivated and insincere in their promises to the Negro. McKitrick sees Johnson as a blundering incompetent whose actions in a fluid situation led to disaster. Scholarship is being aided by the publication of *The Papers* of *Andrew Johnson* (1967–   ), edited by L. P. Graf and Ralph Haskins; the first volume covers 1822–1851. *Stanton* (1962), by B. P. Thomas and H. M. Hyman, is an excellent biography of a major figure. Other significant lives include R. N. Current, *Old Thad Stevens* (1942); F. M. Brodie, *Thaddeus Stevens* (1959); P. W. Riddleberger, *George Washington Julian* (1966); H. L. Trefousse, *Ben Butler* (1957), and *Benjamin Franklin Wade* (1963); and O. H. Olsen, *Carpetbagger's Cru-*

sade: *The Life of Albion Winegar Tourgée* (1969). See also the lectures by R. N. Current, *Three Carpetbag Governors* (1967); and H. L. Trefousse, *The Radical Republicans* (1969).

Legal and constitutional aspects are examined in two important recent monographs: Herman Belz, *Reconstructing the Union: Theory and Policy during the Civil War* (1968); and S. I. Kutler, *Judicial Power and Reconstruction Politics* (1968). See also J. T. Dorris, *Pardon and Amnesty under Lincoln and Johnson* (1953); H. M. Hyman, *Era of the Oath: Northern Loyalty Tests during the Civil War and Reconstruction* (1954); J. B. James, **The Framing of the Fourteenth Amendment* (1956); W. B. Hesseltine, **Lincoln's Plan of Reconstruction* (1960); and William Gillette, **The Right to Vote: Politics and the Passage of the Fifteenth Amendment* (1965).

The southern states during Reconstruction were studied one by one by members of the Dunning school. Best of this group are J. W. Garner, **Reconstruction in Mississippi* (1901); and C. M. Thompson, *Reconstruction in Georgia* (1915). A monument of early revisionist scholarship is F. B. Simkins and R. H. Woody, *South Carolina during Reconstruction* (1932). Other important state studies include R. W. Shugg, **Origins of Class Struggle in Louisiana* (1939); T. B. Alexander, *Political Reconstruction in Tennessee* (1950); W. E. Parrish, *Missouri under Radical Rule, 1865–1870* (1965); Alan Conway, *The Reconstruction of Georgia* (1966); E. S. Nathans, *Losing the Peace: Georgia Republicans and Reconstruction, 1865–1871* (1968); and W. C. Harris, *Presidential Reconstruction in Mississippi* (1967).

The best general surveys of the Grant administration are W. B. Hesseltine, *Ulysses S. Grant, Politician* (1935); and Allan Nevins,

Hamilton Fish: The Inner History of the Grant Administration (1936). Uniquely important is the history of public administration by L. D. White, **The Republican Era, 1869–1901* (1958). C. H. Coleman, *The Election of 1868* (1933), is still standard. On the weird 1872 election, see G. G. Van Deusen, **Horace Greeley* (1953); E. D. Ross, **The Liberal Republican Movement* (1919); and J. G. Sproat, *"The Best Men": Liberal Reformers in the Gilded Age* (1968). On the 1876 election and the end of Reconstruction, see P. L. Haworth, *The Hayes-Tilden Disputed Presidential Election of 1876* (1906); and C. V. Woodward, **Reunion and Reaction* (2nd ed., 1956). An important book which challenges the existence of a monolithic northern business community is R. P. Sharkey, **Money, Class, and Party* (1959). See also G. R. Woolfolk, *The Cotton Regency: The Northern Merchants and Reconstruction, 1865–1880* (1958). P. H. Buck, **The Road to Reunion, 1865–1900* (1937), traces the process of reconciliation between the white people of the North and South. More melancholy is F. G. Wood, *Black Scare: The Racist Response to Emancipation and Reconstruction* (1968).

On Johnson's diplomacy an excellent introduction is G. G. Van Deusen, *William Henry Seward* (1967). On Alaska see Victor Farrar, *The Annexation of Russian America to the United States* (1937); and *Alaska and Its History* (1967), a splendid anthology edited by M. B. Sherwood. Diplomatic themes are also treated by Dexter Perkins, *The Monroe Doctrine, 1867–1907* (1937); C. C. Tansill, *The United States and Santo Domingo, 1798–1873* (1938); D. F. Warner, *The Idea of Continental Union: Agitation for the Annexation of Canada to the United States, 1849–1893* (1960); and M. B. Duberman, **Charles Francis Adams* (1961).

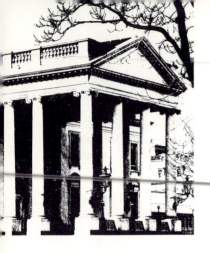

3

FROM HAYES

TO HARRISON

Post-reconstruction politics · Rutherford B. Hayes · Civil service reform · Resumption · Free silver · Bland-Allison Act · Election of 1880 · Garfield and Arthur · The Pendleton Act · The "Mongrel Tariff" · Blaine vs. Cleveland · The tariff · Election of 1888 · Benjamin Harrison · The Fifty-first Congress · The McKinley Tariff · Elections of 1890

Post-Reconstruction Politics

The legacy of the Civil War and reconstruction hung like a heavy cloud over American politics until well toward the end of the nineteenth century. The Compromise of 1877 had settled the sectional controversy for the time being; the North would make no further effort to impose its rule on the South, and the Negro would have to take his chances with the southern whites. But party loyalties remained fixed; the voter looked backward to explain why he was a Republican or a Democrat. The Republican Party had come into existence because of the stand it had taken on slavery, and it had lived on because of its determination to free the slaves, to save the Union, and to punish the South. Now it had carried its program as far as it could go, and its excuse for existence had disappeared.

WHITE HOUSE, *the entrance portico, in 1893.*

The Democrats, likewise, had so long centered their attention upon the issues of slavery, the Civil War, and reconstruction that they had lost contact with the new age. With respect to current developments both parties, most of the time, were completely bankrupt; the issues that divided them were historical merely. In general their platforms revealed few real differences of opinion as to policies, and no real awareness of the problems that confronted the nation. Neither Republicans nor Democrats, as such, seemed to sense the significance of the vast transformation that was coming over American business, nor the critical nature of the relationship between capital and labor, nor the perils that were beginning to beset agriculture, nor the desirability of doing something definite about civil service reform, the money problem, and the tariff. The Republican Party existed to oppose the Democratic Party; the Democratic Party existed to oppose the Republican Party.

Real issues cut across party lines, and even when recognized, which was rare, tended to be evaded or ignored. When the Republican convention of 1880 prepared to adopt the customary meaningless platitudes about civil service reform, a delegate from Texas named Flanagan protested in plain language: "What are we up here for?" What, indeed, if not for the offices? What other purpose could a party serve? But the sterility of party politics during the post-reconstruction years did not mean any abatement of party interest or party activity. Party loyalties remained strong, party discipline was strict, and campaigns were fought as if the very life of the republic hung in the balance.

Rutherford B. Hayes

Rutherford B. Hayes (1822–1893), who succeeded Grant in 1877, was not at the time of his inauguration, and never became, the leader of his party, but he was by no means a nonentity. Like Samuel J. Tilden, his opponent in the election of 1876, Hayes was a lawyer, but unlike Tilden he had never counted many of the country's great corporations as his clients, and he was not a rich man. Also unlike Tilden, who had avoided as nearly as possible any stand on the Civil War, Hayes had served loyally, if without conspicuous distinction, as a volunteer officer in the Union army, and at the close of the war had been brevetted major-general. As governor of Ohio he had made an excellent record: he took his duties seriously, his judgment was good, his word could be trusted, he made appointments for merit even to the extent of naming Democrats to office. During the campaign he astonished reformers by the earnestness with which he denounced the spoils system, and he irritated party regulars by the assertion that "he serves his party best who serves his country best." Deeply opposed to expediency as a rule of political conduct, he confided to his diary during the campaign of 1876 that "if elected, the

firmest adherence to principle, against all opposition and temptations, is my purpose. I shall show a *grit* that will astonish those who predict weakness." As President, however, his good intentions frequently betrayed him into bad politics. His cabinet, for example, which some observers called the ablest since Washington's, contained four men who had voted for Greeley in 1872. As already noted, one of them, Postmaster-General David M. Key, was an out-and-out Tilden Democrat who owed his selection to the bargain that had made Hayes President, but Hayes had even considered naming Joseph E. Johnston, the ex-Confederate General, as Secretary of War. Such unconventional attitudes, however defensible, did not endear Hayes to Republican

Rutherford B. Hayes. *Nineteenth President of the United States. Hayes had commanded a regiment during the Civil War and had been brevetted major-general at its close. His honesty and success as a politician, however, rather than his military record, won him the Republican nomination for the Presidency in 1876.*

regulars, who in no way opposed his determination to become a one-term President.

Civil Service Reform

Hayes's record on the problems of reconstruction has already been reviewed. His next move was in the direction of civil service reform, but to accomplish much along this line he needed a really effective civil service commission, something Congress refused to give him. Nevertheless, Hayes did what he could, unaided by Congress and with comparatively little help from public opinion, to make good appointments. His record in this respect was the best of any President's since John Quincy Adams, but his occasional mistakes annoyed the reformers, who spoke slightingly of his "opportunities and failures," while his successes won him the undying hostility of the most powerful Republican leaders. Early in his administration he engaged in a battle with the Senate over the rule of "senatorial courtesy," according to which every senator of the dominant political party claimed the right to block confirmation of the appointment within his own state of any individual to whom he personally objected. In this fight he won a partial victory. His removal of Chester Alan Arthur, collector of the port of New York, gave great offense to Roscoe Conkling, senator from New York, who succeeded in preventing confirmation of the first man Hayes chose for the place. But with the help of Democratic votes Hayes's second nominee was confirmed.

Resumption

Hayes's tenacious adherence to hard-money views, even in the face of persistent depression, was in keeping with his character. On this issue he saw eye to eye with eastern conservatives, and he approved cordially the action taken by Congress during Grant's administration to bring about the resumption of specie payments. By a law passed early in 1875, before the Democrats took control of the House of Representatives, Congress had authorized the Secretary of the Treasury to prepare for resumption on the first of January, 1879, by building up a gold reserve. John Sherman was chiefly responsible for this measure, and as the designated member of Hayes's cabinet it fell to his lot to carry it into effect. Backed steadfastly by the President, he sold bonds for gold, and ultimately accumulated a gold reserve of $100 million. As this fund grew, confidence that the government would be able to exchange gold dollars for greenbacks on the appointed day grew with it, and the value of the greenback dollar, expressed in terms of gold, also grew. Worth only sixty-seven cents in 1865, the greenback dollars had risen to eighty-nine cents in 1875, to ninety-six cents in 1877, and well before January 1, 1879, to one hundred cents. In 1878 Congress decided that $346,-681,016 in greenbacks should remain a permanent part of the national currency, but the existence of the gold reserve made every greenback, and for that matter every national bank note also, "as good as gold." Accustomed by long usage to a paper currency, no one cared to make the exchange, and with resumption a fact, the Treasury was seldom required to redeem the government's pledge.

Soft-Money Ideas

The steadily appreciating purchasing power of the dollar insured comfortable profits to money lenders, particularly those who made long-term loans. For borrowers, however, the situation was far different. The farmer who mortgaged his farm as security for a five-year loan found to his sorrow when the time for payment came that the dollars he had borrowed were worth far less than the dollars with which he must repay. Dearer dollars meant lower prices for the wheat, or corn, or livestock he had to sell. He must therefore in effect

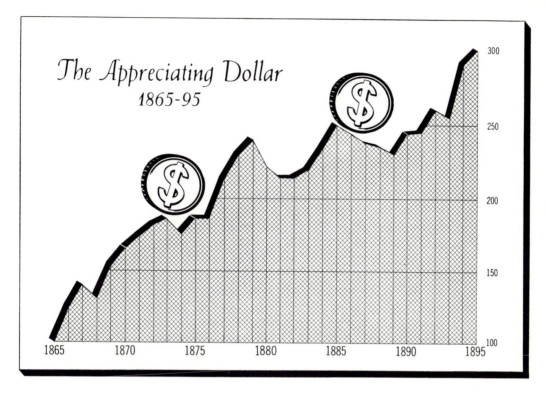

The Appreciating Dollar, 1865–1895. *This chart shows well the steady increase in the purchasing power of the dollar during the three decades after the Civil War. These years were marked by deflation rather than inflation.*

pay back not only principal and interest, but enough more to cover the amount which the dollar had appreciated. When he borrowed, a thousand bushels of wheat might equal in value the amount of his loan; when he repaid, it took from twelve to fifteen hundred bushels of wheat to raise the money he needed, and more for interest. Protests against dearer dollars and lower prices came thick and fast as one depression year after another compounded the gloom, and in the West and the South, where debtors were numerous and creditors were few, soft-money ideas, such as George H. Pendleton's "Ohio idea," found much favor. In general the Democratic Party was more hospitable to soft-money views than the Republican, but in both parties hard-money men, representing the point of view of east-

ern creditors rather than of southern or western debtors, were in the ascendancy. With resumption imminent, the Greenback Party, founded in 1876, won more and more adherents. In the elections of 1878, with some labor support, it polled a million votes, as against eighty thousand two years before, and elected fifteen members of Congress. Western Grangers in search of a remedy for low farm prices accounted in considerable part for the increasing strength of the Greenbackers, and for the Republican loss of the Senate as well as the House.[1]

Free Silver

The success of resumption, and the return of prosperity in 1879, tended to dis-

[1] On the Granger Movement, see pp. 114–117.

credit Greenbackism, and the high-water mark of 1878 was never attained again. In the meantime, however, a new soft-money panacea had been discovered in what was popularly known as "free silver." For ages the two precious metals used as money, gold and silver, had depended for their value, not upon the fiat of government, but upon commercial demand. By a curious and long-sustained coincidence the relative value of the two metals had been almost constant; it took fifteen or sixteen times as much silver to equal in value a given unit of gold. In early times the slight fluctuation in the ratio of value between the two metals had been of small concern. Methods of refinement and of measurement were too crude to make the variations noticeable, and governments themselves were not above deceiving the public all they could. With the progress of modern science, however, the exact amount of silver and of gold in a coin could be easily ascertained, and nations made an effort to establish coinage ratios that would harmonize with the existing commercial ratio. Invariably this proved to be practically impossible, for the commercial ratio was inevitably a variable, while the coinage ratio established by law was a constant. Human nature being what it is, people who knew the difference hoarded the overvalued coins, and spent those undervalued; or, as the ancient Gresham Law expressed it, the cheap money drove the dear money out of circulation. Paper issues, being as a rule less valuable than either gold or silver, rarely had much difficulty in driving both out of circulation. Such had been the case in the United States during most of its history, while during and after the Civil War the rule of the greenbacks and the national bank notes had been supreme.

The "Crime of 1873"

Hopeful that the time had come at last when a metallic currency could be provided for general use, the Secretary of the Treasury obtained from Congress in February, 1873, a new coinage law. This measure took account of the theory, generally observed in European practice, that only one metal could be used as a standard. Accordingly it dropped from the coinage lists the silver dollar, which at the old coinage ratio of sixteen to one contained too much silver to permit it to circulate anyway. This was the famous "crime of 1873," committed, according to a generation of silver orators, as the result of an "international conspiracy to demonetize silver." Actually, no one would have thought of branding this law as a crime had not the ratio of value between silver and gold begun suddenly to change. This was due, no doubt, primarily to the huge outpourings of silver from mines in the American West, although the diminished demand throughout the world for the use of silver as money may also have been a factor.

Whatever the causes, the trend in the world price of silver for the next twenty-five years was downward, a situation which led the despairing silver miners to demand the "free and unlimited coinage of silver at the ratio of sixteen to one" as a remedy. The silver miners were soon joined by the debtor farmers of the Middle West, and to a lesser extent by those of the South, neither of whom had any interest in a higher price for silver, but both of whom were convinced that "free coinage," or "free silver," as they termed the desired policy, would mean a cheaper dollar and higher prices for what they had to sell. Former Greenbackers altered their paper money arguments to fit this new demand. If the government would only take silver from all who offered it, as it still took gold, then coin the silver into silver dollars at the old ratio of sixteen to one and put the new silver dollars into circulation, the country would have more money and cheaper money, just as surely as if more greenbacks had been issued. Free silver thus became the adopted child of the Greenbackers.

The Bland-Allison Act

The silver issue continued as a constant factor in American politics for the rest of the nineteenth century, and during Hayes's administration the silver forces won what they mistook at first for a considerable victory. By the Bland-Allison Act, passed in 1878 over Hayes's veto, the Secretary of the Treasury was ordered to purchase each month from two to four million dollars' worth of silver at the market price, and to coin it into silver dollars at the ratio of sixteen to one. This meant limited coinage, however, instead of unlimited coinage, and while the new silver dollars were made legal tender, Secretary Sherman and others saw clearly that if only they could be backed

by gold, as was the case with the greenbacks, they would be "as good as gold." In practice not only Sherman, but his successors also, whether Republicans or Democrats, completely defeated the hopes of the silverites by standing ready at all times to redeem silver dollars, whatever their "intrinsic value," in gold.

Election of 1880

As the time approached for the election of 1880, it became apparent that the Republicans could count upon that most valuable of all political allies, prosperity. Foreign trade had increased; the United States enjoyed in 1880, not only a greater volume of trade than had ever been recorded in any previous year, but also a favorable balance of trade. Farm prices, particularly wheat and cotton, were up, and

Population Density, 1880. *Except for islands of settlement, the western half of continental United States was still thinly populated.*

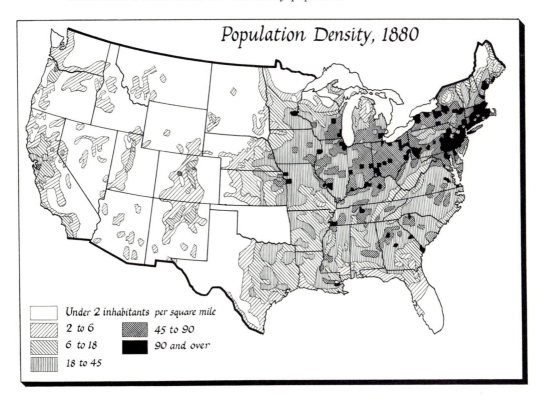

manufacturers were reaping rich harvests from the markets provided by a steadily increasing population. A feeling of confidence replaced the feeling of gloom that had characterized the depression years. But could the Republican Party take advantage of the situation? As everyone knew, it was sadly torn by internal strife. At one extreme were the "Stalwarts," hard-boiled realists who believed in practical politics and scoffed at reform. They were led by Roscoe Conkling of New York, whose great ambition at the moment was to nominate for a third term ex-President Grant. Only a little less conservative were the "Half-Breeds," who regarded James G. Blaine, the "man from Maine," as their leader, and were determined to make him President. In addition to these factions there were many Independents, most of whom were less hostile to Blaine than to Conkling, but had little use for either. Finally there was the President himself, who had no wish or hope for renomination, and his insignificant number of friends. It was obvious that only a compromise could save the day, and the national convention, after many ballots and much heart-burning, produced one. For President the Republicans chose a "dark horse," James A. Garfield of Ohio, a Blaine man who was satisfactory to the reformers, and for Vice-President, Chester Alan Arthur of New York, Conkling's trusted friend and subordinate. The ticket was as strong as compromise could make it.

The Democrats, quite as badly divided as the Republicans, were less successful in achieving a united front. The northern wing of the party was extremely suspicious, and not a little ashamed, of the southern wing; and vice versa. Moreover, in both sections there was internal strife that dated at least as far back as the Civil War. Northern Democrats who had been loyal to the Union during the war had not yet forgiven the "Copperheads" whose desire for peace had almost led them to support the South. Southern Democrats whose devotion to the party stemmed from the leadership of Andrew Jackson had little use for the ex-Whigs and conservative "Bourbons," who now, under the necessity of maintaining white supremacy, called themselves Democrats and sought to monopolize party leadership. Native Americans generally, of whatever section, regretted the dire necessity of cultivating the immigrant vote, particularly the Irish vote, which in many American cities had become a factor to be reckoned with. So long out of power as to have lost its personality, bereft of intelligent leaders, tainted with treason and with pacifism, the Democratic Party floundered helplessly through the campaign. Tilden was too old and too ill to be a candidate, and the nomination went, almost by default, to General Winfield S. Hancock of Pennsylvania, who had won distinction as a Union officer at Gettysburg, and had later pleased the South by the way he conducted himself as military commander of Louisiana during reconstruction. In politics, however, he was only, as one wag expressed it, "a good man, weighing two hundred and fifty pounds." For Vice-President the Democrats named William H. English of Indiana, a political anachronism whose last significant deed had been to promote the admission of Kansas as a slave state during the Buchanan administration. Such a ticket amounted almost to an open confession of political bankruptcy.

The campaign of 1880 presented few realistic issues between the parties. With slight modifications most of the less rhetorical passages of either platform might have served the other party about as well as its own. Since issues were lacking, the campaign turned mainly on personalities. The Republicans, in rejecting the candidacy of General Grant, had freed themselves of the charge of "Bonapartism." Their nominee was, to be sure, a Union officer in the Civil

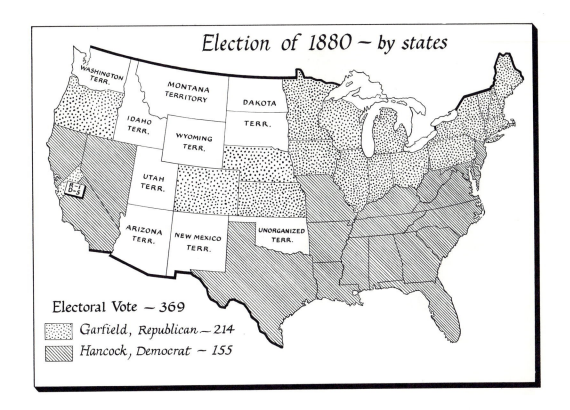

Election of 1880 – by states

WASHINGTON TERR.

MONTANA TERRITORY

DAKOTA TERR.

IDAHO TERR.

WYOMING TERR.

UTAH TERR.

ARIZONA TERR.

NEW MEXICO TERR.

UNORGANIZED TERR.

R–1
D–5

Electoral Vote — 369

Garfield, Republican — 214

Hancock, Democrat — 155

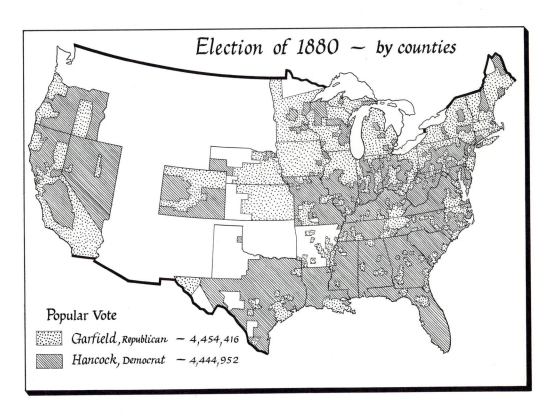

Election of 1880 — by counties

Popular Vote

Garfield, Republican — 4,454,416

Hancock, Democrat — 4,444,952

James A. Garfield. *Twentieth President of the United States. Garfield was born in a log cabin, lived the life of a pioneer farm boy, and drove mules along an Ohio Canal towpath. College educated, and a Disciples of Christ preacher, he made a success of politics only to be cut down by an assassin's bullet.*

War, but he had been, like Hayes, a volunteer officer, and had won distinction in politics rather than in the army. The Democrats, on the other hand, in their effort to shake off the charge of treason, had nominated a professional soldier. If anyone was prepared to play the role of "the man on horseback," it was Hancock, not Garfield. Efforts were made to prove that Hancock, whose exploits on the battlefield had won him the sobriquet, "the Superb," was in reality a coward, and that Garfield, whose record was far cleaner than that of most politicians, had been deeply involved in the Crédit Mobilier and other scandals. Neither charge carried much weight. Garfield,

as a matter of fact, was fairly satisfactory to the reform element in the Republican Party and most Independents gave his candidacy their warm support. The Democratic platform, written by Colonel Henry Watterson of Kentucky, made one unmistakably clear commitment by calling for "a tariff for revenue only." When the Republicans showed a disposition to press this issue, Hancock, possibly aware of the strong protectionist views of some eastern Democrats, declared that the plank was unimportant because the tariff was a "local affair." For this statement he was roundly ridiculed, but he spoke far more truly than he knew. Tariff rates must be levied by Congress, but they have generally been fixed, item by item, because of some local demand.

Election Results

Fought with fury, and as if the result would really be important, the campaign settled nothing much except that Garfield, not Hancock, was to be the next President of the United States. The Republican plurality, out of a total vote amounting to over 9 million, was about nine thousand. Neither of the two leading candidates had a majority of all the votes cast, for James B. Weaver of Iowa, the Greenback candidate, polled over three hundred thousand votes. The Republicans, however, won enough local victories to enable them to recapture the Senate, and, although the membership of the House was so evenly divided as to leave its control in doubt until Congress actually met, the Republicans were finally able to organize it also. For the first time in six years the Presidency and both houses of Congress were under the control of a single party.

James A. Garfield

But as events proved, the Republicans failed signally to capitalize upon their victory. Their first misfortune was the death of the promising new President they had elected. James A. Garfield (1831–1881), like Abraham Lincoln, was a typical product of the American frontier, but he had lived a generation later than Lincoln and had enjoyed advantages, particularly in education, that Lincoln never knew. He served for a time as a volunteer officer in the Civil War, but after 1863 represented an Ohio district in the lower house of Congress. Here he proved to be a finished debater, a tireless committeeman, and a dependable party regular. He arrived at the Presidency prematurely, but had he not achieved the office when he did, it might well have come to him later. Four months after his inauguration he was shot by a disappointed office-seeker. For weeks he lingered between life and death, but finally on September 19, 1881, he died. It cannot be said that with his passing the country lost a great man, but it can perhaps be said that it lost a politician of potential worth at a time when great men in politics were rare.

Chester A. Arthur

Garfield's death elevated to the Presidency Chester Alan Arthur (1830–1886), a New York politician whose record made him the despair of reformers. Early in life Arthur became an organization Republican, and his code of ethics, while calling for the strictest personal honesty, tolerated freely the time-honored custom of rewarding the faithful with the spoils of office. As collector of the port of New York he had, as a matter of course, overstaffed his forces with party workers, and he never hesitated to call upon the men who held their positions through his favor to do their full political duty during campaigns and on election days. As President, however, he was scrupulously on guard against criticism. He bore himself with dignity, refused to indulge in a wholesale proscription of Garfield's appointees, and took up the cudgels for civil service reform, and even tariff revision, with wholly unexpected zeal.

Despite the President's best efforts, Congress showed little disposition to inaugurate any disturbing innovations until after the election of 1882. That year, however, the electorate seemed to register an emphatic rebuke for the ruling party by returning a decisive Democratic majority to the House of Representatives. Was this reverse the result of Republican failure to do something about civil service reform and the tariff? Fearing that this indeed was the case, the Republican leaders in Congress decided to pass laws on both subjects during the "lame-duck" session that began the month after the election and lasted until the fourth of March following. Such a "death-

Chester A. Arthur. *Twenty-first President of the United States. Arthur was the fourth Vice-President to become President because of his predecessor's death. His preparation for the Presidency was inadequate, but he made a far better President than his critics had expected.*

bed" repentance might not be very convincing, but it might in the long run be better than no repentance at all.

Civil Service Reform Again

The need for civil service reform was given added emphasis by the exposure of a series of fraudulent contracts for the carrying of the mails on the western stage routes. These scandals, called the "star-route" frauds because they concerned routes designated by stars on the post-office lists, were denounced by Arthur, and their perpetrators were prosecuted, although there were no convictions. Belatedly eager to demonstrate their opposition to the spoils system, which had made such frauds possible, the Republicans were now ready to establish a civil service commission, but the Democrats were unwilling to permit their opponents to have full credit for such an undertaking. In fact, it was George H. Pendleton, Democratic Senator from Ohio, who introduced and gave his name to the reform measure

"The Merry Star Routers." *Cartoon from* Puck, *September 20, 1882, warning that the fate of Tweed might overtake Dorsey and Brady, two participants in the Star Route Frauds. It didn't.*

which an overwhelming bipartisan majority enacted into law in January, 1883.

The Pendleton Act

The Pendleton Act authorized the President to appoint three civil service commissioners, not more than two of whom should belong to the same political party, whose duty it should be to provide "open competitive examinations for testing the fitness of applicants for the public service now classified, or to be classified." Only the lowest offices were at first classified, but the law provided that the President might extend the classified lists at will to include other executive appointees. President Arthur administered the law in complete good faith. He appointed as the first chairman of the commission Dorman B. Eaton, who as secretary of the Civil Service Reform Association had been an ardent advocate of reform. During the first year of its existence the commission was given jurisdiction over about 14,000 offices out of a total of 110,-000, or about 12.5 per cent. In contrast with the British system, which examined a candidate upon general competence and culture, the American system was based upon strictly practical tests. While it would not be accurate to assume that political considerations had no weight in the making of classified appointments, certainly politics weighed far less than formerly.

Changes of national administration from Arthur's time on worked to the advantage of civil service reform. It happened that Arthur was succeeded by a Democrat, Cleveland; then Cleveland was succeeded by a Republican, Harrison; Harrison in turn was succeeded by a Democrat, Cleveland; and Cleveland, by a Republican, McKinley. Each President, as he was about to retire from office, tended to protect his own appointees by extending the classified lists. Men thus "blanketed" into the civil service were not required to take examinations, but when they died or resigned, their successors received appointments only on recommendation of the commission. By 1893 the number of civil servants under the merit system had reached 45,000; by the turn of the century it was about 100,000; by the time of the First World War nearly half a million — over 60 per cent — of the total of federal employees.

The "Mongrel Tariff"

Tariff reform was as long overdue as civil service reform, and in practice it proved to be much harder to accomplish. During the Grant administration Congress, under the insistent urging of David A. Wells, "Special Commissioner of the Revenue," had made substantial changes in the system of taxation set up during the Civil War. It had eliminated most of the "nuisance" taxes, restricted internal revenues to a few such items as liquor and tobacco, and abolished the income tax entirely. But, out of deference to the manufacturing interests, it had shown little disposition to tamper with the high protective-tariff rates that in some cases were originally levied as offsets to the now abolished excise taxes. Certain minor reductions, made as a campaign gesture in 1872, were practically wiped out in 1875 on the pretext of the depression, and the duties on a few items, such as molasses and sugar, were actually increased. To the reform demands long voiced by Wells, still the nation's outstanding expert on the subject, were now added the arguments of such economists as William Graham Sumner of Yale, and Frank W. Taussig of Harvard; also, the public was becoming increasingly insistent. Finally, on the recommendation of President Arthur, Congress created in 1882 a nonpolitical tariff commission to study the subject, and, in spite of the fact that every one of its nine members was an avowed protectionist, the commission speedily reported back that the existing duties should be cut by as much as 20 per cent. Acting this time without any considerable

James G. Blaine. *The outstanding Republican of his time, and unsuccessful candidate for the Presidency in 1884, Blaine's chief contribution to politics was as a Congressman and as twice Secretary of State.*

Democratic collaboration, the Republicans were able to hurry into law before the adjournment of Congress in March, 1883, what one writer has aptly called the "Mongrel Tariff." Partly because of the necessity for haste, partly because of the effective work of the lobbyists, and partly because of the log-rolling tendencies of congressmen themselves, the measure failed completely to accomplish the purpose for which it had been intended. As Senator Sherman admitted, it retained "nearly all the inequalities and incongruities of the old tariff and yielded to local demands and local interests to an extent that destroyed all symmetry and harmony."

The passage of the "Mongrel Tariff" was not without important political results. Since the Republicans were obliged to defend their handiwork, their party inescapably came to be identified more and more with the policy of protection, whereas the Democrats, who were in duty bound to oppose whatever they could in the Republican program, drifted gradually in the direction of an out-and-out low-tariff policy. When the Democrats in 1883 took control of the House of Representatives, they ignored the claims of Samuel J. Randall, a Pennsylvania protectionist who before 1881 had been three times elected Speaker, in order to place in that office a dependable low-tariff advocate, John G. Carlisle of Kentucky.

James G. Blaine

The campaign and election of 1884 turned less on the tariff, however, than on the personalities of the two outstanding individuals who contested for the Presidency. The Republicans overlooked the claims of Arthur, who had offended the regulars by vetoing in 1882 an $18 million rivers and harbors ("pork-barrel") bill, and had never been able to live down his past to the complete satisfaction of the liberals. Instead, they nominated their outstanding leader, James G. Blaine (1830–1893), whom Garfield had made Secretary of State, but whose resignation from that office Arthur had not hesitated to accept. Blaine was born in Pennsylvania, but had entered politics in Maine. Unlike most politicians his background was journalism rather than the law; he had been connected with both the *Kennebec Journal* and the *Portland Advertiser*. He was deep in state politics before the Civil War, and after 1858 served three terms as a member of the state legislature. When war broke out, he did not join the army, but in 1863 entered the national House of Representatives and remained there until 1876, when he went to the Senate. During Grant's administration he emerged as the outstanding leader of the Republican Party. A firm believer in the righteousness of Radical reconstruction, and a veritable incarnation of Republican prejudice, he appealed strongly to a party-loving age. Both on and off the platform he possessed great personal charm, a quality which he used, no less than Henry Clay, to excite the worshipful support of his followers. Both in 1876 and in 1880 far more sentiment had existed for Blaine than for the men the Republicans had nominated, but Blaine's record had offended the liberals, and lesser lights had won the prize. Known since 1876, the "Mulligan Letters," which revealed that Blaine as congressman had helped obtain a land grant for an Arkansas railroad from which he hoped to make a financial profit, were flaunted as good reason to keep the "man from Maine" in retirement, but the "Blaine or bust" crowd was not to be denied.

Grover Cleveland

The Democrats, as in 1876, nominated a reform governor of New York. Grover Cleveland (1837–1908) was born in New Jersey, but had early removed to New York. After a hard struggle with poverty he had become by 1859 a practicing lawyer in Buffalo. During the Civil War, when other young men were joining the army, he borrowed money to hire a substitute because his meager earnings were needed for the support of his mother and sisters. In 1863 he received a welcome appointment as assistant district attorney, and in

Grover Cleveland. *Twenty-second and twenty-fourth President of the United States. Cleveland was the first non-veteran to achieve election to the Presidency after the Civil War. His record of integrity as mayor of Buffalo and governor of New York paved the way for his election in 1884.*

1870 he was not above accepting a nomination as sheriff of Erie County. Elected, he revealed qualities of scrupulous honesty and unflinching courage that soon made him a marked man. He refused to hire a hangman when two murderers were to be executed, and sprang the trap himself. He made life consistently uncomfortable for local crooks and grafters. In 1881, nominated and elected mayor of Buffalo to placate the "better element," he reorganized the city administration, purged it of venal politicians, vetoed dubious measures, and in general endeared himself to reformers. The fame of the "veto mayor" spread, and when in 1882 the New York Democrats needed a candidate for governor with an unimpeachable record to oppose the Republican candidate, Secretary of the Treasury Charles J. Folger, they turned to Cleveland and elected him by a majority of nearly 200,000 votes. As governor, he struggled irritably against a bewildering accumulation of governmental inefficiency or worse, made some progress and many enemies, particularly among the Tammany leaders of New York City. "We love him most for the enemies he has made," General E. S. Bragg told the Democratic convention of 1884, mindful of Tammany's earnest desire to prevent Cleveland's nomination for the Presidency.

The nomination of Cleveland insured that a large number of Republican liberals, now called "Mugwumps," would swing their support to the Democratic ticket. Ordinarily this would have resulted in his election by a wide margin, but he happened to be a bachelor, and scandalmongers uncovered flaws in his private life which in some minds offset his irreproachable conduct of his public responsibilities. In particular, he refused to deny the charge that he was the father of an illegitimate child. The campaign reached an all-time low in mud-slinging, but the sober second thought of many Americans seemed to coincide with that of a philosophical Mugwump who held that "we should elect Mr. Cleveland to the public office he is so eminently qualified to fill and remand Mr. Blaine to the private life which he is so eminently fitted to adorn." For, whatever might be said of Blaine's public record, his private life was blameless. The Republican candidate may have suffered also from his failure to rebuke on the spot the remark made in his presence by a Protestant clergyman, Doctor Samuel Burchard, who connected the Democratic Party with "rum, Romanism, and rebellion." Blaine had not heard the statement, and repudiated it later, but the Democrats charged him with condoning an offense against the Catholics. Since Blaine's mother was of Irish Catholic ancestry, the Republicans had hoped on this account to win some Irish voters to their standard. Burchard's unfortunate statement may have cost them dear.

Election of Cleveland

The decision in 1884 was almost as close as in 1880. Cleveland's plurality over Blaine in the country as a whole was only 23,000, and the electoral vote stood 219 to 182. Cleveland carried the solid South, Delaware, Indiana, Connecticut, New Jersey, and New York. All the rest of the states voted for Blaine. The Democrats won control of the House of Representatives by a comfortable margin, but the Republicans retained their majority in the Senate. Benjamin F. Butler, the Greenback candidate, received a total of 173,370 popular votes, and John P. St. John of Kansas, Prohibitionist, 150,369. The Prohibitionist vote in New York State alone ran to over 25,000, another factor in the defeat of Blaine. Had the temperance forces not had a candidate of their own, undoubtedly most of them would have voted for Blaine and against Cleveland, whose bibulous habits were well known.

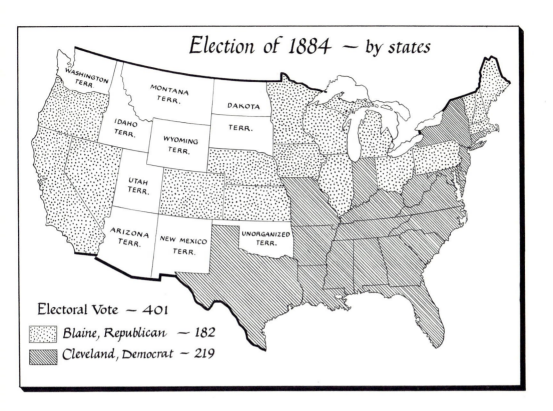

Election of 1884 — by states

WASHINGTON TERR.

MONTANA TERR.

DAKOTA TERR.

IDAHO TERR.

WYOMING TERR.

UTAH TERR.

ARIZONA TERR.

NEW MEXICO TERR.

UNORGANIZED TERR.

Electoral Vote — 401

Blaine, Republican — 182

Cleveland, Democrat — 219

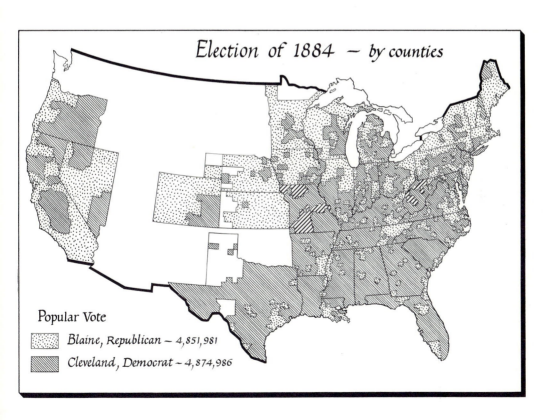

Election of 1884 — by counties

Popular Vote

Blaine, Republican — 4,851,981

Cleveland, Democrat — 4,874,986

Cleveland and Reform

Cleveland's efforts to inaugurate reforms met many obstacles. He protected the Civil Service Commission all he could, and even extended the classified lists, but in order to avoid an outright revolt within his party he was obliged to yield many non-classified offices to the spoilsmen. He had trouble with the veterans of the Civil War, now organized into a powerful society known as the Grand Army of the Republic, because he stood athwart their desires for more and larger pensions. Already the Arrears of Pensions Act of 1879 had permitted pensioners, whatever their service disability, to recover back payments for the period between the time of mustering out and the time a given pension was granted. The abuse of this privilege greatly angered the President, but he could do little about it; on the other hand, he could and did veto a "pauper" pension bill that would have given a pension to all who stood in need of it, regardless of disability. He also vetoed hundreds of the private pension bills that lenient congressmen delighted to push through for the benefit of favored constituents who had seen service, but according to the general law were not entitled to pensions. This attitude on the part of the President, together with his willingness to restore to the states from which they had come all captured Confederate battle flags, won him the undying hatred of the "G.A.R.," sometimes appropriately called the "Grand Army of the Republican Party." While public opinion forced Cleveland to rescind his battle-flag order, he was only a little in advance of the times. The same action, taken by Congress and approved by Theodore Roosevelt in 1905, aroused no public outcry.

The Tariff

Cleveland's chief bid for reform came during the second half of his administration, when he forced both parties to take their stand on the tariff issue. In his annual message of December, 1887, he dealt exclusively with the tariff, presented a well-reasoned, hard-hitting argument against the existing high rates, and, pointing to the annual surplus of about $100 million brought in each year by the Tariff of 1883, declared: "It is a *condition* which confronts us, not a theory." Thus briefed by the President, the Democratic majority in the House of Representatives, with only four dissenting votes, accepted the low-tariff bill presented by Roger Q. Mills of Texas, chairman of the House Ways and Means Committee. This measure called for reductions from an average level of about 47 per cent to an average level of about 40 per cent, and placed such items as wool, flax, hemp, salt, lumber, and tin-plate on the free list. In response to this Democratic challenge, the Senate Committee on Finance, under the leadership of Senator Allison, presented a sample of what the Republicans would be glad to do if only they could win control of the government in the election of 1888. As passed by the Republican majority in the Senate, the Allison bill proposed to maintain a generally high level of duties, but it insured a smaller revenue by resort to prohibitive duties, by the lowering of excises, and by a cut in the duty on sugar. As anticipated, the House would not accept the Senate bill, and the Senate would not accept the House bill. But as Cleveland had foreseen, both parties had been committed to positions that they could not possibly abandon in the coming presidential campaign.

Election of 1888

As was now inevitable, the Democrats renominated Cleveland, and made tariff reform their principal issue in the campaign of 1888. The Republicans, having lost with Blaine in 1884, turned to one of their lesser lights, Benjamin Harrison of

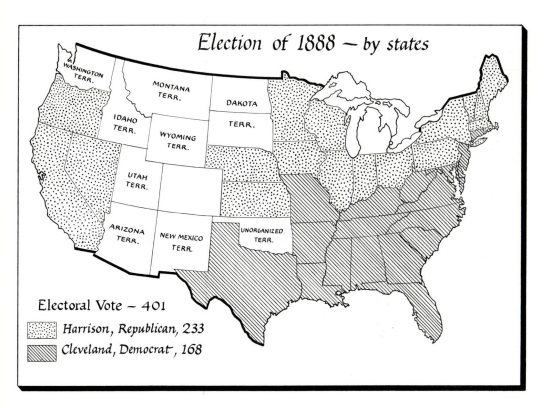

Election of 1888 — by states

WASHINGTON TERR.

MONTANA TERR.

DAKOTA TERR.

IDAHO TERR.

WYOMING TERR.

UTAH TERR.

ARIZONA TERR.

NEW MEXICO TERR.

UNORGANIZED TERR.

Electoral Vote – 401

Harrison, Republican, 233

Cleveland, Democrat, 168

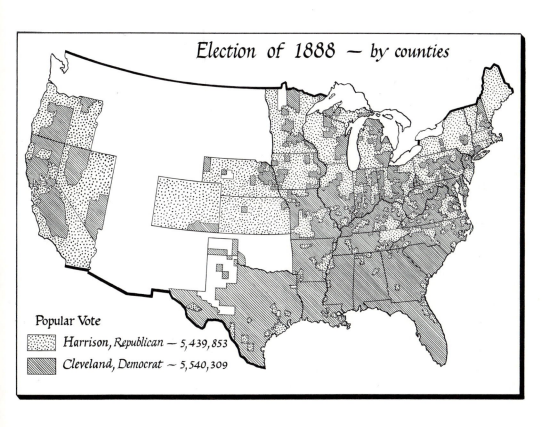

Election of 1888 — by counties

Popular Vote

Harrison, Republican — 5,439,853

Cleveland, Democrat — 5,540,309

Benjamin Harrison. *Twenty-third President of the United States. Harrison was a grandson of the ninth President, and a great-grandson of Benjamin Harrison, signer of the Declaration of Independence. A Civil War officer, and an able lawyer, he was never the leader of his party, even after his election to the Presidency.*

Indiana, who had the triple advantage of a presidential grandfather, residence in a close state, and a clean, if almost empty, political record. The campaign was a revelation to the Republicans, for they learned for the first time how advantageous an issue the tariff could be. Campaign contributions as insurance against Democratic tariff reductions poured into the Republican coffers in a flood. The funds thus collected were used both to carry on an extensive campaign of education, and to "get out the vote." For the former purpose Republican orators and publicists made much of maintaining the high wages of American labor, something that could not be done, they insisted, if the products of low-paid European labor were admitted freely to American markets. When it came

to "getting out the vote," party-workers, particularly in the doubtful states, scrupled at nothing. The scandals of the election, on both sides, were so open and notorious as to give great impetus to the movement for the "Australian" system of secret voting, which down to this time had made little headway in the United States. Harrison won the election by only a slender margin. In the popular vote Cleveland, whose majorities in the South were large, led by more than 100,000, but Harrison, with small pluralities in many of the crucial states, including New York and Indiana, amassed 233 electoral votes to Cleveland's 168.

Benjamin Harrison

Benjamin Harrison (1833–1901) was at the time of his nomination a successful lawyer of great party regularity who had served one term in the United States Senate. He was in no sense the leader of his party, and James G. Blaine, whom he made his Secretary of State, completely overshadowed him. Harrison was a good platform orator, but cold in his personal relationships. "Harrison can make a speech to ten thousand men," said one of his associates, "and every man of them will go away his friend. Let him meet the same ten thousand in private, and every one will go away his enemy." His honesty was probably as unimpeachable as Cleveland's, but he lacked Cleveland's forceful nature. During Cleveland's administration the Democratic Party leaders, one by one, acknowledged the President's supremacy, whereas Harrison from the beginning of his administration to its end, had far less to do with charting his party's course than many another of lesser rank.

Harrison's record on civil service reform and pensions was by no means as courageous as Cleveland's. Like President Grant, he saw fit to allot many minor offices to his indigent friends and relatives. In making other appointments, he leaned on the advice of the politicians, and did what they wanted if he could. His chief contribution to civil service reform was his appointment of Theodore Roosevelt to membership on the Civil Service Commission, an appointment which Roosevelt earned as a reward for serving his party faithfully during the campaign of 1888. As civil service commissioner, however, Roosevelt made it his business to see that no such rewards as he had received were made through the agency of the commission. In the pursuit of this course, he soon fell afoul of the President, whom he came to dislike, and of many of the President's friends, but Harrison retained the obstreperous commissioner in office and when in 1893 Cleveland became President again, he, too, retained Roosevelt. As for pensions, the G.A.R. got exactly what it wanted in the Dependents' Pension Act, which provided that all veterans of the Civil War who had served for as long as ninety days, and who had suffered from any serious mental or physical disability, should receive pensions of from $6 to $12 a month, according to the degree of disability from which they suffered. Widows of veterans, if dependent upon their own labor for support, were awarded pensions of $8 a month, and minor children, $2 a month. As a result of this law the number of pensioners rose from 489,725 in 1889 to 966,012 in 1893, and the amount of money appropriated for pensions in the same period from $89 million to $157 million. By 1911 the total expenditure of the United States for Civil War pensions had exceeded $4 billion, a sum far in excess of the original cost of the war, and the end was not yet in sight.

The Fifty-first Congress

The main business of the Fifty-first Congress was to pass a high protective-tariff bill, but to accomplish this strictly partisan end political strategy of a high order was required. The Republicans had a majority in each house of Congress, but particularly in the House of Representatives the majority depended upon too few votes for comfort. To expedite the business in hand, the Republican Speaker, Thomas B. Reed of Maine, broke traditional rules right and left. Members present, but not voting, were counted to make a quorum, and a powerful Committee on Rules, of which "Czar" Reed was chairman, brought in from time to time whatever special rules were need to push the Republican program along. To bolster up the Republican majority, especially in the Senate, two new northwestern territories, Wyoming and Idaho, were added to the four, North and South Dakota, Montana, and Washington, that the preceding Congress had authorized to take the steps necessary to become states. Since the voters of this region were predominantly Republican, the control of the Republican Party in Congress was greatly strengthened by their admission. Finally, as a sop to the silver Republicans of the West, who refused to vote for a high tariff until something should be done for silver, the Sherman Silver Purchase Act of 1890 was passed. This measure required the Treasury to buy at the market price 4.5 million ounces of silver a month, the estimated output of all the silver mines in the United States. Not all the silver need be coined, but it was to be paid for in Treasury notes redeemable "in gold or silver coin," and so provided for a substantial addition to the amount of money actually in circulation. An attempt to repeal the Compromise of 1877 by the enactment of a Federal Elections, or "Force" bill, which would again give the national government control over voting in the South, as during reconstruction, failed; otherwise, the Republicans might have forged a weapon by means of which they could have controlled the national government for many years.

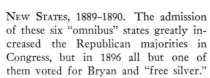

NEW STATES, 1889–1890. The admission
of these six "omnibus" states greatly increased the Republican majorities in
Congress, but in 1896 all but one of
them voted for Bryan and "free silver."

The McKinley Tariff

The McKinley Tariff Act, which became law on October 1, 1890, was the Republican answer to the prayers, and the
contributions, of the American industrialists. It provided first and foremost a set of
duties on manufactured articles higher than
the American government had ever levied
before. Some of these duties turned out to
be, as their authors had intended, actually
prohibitive; others went to the length of
offering protection to nonexistent industries, provided only that responsible persons could demonstrate their intent to begin manufacture. The law also embodied
an impressive list of agricultural duties,
charged against such imports as eggs, butter, potatoes, wheat, and barley. These
items were included primarily for their
psychological effect upon the farmer vote.
Duties levied upon commodities of which
the United States had an excess for export,
and the price of which was fixed on the
world market, amounted, as was well
known, to little more than empty gestures.

The reduction of the revenue, deemed
imperative by both Democrats and Republicans, was accomplished in part by the discouraging effect on importation of the high
duties, but in greater part by placing raw
sugar on the free list. This was in effect

an aid to the manufacturers of refined sugar, whose product was still protected, but who could now buy raw sugar for less, but it was very disturbing to the sugar producers of Louisiana until the idea of a bounty of two cents a pound on all raw sugar of American origin was included. Thus the sugar schedule, figuratively speaking, succeeded in taking money out of the Treasury with both hands. To please the Secretary of State, James G. Blaine, a reciprocity clause was included in the McKinley Tariff, although its provisions were much more restricted than Blaine had hoped. The President was authorized to enforce a specified schedule of tariff rates on items listed as free in case the nations that produced them failed to grant equivalent advantages to American exports.

Public reaction to the behavior of the Fifty-first Congress was far from cordial. Each of its measures made a generous quota of enemies, and the grand total of accumu-lated grievances grew with each succeeding month. To the effect of the McKinley Bill on the revenue, which was sure to be disastrous, was added the orgy of spending in which Congress permitted itself to indulge. Its lavish appropriations for pensions, river and harbor improvements, federal buildings, coast defenses, and other extravagances led the newspapers to refer to it as the "billion-dollar Congress," a description strikingly lacking in political appeal. Unfortunate as a Treasury surplus might have been, a deficit, even less desirable, appeared to be in sight. Consumers found that the higher rates of the McKinley Tariff meant higher prices for what they had to buy; when its rates were made known, John Wanamaker, the storekeeper Postmaster-General, with more business than political acumen, openly urged his customers to "buy now, before prices go up." The attempt to pass a Force bill, which would be certain to revive sectional an-

THE FIFTY-FIRST CONGRESS. *This Congress was notable for its comprehensive program of legislation, not all of which proved to be popular with the voters.*

"THE INSATIABLE GLUTTON." Cartoon from *Puck* calling attention to the amount of fraud that the "pension grabs" promoted.

tagonisms, was unpopular, North as well as South. As Elihu Root phrased it a little later, the whole country was ready to concede "the failure of the plan formulated at the close of the war to elevate the black man by conferring the suffrage upon him."

Elections of 1890

Held only a few weeks after the passage of the McKinley Bill, the congressional elections of 1890 showed how unpopular that measure, and the Congress that passed it, had become. Democratic campaigners did not fail to take full advantage of the opportunity to denounce "Bill McKinley and the McKinley Bill." Peddlers were sent through the country, so the Republicans claimed, to offer tin cups at twenty-five cents each and tin pails at a dollar apiece in order to show the rural voters how much the McKinley duties had increased the cost of living. Merchants and salesmen apologized for high prices, whatever the truth might be, on the ground that the new tariff law had made them neces-

sary. The Republicans, with tea, coffee, and sugar on the free list, had hoped to make much of the "free breakfast table," but the fact that the sugar duties were retained for six months after the passage of the bill made this battle cry seem decidedly premature. When the votes were counted, the Republicans discovered that they had received the most emphatic rebuke in the history of their party. In the Senate the Republican majority was narrowed to eight, and would have been wiped out altogether but for the hold-over senators from the newly admitted states of the Northwest. In the House the Democrats had 235 seats, and the Republicans 88, while nine Farmers' Alliance men, or Populists, refused to vote with either of the older parties. The appearance of this group of independents in Congress marked the beginning of an agrarian revolt in the Middle West and the South, which, with the assistance it received from the silver mining states of the Far West, threatened for a time to bring about a complete realignment of political parties.

BIBLIOGRAPHY

The best survey of the period is J. A. Garraty, *The New Commonwealth, 1877–1890* (1968). Colorful, irreverent, and influential is Matthew Josephson, *The Politicos, 1865–1896* (1938); something of the same viewpoint is expressed in Ray Ginger, *The Age of Excess: The United States from 1877 to 1914* (1965). A full-length effort to overcome the Josephson interpretation is H. W. Morgan, *From Hayes to McKinley: National Party Politics, 1877–1896* (1969). Another effort at revisionism is D. J. Rothman, *Politics and Power: The United States Senate, 1869–1901* (1966). A major influence on a whole generation of students is Richard Hofstadter, *The Ameri-*

can Political Tradition and the Men Who Made It (1948). James Bryce, the distinguished British observer, examines state and local as well as national affairs in *The American Commonwealth* (2 vols., 1888).

Biographical studies of political leaders provide valuable insights, as the era was one of intensely personal politics. In addition to those cited previously, the following are of particular importance: A. C. Flick, *Samuel J. Tilden* (1939); H. J. Eckenrode, *Rutherford B. Hayes* (1930); Harry Barnard, *Rutherford B. Hayes and His America* (1954); R. G. Caldwell, *James A. Garfield* (1931); G. F. Howe, *Chester A. Arthur* (1935); L. B.

Richardson, *William E. Chandler* (1940); D. S. Muzzey, *James G. Blaine* (1934); Allan Nevins, *Grover Cleveland* (1932); and H. S. Merrill, **Bourbon Leader: Grover Cleveland and the Democratic Party* (1957), brief and more critical than Nevins' monumental study. H. J. Sievers, *Benjamin Harrison* (3 vols., 1952–1968), is another monumental work. Other biographies of interest include: C. L. Barrows, *William M. Evarts* (1941); W. A. Robinson, *Thomas B. Reed* (1930); J. A. Barnes, *John G. Carlisle* (1931); E. B. Thompson, *Matthew Hale Carpenter* (1954); Edward Younger, *John A. Kasson* (1955); O. D. Lambert, *Stephen Benton Elkins* (1955); L. L. Sage, *William Boyd Allison* (1956); D. G. Fowler, *John Coit Spooner* (1961); David Lindsey, *"Sunset" Cox* (1959); J. R. Lambert, Jr., *Arthur Pue Gorman* (1953); H. J. Bass, *"I Am a Democrat": The Political Career of David Bennett Hill* (1961); and J. W. Neilson, **Shelby M. Cullom* (1962). Rich and revealing is *Hayes: The Diary of a President, 1875–1881* (1964), edited by T. H. Williams. An important study of a neglected episode is H. J. Clancy, *The Presidential Election of 1880* (1958).

The thorny questions of money and tariff are treated in a number of works. Surveys on money include A. B. Hepburn, *A History of Currency in the United States* (2nd ed., 1924); D. R. Dewey, *Financial History of the United States* (12th ed., 1936); Paul Studenski and H. E. Krooss, *Financial History of the United States* (1952); and Milton Friedman and A. J. Schwartz, *A Monetary History of the United States, 1867–1960* (1963). A major recent work is Irwin Unger, **The Greenback Era* (1964); it can be compared with W. C. Mitchell's classic study, *A History of the Greenbacks* (1903). See also two works by W. T. K. Nugent, **The Money Question During Reconstruction* (1967), and *Money and American Society, 1865–1880* (1968). On the tariff, which has not received much scholarly attention in recent years, the classics are F. W. Taussig, **Tariff History of the United States* (8th ed., 1931); and Edward Stanwood, *Amer-ican Tariff Controversies in the Nineteenth Century* (2 vols., 1903).

C. R. Fish, *The Civil Service and the Patronage* (1905), may now be supplemented by a general survey by P. P. Van Riper, *History of the United States Civil Service* (1958). The background of the Pendleton Act is fully treated by Ari Hoogenboom, **Outlawing the Spoils* (1962). See also A. B. Sageser, *The First Two Decades of the Pendleton Act* (1935). W. E. Davies, *Patriotism on Parade* (1955), treats the G. A. R. and other patriotic organizations. Scholars are giving increasing attention to southern state politics in the post-Reconstruction period. See especially A. D. Kirwan, **Revolt of the Rednecks: Mississippi Politics, 1876–1925* (1951); O. H. Shadgett, *The Republican Party in Georgia: From Reconstruction Through 1900* (1964); W. J. Cooper, Jr., *The Conservative Regime: South Carolina, 1877–1890* (1968); and W. I. Hair, *Bourbonism and Agrarian Protest: Louisiana Politics, 1877–1900* (1969). Some fresh insights are provided in a northern case-study by Geoffrey Blodgett, *The Gentle Reformers: Massachusetts Democrats in the Cleveland Era* (1966).

The fate of the blacks in the post-Reconstruction period has recently become a subject of great scholarly concern. Republican party strategy is discussed by V. P. DeSantis, *Republicans Face the Southern Question* (1959); and S. P. Hirshson, **Farewell to the Bloody Shirt* (1962). A bitter account by a distinguished black historian is R. W. Logan, **The Betrayal of the Negro* (2nd ed., 1965). The influential work of C. V. Woodward, **The Strange Career of Jim Crow* (3rd ed., 1966), has been challenged by other historians; see **The Origins of Segregation* (1968), edited by Joel Williamson, for a collection of conflicting interpretations. Valuable state studies are F. A. Logan, *The Negro in North Carolina, 1876–1894* (1964); M. L. Callcott, *The Negro in Maryland Politics, 1870–1912* (1969); and G. B. Tindall, **South Carolina Negroes, 1877–1900* (1952).

4

THE LAST FRONTIER

*The Far West · California prospectors · Mining booms · Colorado ·
Nevada · The Northwest · The Southwest · Utah · Staging and freighting ·
Evolution of law and order · The Indian wars · The new Indian policy · The
killing of the buffalo · The "sod-house" frontier · The range cattle industry ·
The passing of the cattleman*

The Far West

The exciting events of the Civil War and reconstruction, followed by the manifold problems of depression and recovery, served somewhat to obscure in the minds of contemporaries the importance of what was happening far out on the western frontier. Americans were accustomed to an advancing frontier; there had always been one, and they accepted it as a normal condition of society. But the frontier that came of age after the Civil War differed markedly from its predecessors. It took a Texas historian, Walter Prescott Webb, to observe that civilization east of the Mississippi proceeded comfortably into the West on three legs — land, water, and timber. But beyond the Mississippi on the Great Plains, two of these legs, water and timber, gave out, and thereafter civilization limped along as best it could on only one leg — land.[1] The newest West was a frontier of miners and cattlemen as well as of farmers, a frontier where mounted Indians fought desperately and sometimes successfully to hold back the tide of white invasion. Moreover, it was all that was left of the area within the national boundaries for civilization to conquer. The end of the frontier process, which from the beginning had been a kind of common denominator of American history, was in sight.

California Prospectors

Within a few years after the "forty-niners" had invaded California, they and their successors had exhausted practically all of the free gold that that region had to offer. California mining then became a capitalistic enterprise; expensive machinery was required to do the work that formerly anyone with a shovel and a "washpan"

A LAND OFFICE IN KANSAS. *From a wood engraving, circa 1874.*

[1] W. P. Webb, *The Great Plains* (1931), p. 9.

felt himself adequately equipped to do. As this situation unfolded, some of the adventurers turned to agriculture for a livelihood, others went back to the "States," and still others became "prospectors," men who searched the mountains for signs of gold, and sometimes made a "strike." These prospectors went everywhere, for gold had a way of appearing in the most unlikely places. Not content with having prospected every bleak plateau and every hidden valley of the Rocky Mountains, they found their way to such distant regions as South Africa and Australia, and there, too, they discovered gold. Only rarely did one of them acquire wealth, but thanks to their efforts the world's supply of gold was soon to be doubled.

Colorado

The Pike's Peak gold rush, which occurred just a decade after the rush to California, laid the basis of Colorado. As compared with the forty-niners, the fifty-niners had an easy time of it. Those who came from the East had less than half as far to go, they had no mountains to cross, and the trail they followed was well supplied with ferries, merchants, and even stagecoaches. Denver arrived full-grown almost overnight, and within a matter of weeks other mining camps in the "hills," such as Central City and Idaho Springs, achieved sizable proportions. Horace Greeley, of the *New York Tribune*, who went out merely to see what a gold rush was like, vividly described one of these early camps:

As yet the entire population of the valley sleeps in tents or under booths of pine boughs, cooking and eating in the open air. I doubt that there is . . . a table or chair in these diggings, eating being done on a cloth spread on the ground, while each one sits or reclines on mother earth.

Far sooner than in California the free gold of Colorado gave out, and for a time

it even seemed as if no permanent settlement might result. Covered wagons that had gone west displaying the hopeful legend, "Pike's Peak or Bust," returned east by the same route with the label changed to read, "Busted, by gosh." Some, however, stayed on, as in California, to farm; as early as the summer of 1859 radishes, lettuce, onions, and peas brought high prices on the Denver market. Native grasses were cut for hay; claims were staked out and claims clubs formed; irrigation, after the manner of the Mormons in Utah, was introduced. Soon capitalistic mining replaced the crude efforts of the first comers, and such "valley" towns as Golden, Colorado City, and Pueblo showed sure signs of permanence. Efforts to follow the example of California in making a new state without going through the customary territorial stage came to nought, although an unauthorized Territory of Jefferson existed for a few months. In 1861 Congress made Colorado a territory, and a few years later, in order to obtain more Unionist senators and representatives in Washington, would have admitted it as a state. This offer, however, was wisely declined, for as late as

Pike's Peak or Bust. *The end of the trail, from a sketch by J. C. Beard.*

California Gold Diggers. *An artist's depiction of actual life at the mines. Prospectors carried the same techniques of gold-mining to all the mountain areas that they worked for gold.*

1870 the population of Colorado was only 40,000. Admission as the "Centennial State" came finally in 1876. Shortly afterward the exploitation of silver mines around Leadville inaugurated an era of prosperity that the region had not known before.

Nevada

While the rest of the country resounded to the din of Civil War, the mineral empire of the West expanded with undiminished rapidity. Close on the heels of the Pike's Peak gold rush came a similar rush to the western part of what is now Nevada, where gold had been discovered along the main trail to California. The famous Comstock Lode, discovered in the spring of 1859, brought in no less than 15 million dollars' worth of silver and gold in a single year. Located in the heart of a desert, a less auspicious place for the development of a new area of settlement could hardly have been imagined, but such was the richness of the mines that adventurers by the thou-

sand flocked in from California and Oregon to the West, as well as from the settled regions of the East. Such towns as Carson City and Virginia City fantastically flaunted their wealth in the face of a desert where water was almost as dear as the other liquid refreshments the miners so liberally consumed. In 1861 Congress made Nevada a territory, and three years later, with a population probably greater than it possessed in later years, Nevada accepted the same hasty offer of statehood that Colorado rejected. Unlike most of the mining regions, Nevada offered few opportunities for agriculture and the prosperity of the new state was limited almost exclusively to the exploitation of its mineral resources.

Mining Booms in the Northwest

After the opening of Nevada, mining booms came thick and fast. In the vicinity of Lewiston, Idaho, then a part of Washington Territory, gold was found in 1860, and next year the inevitable boom occurred.

As news of new strikes came in, the miners rushed from place to place founding, as they went, such permanent settlements as Florence and Boise City, but leaving often as suddenly as they had come. "The Idaho miners," said H. H. Bancroft, "were like quicksilver. A mass of them dropped in any locality, broke up into individual globules, and ran off after any atom of gold in their vicinity. They stayed nowhere longer than the gold attracted them." In 1863 the Territory of Idaho was created, but by that time the miners had crossed the Bitter Root Mountains to lay the foundations of Montana. Such mining centers as Bannack City, Virginia City, Deer Lodge, and Missoula not only drew population away from the farther western camps, but also attracted newcomers from the East,

many of whom came up the Missouri River to Fort Benton, which in high water could be reached by steamboats. Among those who came were a number of refugees from the guerrilla warfare that raged along the Kansas-Missouri border during the Civil War, and others who preferred the hazards of the mines to the prospect of being drafted into the army. In 1864 Montana was separated from Idaho as an independent territory.

The Far Southwest

During the same period the Far Southwest, too, had its mining booms. The mineral resources of New Mexico, twin territory with Utah, had long been known, but the Spanish-Mexican population, located mainly in the upper Rio Grande Valley,

Comstock Lode, Nevada. *A diagram showing methods of mining in use on the Comstock, as drawn by T. L. Dawes, 1876.*

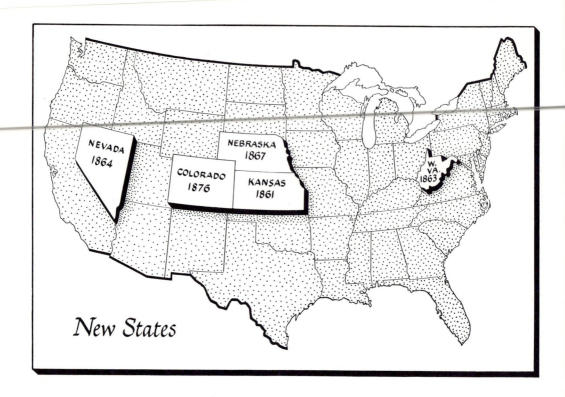

New States

subsisted upon agriculture and ignored the mines. The Americans, however, reopened the ancient diggings near Tucson and Tubac, and found placer gold in considerable quantities in the valley of the lower Colorado. When in 1862 Colonel James H. Carleton attempted to lead a column of eighteen hundred Californian volunteers to the aid of the Union forces in New Mexico, he was plagued by desertions to what he described as "one of the richest gold countries in the world." Thus another mining boom got under way, and in 1863 Congress, as usual, obliged by creating out of the western half of New Mexico the new Territory of Arizona.

Decline of Gold and Silver Mining

The prosperity of these new mountain territories varied markedly in the years that followed the war. As long as the Comstock Lode continued to yield up its riches, Nevada fared best, but by 1880 this magnificent deposit had been worked out, and the desert cities faded as rapidly as they had bloomed. Stocks in Nevada mines valued at $393 million in 1875 could be bought five years later for $7 million. The fate of the mines in Colorado, where the quartz lodes could be reached and reduced only with the aid of heavy financial outlays, fluctuated according to the availability of capital and the intelligence with which it was utilized. In Idaho and Montana the fortune hunters of 1866 numbered probably thirty and forty thousand respectively, but the census of 1870 found that only half that many had seen fit to remain. A dozen years later, the opening of rich copper mines near Butte, Montana, ushered in an era of unprecedented prosperity for that region which the exploitation of other base metals, such as lead and zinc, handsomely reinforced. Ultimately the world's largest copper smelters were to be located at Anaconda, Montana. In the Southwest the exhaustion of placer gold brought the Civil War boom to a quick conclusion, and, in the years that followed, the warlike nature of the Apache Indians tended to discourage even the prospectors. Here, as in Montana, copper presently became a more important product than gold. Always, too, there were agricultural beginnings; indeed, hard as was the lot of the farmer in these regions of inadequate rainfall, Indian raids, and grasshopper plagues, the prosperity of any territory could almost be measured by the number of its inhabitants who forsook the mines for the farms.

The Mining Towns

Social conditions on the mining frontier differed little from place to place. Most mining towns centered about a single long winding street that followed, and occasionally crossed, a mountain stream. Horses hitched along the street testified to the almost universal dependence upon horseback means of communication, and no other criminal was so utterly despised or so certainly punished as the horse thief. Most of the houses were hastily improvised, one-roomed, one-storied structures. In-

variably the most pretentious buildings were occupied by saloons and gambling houses, to which the men turned for amusement after the hard and lonely labor of the mines. Few women reached the early mining camps, and those who came were usually of easy virtue. Drunkenness and debauchery were too common to attract much notice, and for a long time individual vengeance provided almost the only punishment that was meted out for crime. Medical help for the sick and injured was of the crudest sort, or, more likely, was altogether missing, and the death rate was high. The romance of the mines, so dear to the heart of the fictionist, was built on the slenderest possible basis of fact.

Utah

An oasis of civilization at the very center of the mineral empire was Utah, the home of the Mormons, as members of the Church of Jesus Christ of Latter Day Saints were generally called. Here the astute Mormon leader, Brigham Young, had eschewed for himself and his people the quest of gold and silver in order to develop a planned society based on agriculture. The key to Mormon prosperity was irrigation, which the centralized character of the Mormon establishment enabled Young to introduce with a minimum of difficulty. Within less

Irrigation in Utah. *This drawing shows the early irrigation and fencing methods used by the Mormons near Salt Lake City.*

than two decades he succeeded in creating a comprehensive network of irrigation canals that literally made "the desert blossom as the rose." Determined that the new Zion should grow, he sent missionaries all over Europe and the United States, and founded a Perpetual Emigrating Fund Company to supply converts with the money and services they needed for emigration to the promised land. In the early years some of these newcomers actually pushed handcarts the entire length of the Mormon trail, but well before the Civil War wagon trains from Salt Lake City provided a better means of transportation, while after 1869 the Union Pacific Railroad solved the problem permanently.[1]

The coming of the railroad meant closer trade relations with the outside world, and a considerable modification of the self-sufficient economy that Young had promoted. But despite the growing population, which now began to include many non-Mormons, or "Gentiles," the ascendancy of the Mormon church in economic as well as in religious matters long remained in evidence. The Zion's Cooperative Mercantile Institution, for example, which was incorporated in 1869, engaged in almost every type of merchandising, and left most of its competitors far behind. By 1870 the population of Utah was well over 86,000, of whom nearly 13,000 lived in Salt Lake City, a well-planned community with wide streets, comfortable houses, and an impressive Tabernacle, all in marked contrast with the average mining town of crooked streets and vice-infested buildings.

While the Mormon ideal was a theocracy, pure and simple, with an all-powerful church under a divinely-inspired leader, there was no escaping the necessity of making terms with the American government. When President Buchanan decided in 1857

to supplant Brigham Young with a non-Mormon governor of Utah Territory, he could no doubt have implemented his decision without resort to force had he been better advised. But he had been led to believe that the "Saints" were in full rebellion against the authority of the United States, so he sent out a detachment of federal troops to back up his appointee. The resulting "Utah War" was in the main a fiasco, but it prompted a spirit of violence that led to the Mountain Meadows massacre of September, 1857, in which over a hundred non-Mormon emigrants lost their lives.

The principal problem that the Mormons presented, however, was their doctrine of "plural marriages." Hardly more than 3 per cent of the Mormon men had more than one wife, but the existence of polygamy within the nation's borders greatly shocked most Americans, and led to serious efforts to end it. Congress passed an "anti-bigamy" act as early as 1862, but it did not become effective until supplemented by the Edmunds Act of 1882, which provided new and drastic penalties for polygamists. In addition to fine and imprisonment, they might not sit on juries, nor hold public office, nor vote. Rigorously enforced by a federal commission of five members, the new law sent many church leaders to jail, but it took the even more drastic Edmunds-Tucker Act of 1887 to break Mormon resistance. Under this law federal authorities seized the property of the Mormon church, and forced it to pay a high rental even for use of the block on which the Salt Lake Temple stood.

Finally in 1890 Wilford Woodruff, fourth president of the church (Young died in 1877), suspended the practice of plural marriage for the future, while the federal government gave up further efforts to punish persons who had contracted such marriages before November 1, 1890. In due time the church received its property back again, and polygamy began to dis-

[1] See pp. 110–112.

appear. Mormon solidarity in politics gave way to individual alignment with the national political parties, and the quest for economic self-sufficiency yielded to the capitalistic influences which were transforming the American West. With a population which had passed 210,000 in 1890, Utah was now judged qualified for statehood, and in 1896 entered the Union.

Staging and Freighting

Before the coming of the railroad, and to a somewhat lesser extent afterward, enterprising individuals and companies, including many Mormons, made a good thing of supplying the western outposts with the necessities of life and transporting to the East or to some point of the railroad the product of the mines. Stagecoaches and freight-wagons made their appearance on the western plains during the fifties, and by the time the Civil War ended there were few places too remote for them to reach. As early as 1857, when the United States government asked for bids to carry the mail to California, there was no dearth of plains express companies ready to do the work. The contract went to John Butterfield, whose "Overland Mail" operated until 1861 along the southern route, and thereafter by the central route. During the years 1860–1861 the firm of Russell, Majors, and Waddell, without a government subsidy, relayed light mail by "pony express" from St. Joseph, Missouri, to Sacramento, California, in less than two weeks. The pony express and the company that backed it were put out of business by the completion of a telegraph line to the Pacific in 1861, but stagecoach connections, with the aid of generous mail contracts, continued to be multiplied. By 1866 Ben Holladay, into whose monopolistic grasp most of the western routes had fallen, could claim a total of five thousand miles of stage-lines. That same year Holladay sold out to Wells, Fargo, and Company.

Travel by western stage was an experience not to be forgotten. The stage itself, with its high, heavy wheels, its wide, thick tires, and its sturdy leather thorough-braces instead of springs, was no western invention, but rather the product of centuries of experience. It was equipped with three inside seats for passengers, an outside front seat for the driver, and a rear container for baggage. Painted a bright red or green, and drawn by two or more teams of horses, it bowled along the prairies, forded bridgeless streams, ignored wind, sand, and dirt. Dangers abounded from the charges of angry buffaloes, from attacks by hostile Indians, from robberies in a region that long knew no law. Passage through these hazards from the Mississippi to the Pacific cost about $200, with corresponding charges for shorter distances. One articulate traveler, a certain Demas Barnes, who took the stage to Denver in 1865, described his trip as follows:

It is not a *pleasant*, but it is an *interesting* trip. The conditions of one man's running stages to make money, while another seeks to ride in them for pleasure, are not in harmony to produce comfort. Coaches will be overloaded, it will rain, the dust will drive, baggage will be left to the storm, passengers will get sick, a gentleman of gallantry will hold the baby, children will cry, nature demands sleep, passengers will get angry, the drivers will swear, the sensitive will shrink, rations will give out, potatoes become worth a gold dollar each, and not to be had at that, the water brackish, the whiskey abominable, and the dirt almost unendurable. I have just finished six days and nights of this thing; and I am free to say, until I forget a great many things now visible to me, I shall not undertake it again.[1]

Freighting on the western plains was no less important than staging. Little of this went through to the Pacific Coast, for

[1] D. E. Clark, *The West in American History* (1937), p. 517.

Deadwood Coach. *By this picturesque means of transportation passengers journeyed to and from the Black Hills. The stagecoaches also took out the newly mined gold, a principal reason for the many robberies.*

water transportation served that purpose better, but the great interior region opened up by the mines was served, for the most part, by slow-moving freight-wagons, drawn by ox teams from such Missouri River towns as Independence, Leavenworth, Nebraska City, and Omaha. After the building of the Union Pacific the freight-wagons, and the stages also, took off into the interior from such railroad stations as lay nearest the desired destinations, but in any event huge freight charges had to be paid. According to a reliable estimate the total freight bill of the mountain towns for one year, 1866, was $31 million. High prices gave merchants a chance for long profits, and laid the basis for many pioneer fortunes, such, for example, as those amassed by the Creighton brothers of Omaha, and William A. Clark of Montana. Demas Barnes was much impressed with the freighting activities he witnessed:

The great feature of the Plains is the transportation trains, usually consisting of thirty to fifty wagons, five yoke each. . . . As they wind their slow course over the serpentine roads and undulating surface in the distance, a mile in extent (I saw one train five miles long), the effect is poetic, grand, beautiful. They select a high position for camping, draw the wagons in a circle, enclosing say a quarter, half, or full acre, the exterior serving as a

fort, the inside as a camp, and a place wherein to drive the animals in case of danger, and to yoke or harness them for the next trip. One of these camps, seen at sundown, with night fires kindled, and from five hundred to a thousand head of animals feeding near by, is well worth a long visit to behold.

Lawlessness

The traffic of the plains, particularly the cargoes of gold that the stagecoaches took out, led inevitably to many robberies. Gangs of "bad men," drawn together to live by their wits rather than by their labor, terrorized the stage routes, and took a heavy toll, not only in gold but also in lives. The gang led by Henry Plummer, operating during the sixties in what is now Montana, was guilty of over a hundred known murders and an untold number of robberies. But here, as in California, vigilantes, administering lynch law, eventually won out. One might note, indeed, four stages of development on any given mining frontier: (1) peaceful exploitation by the original prospectors; (2) the mining "boom," with its full quota of violence and crime; (3) the establishment of vigilance committees to punish the worst criminals and to introduce a reign of law; and (4) the creation of regular legal governments. In many instances, however, the third and fourth stages were reversed. Legal government sometimes preceded the work of the vigilantes; Plummer himself was a sheriff, and local government throughout the region he terrorized was in the hands of the "bad men" until the vigilantes broke their power.

The Black Hills

In 1876, the last great mining boom of the West broke forth in the Black Hills region of southwestern Dakota Territory — a wild, barren region, long suspected of harboring gold. Deadwood, the principal city, lay in the heart of a wilderness, and depended for the necessities of life upon stagecoaches and freighters from Bismarck to the north and Cheyenne to the south. Bandits and Indians were plentiful, but Wells, Fargo, and Company carried out the gold in steel-lined, heavily guarded coaches that were not lightly attacked. In a single trip, July, 1877, $350,000 in gold was taken out, and before the stage-line surrendered its business to the railroad, the grand total of such shipments had reached $60 million.[1] Deadwood, as the chief supply station for the various mining camps nearby, built up a lively prosperity. Here, too, gathered a notable array of gamblers and outlaws, the backwash of all the mining booms; among them, "Wild Bill" Hickok, who shot from the hip and rarely missed his mark, and "Calamity Jane" Canary, a colossal sinner whose fame spread far and wide. Deadwood was more sophisticated than most of the early mining towns, and boasted, along with its gambling houses and saloons, several theaters, particularly the *Gem*, which provided living quarters for its players and produced numerous plays of merit. During one season, before street carnivals, dance halls, and barroom singers put the theater out of business, the *Mikado* had a run of 130 nights.

[1] Total output of all the western mines, 1860 to 1890, has been set at $1,241,827,032 in gold, and $901,160,660 in silver.

Evolution of Law and Order

For all its seeming tumult, life in the mining camps was founded upon a sound substratum of common sense. Lawlessness eventually was curbed, and the normal institutions of government were evolved. Agriculture, even under the most adverse circumstances, was speedily introduced. Rule-of-thumb arrangements — such, for example, as those which enabled the discoverer of a mine to "stake out his claim," or the first farmer to use the waters of a given stream for irrigation purposes to have a "priority right" over all others — presently received the sanction of law. More women came in, and with them schools, churches, and the amenities of life. Frontier characteristics gradually gave way before the advance of civilization; the individualism of the early miners to the co-operative, capitalistic enterprises that were required to carry on their work; the actual democracy of the boom days to the astounding inequalities between those who "struck it rich," and those whose poverty endured; the radicalism of a new society to the conservatism of one that approached middle age. And yet, the social inheritance from the mining frontier could hardly be called negligible. Throughout the region first opened by the mines, the tendency to paint an overbright picture still reflects the chronic optimism of the prospector, and the ease with which the speculative spirit is fanned into a flame shows that the gambling instinct is not yet quite dead. Here, too, where unruly elements from all over the world broke the "cake of custom" most thoroughly, the old willingness to try anything new remains a hardy perennial. Widely separated from the rest of the country, and for a long time a law unto itself, the Far West retained for many decades a certain aloofness — it was a part of the United States, and yet at the same time apart from it. Californians long spoke, as the

Fort Laramie. *An army post on the Oregon-California trail that was visited alike by emigrants, Indians, and mountain men.*

miners did before them, of going back to the "States."

The Indians

Among the inevitable complications that resulted from the opening of the mining West was the necessity of developing a new Indian policy for the United States. The old policy of leaving the region west of the "bend of the Missouri" for the exclusive use of the Indians had broken down badly in the decade before the Civil War. Thousands of emigrants, crossing the plains to Oregon, to Santa Fe, to Utah, and to California, came into contact and often into conflict with the Indians. Demands for protection of the trails led to the establishment of army posts in the Indian country at such strategic centers as Fort Kearney and Fort Laramie, and to treaties between the United States and most of the Indian tribes, describing the tribal boundaries, and authorizing the government to build both roads and posts wherever it wished. While the Indians received annuities as compensation for the losses they sustained from the white intrusion, they found the new agreements far from satisfactory, and frequently forgot their promises not to molest the emigrants. The requirement of new cessions in Minnesota, in Iowa, in Kansas, and in Nebraska added still further to the unrest, both on the part of the tribes that had to find new homes, and on the part of those who had to make room for unwanted newcomers. Altogether, the time was ripe for trouble from the Indians when the Civil War broke out, while the combing of the mountains for gold that accompanied the conflict furnished still further cause for alarm.

The Sioux Outbreak in Minnesota

In 1862 came the first uprising. The Sioux of Minnesota, reduced by land cessions to a narrow and indefensible reserve along the Minnesota River, had long suffered from the dishonesty of traders and government agents. With the regular army garrisons withdrawn, and their places taken by unsuspecting volunteers, the Indians' temptation to seek revenge was great. Nevertheless, the trouble, when it came, was precipitated by the unauthorized action of a few irresponsible braves who on August 18, 1862, murdered five whites near New Ulm, Minnesota. The white population of the vicinity, sure that a general attack was impending, fled for their lives, while the Indians, no less frightened, divided into two groups, one of which made a hasty retreat to the west, while the other under Little Crow, knowing that the whites would never forgive the murders, took the warpath, burning farmhouses and villages, and killing men, women, and children by the hundreds. In due time the Indians were met by overwhelming numbers of state militia, decisively defeated, and many of them captured. Of the captives some four hundred were tried by court-martial in St. Paul, and over three hundred were sentenced to death. All but thirty-eight of those sentenced were pardoned by President Lincoln, but these unfortunates paid the full penalty for their crime at a great hanging-bee, held at Mankato, Minnesota, the day after Christmas, 1862. Settlers came from far and near to witness the executions, which were made the more weird by the fact that the unhappy Indians during their imprisonment had been converted to Christianity, and had come to be known as the "praying Indians." In 1863 the remnants of the Sioux were harassed by an expedition into Minnesota and Dakota, and the entire Sioux holding in Minnesota was confiscated. Little Crow himself was killed in July, 1863, and his tanned scalp, his skull, and his wrist bones presently became prized exhibits of the Minnesota Historical Society.

The Arapaho and Cheyenne

The rigorous punishment meted out to the Minnesota Sioux failed to deter the plains Indians from following their example. Among the tribes most affected by the coming of the miners were the Arapaho and Cheyenne, who were persuaded in 1861 to make way for the white advance into Colorado by withdrawing into what was generally known as the Sand Creek Reserve, a barren and gameless tract in the southeastern part of the territory. Sullen and resentful, they began by the spring of 1864 to raid the trails along the South Platte, and to push on down into Nebraska. Companies engaged in staging and freighting were put out of business, settlers and travelers were killed, and the whole frontier as far east as the Blue River, was thrown into a panic. Promptly Governor John Evans called out the Colorado militia, but before ordering an attack he urged all peaceable

Indians to concentrate in certain designated posts where they would be safe from harm. Not until fall, when the best fighting weather was over, did any considerable number of Indians choose to accept this invitation, but by that time about five hundred of them, including Black Kettle, their leading chief, had reported to Fort Lyon on Sand Creek, and were encamped nearby. As evidence of their peaceful intentions they flew both a white flag and the Stars and Stripes above their camp.

Meanwhile, however, Major-General Curtis of the United States Army, in command of the West, had telegraphed, "I want no peace till the Indians suffer more," and Colonel J. M. Chivington in command of the Colorado militia made ready to oblige him. Although there were bands of Indians still on the warpath, Chivington chose to ignore them, and instead to make a surprise attack upon the camp at Sand Creek. At the break of day, November 29, 1864, with about nine hundred men he fell upon the unsuspecting camp and murdered in cold blood about one hundred men, women, and children. Following the practice of the savages, the soldiers indulged in indescribable mutilations of the dead bodies, the mildest of which was scalping. Next year the government made a new treaty with the Arapaho and Cheyenne, pushing them farther to the southeast, but the Senate failed to confirm it, and the homeless Indians were sometimes guilty of attacks on settlers and travelers. Expeditions against them in 1867 and 1868 culminated in another massacre, this time on the Washita, near the Texas border, where Lieutenant-Colonel George A. Custer with a detachment of regulars duplicated Chivington's unsavory exploit (November 27, 1868).[1] Black Kettle himself was slain, and his people at length accepted lands assigned to them in the Indian Territory.

[1] Custer lost his rank as Major-General of volunteers after the Civil War ended.

The Western Sioux

The western Sioux, who ranged north of the Platte and east of the mountains, were deeply disturbed, both by the fate that had overtaken the Arapaho and Cheyenne, and by the advent of mining activities in Montana. When, in 1865, the government decided to open a road along the Bozeman Trail, from Cheyenne northwestward to the mouth of the Rosebud in Montana, the Sioux determined to resist this invasion of their finest hunting grounds with all their might. That year General P. E. Connors in command of 1600 men, and guided by Jim Bridger, the noted plainsman, marched over part of the route, but was turned back by the Sioux; and in 1866 a second expedition under Colonel H. B. Carrington succeeded only with the greatest difficulty in building Fort Phil Kearny and Fort C. F. Smith to the east of the Big Horn Mountains. Red Cloud, the Indian leader, and his Sioux warriors risked no open fighting, but they continually harassed wood-trains sent out from the forts, and otherwise hampered the operations. On one occasion, a brash young officer, Captain W. J. Fetterman, was dispatched from Fort Phil Kearny to the aid of a wood-train with definite orders not to take the aggressive. New to western fighting and disdainful of Indians, he disobeyed orders, was ambushed, and in the resulting combat (December 21, 1866) every member of his party was slain. Two years later, when the government made peace with Red Cloud and his warriors, it was on condition that the "country north of the North Platte River and east of the summits of the Big Horn Mountains shall be held and considered to be unceded Indian Territory," and that the forts on the Bozeman Trail should be abandoned. This was one of the few instances in American history in which an Indian treaty registered a white retreat.

The Southwest

The Southwest also had its troubles with Indians. Most peaceable were the Pueblos of western New Mexico and eastern Arizona, relatively civilized tribes who built fort-like houses of adobe brick or stone in remote and inaccessible places. The Pueblos lived primarily from agriculture, especially the growing of corn, they knew something of such arts as weaving and the making of pottery, and they avoided warfare if possible. The Navahos, who dwelt in northwestern New Mexico and northeastern Arizona, learned from the Pueblos about weaving and other arts, but they came to depend for their subsistence mainly upon sheep-raising, and they followed their herds over a wide area. They, too, preferred peace to war, but were ready to defend their lands. The Apaches ranged far and wide throughout eastern Arizona, western Texas, and down into Mexico. They were famous horsemen, skilled warriors, and natural-born plunderers. Their depredations against stagecoaches, ranchers, miners, and emigrants reached a climax during the Civil War, but continued intermittently for many years thereafter. North and east of the Apaches were the Comanches, plains Indians who were also expert riders, and did their share to make life difficult for white men who adventured out on the western plains.

The New Indian Policy

Somewhat belatedly the government began to take steps toward the formation of a new Indian policy. A congressional Committee on the Condition of the Indian Tribes, created in 1865, visited the West, took full testimony on such gruesome events as the Chivington massacre, and revealed how utterly untenable the status of the Indians had become. Its illuminating *Report on the Condition of the Indian Tribes,*

THE KILLING OF THE BUFFALO. This sordid episode, so devoid of sportsmanship, helped starve the Indians into submission, and paved the way for the expansion of the range cattle industry.

THE INDIAN WARS. *For two decades the Indians fought tenaciously on the western plains to preserve their way of life. While they lost in the end, they did not lose every battle.*

LITTLE CROW. "The Hawk that Hunts Walking," or Little Crow, was the principal leader of the Sioux bands that participated in the Minnesota massacres of 1862. From a photograph by A. Z. Shindler, taken four years earlier.

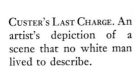

CUSTER'S LAST CHARGE. An artist's depiction of a scene that no white man lived to describe.

made in 1867, led to the creation of an Indian Peace Commission, composed of three generals and four civilians, whose duty it was not only to stop the Indian wars, but also to work out a permanent solution of the Indian problem. The commission planned two great meetings, one for the southern tribes at Medicine Lodge Creek, near the southern border of Kansas, held in 1867, and one for the northern tribes at Fort Laramie, held in 1868. At these councils, treaties were concluded that paved the way for the general adoption of the reservation system. It seemed evident that the Indians could no longer be permitted to roam at will, but must instead be confined to certain specified areas. Confiscation of the western half of the holdings of the Five Civilized Tribes in the Indian Territory, on the ground that the tribes had sided with the Confederacy during the Civil War, made possible the resettlement in that region of the Arapaho and Cheyenne and other plains Indians. In the North the Sioux were left in peaceable possession of southwestern Dakota, and such minor tribes as the Utes, Shoshonis, and Bannocks were concentrated within appropriate narrow limits. Subsidies in the form of annuities, payments for lands, and outright doles helped the dispossessed Indians to eke out a precarious existence, and thus introduced pauperization as a means of insuring docility.

One of the principal defects of American Indian policy was the contradictory attitudes on the one hand of the Bureau of Indian Affairs, created in 1849 within the Department of the Interior, and on the other of the War Department and the army. The Bureau, on the whole, tended to take a paternalistic interest in the welfare of the tribes, sought earnestly to better their conditions of life, and even trusted them with arms for hunting game, arms that were sometimes used instead against the whites. Widespread corruption among the Indian agents coupled with unexemplary behavior on the part of traders, emigrants, and renegades greatly complicated the situation. The War Department, which had to accept responsibility for the pacification of the Indians whenever they got out of hand, took a very dim view of civilian control, and complained bitterly that Indians on the warpath were often better armed than the soldiers sent to fight them. What the government really needed was a separate Indian service, composed of especially trained personnel and endowed with adequate police power, but such an idea was wholly foreign to the times. A new Board of Indian Commissioners, composed of nonpolitical civilians, was created in 1869 to advise with the Bureau of Indian Affairs. Acting on the assumption that eventually the Indians could be turned into peaceful and contented farmers, the makers of Indian policy tried to break down tribal autonomy, and in 1871 they induced Congress to abolish the legal fiction of dealing with the tribes by treaty as if they were foreign nations. This was a definite improvement, but the road to civilization for the Indian was long and hard.

Later Indian Uprisings

By this time most of the Indian fighting was at an end, although occasional outbreaks occurred until as late as 1890. The worst of these was precipitated by the Black Hills gold rush, which brought thousands of whites into the heart of the region reserved for the Sioux. Even before the rush started, military maneuvers, designed merely to check up on the rumors of gold, and wholesale frauds, perpetrated systematically at the Red Cloud Indian Agency, had alarmed the Sioux, and many of them had left the reservation. Led by two able braves, Sitting Bull and Crazy Horse, the fugitives ignored all orders to return and fought bravely when troops were sent to herd them in. During this campaign Colonel

Custer's Expedition. *This Corps of Engineers photograph shows clearly the complicated nature of an army campaign against the western Indians. Such an expedition involved not only fighting men, but also the transportation and protection of essential supplies.*

George A. Custer and his command of over two hundred cavalrymen met the same fate that Custer had meted out to the Indians on the Washita eight years before. Lured into an ambush, Custer and his entire command lost their lives, June 25, 1876. But within a short time General Nelson A. Miles had restored order. Crazy Horse was captured, and Sitting Bull fled to Canada. In 1877, a somewhat similar uprising among the Nez Percés of Idaho came to the same inexorable end. Chief Joseph, the Indian leader, gave a good account of himself, but at length surrendered. "I am tired of fighting," he told his chiefs. "My heart is sick and sad. From where the sun now stands I will fight no more forever." Down in New Mexico and Arizona the Pueblos and the Navahos made terms with the reservation system, but the Apaches were hard to tame, and the campaigns against them

amounted almost to wars of extermination. Not until 1886, when Geronimo, their principal chief, was captured and exiled to Florida, was a lasting peace established. Trouble broke out again later in the decade with the Dakota Sioux. A religious frenzy led to demonstrations by Indian "ghost dancers" that frightened the Indian agents into calling for troops. Fearful of soldiers' vengeance, many Indians left the reservation, only to be massacred at the so-called Battle of Wounded Knee, December 29, 1890. Two weeks before, Sitting Bull, who in 1881 had returned to the United States, had lost his life while resisting, or seeming to resist, arrest.

Lands in Severalty

The wars against the Indians, conducted after 1865 exclusively by regular army detachments, were far from popular with the American people, and protests against the inhuman treatment that the tribes received grew more and more insistent. The publication in 1881 of Helen Hunt Jackson's *A Century of Dishonor,* with its stinging indictment of the American Indian policy, brought public opinion strongly behind all efforts to alleviate the lot of the Indians. Their retention upon reservations, however, was an obvious necessity, and was long continued. In 1887 the Dawes Act paved the way for the gradual extinguishment of tribal ownership of lands, and the substitution in its place of individual allotments of 160 acres each to heads of families, 80 acres each to single adults or orphans, and 40 acres each to dependent children. Only a "trust patent" to the land was given at first, and complete ownership was delayed for twenty-five years. In 1906 the Burke Act gave the Secretary of the Interior a discretionary right to lessen the probationary period, and corrected other defects in the original law. Compulsory education for Indian children was introduced in 1891, and full citizenship was conferred in 1924 upon all Indians in the United States. It cannot be said, however, that the government's policy, granted the best of intentions, was ever an unqualified success. Many of the Indians retained to a degree their tribal identity, and showed remarkable powers of resistance against the white man's way of living. And yet others, particularly in Oklahoma, eventually achieved that full equality with whites that was once only the dream of idealists.

The Killing of the Buffalo

The victory of the whites over the Indians was not won entirely by military means; buffalo hunters, by destroying the princi-

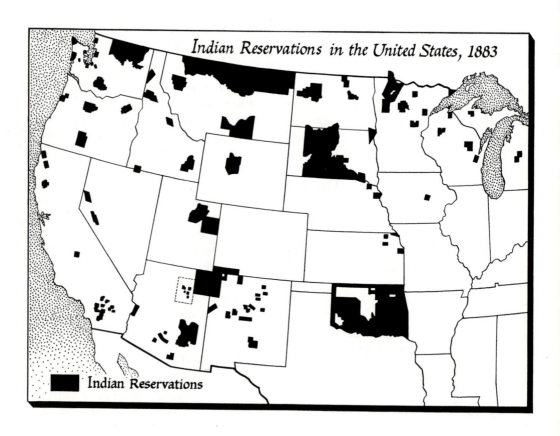

Indian Reservations in the United States, 1883

Indian Reservations

pal food resource of the Indians, also did their rather considerable bit toward bringing Indian resistance to an end. Shortly after the Civil War the killing of the buffalo began. Organized hunting parties equipped with repeating rifles killed them by the tens of thousands to obtain "buffalo robes," soon regarded as almost a necessity in the average American home. Others were killed, by Indians and whites alike, for their meat, but often only the tongue and a few choice cuts would be taken, and the rest of the carcass left to rot. Hunters killed them just for the sport of it, although one English sportsman who came to America primarily to hunt buffalo refused to take part in a game that he described about as exciting as shooting cows in a pasture. The building of the Union Pacific Railroad aided the hunters greatly, and divided the buffalo into two herds, one to the north and the other to the south. By 1870 from 5 to 7 million buffalo still existed, but in the succeeding years the slaughter was terrific. The southern herd was gone by 1875, and in 1883 Sitting Bull and his braves destroyed the last sizable remnant of the northern herd. Probably not more than a thousand head were left alive. For years buffalo bones were gathered for shipment by the trainload to eastern factories, where they were turned into fertilizers, or into carbon for the use of sugar refineries.

The passing of the buffalo, unpleasant as it is to contemplate, was not an unmixed evil. The government purposely did nothing to prevent the tragedy, for as long as the herds remained intact the Indians had a sure food supply, and could the more easily defy governmental control. Some of the later Indian uprisings were caused in part by the Indians' concern at the threatened destruction of their herds, but once the buffalo were gone the end of Indian resistance had been reached. Furthermore, the disappearance of the buffalo, together with the building of the western railroads and the pacification of the Indians, gave western agriculture the chance it needed to grow.

The "Sod-House Frontier"

Directly to the west of the "bend of the Missouri" lay a broad belt of prairie land that invited the settlers in. Here the mapmakers had marked out the boundaries of Dakota Territory to the north, Kansas and Nebraska in the middle, and the unorganized Indian Territory to the south. For the time being white settlers were in law, although not in fact, excluded from the Indian Territory, but from the southern boundary of Kansas to the Canadian border a new agricultural frontier pushed inexorably into the West. Since in general this area was treeless, pioneers found a substitute for the traditional log cabins in sod houses built from the heavy prairie sod turned up by their breaking plows; hence the term, "sod-house frontier." The problem of water was not always so easily solved. In the eastern third of the region rainfall was usually adequate to produce crops, and the water table for wells was not far below the surface. But the western third lay in the high, arid plains, while the middle third was intermediate, with "wet years" when there was no problem of rainfall and water supply, and dry years when the problem was acute.[1]

Federal Land Policy

Generous land legislation did its part to induce the restless farmer, the discontented artisan, the newly-arrived immigrant, and the former soldier to make a try at the West. Not everyone who wished to seek a new home on the "sod-house frontier" could raise the price of the trip, but for those who could do so the acquisition of a farm was made easy. The Homestead Act of 1862, for a few dollars in fees, made it possible for any American citizen, or any alien who had declared his intention of becoming a citizen, to obtain 160 acres of

[1] See p. 170.

The Sod-House Frontier. *With timber for log-cabins lacking, early pioneers on the western prairies and plains built themselves such houses as these.*

unoccupied government land (or 80 acres if within a railroad land grant) by living on it for five years. Or as cynics put it later, the government bet a man a 160-acre farm that "he couldn't live on it for five years without starving to death." An Act of 1870 extended special privileges to soldiers who had fought in the Union army. Any such veteran might count his time of service toward the five-year period required for proving up on a homestead, and any widow of a soldier might count the full term of her dead husband's enlistment in the same way. Furthermore the Preemption Act of 1841, which remained on the statute books until 1891, allowed the settler to locate a claim of 160 acres, and after six months' residence to buy it from the government at the minimum price, $1.25 an acre under ordinary circumstances. In railroad land grants the price was $2.50 an acre on the theory that the coming of the railroad would double the value of the land.

The government even made an effort to adapt its land policy to the conditions of life in the farther West. The Timber Culture Act of 1873, for example, was designed to encourage the planting of trees. Under its terms the settler who would plant 40 acres (later reduced to 10) in trees, and keep them in growing condition for ten years, could obtain title to a quarter section of land. These laws permitted the enterprising settler to extend his holdings far beyond the traditional 160 acres of land. They opened the way also to a veritable orgy of fraud and perjury, both on the part of legitimate settlers and on the part of conscienceless speculators. To cheat the government out of land, as long as plenty of it existed, was regarded on the frontier as a very minor offense, if an offense at all.

The Hazards of Pioneering

The hazards of the new western environment were far greater than most of the pioneers had foreseen. Sometimes in the fall when the high grass was dry, prairie fires swept over the land destroying everything they touched. Lack of timber posed not only a serious problem in the matter of housing, but equally serious problems also in fuel and fencing. For fuel, settlers often resorted to such makeshifts as cow dung, twisted prairie hay (called "cats"), sunflower stalks, and when they were available the far more satisfactory corncobs. Without fencing farming was practically impossible, but out on the prairies the rail fences of earlier frontiers were out of the question. There was much experimentation with hedges, particularly the osage-orange hedge, which was long used to good advantage, but a far better solution was soon supplied by the invention of barbed wire. The trouble with this commodity was that it cost money, a great deterrent for most of the newcomers. There was, too, a great adjustment necessary to meet the weather conditions of the new region. Where the rainfall proved to be inadequate or undependable, windmills were often pressed into use, and, on the high plains, irrigation. Storms of great violence swept over the level terrain, "cyclones" by summer that did terrific damage, blizzards by winter that froze to death both livestock and unsheltered human beings. Most baffling of all were the grasshopper plagues which came every eight or ten years, sometimes oftener. In vast clouds that darkened the sun these insects invaded the prairies, consuming all vegetation, and leaving the farmers' crops a shambles.

They came like a driving snow in winter, filling the air, covering the earth, the buildings, the shocks of grain, and everything. According to one observer their alighting on the roofs and sides of the houses sounded like a continuous hailstorm. They alighted on trees in such great numbers that their weight broke off huge limbs. . . . At times the insects were four to six inches deep on the ground and continued to alight for hours. Men were obliged to tie strings around their pants legs to keep the pests from crawling up their legs. In the cool of the evening the hoppers gathered so thick on the warm rails of the railroad that the Union Pacific trains were stopped. Section men were called out to shovel the grasshoppers off the track near the spot where Kearney, Nebraska, now stands, so that the trains could

Federal Land Policy. *This poster pointed the way for Civil War veterans to desirable land in the West.*

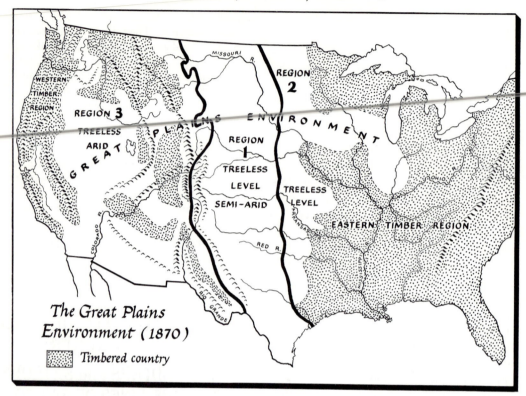

The Great Plains
Environment (1870)

Timbered country

get through. The track was so oily and greasy that the wheels spun and would not pull the train.[1]

Growth of the West

In spite of all these handicaps the settlers kept on coming, aided and abetted by the railroads along whose lines they settled, and for whom their presence meant the difference between solvency and bankruptcy. Veterans of the Civil War flocked to Kansas and Nebraska in such numbers as to give those states for a generation, or even longer, top-heavy Republican majorities. Substantial farmers throughout the North, but more especially those of the upper Mississippi Valley, sold their high-priced holdings to buy the cheaper lands of the West. Farm boys lately grown to manhood, small businessmen who had seen, or who hoped to see better days, and not a few unemployed artisans joined the procession to the West. Europeans, persuaded by railroad and steamship agents to leave their Old World homes, were herded aboard ship, and having reached America were sent by special trains from the port of entry to some prearranged location on railroad lands. As a result of these outpourings the "sod-house frontier" did not last long. Within a single generation a region that had started as wilderness was settled up, and had achieved to a considerable degree the normal paraphernalia of civilization.

The Cow Country

During the same years that the "sod-house frontier" was taking form, a cattlemen's frontier was also developing on the western plains. The various posts that dotted the western trails, some wholly private, and others centered about a garrisoned fort or

[1] Everett Dick, *The Sod-House Frontier, 1854–1890* (1937), pp. 203–4. Quoted by permission of Appleton-Century-Crofts, Inc., and the author.

an Indian agency, got an early start in cattle from the emigrants, who were frequently only too willing to exchange for urgent necessities any livestock they happened to have brought along. It was soon discovered that cattle could fend for themselves on the plains the whole year through, for the wiry "buffalo grass" cured on the ground and remained all winter long as nutritious as hay. There was no temptation, however, to increase these herds beyond immediate needs as long as the plains swarmed with Indians and buffalo, and outside markets were beyond reach.

Beginnings of the Cattle Industry

With the Indians curbed, the buffalo killed, and the transcontinental railroads pushing out upon the plains, the western cattle industry got the chance it needed to grow. But its real beginnings were Mexican rather than American, and dated back for centuries. Both the cattle themselves, and the horses without which the industry would have been vastly different (to say the least), were the descendants of European stock brought over by the Spaniards in the sixteenth century, and allowed to go wild. Survival of the fittest produced by the nineteenth century cattle that were more noted for their speed and endurance than for tender cuts of beef, each blessed also with an incredible spread of horns. The horses, sprung no doubt from noble Arabian forebears, had developed into sure-footed, quick-witted, wiry broncos, well under a thousand pounds in weight, but ideally suited for riding. The technique of cattle-raising, to the last detail, was worked out in Mexico long before it was introduced into the United States, and was practiced for years in New Mexico, Texas, and California. The cowboy's saddle, bridle, bit, lariat, and spurs were adaptations, for the most part, of equipment used by Spanish cavalrymen, while the "round-up" and the use of "brands" to indicate ownership were early invented to meet obvious needs. The unimportance of the cattle industry for so many years was not due to inability to produce cattle. Anyone in the Southwest with a little ambition could have all the cattle he wanted. What the industry needed was a market for its produce, and until that could be found it remained insignificant.

The Long Drive

Attempts to drive Texas cattle to an outside market were made from the time of the Mexican War on, but all such ventures amounted to little until the railroads began to push out across the western plains. Then the idea of the "long drive" from somewhere in Texas to a shipping point in Missouri, Kansas, or Nebraska immediately took hold. Sedalia, Missouri, the railhead of the Missouri Pacific, was the objective of many of the long drives in 1866, but the advantages of a terminal farther west where grazing was better and settlement was not a problem were quickly perceived. Abilene, Kansas, a station on the Kansas Pacific, became noted as early as 1867 as a "cow-town." Here untold numbers of Texas cattle, driven northward through the Indian Territory, or the "Nation," as cowboys called it, were purchased for the use of the newly-established packing-houses. Early each year drovers assembled herds for the "drive," or else individual ranchers rounded up their cattle and threw them upon the trail — a route generally known as the "Chisholm Trail," regardless of where it ran. Grazing the cattle as they went, cowboys moved them slowly northward in herds of two or three thousand head. Such a group required the services of sixteen or eighteen cowboys, a cook with a "chuck-wagon," and a "wrangler" with extra cowponies. Trials on the march included the danger of stampedes due to lightning, buffalo, or Indians.

The Cowboy

On the "long drive" the cowboy developed those peculiar characteristics that made him, like the fur trader, the lumberjack, and the prospector, a unique specimen of the American frontier. He found the revolver indispensable to the protection of his herd, and of great advantage in the actual business of herding. Naturally he became a fair marksman. He sang to the cattle, whether to help him bear the loneliness, or to keep the cattle aware of his presence, or to prevent or promote a stampede. The verses he invented were colorful, they told of the life he led, and they became as authentic a part of the American folklore as the songs of slavery and freedom that the southern Negroes sang. In reality, just a "plain everyday bowlegged human," the cowboy's occasional excesses after periods of long riding and lack of sport caught the eye of the fictionist, and were romanticized out of all proportion to the facts. A wanderer, an adventurer, and sometimes a refugee, the cowboy's actual exploits did make good stories, but most of his life was given over to hard and monotonous labor.[1]

The advance of the frontier into Kansas and Nebraska drove the "Chisholm Trail" farther and farther west, and determined the location of new cow-towns to take the place of those enclosed in settled areas. Dodge City, Kansas, for example, soon replaced Abilene as the leading shipping-point for Texas cattle. Settlement interfered with grazing; moreover, the Texas cattle brought with them the germs of the dreaded "Texas fever" to which they themselves had become immune, but which brought almost certain death to other cattle that caught it. Quarantine laws were passed that pushed the drive still farther into the west. Also, a new market was discovered when the northern plains had been cleared of buffalo. Northern ranchers, eager to expand their herds, paid good prices for the Texas longhorns, bred them up rapidly by the introduction of blooded cattle from the East, and laid the basis for a short, but spectacular, prosperity. Points on the Union Pacific such as Ogallala and Sidney, Nebraska, were visited by western as well as eastern buyers, and Cheyenne, Wyoming, which had once had no other excuse for existence than the railroad, now found itself the center of an exciting cattle industry. Texas cattle were driven northward as far as Dakota and Montana, and even westward into New Mexico, Arizona, Colorado, and Utah.

The Range Cattle Industry

The profits of cattle-growing on a well-policed range, for the use of which the government made no charge, and to which, thanks to the railroads, markets were now easily accessible, did not fail to attract capital, not only from the American East, but also from Europe, particularly England. Ranchers, or "cattlemen," as they were called to distinguish them from their employees, the "cowboys," figured that an original investment of $5000 should pay profits of from $40,000 to $50,000 in four years' time. Ranching companies, some of them with capital investments well up into the millions, were formed to crowd more and more cattle upon the range. Access to water was, of course, essential, and each individual or company engaged in the cattle business took care to obtain title to some land so situated. Here the ranch house and other necessary buildings were located, and from this headquarters operations were carried on over a range bounded by the

[1] The following lines are inscribed on a tombstone in the cemetery at Douglas, Wyoming:
"Underneath this stone in eternal rest
Sleeps the wildest one of the Wayward West.
He was gambler and sport and cowboy too,
And he led the pace in an outlaw crew.
He was sure on the trigger and staid to the end,
But he was never known to quit on a friend.
In the relations of death all mankind is alike,
But in life there was only one George W. Pike."

ARIZONA COWBOY. This photograph dramatically portrays the horse, saddle, equipment, and techniques of the western cow-puncher.

THE RANGE CATTLE INDUSTRY. *Unfenced government lands provided the setting for this agricultural undertaking, which in fact lasted for little more than two decades, but in fiction lives on indefinitely.*

DODGE CITY, KANSAS, in the 1870's. This quiet frontier town came tumultuously to life when cowboys took it over after completing a "Long Drive."

TEXAS LONGHORNS. The "Long Drive" brought uncounted numbers of Texas cattle northward to the railroads for shipment to market and both north and west to stock the ranches of the cattlemen.

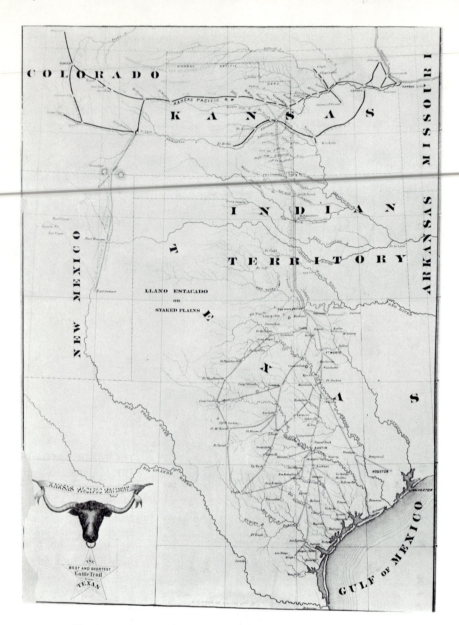

The Long Drive. *This map, published by the Kansas Pacific Railroad in 1875, shows the routes used for driving Texas cattle north for shipment to market.*

distance the cattle were willing to travel to water. Large "outfits," as the companies were called, sometimes had access to water at many different places, and companies existed that claimed the grazing rights to strips of land no less than a hundred miles long and fifty miles wide.

The law of the range, like the law of the mining camp, was to a great extent invented to meet the needs of the situation. Stock-growers' associations were formed, at first for mutual protection, but later to work out rules for users of the range that actually had the effect of law. Indeed, the Wyoming Stock-Growers' Association, formed in 1873, came to have more power than the territorial government of Wyoming, which, as a matter of fact, it controlled. The Association promoted community rather than individual round-ups, regulated the use of brands and recorded them, required that "mavericks" (unbranded cattle, except calves that followed their mothers) should be sold to the highest bidder and the proceeds paid into the Association treasury, discouraged overstocking of the range by refusing membership to outsiders, and made relentless warfare upon all who were suspected of "rustling" (stealing) cattle. Punishment for defiance of the Association might or might not await court action.

The Passing of the Cattleman

The day of the cattleman soon passed. Trouble with rustlers who branded mavericks and "worked" (altered) brands cost the ranchers heavy losses, both in cattle stolen and in fees paid to detectives and inspectors. Trouble with "nesters" (farmers) whose fences interfered with the free access of cattle to water-holes not only caused heavy losses in property, but frequently resulted also in loss of life. Cowboys learned to carry wire-cutters as part of their equipment; and finally, in self-defense, the cattlemen themselves began to fence the land they used but did not own, only to have their fences branded as illegal by the United States government, and ordered down. But the greatest calamity that befell the cattlemen was the overstocking of the range. By the middle eighties so many millions of cattle had been turned loose to pick up a living from the plains that one severe winter was sure to bring disaster, and instead of one such winter most of the range country saw two, 1885–86, and 1886–87. The result was wholesale ruin and bankruptcy, and a complete change in the nature of the cattle industry. After this time, ranchers tended more and more to raise hay for winter feed, and in general to carry on farming as well as ranching activities. On many ranges sheep replaced cattle, although not without resort

to actual warfare between sheepmen and cattlemen. The close-grazing sheep left the range stripped of grass, so when sheepmen came to stay cattlemen had to fight or leave. In some of these conflicts, sheep-herders were slain, the wagons that carried their supplies were burned, and the herds themselves were destroyed.

Short-lived as it was, the range-cattle industry left its mark upon the West and upon the country as a whole. It did its share to promote the growth of the meat-packing industry, so essential to the welfare of the urban East. It made clear the absurdity for the Far West of land legislation devised to meet the needs of the eastern half of the continent, and paved the way for important changes. The Desert Land Act of 1877, for example, permitted the acquisition in the arid states of 640 acres of land at $1.25 per acre on condition that the claimant would irrigate his holding, while the Timber and Stone Act of 1878 made possible the purchase at $2.50 per acre of an additional quarter section valuable chiefly for timber and stone. The cow country also bequeathed to later residents of the plains a breezy, slangy language, cowboy costumes, "dude" ranches, and rodeos. It lived persistently in stories of the "Wild West" such as Owen Wister's *The Virginian,* and the multitudinous works of Zane Grey; in the infinite number of scenarios derived from them for the use of the motion-picture and television industries; in the "Wild West" shows first popularized by "Buffalo Bill" Cody; in the solemn melodies and bungling rhymes of the cowboy songs.

Oh, beat the drum slowly and play the fife
  lowly;
  Play the dead march as you carry me along.
Take me to the green valley and lay the sod
  o'er me.
  I'm just a poor cowboy and I know I've
  done wrong.

BIBLIOGRAPHY

The most convenient guide to the vast literature on the westward movement is R. A. Billington, *Westward Expansion* (3rd ed., 1967); its bibliography is especially full and rich. Other surveys include F. L. Paxson, *History of the American Frontier, 1763–1893* (1924), heavily political; R. E. Riegel and R. G. Athearn, *America Moves West* (4th ed., 1964), lively and strong on cultural matters; and T. D. Clark, *Frontier America* (2nd ed., 1969), emphasizing the region east of the Mississippi. *America's Frontier Story: A Documentary History of Westward Expansion* (1969), edited by Martin Ridge and R. A. Billington, contains valuable documents and truly remarkable photographs.

The significance of the frontier was discussed by Frederick Jackson Turner in essays which can be found in his *The Frontier in American History* (1920), and in *Frontier and Section*, edited by R. A. Billington (1961). Contrasting views on the Turner hypothesis may be found in such works as: G. R. Taylor (ed.), *The Turner Thesis Concerning the Role of the Frontier in American History* (2nd ed., 1956); R. A. Billington (ed.), *The Frontier Thesis* (1966); H. N. Smith, *Virgin Land* (1950); W. P. Webb, *The Great Frontier* (1952); D. M. Potter, *People of Plenty* (1954); W. D. Wyman and C. B. Kroeber (eds.), *The Frontier in Perspective* (1957); and Merle Curti and others, *The Making of an American Community* (1959). Environmental differences between the plains and earlier frontiers are explored in W. P. Webb, *The Great Plains* (1931); and in J. C. Malin, *The Grasslands of North America* (1947).

The most comprehensive one-volume history of the trans-Mississippi west is L. R. Hafen and C. C. Rister, *Western America* (2nd ed., 1950); most of its strength is in the earlier period. *The Works of Hubert Howe Bancroft* (39 vols., 1874–1890) remain the beginning point for study of the Southwest, Rockies, and Pacific Coast in the pioneer period. J. W. Caughey, *Hubert Howe Bancroft* (1946), is both a biography and an introduction to the products of the famous "history factory." A valuable administrative history is E. S. Pomeroy, *The Territories and the United States, 1861–1890* (1947). See also J. E. Eblen, *The First and Second United States Empires* (1968).

Regional and state surveys are numerous but of uneven quality. Among the best regional works are: D. O. Johansen and C. M. Gates, *Empire of the Columbia* (2nd ed., 1967), on the Pacific Northwest; O. O. Winther, *The Great Northwest* (2nd ed., 1950), on the same area; D. W. Meinig, *The Great Columbia Plain* (1968); Earl Pomeroy, *The Pacific Slope* (1965); H. E. Briggs, *Frontiers of the Northwest* (1940), a topical treatment of the upper Missouri Valley; W. E. Hollon, *The Southwest* (1961), defined as Oklahoma, Texas, New Mexico, and Arizona; R. G. Athearn, *High Country Empire* (1960), an impressionistic account of the Missouri Basin; and P. F. Sharp, *Whoop-Up Country: The Canadian-American West, 1865–1885* (1955). In a class by itself is the superb economic history of the Mormons, L. J. Arrington, *Great Basin Kingdom* (1958). On the Mormons see also: S. P. Hirshson, *The Lion of the Lord: A Biography of Brigham Young* (1969); N. F. Furniss, *The Mormon Conflict, 1850–1859* (1960); T. F. O'Dea, *The Mormons* (1957); and William Mulder and A. R. Mortensen (eds.), *Among the Mormons* (1958), a source collection. Useful single-volume state histories include: J. W. Caughey, *California* (2nd ed., 1953); Walton Bean, *California* (1968); R. N. Richardson, *Texas* (2nd ed., 1958); E. C. McReynolds, *Oklahoma* (1954); W. F. Zornow, *Kansas* (1957); J. C. Olson, *History of Nebraska* (1955); and K. R. Toole, *Montana: An Uncommon Land* (1959). Important recent works include H. R. Lamar, *Dakota Territory, 1861–1889* (1956); H. S. Schell, *History of South Dakota* (1961); E. B. Robinson, *History of North Dakota* (1966); T. A. Larson, *History of Wyoming* (1965); L. L. Gould, *Wyoming: A Political History, 1868–1896* (1968); G. M. Ostrander, *Nevada* (1966); R. W. Larson, *New Mexico's Quest for Statehood, 1846–1912* (1968); and H. R.

Lamar, *The Far Southwest, 1846–1912* (1966).

On western mining there are two recent syntheses: R. W. Paul, *Mining Frontiers of the Far West* (1963); and W. S. Greever, *The Bonanza West* (1963). Technical aspects are treated by T. A. Rickard, *A History of American Mining* (1932). A valuable monograph is T. G. Manning, *Government in Science: The U.S. Geological Survey, 1867–1894* (1967). Among the best regional studies are R. W. Paul, *California Gold* (1947); D. A. Smith, *Rocky Mountain Mining Camps* (1967); W. T. Jackson, *Treasure Hill: Portrait of a Silver Mining Camp* (1963), which covers 1848–1873; G. D. Lyman, *The Saga of the Comstock Lode* (1934); W. J. Trimble, *The Mining Advance into the Inland Empire* (1914); and M. G. Burlingame, *The Montana Frontier* (1942). Law and order are discussed in C. H. Shinn, *Mining Camps* (1885). Two fine treatments of later rushes are: Marshall Sprague, *Money Mountain: The Story of Cripple Creek Gold* (1953); and Pierre Berton, *The Klondike Fever* (1958). A rich vein is opened by C. C. Spence, *British Investments and the American Mining Frontier, 1860–1901* (1958).

Pre-railroad transportation problems are dealt with in such works as: Dorothy Gardiner, *West of the River* (1941); O. O. Winther, *Via Western Express and Stagecoach* (1945), and *The Old Oregon Country* (1950). Winther's *The Transportation Frontier: Trans-Mississippi West, 1865–1890* (1964) is an admirable synthesis.

Vivid introductions to the Indian wars are R. K. Andrist, *The Long Death* (1964); and P. I. Wellman, *Indian Wars of the West* (2 vols., 1947). An important study of federal policy is H. E. Fritz, *The Movement for Indian Assimilation, 1860–1890* (1963). See also C. M. Oehler, *The Great Sioux Uprising* (1959); J. C. Olson, *Red Cloud and the Sioux Problem* (1965); Mari Sandoz, *Crazy Horse* (1942); and E. I. Stewart, *Custer's Luck* (1955). An interesting account of Indian war correspondents is Oliver Knight, *Following the Indian Wars* (1960). On military subjects see also R. G. Athearn, *William Tecumseh Sherman and the Settlement of the West* (1956); V. W. Johnson, *The Unregimented General: A Bibliography of Nelson A. Miles*

(1962); and two books by W. H. Leckie, *The Military Conquest of the Southern Plains* (1963), and *The Buffalo Soldiers: A Narrative of the Negro Cavalry in the West* (1967). Other important studies include R. I. Burns, *The Jesuits and the Indian Wars of the Northwest* (1966); E. E. Dale, *The Indians of the Southwest* (1949); and A. M. Josephy, Jr., *The Nez Perce Indians and the Opening of the Northwest* (1965). Rich anthropological data is found in H. E. Driver, *Indians of North America* (2nd ed., 1969); a brief introduction is W. T. Hagan, *American Indians* (1961). H. H. Jackson, *A Century of Dishonor* (1881), is an impassioned indictment of government policies.

On public land policy an important new study is P. W. Gates and R. W. Swenson, *History of Public Land Law Development* (1968). The classic works on the subject are B. H. Hibbard, *A History of Public Land Policies* (2nd ed., 1939); and R. M. Robbins, *Our Landed Heritage* (1942). A suggestive case study is Victor Westphall, *The Public Domain in New Mexico, 1854–1891* (1965).

The best surveys of the cow country are E. S. Osgood, *The Day of the Cattleman* (1929); E. E. Dale, *The Range Cattle Industry* (1930); and Lewis Atherton, *The Cattle Kings* (1961). Andy Adams, *The Log of a Cowboy* (1903), provides a vivid first-hand account. Investment in the range cattle industry is the subject of G. M. Gressley, *Bankers and Cattlemen* (1966). Conflict between cattlemen and "nesters" is stressed in Mari Sandoz, *Old Jules* (1935), the biography of her father; and H. H. Smith, *The War on Powder River* (1966). R. R. Dykstra, *The Cattle Towns* (1968), makes some interesting comparisons. W. P. Webb, *The Texas Rangers* (1935), is both lively and standard. On the bison slaughter, see E. D. Branch, *The Hunting of the Buffalo* (1929); and Wayne Gard, *The Great Buffalo Hunt* (1959). Valuable on one important theme are J. B. Frantz and J. E. Choate, Jr., *The American Cowboy* (1955); and Philip Durham and E. L. Jones, *Adventures of the Negro Cowboys* (1965). The first compilation by the distinguished song-hunter, J. A. Lomax, was *Cowboy Songs and Other Frontier Ballads* (1910); his work has been ably continued by his son, Alan Lomax.

Section Two

THE NEW NATION EMERGES

[1865 - 1898]

With the Civil War there began an era of change in the United States frequently called the economic revolution. Some historians, identifying the war itself with the changes that accompanied it, have called the Civil War the "Second American Revolution." But the war served only to accelerate changes that were already in progress; had there been no war undoubtedly they would have occurred anyway.

Basic in the new dispensation was the revolution in means of communication that centered on the railroads. The railroads were new; until the 1840's they were still in the experimental stage, and only in the 1850's were their full possibilities beginning to be realized. The Civil War, which was the first great railroad war in history, resolved all doubts about them, and after the war the expansion of the nation's railway system proceeded at a rapid rate, too rapid, as events proved, for the economy of the country to stand the strain. But when the depression of the seventies ended, the building was resumed, and by the 1890's the American railway network was virtually complete.

With a national transportation system in the making, American industry was also revolutionized. The system of local manufacture was already

on the way out well before the 1860's, and the necessities of the war finished it off. After the war, manufacturers found in the needs of civilians an adequate substitute for the needs of the military, and in the improving transportation facilities ample means for getting their produce to market. Business on a local scale gave way to business on a national scale; more and more, gigantic corporations tended to drive small operators out of business. Steel supplemented or replaced iron; oil for illumination made possible another great new enterprise; dozens of other opportunities opened the way for a host of entrepreneurs.

The new business world operated at first without the restraint of government; lawmakers could not foresee so vast a transformation, much less make laws to control it. But the great new corporations, although they undoubtedly supplied more jobs for more people, made the achievement of independence for the ordinary individual far more difficult than it had ever been before. Inevitably there was a demand for governmental action. As a result, the full freedom of railway corporations was limited somewhat by the Granger laws and the Interstate Commerce Act; that of other corporations, by state and national antitrust legislation. Even so, the pre-eminence of business leadership in the United States was not seriously threatened during the nineteenth century.

While both labor and agriculture were to a great extent at the mercy of the new industrialism, neither was willing to remain permanently in an inferior status. The Knights of Labor during the 1870's and early 1880's and the American Federation of Labor later on, gave leadership to the cause of union labor, and achieved some results. Peculiarly a problem for labor was the immigrant tide of the late nineteenth century, which brought immense numbers of new workers from the Old World to the New. As for the farmers, they had to adjust both to new and revolutionary means of production, and to the overpowering leadership of industry. Out of their strivings came the Populist revolt in the South and the West, and the search for a panacea in free silver.

The confidence of the nation in its future was greatly shaken by the depression that began in 1873 and lasted until the end of the decade. The hard times, however, were but the growing pains of a new society. The rapid growth of large industry, the astonishing development of great urban centers, the inpouring of ever-increasing numbers of immigrants bringing with them a variety of strange cultures, languages, and religion — all this presented an infinite number of new problems. No less disturbing to the old order of things were the new developments in thought. Darwinism, the rise of science, new trends in religion and the arts were to punctuate the coming years with scores of other social questions. The depression years gave the American people an opportunity to take stock of themselves and perhaps to consider what should be done with their burgeoning and wonderful new material world in order to shape it toward the achievement of a good society. They were to make many false starts in the quest. But start they did to right the worst evils of reconstruction, to attack the prevailing frauds in government and business, to support education and literature once more, and to revive their prewar interest in humanitarian reform.

Casting ingots.

THE ECONOMIC REVOLUTION

Economic changes · The railroads · The Panic of 1873 · The Granger movement · New railroad building · More transcontinentals · Southern and eastern roads · Railroad regulation · The telegraph · The telephone · Edison · Postal changes · The new industrialism · The leadership of steel · The petroleum industry · The meat-packers · Flour-milling · The "New South" · The "trusts" · The Sherman Antitrust Act

Economic Changes

During the Civil War and the decades immediately following there occurred in the United States a series of great economic changes that were virtually to revolutionize the life of the nation. Between 1860 and 1890 the railroads, already expanding rapidly before the Civil War, were extended across the continent to produce a national system of transportation. Almost simultaneously the extension of the telegraph and telephone networks made possible speedy and certain continental communication. The same years witnessed also a spectacular change-over from small factories that had produced only for a local market to great corporate industries that produced for the entire nation. Similarly the banking and financial apparatus upon which all other business depended began to

concentrate in a few strategic centers, with "Wall Street" in New York City as the indispensable center of centers. Inevitably the new industrialism gave rise to urbanization; almost everywhere east of the Mississippi, and even here and there west of it, huge cities appeared into which poured the needed workers, some from rural America, but others from Europe — a veritable avalanche of immigrants whose presence would soon change radically the American pattern of national origins.

The Railroads

The rapidly expanding railroad system was the key to many of the remarkable changes that took place in the last half of the nineteenth century. Manufacturers struggled to produce the almost unlimited

CASTING INGOTS. *One of the processes in the manufacture of Bessemer steel.*

supplies that the railroads required for their own use, then redoubled their efforts to meet the demands of the new markets that the railroads opened up. Agriculture was equally stimulated, and achieved an ever widening base of operations, for the railroads assured the annihilation of every remaining frontier. The immigrant tide rose with the increasing number of jobs. Corporation methods of business and finance, first designed to meet the needs of the railroads, were copied and modified by the rest of the business world.

Greatly overbuilt before the Civil War, at least with respect to the needs of the prewar years, the railroads of the country enjoyed a tremendous prosperity while the war was on. Rates soared, except where the competition of the Great Lakes and the Erie Canal kept them down, and companies that had never made profits before now felt obliged to disguise their heavy earnings by issuing stock dividends. Railroad managers, as long as they could count on a wartime abundance of traffic, showed little interest either in new construction or in improving their equipment. Indeed, by 1865 the number of railroad accidents due to avoidable defects in roadbeds and rolling stock had reached the point where the public would no longer have tolerated such neglect except for the immunity to tragedy that accompanies war. With the return of peace the time was ripe for the renovation of the old roads and the building of new ones. Capital for the purpose was easily obtained by Jay Cooke and other promoters, who convinced investors, both at home and abroad, that railroad securities were among the safest and most profitable of investments.

The First Transcontinental

The federal government, by its generous subsidies to the building of transcontinentals, did much to stimulate the railroad boom. This policy, initiated a number of years before the war broke out but retarded because of southern opposition, was inaugurated in 1862 when Congress chartered the Union and Central Pacific railroads. In addition to the original reasons for building a transcontinental road, proponents could now cite the necessity of connecting California closely enough to the Union to insure its loyalty for all time to come. The Union Pacific was to build westward from Omaha, Nebraska; the Central Pacific eastward from Sacramento, California. Each company, after the completion of an initial forty miles of track, was eligible to receive from the government, for each mile of track laid, ten square miles of land in alternate sections, checkerboard fashion, along the right of way; and also, for each mile of track laid, the loan of $16,000, $32,000, or $48,000 (for plains, foothills, or mountain country, respectively) in government bonds.

Generous as these offers seemed, they proved to be inadequate to attract the modest sums necessary to build the first essential divisions of forty miles each, so in 1864 Congress amended the original terms. The government now doubled the land grant, accepted a second mortgage for the loans it made, and permitted the companies to borrow private capital, up to the amount of the government loans, on first-mortgage bonds. The prospect of title to nearly 20 million acres of land and loans amounting to about $60 million proved to be a sufficient inducement to moneylenders, and building soon began in earnest. At first it was stipulated that the eastern boundary of California should be the dividing line between the two roads, but ultimately they were permitted to race for distance, and in 1869, when they met near Ogden, Utah, the Union Pacific had laid 1086 miles of track and the Central Pacific 689. Problems of construction, particularly in the mountains, taxed to the limit the engineering prowess of the builders, while only by resort to the most unusual expedients were they able to recruit and maintain the manpower needed

First Transcontinental Railroad. After the last spike was driven at Promontory, Utah, the locomotives of the Central Pacific and the Union Pacific touched noses; the engineers exchanged champagne; and the rival leaders shook hands.

THE AGE OF THE TRANSCONTINENTALS.
For three decades, beginning with the 1860's, railroad building into the West was a principal activity of American enterprise.

Palace Car Life on the Pacific Railroad. Woodcut showing the elaborate interiors of early coaches, and the clothing fashions of the times.

to do the work. The Union Pacific employed thousands of Irish immigrants, many of them ex-soldiers who under the efficient direction of General Grenville M. Dodge not only built the road, but also on occasion fought off the attacks of hostile Indians. The Central Pacific, after initial difficulties, resorted to the use of Chinese "coolies," or contract laborers. Unfortunately, as already noted in connection with the Grant scandals, the building of both roads was accompanied by the most shameless profiteering.[1] The fortunes of four leading officials of the Central Pacific, Leland Stanford, Collis P. Huntington, Charles Crocker, and Mark Hopkins, began in this way. But unlike the original owners of Union Pacific stock, most of whom sold out their holdings as soon as the road was built, the "Big Four" of the Central Pacific operated their road for many years, and took excellent profits from it. Each of them left a fortune of $40 million or more.

Other Railroad Construction

When the Union Pacific engine "No. 119" touched noses with the Central Pacific's "Jupiter," a celebration was staged, not only at the meeting place, where speeches were made and gold and silver spikes were driven, but throughout the country. The excitement over the completion of the first transcontinental, however, was doubtless accentuated by the fact that railroad progress was by no means confined to this one project, but was general. Everywhere new rails were being laid, new lines were being planned. The United States itself had chartered two other transcontinentals on terms almost as generous as it had given the Union and the Central Pacific, and was soon to charter a third. These roads received no subsidy in bonds, but they were allowed a double portion of land — twenty sections per mile in the states, and forty in the territories. The

Northern Pacific (1864) was designed to connect the head of Lake Superior with Puget Sound; the Atlantic and Pacific (1866), to build southwestward from Springfield, Missouri; the Texas and Pacific (1871), to cross the continent still farther to the south through Texas, New Mexico, and Arizona.

National assistance to state-chartered railroads, after the pattern set by the Illinois Central grant of 1850, also continued unabated. The Chicago and Northwestern, the Chicago, Rock Island and Pacific, the Burlington and Missouri River, the Chicago, Milwaukee and St. Paul, the Missouri Pacific, the Atchison, Topeka and Santa Fe, the Kansas Pacific, and a host of minor western lines all profited, directly or indirectly, from government aid, and built feverishly. In the East and the South there was not only much new building, but, even more important, the consolidation of many lesser lines into systems that rivaled in their magnificent reaches the projected transcontinentals of the West. By 1873 Commodore Vanderbilt, the ruthless ruler of the New York Central, had extended his control from New York City to Chicago. J. Edgar Thomson, the associate of Andrew Carnegie, had done much the same thing for the Pennsylvania; and Jay Gould, for the Erie, had found a way through Cleveland and Cincinnati to St. Louis. In the South the Chesapeake and Ohio connected Norfolk with Cincinnati, and easy communication through Tennessee linked both Charleston and Norfolk with Memphis. Within five years after the Civil War the South had twenty-five hundred more miles of railroad than ever existed in the old Confederacy, while in the single year, 1873, new construction for this area reached a total of 1,300 miles. For the country as a whole, the eight years following the Civil War saw the laying of about 35,000 miles of new track, an increase during the period of almost exactly 100 per cent.

---

[1] See pp. 38–39.

Railroad Improvements

A great variety of improvements kept pace with the new construction. In 1864 George M. Pullman built his first sleeping-car, the "Pioneer A," at a cost of $20,000, and a few years later he was actively at work on separate dining-, drawing-room, and reclining-chair cars. In 1868 George Westinghouse demonstrated on a Pennsylvania passenger train his epoch-making air-brake, a device which by 1872 became an automatic appliance. During these years steel rails were introduced, although a heated debate continued for some time as to the relative merits of iron and steel for this purpose, and it was not until 1877 that the rapid replacement of iron by steel began. As the roadbeds were improved, heavier locomotives and rolling stock were built and a uniform gauge of four feet, eight and one half inches — the gauge used by the Union Pacific — came into general use. Terminal facilities were greatly improved, union stations made easier the transfer of passengers, and extensive freight yards expedited the traffic in "through freight." Long bridges, after the beginning of work on the Brooklyn Bridge in 1867, became a sort of passion. In 1869 the Missouri River was bridged at Kansas City, and in 1872 at Omaha. Between 1867 and 1874 James B. Eads built the famous bridge that bears his name across the Mississippi at St. Louis. John A. Roebling, the man who planned the Brooklyn Bridge, had first spanned the Ohio River at Cincinnati. These great bridges, and numerous lesser ones, enormously enhanced the speed and ease of railroad transportation.

The Panic of 1873

The burst of railroad expansion that had followed the Civil War ended abruptly with the Panic of 1873. On Thursday, September 18, 1873, the banking firm of Jay Cooke and Company closed its doors in New York, Philadelphia, and Washington. Cooke's fame had risen during the Civil War with his successful flotation of the bond issues by which the North financed its operations. After the war he turned his attention to railway securities, and again demonstrated his ability to win the confidence of investors. In attempting to back the Northern Pacific Railroad, however, he met with disaster. The huge sums needed for this undertaking could not be obtained without European assistance, and after the outbreak of the Franco-Prussian War in 1870 foreign capital became harder and harder to get. The result was that Cooke tied up so much of his firm's resources in advances to the railroad that his partners, without his knowledge or consent, finally took the drastic step of closing. Already a number of bankruptcies had made the business world nervous, and on the day before Cooke's failure there had been a ruinous decline in values on the New York Stock Exchange. But no one dreamed that the firm of Jay Cooke and Company, long regarded as the last word in financial solvency, was in danger. Hence, when the suspension was announced, the Exchange was immediately thrown into a panic so severe that, in comparison, the disturbance of the preceding day looked like nothing at all. The Panic of 1873 had begun. Two days later, with the price of stocks still going down, the Exchange was closed and remained closed for ten days. Bankruptcies followed, factories shut down, business came to a standstill; a depression that was to last for nearly six years had begun. Thus dramatically did the "boom" that the Civil War unleashed come to its inexorable end.

Causes of the Depression

Conditions in Europe had much to do with bringing on the American depression of the 1870's. Long before the United States had lost its political isolation it had developed close commercial ties with the

Jay Cooke, Banker. *The failure of Cooke's firm, J. Cooke & Co., of Philadelphia, on September 18, 1873, resulted from its efforts to finance the Northern Pacific Railroad, and precipitated the Panic of 1873.*

Run on a Bank. *This fanciful representation of what happened when a bank closed well portrays the deep anxiety felt by all concerned.*

Old World, and any large-scale reverse abroad was sure to produce repercussions west of the Atlantic. A sharp panic on the Vienna Bourse in May, 1873, inaugurated a general European depression that could not be kept from America for long. The unloading by European investors of their American holdings had depressed the New York Stock Exchange during the summer of 1873, and had helped prepare for the crash that followed the failure of Jay Cooke and Company. But the depression would not have lasted so long nor been so intense had there not been American as well as European causes for the trouble. Chief among the domestic causes was the huge overinvestment in railroads accompanied by a wild speculation in railroad securities. During the years preceding 1873, especially in the West, many railroads had built in unpopulated regions where for years operations could be carried on only at a loss. Since that fact was known in the financial community, the securities of such unfortunate roads often became the playthings of speculators. Meanwhile, the amount of capital invested in railroads alone during the period had reached $1 billion, while other huge sums had gone into the development of new American industries. To carry on the expansion American corporations had borrowed $1.5 billion from abroad, with interest charges of $80 million. In order to meet these obligations and to remedy an adverse balance of trade, more gold had to be sent abroad each year than the United States could spare. The new national banks yielded to the temptation to overextend their loans, and in five years preceding the panic lent many times as much money as they took in by way of deposits. Insurance companies were hard hit by the Chicago fire of 1871, which cost them $200 million, and the Boston fire of 1872, which added another $73 million to their outlay.

For a period of almost six years after the Panic of 1873 nearly all American business was at low ebb, and new railroad construction almost ceased. Besides having to combat hard times, the railroads were also under vigorous attack for their monopolistic practices. They may not have been more reprehensible than other big businesses, but their public nature made their behavior more easily observable; moreover, with the railroads sooner than with most other enterprises, the breakdown of the competitive system was fully apparent. Among the first to protest against railroad extortions were the grain growers of the upper Mississippi Valley, whose dependence upon the rail-

roads was well nigh complete. Their activities, collectively known as the Granger movement, resulted in the recognition in 1877 by the Supreme Court of the United States that the individual states had a right to regulate the railroads that penetrated their territory, a notable extension of governmental authority.

The Granger Movement

The founder of the Grange, or to use its official name, the Patrons of Husbandry, was Oliver Hudson Kelley, a government clerk in Washington who had intended it to be a cultural and social organization, devoted primarily to spreading ideas on scientific farming, and open alike to both the farmer and his wife. Beginning in 1867, the lodge took hold only slowly, in the South

The Scourge of the West. *Railroad monopolies took a heavy toll from the people who were dependent on them for transportation, and led to persistent demands for regulation.*

as well as in the North, until in the early seventies, when the northwestern farmers seized upon it as a means of attacking the railroads. Granger meetings furnished an ideal forum for the grain growers of the upper Mississippi Valley to speak their minds on the monopolistic tendencies of the railroads through which alone they must ship their produce to market, and through which also they must obtain from the outside world the manufactured articles they had to have. Inasmuch as the number of regions served by competitive lines was few indeed, the ordinary farmer had no choice but to use the road that ran nearest his farm. Competition was a myth; the railroads regularly charged "all the traffic would bear," and dictated at will the terms on which they chose to serve their patrons. Elevators and warehouses, often owned or controlled in turn by the railroads, did likewise; and middlemen, themselves compelled to pay a heavy toll in freight to the roads, were not far behind. Efforts to "get another railroad" so as to restore competition rarely availed; more frequently companies that had once been competitive joined forces and ceased to compete.

The Granger idea — that the state should regulate the railroads, if necessary to the point of fixing maximum rates — was older than the movement. Toyed with gingerly in Massachusetts, its real beginning was in Illinois, where during the late sixties laws were passed to restrain both the elevators and the railroads. These early measures proved unavailing, but a new state constitution, adopted in 1870, specifically stated that the General Assembly should pass laws to correct abuses and to prevent unjust discrimination and extortion by railroads in their freight and passenger rates, and by warehouses in their dealings with the public. Armed with this authority the Illinois legislature of 1871 promptly established maximum rates for the transportation of passengers, required that freight charges should be based entirely upon distance traversed, provided regulations for the storing and shipping of grain, and created a state board of railroad and warehouse commissioners charged with the duty of enforcing the laws. Against these measures the railroads made a determined, and at first a successful, fight, for on the first test case the Supreme Court of Illinois held the laws to be unconstitutional. But the Grangers, now thoroughly aroused, promptly voted out of office one of the judges who had held against them and replaced him with a judge who shared their views. The result was that in 1873 a new law, better drawn but designed to effect the same ends, was sustained.

Granger Legislation

Meantime the Grangers, bent on using the power of the state to curb the railroads, had gone into politics throughout the Northwest. Sometimes they were content merely to vote for Republicans or Democrats who agreed with them, but frequently they chose third-party candidates on separate "Anti-Monopoly" or "Independent" or "Reform" tickets. Independence Day, 1873, was long remembered as the "Farmers' Fourth of July," for on that day hundreds of Granger audiences gave their approval to a *Farmers' Declaration of Independence*, which repeated in well-worn phraseology the grievances from which farmers suffered, and announced in no uncertain way their determination to find relief. Presently Granger legislatures had enacted, not only in Illinois, but also in Wisconsin, Minnesota, and Iowa, measures of drastic regulation for railroads and warehouses.

In each instance litigation followed, and the railroads, despairing of aid from the Granger-minded state courts, at length took their cases to the federal courts. The Granger laws, railroad attorneys claimed, were impairments of contracts that the states had already made in granting charters to the railroads, and they provided for the taking of private property without due process of law. But in the spring of 1877, the United States Supreme Court ruled against the railroads in a series of decisions, the most important of which were *Munn* vs. *Illinois* and *Peik* vs. *the Chicago and Northwestern Railroad*. Thus the "right of a state to regulate a business that is public in nature though privately owned and managed" won striking vindication, and a weapon was forged with which, it was hoped, not only the railroads but other monopolistic enterprises also could be attacked. Most of the early Granger laws were defective and had to be repealed, but the principle on which they were founded endured, and before long railroad and warehouse commissions were hard at work in nearly every state.

Railroad Building

Hard as times were during the 1870's they could not hold back indefinitely the final conquest of the Far West by the railroads. Sure signs of revived business activity appeared as early as 1878 when the Northern Pacific, the misfortunes of which had plunged Jay Cooke and Company into bankruptcy, again prepared to build. Under the leadership of Frederick Billings, a conservative Vermont capitalist, investors were persuaded to put their money once more into Northern Pacific securities, and for three years the westward march of Billings' railroad builders went forward without incident. In 1881, however, Billings' plans came into conflict with those of Henry Villard, a hard-headed German-American whose Oregon Railroad and Navigation Company controlled the railroad and steamboat lines of the Pacific Northwest. Villard had long sought to induce Billings to agree to some traffic arrangement that would prevent competition between the two systems when the Northern Pacific should be finished, but Billings

received all such overtures with cold refusals. Thereupon Villard induced his financial backers in New York to put money into a "blind pool" upon which, for an unrevealed purpose, he might draw at will. With this money he bought up enough stock to secure complete control of both the "N.P." and the "O.R. and N.," and organized a holding company, the Oregon and Transcontinental, through which to manage them. He then deposed Billings as president of the Northern Pacific, took the place for himself, and as president of all three corporations achieved the harmony he desired. On the completion of the Northern Pacific in 1883, by way of celebration he ran a "Golden Spike Special," filled with the most distinguished company of American notables that he could assemble, the entire length of the line.

More Transcontinentals

By this time, however, the American public could no longer be thrilled by news that another transcontinental railroad had been finished. In addition to the Union Pacific, completed in 1869, the Southern Pacific was now running trains to the western coast. The Southern Pacific was a California corporation which had shrewdly acquired the right to build within the borders of that state to meet any eastern land-grant railroad. Owned and managed by the same able group that had built the Central Pacific, it had pushed its lines southward through the state, and was prepared to receive all newcomers at Fort Yuma and the Needles, the two points on the border of southern California where the canyon of the Colorado could be crossed. With the aid of territorial charters from Arizona and New Mexico and a state charter from Texas, the Southern Pacific built eastward from Fort Yuma to meet the old Texas Pacific, which it presently absorbed. By January, 1882, it had through trains running over this route

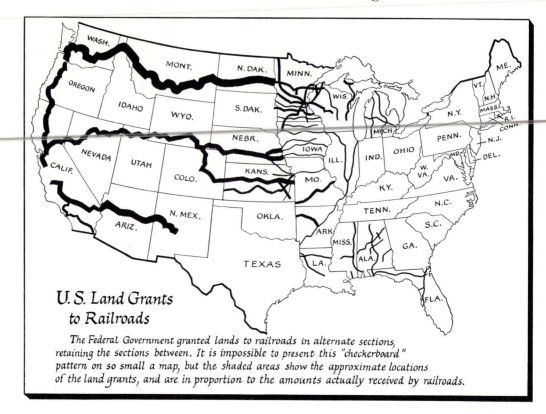

U. S. Land Grants to Railroads

The Federal Government granted lands to railroads in alternate sections, retaining the sections between. It is impossible to present this "checkerboard" pattern on so small a map, but the shaded areas show the approximate locations of the land grants, and are in proportion to the amounts actually received by railroads.

from San Francisco to St. Louis, and by February of the next year it had opened up an alternative route through southern Texas to New Orleans. Alert to every opportunity, the Southern Pacific also connected at the Needles with the Atchison, Topeka, and Santa Fe, which had built westward through Kansas on a state land grant, and from Albuquerque to the Needles on the federal grant of the defunct Atlantic and Pacific. Trains were running the entire length of this route shortly after Villard's "Golden Spike Special" made its much-advertised tour. In 1884 the owners of the Southern Pacific, who were now in a position to monopolize the railroad business of the Southwest, followed the example of Villard and created a holding company, the Southern Pacific of Kentucky, through which to administer their extensive properties. The Southern Pacific owned no railroads in Kentucky, but the

laws of that state were friendly to its purposes, while incorporation in a state far removed from the scene of the road's activities seemed likely to reduce to a minimum the danger of investigation and regulation.

Other western railroads extended their lines during these years with the same feverish speed. The Burlington, the Rock Island, the Northwestern, and the Missouri Pacific competed with the transcontinentals and their branches for the exploitation of the Great Plains. The Denver and Rio Grande built heroically through the Colorado mountains, by way of the Royal Gorge of the Arkansas, to connect with the Union Pacific at Ogden. James J. Hill of Minnesota advanced the fortunes of the St. Paul, Minneapolis and Manitoba slowly but surely until by the time the next panic broke, in 1893, it had become, under a new name, the Great Northern, another transcontinental. North of the United States, in Canada, Donald A. Smith, later known as Lord Strathcona and Mount Royal, brought the Canadian Pacific to completion in 1885, while south of the United States, in Mexico, the Mexican Central, an affiliate of the Santa Fe, had reached Mexico City the year before.

Southern and Eastern Roads

While the most spectacular railroad activities of the period occurred in the trans-Mississippi West, the southern and eastern roads were by no means idle. In the South the Richmond and West Point Terminal Railway and Warehouse Company, a holding company formed in 1881, laid the foundations for what later became the Southern Railway system. The repeal in 1876 of the Southern Homestead Act cancelled all reconstruction restrictions on the disposal of federal lands in the South, and permitted existing and newly-formed railroad companies to take advantage of the land bargains. Both northern and English capital poured into the projects. During the booming eighties the railroad mileage in that portion of the South which lay east of the Mississippi river doubled, while to the west of the river the increase was even higher. Heartening to southern pride was the fact that not a few directors of the new lines were southern born, although by the end of the century northern financiers controlled not less than 90 per cent of the southern mileage. In the East the great systems that had taken form before the Civil War — the New York Central, the Pennsylvania, the Erie, and the Baltimore and Ohio — built or acquired branch lines, consolidated their holdings, and, when well-managed, made money. Everywhere the substitution of steel for iron rails, together with an equally revolutionary improvement of rolling stock and equipment, called for enormous expenditures, funds for which, in spite of much cutthroat competition, the railroads somehow managed to find.

Because of these expensive innovations, statistics on mileage fail to give a complete picture of the railroad development of the period. Nevertheless the statistics are impressive. From 52,000 miles of railroad in 1870 the total mileage in the United States had risen by 1880 to 93,000 and by 1890 to 163,000 — an increase of 70,000 miles in ten years. Construction more than kept pace with the expansion of population. In 1870 the United States had 1,380 miles of railroad per million inhabitants; in 1880 it had 1,858 miles, and in 1890 it had 2,625 miles. By the last-mentioned date the main outlines of the American railroad map were complete; after that date the mileage continued to increase for a time, but such new tracks as were laid served mainly as feeders for existing lines. The age of railroad pioneering was over.

Railway Consolidations and Abuses

The creation of these great railroad systems was not usually accomplished without the elimination of a multitude of lesser lines. Back in the pre-Civil War era more or less accidental connections had played a considerable part in railroad consolidation. In this way the work of Cornelius Vanderbilt in welding together the New York Central had been greatly facilitated. Panics and periods of depression had also done their bit. During the years following 1857, and even more after 1873, the weaker roads had gone into bankruptcy only to emerge as parts of some stronger, and usually much larger, system. During the depression years of the seventies no less than 450 railroads, fully two-fifths of the roads of the country, had suffered this experience. The holding company idea, well exemplified by the Oregon and Transcontinental in the Northwest, and the Southern Pacific of Kentucky in the Southwest, also greatly facilitated consolidation. Great sectional

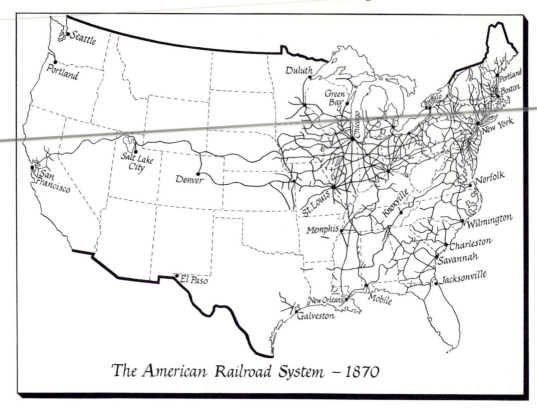

The American Railroad System – 1870

The American Railroad System – 1880

The American Railroad System ~ 1890

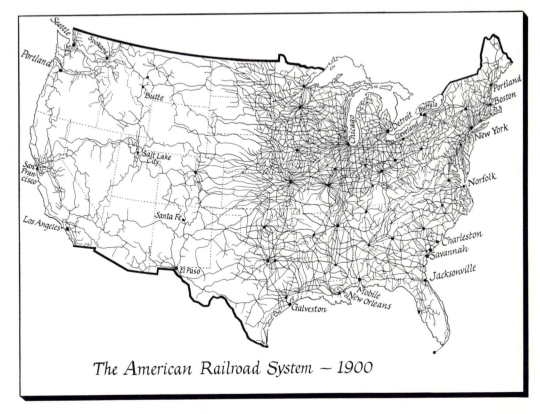

The American Railroad System ~ 1900

systems were thus created that could monopolize the business of the region they covered, and at the same time reduce to a minimum the danger of investigation and regulation. Within these areas competition was stifled, and only the interposition of governmental authority could prevent railroad monopolies from charging for their services "all the traffic would bear."

Competing systems, however, could not always be united, and wherever competition existed it tended to become both ruthless and costly. Rebates were given to favored shippers, particularly to those who shipped large quantities of goods long distances. Regions or cities that were served by more than one railroad were granted cut rates, while those dependent upon the services of a single road were overcharged in an effort to make up the losses from the competing rates. More was charged for a short haul where there was no competition than for a longer haul over the same line when competition between the terminal points existed. Efforts on the part of the roads to eliminate competition, except by one road absorbing another, usually came to nought. Sometimes competing roads, after a disastrous "rate war," made rate agreements, but the temptation to break such self-imposed promises, when to do so meant good profits, was always more than some managers could resist. Pools were tried through which a common treasurer collected all earnings and paid out profits according to a ratio agreed upon, but these, too, led mainly to wrangling and non-observance.

Railroad Regulation

The Granger movement had paved the way for what now became an obvious necessity, the entrance of the national government into the field of railroad regulation. The various state commissions, ill-informed as to the problems that confronted them, and often subservient to the corporations

they were supposed to regulate, accomplished comparatively little. Knowledge, to be sure, came with the years, but it added nothing to the effectiveness of state regulation; by the time a railroad was large enough to need regulation, it was too large for a state commission to regulate it. Local intrastate roads that the commissions could handle were being quietly absorbed into powerful interstate systems that were beyond them. While, according to the Granger decisions, the regulatory authority of a state did not necessarily stop at the state's borders, the fact of the matter was that increasingly it did. Finally, in 1886, the Supreme Court of the United States admitted the inadvisability of its earlier ruling, which permitted states to regulate railroads that extended beyond their borders, and in a case involving the Wabash Railroad and the State of Illinois held in effect that Congress alone had authority to regulate interstate commerce.

Meantime one investigating committee after another had studied the railroad problem. In Granger times a Senate committee, headed by William Windom of Minnesota, had urged that a federal bureau of commerce be created, and twice during the seventies the national House of Representatives had passed bills to that effect. In 1879 the Hepburn committee in New York State submitted a wealth of evidence on the misconduct of the railroads, and inferentially pointed to national regulation as the proper way out. In 1885, the Senate appointed a new investigating committee with a larger range of powers than had been accorded the Windom committee. Headed by Shelby M. Cullom of Illinois, this committee traveled widely and investigated carefully the regulatory efforts of the state commissions. It reported in 1886 that three fourths of the railroad business of the country was interstate in character, hence, under the rule of law laid down in the Wabash decision, beyond the control of state regulation.

Four possible methods of dealing with the situation were listed: (1) the continuance of private ownership and management, but with more effective governmental regulation; (2) government ownership and management; (3) government ownership and private management under public regulations; and (4) government ownership and management in competition with private companies. Noting the widespread opposition throughout the country to government ownership, the committee recommended regulation by the national government as the preferable alternative.

The ICC

Congress was now ready to act, and in 1887 it established an Interstate Commerce Commission to consist of five members, of whom not more than three might belong to the same political party, to be appointed by the President for six-year terms. The law forbade most of the evil practices uncovered by the various investigating committees, and in a sense made national the current trends in state regulation. Rebates, pools, and discriminations were branded as illegal, and the rule that more could not be charged for a short haul than for a longer one over the same line was established. The commission was authorized to investigate complaints against the railroads, and to make decisions which, however, it could enforce only through court action. This provision for a judicial review of its rulings proved to be the undoing of the early commission. Although headed by an eminent ex-judge, Thomas M. Cooley of Michigan, it failed to obtain the judicial backing through which alone its decisions could be made effective. Delays and reversals permitted the railroads to operate about as they had operated before. Not until the Presidency of Theodore Roosevelt did the Interstate Commerce Commission become a really effective body.

Telegraph and Cable

While railroads undoubtedly played the principal role in revolutionizing the means of communication on which Americans depended, they were not alone in the field. When it came to the sending of news and information from place to place, they were far outclassed by the electric telegraph, used for years before the Civil War, but now extended to parallel every railroad right of way and to serve practically every hamlet in the nation. Cable service also steadily improved. The first transoceanic cable, laid in 1858, had soon been destroyed by the use of too strong electric currents, but by 1866, through the persistent efforts of Cyrus W. Field, a better one had been laid, and soon thereafter many others. American newsgatherers, diplomats, and businessmen were thus able to keep in as close touch with London as with New York, and to be far better informed on world affairs than had been possible before. Improvements in ocean-going steamships also helped, for they facilitated foreign travel for Americans, and brought numerous visitors to America from distant shores. Under these circumstances the extremes of provincial-

Scene in a Telegraph Office. *Woodcut.*

ism, so common in the United States of an earlier period, began to disappear.

The Telephone

Of incalculable importance also was the telephone, the invention of Alexander Graham Bell, an American Scot who taught deaf mutes, and had interested himself in acoustics. At the Centennial Exposition of 1876 Bell exhibited his instruments, and made a deep impression on the American public. He was not the first to study the problem of transmitting human speech by electricity, nor the only one to find a solution, but he did develop the first practicable telephone. Even so, it was not easy to induce capital to invest in so fantastic an enterprise, and the successful launching of the telephone owed much to the organizing genius of Theodore N. Vail, later president of the American Telephone and Telegraph Company. During the eighties telephone systems were introduced into virtually every American city, and by the end of the decade no less than 440,000 instuments were in use. Well before the turn of the century successful long-distance connections had been generally established. Among its numerous contributions, the telephone provided at its switchboards a new occupation for women, and through its rural extensions an effective weapon against social isolation.

Thomas A. Edison

In addition to the telegraph and the telephone, electricity was being made to serve many other new uses. Wizard of electrical inventors was Thomas A. Edison (1847–1931), an Ohioan by birth whose formal schooling had been limited to three months, but whose natural ingenuity has probably never been surpassed. At fifteen he had learned to send and receive telegraph messages, but his fondness for experimentation doomed him to frequent dismissals by irritated employers. In 1879 he made his first really revolutionary invention, a practicable

incandescent light. Others had already devised the arc light, which served well enough for street-lighting, but was wholly unsatisfactory for indoor use. By January, 1880, Edison had taken out a patent on his light bulb, which before long he was able to manufacture, in quantities for commercial use, at a factory in Harrison, New Jersey. Improvements in generators followed, and soon business houses and even dwellings were depending for illumination on the new device. The need was for central electric power stations, an opportunity for business expansion so fully appreciated that the number of such stations increased from eight in 1881 to 2,774 in 1898. While Edison, with his numerous inventions, including among others the phonograph, motion pictures, automatic telegraphy, the stock ticker, and the microphone, ranks as the leading electrical engineer of his time, he was by no means the only one. Soon electric railway systems were banishing horse cars from the city streets, electric elevators were adding great numbers of stories to the height of skyscrapers, and electric power was being used to turn a larger and larger proportion of the wheels of industry.

Postal Changes

Meantime the United States Post Office, regardless of deficits, cheapened its rates and amplified its service. Railroad extensions were followed everywhere by postal extensions. Mail delivery at the door was inaugurated in a few American cities as early as 1871, and thereafter was rapidly bestowed upon smaller and smaller communities. Catalogues and printed circulars were accorded special rates to facilitate general distribution, a tremendous boon to advertisers. The penny postal card, introduced into the United States from Europe in 1873, brought the cost of personal mail service to an irreducible minimum; but the two-cent letter rate, inaugurated in 1883,

An Early Light Bulb. One of Edison's most important inventions.

Subscriber's Telephone Set, 1878. Magneto bell with two hand telephones — one used for transmitting and one for receiving.

THOMAS A. EDISON. *By all standards Edison ranks as the greatest of American inventors. During his lifetime he took out 1,097 patents with the United States Patent Bureau. Upon them he built a successful financial career.*

The Youthful Edison. This picture shows Edison, when he was about thirty years of age, seated beside one of his early phonographs.

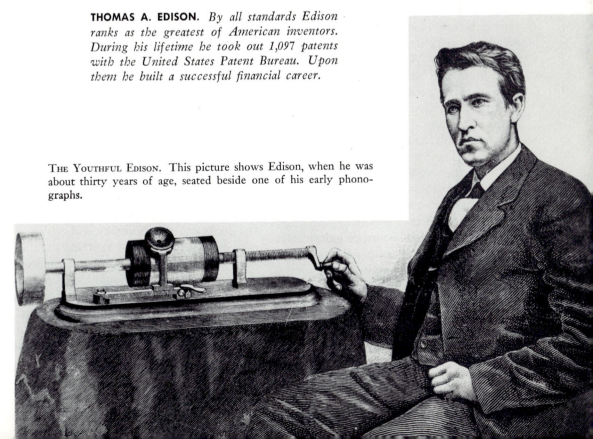

was not far behind. The invention of the typewriter in 1867 (by Christopher Latham Sholes, a Milwaukee printer), and its later extensive exploitation for business purposes, added immensely to the volume of the mails. One result of these changes was to bring the American people closer together than had ever been possible before. The sharper lines of sectionalism were blurred, and the triumph of nationalism was assured. Probably most significant of all, the way was paved for the organization of business along national rather than local or sectional lines. The revolution in means of communication provided a firm foundation for the new industrialism.

The New Industrialism

The beginning of the new industrialism, as already noted, preceded the Civil War.[1] New machines, both during and after the war, did their part toward pushing it forward. The United States Patent Bureau (whose head had contemplated resigning in 1833 because there was nothing left for inventors to do) had granted only 36,000 patents before 1860, but during the three decades from 1860 to 1890 granted approximately 440,000. While by no means all of these inventions were of real significance, some of them were of far-reaching consequence. Americans also borrowed heavily from European ideas, and showed their customary skill in adapting them to American needs. There was plenty of work to do. With the population of the country growing at a prodigious rate, both from the increase in the native stock and from immigration, the needs of more and more people had to be met. Such newly formed industries as steel and oil had to expand and equip their vast establishments. The use of agricultural machinery, greatly expedited during the war, showed no signs of abatement, and new inventions brought more and more

[1] See p. 49.

machines to the farmers' attention. And, as mentioned earlier, the extension and improvement of the railroads produced still more demands for machinery, equipment, and supplies.

With capital abundant, it is not surprising that manufacturing lost none of the momentum it had accumulated during the war. The United States, indeed, became a sort of paradise for industrialists. A dependably high tariff assured them of the right to exploit the steadily growing American market, and the constitutional provision against state control of interstate commerce gave them a vast free-trade zone for themselves. Soldiers returning from the war and immigrants streaming in from Europe supplied a comfortable abundance of labor. One by one the high records of production set up during the war fell below the higher records that came with the first five years of peace. Agricultural America had no chance to keep up the pace being set by industrial America; Jefferson's dream of a nation composed mainly of small free farmers had faded before the realities of the machine age. The America of the future was to be less rural than urban, more factory than farm. The black belt of the cotton kingdom was to recede in importance before a northern black belt, traced by the smoke of factory chimneys, a belt that ultimately was to extend far into the South itself.

The Leadership of Steel

The best barometer of the new industrialism was steel. Before the Civil War the high cost of steel confined its use to the manufacture of such small articles as tools and cutlery in which quality was demanded regardless of price. That anything so bulky as railroad rails, or the heavy locomotives that ran on the rails, should ever be made of steel rather than of iron seemed utterly fantastic. All this was changed as the result of a remarkable discovery made independently and at about the same time by an

American, William Kelly, and an Englishman, Henry Bessemer. Kelly, a resident of Eddyville, Kentucky, who made wrought-iron sugar kettles for his neighbors, observed one day that the effect of an air-blast on molten iron was to make it white-hot. From this he readily deduced that the molten metal itself contained enough carbon to burn out its impurities, if only a strong blast of air could be directed against it. Plainly this "air-boiling" process, if only it could be made practicable, would tend to eliminate the expensive use of charcoal, and so greatly reduce the cost of refinement. In a series of experiments, carried on between 1851 and 1856, Kelly demonstrated the soundness of his idea, although his patrons obstinately insisted upon wrought-iron kettles made in the old-fashioned way.

The Bessemer Process

In 1856 the Englishman, Bessemer, who had been carrying on similar experiments, announced the successful application of a "fuel-less" process, and obtained a United States patent on it. Before the Civil War ended, successful efforts were being made within the United States to make commercial use of the "Bessemer process," as it was generally called, and in 1866 one Alexander Lyman Holley, by obtaining the right to use both the Bessemer and the Kelly patents, paved the way for a phenomenal development. Within a few years the number of Bessemer steel works in the country could be counted by the dozen, and the price of steel had dropped to a figure that made its use instead of iron entirely practicable. Another new method of producing steel, known as the "open-hearth" process, was introduced into the United States from Europe in 1868 by Abraham S. Hewitt, who shared with his father-in-law, Peter Cooper, control of the New Jersey Steel and Iron Company at Trenton. Ultimately far more open-hearth than Bessemer steel was to be made, but until well toward the end of the century Bessemer steel cost less to produce, and so

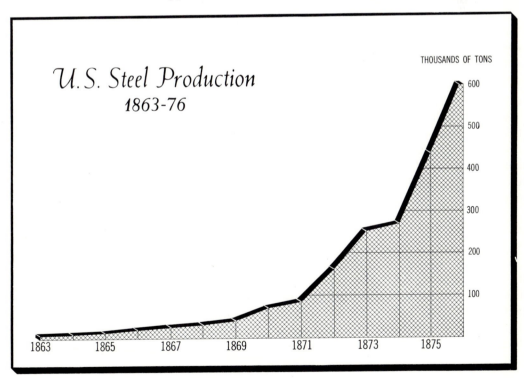

U.S. Steel Production
1863-76

THOUSANDS OF TONS

600
500
400
300
200
100

1863   1865   1867   1869   1871   1873   1875

The Bessemer Process. *This drawing shows the converters at work in the making of Bessemer steel at Pittsburgh, Pennsylvania.*

enjoyed a great advantage. Naturally the steel industry, like the iron industry, tended to concentrate in Pennsylvania, where both iron ore and coal were found in abundance; but by 1873 the Michigan iron mines, little used before the Civil War, were furnishing over half of the ore supply.

Andrew Carnegie

The steel industry was to produce many great names, but none more glamorous than that of Andrew Carnegie (1835–1919), the Scottish immigrant lad whose career became an almost perfect pattern for the typical American success story. The son of a humble, but by no means unintelligent, Dunfermline weaver, young Carnegie was brought to America in 1848 by his parents in the proverbial quest of opportunity. He found it, first as a bobbin-boy at $1.20 a week in a western Pennsylvania cotton factory, then as a messenger at $2.50 a week in a Pittsburgh telegraph office. Soon he was a telegraph operator, one of the first to learn to read "by sound" the messages that came over the wire, and a little later, the private secretary of Thomas A. Scott, a Pennsylvania Railroad official, who was fascinated by the younger man's talents. From that position to railroading was an easy transition; and then from railroading to bridge-building, where he made a specialty of supplanting outmoded wooden construction with iron. Astoundingly versatile, he pursued many side lines, nearly all of which turned out well. He built bridges, made money out of oil, and sold railway bonds in Europe — all at the same time. On one of his trips to England he saw steel being made by the Bessemer process, and returned to the United States determined to put "all of his eggs in one basket," the manufacture of steel. By 1873, the date when he opened the J. Edgar Thomson Steel Mills — named after a powerful partner in the enterprise — his career as a steel magnate had begun.

"Rock Oil"

No less startlingly new than the steel industry, and almost as revolutionary in its possibilities, was the production and refinement of oil. For centuries petroleum, by seeping to the surface in various parts of the earth, had advertised its existence to mankind, but, strangely enough, no one had seemed to realize that it was of any particular value; much less that, by sinking wells, great pools of it could be tapped. Years before the Civil War enterprising farmers in Venango County, Pennsylvania, were accustomed to skim the substance from Oil Creek, a branch of the Allegheny, and use it to grease their wagons. Some even bottled it and sold it as a medicine "guaranteed," when externally applied, to cure rheumatism, and good for almost anything, if taken internally. A Pennsylvania manufacturer, Samuel M. Kier, whose wells persisted in pumping up petroleum as well as salt water, resolved this dilemma by putting "Kier's Rock Oil," a medicine for which he made the most extravagant claims, upon the market. The chief contribution of the salt producers to the oil industry, however, was to be the methods of boring deep wells and of pumping that they had worked out. These methods the early oil men could take over almost without modification.

Oil for Illumination

The possibility that petroleum could be refined into a practical illuminant was not unrealized by the versatile Kier, who made some significant experiments along that line, but the chief credit for this epochal discovery belongs to a graduate of Dartmouth College, named George H. Bissell, who remembered, curiously, some of the experiments with crude oil that one of his teachers had made. Convinced that ultimately he could supplant the old-fashioned tallow candles and whale-oil lamps with something far superior, Bissell leased some land in western Pennsylvania, and sent a sample of the oil it produced to Benjamin Silliman, Jr., professor of chemistry at Yale College, for analysis. In a memorable document, written in 1851, Silliman reported that an excellent illuminant could be made from petroleum, that the cost of refinement would be slight, and that from it a number of important by-products, such as naphtha and paraffin, could also be recovered. Bissell now turned promoter, won sufficient support from capitalists to begin operations, and sent Edwin Drake, a minor but enthusiastic stockholder, out to Titusville, Pennsylvania, to drill for oil. Drake had observed the methods used in operating the salt wells near Syracuse and Pittsburgh,

Andrew Carnegie. *Beginning in 1873 Carnegie devoted his talents as an industrialist to the manufacture of steel. In large part through his efforts, the United States within three decades had replaced Great Britain as the greatest producer of steel.*

AN EARLY OILFIELD. This photograph, taken in 1873, shows what had happened to the James S. McCray & Egbert farm, Petroleum Center, Pennsylvania.

and successfully followed them in his quest for oil. By August, 1859, "Drake's folly," as the incredulous natives called his venture, was producing oil at the rate of twenty barrels a day.

The Petroleum Industry

What followed was hardly less tumultuous than a gold rush. That fabulous sums were to be made from oil, few could deny, and the venturesome flocked to western Pennsylvania by the thousands. Farmers who had known only the extreme of poverty sold their land for fantastic prices, or, by good luck, sometimes became part owners in oil wells that speedily made them rich. Oil derricks dotted the landscape; crossroads became towns, and towns became cities, almost overnight. Pittsburgh, and other strategic centers, found a new source of wealth in the business of oil refining, while the whole country bought the new kerosene lamps, and began to sit up nights. Inasmuch as almost anyone with a little capital could make a start in the oil business, competition for a while was utterly unrestrained. On this account, and also because of the unpredictable nature of both the supply and the demand, the prices of crude oil and of kerosene varied from year to year, from month to month, and even from day to day. Fortunes were lost as well as made. Nevertheless, by 1864 the oil fields around Titusville had expanded to four hundred square miles, and by 1872 not only western Pennsylvania, but parts of West Virginia and Ohio also, were included within the two thousand square miles in the United States devoted to the production of oil. With a total output to date of nearly 40 million barrels, the petroleum industry had in a dozen years climbed to a place of high prominence in the nation's business. In a single year, 1871, foreign purchasers took over 150,000 gallons of American oil, making this commodity the fourth largest item among the country's exports.

John D. Rockefeller

Inextricably intertwined with the history of oil refining in the United States is the name of John D. Rockefeller (1839–1937),

John D. Rockefeller. This portrait of the great industrialist was taken in his old age after his business career was over. His apologists insist that the order he brought to the oil industry justified the ruthless methods by which he achieved his ends.

THE OIL INDUSTRY. *Drilling for oil began in the United States just before the Civil War, but the expansion of the oil industry was primarily a postwar phenomenon.*

a native of Richford, New York, who had moved with his parents to Cleveland, Ohio, when he was thirteen years old. Young Rockefeller had only a common-school education, but he early exhibited extraordinary business talent. Before he had reached his majority he had become a partner in a produce commission firm that took excellent profits, particularly after the outbreak of the Civil War. Shrewd, calculating, and thrifty, he made up his mind in 1862, while other young men of his age were patriotically going off to war, that the "coal-oil" business had a future worth sharing. With characteristic good judgment he first backed a refinery that the inventive genius of one Samuel Andrews had provided with a highly improved process; then, at the end of the war, when it was apparent that he had made no mistake, he gave up his commission business, formed a partnership with Andrews, and started out as an oil refiner on his own. By this time the two chief western centers for the refining of oil were Pittsburgh and Cleveland, but the advantage, as Rockefeller sensed, lay with

Cleveland, which had easy access, both by water and rail, to the East no less than to the West, whereas Pittsburgh, for its eastern market, was wholly dependent upon the Pennsylvania Railroad. Five years later, reinforced by two new allies, H. M. Flagler and S. V. Harkness, Rockefeller had founded the Standard Oil Company of Ohio, which that year refined 4 per cent of the nation's total output. By 1872, with monopoly as his goal, he had acquired twenty out of the twenty-five refineries in Cleveland and was laying plans for further conquests that within a decade were to bring him control over 90 per cent of the oil refineries of the country.

The Standard Oil Company

Rockefeller's ruthless methods left him a rich legacy of hatred. The railroads, hard-pressed for business during the depression, had little choice but to give him the rebates he demanded. Shippers less favored either were ruined by the unfair competition or sold out to Standard Oil. When it came to the marketing of oil, Rockefeller gave no quarter. The United States was divided up into convenient sections, each with its agent and subagents, with every agent under instructions to "sell all the oil that is sold in your district." Agents who succeeded in this undertaking were rewarded with higher salaries and promotions; agents who failed were summarily dismissed. Railroad records were spied upon by Standard Oil men so that the business of competitive refineries could be stolen. Price-cutting was carried to any extreme necessary to put a competitor out of business, and as soon as his defeat was assured the price of oil was set again at a figure as high as or higher than before the price war began. Pipeline companies that carried the crude oil to railway centers, and even hundreds of miles to the refineries, were gathered up by Standard Oil, one by one, usually at its own price. Determined to pay no man profits, Rockefeller built terminal warehouses of his own, established factories to make barrels and other necessary articles, and eliminated hundreds of wholesalers and middlemen. Finally, in order to facilitate centralized control and to insure against unintentional competition among the various Standard properties, the Standard Oil Trust was formed. This device, first adopted in 1879, but revised and more completely applied in 1882, consisted merely of a group of nine trustees to whom was surrendered all the stock of the Standard Oil Company and its various affiliates. Trust certificates were then issued to each Standard stockholder in the proportion of twenty trust certificates for each share of Standard stock. For several years the nine trustees, with John D. Rockefeller at their head, made the decisions for all of the stockholders and all of the companies that were dominated by Standard Oil.

The Meat Packers

Both the steel and the oil industries did their part toward widening the geographic basis of American industrialism by extension into the West, but there also came into existence in that area many industries designed to process the foodstuffs that it produced, or otherwise to serve its particular needs. One of these, the meat-packing industry, owed much of its initial growth to the Civil War demand for "packed" meat, especially salted pork, but urban needs after the war were equally insistent. The meat industry's greatest boon came from the perfection of the refrigerator car, which made possible the shipment of dressed meat for long distances regardless of the weather. Cincinnati, Chicago, and Milwaukee quickly developed into great meat-packing centers, but the western range-cattle industry enabled such Missouri River towns as Kansas City, St. Joseph, Omaha, and Sioux City to provide the older cities with strong competition. Inevitably the trend toward monopoly, so evident in the steel and oil industries, also affected the meat packers, whose activities tended to revolve about the names of Philip Armour, Nelson Morris, and Gustavus F. Swift.

Flour-Milling

The flour millers, like the packers, found it necessary to follow the producers into the West, and by the end of the Civil War showed unmistakable signs of concentrating their principal interests in the upper Mississippi Valley. By 1870 Minnesota ranked fourth among the states of the Union in the manufacture of flour, and Minneapolis had begun the forward march that was to make it within twenty years the leading flour-milling center in the country. Meantime, country millers in southern Minnesota, among them one J. S. Archibald of Dundas, had developed a "new process" that enabled them to manufacture a superior white flour from northern hard wheat. Many hands had a part in the further improvement of this "new process," which George H. Christian, a Minneapolis miller

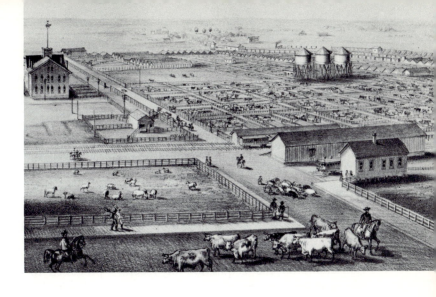

Meat Packing. *This industry grew up when transportation facilities enabled producers to send their livestock to market over long distances. Access to the railroad was as essential to the farmers and ranchers at one end of the line as to the stockyards at the other.*

advertised as "patented," and so gave the name "patent" to the type of flour it produced. Even more revolutionary was the introduction from Hungary of the roller-mill, which during the 1870's, with many American modifications and improvements, began to replace the outmoded mill-stones. John Stevens of Neenah, Wisconsin, one of the principal innovators, obtained in 1880 a United States patent on the roller process. While the manufacture of flour was no monopoly of the Northwest, advertisers soon made the names of such Minnesota millers as C. C. Washburn, John Crosby, and Charles A. Pillsbury familiar to nearly every American household. The small flour mill did not at once disappear, but as time went on the local miller found himself fighting a losing battle against the same forces that were putting his neighbor, the "butcher," out of business.

The "New South"

While these momentous changes were taking place in the North and the West, similar developments had occurred in the "New South." Although the Old South had not been completely without industry (some 160 cotton mills, for example, had been operating in 1860), it was apparent to both northerners and southerners that the lack of manufacturing facilities had been one of the major reasons for the section's

loss of the war. During reconstruction and the depressed seventies there was little that enterprising southerners could do to remedy this deficiency. Local capital was all but nonexistent, northern money was employed elsewhere, and what prewar establishments still existed were run down and in need of repairs. But the situation was far from hopeless. As cotton production resumed its normal course, small amounts of local capital were accumulated, cheap and well-disciplined labor was abundant, and the southern resources of water-power, lumber, coal, and iron ore had scarcely been touched.

The change in southern atmosphere came rapidly after the breakdown of the reconstruction governments and the lifting of the national depression. The "redemption" governments that succeeded carpetbag rule were headed by business-minded men, many of them ex-Whigs, who were eager to cooperate with northern industrialists. For twenty years after reconstruction General John B. Gordon, Joseph E. Brown, and Alfred H. Colquitt practically monopolized political power in Georgia. Scarcely a year of the period passed without two of the three holding the Governor's chair and a seat in the United States Senate. All three were financiers and industrialists. Joseph E. Brown, for example, was an official of the Western Atlantic Railroad, the Southern Railroad and Steamship Company, the Walker Coal and Iron Company, and the Dade Coal Company. The triumvirate, and others like them throughout the South, kept taxes low, especially on new industry, made lavish grants of state lands to new enterprises, and leased out state convicts, among whom were many Negroes, to their own and to other business projects at ridiculously low rates. They also helped obtain the repeal of the Southern Homestead Act of 1866, with its annoying restrictions on the acquisition of federal lands located in the South.

All this favoritism in high places gave southern industry a new lease on life. Strongly backed by northern and English capital, southern railroad, lumber, and mining interests embarked on many new ventures, from which among other things the southern people profited much by furnishing essential labor and supplies. The new, or rebuilt, railroads took the lead in opening up some of the South's rich but hitherto undeveloped natural resources. The Louisville and Nashville Railroad, for example, played a cardinal role in the development of both the southern coal fields and the even more important Alabama iron-ore region. Within a period of twenty years capital estimated at $30 million poured into the southern iron industry, which centered on Birmingham, Alabama, and by the late eighties was producing more pig iron than the entire nation had produced before the Civil War. Surveying the South's progress, Andrew Carnegie in 1889 characterized that section as "Pennsylvania's most formidable industrial enemy." In the seaboard South perhaps the most spectacular development was the rise of the cigarette industry. Aided by the invention in 1880 of a cigarette-making machine and by the increasing production of bright leaf tobacco, the industry grew rapidly, and shifted its center from Virginia to North Carolina. There the Dukes, R. J. Reynolds, and James R.

Day, southerners all, paralleled in their own activities the careers of Carnegie and Rockefeller in the North. During the last twenty years of the nineteenth century the southern cotton industry, likewise, made spectacular headway, accounting by 1900 for about half of the cotton mills and half the production of the country. A natural development from the textile industry was the utilization of cotton seed. Long regarded as almost valueless, by the end of the century the oil-rich seed was being processed to obtain edible oils, fertilizers, and animal food. The making of furniture, chemical fertilizers, cement, and brick products helped further to diversify southern industrialism. By 1900 the per capita wealth of the section was estimated at about one-half that of the North, whereas only twenty years earlier it had been about one-third. Nevertheless, since much of the South's industry was still owned by northerners, the colonial nature of its economy was yet to be overcome.

Close observers of business trends during the eighties did not fail to notice the disturbing trend toward monopoly. With nation-wide competition at work only the ablest, the most selfish, and the most unscrupulous of the competitors could survive. In 1880, for example, the nation had 1,990 woolen mills, in 1890, only 1,311; in 1880 it had 1,934 factories that made agricultural implements, in 1890, only 910. During the same decade the number of iron and steel mills decreased by one third, and the number of leather establishments by three fourths. In every case, however, the total capital investment and the total output of the industry had vastly increased, while ownership, or at least management, had been concentrated far more rapidly than even the reduced number of plants would indicate. What the nation was witnessing was the emergence of a large number of near-monopolies, each aspiring to complete control of some important national necessity.

The "Trusts"

Public awareness of the situation began with the appearance of an article, "The Story of a Great Monopoly," by Henry Demarest Lloyd, in the *Atlantic Monthly* for March, 1881. Lloyd's article was a scathing attack on the Standard Oil Company, and the deep impression it made was fully attested by the fact that that particular number of the *Atlantic* sold out seven editions. "This is the original trust," declared a New York committee that in 1888 began the investigation of Standard Oil. "Its success has been the incentive to the formation of all other trusts or combinations. It is the type of a system which has spread like a disease through the commercial system of this country." What the committee charged was fully borne out by the facts. One after another "an incredible number of the necessaries and luxuries of life, from meat to tombstones," had fallen into the hands of some tightly organized little group that frequently only by the most unscrupulous and underhanded methods had achieved control. Sugar, salt, whiskey, matches, crackers, lead, cottonseed oil, linseed oil, wire and nails, agricultural machinery, electrical supplies, and a host of other items could be obtained only by paying tribute to some such trust or combine. The exact pattern of the Standard Oil Trust was not always followed, but the results were generally about the same. Sometimes the possession of exclusive patent rights promoted the cause of monopoly, and thus made of the liberal patent laws of the United States a kind of subsidy to big business.

The evils of the "trusts," as the public without much discrimination described all big businesses, won much notoriety. Prices were fixed without benefit of competition, and sometimes at higher levels than before the trust was formed. Raw producers were compelled to take what the trust chose to pay, for there was no one else to whom to sell. Labor was forced into line by the closing of troublesome plants, and by the circulation of "blacklists" that made it difficult for "agitators" to obtain employment. Politicians were influenced by free passes from the railroads, by campaign contributions, and by outright bribes. Oliver H. Payne, treasurer of the Standard Oil Company, was reputed to have spent $100,000 to secure the election of his father, H. B. Payne, to the United States Senate in 1886. Powerful lobbies appeared in Washington and in the several state capitals charged with the duty of winning favors from lawmakers and law-enforcers. The Washington lobbyists were sometimes described as the "third house" of Congress. Plants that experience had shown to be well located were en-

Bosses of the Senate. *A cartoon by Keppler which ridiculed the United States Senate for its subservience to the great national monopolies. The "trusts" profited greatly from protective tariffs and other favorable legislation, and their lobbyists sought earnestly to prevent the passage of hampering regulatory laws.*

larged, and others less ideally situated were closed down, without regard to the inevitable unemployment involved or the municipal problems that arose from the concentration of vast numbers of people at whatever centers business leaders deemed strategic. Individual freedom suffered blow after blow as the owners of small establishments became the employees of larger ones, and as the chance to enter business independently grew less and less. Employees were pushed farther from the sight and hearing of employers, and fewer occasions existed for emotions of the "heart" to influence the conduct of businessmen who prided themselves upon their "hardheadedness."

Advantages of the Trusts

And yet the "trusts" were by no means without their good points. Indeed, most business historians have come to believe that the "robber barons" concept of the nineteenth-century industrial leaders was quite mistaken. The time had come when American business, in the interest of the public good, had to be organized along national lines. Much of the competition that the trusts eliminated was sheer waste, and without it prices could be, and often were, reduced. Large-scale businesses were usually far more efficient than the small concerns they supplanted, and were able to make money out of by-products that the smaller operators were forced to throw away. The packers, for example, claimed that they paid more for a live steer than they received for the dressed meat it yielded. Their profits came from the use they made of horns, hoofs, and other materials that the local slaughterhouse wasted. Big business could afford to take heavy initial losses while waiting for ultimate profits. It could bear the cost of advertising and of the slow enlargement of markets. Usually, too, it was better managed, better located, better equipped. Small establishments could not so easily afford to scrap expensive machin-ery because new inventions made better equipment possible. They could not compete with big businesses in paying salaries to the ablest managers. Even without the cutthroat competition to which they were subjected, many of them would have lost out anyway because of their inefficiency.

Legal Status of the Trusts

As public awareness of the trust problem grew, an insistent demand set in that something should be done about it. This meant, to most Americans, that the government should take action against the trusts, but unfortunately governmental action under the existing system was not easily attainable. The Constitution gave the central government only definitely specified powers, and left all others to the states. Since the "founding fathers" had never heard of a trust, the only power to control such organizations that they had lodged with the central government was whatever might be inferred from the right to control interstate commerce. Obviously, the extent to which any such implied power might be exercised would have to be determined by the courts after extensive litigation. The states, on the other hand, had ample power within their several jurisdictions, but their boundaries were too small, for the activities of any important trust extended through many states. Moreover, the requirement of the national Constitution that each state must give "full faith and credit . . . to the public acts, records, and judicial proceedings of every other state" had embarrassing possibilities. Under the terms of this clause special favors obtained in one state might easily be interpreted to mean special favors in every state. Another constitutional advantage enjoyed by corporations flowed from the Fourteenth Amendment which required that the states might not "deprive any person of life, liberty, or property, without due process of law." In 1886 the Supreme Court, reversing an earlier ruling, held that the use of the word person in this clause was meant to apply to corporations as well as to individuals.[1] Thus the states, themselves the creators of the corporations, were restrained by the federal government from any measures of taxation or regulation that the courts chose to regard as depriving the corporations of property "without due process of law."

The Sherman Antitrust Act

Attempts to restrain the trusts were made nevertheless. Just as the Grangers had invoked to good advantage the old rule of common law that a common carrier was subject to regulation because it was quasi-public in nature, so now the states fell back upon the common-law prohibition of conspiracy in restraint of trade. During the later eighties state after state passed statutes based on this principle. Finally, Congress also fell into line, and on July 2, 1890, the Sherman Antitrust Act received the President's signature. This measure, named after Senator Sherman, for no other reason, according to Senator Hoar, "except that Mr. Sherman had nothing to do with framing it whatever," lacked nothing in vigor of language. It branded as illegal "every contract, combination in the form of trust or otherwise, or conspiracy in restraint of trade or commerce among the several states, or with foreign nations." It defined as a misdemeanor any "attempt to monopolize, or combine or conspire with any other person or persons to monopolize, any part of the trade or commerce among the several states or with foreign nations." Penalties for persons held guilty of violating the act were set at a fine not to exceed $5,000 and imprisonment not to exceed a year, one or both, as the court might prescribe. Furthermore, any person injured by

[1] *Santa Clara County* vs. *Southern Pacific Railroad*, 118 United States Reports, 396.

means that the act declared unlawful might recover in court "threefold the damages by him sustained."

Difficulties in Enforcement

Enforcement of these acts was quite another matter. A number of suits were lodged by the states, and a few decisions unfavorable to the corporations were obtained. In New York State, for example, the North River Sugar Refining Company, a part of the sugar trust, lost its charter; and in Ohio, the Standard Oil Company was held guilty of attempting "to establish a virtual monopoly." Since the technical trust was so clear-cut a violation of both the common law and the statutes, that type of organization was generally discontinued, but in its place new devices to accomplish the same end were speedily invented. Chief among these was the holding company, through which a controlling fraction of the stocks in a great number of enterprises was owned and voted by a single corporation, but many of the trusts chose instead to incorporate as a single great company in the most friendly state they could find. As for the Sherman Antitrust Act, for all its brave language, it proved to be unenforceable. Seven out of the first eight attempts to invoke its penalties went against the government, and in the Knight case (1895) the Supreme Court of the United States held that the mere purchase of property, even if it made for monopoly and the restraint of trade, was not in itself illegal; further, that manufacture and production (in this case the refining of sugar) were no part of interstate commerce. Confronted by this interpretation, in which Attorney-General Olney probably concurred, the government made little further effort to enforce the Sherman Act, and lawyers felt free to advise their clients that the Supreme Court of the United States had conceded the legality of private monopoly.

BIBLIOGRAPHY

A lively and provocative introduction to the economic history of this period is E. C. Kirkland, *Industry Comes of Age* (1961); its bibliography is annotated and full. Stimulating, important syntheses may also be found in T. C. Cochran and William Miller, *The Age of Enterprise* (rev. ed., 1961); and in S. P. Hays, *The Response to Industrialism, 1885–1914* (1957), which is an overview of the whole period, and takes note of political as well as economic development. A valuable documentary is *American Economic Development since 1860* (1968), edited by William Greenleaf. The muckraking and readable work of Matthew Josephson, *The Robber Barons* (1934), has been challenged as one-sided and unappreciative of the constructive work of businessmen and financiers. See *The Robber Barons Revisited* (1968), a collection of conflicting interpretations edited by P. d'A. Jones. Significant works in the newer vein include: E. C. Kirkland, *Dream and Thought in the Business Community, 1860–1900* (1956); William Miller (ed.), *Men in Business* (1952); T. C. Cochran, *Railroad Leaders, 1845–1890: The Business Mind in Action* (1953); and E. C. Kirkland, *Charles Francis Adams, Jr.* (1965). On economic thought, see the monumental work of Joseph Dorfman, *The Economic Mind in American Civilization* (5 vols., 1946–1959), III; and the stimulating monograph by Sidney Fine, *Laissez Faire and the General Welfare State, 1865–1901* (1956). On insurance, see Morton Keller, *The Life Insurance Enterprise, 1885–1910* (1963); and R. C. Buley, *The Equitable Life Assurance Society of the United States* (2 vols., 1967). On finance, important works include: G. W. Edwards, *The Evolution of Finance Capitalism* (1938); Henrietta Larson, *Jay Cooke* (1936); and F. L. Allen, *The Great Pierpont Morgan* (1949).

Two recent short works give an overview of railroad development: J. F. Stover, *American Railroads* (1961); and G. R. Taylor and I. D. Neu, *The American Railroad Network, 1861–1890* (1956). Light on a misunderstood subject is shown by Carter Goodrich, *Government Promotion of American Canals and Railroads, 1800–1890* (1960). Rich regional studies include: E. C. Kirkland, *Men, Cities, and Transportation: A Study in New England History, 1820–1900* (2 vols., 1948); H. H. Pierce, *Railroads of New York, 1826–1875* (1953); and J. F. Stover, *The Railroads of the South, 1865–1900* (1955). General works on westward extensions include: R. E. Riegel, *The Story of Western Railroads* (1926); James McCague, *Moguls and Iron Men* (1964); and Julius Grodinsky, *Transcontinental Railway Strategy, 1869–1893* (1962). R. C. Overton, *Gulf to Rockies* (1953), deals with southwestern railroads. Studies of individual western railroads include: Oscar Lewis, *The Big Four* (1938), on the Central Pacific; R. W. Fogel, *The Union Pacific Railroad* (1960); V. V. Masterson, *The Katy Railroad and the Last Frontier* (1952); Stuart Daggett, *Chapters on the History of the Southern Pacific* (1922); R. G. Athearn, *Rebel of the Rockies* (1962), on the Denver and Rio Grande; and R. C. Overton, *Burlington Route* (1965). C. N. Glaab, *Kansas City and the Railroads* (1962), is a model study. Interesting biographies include S. P. Hirshson, *Grenville M. Dodge* (1967); W. J. Lane, *Commodore Vanderbilt* (1942); Julius Grodinsky, *Jay Gould* (1957); George Kennan, *E. H. Harriman* (2 vols., 1922); J. B. Hedges, *Henry Villard and the Railways of the Northwest* (1930); and J. G. Pyle, *The Life of James J. Hill* (2 vols., 1917).

On the impact of railroads, see the essays by R. W. Fogel, *Railroads and American Economic Growth* (1964). *The Railroads: The Nation's First Big Business* (1965), is a brief documentary collection edited by A. D. Chandler, Jr. See also L. H. Haney, *A Congressional History of Railways in the United States, 1850–1887* (1910); and E. G. Campbell, *The Reorganization of the American Railroad System, 1893–1900* (1938). A stimulating revisionist study is Gabriel Kolko, *Railroads and Regulation, 1877–1916* (1965); see also Lee Benson, *Merchants, Farmers, and Railroads* (1955), which emphasizes urban demands for regulation. On taxation of railroad land grants, see L. E. Decker, *Railroads, Lands, and Politics* (1964).

Convenient introductions to the subject of inventions are found in: J. W. Oliver, *History of American Technology* (1956); Roger Burlingame, *Engines of Democracy* (1940); and F. L. Vaughan, *The United States Patent System* (1956), which stresses conflicts. Biographies of great inventors include: Matthew Josephson, **Edison* (1959); H. G. Prout, *A Life of George Westinghouse* (1921); and Catherine Mackenzie, *Alexander Graham Bell* (1928). Industries resulting from inventions are the subjects of several excellent books, including: R. N. Current, *The Typewriter and the Men Who Made It* (1954); A. A. Bright, Jr., *The Electric-Lamp Industry* (1949); H. C. Passer, *The Electric Manufacturers, 1875–1900* (1953); and O. E. Anderson, Jr., *Refrigeration in America* (1953).

The rise of the steel industry is well treated in the monumental work of V. S. Clark, *History of Manufactures in the United States* (3 vols., 1929). An important work is Allan Nevins, *Abram S. Hewitt: With Some Account of Peter Cooper* (1935). On Carnegie, see his revealing *Autobiography* (1920); B. J. Hendrick, *The Life of Andrew Carnegie* (2 vols., 1932); and Gail Kennedy (ed.), **Democracy and the Gospel of Wealth* (1949), an interesting collection. On the oil industry, a recent general survey is H. F. Williamson and A. R. Daum, *The American Petroleum Industry: The Age of Illumination, 1859–1899* (1959). The muckraking classic by I. M. Tarbell, **The History of the Standard Oil Company* (2 vols., 1904), must now be compared with the more sympathetic work of modern scholars, such as: Allan Nevins, *Study in Power: John D. Rockefeller, Industrialist and Philanthropist* (2 vols., 1953); P. H. Giddens, *Standard Oil Company (Indiana)* (1955); R. W. and M. E. Hidy, *Pioneering in Big Business, 1882–1911: History of the* *Standard Oil Company (New Jersey)* (1955); and G. T. White, *Formative Years in the Far West: A History of Standard Oil Company of California and Predecessors through 1919* (1962). Conflicting views are well set forth in Earl Latham (ed.), **John D. Rockefeller: Robber Baron or Industrial Statesman?* (1949). Sample histories of other industries include: R. A. Clemen, *The American Livestock and Meat Industry* (1923); C. B. Kuhlmann, *The Development of the Flour-Milling Industry in the United States* (1929); F. J. Allen, *The Shoe Industry* (1922); A. H. Cole, *The American Wool Manufacture* (2 vols., 1926); and M. T. Copeland, *The Cotton Manufacturing Industry of the United States* (1912).

On the growth of industry in the South, see especially C. V. Woodward, **Origins of the New South* (1951); and *Travels in the New South* (2 vols., 1962), edited by T. D. Clark. Important special studies include: Broadus and G. S. Mitchell, *The Industrial Revolution in the South* (1930); J. P. Baughman, *Charles Morgan and the Development of Southern Transportation* (1968); and J. W. Jenkins, *James B. Duke* (1927). Of interest are biographies of the New South's leading journalists: J. F. Wall, *Henry Watterson* (1956); and R. B. Nixon, *Henry W. Grady* (1943).

On the trusts and efforts to restrain them, a work by a Swedish economist, H. B. Thorelli, *The Federal Antitrust Policy* (1955), is excellent. Still valuable older works include: W. Z. Ripley, *Trusts, Pools, and Corporations* (rev. ed., 1916); J. W. Jenks and W. E. Clark, *The Trust Problem* (5th ed., 1929); J. D. Clark, *The Federal Trust Policy* (1931); and the dependable survey by H. R. Seager and C. A. Gulick, Jr., *Trust and Corporation Problems* (1929).

G. D. Nash, *State Government and Economic Development: A History of Administrative Policies in California, 1849–1933* (1964), is a model study, stimulating and original.

6

LABOR AND THE

NEW IMMIGRATION

Trade unions · The Knights of Labor · The Haymarket riot · The American Federation of Labor · Samuel Gompers · The Homestead and Pullman strikes · Use of the injunction · Coxey's army · Labor in the South · Immigration · Reasons for immigration · Reception of the immigrants · The "new immigration" · Anti-foreigner sentiment · Labor and the immigrant · Demands for restriction · New roots for old

A direct result of the new industrialism was an increased emphasis on labor organization; or, as a later generation might have put it, "big business" gave rise to "big labor." This development was well-nigh inevitable. As the corporations grew in size and strength, the bargaining power of the individual laborer correspondingly decreased. Concentration gave the employer greater power to oppress, by low wages, long hours, and bad working conditions. But concentration meant also a diminishing number of employers, and a proportionately larger number of employees. By acting together and bargaining collectively, laborers might hope to protect themselves against undue exploitation. This they attempted to do through more and stronger trade unions,

MINER'S PAY DAY. *Sketch by Frenzeny for* Harper's Weekly, *1873.*

but even more significantly, by efforts to unite all laborers, of whatever crafts, under one leadership.

Trade Unions

Local labor unions had existed in the United States since the early nineteenth century, and the Jacksonian period had witnessed the development of a well-defined labor movement; but the depression that began in 1837 had been disastrous for labor, and not until the time of the Civil War was any considerable part of the ground lost regained. During the fifties and sixties a few national organizations, formed by such groups as the printers, the locomotive engineers, and the bricklayers, came into existence, but for a long time none of them succeeded in drawing into its ranks any large percentage of those eligible, while

THE EIGHT-HOUR WORK DAY. A Britton and Rey lithograph published in celebration of the eight-hour day for government employees, 1868.

THE SLAVES OF THE "SWEATERS." A drawing by W. A. Rogers, published in *Harper's Weekly*, April 26, 1890, emphasizes the heavy price in human toil exacted by producers of cheap clothing.

THE RIGHTS OF LABOR. *Working conditions in American industry during the post-Civil War period left much to be desired. The prevalence of low wages, the exploitation of women and children, and the employment of cheap immigrant labor led to occasional acts of violence and the beginnings of reform.*

THE GREAT STRIKE. Burning of the Pittsburgh roundhouse during the Railway Strike of 1877. From a sketch by J. W. Alexander in *Harper's Weekly*, August 11, 1877.

attempts at all-labor organizations were even less satisfactory. In August, 1866, a National Labor Union was formed at Baltimore by a group of seventy-seven delegates, representing a great variety of labor interests. This organization lasted half a dozen years, sponsored annual labor congresses that were well attended, and at one time claimed a membership of 640,000. It was soon drawn off into politics, however, and by 1872 had assisted in the formation of the Labor Reform Party, which survived only one presidential election. What little was left of the National Labor Union crashed with the Panic of 1873, but, while it lasted, it had given the movement for an eight-hour day a good start, and had promoted in a variety of ways the study of labor problems. It furnished, also, an example of concerted action by labor that was not forgotten.

Labor troubles came during the seventies in spite of the fact that labor was as yet imperfectly organized. Some of these disorders might actually have been averted had the unions been strong enough to control their men and to bargain successfully with employers. One of the worst outbreaks occurred in the anthracite coal-mining region of Pennsylvania, where for a dozen years after the Civil War a secret society known as the "Molly Maguires" carried more or less legitimate protests against bad working conditions to violent extremes. Finally, in 1877, with the help of a Pinkerton detective, James McParlan, the "Mollies" were broken up by trials and convictions almost as outrageous as the crimes charged. The purpose of the prosecution seems to have been less to obtain justice than to discredit labor organization. The railroad strikes during the summer of 1877 were likewise characterized by much disorder and an unhappy ending. Railroad workers were still unorganized, but a wage cut of 10 per cent announced by the principal northeastern railroads led many men to cease work, even

without union officers to issue strike orders. The efforts of the strikers, however, were unavailing, for at each center of disturbance federal troops were used freely to break the strike. Another example of labor disaffection appeared far out on the Pacific Coast in the area surrounding San Francisco Bay. There the chief difficulties were widespread unemployment and the presence of many Chinese who worked for "coolie wages." But the activities of the leading agitators, who at first seemed headed toward revolution, turned instead to the formation of a local Workingmen's Party, which seemed content with writing some of its principles into the new constitution that California adopted in 1879.

The Knights of Labor

The need for intelligent leadership, so evident in the labor outbreaks of the seventies, was soon supplied by a national organization known as the Noble Order of the Knights of Labor. This society, which was at first a kind of labor lodge, was founded in 1869 by Uriah S. Stephens, a Philadelphia garment-cutter, who provided it with a secret ritual, a password, and a grip. Since the name of the order was at first represented in public notices by five asterisks, it was long known to the uninitiated as "the five stars." Unlike its predecessor, the Knights of Labor built directly upon the individual, rather than upon existing trade unions. "One big union," to which all workers, skilled or unskilled, should belong, was the ideal; indeed, practically anyone, regardless of race, color, or occupation, could become a "Knight." Under these circumstances members of the more exclusive trade unions, who took pride in their craft skills, tended to hold aloof, and for a decade the growth of the Knights was only moderate. The Knights also suffered from the opposition of the Catholic Church to secret societies and to its ritual.

After 1878, when Terence V. Powderly

(1849–1924) of Scranton, Pennsylvania, became its "Grand Master Workman," the order took on new life. Powderly, as his name would indicate, was of Irish origin and a Catholic, but he was a native American, not an immigrant, born in Carbondale, Pennsylvania. At thirteen years of age he joined the ranks of labor as a switch-tender; later as a Scranton machinist he took so prominent a part in the work of the Machinists' and Blacksmiths' Union that he not only lost his job, but also won a place for his name on an employers' blacklist. This happened in 1873, after which he worked for a time in Ohio and western Pennsylvania, but on returning to Scranton won election as mayor of the city in 1878 on the Greenback-Labor ticket. When later a meeting was held at Reading, Pennsylvania, to reorganize the Knights, Powderly dominated the proceedings, and for the next fifteen years his name and the Knights of Labor were almost synonymous terms. Secrecy was done away with, the name of the order was publicly proclaimed, and Powderly, with only the barest apology of a salary, traveled at his own expense wherever he felt he could gain more recruits for the Knights. From a membership of only 28,000 in 1880 the organization shot forward to 52,000 in 1883, 104,000 in 1885, and perhaps as many as 700,000 by 1886.

The ideals of the Knights were by no means new. They believed, with Edmund Burke, that "When bad men combine, the good must associate, else they will fall, one by one, an unpitied sacrifice in a contemptible struggle." Like the National Labor Union they favored the eight-hour day, the "establishment of cooperative institutions productive and distributive," the use of arbitration as a substitute for strikes, and such legal innovations as were calculated to improve the status of labor. Powderly saw especial virtue in the cooperative idea, and under his urging not less than 135 such

Terence V. Powderly, *Grand Master Workman of the Knights of Labor, 1887. The Knights, an industrial union open to all gainfully employed persons, soon lost out to the American Federation of Labor, which was based, not upon individuals, but upon unions of skilled workers.*

ventures were undertaken, some of which for a time seemed destined to endure. But bad management, internal dissensions, insufficient funds, and cutthroat competition accounted for the undoing of most of them. Labor cooperatives proved to be no less difficult to inaugurate than farmer cooperatives.

In spite of their insistence upon arbitration the Knights became embroiled in a series of violent strikes. In 1884 a business recession set in, accompanied by the inevitable increase in unemployment and in labor unrest. Companies that took advantage of the opportunity to discharge union men, particularly Knights, were sometimes fought successfully by boycotts, but the chief weapon of labor proved to be the strike. By use of it, for example, the Missouri Pacific, early in 1885, was forced to restore a wage cut made without warning and without even the excuse of declining

THE SOUTHWEST RAILROAD STRIKES OF 1886. *This labor outbreak was marked by extremes of violence that turned public opinion against the strikers.*

CITIZEN INTERVENTION. This sketch shows a citizens' committee at Forth Worth, Texas, arresting a turbulent striker after a riot on April 3.

MOVING THE FREIGHT. An attempt to start a freight train under guard of U.S. Marshals at East St. Louis, Illinois, during the strike of 1886.

earnings. Public sympathy was almost unanimously with the strikers, and the company in yielding felt obliged to grant its employees time and one-half for overtime, something the strikers had not even asked. In many minor instances during the middle eighties the Knights helped to win such victories.

Strikes of 1886

Sometimes, however, the outcome was far different. In March, 1886, when a foreman in the Texas and Pacific car shops at Marshall, Texas, was dismissed apparently because he was a member of the Knights of Labor, another important strike occurred. Under the leadership of Martin Irons, some nine thousand shopmen employed on the Gould system (of which the Texas and Pacific was a part) quit work, and attempted by sabotage to make all freight-hauling locomotives unfit for duty. So successful were their efforts that along five thousand miles of railroad in the Southwest freight traffic was at a standstill; only passenger trains carrying United States mails were permitted to move. At first popular hatred for Jay Gould worked in favor of the strikers, but when food shortages began to be felt and factories had to close down for lack of coal, the public had had strike enough. Four state governors, strongly backed by public opinion, ordered the strikers to cease interfering with trains, and Powderly himself, hoping for arbitration, intervened to call a temporary halt. When Gould refused to arbitrate, the strike was resumed with renewed violence, but the public was now so definitely against the strikers that their cause was soon lost.

The Haymarket Riot

Excitement over the southwestern railroad strike had scarcely subsided when the May Day strikes of 1886 claimed the attention of the country. The purpose of these strikes, in which perhaps 340,000 men participated, was to promote the cause of the eight-hour day. Although the claim was made that half the strikers won a reduced work day, an episode that occurred in Chicago, the storm-center of the strike, gave organized labor the most severe setback it had yet received. Chicago happened to be the headquarters of a small group of foreign-born anarchists who welcomed the opportunity to expound to the strikers, both orally and in print, their principal tenet, the abolition of the state. To promote this end they were ready to advocate, although far less ready to perform, deeds of violence and terror. On the afternoon of May 3, August Spies, anarchist editor of the *Arbeiter Zeitung*, was addressing a meeting of strikers and strike sympathizers on a vacant lot not far from the McCormick Harvester Works, when the police attempted to disperse the assembly. In the ensuing melee several strikers were killed, and about twenty were wounded. Next day, when the police tried to break up another such assembly at Haymarket Square, the officers of the law were met with a bomb that exploded with terrific violence, killing one policeman and wounding many more. Hard fighting followed, and when the casualties were reckoned it was found that of the policemen seven had lost their lives and over sixty had been seriously wounded, while of the civilians, four were dead and about fifty wounded. In the search for scapegoats that followed, eight well-known anarchists, including Spies, were brought to trial and convicted, more because of the opinions they held than because of any proved connection with the bombing, and four of them were hanged. A few hardy souls condemned the whole proceedings as a miscarriage of justice, and in 1893, Governor John P. Altgeld

The Haymarket Riot, May 4, 1886. *When the police ordered this mass meeting of workers to disperse, someone threw a bomb into the police ranks which killed seven policemen and wounded many more.*

classed himself with this number by pardoning two of the men who had been sent to prison, an act of courage that wrecked his political career.

Decline of the Knights

It was the irony of fate that the public saw in the Haymarket riot occasion for further condemnation of the Knights of Labor. Actually the strike for the eight-hour day had been promoted mainly through local trade unions, and Powderly had counseled against it on the ground that the weapon of the strike should not be invoked until all other means of protest had been exhausted. Nevertheless, the Knights had already won a reputation for violence and they received the blame. Anarchists and other advocates of revolution had found it easy to obtain membership in the order and had used its forums to propagate their views. Powderly even charged that an attorney for one group of employers confessed that anarchists had been paid to become Knights so that "they might stir up the devil and bring discredit upon your whole movement." As the control of the central organization over the behavior of the locals disintegrated, strikes were often undertaken "against the advice of the General Executive Board." The result was that skilled workers, alienated by the ruthless way in which the unskilled precipitated conflicts, tended to withdraw from the Knights in order to build up their own trade unions. By 1888 the membership of the Knights of Labor had declined to less than 260,000, and by 1890 to about 100,000. Within a short time the order had disappeared entirely.

The American Federation of Labor

Meantime a rival organization, which discarded the "one big union" idea in favor of the older federative plan, had begun to make headway. The American Federation of Labor, which was founded in 1881 at Pittsburgh as the "Federation of Organized Trades and Labor Unions of the United States and Canada," shortened its name in 1886, and at about the same time began to lengthen its membership list. While individuals, as such, were excluded from membership, almost any kind of labor organization, whether national, state, or local, might belong. The great bulk of its membership, however, was among the skilled trades, although the United Mine Workers, for example, was an industrial union with mostly unskilled membership. The intent of the new order, however, was in general no less to protect skilled labor from competition by the unskilled than to protect labor as such from the oppression of capital. By way of protecting its individual members against unskilled competition, it sought to limit the number of apprenticeships in each craft, while by way of protecting the organization against possible competitors it warred against what it called "dual unionism." It had no quarrel with capitalism as an economic system, and throughout its history it fought radical or leftist movements among its members. Its mission was to insure that labor should share generously in capitalistic enterprise. To this end it formulated a philosophy which it called economic, or day-to-day unionism, to differentiate its goals from those of the radical political unions of Europe. Among its goals were the practical ones of an eight-hour day, a six-day work week, higher wages, shorter hours, safer and more sanitary working conditions, greater security of job tenure, and the elimination of child labor.

This economic unionism showed little interest in the establishment of labor cooperatives, and it convincingly resisted all efforts to make the Federation over into a separate political party. Instead of going directly into politics as an organization, it supported candidates and platforms, of whatever party, provided only that they were favorable to the program of the Federation. While it hoped to see labor win most of its victories peacefully, either by obtaining favorable legislation or by collective bargaining with employers, the Federation, like the Knights, was willing in case of necessity to rely on the strike and the boycott. Its organization lent itself admirably to the use of the sympathetic strike, by means of which workers in a related craft, even if unwilling to make an issue of their own grievances, might come to the aid of a striking union. A sizable "war chest," supported by a per capita tax levied on members, enabled the Federation's central board of control to aid unemployed strikers and to prolong any conflict it chose to support.

Samuel Gompers

What Terence V. Powderly was to the Knights of Labor, Samuel Gompers (1850–1924) was to the American Federation. Gompers was born in London, the son of a cigarmaker. At ten years of age he began to learn the shoemakers' trade, but he soon gave that up in favor of his father's trade, because the latter was organized and the former was not. In 1863 he came with his parents to America, and a year later he joined the first cigarmakers' union ever organized in New York City. Always an enthusiastic member, when he grew to manhood he became first the union's secretary and later its president. The training that he thus received was of great significance, for in many ways this local New York cigarmakers' union was a model organization. It followed the British system of benefit payments in case of unemployment, sickness, or death; it tried to encourage skill and intelligence among its members; it gained many of its victories by collective bargaining, by arbitration, and by retaining the good will and respect of employers. Gompers never forgot this early training, and much of the conserva-

Samuel Gompers. *Known as the "Grand Old Man" of the labor movement, Gompers was president of the American Federation of Labor for nearly forty years.*

tism of his later career may properly be attributed to it. He was one of the original group of delegates that founded the Federation in 1881, and was even more active in the reorganization of 1886. From 1885 to the time of his death, with the exception of a single year, 1895, he was regularly elected president of the Federation.

Under Gompers' devoted leadership, the Federation scored many successes. It backed the strike for the eight-hour day in 1886, and claimed substantial gains in spite of the unfavorable reaction to the Haymarket riot. It conducted another strike for the eight-hour day in 1890, this time in the carpenters' union, with fairly satisfactory results. It carried on an active public relations campaign that resulted in a growing tolerance, if not outright approval, of unionism. It supported innumerable movements, both in the states and in the nation as a whole, that resulted in the enactment of laws favorable to labor. In part through its activities practically every state in the Union was soon equipped with a bureau of labor statistics, and in 1903 Congress went so far as to establish the Department of Commerce and Labor, with a seat in the cabinet. The Federation encouraged member unions to set up their own systems for sickness and unemployment benefits, and could soon point to many instances in which its advice had been followed. Its assistance could be counted upon, also, in efforts to secure adoption by employers of the "closed shop," which meant that only union labor might be employed in a given plant, and to eliminate "yellow dog" contracts, by which workers were obliged to agree in advance of employment that they would not join labor unions. From a membership of 150,000 in 1886 the Federation by 1900 had grown to more than half a million, by 1905 to a million and a half, and by the outbreak of the First World War to two millions.

The greatest weakness of the American Federation of Labor lay in the fact that it represented only a favored minority of labor. Most unskilled workers were excluded from membership, together with all skilled workers who did not belong to a union. Moreover, a number of labor organizations, including the four great railway unions, refused to affiliate with the Federation on the ground that they were able to take care of themselves, and were not eager to accept responsibility for others. The railway unions, except for sympathetic strikes, could ordinarily be counted on to cooperate with the Federation.

The Homestead Strike

During the depression-ridden years of the nineties the conservative policies of Gompers and the AFL were sorely tested. Gompers himself even lost office for a year during this period when the armies of unemployed men became increasingly radical and impatient of restraint. An omen of what was to come appeared in 1892 when a violent strike broke out in the steel industry, then centered in Pittsburgh, Pennsylvania. The Homestead strike, as this conflict was called, involved on the one hand the Amalgamated Association of Iron and Steel Workers, a well-established labor organization that had been formed as early as 1876 by a merger of several smaller craft unions, and on the other hand the Carnegie Steel Company, perhaps the most powerful of the several American steel corporations. Carnegie three years before had agreed to a satisfactory contract with the union, but at the time trouble broke out in 1892 he had gone to Europe, leaving the affairs of the company in the hands of Henry Clay Frick, a man whose detestation of organized labor was open and unconcealed. The chief point at issue between the company and the workers was a proposed reduction in the pay for piecework. The company argued that such a reduction was justified because more efficient machinery had been installed. The worker who made use of the new tools could turn out more pieces than formerly in a given time without any greater expenditure of energy. Thus, according to the employers, a reduction in the piece rate could be made without reducing the worker's daily or weekly earnings. The union, however, refused to be persuaded, and held that the real intent of the company was a wage cut.

When on July 1 the union refused to accept the company's terms, Frick anticipated the strike by closing the Homestead works. Technically, therefore, what followed was the result of a "lockout" rather than a strike. The union at once began to picket the works, while Frick showed that he meant business by employing Pinkerton detectives to overpower the pickets, an action that led to bloody fighting, July 6, 1892, and the retreat of the Pinkertons. Despite state militia brought in to protect the company's property, the strikers held out for nearly five months, but at length, completely defeated, and with public opinion turning against them, they resumed work on the company's terms. An important factor in alienating the public from the strikers, whose case at first had aroused considerable sympathy, was the mad attack, by Alexander Berkman, a young anarchist, on the life of Frick. For this act the strikers were in no way responsible. Frick, although seriously injured, soon recovered, and Berkman for his crime spent fifteen years in prison.

The Pullman Strike

Of all the many labor disturbances that punctuated the years of depression the Pullman strike of 1894 was by far the most significant. In 1880 George Mortimer Pullman, the inventor and builder of the Pullman sleeping-car, had established for the benefit of his employees the "model town" of Pullman on the outskirts of Chicago. This project carried paternalism to an extraordinary extreme. Model dwellings were built by the company and rented to employees; company stores were opened at which Pullman employees were encouraged to buy; a company church, a company school, a company park, and a company theater ministered to the various social needs of the community. The entire village, indeed, was owned and operated by the Pullman Palace Car Company as a business investment — a kind of modern feudalism, so critics were accustomed to say. The situation was changed somewhat in 1889 when the village was annexed to Chicago, but for the most part the property rights of the Pullman Company remained undisturbed.

Pullman had no use for labor unions, but during the first year of the depression organizers of the American Railway Union made rapid headway with his men. This union was the brain child of Eugene V.

Debs (1855–1926), who was later to become the outstanding leader of the Socialist movement in the United States. Debs was born in Terre Haute, Indiana, of French-Alsatian ancestry, and at the time of the Pullman strike was thus less than forty years of age. He had worked in the railway shops of his home town when he was a boy of only fourteen, and at sixteen he had become a locomotive fireman. A passionate defender of the underprivileged and devoted to the union idea, he held high office in the Brotherhood of Locomotive Firemen, and for a time edited *The Locomotive Fireman's Magazine*. He became increasingly impatient, however, with the unaggressive attitude of the railway brotherhoods and the American Federation of Labor, with which the brotherhoods cooperated, although they would not join it. Convinced that industrial unions were preferable to trade unions and that railroad men should all be members of one organization, in 1893 he founded the American Railway Union, and such was his persuasiveness that within a year the new union had enrolled 150,000 members.

The Homestead Steel Strike. *An illustration showing a shield used by strikers at the Carnegie Steel Works in Pittsburgh when firing on the hated Pinkertons, 1892.*

The Pullman strike was precipitated in the spring of 1894 when the Pullman Company, hard hit by the depression, laid off one-third of its men and cut the wages of the rest from 30 to 40 per cent. No reductions, however, were made in the rent charged for company houses nor in the price of goods at the company stores. In protest the men quit work, and with the demand for sleeping-cars at a standstill Pullman showed no disposition to call them back. With their credit withdrawn at the company stores, the strikers were on the verge of starvation when the American Railway Union came to the rescue with relief money and with the threat of a boycott against the hauling of Pullman cars. On June 26 Debs ordered the boycott to be applied on all the western railroads, and "A.R.U." men obeyed by cutting out Pullman cars from their trains and leaving them on side-tracks. When boycotters were discharged for such acts, the strike became general, and not Pullman cars alone but whole trains stood on side-tracks. From Cincinnati to San Francisco the strike was felt. Traffic between Chicago and the West was virtually paralyzed and hoodlums who joined the strikers stooped to every sort of violence, as the unemployed multitudes poured their accumulated resentment into the strife. Engines were crippled, freight cars were overturned and looted, non-striking employees were driven from their posts.

The railroad operators, faced by this dangerous situation, would normally have been willing to trust the governor of Illinois — the state most seriously involved — to keep order, if necessary by calling out the militia to aid the civil authorities. But the governor of Illinois happened to be John P. Altgeld, already notorious among conservatives for his pardoning of the Haymarket anarchists. The operators, therefore, demanded that federal troops be brought in, and when Altgeld took no steps in that direction they appealed directly to the President for aid. Cleveland was in a quandary, for while the Constitution authorized the President to protect a state against domestic violence, it expressly stated that such action was to be taken "on application of the legislature, or of the executive (when the legislature cannot be convened)."[1] The legislature of Illinois was not in session and the governor of the state had issued no call for help, but the President at length decided that he might intervene on the pretext that the Chicago disorders interfered with the free transport of United States mail. By the fourth of July two thousand regulars, including cavalry and field artillery, had moved into the troubled zone. Having arrived there, they exerted themselves not merely to see that the mails were carried, but also to break the strike. Altgeld protested vigorously that Cleveland's action was unconstitutional and demanded the immediate withdrawal of the federal troops, but Cleveland stood his ground. No doubt Altgeld, had he been given time to do so, would have restored order, but it is very doubtful that he would have tried to break the strike.

Governmental action against the strikers was not confined to the use of troops, for the federal courts soon took a hand. Debs, who had assumed direct supervision of the strike, and several other leaders were arrested by federal officers on the charge of conspiracy to obstruct the mails, and although released on bail were enjoined by federal judges Grosscup and Woods against doing anything to prolong the strike. In direct defiance of this order, Debs urged a group of labor leaders on July 12 to promote a general strike by all the labor organizations of the country. Thereupon he and six others were cited for contempt of court and sentenced to six months in jail. Thus summarily removed from the scene of conflict, Debs was left free to read and to think, and when he

[1] Article IV, Section 4.

emerged from confinement he announced his conversion to socialism. His imprisonment served also to call attention to the fact that the courts were not averse to obtaining results by the use of the injunction that they could not so certainly have obtained had the normal procedure of a jury trial been followed. Criticism of "government by injunction" and of the use of the regular army to break strikes was freely expressed. To many the now familiar Populist charge that a corrupt alliance existed between business and government to suppress the liberties of the people seemed only too well substantiated.

"Bloody Bridles" Waite

That another view of the duty of government could be taken was shown by Governor Davis H. Waite of Colorado, whom the Populists, with Democratic assistance, had elected in 1892. "It is better," he had said, "infinitely better, that blood should flow to the horses' bridles rather than our national liberties should be destroyed." Known thenceforth as "Bloody Bridles" Waite, he did not hesitate to help the striking miners during the so-called "Cripple Creek War" of 1894 instead of giving the customary aid and comfort to the employers. When an army of deputy sheriffs made ready to attack the strikers, Waite called out the entire state militia to preserve the peace, and marched his troops between the opposing forces. Waite was a man of no tact and little judgment, but his attitude, like Altgeld's, gave courage to the forces of labor. Throughout the nineties in Colorado, Idaho, and Montana the Western Federation of Miners battled employers with a degree of violence that bordered on revolution. In May, 1897, the president of this organization urged every union in Colorado and Idaho to arm itself "so that in two years we can hear the inspiring music of the martial tread of 25,000 armed men in the ranks of labor."

"Coxey's Army"

Attempts to induce the government to help solve the problem of unemployment by means of work relief, while not entirely unknown, proceeded usually from the minds of men whom the public regarded as "crackpots." Most famous of these was "General" Jacob S. Coxey of Massillon, Ohio, a Greenbacker and a Populist, who advocated that Congress should issue $500 million in legal-tender notes to be expended at the rate of $20 million a month on the building of good roads. Wages of $1.50 per eight-hour day were to be paid to all who needed employment. Coxey also urged that municipalities desirous of making public improvements should be authorized to issue non-interest-bearing bonds equal to half their assessed valuation. These bonds might then be used as security with the Secretary of the Treasury to obtain loans of legal-tender notes to pay for the construction of schools, courthouses, paved streets, and other worthy projects. Both schemes, on the financial side, were highly inflationary in character, but they aimed at a type of governmental activity that in the next great depression became extremely familiar.

In seeking to promote his ideas Coxey hit upon the expedient of presenting, by means of a march of the unemployed on Washington, a "living petition" to Congress. With the assistance of amused and interested newspapermen, he actually got his march started on Easter Sunday, 1894, and on the first of May following "Coxey's Army," five hundred strong, entered Washington determined to lay its demands before Congress. At the Capitol Coxey and several of his principal adherents suffered ignominious arrest for disobeying an ordinance to keep off the grass. But Coxey's exploit, which attracted wide newspaper attention, was speedily imitated by other marchers, most of whom were stopped far short of Washington.

Coxey's Army. *Part of "General" Coxey's Army, shown on a barge at a lock in the Chesapeake and Ohio Canal. Photograph by Ray Stannard Baker.*

Labor in the South

While these exciting events were occurring in the North, labor in the New South had not yet begun to stir. Within the states of the former Confederacy labor organization was virtually nonexistent, despite the rapid industrial strides being made in some areas. Southern labor, in part because of its rural background and in part because of the racial problem, remained docile and was not easily aroused. Whites from the poorer lands of the piedmont and from the mountains furnished the bulk of the labor supply for the textile mills and such others as required machine operators, while a preponderance of Negroes did the harder work of the mines, the blast furnaces, and the lumber industry. Only in the rarest instances were the two races employed to work side by side at the same tasks; industries that used both whites and Negroes took care that there was a division of labor that separated the races, with the inferior position being regularly assigned to the Negroes. In the textile mills the employment of women and children was practically universal. Nevertheless, one of the chief attractions of the mills to the rural whites was the opportunity they furnished for the whole family to be gainfully employed. Wages were low, at first far lower than wages paid in the northern mills, but with the wife and children at work as well as the head of the house the total income realized was so much larger than could be wrested from a rundown southern farm that the temptation to leave the farm for the factory was well-nigh irresistible. It often turned out that women and children kept their jobs, while the men, less easily adaptable to the new type of work, lost theirs. Not every husband who stayed home while the rest of the family went to work did so of his own volition. Hours of labor were long, sometimes as much as seventy-two hours per week.

Most of the southern mills and factories developed along definitely paternalistic lines. Someone had to provide houses for the workers, and the "company" made it its business to provide them. The company likewise opened stores, and in many instances paid the workers in scrip, good at any time for payments to the company, but redeemable in cash only at infrequent intervals. The company also provided such schools and churches as it deemed desirable, and hired both the teachers and the preachers. To the country people who flocked to the mills these acts of forethought were accepted without suspicion. The houses of the mill villages were better than the houses of the farms, the company stores were easy of access, and charged little more, if any, than other stores; while the schools, the churches, and the factories themselves furnished such an opportunity for community life as the workers had never known before. Throughout the nineteenth century labor organizers were given little encouragement either by employers or by employees. In the twentieth century, however, unionism took strong hold in the South and worked many changes.

Immigration

One principal difference between the industrial North and the industrial South was that the former, unlike the latter, came to depend in large part for its labor supply upon immigrants newly arrived from the Old World. From 1880 onward the immigrant tide swelled to gigantic dimensions. The significance of immigration in American history can hardly be overemphasized; in a sense all the people of the United States, except for a few of Indian blood, are immigrants or the descendants of immigrants. But the so-called "new immigration" of the late nineteenth and early twentieth centuries came from countries in Europe that formerly had contributed only a few of their people to the making of America; hence the newcomers, arriving as they did in such unprecedented numbers, wrought great changes in the proportions of Old World

nationalities represented in the American population. More than ever before the United States became a "nation of nations." It thus becomes virtually impossible to dissociate the history of the nation from the history of immigration.

The migration of peoples from the Old World to the New came in distinct waves. The first great movement came during the seventeenth century and was principally from England. But it is necessary to recall that other nationalities, particularly the Dutch along the Hudson and the Swedes along the Delaware, also participated in this early movement. The next great influx came during the eighteenth century, when the Scotch-Irish and the Rhineland Germans, or Palatines, by the hundreds of thousands reached American shores. "One hundred per cent" Americans of the twentieth century could hardly have been more dismayed at the "new immigration" from southern and eastern Europe than were the English colonials at the coming of the Scotch-Irish and the Palatines. The third wave came during the twenty or so years preceding the Civil War, bringing millions of Celtic Irish and Germans to the country. The fourth wave set in immediately after the Civil War and lasted until the First World War. Included in it were many peoples from all the nationalities that had come before; but as time went on an increasingly large proportion of the newcomers were from southern and eastern Europe, people who were far removed in language and culture from the other Europeans who had preceded them. It was to these later arrivals that the term "new immigration" was applied.

Despite all these waves of immigration, the Anglo-American strain in the civilization of the United States remained dominant. Because they came first, the English immigrants set the original patterns in language, literature, law, government, and religion. These patterns were to be greatly modified by the changed conditions in the New World and by each succeeding wave of newcomers. But the old stock always outnumbered the new, and, reinforced as it always was by a steady stream of migrants from Great Britain, it clung tenaciously to vested positions of power. The less numerous immigrants, therefore, had to learn the English language and bow to Anglo-American customs. These immigrants had a profound influence upon the American way of life, but their influence, like that of the American environment, simply modified the existing culture and did not substitute a new one for it. In one form or another, most of the old traditions lived on.

Reasons for Immigration

Economic opportunity had much to do with the coming of the immigrants. In most years the demand for cheap labor to man the new industries outran the domestic supply. Western lands also existed for those who had means to reach the West. Official stimulation came by the granting of liberal bounties for those who would serve in the army during the Civil War, and by a law of 1864 that permitted the importation of labor under contracts similar to those that in colonial times had brought so many indentured servants to America. Further to encourage immigration, both the federal government and many western states maintained immigration bureaus which vied with the western railroads in issuing pamphlets setting forth the promise of the new lands in the most inviting terms. The new steamship companies of the period, quick to see in the immigrant trade a lucrative source of income, also fostered immigration. Competition among the rival companies was keen, and the rates were correspondingly low. At one time during the seventies it was possible to purchase a ticket from Stockholm to Chicago for only $21, while passage across the Atlantic, port to port, fell to as low as $12, including meals. The existence of such favorable rates was advertised not only by the ship and railroad companies, but also by less responsible agents who made it their business to induce the discontented everywhere to emigrate. These agents, for a commission, sold the emigrants tickets to the New World, herded them westward to farms if they had the

The Lure of American Wages. *A cartoon showing the tug-of-war that immigrants had to face in deciding to leave their homelands for America.*

money with which to buy land, or turned them over to labor contractors if they had not. By word of mouth and by advertising they drew a convincing, but often false, picture of the easy road to wealth in the United States, and for thousands of hard-pressed Europeans the appeal was irresistible.

Within Europe itself, powerful forces goaded many people into emigration. Of all such forces, no doubt population pressure headed the list. About 1750 a remarkable increase in population began. Within one hundred years the total population of the Continent rose by 85 per cent, or from about 140 million to about 260 million. But this was only the beginning. Within the next fifty years Europe's population was to increase by another 54 per cent. And while most of the new population found a living in the industrial cities of Europe itself, there were still many who could not find work either on farm or in factory. Added to the economic urge were other important factors. Dislike of British rule continued as at least a secondary motivation among the Irish, and the revival of reaction that followed the revolutions of 1848 in Central Europe pointed the way to the New World for political nonconformists. Resentment against the requirement of military service, a situation common to most European countries in the last half of the nineteenth century, also sent it quotas. Even religious motives had by no means ceased to count. The Jews of Russia, which then included most of Poland, were subject to severe discrimination and often to bloody pogroms. To escape persecution they came to America in steadily increasing numbers, particularly after the widespread anti-Jewish outbreaks beginning in 1881. Among Christians, too, there were reasons for religious unrest. In most European nations established churches enjoyed special prerogatives that were deeply resented by dissenting sects. There was also widespread criticism of the indifference of the church to the public welfare, and condemnation of the clergy for their worldliness. Religious dissenters, sometimes the converts of American missionaries, found excuses, if not reasons, in such charges for their move to America. Almost everyone knew that in the United States there was no established church and that religious freedom was the rule. "America letters," written to their Old World friends and relatives by immigrants to the New World, exaggerated the blessings attainable by the changes, and drew thousands across the seas.

Reception of the Immigrants

In a moving book, *The Uprooted*, Oscar Handlin tells in general terms the story of the emigrants who left their native villages for what they assumed to be the boundless opportunities of America. In spite of the European trend toward urbanization, most of these people were country folk. To some extent the movement to America was only a part of the more general movement from country to city: most of those who left their homes went to the cities of their own nation, others to the cities of the New World. The peasants of Europe, unlike American farmers, tended to live together in villages from which they went out each morning to their fields. The habits and customs of the village were fixed by centuries of tradition; each person knew his status and felt that he belonged to a community. The act of leaving thus involved a complete break with the past. From then on he was one of the "uprooted"; wherever he went he would probably never again feel at home. Although conditions on the voyage to America were better than they had been earlier in the period, bad food, jammed quarters, and suffering were common throughout the nineteenth century.

Upon arriving in the United States the immigrant found no such warm welcome as he had hoped for. Inscribed on the base

AT ELLIS ISLAND.

OFF TO AMERICA.

of the Statue of Liberty, a gift from France to the United States in 1886, were Emma Lazarus' warming words:

Give me your tired, your poor,
Your huddled masses yearning to breathe free,
The wretched refuse of your teeming shore,
Send these, the homeless, tempest-tossed, to
  me:
I lift my lamp beside the golden door.

But the lifted lamp was a symbol rather than a reality. Certainly the government did nothing to help the new arrivals. An inspector's report for 1871 had this to say:

If Europe were to present us with 300,000 cattle per year, ample agencies would be employed to secure their proper protection and distribution, but thus far the general government has done but little to diminish the numerous hardships of an emigrant's position. . . . All legislation having for its purpose the good of the poor and the lowly, will necessarily be opposed by those who make money off their ignorance and helplessness.[1]

Most of the people who met the immigrant, including many of his own countrymen, were bent merely on cheating him out of what small sums he still retained. They

[1] Quoted in George M. Stephenson, *A History of Immigration, 1820–1924* (1926), 251.

acted as runners for hotels that swindled him, they stole his baggage, cheated him in turning his currency into dollars, sold him railway tickets to nonexistent places, or if they existed, by the most roundabout way. After these greeters were through with him, he walked the city streets in search of a job only to find that most employers were eager to take advantage of his ignorance. Under the urging of self-appointed bosses, or *padrones*, as the Italians called them, he usually contracted to do unskilled pick and shovel labor on some construction job. Or he might find his way to the nation's coal, lead, or copper mines, to its iron foundries or steel mills, to the harder and more menial tasks in all sorts of factories.

We Who Built America is the appropriate title that Carl Wittke gave to his history of the immigrants. Without the labor they furnished it is hard to see how the railroads, the factories, and the cities of the new America could ever have been built, or its rich mineral resources exploited. Members of nearly every immigrant group could be found practically everywhere that hard work had to be done, but there were some recognizable trends in the types of employment they obtained. The Italians, for example, took over in a general sort of way from the Irish the numerous jobs for unskilled labor in the cities; the various Slavic

IMMIGRANTS TO AMERICA.
For those who left the Old World for the New there were incredible difficulties ahead. Baggage was a problem, for the immigrants often started afoot. On arrival they had to line up for inspection, and wait anxiously for such of their belongings as they could not carry. These three photographs are from the Alexander Alland Collection.

IMMIGRANT'S BAGGAGE.

groups accepted stoically the arduous duties of the iron- and steel-works, the stockyards, and the mines; the Jews by the tens of thousands became city sweatshop workers. So each immigrant group in its own peculiar way contributed to the new industrialism.

Immigrants as Farmers

The great majority of the immigrants had no choice but to remain in the cities, but the most favored of them went back to the land. This was especially true of the Scandinavians and Germans, and to a lesser degree of the Finns, the Dutch, and the Czechs. On their arrival in Chicago they were usually met by "land sharks" eager to sell them worthless or nonexistent land. But by this time they had learned to be wary, and some were always fortunate enough to find the land they coveted, land that reproduced as nearly as possible the characteristics of the land they had known at home. Friends and relatives already in America helped the newcomers to settle as close as possible to their own holdings. In general the immigrants were reluctant to push to the farthest frontiers, and preferred to buy or rent land that had already been brought under cultivation. Even so, all was strange and difficult. The soil and crops were different from what they had known, and the American

methods of farming required machinery that was costly to purchase and baffling to use. There was much more buying and selling than in the European village. But since American farmers lived in houses widely separated from those of their neighbors, there was nothing to take the place of the community life of the Old World village. Loneliness told heavily upon the whole family, but especially upon the women. The immigrants also found social discrimination. America might be the land of the free where all men were equal, but many Americans did not act that way. Some thought of themselves always as "more equal than others."

The "New Immigration"

But still the immigrants came. A quarter of a million of them landed on American shores in 1865, and three years later the annual total had reached 326,000, well above the average for the 1850's. By 1873, when more than 460,000 aliens entered the country, the immigrant tide had broken all preceeding records. The census of 1870, which counted 38,558,371 people in the United States, described 2,314,000 of them as immigrants who had arrived during the sixties; while five years later the total number of foreign-born in the population was set at 7,500,000. The total for the decade of the

The Squatters of New York. *A scene near Central Park, New York, by an unknown artist, after a sketch by E. E. Wyand, 1869. This reproduction of a wood-engraving shows the appalling housing conditions on the outskirts of the city. From* American Woodcuts, *Brooklyn Museum.*

seventies, in spite of the depression, was 2,812,191; while during the eighties all previous records were broken by an influx of 5,246,613, an average of more than half a million immigrants a year. By 1905 the million mark had been reached, and until the outbreak of the First World War in 1914 the avalanche continued.

Until the last decade of the nineteenth century, the great bulk of this immigration came, as before the Civil War, from the British Isles and from Germany, but some notable new trends were in evidence. Im-migration from Ireland, although still heavy, never again reached the startling totals of the forties and fifties, and was even exceeded during the seventies by the numbers coming from England. The Scandinavian migration, which had reached only slender proportions before the Civil War, also made spectacular gains; during the seventies the numbers coming from Norway, Sweden, and Denmark averaged about 25,000 a year. The influx from Germany, which up to the middle eighties furnished about one-third of the total, began at that time to drop off, and by the end of the century it furnished not above one-seventh of the whole. Most significant of all was the really "new immigration" from southern and eastern Europe. From the middle eighties on the numbers coming from these areas rose as those coming from northern and western Europe fell. By the later nineties the former exceeded the latter in the proportion of three to two.

Anti-Foreigner Sentiment

The descendants of colonial Americans had long been familiar with immigrants from the British Isles and from Germany, and they found comparatively little difficulty in accustoming themselves to such other northwestern Europeans as the Scandinavians and the Dutch. All these peoples, despite their initial difficulties, took on American ways with a minimum of resistance. But Italians and Poles, Russians and Rumanians, Magyars and Bulgars, Czechs and Croats, Slovaks and Slovenes, Jews and Greeks seemed somehow vastly different. Instead of welcoming amalgamation they seemed almost to set themselves against it. Immigrants of a given language group tended to settle together in the cities, and to retain tenaciously their Old World language and customs. In every sizable city there was likely to be an Italian quarter, a Jewish quarter, a Russian quarter, a Polish quarter, and so on. In each such section the principal language spoken was not English, but the language of the immigrants. Signs over the stores reflected this difference, newspapers published in America but written in the Old World language were for sale in the streets, cities within cities were as numerous as the nationalities represented in the total population. Under these circumstances how could the traditional process of amalgamation be maintained? How could these foreigners resident in America become truly Americans?

Tenements and Slums

There were also the shocking living conditions that characterized the immigrant sections. For these conditions certainly the immigrants were not wholly to blame. The men who built the tenements, refused to repair them, and charged all the traffic would bear were for the most part not immigrants, but native Americans. Nor can the city governments that tolerated such housing conditions be cleared of responsibility. The low rewards of employment in America, not the wishes of the individuals concerned, drove the immigrants into this sordid way of life. With very few exceptions they had not lived so in the Old World, but native Americans rarely seemed to understand. The immigrants, to hear their critics talk, had deliberately reproduced in American cities the same ideal breeding grounds for disease that characterized European slums. In the immigrant sections life expectancy was low and infant mortality was phenomenally high. But it was not this that so much troubled

"Bandit's Roost." A photograph by Jacob A. Riis, showing how the "other half" lived. A print from original plate by Alexander Alland.

the native Americans; what worried them more was that epidemics might, and sometimes did, start in the immigrant sections, then spread to other parts of the city, and even into the country. The immigrants were held responsible, also, for much disorder and violence. They were guilty, no doubt, of a certain amount of drinking and gambling, the inevitable outlets of frustration and despair. But many of the crimes laid to their door were not of their doing.

Religions of the Immigrants

The religions of the immigrants also came in for criticism. Great numbers of them were devout Roman Catholics, and there were always Protestants to express alarm at any increase in the Catholic population. Many Catholics among the immigrants naturally sent their children, when they could afford to do so, to parochial schools instead of to the public schools, and for this they could be denounced. How could they ever expect to be digested into the American population if they neglected the Americanizing influence of the public schools? Out in the agricultural Middle West, where cities were deemed evil anyway and now even more evil because of the coming of the immigrants, the American Protective Association, a secret anti-Catholic order, was founded in 1887 by H. F. Bowers of Davenport, Iowa. Its purpose was to strengthen the bulwarks of nativism against the foreign invaders; to be a good A.P.A. member one must swear not to employ Catholics and not to vote for Catholics. The order spread from the country to the cities in the 1890's, and claimed a million members by 1896. It was probably responsible for such wild tales as that Catholics meant to overthrow the American government, and were collecting arms for the purpose in the basements of Catholic churches. At least, some A.P.A. chapters gave this as an excuse for themselves collecting arms. In the face of the more exciting silver issue of the nineties,

however, the A.P.A., like the pre-Civil War Know-Nothings when confronted by the anti-slavery crusade, soon lost ground and disappeared. But the temporary popularity of the order revealed a spirit of reckless intolerance that made the immigrant a little sceptical of American boasts of freedom of religion.

The Roman Catholics were not the only religious group among the immigrants to be made keenly conscious of their religious affiliations. The Lutherans, both Scandinavian and German, tended to lean toward the most orthodox opinions of their homelands. This was but natural; everything else was so different in America that they would lean over backwards to keep religion just the same if they could. This meant, among other things, that each national group was likely to hold apart from other Lutherans; also, since in the New World the Lutheran clergy grew even more disputatious than in the Old, the number of separate "synods" was multiplied inordinately. The Lutherans aroused the suspicions of other Protestants by holding services in their native languages, by having images, just as the Catholics did, in their churches, and by sending their children, whenever possible, to their own parochial schools, schools which were often conducted in a foreign language. Then there were the Orthodox Catholics from eastern Europe and the Balkans, with practices that seemed particularly foreign to the Americans. The onion-shaped towers of their churches and the ornate robes of their bewhiskered clergy were a far cry from anything the native American sects had produced.

The Jews

Most strikingly different of all were the Jews. There had been Jews in America from the very beginning, but never before in such numbers. The total Jewish population of the United States in 1840 had been about 15,000, but by 1880 it was no less than 250,000. At the latter date most American Jews had come from Germany, but thereafter the overwhelming majority came from Russia, or from the nations of eastern Europe adjacent to Russia; aided by this influx, the Jewish population of the country had increased by 1927 to about 4 millions. In America, as in Europe, the Jews tended to be town- or city-dwellers and often tradesmen; as such, they were naturally objects of suspicion; they suffered from prejudices that were rife in the Old World and were easily communicated to the New. They spoke, or learned to speak, Yiddish; they published newspapers in that language; they lived apart from other immigrants in ghettos; they sent their children to the public schools, but after hours to their own schools to learn Hebrew; they ate different foods; they had a different look. Soon New York City alone had a million Jews, the largest concentration of Jewish population anywhere in the world. Actually, the Jews made the adjustment to New World conditions better than most immigrant groups, but they found to their sorrow that they had not left anti-Semitism behind. It pervaded every aspect of their lives in America hardly less, they sometimes thought, than in Europe.[1]

Criticisms of the Immigrants

Native Americans made a great to-do about the danger to the American system of government from the untutored immigrants. It is true that the newcomers, desperately poor and in need of economic security, did indeed tend to fall in with the wishes of corrupt city machines. This happened in spite of the many mutual aid societies and associations through which they themselves tried hard to look out for each other during such unescapable emergencies as sickness and death; but the politicians could also help, and the immigrants were in no position to reject aid from

[1] See p. 228.

any source. Jobs were an essential, however tedious and soul-searing the work, and the local party leader had some unexplained influence with contractors, especially those who were working on public projects of one kind or another. He could dispense other favors also. If a man found himself or a member of his family in trouble with the law, the party leader could fix it. If he had to have a little cash, the party leader might lend him the money. If Christmas gifts for the children were sparse, at least one could count on a basket from party headquarters. It followed naturally that one voted as the party leader said he should. The city machines might wax fat on the graft they collected in return, but to the immigrant the bargain seemed good. A few immigrants brought to the United States radical European political doctrines, such as socialism, syndicalism, and anarchism, and by advocating them persistently gave all immigrants a bad reputation. Especially after the violent labor troubles of the nineties, altogether too many Americans tended to take seriously the charge made by Senator Chauncey Depew of New York that most Europeans came to America "to destroy our government, cut our throats, divide our property."

Labor and the Immigrant

It might be reasonable to suppose that all labor would stand together, and that the rights of immigrant workers would be no less sacred to the labor leaders than the rights of native Americans. But for a long time this was not so. The trouble was that the coming of so many immigrants built up the labor supply to such an extent that employers could, and did, keep wages down. Strikes proved unavailing when the jobs of the strikers could readily be filled by immigrants; sometimes, indeed, immigrants were brought into the country with this very end in view. Unable to speak or read the English language, the strike-breakers were

The Longshoreman's Noon.
Immigrants usually found it impossible to leave the cities, and considered themselves lucky if they could find jobs on the waterfront.

immune from labor propaganda, while wages that seemed low to the native workers seemed high enough to them.

This was particularly true of two non-European groups of immigrants, the French Canadians and the Chinese. During the last three decades of the nineteenth century the French Canadians came in prodigious numbers to the mill towns of New England, sometimes with the deliberate encouragement of the mill owners, who used them to break strikes and beat down wages. By 1900 there were 134,000 of them in Massachusetts alone, one-sixth the population of the state, and the proportions in the other New England states were not far behind. The Chinese had entered California during gold-rush days. At first their labor was welcomed, particularly in the building of the western railroads. But by the depression years of the seventies, with thousands of whites out of work, the attitude toward them became hostile. Even in the East there was occasion to fear the results of cheap Chinese labor. Once in Massachusetts and once in Pennsylvania during the seventies, Chinese "coolies" were imported from the West and used as strike-breakers. Labor unions, earnestly seeking to obtain higher wages and better working conditions, saw in the horde of immigrants their greatest menace. If the nation's manufacturers could

be protected from foreign competition by a tariff, why not the same sort of protection for the American workingman?

Demands for Restriction

The propaganda in favor of restricting immigration grew with the immigrant tide, and by the end of the nineteenth century it had reached formidable proportions. The strangeness of the immigrants, their foreign accents, their religious idiosyncrasies, their attitudes toward government, their competition in the labor market, all were held against them. Immigrants who had arrived earlier even deplored the coming of those who arrived later. Finley Peter Dunne's Mr. Dooley made this point crystal clear: "As a pilgrim father that missed th' first boats, I must raise me Claryon voice again' the' invasion iv this fair land be th' paupers an' arnychists iv effete Europe. Ye bet I must — because I'm here first." An initial, but not very important, step in the direction of restriction was taken in 1868, with the repeal of the law passed four years before to legalize the importation of labor under contract. But the first really significant triumph of the restrictionists came primarily in response to the insistent demand of the Pacific Coast for Chinese exclusion. In 1879 Congress sought to pass a law that would prohibit any ship from bringing to the United States on a single voyage more than fifteen Chinese passengers. This measure was obviously meant to stop the stream of Chinese migration across the Pacific, and was generally regarded as desirable. But unfortunately the United States had signed a treaty with China in 1868, the Burlingame Treaty, that gave the two powers mutual rights of immigration and emigration. Ultimately, the Chinese government agreed to give the United States the right to "regulate, limit or suspend but not absolutely prohibit" the immigration of Chinese laborers, and in 1882 a Chinese Exclusion Act, which carried this principle to the last possible limit, went into effect.

Legislation on Immigration

The demand for federal supervision of immigration, if not for outright restriction, had by this time grown to such proportions that a general immigration law could be passed. An act of August 3, 1882, placed a tax of fifty cents per head[1] on immigrants brought into the United States by water transporation, the tax to be paid by the carrier, and to be used to defray the expenses of the immigration service. Idiots, lunatics, persons who were likely to become public charges, and convicts, except those who were guilty only of political crimes, were specifically excluded. Steamship companies found guilty of bringing such immigrants to the United States were required to take them back again free of charge. More important still was a law of 1885 which specifically prohibited the importation of immigrants under contract. The law of 1864, which had authorized and even facilitated this practice, had been repealed in 1868, but it was well known that the practice had continued. The new law was specific enough, although the machinery for its enforcement was defective. An

act of 1891, however, created at last the office of "superintendent of immigration," and made possible the establishment of a federal Bureau of Immigration through which the restrictive laws could be enforced. The new law added to the proscribed lists prostitutes, polygamists, and persons suffering from certain types of diseases; it also prohibited under penalty of fine those found guilty of recruiting foreign laborers by advertising or solicitation.

The Literacy Test

For the most part the restrictions that were provided for in these acts were reasonable, and ran equally against all nationals. Demands that legislation be devised to discriminate against immigrants coming from southern and eastern Europe were sufficiently insistent, however, that during the 1890's Henry Cabot Lodge, first as a member of the national House of Representatives and later as a United States Senator, took the lead in advocating a literacy test to be given to all prospective immigrants. According to a bill he introduced in 1896, only those who could read and write either their own or some other language might be admitted. The test, he stated frankly, would "bear most heavily upon the Italians, Russians, Poles, Hungarians, Greeks, and Asiatics, and very lightly, or not at all, upon English-speaking immigrants or Germans, Scandinavians and French." In his opinion, "the mental and moral qualities which make what we call our race" could be preserved only by excluding "the wholesale infusion of races whose traditions and inheritances, whose thoughts and beliefs are wholly alien to ours and with whom we have never assimilated or even been associated in the past." Lodge's measure won a majority in both houses of Congress, but was vetoed by President Cleveland two days before he left office. Cleveland argued cogently that the test proposed was not a test of ability, but only a test of opportunity; it might keep

[1] This tax was raised to $1 in 1894, to $2 in 1903, to $4 in 1907, and to $8 in 1917.

out many who were desirable, and admit many who were not. Similar measures were vetoed later by Presidents Taft and Wilson, but in 1917, during the excitement attendant upon the First World War, the literacy test became law in spite of a second veto by Wilson. Then, shortly after the war ended, Congress adopted a policy of virtual exclusion.

The Process of Assimilation

Wanted or unwanted, most of the immigrants who came to America stayed on to adjust themselves as best they could to the new environment. Some did return, a few whose nostalgia for their homelands drew them back, others who came to America to earn a stake, and had planned all along to return. But of the 14 million immigrants who entered American ports between 1860 and 1900 an overwhelmingly large proportion never again set eyes on their native lands. Some of them did very well, in spite of the pitfalls of the new environment. Country-dwellers did best, for they were used to working with the soil; many of them eventually owned fine farms. City immigrants sometimes emerged as successful shopkeepers and small merchants, as bosses of construction gangs, as policemen and politicians, as labor leaders. Some moved to the outskirts of the city in which they dwelt, and as truck gardeners eked out a precarious existence on what vacant tracts they could find. Most of them worked hard at becoming Americans.

The older immigrants could not always master the language of their adopted land, but the younger ones learned it, and the children who were born of immigrant parents in America usually spoke it with only the accent of their locale, not with the accent of their nationality. Most of the children attended the American schools, and they learned much from them, although in the cities they found little that rang true in the McGuffey-type readers and the other texts they studied. The authors of these books had known only a rural-minded America, and had paid no heed to city dwellers. But the children of the immigrants at least learned to read and write and figure a little. It was easier for them than for their parents to "get on" in the world. Some of them even went on through high school and college to enter the professions. As for the grandchildren of the immigrants, anything might happen. They might, as so often had been the case with their grandparents, be living at the lowest margin of subsistence, or they might have climbed well toward the top of the social and economic ladder, or they might be anywhere in between. In 1961 a great-grandson of Irish immigrants became President of the United States.

New Roots for Old

One of the greatest problems of the immigrants and their descendants was to strike down new cultural roots to replace those so rudely pulled up by removal to America. The original immigrants held on to their Old World language because they could not help themselves, and taught it to their children. Naturally they tried to do the same with such Old World customs as they could transplant. But they found their children increasingly unwilling to do anything that might set them apart from other Americans; and their grandchildren even rebelled at learning the Old World language. In their haste to become Americans too many descendants of immigrants thus put aside their Old World culture before they were able really to replace it with a New World equivalent. This left them dangerously adrift from their moorings. As Carl Wittke so aptly has said: "The man with two cultural homes is much less to be feared than the man who has none at all." Fortunately, as time went on, each immigrant group tended to recover its interest in its natural origins, and to value its contribution as a nationality to American society. Filiopietistic historians often went too far in their claims, but their activities registered an important step in advance. The Old World connection was not something to be ashamed of; rather, it was something in which one could legitimately take great pride.

It would be hard to overestimate the debt that the American nation owes to the millions of immigrants who came latest to its shores. They have left many permanent marks — on how Americans live and think, on their interest in music and the arts, on their agricultural, business, and manufacturing habits, on American literature, law, and politics. It is safe to say that without the richness and diversity of their contributions, not to mention their hard work, the United States could never have achieved the eminent position that it now holds in the world.

BIBLIOGRAPHY

A brief book by a British scholar, Henry Pelling, *American Labor* (1960), provides a good introduction. So does the provocative work by Thomas Brooks, *Toil and Trouble* (1964). J. R. Commons and others, *History of Labour in the United States* (4 vols., 1918–1935), remains indispensable. Useful one-volume texts include: J. G. Rayback, *A History of American Labor* (1959); F. R. Dulles, *Labor in America* (3rd ed., 1966); and Philip Taft, *Organized Labor in American History* (1964). N. J. Ware, *The Labor Movement in the United States, 1860–1895* (1929), remains the best work on the Knights of Labor, but it can now be supplemented by G. N. Grob, *Workers and Utopia: A Study of Ideological Conflict in the American Labor Movement, 1865–1900* (1961). On Gompers and the American Federation of Labor, see: L. L. Lorwin, *The American Federation of Labor* (1933); Philip Taft, *The A. F. of L. in the Time of Gompers* (1957); and Bernard Mandel, *Samuel Gompers* (1963). Important monographs on trade unionism include: Leo Wolman, *The Growth of American Trade Unions, 1880–1923* (1924); I. B. Cross, *History of the Labor Movement in California* (1935); David Brody, *Steelworkers in America: The Nonunion Era* (1960); C. K. Yearley, *Britons in American Labor, 1820–1914* (1957); and G. S. Mitchell, *Textile Unionism and the South* (1931).

On labor subjects, *The Encyclopedia of the Social Sciences*, edited by E. R. A. Seligman and Alvin Johnson (15 vols., 1930–1935), is quite valuable. Important monographs include: P. H. Douglas, *Real Wages in the United States, 1890–1926* (1930); C. H. Wesley, *Negro Labor in the United States, 1850–1925* (1927); and J. A. Hill, *Women in Gainful Occupations, 1870–1920* (1929). See also *The Negro and the American Labor Movement* (1968), edited by Julius Jacobson.

Labor disputes are the subject of a vast literature. Two general works, both strongly pro-labor, are: Samuel Yellen, *American Labor Struggles* (1936); and Louis Adamic, *Dynamite* (2nd ed., 1934). Significant studies of strife in this period include: W. G. Broehl, Jr., *The Molly Maguires* (1964); R. V. Bruce, *1877: Year of Violence* (1959), which treats of the railway uprising; Henry David, *The History of the Haymarket Affair* (1936), a superb work; D. L. McMurry, *The Great Burlington Strike of 1888* (1956); Leon Wolff, *Lockout: The Story of the Homestead Steel Strike* (1965); and D. L. McMurry, *Coxey's Army* (1929). The Pullman affair is carefully treated in Almont Lindsey, *The Pullman Strike* (1942); see also C. E. Warne (ed.), *The Pullman Boycott of 1894* (1955), for conflicting views on federal intervention. A community study is Stanley Buder, *Pullman, 1880–1930* (1967). Important works on the leading figures in the Pullman strike include: Ray Ginger, *The Bending Cross* (1949), a life of Debs; the same author's *Altgeld's America* (1958), which is broader than the title would indicate; and Harry Barnard, *Eagle Forgotten* (1938), the standard life of Altgeld. On the legal aspects of "government by injunction," consult: Edward Berman, *Labor Disputes and the President of the United States* (1924); Felix Frankfurter and Nathan Greene, *The Labor Injunction* (1930); E. E. Witte, *The Government in Labor Disputes* (1932); and the brilliant interpretative study by A. M. Paul, *Conservative Crisis and the Rule of Law: Attitudes of Bar and Bench, 1887–1895* (1960), which is suggestive on other constitutional topics as well.

The saga of the immigrant in America has continued to attract much scholarly interest. Two short works are of particular value: Oscar Handlin, *The Uprooted* (1951), a lyrical account from the immigrant's point of view; and M. A. Jones, *American Immigration* (1960), a competent overall view. The most inclusive book is Carl Wittke, *We Who Built America* (1939), which follows through separately the experiences and contribution of each nationality. Other significant works of a general nature include: G. M. Stephenson, *A History of American Immigration, 1820–1924* (1926); M. L. Hansen, *The Immigrants in American History* (1940); W. C. Smith, *Americans in the Making* (1939); and M. R. Davie, *World Immigration with Special Reference to the United States* (1936), which contains an excellent bibliography. The autobiography of one famous immigrant is *The Americanization of Edward Bok* (1920). D. B. Cole, *Immigrant City: Lawrence, Massachusetts, 1845–1921* (1963), is an exciting monograph.

Interesting collections of writings on immigration policies, stressing divergent viewpoints, are B. M. Ziegler (ed.), *Immigration: An American Dilemma* (1953); and Oscar Handlin (ed.), *Immigration as a Factor in American History* (1959). See also: W. S. Bernard, *American Immigration Policy* (1950); M. T. Bennett, *American Immigration Policies* (1963); Charlotte Erickson, *American Industry and the European Immigrant, 1860–1885* (1957), a study of contract labor; G. W.

Allport, *The Nature of Prejudice* (1954), a basic work; John Higham, *Strangers in the Land* (1955), a probing study of nativism; D. L. Kinzer, *An Episode in Anti-Catholicism* (1964), a study of the American Protective Association; and B. M. Solomon, *Ancestors and Immigrants* (1956), an examination of New Englanders' efforts to secure immigration restriction.

Historians have studied almost all national groups, producing a large literature. On immigration from the British Isles, see: R. T. Berthoff, *British Immigrants in Industrial America, 1790–1950* (1953); W. S. Shepperson, *British Emigration to North America* (1957); Carl Wittke, *The Irish in America* (1956); and Thomas Brown, *Irish-American Nationalism* (1965). On Scandinavian immigration, see: T. C. Blegen, *Norwegian Migration to America* (2 vols., 1931–1940); C. C. Qualey, *Norwegian Settlement in the United States* (1938); and G. M. Stephenson, *The Religious Aspects of Swedish Immigration* (1932). On the Jewish migration, see especially Moses Rischin, *The Promised City: New York's Jews, 1870–1914* (1962). Treatments of other groups of European immigrants include: A. W. Hoglund, *Finnish Immigrants in America, 1880–1920* (1960); Thomas Capek, *The Czechs in America* (1920); D. A. Souders, *The Magyars in America* (1922); R. F. Foerster, *The Italian Emigration of Our Times* (1919); and Theodore Saloutos, *The Greeks in the United States* (1964).

Oriental immigration is beginning to receive the scholarly attention it deserves. F. H. Conroy, *The Japanese Frontier in Hawaii, 1868–1898* (1953), is a basic study. On the Chinese, see Ping Chiu, *Chinese Labor in California, 1850–1880* (1963); Gunther Barth, *Bitter Strength* (1964); and the more general study by R. H. Lee, *The Chinese in the United States* (1960).

An important work on a unique theme is M. L. Hansen and J. B. Brebner, *The Mingling of the Canadian and American Peoples* (1940).

7

THE REVOLT OF THE FARMER

The agricultural revolution · The New West · Collapse of the western boom · The agricultural South · Tenancy · The crop-lien system · The one-crop system · The one-party system · Farmer movements · The Grangers · The Greenbackers · The Free-Silverites · The Farmers' Alliances · The People's Party · Election of 1892

The Agricultural Revolution

The economic revolution that swept through the United States during and after the Civil War involved agriculture quite as deeply as industry. New machines, mostly powered by horses, cut down the amount of hand labor on the farm to a degree comparable with the changes that steam-powered machines had wrought in the factories; by the end of the century, for example, total expenditures for mechanical harvesters exceeded expenditures for every other type of machine except steam engines. Changes in transportation also contributed to the agricultural revolution. With railroads connecting every part of the nation to every other part, and steamship companies opening the way for foreign trade all over the world, the American farmer found it possible to market more and more of his produce at a distance; but he found,

too, that foreign producers were increasingly troublesome competitors. Industrialism in Europe had enlarged the market there for agricultural commodities, but European importers might buy from Canada, or Australia, or the Argentine, or even from Egypt and India, as well as from the United States. Since American farmers produced far more of such items as wheat and cotton than could be consumed at home, prices on the world market determined both the domestic and the foreign price.

Despite this situation, the acreage devoted to agriculture in the United States expanded relentlessly. Between 1860 and 1900 both the total number of farms and the acreage tilled more than doubled. Although some of this expansion lay to the South, the major portion of it was in the North and the West, most especially in the West. Over 3.5 mil-

THRESHING WHEAT *in the Red River Valley of the Dakota Territory (1878).*

THE LEAKY CONNECTION. A Zimmerman cartoon in *Judge*, May 15, 1886, which purported to show "why the poor farmer is so little benefitted by the high price we pay for our living."

THE AGRICULTURAL REVOLUTION. *The transformation of agriculture in the last half of the nineteenth century paralleled the changes in industry during these same years, but made few farmers rich. New machines increased crop yields, new fencing methods helped the stock-growers, but businessmen everywhere "farmed the farmers."*

AGRICULTURAL TRACTOR. This great traction engine and harvester was used in the wheat fields of California in 1898.

BARBED-WIRE FENCING. The invention of barbed wire solved the problem of fencing, but added another heavy expense for farmers and ranchers to bear.

make, but certainly by 1880 total outputs were equal to those achieved before the war, and thereafter the figures rose steadily. In the farther West, with irrigation increasingly effective, the importance of mining diminished relatively, and the importance of agriculture increased. Eastern agriculture, faced with the competition of virgin land, sometimes turned to dairy and truck farming.

No doubt the most basic change that the agricultural revolution brought to the people who lived on the farms was the shift from production for use to production for sale, from subsistence farming to commercial farming. Production for sale meant that the farmer now had to purchase many of the items he had formerly obtained by his own efforts on his own farm. He no longer exchanged his wheat for flour at the local mill, but instead he sold his wheat for cash and bought flour and other groceries at the local store. Farm women no longer devoted themselves to spinning and weaving and the fashioning of garments from home-made cloth; instead, they bought fabrics from the stores, and even ready-made clothing. New and more expensive items also began to appear on the farmer's budget. As farming moved out of the wooded country upon the plains, wire fencing, pumps, windmills, and sometimes even fuel had to be purchased. Furthermore, the farmer must now buy specialized implements if he wished to produce in the quantities necessary for successful commercial farming. According to one estimate, the average northern farmer of the pre-1900 period had to invest about $785 in machinery in order to engage in mixed agriculture. For the times this was a large sum, more than a year's income. The cost of his land and tools, and the manner in which he bought and sold, had thus made the farmer over into a capitalist and a businessman. He could no longer take his living directly from the farm as in earlier

lion new farms were established in the period, including some 600,000 homesteads. By increasing the amount of land under cultivation, by making use of improved machinery, and by accepting better agricultural methods, the average northern or western farmer was producing about four times the amount of wheat and corn he had produced before the Civil War. In the South comparisons between pre- and post-Civil War conditions are more difficult to days; he now had to sell a sizable volume of produce in order to live, and he became increasingly dependent upon a far-away market. In the words of William Jennings Bryan, the farmer was "as much a businessman as the man who goes upon the Board of Trade and bets upon the price of grain." But as a businessman the farmer had one chronic complaint. He himself set no prices. Instead, those to whom he sold set the prices on what he had to sell, while those from whom he bought set the prices on what he had to buy. And always the selling price was too low and the buying price was too high.

The New West

Economic conditions in the farming West differed greatly, depending on the fertility of the soil, the availability of markets, and the yearly pattern of rainfall. One great area of periodic distress was the "Middle Border," a region that stretched from the bend of the Missouri to the Rockies, and had been settled almost entirely after the Civil War. This latest "New West" resulted from two surges of population expansion divided chronologically, more or less, by the depression years of the 1870's. The first surge had filled in the sparsely populated areas in Missouri, Iowa, and Minnesota, and had extended across the Missouri River about as far as the ninety-eighth meridian, which in a general way marks the end of the region where rainfall is adequate for normal farming, and the beginning of an area in which rainfall varies from problematic to totally inadequate. The second surge, aided by a series of wet years, extended far beyond the ninety-eighth meridian into central and western Dakota, Nebraska, and Kansas, and even into parts of Colorado and Montana; also to some extent into the Indian Territory, which by 1889 was legally opened to white settlers.

The New West was the product of the railroads, many of which had received a rich federal land grant, and had used their lands to entice the settlers in. Railroad lands could be purchased on easy terms at low prices, and railroad advertisers left nothing undone to make known the opportunities that existed in the region they wished to develop. Under their facile pens the "legend" of the "Great American Desert" disappeared. Those who could not afford to buy land from the railroads were urged to use their pre-emption rights, to take homesteads, and as the federal land laws were relaxed, to obtain other hundreds of acres for little or nothing by promising to grow timber, or in regions of light rainfall to try irrigation. Veterans of the Civil War, substantial farmers from the upper Mississippi Valley, a few discontented laborers from the cities, and a horde of European immigrants vied with one another to obtain the riches that the railroads promised. Indeed, the vast influx of Scandinavians and other northern Europeans gave a lasting cultural stamp to great portions of the prairie and plains regions. To recount what had happened in figures, the combined population of Kansas, Nebraska, and Dakota Territory in 1870 had been 501,573; ten years later it was 1,583,675; in 1890, it was 3,030,347. And what these states and territories experienced occurred in greater or lesser degree throughout the region.

Thanks to easy credit, the New West in a single generation achieved all the trappings of civilization. The East believed in the West, was convinced that it would grow, and furnished the capital necessary to build it. Farm mortgages at high interest rates bought farmers the tools, livestock, houses, and barns they needed, to say nothing of the extra acres they were often tempted to buy. Counties, by voting bonds, obtained courthouses and jails, roads and bridges, and even more railroads, privately owned to be sure, but paid for in no small part by loans and subsidies of

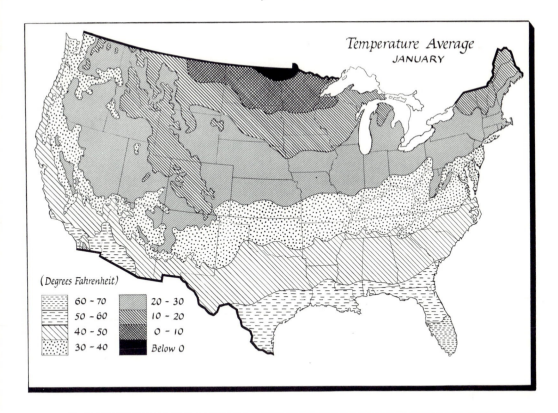

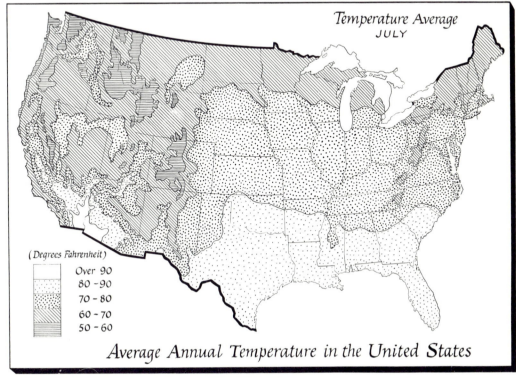

Average Annual Temperature in the United States

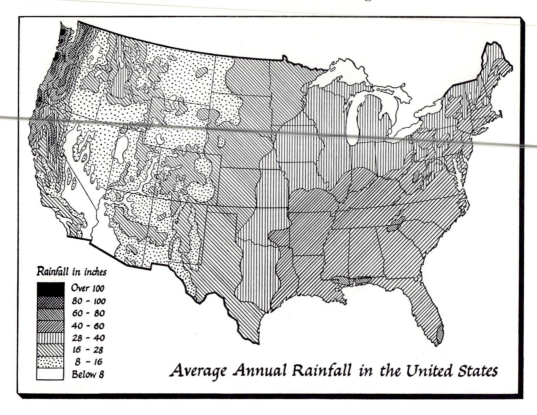

Rainfall in inches

Over 100
80 - 100
60 - 80
40 - 60
28 - 40
16 - 28
8 - 16
Below 8

Average Annual Rainfall in the United States

public money. Cities grew up that reproduced as nearly as possible the conditions that their inhabitants had known in the East. And each sizable center — Omaha, Yankton, Atchison, Topeka, Kansas City — became the scene of a gigantic real-estate boom, and eventually of an equally gigantic "bust."

Collapse of the Western Boom

The collapse of the western boom began with the summer of 1887, the first of a long series of dry seasons. Settlers who had gone hopefully into western Kansas, Nebraska, and Dakota, or beyond, learned to their sorrow that they had gone too far into the area of inadequate rainfall. When the inevitable drought came, eastern financing companies changed their minds about the future of the West, and the once steady flow of easy money came to a halt. Some-

times the same covered wagons that had taken the settlers hopefully west now turned eastward in defeat and despair.

> Fifty miles to water,
> A hundred miles to wood,
> To hell with this damned country,
> I'm going home for good.

The wagons turned back east because, in the settlers' view, there was no longer another West to which to go; the wholesale assault of railroads and individuals upon the lands of the West had all but used them up. The government had handed out its lands as if the supply were inexhaustible, only to discover when it was too late that they were nearly gone. Of mountains and deserts and arid plains there was an abundance, but of land suitable for the traditional types of agriculture perhaps less than 2 million acres remained. Commenting on the government's policy of improvidence, an indignant Nebraska editor complained:

Only a little while ago the people owned this princely domain. Now they are *starving for land* — starving for the right to create from the soil a subsistence for their wives and little children. . . . They would gladly buy land if they could. But the merciless contraction of money and fearful shrinkage of values and prices have put it out of their power to buy land, even though it may be offered at reduced prices. They want *free land* — the land that Congress squandered . . . the land that should have formed the patrimony of unborn generations.

Public alarm over this situation was manifest in deeds as well as in words. When, for example, a 3 million acre tract of former Indian land in what soon became Oklahoma was opened to homestead entry on April 22, 1889, the rush that ensued displayed all the violence of an explosion.

Whole outfits for towns, including portable houses, were shipped by rail, and individual families, in picturesque, primitive, white-covered wagons, journeyed forward, stretching out for miles in an unbroken line. . . . The blast of a bugle at noon on a beautiful spring day was the signal for a wild rush across the borders. Men on horseback and on foot, in every conceivable vehicle, sought homes with the utmost speed, and before nightfall town sites were laid out for several thousand inhabitants each.

Fifty thousand people entered the region the first day, and the city of Guthrie achieved at one fell swoop a population of six thousand. This led to the local saying that "Rome was not built in a day, but Guthrie was." Most of the people who took new land in the West had no desire to retreat to the East. What they wanted was merely a chance to live through the hard years on the land they had taken, without danger of foreclosure by banks, or extor-

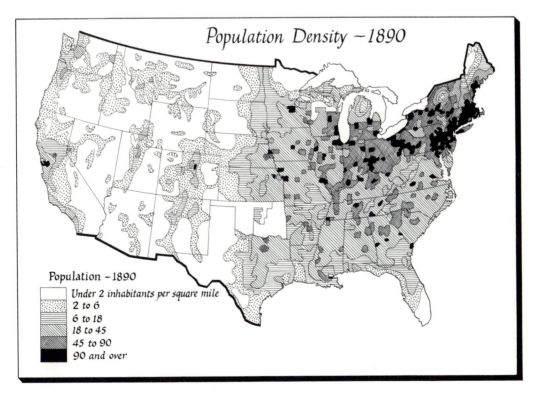

Population Density – 1890

Population – 1890

Under 2 inhabitants per square mile
2 to 6
6 to 18
18 to 45
45 to 90
90 and over

tion by middlemen and railroads. Denied the opportunity of flight to another frontier, and convinced that the ills from which they suffered were not of their own making, they were ripe for revolt.

The "End of Free Land"

Actually there was more myth than reality to the idea that earlier Americans had always had available a plentiful supply of "free land." Throughout most of American history pioneers had had to pay something for the land they had acquired, and for the great majority that situation still continued. The Homestead Act, which provided for outright gifts of land to settlers, dated back only to 1862, and the first homestead claimed lay somewhere in Nebraska. Far more people, even after this date, bought their land from railroads or from speculators or even from the government (which still continued its sales policy) than proved up on homesteads. Furthermore, the granting of homesteads did not cease with the advance of population into the arid West; no doubt overoptimistic homesteaders filed on many more acres (such as they were) during the twentieth than during the nineteenth century. But the people of the 1880's were right in thinking that for the future there would no longer be a plentiful supply of good cheap land — whether to be acquired from the government, or from the railroads, or from speculators — land that was well watered by rain, not by expensive irrigation projects, and that ordinary farmers would know how to farm. Due to its scarcity, such agricultural land would undoubtedly rise in value, and the higher prices would limit more and more drastically the possibilities of land ownership. It was this situation which inspired Henry George, the Californian, to argue that "All who do not possess land are toiling for those who do, and this is the reason why progress and poverty go hand in hand." So in his book *Progress and Poverty* (1879), he proposed to put an end to "unearned increment" by a "single tax"

Opening of Cherokee Strip, 1893. *This photograph catches the drama of the race for desirable homesteads in an Indian area just opened to white settlers.*

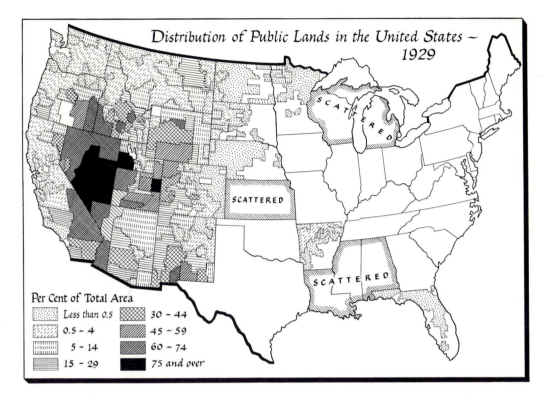

Distribution of Public Lands in the United States ~ 1929

Per Cent of Total Area

Less than 0.5	30 ~ 44
0.5 ~ 4	45 ~ 59
5 ~ 14	60 ~ 74
15 ~ 29	75 and over

on land.[1] Most of the people of the New West were unaware of George's theories, and if they had known them would not have liked them very much. But what they could see and understand was that the kind of land they valued would not much longer be available for the man of little means. This is what they had in mind when they talked about the "end of free land."

The Agricultural South

Meantime the South, despite the transformation wrought in some areas by industrialism, was still dominantly agricultural, and suffered from ills that, if different from those of the West, were equally perplexing. The New South, like the Old, had few large cities, and its annual output of manufactured goods actually accounted for only about one-eighth of the nation's total output. In every southern state far more

people were engaged in agriculture than in any other occupation, while most of its business and professional classes were dependent for their livelihood upon farm income. Southern cotton was still grown after much the same fashion, by nearly the same types of laborers, in approximately the same regions as before the war. The yield had steadily increased. By 1894 the production of cotton in the South exceeded 10 million bales, nearly twice that of the prewar years. Much the same could be said of tobacco, sugar cane, cereals, and livestock, but if the total produce of the South had increased, so also had its population. For the great majority of the southern people, the industrial excitement of the age seemed remote and of no consequence.

Tenancy

Seventy per cent of the farmers of the South, a generation after Appomattox, were tenants. The Negroes, starting as ex-slaves

[1] See p. 252.

with nothing but their labor to sell, could hardly have been expected to do better; but they had made almost as much progress toward individual ownership as the poorest southern whites. For both races the tenant system, once it was well established, tended to become self-perpetuating. In general there were three types of tenants in the South: (1) the cash tenant, who paid rent in money or a specified number of bales of cotton, and was otherwise no different from a landowner; (2) the share tenant, who in lieu of rent paid for the use of his land from one-fourth to one-third of his crop, but furnished his own stock, tools, and foodstuffs; and (3) the sharecropper, who paid a larger proportion of his crop to his landlord, but furnished nothing whatever for himself. Some of the cash and share tenants, who were usually white, were fairly thrifty; the "croppers," on the other hand, among whom most of the country Negroes were numbered, were barely one degree removed from slavery.

The Crop-Lien System

One of the many woeful results of the Civil War was the development of the crop-lien system, which came about largely because so many small farmers had no cash to see them through the season until their crops were mature. Banking facilities in the South had always lagged far behind those of the North. Credit therefore was scarce, and after the war was practically nonexistent in many regions. In Georgia, for example, one hundred counties were without any banking institutions. Faced with these circumstances, the small farmer often bought his food and other supplies on credit from a country store. Gradually the storekeeper, to insure himself against loss, began to take a lien on the crops, and, if possible, also a chattel mortgage. If the farmer chanced to be a tenant, which he often was, the merchant's lien was taken only on the tenant's share of the crop. Immediately

after the war the landlord and the storekeeper were usually two different people. But as time went on they tended to become one and the same. Legal protection for the merchant was soon added by friendly legislatures. If the farmer's purchases exceeded the value of his crop, he was legally bound to trade the following year with the same merchant. Once in debt to a merchant, if he attempted to market even a part of his produce elsewhere, his entire crop might be confiscated for a sheriff's sale. Thus entrapped he became a virtual peon. Without ready cash he had to trade with the same merchant, year in year out. Both the quantity and the kind of goods he bought were subject to some control by the storekeeper. He had to pay whatever price was asked, usually about double that asked from cash customers. He had little or no protection against the merchant who chose to cheat him, a process often aided by his own inability to read or "figure."

Many other harmful results flowed from the crop-lien system. Hopelessly sunk in debt, the farmer often became more and more shiftless, raising only enough to pay his yearly bill at the store. Yet for all his high prices, the merchant himself was not in a very good position financially. Usually in debt, he depended on the yearly deliveries of cotton to meet his own obligations. Sometimes his debtor croppers ran away before the crop was made, sometimes they were lodged in jail. A season of crop failures or exceptionally low prices might seriously endanger the merchant's equity. Existing records indicate that while some merchants prospered, many had only a long list of unpaid bills to show for their efforts, and sometimes bankruptcy.

The One-Crop System

But for the section as a whole, perhaps the greatest evil of the crop-lien system was its encouragement of one-crop agriculture. Almost everywhere throughout the cotton-

CLIPPER

IRRIGATION

SHOWERING THE TREES

SIZING THE ORANGES

Orange Culture. *Florida's semi-tropical climate offered southern agriculturalists this new opportunity, but involved capital outlays too great for the ordinary farmer. The growing of citrus fruit also gained a foothold in California. Illustrations from* Frank Leslie's Illustrated Newspaper, *April 21, 1888.*

growing area the storekeepers tended to insist that the rural debtors raise cotton to the exclusion of all other crops. Being a staple, cotton could be stored without deterioration. It could usually be sold at some price, and it was hard for the farmer in debt to hide it, or to use it for his family as he could use corn and other table crops. Since the merchant had substantial control over what his debtors raised, the growing of corn and other grains tended to diminish, particularly in the Old South. Even the growing of vegetables and of small animals was neglected; by 1900 the great majority of farms in the seaboard South were without chickens or other fowls. As a result the southern cotton farmer came to depend for his foodstuffs upon the storekeeper, to the serious detriment of his diet. Reliance upon the "three M's" (meat, meal, and molasses) had much to do with the widespread prevalence of hookworm, malaria, pellagra, and other diseases. The yearly planting of cotton without crop rotation took its toll from southern soils, while dependence upon

one crop alone meant disaster when the price of cotton plummeted too far downward. A witness before a Senate committee in 1893 testified that over 90 per cent of the cotton growers in some areas of the South were insolvent. This was a part of the price the South had to pay for its undiversified agriculture.

The One-Party System

The one-party system which the reconstruction period had left as a legacy to the South made it extremely difficult for the farmers of that section, whether Negro or white, to seek through political action the amelioration of their ills. The Negroes were virtually powerless, and, because of the peculiar distribution of the white population, the strength of the lower-class rural whites in politics was far less than their numbers would have justified. The best cotton lands lay along the river valleys and close to the sea, precisely the same lands that had grown the cotton of the prewar plantation South. Here the Negroes were concentrated, no longer as slaves but as tenants of a favored few of the whites. In these "black belts" the landlords and the merchants, supported by the votes of the townspeople, and if they chose by the Negroes they "voted," not only ruled supreme over a population predominantly Negro and non-voting, but exercised also a disproportionate influence in the politics of any given state. Since the assignment of membership in the legislature and of delegates in nominating conventions was usually according to population, the representatives of the "black counties" could generally outvote the representatives of the "white counties." And, since white solidarity demanded unfailing support of whatever Democratic candidates were nominated, the "Redeemers," or "Bourbons," of the "black belt," eager servants of the industrialists, the landlords, and the merchants, maintained their uninterrupted sway. Hardly less than before the Civil War the South remained in the hands of a favored ruling caste. Discontent with such a system, followed by an open revolt against it, was sure to come.

Historic antagonisms that stemmed from the Civil War and reconstruction, strong as they were, could not prevent the development of a bond of sympathy between the impoverished farmers of the New West and of the New South. While industry flourished, agriculture, whether western or southern, tended to languish. The downward trend of cotton prices was matched only by the downward trend of prices paid for wheat, corn, and livestock. Railroads made money, banks made money, factories made money; but the farmers barely made a living, and sometimes not even that. The suspicion grew, in both the South and the West, that some sinister force restrained agriculture, while industry climbed steadily to the mountain tops of prosperity. Before the Civil War the agricultural South and the agricultural West, to their own considerable advantage, had stood together

and ruled the country; now industry, with the forces of agriculture divided and ignored, reigned supreme. Could the old agricultural alliance be revived and the political advantages from which industry had fattened be restrained?

Common Grievances

Few people asked themselves that question directly, but common grievances acted powerfully to draw the farmers of the two sections closer together. The western wheat-grower who was convinced that, unless the price of wheat was as much as a dollar a bushel, he could not make money, talked the same language as the southern cotton-grower, who held that any price less than ten cents a pound for cotton meant disaster. The northern farm-owner who was chronically on the verge of losing his property to the mortgage-holder was only a trifle better off than the southern tenant who each year turned over his entire crop to the storekeeper, only to learn, when the books were balanced, that he was still in debt. The West had by far the greater grievance against the railroads. The railroads had built the West, but they had built it for a price. Debts for lands purchased from them were hard to wipe out, and the high cost of transporting bulky western crops to distant markets ate away an alarming proportion of western farm receipts. But the South, no less than the West, knew how railroad companies watered their stock, granted rebates, evaded taxation, bought favors with free passes, and mixed business with politics. Southern farmers, who sold abroad and would have preferred to buy cheap foreign manufactured goods in return, could see more clearly the disadvantages of the high-tariff system than the farmers of the Northwest, but even the Westerners registered their objections to buying in a tariff-protected market and selling against the competition of the whole wide world. Both sections re-

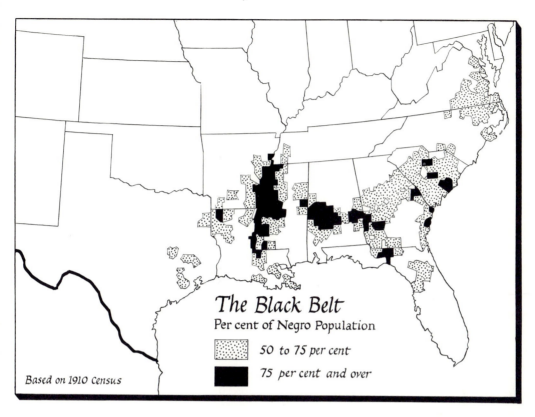

The Black Belt

Per cent of Negro Population

50 to 75 per cent

75 per cent and over

Based on 1910 Census

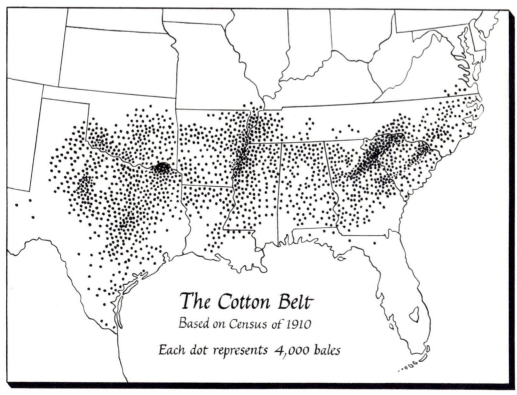

The Cotton Belt

Based on Census of 1910

Each dot represents 4,000 bales

corded heated protests against the tolls paid to trusts and middlemen, the high taxes that for farmlands seemed inescapable, and the steadily appreciating value of the dollar. And, although the West knew it best, both sections were seriously affected by the fact that good cheap lands were rapidly disappearing. The prospect of a new alliance between the dominantly agricultural sections of the country was by no means an idle dream.

Farmer Movements

The farmers' protest went through several phases and involved a series of separate organizations. First in line was the Granger movement, which emerged in the decade following the Civil War, and was primarily directed against railroad extortions. Paralleling but outlasting the Grangers were the Greenbackers and the Free-Silverites, both determined to remedy the farmers' plight by some degree of money inflation. Next came the Farmers' Alliances, one in the Northwest and one in the South, inspired originally with ambitious programs of cooperative buying and selling, but eventually with a determination to seek political as well as economic remedies. Then, as an outgrowth of the Alliances and a final culmination of the agrarian crusade, came the Populist Party, which made a place in its platform for all previously proposed reforms, and added a number of its own.

The Grangers

The anti-railroad activities of the Grangers have already been recounted,[1] but it should not be forgotten that they left other important legacies than the demonstrated right of the states to regulate the railroads. Convinced that they were being robbed by manufacturers and middlemen as well as by the railroads, the Grangers made strenuous efforts to establish cooperative farm-im-

[1] See pp. 115–117.

plement factories, elevators, creameries, and general stores. They experimented with purchasing agencies, and tried cooperative selling. Many of these ventures were unsuccessful, not so much because they were wrong in principle as because of the inexperience and mismanagement of the men who were placed in charge. Their business failures, more than anything else, account for the sudden decline in Granger popularity about 1876, and the relegation of the Patrons of Husbandry once more to the inconspicuous role of a farmers' lodge. But the farmers who had participated in the movement did not soon forget the fright they had given the politicians by their independence, the victory they had won over the railroads, and the good times they had had at lodge meetings and picnics.

The Greenbackers

While articulate farmers rarely failed to protest against the extortions of the railroads, they tended also to listen with respect to soft-money arguments. Inflationary ideas were not often of farmer origin, but they had an almost irresistible appeal for rural voters. The free use of greenbacks during the Civil War had shown what plenty of fiat money could do to raise prices, while the hard money policies that had followed the war had shown equally well what deflation could do to lower them. Philosophical Greenbackers were ready to discard gold and silver as money altogether, and to end all national bank note issues that would circulate as money. Instead, the federal government should issue treasury notes, or greenbacks, which should be legal tender for all debts public and private, and convertible on demand into interest-bearing bonds of the United States. Payments on the national debt should likewise be made as far as possible in greenbacks. In theory the quantity of greenback issues could be so controlled as to keep the purchasing power of the dollar from fluctuating, although in practice the danger of overissues was sure to be great. What the farmers saw in the greenback heresy was a more plentiful money supply, and freedom from the machinations, real or fancied, of the banks and bankers. Greenbackers strongly opposed the resumption of specie payments undertaken by the Hayes administration, and, as already noted, made their influence felt in the elections of 1876, and more especially of 1878.[1] When in many rural communities the Granger meetings faded away, "greenback clubs" often appeared as welcome substitutes.

The Greenbackers did far better in hard times than in good, but they continued to wield substantial influence on into the 1880's. In the election of 1880, they polled over 300,000 votes for James B. Weaver of Iowa, their candidate for the Presidency. In 1884 they nominated the insufferable Benjamin F. Butler of Massachusetts, and their vote fell to 173,000. Four years later they quite generally supported Albert J. Streeter of Illinois, the Union Labor candidate, whose vote was under 147,000. For the next campaign they merged happily with the Populists. But the influence of the Greenbackers was far greater than the votes for Greenback candidates seemed to indicate. They provided arguments and encouragement for the soft-money men in both major parties, and they kept alive a well-merited protest against the steadily appreciating value of the dollar.

The Free-Silverites

The Free-Silverites were not organized as a separate political party, and their activities within the Republican and the Democratic parties have already been discussed.[2] The appeal of free silver to the farmers was the same as the greenback appeal — the

prospect of an expanded currency. If the amount of money in circulation was inadequate to the need, why be particular about the kind of money made available? Why not free silver as well as greenbacks? A sophisticated few no doubt saw that if all the silver currently produced could be coined at the old ratio, and the treasury policy of redeeming all dollars in gold could be stopped, the treasury might ultimately exhaust its supply of gold, and substitute a silver standard for a gold standard, a decidedly inflationary move. Whether the farmers could follow such reasoning or not, they were ready for any kind of money tinkering that would raise farm prices and ease the mortgage burden. So in both political parties the demand for free silver persisted.

The Farmers' Alliances

Meantime the farmers of both South and West had begun again to organize. To some extent they were influenced by the occasional successes of the labor unions; if the workingmen could unite in defense of their rights, why not also the farmer? Eventually, out of the many small orders that were founded, two emerged as dominant, the National Farmers' Alliance of the Northwest, and the Farmers' Alliance and Industrial Union of the South, commonly known, respectively, as the "Northern" (or "Northwestern") Alliance, and the "Southern" Alliance.

The Northern Alliance was founded in 1880 by Milton George, editor of the *Western Rural*, a Chicago farm paper. George's paper made a specialty of denouncing the railroads, especially for the political favors they purchased by means of free passes, and the "Farmers' Transportation Convention" that George called together to launch the Alliance branded the order from its beginning as an anti-railroad affair. Local alliances were multiplied throughout the Northwest, and, as soon as

[1] See pp. 44, 56–57.
[2] See pp. 58–59.

a state could count enough locals to warrant the step, a state alliance was formed. Each state alliance, as it gathered strength, tended to become autonomous, so that in the end the Northern Alliance turned out to be a loose confederation of state orders bound together by only the faintest of ties. The growth of the order was tremendously accelerated by the collapse of the western boom in 1887 and the hard times that followed. By 1890 it was fully organized in ten northwestern states, but the bulk of its strength lay in the wheat-raising sections of Kansas, Nebraska, the Dakotas, and Minnesota, where low prices, high freight rates, oppressive mortgages, and, as a final crushing blow, the drought had driven the long-suffering farmers to despair.

The origins of the Southern Alliance can be traced back to an organization that some frontier farmers in Lampasas County, Texas, formed in the middle seventies to catch horse thieves, round up estrays, purchase supplies cooperatively, and defend their rights against land sharks and cattle kings. Armed with a pretentious secret ritual, the order expanded into a few neighboring counties, but mixed too freely in politics and died out. Revived at the close of the decade in Parker County, it kept clear of politics, and by 1885 it could claim fifty thousand members. Next year a new president, "Doctor" C. W. Macune, furnished the leadership necessary to make the Alliance a really important factor in the life of the South. Macune was a born promoter, not overscrupulous in his methods; as president he dazzled his associates with the vision of transforming the Alliance into a money-saving business venture that every southern cotton-farmer would wish to join. Macune promptly established an Alliance Exchange through which the farmers of Texas were urged to buy and sell cooperatively, and, pointing to the temporary success of the Texas Exchange, he began to spread his gospel of business cooperation throughout the South. With amazing rapidity Macune's organizers captured state after state. Sometimes they found local farm orders in operation and induced them to join forces with the Alliance; sometimes they had little to begin with but the presence of smoldering discontent. But invariably their doctrines won converts, and soon exchanges patterned after the Texas model appeared in nearly every southern state. Unlike the Northern Alliance, the Southern Alliance was a closely knit regional organization in which the state alliances played definitely subordinate roles. For Negro farmers a separate, but affiliated, Colored Alliance was established.

The Alliance in Politics

Circumstances conspired to drive both Alliances, contrary to their expressed intentions, into politics. The Northern Alliance, like the Southern Alliance, made numerous and sometimes successful ventures into cooperative buying and selling, and both orders earnestly stimulated among their members a wide variety of social and educational activities. But in spite of all such efforts farm prosperity failed to put in its appearance. More and more the farmers came to believe that the real trouble with agriculture lay in the unfair discriminations from which it suffered. Because of these evils they were denied the prosperity that their hard labor should have earned. The railroads, the bankers, the manufacturers, and the merchants were somehow robbing the farmer. Only through the power of government could these evil practices be brought to light and corrected, and to influence the government, whether in state or nation, political action was essential.

The Northern Alliance from its beginning had not hesitated to mix its business with politics. Northwestern Alliancemen, on the assumption that what they did as individuals in no way involved the order to which they belonged, made it almost a point of honor to vote for farmers or farmer-minded politicians whenever opportunity offered. Through farmer-controlled legislatures they secured laws to insure the fair grading of grain, to impede the fore-closures of mortgages, and to curb the unfair practices of railroads. Most of this legislation, however, failed of its purpose, whether because of the indifference of administrative officials, the hostility of the courts, or the inability of state laws to deal effectively with nationwide problems. By the year 1890, with the pressure of hard times growing ever more acute, most western Alliancemen were convinced that the only hope of the farmers lay in turning their organization into an out-and-out political party — a party which, at first in the states, and later in the nation, could drive both of the older parties from power. Accordingly, third-party tickets were nominated in every state where the Alliance was strong. As yet the name of the new party varied from state to state, but the Kansans, seeking to dramatize the battle between the people and the "plutocrats," called their organization the People's Party, a name that won increasing acclaim. "Populist" and "Populism" were natural derivatives.

Elections of 1890

In the picturesque campaign that the northwestern Alliancemen waged in 1890, a surprising number of really magnificent orators took up the farmers' cause. Ignatius Donnelly of Minnesota delighted hundreds of audiences with his inimitable wit and his biting sarcasm; James B. Weaver of Iowa hammered home his points with a degree of resourcefulness that suggested comparison with James G. Blaine; "Sockless" Jerry Simpson of Kansas combined the oddities of James Whitcomb Riley with the skill of the trained dialectician; Mrs. Mary Elizabeth Lease, also of Kansas, a hard-bitten pioneer mother who had ex-

The Inflation Balloon. *A cartoon showing how the big boom in business, promoted by monopolistic legislation, failed to help farmers and workers.*

perienced most of the tragedies of frontier life, discovered in herself a rare gift of words that thrilled her hearers to their fingertips. "What you farmers need to do," she is said to have told a Kansas audience, "is to raise less corn and more *Hell*."

But the professional politicians and the oratorical headliners were not the only spokesmen of Populism:

It was a religious revival, a crusade, a pentecost of politics in which a tongue of flame sat upon every man, and each spake as the spirit gave him utterance. . . . The farmers, the country merchants, the cattle-herders, they of the long chin-whiskers, and they of the broad-brimmed hats and heavy boots, had also heard

Jerry Simpson. *The great Populist agitator, "Sockless Jerry," is shown here in a debate with Chester I. Long, at Harper, Kansas, in 1892. Simpson is speaking.*

the word and could preach the gospel of Populism. . . . Women with skins tanned to parchment by the hot winds, with bony hands of toil and clad in faded calico, could talk in meeting, and could talk right straight to the point.[1]

They not only talked, they picnicked, they marched, they sang for their cause. One of their favorite songs, "Good-bye, My Party, Good-bye," which celebrated in forthright verse the break that so many of them had made with a beloved old party, certainly had much to do with the success of Populism in Kansas.

Meantime in the South events had taken a somewhat different course. Macune's effort to solve the problems of the cotton farmer by a policy of business cooperation received a fatal blow with the collapse of the Texas Exchange some eighteen months after it was founded. Discouraged with economic methods, Macune now turned to politics. Laws would have to be passed to improve the status of the southern farmer, the stranglehold of the "Bourbon aristocrats" on state government would have to be broken, a debt-paying system of finance would have to be evolved. Other southerners, too, had similar ideas, among

them Colonel L. L. Polk, editor of a North Carolina farm journal, Benjamin R. Tillman, a hard-hitting back-country South Carolinian, and Thomas E. Watson, a picturesque lawyer-politician of Georgia whose hatred for the governing aristocracy knew no bounds. Under the leadership of such men as these the Southern Alliance, well before the election of 1890, had been transformed into a frankly political order, the chief business of which was to capture the machinery of the Democratic Party, in every southern state. Success in this undertaking, as the leaders well knew, would mean Alliance domination of the South, for there the one-party system insured that candidates once nominated were certain of election.

Alliance Successes

The enormous effectiveness of Alliance activities was mirrored in the election results. In at least four northwestern states, Kansas, Nebraska, South Dakota, and Minnesota, third-party candidates won the balance of power, although in no case did they obtain outright control. In the South, Alliance gains were even more spectacular. Alliance candidates for governor were nominated and elected in three states, South Carolina, North Carolina, and Georgia, while in no less than eight states Alliance-

[1] Elizabeth S. Barr, "The Populist Uprising," in *A Standard History of Kansas and Kansans*, vol. II (1918), pp. 1148–9.

controlled legislatures were chosen. Even in Congress, the evidence of agrarian discontent was emphatically recorded. Two third-party senators, William A. Peffer of Kansas and James H. Kyle of South Dakota, were on hand for the opening session of the Fifty-second Congress, while eight third-party representatives from the Northwest voted for Thomas E. Watson of Georgia for Speaker. Watson was the only southern Congressman to admit that he was now a third-party man, but among the southern delegations there sat perhaps thirty or forty Alliance members and many others who were drawn to the Alliance by bonds of sympathy. Indeed, the *Congressional Directory*, a volume which congressmen regularly compile about themselves, showed that during this period a remarkable number of senators and representatives, regardless of party or section, were at pains to confess their intimate connection with the farm and their deep devotion to farmer interests.

To the third-party men of the Northwest the logical next step was the formation of a new nationwide party of the people, but to southerners such a course seemed fraught with the greatest of peril. The Democratic Party of the South was primarily a symbol of white supremacy. Democratic rule meant white rule. If the white voters of the South were divided, Negro voting might become common, and the supremacy of the white race would be jeopardized. Perhaps even the horrors of reconstruction might be repeated. Southern Alliancemen preferred, therefore, to work within the framework of the Democratic Party, although there was one great objection to such a course. The southern wing of the party, however strong it might become, could hardly hope to dominate the party as a whole. Through an Alliance-controlled southern Democracy a certain amount of useful state legislation might be achieved, but reforms that depended upon nation-wide action would still be out of reach. The so-called "sub-Treasury plan," for example, to which the Southern Alliance was committed after 1889, could never be put into effect without a law of Congress. This plan, much ridiculed then, would seem less radical to a generation familiar with government storage programs. It called for national warehouses in which non-perishable farm produce might be stored and upon which the owners might borrow from the United States government as much as 80 per cent of the "local current value" of their deposits in Treasury notes, issued for the purpose by the United States government, and providing incidentally an unpredictable amount of money inflation.

The People's Party

Southern reluctance was insufficient to restrain the third-party ardor of northwest-

That Wicked Little Farmer Boy. *A cartoon from* Judge, *August 30, 1890, showing the distress that the farmer's revolt was causing both old parties.*

ern Alliancemen, and at Cincinnati, in May, 1891, a mass convention composed mostly of westerners, but attended by a few southerners, formally launched the People's Party as a national organization. The following February in St. Louis a delegate convention representing all the farm orders of the nation tried in vain to achieve organic union, but succeeded in adopting a common platform, the preamble of which, written and read by the versatile Donnelly, reflected with remarkable accuracy the spirit of agrarian revolt:

We meet in the midst of a nation brought to the verge of moral, political and material ruin. Corruption dominates the ballot box, the legislatures, the Congress, and touches even the ermine of the bench. The people are demoralized. Many of the States have been compelled to isolate the voters at the polling places in order to prevent universal intimidation or bribery.[1] The newspapers are subsidized or muzzled; public opinion silenced; business prostrated, our homes covered with mortgages, labor impoverished, and the land concentrating in the hands of capitalists. . . . The fruits of the toil of millions are boldly stolen to build up colossal fortunes, unprecedented in the history of the world, while their possessors despise the republic and endanger liberty. From the same prolific womb of governmental injustice we breed two great classes — paupers and millionaires.

As these eloquent words attested, the Populists sought earnestly to interest labor in presenting a united front with the farmers against a common enemy. But in this effort they were doomed to failure. Only the old and weakened Knights of Labor, struggling valiantly to stave off the day of dissolution, signified any interest in cooperation. The American Federation of Labor, to which increasingly the labor world looked for leadership, adhered tenaciously to its policy of keeping the labor movement free from party politics. It was determined neither to become a political party nor to be absorbed in one. The disappointment of the Populists at the resultant failure of their new People's Party to become a genuine party of all the people was acute.

Four months later, at Omaha, Nebraska, the first national nominating convention of the People's Party came together. Amidst scenes of unprecedented enthusiasm the Populists adopted as their own most of the planks of the St. Louis platform, including a slightly revised version of Donnelly's rhetorical preamble. Land, transportation, and finance furnished the principal issues. Believing, as they did, that the value of the gold dollar had been artificially stimulated to the benefit of the creditor class and to the distress of the debtors, the Populists demanded first and foremost an extensive expansion of the currency — in other words, money inflation. The amount of the circulating medium, they contended, whether by direct paper-money issues or by the "free and unlimited coinage of silver at the ratio of sixteen to one," or by both, should "be speedily increased to not less than fifty dollars per capita." As for the transportation issue, they advocated that the government should own and operate the railroads, and also, for good measure, the telegraph and telephone systems of the country. On the subject of public lands they looked faintly in the direction of conservation by demanding the return to the government by "railroads and other corporations" of all lands received "in excess of their actual needs." Alien landownership the Populists also condemned, and among other reforms favorably mentioned in their platform were the sub-Treasury system, the Australian ballot, a graduated income tax, postal savings banks, shorter hours for labor, the initiative and referendum, election of United States senators by direct

[1] This refers to the Australian system of secret voting, recently introduced into the United States, and strongly supported by the Populists.

vote of the people, and a single term for the President and Vice-President. For their candidates the Populists chose James B. Weaver of Iowa who had fought for the North in the Civil War, to head the ticket, and James G. Field of Virginia, an ex-Confederate, for second place.

Election of 1892

The Populists, while predicting a victory of the "people" over the "plutocrats" in 1896, hoped only to make a good showing in 1892. Circumstances came ably to their assistance. The Republicans, in spite of the overwhelming rebuke they had received in 1890, had little choice but to renominate the unpopular Harrison and to defend the long list of dubious measures, including the McKinley Act, that were associated with his administration; while the Democrats, convinced that another battle must be fought over the tariff, turned for a third time to Cleveland. Signs of dissension in both old parties were apparent. Three days before the opening of the Republican convention, Blaine had resigned as Secretary of State and had permitted his friends to work openly, if unavailingly, for his nomination. Cleveland, likewise, had met with formidable opposition. David B. Hill of New York had sought in every way to discredit the ex-President and to take the nomination away from him; moreover, among soft-money men of the West and the South Cleveland's hard-money views aroused the strongest antagonism.

The Populists went into the campaign as the one party willing to take a radical stand on the money question. Their free-silver plank was less a matter of conviction than of expediency, for the views of the original Populists were derived from the Greenbackers rather than from the Silverites. Nevertheless, "free silver" furnished the one really exciting issue of the campaign. On this issue, primarily, several states of the Rocky Mountain West broke

James B. Weaver. *Populist candidate for President in 1892, Weaver had a long record as third party promoter. His Prohibitionist views made him unpalatable to the Republicans, and he was the Greenbacker candidate for President in 1880. He became an ardent free-silverite.*

from their Republican moorings and voted either for the Populists or, because of Populist secessions from the Republican Party, for the Democrats. Thanks in part to deliberate propaganda on the part of the silver interests, Populist campaigners in the Middle West and in the South found their audiences increasingly interested in the magic of free silver. The "sham battle" over the tariff went on to its logical conclusion, and, quite as the prophets predicted, Cleveland defeated Harrison. But, regardless of what might happen to the Populist Party, it was apparent that the silver issue had a future.

A Democratic Victory

For the moment the triumph of the Democrats seemed complete. Cleveland's popular vote was 5,556,918 to Harrison's 5,176,108 and Weaver's 1,041,028; the electoral vote stood: Cleveland, 277; Harrison, 145; and Weaver, 22. For the first time

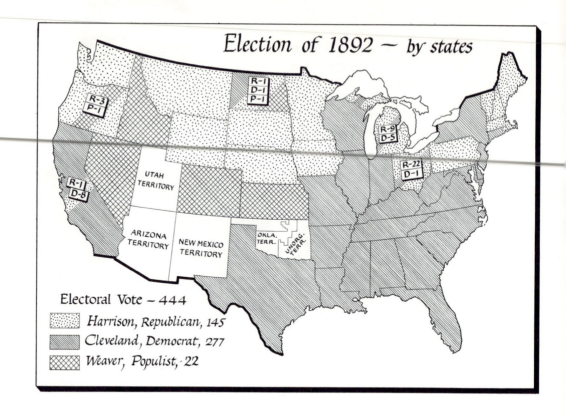

Election of 1892 — by states

R-1
D-1
P-1

R-3
P-1

R-9
D-5

R-22
D-1

R-1
D-8

UTAH
TERRITORY

ARIZONA
TERRITORY

NEW MEXICO
TERRITORY

OKLA.
TERR.

UNORG.
TERR.

Electoral Vote – 444

Harrison, Republican, 145

Cleveland, Democrat, 277

Weaver, Populist, 22

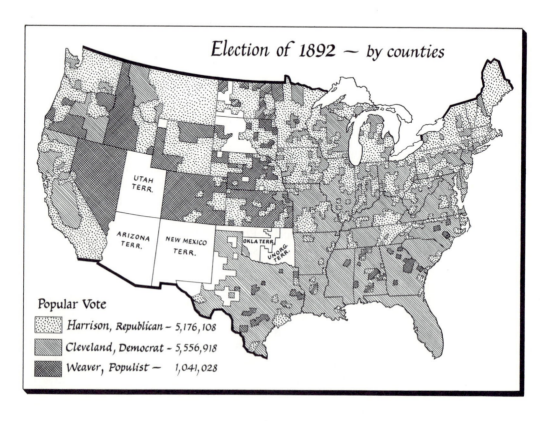

Election of 1892 — by counties

UTAH
TERR.

ARIZONA
TERR.

NEW MEXICO
TERR.

OKLA TERR.

UNORG.
TERR.

Popular Vote

Harrison, Republican – 5,176,108

Cleveland, Democrat – 5,556,918

Weaver, Populist – 1,041,028

since the Civil War both houses of Congress as well as the Presidency were in Democratic hands. The Populists, for all their brave talk, had failed to make a dent in the "solid South," and the votes they had won in the West had been obtained in some instances only by cooperation with the Democrats. The country had again, as in 1890, voted its opposition to the McKinley Tariff; it had again rebuked the Republicans for their two-faced handling of the money question in the Sherman Silver Purchase Act; it had denounced anew the partisanship and extravagance of the Republican pension policy; it had condemned the inadequacy and ineffectiveness of the Sherman Antitrust Act; it had rebuked the President for his wavering attitude toward civil service reform; and it had shown its impatience with the effort to revive the controversies of reconstruction by means of a "Force bill." Significant and interesting was the fact that the six northwestern states admitted by the Republicans in 1889 and 1890 to insure Republican supremacy had actually contributed considerably to Republican defeat.

A casualty of the election was the Farmers' Alliance. In the Northwest it was absorbed into and replaced by the Populist Party. In the South it was torn violently asunder and destroyed by the third-party issue. The smaller faction, convinced that deliverance for the southern cotton-farmer was never to be found under the rule of the Democrats, dared the derision of neighbors and the loss of friends to join hands with the Populists. The larger faction, equally certain that white supremacy was still the one issue to which all others must bow, returned to the Democratic Party. Macune and a few of his adherents tried in vain to restore the Alliance to its former nonpartisan status, but the scandals that pursued Macune's name undermined his influence, and the order he had done so much to create soon passed into oblivion.

Ignatius Donnelly. *Donnelly's wit and rhetoric made him an outstanding Populist spokesman, but he was not a grass-roots farmer, and he did not always represent farmer opinion accurately.*

Ignatius Donnelly

As a matter of fact, neither the Alliances nor the Populists were particularly fortunate in their leadership. Among both Democrats and Republicans party discipline during the last third of the nineteenth century was strong, and politicians who failed to toe the party lines were unceremoniously dismissed. Ignatius Donnelly (1831–1901), for example, by showing too much independence, lost his welcome in the Republican Party in 1868, after three terms in Congress. Since the Democrats showed little interest in turncoats, he had no choice, if he wished to remain in politics, but to align himself with any third party available. Sucessively he became an Anti-Monopolist, a Greenbacker, and a Populist. A brilliant writer and a superb orator, he was also a bit of a crackpot. He wrote one book to prove that civilization had developed originally, as Plato had theorized, from the inhabitants of an island,

Atlantis, which eventually sank into the sea. He wrote another to prove that a great comet, Ragnarok, accounted for the strange deposits of clay, gravel, and silt found upon the face of the earth. He wrote another to prove that Bacon wrote Shakespeare. He also wrote a novel, *Caesar's Column*, in which he seemed to predict that the lower classes, driven desperate by the ills from which they suffered, would join a great Brotherhood of Destruction that eventually would bring down civilization.

Other Populist Leaders

Donnelly was no doubt the most extreme example of the cross the Populists had to bear in their self-appointed leaders, but he was not the only one. Thomas E. Watson of Georgia, a one-term legislator who dared to rebel against the Democratic leadership of his state, showed in his later years unmistakable signs of mental instability, and became a violent detractor of Negroes, Jews, and Catholics. James B. Weaver of Iowa, one of the most sensible of the Populist leaders, had been a minor Republican officeholder until his outspokenly prohibitionist views cost him his party standing. The Populists not only attracted old party politicians out on a limb,

but also writers with unorthodox political or economic views, many of whom were neither farmers nor rural-minded. It is thus a mistake to assume that the opinions of all who professed to speak for Populism really represented the sentiments of the ordinary farmers who voted the Populist ticket. Populist orators might indeed be demagogues who made wild threats and promises, but in this respect they hardly differed from Republican and Democratic orators; it was an age of demagoguery. Nor is there much reason to believe that the ordinary Populist took seriously the charge of a conspiracy against his welfare by "Jewish international bankers." If he believed in any such conspiracy, he at least took the word "Jewish" lightly. Anti-Semitism stemmed from the cities where there were many Jews, and not from the country where there were almost none. What the discontented farmers wanted was higher prices for their produce, and more adequate restraints upon the railroads, the middlemen, and the bankers. To obtain these ends they were willing to turn to the government. Let the people, not the plutocrats, control the government, then let the government control the corporations who gouged the people. To this creed they pinned their faith.

BIBLIOGRAPHY

Two excellent surveys, published a generation apart, are F. A. Shannon, *The Farmer's Last Frontier: Agriculture, 1860–1897* (1945); and G. C. Fite, *The Farmers' Frontier, 1865–1900* (1966). Important special studies are Everett Dick, *The Sod-House Frontier, 1854–1890* (1937); A. G. Bogue, *From Prairie to Corn Belt* (1963); and E. W. Hayter, *The Troubled Farmer, 1850–1900* (1968). A classic study is Joseph Schafer, *The Social History of American Agriculture* (1936). *Readings in the History of American Agriculture* (1960),

edited by W. D. Rasmussen, is a useful collection. E. G. Nourse, *American Agriculture and the European Market* (1924), calls attention to a basic problem not always understood. See also Henrietta Larson, *The Wheat Market and the Farmer in Minnesota, 1858–1900* (1926). A. G. Bogue, *Money at Interest: The Farm Mortgage on the Middle Border* (1955), is an important reinterpretation. Other interesting monographs are J. C. Malin, *Winter Wheat in the Golden Belt of Kansas* (1944); and M. B. Bogue, *Patterns from the Sod*

(1959), a close examination of land use and tenure in eight Illinois counties.

A survey of agricultural movements is C. C. Taylor, *The Farmers' Movement, 1620–1920* (1953). S. J. Buck, *The Granger Movement* (1913), has long been standard. On political movements, see also: F. E. Haynes, *Third Party Movements since the Civil War, with Special Reference to Iowa* (1916), excellent on the Greenbackers; P. R. Fossum, *The Agrarian Movement in North Dakota* (1925); C. McA. Destler, *American Radicalism, 1865–1901* (1946), a book of many strengths and particularly suggestive on Illinois; R. V. Scott, *The Agrarian Movement in Illinois, 1880–1896* (1962); and Nathan Fine, *Labor and Farmer Parties in the United States, 1828–1928* (1928), which is better on the labor than on the farmer side. The changing point of view with reference to the Populists may be followed in these works: J. D. Hicks, *The Populist Revolt* (1931); Richard Hofstadter, *The Age of Reform: From Bryan to F.D.R.* (1955); and Norman Pollack, *The Populist Response to Industrial America* (1962). An interesting rejoinder to those who would "over-revise" Populism is C. V. Woodward, "The Populist Heritage and the Intellectual," which may be found in his *The Burden of Southern History* (2nd ed., 1969). An important case study is W. T. K. Nugent, *The Tolerant Populists: Kansas Populism and Nativism* (1963). Excellent selections from the Populists may be found in *The Populist Mind* (1967), edited by Norman Pollack; and *The Populist Reader* (1968), edited by G. B. Tindall. Conflicting interpretations may be found in *The Populists in Historical Perspective* (1968), edited by R. J. Cunningham; and *Populism: Reaction or Reform?* (1968), edited by Theodore Saloutos.

On agrarian protest in the South, see: Theodore Saloutos, *Farmer Movements in the South, 1865–1933* (1960); and C. V. Woodward, *Tom Watson, Agrarian Rebel* (1938), a superb biography. There are a number of excellent works on southern Populism and near-Populism: F. B. Simkins, *The Tillman Movement in South Carolina* (1926), and *Pitchfork Ben Tillman* (1944); J. B. Clark, *Populism in Alabama* (1927); A. M. Arnett, *The Populist Movement in Georgia* (1922); R. C. Martin, *The People's Party in Texas* (1933); R. C. Cotner, *James Stephen Hogg* (1959), a fine life of the reform Democratic governor of Texas; D. M. Robison, *Bob Taylor and the Agrarian Revolt in Tennessee* (1935); and Stuart Noblin, *Leonidas LaFayette Polk* (1949), a biography of the North Carolina leader. An interesting treatment of a neglected subject is H. G. Edmonds, *The Negro and Fusion Politics in North Carolina, 1894–1901* (1951); in this connection, see also C. H. Nolen, *The Negro's Image in the South: The Anatomy of White Supremacy* (1967). An important large-scale study is H. D. Woodman, *King Cotton & His Retainers: Financing & Marketing the Cotton Crop of the South, 1800–1925* (1968).

A convenient summary of the politics of the 1890's is in H. U. Faulkner, *Politics, Reform, and Expansion, 1890–1900* (1959), which has a good bibliography. See also: G. H. Knoles, *The Presidential Campaign and Election of 1892* (1942); F. E. Haynes, *James Baird Weaver* (1919), the best on that perennial protest candidate; Martin Ridge, *Ignatius Donnelly* (1962); and J. C. Olson, *J. Sterling Morton* (1942), a fine life of a leading conservative Democrat from Nebraska. An important survey is H. S. Merrill, *Bourbon Democracy of the Middle West, 1865–1896* (1953); Merrill's *William Freeman Vilas* (1954) is a case study in Wisconsin Democratic politics.

8

THE SILVER CRUSADE

*The gold reserve · Condition of the Treasury · Panic of 1893 ·
Repeal of the Sherman Silver Purchase Act · Purchases of gold · Tariff
legislation · Rise of the silver issue · Elections of 1894 · William Jennings
Bryan · Plight of the Populists · Election of 1896 · The Dingley Tariff ·
International bimetallism · The return of prosperity*

The Gold Reserve

There is some reason to suppose that, even before his term of office ended, Harrison had occasion to rejoice in his defeat. A nightmare of his administration had been the condition of the "gold reserve." Authorized by the Resumption Act of 1875, and painstakingly assembled by John Sherman during Hayes's administration, this fund had originally amounted to only a little more than $100 million. With that sum the Treasury had successfully resumed specie payments in 1879, although the outstanding issues of greenbacks exceeded the gold reserve in the proportion of about three dollars to one. Businessmen assumed, however, that as long as there was $100 million in gold in the Treasury, the gold standard was secure. Each year the operation of the Bland-Allison Act of 1878 added somewhat to the burden borne by the gold reserve, for successive Secretaries of the Treasury invariably adopted the policy of

UNCLE SAM'S "CROWN OF THORNS." *This cartoon of 1894 may have suggested Bryan's Cross of Gold speech.*

backing the silver dollar, whatever its "intrinsic" value, with gold. But the plentiful revenues and the general prosperity of the eighties steadily increased the gold reserve, until by 1890 the Treasury was able to record that it possessed $190 million in gold, nearly twice the essential minimum.

It was at this point that the financial measures of the Harrison administration began to take effect. In the first place, the McKinley Tariff, as its framers intended, had reduced the annual revenue by about $100 million a year. Secondly, the lavish expenditures of the new administration, particularly for pensions, placed a new and heavy burden upon the Treasury. Thirdly, the Sherman Silver Purchase Act, which replaced the Bland-Allison Act of 1878, not only required the government to purchase nearly twice as much silver as before, but also provided for a new issue of Treasury notes, based on these silver purchases, that all sound-money men agreed must be redeemable in gold rather than in silver. Failure to maintain their parity with gold would mean that the silver standard would succeed the gold standard, and the purchasing power of the American dollar would decline to the commercial value of the silver dollar — a drop of nearly 50 per cent.

Condition of the Treasury

Well before the end of the Harrison administration the condition of the Treasury had begun to excite general alarm. By 1892, the Treasury surplus, which recorded the excess of revenues over expenditures, had almost reached the vanishing point. Far more significant was the fact that the last two years had witnessed heavy withdrawals of gold. Faith that the government could redeem its greenbacks and Treasury notes in gold was obviously shaken, for gold flowed steadily out of the Treasury and paper flowed in. By January, 1893, the gold reserve had dwindled to only $108 million and the Harrison administration, in order to stave off the inevitable crisis until after March 4, was driven to heroic measures. Late in January, Harrison's Secretary of the Treasury successfully implored the New York banks to exchange $6 million in gold for paper, a sum that kept the gold reserve above the $100 million mark until after Cleveland was inaugurated. But when the Democrats took over the Treasury, they found a gold reserve of only $100,982,410.

Panic of 1893

By April 21, 1893, within a matter of weeks after the change of government, the gold reserve dropped below the $100 million mark, and the Panic of 1893 was on. Before six months had passed no less than eight thousand business failures, involving liabilities of $285 million, were recorded. Four hundred banks, most of them in the West or in the South, closed their doors. Railroads followed each other into receivership in a procession that ended only after 156 companies, among them the Erie, the Union Pacific, and the Northern Pacific, had gone into bankruptcy. Panic conditions lasted throughout the summer, after which the country settled down to the long, hard process of waiting out a depression that was to last four full years.

While the condition of the Treasury, which gave rise to the fear that the government would be unable to maintain the gold standard, undoubtedly ushered in the Panic of 1893, there were other reasons in abun-

"Another Prop Needed." *Cartoon from* Puck, *July 9, 1890, suggesting a need for the kind of anti-silver legislation that Cleveland, not Harrison, was later to obtain.*

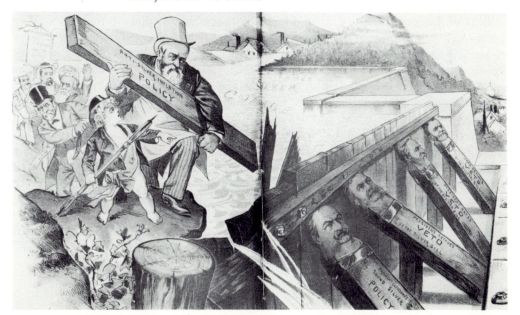

dance that must be taken into account in explaining both the panic and the depression. Well to the front was the long-standing agricultural distress of the West and the South. For both sections the beginning of the depression might better have been set at 1887 than at 1893. The purchasing power of the stricken sections had steadily declined, and in consequence the earnings of all businesses that depended on farm markets or the handling of farm goods had suffered. The eighties, too, had been a period of overexpansion in industry. The great transcontinental railroads, the huge industrial trusts, and the building of the larger cities and the new cities that they had made necessary had drained dry the investment resources of the nation. Furthermore, the depression, far from being a strictly American affair, was of world-wide dimensions. From 1889 on, and particularly after the so-called "Baring panic" of 1890 in England, all Europe had recorded subnormal business conditions; indeed, one reason for the depletion of the American gold reserve was the withdrawal of foreign capital from investment in America in order to bolster up the waning fortunes of European enterprise.

To twentieth-century Americans familiar with the economic activities of the Hoover and Roosevelt administrations, the refusal of Grover Cleveland to regard the problem of business recovery as a direct concern of the government may seem surprising. To Cleveland the depression was a business matter that lay quite outside the realm of politics. He regarded it as his duty, as President, to maintain the historic gold standard if he could, and to keep the government solvent; but beyond that neither he nor the majority he was able to command in Congress dreamed that the government had a duty to perform. The fact that their stand on gold would be helpful to creditors they regarded as purely incidental. Even the radicals of the time — the Populists and the Silverites — confined their demands almost entirely to money inflation of one sort or another. For this attitude Cleveland and his contemporaries are neither to be praised nor censured. They acted as nineteenth-century politicians had always acted. Van Buren, Buchanan, Grant, and Hayes had confronted major depressions during their terms of office, but neither they nor their advisers had conceived of it as the duty of the government to defeat depression and restore prosperity. The business cycle was a strictly business affair.

Repeal of the Silver Purchase Act

On the money question, however, Cleveland acted with vigor. Failure to maintain the gold standard would have seemed to him a breach of public faith. Accordingly, he called Congress at once into special session and asked it to repeal the obnoxious Sherman Silver Purchase Act, which in his judgment had done so much to deplete the gold reserve. He could hardly have thought of a better way to alienate the West and the South, where silver orators were gaining converts every day. The debtor farmers, to whom the gold standard meant low prices and continued agricultural distress, had no desire whatever to save it; for them the fifty-cent dollar had no terrors. The silver interests of the Far West were even more violently opposed to repeal. What silver needed, they insisted, was a larger rather than a smaller subsidy; better still, "the free and unlimited coinage of silver at the ratio of sixteen to one." Congress at length supported Cleveland in his resolve, but only at the cost of a definite split in the Democratic Party. Enough eastern Republicans joined the eastern Democrats to repeal the Sherman Law, but the confidence of western and southern Democrats in the President they had chosen was sadly shaken.

Cleveland's next move alienated the soft-

The New York Stock Exchange. *This picture of a "Recent Flurry in Wall Street," appeared in* Harper's Weekly, *August 12, 1893, and represented an ordinarily busy morning in the Stock Exchange rather than a scene from the Panic of 1893, which occurred the preceding spring.*

money men still further. In spite of the fact that silver purchases were discontinued, the drain on the gold reserve continued. By October the amount of gold in the Treasury was less than $82 million and before the end of the year it was down to $68 million. Faced by this emergency the President, after some hesitation, authorized his Secretary of the Treasury, John G. Carlisle, to invoke the provisions of the still-unrepealed Resumption Act of 1875, and to buy enough gold to maintain the proper reserve. In January, 1894, an issue of $50 million worth of 5 per cent bonds brought $58 million in gold into the Treasury, but of this sum $24 million was immediately withdrawn, and before the end of the year one more purchase of gold was necessary — an "endless chain," for in each case the gold was hardly in the Treasury until it was drawn out again.

Purchases of Gold

By February, 1895, with the gold reserve down to $41 million and currency depreciation once more seemingly in sight, the President saved the situation by a deal with the Morgan and the Belmont banking firms, the latter representing the Rothschilds of Europe. According to the terms of this unusual agreement the favored firms were permitted to purchase a $62 million issue of thirty-year 4 per cent bonds at 104½ instead of at their market value of about 111. Thus the bankers were insured an enormous profit. In return for this special consideration, however, the purchasers guaranteed two things, first, to procure half of the needed gold from abroad, and second, to use their influence to prevent further withdrawals of gold from the Treasury. This deal, while violently and perhaps justly criticized, did serve to restore confidence, and when some months later the government offered $100 million in 4 per cent bonds to the highest bidder, the issue was promptly subscribed five times over. After this transaction all fear that the government could not maintain the gold standard speedily vanished. But to the strongly Populistic South and West the maintenance of the gold standard was more an evil than a good, and worse still, the President had attained this undesired end by "selling out" to Wall Street. The depths of Cleveland's unpopularity knew no bounds.

Tariff Legislation

Part of the price that Cleveland paid for maintaining the gold standard was the defeat of his long-cherished plans for a genuine revision downward of the tariff. Of necessity, or so he thought, he had postponed the tariff battle until after the repeal of the Sherman Act. But when that end had been accomplished, his prestige with the silver wing of his party was so impaired that in that quarter his requests were no longer respected. Moreover, the alliance of eastern Democrats and eastern Republicans, originally called into existence against sil-

Will It Rise? *Or will it drop back to the old place? A cartoon showing the difficulties Cleveland experienced in maintaining the Treasury's gold reserve. From* Judge, *March 7, 1896.*

ver, soon found that it could also function effectively on the tariff. The result was a tariff measure, the Wilson-Gorman Act of 1894, so far removed from the party's pledges on the subject that Cleveland called it a "piece of party perfidy," and obstinately refused to sign the bill, although he did permit it to become a law without his signature.

When William L. Wilson of West Virginia, scholarly chairman of the House Ways and Means Committee, introduced the tariff bill into the House, tariff reformers had good reason to congratulate themselves. The Wilson bill, patterned after the Mills bill of 1888, proposed to put raw materials, such as lumber, wool, and coal on the free list, in part as compensation to manufacturers for the reduced protection they were to receive, and in part as a means of lowering the prices that consumers would have to pay. Sugar, too, both raw and refined, was to be admitted free, and the expensive sugar bounty was to be abolished. On most factory-made items, such as cotton, woolen, and silken fabrics, crockery, and glassware, the duties were to be materially reduced, although their protective character was by no means destroyed. Fearful that the lowered duties might reduce the revenue below the needs of the government, the framers of the bill heeded the Populist demand for an income tax, and levied a flat 2 per cent against incomes over $4,000.

As it passed the House, the Wilson bill was an honest attempt at tariff reduction. In the Senate, however, two eastern Democrats, Brice and Gorman, aided and abetted by log-rolling Democrats from every section, and in particular by the "sugar senators" from Louisiana, joined with the Republicans to attach 633 amendments to the bill, wholly changing its character. The sugar bounty was not revived, but duties that were worth $20 million annually to the Sugar Trust were placed on both raw and refined sugar. Throughout the revised measure the low-tariff principle was all but ignored. Reluctantly the House acquiesced in the wrecking of its work, and the President's attempts at intervention proved unavailing. In general the duties of the Wilson-Gorman Tariff were lower than those of the McKinley Tariff, and not far different from the duties set by the Tariff of 1883. The provision for an income tax, which actually reached the statute books, was declared unconstitutional by the Supreme Court in a five-to-four decision (1895). This was the more remarkable because of the fact that an income tax had been levied and collected during the Civil War without serious question as to its constitutionality. Populists were convinced that the action of the Court was just one more evidence of the unholy alliance between business and government.

Rise of the Silver Issue

The acute labor unrest of 1894[1] drove fear into the hearts of the conservatives, and encouraged the Populists to hope that eventually farmers and laborers would learn to work together. But, as events turned out, whatever union of the working classes was actually accomplished came primarily on the issue of free silver, and more or less without regard for the wishes of party leaders. Propaganda from mine-owners in the silver states of the Far West flooded the country with denunciations of the "crime of 1873" and with innumerable arguments to prove that only "the free and unlimited coinage of silver at the ratio of sixteen to one" was required to restore prosperity. *Coin's Financial School*, a little book written by William H. Harvey and published in 1894, set forth in simple language, and seemingly with unanswerable logic, the doctrines of the silverites. "Professor Coin," as the author called himself, pur-

ported to run a school in Chicago for financiers, and the lectures he gave on the money question were recorded in the book. Illustrated with numerous cartoons and diagrams, and sometimes reduced to the simplicity of a dialogue between the "Professor" and his students, the book appealed to an enormous audience. Silver orators, such as William Jennings Bryan, knew its arguments by heart and spread them far and wide. Soon countless thousands had come to believe that an international conspiracy to set gold above silver was at the root of the economic distress from which the nation suffered. The restoration of prosperity need not await the enactment of a long and complicated series of reforms. By the simple expedient of restoring silver to its historic status as money, all wrong would be righted.

It means work for the thousands who now tramp the streets . . . not knowing where their next meal is coming from. It means food and clothes for the thousands of hungry and ill-clad women and children. . . . It means the restoration of confidence in the business world. It means the re-opening of closed factories, the relighting of fires in darkened furnaces; it means hope instead of despair; comfort in place of suffering; life instead of death.

Unhappily for the plans of the Populists, the silver issue cut across party lines. Silver Republicans in the West and silver Democrats in both the West and South captured the old party organizations in state after state. Even the Populist leaders, caught up in the silver frenzy, were forced increasingly to ignore all the rest of their party's policies and to concentrate on "free silver," a panacea rather than a program.

> The dollar of our daddies,
>   Of silver coinage free,
> Will make us rich and happy
>   Will bring prosperity.

[1] See pp. 149–151.

William McKinley. *Twenty-fifth President of the United States. McKinley had served under Hayes in the Union army during the Civil War, and emerged as a brevet-major, the last Civil War officer to gain the Presidency. A shrewd and kindly regular, he became the conservatives' ideal President. A photograph taken June 7, 1898.*

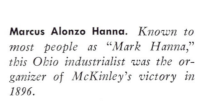

Marcus Alonzo Hanna. *Known to most people as "Mark Hanna," this Ohio industrialist was the organizer of McKinley's victory in 1896.*

Elections of 1894

With the silver forces still divided among three parties, the state and congressional elections of 1894 turned upon hard times and the unpopularity of Cleveland. The Democrats were no more responsible for the depression than the Republicans, if as much so, but it was their misfortune to be in power when the panic broke, and the Republicans drove home the charge that Democratic supremacy and hard times went together. As a result the Republicans obtained a two-to-one majority in the national House of Representatives, greatly reduced the Democratic majority in the Senate, and captured nearly every state government outside the South. The behavior of the Populists during the campaign tended, if anything, to aid the Republicans. In the West the Populists, unable or unwilling to cooperate with the Democrats as fully as in 1892, tended to avoid fusion and to keep "in the middle of the road"; in the South, they unblushingly joined forces with the Republicans. The total Populist vote, however, was more than 40 per cent larger in 1894 than in 1892, and enthusiastic Populists cited the rapid rise of Republicanism before 1860 as evidence of what their party could do by 1896. Leading Republicans held a different view of the situation; some boasted that in 1896 they could "nominate a rag baby and elect it President."

That the original Republican plan for 1896 did not contemplate a straight-out endorsement of the single gold standard was apparent from the record of the candidate slated for first place on the Republican ticket. William McKinley (1843–1901), author of the McKinley Tariff bill of 1890, and governor of Ohio from 1891 to 1895, was a tariff expert with no deep convictions on the money question. Indeed, in so far as he had committed himself, he seemed to have taken the silver side. In 1878 he had voted for the Bland-Allison Act, and in 1890, when the Sherman Silver Purchase Act was being formulated, he again advocated special favors for silver. As a compromise candidate, satisfactory to both the silver and the gold factions of the party, he seemed ideal, for his leanings toward silver were nicely balanced by the fact that he was a thorough-going party regular who could be trusted not to get out of step with party leaders. His availability for the Republican nomination in 1896 was further emphasized by his creditable record as a Union officer in the Civil War, by his chivalrous devotion to his invalid wife, by his suave and genial manners, and by his abiding friendship with Marcus Alonzo Hanna, Cleveland industrialist and boss of the Republican Party in Ohio. Hanna had the normal attitude of his class toward tariff protection, but his regard for McKinley was personal no less than political. He early made up his mind that McKinley must be the Republican standard-bearer in 1896, and long before the convention met had rounded up the necessary votes.

The "Battle of the Standards"

The steady drift of the electorate toward the free-silver "heresy" upset the Republican plan for a fence-sitting campaign on the money question. Southern Democrats, thoroughly frightened by the strength the Populists had shown in 1894, accepted free silver as a means of winning back the ground they had lost. Western Democrats, and frequently also western Republicans, made every effort to outdo the Populists in their devotion to silver. Thirty Democratic state conventions, all in the West or the South, emphatically endorsed "the free and unlimited coinage of silver at the ratio of sixteen to one." Shrewd observers could easily foretell that, in spite of the strenuous efforts of President Cleveland and the gold-standard Democrats of the Northeast, the Democratic Party would be forced to include in its platform an uncompromising demand for free silver. Confronted by this situation, the Republican leaders, Hanna among them, finally determined to commit their party to the single gold standard. They could not hope by a straddling platform to compete with the unequivocal demands of the Democrats for free silver, and they might, by adhering steadfastly to gold, win over the dissident Democratic "gold-bugs" to the support of the Republican ticket. The tariff issue would have to stand aside. Republicans knew full well, when at St. Louis they nailed a "sound-money" plank into their platform, that the "battle of the standards" would dwarf all other party differences to insignificance.

We are unalterably opposed [this plank read] to every measure calculated to debase our currency or impair the credit of our country. We are, therefore, opposed to the free coinage of silver, except by international agreement with the leading commercial nations of the world, which we pledge ourselves to promote, and until such agreement can be obtained the existing gold standard must be preserved. All our silver and paper currency must be maintained at parity with gold, and we favor all measures designed to maintain inviolably the obligations of the United States and all our money, whether coin or paper, at the present standard, the standard of the most enlightened nations of the earth.

The complete conversion of the Republicans to the single gold standard was not accomplished without a party split. More than one hundred votes were cast for an amendment, introduced by Senator Henry M. Teller of Colorado, that favored the "independent coinage of gold and silver at our mints at the ratio of sixteen parts of silver to one of gold." When this amendment was rejected, thirty-four delegates, led by Teller, and including four United States senators and two representatives, left the hall in protest. That they would join the Democrats in case the latter came out for silver seemed a foregone conclusion. But the Republicans adhered steadfastly to their program, nominated McKinley for President, with Garret A. Hobart of New Jersey for Vice-President, and adjourned in the hope that Marcus A. Hanna, their new campaign manager, could find the money and the means to restore their party to power.

The action of the Republicans left the Democrats, whose convention met a few weeks later at Chicago, no logical choice but to endorse free silver. The Democratic National Committee, however, was still in the hands of the men who had helped to nominate Cleveland in 1892, and they made a determined effort to halt the trend toward silver. But when their nominee for temporary chairman, David B. Hill of New York, a "gold-bug," was defeated by Senator John W. Daniel of Virginia, a silverite, 556 to 349, it was apparent that the inflationists were in control. The platform they presented and adopted (628 to 301) on the money question bore no trace of compromise.

We demand the free and unlimited coinage of both silver and gold at the present legal ratio of sixteen to one without waiting for the aid or consent of any other nation. We demand that the standard silver dollar shall be a full legal tender, equally with gold, for all debts, public and private, and we favor such legislation as will prevent for the future the demonetization of any kind of legal tender money by private contract.

William Jennings Bryan. *Sometimes called the "Boy Orator of the Platte," Bryan's pre-eminence as a public speaker was for years almost unchallenged. His favorite subjects in the 1890's were the protective tariff, which he derided, and free silver, which he extolled.*

William Jennings Bryan

The Democrats had produced a platform; they were not long in finding a candidate. Before the convention met, the leading aspirant among the silverites was Richard P. Bland, a congressman from Missouri. But Bland's candidacy had awakened little enthusiasm, and many delegates regretted the constitutional provision that alone would keep them from voting for the far more colorful John P. Altgeld of Illinois, a naturalized citizen of German birth. Among the numerous minor candidates was William Jennings Bryan (1860–1925) of Nebraska, a young man only thirty-six years of age whose reputation for persuasive oratory was already well known. Bryan had served two terms in Congress, 1891 to 1895, and had once attracted nationwide attention by a powerful speech on the tariff. During the depression, without actually becoming a Populist, he had taken up with many of the Populist doctrines, particularly free silver. As Ignatius Donnelly complained, "We put him to school and he wound up by stealing the schoolbooks."

For months before the nominating convention met in 1896, Bryan had been speaking on free silver to western audiences, and had rehearsed many times the ringing phrases that were to bring him fame at Chicago. Fully conscious of his genius as an orator, he knew in his heart that if he could only find the occasion to make the speech he had learned so well the coveted prize would be his.

The opportunity came when he was asked to close the debate on a resolution that would have repudiated free silver and commended the Cleveland administration:

Serene and self-possessed, and with a smile upon his lips, he faced the roaring multitude with a splendid consciousness of power. Before a single word had been uttered by him, the pandemonium sank to an inarticulate murmur, and when he began to speak, even this was hushed to the profoundest silence. . . . He spoke with the utmost deliberation, so that every word was driven home to each hearer's consciousness, and yet with an ever-increasing force, which found fit expression in the wonderful harmony and power of his voice. His sentences rang out, now with an accent of superb disdain, and now with the stirring challenge of a bugle call. . . . The leaderless Democracy of the West was leaderless no more.

The scene enacted in the Convention, as Mr. Bryan finished speaking, was indescribable. Throughout the latter part of his address, a crash of applause had followed every sentence; but now the tumult was like that of a great sea thundering against the dykes. Twenty thousand men and women went mad with an irresistible enthusiasm. The orator had met their mood to the very full. He had found magic words for the feeling which they had been unable to express. And so he had played at will upon their very heartstrings, until the full tide of their emotion was let loose in one tempestuous roar of passion, which seemed to have no end.[1]

Bryan's speech was not a reasoned defense of the silver cause, and was not meant to be. Rather it was a leader's call to action. His closing words, "You shall not press down upon the brow of labor this crown of thorns, you shall not crucify mankind upon a cross of gold," summarized in a sentence all that had gone before. At that moment, had the convention been given the chance, it would doubtless have nominated Bryan by acclamation. When the proper time came, in spite of the fact that more than a hundred and fifty gold Democrats persistently abstained from voting, Bryan obtained the necessary two-thirds majority after only five ballots. For Vice-President the convention chose Arthur Sewall, a wealthy national banker, shipbuilder, and railroad director from Maine, whose views on every issue, except the money question, were in flat contradiction to Populist dogma.

Plight of the Populists

The plight of the Populists when they learned what the Democrats had done was far from pleasant. The Democratic platform had not only appropriated the silver issue; it had denounced with Populistic fervor the "absorption of wealth by the few," and had called for a stricter control of trusts and railroads by the federal government. The Democratic candidate, Bryan, was as dependable on silver as any Populist. The Populist leaders, confident that both the Republicans and the Demo-

---

[1] Harry Thurston Peck, *Twenty Years of the Republic* (1907), pp. 498–502. The quoted sentences are interspersed between long excerpts from Bryan's speech.

crats would be captured by the "gold-bugs," had set the date of the Populist convention later than either of the old-party conventions, and had hoped to rally all free-silver men and all reformers to their standard. Now they were faced squarely with the problem of sacrificing their party by endorsing the Democratic nominee or aiding the Republicans by dividing the silver vote. In general western Populists were willing to accept Bryan and join the Democrats, but to southern Populists such a course, involving, as it did, full surrender to a hated enemy, was extremely painful to contemplate. After a heated battle the Populist convention voted in favor of a compromise. It would name its vice-presidential candidate first on the assumption that a southern Populist would be chosen instead of the wholly unacceptable Sewall. Proponents of the plan argued that the convention might then nominate Bryan for President, if it chose, with the full expectation that the Democrats would withdraw Sewall, accept the Populist nominee for Vice-President, and so emphasize the separateness as well as the temporary fusion of the two parties.

The Populist choice for Vice-President fell on Thomas E. Watson, the fiery Georgian, after which there was no further chance to stop Bryan for first place. Had the Democrats then substituted Watson for Sewall, the Populists could have held up their heads during the campaign. But the Democrats were satisfied that they had won what they wanted, and ignored Watson, who nevertheless remained in the race and campaigned vigorously. Bryan accepted the Populist nomination, but paid no attention to Watson's candidacy. The anomaly of the situation led to endless confusion in the balloting, and many Populists voted the Democratic ticket in order to be sure that their ballots would count. The Populist Party, indeed, practically dissolved during the campaign.

The gold wing of the Democratic Party subsequently held a convention and nominated John M. Palmer of Illinois for President and Simon B. Buckner of Kentucky for Vice-President. Cleveland supported this ticket, but like most of the "Gold Democrats" hoped for a Republican victory.

Campaign of 1896

By repudiating Cleveland and absorbing Populism, the Democrats had placed

POLITICS IN THE TENEMENTS. While the parade moves by, a "coat-tail orator" has his say. *Harper's Weekly*, October 31, 1896.

THE CAMPAIGN OF 1896. *The "Battle of the Standards," as this campaign was often called, was fought with every weapon in the political arsenal, and aroused intense excitement.*

their party in a position to challenge seriously the Republican expectation of an easy victory. Bryan as a campaigner was a riot. "Probably no man in civil life," observed the New York *Nation*, "had succeeded in inspiring so much terror, without taking life, as Bryan." Between the time of his nomination and election day he traveled eighteen thousand miles and spoke to hundreds of audiences. Inspired by the endless vitality of their leader, a host of lesser orators spread the gospel of free silver to every village and crossroads in the country. The Democratic campaign chest, however, was slender, for the only large contributions came from the hard-pressed silver interests of the Far West. It was at this point that the Republicans proved invulnerable. Conceding privately that "the Chicago convention has changed everything" and that the campaign "will be work and hard work from the start," Hanna, the Republican campaign manager, began an earnest solicitation of funds from all the important business interests that had a financial stake in Republican success. Exactly how much money he and his subordinates collected will never be known, but Hanna later admitted receiving gifts of not less than $3.5 million, a huge sum for the times, and particularly for a lean year. With ample funds at his disposal and more always to be had for the asking, Hanna embarked upon a "campaign of education" well calculated to discredit the reasoning of the silverites. Hundreds of well-paid orators challenged the tenets of Bryan and his underpaid volunteers, tons of shrewdly phrased pamphlets exploded the theories of "Professor Coin," batteries of skillful writers provided news and editorials for subsidized newspapers.

By staking everything on so dubious an issue as free silver, the Democrats had laid themselves wide open to this kind of attack. No doubt the "bimetallists," as they called themselves, in contrast with the gold "mon-

McKINLEY BANNERS. According to this *Harper's Weekly* illustration, October 24, 1896, the American flag was involved in the fight for sound money.

ometallists," were sincere in their conviction that the need for free silver exceeded every other reform in importance, but they found few orthodox economists who would agree with the arguments by which they defended it. Republican pampheteers dwelt upon the absurdity of trying to maintain two different "yardsticks" with which to measure money, and featured the downright dishonesty involved in paying off valid debts with "fifty-cent" silver dollars. Among the reformers themselves there was much dissent from the free-silver hypothesis and some genuine dismay at the overemphasis it received. Henry Demarest Lloyd, the author of *Wealth Against Commonwealth* (1894), a powerful indict-

The Silver Argument Explodes. *A rise in the price of wheat during the campaign of 1896 encouraged the Republicans. According to this cartoon, as wheat went up in value, Bryan and free silver went down in public esteem. From* Leslie's Illustrated Weekly, *October 29, 1896.*

ment of the existing economic order, described free silver as a "fake" and called it the "cowbird of the reform movement. It waited until the nest had been built by the sacrifices and labors of others, then laid its eggs in it, pushing out the others which lie smashed on the ground."

Republican Tactics

No doubt the Republican propaganda actually won over many free-silverites to Republican views, but not all that Hanna's lieutenants did was strictly educational. Every time-tested device for gathering in the votes was utilized — parades led by brass bands, torchlight processions, flaming posters, campaign caps and buttons. As the end drew near, threats were passed out freely. Workingmen were told that the election of McKinley would mean high wages and prosperity, but the election of

Bryan, the loss of their jobs. Employers were known to reinforce this argument by telling their employees that if Bryan were elected they need not come back to work. Farmers were informed that in case there was a Democratic victory their mortgages would not be renewed. Nor was there any lack of funds among the Republicans on election day to keep on duty a full quota of "workers at the polls." Not among the least of Hanna's shrewd moves was to keep McKinley discreetly in the background. Hanna well knew that in a rough-and-tumble campaign the Republican candidate would have been no match for Bryan. Small delegations were permitted to visit McKinley at his home in Canton, Ohio, and to be charmed by his personality, but they were given no fighting message. McKinley's famous "front-porch" speeches mainly recorded calm confidence; the others could do the fighting. Widely advertised as the "advance agent of Prosperity," he was never once really required to defend the title he had received.

Election Results

It was a common statement that, if the election had been held in August instead of November, Bryan would have been the victor. No one knows. Possibly a rise in the price of wheat due to a short crop abroad, whereas the American crop was abundant, seriously affected the results. However that may be, the Republicans undoubtedly picked up many votes as the campaign neared its close, and in the end they won an overwhelming victory. In general the agricultural South and West supported Bryan, while the industrial Northeast supported McKinley; but McKinley's Northeast extended as far west as Iowa, Minnesota, and North Dakota, while Bryan's solid South and West were broken by such notable Republican exceptions as Maryland, Delaware, West Virginia, Kentucky, California, and Oregon. McKinley

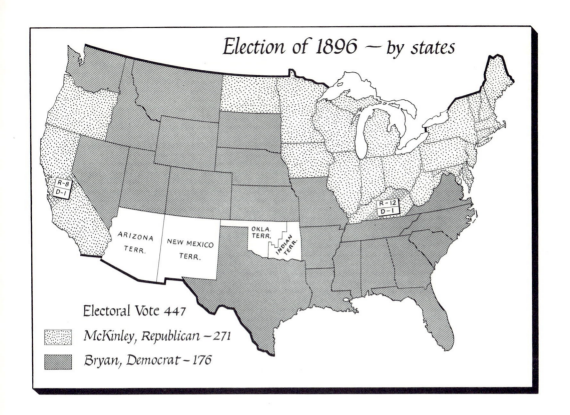

Election of 1896 — by states

R-8
D-1

R-12
D-1

ARIZONA
TERR.

NEW MEXICO
TERR.

OKLA.
TERR.

INDIAN
TERR.

Electoral Vote 447

McKinley, Republican — 271

Bryan, Democrat — 176

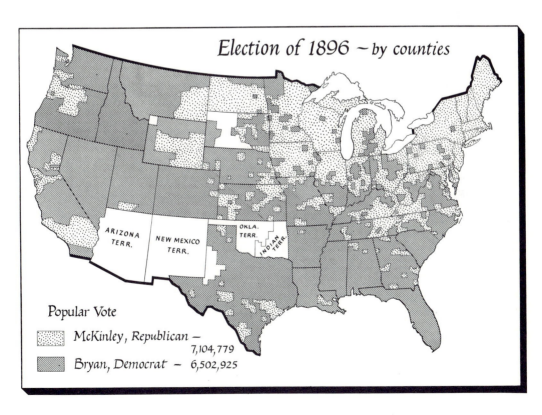

Election of 1896 — by counties

ARIZONA
TERR.

NEW MEXICO
TERR.

OKLA.
TERR.

INDIAN
TERR.

Popular Vote

McKinley, Republican —
7,104,779

Bryan, Democrat — 6,502,925

received more than 7 million popular votes to 6.5 million for Bryan, while the electoral vote stood 271 to 176. The real meaning of the election was somewhat obscured by the unfortunate issue on which it had been fought. In actual fact Bryan represented the forces of agriculture, both in the South and in the West, and to a lesser extent the forces of labor. McKinley, on the other hand, was the candidate of northeastern industry, which, ever since the Civil War, had been well-entrenched in the control of the national government and meant to hold its ground. The defeat of Bryan and the downfall of Populism freed the industrial leaders, temporarily at least, from the menace of popular interference with their monopolistic ambitions. Tom Johnson, soon to become mayor of Cleveland, Ohio, described the election as "the first great protest of the American people against monopoly — the first great struggle of the masses in our country against the privileged classes. It was not free silver that frightened the plutocrat leaders. What they feared, then, what they fear now, is free men."[1]

McKinley was inaugurated to the accompaniment of brightening economic skies and promptly took the necessary steps to identify Republican policies with the return of prosperity. Congress, being safely Republican in both houses, was called immediately into special session, not, as one might have supposed, to enact a gold-standard law, but rather to revise the tariff along strictly protectionist lines. In the preceding session the Republicans had already framed and presented a tariff bill, so within record time a measure introduced by Representative Nelson Dingley, Jr., of Maine was enacted into law. The rates it established quite outdid all previous efforts at tariff protection. Its purpose, as one inspired observer pointed out, was not to produce revenue and incidentally to afford

protection, but rather to afford protection and incidentally to produce revenue.

The Dingley Tariff

The Dingley rates were so high as to discourage importation. During the first year they were in force the total revenue collected from tariffs dropped $25 million below the returns for the preceding year under the Wilson Act. Duties were reimposed on wool and hides, which formerly had been on the free list; an intricate sugar schedule was devised to suit as precisely as possible the desires of both the growers and the refiners of sugar; and the high duties of 1890 on woolens, cotton, linen, silk, crockery, and steel products were either restored or increased. So ample was the duty of $7.84 a ton on steel rails that American steel manufacturers were able to charge a higher price for the rails they sold in the United States than for those they shipped to London and sold, presumably at a profit, in connection with English rails.

The establishment of limited reciprocity, as in 1890, was also provided for in the new law. A few items such as tea and coffee were put on the free list with the understanding that the President might proclaim specified duties in force if the nations that exported them failed to make similar concessions to American goods. Other items, such as brandies, wines, and works of art, carried duties that the President might reduce to designated levels, also by proclamation, if he could obtain adequate favors in return. Finally, on all tariff-bearing articles, the President might negotiate treaties with foreign nations to scale down the American rates as much as 20 per cent, but all such treaties required ratification by the Senate before they could become effective. By presidential proclamation some minor breaches were made in the high-tariff wall, but the eleven reciprocity treaties negotiated by the administration were all rejected by the Senate.

[1] Tom L. Johnson, *My Story* (1911), p. 109.

International Bimetallism

McKinley's failure to ask Congress for a rigid gold-standard law is not difficult to explain. The Senate, while safely Republican on the tariff, contained too many hold-over silver Senators to be regarded as trustworthy on the money question. McKinley therefore took advantage of the clause in the Republican platform that called for an international conference on bimetallism to substitute diplomacy for legislative action. That he would maintain the gold standard, with or without the sanction of law, was apparent from his choice of a conservative Chicago banker, Lyman J. Gage, as his Secretary of the Treasury. To give plausibility to the negotiations on silver, which were almost certain to fail, McKinley chose as his Secretary of State the aged John Sherman, whose historic connection with American monetary problems made his selection seem ideal. Sherman's memory was known to be failing, but this slight disqualification was more than offset by the fact that his seat in the Senate was coveted by McKinley's friend and patron, Marcus A. Hanna. On April 12, 1897, McKinley named a commission of three ardent bimetallists, headed by Edward O. Wolcott of Colorado, to visit Europe in the interest of international bimetallism. At Paris the commission was received with some show of cordiality, but at London it learned that Great Britain positively would not open her mints to silver on any terms satisfactory to the Americans. The final failure of "international bimetallism," coupled with heavy Republican gains in the election of 1898, enabled Congress at last to pass the long-promised gold-standard law on March 14, 1900.

The Return of Prosperity

The close coincidence between the return of prosperity and the return of the Republicans to power furnished a valuable weapon to Republican campaigners for many years to come. It is possible, of course, that the prospect of Republican victory promoted business confidence and led to business expansion. Good times were on the way back, however, even before the election, and it seems reasonable to suppose that the course of events would not have been far different, even if Bryan had been elected. Undoubtedly one reason for the upward surge was an increase in the money supply. It is a curious fact that monetary inflation actually occurred in spite of all the Republicans had done to prevent it, and it occurred in a way they had least expected, by means of an increase in the world's supply of gold. For a quarter of a century before 1890 the amount of new gold mined each year was practically constant. Then a steady increase began which by the end of the nineties had reached spectacular proportions. In the year 1897, approximately twice as much gold was produced as in the year 1890; in 1898 nearly two and one half times as much. The cyanide process by which more gold was extracted from the ore mined, coupled with new discoveries of gold in Australia, South Africa, and the Klondike, accounted for the increase. Bryan was doubtless right when he first began to assert that the amount of gold in existence was inadequate to transact the world's business, but his arguments were less convincing with each succeeding year. Before Bryan became active in politics American business had to overcome the handicap of a steadily appreciating dollar, which meant also steadily diminishing price levels; by the time Bryan began to run for President, the value of the dollar had begun to diminish, and prices were on the rise.

Fortunately for the farmers, agriculture shared generously in the new prosperity. The stimulus of gold inflation affected both farm and factory, while the drought in the

A TYPICAL CABIN IN DAWSON.

MEAT MARKET IN DAWSON.

THE KLONDIKE GOLD RUSH.
Gold strikes in north-western Canada rekindled memories of the gold rush to California a half century before, and reproduced some of the same primitive scenes.

West at long last came to an end. Good harvests in the United States were matched by poor harvests abroad, with a consequent strengthening of the overseas demand for American farm produce. Even more significant was the growing home demand that stemmed from the rapid influx of immigrants and the steady trend toward urbanization. Rising prices for farm produce were accompanied by rising prices for farm land; the competition of cheap land on new frontiers was at an end. Some farmers, and many real estate operators, waxed rich on unearned increment. The Spanish-American War, the Philippine Insurrection, and the Boer-British War, while they lasted, also added their quotas to the agricultural boom. With the turn of the century American farmers had entered into a period of good times that would outlast the First World War.

The Populist Contribution

As for the Populist Party, its vitality as an organization was sapped by the election of 1896. It continued to nominate candidates as late as 1912, but, betrayed by fusion and rent with internal dissension, it was never again a serious factor in American party politics. Nevertheless, if the Populist Party itself lost its life, many of the principles for which it stood lived on and in later years won substantial victories. This, indeed, had been, and continued to be, the fate of third parties in American history; the third party, almost certainly, would be absorbed into one or the other or both of the older parties, but such of its ideas as had merit would survive, and win eventual acceptance. The Populists believed firmly in making the government more responsive to popular rule, and they earnestly favored such measures as the Australian secret ballot, the initiative and referendum, and the election of United States senators by direct vote of the people. These reforms, together with others pointing in the same direction, were soon adopted. The Populists also insisted that the national government should use its power to bring about the more active control of the railroads and the trusts, reforms that both the Theodore Roosevelt and the Woodrow Wilson administrations made every effort to achieve. The Populists likewise called emphatic attention to the defects of the American banking and currency system; if they were better on diagnosis than on prescription, the agitation for reform that they began certainly had something to do with the subsequent study of the problem,

and the eventual adoption during the Wilson administration of the Federal Reserve System. It is noteworthy in this connection that William Jennings Bryan himself, twice nominated by the Populists for President, played a conspicuous part in the drafting of the Federal Reserve Act. The Populists were also aware of the need for some better system of rural credits, an end ultimately served by the Federal Farm Loan Act of 1916. They struggled with the problem of agricultural marketing, and devised the "sub-Treasury plan" which set interesting precedents for the marketing measures of the 1920's and the 1930's. They wanted a more equitable system of taxation, and in due time the graduated income tax they favored became the cornerstone of the federal taxation system. They were frightened by what they termed "the end of free land," and their resentment against the defects in the national land policy contributed to the adoption later of conservation and reclamation projects of vast importance. It would be absurd to argue that Populism alone was responsible for all these achievements, but it would be equally absurd to deny that third-party activities were important in bringing them about.

BIBLIOGRAPHY

On economic conditions leading to the Panic of 1893 and the depression that followed, the basic monograph is still F. P. Weberg, *The Background of the Panic of 1893* (1929). But see also Rendigs Fels, *American Business Cycles, 1865–1897* (1959), which benefits from a new generation of economic analysis. Among the many contemporary studies that involve the silver question, F. W. Taussig, *The Silver Situation in the United States* (1893), is probably the best. For the inflationists' more spectacular arguments, see W. H. Harvey, *Coin's Financial School* (1894), a classic in protest. One of the finest books ever written about tariff-making is F. P. Summers, *William L. Wilson and Tariff Reform* (1953).

The vast literature on the great 1896 campaign may be sampled in *William Jennings Bryan and the Campaign of 1896* (1953), edited by G. F. Whicher. An excellent documentary collection is *Issues of the Populist and Progressive Eras, 1892–1912* (1969), edited by R. M. Abrams. No less than three recent books focus on the election: S. L. Jones, *The Presidential Election of 1896* (1964); P. W. Glad, *McKinley, Bryan, and the People* (1964); and R. F. Durden, *The Climax of Populism* (1965). On the Republican candidate the most balanced study is H. W. Morgan, *William McKinley and His America* (1963); Margaret Leech, *In the Days of McKinley* (1959), is impressionistic. The best work on Hanna is Herbert Croly, *Marcus Alonzo Hanna* (1912); but see also Thomas Beer, *Hanna* (1929). Two interesting journals of the period have been published: C. G. Dawes, *A Journal of the McKinley Years* (1950), edited by B. E. Timmons; and *The Cabinet Diary of William L. Wilson, 1896–1897* (1957), edited by F. P. Summers.

The Democratic candidate has at last been accorded a full-length scholarly biography, P. E. Coletta, *William Jennings Bryan* (3 vols., 1964–1969). An excellent short study is P. W. Glad, *The Trumpet Soundeth: William Jennings Bryan and His Democracy, 1896–1912* (1960). Glad has also edited *William Jennings Bryan: A Profile* (1968). See also Bryan's own book on 1896, *The First Battle* (1897), and the posthumous *Memoirs of William Jennings Bryan*, published by his widow in 1925. *Selections from William Jennings Bryan* (1967), edited by Ray Ginger, is the work of a vehement non-admirer.

Valuable books on the politics of this and the succeeding period include W. A. White, *Masks in a Pageant* (1928), which contains an intriguing sketch of McKinley; Matthew Josephson, *The President Makers, 1896–1919* (1940), a disillusioned liberal survey; R. B. Nye, *Midwestern Progressive Politics* (1951);

and J. R. Hollingsworth, *The Whirligig of Politics: The Democracy of Cleveland and Bryan* (1963). From this point onward the basic compilation of election statistics is E. E. Robinson, *The Presidential Vote, 1896–1932* (1934).

Attention should be given to other aspects of protest politics in the period. On the Single Taxers, see the classic statement by Henry George, *Progress and Poverty* (1879); and C. A. Barker, *Henry George* (1955), the standard biography. C. A. Lloyd, *Henry Demarest Lloyd* (2 vols., 1912), is by a devoted daughter; see also the scholarly work of C. M. Destler, *Henry Demarest Lloyd and the Empire of Reform* (1963). On the Nationalist Movement, the best book is A. E. Morgan, *Edward Bellamy* (1944); but Bellamy's novel, *Looking Backward, 2000–1887* (1887), is of fundamental importance for all its stylistic limitations. The basic guide to Socialism in the United States is the splendid cooperative work edited by D. D. Egbert and Stow Persons, *Socialism and American Life* (2 vols., 1952); its second volume is a massive bibliography put together by T. D. S. Bassett. An able survey of the movement to 1900, in all its significant aspects, is Howard Quint, *The Forging of American Socialism* (1953). An excellent case-study is H. F. Bedford, *Socialism and the Workers in Massachusetts, 1886–1912* (1966). Interesting treatments of leading figures and their thoughts may be found in Daniel Aaron, *Men of Good Hope* (1951); and C. A. Madison, *Critics and Crusaders* (2nd ed., 1958). *Late Nineteenth-Century American Liberalism: Representative Selections, 1880–1900* (1962), edited by Louis Filler, is a useful collection.

9

SOCIETY IN THE GILDED AGE

The rise of the city · The urban South and West · Urban uniformity · Tenements and slums · The vulgar rich · City government · Tammany and Tweed · Municipal corruption · Business ethics · Rural and village life · Practical Christianity · Roman Catholicism · Judaism · Godkin, Curtis, and Schurz · Pulitzer and Hearst · Urban reform · Women's rights · Educational changes · The Centennial Exposition

The Rise of the City

In 1874 Mark Twain, in collaboration with Charles Dudley Warner, published *The Gilded Age*, a satire on the corruption and fortune-chasing of the times that gave its name to the next twenty years. Twain was raised in a Missouri village, and most of his writings involved the people of the Mississippi River countryside. Despite Twain's concern with the rural life of the Middle and Far West, the most startling development of post-Civil War America, and the one most portentous for the future, was the almost astronomical growth of the industrial city. Before the war America's few great cities had been largely commercial. With some notable exceptions the markets for the goods they produced were in their own immediate surroundings.

The elements producing the national market for manufactured goods, and in large part responsible for the rise of the metropolis, were numerous. Among the more potent were: (1) the development of the stationary steam engine; (2) the great wave of impoverished European immigrants to supply the power needed for mass production; (3) the national network of railroads to convey goods to all parts of the country; and (4) the mentality of the new industrialists which was national in sweep instead of provincial, and was willing to take large chances in the hope of large rewards. The goods produced by such a national system, although not necessarily better than homemade articles or those produced by local artisans, were certainly more novel, and in the end far cheaper both in money and time required for manufacture. The new production was accepted with enthusiasm by consumers, and almost every town and city in the country avidly hailed the growth of new factories.

LAWN TENNIS on Staten Island (1899).

The City of Chicago, 1892. *This print shows the Lake Michigan waterfront, the harbor, and the Chicago River, as well as the square-block plan of the city. Note the relatively large proportion of sailing craft to steamships.*

The Urban South and West

While the Northeast led the way in urbanization, other sections were excellent imitators. The South, during and after reconstruction, attempted eagerly to crowd itself with factories and cities. As Henry Watterson put it, "The South having had its bellyful of blood, has gotten a taste of money, and is too busy trying to make more to quarrel with anybody." The new industrialism became almost a religion throughout the reviving section. "Next to God, what this town needs," said an evangelist in the 1890's of Salisbury, North Carolina, "is a cotton mill." The West, too, tried hard to be free of its heavy dependence on agriculture, which made no one rich, and to embrace industry, which offered wealth to at least a few. In 1871 the Milwaukee Chamber of Commerce lamented:

We are sending our hard lumber east to get it back as furniture and agricultural implements, we ship ore to St. Louis and New York, to pay the cost of bringing it back as shot, type, pipe, sheet lead, white lead, paint, etc., we ship away our wool crop and import cloth, carpets, blankets and other fabrics; we give rags for paper, and hides for boots and harness, and iron-ore for stoves — and our consumers all the while are paying the double costs of this unnecessary transportation.

What this Chamber of Commerce really wanted for Milwaukee was factories, of whatever kind, and Milwaukee soon got them. So also did every other enterprising western city with good railroad or water connections. In 1870 only 20.9 per cent of the American population lived in places of eight thousand inhabitants or more, whereas by 1903, 33.1 per cent were so situated. In the East the percentage of city dwellers ran well above this figure; in the South, the Middle West, and the Far West, well below it. But the trend toward urbanization was national, not sectional, and it affected every part of the country. By 1900 twenty-five million Americans had become city dwellers in a nation that only a few decades earlier had been one largely of farms and woods.

While in every section villages were rapidly becoming towns and towns cities, in

HOME INSURANCE BUILDING. This Chicago skyscraper, located at the northeast corner of LaSalle and Adams Streets, was erected in 1884, the first of its kind.

FLAT IRON BUILDING. This early contribution to skyscraper architecture has long been a landmark at Madison Square, New York, where Broadway, Fifth Avenue, and Twenty-third Street converge.

THE SKYSCRAPER ERA. *The use of structural steel and the electric elevator enabled architects to erect such "cathedrals of commerce" as these. Probably the skyscraper was the most distinctive American contribution to architecture.*

the post-Civil War decades it was the half dozen or so great metropolitan centers that most attracted attention. This occurred in part because of their spectacular growth. Chicago, still a small town of 30,000 in 1850, reached a half million in 1880, and twenty years later had become the second city in the nation with a population of 1.7 million, compared to that of over 3 million for New York. By the same date Minneapolis and Los Angeles, virtually villages at the start of the Civil War, were cities of 200,000 and 100,000. Birmingham, Alabama, nourished by the coal and iron industry, had grown from nothing in 1871 to 38,000 by 1900. The smaller part of this new population had come from the natural increase of native urban dwellers; perhaps a third more were Americans attracted from native farms and villages. But about 50 per cent of the total urban growth from 1870 to 1900 came from abroad. By the end of the century three-fourths of Chicago's population had been born abroad, and for New York, an even larger fraction.

In the face of such developments it was not strange that native-born Americans were asking whether the nation's traditions and institutions could long be preserved.

Urban Uniformity

The new cities and the rejuvenated old ones showed remarkable similarities. According to James Bryce, "American cities with eight or nine exceptions differ from one another only herein, that some of them are built more with brick than with wood, and others more with wood than brick." The checkerboard of "squares" in which William Penn had laid out Philadelphia became the favorite American pattern for city development, and each new "addition" strove valiantly to be exactly like the rest. Pavements rarely kept up with expansion, and while asphalt and brick won increasing popularity, cobblestone, stone block, wood block, and macadam continued in general use. Telephone, telegraph, and electric light poles and wires, all rare or missing in the seventies, were common by the nine-

The Bowery at Night, 1896.
Electric illumination did much to dispel the darkness and lessen the danger of city streets, but the increased traffic in crowded centers offered new, if brighter, hazards.

ties, and competed with trees and fences for space at the sides of roads and railroads. Business districts at any given time were everywhere much alike, but each decade saw the height of downtown buildings increase. The first of the skyscrapers, made possible by the use of structural steel and iron, was the ten-storied Home Insurance Building of Chicago, completed in 1885. Thereafter, with one accord, city skylines rose, while traffic congestion increased in spite of the best efforts of horsecars, cable cars, and elevated railways to keep pace with it.

The Urban Worker

Behind these externals lay a pattern of life that varied little from city to city. The great majority of city-dwellers were employees of industry or trade, dependent upon wages for their daily bread. Wages, judged by present-day standards, were incredibly low; by 1900 American workers, on an average, earned between $300 and $400 a year at a time when a dollar might be worth perhaps only four or five times what it is worth today. The unskilled worker might receive as much as $1.50 a day for his efforts, but he was often unemployed; a total take of $4 or $5 a week was not unusual. For such persons there were then no unemployment benefits; if one were out

of work for long, he begged, borrowed, stole, or starved. The working day was ordinarily ten hours, and the six-day week was taken for granted. Accidents among industrial employees were numerous, and too lightly regarded by employers. The employment of women and children in industry tended to hold wages down, but was for many families an absolute necessity. While a few women in the upper strata of society grumbled that the opportunity for "careers" was still in large measure denied them, those on the lower levels suffered no such privations. The percentage of women gainfully employed rose from 15 per cent in 1870 to 20 per cent in 1900. In Philadelphia, by the latter year, one third of all women (counting girls over ten years of age) worked for wages away from their homes. Wherever it could be used to advantage, child labor was ruthlessly exploited — in the cotton mills of the South, in the sweatshops of the East, in the packing-plants of the West. According to one estimate, there were not less than 10 million people in the United States living in abject poverty, people who, "though using their best efforts, are failing to obtain sufficient necessaries for maintaining physical efficiency."

Poverty existed abundantly in the city even during normal times. In periods of

An Early Telephone Exchange. *This 1888 photograph of a "central" office on Cortland Street, New York, is a far cry from the automation in use today. Note also the differences in styles of dress, hair arrangements, and furniture.*

sharp economic reverse, it doubled and trebled and was accompanied by acute distress and actual starvation. The business cycle with its sharp ups and downs had, of course, operated before the Panic of 1873. The financial panics of 1837 and 1857 had had serious repercussions in the financial and commercial community, but unemployment and starvation on any large scale did not occur because America was still a land pre-eminently devoted to farming, and while the farmer might have had little money in his pocket during hard times and might even lose title to his land, he was still able to provide food and shelter for his family. This was often impossible for the industrial worker in the grim years after 1873, and as a result the stricken cities spawned privation, breadlines, and radicalism.

Tenements and Slums

The long depressions of the seventies and the nineties served to emphasize the incredibly wretched living conditions of the industrial worker in American cities. About 90 per cent of the workers lived in rented quarters, the best of which were none too good and the worst, usually known as tenements, indescribably noisome. Since no major cities had effective building codes

and the price of real estate was mounting yearly, owners sought to get as much return from every square inch of property as possible. The usual tenement, the pattern for which probably originated in New York in the 1840's, was a three to six story structure of brick or wood. Cold water was usually provided from one tap on the ground floor, and there might be one toilet, often in the cellar, although in the early days it was usually located outside the building. Until the 1890's the tenements were often without fire escapes, and access to the upper floors was by a single staircase. Many of the rooms were miserably lighted, since the next tenement building was but two or three feet away, and many interior rooms had no outside ventilation. A New York housing commission of 1888 found that into one, two, or three of these "small dirty pen-like rooms" were often packed families of ten or fifteen people. No comparable living conditions could be found, the New York Commission concluded, even "in the worst slums of Europe." In an age when ignorance of the simplest sanitary precautions was rivaled only by indifference to those that were known, preventable diseases such as smallpox, typhoid, and typhus took a heavy toll

THE INSIDE OF A CHICAGO SLUM, 1891.

CITY TENEMENTS. *The miserable conditions of life in the slum districts of American cities toward the end of the nineteenth century are here graphically portrayed.*

"DENS OF DEATH AT THE FIVE POINTS."
From a photograph in the Jacob A. Riis collection.

from even the more fortunate part of the population. In the slums the death rate was staggering. At any one time three-fourths of the sickness and death in New York City occurred among the less favored half of the population.

The Vulgar Rich

Hardly less distressing than the plight of the poor was the vulgar ostentation of a small army of *parvenu* rich. War profiteers, successful speculators, oil men and miners who had "struck it rich," flocked to the cities to display their wealth. Few could approximate the extravagances of the notorious Jim Fisk, but many tried. Fisk, at the height of his glory, had sumptuous offices in "Castle Erie," a huge marble building on Eighth Avenue in New York that also housed his privately owned and operated Grand Opera House. From his theatrical stars and dancers, many of whom were imported, he recruited a harem that might well have been the envy of an Oriental potentate. The chief recipients of his favor lived in palaces, and took the air in fine carriages, drawn sometimes, when Fisk went along, by three teams of splendid horses, whites to the left and blacks to the right. Among Fisk's other fancies were canary birds, hundreds of which, in gilded cages, adorned his rooms, and the well-appointed steamboats that he owned and loved. On occasion he would dress himself in the gold lace of an admiral's uniform, and once, when so arrayed, he contrived to receive President Grant. The colonelcy of the Ninth Regiment of the New York National Guard, a position he obtained by means of generous gifts, furnished him with another opportunity for gaudy pageantry. During the summer of 1871 he took the entire regiment to Boston at his own expense to celebrate the anniversary of the battle of Bunker Hill. He died on January 7, 1872, from bullet wounds inflicted by one of his own kind, Edward S. Stokes, a "business and amatory rival." Stokes, for

THE GEORGE WASHINGTON JONES FAMILY EN ROUTE TO PARIS.

THE VULGAR RICH. *What sudden wealth and foreign travel could do to simple-minded Americans is the theme of these two drawings by A. B. Frost, published in* Harper's Weekly, *August 24, October 12, 1878.*

THE GEORGE WASHINGTON JONES FAMILY RETURNS FROM PARIS.

his crime, was sentenced to four years in the penitentiary at Sing Sing, but there he received many special privileges, such as being permitted to drive about at night with the span of horses he kept for the purpose at a local livery stable. On his release he became the proprietor of the Hoffman House at Broadway and Twenty-sixth Street, New York, a hotel chiefly noted for the daring paintings on its barroom walls.

The Plutocracy

Even more alarming to many thoughtful Americans than the vulgar exploits of men like Fisk were the more restrained but perhaps more socially significant actions of "the new plutocracy," as it was called. To demonstrate their wealth, these people built enormous mansions and attempted to live like the nobility of the old world. Their entertainments were princely in extravagance. The apogee of such spectacles was probably reached in 1897 when the Bradley Martins rented much of the Waldorf Astoria Hotel and converted it at a cost of over $100,000 into a replica of Versailles. The arriving guests, dressed in what they thought the proper costumes for the court of the Sun King (Louis XIV), were led by August Belmont, whose suit of gold inlaid armor cost a small fortune. Since the close of the Civil War the jeweler Tiffany had done a booming business in designing family crests. And after 1874 when Jennie Jerome, daughter of a Wall Street broker, married Lord Randolph Churchill, many other American families of the "upper crust" sought to insure their place in this incontestable elite by similar international exchanges. William Waldorf Astor, whose ancestor had arrived in the United States as a penniless immigrant, even settled in England, where by the judicious use of money he soon acquired a seat in the House of Lords. At home his relative, Mrs. William Astor, contented herself by leading the *creme de la creme* of American society, or "the four hundred," as it was called, after the remark of her friend Ward McAllister, who intimated in 1888 that there were only about four hundred people in New York who really counted. Mark Twain's dry comment that we were "all descended from Adam" reflected the dominant sentiment, but it did not dispel the fear that the old egalitarian and democratic American traditions were threatened with extinction.

John Jacob Astor IV's Mansion *at the northeast corner of Fifth Avenue and Sixty-fifth Street, New York, from a photograph taken about 1901. The mansion was designed by R. M. Hunt.*

City Government

The burgeoning city was regarded as a sinkhole of iniquities by the average rural citizen. The character of its population, the great economic and social disparities between its classes, the activities of its very rich and very poor, and the conditions of its slums all excited censure and revulsion. But perhaps the most striking urban failure was that of city government. After a study of American governments preparatory to writing his famous *The American Commonwealth* (1888), James Bryce called city administration "the one conspicuous failure in the United States." Everywhere from New York to San Francisco the condition seemed the same. In almost every sizable city a corrupt city boss, usually not himself holding office, controlled the elected mayor and the city council, who in turn levied taxes and let clusters of contracts for paving streets, laying sewers, building schools, and other public works. These officials also had the power to grant lucrative utilities franchises to private enterprisers for street railways, the supply of gas, electric power, and water. A long-term franchise — sometimes running for fifty years — giving a monopoly to a street railway company, with guaranteed incomes double and treble a fair return on the capital invested, offered the chance for millions of dollars in profits which were usually split between the fortunate capitalist and the boodling ring of city officials. A good portion of the returns were channeled to the boss, who divided the spoils among his followers in the city wards and precincts. They, in turn, used a part of the funds to help the poor and provide them with cheap entertainment and drink. The rest was pocketed. The precinct and ward captains parcelled out city jobs among the faithful and interceded with friendly judges, often members of the machine, when their clients fell afoul the law. Often the local ward boss was the only friend in power whom the poor immigrant had, and the clubhouse of the political machine the only social service agency he knew. For such benevolent activities the machine asked for only one thing, votes on election day; and if gratitude was unlikely to move a citizen, there was usually money to buy his franchise. So the machines repeatedly triumphed at the polls, despite reformers who declaimed for lower taxes, abolition of graft, and the regulation or abolition of saloons. Since the numerous poor had no property to tax, since a portion of the graft helped ease their lot, and since liquor was in times of complete disaster often their only solace, they voted the ticket straight.

Tammany and Tweed

As befitted its size and prominence, New York City furnished the country with the outstanding example of municipal corruption. There the Tammany Society, a political organization that dated back to the eighteenth century, controlled the local machinery of the Democratic Party, and regularly rolled up huge majorities. Tammany Hall, as the society was usually called (after its meeting-place on Fourteenth Street), won the support of the masses by providing the services mentioned above. When Grant became President of the United States the "Grand Sachem" of Tammany Hall was William M. Tweed, a thoroughgoing corruptionist who had worked his way up in politics from membership in a volunteer fire department. Tweed's opportunity for wholesale graft came after he and his associates by the most barefaced bribery had secured from the state legislature a city charter specifically designed to let them avoid responsibility for their crimes. The principals of the "Tweed Ring" were "Boss" Tweed himself, whose presidency of the board of supervisors of New York County (coterminous with New York City) had obvious possibil-

THE TAMMANY TIGER LOOSE. Nast's portrayal of the mauling of the Republic, one of his most memorable cartoons, was credited' with bringing about the downfall of the Ring. From *Harper's Weekly*, November 11, 1871.

THE TWEED RING. *This group of New York City grafters showed the depths to which political depravity could fall, even in a democracy. But these cartoons indicate also how public opinion could be aroused against such offenders. In the end the Ring had to go.*

WHAT ARE YOU LAUGHING AT? TO THE VICTOR BELONG THE SPOILS. Another Nast cartoon, this time celebrating the collapse of the Ring. From *Harper's Weekly*, November 25, 1871.

ities; A. Oakey Hall, the mayor, an aspirant for social recognition whose fastidious appearance won him the sobriquet, "Elegant Oakey"; Peter B. Sweeny, treasurer of both city and county, useful for his position, and for his unquestioned ability as a lawyer; and Richard B. Connolly, the controller, otherwise and appropriately known as "Slippery Dick." In 1869 this crew began a series of peculations that mounted year by year until at the height of their power they were dividing among themselves and their confederates 85 per cent of the total expenditures made by the city and county. Tweed received as his share 24 per cent of the "take," and the rest was apportioned by prearranged plan. The actual cost of maintaining the city's armories, for example, totaled for a given period $250,000, but the amount paid out allegedly for that purpose was $3.2 million. Building a courthouse cost about $3 million, but the county's books showed expenditures of about $11 million. Plastering alone cost the taxpayers nearly $2.9 million and carpeting $350,000 — "enough to cover the whole City Park three times." In one period of thirty months the city and county printing bill ran to over $7 million. It is probable that the loot taken by the Tweed Ring reached a staggering $100 million.

At last, scathing editorials in the *New York Times*, and cartoons by Thomas Nast in *Harper's Weekly*, began to take effect, and the public was aroused. George Jones, the owner of the *Times*, was offered a million dollars to quiet his paper, and Nast, a half million to go to Europe and give up his campaign of caricature. Long baffled for lack of direct evidence, the *Times* finally got the proofs it needed from an insider with a grievance. The exposure that followed was complete and devastating, the more so when the efforts of Tweed, Hall, and Sweeny to lay the entire blame on Connolly drove the latter to open his records to the reformers. Under the brilliant leadership of Samuel J. Tilden and Charles O'Conor, they were able by the end of 1872 to drive every member of the "ring" out of office. Tweed himself died in jail.

Municipal Corruption

Since almost every sizable city had its variation of Tammany Hall, some of the nation's rural minded reformers came to believe that the city was the natural habitat of corruption and vice. More serious students of government, like James Bryce, felt that the explanation lay in the large proportion of immigrants in the American urban population. The immigrants, Bryce explained, impoverished, uneducated, and with little or no democratic experience in their native countries, were the natural prey of political bosses. But such explanations were hardly fair either to the city or to the immigrants. For Cincinnati, St. Louis, Minneapolis, and San Francisco, where the older stock of Americans were in the majority, exhibited much of the same blight. And if the city as an institution was corrupt, it did not hold a monopoly on dis-

honesty. The Grant administration was known, even before it ended, as the most corrupt that the republic had yet experienced. Reconstruction, with its attempt to maintain the power of the northern Radicals by forcing alien rule on the South, would have been a scandal even if honestly carried out, but the number of honest officials in the "carpetbag" South seems to have been minimal. Yet the scandals that rocked the country were as frequently associated with the North or the West as with the South. The Crédit Mobilier, the Whiskey Ring, the frauds in the Indian Service, had no Southern nor strictly urban connotation. Obviously, the moral standards of the entire nation during the postwar years sank to a new low.

Moral Laxness

Illustrating the trend of the times was the notorious Beecher-Tilton divorce trial. Henry Ward Beecher was one of the most influential ministers in the country. Discarding the orthodox views of his well known father, Lyman Beecher, he preached a mixture of the new liberal theology and a strictly orthodox economic and social policy, a combination which pleased not only his own wealthy Brooklyn congregation but many influential Protestant lay and clerical leaders throughout the country. His sermons were reprinted and often cited as the last word in matters where theology and social policy merged. A good portion of the nation was aghast, and the rest perhaps titillated, when in 1875 a member of Beecher's congregation, Theodore Tilton, brought suit against him for alienation of his wife's affections, charging adultery. Verbatim accounts of the trial, together with Beecher's letters to Mrs. Tilton, were widely circulated. And although the jury could come to no decision, the effect of the case upon the nation was hardly conducive to the raising of ethical standards.

Henry Ward Beecher. *This eminent clergyman was the son of Lyman Beecher, the well-known pre-Civil War Presbyterian minister, and the brother of Harriet Beecher Stowe. The doubts cast on his personal behavior in the Beecher-Tilton adultery case came as a shock to the entire nation.*

Business Ethics

A similar lack of ethics permeated business. The almost universal devotion of Americans to the pursuit of wealth was in itself notorious, but the devious means men used to gain it hit at the very foundations of society. In part this laxity of conduct could be blamed on the war, during which millions of young people learned their first lessons in adult morality, lessons they naturally took with them into private life. But the war can hardly be blamed for every evil practice of the business world. Far more important was the utter novelty of large-scale business operations. Before the war most business was small and its activity local. Standards of conduct existed which the prudent businessman, to retain the good will of his customers and the public, felt obliged to recognize. But for national large-scale business no code of ethics had yet been evolved. With monopoly, or at least near-monopoly, as a goal, the struggle for survival among competitors was intense, and usually only the ruthless had a chance to win. The law offered no restraints, for,

since such problems had not been faced before, laws to meet them had not been devised. Furthermore, as business organizations grew in size and power they found that they could, when they chose, have a hand in both the making and the enforcement of laws. The situation was not unlike that on the high seas in the days when piracy and buccaneering, unchallenged by international law, amounted almost to legitimate occupations.

Corporation methods of finance offered an opportunity, never long neglected, for astounding frauds in the issuance and manipulation of stocks and bonds. "Wild-cat" or "blue-sky" securities were easily sold to a public made gullible by the unprecedented number of fortunes that the "boom" times actually produced. Oil companies were organized that never drilled a well, mining companies that never sank a shaft, railroad companies that never laid a rail — all for the sole purpose of separating careless investors from their savings. General Robert C. Schenck, an ex-congressman from Ohio whom Grant sent as Minister to England, gave his support to the promoters of a mining venture that sold $50,000 worth of worthless stock to British investors. Schenck further distinguished himself by writing a treatise on poker-playing. General George B. McClellan, more innocently, backed a $10 million corporation that proposed to exploit a mythical diamond and ruby field in California.

Even the most substantial corporations were frequently led to "water" their stock and to incur bonded indebtedness altogether out of proportion to their assets. Daniel Drew, a pious old fraud who hoped to purchase pardon for his sins by making generous pledges, seldom paid, to Drew Theological Seminary, wormed his way into the directorate of the Erie Railway, became its treasurer, and for years manipulated the price of its stock in order to make himself rich. According to a current

Wall Street saying: "Dan'l says up — Erie goes up. Dan'l says down — Erie goes down. Dan'l says wiggle-waggle — Erie bobs both ways." In 1868 Cornelius Vanderbilt, who already controlled the New York Central and the Hudson River railroads, proposed to add the badly run-down Erie to his domain. A battle royal followed in which Drew, supported by his apt "pupils," Jay Gould and Jim Fisk, finally won. To do so, however, Drew and his associates found it necessary to issue 50,000 shares of fraudulent stock, to flee to New Jersey in order to escape arrest, and to bribe the New Jersey legislature to legalize their transaction. But Drew's luck did not hold. His two "pupils" raised the price of the Erie stock by sales abroad, thanklessly cornered their teacher, and trimmed him of a million and a half. The Panic of 1873 also hit him hard, and by 1876 he was bankrupt with liabilities of over a million dollars and no assets to speak of.

Not many types of sizable business enterprise came through the cycles of boom and depression with clean records. Three new York savings banks failed in 1872 under the most scandalous circumstances; while small investors suffered acutely, the former bank officials continued to live in luxury. During the first eight years of the seventies, twenty-eight New York life insurance companies failed outright, or avoided failure by amalgamation with stronger concerns. Losses to policy-holders amounted to a nominal total of $158 million in insurance. Even the solvent companies unblushingly "froze out" aged and undesirable policy-holders, usually by increasing rates. "The whole chapter," said the *Commercial and Financial Chronicle*,[1] "is so dark a record of betrayal of corporate trust —incapacity being so blended with dishonesty that it is impossible to separate them — that if we had the space and the data, we should

not have the desire to expose its details."

In the city, the state, and the nation, in business and in private life, wherever the citizen looked he saw graft, corruption, and unethical conduct. James Russell Lowell expressed the national sense of humiliation when he wrote, apropos of the opening of the Centennial Exposition at Philadelphia in 1876:

Columbia, puzzled what she should display
Of true home-make on her Centennial Day,
Asked Brother Jonathan; he scratched his head
Whittled awhile reflectively, and said,

.   .   .   .

Show your State Legislatures; show your
    Rings;
And challenge Europe to produce such things
As high officials sitting half in sight
To share the plunder and to fix things right;
If that don't fetch her, why you only need
To show your latest style in martyrs — Tweed.
She'll find it hard to hide her spiteful tears
At such advance in one poor hundred years.

Rural Life

Lowell's bitter sarcasm well expressed the hopelessness that overcame so many Americans when they listed the nation's shortcomings. Nevertheless, there was a brighter side even if most men failed to see it. For the United States was not merely a nation of corrupt political machines, of slums, and of grafters in low and high places. The great majority of city dwellers were, of course, honest, and more than 60 per cent of the people, as late as 1900, still lived in the country, or in towns of less than 4,000 inhabitants. Practically all of these, and many more besides, depended directly or indirectly upon agriculture for their livelihood. Even the cities owed much to the farms, for throughout the nineteenth century an abundant farm demand, restrained from foreign purchases by a protective-tariff policy, absorbed the products of the city factories, and spared American manufacturers the necessity of finding

[1] April 19, 1879.

in foreign markets an outlet for their goods. For agriculture, as for industry, these were revolutionary years. New tools had to be devised and used, new types of crops raised to suit city markets, experiments with diversification and standardization had to be carried through, a rising price for farmlands had to be faced. Less and less, the American farmer farmed according to ritual; more and more he used his intelligence and the reports of scientific investigators to improve his profits. Caught securely in the meshes of the prevailing economic system, he made every effort to understand it and to bend it to his needs. The farmer movements of the period were not the work of wild-eyed radicals; the farm leaders and a host of well-informed followers based their arguments upon reasoning as sound as that which guided the actions of the prudent industrialists. The interests of the farmers perhaps collided with those of the industrialists, but that did not necessarily make farm policies radical.

Village Life

Farm life tended gradually to merge with village life. On Saturdays farmers went to town to trade; on Sundays they went to town to church; on other days when work was not too pressing they went to town, with or without excuses. Retired farmers went to town to live and to be visited by their children, who in many cases were now their tenants. Farm boys and girls went to school in town, got jobs in town, and, when they could, set out with the town boys and girls for the city. Farmers and farm wives borrowed from the town the conveniences that the town had borrowed from the city. Steadily, the isolation of farm life broke down — a process that the rural free delivery of mail, rural telephones, rural electrification, the automobile, and the radio were soon to accelerate immeasurably.

Country towns and villages enjoyed an importance during most of the nineteenth century that they have since entirely lost. As centers of trade for the surrounding countryside, they could almost count on a steady amount of weekly business. The stores might be strung along a single "Main Street," or they might surround a central "square" on which, in county-seats, the courthouse was certain to be located. Only in the business districts of the larger towns were the streets paved, and both horses and

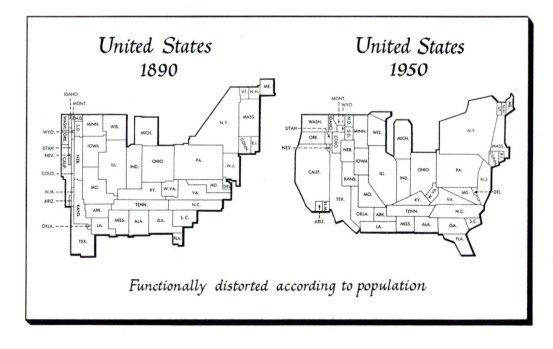

Functionally distorted according to population

The Country School. *This painting by Winslow Homer lacked only more children — many more — to make it truly authentic. These "little red schoolhouses," according to James Russell Lowell, were the "Martello Towers" that protected American democracy.*

The One-Room Country School *sometimes took this form in the Rocky Mountain West. This picture is of a Johnson County, Wyoming, schoolhouse in use, 1906–1907.*

drivers took mud, ruts, and dust philosophically. The dwellings, at least on one side of the inevitable railroad tracks, were commodious, set well back from tree-lined streets, and surrounded by large lawns. Barns and outbuildings were numerous, for many townspeople kept a horse or two to draw the family "buggy," a cow, a pig to butcher in the fall, and some poultry. There was usually room for a few fruit trees and a vegetable garden. The incomes of villagers were not large, but they had no need to be to provide a decent and adequate life.

All the town paid deference to the railroad. Incoming passenger trains were met by as many of the inhabitants as were footloose, and arrivals and departures were carefully noted. The station agent was an individual of importance who often asserted his dignity by a superb indifference to the wants of customers. For over the railroad all of the town's foreign commerce was conducted, and by means of it and the telegraph line that seemed a part of it, contact with the rest of the world was maintained. Resentment against railroad extortion was rife, especially in the West, and campaigns for railroad regulation merged into demands for government ownership. But the awe-inspiring importance of the railroad was never forgotten. Not infrequently the railroad companies played leading roles in local as well as in state and national politics.

Crime and misdemeanors were not unknown in the countryside and the village, as any reading of the court files in a county courthouse will attest. Throughout the western part of the Middle West, and especially from West Virginia to Arkansas, the region over which much of the Civil War had been fought, bands of ruffians continued their wartime habits and for years escaped arrest. Most noted of these outlaws was Jesse James, who in 1872 robbed the Kansas City Fair of $10,000, and until the time of his death a decade later kept the Kansas-Missouri border in a state of frightened expectancy.

Rural Religion

But on the whole there were only two social classes, usually clustered around three institutions, the saloon and the pool hall on the one hand, and the church on the other. Although economic standing had little to do with the division, almost invariably the leading professional, business, and tradespeople belonged to the sober, moral, church-going majority, and if they felt the impulse to transgress they usually left for a holiday in the distant city. At the center of the town's social life was the church. In every village on a Sunday morning the calm was shattered at regular intervals by the jangling of bells of not less than three or four rival Protestant denominations. Church services went on all day, and attendance was good: Sunday school at ten, preaching at eleven, children's services in the afternoon, young people's meetings at seven, evening worship with liberal congregational singing at eight. Weekday services included prayer-meetings on Wednesday evening, to which only a handful of the most devout repaired; better attended meetings of ladies' aid societies, missionary societies, and guilds, all absorbed in money-raising efforts; choir-practice for the faithful, if somewhat storm-tossed, musical contingent; and "protracted meetings," or "revivals," held night after night for several weeks once or twice each year. For these long meetings evangelists were often called in to aid the local pastors, and with good luck hundreds might be induced to "make their profession of faith." The old emotionalism of the frontier was not quite dead. "Shouting" was not unusual, "conversion" was for many an intensely exciting experience, and preaching reached the pinnacle of success when "not a dry eye was left in the house." A few country churches, each in its mournful setting of tombstones, still managed to survive, as the long rows of teams tied each Sunday to the church's hitch-racks well attested. Farm families, however, preferred increasingly to attend church in town, and so the country congregations dwindled.

But whether in country churches, or those in the towns and cities, many of these old Americans clung fast to many of their ethical ideas, a fact that perhaps in part explains the religious revival that swept through Protestant America during the 1870's. Poured forth from thousands of pulpits, the doctrine that the depression was but a just judgment upon men for their sins produced a multitude of penitents. Rivalry with the Roman Catholics and the Jews, whose numbers were being enormously increased by immigration, and rivalry among the various Protestant denominations themselves, spurred religious workers to greater and greater activity. Leadership was furnished less by the great preachers of the day, such as Henry Ward Beecher and Phillips Brooks, than by the evangelists, among whom Dwight L. Moody, the exhorter, and Ira D. Sankey, the singer, were pre-eminent. In 1875 Moody and Sankey, just returned from a series of successful revivals in the British Isles, began a meeting in Philadelphia that lasted three months, and then went on to New York, Chicago, Boston, and other great cities. In Chicago for four months their "tabernacle" was crowded daily by an audience of from five to ten thousand persons. The traditional doctrines of these evangelists, and of the host of lesser lights who imitated them, had little direct bearing on the social problems of the time, but they at least extolled the Christian virtues and filled "converts" with an earnest if unguided desire to better the lot of their fellow men.

Practical Christianity

The continued vitality of Protestantism which had sired so many new sects in the past was evidenced by the rapid spread of three organizations devoted to practical Christianity, and the birth and growth of still another important American creed. Far more conscious than the churches of the needs of the time were the Young Men's and Young Women's Christian Associations, both of which dated back to the middle of the century, but began to be really effective only during the seventies. Religion, for them, meant wholesome recreation, study classes, and even musicals, far more than the inculcation of Christian theology. Immediately effective among the submerged classes was the Salvation Army, which invaded the United States from England in 1879, and soon extended its interest from saving the souls of the down-and-out to an extensive program of social activity.

Quite at the other extreme of society was Christian Science, which took its tenets from *Science and Health with Key to the Scriptures*, a book published by Mrs. Mary Baker G. Eddy in 1875. Rejecting medicine, and claiming for the Divine Mind an absolute superiority over matter, the Christian Scientists preached a doctrine which, they claimed, wrought many healings of all types of disease and discord, and which, for a certainty, wrought notable cures among those whose nerves were unstrung by the increasing tempo of modern life. Its influence also reached over into other denominations and into medicine itself. While Christian Scientists were at pains not to ascribe their cures to the human will, the belief grew among those who made this assumption that a vigorous will had much to do with the attainment of happiness and health.

Roman Catholicism

Religious life was further stimulated by an old group in America, the Roman Cath-

Moody and Sankey. *These two noted evangelists held revival meetings in most large American cities. The picture shows them at their opening service in the Brooklyn "Rink." From* Harper's Weekly, *November 6, 1875.*

olics, whose numbers had materially grown with the Irish immigration of the forties and and fifties. In 1860 American Catholics, the largest group of which was Irish in extraction, numbered about 3.5 million or about 11 per cent of the population. Through the last half of the century the Catholic Church grew rapidly as thousands of its adherents from southern and eastern Europe poured into the country yearly. By 1890 Catholics constituted the largest single religious group in thirteen states. The enhanced stature of American Catholicism was acknowledged by the appointment of James Gibbons, Archbishop of Baltimore, in 1886 as the second American cardinal. For a time the church was internally divided over the questions whether good Catholics should or should not adapt their religious ideas to American beliefs, and whether each of the national groups in the rising church should have officials of its own nationality. Cardinal Gibbons was largely instrumental in upholding the doctrine of the separation of the church and state so that Catholics were comfortably able to fit their religion into the political ideas of their new country. Gibbons also took the position that the church should be unified and not separated into ethnic groups, a development which helped to explain the continuing strength of the Irish clergy in the hierarchy. Gibbons also did much to infuse the Catholic Church with a concern for the social and economic betterment of the laboring classes, a cause which was greatly aided in 1891 by Pope Leo XIII in his well known encyclical *De rerum novarum*, which emphasized the obligation of the state to the workingman. Catholicism, in fact, never lost its hold over its communicants in the working classes to the extent that Protestantism did during these years. Nor did this loyalty escape the observation of the anti-Catholic fanatics.[1]

[1] See p. 160.

Judaism

For most of the nineteenth century the Jewish communities in the nation remained relatively small. The heavy immigration from Germany before 1860 had added sizable numbers to the older colonial Jewish population. From this latter group came much of the impetus for a reform movement which closely paralleled the main developments in Protestantism. Led by Isaac Wise of Cincinnati, Reform Judaism looked toward "Americanization." Sunday instead of Saturday was adopted as the day of worship, the importance of traditional dogma was de-emphasized, and many of the old European customs were dropped. Beginning about 1890, however, the quickening stream of Jewish immigration from central and eastern Europe brought opposition to the reform movement. The great majority of these newcomers were impoverished and relatively uneducated people who, grouped together in city ghettos, became a force for conservatism. And since many of them continued to preserve their old ways and customs, most of which were utterly strange to native Americans, they became the object of bigotry. Anti-Semitism was almost absent from the nation before 1890. After that it grew rapidly, giving back-handed support to Conservative Judaism and the new Zionism founded in 1897 in Basle, Switzerland, by Theodor Herzl, which sought to re-establish a Jewish state in Palestine.

Godkin, Curtis, and Schurz

This intensification of religious life in the postwar decades was paralled by a quickening of social criticism that aimed its shafts not only at corruption and immorality but also at the prevailing spirit of materialism. Edwin Lawrence Godkin, George William Curtis, and Carl Schurz were three critics who deserve particular mention. A nation that could list such men among its leaders

CURTIS   GODKIN   SCHURZ

THREE REFORMERS. *George William Curtis, editor of* Harper's Weekly, *E. L. Godkin, editor of* The Nation, *and Carl Schurz, politician and publicist, played outstanding roles in developing a healthy public reaction against dishonesty in government, business, and private life.*

of thought had little reason to despair. Godkin (1831–1902) was of English stock, the son of a distinguished Protestant clergyman and journalist. After a brief newspaper career in England and Northern Ireland he emigrated in 1856 to America. Nine years later he established *The Nation*, a weekly newspaper, which rapidly became a major influence in American life and thought. According to James Bryce, *The Nation* was "the best weekly not only in America but in the world." Godkin was a stout defender of sound money and a laissez-faire social policy which included free trade. He also fearlessly denounced political corruption and business rascality, and was an ardent supporter of civil service reform. His weekly pronouncements on both politics and society were eagerly awaited by ministers, editors, and minor publicists who pushed the radius of *The Nation*'s influence far beyond the number of its readers.

George William Curtis (1824–1892), a New Englander by birth and intellectual tradition, in 1863 became editor of the strongly pro-northern *Harper's Weekly*, which in the ascendancy it soon gained over men's minds was rivaled only by *The Nation*. Although *Harper's Weekly* appealed to a far wider audience than *The Nation*, possibly because of its broader interests and because of its pictorial representations including the cartoons of Thomas Nast, it never was as militant or comprehensive in its demands for reform. Curtis' influence, however, was exerted from the lecture platform almost as actively as from the editor's desk. Scores of audiences heard his speech on "Political Infidelity," and scores more his excoriation of America for its worship of materialism.

But perhaps the most influential reforming voice from the platform belonged to Carl Schurz (1829–1906). German-born and educated, Schurz had to flee from his native country because of his part in the liberal revolutionary movements of 1848–49. Expelled from France as a radical, he

Joseph Pulitzer and the St. Louis Post Dispatch, *May 8, 1898. The headlines report Dewey's victory at Manila Bay. Portrait by John Singer Sargent, 1905.*

joined the German colony in Wisconsin, where he soon became a leader of the antislavery movement. A major-general in the Northern forces during the war, he afterwards made an official tour of the South at the behest of President Johnson. Subsequently he was a leader of the Liberal Republicans; for six years, 1869–1875, he represented Missouri in the United States Senate; after that he became Hayes's Secretary of the Interior. Schurz was a born orator, an intense democrat, and an ardent foe of business wrongdoing and political corruption. When he spoke in the Senate the galleries were packed, and great crowds turned out to hear his public lectures, which he always memorized and delivered impressively. He was an ardent civil service advocate, opposed Bryan in 1896 on free silver, but supported him in 1900 on antiimperialism.

Pulitzer and Hearst

By the 1890's two other powerful voices of a rather different nature had been added

to the swelling demand for reform. Joseph Pulitzer and William Randolph Hearst were the originators of the new mass chain newspapers that were to revolutionize urban journalism. Until their rise the most influential newspapers of the country had been identified with great editors like Horace Greeley of the *New York Tribune*. Educated and cultured, such men wrote and edited their newspapers for the literate middle and upper classes. Pulitzer and Hearst, on the other hand, deliberately set the tone of their papers to attract the masses of the cities. An impecunious Hungarian immigrant in 1864, Pulitzer acquired control of the *St. Louis Post-Dispatch* in 1878 and of the *New York World* five years later. Hearst was given the *San Francisco Examiner* by his wealthy father in 1887 and in 1895 acquired the *New York Journal*. Already Pulitzer had devised the new formula for "yellow journalism." Lowering the prices of his papers radically, he sprinkled them with a combination of sin, sex, and sensation, together with strident

Sport News. *From the front page of* The Daily Examiner, *July 9, 1889, Hearst's San Francisco paper.*

William Randolph Hearst

demands for reform. Hearst answered with even more sensationalism and more radicalism. Whatever else they might have done, the two men and their newspapers reached the great city masses and stimulated the growing reform spirit.

In the business and political world the work of Godkin, Curtis, Schurz, and later Hearst and Pulitzer, was not wholly without effect. Scandals were ruthlessly exposed, and sometimes, as in the case of Tweed, the guilty were punished. A governor in Nebraska and a state treasurer in Minnesota were impeached and removed from office. A member of the Kansas legislature laid on the speaker's desk $7,000 that he had been paid to vote for the re-election of Samuel C. Pomeroy to the United States Senate, and Pomeroy was not re-elected. The Whiskey Ring was put out of business; thievery in the Indian Service was restrained; wholesale attempts to bribe Congress, as in the Crédit Mobilier, were not again attempted; the Star Route frauds were denounced; a beginning was made

with civil service reform; corporation misconduct was brought into the open; and the people showed a disposition to use the power of government to restrain practices which interfered unjustly with the personal and property rights of individuals.

Urban Reform

Simultaneously both technology and a growing awareness of the evils of urban life were making the city a better place in which to live. The carbon arc electric lamp, and Thomas A. Edison's new incandescent bulb introduced in 1879, not only improved the lighting of the streets but resulted also in a noticeable reduction in crime. The construction of steam elevated railroads in New York during the late sixties, and the perfection of the electric trolley car at the end of the eighties, helped solve the problem of urban transportation. Better paving, more concern with pure water, and improved sanitation facilities followed, especially after the great typhoid outbreaks in Philadelphia and Chi-

Jane Addams. *One of America's greatest humanitarians and social reformers, Jane Addams was the founder of Hull House, Chicago, a slum-located center for the improvement of the city's community and civic life.*

cago in the eighties and nineties. Frederick Law Olmsted, an architect, had started a campaign before the Civil War to beautify cities and provide places for healthful relaxation through the construction of parks after European models. At the same time came a movement to establish playgrounds and playing fields where children and adults could get healthy exercise away from dirty and crowded streets.

Sports

Along with these developments came the rapid rise of organized sports. Baseball had its origins in what the English called "rounders," a game which, after considerable modification, the Americans called "town ball." As early as 1845 the Knicker-

bocker Club of New York provided a rule book for the game, but its popularity really dates from the Civil War, during which it was played with enthusiasm by both the wearers of the Blue and the wearers of the Gray. After the war, its devotees carried it to every part of the nation, North and South alike. During the seventies and eighties it developed into the "great American game," with a complicated system of major and minor leagues that every boy and youth in America understood. Football, which was introduced into the United States during the seventies as an adaptation of English Rugby, had by the nineties conquered most of the American colleges and universities. Professional boxing approached the level of respectability when "Gentleman Jim" Corbett won the heavyweight championship in 1892. By this time, too, the bicycle had been tamed, and bicycling had become a fad that women and children as well as men could enjoy. For devotees of the less strenuous life there were such milder activities as lawn-tennis, roller-skating, and croquet. The poor no less than the rich, town- and country-dwellers no less than city-dwellers, found in sports a satisfying refuge from the workaday world, which replaced, in a sense, the excitement once associated with a developing frontier. And, at least for masculine America, the activities recorded on the "sports page" furnished lively topics of conversation when all else failed.

By the end of the century most large cities had responded to the growing popular demand for parks and playgrounds. By that time also at least a start had been made to improve conditions in the squalid tenements. In 1879 a new type of tenement, with better toilet facilities and lighting, was introduced in New York, and during the next twenty years a number of housing committees made surveys and reports which were too often ignored. Perhaps more than any other man, Jacob Riis, an immigrant and a New York reporter, inspired reform by publishing *How the Other Half Lives* (1891), a book which had a national sale. Finally, in 1900 the New York Committee of Fifteen, which included John D. Rockefeller, Jr., Jacob H. Schiff, and George Foster Peabody, made a thorough study of slum housing which led to the first effective New York building law.

Women's Rights

Along with movements for honesty in politics, and business and urban reform, came a definite upsurge of humanitarianism. To a great extent this can be accounted for on the ground that exactly the same interest had preceded the Civil War, and with war out of the way the old American desire to better the lot of the unfortunate reasserted itself. But the rising criticism and the growth of a group of educated middle-class women, and to an extent leisured women, in the cities was not without influence. Women were especially concerned with the settlement house movement, which sought to establish social service institutions among the worst slums of the cities. Origi-

nating in London's Toynbee Hall in 1884, the idea was soon carried across the Atlantic, where settlement houses were established in most of the major cities. Among the leaders of the movement that inaugurated social work in the United States were Jane Addams of Hull House in Chicago and Lillian Wald of the Henry Street settlement in New York. Women also played an important part in the campaign against alcohol. The evangelical churches, especially the Methodists, the Baptists, and the Presbyterians, presented a united front against the "demon rum." They were joined in 1874 by the Women's Christian Temperance Union, for years headed by Frances E. Willard. Both the churches and the lay organization crusaded for temperance instruction in schools, for local option for counties and towns, and for statewide prohibition. By the end of the eighties the temperance forces could point to only a few victories, but they were confident of the future.

Because women seemed to be more easily aroused against intemperance than men, temperance advocates very generally fa-

The Temperance Movement. *WCTU members singing in front of a bar room. From Frank Leslie's Illustrated Newspaper, February 21, 1874.*

vored the "emancipation of women," particularly with respect to conferring upon them the right to vote. The woman suffrage movement, like the temperance movement, had attracted attention long before the Civil War, but the attainment of suffrage by the illiterate freedmen of the South had spurred the women reformers to renewed activity. The argument was made that women were as fit to cast a ballot as ex-slaves. Led by such intrepid workers as Susan B. Anthony and Elizabeth Cady Stanton, and joined by a host of professional reformers who before the Civil War had centered their attack upon slavery, the suffragettes made a little progress. A few states reluctantly conceded to women the right to vote in school elections, and the two territories of Utah and Wyoming established complete political equality. Eventual victory for the suffragettes was forecast by the increasing freedom with which women

Elizabeth Cady Stanton and Susan B. Anthony. *These two outstanding advocates of woman suffrage spent their long lives in pursuit of social reform in general and equality for women in particular.*

attended college, entered such professions as the ministry, the law, and medicine, and organized women's clubs.

Other Reformers

That the zeal for reform so characteristic of Americans during the generation preceding the Civil War had been eclipsed rather than destroyed by that struggle was apparent in a multitude of ways. Dorothea L. Dix, to mention a single name, laid down her war work only to resume her earlier efforts for the improvement of conditions among criminals, paupers, and the insane. In state after state, boards of charities were set up to deal with the problem of relief. State schools for the deaf and blind were established, and occasional efforts were made to deal separately with the problem of juvenile delinquency. In Massachusetts, for example, an industrial school for delinquent girls was opened during the seventies at Lancaster. Even the humane treatment of animals was demanded, and an American Society for the Prevention of Cruelty to Animals, founded in 1866 by Henry Bergh on the model of the British Royal Society for the same purpose, made rapid progress. Through its efforts American children by the million read the well-told tale, *Black Beauty* (1877), by Anna Sewell, an English writer. More important still, the Society interested itself in the well-being of children as well as animals, and did much to rescue the unfortunate from conditions that were sure to drag them down. All such efforts, however, were at best only piecemeal, and comparatively little thought was given to the underlying causes of insanity, poverty, and crime. Some light was shed on the subject by the work of R. L. Dugdale, *The Jukes: A Study in Crime, Pauperism, Heredity, and Disease* (1877), which traced the history of a feeble-minded and diseased family that had cost the state of New York a million dollars since 1800.

Educational Changes

Another trend indicating growing social awareness was the increase in philanthropic activities. Not all the profits of the new industrial age went to individuals; millions of dollars were given to education. Before the Civil War such a gift as that of Stephen Girard, who left $2 million to found a boys' school in Philadelphia, was so rare as to brand its donor as an eccentric. After the war such gifts became increasingly common. In 1865 Ezra Cornell gave $500,-000 to found Cornell University in Ithaca, New York. Two years later George Peabody established the Peabody Fund to improve Southern education, and within a few years both Vanderbilt University in Tennessee and Johns Hopkins University of Baltimore opened their doors through the generosity of rich donors. Supplemented subsequently by the immense outpourings of such philanthropists as John D. Rockefeller, Andrew Carnegie, and Edward Stephen Harkness, the total endowment of colleges and universities in the United States reached an enormous figure.

A new interest in education was signalized in 1867 by the appointment of the first United States Commissioner of Education. From that time rapid developments took place on all educational levels. In 1873 St. Louis introduced the European institution of the kindergarten. More and more, graded elementary schools, with a separate room and a teacher for each grade, took the place of the old one-room school. And the number of high schools rocketed. Before the Civil War only about 100 public high schools existed, and most of the training for college was given by private academies. By 1870 the number of high schools had risen to 600, and by 1900 to 6,000.

Higher Education

All American educational institutions were revitalized in the period, but the most notable changes and the most portentous for the future took place in the colleges and universities. Perhaps even more important than private philanthropy in the stimulation of higher education was the effect of the Morrill Act of 1862. Under its terms each state in return for a federal land grant of as many times 30,000 acres as it had senators and representatives, was required to establish at least one college to "teach such branches of learning as are related to agriculture and the mechanic arts." The terms of the act had interesting implications. First, they attacked the prevailing assumption that only the traditional classical subjects were suitable for a college curriculum, and, second, they implied that any able citizen, whatever his intended occupation, might profit from a higher education and that the cost of such was a proper charge on government. Many of the western state universities rose to preeminence as a result of the Morrill Act, and ultimately not less than sixty-nine "land-grant colleges" profited from its terms.

Equally important in the broadening of university horizons was the work of Charles W. Eliot, the brilliant young chemist who in 1869, at the age of thirty-five, became president of Harvard University. In a few years Eliot had substituted the elective system for the old required classical curriculum with its heavy emphasis upon languages, mathematics, ethics, rhetoric, and theology. His reform opened the way for the advance of the new social and physical sciences, which were to play such an important part in the twentieth-century world. It also permitted the introduction of many bread and butter courses as well as others more properly characterized as the sawdust and lard variety, which, carried to an extreme, have plagued modern higher education ever since. The elective idea spread like wildfire and awakened both enthusiastic approval and fierce denunciation. But for

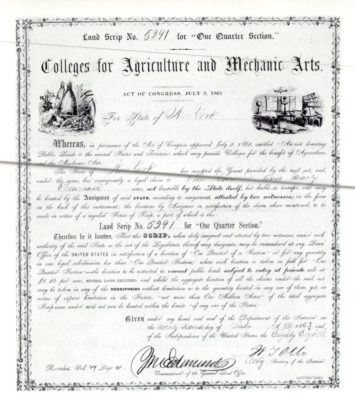

LAND SCRIP. Facsimile of grant to the State of New York.

PRESIDENT ELIOT

HIGHER EDUCATION. *This cause was greatly advanced by the enlightened policies of Charles W. Eliot, President of Harvard University, 1869–1900, and by the action of Congress during the Civil War in granting public lands to the states for aid in the teaching of Agriculture and the Mechanic Arts.*

good and for ill it had come to stay, although most institutions ultimately insisted upon a central core of required "liberal" subjects, especially in the first two years of college.

Among other striking changes in higher education was the start that was made to achieve equality in opportunity for women and for Negroes. Women's right to equal treatment in elementary and secondary schools was acknowledged, in theory at least, before the Civil War, but their chances of entering a collegiate institution remained slight. In 1865 Vassar opened its doors at Poughkeepsie, New York, and was followed shortly by Wellesley, Smith, Bryn Mawr, and Radcliffe, all in the East. It should be noted, however, that Mt. Holyoke at South Hadley, Massachusetts, had

existed since 1837. Later, women's colleges were organized in the West and the South.

More important to the advance of women's education, however, was the development of co-education, pioneered by Oberlin, Antioch, and Iowa before the Civil War. The University of Wisconsin set up a special department for women in 1863, and when Ohio State admitted them from its foundation in 1870, the idea was rapidly copied not only by state universities but by private institutions as well.

Colleges for Negroes

Higher education for the Negro made progress in 1867 with the incorporation of Howard University in Washington, named after one of its most active promoters, General O. O. Howard; and in quick succession such other institutions as Fisk University in Nashville, Straight University in New Orleans, and Shaw University in Raleigh began to function. For these and similar schools northern philanthropy retained for a time a certain fondness, born of the abolitionist crusade. The Peabody Fund was administered mainly with a view to the improvement of common schools for Negroes, but the Peabody Normal College in Nashville, which it aided generously, also served notably the cause of education among the whites. Quite naturally some Negroes at first thought of education, particularly higher education, primarily as a means of escape from manual labor, and showed little interest in the more "practical" subjects that were crowding into the curricula of the northern colleges and universities.

Nevertheless, the Hampton Normal and Agricultural Institute, which opened at Hampton, Virginia, in 1870 with funds provided by the American Missionary Association, struck out along new and bold lines. Its purpose was to emphasize the dignity and importance of skill in labor with the hands, and to prepare its students as well as possible for the type of work that was actually available to them in the South. Means were provided at the Institute whereby the poorer students might "work their way through," and in 1872 Hampton's most distinguished student, Booker T. Washington, walking and begging rides to make a five-hundred-mile journey from his home in West Virginia, arrived with fifty cents in his pocket to take advantage of the opportunities which the Institute offered. Less than ten years later, Washington was chosen to head a school for Negroes at Tuskegee, Alabama, which under his leadership was soon to rival Hampton in its success with the same type of instruction. Critics of industrial education for Negroes complained that it was designed merely to keep the colored race in a permanently inferior status, but in the

Booker T. Washington. *As founder of the Tuskegee Normal and Industrial School for Negroes, Washington advocated for his race an initial emphasis upon industrial education and a gradual approach to civil and political equality.*

main the aims and efforts of Hampton, Tuskegee, and their imitators were applauded by both Negroes and whites.

The Graduate Schools

Not the least important of the changes made in higher education was the establishment of graduate work and graduate schools — perhaps the best evidence that American scholarship was reaching maturity. Before this time the devotee of advanced learning had little recourse but to study abroad. Most American scholars were European made. Some obtained their training in England, but an apparent disdain of English savants for Americans who pretended to scholarship led the latter to prefer the Continent, especially Germany, where they were more cordially received. When the time came for the establishment of American graduate schools, therefore, they followed the German, not the English, model, and presently the Ph.D. (Doctor of Philosophy) degree, then virtually unknown in England, was to become in America, as in Germany, the heart's desire of every budding scholar. The first Ph.D conferred in America was given by Yale in 1861, but the Yale graduate school was not organized until ten years later. By 1872 Harvard had established a graduate school, and in 1876 the Johns Hopkins University set a new precedent by making graduate work its main concern. Before long even the new state universities of the West were emphasizing the importance of research and the training of scholars, and the day had passed when advanced work could be done only in Europe.

The introduction of graduate studies in so many American institutions almost at once emphasized research and scholarly writing as qualifications for teachers and means to advancement. While the teaching of undergraduates may have suffered because of these new interests, in the end the influence of the university and the college upon society grew amazingly. In the astounding transition from a raw industrial nation which was still largely rural in its ways and attitudes to an urban, scientific, and socially-minded country, the academic philosophers, the social scientists, and the men of the laboratories played an amazing and still undervalued part. Indeed, without some comprehension of the ideas supplied and propagated by such academicians as William James and John Dewey, Thorstein

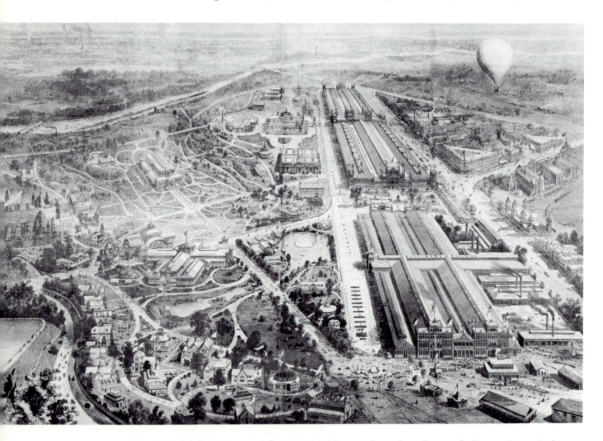

The Philadelphia Centennial, 1876. *This woodcut, based on a balloon view of the Fair Grounds, shows clearly the ambitious nature of the undertaking.*

Veblen and John R. Commons, Albion Small and E. A. Ross, Frederick Jackson Turner and Charles A. Beard, Josiah W. Gibbs and Charles Michelson, to name only a few, it is difficult to understand twentieth-century America.

The Centennial Exposition

Probably few Americans were able to take comfort during the dismal seventies from the fact that an educational quickening seemed imminent, or from knowing that their humanitarian instincts were still alive. But a great many had their faith in their country restored by a visit to the Centennial Exposition, held in Philadelphia from May to October, 1876. Similar "world's fairs" had recently been staged in Europe, notably at London, Paris, and Vienna, but the Philadephia Exposition was the first to be undertaken in the United States. Preparations for it had been begun before 1873, and in spite of bad business conditions the project was not abandoned. Interested individuals gave heavily of their time and money, the city of Philadelphia contributed generously, and still further assistance was obtained from the various states and from the government of the United States. The railroads, famishing for lack of business, offered greatly reduced rates to Philadelphia and from all over the country the people came. By the time the Exposition closed, more than 9 million visitors had entered its gates, and on a single day as many as 275,000. With total receipts of $3 million the fair was a brilliant financial success.

Compared with later exhibitions, the Philadelphia Centennial had little to offer. Its architecture was mediocre, and its art exhibits, while representative of the best that the United States could then supply, suffered from the unwillingness of foreign nations to send their treasures to America. England, however, was more generous than her Continental neighbors, and for the first time thousands of Americans were able to view the works of such masters as Gainsborough and Reynolds. English furniture and household decorations, German porcelain, French textiles, Japanese bronzes and lacquer wares, and Indian shawls and jewels were also freely displayed. These foreign exhibits greatly impressed the common run of visitors, whose provincialism had always made them slow to recognize that Americans in some ways might possibly be excelled by foreigners. Such exhibits also stimulated interest in foreign lands, and more than ever before Americans began to seek opportunity for travel abroad.

Successes of the Fair

The greatest success of the fair was along materialistic rather than artistic lines. Its very size was impressive. The Main Building, covering twenty acres of land, was reputed to be the largest building in the world. Numerous other buildings, four of them also of large dimensions, occupied an enclosure of 236 acres in Fairmount Park, overlooking the Schuylkill River. Machinery Hall housed a magnificent Corliss engine and numerous other symbols of the triumphs of American industry. When it came to commercial and industrial exhibits, European nations, eager to advance their trade in America, vied with the United States in the richness of their offerings, but Americans were able to feel pleasantly elated as they observed that in such matters as these their own country was more often than not in the lead. Agricultural, mining, and educational exhibits illustrated the nation's achievements in these fields. But if the Exposition brought one thing home to the observant visitor, it was the fact that already the United States had become one of the world's important industrial nations, and that inevitably the future pointed toward an urban, industrial society, a society which would differ radically from the old agrarian culture of the past.

BIBLIOGRAPHY

A. M. Schlesinger, *The Rise of the City, 1878–1898* (1933), is an important pioneering study. It may now be supplemented by several useful surveys, including C. N. Glaab and A. T. Brown, *A History of Urban America* (1967); Blake McKelvey, *The Urbanization of America, 1860–1915* (1963); and two books by C. M. Green, *American Cities in the Growth of the Nation* (1957), and *The Rise of Urban America* (1965). Lewis Mumford, *The Culture of Cities* (1938), offers provocative insights. Conflicting interpretations are collected in *The Challenge of the City, 1860–1910* (1968), edited by L. W. Dorsett. Ten scholars reappraise the era in *The Gilded Age* (1963), edited by H. W. Morgan. Excellent documentary collections include *The Gilded Age* (1969), edited by R. A. Bartlett; *The Nation Transformed* (1963), edited by Sigmund Diamond; *The Transformation of American Society* (1968), edited by J. A. Garraty; and *The Nationalizing of American Life* (1965), edited by Ray Ginger.

Several cities have been studied in depth; see B. L. Pierce, *A History of Chicago* (3 vols., 1937–1957); Blake McKelvey, *Rochester* (4 vols., 1945–1961); and Bayrd Still, *Milwaukee* (1948). H. M. Mayer and R. C. Wade, *Chicago: Growth of a Metropolis* (1969), is the collaboration of an urban geographer and a historian; it is studded with maps and hundreds of photographs. C. M. Green, *Washington: Capital City, 1879–1950* (1963), is another valuable work. Among the most important recent studies in urban history are S. B. Warner, Jr., *Streetcar Suburbs: The Process of Growth in Boston, 1870–1900* (1962); Stephan Thernstrom, *Poverty and Progress: Social Mobility in a Nineteenth Century City* (1964), a close look at the workers of Newburyport, Mass., 1850–1880; and J. W. Reps, *The Making of Urban America* (1965), a history of urban planning. Rural life is well portrayed by John Ise, *Sod and Stubble* (1936); small town life is described by Lewis Atherton, *Main Street on the Middle Border* (1954).

The working and home conditions of the poor are well described in the important scholarly work of R. H. Bremner, *From the Depths* (1956). But one should consult the contemporary works, notably two books by Jacob Riis, *How the Other Half Lives* (1890), and *The Battle with the Slums* (1902); and Robert Hunter, *Poverty* (1904). On the social work movement, see A. F. Davis, *Spearheads for Reform* (1967); and two works by Roy Lubove, *The Progressives and the Slums* (1962), and *The Professional Altruist* (1965). The starting point for study of Jane Addams is her own *Twenty Years at Hull-House* (1910); but see also J. W. Linn, *Jane Addams* (1935); and J. C. Farrell, *Beloved Lady* (1967). A brief study of another important figure is D. R. Blumberg, *Florence Kelley: The Making of a Social Pioneer* (1966).

A picture of high society and its aristocratic pretensions is in Dixon Wecter, *The Saga of American Society* (1937). A lively biography of one of the more uninhibited men of wealth is W. A. Swanberg, *Jim Fisk* (1959). A. B. Callow, Jr., *The Tweed Ring* (1966), is a superb scholarly study of one of the most notorious machines. But see also Seymour Mandelbaum, *Boss Tweed's New York* (1965), for a close examination of the milieu; and W. L. Riordan, *Plunkitt of Tammany Hall* (1905), for an inside view. Morton Keller, *The Art and Politics of Thomas Nast* (1968), reproduces some of the work of the greatest political cartoonist of the age. An interesting picture of the social scene in the national capital is *Carp's Washington* (1960), edited by Frances Carpenter.

On the religious trends of the period, consult: W. W. Sweet, *Revivalism in America* (1944); W. S. Hudson, *American Protestantism* (1961); B. A. Weisberger, *They Gathered at the River* (1958); and J. F. Findlay, Jr., *Dwight L. Moody* (1969). Sibyl Wilbur, *The Life of Mary Baker Eddy* (5th ed., 1923), is the official and favorable account of Christian Science. More critical is E. F. Dakin, *Mrs. Eddy: The Biography of a Virginal Mind* (1929). Robert Peel, *Mary Baker Eddy: The Years of Discovery* (1966), by a Christian Scientist, stresses intellectual aspects. A stimulating general work which treats Mrs. Eddy in context is D. B. Meyer, *The Positive Thinkers* (1966).

Two excellent surveys of the Roman Catholic Church are Msgr. J. T. Ellis, *American Catholicism* (2nd ed., 1969); and Theodore Maynard, *The Story of American Catholicism* (1941). Some historical material is also to be found in T. T. McAvoy (ed.), *Roman Catholicism and the American Way of Life* (1960). For the liberal movement, see R. D. Cross, *The Emergence of Liberal Catholicism in America* (1958). David Philipson, *The Reform Movement in Judaism* (2nd ed., 1931); and Nathan Glazer, *American Judaism* (1957), are best on the early days of Judaism in the United States.

The literature on reform and reformers is fairly extensive. Two excellent general works are E. F. Goldman, *Rendezvous with Destiny* (1952); and T. H. Greer, *American Social Reform Movements: Their Pattern since 1865* (1949). Other books of merit are: Arthur Mann, *Yankee Reformers in the Urban Age* (1954); F. M. Stewart, *The National Civil Service Reform League* (1929); C. W. Patton, *The Battle for Municipal Reform: Mobilization and Attack, 1875–1900* (1940); and Gordon Milne, *George William Curtis & the Genteel Tradition* (1956). C. V. Easum, *The Americanization of Carl Schurz* (1929), treats of Schurz's pre-Civil War career; Joseph Schafer, *Carl Schurz, Militant Liberal* (1930), his whole life. On journalism, see B. A. Weisberger, *The American Newspaperman* (1961); and W. A. Swanberg, *Citizen Hearst* (1961). Pulitzer has recently interested several writers including George Juergens, *Joseph Pulitzer and the New York World* (1966); J. S. Rammelkamp, *Pulitzer's Post-Dispatch* (1966); and W. A. Swanberg, *Pulitzer* (1967).

The feminist movement has recently been subjected to much scholarly scrutiny. Notable general works are Eleanor Flexner, *Century of Struggle* (1959); R. E. Riegel, *American Feminists* (1963); Andrew Sinclair, *The Better Half* (1965); and W. L. O'Neill, *Everyone Was Brave* (1969). A valuable documentary collection is *Up from the Pedestal* (1968), edited by A. S. Kraditor. Other important works include the biographies of Susan Anthony by Katharine Anthony (1954); and Alma

Lutz (1959); Alma Lutz, *Created Equal* (1940), a study of Mrs. Stanton; Mary Earhart, *Frances Willard* (1944); Mary Peck, *Carrie Chapman Catt* (1944); and C. C. Catt and N. R. Shuler, *Woman Suffrage and Politics* (2nd ed., 1926). Important recent monographs include A. S. Kraditor, *The Ideas of the Woman Suffrage Movement, 1890–1920* (1965); and A. P. Grimes *The Puritan Ethic and Woman Suffrage* (1967).

An influential work on black history is August Meier, *Negro Thought in America, 1880–1915: Racial Ideologies in the Age of Booker T. Washington* (1964). A classic is Washington's autobiography, *Up From Slavery* (1901); see also S. R. Spencer, Jr., *Booker T. Washington and the Negro's Place in American Life* (1955), a brief biography; and *Booker T. Washington and His Critics* (1962), a collection of documents and conflicting interpretations edited by Hugh Hawkins. An exposé notable both for its melancholy details and for its mild recommendations is R. S. Baker, *Following the Color Line* (1908). A rich study of the blacks in New York City from 1865 to 1920 is S. M. Scheiner, *Negro Mecca* (1965). On black education, see H. A. Bullock, *A History of Negro Education in the South* (1967); R. H. Bremner, *American Philanthropy* (1960); H. L. Swint, *The Northern Teacher in the South, 1862–1870* (1941); and two books by H. M. Bond, *The Education of the Negro in the American Social Order* (1934), and *Negro Education in Alabama* (1939).

General histories of education include E. P. Cubberley, *Public Education in the United States* (2nd ed., 1934); and E. W. Knight, *Education in the United States* (3rd ed., 1951). An interesting study of nineteenth-century schoolbooks is R. M. Elson, *Guardians of Tradition* (1964). Long a standard work is Thomas Woody, *A History of Women's Education in the United States* (2 vols., 1929). A comparison of Edward Eggleston, *The Hoosier Schoolmaster* (1871), with Herbert Quick, *One Man's Life* (1925), shows how rapidly conditions were changing. L. A. Cremin, *The Transformation of the School: Progressivism in American Education, 1876–1957* (1961), is good. Still useful is E. W. Knight, *Public Education in the South* (1922).

On higher education, see G. P. Schmidt, *The Liberal Arts College: A Chapter in American Cultural History* (1957); Frederick Rudolph, **The American College and University: A History* (1962); and L. R. Veysey, *The Emergence of the American University* (1965).

Fabian Franklin, *The Life of Daniel Coit Gilman* (1910), furnishes excellent insight into the way in which a great university was built; but on the same theme, see also C. W. Eliot, *A Late Harvest* (1924); and Ferris Greenslet, *The Lowells and Their Seven Worlds* (1946). Many of the great universities have produced histories by their own historians, among them James Gray, *The University of Minnesota, 1851–1951* (1951); M. E. Curti and Vernon Carstensen, *The University of Wisconsin: A History, 1848–1925* (2 vols., 1949); Jonas Viles, *The University of Missouri* (1939); S. E. Morison, *Three Centuries of Harvard, 1636–1936* (1936); Horace Coon, *Columbia, Colossus on the Hudson* (1947); R. J. Storr, *Harper's University: The Beginnings: A History of the University of Chicago* (1966); J. T. Ellis, *The Formative Years of the Catholic University of America* (1946); E. P. Cheyney, *History of the University of Pennsylvania, 1740–1940* (1940); S. W. Rudy, *The College of the City of New York* (1949); J. F. Hopkins, *The University of Kentucky: Origins and Early Years* (1951); Hugh Hawkins, *Pioneer: A History of the Johns Hopkins University, 1874–1889* (1960); and C. M. Gates, *The First Century at the University of Washington* (1961).

E. D. Ross, *Democracy's College: The Land-Grant Movement in the Formative Stage* (1942), describes the Morrill Act and its results. It is supplemented by John Ise, *The United States Forest Policy* (1920); P. W. Gates, *The Wisconsin Pine Lands of Cornell University* (1943); C. L. Becker, **Cornell University: Founders and the Founding* (1943); Morris Bishop, **Early Cornell, 1865–1900* (1962); and E. D. Ross, *A History of Iowa State College of Agriculture and Mechanic Arts* (1942).

A. C. Cole, *A Hundred Years of Mount Holyoke College* (1940); and J. M. Taylor and E. H. Haight, *Vassar* (1915), are histories of two women's colleges. See also Leon Richardson, *History of Dartmouth College* (2 vols., 1932); N. C. Chaffin, *Trinity College, 1839–1892: The Beginnings of Duke University* (1950); and Edwin Mims, *History of Vanderbilt University* (1946).

IO

SCIENCE, SOCIAL IDEAS,

AND THE ARTS

World's Fair of 1893 · Charles Darwin · Social Darwinism · Social Christianity · James and pragmatism · John Dewey · Pragmatic education and law · Reform Darwinism · Henry George · Edward Bellamy · The new economics · Historians · Mark Twain · Henry James · William Dean Howells · Naturalism and determinism · Poetry and music · Painting · Architecture

World's Fair of 1893

In the spring of 1893 Chicago opened the World's Columbian Exposition. Celebrating the four hundredth anniversary of the discovery of America, the Fair commemorated the startling progress of the nation in industry, agriculture, and the arts. Here was a thirty-years' record of the nation's amazing technological and scientific progress, as well as innumerable portents of the shape of things to come. At night the Fair was dazzling with the new electric lights, and Henry Adams saw in the whirring dynamos that produced the electric current the power symbol of the new urban mass and the ever more centralized civilization of the future. And as the Fair both recorded the past and hinted at the future of material America, just so did it suggest the revolutionary changes that had been and

were to be made in the realm of ideas and the creative arts. A series of national "congresses" accompanied the Fair for the purpose of discussing the most vital scientific, cultural, literary, and religious problems of the day. Imbedded in these conferences is the record of a nation converting old comfortable ideas that had worked well in the nineteenth-century agrarian world to others more suitable for a newer urban, industrial, and scientific civilization. Impregnating many of the conference papers attacking the accepted ideas of the older civilization was the spirit and method of the great English scientist, Charles Darwin (1809–1882). Darwin was only one of many thinkers and scientists whose ideas helped bring about the great intellectual upheaval that accompanied the birth of the twenti-

SKYSCRAPERS *began their upward reach, which was to alter the American skyline, at the end of the nineteenth century.*

eth-century world. But in his book *The Origin of Species* (1859), Darwin used the new scientific method to challenge some of the most ancient and cherished ideas of western civilization. Thus his name became forever linked with the rise of the new scientific thought.

Charles Darwin

Before writing *The Origin of Species* Darwin had spent years patiently studying animal life in various parts of the world. From his observations he concluded that existing life had not been created by God in six days in the forms it now exhibited, but had evolved slowly over millions of years from the simplest of origins by a process of natural selection. All life was in fierce competition for survival, and those species survived and flourished that were best adapted to their environment. Since the natural environment was continually changing, species likewise had to change or die. This had resulted in the utter extinction of untold numbers of kinds of life, but the fittest — those best adapted to the conditions in which they had to live — had passed on their characteristics to new generations. And thus the struggle for existence had produced over great spans of time entirely new species.

Some of the precepts of Darwinism obviously challenged a literal interpretation of the Biblical story of creation. The result, together with the impact of the new so-called higher criticism, subjecting the Bible to the test of historical knowledge, started a controversy between "fundamentalist" and "liberal" Christians which often ended in heresy trials and the driving of many ministers from Protestant pulpits. But the reasonableness of the evolutionary hypothesis could not be lost indefinitely on a world that owed so much to scientific discovery. Thomas Henry Huxley, the English biologist, and Herbert Spencer, the English philosopher, both of whom visited America, greatly influenced American thinking toward the acceptance of Darwinian concepts, and John Fiske, the American historian, argued earnestly that, far from undermining religion, Darwinism made possible "a higher view of the workings of God and of the nature of Man than was ever attainable before." Prominent clerics, among them Henry Ward Beecher and Lyman Abbott, also attempted to reconcile science and religion, and the popular defense of evolution made by a Scot, Henry Drummond, in his book *Natural Law in the Spiritual World* (1884), profoundly impressed the American reading public. In most churches religion was never quite the same after Darwin. As the modernists gradually won, the result was less and less emphasis upon dogma, upon Old Testament and original sin. And in the more advanced churches the doctrine of hell itself was abandoned, as was most supernaturalism.

Social Darwinism

Outside the clergy Darwinism was enthusiastically received for two related reasons. First, its main defenders drew from it a doctrine of progress which exactly suited the spirit of the times. Second, they used it to defend the existing economic and political order. This application of Darwinism to human society was first made by Herbert Spencer, who argued that the evolutionary process not only meant ceaseless slow change but also ceaseless slow progress. Moreover, Spencer argued, human society was subject to the same natural laws of fierce competition that governed the destinies of all other species. Man might ignore or violate these laws to his own peril. But if he accepted the "great design" and established the "pure competitive society," then by the workings of the survival of the fittest, the able would rise to the top of the social heap and the unfit would be discarded. In such a "pure" economic society the business or financial ty-

THE WORLD'S COLUMBIAN EXPOSITION. *The Chicago World's Fair, celebrating the 400th anniversary of the discovery of America, was housed in buildings that, according to one observer, were "what the Romans would have wished to create." It stimulated a classical revival in architecture.*

THE IOWA BUILDING. These decorations were made of corn and small grain.

THE COURT OF HONOR. A view looking eastward over the main basin.

coon was by the process of natural selection a true leader and prophet, and government only an encumbrance. Government should keep the peace and perform a few other necessary functions like distributing the mails, but it should neither help the underprivileged nor restrict the actions of the rich. Thus public education, poor relief, or any system of social insurance was a drag on the wheels of progress and a violation of natural law.

This Spencerian version of *laissez faire* was quickly spread through America by John Fiske and other ardent apostles in the late sixties and early seventies. Clerical leaders, especially the early "modernists"

William Graham Sumner. *As a professor of political and social science at Yale from 1872 to 1910, Sumner objected strenuously to governmental interference with private enterprise, and ridiculed reformers; but his opposition to a high protective tariff won more applause from reformers than from businessmen.*

led by Beecher, favored this Social Darwinism, and universities hailed it as the "one unvarying and basic law of an enlightened political economy." By 1880 one university president remarked that in choosing a new staff member for his economics department *laissez faire* was not a test for orthodoxy but one "used to decide whether a man was an economist at all." And of course it was cordially embraced by industrialists and financiers. Andrew Carnegie even remarked that Herbert Spencer was "the man I owe most to." Carnegie was so enamored of the system which proved that he had been selected by natural law to lead society that he devised his own "laws of wealth," and published them in *The North American Review.*

But the ablest and most consistent

Social Darwinist in America was Professor William Graham Sumner of Yale (1840–1910), a sociologist and a political economist. Sumner was an unusually trenchant writer and a coiner of memorable phrases. Seeing all life, including human society, as engaged in one great grim struggle for existence, he believed that "absolute competition" was the only weapon by which a species sharpened its faculties sufficiently, and pared off enough of its slothful nature, to survive. He was thus scornful of all reformers and implacably opposed to any government intervention in economic life. Such activity was not only harmful, but in the end useless. For the laws of economics were as fixed as those of physics, he argued, and the attempts of reformers to change them were comparable to those of an ant trying to "deflect a mighty river." Sumner celebrated the millionaires as makers of progress. But he was such an outspoken foe of the tariff as a prime example of harmful governmental intervention that he almost lost his position at Yale. In an age dominated by tariff-made monopolies and ridiculous concern with the poor, he declared, the "forgotten man" in America was the middle-class factory owner or merchant who stood on his own feet in the competitive race and asked neither aid nor restriction. At his death in 1910 Sumner was distinctly out of favor with the majority of reformers and even with most conservatives. His most lasting contribution was his sociological study *Folkways* (1907), which, by insisting that human institutions had always been relative to a time and place, helped overthrow his own rigid and deterministic philosophy of economics.

The emphasis of Social Darwinism on competition and the survival of the fittest had interesting developments in the area of international relations. If what was true of single societies was true of the struggle between nations, then it was obvious that Great Britain, the rapidly rising German

Empire and, of course, the United States had come to world leadership because of a natural, inherent vigor and superiority. Moreover, the continued expansion of these powers at the expense of their weaker and more "unfit" neighbors was in the scheme of things, and in fact hastened progress. Both German and British writers contributed to this Teutonic and Anglo-Saxon myth, and Americans were not far behind. Herbert Baxter Adams, the German-trained historian at Johns Hopkins, John W. Burgess, the Columbia political scientist, and the Reverend Josiah Strong, as well as many popular writers, contributed to this form of Social Darwinism. The movement in turn had important effects upon the rising imperial temper of America, as well as upon the American attitude toward the new immigration. Frank Norris' glorification of football as a "true Anglo-Saxon game," too competitive and rugged for lesser and more pigmented races, says much about the temper of the times — as well as about man's inability to predict the future in sports as in other activities.

Social Christianity

Although Social Darwinism was extremely popular in the two decades after 1870, counter-developments were already undermining it. By the late 1880's a Protestant religious movement called "the Social Gospel," or, more simply, "Social Christianity," was challenging the logic of applying biological principles to human society. Christianity had always insisted that man as a moral being was separate from the rest of nature, and Spencer's jump from animals to man was scarcely consistent with this precept. In part, the Social Gospel probably grew from the renewed emphasis on the ethics of Christianity by clergymen who, as modernists, had discarded much of the older supernaturalism. Perhaps also the Protestants' growing sense of competition with Roman Catholicism for the loyalty of

Charles Darwin. *Father of modern biological thought, Darwin provided a rationale for economic, social, and religious thinkers who helped to bring about the break from tradition which ushered in our era.*

the working classes played its part. By the 1890's it was apparent that while many Protestant workers were becoming hostile to the church, the loyalty of both the old Catholics and the innumerable immigrants seemed to remain unchanged. At least the followers of the Social Gospel could never be criticized for ignoring the plight of the poor. Central to the new doctrine was the belief that the church should become an active leader in a movement for social and economic reform which would implant the ethics of Christ in the factory and the marketplace. The pietism of the old individualists, wrote Washington Gladden, a leader of the Social Gospel, no longer had an appeal for many Christians. What was needed was "a religion that laid hold on life with both hands." Gladden, Shailer Matthews, and Lyman Abbott — one of the editors of the influential *Outlook* — were among the more moderate clerical leaders of the Social Gospel. Their aim was a Christian capitalism dominated by ethical considerations. Much farther to the left were George D. Herron, until 1899 Professor of Applied Christianity at Iowa College, and Walter Rauschenbusch of the

JAMES

DEWEY

Rochester Theological Seminary, who described capitalism as "essential atheism" and believed that the abolition of private property was the only basis on which a "Christian democracy" could be established.

A movement with similar aims got under way in the Roman Catholic Church, especially after Pope Leo XIII issued in 1891 his *De rerum novarum*. This famous encyclical pointed to the critical problem created by vast wealth, and attendant poverty among the masses, and called upon both church and state to find a remedy. With the blessings of Archbishop James Gibbons, Father John A. Ryan, born and raised in Populist North Dakota, took up the challenge. Both as a university professor and as an author, Father Ryan devoted his great energies to the study of labor problems. Within a short time he had formed a considerable group of like-minded people intent on using the Catholic Church as an instrument of social justice.

Although the advocates of the Social Gospel probably remained a minority among the clergy, their efforts had a profound effect on the reform movement in the first years of the twentieth century,

and especially on the character of modern Protestantism. Social Christianity achieved one of its more immediate ends by bringing back to the fold many workingmen who had been alienated by the seeming indifference of the church to their plight. And it started the development through which the social service agencies of the church became a major part of its activities.

James and Pragmatism

Simultaneously with the growth of Social Christianity, William James (1842–1910), brother of the novelist Henry James, was developing his philosophy of pragmatism. William and Henry James grew up in a most unorthodox family. Their father had hobnobbed with the intellectuals of Brook Farm and later traveled widely and became interested in a variety of religious and philosophical thought. Despite this background, or perhaps because of it, William James received a good education, and after studying science was appointed professor of psychology and philosophy at Harvard. His *Principles of Psychology* (1890) was a pathmaking book in America,

GREAT AMERICAN THINKERS. *These three leaders of American thought, although by no means of one mind, may properly be classed as pragmatists. William James made his contribution through his perceptive approach to psychology. John Dewey was for many years the outstanding leader in the field of American education. Oliver Wendell Holmes was a philosopher of the law.*

HOLMES

and his later volumes, most of them dealing with philosophy, were even more important. His association at Harvard with Chauncey Wright and Charles Sanders Peirce introduced him to the speculations of these two men about chance and indeterminism in the universe. By the time he was a mature scholar, James was opposed to the closed deterministic universe of the nineteenth century, including that of Darwin. Instead, he emphasized chance, human thought, deed, and free will. Man was neither a prisoner of the past nor of some exact and awe-inspiring natural law. Instead he was a relatively free agent in an unpredictable universe. James's pragmatism has sometimes been called the opposite of a philosophy, in that it gave no final answers about the universe, how it operated, or where it was going. Pragmatism was centered on man, principally on the thought process and its relation to events. For James, thought was never separate from the act, but was a part of it. Indeed the validity of the thought could be tested not by reference to some theological or philosophical system but by the action it inspired and the consequences of that action.

John Dewey

James's most illustrious follower, John Dewey (1859–1952), spent most of his adult life as a professor at Chicago and Columbia Universities. Like James, Dewey was a convinced democrat. He was also an ardent reformer who believed intensely that through intelligence man could partly control his natural environment and build a democratic society far more productive of human happiness than any culture had yet produced. Seizing upon James's concept that speculation was merely an instrument, he developed his own variety of pragmatism which he called "instrumentalism." Far more than James, he insisted that thought of any value inspired action. In fact, it was only by using thought as an instrument of action that man arrived at what was true and valid. Learning then came from going through almost a laboratory process in which thought was tested in the crucible of the act and its validity was determined by the results of the act. True to his own philosophy, Dewey was an activist all his life, concerning himself with immediate and emergent issues. His more formal philosophic thought may be found in a series of scholarly books starting with *Experience and Nature* (1925), but to understand the whole man one must also read his innumerable magazine articles and tracts, which he wrote on a host of current social and educational problems.

Both James's and Dewey's varieties of pragmatism have been severely criticized for so emphasizing action that they all but excluded ethical and aesthetic considerations. Their pragmatism also practically ignored the vast speculative systems of the past and questioned the value of history as an aid to discovering what was true for the present. But the most damaging criticism was that pragmatism included no system of human values. By insisting that truth was to be measured largely by the consequences of a belief, pragmatism came dangerously close to admitting that the end justified the means, and hence that for both individuals and societies, expediency was a better guide than principle.

Pragmatic Education and Law

James's influence, until after 1900, was largely confined to his students, the university and college world, and his rather small reading public. But Dewey became a public figure very early in his career, and his continuing preoccupation with current issues gave pragmatism a popularity that few philosophies have enjoyed. Despite its critics, the public welcomed Dewey's doctrine, perhaps because so much in it was ingrained in the American mind. The practical and experimental approach, the emphasis upon the present and the future, the rather cavalier treatment of the past, and especially the emphasis upon the free and creative role of man — all these views were closer to actual American experience than were the assumptions behind the nineteenth century deterministic systems. More specifically, pragmatism-instrumentalism had profound effects on American education.

Dewey's doctrine of "learning by doing" was first applied in Chicago, and its widespread acceptance by "progressive" educators started a debate that still continues.

Dewey's instrumentalism also had an impact upon law, for it undermined the assumption that judges decided cases according to a set of immutable principles. In 1881 Oliver Wendell Holmes, Jr. (1841–1935), a close friend of William James, published his *Common Law*. Holmes, then a justice of the Massachusetts Supreme Court and after 1902 of the United States Supreme Court, held that the great decisions of American constitutional law had not been reached mainly by applying logic to the immutable principles of the Constitution; instead "The felt necessities of the time, the prevalent moral and political theories, intuitions of public policy avowed or unconscious, even the prejudices which judges share with their fellow men, have had a good deal more to do than the syllogism in determining the rules by which men should be governed." Other legal theorists argued that if the present so influenced judicial decisions, then why not look at the social and economic facts surrounding a case before applying a general principle of law? Outright pragmatists went further and maintained that if justice were to be served, any legal decision had to be considered for its social and economic effects. Thus in 1908, Louis D. Brandeis made judicial history when in presenting a brief before the Supreme Court in the case of *Muller* vs. *Oregon* he cited the opinion of experts that the hours women worked affected their health and therefore the health of the community. On the basis of the social facts presented, the Court overturned previous decisions and held the Oregon ten-hour law constitutional. Brandeis became a Supreme Court Justice in 1916, and thus was able to accelerate the movement toward the pragmatic interpretation of constitutional law.

The effect of pragmatism on areas outside education and the law is more difficult to measure. But its assumption that man was free to act, its refusal to accept dogma, its experimental and tentative spirit, its emphasis on facts and results, and its bent toward democratic reform, encouraged or at least seconded the reforming spirit of many intellectual rebels who in the last quarter of the nineteenth and the first decade of the twentieth centuries were weakening the influence of post-Civil War conservatism.

Reform Darwinism

Some who rejected Social Darwinism showed the influence of pragmatism. Others were moved as much by the ethical impulse of the Social Gospel. At the same time a logical attack against the conservative position was drawn from Darwinism itself. As a method, Darwinism had stressed the importance of empirical research and thus encouraged the rising social sciences to take a hard look at the facts before they made sweeping judgments about society as Herbert Spencer had done. In effect Social Darwinism sanctioned unrestrained private enterprise and the pursuit of gain as beneficent social goals. The thirty years following the Civil War, with two depressions and ever-increasing rural misery, did not bear out that view. In the light of the facts it was natural for empirically-minded social critics to reach the opposite conclusion, that cooperation and social planning might best benefit America. Once made, these assumptions could be defended even from Darwinism. For this "reform Darwinism," as it has recently been called, stressed both the element of change and the importance of environment in the theory of evolution. If change was the rule for the animal kingdom, why not also for human society? And if environment was so important in creating new species, why could not human nature be altered by change in the social environ-

ment? Reform Darwinists ardently believed so, and set about to prove it.

Among the earliest and most vigorous advocates of reform Darwinism was Lester Ward (1841–1913). Born of a poor Illinois family and hardened by manual labor, Ward educated himself, became a paleobotanist in the government service, and eventually, in 1906, secured a professorship at Brown University. Meanwhile through his writings he founded American sociology, and gave it a reforming bias which it long retained. Central to Ward's thought was a sharp distinction between the life of the species and human society. The former, he argued, was controlled by blind "genetic" or inherited forces, which were neither logical nor efficient. Ward pointed out the enormous wastage in nature and the stunted and misshapen varieties of life it brought forth. On the other hand, the evolution of human society was mainly sparked by "teleic" or mental powers. Not Spencer's laws, but rather "man's intellectual capacity" to produce change and thus "to shape the environmental forces to his own advantage" had been responsible for most of the great social gains.

The long list of Ward's books, which included *Dynamic Sociology* (1882) and *Outlines of Sociology* (1898), attracted little public notice, possibly because of the author's awkward and difficult style. But their point of view influenced a whole generation of sociologists, among the more important of whom were Albion Small and Edward A. Ross. Small was the editor of the *American Journal of Sociology* for thirty years after its founding in 1895. The directions in which he pointed the journal are clear from his statement in the opening number. "The entire spirit of sociology," he wrote, "is a deep loyal impulse of social service. Its whole animus is constructive, remedial and ameliorative." Ross, born in Iowa and educated at Johns Hopkins, spread the gospel of reform Darwinism.

When he started teaching in 1891, Ross argued for a sociology based upon a "real Darwinism" with reform as its objective. In *Sin and Society* (1907), which contained a preface written by Theodore Roosevelt, Ross demanded "an annual supplement to the Decalogue" so that the majority of citizens would appreciate the fact that sin evolved along with society, and that tax dodging was "larceny," child labor "slavery," and adulteration of foods "murder."

Henry George

Three years before Ward's first book on sociology appeared, Henry George (1839–1897) published his influential *Progress and Poverty*. Born in Philadelphia, George spent most of his young life working as a printer and a journalist in San Francisco. There, in a few short years, he watched a virtual frontier trading post converted into a sophisticated urban society. At the same time he saw both wealth and poverty rapidly compounded. What caused this paradox, George asked himself, and found the answer in the fast growing monopoly of land in the hands of the few, and constantly increasing land rents and land value. The individual owners, however, had little to do with the process. What gave land its value was the growth of the society upon it, the number of people using it and needing it. A frontier farm was worth little; the same site forty years later, in the heart of a bustling city, appreciated enormously in price because of its social value. The difference between the value in such land was a social and an "unearned" increment. Therefore George proposed a "single tax" upon this unearned increment which would pay all the costs of government, thus making other taxes unnecessary, and at the same time destroy the monopoly of land by making it too expensive to hold in large quantities. This basic monopoly gone, and with it the possibility of making great fortunes, equal opportunity would return and the monopoly problem, George believed, would be solved.

Along with his economic interpretation of the social crisis and his remedy in the form of the single tax, George launched a searing indictment of Social Darwinism. "The injustice of society," he wrote, "and not the niggardliness of nature, is the cause of . . . want and misery." The inequality between men was not an evidence of the survival of the fittest, but rather a basic inequality in opportunity. Once the existing monopoly of land and rents had been abolished, the great inequalities between men would disappear, and a new era of brotherhood and religious faith would dawn. George's *Progress and Poverty* attracted an amazingly large reading audience, and single-tax societies flourished not only in the United States but in many foreign countries. But perhaps in the long run George's most important influence lay not in the answers he proposed but in the questions he raised about the existing social system. Nearly every important reformer in the next thirty years read George's book, and a surprising number of them confessed that their interest in changing the social system was born on reading *Progress and Poverty*.

Edward Bellamy

Edward Bellamy (1850–1898), in his attack on reigning social beliefs, was animated by much the same Christian and egalitarian ethics that had moved Henry George. With a long New England family background, Bellamy was clearly influenced by that section's utopian tradition. Although a professed Christian, he was so incensed by church defenses of the industrial system that he refused to attend services and forbade his children to attend. Socialism, he finally came to believe, was the only form in which an industrial society could practice and preserve Christian ethics. He embodied his themes in *Looking Backward* (1888), a novel whose hero suddenly found himself projected forward in time, living in a Christian socialist Boston of the year 2000. In Bellamy's utopia private ownership of production had been peacefully abolished and everyone lived in a sort of great industrial army, eating in huge cafeterias and spending their state script in a super-department store. Although both young men and women were obliged to work at manual labor a certain number of years, throughout this highly technical society there was a great amount of individual choice and a remarkable absence of coercion. As a novel, *Looking Backward* was hardly an artistic triumph, but as a tract for the times it was an overwhelming success. Inspired by Bellamy's "Nationalism," hundreds of thousands of Americans read the book and promptly organized "Nationalist" clubs to work for the inception of the new state. During the turbulent nineties the movement died almost as quickly as it had grown, but Bellamy's short-lived success clearly indicated that great numbers of Americans, thoroughly disenchanted with the *laissez-faire* industrial society as it then existed, demanded change. *Looking Backward* also introduced to many Americans an ethical socialism which, stripped of its Marxist overtones of materialism, violence, and class warfare, was acceptable to many. Clearly, after Bellamy such things as municipal ownership of utilities and state regulation of private enterprise never carried with them the onus they once had for numerous Americans.

The New Economics

Henry George and Edward Bellamy were publicists rather than economists and had arrived at their economic ideas in a most informal way. Meanwhile a group of young professional economists, most of them trained in German universities, were also challenging the validity of the prevailing *laissez-faire* concepts. The leaders of this group, Richard T. Ely of Johns Hopkins and Wisconsin, Simon Patten of Pennsylvania, and John R. Commons of Wisconsin, acted from more or less the same assumptions. Instead of viewing man as a quarreling competitive animal, they saw him as an ethical creature, "full of noble instincts," as Patten believed, "and swift accurate reactions to duty. . . ." Both Ely and Commons were lay leaders in the Social Gospel movement, and both helped to organize the Brotherhood of the Kingdom, a society dedicated to infusing the industrial world with Christian ethics. All of them firmly believed in man's ability to reorder nature and human society through the agency of the state. In founding the American Economic Association in 1885, these young rebels wrote into its credo a denunciation of *laissez faire* as "unsafe in politics and unsound in morals," as well as their aspirations for the state: "We regard the state," their document read, "as an educational and ethical agency whose positive aid is an indispensable condition to human progress."

Perhaps the most original of all the young economists of the period, and certainly one who was less imbued with their ethical and reforming urge, was Thorstein Veblen (1857–1929). Son of a Norwegian immigrant to Wisconsin, Veblen studied formal economics both at Yale under Sumner and later at Johns Hopkins. A natural rebel against conventions and a self-confessed "disturber of the intellectual peace," Veblen was not able to obtain a university position until he was almost forty. Thereafter his unconventional morals and ideas, and his difficult personality, made his short academic career a stormy one. Veblen's books, among the most important of which are *The Theory of the Leisure Class* (1899) and *The Engineers and the Price System* (1921), did not command a wide reading public. They were too far off beat, too ironic in spirit, and too prolix in style to interest even most scholars.

BEARD

TWO LEADING HISTORIANS. *The writing of interpretative history gained much impetus from the work of these historians. Charles A. Beard emphasized economic factors in history, and was sometimes charged, quite incorrectly, with being an economic determinist. Frederick Jackson Turner rang the changes on the frontier theme in American history.*

TURNER

THE FRONTIER HYPOTHESIS. An irreverent student cartoon.

But some of his ideas became influential, and the most original of his phrases passed into the common vocabulary.

Veblen always contended that he was not a reformer but that his efforts were directed at depicting the American economy exactly as it existed. But in his so-called "descriptive studies" he denied practically all the fundamental postulates of Social Darwinism, as well as aiming shafts of ridicule at the owning classes. Dealing often in psychological and anthropological data, he argued that basically most men were moved by an "instinct of workmanship," which if untrammelled, would result in efficient, aesthetically pleasing production. But in the "pecuniary society" that dominated America the business man, as distinct from the pure industrialist, was animated almost entirely by the "acquisitive instinct" which he satisfied by manipulating the price system and which thus throttled and debased productive facilities. Veblen saw increasing friction in the advancing industrial society between the men who wanted to produce and the small owning class that was interested solely in accumulating wealth. The end product, he predicted, would probably be revolution and dictatorship. The only alternative he offered was a society run by an educated elite of engineers and technicians. In *The Theory of the Leisure Class* Veblen had a good deal of savage fun in examining the customs and mentality of the American rich. And he related his concepts of "conspicuous consumption" and "pecuniary emulation," involving the search for status symbols, to similar phenomena in "other savage and barbarous societies." After Veblen's diagnosis it was difficult to consider the very wealthy as cultural heroes, the end product of the survival of the fittest.

Historians

Evolutionary science, especially in its claim to establishing a law of development for the species and its emphasis upon environment, also influenced the teaching and writing of American history. For a number of years the effort of many historians to be scientific led to the production of fact-heavy manuscripts which their authors fancied were objective because they were innocent of both interpretation and literary value. On the other hand, the search for a causal law in history similar to the law of natural selection produced a number of works which stimulated historical thought even if they did not totally convince. The racist views of Herbert Baxter Adams of Johns Hopkins were optimistic. The democratic seed that had been planted in the primeval German forests, Adams argued, had reached its flowering in the Anglo-Saxon civilization of the United States. The conclusions of Brooks and Henry Adams, grandsons of the sixth President, were extremely pessimistic. For Brooks civilization in the past had alternated between a masculine, military, creative phase and a feminine, pecuniary, sterile one. Equating the civilization of the United States in 1890 with the latter phase, Brooks waited for disaster. His brother Henry, who had already written his brilliant *History of the United States during the Administrations of Jefferson and Madison* (1889–1891), applied Kelvin's second law of thermodynamics to the historical process and looked ahead to the dreary day when all the energy of society would be dissipated.

More profound in their influence on the future course of American historical thought were the historians who looked not for an over-arching law but to the immediate environment as an explanation of the development of American society. Charles A. Beard (1874–1948) led the group which emphasized economic factors as most important in determining men's political and social views. In *An Economic Interpretation of the Constitution* (1913)

Beard sought to show a close relationship between the personal economic interests of the founding fathers and their votes in the Constitutional Convention. From the date of its publication the work drew excited denunciations from the nation's conservatives and equally warm praise from its radicals. And although Beard's findings have subsequently been questioned by professional historians, his economic approach has continued to influence the writing of American history down to the present.

Frederick Jackson Turner

But of all the environmentalists Frederick Jackson Turner (1861–1932), left the most persistent imprint on subsequent historical thought. Born in post-frontier Wisconsin, Turner had seen the Indian and the forest disappear before the pioneer's plow, and the pioneer replaced by a settled agriculture. As a student of history and a young professor at the University of Wisconsin, Turner was not convinced that most of the distinctive traits of American civilization had been born in the early German forests, or in Great Britain, or even in the long settled parts of the Atlantic seaboard. At the Chicago World's Fair history conference in July, 1893, Turner read what probably still remains the single most influential paper in American historical writing, "The Significance of the Frontier in American History." Pointing out that "the germ theory of politics" had been sufficiently emphasized, and that the evolution of institutions along the Atlantic coast was, after all, a fairly "familiar phenomenon," he urged historians of the United States to study the West as well as the East.

American social development has been continually beginning over again on the frontier. This perennial rebirth, this fluidity of American life, this expansion westward with its new opportunities, its continuous touch with the simplicity of primitive society, furnish the forces dominating American character. The true point of view in the history of this nation is not the Atlantic coast, it is the Great West. . . . What the Mediterranean Sea was to the Greeks, breaking the bonds of custom, offering new experiences, calling out new institutions and activities, that and more, the ever retreating frontier has been to the United States directly, and to the nations of Europe more remotely.

Turner's words were heeded, and soon a veritable cult of the West had sprung up among the writers of American history. The American Historical Association, founded in 1884 by scholars with unimpeachable eastern connections, was accurately, if facetiously, described as the "Turner-verein." Turner's disciples outdid their master in claiming significance for the frontier, and they often claimed too much. Nevertheless, it seems clear that the influence of a succession of frontiers, with their free land, free natural resources, and expansive environment, had much to do with molding the character of American civilization. De Tocqueville had recognized the importance of the great open land frontier in his perceptive *Democracy in America* (1835). So had E. L. Godkin and a number of others. But none had rounded out their observations with such completeness or had put them in such a philosophical frame of thought as Turner.

Turner had one other advantage over his earlier competitors in obtaining a hearing for his theories. He spoke at the right time. For, as he noted in 1890, the federal Census Bureau had announced that the continuous frontier line in the United States had disappeared. Five years later the United States began to undersell British-made steel in the world market. As he spoke at Chicago, Turner stood at a great time divide: behind him were the frontier and the farmer; ahead, industry and the city. By the logic of his own environmentalism, the influence of the former was bound to wane, that of the latter to wax.

HAMLIN GARLAND. In such books as *Main Travelled Roads* (1891), and *A Son of the Middle Border* (1917), Garland portrayed life as he found it in the western Middle West. This photograph of Garland in his old age shows his conscious effort to look like Mark Twain.

REGIONAL LITERATURE. *The size and diversity of the American nation produced many writers who exploited local and regional themes.*

BRER RABBIT AND BRER B'AR. An illustration from *The Honey Orchard*, one of Joel Chandler Harris's Uncle Remus stories. Here Brer Rabbit persuades Brer B'ar that a hurricane is coming, and that for his protection he must be tied to a tree, thus ending his depredations on Brer Rabbit's honey supply. These stories transferred to the animal kingdom the problems southern Negroes experienced in living with the dominant southern whites, and show how by subtlety the Negroes often got their way.

Regional Literature

The Civil War and the years immediately afterward seem to have had a blighting effect on the American arts. Immediately before the war distinguished American music and painting were practically nonexistent, and architecture was largely derivative. But Emerson, Thoreau, Hawthorne, Poe, Melville, and Whitman had created a distinguished literature. After the war all these were either dead or silent except for Whitman, and even his works went unnoticed and unread for many years. Taking the place of these giants immediately after the war were a group of "genteel writers" whose names are now unimportant. Possibly reacting to the barbarity of the new industry and the city slums, and to the vulgarity and chicanery of polite and political society, these writers retreated into a never-never world of fancied prettiness and sentimental confectionery. For over two decades they set the standards of taste for an overwhelmingly feminine audience, and effectively prevented the rise of a literature that concerned itself with the joys, problems, and tragedies of real people.

Much more realistic and vital in their writings, even though many of them were not greatly talented, were the regionalists who dealt extensively in local color and customs peculiar to their own sections of the country. Among the best of these were Joel Chandler Harris (1848–1908) and George Washington Cable (1844–1925), both of whom wrote about the South; Hamlin Garland (1860–1940), whose tales of the Middle Border depicted the northern plains; Bret Harte (1836–1902), who wrote of life in the mining regions of California; and Sarah Orne Jewett (1849–1909), with her novels of rural New England. While these regionalists have been discounted by critics, they did stimulate both the production and the appreciation of better writing in their own sections of the country, and they served as a token of a significant development in American literature. Previous to the war almost all of the country's first-rate authors had come from the Atlantic seaboard, with a majority from New England and New York. But after 1870 almost the reverse occurred. Creative writers came from every portion of the country, and fewer came from New York and New England than from any other major section.

Mark Twain

The best evidence that the eastern monoply of talent had been broken was the spectacular literary career of Samuel Langhorne Clemens, more familiarly known as Mark Twain (1835–1910). Brought up in the small village of Hannibal, Missouri, on the Mississippi River, Twain spent his youth

HUCKLEBERRY FINN

MARK TWAIN

SAMUEL LANGHORNE CLEMENS. *Better known as Mark Twain, Clemens was the first westerner to gain prominence in the American literary world. The early editions of his* Tom Sawyer *and* Huckleberry Finn *were replete with illustrations, such as this 1885 sketch of Huckleberry Finn, by E. W. Kemble.*

For some time after the Civil War American painters, like most of their countrymen, remained preoccupied with the national scene, westward expansion, the mores and growth of new country and a new nation. But Europe beckoned, and the promise of a richer culture drew some to an expatriate life and first influence from the greatest painting of the time, French impressionism. And with the famous exhibit in 1908 of the "Ashcan School," the growing wave of self-criticism and social consciousness, already manifest in the muckraking journalists and realistic novelists like Norris and Dreiser, found its way into painting. The result was that by the 1930's there was a remarkable eclecticism, a wide variety of influences, styles, and interests.

Edward Lamson Henry, *The 9:45 Accommodation, Stratford, Connecticut.* 1867. The Metropolitan Museum of Art, Bequest of Moses Tanenbaum, 1937.

George Inness, *Summer At Medfield*. Boston Museum of Fine Arts.
Photographed by Barney Burstein, Boston.

James A. McNeill Whistler, *Old Battersea Bridge: Symphony in Brown and Silver*. c. 1865. Addison Gallery of American Art, Phillips Academy, Andover, Massachusetts.

Mary Cassatt, *Mother and Child.* Anonymous
Loan to Boston Museum of Fine Arts.

John Singer Sargent, *The Wyndham Sisters:
Lady Elcho, Mrs. Tennant, and Mrs.
Adeane.* 1899. The Metropolitan Museum
of Art, Wolfe Fund, 1927.

William J. Glackens, *Chez Mouquin*.
1905. The Art Institute of Chicago,
Friends of American Art Collection.

Robert Henri, *West 57th Street*. 1902. Yale University
Art Gallery. Mabel Brady Garvan Collection.

Maurice Prendergast, *May Day*, *Central Park*. 1901. Collection of the Whitney Museum of American Art, New York.

Charles Burchfield, *Old House and Elm Trees,* 1933. Collection of the
Virginia Museum of Fine Arts, John Barton Payne Endowment Fund, 1942.

John Steuart Curry, *The Line Storm.* 1935. Collection of Mrs. Sidney Howard.
Reproduced by permission of Mrs. John Steuart Curry.

George Bellows, *Both Members of This Club.* 1909. National
Gallery of Art, Washington, D.C. Chester Dale Collection (Gift).

Albert Pinkham Ryder, *The Race Track or Death on a Pale Horse.* c. 1910.
The Cleveland Museum of Art. Purchase from the J. H. Wade Fund.

Thomas Hart Benton, *Boom Town*. 1928. Collection of The
Memorial Art Gallery of the University of Rochester.

Edward Hopper, *Early Sunday Morning*. 1930. Collection of the
Whitney Museum of American Art, New York.

in a variety of pursuits including those of river steamboat pilot, gold miner in California, newspaper editor, and public lecturer. It was as a humorist that he offered his first popular book, *The Innocents Abroad* (1869), and he returned to the role repeatedly in novels, short stories, and numerous public lectures. But Twain is most widely remembered for his accounts of boyhood along the Mississippi River. *The Adventures of Tom Sawyer* (1876) and *Adventures of Huckleberry Finn* (1884) remain his best recognized works and the ones for which he was saluted at Oxford University with an honorary degree. As in so many humorists, there was an ambivalence in Twain. Intensely disliking the materialistic spirit of the new industrialism, he was also attracted to its glitter and its rewards. While he continually satirized the *nouveau riche* and their lack of taste and manners, he himself lost heavily in speculative attempts to establish a fortune. Although celebrating the western spirit, he lived most of his adult life in the East. An ardent democrat, his bleak estimate of human nature is revealed in a superb short story, "The Man Who Corrupted Hadleyburg." As he became older, his pessimism grew, and few bleaker notes were struck in American literature until after the First World War, than in his *The Mysterious Stranger* (1916), published posthumously.

Henry James

In two of his works, *The Innocents Abroad* and *A Connecticut Yankee at King Arthur's Court* (1889), Twain brought Americans in humorous juxtaposition with the peoples of the Old World, but much more serious in attempting an international comparison were the works of another American, Henry James (1843–1916). Born in New York, James spent much time abroad accompanying his restless father, and unlike his philosopher brother William,

Henry James. *If Mark Twain was typically American, his contemporary, Henry James, certainly was not. While literary critics and sophisticated Americans greatly valued James's writings, ordinary people rarely appreciated them, and disliked his admiration for England.*

never felt really at home in America. He was repelled by the American lack of refinement, by the crass materialism of his age, and by an atmosphere which he felt was thoroughly uncongenial to artistic and creative pursuits. After a fruitless try at the law in 1882, he settled in England permanently. Without being blind to their weaknesses, James admired the English upper classes for their subtle intellectual sophistication, their devotion to literature and the arts, and their cultivated manners. In thorough sympathy with Britain's position after the start of the First World War, he officially gave up his American citizenship and became a British subject.

But James never became entirely detached from his birthright. A major theme in many of his novels is the interaction born of the encounter between the sophisticated, cultured, and morally complex European and the rather gauche, vigorous, and often puritanical American. Two of his earlier books, *Daisy Miller* (1879), and *The Europeans* (1878), depict such a meeting, the one describing Americans in Europe, the other, the cultivated European in New England. For a period in his middle life James not too successfully drew his inspiration almost entirely from his new-found home in England. Then in *The Ambassadors* (1903), and *The Golden Bowl* (1904), he went back to a study of the impact of Europe and Europeans upon the American character and mind. It was mostly in these later works, by his acute inquiry into the minds of his characters, that James established his place among the most gifted of American novelists — and started a major trend in modern American writing, the psychological and stream-of-consciousness novel. Until recently James has not been fully appreciated by Americans. Besides, the complexity of his style, his criticism of his countrymen, and his taste for European aristocrats, made him unpopular on this side of the Atlantic.

William Dean Howells

Much more congenial to American taste at the time, both in his choice of subject matter and in his treatment of characters, was William Dean Howells (1837–1920). Born in an Ohio village and trained in a newspaper office, Howells became a magazine editor in both Boston and New York. As an editor Howells acquainted Americans with the twin schools of naturalism and determinism, then flourishing in France and Russia. The naturalists, responding to the urban and democratic tides, argued that writers should forget the upper classes and concentrate on the lives of the masses, depicting them, even those from the lower depths, as faithfully as possible. The determinists, Darwinian in emphasis, tried to show that man's life, mind, and character were all products of his environment, and that free will was mostly a fantasy. Howells had an uncanny knack of spotting literary ability. This and his broad sympathy led him to befriend many a young and struggling author. It is probably his discovery and aid of young writers more than the merit of his own writing that won him the title of "the dean of American literature."

Yet Howells was something of a pathbreaker in his own novels. In *The Rise of Silas Lapham* (1885) and *A Hazard of New Fortunes* (1890), he became the first serious American writer to deal with some of the central social problems of his times. Concerning himself with the class and individual tensions released by the movement of Americans from village to city, by the newly rising rich, and by the new place of women in society, he became the originator of American naturalism. Later in his career he was interested in economic questions. *Through the Eye of a Needle* (1907) and similar works were the best written of the many utopian novels that appeared around the turn of the century. Yet Howells' preference for upper-middle-class characters, and his squeamishness about sex and violence, prevented him from going far along the road to naturalism.

Naturalism and Determinism

Far more uninhibited than Howells were four much younger men of the next generation. Stephen Crane (1871–1900) and Frank Norris (1870–1902) both died quite young, and Jack London (1876–1916), at the age of forty. But Theodore Dreiser (1871–1945), pursued a long literary life reaching well into the second quarter of the twentieth century. Most of the new forces and trends in literature can be seen in the work of this quartet. In their work realism shaded into naturalism, and they were frank and objective in discussing the seamy side of life. With a wealth of vivid language for one so young Crane investigated the ordinary human mind under great stress. *The Red Badge of Courage* (1895) explored the mental strains of a common soldier in battle for the first time. Norris, Dreiser, and London also treated of such common clay. Norris in *The Octopus* (1901), explored the plight of the California wheat farmer besieged by the railroad. Dreiser in *Sister Carrie* (1900) shocked the nation by portraying an amoral girl who was not punished for her sins. And London realistically drew a host of characters from the waterfront bum to the working stiff of the western wheat fields. Norris, and especially Dreiser, emphasized the social environment in the shaping of their characters. By introducing violence into their plots all four of these writers broke the moral and literary canons of their time. Dreiser's *Sister Carrie* not only depicted the squalid life of a slum girl's attachment to several dubious males, but also in the end saw her attain money and a respectable career. So shocked was 1900 America that the book was withdrawn from sale. In *The Iron Heel* (1908), London described the coming class war and the advent of a particularly violent dictatorship. Before the advent of this group most of America's writers had been drawn from the more or less comfortable middle class. And although Crane and Norris followed that pattern, Dreiser came from a Catholic working family in Indiana and Jack London was born a waif on the Oakland, California, waterfront.

Poetry and Music

The years between 1870 and 1914 also witnessed the rebirth of American poetry and the rise of women as serious literary artists. Emily Dickinson (1830–1886) in New England and Sidney Lanier (1842–1881) in the South were writing finely

Jack London. *In his writings, as in his life, London took an almost pathological interest in the primitive traits of man, his tendency to revert to savagery, and his delight in the triumph of brute force.*

wrought verse immediately after the Civil War, and Edward Arlington Robinson (1869–1935) became the first significant American poet of the twentieth century. The advent of Ellen Glasgow (1874–1945) and Edith Wharton (1862–1937), as first-rate novelists was a revolution of the sexes in American letters. Ellen Glasgow's studies of decaying Virginia aristocracy, of the unmannered and uncultured rising lower classes, of the southern feminine tradition which she deplored, and of the disfigurement of city and countryside by industry all have much to say about the modern South. Edith Wharton's books are as eloquent about life among old New York families, which she cordially disliked. As literary craftsmen neither woman had a superior in the years before the First World War.

Despite the country's Germanic heritage, serious native music was practically nonexistent during the nineteenth century, mainly for the want of an appreciative public. But better times were ahead. Before the Civil War the New York Philharmonic was the only orchestra giving regular concerts. Within the next fifty years most major cities had established symphony orchestras, and within a short time there were flourishing groups in Boston, Philadelphia, Pittsburgh, Cleveland, Minneapolis, San Francisco, and Los Angeles.

Painting

Painters and sculptors labored under much the same difficulties as musicians. Few of the new millionaires were men of taste and most of them who collected art favored the recognized European masters. This was unfortunately also true at first of the Metropolitan Museum in New York, established in 1870, and of similar public galleries subsequently organized elsewhere. Most artists of ability preferred to be trained in Europe and some of these decided either to remain there or to return abroad after they had tried unsuccessfully to find favor and patronage in their native country.

Mary Cassatt, of Philadelphia, was trained in France and chose to stay there, and both James McNeill Whistler and John Singer Sargent eventually settled in England, where Whistler, especially, acquired a reputation both for his fog-shrouded riverscapes and his belligerent thrusts at hostile critics. The three expatriates were all more or less influenced by the reigning French school of impressionism, as were the majority of less able painters working at home. But George Inness, Thomas Eakins, Winslow Homer, and Albert Pinkham Ryder, were doing non-derivative and genuinely American work which both by its originality and its aesthetic appeal deserved to be remembered. Ryder, almost ignored in his own time, has particularly attracted the attention of critics today because his eerie dreamlike canvases shot full of symbols

pointed unerringly toward the post-impressionist and abstract art of the twentieth century.

Something of a landmark in American painting occurred in 1908 when a group of Philadelphia artists labelled by critics the "Ashcan School" held a show in New York which elicited widespread public discussion. Hitherto public artistic debate of such dimensions had been aroused only by controversies over whether a particular painting or statue was so indecent as to be unsuitable for public exhibition. The Philadelphia group, most of whom had to work at illustrating to make a living, were led by Robert Henri, John Sloan, and Robert Prendergast, and the debate was over their manner of painting and the subjects they chose to paint. Influenced perhaps both by the camera and by a cult of scientific naturalism akin to that developing in the novel, they executed a variety of urban subjects including dirty streets and trash-filled alleys with a precision that dismayed the more romantic critics who held that only the beautiful should be painted, and that most of the beautiful was natural and not man-made. The camera-like precision of the group was soon forgotten, but their liberal ideas about what made suitable subjects for painting were extremely influential. And the public discussion which the "Ashcan" exhibition excited indicated a new-found American interest in painting that augured well for the future.

Architecture

Of all the fine arts architecture is the one that demands the closest meeting of the aesthetic and the useful, and the one that must be supported willy-nilly by any society worthy of the name. American architecture after the Civil War was the essence of inutility, ugliness, and banality. Some of the bumptious spirit of the gilded age with its ignorance of standards and lack of taste was expressed by the architects of

Saturday Afternoon on the Roof. *By John Sloan, one of the "Ashcan School" of American painters.*

the period, but many of the models for the 1870 American "chambers of horrors" came from abroad. Most of the public and private buildings of the period, which borrowed simultaneously from almost every historic style, and then added an improbable mélange of decorated towers, turrets, balconies and ornamented gingerbread, are now mercifully gone. Hastening their departure was Henry Hobson Richardson (1838–1886), who began to design public buildings in the late 1870's after the Romanesque style which had preceded the Gothic movement in early medieval Europe. With their spare and clean exteriors, and their well-lighted and useful interiors, such buildings were a welcome relief from the monstrosities of the age before. During the nineties a brief return to the columned and porticoed classical

school, a movement aided by the pseudo-classical buildings of the Chicago Fair, was headed by Stanford White. Ralph Adams Cram, another leading New York architect of the time, preferred a simplified Gothic for his structures. But even though the buildings of both men were far superior to those of the seventies, their reliance on the aesthetic expressions of the past exhibited a lack of originality and a failure to comprehend that the new industrial and urban age demanded a new type of building.

Meanwhile modern technology made possible radical changes in the building art. The employment of steel by John and Washington Roebling in the beautifully designed Brooklyn Bridge completed in 1883 illustrated both the great utility and the aesthetic possibilities of this new material.

WAINWRIGHT OFFICE BUILDING, ST. LOUIS (1890). In this building, tall for its time, the architect, Louis Sullivan, emphasized vertical as well as horizontal lines.

TRINITY EPISCOPAL CHURCH, BOSTON. In this building Henry Hobson Richardson modified the traditional French and Spanish Romanesque in so unique a manner that the style came to be termed "Richardsonian."

It was shortly discovered that by the use of a steel skeleton, and later of steel reinforced concrete, the weight of a building no longer demanded bearing walls of massive thickness. Together with the invention of the electric elevator, the new steel and concrete shell greatly raised the permissible height limit, and the American skyscraper was made possible.

Simultaneously with these developments a school of Chicago architects was advocating a new style of building conforming to the peculiar needs and spirit of the age. At the center of this new group was Louis H. Sullivan (1856–1924) with his doctrine that "form follows function." Sullivan first applied his dictum in 1890 by designing the Wainwright office building in St. Louis, a structure equally innocent of the traditional thick walls at the bottom and of elaborate ornamentation. Other able inventive architects, like John W. Root, cooperated with Sullivan in working out the possibilities of the new style. But by far the ablest of the Chicago group, and one of the world's great creative architects, was Sullivan's student, Frank Lloyd Wright (1869–1959). Wright was a fierce opponent of the new skyscraper on the grounds that in a continent so broad, buildings should be parallel, not vertical to the earth. At his two schools, Taliesin East and Taliesin West, Wright argued for an organic architecture in harmony with the site and using native materials. Until after the Second World War, Wright was largely unhonored in his own country, but he probably contributed as much to modern building as any western European architect.

BROOKLYN BRIDGE UNDER CONSTRUCTION. This famous bridge, planned by John A. Roebling in the late 1860's and completed by his son, Colonel Washington Roebling, was dedicated May 24, 1883. An engineering triumph, it set the pattern for other suspension bridges throughout the nation.

ARCHITECTURE AND ENGINEERING. *The freedom that American architects won from traditional restraints during these years was made possible by rapid advances in the field of engineering. The upward thrust of American skylines began well before World War I and was accelerated after its close.*

Although Wright was vehemently opposed to skyscrapers, and though many critics have damned such buildings for creating urban congestion and for removing man further from his natural habitat of earth, sunshine, and air, they are considered by many foreigners to be the most typical expressions of modern American civilization. In many ways perhaps they are. For these long clean pencils of steel and concrete, symphonies of science, engineering, and design, are at once a historic symbol of American society's triumph over a raw continent, and at the same time towering tokens of an undisclosed collective future.

THE NEW YORK SKYLINE IN 1912. This view of lower New York contrasts markedly with those of a half century later. Many now familiar landmarks are missing.

BIBLIOGRAPHY

The best general works on post-Civil War social ideas and intellectual life are: M. E. Curti, *The Growth of American Thought* (3rd ed., 1964); R. H. Gabriel, *The Course of American Democratic Thought* (2nd ed., 1956); Stow Persons, *American Minds: A History of Ideas* (1958); and H. S. Commager, *The American Mind* (1950). M. G. White, *Social Thought in America* (2nd ed., 1957), should also be consulted.

The general impact of Darwin and Darwinism is best obtained from the excellent study of one of the nation's early important scientists, A. H. Dupree, *Asa Gray, 1810–1888* (1959); but see Perry Miller (ed.), *American Thought: Civil War to World War I* (1954). For the impact of evolution on social ideas, see Richard Hofstadter, *Social Darwinism in American Thought* (2nd ed., 1955). One major theme is explored in I. G. Wyllie, *The Self-Made Man in America* (1954); J. G. Cawelti, *Apostles of the Self-Made Man* (1965); and *The American Gospel of Success* (1965), an anthology edited by Moses Rischin. Important recent monographs include M. H. Haller, *Eugenics* (1963); F. C. Jaher, *Doubters and Dissenters: Cataclysmic Thought in America, 1885–1918* (1964); and J. C. Burnham, *Psychoanalysis and American Medicine, 1894–1918* (1967).

On religion generally, see Sidney Warren, *American Freethought, 1860–1914* (1943); and E. A. White, *Science and Religion in American Thought: The Impact of Naturalism* (1952). The Social Gospel movement and the influence of industrialism and urbanism on religion are well studied in: C. H. Hopkins, *The Rise of the Social Gospel in American Protestantism, 1865–1915* (1940); Henry May, *Protestant Churches and Industrial America* (1949); A. I. Abell, *The Urban Impact on American Protestantism, 1865–1900* (1943); and J. H. Dorn, *Washington Gladden* (1967). J. A. Ryan, *Social Doctrine in Action* (1941), the autobiographical account of the priest who led a similar movement in the Roman Catholic Church, should be supplemented by A. I. Abell, *American Catholicism and Social Action: A Search for Social Justice, 1865–1950* (1960).

R. B. Perry, *The Thought and Character of William James* (2 vols., 2nd ed., 1948), is the standard biography of the father of pragmatism. See also E. C. Moore, *William James* (1966); John Wild, *The Radical Empiricism of William James* (1969); and Sidney Hook, *John Dewey* (1939), a study of James's leading disciple. *The Mind and Faith of Justice Holmes* (1943), edited by Max Lerner, is important for legal thought. Studies of social scientists include Samuel Chugerman, *Lester F. Ward* (1939); Joseph Dorfman, *Thorstein Veblen and His America* (1934); and D. M. Fox, *The Discovery of Abundance* (1967), on Simon Patten. *Lester Ward and the Welfare State* (1967) is a selection from Ward, edited by H. S. Commager. Studies of social thought in the period include Charles Page, *Class and American Sociology* (1940); and R. J. Wilson, *In Quest of Community* (1968). *Social Darwinism* (1963) is a collection of W. G. Sumner's writings edited by Stow Persons. One major theme is explored by Clinton Rossiter, *Conservatism in America* (2nd ed., 1962); and R. G. McCloskey, *American Conservatism in the Age of Enterprise* (1951).

General works on the course of American historical writing are H. H. Bellot, *American History and American Historians* (1952); Harvey Wish, *The American Historian* (1960); and Michael Kraus, *The Writing of American History* (1953). But see also W. T. Hutchinson (ed.), *The Marcus W. Jernegan Essays in American Historiography* (1937). Modern controversies about the writings of Turner and Beard have produced a voluminous periodical literature. The pro and con of the "frontier thesis" can be found in the works cited in the bibliography following Chapter 4. See C. A. Beard, *An Economic Interpretation of the Constitution of the United States* (2nd ed., 1935); Lee Benson, *Turner and Beard* (1960); and Richard Hofstadter, *The Progressive Historians* (1968). On one great historian, see: Ernest Samuels, *Henry Adams* (3 vols., 1948–1964); Elizabeth Stevenson, **Henry Adams: A Biography* (1955); and W. H. Jordy, *Henry Adams, Scientific Historian* (1952). These should be supplemented with Adams' own **Education of Henry Adams* (1918), which is at once an autobiography and a seminal book for an understanding of the period. For Brooks Adams, see A. F. Beringause, *Brooks Adams: A Biography* (1955). Interesting recent studies of historiography include Jurgen Herbst, *The German Historical School in American Scholarship* (1964); and R. A. Skotheim, *American Intellectual Histories and Historians* (1966). Useful anthologies of historical writing are *Paths of American Thought* (1963), edited by A. M. Schlesinger, Jr., and Morton White; and **The Historian and the Climate of Opinion* (1969), edited by R. A. Skotheim.

General works on the literature of the period include two books by Van Wyck Brooks, **New England: Indian Summer* (1940), and *The Confident Years* (1952); Alfred Kazin, **On Native Grounds* (1942); and Maxwell Geismar, **Rebels and Ancestors* (1953). More specialized are R. W. Schneider, *Five Novelists of the Progressive Era* (1965); Larzer Ziff, **The American 1890's* (1966); and Franklin Walker, **San Francisco's Literary Frontier* (2nd ed., 1969). On Twain, see Justin Kaplan, **Mr. Clemens and Mark Twain* (1966); and **Mark Twain's "Huckleberry Finn"* (1959), a collection of conflicting interpretations edited by B. A. Marks. On James, see the major biography by Leon Edel, *Henry James* (4 vols. to date, 1953–   ); and F. O. Matthiessen, **Henry James* (1944). On

Crane, see John Berryman, **Stephen Crane* (1950); and R. W. Stallman, *Stephen Crane* (1968). On Howells, see two books by E. H. Cady, *The Road to Realism* (1956), and *The Realist at War* (1958); and Kermit Vanderbilt, *The Achievement of William Dean Howells* (1968). Discussions of other major writers are Ernest Marchand, *Frank Norris* (1942); Joan London, **Jack London and His Times* (1939); and W. A. Swanberg, *Dreiser* (1965).

For painting and architecture, see O. W. Larkin, *Art and Life in America* (2nd ed., 1960), a rich book. An important new monograph is R. B. Stein, *John Ruskin and Aesthetic Thought in America, 1840–1900* (1967). A study of painting is Jerome Mellequist, *The Emergence of an American Art* (1942). Three important surveys of American architecture are C. W. Condit, *American Building* (1969); J. M. Fitch, *American Building* (2nd ed., 1966); and John Burchard and Albert Bush-Brown, **The Architecture of America* (1961). A brief study of the growth of cities is Christopher Tunnard and H. H. Reed, **American Skyline* (1955). An influential work is Lewis Mumford, **The Brown Decades* (1931). A major new work is C. W. Condit, *The Chicago School of Architecture* (1964). L. H. Sullivan, **Autobiography of an Idea* (1924); and F. L. Wright, *An Autobiography* (1943), are two personal statements by influential architects. Works on important individuals include: Lloyd Goodrich, *Thomas Eakins* (1933); F. F. Sherman, *Albert P. Ryder* (1920); and two books by H. R. Hitchcock, **The Architecture of H. H. Richardson and His Times* (1936), and *In the Nature of Materials* (1942), a study of Wright.

Section Three

EXPANSION AND REFORM

[1890 - 1917]

The closing decade of the nineteenth century showed the United States reaching maturity as a nation. The national boundaries, long merely geographic lines, now marked also the extent of population expansion. The frontier line, long of interest to cartographers and more recently also to historians, could no longer be traced from north to south between territory that was already settled and territory that was yet to be settled. But the westward movement had been a constant factor all through American history; was the national habit of expansion so strong that it would continue even at the expense of new acquisitions?

Undoubtedly the United States was beginning by the 1890's to show an interest in distant lands, greater perhaps than it had ever known before; but it would be too simple an explanation to attribute this entirely to a persistence of the westward movement. The United States as a full-grown nation could not much longer avoid close contacts with all the rest of the world. Trade relationships were growing. Americans, especially since manufacturing had flowered, had more to sell than formerly, which to some observers suggested the need for colonies. The spirit of imperialism had affected other nations, and a mad scramble for empire was on, with

Great Britain, France, Germany, and Russia leading the way. Nationalistic Americans, proud of their country's newly-achieved greatness, were not unaffected by what they saw. If other nations to flatter their self-esteem must have colonies, why not also the United States? Nor should the missionary impulse be overlooked. Americans were sure they had a way of life worth teaching to others; indeed, they were not sure but what they were under a deep moral obligation to share their blessings with peoples less favored. Politicians, possibly eager to divert attention from unpleasant domestic conditions, rang the changes on foreign affairs.

Some such motives as these lay back of the diplomacy of the 1890's. Harrison's Secretary of State, James G. Blaine, showed an interest in the Pacific, and sought a closer relationship with Latin America. Grover Cleveland belligerently invoked the Monroe Doctrine, even against Great Britain, whose navy in earlier years had been its chief defense. William McKinley, albeit somewhat reluctantly, intervened in Cuba to prevent Spain from suppressing a colonial insurrection, and emerged from the resulting war with the remnants of the Spanish empire, both in the Caribbean and in the Pacific, as American possessions. Then, in order to keep the Philippines, the United States had to suppress the same kind of insurrection that had faced the Spanish in Cuba. Under Theodore Roosevelt the new American empire was consolidated, and the essential diplomatic and military measures taken for its defense.

But the American people, after the first taste of empire, found that they did not like it, and turned with far greater relish to the task of domestic reform. From the first years of the century to the time the United States was caught up in the First World War, the progressive movement held the center of the stage. Its roots lay in part with Populism; many of its principal tenets had been expounded earnestly by Ignatius Donnelly and William Jennings Bryan. But they could be traced also in part to the ideas of European socialism, ideas that had caught on with a few earnest labor leaders, such as Eugene V. Debs. With the need for reform fully exposed by the muckrakers, many reform governors such as Robert M. LaFollette of Wisconsin, and two reform Presidents, Theodore Roosevelt and Woodrow Wilson, achieved notable results. The power of private monopoly over government was severely shaken, although by no means broken.

The course of the progressive movement saw many political changes. The Republican Party under Roosevelt's leadership leaned toward reform, but under Taft's leadership made little progress. The result was a party split in 1912, with Roosevelt heading a new Progressive Party. But the Democrats, thanks to the divided opposition, won the election, and with Wilson as their leader put through much of the progressive program. In so doing they branded the Democratic Party as the party of reform and tended to absorb the more aggressive supporters of the Progressive Party, an organization which promptly died. For the Republicans there was little choice but to accept the mantle of Taft conservatism that had been thrown their way.

II

THE PATH OF EMPIRE

Diplomatic isolation · Blaine's foreign policy · Hawaii and Samoa ·
Chile · The Venezuelan controversy · Cuba · American intervention ·
Dewey at Manila · Santiago · Treaty of Paris · The United States as a world
power · Election of 1900 · The "insular cases" · Hay's "open door" policy ·
The Boxer Rebellion · Minor American possessions · Decline of interest in
colonies

Diplomatic Isolation

Until well toward the end of the nineteenth century the foreign policy of the United States reflected primarily the interest of the American people in westward expansion. Washington's policy of isolation was designed to keep the new nation free from any European entanglements that might distract its attention from the main business in hand — the conquest of a continent. The Monroe Doctrine, by which European governments were warned to keep out of American affairs, was merely the converse of the same proposition. By it the United States hoped to end for all time the threat of outside interference with the workings of "manifest destiny." The War of 1812 and the war with Mexico were both expansionist wars, and the Civil War was fought, in considerable part at least, to decide whether the North or the South should have the advantage in the formation of new western states. During all these years the United States was busy at home.

It cared little about the doings of other nations so long as they showed no desire to block the American policy of expansion. American political development was self-centered and introspective. American economic development was a frantic struggle to exploit the rich natural resources that the continent had divulged, and to satisfy, mainly by domestic production, the needs of a rapidly growing people. American diplomacy, especially during the quarter-century that followed the Civil War, was episodic and inconsequential.

By the last decade of the nineteenth century a change had set in. The era of continental expansion was over, the United States was full grown, the time-honored frontier process was fading from the picture. Good free lands and good cheap lands were nearing exhaustion. Population penetration into the High Plains and the Rocky Mountain plateau all but eliminated from census maps the zone of uninhabited

ANOTHER EXPLOSION AT HAND. *A cartoonist's prediction for the rapidly expanding American empire.* Puck, *1900.*

The British-American Joint High Commission, 1898. *This meeting in Quebec of representatives from Great Britain and the United States considered about a dozen items of international difference between the United States and Canada, but failed to reach an agreement on the Alaskan boundary dispute which the discovery of gold in the Klondike had precipitated. See p. 306. From* Harper's Weekly, *September 24, 1898.*

territory that until 1890 had stretched unbroken from the Canadian to the Mexican border. American industry was catching up on its assignment. Already, for many mines and factories, the time had come when the needs of the domestic market could be fully supplied, with a margin left over for sale abroad. American capital had been multiplied many times over, and considerable sums now sought foreign investment. The interest of the United States in itself alone began to give way to an active American interest in the whole wide world. Diplomatic aloofness had lost its charm; increasingly the American government felt called upon to play an important part in international affairs.

Blaine's Foreign Policy

James G. Blaine, twice Secretary of State (1881, 1889–92), has often been spoken of as the "harbinger of the new era." This, no doubt, is an exaggeration, but Blaine did attempt to widen the sphere of American influence to include, in fact as well as in theory, all of the Americas. Toward European nations with an interest in the western hemisphere, but most particularly toward

Great Britain, he adopted an uncompromising, almost belligerent, attitude. While serving under Garfield, for example, he made a blustering, but unavailing, demand that the British government give up its rights under the Clayton-Bulwer Treaty of 1850 to joint control of any interoceanic canal that should be built. Likewise, during his second term in office he tried to establish a kind of prescriptive right for the United States to the fur-seal fisheries of the Bering Sea, a contention that a joint Anglo-American arbitration commission was unable to approve. Most important of all, he sought consistently to promote the cause of "Pan-Americanism."

Pan-Americanism

Blaine's fondest dream was to induce the Latin-American republics of North and South America to enter a kind of informal federation, with the United States as an interested and friendly "elder sister" at its head. Through such a union Blaine hoped to eliminate wars between the lesser American nations and to promote better commercial relationships between them and the United States. As Garfield's Secretary of State, he had invited the Latin-American nations to a peace conference in Washington, scheduled for 1882, but his successor, Frederick T. Frelinghuysen, had revoked the invitation. Shortly before Blaine took over the State Department for the second time, Cleveland's Secretary of State, Thomas F. Bayard, with the prior approval of Congress, had issued an invitation similar to the one Blaine had issued years before. It therefore fell to Blaine's lot to receive in Washington on October 2, 1889, the representatives of nineteen independent American republics. Nothing could be accomplished on so important a subject as arbitration, but the First Pan-American Congress, as this meeting came to be called, made considerable progress in the discussion of such important problems as the standardization of sanitary regulations, the building of an intercontinental railroad, and the adoption of uniform weights and measures, including a common silver coin. One permanent result of the Congress was the establishment of an International Bureau of American Republics, with headquarters in Washington. Another was the precedent set for the holding of such meetings; similar Congresses have been held from time to time ever since.

Hawaii and Samoa

It is possible to discern in Blaine's foreign policy an effort to reserve the Pacific as a region for future American exploitation. Blaine cultivated good relations with Japan, and at the same time managed to keep friendly with China in spite of the deepening antagonism between the two great Oriental nations that led to open war in 1894. Nor was Blaine displeased at the prospect of the speedy annexation to the United States of Hawaii, for generations the chief stopping-place in the mid-Pacific for vessels bound to Asia, and a center of steadily increasing importance for the production of sugar. These conditions, indeed, inspired the American State Department to negotiate a reciprocal trade treaty with Hawaii as early as 1875, which was renewed in 1884 and so amended (1887) as to give the United States an exclusive right to develop a fortified base at Pearl Harbor. When in 1893 Americans in Hawaii staged a revolution with annexation to the United States as their goal, Blaine had left office, but he would certainly not have objected to the treaty of annexation that was signed, but never ratified. Not until McKinley became President, in 1898, was annexation actually accomplished, but Blaine had favored it, and had hoped for it. Blaine also sought to retain for the United States a foothold in the Samoa Islands, first tentatively marked out as early as 1872. Both Germany and Great Britain had interests in the Samoas, however, and international rivalry for commercial privileges became acute. A conference of the three contending parties, called by Bismarck, met in Berlin in 1889, and decided on a tripartite protectorate, but this worked badly and was abandoned in 1899. The islands were then divided between the United States and Germany, while Great Britain was indemnified for her withdrawal by title to the Gilbert and Solomon Islands, which had formerly belonged to Germany. These negotiations, from beginning to end, showed small regard for the traditional American policy of isolation.

Chile

While Blaine's policy in the Pacific was later to pay substantial dividends, his plans for Pan-Americanism fell far short of the goals he had set. The United States minister to Chile, Patrick Egan, for whose appointment Blaine was responsible, openly took sides in a Chilean revolution, and even more unfortunately gave his support to the side that lost. While feeling against the

United States was still high in Chile, American sailors on shore leave at Valparaiso became involved in street fighting that cost two of them their lives and others, serious injuries. By threat of military reprisals, the United States collected an indemnity of $75,000 for this "outrage," and built up an amount of ill-will throughout all Latin America that could not be measured. These incidents undid nearly everything Blaine had accomplished. Under the terms of the McKinley Act he negotiated a few useful trade treaties, and no doubt the Pan-American Congresses served a valuable end, but for the most part Blaine's high hopes of international accord among the American nations were long to remain unrealized.

The Venezuelan Controversy

That the aggressive nature of American diplomacy was neither a personal policy of Blaine's nor a party policy of the Republicans was made evident shortly after Harrison left office by Cleveland's handling of the Venezuelan boundary dispute. The boundary line between Venezuela and British Guiana lay in a tropical wilderness and had never been properly delimited. Long a subject of desultory controversy, the subject became really interesting when the news came out that gold had been discovered in the disputed territory. To Cleveland the prospect of the British government enforcing its will upon Venezuela, as the American government had recently enforced its will upon Chile, was extremely disquieting. He had made up his mind that, in case such action resulted in the taking of territory properly belonging to an American nation, the Monroe Doctrine would clearly have been violated. In his message to Congress of 1894, he therefore expressed his hope that the matter would be arbitrated, and Congress by resolution promptly echoed his sentiments. The British government, however,

refused to submit the whole question to arbitration, although pointing out that it had long been willing to arbitrate within certain specified limits. This attitude satisfied neither Cleveland nor his aggressive Secretary of State, Richard Olney, who took the matter up with Lord Salisbury, the British Foreign Minister, in a dispatch of July 20, 1895. "Today," said Olney, "the United States is practically sovereign on this continent, and its fiat is law upon the subjects to which it confines its interposition." Any advances of the British boundary at the expense of Venezuela, Olney claimed, would "greatly embarrass the future relations between this country and Great Britain."

At first the British showed no signs of backing down, and Cleveland plainly threatened war. Eventually, however, a plan of arbitration satisfactory to the United States was accepted, and Americans talked loudly of their diplomatic triumph. Undoubtedly the British right-about-face was due to other circumstances than the American representations. The British people were in no mood to fight the United States; furthermore, a telegram of congratulations sent by Kaiser Wilhelm II of Germany to Paul Kruger, the anti-British Boer leader in South Africa who had successfully repulsed Jameson's raid of "outlanders" into Boer territory, emphasized the fact that the future enemy of Great Britain might be Germany, rather than the United States. Indeed, friendship with the United States became from this time forward an earnest objective of British diplomacy. The strong stand that the United States had taken on behalf of a Latin-American republic should have made for better relations between the United States and her neighbors, also, but Olney's bombastic words robbed the American victory of its chance to bear such fruit. The "Colossus of the North" was still mistrusted.

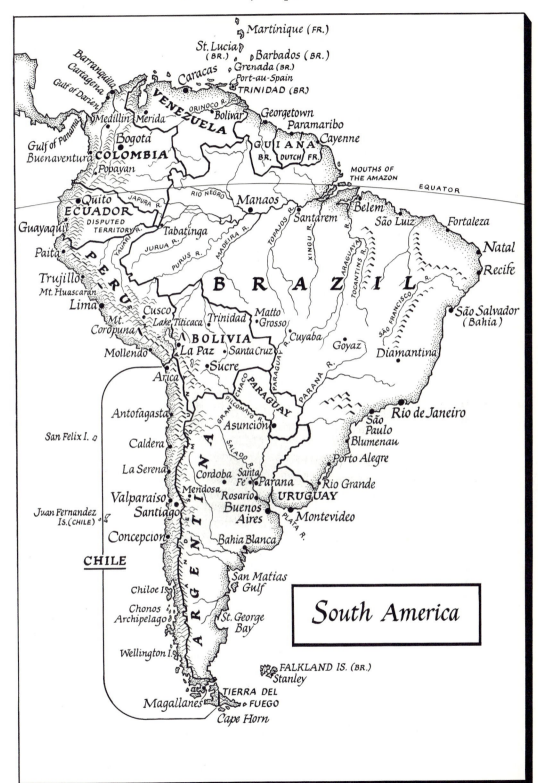

Martinique (FR.)
St. Lucia (BR.)
Barbados (BR.)
Grenada (BR.)
Port-au-Spain
TRINIDAD (BR.)
Caracas
Barranquilla
Cartagena
Gulf of Darien
VENEZUELA
ORINOCO R.
Bolivar
Georgetown
Paramaribo
Cayenne
GUIANA
BR. DUTCH FR.
Medillin Merida
Gulf of Panama
Bogota
Buenaventura
COLOMBIA
Popayan
MOUTHS OF THE AMAZON
EQUATOR
Quito
ECUADOR
DISPUTED TERRITORY
JAPURA R.
RIO NEGRO
Manaos
Belem
São Luiz
Fortaleza
Guayaquil
Paita
PERU
Tabatinga
YAVARY R.
JURUA R.
PURUS R.
MADEIRA R.
TOPAJOS R.
Santarem
XINGU R.
PARAGUAY R.
TOCANTINS R.
Natal
Recife
Trujillo
Mt. Huascarán
Lima
B R A Z I L
SÃO FRANCISCO R.
São Salvador (Bahia)
Cusco
Lake Titicaca
Trinidad
Matto Grosso
Cuyaba
Goyaz
Diamantina
Mt. Coropuna
BOLIVIA
La Paz
Santa Cruz
Mollendo
Sucre
PARAGUAY R.
Arica
CHACO
PARAGUAY
PARANA R.
Rio de Janeiro
Antofagasta
PILCOMAYO R.
Asuncion
São Paulo
Blumenau
San Felix I.
Caldera
ARGENTINA
SALADO R.
Porto Alegre
La Serena
Cordoba
Santa Fe
Parana
Rio Grande
Valparaiso
Mendosa
Rosario
URUGUAY
Juan Fernandez IS.(CHILE)
Santiago
Buenos Aires
PLATA R.
Montevideo
Concepcion
Bahia Blanca
CHILE
San Matias Gulf
Chiloe IS.
Chonos Archipelago
St. George Bay
Wellington I.
FALKLAND IS. (BR.)
Stanley
Magallanes
TIERRA DEL FUEGO
Cape Horn

South America

Cuba

Great Britain was not the only European power, however, whose concern with American affairs led to diplomatic difficulties with the United States. Spain still held a remnant of her once great American empire, notably the two islands of Cuba and Puerto Rico just south of the Atlantic seaboard of the United States. Cuba had long been a storm-center in Spanish-American relations. Before the Civil War southern expansionists had coveted the island; after the war Cuban insurrectionists had repeatedly sought to involve the United States in their struggles. For ten years, from 1868 to 1878, the island was in constant turmoil, and in 1895 another revolt broke out. This second insurrection came about in no small part as a result of American tariff legislation. The McKinley Tariff of 1890, which admitted raw sugar free of duty and compensated American growers by a bounty, had enormously stimulated the Cuban sugar industry. Much new foreign capital was poured into Cuban plantations, and for a brief period the island enjoyed unusual prosperity. When, in 1894, the Wilson-Gorman Act again made raw sugar dutiable, Cuban sugar prices declined precipitately, and the era of prosperity vanished as rapidly as it had come. With the American market for other Cuban commodities, notably tobacco, also weakened by the depression, hard times and unemployment provided a convenient setting for insurrection. Even in prosperous times the ordinary Cuban, whose lot as a peon was only a little better than that of a serf, had abundant reason for discontent. Spanish policy discriminated not only in favor of the mother country, but also in favor of the small ruling caste of pure-blood Spaniards in Cuba. The Cuban "native," colored by a strong infusion of Negro blood, did most of the work, while the upper-class whites took most of the profits.

Furthermore, the Spanish officials in Cuba were notably inefficient and corrupt.

Nature of the Cuban Revolt

It is an exaggeration to speak of the disorder in Cuba that broke out in 1895 as a revolution, although citizens of the United States tended to view it in that light. Maximo Gomez, the Cuban leader, was utterly unable to maintain a government, or even to keep an army in the field. What he promoted was insurrection rather than revolution, and his chief weapon was devastation. Small guerrilla bands, often operating by night rather than by day, destroyed sugar mills, laid waste plantations belonging to Spanish loyalists, and sought in every way to starve and demoralize their enemies. Carrying on at first almost without military equipment, the Cuban *insurrectos* were soon receiving aid from other Cubans who resided in the United States, and from American sympathizers, most of whom thought of Gomez and his guerrillas in terms that might have been applied to George Washington and the patriot army of 1776. In New York a Cuban junta, which called itself the Cuban government, sold bonds, and with the proceeds bought and shipped arms to the insurrectionary forces.

Spanish methods of dealing with the insurrection were both brutal and effective. "Butcher" Weyler, the Spanish commander in Cuba, built "corrals" of barbed wire and blockhouses to separate the more peaceful sections of the island from the more warlike, and herded all the population suspected of disloyalty into *reconcentrado* camps, which were policed by Spanish troops. This policy was well advanced toward the pacification of the island when the Cuban situation began to make the headlines in American newspapers. In the camps the suffering was indescribable, for the Spanish were unable to provide adequate food and housing for the people whose freedom they curtailed. Reporters told lurid tales of the bad conditions they saw, and Americans who resided in Cuba or who visited the islands for the sights they could see corroborated the newspaper accounts. The American public, long unaccustomed to the horrors of war, began to feel that the government of the United States should take a hand in the situation, and do something to "reform" the war. Both Cleveland and McKinley tried hard to keep the peace, and the latter had only this object in mind when he made strong representations to the Spanish government "against the uncivilized and inhuman" conduct of Weyler's campaign. The Spanish government, conscious of the fact that the proximity of the United States to Cuba gave the Americans an immense military advantage, made every effort to comply with McKinley's request, even ordering the abandonment of the *reconcentrado* policy, and the recall of Weyler. In fact, the American minister to Spain informed his government that the Spanish officials, if given a little time, would agree to whatever demands the United States cared to make.

Whatever chance there was of peaceful settlement evaporated as a result of two untoward incidents. The first was the publication of a private letter written by Dupuy de Lôme, the Spanish minister in Washington, to a friend in Cuba. This letter, purloined from the mails by a clerk in the Havana post office and published in the newspapers, described McKinley as a "spineless politician." Inasmuch as the original one-hundred-per-cent American, Theodore Roosevelt, held that the President had "no more backbone than a chocolate éclair," de Lôme's statement may not have been altogether inaccurate, but it was one thing for an American citizen to speak his mind about the President, and quite another for a foreign minister to make such a statement. De Lôme's recall was immediately requested, and the offending minister resigned.

The other unfortunate incident was the destruction of the battleship *Maine* in Havana Harbor, February 15, 1898, with heavy loss of life. The *Maine* had been sent to Cuban waters the preceding January, ostensibly on a "courtesy call," but actually to protect Americans and American interests in the troubled area. That the Spanish government could have promoted such a catastrophe at a time when its officials were making every effort to keep on good terms with the United States seems incredible, but the American public jumped immediately to the conclusion that Spain was responsible The battle cry, "Remember the *Maine*," rent the air, and the demands on Spain made by the American government became more and more peremptory.

American Intervention

It is possible that war might have been averted had McKinley had the same sort of courage that John Adams exhibited in 1798, when he prevented hostilities between the United States and France from going the full length of declared war. Nor would McKinley have had to abandon the island to Spanish rule; he could have named his own terms. Had the President decided to make a firm stand for peace, he would have received the cordial support of Marcus A. Hanna and many another leading capitalist who feared the economic unsettlement that war might bring. But McKinley knew that opposition to following the lead of the "plutocrats" on this, or on any other matter, was already rife among the young Republicans, and he believed that only by yielding to the popular clamor for war could he be certain of holding his party together. Finally, on April 9, the Spanish government, in response to a joint peace plea, delivered by the great powers of Europe to both Spain and the United States, ordered the cessation of hostilities in Cuba and gave in to the American contentions on every essential point. Nevertheless, the President on April 11 sent a war message to Congress. Six days later Congress by joint resolution demanded that Spain withdraw from Cuba, and authorized the President to use the military and naval forces of the United States to effect that end. Expressly disclaiming any intent to add Cuba to the United States, the resolution went on to assert that the people of the island were "and of right ought to be free and independent."

The outbreak of hostilities in this "needless war," as James Ford Rhodes, the historian, later described it, did not take place because of the failure of American diplomacy. War came in spite of the complete success of American diplomacy, and primarily because the American people wanted a war and President McKinley bowed to the public clamor. In part this demand came from Americans who wanted protection for their investments in Cuba, now totalling over $50 million. But in part it arose from a state of mind that permeated the public as a whole. It is significant that American business leaders generally opposed the idea of war, while innumerable journalists, politicians, admirals, and even clergymen demanded it in the name of nationalism, inevitable growth, and humanity. The American frontier was exhausted; where else could Americans look for new conquests if not beyond the national borders? Empire-building was in the air. The great European powers had already divided up much of Africa and Asia, and they were rapidly foreclosing on the rest. Darwinism, as applied to the the life of nations by Admiral Alfred Thayer Mahan and Senator Henry Cabot Lodge, seemed to urge expansion as an inevitable manifestation of the survival of the fittest. With a somewhat different motivation, preachers argued for imperialism as a means of Christianizing and civilizing the world's "little brown brothers"; it was all a part of the "white man's burden." Nor should it be for-

gotten that the American people had lived through a harrowing depression and an election in which radical social changes had been proposed, with the upper and the lower classes ranged in strong opposition to each other. What better means of restoring national unity could there be than a foreign venture which would cost so little by way of expenditure in blood and treasure, but promised so much in hope and glory?

Nor can one overlook the lasting legacy of the Civil War, a struggle which for more than thirty years had colored almost every aspect of American thought and action. Veterans of the Civil War were held in honor because of their war record, and particularly in politics they tended to fare better than the men who had stayed at home. As the old soldiers grew older, they forgot the seamy side of war, and told tall tales of heroics and adventure. Young Americans, typified by Theodore Roosevelt, had grown to manhood on a steady diet of Civil War glorification. They envied the boys in blue or gray, and felt cheated that they had had no chance to win distinction for themselves in war.[1] Older Americans saw certain advantages in letting youth have its way. They took pride in the great new nation that they had seen emerge, but their faith was somehow tinctured with doubt. Had the United States really arrived as a nation, or was it only on its way? Perhaps by a baptism of blood the country could prove to itself and the rest of the world that it was really great. If the United States could win a war, who could deny it the high station among the nations of the world to which it aspired? Years later, Theodore Roosevelt recaptured

[1] It is interesting to note that in England Winston Churchill and other ambitious young men were complaining also of the lack of a war, especially a war that would give them the chance to shoot at other white men. See Robert Lewis Taylor, *Winston Churchill: An Informal Study of Greatness* (1952), p. 90.

The Battleship *Oregon*, pride of the United States Navy.

THE NAVY AND THE WAR. *The United States Navy, in contrast with the Army, was well prepared for war in 1898, both as to personnel and fighting ships.*

Admiral George Dewey. The hero of Manila Bay, from an engraving by E. S. King in the Mariners' Museum.

the atmosphere of 1898 when, if correctly reported, he mourned apologetically, "It wasn't much of a war, but it was the best war we had." And, in his eyes, and in those of most Americans, it had freed a subject people from foreign rule.

The American Navy

As the American people entered the war, they were extremely conscious and proud of the new "white navy" by means of which they hoped to win it. The construction of steel ships had begun in the eighties, in part as a means of reducing the then vexatious surplus, but even in the "heart-breaking nineties," when funds were low, more and more new units were added to the navy. By that time Admiral Mahan had begun the publication of a series of books which demonstrated conclusively that the influence of sea power on a nation's desti-

nies, particularly in wartime, was decisive. Mahan made important converts, among them Theodore Roosevelt, whom McKinley appointed Assistant Secretary of the Navy in 1897. In office Roosevelt made a fetish of naval efficiency, and insisted above all else on target practice. Ten days after the *Maine* went down, he took advantage of his superior's absence from Washington to put the entire navy on a war footing. "The very devil seemed to possess him," the outraged Secretary of the Navy, John D. Long, confided to his diary. It was possibly due to Roosevelt's planning, also, that Commodore George Dewey was in command of an American squadron in Asiatic waters — in striking distance of the Spanish fleet in Manila Bay — when war broke out. The stronger portion of the American navy, however, was mobilized off Chesapeake Bay under command of Captain (later Rear-Admiral) William T. Sampson, who was advanced to his post over a dozen ranking senior officers. A new battleship, the *Oregon*, uselessly located in the North Pacific, was ordered to the Atlantic, and on March 19 began a voyage around Cape Horn that for two months whetted the interest of the newspaper-reading public.

The Army

If the navy was well prepared for war, the army was not. Its 27,000 officers and men were scattered over the country in small garrisons; it lacked a central planning board comparable to the present general staff; its ranking officers owed their positions to seniority rather than to efficiency. The second line of defense, the National Guard of the states, was of uncertain size and merit, but capable of great expansion in case of need. Everyone took it for granted, however, that in a really important war a volunteer army, organized along the lines of the Union army in the Civil War, would do most of the fighting. And yet Congress, for all its impatience to get on with the war, did little to make ready for it before it came. Fifty million dollars was appropriated for the national defense in March, 1898, but not until late in April, after the war resolutions had been passed, were extensive army increases authorized. At that time Congress voted an expansion of the regular army to 62,597 men, and the creation of a volunteer army of 125,000. While most of the volunteers were to be raised through the states, as in the Civil War, the law also provided that the President might accept directly into the national service three regiments of volunteer cavalry. This provision was included primarily to enable Theodore Roosevelt, who now resigned as Assistant Secretary of the Navy, to lead a regiment into battle. With the help of Captain Leonard Wood, an officer of the medical corps, Roosevelt brought together a motley array of ex-cowboys, college athletes, and adventurers to form the First United States Volunteer Cavalry, or, as they were generally called, the "Rough Riders." Since Roosevelt had had no military experience whatever, he modestly accepted only a lieutenant-colonelcy, while the command of the regiment went to Wood.

Dewey at Manila

The first blow of the war was struck by Commodore Dewey at Manila Bay, into which the American commander had led his little fleet of four cruisers and three minor craft early on the morning of May 1. There, in leisurely fashion, with time out for breakfast, Dewey's ships methodically destroyed the Spanish ships, which their commander, Admiral Montojo, knowing full well what was in store for him, had thoughtfully stationed at some distance from the defenses of Manila so that the city might be spared the danger of shell-fire, and in shallow water where as many as possible of his men might escape. The Spanish losses in this one-sided battle included 381 killed, besides numerous wounded, while not an American was killed and only seven or eight were wounded.

Popular rejoicing in the United States on the receipt of the news from Manila Bay was unrestrained, but Dewey's position was in reality far from comfortable. He had possession of the Bay, but not one foot of land. Naturally he lost no time in urging the American government to send an expeditionary force to his aid, but the needed land forces did not arrive until the end of July. Meantime, Dewey had had a misunderstanding that might have been serious with Admiral Otto von Diedrichs, commander of a German fleet that had anchored in the harbor, but, thanks to hearty cooperation from Captain Edward Chichester, commander of a British squadron, the affair was settled amicably. When finally General Wesley Merritt arrived, with a force of nearly 11,000 men, the city of Manila was captured with little more than token resistance. By that time both the Spanish and the Americans were less worried about each other than about the presence of a large army of Philippine insurgents under Emilio Aguinaldo, a native leader whom the Spanish had once exiled, but whom Dewey had brought back home. Curiously, the surrender of Manila to the Americans occurred August 14. with both parties unaware of the fact that on the other side of the world, two calendar days before, an armistice had been signed.

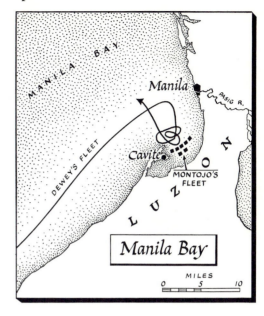

Santiago

Events in the Atlantic theater had moved less swiftly than in the Pacific, but the outcome was quite as decisive. The first concern of the American fleet was to intercept and destroy a Spanish squadron, known to have set sail from the Cape Verde Islands on April 29 for American waters. But the Spanish commander, Admiral Pascual Cervera, succeeded in reaching the port of Santiago de Cuba without being challenged by the Americans on the high seas. There he was presently blockaded by Admiral Sampson's entire fleet, including the lately arrived *Oregon*. The Spanish ships were no match for the Americans, and Cervera on this account seemed bent on avoiding battle. Sampson planned to block the narrow entrance to the harbor by sinking an old collier, the *Merrimac*, in its channel. This feat of seamanship was accomplished by Lieutenant Richmond Pierson Hobson and a crew of seven men; but the *Merrimac* went down in such a position as to permit the Spanish fleet to come out, or the Americans to go in, if either cared to try.

Unwilling to risk his ships to the mines and fortifications of the harbor's entrance, Sampson, like Dewey before him, asked for a land expedition to come to his aid. The plans of the army, prepared by the senior major-general, Nelson A. Miles, were to take Puerto Rico during the summer, and later, when the danger from tropical diseases would be less, to make a frontal assault on Havana. All this had now to be changed, and an expeditionary force had to be dispatched without further preparation to Santiago. Amidst literally indescribable

The Invasion of Cuba. *The unpreparedness of the army for foreign war resulted in much confusion, but the fighting men acquitted themselves well. This photograph shows troops going ashore in men-of-war's boats. From* Harper's Weekly, *July 16, 1898.*

confusion, some 6,000 troops, all from the regular army except Theodore Roosevelt's Rough Riders (without their horses), were dispatched from Tampa Bay, Florida, on June 14, and six days later appeared off Santiago. From their first meeting, General William R. Shafter, in command of the army, and Admiral Sampson, in command of the navy, misunderstood each other perfectly. Nevertheless, the troops somehow got ashore several miles to the east of the harbor, and with the Rough Riders ever in the thick of the fray began an advance that by the first days of July had led them to the storming of San Juan Hill, close to the city's last defenses. By this time, however, the American striking power was almost spent, and the officers in command scarcely knew whether to advance or retreat. "We are within measurable distance of a terrible military disaster," wrote Theodore Roosevelt.

San Juan Hill. *A portion of the American line held by the 9th United States Infantry. From* Harper's Weekly, *July 30, 1898.*

Sampson or Schley?

But as events proved the Spanish were even more thoroughly disheartened than the Americans. Their army was short of ammunition and the city was on the verge of famine. Nothing, it seemed to them, could halt the American advance. Ultimate surrender was inevitable. Under orders from Madrid, Admiral Cervera made a brave attempt on July 3 to escape with his squadron from the harbor, but American shells set his wooden-decked ships afire, and one after another they had to be beached. When the fight was over he had lost every ship, and had casualties of about 400 killed and wounded; the American fleet was practically unharmed, and had lost one man killed and one man wounded. At the time the battle began, Admiral Sampson was several miles away in conference with General Shafter, and the highest ranking officer on the scene was Commodore W. S. Schley. Before the battle ended, Sampson's flagship was in the fight, and the American ships, with the exception of the one on which Schley was stationed, had throughout obeyed Sampson's orders and ignored Schley's. Nevertheless, the debate long raged in the newspapers, "Was it Sampson, or was it Schley?" Theodore Roosevelt's verdict that there was "glory enough for all" probably overstated the facts, and certainly made few converts.

Armistice Terms

With Cuba's naval protection gone and communications with Spain cut, there was nothing left for the Spanish government to do but to sue for peace. This it did through the French embassy at Washington, which opened negotiations for an armistice on July 13. Three days later, General José Velazquez Toral, in command of the Spanish forces at Santiago, signed articles of capitulation with Shafter. By this time General Miles, lest he be too late,

was beginning his expedition to Puerto Rico, which, lacking opposition, proved to be in comparison with the Santiago campaign a model of efficiency. The chief purpose of the expedition was to enable the United States with better grace to lay claim to the island, for the French ambassador, as intermediary, soon learned that before the United States would make peace, Spain must agree to withdraw entirely from the western hemisphere. Spanish sovereignty over Cuba must be relinquished, and all the rest of the Spanish West Indies, including Puerto Rico, must be ceded to the United States. On the other side of the world the American government demanded the cession of Guam (midway between Hawaii and the Philippines), and possession of the city, harbor, and bay of Manila, pending determination in the treaty of the "control, disposition, and government" of the Philippines. In view of these somewhat extraordinary territorial demands, the United States promised to waive for the time being "any demand for pecuniary indemnity." On these terms an armistice was signed on August 12, and the war was over.

Treaty of Paris

Commissioners from the United States and Spain met in Paris, October 1, 1898, to work out the details of peace. The American delegation consisted of William R. Day, chairman, who was required to resign as Secretary of State to accept the assignment, three leading senators of whom one was a Democrat, and a prominent Republican newspaper editor. McKinley's instructions gave the commissioners no option as to the expulsion of the Spanish Empire from America, but the Spanish delegation argued plausibly that, inasmuch as there was no government in Cuba worthy of the name, that island should be ceded directly to the United States, which would thereby become responsible for the Cuban debt.

End of the War. *John Hay, Secretary of State, signing the memorandum of ratification on behalf of the United States. President McKinley stands to his right. From* Harper's Weekly, *April 22, 1899.*

The Americans refused this dubious offer. They agreed that the United States should occupy the island temporarily, but they successfully insisted that Spain should assume the island's debt. The most heated dispute was over the Philippine Islands, which McKinley soon informed the American commissioners they must somehow obtain. Since the total area of the Philippines was about 7,000 square miles greater than that of the British Isles, and since in all this vast space the United States had occupied only one city, the demand seemed utterly unjustified on military grounds. Spanish protests were long drawn out, and in the end the Spanish commissioners won an extraordinary concession. Without exactly explaining why it was to be done, the United States agreed to "pay to Spain the sum of $20 million within three months after the exchange of the ratifications of the present treaty." Money payments were usually demanded of vanquished powers instead of being accorded to them, but, in view of the extensive territorial cessions the United States had obtained, a money indemnity could hardly have been required. The American payment was variously explained as representing the difference in value between what the United States had

actually conquered and what it insisted on taking, or the investment the Spanish government had made in the Philippines, or what it was worth to the United States in satisfaction just to have a war and win it. On December 10, 1898, the treaty was finally signed, and early next month the President submitted it to the Senate for ratification.

Ratification

For a time there was danger that the necessary two-thirds majority could not be obtained. Led by the "peerless" William Jennings Bryan, "anti-imperialists" gave battle the whole country over against so wide a departure from American tradition as was involved in the acquisition of the Philippines. Not Democrats merely, but many prominent Republicans also, including Senator Hale of Maine and Senator Hoar of Massachusetts, objected strenuously to the terms of the treaty, and when the time came voted against ratification. Speaker Thomas B. Reed was "terribly bitter" in his opposition, and according to Senator Lodge was "saying all sorts of ugly things about the Administration and its policy." Ultimately Reed resigned his seat in the House and retired from politics rather than stand with his party on such an issue. Andrew Carnegie went to Washington and lobbied against the treaty. Strange as it may seem, the man who finally saved the treaty was Bryan. According to one point of view, the "Great Commoner" was convinced that free silver would not provide the Democrats with a winning issue in 1900, and saw in a battle over imperialism the best chance for a Democratic victory. But according to another point of view he was not seeking primarily to create an election issue; all he wanted to do was to insure that so important a question as Philippine independence should be decided separately from the rest of the treaty, and solely on its own merits. Whatever his motives may have been — some say he was merely "dumb" — he maintained that the proper policy was first to accept the treaty, and then to demand that the Philippines be set free. Without the efforts of Bryan, who conferred in Washington with wavering Democrats and Populists, it seems certain that the administration would have lost. As it was, ten Democrats and eight Populists voted with thirty-nine Republicans to give the treaty one more than the two-thirds majority required for ratification.

The United States as a World Power

By any standards of measurement, the United States emerged from the Spanish-American War a world power. It had defeated a European nation in war, and, thanks to the war and other expansionist efforts, it had added to its possessions regions distant enough and different enough that none could deny the existence of an American empire. Alaska, the Hawaiian Islands, the Philippines, and Puerto Rico, all these and a number of minor islands, together with the temporary occupation of Cuba, satisfied for the moment the ambitions of the most rabid of expansionists. Of these possessions Alaska and Hawaii seemed most easily as-

similable. Alaska the United States had owned since 1867, but only since 1896, when gold was discovered in the Klondike, a nearby district in Canada, had the possibilities of "Seward's Folly" been realized. Thereafter, the discovery in Alaska itself of gold, and the exploitation of its other vast national resources, had proved the acquisition to be an extremely profitable investment. As for Hawaii, the need for a mid-Pacific base, following Dewey's victory at Manila Bay, paved the way for annexation by joint resolution of Congress, signed July 7, 1898. The mid-Pacific islands thus acquired had a population of more than 150,-000, and enormous sugar-producing possibilities. Not more than one-fifth of their residents were native Hawaiians; nearly another fifth were Caucasians, and the remaining three-fifths were Orientals. Here long-standing American investments were important, and the wishes of American residents were given careful consideration. Both Alaska and Hawaii became territories of the United States after the traditional pattern, although Alaska was much slower than Hawaii in achieving full territorial status. For both, statehood long seemed out of the question.

Freedom for Cuba

The Spanish cessions presented many perplexing problems. Cuba had to be occupied, made more sanitary, and provided with a government before it could be set free. Under General Leonard Wood as governor, and with the assistance of many American medical men, notably Majors William C. Gorgas and Walter Reed, the pacification and sanitation of the islands was accomplished with praiseworthy speed. As an incident to this task the mosquito carrier of yellow fever was identified, and the pestilence it spread brought under control. By 1901 the Cubans had formed a constitution, patterned after that of the United States, and were ready to begin

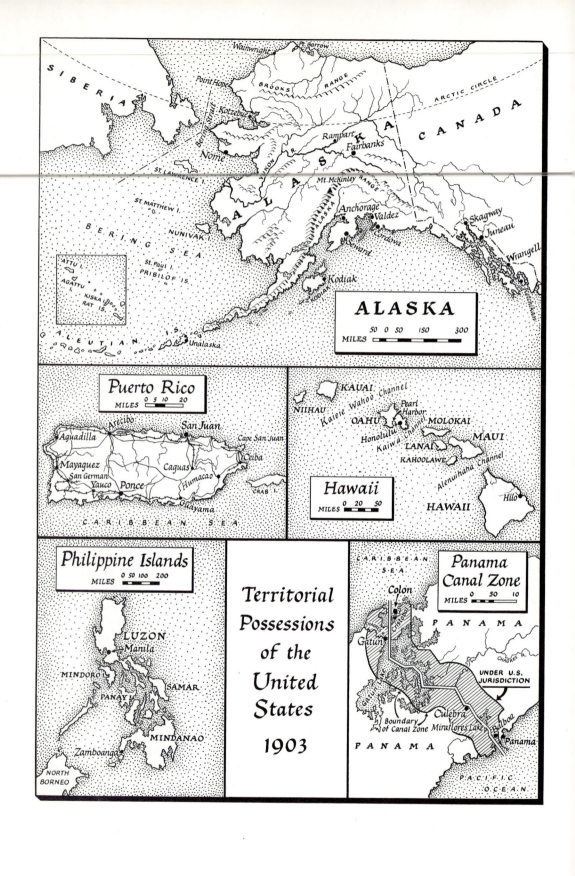

ALASKA

MILES 50 0 50 150 300

Puerto Rico

MILES 0 5 10 20

Hawaii

MILES 0 20 50

Philippine Islands

MILES 0 50 100 200

Panama Canal Zone

MILES 0 50 10

Territorial
Possessions
of the
United
States

1903

self-rule. Before this could be accomplished, however, they were required by the United States to subscribe to the famous "Platt Amendment," which seriously limited the sovereignty of the new republic. Cuba might not make any treaty that would impair its independence, it must keep its debt within its capacity to pay, it must permit the United States to intervene with force in case that should be necessary to keep order, and it must carry out the plans of sanitation the United States had begun. When an insurrection broke out in Cuba in August, 1906, the United States exercised its right of intervention, and sent William Howard Taft to Cuba to "sit on the lid." For more than two years the American occupation continued. On several other occasions the United States made use of its right of intervention, but in every such instance stopped short of annexation. Finally, under Franklin D. Roosevelt, the Platt Amendment was abrogated.

The Philippines

The problem of Cuba was as nothing compared to the problem of the Philippines, for in annexing the latter the United States acquired also a full-blown insurrection. The Philippine population, which was a mixture of native races and immigrants from the Asiatic mainland, included about 7 million Spanish-speaking and Roman Catholic Filipinos, besides perhaps two-thirds of a million wild and uncivilized Igorrotes and Moros. Under Spanish rule the islanders had suffered from neglect, exploitation, and oppression, and, when the Spanish-American War broke out, Filipino insurgents were seriously challenging Spanish supremacy. The insurrection was immensely aided by Dewey's return of its exiled leader, Emilio Aguinaldo, whose forces, by the time the United States had acquired title to the islands, actually held the upper hand

Taft Sitting on the Lid. *This cartoon shows William Howard Taft, a favorite foreign envoy of President Theodore Roosevelt, "Home Again," with plenty to do. W. A. Rogers in* Harper's Weekly, *May 13, 1905.*

everywhere except in Luzon. At first the Filipinos had assumed naively that the American promise of freedom for Cuba carried with it by implication the promise of freedom for the Philippines. When they learned that the United States had no such intentions, they turned in full force against the new invaders, and for two and one-half years fought hard for their independence. Not until October 1, 1901, did the United States find it possible to announce the complete suppression of the insurrection, and for many months longer the facts failed to justify the statement.

The Philippine Insurrection. *In this conflict American troops experienced most of the hazards of guerrilla warfare. In the picture American volunteers are shown taking the offensive against the enemy. From a United States Army photograph.*

Puerto Rico

The occupation of Puerto Rico[1] involved fewer perplexities than confronted American officials either in the Philippines or in Cuba. The population of the island was less than a million, nearly two-thirds of whom were white, and the rest of Negro extraction. There had been no revolution and no war damage of consequence. American rule was accepted without enthusiasm, but without protest. Even under the military regime rapid strides were made toward better sanitation, the building of roads, and the reordering of public finance. So smooth was the transition that as early as April 12, 1900, Congress passed the Foraker Act establishing a civil government for Puerto Rico, the first to be accorded any of the new possessions. The pattern of government thus set for the dependencies was similar to that of the traditional American territory, but with fewer privileges of self-government. Furthermore, residents of

[1] By an act of Congress, signed May 17, 1932, the name Puerto Rico was officially substituted for Porto Rico.

the island were not yet accorded full American citizenship, but were described instead as citizens of Puerto Rico. Later on, important changes occurred. An act of Congress signed March 2, 1917, provided the island with the customary territorial form of government, and declared its citizens to be citizens of the United States. Another act, signed July 3, 1950, recognized the right of the Puerto Ricans to adopt a constitution, and establish a government of their own. After this was done, Puerto Rico was correctly described as a self-governing commonwealth voluntarily associated with the United States. Its people elected their own governor as well as legislature, and and on local matters its government was completely autonomous.

Election of 1900

Republican successes in the elections of 1898 denoted little more than general satisfaction at the victories won by Americans in the war with Spain, but the presidential election of 1900 was a pitched battle, with imperialism, in Bryan's words, the "paramount issue." The Republicans, with William McKinley once more their standard-bearer, and with Theodore Roosevelt, the hero of San Juan Hill, as their candidate for Vice-President, rejoiced in the "new and noble responsibility" that had come to the American people, and asserted that "no other course was possible" in the Philippines than the one that had been taken. The Democrats, still under the spell of Bryan's oratory, also renominated their leader of the preceding campaign, but for second place they had no war hero, only the time-worn Vice-President of Cleveland's second administration, Adlai E. Stevenson of Illinois. Bryan himself had been a colonel of Nebraska volunteers, but he had had no such luck with the War Department in obtaining a chance to fight as had the colonel on the Republican ticket.

Imperialism the Paramount Issue

During the campaign the Democrats saw to it that debate on imperialism held the center of the stage. The arguments were not new; they had all been used while the Treaty of Paris was before the country. Nor was the decision ever in doubt. McKinley, as the cartoonists so graphically portrayed, always had his "ear to the ground," and he knew full well that he had read the public mind aright. Nevertheless, Democratic orators dwelt long upon the inconsistency of a democracy such as the United States fighting to suppress the ambitions of another people to be free. They cast William McKinley in the role of George III, and Aguinaldo in that of George Washington. They pointed out the practical difficulties involved. The United States was wholly without experience in the governing of colonies. How could it hope to solve the problems of a distant and alien race? A great navy and a great army would be necessary to protect the new possessions. Once the United States had depended upon the Atlantic Ocean and the Pacific Ocean for its defense. But with Asiatic possessions American military might must be expanded to reach far across the seas.

Republican orators had no difficulty in defending all that had been done. The Philippines, they claimed, offered an inviting missionary field. The United States had at last an opportunity to extend the blessings of American civilization. The Filipinos were not yet capable of governing themselves; freedom would mean only anarchy and misrule, or perhaps conquest by some predatory commercial nation, such as Germany or France. The United States had become a great power, and it must accept the responsibilities of greatness, or

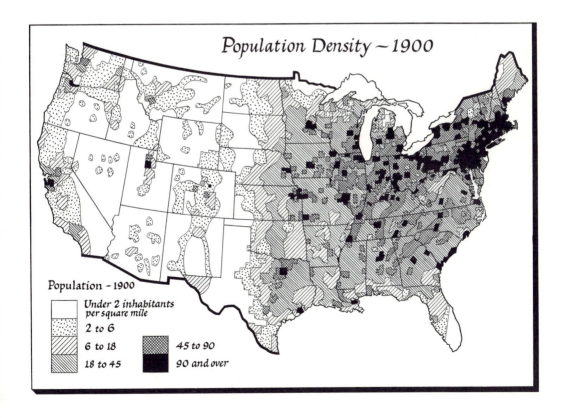

Population Density – 1900

Population – 1900

- Under 2 inhabitants per square mile
- 2 to 6
- 6 to 18
- 18 to 45
- 45 to 90
- 90 and over

as Kipling phrased it, "Take up the White Man's Burden." There would be profits, too, good profits, from colonial trade. The Philippines were pictured not only as a land inviting investments, but also as a steppingstone to the "illimitable markets" of China. In the spirit of European imperialists Senator Beveridge exclaimed, "The trade of the world must and shall be ours." Besides, how could the United States be a really great nation if it had no colonies? Other great nations had colonies and were engaged in a mad scramble for more. Why should Americans deny themselves whatever glory colonial possessions would bring?

Other Issues

But imperialism was not the only issue of the campaign. On free silver and the tariff both parties defended the positions they had taken in 1896, and these issues swayed many voters. Cartoonists made merry with the "hold-your-nose-and-vote" crowd. Some gold-standard men "held their noses" and voted for Bryan because they agreed with him on imperialism; some free-traders "held their noses" and voted for the obnoxious McKinley because they believed in expansion; in a variety of ways the old adage that "politics makes strange bedfellows" was proved to be true. Shrewdly, Republican campaigners turned attention away from these discordant issues all they could, and rang the changes on prosperity. By comparing the hard times of Cleveland's second administration with the good times of the McKinley era, they were able to associate prosperity with Republican policies and to blame adversity on the Democrats. Slogans such as "The Full Dinner Pail," and "Let Well Enough Alone," pressed home the point.

Re-election of McKinley

In the end McKinley won a more overwhelming victory than in 1896. He had again the advantage of a huge campaign fund, while Bryan's backers had even less to spend than four years before. Bryan carried only the "solid South," and four silver states, Colorado, Nevada, Idaho, and Montana, while McKinley carried all the rest, including Bryan's home state, Nebraska. The popular vote stood 7.2 million to 6.3 million and the electoral vote, 292 to 155. The election was notable for the large number of minor parties that had presidential tickets in the field, but the number of voters they attracted was so small that McKinley received a majority of the popular as well as of the electoral vote. Both houses of Congress were also assured to the Republicans by substantial majorities, and, except in the South, Republican candidates for state office were generally the victors. In so far as an election could decide anything, the country had given its approval to imperialism, the gold standard, and a high protective tariff.

Constitutional Problems

A problem of imperialism as yet unsettled at the time of the election was how to reconcile the exigencies of empire with the Constitution of the United States. According to the treaty of cession, "the civil rights and political status of the native inhabitants of the territory . . . ceded to the United States" were left to the determination of Congress. Did this mean that Congress could do as it pleased without extending the liberties guaranteed by the Constitution to its island possessions, or was the freedom of Congress in this respect as much subject to the Constitution in the new territory as in the old? In other words, as the public phrased the question, Does the Constitution follow the flag?

From the first, Congress assumed that it was free from all embarrassing constitutional limitations. In the Foraker Act, for example, it levied a tariff against Puerto Rican imports into the United States equal

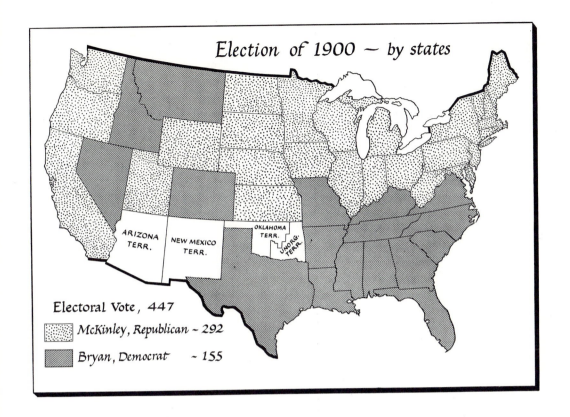

Election of 1900 — by states

ARIZONA TERR.

NEW MEXICO TERR.

OKLAHOMA TERR.

UNORG. TERR.

Electoral Vote, 447

McKinley, Republican – 292

Bryan, Democrat – 155

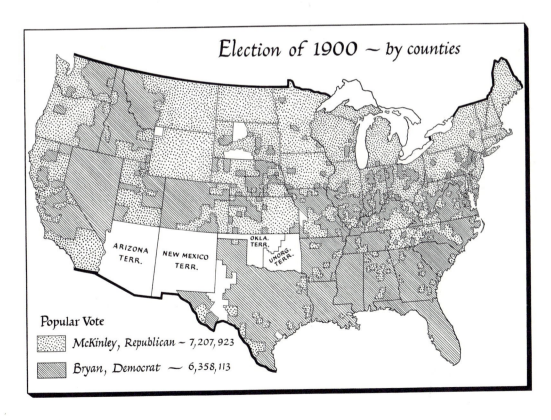

Election of 1900 — by counties

ARIZONA TERR.

NEW MEXICO TERR.

OKLA. TERR.

UNORG. TERR.

Popular Vote

McKinley, Republican – 7,207,923

Bryan, Democrat – 6,358,113

to 15 per cent of the regular import rates. If Puerto Rico had become a part of the United States this provision was clearly contrary to the constitutional requirements that "all duties, imports, and excises shall be uniform throughout the United States." Obviously, therefore, Congress did not regard the island as a part of the United States in the constitutional sense of the term, nor did the President who signed the law. But what would be the attitude of the federal courts, which since the time of John Marshall had felt free to set aside laws of Congress that in their judgment did not harmonize with the Constitution?

The "Insular Cases"

In a series of five-to-four opinions on what came generally to be known as the "insular cases" the Supreme Court decided in 1901 not to interfere with the stand that Congress and the President had taken. The first of these cases, *De Lima* vs. *Bidwell*, was brought by an importer of Puerto Rican sugar against the collector of the port of New York who *before* the enactment of the Foraker Act, but *after* the acquisition of Puerto Rico by the United States, had charged the full import duties. In this case the Court held that the money collected must be refunded, for Puerto Rico was no longer foreign territory. In another case, however, *Downes* vs. *Bidwell*, where the collections had been made *after* the passage of the Foraker Act and according to its terms, the Court held that a refund was unnecessary, for Puerto Rico was not exactly a part of the United States. To eight justices these decisions seemed utterly contradictory, for the result was achieved by Mr. Justice Brown changing sides, and voting in the second decision with the four justices who had constituted the minority in the first decision. The reasoning by which he sought to explain this shift of opinion no one but himself seemed to understand. But his decision, that Puerto Rico

and the other dependencies were "territory appurtenant — but not a part — of the United States," stood. "Mr. Dooley," the popular newspaper commentator of the time, probably got the idea clearly enough when he said: "No matter whether the constitution follows the flag, or not, th' Supreme Court follows th' illiction returns." In another case, *Hawaii* vs. *Mankichi*, the Court decided that in the period after annexation, but before the passage of an organic act of government, the inhabitants of the Hawaiian Islands could not claim the right of trial by jury as secured by the Fifth and Sixth Amendments. The reasoning in this case was even more stratospheric, for the Court held that the "rights alleged to be violated . . . are not fundamental in their nature."

Progress toward Self-Government

Following the British example, American colonial policy differed from the European. Cuba was set free, or at least relatively free, although the United States, had it chosen to do so, might easily have retained the island as a dependency. Even the Philippines were promised ultimate independence, by the Republicans no less than by the Democrats. On this issue the two parties differed merely as to when independence should be granted. What the Democrats said should be done immediately, the Republicans proposed to do later, after the Filipinos had enough experience in self-government to cope with the problems of independence. Philippine policy, therefore, worked toward increasing autonomy regardless of the party in power. McKinley sent William Howard Taft to the Philippines to institute civil government, and under his administration the beginnings of self-rule took place. By 1907 the Filipinos were electing the lower house of their legislature; by 1916, under the Jones Act, they were permitted virtual autonomy, although during the twenties, with the Re-

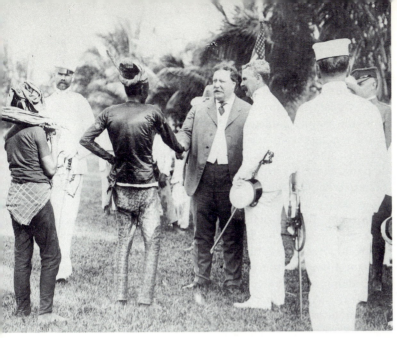

Taft in the Philippines. *Secretary Taft is shown here on his last visit to the Philippines greeting some of his old friends.*

publicans again in the ascendancy, some of the privileges acquired while Wilson was President were lost. By 1934, with the Democrats in power, the Tydings-McDuffie Act offered independence after ten years, an offer that the Philippines were willing to accept two years later. Soon after the Islands were recovered from Japan following the Second World War they became an independent republic.[1]

Dominion over the Philippines carried with it also many other familiar aspects of American culture. One of the most important innovations was the American public school system. In 1898 perhaps five thousand Filipino children were in school; by 1920, over a million. At first American teachers were placed in charge, but adequately trained Filipinos, many of them educated in the United States, were soon available to take over the work. By 1920 the number of American teachers had dwindled to three hundred, and the English language rivaled the Spanish as the most generally understood tongue in the islands. American notions of sanitation also reached the Philippines. Smallpox and cholera were stamped out, lepers were isolated in colonies and treated instead of be-

[1] See pp. 609–610.

ing permitted to roam at will, and the infantile death rate was sharply reduced. Good roads, too, were built, and improved methods of transportation were introduced. Most significant of all, the modified tariff barriers that had at first restricted trade between the Philippines and the United States soon gave way to virtual free trade, thus opening the rich American markets to Philippine sugar, coconut oil, rice, tobacco, and hemp. The result of this favored economic status was a degree of prosperity such as the Phliippines had never known before. Whatever their political differences, the economic ties that bound the islands to the United States became closer with each succeeding year. By the 1930's the United States was by far the most important market of the Philippines, and the source of most imports into the islands. It was because these ties would be hard to break that the probationary period of ten years, during which the American customs barriers were to be raised gradually, was stipulated in the Tydings-McDuffie Act.

China

While trade helped to sustain good relations between the United States and the

Philippines, it also helped to involve America seriously for the first time with the Oriental mainland. The threat to American isolation involved in the acquisition of a great overseas empire was more formidable than most Americans understood. Possession of the Philippines, in particular, made the United States, whether it so desired or not, a power in Asia with an interest in whatever went on there. But the great powers of Asia, with the exception of Japan, were also the great powers of Europe. By 1895 Great Britain, France, Russia, and the Netherlands dominated most of the non-Chinese Orient. And within a few years it was apparent that they, together with Japan and Germany, were intent upon completing the process with a division of China. "Spheres of influence" were already marked out, in which the various nations enjoyed special "concessions," and which they obviously hoped to absorb. When the United States became an Asiatic power, Great Britain held Hong Kong; Japan, Korea; Germany, a ninety-nine year lease on the port of Kiao-Chau, together with special rights in the entire Shantung Peninsula; France, Kwangchau Bay; and Russia, Port Arthur together with special privileges in Manchuria. If the process of dismembering China were completed, the old American trade with China would rapidly diminish and the imperialist hope that the Philippines would act as a way-station in a greatly expanded Oriental commerce would entirely dissolve. On the other hand, how could the United States maintain her traditional isolation from Europe and at the same time preserve her position and her aspirations in the Far East?

Hay's "Open Door" Policy

To counter the trend, John Hay, who had succeeded William Day as Secretary of State, seized upon a British suggestion and asked the great powers to agree to an "open door" in China. Each power was invited in the fall of 1899 (1) to respect the trading privileges of all other nations within its sphere of influence, (2) to permit Chinese officials to collect the existing tariff under which the United States was a most favored nation, and (3) to avoid discrimination against the nationals of other countries in port dues and in railroad rates. Great Britain, alone among the powers, accepted the Hay proposal outright, although excepting Hong Kong and Kowloon from the commitment. The others professed to agree in principle, but would accept only on condition that all other powers would do the same. Thereupon Hay blandly announced that, since all had agreed in principle, the United States now considered the policy approved. But it was a verbal victory only; events soon proved that very little had been changed.

The Boxer Rebellion

The outbreak of the Boxer Rebellion in the spring of 1900 furnished an excellent opportunity for the aggressive powers to pursue their ends. This nationalistic movement, led by a Chinese patriotic society called the Boxers, was directed against all foreigners and foreign property. With the Chinese police unable or unwilling to restore order, many foreigners were killed, and eventually the whole diplomatic corps was surrounded and besieged in Peking. Armed intervention by the foreign powers was now inevitable, and after much negotiation a joint international expeditionary force was sent to Tientsin, whence it set out for Peking to relieve the besieged diplomats, arriving August 14, 1900. Since this force included Japanese, Russian, German, and French troops, as well as British and American, most well-informed observers took it for granted that the affair would end in the complete partition of China.

That such a partition was avoided was

due largely to the stand taken by the United States, supported by Great Britain and eventually by Germany. While the fighting was still in progress Secretary Hay stated that it was a cardinal policy of the American government to "preserve Chinese territorial and administrative entity [integrity]," together with the "open door" for the commerce of all nations. In pursuit of these aims, Hay subsequently obtained an agreement among the participating nations to accept a money indemnity from China rather than the territorial cessions that some of them would have preferred. Of the total $333 million indemnity required of China, the share awarded to the United States amounted to less than $25 million. When later investigations indicated that even this sum was excessive, Congress in 1908, on recommendation of President Roosevelt, reduced the obligation to approximately half its original size, and in 1924 remitted also an unpaid balance of $6 million. In appreciation of these friendly acts the Chinese government announced that it would devote the first remission to the education of Chinese students in the United States, and the second to educational and scientific work in China. For a generation the Chinese tended to regard the United States as a kind of moral, if not political, ally.

The United States recognized no political alliance, with China or any other nation, but the Boxer negotiations betrayed clearly how significantly the acquisition of empire had altered the basic assumptions of American diplomacy. The decision to take part in an international military expedition was hard to reconcile with the traditional policy of no entangling alliances, while the demand for the preservation of Chinese territorial integrity, in view of the rapacious desires of some of the world's greatest nations, was an even more startling innovation. To guarantee this latter end, the American government would either have to rely upon military force, a course the whole world knew that the American people would oppose, or, more likely, upon diplomatic maneuverings toward a balance of power in the Orient. Either course would involve a virtual abandonment of long-established traditions.

Minor American Possessions

Recounting the spoils of imperialism, Americans were aware that certain minor possessions also formed a part of their new empire. Besides Alaska, Hawaii, the Philippines, and Puerto Rico, American sovereignty also extended to Guam, some fifteen hundred miles east of the Philippines, to American Samoa, which consisted of the island of Tutuila and several lesser islands in the Samoan group, and to numerous uninhabited Pacific islets over which no other nation had chosen to raise its flag. Until otherwise directed, these possessions remained under the absolute control of the President as commander-in-chief of the army and navy. Under his authority, the United States Navy, aided in each case by a local advisory legislature, administered both Guam and American Samoa until well after the Second World War. By an act of Congress, approved August 1, 1950, Guam became an unincorporated territory of the United States, and thereafter its administration was vested in the Department of the Interior. By an order of July 1, 1951, President Truman transferred the administration of American Samoa also to the Department of Interior. Both the Guamanians and the American Samoans became American citizens.

Also, the United States acquired two other tiny colonies as a result of the decision to build a canal across the Isthmus of Panama. The Canal Zone, ten miles wide, obtained by treaty with Panama in 1903, came to be inhabited principally by government employees, and was eventually left to the government of Congress, the

AN ESKIMO HOUSE MADE OF SKINS.

AN ALASKAN ESKIMO.

QUEEN LILIUOKALANI. The last native ruler of the Hawaiian Islands.

ALASKA AND HAWAII. *Alaska had long been an American possession, but interest in the area grew rapidly after the Klondike Gold Rush of 1897. Hawaii was ruled by a native dynasty until 1893, when the dynasty was overthrown by a revolution. From this time, until annexed by the United States in 1898, Hawaii was an independent republic.*

AN HAWAIIAN GRASS HOUSE.

President, and the national courts. The Virgin Islands, acquired by purchase from Denmark in 1917, were deemed of value for the proper defense of the Canal. To govern the impoverished 25,000 inhabitants, most of whom were of Negro descent, the President was authorized to appoint a governor, subject to the approval of the Senate. The Danish code of laws, already in force, was retained. President Truman, in 1950, appointed the first Virgin Islander to the governorship, while by a revised Organic Act of 1954, local legislative authority was vested in a unicameral legislature composed of eleven senators.

Imperial Defense

Just as the opponents of imperialism had predicted, the United States could not avoid the rapid expansion of its military might. If there was to be an American empire, that empire had to be defended. Under Elihu Root as Secretary of War the United States Army underwent a reorganization so thorough that the scandals of inefficiency that marred the prosecution of the war against Spain could not soon be repeated. In keeping with modern practice a general staff was created to take the place of the senior major-general in command of the army, and to lay plans for the proper defense of the United States and its possessions. By means of the Army War College, established in 1901, and other service schools, an attempt was made also to carry on the military education of officers after they had been commissioned. The size of the army was not greatly increased, but a new militia law, designed to make of the National Guard a more efficient second line of defense, was placed on the statute books in 1903. Even more striking than the reorganization of the army was the rapid expansion of the navy, to which one or two new battleships were added every year.

Decline of Interest in Colonies

Quite as striking a fact as the sudden acquisition of a colonial empire by the United States was the equally sudden subsidence of the expansionist urge. After the first excitement, interest in the newly acquired possessions diminished, and the public showed not the slightest appetite for more. When the United States entered the First World War in 1917, one of the certainties, unchallenged by any political party, was that the American nation would not emerge with more colonies. At the Paris Peace Conference the United States, almost alone among the victors, made no demands for territory, and all efforts to saddle the American government with disagreeable mandates came to nought. From the financial point of view colonial empire had proved to be almost a total loss; the Philippines in particular had cost the government huge sums, and had brought in next to nothing by way of profit. This, perhaps, need not have been so; other nations took a heavy toll from their possessions. But neither the American government nor the American people showed great aptitude along this line. Americans with a taste for foreign trade and investments were not lacking, and in the sense of expanding commercial interests, American imperialism was by no means dead. But American traders made as good profits, if not better, in lands outside rather than inside the American empire. Discouraging, too, was the discovery that distant possessions meant involvement in world politics, and the consequent danger of war.

BIBLIOGRAPHY

Two works by E. R. May provide a fresh examination of several of the main subjects in this chapter: *Imperial Democracy* (1961), and *American Imperialism: A Speculative Essay* (1968). An influential monograph which finds traces of imperialism much earlier is Walter La Feber, *The New Empire: An Interpretation of American Expansion, 1860–1898* (1964). The shifting views of one major historian can be followed in two books by W. A. Williams: *The Tragedy of American Diplomacy* (2nd ed., 1962), and *Roots of the Modern American Empire* (1969); Williams was admittedly influenced by La Feber. A brief economic determinist's essay is *The Roots of American Foreign Policy* (1969) by Gabriel Kolko.

Several works by "realists" discuss episodes in turn-of-the-century foreign policy. Notable among these are: G. F. Kennan, *American Diplomacy, 1900–1950* (1951); R. E. Osgood, *Ideals and Self-Interest in America's Foreign Relations* (1953); and Hans Morgenthau, *In Defense of the National Interest* (1951). These may be contrasted with the more idealistic approach of F. R. Dulles, in his *Prelude to World Power* (1965), *The Imperial Years* (1956), and *America's Rise to World Power, 1898–1954* (1955). The expansionist sentiment that dominated some American thinking during these years is the subject of J. W. Pratt, *Expansionists of 1898* (1936); and it also receives attention in the more inclusive work of A. K. Weinberg, *Manifest Destiny* (1935). See also the important surveys by S. F. Bemis, *The Latin American Policy of the United States* (1943); and Dexter Perkins, *A History of the Monroe Doctrine* (2nd ed., 1955).

The best analysis of Harrison's foreign policy is A. F. Tyler, *The Foreign Policy of James G. Blaine* (1927). D. M. Pletcher, *The Awkward Years: American Foreign Relations under Garfield and Arthur* (1962), treats the earlier period. Valuable also is G. R. Dulebohn, *Principles of Foreign Policy under the Cleveland Administrations* (1941). Walter Millis, *Arms and Men* (1956), is a discerning general survey of American military policy.

The drive for naval preparedness is well presented in Harold and Margaret Sprout, *The Rise of American Naval Power, 1776–1918* (3rd ed., 1944); on the navy, see also: W. D. Puleston, *Mahan* (1939); W. R. Herrick, Jr., *The American Naval Revolution* (1966); and G. C. O'Gara, *Theodore Roosevelt and the Rise of the Modern Navy* (1943).

On some of the episodes of pre-Spanish War imperialism, see: G. H. Ryden, *The Foreign Policy of the United States in Relation to Samoa* (1933); H. C. Evans, Jr., *Chile and Its Relations with the United States* (1927); and A. L. P. Dennis, *Adventures in American Diplomacy, 1896–1906* (1928). The literature on Hawaii is large; among the best works for this period are: S. K. Stevens, *American Expansion in Hawaii, 1842–1898* (1945); R. S. Kuykendall, *The Hawaiian Kingdom*, III, *1874–1893* (1967); Jacob Adler, *Claus Spreckels* (1966); E. M. Damon, *Sanford Ballard Dole and His Hawaii* (1957); two books by W. A. Russ, Jr., *The Hawaiian Revolution (1893–94)* (1959), and *The Hawaiian Republic (1894–98) and Its Struggle to Win Annexation* (1961); and Gavan Daws, *Shoals of Time* (1969). Discussions of Anglo-American relations are contained in: Kenneth Bourne, *Britain and the Balance of Power in North America, 1815–1908* (1967); H. C. Allen, *Great Britain and the United States* (1955); L. M. Gelber, *The Rise of Anglo-American Friendship, 1898–1906* (1938); R. H. Heindel, *The American Impact on Great Britain, 1898–1914* (1940); C. S. Campbell, Jr., *Anglo-American Understanding, 1898–1903* (1957); R. G. Neale, *Great Britain and United States Expansion: 1898–1900* (1966); and Bradford Perkins, *The Great Rapprochement* (1968).

A short, lively account of the Spanish-American War, magnificently illustrated, is Frank Freidel, *The Splendid Little War* (1958). The most entertaining account of American intervention in Cuba is Walter Millis, *The Martial Spirit* (1931). A brief synthesis is H. W. Morgan, *America's Road to*

Empire: The War with Spain and Overseas Expansion (1965). The role of newspapermen in promoting the war is well set forth in J. E. Wisan, *The Cuban Crisis as Reflected in the New York Press* (1934).

The debates over the question of Empire are well covered in *American Imperialism in 1898* (1955), edited by T. P. Greene. Conflicting interpretations by historians appear in *American Expansion in the Late Nineteenth Century* (1968), edited by J. R. Hollingsworth. Claude Bowers, *Beveridge and the Progressive Era* (1932), recounts the thinking and activities of a leading imperialist. The anti-imperialist argument is given in Merle Curti, *Bryan and World Peace* (1931); W. M. Armstrong, *E. L. Godkin and American Foreign Policy, 1865–1900* (1957); M. A. D. Howe, *Portrait of an Independent, Moorfield Storey* (1932); and R. L. Beisner, *Twelve Against Empire: The Anti-Imperialists, 1898–1900* (1968). Elmer Ellis, *Mr. Dooley's America: A Life of Finley Peter Dunne* (1941), is the biography of a political humorist who viewed the whole imperialistic venture with considerable misgivings. On the Treaty of Paris, see C. E. Hill, *Leading American Treaties* (1922); and Royal Cortissoz, *Life of Whitelaw Reid* (1921).

J. W. Pratt, *America's Colonial Experiment* (1950), is a convenient summary. Much has been written on individual dependencies and protectorates, including: J. P. Nichols, *Alaska* (1924); E. S. Pomeroy, *Pacific Outpost: American Strategy in Guam and Micronesia* (1951); L. H. Evans, *The Virgin Islands* (1945); and E. J. Berbusse, *The United States in Puerto Rico, 1898–1900* (1966). On Cuba, see: R. H. Fitzgibbon, *Cuba and the United States, 1900–1935* (1935); D. F. Healy, *The United States in Cuba, 1898–1902* (1963); and A. R. Millett, *The Politics of Intervention: The Military Occupation of Cuba, 1906–1909* (1968). On the Philippines, important works include: G. L. Kirk, *Philippine Independence* (1936); Moorfield Storey and M. P. Lichauco, *The Conquest of the Philippines by the United States, 1898–1925* (1926); A. S. Pier, *American Apostles to the Philippines* (1950); and Leon Wolff, *Little Brown Brother* (1961), a severely critical account of the putting-down of the Philippine insurrection.

A. W. Griswold, *The Far Eastern Policy of the United States* (1938), is standard and reliable. Tyler Dennett, *John Hay* (1933), is valuable for the Open Door policy. Also useful in this connection is Tyler Dennett, *Americans in Eastern Asia* (2nd ed., 1941). Monographs treating the Open Door policy and its implications include: C. S. Campbell, Jr., *Special Business Interests and the Open Door Policy* (1951); Charles Vevier, *The United States and China, 1906–1913* (1955); and three works by P. A. Varg, *Open Door Diplomat: The Life of W. W. Rockhill* (1952), *Missionaries, Chinese and Diplomats: The American Protestant Missionary Movement in China, 1890–1952* (1958), and *The Making of a Myth: The United States and China, 1897–1912* (1968). See also the important revisionist work by M. B. Young, *The Rhetoric of Empire: America's China Policy, 1895–1901* (1969).

12

WORLD POLITICS

Toward world power · Roosevelt's foreign policy · Japan's ambitions · Russo-Japanese War · Root-Takahira Agreement · Taft's "dollar diplomacy" · Anglo-American relations · The Panama Canal · Colombian resentment · The tolls controversy · Caribbean control · Mexico · The Mobile doctrine · "Watchful waiting" · The peace movement · Algeciras and after

Toward World Power

The United States at the turn of the century had become the center of an empire that stretched some ten thousand miles across the surface of the earth. By virtue of that fact it was forced to concern itself during the succeeding years not only with Latin-American affairs, but also with the politics of eastern Asia, and even with the balance of power in Europe. Superficially, the American nation was well fitted to play an important role in world politics; in population, trade, iron and steel production, naval power, and even size of empire, it had achieved an impressive eminence. Nevertheless, it still lacked one important requisite for the exercise of world power, namely, popular acceptance of the obligations that such a course involved. Mr. Dooley probably reflected faithfully the sentiment of the American people when, apropos the "insular cases," he objected to the Constitution following "the flag to all th' tough resorts on the Passyfic Coast."

THE PEACE PALACE AT THE HAGUE *housed the arbitration tribunal set up in 1899.*

"Ye can't make me think th' constitution is goin' trapezin' around ivrywhere a young leftinant in th' ar'rmy takes it into his head to stick a flagpole. It's too old. It's a home-stayin' constitution with a blue coat and brass buttons on to it, an' it walks with a goold-headed cane. It's old an' it's feeble an' it prefers to set on the front stoop and amuse the childer. It wudden't last a minyit in thim thropical climes."

The public, in fact, often overlooked the existence of an American empire, and with perfect composure roundly berated European nations, particularly Great Britain, for imperialistic practices of which their own country was equally guilty. Despite all the facts to the contrary, the American people treasured in their hearts the myth that the relationship of the United States to the rest of the world was exactly the same as it had been in the nineteenth century. Whatever the new conditions, the people thought in terms of the old traditional cautious policy of isolation.

Death of McKinley

But if the American people could believe that nothing had changed in the nation's foreign policy, the President and the Department of State knew better. While in the main William McKinley had been the architect of the new empire, it fell to his successor, Theodore Roosevelt, to deal with most of the new foreign involvements. McKinley was the fifth American President to die in office. Six months after his second inauguration he visited the Pan-American exposition at Buffalo, New York, and on September 5, 1901, made a speech in which he emphasized the end of American isolation and the importance of reciprocity as a means of promoting foreign trade. Next day, during a reception, he was shot by an anarchist, and eight days later died. Thereupon the youthful Vice-President, Theodore Roosevelt, became on September 14, 1901, the twenty-sixth President of the United States. For the time being the new President retained the entire McKinley cabinet, including John Hay, who held office as Secretary of State until the time of his death in 1905.

Roosevelt's Foreign Policy

On the surface, at least, Roosevelt seemed completely at odds with the American people in their desire for a cautious foreign policy. As much as any man he had contributed to the imperialist wave that had culminated in the Spanish-American War. As President he often acted as his own Secretary of State, and apparently he believed in the strenuous life for nations no less than for individuals. "The great national virtues," he wrote, "are the fighting virtues," without which a nation would be doomed to stagnation. War at times, he believed, was good, and always preferable to a loss of national honor. Expansion was not to be despised, but prized, for every expansion of a great civilized power meant "a victory for law, order and righteousness." Roosevelt sensed, moreover, the growing international insecurity of his age. During his two administrations he was continually worried about his nation's defenses, and he saw enemies everywhere. He was extremely suspicious of Germany's intentions in the Western Hemisphere; Great Britain annoyed him; and both Russia and Japan exasperated him by their actions in the western Pacific. From such a man one might have expected an extremely active and even adventurous foreign policy, but Roosevelt in fact was often a very different person from Roosevelt in theory. In practice he acted precipitately only when American security was involved, and then only when the adversary was a small country. In the one international situation during his term when war might have resulted, that involving Japan, he was extremely moderate, and his speeches on foreign policy were models of propriety. There is reason to believe that Roosevelt was never altogether happy with the Far Eastern policy he had inherited, and in some ways his actions constituted a retreat from the principles of John Hay and the McKinley administration. He firmly believed in holding and defending the Philippine Islands, but near the end of his term he regretted their acquisition and wished there were some honorable way of getting rid of them. He also supported the principle of commercial opportunity in China, but not at the risk of serious conflict. There were times, too, when he doubted the wisdom of having committed the United States to the maintenance of Chinese national integrity, as John Hay had done at the outbreak of the Boxer Rebellion.

Japan's Ambitions

After the Boxers were suppressed and order was restored, the withdrawal of the expeditionary forces from China was set for the fall of 1901, and was carried out ac-

RUSSO-JAPANESE WAR. *In this conflict the sympathy of the American people lay principally with the Japanese, but President Roosevelt, as mediator, showed a high degree of impartiality.*

CONFERENCE AT PORTSMOUTH, New Hampshire, September 5, 1905. The Russian delegates are seated to the left, and the Japanese to the right.

THE WRECK OF A RUSSIAN SHIP. This photograph shows the wreck of the Russian merchant steamer, *Sungari*, sunk by the Russians at Chemulpo to prevent her from falling into the hands of the Japanese.

cording to agreement by all the nations except Russia, which maintained a special concentration in Manchuria with a view to exacting further favors from China. To prevent this course of action, only the Japanese were prepared to strike. Japanese students of western civilization had reached the conclusion that the enormous and growing population of Japan could be supported only by the rapid expansion of manufacturing. But to accomplish this end Japan needed access to a greater supply of mineral resources than existed in the Japanese homeland, and in addition an opportunity to exploit extensive external markets. Both of these needs China could be persuaded in one way or another to supply, provided only that some outside nation did not interfere. Since at the moment Russia's operations seemed to be endangering the "lifeline" between Japan and China, Japanese statesmen made deliberate plans for the expulsion of Russia from Manchuria. On January 30, 1902, Japan signed a treaty of alliance with Great Britain,

which recognized the independence of Korea and China, and applied the open-door policy to both. It was further agreed between the two contracting powers that if either should be attacked in defense of its legitimate interests by a single nation, then the other party to the alliance would remain neutral; but if either should be attacked by more than one nation, then the other ally must come to its aid. One advantage of this alliance from the British point of view was that it would permit the withdrawal of British naval units from the Far East for concentration in European waters where the naval might of Germany was on the rise. The fundamental consideration so far as Japan was concerned was that the Japanese army might now drive the Russians out of Manchuria without fear of attack from any other power.

Russo-Japanese War

The Russo-Japanese War broke out February 5, 1904, when the Japanese attacked the Russians at Port Arthur without a previous declaration of war. The fighting occurred on Chinese soil, although China, strongly supported in this endeavor by the United States, succeeded in remaining neutral. Naturally American sympathy ran with Japan, for it was the Russians, rather than the Japanese, who had most openly flouted the "open door." Roosevelt looked upon Japan as a "counterpoise" against Russia, felt that Japan was "playing our game" when it destroyed Russian sea power, and even went so far as to send a private warning to France and Germany that if either of them entered the war on the side of Russia he would bring the United States to the aid of Japan. But, following a series of Japanese victories in Manchuria, the President became worried lest the war should result merely in Japan's taking over Russia's interests in the province rather than in freeing it from foreign influence. Consequently, when he was asked to mediate the struggle, he declined to do so unless Japan would first promise that she would respect the "open door" policy in Manchuria, and indeed return the province to China. This promise Japan was obliged to give, for if a revolution at home and Japanese victories in the Far East had made peace a necessity for the Russians, financial exhaustion had made it equally imperative for the Japanese. With his objective achieved, Roosevelt then received Russian and Japanese delegates at the Portsmouth (New Hampshire) Naval Yard on August 9, 1905, to discuss peace. For a while it seemed as if the conference would fail, for the Russians refused to consider the Japanese demands for the island of Sakhalin and a large money indemnity. Largely because of Roosevelt's pressure the Japanese gave up their monetary demands, and Russia agreed to cede the southern half of Sakhalin to Japan. In the treaty signed September 5, 1905, both sides agreed also to evacuate Manchuria, but as a result of the war Japan got a firmer hold on Korea, and

took over from Russia the South Manchuria railroad. Roosevelt, for his services to the cause of peace, received the Nobel peace prize and the plaudits of his countrymen.

Japanese-American Relations

Although Roosevelt labored to save the "open door" in Manchuria, he agreed to its being shut in Korea. Two things were apparent by 1905; first, that Japan probably could not be stopped in its penetration of Korea except by force; second, that the Philippines might become a logical place for Japanese expansion in the future. Since Roosevelt believed that to stop Japan in Korea was impractical, if not impossible, he decided that the next best thing was to acknowledge the inevitable and obtain compensation. Accordingly, in July, 1905, William Howard Taft, acting as Roosevelt's agent, negotiated in Tokyo an executive agreement by which the United States recognized Japan's "suzerainty" over Korea in return for a Japanese disavowal of any aggressive activities in the Philippines. Four months later the United States removed its legation from Seoul, and thereafter conducted all matters that related to Korea through the Japanese foreign office.

Notwithstanding this generous gesture, the relations between the United States and Japan grew increasingly critical after the Peace of Portsmouth. The Japanese people held American intervention responsible for the terms of the treaty, which they regarded as much too favorable to Russia. They resented also the American patrol of the sealing waters off the Pribilof Islands, a practice that in July, 1906, resulted in the death of five Japanese nationals. But their most irritating grievance was the treatment accorded Japanese residents of the Pacific Coast states, especially California. Despite a Japanese commitment of 1900 to withhold passports to emigrants bound for the American mainland (although permitting them to Hawaii), the number of Japanese in the United States had increased rapidly — by 1906 there were perhaps 75,000 of them in California alone. Their presence gave rise to the same kind of race prejudice that had manifested itself earlier against the Chinese. When, in October, 1906, the San Francisco school board issued an order requiring all of the ninety-three Japanese school children in the city to attend a separate school, Japan's national pride, bolstered by her recent victory over a great European power, was deeply wounded. Some of her newspapers demanded war, and the government sent strongly worded protests to Washington. Roosevelt was furious at the "infernal fools" in California, as were most eastern Americans. After strong and persistent pressure, he succeeded in obtaining a repeal of the school measure, promising in return to put an end to the unwanted immigration. He then negotiated what came to be called the "Gentlemen's Agreement." The Japanese government promised not to issue passports to laborers wishing to emigrate to the American mainland, while the President, in return, under authority of a 1907 amendment to the immigration act, denied entrance to continental United States of Japanese immigrants not coming directly from Japan. This agreement, as was intended, permitted the continuation of Japanese immigration into Hawaii, a policy the sugar planters of the island desired, but Japan in practice also cut down on passports to Hawaii.

Root-Takahira Agreement

Roosevelt, by including in his 1907 annual message to Congress a strong indictment of the Californians, somewhat mollified the Japanese government, but he now feared lest the Japanese might interpret his "righteous action" as an indication of weakness. He therefore determined to send the American fleet, now the second largest in the world, around the globe by way of Japan to dispel such feelings. As the fleet

neared Japan a real war scare was whipped up in the United States by the sensational press, but both ships and men were so enthusiastically welcomed in Tokyo that the voyage, in addition to displaying America's newborn naval power to the world, set the stage for a short period of better relations with Japan. This period culminated in the signing of the Root-Takahira Agreement on November 30, 1908. This was not a treaty, but merely an executive agreement that bound only the Roosevelt administration and the then current government in Japan. According to this document: (1) the two nations asserted a common desire to develop their commerce on the Pacific freely and peacefully; (2) they agreed to maintain "the existing *status quo*" in the Far East, including the open door in China; (3) they stood together in support of the independence and integrity of China; and (4) they promised, in the event of any threat to existing conditions, to consult with each other as to what measures they should take.

There has been much subsequent argument over just what the Root-Takahira Agreement really meant. On the surface it looked as if the United States had won a sweeping victory by obtaining from Japan a promise to respect the Philippines and to support the principles of the "open door" and the integrity of China. But, as both governments knew, the agreement was utterly unenforceable on Japan, for the United States, without allies and unwilling to have them, was powerless to implement the promises it had received. Furthermore, the second part of the agreement could be interpreted to mean an American acknowledgment of the special economic and political position of Japan in Manchuria and North China, in effect a complete reversal of American Far Eastern policy.

Railroads in Manchuria

Whatever the actual intent of the Root-Takahira Agreement, the Japanese apparently interpreted it as giving them a free hand to develop their already large interests in Manchuria. Russia, not to be outdone by her Asiatic neighbor, also stepped up her activity in North China. Both countries, in their attempts to win economic and political control of desired territory, relied upon the holding of treaty ports and the construction of railroads in the interior. Whereas in 1895 there were only two hundred miles of Chinese railroads, in 1913 there were 6,000 miles. The major part of the new construction was in Manchuria, precisely where the Chinese population was smallest. The obvious aim of this construction was first announced by Russia, when she boldly claimed in 1908 that "railroad concessions convey absolute sovereignty" in China. To this doctrine, obviously, the United States could not agree. But since neither Roosevelt nor Root, his then Secretary of State, was willing to support any logical countermeasure, the answer to this new type of empire building had to await the inauguration of Roosevelt's successor, William Howard Taft, who became President on March 4, 1909.

Taft's "Dollar Diplomacy"

Taft was better acquainted with the Far East than any President before him. His long residence in the Philippines and his tours of eastern Asia had made him many friends throughout the region, among them Willard Straight, the American Consul-General at Mukden, Manchuria. Straight had long believed that Japan, if not stopped, would eventually seize all of North China and freeze out American trade in this area. Consequently he argued that the United States should checkmate Japan in Manchuria by supporting the construction of American-financed railroads. Taft and his Secretary of State, Philander C. Knox, accepted the idea, and promoted it into a policy generally known as "dollar diplomacy." Taft lauded the plan as a means of

Elihu Root. *Outstanding as an organizer of the new American empire, Root was first Secretary of War, then Secretary of State in Theodore Roosevelt's cabinet.*

"substituting dollars for bullets," and maintained that the government of the United States was duty bound to "extend all proper support to every legitimate and beneficial enterprise abroad." Since American capital had never been acutely interested in Manchuria, the State Department had to bring pressure to bear upon the reluctant New York bankers before they would agree to risk American resources in a region where they did not normally desire to invest. The new doctrine reversed the cautious Far Eastern policy of Theodore Roosevelt, and made the United States a frank competitor of Japan and Russia on the mainland of Asia.

The Taft policy, on the whole, was not a success. The State Department was able to induce a group of New York financial houses to contribute a small capital pool for Far Eastern investment, and, over the mild objections of the British, French, and German governments, the group was permitted to join with European bankers in making a loan for the construction of railways in central and southern China. But the major American proposal, one designed specifically to counter Japan and Russia in Manchuria, met a different fate. In December, 1909,

Knox proposed to all the interested powers a scheme for organizing a great international consortium of private capital, the money so contributed to be lent to China for the purchase of all the railroads of Manchuria then owned and operated by Japan and Russia. Until China should repay the loan, the railroads were to be directed by an international board. Naturally this scheme met the determined opposition of both Japan and Russia, and since British support was not forthcoming, it was dropped. Probably Theodore Roosevelt sized up the situation wisely when he wrote to Taft, late in 1910: "as regards Manchuria, if the Japanese choose to follow a course of conduct to which we are adverse, we cannot stop it unless we are prepared to go to war, and a successful war about Manchuria would require a fleet as good as that of England, plus an army as good as that of Germany." Taft's policy of "dollar diplomacy" for China was abruptly discarded after Wilson took office in 1913. American bankers had never been enthusiastic investors in Chinese railroads, and after the Wilson administration denounced the program they hastily withdrew what small loans they had made Some six years later, ironically enough, President Wilson reversed himself, and urged without success the return of American capital to China as a means of checking the growing power there of Japan.

American Position in the Orient

Thus by 1913 the American position in the Far East was not very satisfactory. To summarize, John Hay had no doubt hoped that his support of the open door and the territorial integrity of China would greatly promote American commercial expansion in the Far East. But since the United States was unwilling to use force in maintaining Hay's policies, their survival depended upon the preservation of a balance of power in the Orient. For a time Theodore Roosevelt had attempted to use Russia

and Japan as makeweights against each other, while relying upon the good will of Great Britain to help achieve a true balance. But by 1905 the rapid rise of Japan had crippled this policy so much that Roosevelt was willing to retreat from the "open door" principle in Korea in order to obtain in return a promise of protection for the Philippines. Moreover, Great Britain, threatened in Europe by the growing might of Germany, conceded to Japan after 1905 a free hand in North China, and by 1907 reached a world understanding with Russia. Spurred on by the American proposal to internationalize the railroads of Manchuria, Japan and Russia, to the delight of the British, actually planned in 1910 and in 1912 a secret division between themselves of Manchuria and Mongolia, and promised to resist the efforts of any other nations to exploit these provinces either commercially or politically. By the end of the Taft administration there was no longer a balance of power in Eastern Asia. Without it, the United States stood isolated in the Orient, and virtually helpless to maintain the integrity of China or to preserve the open door.

Anglo-American Relations

While the American adventure into Far Eastern diplomacy was meeting with little success, a gratifying record of triumphs was being recorded in the Western Hemisphere. Here the United States had a better understanding of the problems that arose, and ordinarily no such powerful antagonists to deal with as in the Orient. Furthermore, events soon proved that on most matters of consequence in the New World the United States could count on firm British support. For example, in the settlement of the dispute with Canada over the Alaskan boundary, finally achieved in 1903, the British government showed more concern for the maintenance of cordial relations with the United States than for pleading the cause

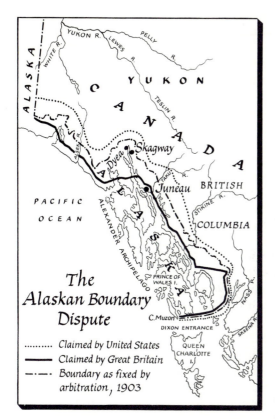

The Alaskan Boundary Dispute

.... Claimed by United States
———— Claimed by Great Britain
—·—·— Boundary as fixed by arbitration, 1903

and Lord Alverstone, the British Chief Justice. With Alverstone voting consistently with the Americans, the Commission by a four-to-two vote upheld every important American contention.

The Panama Canal

Similarly, the British gave way to American desires in the matter of constructing a transoceanic canal through Central America. The United States, to protect its new outposts of empire in the Atlantic and the Pacific, now regarded such a canal as a cardinal necessity. Such a waterway would reduce the ocean trip between San Francisco and New York by almost two-thirds, and would thus save many precious days in transferring the American fleet from one ocean to the other. Unfortunately the Clayton-Bulwer Treaty of 1850 gave the British equal rights with the Americans in any canal to be constructed. The American government therefore asked British consent to a revision of the treaty that would enable the United States to construct and operate a strictly American canal. At first, since the Americans offered no compensating advantages, the British demurred, but eventually, when it appeared that Congress might well vote to go ahead with the canal regardless of treaty provisions, they gave in. The resulting Hay-Pauncefote treaty of February 5, 1900, satisfied the American negotiator, Secretary Hay, but it lost in the Senate because it prohibited the United States from fortifying the canal. Thereupon a second Hay-Pauncefote treaty, concluded November 18, 1901, eliminated the obnoxious clause. The only reservation the British insisted upon was that the canal should be "free and open to the vessels of commerce and of war of all nations . . . on terms of entire equality"; nor were there to be any discriminations "in respect of the conditions or charges of traffic."

of Canada, an important part of the British Empire. By a somewhat dubious reinterpretation of the original treaty line agreed upon between Great Britain and Russia in 1825, the Canadians laid claim to a corridor across the Alaskan panhandle that would have given them direct access to the ocean from the gold-bearing Klondike. Irate at a claim he deemed fantastic, President Roosevelt threatened to maintain American sovereignty in the disputed area by force, if necessary. But he agreed instead to a plan of settlement through which the United States stood no chance to lose. Each side was to appoint three commissioners who would jointly arbitrate the dispute, and decisions could be made only by a majority vote. As finally constituted, the Commission consisted of three Americans whose minds were already made up, two Canadians who were equally committed,

Hay's success in the canal undertaking was probably due more to the inclinations of the British than to his own undoubted ability. Under heavy diplomatic attack from the major European nations and isolated in an increasingly warlike world, Great Britain at the turn of the century was seeking dependable friends. A strong United States in the Caribbean might be persuaded to protect British interests there, thus freeing British sea power to concentrate nearer home against the rising German navy. Within a few years Great Britain tacitly acknowledged American supremacy in the Caribbean by reducing her naval and land forces in that region to a mere token. As in the Spanish-American War and again in the Alaskan boundary dispute, British diplomacy seemed determined to obtain American friendship, even at considerable cost. While the American public in general distrusted Great Britain and refused to think British friendship desirable, there is good evidence to indicate that the American government took a far different view. Since, as the decade progressed, the growing naval strength of the United States was based increasingly in the Pacific, it seems reasonable to suppose that responsible American officials felt satisfied to entrust the policing of the eastern Atlantic to the British.

Two possible routes were available for the new canal, one through Panama, a part of Colombia, where a French canal company had previously gone bankrupt in attempting to dig a waterway, and the other through Nicaragua. A commission appointed by the President, the Walker Commission, had reported in favor of the Nicaraguan route, and the House of Representatives had so voted, both influenced (1) by the possibility of building a water-level canal through Nicaragua, and (2) by the extremely high price, $109 million, which the French company had set for its Panama concession. Alarmed by these developments, the French company quickly reduced its price to $40 million, and sent a remarkable representative to the United States in the person of Philippe Bunau-Varilla, who was joined, in his task of persuading the American government to favor the Panama route, by William Nelson Cromwell, a New York attorney. Cromwell, incidentally, had contributed $60,000 to the Republican campaign fund of 1900. Led by Mark Hanna, the Senate on June 28, 1902, voted for the Panama route, but instructed the President to negotiate with Nicaragua in the event that a right of way through Panama could not be secured in "a reasonable time."

Canal Diplomacy

Using the threat of the Nicaragua alternative, Secretary Hay drove a sharp bargain with Thomas Herran, the Colombian representative at Washington. The United States was to receive a canal zone six miles wide across the isthmus in return for a cash payment of $10 million, and a yearly annuity of $250,000. Within this zone, stretching from Panama City to Colón, but not including those cities, the United States was to have virtually sovereign rights. The treaty contained one other most remarkable provision: Colombia agreed not to negotiate with the French company, and thus forfeited any chance it might otherwise have had to obtain part of the $40 million that the French company expected to receive from the United States. The United States Senate promptly ratified the treaty, but the Colombian government, resenting both the terms and the manner in which they had been imposed, refused to ratify.

The chief Colombian objection to the treaty, apparently, lay in its monetary clauses, for Washington soon learned that, if $15 million each could be obtained from the United States and from the French company, the path of the treaty would be smoothed. This sum was perhaps not unreasonable, for the French concession expired in October, 1904, after which all its interests and property in Panama would revert to Colombia. Thus by waiting only a short time Colombia might claim the entire $40 million. Moreover, Panama belonged to Colombia, and the seller presumably had the right to place his price on his own merchandise. The Department of State, however, told Colombia that it would consider any modification of the treaty "a breach of faith," and there the matter rested.

Up to this time President Roosevelt had not been strongly prejudiced for either the Panama or the Nicaragua route. Now, in the face of Colombia's refusal, he became a zealous advocate of the Panama route. Calling Colombia a "pithecoid community" and its government everything from "blackmailers" to "homicidal corruptionists," he penned an angry message to Congress demanding that the canal zone be taken by force. On second thought, he filed the message away among his manuscripts and turned to his advisers to explore other ways of securing the canal. One such idea came from Bunau-Varilla, who sent the President a newspaper containing a marked story of a possible revolution in Panama against Colombian control.

Revolt in Panama

The revolution in Panama was fomented and financed in New York City by officers of the French company, but its success was unquestionably due to the cooperation of the American navy. Back in 1846 the United States and Colombia (then New Granada) had signed a treaty in which the government at Washington had recognized the "rights of sovereignty and property" that New Granada had in Panama. By the same instrument both countries agreed to protect the right of free transit across the isthmus. Obviously the latter clause was aimed at the possible intrusion of some third power, and was not meant to confer on the United States the right to obstruct the movements of Colombian troops. Until

Philippe Bunau-Varilla. *This skillful manipulator played a leading role in the diplomacy that preceded the building of the Panama Canal.*

1903 the United States had so interpreted the treaty, and had obtained the consent of Colombia whenever American troops were used in the Panama area during times of disorder. But on October 30, 1903, the commander of the U.S.S. *Nashville,* then in nearby waters, was told that, in case there should be a rebellion in Panama, he should seize the Panama Railroad and "prevent the landing of any armed force with hostile intent" within fifty miles of Panama. Late in the afternoon of November 2, the *Nashville* steamed into Colón. Since the only possible route by which Colombia could bring troops to Panama was by sea, the revolution took place the next day without the usual violence. Three days later Secretary Hay accorded diplomatic recognition to the new republic of Panama.

With Colombia disposed of, and with Philippe Bunau-Varilla appointed the first minister of Panama to the United States, a new Hay-Bunau-Varilla Treaty of November 18, 1903, quickly cleared the way for the

Building the Panama Canal. *The magnitude of the United States' engineering achievement is conveyed in this lithograph by Joseph Pennell, dated February 14, 1912. Construction equipment was then primitive in comparison with the machinery used today in the building of American highways.*

construction of the canal. The United States acquired a zone five miles wide on each side of the canal "as if she were sovereign," an area which she could fortify at will. Panama received an initial payment of $10 million and $250,000 a year, beginning nine years after date. The United States guaranteed the independence of Panama, but the principles of the Platt Amendment, including the right of intervention, were applied to the new republic. Between 1846 and 1903 Panama had been the scene of no less than fifty-three insurrectionary outbursts. Thereafter they ceased abruptly.

Roosevelt defended his Panama action on the ground that the canal was desperately needed by the world, and that in delaying its construction Colombia had been, in effect, an enemy of civilization. All the canal negotiations, he said, were conducted "by the highest, finest and nicest standards of public and governmental ethics." Years later at Berkeley, California, he boasted, "I took Panama." The American people, if one is to credit the newspapers, were delighted with the President's course, while Europe, having had much experience with such things, was united in its criticism. Latin-American countries, of course, bitterly condemned the "rape" of a sister republic and expressed a widespread distrust of American intentions. This fear of the "Colossus of the North" was destined for further increase as the new Latin-American policies of the United States unfolded.

Colombian Resentment

Colombia's deep resentment at the way it had been treated soon became a matter of real concern to the United States. Not only Colombia, but other Latin-American nations, also, saw in Roosevelt's action a precedent that might be used for other imperialistic ventures at their expense. To alleviate the tension, Secretary Root proposed in 1909 a series of three treaties, between the United States and Panama, the United States and Colombia, and Panama and Colombia. By their terms the first ten installments of the $250,000 quit-rent would have been assigned to Colombia. But Colombia would have nothing to do with the suggestion. While Taft was President another effort at appeasement was made. Would Colombia accept $10 million for a coaling station and any other canal route that might be available through her territory? Colombia would not. Even when the United States suggested informally that the sum might be raised to $25 million, Colombia remained obdurate and asked for arbitration, something the United States dared not risk. During Wilson's administration Secretary Bryan negotiated a treaty with Colombia which expressed regrets for what the United States had done, and offered $25 million by way of compensation. This proposal, which Colombia was ready to accept, was rejected by the United States Senate, in which sat many of Roosevelt's loyal friends. After Roosevelt's death, with Harding as President, a treaty very similar to the one Bryan had proposed, but with the "regrets" clause omitted, was ratified by both nations. By that time the fear that European syndicates would be able to monopolize the rich oil resources of Colombia to the exclusion of American firms made the purchase of Colombian good will more attractive.

Building the Canal

The actual building of the canal was an engineering feat of extraordinary magnitude. The impracticability of a sea-level canal was soon discovered and a lock canal, which would cost less to build both in time and in money, was decided upon. At first sanitation threatened to be an even greater problem than excavation, but the work of Colonel W. C. Gorgas in making the canal zone a fit place in which to live was so well

done that trouble from that source was soon practically eliminated. Administrative difficulties arising from the fact that Congress insisted on delegating the control of operations to a commission instead of to an individual hampered work for a while, but Roosevelt at length made Major George W. Goethals, an army engineer, chairman of the commission, and extracted a promise from all other members of the commission never to disagree with the chairman. After that the work proceeded satisfactorily, and on August 15, 1914, the first ocean steamer passed through the canal. The cost of building it ran to $275 million, which the government raised by floating bonds, together with another $113 million for fortifications; but receipts during the first fifteen years of operation brought in large enough net earnings to meet in full the interest on the bonds floated. Roosevelt always considered the building of the Panama Canal the greatest achievement of his administration.

The Tolls Controversy

In 1912 Congress, looking forward to the opening of the canal, passed a law exempting American coastwise shipping from the payment of tolls. This law was signed by Presi-

The Canal Finished. *Aerial view of Gatun locks, April 21, 1961.*

dent Taft, who was certainly a good lawyer, but was immediately protested by Great Britain on the ground that the tolls exemption violated that clause of the Hay-Pauncefote Treaty which opened the canal to the vessels of "all nations" on terms of "entire equality." The British government offered no objection to the United States returning tolls to American shippers as rebates or subsidies; what it did object to was the prospect that with the exemption in force the rates would be so set as to require foreign shipping to pay the entire cost and upkeep of the canal. American railroad interests, who foresaw the diversion of much transcontinental traffic from the railroads to the new sea route, also had legitimate grounds for complaint, but Congress let the law stand until June, 1914, when President Wilson successfully insisted on its repeal. Although the President at the time stated no other reason for demanding repeal than that diplomatic negotiations of a very delicate nature were involved, it seems that he was primarily interested in obtaining the acquiescence of the British government in his Mexican policy.

The "Big Stick" Policy

Before he became President, and with his thoughts on the New York Republican machine, Theodore Roosevelt had once quoted an old adage: "Speak softly and carry a big stick, and you will go far." Later this statement was resurrected and fittingly applied to his policy in Latin America. As American statesmen watched the rising tensions in Europe prior to the First World War, they became increasingly apprehensive about the defense of the Western Hemisphere and the canal so vital to its protection. Consequently the Monroe Doctrine took on new significance. Elihu Root, Secretary of War in 1900, revealed the American preoccupation with that treasured formula when he remarked that "the American people will within a few years have to either abandon the Monroe Doctrine or fight for it, and we are not going to abandon it." The administration of Theodore Roosevelt, and hardly less the administrations of his successors, Taft and Wilson, successfully broadened the scope of the doctrine until Monroe and John Quincy Adams would have had difficulty in recognizing their creation. Simultaneously, the doctrine gained added vitality by the growing respect with which it was held abroad.

The Venezuelan crisis in 1902–1903 offered the first occasion for the use of the "big stick." At the turn of the century Venezuela was burdened by a huge debt held in Europe, upon which the nation was currently paying neither interest nor principal. After all peaceful efforts to obtain settlement had been blocked by the Venezuelan dictator, Cipriano Castro, the interested European powers determined on armed intervention. But before cooperating, Germany significantly asked what the attitude of the United States would be toward the joint project. Roosevelt, who privately referred to Castro as an "unspeakable villainous little monkey," felt that a "spanking" was due Venezuela, and Hay replied that the Monroe Doctrine applied only to territory, and did not prohibit policing action for the collection of valid debts. Two years later, however, after Great Britain, Germany, and Italy had instituted a blockade of Venezuelan ports, the President began to change his opinion on the desirability of European policing action in the Western Hemisphere. In part, this change of attitude was undoubtedly due to Germany's aggressive tactics in bombarding the Venezuelan fort and village of San Carlos. Probably more fundamental was his fear that such European operations might eventually result, as they had in China, in territorial seizures. Castro at length agreed to arbitrate the claims against his government, and the European powers accepted this solution, encouraged perhaps

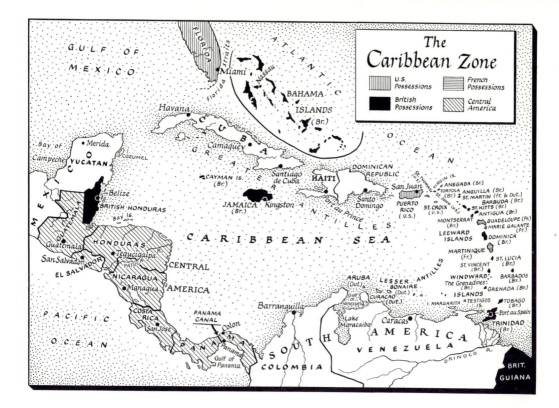

The Caribbean Zone

U.S. Possessions		French Possessions
British Possessions		Central America

by some behind-the-scenes pressure from Roosevelt. When finally the Hague Tribunal settled the case, it reduced the foreign claims against Venezuela from $40 million to $8 million.

The Drago Doctrine

Eventually Roosevelt reached the conclusion that the United States must itself be prepared to intervene in Latin-American affairs if it wished to be sure of keeping other nations out. In 1902, while the Venezuelan crisis was on, the Argentinian Foreign Minister, Luis M. Drago, expressed the opinion that "the public debt cannot occasion armed intervention nor even the actual occupation of the territory of American nations by a European power," a doctrine that was later endorsed by the Second Hague Conference. This doctrine had never been maintained by the United States, but the Venezuelan crisis had brought the matter into sharp focus, and had helped Roosevelt to make up his mind. Could the United States tolerate European intervention in the Western Hemisphere, even when such intervention was ostensibly limited to the collection of debts? Roosevelt answered this important question by first taking action in the Dominican Republic, and later formulating the Roosevelt corollary to the Monroe Doctrine.

The Roosevelt Corollary

The Dominican Republic was ruled from 1882 to 1899 by a dictator, President Ulises Heureaux. Famed alike for his ruthlessness and his lavish expenditures, Heureaux had borrowed to the hilt on his nation's credit at ruinous rates of interest. By the time of his assassination in 1899 the resources of the small country, including the customs duties and railroad receipts, were pledged for years ahead. When a revolution broke out in 1903, several European powers threatened to land troops in the troubled republic. Meanwhile, the current Dominican president, believing that one intruding nation was preferable to many, asked the United States to intervene. For over a year

Roosevelt delayed. Then fearing that extensive European intervention might be the prelude to annexation, he acted. Even as American troops were landing in the island republic, Secretary of War Elihu Root justified his nation's course by stating: "What we will not permit the great Powers of Europe to do, we will not permit any American Republic to make it necessary for the great Powers of Europe to do." President Roosevelt later amplified Root's remarks in his annual message to Congress of December, 1904:

If a nation shows that it knows how to act with reasonable efficiency and decency in social and political matters, if it keeps order and pays its obligations, it need fear no interference from the United States. Chronic wrongdoing, or an impotence which results in a general loosening of the ties of civilized society may in America, as elsewhere, ultimately require intervention by some civilized nation, and in the Western Hemisphere the adherence of the United States to the Monroe Doctrine may force the United States, however reluctantly, in flagrant cases of such wrongdoing or impotence, to the exercise of an international police power.

Roosevelt's "corollary" thus made it clear to Europe that the United States would no longer tolerate any European armed intervention in the Western Hemisphere, and at the same time warned Latin-American nations that they must keep the peace and honor their international obligations, or else run the risk of intervention by the United States. What transpired within the Dominican Republic revealed exactly how Roosevelt meant to apply his new interpretation of the Monroe Doctrine. He obtained from the Dominican government, acting under the shadow of American troops, an agreement that made it a virtual protectorate of the United States. The collection of Dominican customs was handed over to an agent of the United States, who would then apportion the receipts, according to a fixed ratio, between the current governmental expenses of the republic and the reduction of its national debt. The Dominican government also agreed not to increase its debt nor change its customs rates without the consent of the United States. At first the United States Senate refused to approve this high-handed arrangement, but Roosevelt carried it out as an executive agreement until 1907, when the Senate finally ratified a treaty embodying its terms.

Caribbean "Dollar Diplomacy"

The Taft administration continued, and even extended, the Roosevelt policy of Caribbean control. Taft's Secretary of State, Philander C. Knox, made every effort to push American intervention into the financial affairs of two Central American nations, Honduras and Nicaragua, a step further than Roosevelt had gone in the Dominican Republic. If, as seemed apparent, unpaid European loans to these Central American powers constituted a menace to American interests, why not transfer the loans to American banks? Both public policy and the private banking interests of the United States would profit from the transaction, another victory for "dollar diplomacy." Accordingly Knox negotiated with the two powers agreements patterned on the Dominican model, but involving also the refunding of their debts through New York bankers. The United States Senate rejected both treaties, but in the case of Nicaragua the Department of State induced American bankers to make private arrangements looking toward the same ends. When disorder continued to plague Nicaragua, the United States intervened in 1912 with 2,700 marines, and thereafter, without benefit of treaty, policed the country, turned its financial affairs over to an American collector, and put its government on a dole.

"Guard Mount." *Marines changing guard in barracks yard, Port-au-Prince, Haiti, 1915, during American occupation.*

Wilson's Caribbean Policy

Although Woodrow Wilson orally denounced "dollar diplomacy," and temporarily abolished it in the Orient, he continued to observe the Roosevelt-Taft formula for the control of the Caribbean. The Lansing Memorandum of November 24, 1915, containing the statement that the United States would "not tolerate control over or interference with the political or financial affairs of these republics by any European power or nationals," became the classic statement of American Caribbean policy. In Nicaragua American intervention under Wilson went to new lengths. For years the United States had been interested in securing exclusive rights for the construction of a canal through that nation, but when Knox had obtained such an agreement in 1913 the Senate had turned it down. A year later Wilson's Secretary of State, William Jennings Bryan, negotiated the Bryan-Chamorro Treaty, which contained all of the concessions Knox had sought, and a "Platt Amendment" as well. This time the Senate accepted the treaty, except for the Platt Amendment. As finally ratified, it gave the United States, in return for $3 million, exclusive rights to construct a canal and to lease sites for naval bases on both the Atlantic and the Pacific coasts of Nicaragua. Two of Nicaragua's neighbors, Costa Rica and Salvador, objected to the treaty as a menace to their security, and eventually carried their cases to the Central American Court of Justice, a court that the United States and Mexico had helped create to keep the peace in Central America. When the court decided in favor of the two protesting nations, the United States and Nicaragua ignored its decision. The court soon ceased to function.

With the outbreak of the First World War, the defense of the Panama Canal became a matter of vital concern to the United States, and led to further drastic action in the Caribbean. Hoping to end an era of revolution and anarchy in Haiti, the United States in 1914 offered that nation the same type of financial receivership that Roosevelt had instituted in the Dominican Republic, its closest neighbor, nearly ten years before. This offer Haiti chose to reject, but when serious rioting broke out in 1915, the United States landed marines at Port-au-Prince, restored order, and forced on the Haitian government the treaty it had previously refused. The treaty was to run for ten years, and for an additional ten years if the United States so desired. American officers, backed by American marines and a native constabulary, soon supplanted the Haitian authorities in the discharge of their duties, and eventually the Haitian government was entirely suspended. Meantime, in 1916, the United States also substituted military government for native rule in the Dominican Republic, despite local protests, and, as previously noted, acquired the Virgin Islands by purchase from Denmark.

By this time the Caribbean Sea had become to all intents and purposes an American lake. Property rights acquired by the United States on its borders included: (1) Puerto Rico, the Canal Zone, and the Virgin Islands; (2) convenient sites for naval bases at Guantánamo in eastern Cuba, on the Corn Islands off Nicaragua, and elsewhere; and (3) a concession from Nicaragua giving the United States the sole right of constructing a canal through her territory. Cuba and Panama, thanks to the principles of the Platt Amendment, were virtual protectorates of the United States, while the application of the Roosevelt corollary eventually brought the Dominican Republic, Haiti, and Nicaragua quite as completely within the American orbit. Other territory in the Caribbean zone was either in the hands of friendly European nations who made no effort to match the strength of the United States in the region, or of independent Latin-American nations whose conduct was tempered by fear of the "big stick."

American Motives

Ruthless as American Caribbean policy seems, in retrospect, to have been, it must not be forgotten that protection of the canal as a vital artery of American sea power was the main reason for the creation of this extensive system of possessions and protectorates. It is quite incorrect to assume that all this penetration of the Caribbean world was motivated by American economic greed. While the grasping forces arising out of a maturing American capitalism may have helped fashion the policy, they were much less important in determining the actions taken than considerations of national defense and security. Moreover, the impoverished and backward areas in which the United States intervened were not very attractive places for investment and trade. In the Dominican Republic, for example, American investments by 1913 totalled only $4 million, and American trade only $11 million. If the American government had any other objectives in mind than the defense of the canal, they were principally the protection of American lives and property already in the troubled areas, and the abatement of governmental nuisances that threatened to become international scandals.

Mexico

Had the United States really wished to promote commercial expansion by military intervention, it could have found a far better opportunity in Mexico, where a devastating revolution broke out in 1910. Here American investments bulked larger than in all the rest of the Caribbean combined, amounting in President Taft's opinion to not less than a billion dollars. American capital controlled approximately 78 per cent of the mines, 72 per cent of the smelters, and 58 per cent of the oil production within Mexican borders. The Wilson administration, to which fell the working out of a Mexican policy, was under heavy pressure to use military force in Mexico as a means of protecting American trade and investments, but it would be difficult to maintain that such force as it chose to use was designed primarily to aid American capitalistic interests.

For a third of a century before 1910 an iron-handed dictator, Porfirio Diaz, had ruled in Mexico, supported by the army, the church, and a few large landowners. During his long tenure of office Diaz had effectively destroyed the traditional communal land system, and had turned most of his people either into landless peasants who earned a meager living by working on the great estates, or into impoverished employees of the foreign-controlled industries, most of which, as noted above, were owned by United States investors, although European investors, particularly the British, also had substantial stakes in Mexico. While the wealth of Mexico was thus being channeled to foreigners and a few favored Mexicans, the masses of the people were held in the bondage of illiteracy and poverty. Finally, late in 1910, the long-smoldering discontent broke out into open revolution under the leadership of Francisco Madero,

a man of strongly democratic inclinations who had been educated in the United States. Warmly supported by the peasantry and a small group of middle-class merchants, the revolutionary movement sought to destroy the feudalistic system of Mexican society, to divide the land among the Mexican people, to curtail drastically the foreign exploitation of the nation's wealth, and to establish a real democracy. The ideals of the revolution were ultimately embodied in the Constitution of 1917, which stated significantly in its Clause 27 that the ownership of all the lands, waters, and sub-surface wealth of Mexico was vested in the nation, and existing concessions might be expropriated.

The forces behind Madero were strong enough to drive Diaz from office in May, 1911, and to enable Madero to assume the Presidency. But Madero found it extremely difficult to keep order; indeed, many of his

VILLA TROOPS AT CHIHUAHUA.

PANCHO VILLA. Described by a contemporary as "the greatest gunman and bandit in the whole world." 1915.

ANTAGONISTS IN MEXICO. *Because of internal disorders, Mexico was more in the American news during Wilson's first administration than at any time since the Mexican War.*

local leaders were far more interested in looting than in reform. Counter-revolutionary forces, composed principally of the disgruntled feudal elements, and strongly backed by the representatives of foreign capital, sought therefore to replace his government with one more to their liking; they also received the support of many members of the diplomatic corps, including Henry Lane Wilson, Ambassador from the United States. Although the Taft administration had recognized Madero's government, and had placed an embargo on the shipment of arms to his opponents, Ambassador Wilson showed great partiality for General Victoriano Huerta, leader of the reactionary forces, who in February, 1913, seized control of the government and threw Madero in jail, where after a few days he was murdered. Recognition of the Huerta

regime, as Ambassador Wilson strongly recommended, would have helped it greatly in warding off the attacks of rival factions led by Francisco ("Pancho") Villa, Emiliano Zapata, and Venustiano Carranza, but President Taft refused to act during his last few weeks in office, and turned the whole problem over to his successor, Woodrow Wilson.

The Mobile Doctrine

On the basis of precedent, recognition by the United States of an existing, or *de facto,* Latin-American government would have been almost automatic, regardless of how it came to power; moreover, since the Huerta government seemed to be the best fitted to restore order and protect foreign lives and property, it was promptly recognized by interested European nations, including

AMERICAN PUNITIVE EXPEDITION IN MEXICO. The 13th Cavalry marching out of El Vallo, April, 1916.

BRIGADIER-GENERAL JOHN J. PERSHING. Photograph of the General while he was in command of the El Paso patrol district, 1914.

Great Britain and France. But President Wilson soon let it be known that in this case he did not intend to act according to precedent. He was shocked at the violent and undemocratic way in which "that scoundrel Huerta" had seized power, and he regarded Huerta's "despotism" as a threat to Mexico's "submerged people" who were "struggling toward liberty." He announced publicly, March 11, 1913, that the American government had no sympathy "with those who seek to seize the power of government to advance their own personal power." He recalled Ambassador Wilson and sent John Lind of Minnesota to Mexico as his special agent, charged with the task of obtaining an armistice among the warring factions, and their consent to a free election in which all who were seeking the Mexican Presidency might participate except Huerta.

If this course were followed, Wilson would be willing to back the winner, and to encourage American bankers to do likewise. When, not surprisingly, Lind failed to achieve adoption of this idealistic but impracticable plan, Wilson instituted an arms embargo against all the warring parties, including Huerta, and warned American citizens to leave Mexico. The policy of the United States toward Mexico, he announced presently, would be one of "watchful waiting." As a rebuke to powerful American business interests, which demanded military intervention instead, Wilson announced in a speech delivered at Mobile, Alabama, October 27, 1913, that the "United States will never again seek one additional foot of territory by conquest." He seemed not to realize, however, that his refusal to recognize Huerta amounted in fact to diplomatic intervention by the United States in Mexico's domestic affairs.

"Watchful Waiting"

"Watchful waiting" was easier to defend as an ideal than to live up to in practice. When Wilson announced his famous "Mobile Doctrine," strong detachments of the regular army were already mobilized along the Mexican border as if to strike, and impressive naval units were stationed in Mexican waters. These measures, the first of which was taken before Taft left office, were regarded as essential for the protection of American territory from Mexican marauders, and for the assistance of American citizens desirous of escaping from Mexico to the United States. Wilson's determination to be rid of Huerta led him also to lift the embargo on Huerta's opponents, while retaining it against Huerta. The danger of foreign intervention was lessened by American surrender to Great Britain on the Panama Canal tolls controversy.[1] Finally, on the pretext that Huerta had failed to apologize properly for the arrest at Tampico of a boatload of American sailors, Wilson asked and obtained of Congress permission to take such military measures as might be necessary to bring Huerta to terms. On April 22, 1914, American marines and bluejackets took Vera Cruz, occupied the customs house, and prevented the landing of munitions for Huerta from a German ship. Eighteen Americans and many more Mexicans were killed in the clash. Huerta promptly handed the American chargé d'affaires at Mexico City his passports, and the army and navy of the United States prepared for war.

The Niagara Conference

The complete shipwreck of "watchful waiting" was prevented by the action of the three leading Latin-American nations,

Argentina, Brazil, and Chile, who promptly offered mediation. This Wilson as promptly accepted, and instead of the war a conference was held at Niagara Falls, Canada, in which representatives of the United States and the two leading Mexican factions participated. The Niagara recommendations were of little consequence, but the conference at least afforded the United States an opportunity to welcome the assistance of other American nations in solving the Mexican problem, and, by postponing military action, it made possible the peaceful elimination of Huerta, who now realized that he could never win. In July, Huerta resigned and left the country, and in August, Carranza, increasingly the favorite of the United States as the best hope of peace, entered the capital. By this time the outbreak of the First World War ended with finality any prospect of European intervention. In November of the same year the American occupation of Vera Cruz was terminated, but not until the summer of 1915, after a conference with what newspapermen called the "A B C" (Argentina, Brazil, Chile) and the "B U G" (Bolivia, Uruguay, Guatemala) powers, did the United States accord Carranza's government full recognition. Arms that Carranza was permitted to purchase in the United States helped the new President to restore order, much to the disgust of other revolutionary factions to whom American manufacturers were forbidden to sell. Carranza's chief opponent, Francisco Villa, vented his rage at the United States for this affront by twice crossing the international border in 1916, and murdering American citizens upon American soil. With the consent of Carranza an American military expedition under the command of Brigadier-General John J. Pershing advanced into Mexico in search of Villa, but it failed to catch him, and was presently withdrawn at Carranza's insistence.

Wilson, both at the time and later, was

[1] See p. 307.

subjected to severe criticism for his initial interference in the Huerta affair, and for his seemingly spineless policy of "watchful waiting." But Wilson's critics should not forget that American involvement in the Mexican revolution actually began with the activities of Henry Lane Wilson well before Woodrow Wilson became President of the United States. Ambassador Wilson had tried as hard to commit his government to the support of Huerta as ever President Wilson tried to bring about the Mexican usurper's downfall. Wilson's subsequent policy on the whole served the cause of peace. It may have resulted in the loss of a few hundred American lives, and perhaps $200 million worth of property, but it fell far short of outright military intervention. What a full-scale war might have cost in lives and money would be hard to estimate. Peace with the United States at least permitted the Mexican people to work out their national destiny for themselves. It also freed the United States on the eve of its entrance into the First World War from a most serious encumbrance at its back door. In general, it seems reasonable to conclude that Wilson's readiness to intervene in the Caribbean whenever serious European complications threatened, coupled with his reluctance to use a strong policy in Mexico, constitute rather convincing evidence that the over-all American Caribbean policy was dictated largely by strategic considerations, and only secondarily by the need of supporting private American investments.

The Peace Movement

While the United States, before 1914, still believed in its historic policy of isolation and tried in general to hold aloof from European political disputes, many thoughtful Americans had begun to fear that the nation's new overseas commitments might conceivably result in involvements that would lead to war. How then could peace be maintained? It did not require much logic to deduce that the surest way to keep the United States out of war was to keep war out of the world, and a strong movement for world peace began. The first Hague Conference, called by the Tsar of Russia in 1899, had already struggled with this problem, and had recommended three means for settling disputes without resort to war: (1) through good offices and mediation, which, when offered by a third party to powers at war or about to go to war, must not be considered an unfriendly act; (2) through international commissions of inquiry, for which so many precedents existed, particularly in the relations between Great Britain and the United States; and (3) through submission to a new court of arbitration to be established at the The Hague. Not only did the United States accept the recommendations of the Hague Conference, but President Roosevelt submitted the first case for the Hague Tribunal to decide — the old and unimportant Pious Fund controversy with Mexico — and agreed to the decision.

At the second Hague Conference, held in 1907, the United States began a persistent campaign to commit the nations of the world to the settlement of their disputes by peaceful means. The American delegation worked strenuously, although unavailingly, for the creation of an international court of justice comparable to the United States Supreme Court, to which cases could be referred for adjudication. The conference, and a subsequent one at London, drew up a set of rules for the conduct of war on land and sea, but both failed of ratification. Even the United States refused to support a ban on poison gas in armed combat. More fruitful was a model arbitration treaty which all the nations of the world were urged to follow. While Roosevelt was President, Secretary Root negotiated twenty-five treaties providing for the reference of disputes between the signatory nations to the Hague Tribunal, but these agreements were weakened by excluding all questions of "national honor or of grave national interests," precisely the kind of differences that caused most wars. President Taft was also an earnest advocate of arbitration, and during his administration Secretary Knox obtained two treaties, with Great Britain and France respectively, of a more general nature than their predecessors; but unfortunately the United States Senate amended them to death.

Wilson's Secretary of State, Bryan, had spoken to Chautauqua audiences all over the country on the subject of peace, and regarded his cabinet appointment as a direct invitation to further the cause of arbitration. More successful than any of his predecessors, he obtained the ratification of no less than thirty arbitration treaties, most of them based on what newspaper men called the "twenty minutes before you spank" principle. Bryan believed that war, if postponed until the period of acute tension had ended, could be averted. His treaties provided for the arbitration by international commissions of all disputes "of whatever character and nature." While the arbitration proceedings were in progress, the participating nations might neither increase their armament nor resort to war. It is worthy of note that by 1914 Bryan had obtained treaties of this nature with every one of the European nations allied against Germany in the First World War, while Germany, Austria, and Turkey had rejected his proposals.

The Algeciras Conference

In general, the United States sought during these prewar years to avoid any direct participation in European diplomacy, but Theodore Roosevelt no doubt involved his country far more deeply in European affairs than most Americans realized when he took part in the settlement of the Moroccan crisis of 1905–1906. This threat to European peace was precipitated when the German

Emperor made a saber-rattling speech at Tangier in March, 1905. By a secret understanding Great Britain and France had agreed to support each other in their determination to dominate the political and economic life of Egypt and Morocco, respectively. But in Morocco the French intentions ran squarely against an old treaty which Germany and even the United States had signed, the terms of which guaranteed a commercial open door in the North African country to all nations. War appeared likely when Germany demanded an international conference on the subject and France refused to agree. After much belligerent talk from each side, the Kaiser asked the United States, as the foremost defender of the open-door principle, to help promote the conference, and this Roosevelt eventually did. But in his instructions to Henry White, the representative of the United States at the conference, the President directed that nothing should be done to break up the Anglo-French entente, and that White should help France "get what she ought to have."

When the conference finally took place at Algeciras, Spain, in January, 1906, it decided against the open-door principle and accorded to France a victory on all important points. For one of its decisions, that the port of Casablanca should not be turned over to Germany, Roosevelt took personal credit. He had a deep distrust of Germany, and was strongly opposed to the establishment of such a German outpost so close to the Western Hemisphere. Whether Roosevelt actually helped to avert the outbreak of a general European war, as he thought, will never be known, but undoubtedly one of his motives for taking part in the affair was to help preserve the peace. Nevertheless, by consistently supporting Great Britain and France, Roosevelt probably made Germany more fearful of encirclement than ever, and his action served notice on her that in the future she would probably be outvoted in any similar world conference. Without knowing at the time how partisan the United States had been at Algeciras, many Americans were plainly uneasy about the affair. In ratifying the Algeciras convention the Senate emphasized this feeling by stating that the United States took no responsibility for the enforcement of the pact, and further that the action did not in any way change the historic American policy "which forbids participation by the United States in settlement of political questions which are entirely European in their scope."

Roosevelt's successors retreated somewhat from the advanced position he had taken, and showed a greater reluctance to break with long-established tradition. Taft no-

tably abstained from interfering either in the second Moroccan incident of 1911 or in the Turko-Italian war that followed. To him these matters were not of "direct political concern" to the American nation. Woodrow Wilson followed the same course during the Balkan wars of 1913. Except for the Algeciras episode the United States thus clung to its traditional isolation from purely European disputes until after the outbreak of the First World War.

American diplomatic policy before 1914, as summed up by a distinguished student of the subject, sought three principal objectives, (1) continued predominance in the Caribbean, (2) equal participation with other powers in the Orient, and (3) abstention from the affairs of European nations.

BIBLIOGRAPHY

H. K. Beale, *Theodore Roosevelt and the Rise of America to World Power* (1956), is a series of valuable lectures; the author's untimely death cut short a projected multivolume biography. H. F. Pringle, *Theodore Roosevelt* (1931), was for many years the most influential biography; it is severely critical in tone, especially in foreign policy. W. H. Harbaugh, *Power and Responsibility: The Life and Times of Theodore Roosevelt* (1961), is an excellent study, more friendly than Pringle, yet not uncritical. G. E. Mowry, *The Era of Theodore Roosevelt, 1900–1912* (1958), is a general survey of the period; it contains chapters on foreign policy and a full bibliography. Of great scholarly importance is *The Letters of Theodore Roosevelt*, superbly edited by E. E. Morison and others (8 vols., 1951–1954). A brief, brilliant reinterpretation is *The Republican Roosevelt* (1954), by J. M. Blum, one of those who worked on the *Letters* project. A convenient brief life is *Theodore Roosevelt and the Politics of Power* (1969), by G. W. Chessman, who has also written *Governor Theodore Roosevelt*

(1965). See also the reappraisal by D. H. Burton, *Theodore Roosevelt: Confident Imperialist* (1968). *Theodore Roosevelt: A Profile* (1967), edited by Morton Keller, contains writings by and about TR. *The Writings of Theodore Roosevelt* (1967), edited by W. H. Harbaugh, is a valuable supplement to Roosevelt's *Autobiography* (1913). Useful for foreign affairs in TR's second term is P. C. Jessup, *Elihu Root* (2 vols., 1938); a brief synthesis is provided by R. W. Leopold, *Elihu Root and the Conservative Tradition* (1954).

On relations with Japan, see F. R. Dulles, *Yankees and Samurai: America's Role in the Emergence of Modern Japan, 1791–1900* (1965); and P. J. Treat, *Diplomatic Relations between the United States and Japan, 1895–1905* (2 vols., 2nd ed., 1938). A. L. P. Dennis, *The Anglo-Japanese Alliance* (1923), can now be supplemented by J. A. White, *The Diplomacy of the Russo-Japanese War* (1964). On the perennially interesting question of Roosevelt's involvements with Japan, the following are noteworthy studies: Tyler Dennett, *Roosevelt and the Russo-Japanese War* (1925); T.

A. Bailey, *Theodore Roosevelt and the Japanese-American Crises* (1934); R. A. Esthus, *Theodore Roosevelt and Japan* (1966); and C. E. Neu, *An Uncertain Friendship: Theodore Roosevelt and Japan, 1906–1909* (1967). An interesting monograph on a related subject is E. H. Zabriskie, *American-Russian Rivalry in the Far East, 1895–1914* (1946).

On Canadian relations, helpful recent books include R. C. Brown, *Canada's National Policy, 1883–1900* (1964); and G. M. Craig, *The United States and Canada* (1968). See also C. C. Tansill, *Canadian-American Relations, 1895–1911* (1943); and P. E. Corbett, *The Settlement of Canadian-American Disputes* (1937). Allan Nevins, *Henry White: Thirty Years of American Diplomacy* (1930), sheds light on the subject of the Alaskan boundary dispute. An important episode in the Taft administration is treated in L. E. Ellis, *Reciprocity, 1911* (1939).

On inter-American problems, interesting fresh material may be found in T. F. McGann, *Argentina, the United States, and the Inter-American System, 1880–1914* (1957). Generally useful on the Caribbean region are: J. F. Rippy, *The Caribbean Danger Zone* (1940); W. H. Callcott, *The Caribbean Policy of the United States, 1890–1920* (1942); and D. G. Munro, *Intervention and Dollar Diplomacy in the Caribbean, 1900–1921* (1964). Also valuable are: H. C. Hill, *Roosevelt and the Caribbean* (1927); E. T. Parks, *Colombia and the United States* (1935); J. F. Rippy, *The Capitalists and Colombia* (1931); A. P. Whitaker, *The United States and South America: The Northern Republics* (1948); and D. G. Munro, *The Five Republics of Central America* (1918).

The literature on the Panama Canal is extensive. Among the more important diplomatic studies are: N. J. Padelford, *The Panama Canal in Peace and War* (1942); M. W. Williams, *Anglo-American Isthmian Diplomacy, 1815–1915* (1916); and W. D. McCain, *The United States and the Republic of Panama* (1937). On the building of the canal see: J. B. and Farnham Bishop, *Goethals* (1930); M. C. D. Gorgas and B. J. Hendrick, *William Crawford Gorgas* (1924); J. M. Gibson, *Physician to the World: The Life of General William C. Gorgas* (1950); and M. P. DuVal, Jr., *And the Mountains Will Move* (1947), which emphasizes the engineering problems.

On Mexican relations, a valuable general survey is H. F. Cline, *The United States and Mexico* (2nd ed., 1963). A popularly written, highly critical biography is Carleton Beals, *Porfirio Diaz, Dictator of Mexico* (1932). Interesting sidelights are contained in Edith O'Shaughnessy, *Intimate Pages of Mexican History* (1920). Case studies are set forth in D. M. Pletcher, *Rails, Mines, and Progress: Seven American Promoters in Mexico, 1867–1911* (1958). Special studies treating Wilson's Mexican policy include: G. M. Stephenson, *John Lind of Minnesota* (1935); C. C. Clendenen, *The United States and Pancho Villa* (1961), and *Blood on the Border: The United States Army and the Mexican Irregulars* (1969); and R. E. Quirk, *An Affair of Honor: Woodrow Wilson and the Occupation of Vera Cruz* (1962). See also J. M. Callahan, *American Foreign Policy in Mexican Relations* (1932); and Harold Nicolson, *Dwight Morrow* (1935). Important studies of the Mexican Revolution include: Ernest Gruening, *Mexico and Its Heritage* (1928); Frank Tannenbaum, *Mexico, the Struggle for Peace and Bread* (1950); and Anita Brenner, *The Wind That Swept Mexico* (1943).

On the Algeciras Conference, see E. N. Anderson, *The First Moroccan Crisis, 1904–1906* (1930). On the Hague Conferences, the fullest account is J. B. Scott, *The Hague Peace Conferences of 1899 and 1907* (2 vols., 1909). But see also the prize-winning monograph by C. De A. Davis, *The United States and the First Hague Peace Conference* (1962). An important theme is developed in Peter Brock, *Pacifism in the United States from the Colonial Era to the First World War* (1968).

13

THE PROGRESSIVE MOVEMENT

The reform spirit · The "muckrakers" · Conservatism and progressivism · Municipal and state reforms · Robert M. LaFollette · The direct primary · Prohibition · Woman suffrage · Roosevelt as President · The trust problem again · Railroad regulation · The Pure Food Act · Labor and the "square deal" · Conservation · Election of 1904 · The Panic of 1907

The Reform Spirit

The years from 1900 to 1916 saw the rise of a reform movement in the United States that affected every aspect of American life, city and state as well as national, social no less than political. Just as during the Jackson period, now again reform was in the air. Much of the momentum for this new reform came from the Populists, whose party had practically disappeared by the turn of the century, but whose ideas won some support from both Bryan Democrats and Roosevelt Republicans. But whereas the Populists won little support for their movement from outside the rural classes, the reformers of the progressive age were backed principally by members of the urban middle classes, including many individuals of considerable wealth. The leadership of the Populists and of the progressives showed a similar divergence. Instead of the broken-down third party politicians and the grass-roots farmers who had represented

the Populists, the progressives recruited their leaders principally from the ranks of the professions and the small businessmen. Just why so many well-to-do individuals should have chosen to devote their time and talents to reform causes during a period of relative prosperity may seem at first glance difficult to understand. But one should remember that the spectacular rise of big business during the last third of the nineteenth century had presented the urban middle classes with two serious threats. What chance had little business to survive in the uneven competition with big business? And how far would big business go in taking over the actual control of government itself? From another direction also the small owner felt himself to be threatened. How was he to deal with the growing power of the labor unions, and with the inroads that European socialism was making upon American thought? As he saw it, reform was

"FIGHTING" BOB LAFOLLETTE, an indefatigable reformer, making a sidewalk speech.

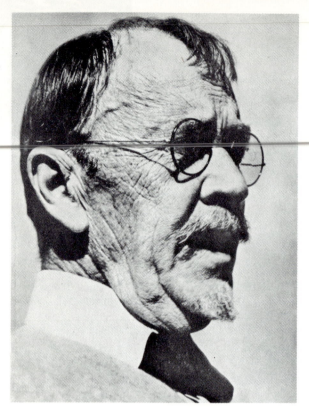

Joseph Lincoln Steffens. *Usually known as Lincoln Steffens, this outstanding journalist, in a series of articles later published as a book, called attention to the widespread corruption in American city government.*

needed both to curb the power of the great corporations and to arrest the progress of union labor and socialism among the city workers. The progressive movement was thus in considerable part an attempt to preserve small business in the United States as a way of life, and as a political and economic power in the nation. At the same time the progressives sought also to redirect American thinking, long dominated by agrarian doctrines, toward the pressing new urban and industrial problems of the age. Other factors that help explain the rising middle-class interest in reform include (1) the development of Social Christianity, (2) the emphasis that Darwinism gave to environment as a determinant in life, and (3) the growing power of women in social and moral questions.

The "Muckrakers"

The new awakening owed much also to the "muckrakers," a group of energetic journalists who made it their chief concern to discover and exploit in popular articles the seamy side of business and political behavior. They owed their name to Theodore Roosevelt, who was by no means unsympathetic with their work, but who compared some of the most sensational of them to the character in *Pilgrim's Progress* "who could look no way but downward with the muck-rake in his hands." A vehicle was available for the muckrakers in the popular magazines that the nineties had produced, *McClure's*, the *Cosmopolitan*, *Everybody's*, the *American*, *Pearson's*, *Munsey's*, the *Arena*, and a number of others. Through these journals Ida M. Tarbell exposed the "History of the Standard Oil Company," Lincoln Steffens, "The Shame of the Cities," Thomas Lawson, "Frenzied Finance," Charles Edward Russell, "The Beef Trust," Ray Stannard Baker, "The Railroads on Trial," and so on through an almost interminable list of titles. Supplementing and often corroborating the findings of the muckrakers were the volumes of the census of 1900, which soon began to appear, and the compendious *Report of the Industrial Commission* (19 vols., 1900–1902), an investigating committee set up by Congress in 1898. Unread by the public at large, but of notable perspicacity, were the philosophical treatises of Thorstein Veblen, which provided reformers with some of their most cogent arguments against "predatory wealth."[1]

Conservatism in America

During the last half of the nineteenth century a majority of Americans had believed that social health depended upon a minimum of governmental interference with business

[1] See pp. 253–255.

and the individual. According to this theory, the "natural law" of competition operating in a free market would send the able and virtuous men to the top, while the misfits would sink to the bottom. Since they were able, the group at the top would naturally expect to dominate the government, either directly or through their agents. Anything that threatened this rule of the elite, either in the economic or the political sphere, was considered socially bad. In denouncing the unions as evil, during the coal strike of 1902, the capitalist George F. Baer was quite sincere. Rather than rely upon union organizations, Baer told the workers, they should put their trust in the "Christian men to whom God in His infinite wisdom has given control of the property interest of the country." Men of such beliefs naturally felt increasingly that the government should help economic and moral laws along by granting such aids as tariff protection to aspiring businessmen. In broad terms, such was the prevailing view among conservatives at the turn of the century.

The Progressive Creed

Opposing this conservative formulation, the Populists had believed that unrestrained governmental friendliness to big business, coupled with a general indifference to the welfare of the masses, was as unfair individually as it was harmful socially. What was needed, the Populists argued, was a government dominated by a majority of the people who would use it to help them out when they were in trouble. With this Populist view the progressives agreed. However much they differed on the means to achieve their ends, practically all of them insisted that government should clearly reflect the majority will, and that the often corrupt control of business over government should be broken. Most progressives also felt that the economic activity of big business should be curbed of its ruthless-

ness, and that opportunity for the small businessman, the farmer, and the laborer to make their way up in the world should be increased. Groups who could not fend for themselves in a harsh competitive urban world, including women and children, should receive governmental protection. Some of the more morally minded of the progressives even insisted that individuals should be restrained from such harmful conduct as drinking and gambling. To serve such socially useful ends, progressives believed that the state should intervene as a regulatory and protective agency.

There was, of course, much difference of opinion among progressives on just how far the state should interfere in the life of its citizens. Some insisted that it should go only so far as to break up monopolies by effective antitrust laws. Others, at the opposite extreme, accepted many socialist ideas that had been brought to America from Europe far back in the nineteenth century, and popularized by such writers as Edward Bellamy. Opportunity in America was still too widespread for many Americans to take seriously the fundamental tenet of socialism, that an all-powerful state should own and operate all the agencies of production and distribution, and the aggressive radicalism of Daniel De Leon's Socialist-Labor Party, which was active in national campaigns throughout the nineties, made few converts. Far more influential were the moderate socialists, who broke away from De Leon's leadership to found the Social Democratic Party, which in 1900 nominated Eugene V. Debs for the Presidency. The next year it was formally organized as the Socialist Party of America. The moderates, while differing little from the radicals in theory, tended to emphasize measures of "immediate interest" that would "lessen the economic and political power of the capitalist." Pending more fundamental reforms, they were willing to support such halfway measures as public works for the relief of the unemployed; the public ownership of the railroads, public utilities, and all existing national monopolies; the improvement of the industrial condition of the workers; the extension of inheritance taxes; a graduated income tax; woman suffrage; the initiative and the referendum; the abolition of the doctrine of judicial review; the election of judges by the people for short terms; and the enactment of further measures for general education and the conservation of health. Many so-called socialistic policies had an ancestry quite separate from the Socialist Party, but whatever their origin they had a way of seeping over into the platforms of other reformers, and even into those of the old parties themselves.

Municipal Reform

Reforms in municipal government marked the beginnings of the progressive movement. Lincoln Steffens' articles made the "shame of the cities" better known than ever before, but reformers had already arisen. In Toledo Samuel M. Jones, better known as "Golden Rule" Jones, made successful war upon the private-contract system, and advocated the municipal ownership of public utilities. Elected to office in 1897, Jones was repeatedly re-elected, and in 1904 was succeeded by his friend and disciple, Brand Whitlock, who continued the good work. In Cleveland Tom Loftin Johnson became mayor in 1901. A convinced "single-taxer," he secured among other reforms a long-overdue re-assessment of property values, municipal control of the streetcar system, and a three-cent fare. Under his regime Cleveland could claim to be the "best governed city in the United States," a claim that Milwaukee, under the Socialist leadership of Emil Seidel and Daniel W. Hoan, was soon to challenge. The "gas and water socialism" of the reform mayors was often inspired as much by the desire for clean government as by a demand for more economical and efficient service.

To many thoughtful critics the reform of city government could best be promoted by a change in the system. City administration was primarily a business affair; why should it be hampered by a form of government patterned after that of the United States? Why should the Democrats and the Republicans run opposing tickets for city offices? What difference did it make whether a candidate for mayor or alderman believed in a high tariff or a low tariff, in imperialism or in isolation, in free silver or the single gold standard? In 1901 the city of Galveston, Texas, which the year before had been destroyed by a tidal wave and was in desperate need of efficiency in government, tried to obtain it by turning over the whole problem to a commission of five, each of whom would administer, under rules laid down by a majority vote, some department of city affairs. Soon many other cities were experimenting with the "commission form" of government, and out of it grew an even more reasonable scheme, the "city manager" plan. This system, which originated probably in Staunton, Virginia, sought to duplicate the methods of the business corporation. The elected board or commission employed a manager, who ran the city with the same freedom of action that was normally accorded a business executive. Soon hundreds of American cities, large or small, were being administered, usually more efficiently than ever before, by commissions and city managers. Thousands, however, adhered to the old systems, and in all too many instances to the old ways.

State Reforms

The most spectacular of the reforms of this period occurred in the realm of state, rather than city, government. Theodore Roosevelt, as reform President of the United States, had many precursors and imitators among the state governors, each with a vision of reform. They found the state governments almost completely in the control of whatever big business corporations happened to be most powerful in their particular part of the country. Well-oiled party machines in each state did the bidding of the state "boss," and the "boss" in turn did the bidding of the business interests that furnished the oil for his machine. Speaking before the New York Constitutional Convention of 1915, Elihu Root, an excellent authority, remarked:

Mr. Platt ruled the state; for nigh upon twenty years he ruled it. It was not the governor; it was not the legislature; it was Mr. Platt. And the capital was not here [at Albany]: it was at 49 Broadway. . . . The ruler of the state during the greater part of the forty years of my acquaintance with the state government has not been any man authorized by the constitution or by law. . . . The party leader is elected by no one, accountable to no one, bound by no oath of office, removable by no one. . . . I don't criticize the men of the invisible government. . . . But it is all wrong.

For a reformer to be elected to a governorship under such conditions was in itself a revolution; once in office his only chance of remaining there was to break the power of the machine.

Robert M. LaFollette

Outstanding among the reform governors was Robert M. LaFollette (1855–1925) of Wisconsin, a man whose influence upon the course of political events during his lifetime was more fundamental than that of many Presidents. "Fighting Bob," as he came to be called, had entered politics, without benefit of machine assistance, soon after his graduation from the University of Wisconsin in 1879. As county prosecutor of Dane County he made an excellent record, and in 1884 was nominated and elected for the first of three successive terms in the national House of Representative. He was

Robert Marion LaFollette. *After serving as governor of Wisconsin, LaFollette was elected in 1905 to the United States Senate, and served there until the time of his death. From a 1917 photograph.*

an indefatigable canvasser, delighted in controversy, and developed political speechmaking into a fine art. Like many another Republican he was left at home by the election of 1890, and but for a controversy with the all-powerful Senator Philetus Sawyer, who was both a politician and a lumber baron, his ambitions for a career in state politics might easily have been gratified. When the Democrats took over the government of Wisconsin in 1891, they found that for years the Republican state treasurers had made a practice of depositing the state's funds, interest free, in certain favored banks. The new attorney-general promptly brought suit to recover this interest money for the state, and Sawyer, because he had acted as bondsman for the treasurers, came in for his share of the trouble. According to the LaFollette version of the story, Sawyer attempted through LaFollette to bribe the judge before whom the case was to be tried — a Democratic brother-in-law of LaFollette's. Deeply incensed, LaFollette made the whole matter public, and helped the state recover the funds of which it had been defrauded.

From that time on LaFollette was a crusader for reform. Determined to win the governorship, he was repeatedly denied the nomination in spite of a growing popular sentiment in his favor; not until 1900 was he able to line up a majority of the convention delegates. Elected, and twice re-elected, he forced through reluctant legislatures laws for the more effective taxation of the railroads and other corporations; for the establishment of direct primaries through which the people, not boss-ridden conventions, could select their own candidates for office; for the termination of the free-pass evil by prohibiting state officials from accepting them; and for the conservation of the natural resources of the state in forests and water power. In his quest of good government he enlisted the aid of experts from the University of Wisconsin, whose new president, Charles R. Van Hise, was his close personal friend and his choice for the office. He was instrumental, also, in the creation of a Legislative Reference Bureau through which legislators might obtain expert advice on the drafting of bills. In a sense LaFollette and many of the other reform governors built up political machines, but the organizations they developed were generally free from corruption.

Other Crusaders

The "Wisconsin idea," which was fundamentally to free the state from business domination through venal party bosses and to turn over public administration to popularly chosen leaders willing to seek the advice of experts, exactly suited the temper of the times. Other governors in other states duplicated in varying degrees the LaFollette record in Wisconsin. In Missouri Joseph

W. Folk won public attention as circuit attorney by successfully prosecuting the corrupt ring of St. Louis "boodlers," the current term for grafters, that for years had fattened on municipal spoils. As governor for four years after 1905, he sought with moderate success to repeat in the state arena what he had done for his home city. In New York Charles Evans Hughes won deserved acclaim as counsel for a legislative investigating committee that examined into the methods of the New York life insurance companies. Hughes's sensational disclosures brought about a revolution in the insurance business and led to his election as governor in 1906. Out in California the star of Hiram Johnson began to rise when, in 1906, he attracted attention as a member of the staff of prosecuting attorneys in charge of some San Francisco "boodling" cases. In 1908 he secured the conviction of Abe Ruef, grafting municipal boss of San Francisco, after Francis J. Heney, the original prosecutor, had been shot in the line of duty. In 1910 Johnson was elected governor, determined above all else to end the domination of the state by the Southern Pacific Railroad.

The roll of reform governors was a long one, including, besides such prominent individuals as A. B. Cummins of Iowa and John A. Johnson of Minnesota, many lesser lights whose names never became nationally well known. Private individuals, such as William S. U'Ren of Oregon, crusader for "the Oregon system," which featured popular participation in government, also took a hand, while the public at large, fully aroused by the revelations of the muckrakers, demanded and obtained results.

The Direct Primary

The most fundamental of the political reforms effected during these years was the substitution of the direct primary for the convention system of making nominations. Under the old system only a small fraction of the voters, certainly never more than 15 per cent, attended the original caucuses or "primaries" by which convention delegates were chosen. A large proportion of those who attended were local officeholders and aspirants to office. It was thus easy for the machine to secure a working majority of the delegates to almost every convention, and to put through the "slate" of nominees agreed upon by the leaders in advance. The direct primary, however, substituted voting at the polls by secret ballot for the caucus-convention system, and reduced immeasurably the chances of machine manipulation. Within a comparatively short time after the passage in 1903 of the Wisconsin primary law, similar laws had been enacted by nearly every state in the Union. The results were revolutionary, at least for the time being. It would be idle to claim that the direct primaries completely eliminated either business domination of government or the power of venal party bosses. But the new laws greatly promoted the possibility of successful popular uprisings against corrupt machines, and because of them in state after state men were elected to office who under the old system would never have had a chance. Later on, politicians found many ways to "work" the primaries, particularly the "presidential" primaries that were provided in some states for the selection or instruction of delegates to national nominating conventions.

Initiative and Referendum

The initiative and referendum were twin measures of popular government that might be used as clubs over legislatures unresponsive to the popular will. By these devices laws could be initiated by petition, and voted on by ballot, or "held up" to a popular vote by petition, after passage by the legislature. The use of the referendum for constitutional provisions and for such local legislation as the flotation of bond issues was by no means new, but its application

to ordinary law-making, coupled with the power of popular initiative, was decidedly an innovation. The initiative and referendum were first adopted in South Dakota, in 1898, but obtained their best test in Oregon, where from 1902 to 1910 no less than thirty-two measures were referred to the people for a vote. In Oregon, too, the recall, a measure by which criticized officials, on petition of a stipulated number or percentage of the voters, were required to stand for re-election at special elections, was given a thorough trial. Indeed, "the Oregon system" came to be the term most commonly used to describe the new adventures in popular government. Largely because of U'Ren's effective leadership, Oregon had adopted the Australian ballot in 1891, a registration law in 1899, the initiative and referendum law in 1902, the direct primary in 1904, a sweeping corrupt practices act in 1908, and the recall in 1910. "In Oregon," so it was said, "the state government is divided into four departments — the executive, judicial, legislative, and U'Ren — and it is still an open question who exerts the more power." Within a decade nearly twenty states had the initiative and referendum, and nearly a dozen the recall. Acceptance of "the Oregon system" moved in general from west to east, and in the older states often met unyielding opposition.

Direct Election of Senators

That even the federal government might be affected by state reforms was proved when preferential primaries were introduced whereby the voters might express their choices for United States senators. These laws assumed that in senatorial elections state legislatures would be guided solely by the popular mandate, and regardless of personal or party considerations would elect the primary winner to the senatorship. The movement for direct election of United States senators dated far back into the nineteenth century, and had won warm support not only from reform politicians such as the Populists, but from many conservative citizens as well. Four times, in 1894, 1898, 1900, and 1902, the national House of Representatives had supported a constitutional amendment for the direct election of senators, but each time the Senate had refused to concur. Meantime the scandals involved in legislative elections became increasingly evident. At best state legislation tended to be treated as of secondary importance in years when a senator was to be chosen; at worst open bribery was resorted to by individuals and corporations hoping to elect a candidate friendly to their interests.

Undoubtedly the framers of the Constitution had intended that the upper chamber should represent not merely the individual states, but also the wealth of the nation. They had builded better than they knew. By the twentieth century the United States Senate could be spoken of, not without considerable truth, as a "millionaire's club." Men of great wealth aspired to a seat in it as a crowning evidence of success. Corporations with privileges to protect made every effort to secure a senatorship for one of their directors, or at least for one of their attorneys. Party bosses themselves often sought and obtained election to the Senate. The general level of intelligence in the upper chamber therefore was high — has perhaps never been higher — but the senators, so critics insisted, represented the vested interests of the country rather than the people as a whole. Naturally the Senate refused, as long as it dared, to risk the results of popular election. But the preferential primaries, which eventually were adopted by more than half the states, brought about by indirection the change that the Senate had tried to avoid. In this development U'Ren and "the Oregon system" pioneered the way. Further, as popularly chosen senators took their seats, the opposition to direct election was broken down. By 1912 the Senate submitted to the inevitable and

agreed to the Seventeenth Amendment, which a year later became a part of the Constitution.

The reforms of the Roosevelt era in state and city government greatly facilitated the efforts of those who wished to enlist the aid of the law in the improvement of social conditions. No longer so deferential to the rich man's point of view, and unhampered by the constitutional limitations that so restricted the activities of the national government, the states crowded their statute books with laws that had rarely or never been obtainable before. A large part of the new legislation was designed to promote the interests of labor, but other subjects, particularly the prohibition of the liquor traffic, received careful consideration.

Labor Legislation

Most important of the new labor legislation, perhaps, was the series of employer's liability, or workmen's compensation, acts that followed Maryland's first feeble beginning in this direction in 1902. These laws were designed to reverse the old common-law rule that a workman had to prove negligence on the part of his employer in order to obtain compensation for injuries, and that even this might be insufficient if he himself, or any "fellow-servant," had been guilty of contributory negligence. The new principle, which by 1921 had been accepted in all but six states, was that in hazardous occupations the employer was liable for all injuries that occurred to his employees while they were at work. As a result of the new laws millions of dollars were soon paid out each year in benefits to injured workmen or their families.

Efforts were made also to increase the protection given to women and children in industry. Most of the states eventually adopted laws forbidding in certain types of industry the employment of children under fourteen years of age, while laws for compulsory school attendance accomplished the

LABOR PROBLEMS. *The progressives took a deep interest in the welfare of labor, but more as humanitarian reformers than as instigators of direct action by organized labor.*

CHILD LABOR IN A GLASS FACTORY. An interior view photographed by Lewis W. Hine, June, 1911. From the Jacob A. Riis collection in the Museum of the City of New York.

A WOMAN WORKER. From a photograph of a woman working with spools in a North Carolina factory, about 1912.

EUGENE V. DEBS. The perennial Socialist candidate for President is shown here addressing a railroad yards audience.

"I Cannot Tell a Lie — I Did It with My Little Hatchet." *A cartoon showing Mrs. Carry Nation, the Kansas temperance crusader, in a belligerent pose.*

same purpose in another way. Opposition from the southern textile industries caused some of the southern states to lag either in the enactment or in the enforcement of child-labor laws, and as early as 1906 a movement was begun to give Congress authority over child labor by a constitutional amendment. Such an amendment was actually submitted in 1924, but it failed of ratification. Laws limiting the number of hours per day that women and children might be employed, and fixing minimum-wage schedules that they must be paid, were also enacted by some of the states. Attempts to extend these same principles to employed men met with stronger opposition, but a few successes were recorded. In the whole field of labor legislation the United States lagged far behind European nations. Unemployment insurance and old-age pensions, for example, while common enough else-

where, were hardly more than talked about in the United States.

Prohibition

Attempts by prohibitionists to do away with the liquor traffic date far back into the nineteenth century, but the era of successful activity began with the formation of the Anti-Saloon League in 1893. This organization received the active support of all the evangelical denominations, and was maintained by the funds its agents were permitted to collect at regular church services. Its methods came to be quite as hard-boiled as those of the politicians with whom it had to deal. It knew one test, and only one test, for fitness to hold office. If a man favored the liquor traffic, the Anti-Saloon League was against him; if he opposed the liquor traffic, the Anti-Saloon League was for him. With a budget that by 1903 had

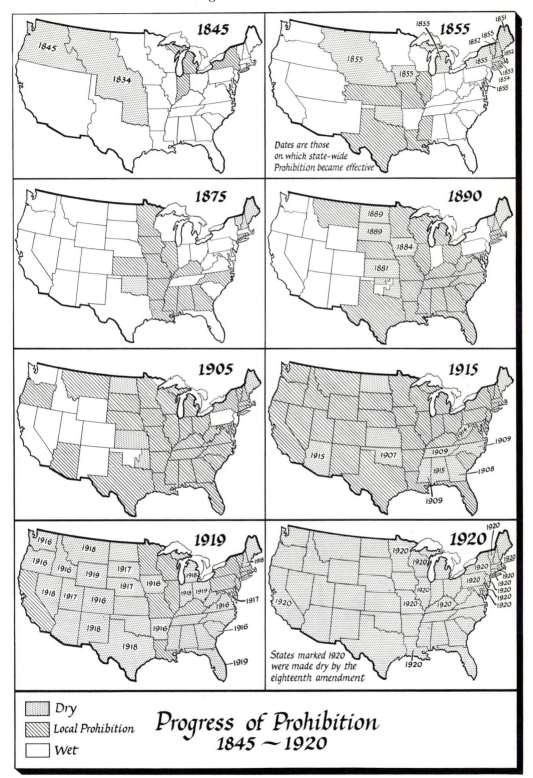

Progress of Prohibition
1845 — 1920

Dry
Local Prohibition
Wet

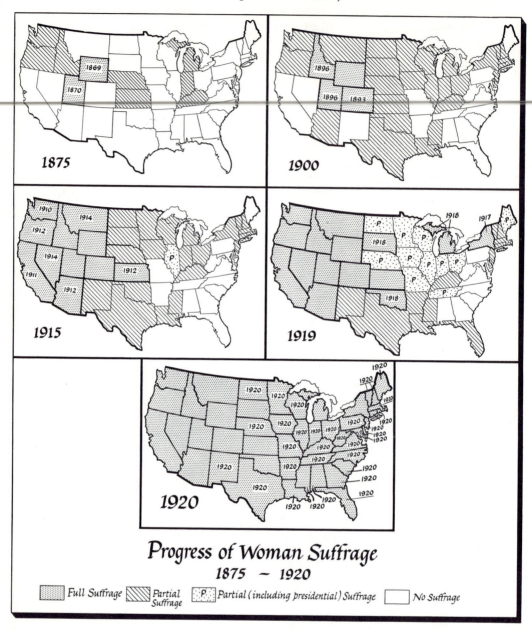

Progress of Woman Suffrage
1875 – 1920

Full Suffrage   Partial Suffrage   P. Partial (*including presidential*) Suffrage   No Suffrage

reached $400,000 a year, the League was in a position to hire hundreds of organizers and to maintain scores of offices. For a generation, under the leadership of Wayne B. Wheeler and William H. Anderson, it sought to make the issue, "wet" or "dry," take precedence over nearly every other issue in state and local politics. As between low license and high license, the League favored high license. As between high license and "local option," whereby a town or county might vote to exclude saloons, it favored local option. As between local option and statewide prohibition, it favored statewide prohibition. And as between statewide prohibition and national prohibi-

Suffragettes. *This unlovely epithet was applied to women who in the Wilson period actively sought the right to vote for members of their sex. "Feminists" of the nineteenth century were somewhat less militant, but no less determined. Victory came in 1920.*

tion, it favored national prohibition. Never too squeamish about its methods or its political bedfellows, it took what it could get.

It got a great deal. The liquor business was open to attack for all the same reasons that other big businesses were vulnerable, and for many more besides. A veritable barrage of tracts, sermons, orations, and temperance journals set forth its shortcomings with a degree of passionate enthusiasm reminiscent of the abolitionists. The efforts of brewers, distillers, and wine-makers to obtain business favors from legislatures, county boards, and city councils were skillfully used to classify the liquor interests with the corruptionists. Local liquor dealers' associations were taunted as defenders of lawlessness and vice, and crooked politics was traced with an unerring eye to the door of the saloon. In the South the mistakes of the Negro were blamed upon liquor, and prohibition was demanded as a necessary preliminary to good relations be-

tween the races. At first the successes of the Anti-Saloon League were mainly confined to the rural districts and were obtained by local option, but before 1909 four southern states had voted dry, and within the next few years many others, northern as well as southern, were to follow. By the time the First World War broke out, nearly half the people of the United States lived in "dry" territory, while in three-fourths of its total area the saloon had been outlawed. The ratification of the Eighteenth Amendment to the Constitution in 1919 merely completed a process that had been long under way.

Woman Suffrage

Woman suffrage was a companion reform to prohibition. If women obtained the vote, so prohibitionists reasoned, they would with certainty aid the temperance cause. In 1869 the Territory of Wyoming had conferred the suffrage on women, and by 1911 six western states, Wyoming, Colorado, Utah, Idaho, Washington, and California, had accepted the innovation *in toto*, while many other states gave women the right to vote in certain elections. Like the prohibitionists the suffragists hoped to crown their efforts by obtaining an amendment to the Constitution that would end the denial of the suffrage to women, and, while adding state after state to their list of converts, they continued to work on Congress. An outbreak of "militancy," borrowed from Great Britain before the First World War, may have had something to do with bringing Congress to yield in 1919. The Nineteenth Amendment became a part of the Constitution in 1920.

The movements for prohibition and woman suffrage carried along in their wake a great variety of reforms designed to promote the public health and happiness. New building codes were devised, and public parks and playgrounds were multiplied. Renewed efforts were made to wipe out gambling and prostitution. Special courts were established to deal with the problem of juvenile delinquency. Divorce laws were relaxed. Legal discriminations against women, aside from the suffrage, were brought near the vanishing point. Most of these laws, like prohibition and the labor codes, depended for their constitutionality upon the "police power"; that is, the right of the state to do whatever might be necessary to promote the health, happiness, and morality of its citizens. Such laws frequently interfered seriously with the full freedom of individuals, and led to an enormous amount of litigation. The courts, almost invariably hostile in the beginning, eventually relented, and in nearly every instance granted a grudging approval to the measures that the public desired.

Theodore Roosevelt

Just as this broad reform movement was getting under way, the youthful Theodore Roosevelt (1858–1919) became President of the United States, following the death of William McKinley, September 14, 1901. Well-born, well-educated, well-to-do, the new President in his youth had disdained the life of a rich man's son, and in 1881, as a representative in the state legislature of New York, had entered politics "at the bottom of the ladder." A few years later, after the death of his mother and his young wife on the same day, he thought himself ready to turn his back on a political career, and began to spend part of each year on a Dakota ranch. The new life was like a tonic; he loved it. His western experience was brief, but it was also deep. Actually, however, he was never really out of politics, although he had been disappointed at the nomination of James G. Blaine in 1884, and questioned whether there was a place in political life for a reformer such as he thought himself to be. Nevertheless, he consented to make the hopeless race as Republican candidate for mayor of New York in 1886, and he campaigned for Harrison in 1888 with such earnestness that he was rewarded by appointment to the Civil Service Commission. Here for six years he did outstandingly effective work, but in 1895 he accepted an even humbler post as president of the New York Police Board, a position that served greatly to broaden his social horizon. He emerged from these experiences with a habit of mind that was to remain strongly in evidence throughout his career. Both as civil service commissioner and as police commissioner, he had found that those who opposed his views were almost invariably insincere, or dishonest, or worse, while he himself was cast in the role of righteousness. Inevitably he became accustomed to thinking of himself as always right, and his opponents, whatever their views, as always wrong. In spite of his active political life, he wrote extensively, sometimes of his ranch and hunting exploits, but more often of American history or biography. His best work was a four-

As a Rough Rider at San Juan Hill.

THEODORE ROOSEVELT, *twenty-sixth President of the United States. The rapid rise of Roosevelt in politics owed much to the effective way in which he could dramatize his activities.*

As Assistant Secretary of the Navy.

As President, Delivering a Flag Day Speech.

volume series, *The Winning of the West*, which traced in exciting detail the story of the white man's conquest of the region from the Appalachians to the Mississippi.

Roosevelt re-entered national politics in 1896 by campaigning for McKinley with more enthusiasm than his understanding of the money question warranted, and after McKinley's inauguration served as Assistant Secretary of the Navy. As a hero lately returned from the war, he was elected governor of New York in 1898, and Vice-President in 1900. Given to impetuous statements on all manner of questions, and sometimes to unpredictable actions, the new President was immediately suspect by the more conservative element of his party. This group disliked his almost mystical sense of nationalism, his often expressed sympathy for the disinherited, and his obvious preference for men of letters, artists, and soldiers over businessmen and financiers. They were also apprehensive about his gradually evolving view that the state should protect large segments of the population from the effects of ruthless competition, and they disliked his Jacksonian conviction that the President, representing all the people, should take a major part in the formulation of legislative policy. Roosevelt was not a radical. But whether from a fear of rising socialism or of a dominant corporate collectivism, or simply from his own sense of justice, he became convinced that many changes had to be made in American political life. Conservatives, of course, could be expected to oppose most of these views and, indeed, some of them had helped to make him Vice-President in the hope of bringing his political career to an untimely end.

Roosevelt as President

To the confusion of his critics, Roosevelt took over his duties as President in perfect good taste, and even promised "to continue absolutely unbroken the policies of President McKinley for the peace, prosperity, and honor of our beloved country." Especially reassuring was the decision to retain McKinley's cabinet, for whatever his faults McKinley had proved himself to be an able judge of men. Two of the advisers on whom Roosevelt was to depend most, John Hay, Secretary of State, and Elihu Root, Secretary of War, were already in the cabinet, while a third, William Howard Taft, had been picked by McKinley for the difficult task of inaugurating civil government in the Philippines. Roosevelt even sought with some success to appease Mark Hanna, although, as both knew, the gulf between them on most matters of consequence was very wide. It was inevitable that eventually Roosevelt was to be his own President. For the most part McKinley had been content to follow public opinion, but aggressive leadership was an integral part of the Roosevelt personality, and the times were ripe for the type of leadership he could provide.

The Trust Problem Again

Economics was definitely not Roosevelt's principal forte, but he would have been blind indeed if he had not recognized in the emergence of "big business" a problem of fundamental importance to his administration. By the beginning of the twentieth century "rugged individualism" had run riot in the United States. In one industry after another great corporations, successfully claiming the rights of persons before the law, had grown to monopolistic proportions. The total capital of million-dollar corporations had increased from $170 million in 1897 to $5 billion in 1900, and to $20.5 billion in 1904. Railway mergers, such as the one by which E. H. Harriman brought the Union Pacific and the Southern Pacific together in 1900, had become the order of the day. Concentration in industry was effected both by means of "horizontal" combinations through which several industries of the same kind were united, and by means of "vertical" combinations, through which businesses of allied interests joined forces. Of the latter type was the United States Steel Corporation, the first of America's billion-dollar companies, which J. P. Morgan helped knit together in 1901. But what happened to steel happened also in greater or less degree to tobacco, petroleum, sugar, copper, beef, starch, flour, whiskey, and innumerable other commodities. Among the rulers of these great corporations there was a close community of interest, and since most of the mergers were arranged by financiers, a few great banking firms, notably the house of Morgan, came to occupy a commanding position in the nation's business structure.

Northern Securities Case

Roosevelt's first action against the trusts was taken in February, 1902, when his Attorney-General announced that suit was being brought under the terms of the Sherman Antitrust Act to dissolve the Northern Securities Company through which the year before a merger of three northwestern railroads, the Great Northern, the Northern Pacific, and the Chicago, Burlington & Quincy, had been attempted. If the government could induce the Supreme Court to support it in this instance, Roosevelt believed that he might later make the Sherman Act a really effective weapon in arresting the trend toward monopoly that had set in. The organizers of the Northern Securities Company, James J. Hill and J. P. Morgan, believed that they had remained within the letter of the law, but the Supreme Court, by a decision reached in 1904, ruled otherwise, although to reach this conclusion it had to abandon the reasoning of the Knight case. According to the majority of the Court, the Northern Securities Company was a violation of free competition within the meaning of the Sherman Act, and must be dissolved. Economically

the Northern Securities decision meant little, since business leaders soon found other ways to achieve cooperation, but the psychological effect on the public was profound.

Gleeful at having induced the Court to "reverse" itself, and acclaimed by the public as a "trust-buster," Roosevelt went ahead with other prosecutions. Actually, since the Northern Securities Company was not engaged in manufacturing, the Knight decision was not reversed technically until the Standard Oil and American Tobacco Company decisions of 1912. A total of twenty-five indictments were brought by the Department of Justice during his administration, and in a few instances the government scored victories. Perhaps the most notable of them was the dissolution of the "beef trust," which counted among its sins an agreement whereby six-tenths of the nation's dealers in fresh meat avoided bid-

J. Pierpont Morgan. *As the leading American financier, Morgan devised the Northern Securities Company, which in 1904 the Supreme Court ordered to be dissolved. This decision registered one of Morgan's few defeats.*

"Get Rid of Your Friends." *A cartoon showing the result of Roosevelt's revival of the Sherman Antitrust Act.*

ding against one another in the purchase of livestock. Eventually Roosevelt came to distinguish between "good trusts," which showed a proper concern for the welfare of the consumer, and "bad trusts," which sought only selfish ends. The latter he prosecuted, the former he let alone. The Supreme Court, in the rule of reason it adopted in 1911, came to about the same conclusion. Only when the monopolistic actions of trusts "unreasonably" interfered with interstate commerce would the Court hold against them. By allowing itself this wide latitude, the Court was free to ignore mere "bigness," while at the same time punishing the misuse of power that great size made possible. But this more selective use of the Sherman Act failed to achieve the desired results. As the government proceeded against one trust after another, monopolies seemed only to grow and prosper the more. Long before Roosevelt left office, he had de-emphasized "trust-busting" by asking for federal incorporation and federal regulation of all interstate business.

Railroad Regulation

Roosevelt's efforts to obtain regulatory laws from Congress most nearly approached success with reference to the railroads. The Interstate Commerce Act of 1887 had taken a step in this direction, but its primary purpose after all had been the maintenance of free competition. Even in that sphere the Interstate Commerce Commission, hampered repeatedly by court decisions, had been singularly ineffective, and without a new grant of powers it could never hope to cope with the great mergers that had taken place since its creation. First, the rebate evil was curbed by the Elkins Act of 1903. Then a new Department of Commerce and Labor was set up, within which a fact-finding Bureau of Corporations was designed to ferret out questionable corporation practices. Finally, with strong presidential support, the Hepburn Act, which added immeasurably to the power and prestige of the Interstate Commerce Commission, became law in 1906. No longer did the Commission have to go to court to enforce an order; now the carrier had either to accept the rates set by the commission or go to court itself. Furthermore, the law also extended the jurisdiction of the commission to include other common carriers, such as express companies, pipe lines, sleeping-car companies, bridges, and ferries; it forbade the granting of free passes; it prohibited railroads from carrying commodities, except for their own use, that they had produced themselves — coal, for example — and it empowered the commission to prescribe a uniform system of bookkeeping for all railroads, a provision of fundamental importance. Owing to the various methods of accounting in use among the railroads, it had been virtually impossible to arrive at dependable comparative statistics. Within a few years, under the operation of the new law, the ICC had not only effected drastic reductions in rates,

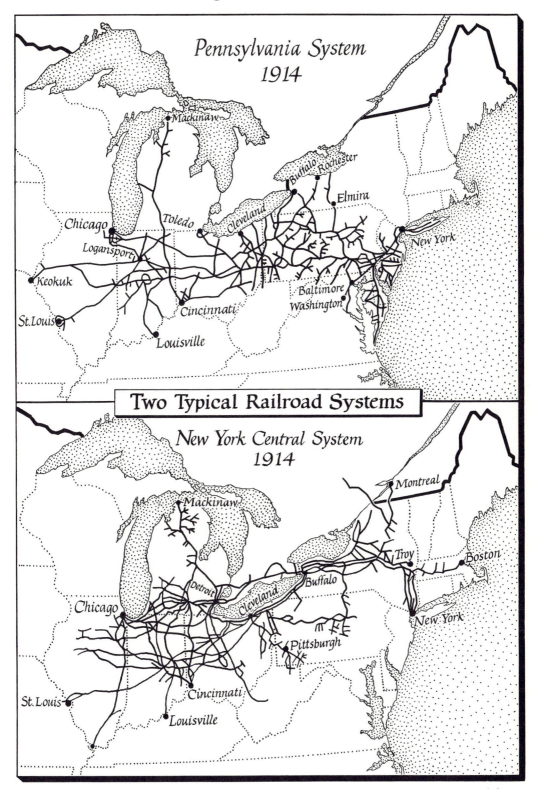

Pennsylvania System
1914

Two Typical Railroad Systems

New York Central System
1914

but it had also won the respect of the public, the courts, and even the carriers themselves, who increasingly tended to accept its decisions as final.

Pure Food and Drug Act

The railroads were not the only trusts to feel the force of national regulation. The meat-packers, the food-processors, and the producers of drugs and patent medicines had much to explain when the muckrakers got through with them. Precedents for federal action in this field were not altogether lacking, for laws dating back to the 1880's required inspection by the Bureau of Animal Husbandry of all meats designed for export. A law of 1906 extended federal inspection to all meats destined for interstate commerce, and a Pure Food and Drug Act, passed the same year, placed some restrictions, but not nearly enough, on the producers of prepared foods and patent medicines. An amendment to this act, passed in 1911, prohibited also the use of misleading labels, but events proved that the gullible public bought about as freely when the unpleasant truth was printed on the label as when it was not. The real root of the difficulty, fraudulent advertising, escaped unscathed. All such regulation, when undertaken by the federal government, depended for its validity upon the powers of Congress over interstate commerce, and the exact line of demarcation between state and national authority could be drawn only by the courts. Roosevelt, annoyed at the existence of this "twilight zone," strongly favored resolving all doubts in favor of the national government.

The "Square Deal"

Always a happy phrase-maker, Roosevelt's insistence on a "square deal" for labor, capital, and the public gave him the advantage of an attractive label for his labor policy. Naturally the rapid development of industrial concentration aroused the fears

of labor, and as the strength of organized capital grew, the strength of organized labor grew also. By 1905 the American Federation of Labor claimed for its affiliates a total membership of two millions, with perhaps six hundred thousand unaffiliated, but cooperating, union members. Under the circumstances a test of strength between labor and capital was almost inevitable. It came, reasonably enough, in the coal-mining region of Pennsylvania, where in spite of deplorable labor conditions the operators were stubbornly determined to resist reform. Demanding recognition of their union, a wage increase of 20 per cent, an eight-hour day, and other fringe benefits, the anthracite coal miners quit work on May 12, 1902, and at a cost of perhaps a million dollars to all concerned held their lines intact until October 23. John Mitchell, the strike leader, kept his men from violence, and won much sympathy for the strikers' cause. President George F. Baer of the Philadelphia and Reading Coal and Iron Company, who spoke for the operators, was far less skillful in handling public opinion. He insisted from the first that the companies would not even so much as meet with the union representatives, and refused an invitation to attend a White House conference with the labor leaders.

Fully conscious of the widespread suffering that the coal shortage was sure to bring, Roosevelt used his influence with both sides in favor of a compromise solution. He found the miners ready enough to talk terms, but the operators remained obdurate. Only after the President had threatened to send in a "first-rate general" with sufficient federal troops "to dispossess the operators and run the mines as a receiver" would the owners consent to governmental mediation. Even so the operators agreed to accept the findings of a commission appointed by the President only if a sociologist and not a union man should be selected to represent

THE CONSERVATION MOVEMENT. *These two pictures show well one problem of conservation with relation to the nation's forests.*

MOUNT ST. HELENS. This view looks across twenty-five miles of virgin Douglas fir timber in the Lewis River Valley to Mount St. Helens (9,671 feet) in southern Washington.

COEUR D'ALENE NATIONAL FOREST, IDAHO. The devastation wrought here on a heavy stand of white pine came as the result of a hurricane and fire.

the union point of view. Thereupon work was resumed at the mines. Roosevelt appointed E. E. Clarke, president of the Brotherhood of Railroad Conductors, as the "eminent sociologist" on the commission, and in March, 1903, a decision was announced that in the main favored the unions. Roosevelt's actions in the 1902 coal strike were in sharp contrast with those of his predecessors in the Presidency. They had invariably assumed that a strike was a strictly private affair, and that governmental intervention was only warranted to prevent federal services from being disrupted or to protect private property in the case of wide disorder. Roosevelt set an important precedent when he insisted that the public was an interested third party in any large strike.

Nor was this all. Repeatedly the President recommended to Congress legislation favorable to labor, such as the protection of women and children in industry, limitations on the use of injunctions in labor disputes, and employer's liability laws for workers on interstate railroads. Only the last-mentioned of these recommendations received the favorable action of Congress, and the first such law, passed in 1906, was annulled by the Supreme Court. A law of April, 1908, met the Court's objections. In general Roosevelt's thinking on the labor problem was not far in advance of his times, but his actions on the anthracite coal strike certainly registered a marked improvement over the positions taken by his predecessors.

Conservation

Another policy dear to Roosevelt's heart was the conservation of the nation's natural resources. When he became President, the United States was "somewhat in the position of the man who had unexpectedly lost most of his fortune." Its greatest resource throughout its history, or so the people had always thought, had been its vast reservoir of public lands. Now the best of these had been used up; although at the turn of the century more than 500 million acres still remained open to settlement, only a small fraction of this vast area could ever be farmed in the traditional American way. Moreover, even after the lands had passed into private or corporate hands the tendency had been to exploit them rather than to preserve their fertility. Millions of acres, particularly in the East and the South, had been returned, thoroughly despoiled, to nature, or could be farmed only by the constant use of fertilizer. What had happened to the lands had happened also in varying degrees to other natural resources. Four-fifths of the nation's forests had been chopped down without thought as to their replacement, and many of those that remained had been acquired by a few large lumber companies bent on using them up. Mineral resources, too, whether of metals, coal, gas, or oil, had been exploited with the utmost wastefulness. Water-power sites, in return for next to nothing, had been al-

lowed to pass into the hands of private companies who had developed their possibilities along profit-making lines, without regard for the destruction of beauty or prevention of floods. By the turn of the century, pessimists were predicting that the rich resources of the United States would soon be exhausted, and the poverty of the Old World would extend to the New.

During Roosevelt's administration conservation activities were many and varied. The Reclamation Act of 1902 put the federal government into the business of building the dams, tunnels, flumes, and ditches necessary for irrigation projects. An Inland Waterways Commission, appointed in 1907, stressed the interrelation of all conservation problems, and urged the President to call a national conference on conservation, to which representatives from all sections and from both parties should be invited. As a result, on May 13, 1908, Roosevelt met at the White House with an assembly of notables that included state governors, cabinet members, Supreme Court justices, members of Congress, businessmen, and a wide range of experts. For three days he kept the conference in session, and from it he obtained support for such important policies as the protection of the water supply of navigable streams, the control of forest fires, government regulation for the cutting of timber, the granting of surface titles to public lands separate from the right to exploit the minerals that lay below the surface, and the withdrawal from entry of lands bearing coal, oil, natural gas, and phosphate. On Roosevelt's order, the Secretary of the Interior added to the forest lands already withdrawn from entry some 80 million acres of coal lands, 1.5 million acres of lands adjacent to water-power sites, and nearly 5 million acres of phosphate lands.

There was a direct relation between Roosevelt's policy of governmental interference in the affairs of business and his

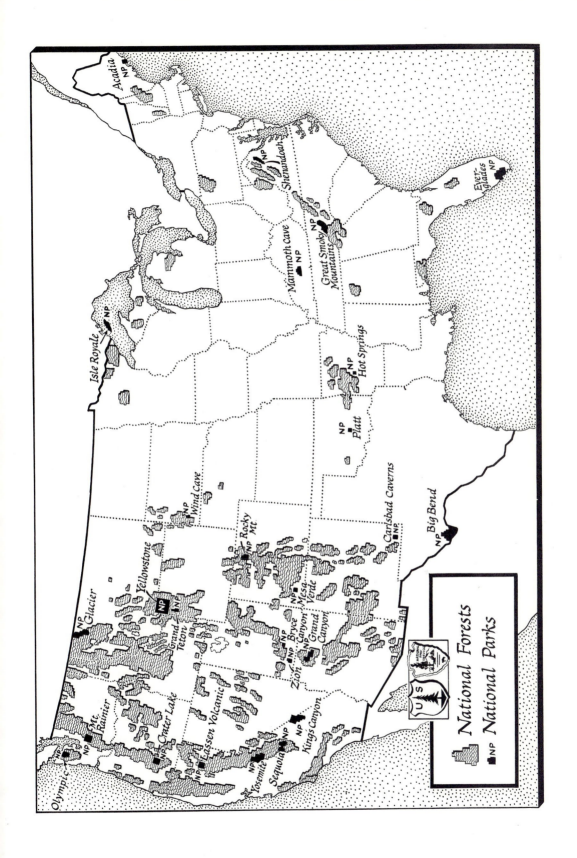

Acadia
NP

Shenandoah
NP

Everglades
NP

Mammoth Cave
NP

Great Smoky
Mountains
NP

Isle Royale
NP

Hot Springs
NP

Platt
NP

Wind Cave
NP

Rocky
Mt.
NP

Carlsbad Caverns
NP

Big Bend
NP

Yellowstone
NP

Glacier
NP

Grand
Teton
NP

Mesa
Verde
NP

Bryce
Canyon
NP

Grand
Canyon
NP

Zion
NP

Mt.
Rainier
NP

Crater Lake
NP

Lassen Volcanic
NP

Kings Canyon
NP

Olympic
NP

Yosemite
NP

Sequoia
NP

National Forests
National Parks
NP

policy of conservation. In the former he brought businessmen face to face with the specter of effective governmental regulation; in the latter he served notice that in certain spheres, previously left open to private initiative, the government either would act itself, or would permit individuals to act only on terms laid down by the government in advance. The day of rampant individualism was almost done. No doubt Senator Robert M. LaFollette, never a very devoted admirer of Roosevelt, had these considerations in mind when he described conservation as Roosevelt's greatest work. According to the Wisconsin Senator, Roosevelt deserved unstinted praise "for staying territorial waste" and for saving the things "on which alone a peaceful, progressive and happy race life can be founded."

Election of 1904

Roosevelt as President enjoyed a tremendous popularity. This was due not only to the issues he embraced, but even more to the type of man he was. To a phenomenal degree he exhibited in his personality the traits that the average American most admired; the President, indeed, was the ordinary citizen as he might have appeared under a microscope. What Roosevelt actually became, the ordinary citizen wished to be. His prominent teeth, his spectacles, his cowboy hat, and his general air of belligerency made him the cartoonist's delight, and his knack of clothing his every deed in an aura of righteousness did him no harm.

T. R. is spanking a Senator,
T. R. is chasing a bear,
T. R. is busting an awful Trust,
And dragging it from its lair.
They're calling T. R. a lot of things —
The men in the private car —
But the day-coach likes exciting folks
And the day-coach likes T. R.[1]

[1] "Theodore Roosevelt" by Stephen Vincent Benet. From *A Book of Americans* (1933) by Rosemary and Stephen Vincent Benet.

Roosevelt's popularity had much to do with the overwhelming victories scored by the Republicans in the four elections (1902, 1904, 1906, 1908) held during his administration, and his renomination and re-election in 1904 was a great personal triumph. Eager to be President in his own right, Roosevelt was unduly distressed at the tendency of ultra-conservative Republicans to rally around Mark Hanna for the nomination, but Hanna's death in February, 1904, left him a free field. Chosen to serve with him as Vice-President was Charles W. Fairbanks, an Indiana conservative. To oppose Roosevelt the Democrats turned to a conservative New York judge, Alton B. Parker, whose orthodoxy on all issues affecting business was as dependable as Roosevelt's was uncertain. For Vice-President they nominated Henry Gassaway Davis, a rich octogenarian from West Virginia, who was expected to contribute heavily to the Democratic campaign chest, but proved to be a disappointment. To clinch the Democratic bid for "Wall Street" support, Parker came out openly for the gold standard, and completely repudiated Bryan's record on free silver. Nevertheless, when the votes were counted it appeared that he had suffered a worse defeat than Bryan had met in 1896 and in 1900. The electoral vote stood 336 for Roosevelt and 140 for Parker. Elated by the returns, Roosevelt immediately issued a dramatic statement that he must have regretted later many times: "The wise custom which limits the President to two terms regards the substance and not the form, and under no circumstances will I be a candidate for or accept another nomination."

Panic of 1907

Roosevelt's second administration came near to disaster in connection with the Panic of 1907, which was the result, many claimed, of his unwarranted attacks on business. His prosecution of the trusts and his attempts to

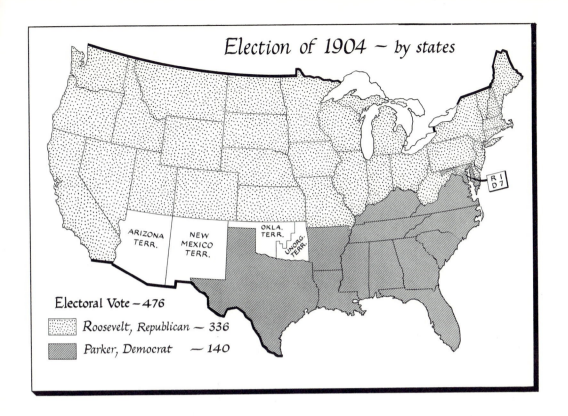

Election of 1904 ~ by states

ARIZONA
TERR.

NEW
MEXICO
TERR.

OKLA.
TERR.

UNORG.
TERR.

R I
D 7

Electoral Vote — 476

Roosevelt, Republican — 336

Parker, Democrat — 140

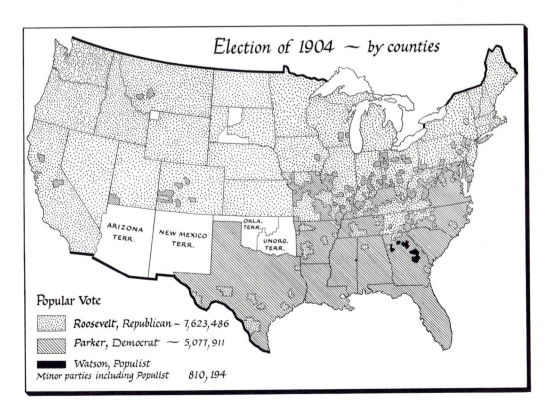

Election of 1904 ~ by counties

ARIZONA
TERR.

NEW MEXICO
TERR.

OKLA.
TERR.

UNORG.
TERR.

Popular Vote

Roosevelt, Republican ~ 7,623,486

Parker, Democrat — 5,077,911

Watson, Populist
Minor parties including Populist   810,194

regulate the railroads, hostile critics declared, endangered legitimate profits; the "square deal" encouraged labor to make unreasonable demands; and conservation called a halt to the lucrative exploitation of natural resources. Roosevelt was deeply sensitive to the criticism that his policies were undermining confidence, but he claimed that the fault lay with business and not with him. "If trouble comes from having the light turned on," he told a cabinet member, "remember it is not really due to the light, but to the misconduct which is exposed." He came, indeed, to believe that the Panic of 1907 was purely psychological; that it had been intentionally precipitated by "malefactors of great wealth," bent on discrediting his policies.

Undoubtedly an important factor in bringing on the panic was the wholesale multiplication of securities that had taken place in the early years of the century. United States Steel, for example, was capitalized at a sum far in excess of the total capital of the companies it incorporated. These securities were often sold at higher prices than the earning power of the corporations they represented would justify, and eventual disillusionment was sure to come. Another factor was the inelasticity of the currency and of credit. The United States government had no way of providing an extra supply of money to meet an emergency. The total amount of gold and silver, national bank notes, and Treasury notes that composed the money of the country was relatively fixed. If confidence lagged and money was hoarded, there was sure to be a shortage. Much the same thing was true of credit, which was limited primarily by the willingness of a few great New York bankers to lend. Practically every financial institution in the country was connected in one way or another with the Wall Street bankers, and was amenable to discipline by them. They thus constituted a kind of "money trust" that almost

at will could grant or withhold the credit necessary to keep the nation's business moving.

The panic began on October 22, 1907, with a run on the Knickerbocker Trust Company, the third largest bank in New York City. Disastrous runs occurred also on other New York banks, and stock exchange values plunged rapidly. To help meet the emergency, George B. Cortelyou, Secretary of the Treasury, deposited $25 million of Treasury funds with hard-pressed New York banks, while the President, at the suggestion of J. P. Morgan, promised the United States Steel Corporation immunity from prosecution so that it could absorb, and save from collapse, the Tennessee Coal and Iron Company. This course, Morgan told Roosevelt, was necessary to save an important New York bank, and would stave off a really major disaster. As it turned out, the storm was soon over, and in its wake came no long period of depression comparable to the aftermath of 1873 and 1893. Convinced that the panic might have been averted, had the banking and currency system of the United States been on a sounder footing, Congress in 1908 passed the Aldrich-Vreeland Act, which empowered the national banks of the country for a period of six years to issue emergency currency in times of financial stringency. This was but a stop-gap measure. The most important part of the act was the creation of a National Monetary Commission to investigate the banking and currency systems of the world, and to lay plans for a thoroughgoing reform in the American system. The Federal Reserve System that ultimately resulted from this investigation was not created until Wilson's administration, but was in line with Roosevelt's actions on other matters. No President before Roosevelt had urged such large-scale federal intervention into areas that formerly had been reserved for the states or for private action.

BIBLIOGRAPHY

A convenient guide to the vast literature on this period is *The Progressive Era and the Great War, 1896–1920* (1969), compiled by A. S. Link and W. M. Leary, Jr. Conflicting interpretations are gathered in *The Progressive Era* (1963), edited by Arthur Mann. R. H. Wiebe has published two provocative books of reinterpretation, *Businessmen and Reform* (1962), and *The Search for Order, 1877–1920* (1967). The view that the progressives were doing the work of conservatives, wittingly or not, is given in such works as John Chamberlain, *Farewell to Reform* (1932); Gabriel Kolko, *The Triumph of Conservatism* (1963); and James Weinstein, *The Corporate Ideal in the Liberal State* (1968). Valuable readings are contained in *The Progressive Years* (1962), edited by Otis Pease; *The Progressive Movement* (1963), edited by Richard Hofstadter (1963); and *The Progressives* (1967), edited by Carl Resek. A survey of social history is provided by H. U. Faulkner, *The Quest for Social Justice, 1898–1914* (1931). W. L. O'Neill, *Divorce in the Progressive Era* (1967), treats an often-neglected social reform. On child labor reform, see J. P. Felt, *Hostages to Fortune* (1965); and S. B. Wood, *Constitutional Politics in the Progressive Era* (1968).

On the muckrakers, see especially C. C. Regier, *The Era of the Muckrakers* (1932); Louis Filler, *Crusaders for American Liberalism* (1939); and D. M. Chalmers, *The Social and Political Ideas of the Muckrakers* (1964). For samples of the writings of these journalists, see D. G. Phillips, *The Treason of the Senate* (1906); *The Muckrakers, 1902–1912* (1961), edited by A. M. and Lila Weinberg; and *Years of Conscience* (1962), edited by Harvey Swados. *The Muckrakers and American Society* (1968), edited by Herbert Shapiro, contains conflicting interpretations. Notable memoirs include *The Autobiography of Lincoln Steffens* (2 vols., 1931); R. S. Baker, *American Chronicle* (1945); and *The Autobiography of Upton Sinclair* (1962). See also R. C. Bannister, Jr., *Ray Stannard Baker*

(1966); and Peter Lyon, *Success Story* (1963), a biography of S. S. McClure.

On socialism, D. A. Shannon, *The Socialist Party of America* (1955), is a fine study, notable for its appreciation of regional differences. Different interpretations are given by Ira Kipnis, *The American Socialist Movement, 1897–1912* (1952); and James Weinstein, *The Decline of Socialism in America, 1912–1925* (1967). A study of the Socialist campaigns of the period is H. W. Morgan, *Eugene V. Debs: Socialist for President* (1962). The best study of Emma Goldman is Richard Drinnon, *Rebel in Paradise* (1961).

On LaFollette and the Wisconsin leadership in reform, there are several admirable books. His detailed *Autobiography* (1913) is of fundamental importance. See also *LaFollette* (1969), edited by R. S. Maxwell. A full-length biography written by his widow and his daughter, B. C. LaFollette and Fola LaFollette, *Robert M. LaFollette, 1855–1925* (2 vols., 1953), is based upon his papers. More critical in tone is R. S. Maxwell, *LaFollette and the Rise of the Progressives in Wisconsin* (1956); and H. F. Margulies, *The Decline of the Progressive Movement in Wisconsin, 1890–1920* (1968). Charles McCarthy, *The Wisconsin Idea* (1912), is the statement of an enthusiastic LaFollette supporter, while McCarthy's own part is told in E. A. Fitzpatrick, *McCarthy of Wisconsin* (1944). Biographies of some LaFollette enemies include R. N. Current, *Pine Logs and Politics: A Life of Philetus Sawyer, 1816–1900* (1950); and R. S. Maxwell, *Emanuel L. Philipp, Wisconsin Stalwart* (1959).

Progressive efforts in the states are examined by a strong supporter in B. P. DeWitt, *The Progressive Movement* (1915), a valuable book. Sprightly articles on state and municipal reform by Lincoln Steffens are contained in *The Struggle for Self-Government* (1906), and *Upbuilders* (1909). Studies of individual states include: W. A. Flint, *The Progressive Movement in Vermont* (1941); H. L. Warner, *Progressivism in Ohio* (1964); R.

M. Abrams, *Conservatism in a Progressive Era: Massachusetts Politics, 1900–1912* (1964); R. E. Noble, Jr., *New Jersey Progressivism before Wilson* (1946); E. F. Goldman, *Charles J. Bonaparte* (1943); L. G. Geiger, *Joseph W. Folk of Missouri* (1953); C. O. Johnson, **Borah of Idaho* (1936); G. E. Mowry, **The California Progressives* (1951); and S. C. Olin, Jr., *California's Prodigal Sons* (1968).

The battle for municipal reform may be followed in Lincoln Steffens' muckraking classic **The Shame of the Cities* (1904), as well as in some notable memoirs, including: T. L. Johnson, **My Story* (1911); Brand Whitlock, *Forty Years of It* (1914); Fremont Older, *My Own Story* (1925); and F. C. Howe, **The Confessions of a Reformer* (1925), which should be compared with his optimistic **The City* (1905). Important scholarly works on municipal reform include W. E. Bean, **Boss Ruef's San Francisco* (1952); Z. L. Miller, **Boss Cox's Cincinnati* (1968); Jack Tager, *The Intellectual As Urban Reformer* (1968), a study of Whitlock; J. B. Crooks, *Politics & Progress* (1968), on Baltimore reformers; and M. G. Holli, **Reform in Detroit* (1969), an account of the work of Hazen Pingree.

On prohibition, a great classic is P. H. Odegard, *Pressure Politics: The Story of the Anti-Saloon League* (1928). Two recent reinterpretations are J. H. Timberlake, *Prohibition and the Progressive Movement, 1900–1920* (1963); and J. R. Gusfield, **Symbolic Crusade* (1963). Among the growing number of state studies especially notable are G. M. Ostrander, *The Prohibition Movement in California* (1957); and N. H. Clark, *The Dry Years: Prohibition and Social Change in Washington* (1965). References on the feminist movement were listed in the bibliography following Chapter 9.

The standard survey of economic history in this period is H. U. Faulkner, **The Decline of Laissez Faire, 1897–1917* (1951). In addition, the following works should be noted: I. M. Tarbell, *The Life of Elbert H. Gary* (1925); Herbert Croly, *Willard Straight* (1924); J. A. Garraty, *Right-Hand Man: The Life of George W. Perkins* (1960); and A. K. Steigerwalt, *The National Association of Manufacturers, 1895–1914* (1964). Important criticisms of the economic order include: H. D. Lloyd, *Wealth against Commonwealth* (1894); and three works by Thorstein Veblen, **The Theory of the Leisure Class* (1899), **The Theory of Business Enterprise* (1904), and *The Instinct of Workmanship* (1914). On Roosevelt and labor, see H. L. Hurwitz, *Theodore Roosevelt and Labor in New York State, 1880–1900* (1943); and R. J. Cornell, *The Anthracite Coal Strike of 1902* (1957). Interesting works showing the need for pure food and drug reform are: J. H. Young, *The Toadstool Millionaires* (1961); O. E. Anderson, Jr., *The Health of a Nation: Harvey W. Wiley and the Fight for Pure Food* (1958); and Upton Sinclair's classic muckraking novel **The Jungle* (1906).

General introductions to conservation include: C. R. Van Hise, *The Conservation of Natural Resources in the United States* (2nd ed., 1915); and E. R. Richardson, *The Politics of Conservation* (1962). S. P. Hays, **Conservation and the Gospel of Efficiency: The Progressive Conservation Movement, 1890–1920* (1959), is a provocative reinterpretation. Other important works include: A. H. Dupree, **Science in the Federal Government* (1957); M. M. Vance, *Charles Richard Van Hise* (1960); John Ise, *Our National Park Policy* (1961); and W. E. Smythe, **The Conquest of Arid America* (2nd ed., 1905), the handbook of the irrigation crusade.

14

TAFT AND WILSON

Roosevelt's Renunciation

During his troubles with the Panic of 1907, Roosevelt was confronted with the more personal problem of what he would do about the presidential election of 1908. He knew very well that the Presidency could have been his again almost for the asking, and he knew too the wrench it would give him to renounce the position he so much enjoyed. But there were other considerations, among them his statement, after the election of 1904, that he would abide by the "wise custom" which had limited his predecessors to eight years. Beyond this promise he had grave theoretical scruples about the too long continuation of a President in office. He was emphatic in his approval of a very strong executive, but to avoid the dangers of a possible dictatorship he believed just as strongly in limiting the duration of the President's power. "I don't think," he wrote to a British historian, "that any

harm comes from the concentration of powers in one man's hands, provided the holder does not keep it for more than a certain definite time, and then returns to the people from whom he sprang. . . ." Consequently, in order to head off the danger that his devotees might draft him, he decided to work actively for the nomination and election of someone else, but someone whom he could trust to carry out the Roosevelt policies. Among the individuals most eligible for the Republican nomination, aside from the President himself, were Charles Evans Hughes, the reform governor of New York, Elihu Root, the Secretary of State, and William Howard Taft, the Secretary of War. Roosevelt did not particularly like Hughes, he doubted Root's ability to appeal to the masses, and his choice finally fell on Taft, one of his close personal friends.

U. S. CAPITOL. *Here, both Taft and Wilson won victories and suffered defeats at the hands of Congress.*

William Howard Taft

William Howard Taft (1857–1930) had already served his country long and well. His family had played a prominent role in the affairs of Cincinnati, Ohio, and Taft's father, Judge Alphonso Taft, had once been a member of Grant's cabinet. Taft's rise up the political ladder came principally by the appointive route. An honor graduate of Yale, he became successively a judge in the superior court of Ohio, solicitor-general in the federal Department of Justice, federal judge, commissioner to the Philippines and governor-general, and finally Secretary of War. A consistently able administrator and Roosevelt's favorite envoy abroad, he had had what seemed to be an almost ideal training for the Presidency. His personal inclinations lay toward the Supreme Court, but more than once he felt obliged to reject the appointment he craved in the interest of the unfinished business he had in hand. His family was more ambitious for him than he was for himself. His wife wanted him to be President, and so also did his wealthy brother, Charles P. Taft. He was a huge man weighing three hundred and fifty pounds, good-natured and affable, and blessed with an infectious chuckle. Presidential support can be, and in this case it was, extraordinarily effective, and as a result Taft was nominated on the first ballot by a convention that would have preferred Roosevelt. Second place on the ticket went as a consolation prize to the conservatives, who counted the nominee, James S. Sherman of New York, as one of the most dependable of their number.

The Democrats Name Bryan

The Democrats, disastrously defeated four years before with the conservative Parker, renominated Bryan who was still young, vigorous, and hopeful. For Vice-President they nominated John W. Kern of Indiana. Bryan as a favorite Chautauqua orator had probably been heard by more Americans than any other man in public life, and his adherents gave him the same unstinted devotion that Henry Clay and James G. Blaine had once commanded. In 1906 Bryan had made a trip around the world, had been well received, and had returned with his self-confidence restored. Ready at last to admit that free silver was a dead issue, he proposed in August, 1906, a new program for curbing the trusts. Corporations should be barred from contributing to campaign funds, interlocking directorates should be prohibited, and a federal license should be required of all engaged in interstate business. For the railroad problem he reverted to the Populist remedy, government ownership, "not as an immediate issue, but as an ultimate solution of the controversy." The trouble with Bryan's program was that it was so like Roosevelt's; indeed, well before election time Congress had passed and Roosevelt had signed a measure forbidding corporations to contribute toward the election of nation officers, while Bryan had materially modified his views on the railroad question.

Election of 1908

The real issue in the campaign of 1908 was whether Bryan or Taft could be the better trusted to carry out the Roosevelt policies. In the end Taft won by an electoral vote of 321 to 162. Besides the "solid South" Bryan carried only Nebraska, Colorado, and Nevada, but he at least surpassed Parker's record of four years before. An "Independence League" ticket, sponsored by William Randolph Hearst, served to enliven an otherwise dull campaign, but polled only a negligible number of votes. Republican conservatives, looking carefully into Taft's record as a judge, concluded that they had little to fear from Roosevelt's political legatee. Later, not without a show of justice, Bryan complained that the Republicans had enjoyed an unfair advantage

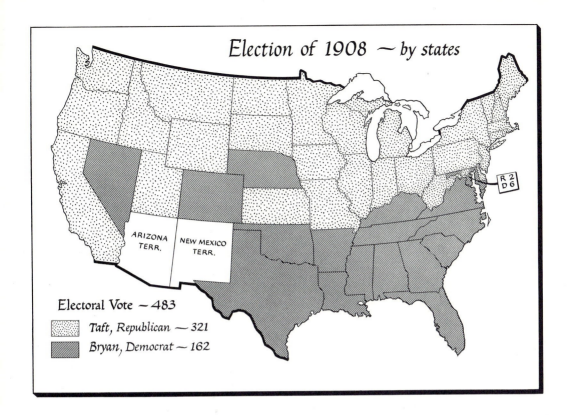

Election of 1908 — by states

R 2
D 6

Electoral Vote — 483

Taft, Republican — 321

Bryan, Democrat — 162

ARIZONA TERR.

NEW MEXICO TERR.

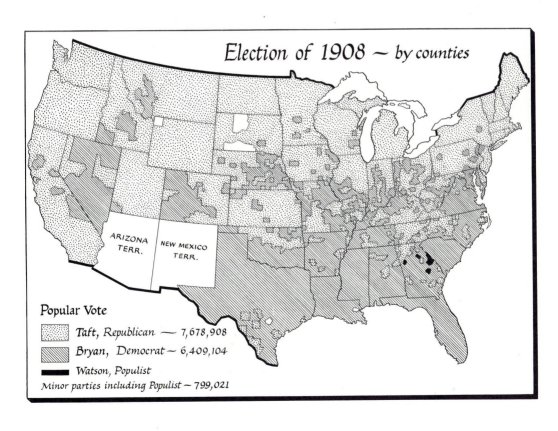

Election of 1908 — by counties

ARIZONA TERR.

NEW MEXICO TERR.

Popular Vote

Taft, Republican — 7,678,908

Bryan, Democrat — 6,409,104

Watson, Populist

Minor parties including Populist — 799,021

in the campaign. Taft the progressive carried the West, while Taft the conservative carried the East. Forty-six states participated in the election of 1908; for in 1907 the majority party in Congress had at last decided that Republican supremacy was well enough established to risk the admission of Oklahoma, an almost certainly Democratic state. A similar offer to admit New Mexico and Arizona as one state failed because of the opposition of Arizona to such a scheme.

Taft Takes Office

When Taft took office as President in 1909, the reform spirit was at high pitch, and reformers confidently expected that the new administration would carry forward actively the program Roosevelt had begun. In his inaugural address Taft pledged himself to such a course, and in making up his cabinet he chose three of Roosevelt's chief advisers. Philander C. Knox, once Roosevelt's "trust-busting"

Attorney-General, but now a Senator from Pennsylvania, became Secretary of State, while George von L. Meyer, Roosevelt's Postmaster-General, took over the Navy Department, and James Wilson stayed on as Secretary of Agriculture. "Never before in our time," said the *New York Tribune*, "has the entry of a new President into office marked so slight a break politically between the present and the past." In order the better to give his successor a free hand, Roosevelt took off immediately on a hunt for big game in Africa, and for a full year was lost to the civilized world. Unfortunately, Taft was unable to live up to the reputation as a reformer that Roosevelt had made for him. An able constitutional lawyer, he had more respect for the independence of Congress than Roosevelt had ever had, and often it was Congress rather than the President who determined the course of national policy. Furthermore, Taft was not a disciple of the "strenuous life," and tended to avoid rather than to embrace political warfare; Roosevelt, on the other hand, was never happier than in the midst of an "elegant row." Before long the public began to grumble that Taft had been elected to carry out the Roosevelt policies, and had "carried them out on a stretcher."

Payne-Aldrich Tariff

Taft's first failure was with tariff revision, a subject which Roosevelt had consistently avoided, but which was vaguely promised in the Republican platform. Taft, moreover, had pledged himself during the campaign to call Congress into special session for the specific purpose of revising the tariff, and this he promptly did, for March 15, 1909. A few weeks later, on April 9, the Payne bill, providing for moderate reductions in duties, had passed the House. When the bill reached the Senate, it was taken in hand by Senator Nelson W. Aldrich of Rhode Island, chairman of the Sen-

UTAH
1896

ARIZONA
1912

NEW
MEXICO
1912

OKLA.
1907

New States

ate Committee on Finance, and rewritten to fit the high-protectionist views of the multimillionaire industrialists, of whom Aldrich himself was one. But Aldrich's plans for the speedy passage of the bill were interrupted by a little group of middle-western insurgents, led by Robert M. LaFollette of Wisconsin, who had entered the Senate in 1906. Determined that the bill should not be passed before the public could find out how complete a betrayal it was of the Republican campaign pledges, LaFollette, ably assisted by Dolliver and Cummins of Iowa, Beveridge of Indiana, Bristow of Kansas, and a few others, studied it by night and debated it by day. They were unable to prevent its passage, but ten of them joined with the Democrats in refusing to vote for it. Known now as the Payne-Aldrich bill, the measure at length was accepted by the House and sent to the President for approval.

Taft and the Tariff

Meantime the President, who had really wanted an honest revision downward, had at first encouraged the insurgents, thinking that they might obtain a better bill, but finally, dismayed at the prospect of a split in his party, had joined forces with the conservative majority. The Payne-Aldrich bill that emerged from the joint House and Senate conference committee was a complete betrayal of Taft's campaign promises, but he signed it nevertheless. It provided for more decreases than increases in duties, but the decreases were rarely on items of significance, and far more duties were left untouched than were changed. The average rate on dutiable goods was about 1 per cent higher under the new law than under the Dingley Act of 1897. Taft's attitude amazed and disappointed the public, which during the preceding regime had become

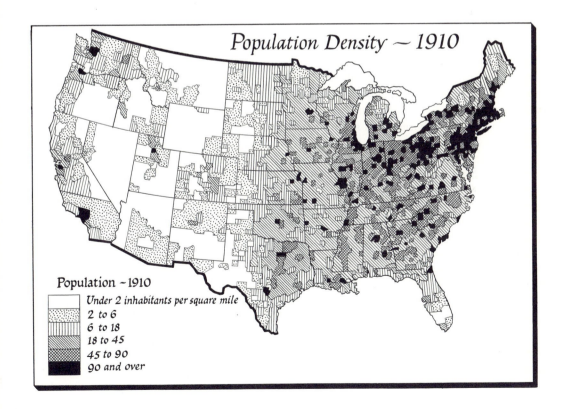

Population Density — 1910

Population ~ 1910

	Under 2 inhabitants per square mile
	2 to 6
	6 to 18
	18 to 45
	45 to 90
	90 and over

Gifford Pinchot. *As first Chief of the Forestry Service, Pinchot, next to Roosevelt, became the nation's outstanding conservationist.*

taxation as a means of regulation.

Separately adopted, but related to the tariff by its bearing on national finance, was a resolution submitting to the states a constitutional amendment for the legalization of a federal income tax. Submitted on July 12, 1909, the Sixteenth Amendment was fully ratified and declared in force on February 25, 1913, just before Taft left office.

Taft, painfully aware of his ebbing popularity, sought by a "swing around the circle" to rehabilitate himself with his western critics. In the fall of 1909 he traveled 16,000 miles, and spoke repeatedly to large, but unenthusiastic, audiences. At Winona, Minnesota, he made the strategic blunder of defending the Payne-Aldrich Tariff, insisting that it was the best tariff bill that the Republican Party had ever passed. This was small consolation to a public that had come to believe, not without reason, that the tariff was "the mother of the trusts."

Ballinger-Pinchot Controversy

Circumstances soon made it appear that on the subject of conservation the new President was no more to be trusted than on the tariff. Taft's Secretary of the Interior, R. A. Ballinger of Washington, was not unaware of the skepticism common to his section about the retardation of western development for the benefit of generations yet unborn. Nevertheless, he claimed that his actions in restoring to private entry some water-power sites in Montana and Wyoming and some coal lands in Alaska were due to legal scruple rather than to unconcern about conservation. As President, Roosevelt was accustomed to follow the dictates of his conscience, if no law stood in the way, whereas Ballinger and Taft both felt obliged to seek legal justification for their acts. Ballinger's behavior was vigorously protested during the summer and fall of 1909 by one of his subordinates, Louis R. Glavis, and by the chief

accustomed to presidential leadership, and had expected him to bring enough pressure to bear on Congress to get what he and the country wanted.

While Taft himself regarded some of the bill, particularly the woolens schedule, as indefensible, there were parts of it that were legitimately entitled to praise. The European system of maximum-minimum rates, which it incorporated, enabled the President to apply a higher schedule of rates against nations discriminating against American trade. A bipartisan tariff board was also established, the duty of which was to study the relative costs of production at home and abroad and to give Congress expert advice as to the rates it should set. Furthermore, a 1 per cent tax on the net income of corporations in excess of $5,000 opened up new possibilities both for the production of revenue and for the use of

Ballinger-Pinchot Controversy Cartoon. *"There is only a little difference between them." Only, that is, the public lands.*

of the forestry service, Gifford Pinchot, whose division lay within the Department of Agriculture. Taft, after careful investigation, decided that there was nothing against Ballinger, and dismissed both Glavis and Pinchot from office. In the case of Pinchot, he took action with great reluctance, for Pinchot, as everyone knew, was a close friend of Roosevelt's. Dismissal, however, was an administrative necessity, for Pinchot by writing Senator Dolliver in defense of Glavis had violated a rule prohibiting subordinates from corresponding directly with members of Congress. "There is only one thing for you to do," Senator Root had told the President, "and that you must do at once." But to the ever more hostile public, however well-founded the action, it appeared that Taft had lined up with the anti-conservationists.

Insurgency in the House

Meantime insurgency had broken out in the House, where a small group of progressive-minded Republicans had discovered that with Democratic cooperation they could outvote the Republican regulars. This power they determined to use against the autocratic sway of the Speaker, Joseph G. Cannon of Illinois, an ultra-conservative

who consistently and effectively stood in the way of all progressive legislation. Ably led by Representative George W. Norris of Nebraska, they presented an amendment to the House rules designed to take the appointment of the Rules Committee out of the Hands of the Speaker, and to make it elective by the House. With every parliamentary device in his possession, Cannon fought back, but eventually the insurgent-Democratic combination won out. When the next Congress met, the rules were still further amended. No longer was the Speaker permitted to appoint all committees and to designate their chairmen; instead, committees were made elective by the House itself, with the Ways and Means Committee acting as a committee on committees. Nor could it now be said that the Speaker, next to the President, was the most powerful American official; moreover, the chief agency for maintaining party discipline in the House was destroyed. Members felt free to vote as their consciences or their constituents might direct, regardless of party pressure. (Subsequently, the practice of awarding committee appointments in accordance with seniority posed another threat to legislative freedom.) By the spring of 1910 the group of middle-western Republican senators who had opposed the

ROOSEVELT, THE HUNTER. In the foreground are three water buffalo heads. To Roosevelt's right is his son, Kermit.

tariff bill were now in direct conflict with the President. They openly criticized Taft's stand on the tariff, on the Ballinger-Pinchot controversy, and on numerous other issues. Taft in return denied them patronage and even attempted without success to defeat some of them in the Republican primaries.

With insurgency rampant both in the Senate and the House, it was obvious that the party split which Taft had sought to avoid had come about. On the one hand were the conservatives led by Aldrich and Cannon, a faction with which the President, willy-nilly, had come to be allied. On the other hand were the insurgents, who stood for popular, not boss, control of the party, and believed that when the direct primary was established in every state their faction would be in the majority rather than in the minority. They stood also for real tariff revision, for genuine conservation, and for the expansion of governmental control over trusts and railroads. For leadership they looked beyond Norris and LaFollette to Africa:

Teddy, come home and blow your horn,
The sheep's in the meadow, the cow's in the
    corn.

The boy you left to 'tend the sheep
Is under the haystack fast asleep.[1]

Roosevelt Emerges from Africa

On March 14, 1910, the Roosevelt hunting party disbanded at Khartum in the Anglo-Egyptian Sudan. Not without some assistance, Roosevelt had accounted for nine lions, five elephants, thirteen rhinoceroses, seven hippopotamuses, and no less than two hundred and sixty-two other specimens. In Egypt he observed the symptoms of mounting discontent, and two months later in London he told the British either to get out of there or else to stay in and do their duty. In Italy he missed an audience with the Pope because the Holy Father insisted on knowing in advance that Roosevelt would not visit the Methodist mission in Rome; for good measure the ex-President passed up the Methodists also, but he met the King and Queen. In Austria-Hungary he was banqueted by the Emperor; in Germany he helped the Kaiser review his army; in England, as the official representative of the United States at the funeral of

[1] *Life*, May 26, 1910, quoted in Mark Sullivan, *Our Times*, IV, 441.

ROOSEVELT IN NEW YORK, June 18, 1910. To his right is Mayor William Jay Gaynor of New York; in the front seat is Cornelius Vanderbilt.

Edward VII, he vied for attention with all the assembled royalty, dead and alive. He delivered carefully prepared addresses at the Sorbonne, at Christiania, at Berlin, and at Oxford. And between times he read letters and newspapers from home that featured the Taft betrayal. He had, too, more direct information; Gifford Pinchot had crossed the ocean to meet him.

Eventually Roosevelt landed at New York, June 18, 1910, amidst a huge public celebration. It was soon apparent that the old cordiality between him and his successor was gone, although in the campaign of 1910 Roosevelt made every effort to heal the breach in the party and to bring about a Republican victory. It was with party success in view, not the discomfiture of Taft, that in August, 1910, he took the temporary chairmanship of the New York State nominating convention away from Vice-President Sherman, whom the conservatives had favored, and helped in the nomination of a liberal candidate, Henry L. Stimson, on a liberal platform for governor. Only by such a course, he believed, could the Republicans hope to hold the party together and maintain their control of the state. He made two speech-making tours, one through the West and another through the South, as he thought, in the interest of party harmony and Republican success at the polls. At Osawatomie, Kansas, he gave a name, the New Nationalism, to the principles for which he stood, and to which he believed that he had committed the Republican Party. While the progressive direction of his sympathies was apparent, he made numerous efforts to conciliate the conservatives. With even-handed justice he endorsed Beveridge, the insurgent, for re-election to the Senate from Indiana, and Warren Gamaliel Harding, a consistent conservative, for the governorship of Ohio. In his address before the New York convention he praised the Taft administration in the highest terms, and in September he again called on the President.

Elections of 1910

All this was of no avail, for the country was in a mood to rebuke the Republicans by voting the Democratic ticket. Stimson, Beveridge, and Harding alike went down to defeat, and the House of Representatives fell to the Democrats with 228 members to 161 for the Republicans and one for the Socialists, Victor L. Berger of Milwaukee. The Senate remained Republican by a vote of 51 to 41, but this majority was so slender that the insurgents, of whom there were a dozen or more, by voting with the Democrats, could easily overturn it. The conservative Republicans had thus lost control of both houses of Congress. In the states the trend was equally pronounced. Not only in New York and Ohio, but in such other Republican centers as Massachusetts, Connecticut, and New Jersey, the Democrats emerged triumphant. Hiram Johnson's victory in California was an exception to the rule.

There can be no doubt that the election was intended as a rebuke to the Taft administration, but in many ways it was undeserved. In reality, Taft had carried out the Roosevelt policies with considerable success. He had secured action on the tariff, something that Roosevelt had not even dared to attempt. He had prosecuted the trusts with vigor and persistence; before his administration ended he had brought more than twice as many suits against them as were undertaken by Roosevelt, and in shorter time. He had sponsored the Mann-Elkins Act of 1910, which gave the Interstate Commerce Commission jurisdiction over terminals and services of communication by telegraph, telephone, and cable. It also placed upon the carriers the burden of proving the justice of contemplated changes, for under its terms the commission might suspend new rates for ten months, pending investigation. It included, too, a plan that was essentially Taft's own, to create a special Commerce Court, composed of experts in the law of commerce, to which appeals from the decisions of the commission might be made. Taft's services to conservation were similarly notable. He replaced Pinchot by the head of the Yale School of Forestry, who added to the national forests by the purchase of timbered tracts in the Appalachians. Taft also got authority from Congress that Roosevelt lacked to withdraw coal lands from entry, and he was the first President to withdraw oil lands. Other reform measures enacted during the Taft administration, but generally ignored by his critics, included the improvement of the public land laws; the requirement of safety appliances on railroads; the establishment of a Bureau of Mines charged among other things with the duty of studying the welfare of the miners; a postal savings law; a parcel post law; and the separation of the Department of Commerce and Labor into two departments.

Taft's Political Ineptitude

Much of Taft's unpopularity may be attributed to his political ineptitude, and

much of it merely to hard luck. He got little credit for the reforms of the Mann-Elkins Act, for the measure as finally passed was more radical than he had dared to recommend. His Commerce Court was well conceived, but it showed too great friendliness for the corporations to suit the public, and one of its judges, R. W. Archbald, had to be impeached. In 1913 it was abolished. He signed long overdue measures for the admission of Arizona and New Mexico, but when Arizona included the recall of judges in her constitution he refused to proclaim its admission until the obnoxious clause had been taken out. Once in the Union, Arizona ostentatiously readopted the clause it had been compelled to delete.

Taft even had trouble about his appointments to the Supreme Court. When Chief Justice Melville W. Fuller died in 1910, Taft promoted Associate Justice Edward Douglass White of Louisiana to fill the vacancy. This was a graceful compliment to a hard-working judge and a political opponent, but White, besides being a Democrat, was a Roman Catholic, an ex-Confederate, and a conservative. To appoint him Taft had to overlook the claims of Associate Justice J. M. Harlan of Kentucky, who was a Republican, a Protestant, a veteran of the Union army, and a liberal. Altogether President Taft appointed five new members to the Supreme Court, all able jurists; and his choices included liberals and conservatives, Democrats and Republicans. But even the appointment of Charles Evans Hughes in 1910 failed to win the applause it merited. Some said Hughes should have been made Chief Justice; others, that the appointment was designed merely to sidetrack a possible competitor for the Republican nomination in 1912.

Reciprocity with Canada

Reciprocity with Canada was a favorite Taft policy, and seemingly quite in line with the views of the tariff reformers. At length, after persistent effort, he obtained an agreement in 1911 that noticeably lessened the trade barriers between the Dominion and the United States. The proposed schedules, however, reduced the tariff on agricultural imports into the United States from Canada, and offended the middle-western insurgents, whose interest in tariff reform concerned industry more than agriculture. Only with the assistance of Democratic votes was the President able to obtain the endorsement of his program in Congress. But this, events proved, was not enough. Unwisely the President had said in defense of reciprocity that its ultimate result would be to "make Canada only an adjunct of the United States." "Champ" Clark, Democratic Speaker of the House and also a supporter of reciprocity, even looked forward to the time when Canada would become a part of the United States. All this was too much for the Canadians, who voted out of power the party that had negotiated the agreement, and refused ratification.[1]

In the last half of the Taft administration, Congress, under the control of the Republican insurgents and the Democrats, did not hesitate to plague the President openly by passing piecemeal revisions of the tariff that he was certain to veto. A new woolens schedule to replace the unspeakable Schedule K, a farmers' free-list bill, and a cotton bill were sent to his desk in quick succession. As expected, the President took the stand that constant tariff tinkering was unsettling to business, and that if the tariff were to be revised at all, it must be revised as a whole, and not bit by bit. No doubt his opponents were interested primarily in forcing him to multiply vetoes that would add to his unpopularity.

[1] It will be recalled that Taft's foreign policy in the Far East and in Central America won him much criticism. See pp. 305–6, 314.

The LaFollette and Roosevelt Candidacies

The original program of the Republican insurgents was not the formation of a new party, but the capture of the party to which they still belonged. This was made clear as early as January 23, 1911, when a group of them, meeting at Senator LaFollette's house in Washington, formed the National Progressive Republican League. Included in their program were the reforms designed to enable the people to defeat boss rule, such as the direct election of United States senators, direct primaries, the direct election of delegates to national nominating conventions, the initiative, the referendum, and the recall in the states, and a thoroughgoing corrupt practices act. On the assumption that Roosevelt would not consider a third term, they rallied around LaFollette as the "logical man" to defeat Taft for renomination. But to the intense disappointment of LaFollette, who claimed that he had been used only as a "stalking horse," Roosevelt announced on February 24, 1912, that he was ready to throw his "hat in the ring." From this day the LaFollette candidacy was a lost cause, and the progressive wing of the party turned with unbounded enthusiasm to Roosevelt.

It soon developed that the ex-President, for all his popular appeal, had entered the campaign too late. The party machine was in the hands of the conservatives, who were determined to renominate Taft. They had already lined up many of the southern delegations, which because they were so largely composed of federal officeholders could always be trusted to follow the will of the President, and they now made haste to gather in the rest. Where the old convention system of choosing delegates was in force, the party regulars were almost invariably in control, and obediently delivered their delegations to Taft. On the other hand, wherever the new system of presidential primaries existed, Roosevelt generally won; indeed several states made haste to adopt such laws in order to promote his chances. When the Republican convention met in Chicago on June 18, it was apparent that the Roosevelt forces were approximately 100 votes short of a majority. To make up this deficiency they had brought contests involving about 250 seats, some fairly reasonable and others merely for "moral effect." But the pro-Taft national committee had already turned most of their contests down, and the convention, effectively controlled by a conservative "steam-roller," gave nearly all the disputed seats to Taft, a "naked theft," according to Roosevelt. Taft was nominated on the first ballot, although 107 delegates voted for Roosevelt and 344 others sat silent in protest.

The Progressives Name Roosevelt

Even before the Republican convention met it was obvious that Roosevelt was in no mood to accept defeat. If he lost the Republican nomination, he would run anyway. On June 22 he told a rump conven-

Listening For The Call to Arms. *According to this cartoonist the popular demand for Roosevelt to run again was not wholly spontaneous. Ketten in the* New York World.

tion that met in Orchestra Hall, Chicago, "If you wish me to make the fight, I will make it, even if only one state should support me." Six weeks later, an uproarious Progressive Party convention assembled, again in Chicago, to select Roosevelt as its standard-bearer. Already the new third party had a symbol with which to match the Republican elephant and the Democratic donkey — the "bull moose." This was a favorite term with Roosevelt, one he had used as far back as 1900, when he had boasted to Hanna that he was "as strong as a Bull Moose." An enthusiastic audience of 20,000 people heard the Progressive leader denounce both old parties as "husks, with no real soul within either, divided on artificial lines, boss-ridden and privilege-controlled, each a jumble of incongruous elements, and neither daring to speak out wisely and fearlessly what should be said on the issues of the day."

On a great variety of issues the new party spoke out. Its program, called the "New Nationalism" after the title of Roosevelt's Osawatomie speech, demanded great increases in the powers of the federal government to regulate big business in the interest of the public, and to care for the weak and unfortunate members of society. Its policy on trusts recognized corporations as "an essential part of modern business," and in lieu of dissolving them it demanded effective regulation through "a strong federal administrative commission." This body, according to Roosevelt, should even have the power to set prices on goods made by monopolies. The platform also proposed a federal securities commission to supervise the issuance of stocks and bonds, and called for an immediate revision of the tariff in favor of the consumer, for a land monopoly tax, and for government ownership of the Alaskan railroads. It endorsed, too, all the current reforms such as the direct primary, woman suffrage, an easier way to amend the Constitution, better working conditions in the factories, the prohibition of child labor, the better regulation of women's labor, minimum wage standards, and an eight-hour day. The Bull Moose program, in short, looked away from the old individualistic, antitrust, small-business type of progressivism, and toward a new corporate type of society in which big business and big labor were to be policed by big government. Its humanitarian aspects delighted social workers such as Jane Addams, and gave the new party a crusading character that well became its leader. With a fervor reminiscent of Populism the Progressive convention sang "Onward Christian Soldiers," and quoted Roosevelt's challenge to the Taft forces at Chicago: "We stand at Armageddon and we battle for the Lord."

The Democrats Name Wilson

Meanwhile, the Democrats, convinced that the Republican split would insure their triumph at the polls in November, had met in Baltimore, July 25, to choose their candidate from a long list of favorite sons. After the tenth ballot it seemed certain that J. Beauchamp ("Champ") Clark of Missouri, Speaker of the House, would be the nominee, for he had obtained a majority of the votes, although not yet the two-thirds majority then necessary for a Democratic nomination. But William Jennings Bryan, still the dominant personality in the Democratic Party, switched from Clark to Governor Woodrow Wilson of New Jersey on the fourteenth ballot. The Tammany delegation from New York had voted for Clark since the tenth ballot, and Bryan's explanation of his conduct was that he could not support anyone who would owe his nomination to Tammany. Cynics insisted that Bryan was only trying to deadlock the convention so that it would again turn to him, but on the forty-sixth ballot it chose Wilson.

The campaign provided plenty of excitement and the public enjoyed it thoroughly.

Roosevelt and Taft, throughout the primary contests and on into the election campaign, belabored each other as only two friends fallen out can do. Wilson proved to be an admirable public speaker, and defended the "New Freedom," as he called his program, with a felicity that won him many votes. Assailing Roosevelt's concept of a powerful regulatory state, Wilson predicted that it could only lead to the rule of exploiting monopolies sanctified by government. What was needed, Wilson asserted, was the destruction of "illicit competition" by big business through the ruthless use of the antitrust law, and a return to the "old competitive democratic principles." "The history of liberty," he remarked in one of his most important speeches, "is the history of the limitation of governmental power."

Election Results

The results of the election were what all astute observers were able to foresee. Wilson, with fewer popular votes than Bryan had received in any of his three defeats, amassed an electoral vote of 435 to Roosevelt's 88 and Taft's 8. With the Democrats equally victorious in the House of Representatives and the Senate, the new President would be assured also of a comfortable working majority in Congress. In most of the state contests the Democrats also scored victories, the cleanest sweep their party had made since before the Civil War. Those who looked behind the more obvious results made two significant observations. One was that Eugene V. Debs, the hardy perennial of socialism, received 897,000 popular votes, more than twice as many as in 1908; to a large block of voters, it would seem that neither Roosevelt nor Wilson went far enough in their liberalism. The other was that in the state and local contests the Progressives made almost no impression whatever. The Democrats and the Republicans had all the offices. This portent was not lost on Roosevelt. "The fight is over," he told a friend. "We are beaten. There is only one thing to do and that is to go back to the Republican Party. You can't hold a party like the Progressive Party together . . . there are no loaves and fishes."

Woodrow Wilson

It was somewhat ironic that the reform policies which Roosevelt had begun, and which Taft had sought with only partial success to continue, would be carried to fruition, if at all, by a Democratic President. Woodrow Wilson (1856–1924), upon whom this task developed, had an unusual preparation for the Presidency. He was a native of Staunton, Virginia, the first President of southern birth since Andrew Johnson. His father, a prominent southern Presbyterian clergyman, was of Ohio birth and Scotch-Irish ancestry. His mother, Janet Woodrow, was the daughter of a Scottish Presbyterian minister, who had come to America in 1836, when she was only nine years old. Wilson thus came naturally by his unbending Presbyterianism. In his youth he studied law, but gave it up to become a college professor, and as a political scientist at Princeton University achieved international recognition for his studies in comparative government.

Drawing his early principles from such English statesmen as Burke, Cobden, and Bright, Wilson, like so many other progressive leaders in both parties, started his political life as a conservative, or, more accurately, as a "classical liberal." He had defended the open shop in the nineties, had opposed the Populists, and as late as 1908 had regarded both Bryan and Roosevelt as dangerous radicals. On the expansion of the presidential power, however, he agreed with Roosevelt completely. Deeply impressed with the vast powers wielded by the prime ministers in Great Britain and elsewhere, he became convinced that the principle of executive leadership must somehow be grafted into the American system. "The President," wrote the professor, "is at liberty, both in law and conscience, to be as big a man as he can. His capacity will set the limit." Promoted to the presidency of Princeton, Wilson made an effort that was totally unappreciated by the governing board to democratize the institution. Hence, when the Democratic "boss" of New Jersey, in search of window dressing for his ticket, offered Wilson the nomination as governor in 1910, he accepted gladly, made an earnest campaign, and was elected.

To the consternation of the party bosses, Wilson, once in office, insisted on carrying out the liberal promises of the state Democratic platform. Turning against the people who had nominated him, the governor put into practical effect the doctrine of executive leadership he had taught so long. By appealing to the people both directly and through the press, he soon had the legislature doing his bidding and not that of the party machine. On pressure from the governor's office, the legislature of New Jersey passed measures to establish employer's liability, to punish corrupt practices, to control public utilities, and to reform the election machinery. These victories in a state that had long been known as the "home of the trusts" made Wilson a marked man. He was soon deserted by the bosses and some conservatives who had previously supported him, but his record won increasing admiration among the progressives. Adroitly presented to the public outside New Jersey by Colonel Edward M. House of Texas, he had become by 1912 the favorite candidate of the progressive wing of his party.

Having achieved the Presidency, Wilson was determined to be the prime-minister type of President. With this end in view he included in his cabinet as Secretary of State the man whose influence with the rank and file of the Democratic Party was still

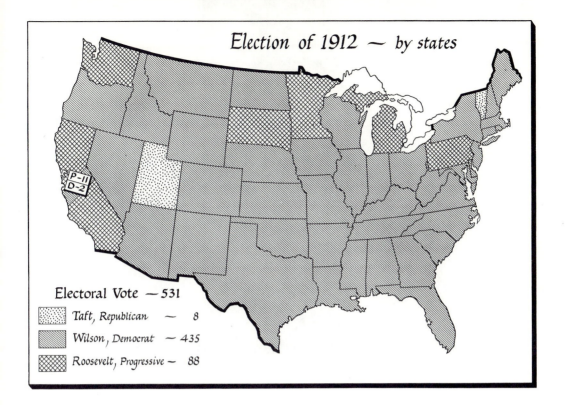

Election of 1912 — by states

Electoral Vote — 531

- Taft, Republican — 8
- Wilson, Democrat — 435
- Roosevelt, Progressive — 88

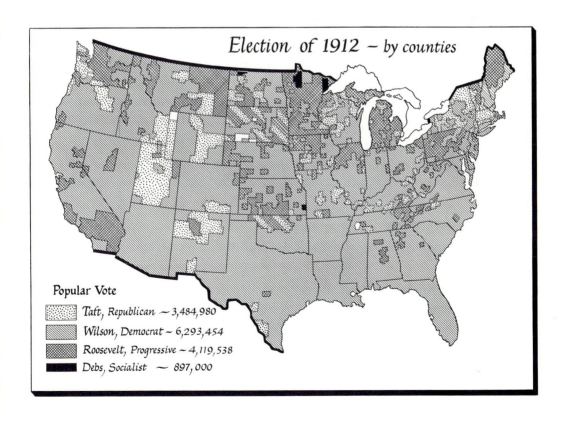

Election of 1912 — by counties

Popular Vote

- Taft, Republican — 3,484,980
- Wilson, Democrat — 6,293,454
- Roosevelt, Progressive — 4,119,538
- Debs, Socialist — 897,000

William Howard Taft and Woodrow Wilson. *Here the twenty-seventh and twenty-eighth Presidents of the United States meet at Wilson's first inauguration.*

second to none, William Jennings Bryan. Other appointments were made, not only with an eye to the fitness of the candidate, as might have been expected of such a President, but also with an eye to achieving party cohesion. It was soon clear that Wilson meant to become the unchallenged leader of his party. He broke a precedent more than a century old by appearing in person to read his messages to Congress, short messages that the public would also read and expect to see speedily translated into law. He took the people constantly into his confidence, and made the most of newspaper publicity. The President, he had once said, "has no means of compelling Congress except through public opinion." But he also used his influence directly upon congressmen in personal interviews, and unhesitatingly accorded patronage favors to the faithful, while denying them to others. Behind the scenes he relied heavily upon the advice of Colonel House, who was not

a military man at all, but a shrewd political observer with whom Wilson discussed most matters of consequence. The President also listened attentively to his faithful private secretary, Joseph P. Tumulty, a Roman Catholic and a keen practical politician.

Underwood-Simmons Tariff

Wilson's first efforts were directed toward the downward revision of the tariff, an end his predecessor had failed to achieve. Under steady pressure from the White House, the Underwood-Simmons Tariff Act was ready for the President's signature on October 3, 1913. When during the debate on the bill lobbyists had swarmed into Washington to protect special interests, Wilson appealed to the people through the press for help. "Washington," he said, "has seldom seen so numerous, so industrious, or so insidious a lobby." An aroused public opinion came promptly to the rescue, and the lobbyists were soon more embarrassed than embarrassing. The new tariff law was neither a free-trade measure nor a low-tariff measure, and was not meant to be either. Its schedules of duties, however, were on the average about 10 per cent lower than those of the Payne-Aldrich Tariff, and it placed a hundred new items, mostly raw materials or foodstuffs, on the free list. What these duties might have done for business and for the revenue will never be known, for the outbreak of war in Europe drastically reduced importations. To make up for the resulting loss of revenue, the government was obliged to fall back on an income tax, made possible by the recent adoption of the Sixteenth Amendment, and provided for in the Underwood-Simmons Act to offset any possible loss of revenue from the new rates. A tax of 1 per cent was charged against all incomes in excess of $3,000, or, in the case of married couples, $4,000; while on incomes above $20,000 a surtax, beginning with an additional 1 per cent, was gradually stepped up to a maximum of 6 per cent on incomes above $500,000. At the time these rates were devised the possibilities of the income tax were only faintly realized, but within a few years it became the federal government's chief reliance for revenue.

Federal Reserve System

On the heels of the tariff act came banking and currency reform on a scale never before attempted in the United States. The National Monetary Commission that Congress had created as a result of the Panic of 1907 reported in 1912 that the only sure cure for the financial ills from which the country suffered would be a centralized banking system, substantially a third Bank of the United States. The subject was again investigated during the second half of the Taft administration, this time by a committee of the Democratic House of Representatives, headed by A. J. Pujo of Louisiana. The Pujo Committee, while fully convinced

that there was a "money trust" controlled by the whims of a few great bankers, balked at the idea of creating the same kind of bank that a great Democratic President, Andrew Jackson, had felt obliged to destroy. Under Wilson's leadership, Congress eventually hit upon the expedient of creating a series of sectional banks, held together only by a Federal Reserve Board. This board, which Wilson thought of as analogous to the Interstate Commerce Commission, was to consist of seven members, two of whom, the Secretary of the Treasury and the Comptroller of the Currency, were to be members ex officio, while the others (increased to six in 1922) were to be appointed by the President and confirmed by the Senate for ten-year terms. One of the nonpolitical members was to be designated governor of the board. The United States was to be divided into twelve districts, each of which would contain some natural metropolitan center in which a Federal Reserve Bank would be established. The new banks were not to do business with individuals, but were to be strictly "bankers' banks," with which every national bank must deposit its reserve, and which state banks might also use at their option. The hope of the men who framed the measure was that in times of crisis the strength of the total reserves could be mobilized to sustain any one bank.

The law also provided for a new type of currency, Federal Reserve notes. These new notes were based upon the commercial loans made by member banks to businessmen. Thus the total amount of bank notes in circulation could vary with the amount of business conducted in the country, and so overcome the inelasticity of the currency, a chronic complaint under the old system, which had tied the amount of the national bank notes to the quantity of government bonds owned by the national banks. It was also hoped, as the system developed, that through the sale or purchase of government bonds and through changing the so-called "rediscount" rate, the Federal Reserve Board could alter the amount of credit in the country and thus help to prevent wild speculative booms and sharp depressions. Wilson signed this measure, known as the Glass-Owen Federal Reserve Act, December 23, 1913.

When the Federal Reserve System was first proposed, the bankers of the country were extremely suspicious of it, and the fact that Secretary Bryan openly supported it was well calculated to exaggerate their fears. But before the measure reached final passage, the bankers had begun to see its advantages, and within a short time the best of them were enthusiastic in its praise. While it is a fact that, at the time the Great Depression began in 1929, only about one-third of the banks of the country were members of the Federal Reserve, it is an even more striking fact that by that time the combined assets of the "member banks" accounted for more than four-fifths of the nation's banking resources.

Wilson's Trust Policy

When Wilson appeared before Congress on January 20, 1914, to direct attention to the trust problem, he had information available that his predecessors had lacked. The nature of modern business had been better studied. The Bureau of Corporations established in Roosevelt's time had begun to bear fruit, while economics had elbowed its way to the front in the colleges and universities as the most significant of the social studies. Whatever his earlier attitudes, Wilson now knew, better than either Roosevelt or Taft had known, the hopelessness of trying merely to turn big business into little businesses. Such efforts were like trying to turn back the clock. What Wilson now sought of Congress was a clear definition of what was fair and what was unfair in business activity; further, a more complete recognition of the fact that the government through proper agencies should have the right to enforce the regulations laid down by Congress. Before the midterm elections

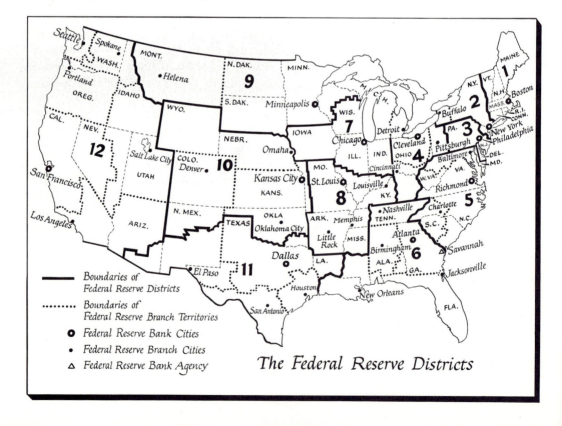

Boundaries of
Federal Reserve Districts

Boundaries of
Federal Reserve Branch Territories

◉ Federal Reserve Bank Cities

• Federal Reserve Branch Cities

△ Federal Reserve Bank Agency

The Federal Reserve Districts

of 1914, Congress had enacted two significant measures, the Clayton Antitrust Act and the Federal Trade Commission Act. The Clayton Act added various new prohibitions to the already long list of practices forbidden to corporations, and the Federal Trade Commission Act created a new board of five members to investigate the origin and management of corporations, and to seek the assistance of the courts in putting an end to such "unfair methods of competition in commerce" as it might discover. Some progress was made with the enforcement of these laws during Wilson's first administration, but the work thus begun was adversely affected by the entrance of the United States into the First World War. While that struggle was on, little attempt was made to enforce the restrictions of the Clayton Act, and after the Republicans returned to power in 1921 there was little desire to enforce them.

A "Magna Carta" for Labor

The attitude that the Wilson administration meant to take toward labor was clearly revealed by the incorporation in the Clayton Act of what Gompers hailed as labor's "Magna Carta." Section 6 of that measure seemed specifically to exempt labor and agricultural corporations from prosecution under the terms of the antitrust laws, while Section 20 sought to limit the use of injunctions in labor disputes, prescribed trials by jury in contempt cases, and legalized such labor weapons as strikes, picketing, peaceable assembly, boycotts, and the collection of strike benefits. The framers of the Sherman Antitrust Act had probably not meant to extend its provision to labor unions, but in the Danbury Hatters decision of 1908 the Supreme Court had read that interpretation into the law.[1] Until the passage of the Clayton Act, labor unions had to take particular care lest they be held guilty of "interstate boycotting." Judicial

[1] *Loewe* vs. *Lawler*, 208 U.S., 274.

His Majesty the Toiler. *By Frank C. Kirk.*

obstacles had been placed in the way of nearly every other labor practice also, and "government by injunction" had become a fact. The provisions of the Clayton Act were therefore hailed as a great boon to labor, although time was to prove that some of the supposed guarantees were far more effective as rhetoric than as law. During the war years labor, like business, was relatively free from discriminatory pressures, but after the war was over many of the old anti-labor practices were revived, and some of the supposed restraints of the Clayton Act were interpreted away by the courts.

The *Titanic* Leaving Liverpool. *On her maiden voyage the White Star liner* Titanic *struck an iceberg southeast of Cape Race and sank, April 15, 1912. Of the 2,224 passengers and crew aboard, 1,513 lost their lives.*

The friendliness of the Wilson administration toward labor was manifested in many ways. A Children's Bureau in the new Department of Labor sought to extend at least as good advice on the care of the nation's youth as the Department of Agriculture had long made available to farmers for the care of livestock. Twice Congress attempted to prohibit child labor, and when the Supreme Court declared these measures unconstitutional, it sought, also in vain, to secure by an amendment to the Constitution the power that the Court had denied it. Spurred on by revelations that carelessness on the part of the shipping interests had had much to do with the sinking in 1912 of the passenger liner, *Titanic*, Congress in 1915 passed the LaFollette Seamen's Act, which required better working conditions for ships' crews, and ended the tyrannical control over their men that sea captains had exercised since long before the days of Captain Bligh. Such measures as these, however, fell far short of the revolutionary goals set by small but tempestuous groups of extreme radicals. When Wilson became President the furor over the bombing in 1911 of the building which housed the *Los Angeles Times*, a rabidly anti-union newspaper, had barely died down. Two brothers named

McNamara were accused of the crime, and in spite of generous labor contributions to their defense, they ultimately confessed, and were sentenced, while thirty-eight labor leaders were later convicted as their accomplices. Most difficult of the radical groups to deal with was the Industrial Workers of the World, commonly called the "IWW," or "Wobblies," who had their greatest strength in the far Northwest. Their warlike methods resulted in the passage by sixteen states of criminal syndicalist laws, the ruthless enforcement of which crippled seriously radical activities. Since many of the extremists were recent immigrants, a strong impetus was given to the ever-smoldering demand for immigration restriction, and in 1917 Congress passed a bill which required ability "to read the English language or some other language" for admission to the United States. The measure became law over President Wilson's veto.

Rural Credits

In his inaugural address Wilson had given prominent mention to the needs of agriculture, and had particularly stressed the importance of providing some system of rural credits. The Federal Reserve Act authorized short-term loans up to six months on farm mortgages, but the pressure for long-term loans, by means of which the purchase of farm lands could be financed, grew steadily more insistent. After two years' consideration, Congress finally agreed to the Federal Farm Loan Act of 1916, which created a farm loan system patterned closely on the model of the Federal Reserve System. A central board consisting of the Secretary of the Treasury and four appointive members was given general control over a dozen Federal Farm Land Banks operating in as many different districts. Out of deference to the wishes of private moneylenders, who objected to the government monopolizing the business of supplying rural credits, the law provided also for the estab-

Labor Violence. *The* Los Angeles Times *Building, after its bombing on October 1, 1911, was gutted by a fire in which nineteen persons lost their lives.*

lishment of joint-stock land banks, privately financed. By 1930 the two types of banks created by the Federal Farm Loan Act had together lent over $2 billion to farmers at interest rates of from 5 to 6 per cent.

"Dollar-Matching"

Before the exigencies of war halted the course of domestic reform the Wilson administration inaugurated another notable policy. Gifts from the federal government to aid the states in such matters as education and internal improvements were almost as old as the Constitution, but throughout the nineteenth century these gifts had been made primarily in the form of land or the receipts from land sales. By the time Wilson became President this source of supply had so nearly approached exhaustion that some new form of subsidy had to be found. It was discovered in the form of the heavy receipts that came in, or could be made to come in, from the income tax. This revenue, it turned out, was collected from a comparatively small fraction of the total

population, most of whom lived in the Northeast. But there was no gainsaying the fact that the earnings from which the income tax was paid were drawn from all over the nation. Coupled with the demand for better educational facilities and better transportation in the larger, poorer, and less densely populated states of the West and the South was the belief that in some fashion the government should attempt to redistribute among all the states the heavy earnings that were being piled up in the industrial areas of the Northeast. Southern and western votes on behalf of such a policy were easily accumulated, and the South and the West controlled the Democratic Party.

The new type of federal grants in aid of education began in 1914 with the passage of the Smith-Lever Act, which provided that the United States should match, dollar for dollar, the contributions of such states as chose to cooperate in a program of agricultural extension for the direct education of the farmers through county agents. The supervision of this program was left to the Department of Agriculture, working through the land-grant colleges. This measure was followed in 1917 by the Smith-Hughes Act, which appropriated funds, again on a dollar-matching basis, for education in commercial, industrial, and domestic-science subjects in schools of less than college grade. A board of vocational education, created by the act, was given the right to pass on the merits of the projects for which the various states proposed to use their allotments. The impetus which these acts gave to agricultural and vocational education, supplemented by the work of the Bureau of Education, the Children's Bureau, and other federal agencies, was felt in a steadily mounting number of the nation's high schools. Talk began in educational circles of the need for a federal Department of Education with a seat in the cabinet, but opponents of the idea argued that federal control over state educational policies must not be carried too far.

Federal Highways Act

The Federal Highways Act of 1916 carried the dollar-matching principle into the field of road-building. The automobile, which was at first condemned because it tore up the roads, soon led to a demand for better roads that completely overtaxed the resources of the states. It was only natural in such an emergency to turn to the federal government for aid, and Democrats who could remember well Jackson's war on the Bank soon demonstrated that they had quite forgotten his Maysville veto. Aid was needed for a Lincoln Highway, just marked out from coast to coast, for a Dixie Highway from Lakes to Gulf, and for half a hundred other projects. Yielding to the general pressure, Congress appropriated $5 million the first year for distribution among the states. Size, population, and existing mail routes were all to be taken into consideration in determining the amounts al-lotted to each. Moreover, every dollar contributed by the federal government must be matched by a dollar from the state which received it, and federal control must be accepted in all such dollar-matching expenditures. When Congress made this first appropriation it knew little of the cost of road-building, but it soon found out a great deal. Nor could the process it had begun be ended until a complete set of federal highways, connecting every important center with every other, had been built. The dollar-matching principle, together with its attendant federal control, was rapidly extended during the First World War and even more during the New Deal period. The process accounts for much of the increase in federal power at the expense of that of the states.

Wilsonian vs. Jeffersonian Democracy

The contrast between Wilson's Jeffersonian pre-election demand for a "New Freedom" and his later legislative program is marked indeed. Instead of limiting the power of the federal government, as his attack on the Progressive program had implied must be done, the Wilson measures actually added greatly to it. With Hamiltonian thoroughness, the Wilsonians had devised a great national banking system that gave the national government extensive power in regulating the currency and credit system of the entire nation. In their attempts to "restrain men from injuring one another," they had circumscribed the area in which private industry might regulate its own activities. In protecting the rights of labor and children, they had seriously limited the freedom of individuals to do as they pleased. In concerning themselves about the public welfare, they had assumed wide paternalistic privileges for the national government. By the end of Wilson's first term, the Wilsonians had enacted into law much of the "Bull Moose" program of "New Nationalism."

Muddy Roads. *The automobile, denounced at first as a destroyer of good roads, became eventually the most important influence in stimulating the construction of an effective American highway system. The picture shows an early Winton car on a transcontinental tour stuck in a mudhole (about 1904).*

A part of the explanation of the inconsistency displayed by Wilson and his followers lay in their devotion to the twin Jeffersonian ideals of equal opportunity for all men and individual freedom as well. The two ideals, by Wilson's time, had become increasingly incompatible in a world of big business and big cities. By infringing a little on freedom the Wilsonians hoped to strengthen equality of opportunity. As so often happens, the responsibility of office had forced the Wilsonians to compromise their theory with hard facts. Before the outbreak of war in 1914 Wilson had already begun to compromise on domestic issues; thereafter this man of peace was obliged to compromise also on foreign policy.

BIBLIOGRAPHY

Indispensable for this period is H. F. Pringle, *The Life and Times of William Howard Taft* (2 vols., 1939), based upon Taft's papers and highly sympathetic. For the conservative viewpoint, in addition to the works previously mentioned on Root, the following are of value: J. B. Foraker, *Notes of a Busy Life* (2 vols., 3rd ed., 1917); Everett Walters, *Joseph Benson Foraker* (1948); N. W. Stephenson, *Nelson W. Aldrich* (1930); Blair Bolles, *Tyrant from Illinois: Uncle Joe Cannon's Experiment with Personal Power* (1951); and W. R. Gwinn, *Uncle Joe Cannon* (1955). There are two important biographies of H. L. Stimson, moderate progressive and Secretary of War: H. L. Stimson and McGeorge Bundy, *On Active Service in Peace and War* (1948); and E. E. Morison, **Turmoil and Tradition* (1960). The standard, if rather uncritical, biography of the 1916 Republican presidential candidate is M. J. Pusey, *Charles Evans Hughes* (2 vols., 1951). It may now be supplemented by R. F. Wesser, *Charles Evans Hughes: Politics and Reform in New York, 1905–1910* (1967). The literature on the Ballinger-Pinchot affair, already vast, continues to grow. Pinchot's side is argued in his own *The Fight for Conservation* (1910), and *Breaking New Ground* (1947); and in A. T. Mason, *Bureaucracy Convicts Itself* (1941). Ballinger's position is best set forth in Pringle's life of Taft. Relatively dispassionate are J. J. Penick, *Progressive Politics and Conservation* (1968); and M. N. McGeary, *Gifford Pinchot, Forester-Politician* (1960), a full-length biography based upon Pinchot's papers. A new study of Pinchot's career between 1910 and 1917 is M. L. Fausold, *Gifford Pinchot, Bull Moose Progressive* (1961). A valuable study of twentieth-century land policy is E. L. Peffer, *The Closing of the Public Domain* (1951).

Two dependable guides to the Progressive revolt against Taft, both based upon wide research, are K. W. Hechler, *Insurgency: Personalities and Politics of the Taft Era* (1940); and G. E. Mowry, *Theodore Roosevelt and the Progressive Movement* (1946). A careful study which gives full attention to the aftermath is James Holt, *Congressional Insurgents and the Party System, 1909–1916* (1967). Richard Lowitt, *George W. Norris: The Making of a Progressive, 1861–1912* (1963), is the first volume of the definitive biography of the great insurgent leader of the House. *The Autobiography of William Allen White* (1946) is rich and vivid; it may be supplemented by Walter Johnson, *William Allen White's America* (1947). Other important biographies of progressives include: A. T. Mason, *Brandeis* (1946); T. R. Ross, *Jonathan Prentice Dolliver* (1958); and A. B. Sageser, *Joseph L. Bristow* (1968). An interesting collection of pronouncements from Oyster Bay is Theodore Roosevelt, *The New Nationalism* (1910). A detailed and opinionated work, which lays most of the blame for the failures of the Progressive Party on the head of George Perkins, is A. R. E. Pinchot, *History of the Progressive Party, 1912–1916*, edited by H. M. Hooker (1958).

Woodrow Wilson and the Progressive Era, 1910–1917 (1954), by A. S. Link, is a fine introduction, with a superb bibliography. Professor Link is engaged in the production of a full-length biography, based upon multi-archival research. Five volumes of his *Wilson* have appeared since 1947; he now has reached the declaration of war. He is also editing Wilson's papers for publication; seven volumes have appeared since 1966, reaching 1892. Also edited by Link is *Woodrow Wilson: A Profile* (1968), a collection of writings by and about Wilson. The best single-volume Wilson biographies are H. C. F. Bell, *Woodrow Wilson and the People* (1945); and Arthur Walworth, *Woodrow Wilson* (2nd ed., 1965). Neither Bell nor Walworth is as critical of his subject as Link is. J. M. Blum, *Woodrow Wilson and the Politics of Morality* (1956), sees Wilson as an anachronism. An interesting collection of centennial essays by various authorities is *The Philosophy and Policies of Woodrow Wilson*, edited by Earl Latham (1958). A highly useful historiographical essay is R. L. Watson, Jr., "Woodrow Wilson and His Interpreters," *Mississippi Valley Historical Review*, XLIV (1957), 207–236.

The history of the Wilson administration by F. L. Paxson, *American Democracy and the World War* (3 vols., 1936–48), is detailed, factual, and chronological. A brilliant brief survey of these years is contained in W. E. Leuchtenburg, *The Perils of Prosperity* (1958). Wilson's 1912 speeches have been edited by J. W. Davidson and published with the title, *A Crossroads of Freedom* (1956); these should be compared with the volume which appeared with Wilson's own name, *The New Freedom* (1913). An interesting collection of materials focusing upon the apparently divergent attitudes of the major 1912 candidates upon a single issue is E. C. Rozwenc (ed.), *Roosevelt, Wilson, and the Trusts* (1950). The early career of Wilson's closest political friend is fully described in R. N. Richardson, *Colonel Edward M. House: The Texas Years, 1858–1912* (1964).

The Wilson cabinet proved to be particularly fruitful in autobiography: W. G. McAdoo, *Crowded Years* (1931); D. F. Houston, *Eight Years with Wilson's Cabinet* (2 vols., 1926); W. C. Redfield, *With Congress and Cabinet* (1924); *The Letters of Franklin K. Lane*, edited by A. W. Lane and L. H. Wall (1922); and Josephus Daniels, *The Wilson Era: Years of Peace, 1910–1917* (1944). *The Cabinet Diaries of Josephus Daniels* (1963), edited by E. D. Cronon, provides more evidence. See also J. L. Morrison, *Josephus*

Daniels (1966). J. M. Blum, *Joe Tumulty and the Wilson Era* (1951), is an informative biography of Wilson's principal secretary.

Wilson's legislative program has attracted the attention of many writers. Sidney Ratner, *American Taxation* (1942), is both readable and reliable, and is especially good on the income tax. Basic is P. M. Warburg, *The Federal Reserve System* (2 vols., 1930). On the trust problem, see G. C. Henderson, *The Federal Trade Commission* (1924); and D. D. Martin, *Mergers and the Clayton Act* (1959), which assays the results. D. W. Grantham, *Hoke Smith and the Politics of the New South* (1958), treats the career of an influential Senator of the Wilson era. See also the richly detailed synthesis by G. B. Tindall, *The Emergence of the New South, 1913–1945* (1967). One of the most exciting episodes of the Wilson period is treated by A. L. Todd, *Justice on Trial: The Case of Louis D. Brandeis* (1964).

Labor historians have produced some important studies in recent years. Among these are: Hyman Weintraub, *Andrew Furuseth, Emancipator of the Seamen* (1959); G. H. Stimson, *Rise of the Labor Movement in Los Angeles* (1955); Robert Knight, *Industrial Relations in the San Francisco Bay Area, 1900–1918* (1960); J. O. Morris, *Conflict within the AFL, 1901–1938* (1958); Marc Karson, *American Labor Unions and Politics, 1900–1918* (1958); Marguerite Green, *The National Civic Federation and the American Labor Movement, 1900–1925* (1956); Irwin Yellowitz, *Labor and the Progressive Movement in New York State, 1897–1916* (1965); G. J. Adams, *Age of Industrial Violence, 1910–1915* (1966), an examination of the Commission on Industrial Relations; and Melvyn Dubofsky, *When Workers Organize: New York City in the Progressive Era* (1968). Two books examine the "scientific management" movement: M. J. Nadworthy, *Scientific Management and the Unions, 1900–1932* (1955); and Samuel Haber, *Efficiency and Uplift* (1964).

The Industrial Workers of the World have received an enormous amount of study in recent years. Melvyn Dubofsky, *We Shall Be All* (1969), is a full-length study; it largely supersedes the former standard work by P. F. Brissenden, *The I. W. W.* (2nd ed., 1920). A lively popular account is Patrick Renshaw, *The Wobblies* (1967). *Rebel Voices: An I. W. W. Anthology* (1964), edited by J. L. Kornbluh, is a superb documentary. Biographies of leaders include J. R. Conlin, *Big Bill Haywood and the Radical Union Movement* (1969); and G. M. Smith, *Joe Hill* (1969). R. L. Tyler, *Rebels of the Woods* (1967), is a study of the I. W. W. in the Pacific Northwest.

Recently historians have begun to concern themselves with the intellectual currents of the Progressive Era. In addition to the works of Hofstadter, Mowry, and Goldman, already mentioned, two comprehensive analyses reaching rather different conclusions have appeared: D. W. Noble, *The Paradox of Progressive Thought* (1958); and Charles Forcey, *The Crossroads of Liberalism: Croly, Weyl, Lippmann, and the Progressive Era, 1900–1925* (1961). Daniel Levine, *Varieties of Reform Thought* (1964), is a series of succinct case studies. Henry May, *The End of American Innocence: A Study of the First Years of Our Own Time, 1912–1917* (1959), is a reinterpretation of the period. Christopher Lasch, *The New Radicalism in America, 1889–1963* (1965), is an impressionistic study of intellectual radicals and near-radicals. Basic works with which intellectual historians must concern themselves include: Herbert Croly, *The Promise of American Life* (1909); Walter Rauschenbusch, *Christianity and the Social Crisis* (1907); Walter Weyl, *The New Democracy* (1912); L. D. Brandeis, *Other People's Money* (1914); and two books by Walter Lippmann, *A Preface to Politics* (1913), and *Drift and Mastery* (1914).

Section Four

WAR AND PEACE

[1914 - 1929]

The Wilson administration marks both the climax of an era of reform and the end of an era of relative peace. With the entrance of the United States into the First World War the progressive reforms that had seen their beginnings during the Presidency of Theodore Roosevelt came to an end; all else had to be sacrificed to the winning of the war. When the war was over, somehow, somewhere, the reform ardor of the earlier years of the century had abated. For more than a decade the country was in the grip of conservatism.

The outbreak of general war in Europe made a far greater difference to Americans than most of them had foreseen. They were aware of the fact that the United States was full-grown as a nation, but they had not yet realized that the new status meant new responsibilities and new involvements. Wilson himself, when he undertook to defend the rights of a neutral nation, and incidentally the rights of all neutral nations, was not fully aware of the consequences that would follow his actions. The struggle to maintain neutrality was unavailing; the United States was caught up in the war whichever way it turned. By abandoning its neutral rights it would have helped the Central Powers to victory; by asserting them, it presently

ceased to be a neutral, and ended up as a partner of the Allies. There was really no such thing as neutrality for a nation as large and powerful as the United States. Faced by that fact, the nation fought on the side from which it had little to fear, and against the side from which it had much to fear.

Wilson realized more fully than most of his countrymen that the only way to keep the United States out of war was to prevent the outbreak of war anywhere, at least war on a general scale, involving the great powers. His earnest fight for the League of Nations had this as its objective. It is by no means certain that the kind of League Wilson was able to have written into the Treaty of Versailles would have saved world peace, but it was the only comprehensive plan for world cooperation there was, and, looking backward, it is hard to see how giving it a try could have done any harm. The United States killed any chance that the League might prevent war when it refused adherence to the Covenant Wilson had drawn. This verdict at first was shot through with politics, but eventually it came to represent the will of the nation. Weary of war, unwilling to look its destiny in the face, the nation convinced itself that it could be a great power and at the

379

same time enjoy the isolation it had known as a minor power. It turned its back on world leadership, and devoted itself to its own enrichment.

For a time this unrealistic retreat from the world seemed to bear pleasant fruit. American political leaders took the advice of American industrial leaders almost as completely as in the nineteenth century. In consequence, after a brief period of postwar readjustment, the nation — except for the staple farmers and some elements of labor — enjoyed a period of lush prosperity. But before the decade of the twenties ended, it became apparent that the lush times were only the boom period of the old business cycle. With the year 1929 the crisis had come, and following it a depression as deep and dark as the preceding wave of prosperity had been high and handsome.

Although the 1920's was a period of political conservatism and even reaction, it was also one of rapid and far-reaching social changes, powered not by politicians, but rather by a series of fundamental shifts in the nature of American life and the nation's economy, and by the diffusion of many new and influential ideas. By 1920 the United States had become predominantly an urban country, and during the next decade the resulting sharp conflict between its traditional agrarian beliefs and the new urban ideas was clearly evident. Simultaneously, the nation's economy had become dedicated to mass production and thus by necessity to mass consumption, an economic revolution that resulted in profound changes, not only in prevailing economic philosophy but also in many basic social attitudes and folkways. Responding partly to the currents of new thought flooding into the country from Europe, and partially to massive domestic changes, the country's intellectuals were reassaying both their beliefs about the past and their hopes and fears for the future; and their conclusions differed sharply from those of preceding generations. At the same time the nation's creative artists were producing a brilliant series of literary and artistic works which for the first time could be compared favorably with those emanating from the older cultures across the ocean. Far from being either static or sterile, the 1920's in their totality were a decade of rapid and significant change fraught with meaning for the future.

15

THE DEFENSE OF NEUTRALITY

War in Europe · House's "great adventure" · American neutrality ·
Sympathy for the Allies · Propaganda · Economic ties with the Allies · In-
ternational law and the war · Relations with Great Britain and Germany ·
Submarine warfare · The Lusitania · Preparedness · Election of 1916 · Con-
gress declares war · Why America fought · The balance of power

War in Europe

Neither President Wilson nor most of his official family were prepared for the startling news that came to Washington July 28, 1914, from the American ambassador to France, Myron T. Herrick. The "minor Balkan struggle" between Austria and Serbia, Herrick warned, had got out of hand, and a good part of Europe was already mobilizing for a general war. This development was something that Wilson had not anticipated. In taking over the Presidency he obviously had had little expectation of becoming a diplomat. His administration was organized for domestic reform, a policy reflected in his choice of a Secretary of State. He had not so much as mentioned foreign affairs either in his inaugural address or in his first message to Congress. For the majority of Americans the news from abroad was dumfounding. Engrossed in the affairs of their own hemisphere, they had little comprehension of the true state of European national rivalries or of the great system of alliances that

threatened to turn any local quarrel into a general conflict that inevitably would have serious repercussions on the entire world.

The European Alliances

Faced by this frightful prospect, the American public brushed up on its European history. Europe, it appeared, had depended for years on a "balance of power" between two large blocks of contending powers to keep the peace. On the one side were Germany, Austria, and Italy, whose agreements on military cooperation dated back to the days of Bismarck; on the other were Great Britain, France, and Russia, ancient enemies whom the rise of modern Germany had driven together. France and Russia had been allies since 1891, but the entente that bound Great Britain to France dated no further back than 1904, while the agreement between Great Britain and Russia came as late as 1907. Each set of partners made every effort to line up the lesser nations of Europe on its side. Some, like

THE TORCH OF LIBERTY. *Neutrality or war — which would preserve America's freedom?*

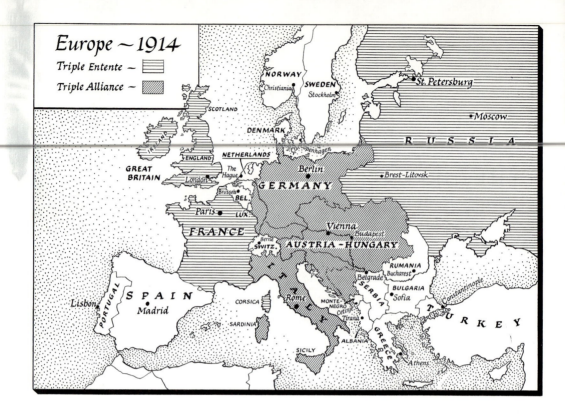

Switzerland, Belgium, the Netherlands, and the Scandinavian countries, maintained a rigid aloofness, but others more or less unofficially chose sides. The Triple Alliance, as the combination led by Germany was generally called, could count with some certainty on the support of Bulgaria and Turkey, while the Triple Entente, led by Great Britain, was on friendly terms with Spain and Portugal, and hoped for support from some of the Balkan nations.

Imperial Rivalry

Imperial rivalry was one of the forces bringing these combinations of powers into conflict all over the world. England, France, and Russia had old established empires to which they had added liberally in the last quarter of the nineteenth century. Germany, too, wanted a "place in the sun," but she had entered the competition too late to obtain the share of spoils to which she felt herself, as a great nation, entitled. She had a few colonies, but they were definitely second-rate. The Triple Entente, she believed, was created only to draw a "ring of iron" about her that would prevent the legitimate fulfillment of her desires. Italy, too, had strong colonial ambitions. Imperial rivalry went further, however, than the mere acquisition of colonies. In the development of backward nations lay an equally inviting field. Rivalry for concessions in China, Persia, Morocco, Turkey, and the Balkans, everywhere that money could be invested and profits taken, was acute, with sometimes one nation ahead and sometimes another.

The Balkans

In no region was the atmosphere more tense than in the Balkans and the Near East. Here, in addition to the ever-present activities of the British and the Germans, the Austrians, the Italians, and the Russians all claimed special interests based on proximity, while the Russian government, as a cloak for its ambition to secure free access to the Mediterranean, essayed the additional role of protector to Greek Orthodox Christians wherever they might be found. In 1908 Austria had annexed Bosnia and Herzegovina, two Serbian provinces handed her for administration in 1878 after the Russo-Turkish War; Russia had protested, but had been compelled to withdraw her objection when warned that an attack upon Austria-Hungary would lead to a war with Germany also. She promised Serbia, however, that she would not yield in such a fashion again. In 1911 Italy had fought a war with Turkey to justify her conquest of Tripoli; and in 1912–1913 two wars had been fought among the little Balkan countries themselves, as a result of which both Turkey and Bulgaria had lost much territory to Greece, Serbia, and Rumania. America did not know it, but for months before the war broke out the Balkan situation had European diplomats all on edge.

Nationalism

Another factor in the situation was the exaggerated nationalism that the nineteenth century had bequeathed to the twentieth. Anthropologists were able to prove conclusively that most European nations, certainly all the great powers, were peopled by mixed populations with no faint title to racial purity, and that nationalism owed more to a common language and history than to race. Each nation prided itself upon its cultural heritage, perverted its history to make its glories seem greater, and aroused the patriotism of its people to the highest possible pitch. It became, therefore, a matter of national pride to draw within the boundaries of any given nation all who spoke its language or shared its culture. France looked forward to the time when Alsace-Lorraine, taken from her by Germany in 1871, should be again a part of France; Italy dreamed of drawing all of Dalmatia within her borders; nearly every Balkan nation claimed a part of every other;

subject nations like the Poles and the Czechs longed to be free. Austria-Hungary, a polyglot of nationalities, was every neighbor's envy.

All this was bad enough, but the dangers of the situation were compounded again and again by the rampant militarism and navalism that affected every European nation. Universal military training had long been a policy of all the great powers of Europe except Great Britain, and most of the lesser ones. Huge standing armies made every nation an armed camp, with preparedness a national watchword. The insular character of the British Isles saved Great Britain from the necessity of keeping pace in land armament with her rivals on the Continent, but she prided herself upon her navy, which she meant to keep overwhelmingly stronger than any other. Germany's challenge to British supremacy on the high seas following the greatly enlarged German naval appropriations of 1898, not only aroused Great Britain to new building, but also led her to abandon her position of "splendid isolation," and to seek allies. On this account she had ended her age-old rivalries with France and Russia, had made an alliance with Japan, and had sought with great earnestness to win the friendship of the United States.

House's "Great Adventure"

In Europe the danger that war might break out at any moment was fully realized by the well-informed, and a few Americans understood the situation. Among them was Colonel House, the intimate adviser of the President, who in the spring of 1914 undertook what he called "the great adventure," a trip to Europe to promote the reduction of land and naval armament. House visited the Kaiser and talked with him for half an hour, established close connections with Sir Edward Grey and others in England, and had a try at Paris only to be frustrated there by the customary cabinet crisis. Every-

Colonel Edward M. House. *A non-military Texas colonel and a shrewd politician, Colonel House was Wilson's close adviser at home and frequent representative abroad.*

where he found "militarism run stark mad," but the British told him they were ready to talk reduction, and he so reported to the Kaiser. On June 28, 1914, shortly before he sailed for the United States, he learned that the heir to the Austrian throne, the Archduke Franz Ferdinand, and his wife had been assassinated at Sarajevo, in the province of Bosnia, but neither House nor his English hosts appeared to realize that this by no means unusual Balkan incident would lead to war. But war came nevertheless by the time House reached home. His "great adventure" was undertaken too late.

Immediate Causes of the War

The incidents which led actually to the outbreak of war seemed trifling to Americans. The assassination of the Austrian heir-apparent looked like the work of some superpatriotic young Bosnian Serbs who disliked the Archduke's plan for making

the "dual monarchy" of Austria and Hungary into a "triple monarchy" that would extend to the Slavs in the empire a right of participation comparable to that enjoyed by the Austrians and the Magyars. Should such a plan succeed, the creation of a greater Serbia might be long delayed, and it was apparently with this thought in mind that the fatal shots were fired. Naturally the Austrian government took a serious view of the situation, the more so because it claimed, probably with good reason, that the Serbian government had guilty knowledge of the plot and had made no effort to prevent its execution. On the assumption that Serbian officials were in reality responsible for what had happened, the Austrian government decided upon punitive measures against its diminutive neighbor, and on July 5 obtained the German Kaiser's permission to go ahead. On July 23 an Austrian ultimatum was delivered to Serbia, which was purposely made so strong as to prevent complete acceptance, and when the Serbian reply proved "evasive," Austria began to mobilize for war.

The ramifications of the European network of alliances now came quickly into play. Russia, in her role of protector to all Greek-Orthodox nations, professed to fear that Austria's real intention was annexation rather than punishment, and supported Serbia's plea that the affair should be settled by the Hague Tribunal. Some such settlement was also strongly urged by Great Britain, France, and Italy, but Austria remained obdurate, while Germany, although bending every effort to localize the affair, refused to abandon her ally. On July 28, Austria declared war on Serbia, and on the following day Russia began mobilization. At this point the German Kaiser telegraphed frantically to his kinsman, the Tsar, to use his influence for peace, and the Tsar ordered that mobilization should be confined strictly to the Austrian frontier. But the Russian military leaders easily per-

Archduke Franz Ferdinand and Wife. *This photograph was taken only an hour before the assassination, an event that precipitated World War I.*

suaded the Tsar to reverse himself, and on July 30 he gave the command for general mobilization. Thereupon the German government delivered an ultimatum to Russia, requiring the cessation of mobilization within twelve hours. When this demand fell on deaf ears, Germany on August 1 declared war on Russia.

France was the ally of Russia, and Germany now demanded to know in eighteen hours what France intended to do. Bound by her treaty with Russia and ready to have a try at getting back Alsace-Lorraine, France replied that she would consult her own interests. Thereupon, on August 3, Germany declared war upon France and began at once to move troops toward the Belgian frontier. The German plan of campaign was to avoid the heavily fortified Franco-German frontier, demand passage through Belgium, and by speedy action outflank and destroy the French army before the anticipated Russian invasion of eastern Germany could do any vital damage — a plan that failed, for the Belgians resisted valiantly and the French re-formed their lines and eventually stopped the invaders. Because the Belgians resisted, Germany, although bound by treaty to protect Belgian neutrality, declared war on Belgium. Great Britain, meantime, had been debating her obligations to France, which might mean less than aid in time of war, but the attack on Belgium, whose neutrality she, too, was pledged to defend, decided her. On August 4 she declared war on Germany.

American Neutrality

The breath-taking speed with which Europe thus plunged into the abyss of war left Americans aghast. The American course, however, was clear. Neutrality, since the days of George Washington, had become an American tradition. The only exception to the rule had been the War of 1812, an unconfessed blunder that no one expected to see repeated. On August 4 the President issued the first of a series of proclamations of neutrality by means of which the State Department struggled to keep abreast of the rapidly spreading war. Two weeks later he urged the American public to be "neutral in fact as well as in name during these days that are to try men's souls. We must be impartial in thought as well as in action." Wilson's neutral course and the frenzied efforts of the government to bring stranded American tourists back from Europe met with universal approval. This was Europe's war, not America's, and with the help of a sizable army of war correspondents the American public prepared to stand by and watch while the fire burned itself out.

But the composite character of the American population insured from the start that neutrality in thought and deed would be far easier preached than practiced. Practically all Americans were of European descent, and many of them were either immigrants or the children of immigrants. The census of 1910 showed over 13 million persons of foreign birth living in the United States, and another 19 million with one or both parents born abroad. Understandably, many of these people had a double loyalty; they were loyal to the United States, but they were loyal also to the foreign nations from which they had sprung. Some of them, whose family memories ran back to the Central Powers, as Germany and the nations associated with her in the war came to be called, were outspoken in their bias. Joined by a number of Irish-Americans who hated England more than they liked Germany, by a few native Americans who greatly admired German efficiency and industrial skill, and by a handful of professional Anglophobes, they constituted a considerable minority group favorable to German success. Soon the general public was branding German sympathizers of recent foreign origin as "hyphenates," a term rarely, if ever, applied to persons of British descent who ardently hoped for a British victory.

Sympathy for the Allies

For from the very outbreak of the war the bulk of popular sympathy in the United States ran with the Allies, as the nations opposed to Germany and Austria were called, and against the Central Powers. Austria and Germany had issued the first declarations of war; they were apparently the aggressors. Germany was the one nation ostensibly prepared for war. Her violation of her treaty with Belgium, called by one German diplomat a "scrap of paper," was hard to overlook. The ruthless progress of German troops through Belgium and northern France produced a deep feeling of sympathy for the underdogs in the fight. But perhaps even more important in explaining the pro-Allied bias of the American people was their cultural solidarity with the people of the British Empire. A common language and literature, together with many kindred institutions, fostered a community of interest between the Americans and all the other English-speaking peoples. No doubt this sentiment was strongest with the more educated and more articulate Americans, but they were also the more influential. Few of them had escaped courses in English literature, English gov-

War in Europe? *The photograph shows the crowd that gathered in front of the* New York Tribune *office to read the war bulletins, July 31, 1914.*

ernment, and English history, but few of
them had taken comparable courses in the
institutions and literature of Germany and
Austria. It was true, too, that the British
Isles had long traded extensively with the
United States, and that such powerful financial houses as J. P. Morgan and Company had closely integrated connections
with London, and through London with
the rest of the world. In addition, the
obvious friendliness of British foreign policy toward the United States had been
strongly in evidence ever since the Spanish-
American War, and had at last borne fruit.
While German expansion had appeared to
threaten American interests both in the
Caribbean and in the Pacific, British policy
seemed pointed toward a trans-Atlantic
understanding, closely bordering on an alliance.

HERRICK

PAGE

American Leaders on the War

American sympathy for Great Britain
was particularly strong in high places.
Theodore Roosevelt, for example, when
arguing in 1911 against Taft's over-eager-
ness to promote the signing of all-inclusive
arbitration treaties, wrote significantly that
he was opposed to signing a compulsory
treaty of arbitration with any country except Great Britain. Throughout the war
he was a devoted partisan of the Allies.
Even President Wilson, despite his desire to
keep the United States neutral, shared the
dominantly pro-British sentiment. This attitude might have owed something to his
ancestry, which was Scottish and Scotch-
Irish, but certainly as a scholar he had acquired a deep interest in English history,
and had written in praise of the English
parliamentary system. In January, 1915,
just five months after the war began, he
told his secretary, "England is fighting our
fight." His advisers, with few exceptions,
were similarly pro-Allied in spirit. Not one
favored the German side. Leading the pro-
Allied group in Washington were the in-

GERARD

THREE WARTIME AMBASSADORS. *Upon these
men, Walter Hines Page in London, Myron T.
Herrick in Paris, and James W. Gerard in
Berlin, fell the principal task of representing
the United States to the governments of the
belligerents. All three of them became ardently pro-Ally.*

fluential Colonel House, Secretary of the
Treasury McAdoo, and Robert Lansing,
State Department Counselor, who became
Secretary of State after Bryan's resignation.
Lansing later admitted in his memoirs that,
in the argument over the British blockade,
he had softened his notes to London be-
cause he was sure that eventually the
United States would enter the war on the
side of the Allies. The representatives of
the United States abroad held similar views.
Myron T. Herrick in France, James W.

Gerard in Germany, and Brand Whitlock in Belgium were anything but neutral in spirit. Walter Hines Page in London was so rabidly pro-British that he became less an American ambassador than a British propagandist, despite his official position. Early in the war he expressed his gratitude that he had been born of English "race and blood."

Propaganda

Despite this initial advantage, which in itself almost guaranteed that majority sentiment in the United States would favor the Allies, the Allied governments made every effort to sell their cause to the American public. Sir Gilbert Parker, a Canadian novelist familiar with the United States, headed the American section of the official propaganda institute in London, from which came a free news service, including prepared editorials, for the use of American newspapers, and thousands of pamphlets designed for American distribution. The feat of the British navy in cutting all trans-Atlantic cables connecting the United States with the Central Powers provided an additional aid to Allied propaganda; thereafter most of the war news reached America through London, where it was carefully edited to give it a pro-Allied slant. In addition, the British propagandists showed far more ingenuity than their German counterparts in appealing to American public opinion. Thousands of Americans read and believed the British representations that Germany was the proved aggressor in the war, that the German aim was the conquest of the world, and that German military forces pursued a calculated policy of *Schrecklichkeit*, or terror, toward noncombatants. The destruction of the Belgian library at Louvain, the shooting of the English nurse, Edith Cavell, as a spy, and the British report on atrocities in Belgium were all presented to Americans as proof of German barbarism.

German efforts at propaganda in the United States, in comparison with the British, were ineffective indeed. Actually the German views got through in spite of British censorship, and were quite generally published in the American German language press, from which the English language papers were free to copy at will. But the American public, in general, was not interested in the German side of the argument. The German campaign, headed at first by the American poet, George Sylvester Viereck, and promoted by the German embassy in Washington, was eventually given up because of its acknowledged failure. German agents then sought, perhaps as a kind of substitute for propaganda, to hamper American trade with the Allies by sabotaging American industrial plants and trading facilities. As early as January, 1915, they destroyed a railroad bridge in Maine, over which artillery sold to Canada was to be moved. Following this "outrage" came a series of explosions on ships moving out of American harbors for British ports, and in American factories engaged in the production of military goods for the Allies. A German attempt to blow up the Welland Canal was unsuccessful. Unfortunately for the German operations, the identity of the foreign agents engaged in these plots became known; among those implicated were the Austrian ambassador, Constantin Dumba, and several attachés of the German embassy in Washington, all of whom were ordered to leave the country. Not only did the German efforts at sabotage fail to stop American shipments to the Allies, but they also tended inevitably to strengthen anti-German feeling among the American people.

Economic Ties with the Allies

The thriving war trade between the United States and the Allies, which the German saboteurs were trying unsuccess-

Dr. Constantin Dumba. *Wilson sent the Austrian ambassador home when it was discovered that Dumba was trying to interfere with production in American munitions plants.*

fully to reduce, was in itself an extremely important factor in the conditioning of American public opinion. Just before the outbreak of war the American economy seemed to be slipping rapidly into depression; during the year 1914 some 16,000 American business firms went bankrupt, and unemployment mounted steadily. But Allied purchases in the United States, which began immediately after the war broke out, reversed this trend in a matter of months. American exports to the Allied nations increased from $824 million in 1914 to $2 billion in 1915, and to $3.2 billion in 1916. At first this trade was mainly in foodstuffs and other civilian goods, but after a British disaster on the western front in 1915 due to the shortage of shells, orders for military supplies began to pour in upon American factories. For the most part American producers were unprepared to supply the Allies with heavy military equipment, but they could, and did, ship abroad great quantities of ammunition and explosives. "The Allies," according to Viscount Grey, who as Sir Edward Grey had been the British foreign minister, "became depend-

ent for an adequate supply on the United States." At the same time, because of British control of the seas, Germany's trade with the United States virtually vanished. American exports to the Central Powers diminished from $169 million in 1914 to $11 million in 1915, and only a little over $1 million in 1916.

A few Americans from the very start of the war questioned the wisdom, and even the legality, of selling military supplies to any of the belligerents. To carry on trade in war goods, the argument ran, would be unneutral, for with the British navy on guard to prevent similar trade with the Central Powers the United States could not sell equally to both sides. In keeping with this view, Senator Hitchcock of Nebraska introduced an embargo measure in December, 1914, but even Secretary of State Bryan opposed it, maintaining that to institute such action after war had been declared would be in itself a breach of neutrality. When businessmen, farmers, and workers alike joined in the protest, the Hitchcock proposal was soundly beaten, and the exports of war goods continued, rising from a value of $6 million in 1914 to $467 million in 1916.

Trade with the Allies, the people soon came to realize, was the key to American prosperity; without it the descent toward depression might begin all over again. The *Financial Annalist*, commenting on this trade, voiced the sentiments of most Americans of all classes when it asserted: "We need it for the profits it will bring." Nor did the American public regard trade with the Allies, whether in military or in civilian goods, as unneutral. They agreed rather with Secretary Lansing, who observed that "If one belligerent has by good fortune a superiority in the matter of geographical location or of military or naval power, the rules of neutral conduct cannot be varied so as to favor the less fortunate combatant." No doubt this position was correct both in law and in precedent. It was not the fault of the United States that the British navy could control the seas.

Loans to the Allies

At first the suggestion that American bankers be permitted to lend the Allies the money they needed to buy American goods met with strong official objection. As early as August 10, 1914, J. P. Morgan and Company, later selected as the purchasing agent of the Allies in the United States, inquired about the attitude of the American government toward such loans. Secretary Bryan, declaring that "money is the worst of all contraband because it commands everything else," vehemently opposed any loans to warring powers. "In the judgment of this government," he wrote, "loans by American bankers to any foreign nation which is at war are inconsistent with the true spirit of neutrality." And for a time this ruling held.

But, as the bankers had foreseen, it was not long before the Allied nations began to run short of international exchange with which to balance their accounts. Within a few months the administration was willing to facilitate continuation of the trade by permitting American bankers to advance needed credits. But this was not enough. By the fall of 1915, with trans-Atlantic shipments now reaching staggering proportions, it was apparent that both Great Britain and France would either have to float huge American loans, or else curtail their purchases in the United States. In consequence, the New York financial houses, backed strongly by such important officeholders as Secretaries McAdoo and Lansing, as well as by a growing public opinion, brought pressure to bear upon the American government to change its attitude, and to permit the loans necessary for the continuation of trade with the Allies. Unquestionably the swing in American sentiment toward the Allies, following the sinking of the *Lusitania* in May, 1915, was of great importance in bringing about a revision in the American policy on loans. By September, 1915, the administration let it become known in financial circles that the government would no longer oppose loans to the Allies. Shortly thereafter the first loan was made, to the amount of $500 million, a large part of it taken by corporations engaged in producing for the Allies. Later Allied loans were floated by popular subscription; by April, 1917, Great Britain, France, and Russia together had borrowed $2.3 billion from American investors, of which the larger part went to pay for Allied purchases in the United States, and consequently never left American shores. Cut off by the British navy from purchasing in the United States, Germany had small need of American exchange. By 1917 the total German loan from American investors was a paltry $27 million.

Many years later, in 1934, the so-called Nye Committee of the United States Senate investigated the connection between the international bankers and American entrance into the war. The investigation produced evidence to show that the New York financial community was heavily committed to Allied victory. "The meaning of Allied success is plainly shown by the action of the stock market," ran one wartime editorial in a financial journal. "From now on there can be no doubt that the collective American mind will interpret anything that points to defeat of Germany as favorable to American business." Undoubtedly this Wall Street position had its influence among businessmen, a portion of the press, and perhaps a few high American officials. But the assumption that Wall Street was mainly responsible for changing the administration's mind, and thus shoving the nation toward war, cannot be supported by existing evidence. Wilson's whole career indicated that he had little respect for the opinions of the New York bankers on any subject. As President he had fought them repeatedly. If anything, after the loans were made, Wilson became more rather than less neutral in his attitude toward the European struggle, a position he did not change until after the resumption of unrestricted submarine warfare by Germany in January, 1917.

Whatever the government's attitude, the close trading and financial connections between the Allies and the United States were of vast and continuing importance, both abroad and at home. Allied victory, perhaps even Allied continuation in the war, came more and more to depend upon the steady stream of military and civilian goods across the Atlantic. This situation greatly strengthened the argument of the German militarists in favor of the unrestricted use of German submarines along the sea lanes. Also, it tied the sympathies of the business interests in the United States, and everyone they could influence, irrevocably to the Allied cause. By 1916 many American firms had invested far too heavily in the Allied cause to permit of retreat. Speaking after the war for the House of Morgan, Thomas

W. Lamont declared: "Our firm had never for one moment been neutral; we didn't know how to be. From the very start we did everything we could to contribute to the cause of the Allies."

For most Americans, however, sympathy with the Allies was one thing, and the involvement of the United States in the war was quite another. Americans were ready to reap a golden harvest by selling goods to whatever foreign buyers could afford them, but they had no notion of surrendering American neutrality, and they relied confidently on the rules of international law to protect them in their lucrative wartime trade.

International Law and the War

International law was at least as old as Hugo Grotius, whose book, *De Jure Belli ac Pacis*, was published in 1625. Its rules had nothing more behind them than custom and the common consent of sovereign states. There was a law of peace that was rarely broken, and a law of war that was rarely kept. Invariably in time of war disputes broke out as to what the law really was, and how it should be construed. The rights of neutrals were particularly subject to debate. In general, Great Britain, who expected always to control the seas, was inclined to interpret neutral rights as narrowly as possible, whereas the United States, whose policy was permanent neutrality, and most other nations whose navies were inferior to the British, exaggerated the privileges of neutrals all they could. Attempts to obtain agreement on the meaning of the rules or to amend them met with no success. Neither the code of land warfare adopted by the Second Hague Conference, nor the Declaration of London with respect to naval warfare, was fully ratified. Promptly on the outbreak of the war Wilson asked the belligerents to adhere to the Declaration of London, and the Central Powers agreed to do so if the Allies would bind themselves similarly. But the British feared the limitations on sea power contained in the new rules and refused to accept them. The United States, therefore, in defending its neutrality had nothing better to depend on than the jumbled mass of precedents and opinions that had accumulated since the time of Grotius. Many of these rules were utterly unrelated to the conditions of modern warfare, but obsolete as they were, they were the only rules that existed.

It was immediately apparent that the British had no notion of allowing the vast amount of American goods and shipping that soon took to the seas to fall into the hands of their enemies. This trade represented not merely, or mostly, the ordinary exports of the United States to Europe, but rather millions of dollars' worth of goods shipped purely in response to the wartime needs of the belligerents. The products of American farms and factories were earnestly coveted by both sides, and the United States was eager to sell. All this was entirely satisfactory to the British, with the single important exception that they were determined to prevent anything of value from reaching the Central Powers. To accomplish their purpose the British had only to use their naval strength, but, unlike the Germans, they did what they could to reconcile wartime necessities with the existing rules of international law. For authority in dealing with neutral trade, they invoked three well-recognized belligerent rights: (1) the stoppage of trade in contraband goods, (2) the doctrine of continuous voyages, and (3) the blockade.

Relations with Great Britain

In each instance, however, British policy trod heavily on neutral toes. The British definition of contraband — that is, goods that might be of direct (absolute contraband) or indirect (conditional contraband) use to the enemy — was so generous as to include every commodity that the Central Powers might wish to import. This, the American State Department claimed, was going too far. Further, British ships inspected trade between the United States and such neutrals as bordered on Germany, or on any of her partners, to make sure that none of it was ultimately intended for the enemy. If that was deemed to be the case, the trip was regarded as one continuous voyage which might be interrupted anywhere in its progress. This, too, was protested, although in the American Civil War the United States had done practically the same thing to prevent British commodities from reaching the South. Finally, a Ministry of Blockade was set up, which took good care that all shipping found anywhere on the high seas was carefully scrutinized to prevent the Central Powers obtaining anything that the British did not wish them to have. Such a blockade, the United States maintained, was illegal. It was enforced at long distance; it was applied against neutral as well as against belligerent coasts; and it was unenforceable against the countries that bordered on the Baltic Sea, because there the German navy, not the British, was supreme. But the British, while admitting that their methods might be somewhat unusual, argued that they were living up to the spirit, if not the letter, of the law.

The list of protests lodged by the United States against Great Britain included also vigorous denunciations of the British practice of taking neutral ships to Allied ports to be searched. The old rules contemplated search on the high seas, but with modern shipping such a practice was difficult, and after submarine warfare began, extremely dangerous. Sometimes American ships were held up for months at Allied ports. The British practice of searching American mail, both to and from Europe, also drew criticism. The British held that American mail pouches, even when consigned to neutral

Europe, 1916. *In this grim* Masses *cartoon (October, 1916), Boardman Robinson drew the "European ass moving toward a precipice, astride his back the dark hooded figure of Death holding the carrot of Victory before his nose."*

countries, often contained things of value intended for the enemy, and they proposed also to know what information was going into and coming out of Germany. Exports from the Central Powers were given as scant courtesy as imports, and for long periods American industry was shut off from supplies obtainable only from Germany, such as dyestuffs, drugs, and sugar-beet seed.

The American State Department, probably with the original intent of collecting damages after the war, fully and conscientiously stated its case against British violations of American neutrality. As early as September 26, 1914, Washington protested against a British proposal to lengthen the contraband list. Action "so prejudicial to neutral rights," the American note warned, might provoke "bitter feeling" between the two nations. The State Department also registered its objections to each extension of the unneutral practices connected with the British blockade. But somehow the American arguments, although usually based on good historical precedent, were too mildly stated to produce results. Obviously, neither Wilson nor Lansing wished to embarrass the British government unduly, and they even toned down some of their protests with this thought in mind. If the United States had threatened an embargo on exports to the British Isles, or had proposed to convoy across the Atlantic goods intended for the Central Powers, the British might have taken more seriously the American representations. What happened instead was that American shippers learned to avoid trouble by conforming to the British rules. And, since Allied needs were sufficient to absorb all the surplus commodities the United States could produce, there were few seizures of American goods, especially from 1915 on. Such shipments

A GERMAN SUBMARINE. This is the type of submarine used by Germany in World War I.

A SUBMARINE VICTIM. Sinking of the *Illinois*, an army tanker, March 18, 1917. Photograph taken by the submarine that did the sinking.

as were interrupted were almost wholly owned by foreigners before they left American shores. It was evident that the American government had decided that saving the traditional concepts of American neutrality was not worth the threat of a German victory.

The close community of interests between the United States and the Allies was an object of great concern to the Germans, whose economy was seriously hurt by their inability to trade with America. The German Foreign Office was frantic with rage, and lodged frequent and vehement protests with the State Department, all to no avail. It also gave encouragement to the German agents who were seeking to sabotage such American industries as were aiding the Allies. German sympathizers in the United States were similarly disturbed at American acquiescence in the British trade regulations, among them Senator William J. Stone of Missouri, chairman of the Senate Committee on Foreign Relations. Stone was one of those who favored an embargo on the shipment of military supplies, particularly ammunition, outside the national borders, but he could not budge the State Department from its insistence that trade of this kind was not a violation of neutrality.

Submarine Warfare

Germany's most effective means of retaliation against the pressure of Allied sea power proved to be the submarine, a type of craft her engineers had brought to extraordinary efficiency. On February 4,

1915, in protest against the British stoppage of food shipments to Germany, the German government drew a "war zone" about the British Isles, and announced its intention to sink on sight every enemy merchantman within the area. The United States was warned to keep American shipping out of the danger zone lest by mistake American ships and lives might be lost. Against this new type of warfare the American government lodged an immediate protest. Its illegality was obvious even to the German government, which defended it only on the ground of retaliation for allegedly illegal actions by the Allies, and the willingness of neutrals to acquiesce in them. The war-zone decree could not be defended as a blockade, for a blockade, to be binding on neutral nations, must effectively stop a major part of the shipping plying to and from the blockaded ports, whereas German submarines could not hope to intercept more than an occasional ship. Visit and search by a submarine to ascertain the character of the ship and the nature of its cargo would be a virtual impossibility. Sinking on sight defied all the rules that required the attacking warship to provide for the safety of noncombatant passengers and crews. Reciting the evidence as to the illegality of the war-zone decree, Wilson's note of protest declared that the United States was "reluctant to believe" that the warfare contemplated would ever be carried into effect, and warned that in case American ships or lives were lost the German government would be held to a "strict accountability."

The *Lusitania*

The threat to American neutrality posed by the submarine blockade led Wilson to dispatch Colonel House to Europe on a "quest for peace." House cherished the chimerical hope that he might persuade the British to give up their blockade and the Germans their submarine attacks on

merchantmen — the very weapons by which the two leading contenders hoped to win the war. Naturally his "quest" was

OCEAN STEAMSHIPS.

CUNARD

EUROPE VIA LIVERPOOL
LUSITANIA

Fastest and Largest Steamer now in Atlantic Service Sails
SATURDAY, MAY 1, 10 A. M.
Transylvania, Fri., May 7, 5 P.M.
Orduna, - - Tues., May 18, 10 A.M.
Tuscania, - - Fri., May 21, 5 P.M.
LUSITANIA, Sat., May 29, 10 A.M.
Transylvania, Fri., June 4, 5 P.M.

Gibraltar—Genoa—Naples—Piraeus
S.S. Carpathia, Thur., May 13, Noon

ROUND THE WORLD TOURS
Through bookings to all principal Ports
of the World.
Company's Office. 21-24 State St., N. Y.

NOTICE!

TRAVELLERS intending to embark on the Atlantic voyage are reminded that a state of war exists between Germany and her allies and Great Britain and her allies; that the zone of war includes the waters adjacent to the British Isles; that, in accordance with formal notice given by the Imperial German Government, vessels flying the flag of Great Britain, or of any of her allies, are liable to destruction in those waters and that travellers sailing in the war-zone on ships of Great Britain or her allies do so at their own risk.

IMPERIAL GERMAN EMBASSY
WASHINGTON, D. C., APRIL 22, 1915.

The *Lusitania* Warning. *This newspaper notice was widely regarded as a bluff or a hoax, and kept few passengers off the liner. Such a warning had no standing in international law.*

fruitless, and on May 7, 1915, the British passenger liner, *Lusitania*, on which he had sailed to Europe a few weeks before, was torpedoed without warning and sunk off the Irish coast on her way to England. More than 1,100 persons lost their lives, including 128 Americans. The sinking was a perfectly clear violation of neutral rights. Warning had not been given by a shot across the ship's bow, or in any other manner prescribed by sea usage. The fact that an advertisement in a New York paper had warned passengers of what might happen if they sailed on the *Lusitania* proved merely that the act was premeditated; no known rule of international law provided for a newspaper warning, and the advertisement was generally regarded as a hoax. The fact that the *Lusitania* carried ammunition designed for Allied use was equally irrelevant. The Germans had a perfect right to capture and confiscate the ship, even to sink it, but according to the existing rules they must first find out by a search what its cargo contained, and make satisfactory provision for the safety of noncombatants. The failure of the captain to zigzag his ship, as ordered, and to proceed at high speed through the submarine-infested zone, has led some persons to conclude that an unrevealed conspiracy existed to tempt the Germans to sink the *Lusitania*, so that the United States would be drawn into the war. There is no real evidence to support such a contention. The argument, sometimes made, that the *Lusitania* by carrying British military supplies had forfeited her neutral rights and had become in effect a warship also strains the facts considerably.

American opinion on the *Lusitania* disaster was not entirely unanimous. Theodore Roosevelt, the most bitter of the anti-German leaders in the United States, described the attack on the *Lusitania* as an "act of piracy," and demanded immediate war. Many agreed with him, particularly along the Atlantic seaboard where the importance of keeping open the sea lanes to Europe was most keenly felt, but in the West and the South there was a tendency to ask why American citizens needed to venture into the danger zone. Should the American government not prevent such incidents in the future by prohibiting its nationals from sailing on belligerent merchant ships, or on ships carrying munitions? Bryan himself took this attitude, which easterners called "provincial," and he would have been willing even to submit the *Lusitania* incident to arbitration. He signed the first note of protest that Wilson wrote, but the next one was too much for him, and he resigned from the cabinet rather than be party to a policy which in his judgment might easily lead to war. The same sentiment appeared in Congress, where only the vigorous intervention of the President prevented the passage of resolutions, sponsored in the House by McLemore of Texas and in the Senate by Gore of Oklahoma, forbidding American citizens to travel on belligerent merchantmen, except at their own peril.

Germany Backs Down

The *Lusitania* incident led to a diplomatic correspondence between the United States and Germany that lasted all through the summer of 1915. Wilson's statement, made in a public address just before his first note was sent, "There is such a thing as a man being too proud to fight," seemed to betoken an attitude of weakness, but in three successive notes he argued the case with Germany, taking stronger ground each time. The submarine, he held, used as Germany was using it, was an illegal weapon, and any repetition of the *Lusitania* offense would be regarded as a "deliberately unfriendly" act. This was a threat of war, as the German ambassador to the United States, Count von Bernstorff, well knew, but the offense was repeated on August 19,

1915, when the *Arabic* was sunk with the loss of two American lives. Thereupon von Bernstorff, acting on his own initiative, promised the American State Department, in writing, that liners would not be sunk "without warning and without safety to the lives of noncombatants, provided that the liners do not try to escape or offer resistance." Eventually the German government agreed to back up von Bernstorff's words with deeds. Wilson had scored a signal diplomatic triumph, but he had won his victory only by the threat of war. When, either by accident or intent, a few more sinkings occurred, notably the *Sussex*, on March 24, 1916, Wilson in a spectacular appearance before Congress renewed his threat and forced from the German government a reiteration of its promise. The "Sussex pledge," as it was sometimes called, was made on the condition that the United States should also force the Allies to abide by the rules of international law, a condition that Wilson promptly rejected. "Responsibility in such matters, he maintained, "is single, not joint; absolute, not relative." And for nine months, while the Allies carried on as usual, the German government, whether because it feared hostile action by the United States, or because it needed to build more submarines, kept its promise.

Preparedness

In part, at least, to implement his threats, Wilson now put himself at the head of a strong demand for military preparedness that, in spite of much "pacifist" protest, was sweeping the country. On the very day that he dispatched his third *Lusitania* note he authorized the Army and Navy Departments to draft plans for the strengthening of the national defenses, and in his annual message to Congress of December, 1915, he called emphatic attention to these proposals. Early in 1916 he toured the country to speak for preparedness, and on Flag Day, June 14, he led a preparedness parade down

Count Johann-Heinrich von Bernstorff. *As German ambassador to the United States, Count von Bernstorff opposed Germany's unrestricted use of the submarine, and made every effort to prevent his government from bringing the United States into the war.*

Pennsylvania Avenue. Similar demonstrations took place all over the nation. Most famous of them, no doubt, was the San Francisco parade, July 22, 1916, during which a bomb exploded, killing a number of people. Thomas J. Mooney and Warren K. Billings, two radical labor leaders, were indicted for the crime, and were convicted on what was later proved to be perjured testimony. Later, with the rise of Communism in Russia, this episode was to have strong international repercussions, but for the time being it served mainly to reinforce the determination of the preparedness advocates. California courts consistently refused to set aside the verdict by which the accused men had been convicted. While the sentence was commuted from death to life imprisonment, not until 1939 was a governor of the state, Culbert L. Olson, willing to take the political risk of freeing the prisoners.

Wilson's willingness to embrace preparedness was strengthened by the failure of another House mission to Europe, this time in order to offer the Allies a "plan to compel peace." The idea was that Wilson, with Allied foreknowledge, should demand the cessation of hostilities and a conference of the belligerents to discuss peace terms. If the proposals of the Allies — to be agreed upon in consultation with the United States — were not accepted by Germany, then the United States would "probably" join the Allied war effort. Wilson's use of the word "probably," as an afterthought, no doubt wrecked the plan, and the war went on. It was Wilson's fear that if the war should continue the United States would be drawn into it that had led him to accept House's scheme in the first place; now with the failure of the plan the President was even more fearful of war and determined to be ready for it.

The battle of Jutland, fought May 31–June 1, 1916, gave Americans a rude jolt. In that engagement the German High-Seas Fleet boldly challenged the British Grand Fleet in the North Sea and inflicted such serious damage upon it as to serve warning that British command of the seas might soon be threatened. Already the *Chicago Tribune*, persistent champion of a foreign policy based on national self-interest, had warned its readers of the dire consequences to the United States in case the British fleet should be destroyed. "British naval supremacy," it pointed out editorially, "has been the stable factor in world diplomacy for so many years that all but diplomats are inclined to forget it." Americans were reminded that the Monroe Doctrine had been "largely built upon it" and that even the Oriental policies of the United States "had to look to it for sanction." If the British fleet were annihilated, every item of American foreign policy "would have to be scrutinized in the light of unknown conditions," and the nation's future might be gravely imperiled. To forestall such a calamity, many Americans, including apparently some of the makers of *Tribune* policy, were ready to form a definite alliance with Great Britain and enter the war.

Opposition to preparedness in Congress now lost ground steadily, for even those who were unwilling to concede that the British navy was the first line of defense for the United States were not unaware of the dangers to America that might flow from German control of the seas. A National Defense Act which authorized the increase of the standing army to 175,000, and the National Guard to 450,000, became

Preparedness Parade. *Wilson was a slow convert to preparedness, but early in 1916 he toured the country to advocate, along with other defense measures, that the United States should build "incomparably the greatest navy in the world." He is shown here, with other dignitaries, leading a preparedness parade in New York City.*

Launching the USS *Nevada*. *This photograph shows the hull of the battleship just after it left the ways, July 11, 1914. Its building thus preceded the preparedness drive that Wilson opened. The American navy was proportionately stronger in capital ships than in auxiliary craft.*

law early in June. Even more important was the Naval Appropriation Act, passed two months later, which provided for the immediate construction of four dreadnoughts and four battle cruisers. The total appropriation carried in this measure ran to $313 million, the largest sum Congress had ever voted at any one time for naval purposes. Three capital ships, the *Nevada*, the *Oklahoma*, and the *Pennsylvania*, had just been completed. As two further means of promoting the national defense, Congress created (1) a Council of National Defense, to consist of six cabinet officers and seven unpaid civilian experts, and (2) a United States Shipping Board, which might build, or otherwise acquire, and operate a fleet of merchantmen. The nation was preparing for war as it had never prepared for war before.

Election of 1916

The campaign and election of 1916 occurred during the months immediately following Wilson's diplomatic victory over Germany. That he would be a candidate to succeed himself in spite of the fact that the platform on which he was elected opposed a second term was universally taken for granted. Wilson was the leader of his party. Even the defection of Bryan gave the President no cause for alarm, for by the time Bryan quit the cabinet Wilson had wholly eclipsed him. The congressional

elections of 1914 had found most of the Progressives back in the Republican fold, but the Democrats emerged triumphant in a straight-out two-party contest. The reason for this, everyone knew, was Woodrow Wilson. When the Democratic convention met in St. Louis on June 14, it had nothing to do but to renominate both Wilson and his running-mate of four years before, Thomas R. Marshall of Indiana, by acclamation, and to record in its platform complete approval of every action the administration had taken.

In a shrewd effort to unite all forces opposed to Wilson, the Republicans turned for their candidate to Associate Justice Charles Evans Hughes of the United States Supreme Court. With the discretion permitted to justices, Hughes had not openly taken sides for or against Germany, for or against intervention in Mexico, for or against preparedness. Nor had he been involved in any way in the disastrous split of four years before. His background as governor of New York was satisfying to the Progressive wing of the party, and his decisions as associate justice had caused the conservatives no alarm. Hughes's availability was so obvious that the Republicans, meeting at Chicago, June 7, named him on the first ballot, although he had done nothing to advance his candidacy and had not even said that he would accept the nomination. For Vice-President they chose Charles W. Fair-

Charles Evans Hughes. *The Republican nomination came to Hughes in 1916 without solicitation, a rarity in American politics. Hughes resigned as Associate Justice of the Supreme Court to make the race. Before his appointment to the Court he was a reform governor of New York, and after the war he served first as Secretary of State, then as Chief Justice. The photograph is dated June 12, 1916.*

banks, who had held the office under Theodore Roosevelt. All fell out as planned. Roosevelt, by declining a Progressive nomination and supporting Hughes, dealt a deathblow to the party he had founded. Pro-Germans who thought Wilson had been unfair to Germany, anti-Germans who condemned his soft treatment of wanton aggressors, pacifists who were for peace at any price, war advocates who demanded, sometimes in the same breath, intervention in both Mexico and Europe, all rallied to the Republican standard. The day Hughes resigned from the Supreme Court to accept the proffered nomination he might have been elected, for then all factions could have claimed him as their own.

As the campaign progressed, the President's chances improved. His followers proclaimed truthfully that he had "kept us out of war," forgetting, perhaps, that he had a threat out that might draw the nation in. Many Progressives who had supported Roosevelt in 1912 were ready to change their allegiance to Wilson, for under his dynamic leadership a spectacular and comprehensive program of domestic reform had been achieved. Wilson got the "breaks" of the campaign. When a "hyphenated American," Jeremiah A. O'Leary, whose object was to induce Irish-Americans and German-Americans to vote the Republican ticket, sent a long telegram to Wilson denouncing him for unfairness to Germany, the President's reply was tart: "I would feel deeply mortified to have you or anybody like you vote for me. Since you have access to many disloyal Americans and I have not, I will ask you to convey this message to them."

The Adamson Act

Hughes, on the other hand, was obliged to conduct a campaign of carping criticism, while not being free to take sides on anything. He had only one stroke of luck. The four great railway brotherhoods chose the Labor Day immediately preceding the election as a desirable time to strike for recognition of the basic eight-hour day and time and a half for overtime. Such a strike in an age when there was virtually no such thing as transportation by truck would have throttled business and seriously hampered the President's efforts to speed up preparedness. Faced by this emergency, Wilson asked Congress to prevent the strike by enacting into law the demands of the brotherhoods. Congress obeyed with the passage of the Adamson Act, which became a law on September 1. Here Hughes had ample ground for criticism, and he made the most of it, but when asked if he would favor repealing the law, he could only reply, "You can't repeal a surrender."

Wilson's Narrow Victory

The night of election day it appeared certain that Hughes had won. He had carried the East almost solidly, including the state of New York. He had carried also every state in the old Northwest except Ohio. But the returns from the South and the farther West told a different story. The solid South was conceded to the Democrats, but nothing of the kind was expected from such dependable Republican centers as Kansas and California. Nevertheless Wilson carried every state west of the Mississippi except Minnesota, Iowa, South Dakota, and Oregon, each of which he lost by a slender margin. In the electoral college the vote stood 277 to 254, the closest division since 1876, but the popular vote gave Wilson a lead of 9,129,606 to 8,538,221. Again the Democrats captured both houses of Congress. Significantly the protest vote of nearly a million that had been cast for Eugene V. Debs, the Socialist candidate in 1912, dropped to 585,113 for Allan Benson, in 1916.

Wilson's Bid for Peace

Deeply impressed by the popularity of the slogan, "He kept us out of war," Wilson made another attempt shortly after the election to bring the war to an end. In a note released December 20, 1916, he asked the fighting powers for "an avowal of their respective views" as to terms upon which the war might be concluded. Both sides, he observed, claimed to be fighting for "virtually the same" things, the rights of small nations and security for themselves. Perhaps if they would state their war aims more precisely, the differences between them would not be too great to bridge. Anticipating Wilson's offer, and with the military situation running strongly in their favor, the German authorities had already let it be known on December 12 that they were willing to enter a peace conference. They thus made Wilson's call for a statement of war aims appear to be a reinforcement of their offer. The Allies indignantly rejected the idea of treating with a victorious Germany, but, although deeply offended that Wilson should have made a move for peace at a time when Germany was winning, they replied at length to his inquiry. Peace, they said, must carry with it the restitution of conquered territories, full reparations for damages done, and guarantees that nothing of the kind would happen again. The Germans, however, refused to state specific aims, reserving for themselves full freedom of action at the council table.

Reading these replies, it seemed to Wilson that there could be no hope of a lasting peace if either side were permitted to have its way. On January 22, 1917, in an address before the Senate he began to argue the case for a "peace without victory," hoping that eventually the warring nations would heed the wisdom of his words. Such a peace as the victor might impose upon the vanquished, he said, "would be accepted in humiliation, under duress, at an intolerable sacrifice, and would leave a sting, a resentment, a bitter memory upon which terms of peace would rest, not permanently, but only as upon quicksand. Only a peace between equals can last." He even outlined the terms of what he thought would constitute a just peace: equality of rights for small and great nations; universal recognition of the principle that governments derive their just powers from the consent of the governed; the right of every great people to have an outlet to the sea; the freedom of the seas "in law and in fact"; the limitation of armaments; and the avoidance by all nations of entangling alliances. Already he had made known his belief that there must be a league to enforce peace, and he told the Senate that if such a peace as he had outlined could be made the United States must do its part to maintain it.

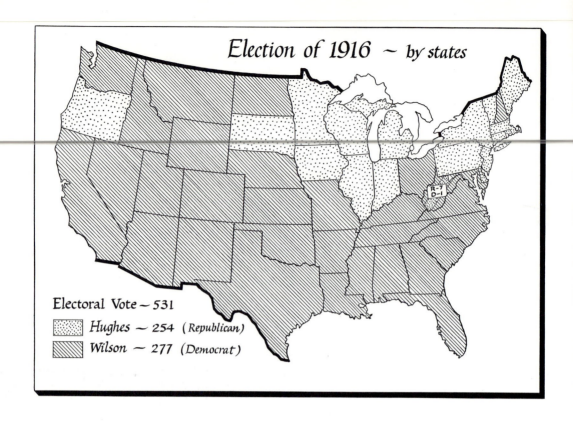

Election of 1916 ~ by states

R—7
D—1

Electoral Vote ~ 531

Hughes ~ 254 (Republican)

Wilson ~ 277 (Democrat)

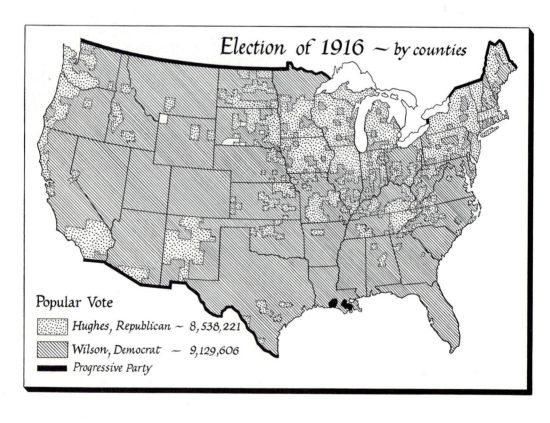

Election of 1916 ~ by counties

Popular Vote

Hughes, Republican ~ 8,538,221

Wilson, Democrat ~ 9,129,606

Progressive Party

The Submarine Again

These were brave words, but before they were spoken the German government had already decided upon the policy which was to rob them of their effect. Convinced by the German admiralty that unrestricted submarine warfare would speedily destroy enough shipping to isolate Great Britain and force her to sue for peace, the German government announced on January 31, 1917, that its submarines would sink on sight all ships found within specified war zones, whether neutral or belligerent. Its promise to the United States not to sink without warning and without making provision for the safety of noncombatants it withdrew on the ground that the United States had failed to stop the illegal practices of the Allies. Wilson had no choice now but to break off diplomatic relations with Germany, and this he promptly did.

For a time it seemed that the President was seeking a formula short of outright war to resolve the situation. Harking back to the undeclared naval war between France and the United States in 1798, he spoke of "armed neutrality," and asked Congress to grant him authority to provide American merchantmen with guns for their defense. A "little group of willful men," as the President called them, filibustered this measure to death, but the needed authority was found in an unrepealed law of 1797, and the merchantmen were armed. It was clear that if either the United States or Germany struck a blow there would be war. Wilson professed to believe that the Germans would never carry out their threats, but when, on March 18, German submarines sank three ships with loss of American lives war became inevitable.

Why America Fought

Despite the prominence of the submarine issue, many factors worked together to draw the United States into the war. Undoubt-edly the diplomatic impasse over submarine warfare did in fact precipitate hostilities, and he who says that the United States would have entered the war even if illegal sinkings had not been resumed says far more than he can prove. But undoubtedly other considerations also influenced the American people, among them the deep sympathy most Americans felt for the Allied cause, reinforced as it was by British propaganda, and by the strong economic ties that bound the United States to the Allies. How closely the American economy was geared to Allied trade became apparent when the German submarine threat of January, 1917, brought about a sudden stoppage of shipments from Atlantic ports. Thoroughly frightened by the German sinkings, neutral shipping refused to put to sea. Belligerent merchantmen continued to come and go, but they were utterly unable to handle the traffic that cluttered the docks and warehouses of the eastern seaboard, and tied up the railroads with unloaded freight as far west as Pittsburgh. Out of the transportation snarl a food and fuel shortage developed in some metropolitan areas; from the lower East Side in New York City, quite in the best revolutionary tradition, there was a march of angry women on the City Hall demanding food. Without American shipping to move American goods overseas, the United States faced a severe economic reverse. And Great Britain faced the loss of the war.

In the spring of 1917 the Germans seemed to have victory within their grasp. German offensives, particularly in the East, had been overwhelmingly successful; Allied offensives were invariably followed by "strategic retreats." Nearly all of Belgium and a large share of northern France lay in German hands. The Russians had lost most of Poland, while Rumania was no sooner in the war on the Allied side than her army was defeated and her territory occupied. Much of Serbia had long since been overrun. With Austria, Bulgaria, and Turkey completely subservient to the German will, the long-dreamed-of *Mitteleuropa* had become a fact. Germany had lost her colonies, and she was beginning to suffer from the Allied blockade, but with the assistance of the submarine she had good reason to believe that her road to victory was clear. From its inception unrestricted submarine warfare took a terrific toll. For weeks one ship out of every four that left British ports failed to return. Neutral shipping tended more and more to stay out of the war zone. Even if the British navy remained afloat, Great Britain could be starved into submission.

The Balance of Power

Looking backward, it seems apparent that the one outcome of the war completely unacceptable to most Americans was a German victory. No doubt they would have preferred Wilson's "peace without victory" to American intervention in the war, provided that such a peace would have left Great Britain strong, with its navy able to control the Eastern Atlantic. But they feared the consequences of substituting Germany for Great Britain as an Atlantic neighbor. As Elihu Root pointed out, on September 14, 1917, "If we had stayed out of the war, and Germany had won, there would no longer have been a balance of power in Europe, or a British fleet to support the Monroe Doctrine and to protect America." From its infancy the United States had relied upon the balance between the British navy on the one hand and the continental armies of Europe on the other as a sure means of protection for the western hemisphere from European invasion. Always the two forces had checkmated each other. Continental armies could threaten the security of the British Isles if the British navy should be committed too far away from home, while the British navy could make the huge continental

armies ineffective beyond European shores. It was a military truism that a nation with a great navy but a weak army could strike far but not hard, while a nation with a great army but a weak navy could strike hard but not far. But a nation with a great navy *and* a great army could strike both hard and far. If the Allies lost the war, Germany would be such a nation.

Within the American government many officials freely admitted their uneasiness at the thought of a German victory. As early as 1913 Lewis Einstein, in an article sanctioned by the State Department, pointed out that a future shift in the European balance of power would be of great concern to the United States, and that British naval superiority was an essential element in the existing favorable balance. After the outbreak of war both Lansing and House warned Wilson repeatedly that a German victory, by destroying British sea power, would threaten American security. "It is safer and surer and wiser for us to be one of many enemies," Lansing wrote in 1916, "than to be in the future alone against a victorious Germany."

Anglo-American accord had made possible the location of most of the new American navy in the Pacific, as a guarantee against the danger of Japanese aggression. Germany had been long restive under the restraints of the Monroe Doctrine, and had cast jealous eyes upon Latin America as a field for colonial expansion. If Germany drove the British navy from the Atlantic, what would be her next move? As if to provide an answer to this question, intercepted dispatches that the British secret service had turned over to the American government revealed that on March 1, 1917, the German Foreign Minister, Alfred Zimmermann, had offered Mexico an alliance on the following terms:

That we shall make war together and together make peace. We shall give generous financial support, and it is understood that Mexico is to reconquer the lost territory in New Mexico, Texas, and Arizona.

Further, the President of Mexico was to urge Japan to shift from the Allies to the Central Powers, presumably in return for what spoils Japan might desire at the expense of the United States. After the news of the "Zimmermann plot" reached the public, an American declaration of war on Germany was almost a certainty.

Wilson Asks for War

Wilson called Congress into special session for April 2, and on the evening of that day read his call to arms. Everything else had been tried, he claimed, and now the only recourse was war. The President disclaimed any desire to fight against the German people, and distinguished between them and their government. That govern-

ment, however, had challenged the security of democracy throughout the world. The United States was glad to fight it, he said,

for the ultimate peace of the world and for the liberation of its people, the German peoples included: for the rights of nations great and small and the privilege of men everywhere to choose their way of life and of obedience. The world must be made safe for democracy. Its peace must be planted upon the tested foundations of political liberty.

The response of Congress to the President's eloquent appeal was not unanimous, but it was overwhelming enough to be convincing. On April 4 the Senate passed the war resolution by a vote of 82 to 6, and on April 6 the House concurred by a vote of 373 to 50. Diplomatic relations with Austria-Hungary were promptly broken, but war was not declared until December

Wilson's War Message. *By delivering in person his messages to Congress, Wilson broke a long precedent. His war message not only recounted the events of German warfare against neutral commerce, but it charged also that the German government had become the enemy of liberty. Autocracies must go. "The world must be made safe for democracy."*

7. Against Germany's other allies, Turkey and Bulgaria, the United States issued no declarations of war. Claiming that the war against Germany was being fought on behalf of neutral rights generally, the United States urged other neutrals also to join in the crusade. As a result Cuba, Panama, Siam, Liberia, China, and Brazil entered the war on the Allied side, and several other nations broke off diplomatic relations with the Central Powers. Long before, Japan and Portugal had joined the Allies in order to fulfill their treaties with Great Britain, while Italy by generous promises and Greece by threats had also been brought into the Allied camp. Thus the war became in fact as well as in name a World War.

The "War to End War"

President Wilson was an idealist who rarely talked or thought about foreign affairs in terms of "power politics." To have done so would have been inconsistent with his character and ethical outlook, although his actions, as for example in his Caribbean policy, were not always in harmony with his words. His argument that "we entered the war as the disinterested champions of right" was a rationalization.

More probably the United States entered the war because so many Americans felt that continued neutrality would imperil the future security of the nation. But Wilson's high principles had a strong appeal for the masses. He touched a magic chord when he said, "The world must be made safe for democracy." With Russia in the throes of a democratic revolution, a fair case could be made for the assertion that the war was a conflict between autocracies and democracies. As long as autocratic rulers were free to build up military machines and to declare war at will, the less militant democracies of the world were at a serious disadvantage. While autocracy was enthroned among any of the great nations, there could be little reason to hope for a just and lasting peace. In line with this argument, the war became in Wilson's mind and words not only a war to make the world safe for democracy, but also a "war to end war." With these emotional overtones ringing in their ears, the American people went to war in a mood of the highest idealism. They fought — or at least great numbers of them so believed — for the survival of democracy and for peace on earth.

BIBLIOGRAPHY

An excellent introduction is provided in a brief essay by D. M. Smith, *The Great Departure: The United States and World War I, 1914–1920* (1965). A short reinterpretation of the origins of the war is Laurence Lafore, *The Long Fuse* (1965). The leading works on the background of the European conflict are S. B. Fay, *The Origins of the World War* (2 vols., 2nd ed., 1930); and B. E. Schmitt, *The Coming of the War, 1914* (2 vols., 1930). While Fay and Schmitt do not agree completely, both contend that some blame should go to each side. H. E. Barnes, *The Genesis of the World War* (3rd ed., 1929), a pioneer "revisionist" book, puts most of the blame on France and Russia. The literature on the war itself is immense, and continues to grow. Dependable overall surveys are B. H. Liddell Hart, *The Real War, 1914–1918* (1930); and Cyril Falls, *The Great War* (1959). A study which depicts in vivid detail the horror of the war's opening weeks is B. W. Tuchman, *The Guns of August* (1962). A close analysis based upon multi-archival research is Marion Siney, *The Allied Blockade of Germany, 1914–1916* (1957). An exciting episode is related by

B. W. Tuchman, *The Zimmermann Telegram* (1958).

E. R. May, *The World War and American Isolation, 1914–1917* (1959), is a superb reinterpretation, based upon European as well as American sources; it is generally pro-Wilson in its conclusions. A. S. Link, *Wilson the Diplomatist* (1957), is a stimulating series of lectures by the leading Wilson scholar of our time. Interesting discussions of Wilson's diplomacy may be found in Harley Notter, *The Origins of the Foreign Policy of Woodrow Wilson* (1937); and E. H. Buehrig, *Woodrow Wilson and the Balance of Power* (1955). Collections of varying interpretations include *America's Entry into World War I* (1964), edited by H. J. Bass; *Intervention, 1917* (1966), edited by W. I. Cohen; and *American Intervention, 1917* (1966), edited by D. M. Smith.

Charles Seymour defended the Wilson position on neutrality and intervention in *American Diplomacy during the World War* (1934), and *American Neutrality, 1914–1917* (1935). The same is true of the scholarly legal study by A. M. Morrissey, *The American Defense of Neutral Rights, 1914–1917* (1939). Seymour and Miss Morrissey emphasize the German submarine as the decisive factor in bringing about American intervention. Edwin Borchard and W. P. Lage, *Neutrality for the United States* (2nd ed., 1940), one of the many books designed to keep this nation out of another world war, argues that the United States was not truly neutral in 1914–1917, and that the submarine was something of an excuse for formal entry into the war. Criticism of American neutrality was first effectively stated in C. H. Grattan, *Why We Fought* (1929). It was continued by C. C. Tansill in *America Goes to War* (1938), which is marred by Anglophobia. Walter Millis, *Road to War, America, 1914–1917* (1935), is the most clearly written of all the revisionist works; Millis seems not to have objected so much to American intervention as to the way it came about. An excellent historiographical study is W. I. Cohen, *The American Revisionists* (1967). A re-evaluation is S. R. Spencer, Jr., *Decision for War, 1917* (1953). A valuable historio-

graphical essay is R. W. Leopold, "The Problem of American Intervention, 1917," *World Politics*, II (1950), 405–425.

On American involvement with the war, *The Intimate Papers of Colonel House*, edited by Charles Seymour (4 vols., 1926–1928), provides a running commentary from the pen of an insider. B. J. Hendrick, *Life and Letters of Walter H. Page* (3 vols., 1922–1925), reveals clearly the strongly pro-British sympathies of the American Ambassador to the Court of St. James. Robert Lansing, *War Memoirs of Robert Lansing, Secretary of State* (1935), a valuable source, should be supplemented by the scholarly analysis of D. M. Smith, *Robert Lansing and American Neutrality, 1914–1917* (1958).

H. C. Peterson, *Propaganda for War* (1939), examines closely and critically the effects of British propaganda in the United States. In this connection, see also the broader work by H. D. Lasswell, *Propaganda Techniques in the World War* (1927). Three substantial works on different topics all involve Anglo-American relations: Forrest Davis, *The Atlantic System: The Story of Anglo-American Control of the Seas* (1941); Armin Rappaport, *The British Press and Wilsonian Neutrality* (1951); and L. W. Martin, *Peace Without Victory: Woodrow Wilson and the British Liberals* (1958).

The plight of German-Americans has been carefully studied by Carl Wittke, *German-Americans and the World War* (1936); and C. J. Child, *The German-Americans in Politics, 1914–1917* (1939). The attitudes of influential antipreparedness members of Congress may be found in A. M. Arnett, *Claude Kitchin and the Wilson War Policies* (1937); and M. L. Billington, *Thomas P. Gore* (1967). F. C. Howe, *Why War?* (1916), is a vigorous anti-interventionist argument by an eminent reformer who held a post in the administration. *War and the Intellectuals: Essays, 1915–1919*, by R. S. Bourne, is a valuable collection edited by Carl Resek (1964); it illustrates the bitter tone of some opponents of war. R. H. Frost, *The Mooney Case* (1968), is a superb account of the most celebrated victim of the preparedness campaign.

16

THE FIRST WORLD WAR

The American army · Financing the war · Restriction of civil liberties · The Creel Committee · The wartime government · The "home front" · The navy in the war · The AEF · The Russian Revolution · The American contribution to victory · The debate on war aims · Defeat of Germany · The armistice

Before the entrance of the United States into the war most Americans had taken it for granted that geographic conditions would limit American participation primarily to naval and financial aid. A succession of missions to Washington from the Allied governments soon indicated that the Allies needed everything — money, ships, supplies, men — if the Central Powers were ever to be defeated. Nor could they wait. The United States must act quickly, and avoid mistakes.

The American Army

Because the Allies needed men the plans of the General Staff for raising an army in leisurely fashion were immediately speeded up. Convinced that the principle of volunteering, upon which both Great Britain and the United States had relied mainly in earlier wars, had been proved by England's recent experiences to be inadequate, the military leaders persuaded Congress to ap-

ENLISTMENT POSTER, 1917. *By James Montgomery Flagg. Collection, Museum of Modern Art.*

prove in May, 1917, a Selective Service Act. This measure required all men between the ages of twenty-one and thirty (later eighteen and forty-five) to register for military service. The registrants were then divided by local civilian boards into five classes, the first of which consisted of able-bodied, unmarried men, without dependents. The 2,810,296 men actually selected for service during the war came from this group alone. An elaborate lottery system determined the order in which they were called. Not all of the American army, however, was raised by the draft. The combined strength of the regular army and the National Guard stood at about 750,000 men when the Selective Service Act went into operation, and from this pool of trained and partially trained men the military leaders drew heavily in creating the various units that composed the new National Army. By the end of the war the continuous transfer of individuals and units from one division to another had broken down fairly completely distinctions as to origin. For the training of the men thirty-two camps and cantonments, mainly located in the South, were hastily constructed.

Officer Training

Almost as difficult as the problem of obtaining the men was the problem of supplying the army with competent officers. For the higher ranks, officers of the regular army and the National Guard were promoted, but for the lower grades the army depended upon the graduates of hastily organized officers' training camps from which "ninety-day wonders" were soon being turned out in profusion. At first only volunteers of excellent promise were accepted for officer training, but later, candidates were selected on merit from among the drafted men. Political appointments, such as had disgraced the formation of the Civil War armies, both North and South, were deliberately avoided. This decision was a great disappointment to Theodore Roosevelt, who had aspired to emulate his performance in the Spanish-American War, and lead a division of volunteers to France. The war, he complained, was a "very exclusive war," and his hatred for Wilson, already burning brightly, flamed up anew after his rejection.

Financing the War

Financing the war would have been difficult had the United States had only her own expenditures to consider, but she had also largely to finance her Allies. Economists urged a "pay-as-you-go" system, with taxation of wartime profits and earnings furnishing most of the revenue, but such a system was a practical impossibility. For one thing, money was needed immediately, and newly devised taxes would take months, or even years, to produce the needed funds. Congress therefore resorted to loans, as well as taxes. The first loan act, which became law on April 24, authorized the borrowing of $5 billion and subsequent credits were voted as needed. Five huge bond issues were floated, the first four known as "Liberty Loans," and the last, which was offered after the fighting had ended, as the "Victory Loan." The total amounts so subscribed reached nearly $21.5 billion and drew upon the savings of over 65 million individuals. Each loan was accompanied by a great "drive," in which every conceivable device was used to induce both those who had the means and those who had not to subscribe. The bonds were issued in denominations as low as $50 and $100, and the purchase of such a bond, on the installment plan if need be, was made almost a test of loyalty. Individuals who were suspected of being "pro-German" were compelled to prove their patriotism by particularly generous contributions; if they did not, their houses might be decorated with yellow paint, or they might even be subjected to rough handling. Corporations with large payrolls put pressure upon their employees to subscribe. Thrift stamps and war-savings certificates were devised to tap even the savings of the children. Unfortunately the securities marketed by the government were negotiable, and because the government refused to buy them back ahead of maturity dates they depreciated materially in value. Speculators made excellent profits; worse still, the bonds, unlike the nontransferable bonds issued during the Second World War, served, when they fell into the hands of banks, to promote rather than to restrict inflation. Prices rose rapidly, and without serious attempt on the part of the government to hold them down.

The income tax, with its surtax feature, offered an easy means of expanding the national revenue. The Revenue Act of 1916 had already doubled the normal income tax, but the War Revenue Act of 1917 doubled it again, bringing it to 4 per cent, and taxed incomes as low as a thousand dollars. The graduated surtax and the tax on corporation earnings were also raised, and a new graduated excess profits tax took from 20 to 60 per cent of such business earnings as exceeded the average for the years 1911–1913. The excise taxes on liquor and tobacco were steeply increased, and a host of "nuisance taxes" introduced — on railroad and sleeping-car tickets, on theater tickets and club dues, on telephone and telegraph messages, and on numerous other "luxuries." Postage rates went up, the ordinary letter rate from two to three cents. These were the beginning, and still higher taxes were written into the Revenue Acts of 1918 and 1919. Altogether the United States raised a total of $11.3 billion from taxation, less than one third the amount spent or lent during the same period. The total expenditures from April, 1917, to October, 1919, aggregated $35.4 billion of which $9.4 billion was lent to the Allies.

Private Benevolence

The contribution of the American people to the cost of the war included also millions of dollars expended for private benevolence. Probably the Red Cross, with its emphasis on medical care and hospitalization, was most appreciated by soldiers and public alike. Its first drive for funds, held immediately after the flotation of the First Liberty Loan, netted over $100 million and subsequent drives brought in other huge sums. The Young Men's Christian Association, the Knights of Columbus, the Jewish Welfare Board, and the Salvation Army also solicited contributions for wartime activities, and spent lavishly in their efforts to make life in the army camps and overseas more bearable. Besides all this, women's organizations knitted socks, prepared bandages, and provided numerous

First Liberty Loan of 1917. *This facsimile of a First Liberty Loan small denomination bond lacks the non-transferable, redemption on demand, clauses of the "E" bonds issued during and after World War II.*

other items of consequence to the soldier's comfort. Undoubtedly the benevolent agencies did much to substitute harmless amusements for the traditional resort of the soldier to intoxication and immorality, and they sought also to bolster up army morale. The "Y" suffered much criticism, partly because it accepted the task of vending such supplies as candy and cigarettes, instead of confining its efforts more exclusively to straight-out gifts. Nearly all of the work supported by benevolence had to be done; if private agencies had not undertaken it, the government itself would have been obliged to do so. So valuable did this work seem that the government encouraged all drives for funds by benevolent societies while the war was on. Gifts to churches, colleges, hospitals, and endowment funds, whether directly concerned in the war or not, at least cultivated the habit of giving.

War Risk Insurance

In general the government itself took care of the dependents of soldiers, and made what provision it could to prevent the men who fought the war from becoming objects of charity in the future. By rigorous examinations it kept out of the service all those who might reasonably be expected to break under the physical and mental strain of war. Men who had families dependent on them for support were given deferred classification, which amounted in effect to exemption from the draft. The Bureau of War Risk Insurance, established originally in 1914 to write marine insurance, was enlarged in October, 1917, so as to permit it to assume for the military forces of the United States the obligations ordinarily associated with employers' liability. A soldier who had dependents was obliged to allot a part of his pay to his family, and to this sum the government, in accordance with a prescribed schedule, added more. If a soldier died in service, his widow received $75 a month until remarriage. If he

"Americans All." *The final issue of war bonds came after the war was won, hence the term, Victory Bonds. The list of names to the right emphasizes the variety of national origins represented in the American armed forces. A Howard Chandler Christy poster, 1919.*

were disabled, he received compensation commensurate with the degree of his disability. If he were maimed in such a way as to need re-education, the government accepted the responsibility for that also, and charged the Federal Board for Vocational Education with the duty of providing the necessary training. And for all who would take it the government offered an insurance policy of from one to ten thousand dollars, at cost, the premiums to be deducted from the soldier's pay. By 1919 over 4.5 million such policies had been written, representing an aggregate of $38 billion. The pay of the American private was $30 a month, the highest in the world, and it was supposed that the insurance system adopted by the government would forestall the customary drive for pensions at the end of the war. This hope, as events proved, was vain.

Public Opinion on the War

The raising of huge armies, the flotation of unprecedently large loans, and the ruthless expansion of taxation were tasks that in a democracy would have been impossible but for the support of a thoroughly aroused public opinion. When war was declared in 1917, it is reasonable to suppose that the action was approved by a majority of the people as well as by a majority of Congress. But the popular majority was by no means so overwhelming as the vote in Congress indicated; indeed, many a congressman would have voted the other way had he dared. Most of those who doubted the wisdom of American entrance into the war were sympathetic with the Allied cause and ripe for conversion, but a small minority, composed of pro-Germans, Socialists, and pacifists, were bitterly opposed. Many of them were in complete agreement with Senator LaFollette, who in casting his vote against the war resolution maintained, "I say Germany has been patient with us," or with Morris Hillquit, the Socialist, who asserted, "The country has been violently, needlessly, and criminally involved in war."

Restriction of Civil Liberties

It seemed essential to Wilson and his advisers that, if the sacrifices necessary to win the war were to be borne, public opinion should support the war with virtual unanimity. Accordingly, Congress passed the Espionage Act of June 15, 1917, which levied stiff penalties on persons making false statements that might obstruct the prosecution of the war, incite disloyalty, or hinder recruiting. It also authorized the Postmaster-General to bar from the mails any printed matter violating the act. In the Trading-with-the-Enemy Act of October 6, 1917, the Post Office Department was granted further power to set up a virtual censorship on foreign-language newspapers. By far the most stringent of all wartime measures against dissent was the Sedition Act of May 16, 1918, providing stiff penalties for persons uttering disloyal, scurrilous, or abusive language about the Constitution, the government of the United States, the armed forces, and the flag, or language calculated to be such or to interfere with war production. How far repressive sentiment had moved was indicated when the Senate struck out an amendment to the act stating that it did not prohibit people from speaking or publishing what was true if their motives were good and the end justifiable.

Despite the fact that relatively few serious acts of disloyalty occurred, both Attorney-General Gregory and Postmaster-General Burleson were vigorous in their use of the Espionage and Sedition Acts. Over fifteen hundred persons were arrested for disloyal utterances, among them the gentle Eugene V. Debs, who for years had led the Socialist cause in the United States. Some of the proceedings were against actual pro-Germans, but the majority, as in the Debs trial, were against economic and political radicals who supported the Socialist position that the war was imperialistic and a direct result of capitalism. An even more direct blow to freedom of discussion was struck by the Post Office Department. Postmaster-General Burleson not only curtailed the mailing privileges of radical and foreign-language newspapers, but from time to time also seized issues of palpably loyal publications that happened to contain criticism of administration policy. An edition of *The Nation* was held up because it carried the caption "Civil Liberties Are Dead," and an issue of *The Public* was con-

The American Red Cross.
An example of Red Cross activities during World War I came after the sinking of the troop transport, Otranto, off the coast of Islay, Scotland. The picture shows Red Cross supplies being distributed to the Scottish villagers who took the survivors into their homes and cared for them.

fiscated because it suggested that the wartime taxes on large incomes were too low. In prosecuting the Espionage and Sedition Acts, both the Department of Justice and the Post Office Department probably went beyond the limits that Congress intended when it passed the legislation. But both were no doubt accurately reflecting a hysterical demand from the majority for the repression of all dissent.

The harm done to freedom of speech and the press by these repressive measures illustrates the cruel dilemma of a democracy at war. Just where the line should be drawn between preserving the traditional freedoms and the nation's demand for unity is a difficult question. Perhaps no better answer is to be found than in Supreme Court Justice Holmes's opinion in the case of *Schenck* vs. *the United States*. Schenck, a Pennsylvania German, issued pamphlets against the war and conscription. When arrested for treason, he insisted that he was within the rights guaranteed him by the Constitution. But in a unanimous decision written by Holmes, the Court found him guilty. While the Court admitted that the defendant would have been within his rights in ordinary times, it pointed out

that "the character of every act depends upon the circumstances." Thus no guarantee of free speech could protect a man who falsely cried fire in a crowded theater and thus caused a riot. It was a question of the "proximity and degree" of the danger to society. "When a nation is at war," Justice Holmes stated, "many things that might be said in time of peace are such a hindrance to its effort that their utterance will not be endured so long as men fight, and that no court could regard them as protected by any constitutional right." The Court's admission that the Constitution was suspended when the nation was faced with a clear and present danger threw a tremendous responsibility upon the good sense and moderation of administrators then and for the future.

The Creel Committee

In its attempt to achieve national solidarity, however, the Wilson administration relied more upon persuasion than upon coercion. Just eight days after the declaration of war, the President created the Committee on Public Information, naming as its head George Creel, a former editor and free lance writer. The Creel Com-

Official Bulletin

PUBLISHED DAILY UNDER ORDER OF THE PRESIDENT BY THE COMMITTEE ON PUBLIC INFORMATION
GEORGE CREEL, CHAIRMAN

Vol. 1.   WASHINGTON, THURSDAY, MAY 10, 1917   No. 1.

PRESIDENT'S WELCOME TO STATES' DEFENSE COUNCIL

The President to governors and representatives of State councils of national defense, the White House, 2 May, 1917:

"Mr. SECRETARY (SECRETARY OF WAR) AND GENTLEMEN:

"It goes without saying that I am very glad to see you and very glad to see you on such an errand. I have no homily to deliver to you, because I know you are as intensely interested as I am in drawing all of our efforts and energies together in a common action. My function has not of recent days been to give advice but to get things coordinated so that there will not be any, or at any rate too much, lost motion, and in order that things should not be done twice by different bodies or done in conflict.

"It is for that reason that I particularly welcome a conference such as this you are holding to-day and to-morrow—the conference which will acquaint you with exactly the task as it is conceived here in Washington and with the ways in which cooperation can be best organized.

POST THE BULLETIN.

Postmaster:

Your particular attention is called to THE OFFICIAL BULLETIN which is to be issued as the official news medium of the Government under the direction of the Committee on Public Information appointed by the President of the United States for the purpose of disseminating official news during the present war crisis. All postmasters are directed to post this BULLETIN daily in a conspicuous place in the lobby or other portion of their respective post-office buildings where the public can read it; and, without expense to the Government, each and every postmaster is earnestly urged to see that this BULLETIN is made available to as many people as possible in the manner suggested.

A. S. BURLESON,
Postmaster General.

OFFICIAL BULLETIN WILL GIVE PUBLIC DETAILED WAR NEWS.

The OFFICIAL BULLETIN, of which this is the first issue, is designed to inform the

---

TREASURY FORCE GIVING LIBERALLY TO RED CROSS

There has been a general response to the call of the Secretary of the Treasury, to the officers and employees of the Treasury Department issued April 24, 1917, to give liberally to the Red Cross, and to date $7,724.10 has been received and deposited on account of this fund. Many of the offices located in the field have not yet made their returns and the final time limit for such returns is May 18. Subscriptions are coming in from the field offices at the rate of approximately $1,000 a day. The Secretary is very much gratified over the enthusiastic manner in which all employees of the department are responding to his appeal.

The call was as follows:

To the officers and employees of the Treasury Department:

Now that our country is engaged in a war which has been thrust upon us by Germany through defiance of our international rights and the laws of humanity, it behooves every American citizen, no matter of what descent or shade of opinion, to give evidence of the most loyal and whole-hearted support of the Government in the present conflict. I like to believe that there is not a man or woman among the more than 30,000 employees of the Treasury Department

---

mittee early conceived of itself as having a double function—not only to keep the American public informed about the progress of the war, but also to formulate and state the official view of why the nation went to war and what it was fighting for. The Committee was thus both a news-gathering agency and a propaganda machine. Obtaining many of its ideas from a previously established British organization, it offered free to national publishers a day-to-day account of the war's progress. It turned out a stream of persuasive books, pamphlets, and throwaways on such diverse subjects as *Why the War Came to America, Why Working Men Support the War, The Government of Germany,* and *German War Practices.* At the same time the CPI organized a bureau of "four-minute men," who harangued theater, church, school, and club audiences on the iniquities of the Germans, and the necessity of winning the war. When the fighting was over Creel estimated that the Committee had issued over 75 million pieces of propaganda and that 75,000 volunteer speakers had addressed 7.5 million separate audiences.

The Creel thesis on the origins of the war was a simple one taken over from the Allies. It pictured a militarized and Prussianized German state seeking to dominate the world, planning the war years in advance, and setting the exact date of *Der Tag* for the beginning of hostilities. The war was thus against autocracy, and "to make the world safe for democracy." Later the Creel Committee fully adopted Wilson's war aims, and spread the word both at home and abroad that the United States was seeking no material gains, but was waging a war to end war, to secure eternal peace among men. Such black and white explanations of the aims of the struggle could hardly be precisely true. Nor could such broad aspirations be achieved. These propaganda statements became targets for criticism when peace finally came on far less idealistic terms. But during the struggle most Americans accepted them as true, and the will to victory was strengthened accordingly.

Council of National Defense

Neither the political nor the economic organization of the United States was fitted to meet the emergencies of war, and drastic changes had to be effected in both. Fortunately the defense measures of 1916 had provided for a planning board known as the Council of National Defense. The six members of this council were cabinet officers with an abundance of other work to do, but they were expected to follow the recommendations of an Advisory Commission of seven civilians, also provided for in the law. Headed by Daniel Willard, president of the Baltimore and Ohio Railroad, and assisted by as many "dollar-a-year" volunteers as it could use, the Advisory Commission soon became what Professor Paxson has aptly called a "civilian general staff." Largely through the plans it devised, the government of the United States was reorganized for wartime efficiency, while industry, agriculture, labor, and every other form of American economic life were forced to operate with the single-minded purpose of winning the war. Temporarily the United States ceased to be a democracy, and the freedom of the individual was sacrificed to the larger necessity of a military victory. New and powerful administrative agencies, responsible only to the President, told the people of the nation what they might and might not do, and what they had to do.

Bernard Baruch. *As head of the War Industries Board, Baruch was sometimes described as the economic dictator of the United States. This might have been an exaggeration, but his power was undeniably great.*

The Wartime Government

Before the war was over, six great wartime agencies had taken over the chief responsibility for adjusting American economic life to the necessities of the struggle. The oldest of these was the United States Shipping Board, which had been created the year before the war broke out. Through its Emergency Fleet Corporation it struggled valiantly, and with considerable success, to build ships faster than the submarines could sink them. A second agency, the Food Administration, had as its responsibility the supply of food, both for soldiers and for noncombatants, overseas. As Food Administrator, Herbert Hoover preached the "gospel of the clean plate," persuaded the American people to accept "wheatless" and "meatless" days, and encouraged all who could to plant "war-gardens." More important still, Hoover's Grain Corporation set high prices for wheat that led to a remarkable expansion of the nation's wheat acreage, with a corresponding increase in production. Unlike the OPA in the Second World War, the Food Administration had little coercive power, and relied mainly upon persuasion. A Fuel Administration dealt similarly with the pressing coal and oil problem; a Railroad Administration took over all the railroads of the country and operated them as if they were a single system; a War Trade Board licensed foreign trade and took care that American commodities did not reach the enemy; and a War Industries Board, most powerful of all, took full command of American production. Under Bernard Baruch as chairman, the WIB told manufacturers what materials they could use, and what materials they must save. It could order them to undertake totally new endeavors. It could determine priorities, and so give or withold both the raw materials and the transportation upon which every manufacturer depended. It could standardize products, and with the President's approval it could, and did, fix prices, although primarily on raw materials rather than completed products. Of great assistance in working out the orders of the War Industries Board was the War Finance Corporation, which, operating with a half-billion dollar revolving fund granted by Congress and such other sums as it could borrow, lent to businesses that needed encouragement, while restraining vigorously all nonessential demands for capital.

Through these six great "war boards," which the President, until six months after alone, the government of the United States was soon exercising powers that in ordinary times would have been deemed incompatible with democracy. Beginning in March, 1918, the heads of these boards met with him weekly as a kind of war cabinet. Such legislation as they required, Congress ordinarily felt obliged to supply. The most sweeping of these grants was contained in the Overman Act, signed May 20, 1918, by which the President, until six months after the war should end, was given free rein "to utilize, coordinate, or consolidate any executive or administrative commissions, bureaus, agencies, offices, or officers" at will; to create new agencies and abolish old ones, and to utilize funds voted for any purpose in whatever way he deemed that purpose best served. One critic of the bill suggested ironically an amendment: "If any power, constitutional or not, has been inadvertently omitted from this bill, it is hereby granted in full." Working closely together under the President, and assured of support by state councils of defense locally maintained, the war boards all but supplanted the ordinary civil authorities.

Had the war lasted a year longer, war boards would have exercised much more power in directing the American economy. By Armistice Day plans had been made, for example, to clothe all Americans in a common street uniform. But even under the existing regulations of 1918 the traditional free economy was practically shelved. The American economic system at the end of the war was a virtual state capitalism, in which most of the power of decision rested strictly with government.

If a change had occurred in the locus of economic control, little had taken place in the personality of the controllers. Faced with innumerable technical and industrial problems, the war boards were staffed with businessmen and industrialists, many of whom offered their services to the government on a dollar-a-year basis while retaining their permanent positions in private industry. While much postwar criticism was focused on the dollar-a-year men who were in a position to favor their own industries in the race for war contracts, it is also generally acknowledged that the system performed many near miracles in the production of essential war goods. According to the testimony of the German General Ludendorff, American industrial production, as much as any other single element, accounted for the Allied victory.

Labor and the War

The support of organized labor for the war was greatly promoted by the earnest efforts of Samuel Gompers, one of the seven members of the Advisory Commission, whose insistence that the war must not be used to depreciate wages or labor standards became a governmental policy on the understanding that labor would not embarrass the government by "basic strikes." Indeed, the draft, which took many men out of the labor market, and the cessation of immigration, which cut off a historic source of supply, led to a labor scarcity that drove wages to unprecedented heights. By 1918 the average worker was earning nearly twice as much as in 1914, and even allowing for the mounting costs of living he was fully 20 per cent better off than he had been when hostilities began. High wages and steady employment meant also prosperity for the labor unions, whose membership shot upward during the war by no less than 37 per cent. To facilitate the mobility of labor the government greatly expanded the United States Employment Service of the Labor Department, and to fill labor shortages it encouraged the use of women in industry. Labor disputes were kept at a minimum. A War Labor Conference Board, created in 1918, laid down the rules that should govern the relationship of capital and labor, and a National War Labor Board, under the co-chairmanship of William Howard Taft and Frank P. Walsh, acted as a court of last resort in the settlement of labor disputes. The formulation of labor policies in the new war industries was handed over to a War Labor Policies Board of which Felix Frankfurter became chairman.

The Standard of Living

Perhaps more important than the immediate effects of the war were the enduring changes it created in American society. The intense demands upon American farmers and manufacturers greatly stimulated the productive resources of the nation. The number of acres under cultivation increased by 10 per cent between 1914 and 1920, the production of mines about 30 per cent, total manufactures about 35 per cent. While much of the gain was temporarily sent abroad, the resulting increase in basic productive facilities presented the possibility of a sizable elevation in the national standard of living during the postwar years. Even more dramatic was the impact of the war upon the international economic position of the United

States. As late as 1914 the United States had been a debtor nation, that is, the government and citizens owed more to Europeans than Europeans owed to the United States and its people. But the costs of the war had forced European capital to withdraw from America and elsewhere in the world. Into this void American investors had stepped. They not only took over many European holdings in America, but they repeated the process in many colonial areas, and lent huge sums to Europe as well. Whereas Great Britain, France, and Germany had before the war been the chief investors across international boundaries, the United States, with almost $20 billion lent abroad when the war ended, had become the foremost creditor nation of the world. This sudden shift in the nation's international credit position was to have profound effects upon both its international and its domestic policies.

Despite government statistics it is impossible to say precisely how the increase in national wealth during the war was divided among the various classes of Americans. Certainly most manufacturers and the owners of large capital fared well, and the farmer and the laborer took a relatively larger proportion of the national income than they had had before. But because of price inflation, salaried workers and people living on fixed incomes suffered. Another hint of what had happened in America is the fact that many iron and steel firms had earned over three times their original capital outlay in the war years. Income tax returns in 1918 indicated that over 25,000 people in the United States, exactly four times as many as before the war, had a yearly income of over a million dollars.

The war made other major changes in American society. Because of the dire need for labor in manufacturing establishments, southern Negroes came to northern cities in vast numbers. Their adjustment to

Women War Workers. *The photograph shows two women at work in a munitions factory.*

northern urban life, and the new problem of relationship with the white population, was to spell trouble for both races. The war also speeded up the invasion by women of factory and office. By the end of 1917 almost 2 million women were working in manufacturing establishments, not to mention other types of employment. Once freed from the hampering environment of the home, American women rapidly changed their attitudes toward society and their own place in it. The war also had serious repercussions upon the nation's health. With many physicians mobilized for the war, the influenza epidemic of 1918 became a serious plague. The "flu," indeed, baffled medical science, and took a heavy toll both in the cantonments and among civilians. For the most part the educational system of the country carried on as usual, although higher education was hard hit by enlistments, and, after the service age was lowered from twenty-one to eighteen, by the draft. In an effort to combine education and military training the Students' Army Training Corps was established in practically all the colleges during the fall of 1918. Young men of draft age were allowed to continue their studies in uniform and at the expense of the government, while learning the art of war from army officers. The compensation paid the colleges by the government for the use of

their facilities saved many of them from financial collapse, but as an educational experiment the SATC was a failure.

The "Home Front"

Undoubtedly the most unlovely feature of the "home front" was the ugly intolerance bred by the war. Americans of foreign extractions suffered from it more acutely than any others, especially when they had been "pro-German" in the period of neutrality. Most of the acts of intolerance were not the acts of the government, but of the people. The German language, which before the war had been more widely taught in America than any other foreign language, was all but eliminated from the public schools, and suffered from drastic restrictions in the colleges. Printing, preaching, teaching, even talking in the German language were treated as if criminal offenses, and were sometimes made so. Musicians of German or Austrian origin, such as Frederick Stock and Fritz Kreisler, were publicly humiliated. Honorary degrees granted to such nationals before the war were revoked by the universities that had granted them. All aliens and all citizens of recent alien origin were made to feel their inferiority to the so-called "native Americans." It was as Wilson himself had said on the eve of war:

Once lead this people into war and they'll forget there ever was such a thing as tolerance. To fight you must be brutal and ruthless, and the spirit of ruthless brutality will enter into every fiber of our national life, infecting Congress, the courts, the policemen on the beat.

Conformity, as the President had foreseen, became the only true virtue, and the man who refused to conform had to pay a severe penalty. All this was scarcely compatible with Wilson's plans for a democratic and peaceful world. But the American people, like the President, went on practicing one thing during the war years and believing in another, leaving the great contradiction unresolved.

The Navy in the War

For actual combat duty the navy preceded the army to Europe by many months. Indeed, Rear-Admiral William S. Sims, who was chosen for overseas command, was in London before the United States entered the war, and by May 4 the first

detachment of American destroyers had crossed the Atlantic. Ultimately 300 warships, large and small, and 75,000 officers and men were serving in the overseas detachments of the American navy. Their activities extended from the vicinity of the British Isles to the Mediterranean. No doubt these reinforcements were partly responsible for the fact that the experiment of Jutland was not repeated. The American naval forces made no effort to operate separately, but became in effect a part of the British Grand Fleet. American ships were used, among other things, to enforce the very rules of blockade against which the United States as a neutral had protested so vigorously.

The greatest single concern of the combined navies when the United States entered the war was the defeat of the submarine. This was eventually accomplished by a variety of means. American insistence had much to do with the laying of a mine field across the opening of the North Sea, between the Orkney Islands and the coast

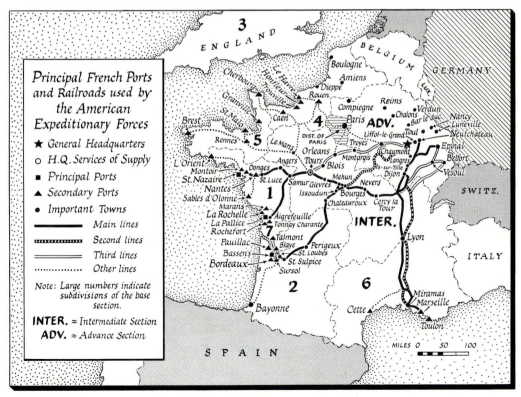

Principal French Ports and Railroads used by the American Expeditionary Forces

★ General Headquarters
○ H.Q. Services of Supply
■ Principal Ports
▲ Secondary Ports
● Important Towns

━━━━━ Main lines
▬▬▬▬▬ Second lines
═══════ Third lines
··············· Other lines

Note: Large numbers indicate subdivisions of the base section.

INTER. = Intermediate Section
ADV. = Advance Section

AN AMERICAN CONVOY. Aerial view of a convoy approaching the coast of France.

of Norway. This, and a similar mine field across the Straits of Dover, seriously crippled submarine activities. Cruising destroyers, armed with improved means of detection, also hunted down the "U-boats," and sank them with depth charges. By the end of the war about half the German submarine flotilla had been destroyed. American ships likewise played a leading role in convoying merchantmen and troop ships through the danger zone, thereby cheating the submarines of their prey.

The AEF

The frantic pleas of the Allies for American troops in France led the General Staff to revise its plans with respect to the training of the American army. It was decided that troops would have to be sent overseas only partly trained and partly equipped. The rest of the work could be done over there. Mainly as an earnest of good intentions General John J. Pershing was ordered to France in May, 1917, as head of the American Expeditionary Force, and next month the first of the American detachments began to arrive. The American plan called for more than the mere transporting of troops. Already the facilities of France and her allies were being taxed to the limit to support their own armies, and the American contingent must be a help, not a burden. Ten thousand tons of wheat reached France in advance of the troops it was supposed to sustain, and, to make

way for the coming of further detachments of the AEF, harbors had to be dredged, docks constructed, debarkation depots created, railroads made over, freight yards laid out, telegraph and telephone lines erected, hospitals, barracks, and warehouses put together. All this was done by American labor, in accordance with American methods, and for the most part with American materials, although American sawmills sometimes condescended to turn European logs into lumber. Over 5 million tons of supplies were sent abroad by the United States before the armistice was signed. As to manpower, the American records show that 2,079,880 men were transported overseas. Not all of these were fighting men, but from them Pershing netted forty-two combat divisions.

From the first General Pershing, who had himself written the orders under which he operated, insisted upon the creation of a separate American command. This did not please the Allies, who wished to use the American troops as replacements, to be brigaded with French or British units. But Pershing was convinced that three years of defensive fighting had weakened the Allied armies for effective offensive tactics, and finally forced the Allied leaders to give in. The American army thus became a wholly independent unit, and in October, 1917, began to take over a quiet sector of the battle line. American combat participation began as early as October 21,

THE AMERICAN NAVY AT WAR.
These three photographs show some of the many activities in which the navy participated during the war. Naval units convoyed ships to European ports where American troops and supplies were landed; and they also helped hold the German submarines at bay, in large part by the use of depth bombs and mines.

MINE LAYING IN THE NORTH SEA.

AMERICAN SHIP UNLOADING AT ST. NAZAIRE, FRANCE. This cargo consisted of hay, iron, and canned goods.

1917, when battalions of the First American Division joined the French forces for a time on the Sommerville sector. When in March, 1918, Russia made a separate peace and the Germans began a great *Friedensturm* designed to end the war, Pershing lent still more troops to the hard-pressed French. In the summer fighting before Paris, especially at Château-Thierry early in June, the Americans gave a good account of themselves. Surprised and pleased, Marshal Foch, now Allied commander-in-chief, saw the point to Pershing's insistence on a separate army and separate training, and cooperated cheerfully in promoting these ends. Pershing was never able to supply from American sources all the matériel of war necessary for a complete army. The ordnance, the tanks, and the airplanes he used were in considerable part of Allied manufacture. But the men were all Americans, and they did Pershing's bidding, subject only to the supreme command of Foch. Before the war ended, American troops held one fourth of the battle line, more even than the British.

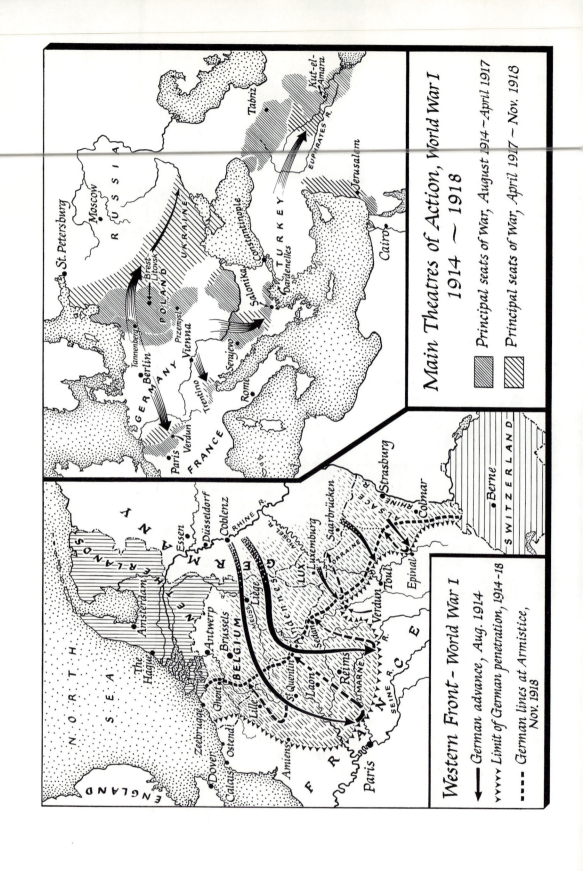

Main Theatres of Action, World War I
1914 ~ 1918

▨ Principal seats of War, August 1914 – April 1917

▨ Principal seats of War, April 1917 – Nov. 1918

Western Front – World War I

—— German advance, Aug. 1914

vvvvv Limit of German penetration, 1914–18

- - - German lines at Armistice, Nov. 1918

The American Army Overseas. *Getting supplies to the American Expeditionary Force was a colossal and exasperating task. This photograph shows a typical traffic jam on a road back of the American line in Argonne, northwest of Verdun.*

The Saint-Mihiel Salient

Pershing's first action as an independent commander was the reduction of the Saint-Mihiel salient, where the German line protruded sharply across the Meuse River southeast of Verdun. With some French assistance, but following his own plans, he attacked both flanks of the salient and in two days had it straightened out. Half a million American troops participated in the battle; they suffered 7,000 casualties, and took 16,000 German prisoners. Had they been permitted to do so, the Americans would gladly have pushed ahead toward Metz, across the German frontier, but no farther away than they had already come. Metz was a key city in the German defenses, and had it fallen the war might have ended in September rather than in November. Pershing was ready with his plans, but Haig, who headed the British forces, favored a different strategy, and Foch listened to Haig instead of Pershing. The American army was shifted to the west, and directed down the Meuse River and through the Argonne Forest toward Sedan. The war ended before Sedan was taken, but by November 11, Pershing explained later, the American troops "had cut the enemy's main line of communications, and nothing but surrender or an armistice could save his army from complete disaster."

The Meuse-Argonne

The advance of the American army in the Meuse-Argonne was only a part of the larger campaign by which Foch smashed his way to victory through the supposedly impregnable Hindenburg Line, behind which the Germans had taken refuge. Three other major offensives, the Ypres-Lys, the Somme, and the Oise-Aisne, preceded and accompanied the American drive. With the Allied forces acting for once in complete coordination, an Allied drive was begun north of Salonika against Bulgaria, another against the Turks in Palestine, and a third against the Austrians in Italy. Everywhere the Allied arms were successful. Before the end of September, Bulgaria was out of the war; Turkey quit in October; Austria surrendered early in November; on November 11 Germany, too, with her armies everywhere in full retreat, gave up the fight.

American participation in the war was not wholly confined to the fighting in France. In July, 1918, an American regiment was sent to Italy, and in October

Outpost in Alsace. *A team of American soldiers holds out against the enemy in the Amphershock sector of Alsace. They have resorted to a French machine gun for cover. August 29, 1918.*

two American divisions were lent to the French for use in Belgium. More debatable was the part played by American troops in Allied maneuvers against Bolshevik Russia. Without authority of a declaration of war against Russia, 5,000 Americans fought with the Allies in the Archangel-Murmansk campaign that lasted from September, 1918, to May, 1919; while 10,000 Americans joined an Allied expedition to Vladivostok and eastern Siberia that lasted until January, 1920.

The Russian Revolution

Meantime, the American people watched with varying emotions the revolutionary experiment in Russia. As soon as possible after the overthrow of the Tsar in March, 1917, an American mission headed by Elihu Root, former Secretary of State, and Hugh L. Scott, chief of staff of the United States Army, was sent to Petrograd to help the new government to a good start, and to encourage it in the continued prosecution of the war against Germany. But the wheel of revolution in Russia turned rapidly to the left, and before the end of the year Nicolai Lenin and Leon Trotsky, leaders of the most extreme advocates of Communism, the Bolsheviks, had climbed to power with the assistance of German gold, and on the promise to the Russian people of peace. Late in December, 1917, at Brest-Litovsk, the Bolsheviks signed an armistice which meant closing out the war on German terms. They were convinced, no doubt, that when the time of world revolution came, it would make little difference what nation held what territory. Finland had declared its independence in July, 1917, and when the Treaty of Brest-Litovsk was finally signed in March, 1918, Poland, Lithuania, and the Ukraine were also separated from Russia, preparatory to leisurely German assimilation. It was clear from this peace that Germany at the moment, whatever her original intent, was engaged in a war of conquest. Should the fighting on the western front end in a German victory, it seemed reasonable to suppose that similar terms would be imposed upon the rest of the Allies. The defection of Russia thus was a great help to Germany, and the repudiation by the Bolsheviks of their foreign debts by no means improved the feelings of the Allies. Naturally, the Allies wished to bring to power in Russia a government that would resume the war against Germany and would agree to meet its financial obligations. The military activities on Russian soil, in which the United States participated, were parts of the ill-fated Allied projects for bringing about these results.

America's Contribution to Victory

The military contribution that the United States made to the winning of the war was not inconsiderable. An army of 3.5 million men was raised, of whom 1.4 million saw active service overseas. Had the hostilities lasted into 1919, as the Allied plans anticipated, the American activities would have been still more impressive. As it was, the "Yanks" captured 44,000 prisoners, took 1,400 guns, and brought down 755 enemy airplanes. The American contribution in the air was somewhat disappointing. In spite of the earnest activities of the Aircraft Production Board, and the creation of the new "Liberty engine," "the eyes of the army went aloft in foreign planes." But 11,000 aviators had been trained by the time of the armistice, and 4,300 of them were in France. American casualties, considering the short period of time Pershing's troops were engaged, were heavy — heavier, probably, than in corresponding French and British units where the troops were better trained and where by this time the utmost effort was being made to hold down losses in manpower. But the total number of deaths suffered by the American army from all causes was under 125,000 and of these less than half were battle deaths. Compared with the 1.7 million battle deaths suffered by the Russians, the 1.6 million by the Germans, the 1.4 million by the French, the 900,000 by the British, and the 800,000 by the Austrians, the American losses seemed inconsequential, but they were sustained during only about six months of actual fighting, while for the European belligerents the war lasted over four years. Excellent health precautions practically eliminated such filth diseases as dysentery and typhoid, from which so many American soldiers had died in previous wars, and skillful surgery and hospitalization returned five-sixths of those wounded to their regiments. The worst scourge came from the influenza, which took as heavy a toll among civilians as among soldiers.

The Will to Win

But it would be quite unfair to judge the part that the United States played in the war wholly from the military angle. The American troops came to Europe with a will to win, and their coming bolstered enormously the morale of the war-wearied Allies. Confidence in victory was standard

Brest-Litovsk Peace Conference. *The arrival of the Russian delegation to treat with the Germans is shown here. In the center is Trotsky (profile), and just emerging from the train are Joffe and Kamenev. January, 1918.*

equipment for all Americans, and it was systematically whipped up at every training camp, both in the United States and in Europe. It was a singing war, with tunes and verses inspired by cocksureness. The men went to camp, embarked and disembarked, marched and relaxed to "It's a long way to Tipperary," "Over There," and a dozen similar "hits." The American "doughboy" was not easily depressed by the petty vexations of army life. He made fun of them in the stories passed along by word of mouth, and in the *Stars and Stripes,* a newspaper that the soldiers of the AEF themselves edited in a style that combined the best and the worst of the college daily and the American sports page. Punctilious officers saw themselves as privates saw them in cartoons and comic strips drawn by professionals. The unlimited assurance with which the American army tackled its task impressed even the Germans. Women served not only as nurses, but also as substitutes on the home front for messenger and elevator "boys," as streetcar conductors, railroad workers, and factory hands, and even as "farmerettes." When Secretary of the Navy Daniels ruled that a yeoman need not necessarily be a man, about 11,000 "Yeomanettes" signed up for service, along with some 269 women marines, generally called "Marinettes."

Unity of Command and Supply

There was much more for which the United States could claim credit. Pershing was quick to point out that the Allies needed above all else a unified command. "When one was attacking, the other was usually standing still." American insistence, together with the grave threat of German victory as a result of the *Friedensturm,* helped pave the way for the assumption of supreme command in France by Marshal Foch. The American genius for business organization led to another almost equally important reform—a unified system of supply. The American idea was that all resources—shipping, food, munitions, and other supplies—should be pooled, and drawn upon as needed. To accomplish this end much inertia had to be overcome, but before the war was over a remarkable transformation had been wrought. For this change much credit was due to General Charles G. Dawes, Pershing's purchasing agent. Last, but not at all least, came the ideal of a peace so even-handed in its justice toward all nations, great and small, victor and vanquished, that the causes of war would be forever abolished. Six thousand years of history proclaimed the illusiveness of such a hope, but the eloquent arguments of the American President tended to dispel the reality of the past. Long before the entrance of the United States into the war, Wilson had been urging such a settlement, and before its close his preachments had gained an almost miraculous ascendancy over world opinion. What he stated in general terms every nation translated into the specific terms its national aspirations demanded. A "peace of justice" meant something quite different to each people, but in every case it meant something worth fighting for. And if this war should be indeed the war that would end all war, the goal was doubly worth the effort. Wilson's idealism became a two-edged sword. On the one hand it provided the Allies with a unified purpose in the war; on the other it tended to break down enemy morale. Why fight against a peace of justice?

The Debate on War Aims

Wilson's interest in a peace of justice had been stated clearly in his "peace without victory" speech of January, 1917. After the entrance of the United States into the war, he modified his stand only by insisting on a complete victory over the autocratic rulers of the Central Powers, but for the *people* of Germany and of her

American Training Planes, 1917. *These "Curtis Jennies" were used only for training and in America. In Europe airplanes at first did reconnaissance duty primarily, but they were soon armed with machine guns and bombs. When the war began planes could fly not more than 60 to 70 m.p.h. By its end fighter planes could fly 120 m.p.h., and bombers, 80 to 90 m.p.h.*

allies, as distinguished from their *governments*, he still adhered to generous terms. When Pope Benedict XV urged a negotiated peace in August, 1917, Wilson in reply drew this distinction clearly. The United States, he said, wished neither punitive damages, nor the dismemberment of empires, nor the establishment of exclusive economic leagues after the war, but the autocratic rulers must go. That his ideas comported ill with the network of semi-secret treaties on the postwar world that the Allies had agreed to among themselves, the President must have known. These treaties planned a victor's peace rather than a peace of justice, but Wilson seemed to believe that the popularity of his views with the masses in all countries would bring the Allied governments eventually to his program. As a matter of fact, Lloyd George, the British Prime Minister, while fully aware of his country's commitments, echoed the President faithfully, although Clemenceau, the French Premier, admitted frankly, "My war aim is to conquer."

Wilson gave classic statement to his views in a speech delivered before Congress in January, 1918. If the world were to become "a fit and safe place to live in," the peace should embody these "Fourteen Points":

1. Open covenants of peace openly arrived at.

2. Freedom of navigation upon the seas, alike in peace and in war.

3. Equality of trade conditions among all nations consenting to the peace.

4. Guarantees that national armaments will be reduced.

5. The adjustment of colonial claims in the interests of the populations concerned.

6. The evacuation of all Russian territory.

7. Belgium must be evacuated and restored.

8. French territory should be freed and restored, and the wrong of Alsace-Lorraine should be righted.

9. Readjustment of Italian frontiers along clearly recognizable lines of nationality.

10. The peoples of Austria-Hungary should be accorded opportunity for autonomous development.

11. Rumania, Serbia, and Montenegro should be evacuated and restored, and Serbia secured an access to the sea.

12. The Turkish portions of the Ottoman Empire should be assured a secure sovereignty, but other nationalities under Turkish rule should have autonomy.

13. An independent Polish state with free and secure access to the sea.

14. A general association of nations for mutual guarantees of political independence and territorial integrity.

Wilson's program was not the product merely of his own thinking. In the main, it was suggested to him by the "Inquiry," a group of scholars drawn together by Colonel House to provide the American

State Department with the specific data it would need at the peace conference. It was never formally accepted by the Allies as their own. Wilson spoke for himself and for the government he headed, but he could not speak officially for the nations he usually referred to as the "Associates" of the United States in the war.

German Aspirations

The German government in repeated state papers showed that it had no interest whatever in the type of peace Wilson sought. Its real answer to the Fourteen Points was the Treaty of Brest-Litovsk with Russia in March, 1918. This treaty sheared off from Russia over 300,000 square miles of territory, with a population of 56 million people. It took away one third of Russia's railway mileage, 73 per cent of her total iron output, 89 per cent of her coal production, 5,000 factories, mills, distilleries, and refineries. By a supplementary agreement signed in August, 1918, Germany exacted also an indemnity of 6 billion marks. There is no reason to suppose that the terms of this treaty were unpopular with the people of Germany. Probably the people, no less than the government, were ready for a peace of violence, similar to the Treaty of Brest-Litovsk, against the western nations. Wilson's Fourteen Points were described by one German writer as a "real symphony of a will to no peace." It was only in defeat that either the German government or the German people began to show an interest in a "just peace."

Defeat of Germany

The German defeat, when it came, was thoroughgoing and complete in a strictly military sense. Later the German people were persuaded to believe that they had laid down their arms in the hope of a just peace when they might have fought on indefinitely. The Creel Committee had seen to it that the Wilson proposals were widely circulated within Germany, and undoubtedly the American propaganda had some effect. But the German armies were badly beaten, and their commanding officers knew it. Their allies had been knocked out, one by one. Their supposedly impregnable Hindenburg Line had cracked. Their submarine campaign had failed. Their services of supply were breaking down. The morale of their troops, in full retreat, was declining. Revolution, born less of Wilson's promises than of military disaster, was in the air. Ludendorff and Hindenburg informed the German Emperor in September that all was lost, and that peace must be made at once. Ludendorff had a nervous breakdown. It was the hopelessness of the military situation and the certainty of Allied victory that led the German government, like a drowning man grasping at a straw, to ask Wilson for an armistice on the basis of the Fourteen Points. It was the impending collapse of the military front, and not merely unrest at home, that forced Germany to sue for peace. In the words of Count Bernstorff,

The charge that Wilson purposely betrayed us over the Fourteen Points acquired greater prominence from the fact that a legend was fostered in Germany to the effect that we laid down our weapons in reliance on the Fourteen Points. This legend is a flat falsification of history, as everyone knows who then took any part in the negotiations. We had to lay down our arms because the Supreme Command insisted that we should do so in order to avoid a catastrophe, and then we invoked Wilson's help with an appeal to the Fourteen Points.[1]

The Armistice

The negotiations for an armistice were begun early in October, 1918, by a new German Chancellor, Prince Max of Baden, known to be a liberal, who professed to

[1] *Memoirs of Count Bernstorff* (1936), p. 136.

The Allied Military Leaders. *The photograph shows from left to right Marshal Joffre, Marshal Foch, Marshal Haig, and General Pershing. The problem of achieving a unified war effort, with so many nations participating in the decisions, led to the appointment of Marshal Foch as the Allied Supreme Commander in France.*

Wilson that he spoke "in the name of the German government and the German people." Even so, the pre-armistice negotiations were long drawn out. Wilson's Fourteen Points were accepted by the Allied leaders only after elaborate interpretations and amendments, to all of which the Germans were obliged, because of the military situation, to consent. Among other things, Wilson's second point, the "freedom of the seas," was ruled out altogether at the insistence of the British, while with reference to invaded territories, it was expressly stipulated that full compensation must be made for all damage done "by land, by sea, and from the air." When the German envoys signed the armistice they knew, therefore, that they were obtaining substantially less than the Fourteen Points, but they knew also that failure to sign meant only the substitution of unconditional surrender for what was left of the Wilson program. Even so, the armistice was not actually signed until the German fleet at Kiel had mutinied rather than put to sea for a final test of strength, the Kaiser himself had been forced to abdicate, and leaders who owed no allegiance to the former "autocratic rulers" were in complete control. With the signing of the armistice, November 11, 1918, the war came to an end.

Military Terms of the Armistice

The military terms of the armistice revealed still further the extremity of the German collapse. No nation with the faintest hope of victory could have accepted them. The German army must retire to the left bank of the Rhine, surrendering huge stores of military supplies and railroad equipment; the bridgeheads at Cologne, Coblenz, and Mainz must be occupied by Allied troops; Allied prisoners of war and deported inhabitants of occupied territory must be returned without reciprocity; the German submarines and battle fleet must be taken to a neutral or Allied port for internment (the Germans took their ships to Scapa Flow as required, but ultimately scuttled them); and the predatory treaties of Brest-Litovsk and Bucharest with Russia and Rumania respectively, must be cancelled. The Allies on their part were at liberty to requisition such German property as their armies of occupation might need, and to maintain the blockade of Germany that they had

Armistice Day Celebration. *This photograph of New York City was taken in 1918 on Fifth Avenue looking downtown from the Library.*

set up during the war. All this the German leaders knew and agreed to when they signed the armistice.

Alone among the Allied commanders, General Pershing had opposed any armistice at all. He believed that only by a knock-out blow delivered on German soil could the German people be made to realize the completeness of their defeat. Subsequent events seemed to prove that in this opinion he may have been correct. After the war such irresponsible demagogues as Hitler, with the aid of the unreconciled military caste, were able to convince the German people that they had been tricked into making peace when their armies were still unbeaten. Undoubtedly this state of mind had much to do with determining the course of events that led to the Second World War. As matters stood, the demagogues could make a plausible cause.

BIBLIOGRAPHY

American participation is superbly narrated and analyzed by E. M. Coffman, *The War to End All Wars* (1968). A vivid illustrated account of the A. E. F. is Frank Freidel, *Over There* (1964); see also Laurence Stallings, *The Doughboys* (1963). T. G. Frothingham, *The American Reinforcement in the World War* (1927), is clear and satisfactory. In a special category is the interesting work of Emmet Crozier, *American Reporters on the Western Front, 1914–1918* (1959). Much fresh material has been used by W. B. Fowler, *British-American Relations, 1917–1918: The Role of Sir William Wiseman* (1969). An interesting account of an experiment that never amounted to much is D. F. Trask, *The United States in the Supreme War Council* (1961). L. E. Gelfand, *The Inquiry: American Preparations for Peace, 1917–1919* (1963), is careful and probably definitive on one important subject.

The mobilization of American resources to win the war has received much attention. *How America Went to War*, edited by Benedict Crowell and R. F. Wilson (6 vols., 1921), is an elaborate account from official sources of the various activities of the nation. W. F. Willoughby, *Government Organization in War Time and After* (1919), is a valuable survey of the federal agencies created for the prosecution of the war. Activities of the WIB are discussed in B. M. Baruch, *American Industry in the War* (1921); M. L. Coit, *Mr. Baruch* (1957); and Baruch's autobiography, *Baruch: The Public Years* (1960). On price controls, see Herbert Stein, *Government Price Policy in the United States during the World War* (1939); and G. P. Adams, Jr., *Wartime Price Control* (1942), which relates the experience of the first war for the benefit of another wartime generation. On food, see Herbert Hoover, *Years of Adventure, 1874–1920* (1951), the first volume of his *Memoirs;* and W. C. Mullendore, *History of the United States Food Administration, 1917–1919* (1941). On the financing and cost of the war, see J. M. Clark, *The Costs of the World War to the American People* (1931). F. R. Dulles, *The American Red Cross: A History* (1950), narrates the contribution of that organization.

Josephus Daniels, *The Wilson Era: Years of War and After, 1917–1923* (1946), is the reminiscence of the Secretary of the Navy. For the role of Daniels' energetic assistant, see Frank Freidel, *Franklin D. Roosevelt: The Apprenticeship* (1952), the first of a multivolume biography of the highest quality. The relations between these two colorful characters are explored further in Jonathan Daniels, *The End of Innocence* (1954), by the Secretary's son. On the part of the Navy in the war, there are a number of excellent accounts, among them E. E. Morison, *Admiral Sims and the Modern American Navy* (1942); Louis Guichard, *The Naval Blockade, 1914–1918* (1930); T. G. Frothingham, *Naval History of the World War*, III: *The United States in the War, 1917–1918* (1926); and T. A. Bailey, *The Policy of the United States toward the Neutrals, 1917–1918* (1942).

On the Secretary of War, see C. H. Cramer, *Newton D. Baker* (1961); and D. R. Beaver, *Newton D. Baker and the American War Effort, 1917–1919* (1966). The work of the Army is told with greatest completeness in the *United States Army in the World War, 1917–1919* (17 vols., 1948), a work prepared by the Historical Division, Department of the Army. J. J. Pershing, *My Experiences in the World War* (2 vols., 1931), is an excellent memoir, although far less charitable toward the General's superiors than they were toward him; his best biography is Frederick Palmer, *John J. Pershing, General of the Armies* (1948). Other valuable memoirs by high-ranking officers are J. G. Harbord, *The American Army in France, 1917–1919* (1936); Hunter Liggett, *Commanding an American Army: Recollections of the World War* (1925); P. C.

March, *The Nation at War* (1932); and M. M. Patrick, *The United States in the Air* (1928). An interesting biography is D. A. Lockmiller, *Enoch A. Crowder* (1955), on the founder of "selective service." See also E. M. Coffman's life of General March, *The Hilt of the Sword* (1966).

An excellent account of society on the home front is in P. W. Slosson, *The Great Crusade and After, 1914–1928* (1930). On the part played by labor, see John Steuben, *Labor in Wartime* (1940); and Samuel Gompers, *American Labor and the War* (1919). On wartime education, see L. P. Todd, *Wartime Relations of the Federal Government and the Public Schools, 1917–1918* (1945); and P. R. Kolbe, *The Colleges in War Time and After* (1919). On the mobilization of public opinion in favor of the war, there are several books by the head mobilizer, George Creel: *The War, the World and Wilson* (1920), *How We Advertised America* (1920), and *Rebel at Large* (1947), his bitter memoirs. On the same subject, see J. R. Mock, *Censorship, 1917* (1941); J. R. Mock and Cedric Larson, *Words That Won the War* (1939); and G. F. Bruntz, *Allied Propaganda and the Collapse of the German Empire in 1918* (1938).

H. C. Peterson and G. C. Fite, **Opponents of War, 1917–1918* (1957), is a horrifying catalogue of the abuses of liberty in wartime; perhaps no other work portrays so vividly the hysteria of the home front. See also the classic account by Zechariah Chafee, Jr., *Free Speech in the United States* (1941). On some radical victims, see H. M. Hyman, *Soldiers and Spruce* (1963); Oscar Ameringer, *If You Don't Weaken* (1940); R. L. Morlan, *Political Prairie Fire: The Nonpartisan League, 1915–1922* (1955); and Donald Johnson, *The Challenge to American Freedoms: World War 1 and the Rise of the American Civil Liberties Union* (1963). S. W. Livermore, **Woodrow Wilson and the War Congress, 1916–1918*, which was first published as *Politics Is Adjourned* (1966), shows how precarious Wilson's political position was even before the fateful 1918 general election.

17

THE RETREAT FROM EUROPE

Elections of 1918 · The Paris Peace Conference · The League of Nations · The Peace of Paris · The Senate and the Treaty of Versailles · Election of 1920 · The return to isolation · The Washington Conference · The World Court · The war debts controversy · Reparations · The Kellogg-Briand Peace Pact · Latin-American relations · Mexico · The Caribbean

Winning a war and winning the ensuing peace, as Americans now know well, are two very different things. Will Rogers overstated the case when he contended that the United States had won every war in which it had fought, and had lost every peace. But after the fighting died down in 1918 circumstances conspired to make the transition from war to peace peculiarly difficult.

Elections of 1918

To begin with, President Wilson, despite the high esteem in which he was held abroad, had suffered a disastrous political defeat at home. In the midterm elections of 1918 the Republicans won the House of Representatives by a majority of twenty

ONE AT A TIME. *Ultimately, the Senate voted down the peace treaty, and so kept the U.S. out of the League. Orr, Chicago Tribune.*

votes, and the Senate by a bare majority. Wilson himself had contributed to the Democratic defeat by an appeal on October 25 for a Democratic majority in Congress through which alone, he maintained, he could hope to carry on his policies. The Republicans skillfully turned this statement, which contrasted markedly with the President's earlier insistence on nonpartisanship for the duration, into a charge that they had not supported the war, and undoubtedly they gained many votes as a result. But the Wilson administration had already accumulated about all the enmity it could hope to carry; every European nation that participated in the war had already had at least one change of government since it began. Wilson's propaganda for an early peace and a just peace had small appeal for the "bitter-enders," who with Theodore Roosevelt at their head blamed the President for his delay in getting into the war, and made fun of his notewriting and idealism. The fact that he had led the country into the war at all was equally offensive to the pacifists and the German-Americans. To critics of his war policy were added those who disliked the liberal legislation of his first administration, his surrender to labor in the Adamson Act, and his attitude toward Mexico. Most important of all, the Republican politicians after six long years of separation from the spoils of office were alert to every opening that would facilitate their return to power, and directed their campaign with skill.

The logical place for the making of the treaty of peace, as had so often been the case after previous wars, proved to be Paris. Unwisely, perhaps, Wilson chose to represent the United States in person at the Conference, and to take along with him a delegation that would in no way interfere with his wishes. The other members of the American delegation were Robert Lansing, Secretary of State; Colonel House, the President's intimate friend; General Tasker H. Bliss, a military adviser; and Henry White, a Republican who had long since retired from active political life. So many experts, however, some of whom had been active in Colonel House's "Inquiry," accompanied the official delegates, that a large liner, the *George Washington*, was required to transport them all to Europe. The President's party reached France on December 13, 1918, but the Paris Peace Conference did not actually convene until January 18, 1919. In the meantime Wilson paid official visits to Paris, London, and Rome, and inspected some of the battlefields of the war. Everywhere he was received with the most wholehearted enthusiasm on the part of the people, and with every show of hospitality on the part of the heads of the Allied governments, although many of them regretted the necessity of having to deal with him personally.

The Paris Peace Conference

The Paris Peace Conference was an extraordinary gathering. All the Allies were represented, including such nonparticipating belligerents as China and Brazil, but the Germans for understandable, if not necessarily justifiable, reasons were denied any voice whatever in the proceedings. It was clear that the problem of reconciling conflicting Allied opinions would be a serious enough task without a German delegation ready to take every advantage of Allied disagreements. The Conference, of course, was too large to carry on the actual negotiations, and met only for plenary sessions to confirm what had already been agreed upon behind the scenes. All matters of consequence were settled by the "Big Four," Clemenceau of France, Lloyd George of Great Britain, Orlando of Italy, and Wilson of the United States. Of this group, Wilson was still committed in principle to the Fourteen Points, although some of his points had been seriously modified in the pre-armistice negotiations. But Clemenceau, Lloyd George, and Orlando considered themselves bound primarily by the secret treaties which the Allies had negotiated with each other early in the war. These treaties promised France Alsace-Lorraine, the Saar Basin, and an independent government for the rest of the German territory west of the Rhine. Great Britain was to receive most of the German colonies, and a free hand in Egypt, Persia, and Mesopotamia. Italy was assured her *Italia Irredenta* — the Trentino, the southern Tyrol, and control of the Adriatic. Rumania had been assigned Transylvania and other territorial acquisitions. Japan was to succeed Germany in Shantung and in the islands of the central Pacific north of the equator. Russia, who had forfeited her claims by withdrawing from the war, was to have been given Constantinople and the Dardanelles. To the Allies these terms signified their rightful spoils of victory, and they proposed to obtain them as nearly as they might.

The Treaty of Versailles

Wilson had hoped that the influence of an aroused world opinion would enable him to persuade the Allies to forget their harsh terms, and to accept more literally his Fourteen Points program. In the end he won only a compromise. When delegates from the new German republic agreed to this treaty on June 28, they surrendered Alsace-Lorraine to France; gave up to Poland generous blocks of territory including a corridor to the sea along the Vistula; and ceded border rectifications to Belgium and Denmark. The German colonies were all taken away, and handed over to the Allied countries, not for outright annexation, but under a League of Nations mandate system that in practice amounted to the same thing. The Saar Basin, Germany's richest coal-mining area was turned over to French exploitation for a period of fifteen years, during which time it was to be under the political control of an international commission; at the end of the stipulated period the people of the Saar might decide by plebiscite whether the region should be returned to Germany, continued under international control, or ceded to France.

Reparations for the damages done by the German armies had been agreed to in the pre-armistice terms, but the Conference was unable to fix upon the amount due, and left this to be decided by a Reparations Commission after peace was restored. In May, 1921, the Commission set the German bill for damages at about $33 billion, well beyond the ability of Germany to pay. In 1922, on the ground that Germany had defaulted in her payments, the French seized the Ruhr Valley coal fields. Finally, after several fruitless efforts to solve the problem by international agreement, Germany under Hitler openly repudiated her obliga-

tions, and the Allies were unwilling to fight about it. France relinquished the Ruhr in 1925. Ten years later, the Saar voted by an overwhelming majority for reunion with Germany.

In some ways harder for the Germans to bear than the reparations bill (most of which was never paid anyway) was the assertion in the treaty that their country and her allies were responsible "for causing all the loss and damage to which the Allied and Associated governments have been subjected as a consequence of the war." This "war-guilt" clause, they maintained, quite indefensibly placed full blame upon the Central Powers for the outbreak of war in 1914.

The Treaty of Versailles also provided for the complete disarmament of Germany. Her standing army was reduced to 100,000 men and conscription was abolished; frontier fortifications not in Allied hands were to be razed; the manufacture, importation, or exportation of war materials was virtually prohibited; and the German navy was reduced to insignficance.

The League of Nations

Harsh as these terms were, they did not satisfy Clemenceau, who conceded even this much only on condition that there be a separate alliance between Great Britain, the United States, and France to repel jointly any future attacks on France. Wilson consented to the alliance, but the Senate, as he should have foreseen, refused to accept so forthright a departure from the American tradition of nonintervention in European affairs. Wilson pinned his hope for future peace, however, less on the proposed alliance than upon the League of Nations, which by his persistent efforts the Allies were at length induced to include in the Treaty of Versailles. Through this organization, he hoped, many of the injustices of the treaty could be righted later, when wartime fevers should have abated. The

The Big Four. *Lloyd George of England, Orlando of Italy, Clemenceau of France, and Wilson of the United States, as the political leaders of the major victorious nations, decided all important questions at the Peace Conference.*

Covenant of the League described three principal agencies: (1) a permanent Secretariat with headquarters established at Geneva, Switzerland; (2) a Council of nine members (later enlarged), to consist of one representative from each of the great powers, France, Great Britain, Italy, Japan, and the United States, and four others to be chosen by the Assembly; (3) an Assembly in which every member nation was to have a representative and a vote. The members of the League agreed by the famous Article X "to respect and preserve as against external aggression the territorial integrity and existing political independence" of all other members, and to recognize the right of every member nation to bring problems that might disturb the peace to the attention of the Assembly or the Council. Peace was to be achieved primarily by arbitration or adjudication, and the establishment of a permanent court of international justice was contemplated; but disputes not so adjusted must be submitted for settlement either to the Council or to the Assembly. Against nations making illegal war the Council might impose drastic economic sanctions, and in case it deemed military measures necessary to check aggressors it might make appropriate recommendations to members of the League.

The Peace of Paris

The Treaty of Versailles was only one of many treaties that taken together may properly be called the Peace of Paris. Wilson's tenth point had expressly stated that he wished to see the place of Austria-Hungary among nations "safeguarded and assured," but the disintegration of that unhappy power had been so complete that its resurrection as one nation was beyond possibility. Each of the many national groups that composed the old Empire was now determined to be free, except, possibly, the German-speaking portion of Austria, which would have preferred union with Germany. But the Treaty of Saint-Germain, signed September 10, 1919, warned the new "Republic of Austria" to "abstain from any act which might directly or indirectly or by any means whatever compromise her independence." This action was taken partly in order to prevent Germany from being strengthened by the addition of so many Austrians, and partly to prevent the new

state of Czechoslovakia from being nearly encircled by Germany. The Treaty of Trianon with Hungary was not signed until June 4, 1920. It cut down the domain of the Magyar kingdom to an irreducible minimum. The Treaty of Neuilly with Bulgaria, signed November 27, 1919, trimmed off in similar fashion the borders of Germany's smallest ally, and the Treaty of Sèvres with Turkey, signed August 10, 1920, left little non-Turkish territory to the Turks.

The "Balkanization" of Central Europe

Through these and numerous supplementary treaties the "Balkanization" of Central Europe was completed. The states that had aided the Allies were rewarded by territorial gains; those that had supported the Central Powers were punished by territorial losses. Numerous new states appeared on the map of Europe: Finland, Estonia, Latvia, Lithuania, Poland, Czechoslovakia, Yugoslavia, Albania. Everywhere the problem of "minorities" threatened the permanence of peace, for boundary lines that would separate every nationality from every other simply could not be drawn. Even the victors were not wholly satisfied. During the Peace Conference Wilson had insisted that the Italians were not entitled to Fiume on the eastern coast of the Adriatic, and as a result the Italian delegation had left the Conference. Ultimately they came back, and by a *coup* Italy obtained the coveted port later

on. But the Italians never forgave Wilson, although he consented to the inclusion within Italian borders of several hundred thousand Austrian Germans in the Trentino. This, like many another such decision, was condoned on the ground that it was necessary to provide the nation concerned with a defensible frontier. By the time these treaties were written, Wilson must have realized that in much of Europe "clearly recognizable lines of nationality" simply did not exist. Even less attainable was the hope seemingly cherished by each of these little states of achieving economic self-sufficiency. Instead of creating a world community, as Wilson had hoped, the Peace of Paris accelerated in many ways the old forces of nationalism.

The completed Peace of Paris was severely criticized in many quarters. In Germany it was looked upon as a hypocritical violation of the promised peace of justice based upon the Fourteen Points. The "Diktat of Versailles" became a hated phrase throughout the defeated country and was used to whip up the rising wave of German nationalism. Many victorious Allies denounced the peace for not giving them all they had been promised in the secret treaties of 1915 and in Wilson's Fourteen Points. Nationalists among the victorious powers denounced the peace for being too soft toward the defeated, while idealists, especially in the United States, considered the settlement much too harsh.

Defects of the Peace

Admittedly the Peace of Paris was far from perfect and could not be squared on many counts with the Fourteen Points. As things turned out, the mandate system of parcelling out former German colonies among the victorious powers looked like a hypocritical form of the old colonialism. The reparations eventually charged to Germany were certainly not in the spirit of peace without victory. Because of British opposition, Wilson's demand for freedom of the seas was lost, and the promise of disarmament fell before the French insistence on military security. The doctrine of self-determination, while honored more than critics would confess, was seriously violated in northern Italy, and could not be applied in eastern Europe simply because in many localities no clear national majorities existed. Where it was applied most extensively, in the old Austrian empire, it dismembered a self-contained economic unit and by so doing insured future distress. The absence from the conference of revolutionary Russia, already hostile to the West, and vice versa, was also ominous for the future stability of eastern Europe. Nor did the well-known anti-Japanese sentiment of the Australians augur well for an enduring peace in the western Pacific.

Yet for all the faults of the Peace of Paris, one might ask whether a better peace could have been obtained at that time, and whether, if so, it could have won the needed support on both sides of the Atlantic. In a world dominated by fear, hate, and intolerance, the European allies were demanding some reward for their years of suffering and some security for the future. As usual, the material rewards were not enough to satisfy all the victorious claimants. And the road to security was a debatable one. To a Frenchman who had seen his country invaded and devastated twice in his lifetime, reliance upon a League of Nations had to grow out of faith rather than experience. Had the peoples of Europe instead of their governments made peace, the settlement would have been much harsher, judging by the vengeful slogans popular in all nations from Great Britain to Italy. But such a so-called practical and realistic peace would have alienated Wilson and the majority of Americans who were halfway expecting a millenium, but who were in the last analysis not willing to pay for it by pledging their own armed strength to France or even to the League to stop further aggression.

The Peace of Paris was a compromise between European memories and American expectations, between theoretical justice and the realities of the time. It was a much more moderate peace than the one the Germans had exacted from Russia at Brest-Litovsk. Much can be said for Lloyd George's observation that the chief trouble was not with the peace written in Paris, but with its administration afterwards when the United States was absent from the world's councils. It may well have been, as Wilson commented about the Far Eastern settlement, the best that could be wrung "from a dirty past." Certainly most of the forward looking elements incorporated in the peace were there because of the American President's long and dogged struggles in Paris.

The Senate and the Treaty

The seeds of future wars were strewn throughout the Peace of Paris, but Wilson hoped that the League of Nations might prevent their growth. Unfortunately, he was soon to discover that for this innovation he was unable to win the support of his own government. The election of 1918 had given the Senate to the Republicans by the narrowest possible margin, and Henry Cabot Lodge of Massachusetts had become Chairman of the Senate Committee on

Foreign Relations, to which the Treaty of Versailles was referred, after its submission to the Senate, July 10, 1919. All through his public life Lodge had been a conservative, an ardent Republican partisan, and a nationalist. He was thus bitterly opposed to practically everything Wilson stood for and disliked the President intensely — a feeling which Wilson cordially reciprocated. In 1916 Lodge had believed that a world organization might be able to preserve the peace, but in 1918 he changed his mind. He was not willing publicly to join the "bitter enders," such as LaFollette of Wisconsin, Reed of Missouri, and Johnson of California, who were adamant against any world organization. But he did feel that securing world peace was impossible "by any of the methods proposed." As a knowing politician, however, Lodge recognized the popular support for the League over the country. Accordingly, he announced that he was for a League, but not Wilson's League. His strategy was to "Republicanize the treaty" by attaching to it a series of reservations or interpretations, most of which would have reduced the obligations of the United States to the world organization. By such a course he hoped to keep unity between the pro- and anti-League factions of his own party and also claim credit for the final result. If the treaty were accepted with his amendments, it would then be in part a Republican treaty; if it were rejected, much of the blame for its defeat could be placed upon Wilson and the Democrats. Either result, Lodge calculated, would aid the Republican Party, and damage Wilson and the Democrats in the coming presidential election. To help insure such results, Lodge contrived the appointment to his committee of four bitterly anti-League and anti-Wilson Republicans, thus ignoring the moderates in his party.

Unfortunately, the President himself had opened the way to a partisan struggle by refusing to take to Paris any pro-League Republicans of national stature. Moreover, on his return to the United States he continued to ignore such powerful Republican friends of the League as Taft, Root, and Hughes. Throughout the long fight Wilson never really attempted to conciliate either the moderate Republicans or the Senate. Nor would he compromise on any important part of the agreement made at Paris. He felt, probably correctly, that the people, if thoroughly aroused, could force their rulers to heed the popular will. The Senate might prefer not to ratify the treaty, but in the end, he remarked, it would have "to take its medicine."

Accordingly when the Lodge group sought to amend the treaty radically, a process described by some observers as "death by strangulation," the President took his case to the people on an extensive speaking tour. Had the radio then been available, or television, this hot summer trip, which completely sapped his vitality, would not have been necessary. Later Presidents, from an air-conditioned White House room, were able to reach far larger numbers than Wilson's speaking tour enabled him to reach in 1919. For the President and his cause the trip proved to be disastrous. Already badly shattered by an attack of influenza in Paris, Wilson broke down physically under the ordeal and was obliged to return to Washington, where he suffered a stroke of paralysis. For months he was almost totally incapacitated, and when he did recover enough to carry on the more essential duties of his office, he lacked the physical vigor necessary to deal with his foes.

Defeat of the Treaty

The Treaty of Versailles was twice before the Senate, and both times failed to achieve the two-thirds majority necessary for ratification. At first with fourteen reservations to match Wilson's Fourteen Points, but finally with fifteen, the Republican majority stood ready to ratify, but the Democratic minority following Wilson's own recommendation declined, although it was well known that the leading European powers would have preferred ratification with the reservations to no ratification at all. On the final vote, March 20, 1920, the Senate voted, forty-nine to thirty-five, to accept the treaty with the reservations attached. But Wilson had asked the Democrats to stand by him and vote down the treaty with the Republican reservations. Recorded against the treaty were the "bitter-end" isolationists and many of Wilson's closest supporters, Democratic regulars who were willing to accept the treaty precisely as the President had submitted it, but in no other form. Thus the treaty failed with an overwhelming majority of the Senate favoring its adoption, although some wanted it with reservations, and others only without. As one historian has summarized the result, men on both sides consistently voted their party instead of their conscience.

Who really killed the treaty? Some observers believe that if Wilson had been more pliable a compromise could have been reached, but others insist that the reservations were designed to kill the treaty, and would have been made stronger had they been acceptable to the President. As a sequel, it is interesting to note that once the Republican Party came to power, Henry Cabot Lodge, still chairman of the Senate Committee on Foreign Relations, was opposed to the League with or without reservations, and, in fact, became the leader in his party's flight toward complete isolation. What would have transpired had Wilson followed the advice of Colonel House to resign the Presidency and leave the battle to Vice-President Marshall may only be surmised. By this time the friendship between the President and his former intimate had cooled, and House's letter, embodying this advice, was never an-

Henry Cabot Lodge. *As chairman of the Senate Committee on Foreign Relations, Senator Lodge, a bitter foe of Wilson, led the fight on the Treaty of Versailles.*

swered. Wilson's break with House has sometimes been attributed to his second wife, Edith Bolling Galt, whom he married in December, 1916, following the death of his first wife in August, 1915. Particularly during his illness, the influence of the second Mrs. Wilson over the President was very great. Himself a casualty of the war, Wilson could not yet understand how thorough was his defeat. From the news that filtered into his sickroom he continued to believe that the American people, who were now in reality drifting rapidly back to isolationism, were still with him. When Congress by joint resolution sought to declare the war with Germany at an end, he interposed his veto, charging that such a course would be an "ineffaceable stain upon the gallantry and honor of the United

The Second Inauguration. *The President and Mrs. Wilson are shown here returning from the Capitol after the inauguration, March 5, 1917, a Monday.*

States." The election of 1920, he maintained, must be made a "solemn referendum" to decide whether the American people would accept or reject the obligations of the treaty and the League.

Significance of Wilson's Defeat

Looking backward, after the experience of a Second World War, it would seem that the United States, by its half-hearted refusal to support the League of Nations, destroyed whatever chance there was to prevent another general war. Had the American nation shown itself willing to accept the responsibilities of world leadership, it is possible that the return to international anarchy which marked the next two decades might have been forestalled. Conceivably, also, the mistakes and the injustices of the treaty, of which there were many, might have been ironed out through instrumentalities provided for in the League. But when the richest and most powerful of all the nations refused to cooperate in any effective way for the maintenance of peace, the possibility of another world war became a certainty. Essentially

what the United States had done in its European adventure was to create the alliance of power that had won the war, had written the peace, and was necessary for the enforcement of its terms. By refusing to support the peace it had made possible, the United States materially weakened the victors and correspondingly strengthened the losers. During the fight on the League, Wilson had recorded his conviction that, in case his efforts failed, the war would have to be fought all over again. What might have happened can never be known, but a generation later the war that Wilson predicted came to pass. It was this return of the United States to isolation which, according to Winston Churchill, made possible the Second World War:

It is my opinion that this war would have been prevented if the United States had been in the old League of Nations or, even if it had not, if a strong position had been taken by the leaders. Instead it was led by weak and feeble forces until the hostile forces seized control elsewhere and brought war down upon the world once more.

Election of 1920

The election of 1920 was hardly the "solemn referendum" on the treaty and the League for which Wilson had called, but it did its part toward contributing to those "weak and feeble forces" that Churchill later had occasion to regret. The death of Theodore Roosevelt in 1919, to whom the Republican nomination almost certainly would have gone had he lived, precipitated a lively contest among General Leonard Wood, upon whom Roosevelt's mantle had fallen, Governor Frank O. Lowden of Illinois, and Senator Hiram Johnson of California. But in the end the leading contenders killed themselves off, and the nomination went to Senator Warren G. Harding of Ohio, the choice of the Republican leaders in the Senate. Harding's limited talents made it seem certain that the charge of "executive usurpation" would never need be brought against him. He was a reservationist during the fight of the Treaty of Versailles, and always a dependable regular. For Vice-President the Republicans chose Calvin Coolidge of Massachusetts, who first won a national reputation when he called out the state militia in 1919 to suppress the Boston police strike. To oppose this ticket the Democrats nominated Governor James M. Cox of Ohio for President, and Franklin D. Roosevelt, Wilson's Assistant Secretary of the Navy, for Vice-President. On the Treaty of Versailles and the League of Nations the Democratic platform stood earnestly by Wilson's record, and the Democratic candidates stood on their platform. But the Republican platform was vague on this issue, and the Republican candidates even vaguer. Such League advocates as Hughes, Root, and Taft were able to maintain that the election of Harding would be the surest way to get the United States into the League, while such irreconcilables as Johnson and Borah could declare with equal certainty that

Warren G. Harding. *As twenty-ninth President of the United States, Harding conspicuously lacked the ability to fulfill the duties of his high office. A 1962* New York Times Magazine *poll of seventy-five American scholars, most of them historians, ranked him as one of the nation's two failures as President. The other failure was Ulysses S. Grant.*

Harding would keep the United States out of the League. Exactly what the public was thinking on this issue when it went to the polls would be hard to state, but the "League to Elect Harding" held together during the campaign and scored a decisive victory. The last few months of the Wilson administration had witnessed a sharp economic decline, and the voters tended as usual to hold hard times against the party in power, which in the public mind meant the party that held the Presidency. Moreover, the country was no longer in a reform mood. It resented having had to fight a war; it was tired of the long debate over the Treaty of Versailles; it was eager for a return to "normalcy." Harding's popular majority was over 7 million, and in the electoral college he received 404 to Cox's 127. He was assured, also, of a Congress that would be overwhelmingly Republican in both houses.

The Return to Isolation

The new President, despite his votes as Senator for the treaty with reservations, and despite his temporizing during the campaign, chose to interpret his election as a mandate against ratification. The Treaty of Versailles, he maintained, was dead. Following a July, 1921, joint resolution of Congress, which once more declared the war at an end, the American Department of State began negotiations with Germany that led to a separate treaty, signed August 25, 1921, and later duly ratified. By this document the United States obtained every possible advantage of the Treaty of Versailles, but accepted none of its responsibilities. The Department of State also negotiated and the Senate ratified similar peace treaties with Austria and Hungary, together with treaties establishing normal relations with the "succession states" of Central Europe,

and with Turkey. As for Soviet Russia, the new administration agreed with the stand already taken by the Wilson administration that the United States should have no diplomatic relations with a government that was determined "to conspire against our institutions," and "whose diplomats will be the agitators of dangerous revolt." For a time the Department of State seemed also to extend this policy of non-recognition to the League of Nations, and refused even to acknowledge communications that the United States received from it; but from this extreme position it eventually retreated. And yet, as one observer remarked, the United States had about completed a full cycle, "from isolation to leadership and back again."

President Harding, in taking his firm stand for isolation, was no doubt influenced by the bitter-enders in his party, some of whom had threatened to wreck his admin-

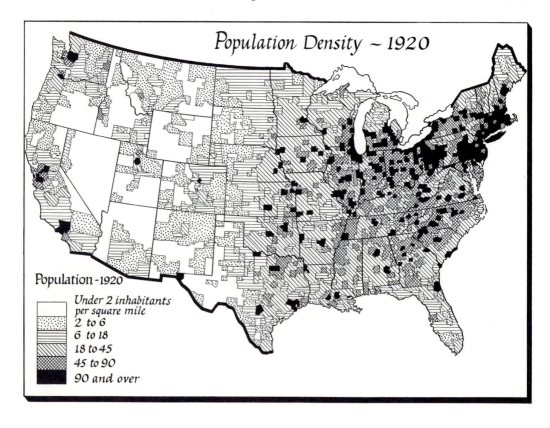

Population Density ~ 1920

Population - 1920

Under 2 inhabitants per square mile
2 to 6
6 to 18
18 to 45
45 to 90
90 and over

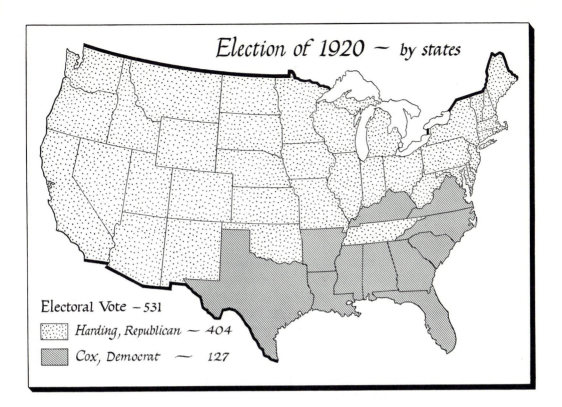

Election of 1920 ~ by states

Electoral Vote ~ 531

Harding, Republican ~ 404

Cox, Democrat ~ 127

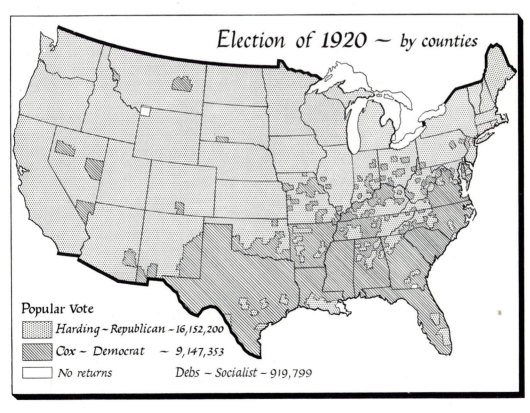

Election of 1920 ~ by counties

Popular Vote

Harding ~ Republican ~ 16,152,200

Cox ~ Democrat ~ 9,147,353

No returns   Debs ~ Socialist ~ 919,799

istration if he dared do otherwise. But it is also true that he was extremely unversed in foreign affairs, and even unaware of the full significance of his decision. Perhaps, too, he sensed the fact that the American people were fast losing their interest in the international scene; to have reversed this tide would have required far more dedication to the cause and far greater qualities of leadership than he possessed. Such a man as Hoover or Hughes as President might once more have aroused the nation to a recognition of its world commitments, but Harding did not compare with either in understanding and ability. He did indeed make Hughes his Secretary of State, and Hughes no doubt would have preferred to revise and accept the Treaty of Versailles, or perhaps to create a new and more acceptable League of Nations. But on foreign policy Hughes was not a free agent, and had to abide by the President's decision. Calvin Coolidge, who succeeded to the Presidency when Harding died in 1923, was as unfitted as his predecessor to cope with foreign problems, and Frank B. Kellogg of Minnesota, whom Coolidge made Secretary of State when Hughes resigned in 1925, was as helpless as Hughes to reverse presidential policy. Furthermore, by the time Kellogg took office, if not sooner, the majority of the American people were fully sold on the principle of no foreign entanglements, and a reversal of the Harding decision had become impossible.

At the time it was made, however, Harding's break from Wilsonian idealism was too abrupt for many Americans to accept without protest, and even the most hardboiled reactionaries could see that some satisfactory substitute had to be found. To meet this need the current interest in naval reductions seemed to offer a ready-made opportunity. The program of naval expansion begun by the United States, Great Britain, and Japan during the war had de-

veloped at its close into an unhealthy and expensive rivalry that threatened to continue indefinitely. Senator Borah, an outstanding "bitter-ender" in the treaty fight, became the most prominent advocate of naval limitation, and it was due in no small part to his efforts that President Harding was persuaded to call an International Conference on Limitation of Armaments to meet on Armistice Day, November 11, 1921. Every possible device was employed to build up the Conference as the Republican counterpart of the Wilsonian program. It was persistently spoken of as the "Peace Conference," although it was nothing of the kind, and a great to-do was made over its opening. At eleven o'clock on the appointed day the whole nation paused in commemoration of the restoration of peace, while at the Arlington National Cemetery the body of an unknown American soldier was ceremoniously interred.

The Washington Conference

Next day, after the formal welcome by President Harding was over, Secretary Hughes presented a program of naval reduction so drastic as to startle the Conference. Exhibiting a knowledge of detail that was in itself amazing, he advocated that the naval strength of the great powers should be fixed at stipulated ratios, that naval tonnage in excess of specified maxima should be scrapped, and that no new ships should be constructed for a period of ten years. In the end five powers, the United States, the British Empire, Japan, France, and Italy, agreed to limit their strength in capital ships to total tonnages that bore to each other roughly the ratios of 5 : 5 : 3 : 1.7 : 1.7, respectively. Unfortunately this agreement left unsolved the important problem of lesser craft. Some critics said that the elimination of capital ships was inconsequential, since the battle of Jutland had proved that they were no longer of value; others, that the agreements failed to

The Washington Conference, 1921. *Left to right the participants in the conference shown here are: J. S. Garrett, Secretary General of the Conference; Jonkheer H. A. Van Karne-Beek, Netherlands; Sao Ke Alfred Sze, China; Arthur James Balfour, United Kingdom; Charles Evans Hughes, United States; Aristide Briand, France; Carlo Schanzer, Italy; Baron de Cartier de Marchienne, Belgium; Prince Ivesato Tokugawa, Japan; Viscount D'Alte, Portugal.*

provide for any inspection or enforcement. But the limitations adopted at least resulted in tremendous budgetary savings for the nations concerned, and naval experts generally refused to concede that dreadnoughts and battle-cruisers were obsolete. In 1927, at the suggestion of President Coolidge, a conference met at Geneva to discuss the limitation of auxiliary ships, but failed to reach an agreement. In 1930 at London, a conference called by President Hoover fared somewhat better. Some limitations were imposed on the building of lesser craft, Japan was appeased by a more generous quota on cruisers and destroyers, and the naval holiday in capital ships was extended to 1936.

An unforeseen, and perhaps unforeseeable, result of the disarmament program was to leave Japan relatively stronger in the Far East, and the United States and Great Britain relatively weaker. The Washington agreement actually referred only to capital ships, and placed no limitations on

the building of auxiliary craft of any kind, but the United States for a period of three years following the conference failed to lay down a single keel, and for three years more did little building of consequence. Only after Japan, followed by some of the other powers, had begun to build cruisers again did the United States in 1928 re-enter the rivalry. Even after the agreement of 1930, the United States, and to a lesser extent, Great Britain, failed to build up to their treaty limitations. Japan, on the other hand, built to the very limit of her quotas, and in 1934, when she began to feel cramped by them, denounced the agreement that bound her until 1936. After that date the race for naval supremacy was resumed in earnest, but Japan started it in a far stronger position, relatively, than she had been in before the negotiations on limitation of armaments had begun. It is possible that the Washington Conference and the agreements that flowed from it, instead of promoting peace by disarmament as the western powers intended, may actually have furnished Japan the necessary incentive to start her on the road to Pearl Harbor.

The Four-Power Pact

The Washington Conference resulted in the drafting of two other noteworthy treaties, one signed by four powers, and the other by nine. The Four-Power Pact, agreed to by the United States, the British Empire, France, and Japan, paved the way for the abrogation of the Anglo-Japanese Alliance, which had become distasteful to both Great Britain and the United States. The new pact proposed to preserve the peace in the Pacific by pledging the contracting powers mutually to respect one another's rights "in relation to their insular possessions and insular dominions in the region," and to refer to a joint conference such disputes as might cause trouble. The four powers also bound themselves to "communicate with one another fully and frankly" on the action to be taken in case their rights were "threatened by the aggressive action of any other power." Had the pact ever been taken seriously, as it was not, it might have constituted almost as decisive a departure from the American policy of isolation as if the United States had entered the League of Nations. Closely connected with it was Article XIX of the Treaty on Naval Limitation which bound the United States, the British Empire, and Japan to maintain the *status quo* with respect to "fortifications and naval bases in the Pacific." But, inasmuch as both the Japanese "home islands" and Hawaii were excluded from this provision, the Japanese were left free to build up their naval strength further in East Asia.

The Nine-Power Treaty

The Nine-Power Treaty related to "principles and policies to be followed in matters concerning China," and was signed by the United States, Belgium, the British Empire,

China, France, Italy, Japan, the Netherlands, and Portugal. The situation in the Far East had changed materially as a result of the First World War. In 1915 Japan had in effect repudiated the doctrine of the open door by presenting to China twenty-one offensive demands for special privileges, many of which China was forced to concede. In 1917, by the Lansing-Ishii Agreement, Japan once more gave lip-service to the open door, but won from the United States recognition "that territorial propinquity creates special relations between countries." At the Paris Peace Conference, Japan insisted on being awarded the German concessions in Shantung, although the Japanese delegates promised Wilson that Japan would eventually withdraw from the peninsula, which, at least in a military sense, she did. The purpose of the Nine-Power Pact was to reconcile this situation, as nearly as possible, with the open door for world trade in China and the integrity of the Chinese Republic. In words the new treaty seemed to administer a strong rebuff to Japanese policy, for it pledged the signatory powers to respect Chinese sovereignty, to aid China in maintaining an effective government, to use their influence in favor of "equal opportunity for the commerce and industry of all nations" in China, and to "refrain from taking advantage of conditions in China to seek special rights." But Japan by the decade of the thirties was violating all these pledges with impunity, and the treaty provided no means whereby an offending power could be restrained.

Minor Agreements

Certain minor agreements were not written into the Nine-Power Treaty. A separate treaty provided for the return of Shantung to China on condition that China should buy from Japan the former German railway line serving the peninsula, and should also honor numerous private contracts obtained by the Japanese during the occupation. The United States had objected also to the status of the island of Yap, which the League of Nations had handed over to Japan as a mandate, together with numerous other Pacific islands north of the equator that Japan had seized from Germany during the war. Yap, because of its importance as a cable station, should have been internationalized, according to the American contention. The result was a separate treaty between the United States and Japan, signed during the Conference, that gave the United States the cable privileges it desired on the island. Although Japan withdrew from the League of Nations in 1933 (effective 1935), she retained her mandates in the Pacific islands, and fortified them well, as many "G.I.'s" who fought in the Second World War can testify. Resolutions of little binding force called also for the removal of foreign post offices and radio stations from China, the acknowledgement of her right to tariff autonomy, and a study of extra-territoriality.

Harding's formula of peace by disarmament proved to be a poor substitute for Wilson's formula of peace by international cooperation. But it satisfied the growing isolationist spirit of the times. For over a century before the First World War the United States had held aloof from world affairs; now it was ready to return to its traditional policy and let the nations of Europe and Asia go their own way. With adequate naval disarmament, Harding's apologists reasoned, the United States need not fear an aggressor, and it never meant to be one. Pleased with this easy approach to perpetual peace, they overlooked the inadequacy of the disarmament actually achieved, and failed to observe the even more important fact that a great and powerful nation in an increasingly interdependent world had no chance to escape outside responsibilities.

The World Court

The Washington Conference was not the only Republican effort, however, to promote world peace. The idea of a permanent court of international justice had been advocated by the American delegation to the Second Hague Conference in 1907, and was far more closely identified with Republican than with Democratic policy. When, therefore, under Article XIV of the League of Nations Covenant, plans were drawn in 1920 for such a court, there seemed no good reason why a Republican administration should not give the new institution its blessing. Indeed, Elihu Root, respected elder statesman of the Republican Party, had assisted in drafting the World Court protocol, and John Bassett Moore, America's foremost authority on international law, was slated for a place on its bench of eleven (later fifteen) judges. The only difficulty in the way of American participation seeemd to lie in the fact that

John Bassett Moore. *This distinguished American authority on international law was one of the original members of the World Court. He was succeeded in 1928 by Charles Evans Hughes.*

the judges were to be chosen by the Council and Assembly of the League of Nations, but it was proposed that for this purpose only, the United States might have a voice in the proceedings. Certain that public opinion was "overwhelmingly in favor of participation," President Harding urged American adherence to the Court, only to be rebuffed by the Senate, in which the irreconcilables were able to prevent any action whatever. Extreme isolationists professed to fear that adherence to the Court would be only the entering wedge to further involvement in world affairs, and the still-embittered critics of "Wilsonism" would have nothing to do with anything even remotely connected with the League. Harding was not the last American President to advocate the adherence of the United States to the World Court. Coolidge, Hoover, and Roosevelt all urged the Senate to ratify its protocol, but they all failed to get results. In spite of nonparticipation by the United States, an American judge always sat on the court. Moore was succeeded by Charles Evans Hughes in 1928; Hughes, by Frank B. Kellogg in 1930; Kellogg, by Manley O. Hudson in 1936.

America and the World

In spite of the continuing devotion of most Americans to the policy of diplomatic isolation, evidence that the United States must play a leading role in international affairs accumulated rapidly during the twenties. As a result of the war, the American nation had enormously expanded its industrial plant; it had discovered unsuspected possibilities by way of agricultural production; it had accumulated out of its profits huge sums for new investment. Moreover, if the high speed to which its economic machine had been geared were to be maintained, the country must import many materials which it could not produce, such as rubber, silk, nickel, and tin, and many others which it could produce only

in limited quantities, such as sugar, wool, hides, and nitrates. What the United States really needed was a peaceful and friendly world generally committed to the open door. That American statesmen of the twenties failed to achieve this goal should have occasioned no surprise. They were faced at home by a sentimental regard for political isolation and a deep-rooted belief in the protective-tariff system; they were faced abroad by the jealousies and hatreds engendered by the war and the peace, feelings compounded so far as they concerned the United States by the conviction that the American people had escaped most of the war's ravages, but had taken most of its profits.

The War Debts Controversy

Among the most perplexing of the problems before the American government during the twenties was the collection of the loans by which the United States had so largely financed the Allied cause after 1917, and the work of reconstruction after the war. To the American people these intergovernmental loans seemed no different from the loans of one individual to another, and their repayment was regarded as a matter of simple honesty. Europeans took a somewhat different view of the situation. The war, they argued, was a common endeavor, in which each nation had given all that it had to give. The United States had entered the conflict late, and its casualty list was short; why should it begrudge the dollars it had spent? Why should it not forgive its debtors, especially since American prosperity so far outstripped European? Moreover, most of the money lent had been expended in the United States, and goods rather than gold had been sent abroad. Was it fair to ask European nations to pay back gold that they had never seen; indeed, half the world's supply of gold was already in the United States. Nor could European nations hope to build up large balances in

"Paying for a Dead Horse."
The American people, although convinced that the Allies should pay their war debts to the United States, showed much sympathy for Germany in her problem of reparations.

America by the shipment of goods; the high American tariff forestalled that. To the war-heated imaginations of European critics "Uncle Sam" became "Uncle Shylock," and hostile feeling ran high.

Nevertheless, in 1922 Congress created a World War Foreign Debt Commission which opened negotiations with the various Allied nations, and ultimately succeeded in reaching refunding agreements with fifteen of them. American policy called for settlements in accordance with ability to pay; hence the interest charges ranged from as low as 0.4 per cent in the case of Italy to the normal 3.3. per cent required of Great Britain and the more solvent states. The British settlement was effected as early as June, 1923, and the others during the next few years. Opposition to repayment reached its maximum in France, where the costly work of reconstruction threatened to bankrupt the government, but an agreement was signed in April, 1926, which set the interest rate at 1.6, and allowed a period of sixty-two years for payment. The grand total of all the funded debts was increased by postwar loans for rehabilitation purposes and by unpaid interest to more than $11.5 billion, with 90 per cent of the amount owing by Great Britain

($4.6 billion), France ($4.02 billion), and Italy ($2.04 billion). Repayments by December 31, 1930, amounted to about $2.5 billion, of which more than 70 per cent came from Great Britain. Next year, following the Hoover moratorium, a few nations met their obligations, but thereafter payments from all nations except Finland, whose debts were strictly postwar, virtually ceased.

Russia alone among the European nations that had borrowed from the United States refused to consider the funding of her debt. The Soviets, in keeping with their views on capitalism, repudiated all financial obligations incurred by preceding Russian governments, and denied the claims for indemnification lodged by foreigners whose property had been confiscated or destroyed during the revolutions of 1917. It was in part on this account that the American government so long refused to accord recognition to the Soviet government. No attempt was made, however, to prevent American firms from trading with Russia at their own risk. It should be noted that the Russian debt to the United States was very small, only $192 million, whereas the repudiated Russian debt to Great Britain was $4.3 billion.

Charles Gates Dawes. *This Chicago banker served his government in many capacities, as purchasing agent during World War I, as its first budget director, as head of the commission on German reparations, as Vice-President, as president of the RFC, and as Ambassador to Great Britain.*

Reparations

Inevitably the problem of war debts became closely intertwined with the problem of German reparations. If Germany could meet her obligations to the Allies, then the Allies could make their payments to the United States. Any connection between these two problems was vigorously denied by the American government, but its existence in fact if not in theory was abundantly clear. The difficulties experienced by Germany in paying the extortionate sums required by the Reparations Commission in 1921 led to two efforts at readjustment, one in 1924, and another in 1929. It was significant that in each case the commission of experts entrusted with the negotiations was headed by an American, in the first instance by Charles G. Dawes, and in the second by Owen D. Young. The Dawes Plan reduced the sums required from Germany each year, arranged for a foreign loan to support the German monetary system, and required French withdrawal from the Ruhr Valley, a district into which France had sent her troops in 1922 because of German failure to make repara-

tions payments. For four years, in large part by borrowing private funds in the United States, with administration approval because this was regarded as a strictly business deal, Germany was able to meet the new payments, but by 1928 she was again in trouble. The Young Plan proposed another set of annuities to run for a period of 58.5 years, the capitalized value of which would amount to only a little more than $8 billion, approximately the sum still due from the Allies to the United States. Further, it stipulated that additional reductions might be made proportional to any readjustments in the inter-Allied war debts; in other words, if the United States would reduce its demands, the Allies would also reduce theirs. But the Young Plan, too, overestimated either the ability or the willingness of Germany to pay, and after 1931 all payments were discontinued. Altogether Germany had paid the Allies about $4.5 billion, more than half of which she had borrowed from American investors.

The Quest for Peace

The search for a means to insure world peace went on insistently throughout the Coolidge years. Unfortunately the organizations most actively concerned with such problems were in complete disagreement as to the best means to promote the cause they held so dear. Peace-lovers of the Wilson school kept up the fight for American entrance into the League as the surest way to prevent the outbreak of war. They rejoiced when the representatives of the United States, at first unofficially, but later on terms of entire equality, sat in on the non-political discussions of League committees, such, for example, as the conference on the opium traffic. Ultimately, they asserted, the United States could no longer ignore the obligations of membership. Others who still saw in the League nothing more than a convenient instrument for enforcement of an unjust peace urged that the United States should give its full support to the World Court. Still others, perhaps with greater faith than wisdom, believed that the peace could best be maintained by a simple declaration on the part of every nation that it would not resort to war. Chief leader of the third group, whose panacea was labeled the "outlawry of war," was Senator William E. Borah of Idaho. Most American politicians, including the President, were inclined to regard the "outlawry" scheme as impractical, and possibly contrary to the Constitution of the United States which specifically gave Congress the right to declare war, but a pact signed by seven European nations at Locarno in 1925 seemed to indicate a certain willingness on their part to flirt with the idea. By that document Germany, Belgium, France, Great Britain, and Italy undertook to guarantee the western boundaries of Germany and the demilitarization of the Rhineland. Germany agreed also to arbitrate her disputes with France, Belgium, Poland, and Czechoslovakia. Further, the three powers most directly concerned, France, Belgium, and Germany, agreed not to attack each other, not to invade each other's territory, and not to resort to war against each other, except for purposes of defense or in response to their obligations under the League of Nations, to which, it was decided, Germany must be admitted.

Hailed as at least a partial renunciation of the "right to make war," the Pact of Locarno stimulated the "outlawry" advocates in the United States to renewed endeavors. The United States, they pointed out, stood now almost alone in its resistance to every plan for world peace. They were soon aided by Aristide Briand, French foreign minister, who on April 6, 1927 — tenth anniversary of the entrance of the United States into the First World War — urged a treaty between France and the United States similar to those agreed upon by the European nations at Locarno. What Briand

William E. Borah. *Repeatedly re-elected Senator from Idaho, Borah, despite his extreme provincialism, came to exert a powerful influence over American foreign affairs. He took a leading part in defeating the Treaty of Versailles, and he successfully opposed American adherence to the World Court. But he also forced Harding to call the Washington Conference, and he promoted the idea of the "outlawry of war" so vigorously that it was embodied in the Kellogg-Briand Pact.*

really had in mind was to replace the Root Arbitration Treaty of 1908, which was due to expire in 1928, with a stronger one, but "outlawry" enthusiasts were quick to seize the opportunity he had given them. They persuaded the Secretary of State, Frank B. Kellogg of Minnesota, who had succeeded Hughes in 1925, to expand the scope of the negotiations. Replying to Briand, Kellogg said:

It has occurred to me that the two governments, instead of contenting themselves with a bilateral declaration of the nature suggested by M. Briand, might make a more signal contribution to world peace by joining in an effort to obtain the adherence of all the principal Powers of the world to a declaration renouncing war as an instrument of national policy.

The Kellogg-Briand Pact

Kellogg's proposal resulted in prolonged negotiations which led finally to the signing at Paris, on August 27, 1928, of a general treaty along the lines he had proposed. The representatives of fifteen nations, including Japan, Italy, and Germany, affixed their signatures to a document which condemned war as a means for "the solution of international controversies," and renounced it as "an instrument of national policy in their relations with one another." The contracting parties also agreed that "the settlement or solution of all disputes or conflicts of whatever nature or of whatever origin they may be, which may arise among them, shall never be sought except by pacific means."

Ultimately sixty-two nations gave their adherence to the Kellogg Pact; but the futility of all such declarations, unless buttressed by positive means to enforce them, was demonstrated presently by the attacks of Japan on China, Italy on Ethiopia, and Germany on Poland, Denmark, Norway, the Netherlands, Belgium, and Luxembourg. The pact may, indeed, have lulled into a sense of security nations that might otherwise have been better prepared for the assaults of their predatory neighbors. Nevertheless, European statesmen saw significance in the willingness of the United States to cooperate at last, however faintly, in the effort to maintain world peace, but the customary Senate reservations revealed the microscopic nature of the involvement. Although the Senate ratified the treaty with only one dissenting vote, it insisted that there could be no curtailment of America's right of self-defense, that no obligations had been assumed which were incompatible with the Monroe Doctrine, and that the United States was not bound to take action against states that broke the treaty. Kellogg did the best he could to make the pact to which he had given his name a success. He negotiated supplementary treaties of arbitration with such nations as would consent to them, and took particular pains to make arbitration compulsory between the United States and other American nations.

Latin-American Relations

The relations between the United States and her Latin-American neighbors after the First World War were seriously affected by two new factors: (1) the defeat of Germany had reduced to insignificance whatever danger had existed, if any, of further European colonization in the New World; and (2) the United States had supplanted Great Britain as the outside nation upon which Latin America relied principally for capital and trade. United States investors bought up Latin-American securities; United States importers brought in from Latin-American countries such items as coffee, rubber, tin, copper, nitrates, sugar, bananas, and lumber; United States exporters sent in return manufactured goods of all kinds, particularly automobiles and machinery. How free could these lesser republics remain when they must depend so much on the "Colossus of the North"? How willing would the United States be to permit European corporations to compete on equal terms with American corporations on such a significant item, for example, as oil? Was the Monroe Doctrine now to become a mere cloak for commercial domination?

A somewhat disturbing answer to this question came early in the Harding administration when the United States ended its long dispute with Colombia over the part Theodore Roosevelt had played in the Panama Revolution of 1903. Colombia had rich oil resources, and American oil interests feared that the resentment Colombians felt for Roosevelt's action might play into the hands of their British competitors. Harding had been only a few days in office when he informed his cabinet and the press that the Thompson-Urrutia treaty with

Colombia, which proposed the payment of $25 million to Colombia for whatever damage she might have suffered, would be resubmitted with the "sincere regret" clause stricken out. This treaty had been negotiated early in the Wilson administration, but had failed of ratification by the Senate, both before and after the death of Theodore Roosevelt. Advocates of ratification frankly admitted that the object of the treaty was to help along the American oil interests that were seeking concessions in Colombia. Senator Lodge, the close friend of Theodore Roosevelt, who had at first been violently opposed to anything that might look like the appeasement of Colombia, now led the fight for the treaty, pointing out that "the question of oil is one that is vital to every great maritime nation," and urging that the United States should stand behind its overseas investors. On the other side, Senator Watson of Georgia complained that the payment to Colombia amounted only to "an indirect subsidy to the oil interests." But the treaty was ratified, April 20, 1921, by a vote of 69 to 19. In Colombia there was still opposition to any settlement with the United States that failed to include an outright apology, but the money payment in itself could be so construed, and at length the treaty was accepted. It was proclaimed in force March 1, 1922, and worked as had been intended to the considerable advantage of American oil interests.

Mexico

Latin-American resentment against financial and commercial domination of their economies by the United States reached a high level in Mexico during the presidency of Plutarco Elías Calles, who attempted to put into effect the anti-foreigner provisions of the Constitution of 1917, adopted under Carranza, but never fully enforced. Two laws enacted in 1925 greatly disturbed American investors in Mexico. One of them, an alien lands law, permitted foreigners to acquire land in Mexico only on condition

Dwight W. Morrow. *As American Ambassador to Mexico, Morrow succeeded, where normal diplomacy had failed, in smoothing out the relations between the United States and Mexico. Later he was elected to the United States Senate, but died before taking office.*

that for this purpose they renounce the protection of their own governments, and acquire holdings on precisely the same terms as if they were Mexican citizens. The other, usually spoken of as the petroleum law, declared that the subsoil rights were the "inalienable and imprescriptible property of the nation," and that concessionaires must renew their rights on these terms or suffer confiscation. The anti-Catholic program of the Calles government, which nationalized Church property, expelled foreign clerics, and otherwise limited the privileges of the Church, still further annoyed Americans, particularly Roman Catholics, and posed a difficult problem for the Department of State. In this emergency, with many Americans who had investments in Mexico actually demanding war, President Coolidge sent his personal friend, Dwight W. Morrow, to Mexico to work out a solution. Morrow proved to be an ideal man for the task. He persuaded Calles to have some of the more objectionable provisions of the anti-foreign legislation declared unconstitutional by the Mexican courts, and, with the help of an American Catholic priest, Father John J. Burke, he also induced Calles to open negotiations for a new accord between the Mexican government and the Mexican Church. The settlements achieved were not entirely satisfactory to American investors in Mexico, but they made it clear to all Latin Americans that the United States had no intention of pushing the claims of its citizens by resort to war.

The Caribbean

There were signs, also, that the American government was ready to retreat from the aggressive Caribbean policy begun by Theodore Roosevelt and perpetuated by Taft and Wilson. When in 1923 a revolution broke out in Honduras, the United States avoided acting alone, and joined with the four Central American neighbors of Honduras in setting up and recognizing a provisional government. In Nicaragua, with the nation at peace and payments on its debt being made regularly, President Coolidge in 1925 ordered the token force of marines that remained in the country to come home. This proved to be a mistake, for fighting at once broke out, and many more United States marines went back than had been withdrawn. But in 1927 Henry F. Stimson, acting as Coolidge's agent, arranged for a peaceful election under American supervision, and by 1933 the marines were out again, this time to stay out. Similarly, with the help of Sumner Welles, the United States managed to get the marines out of the Dominican Republic in 1924, but they stayed on in Haiti, where their removal would have been merely an "invitation to bloodshed," until 1933.

More important than all this in the eyes of Latin Americans was the disavowal of the Roosevelt corollary to the Monroe Doctrine, according to which the United States had claimed the right to intervene in Latin America to keep order, and so to prevent intervention for that purpose by any European nation. During the 1920's there seemed to be no serious danger that any European power would attempt such an intervention, and both the Monroe Doctrine itself and the Roosevelt interpretation seemed anachronistic. Finally, in the so-called Clark Memorandum, the United States Department of State denied the validity of the Roosevelt argument, and asserted that the American government no longer felt obliged to supervise the behavior of the Latin-American republics. It still stood ready to guarantee their freedom and territorial integrity as against European aggressors, but otherwise their internal and external affairs were their own business. This document was dated December 17, 1928, while Coolidge was still President, but it was not officially published until 1930. In a further effort to cultivate better Latin-American relations, Herbert Hoover, following his election to the Presidency in 1928, visited eleven Latin-American republics. But despite the gospel of good will he preached, the old fear of Yankee imperialism refused to die. It might drop out of sight from time to time, but it was always sure to rise again.

BIBLIOGRAPHY

A stimulating recent interpretation is N. G. Levin, Jr., *Woodrow Wilson and World Politics* (1968). Two striking revisionist books are by A. J. Mayer: *Political Origins of the New Diplomacy, 1917–1918* (1959), which bears the paperback title of *Wilson vs. Lenin*, and *Politics and Diplomacy of Peacemaking (1968). A massive documentary collection is *A History of the Peace Conference of Paris* (6 vols., 1920–1924), edited by H. W. V. Temperley. R. S. Baker, *Woodrow Wilson and the World Settlement* (3 vols., 1922), gives a valuable inside picture in immense detail. Other memoirs of importance include: Harold Nicolson, *Peacemaking, 1919* (1933); J. T. Shotwell, *At the Paris Peace Conference* (1937); D. H. Miller, *The Drafting of the Covenant* (2 vols., 1928); and Stephen Bonsal, *Unfinished Business* (1944). David Lloyd George, *Memoirs of the Peace Conference* (2 vols., 1939), can now be supplemented with a scholarly monograph by S. P. Tillman, *Anglo-Saxon Relations at the Paris Peace Conference of 1919* (1961).

Controversy has surrounded the Peace Conference from its inception. Collections illustrating conflicting views include: *Wilson at Versailles* (1957), edited by T. P. Greene; *The Versailles Settlement* (1960), edited by I. J. Lederer; *Versailles, 1919* (1964), edited by Ferdinand Czernin; and *Wilson and the League of Nations* (1967), edited by R. A. Stone. Much of the early controversy was touched off by J. M. Keynes's savage indictment, *The Economic Consequences of the Peace* (1919). Paul Birdsall, *Versailles Twenty Years After* (1941), is a careful re-evaluation, reaching rather favorable conclusions about the conference and its work. Special studies of Wilsonian peace diplomacy include: L. A. R. Yates, *The United States and French Security, 1917–1921* (1957); L. L. Gerson, *Woodrow Wilson and the Rebirth of Poland, 1914–1920* (1953); R. H. Fifield, *Woodrow Wilson and the Far East* (1952); R. W. Curry, *Woodrow Wilson and Far Eastern Policy, 1913–1921* (1957); B. F. Beers, *Vain Endeavor: Robert Lansing's Attempts to End the American-Japanese Rivalry* (1962); and *The Immigrants' Influence on Wilson's Peace Policies* (1967), essays edited by J. P. O'Grady.

On the establishment of the League of Nations, see the comprehensive treatment by D. F. Fleming, *The United States and the League of Nations, 1918–1920* (1932). An important study of the American background of the League idea is R. J. Bartlett, *The League to Enforce Peace* (1944). T. A.

Bailey, *Woodrow Wilson and the Lost Peace* (1944), and *Woodrow Wilson and the Great Betrayal* (1945) are brilliantly written and have had an enormous influence on historians. Although he himself holds internationalist views, Bailey places much of the blame for the defects of the peace and the failure of the treaty on Wilson. Recent and critical is George Goldberg, *The Peace to End Peace* (1969). A horrifying picture of Wilson's collapse is provided by Gene Smith, *When the Cheering Stopped* (1964). A close study of the controversy over Article Ten of the League is J. C. Vinson, *Referendum for Isolation* (1961). On Wilson's chief Senate opponent, see J. A. Garraty, *Henry Cabot Lodge* (1953), judicious and objective.

W. M. Bagby, *The Road to Normalcy* (1962), is a full-scale, scholarly work, based upon archival research. Frank Freidel, *Franklin D. Roosevelt: The Ordeal* (1954), the second volume of a model biography, contains an excellent account of the 1920 campaign. Important memoirs include J. M. Cox, *Journey Through My Years* (1946), by the Democratic standard-bearer; and *The Memoirs of Will H. Hays* (1955), by the masterful Republican National Chairman. Other references on political history will be found in the next bibliography.

A strongly revisionist work is R. N. Stromberg, *Collective Security and American Foreign Policy* (1963); it argues that "collective security" was only a myth. Brief general studies of foreign relations include Selig Adler, *The Uncertain Giant, 1921–1941* (1965); and L. E. Ellis, *Republican Foreign Policy, 1921–1933* (1968). Another useful survey is Allan Nevins, *The United States in a Chaotic World, 1918–1933* (1950). The careers of the Harding-Coolidge Secretaries of State are recounted in Dexter Perkins, *Charles Evans Hughes and American Democratic Statesmanship* (1956); Betty Glad, *Charles Evans Hughes and the Illusions of Innocence* (1966); L. E. Ellis, *Frank B. Kellogg and American Foreign Relations, 1925–1929* (1961); and R. H. Ferrell, *Frank B. Kellogg/Henry L. Stimson* (1963). An interesting and provocative synthesis is Selig Adler, *The Isolationist Impulse* (1957). Interesting special studies include J. A. DeNovo, *American Interests and Policies in the Middle East,*

1900–1939 (1963); and A. H. Taylor, *American Diplomacy and the Narcotics Traffic, 1900–1939* (1969).

The literature on continuing diplomatic problems of the 1920s is very large, and can only be treated briefly here. On the League and Court issues, see two books by D. F. Fleming, *The United States and World Organization, 1920–1933* (1938), and *The United States and the World Court* (1945); and F. P. Walters, *A History of the League of Nations* (1952). On the Far East, consult G. E. Wheeler, *Prelude to Pearl Harbor: The United States Navy and the Far East, 1921–1931* (1963); Eleanor Tupper and G. E. McReynolds, *Japan in American Public Opinion* (1937); and Dorothy Borg, *American Policy and the Chinese Revolution, 1925–1928* (1947). G. F. Kennan, *Soviet-American Relations, 1917–1920* (2 vols., 1956–1958), is a monumental work. An important monograph is P. G. Filene, *Americans and the Soviet Experiment, 1917–1933* (1967). *American Intervention in the Russian Civil War* (1969), edited by B. M. Unterberger, is a collection of conflicting interpretations. Other works dealing with American intervention are J. A. White, *The Siberian Intervention* (1950); and B. M. Unterberger, *America's Siberian Expedition, 1918–1920* (1956). See also the survey by W. A. Williams, *American-Russian Relations, 1781–1947* (1952), which is sympathetic with the Soviet position.

On the Washington Conference, an important monograph is J. C. Vinson, *The Parchment Peace* (1955). The best work on the naval aspects is Harold and Margaret Sprout, *Toward a New Order of Sea Power* (1940). Herbert Feis, *The Diplomacy of the Dollar: First Era, 1919–1932* (1950), is a valuable study by an expert with a flair for writing clear prose. See also Joseph Brandes, *Herbert Hoover and Economic Diplomacy: Department of Commerce Policy, 1921–1928* (1962). On the knotty problems of war debts and reparations, see B. H. Williams, *Economic Foreign Policy of the United States* (1929).

On the Peace Pact, the best book is R. H. Ferrell, *Peace in Their Time* (1952). But see also M. C. McKenna, *Borah* (1961); J. C. Vinson, *William E. Borah and the Outlawry of War* (1957); and J. E. Stoner, *S. O. Levinson and the Pact of Paris* (1942).

On Latin American relations, many of the works noted in the bibliographies for Chapters 11 and 12 are pertinent here. See also three recent monographs: E. A. Rice, *The Diplomatic Relations between the United States and Mexico, as Affected by the Struggle for Religious Liberty in Mexico, 1925–1929* (1959); R. F. Smith, *The United States and Cuba: Business and Diplomacy, 1917–1960* (1960); and William Kamman, *A Search for Stability: United States Diplomacy Toward Nicaragua, 1925–1933* (1968).

18

THE ROAD TO PROSPERITY

*Decline of the Presidency · Harding · The Harding scandals ·
Coolidge · Pressure for pensions · Immigration restriction · The red scare ·
The Ku Klux Klan · Postwar business · Strikes of 1919 · Agricultural con-
ditions · The Republican recovery program · Farmer-labor discontent ·
Elections of 1924 and 1928*

Decline of the Presidency

The decline in importance of the Presidency, so evident during most of the 1920's,
actually began during the Wilson administration. The fighting had no sooner ended
in Europe than Congress made all convenient haste to withdraw the unusual
wartime powers of the President and to
scrap war boards through which, under
his leadership, the nation had mobilized its
economic resources to win the war. Also,
the absence of the President in Europe during the writing of the Treaty of Versailles
left many loose ends at home. The world
of 1919 lacked the easy means of international communication so commonplace today, and without the President's actual
presence in Washington his leadership in
domestic matters suffered acutely. This
situation was rendered infinitely worse by
Wilson's illness during the last year and
a half he was in office. For months of this
time only his wife, his physician, and at rare

intervals his private secretary, Joseph
Tumulty, saw him regularly, and all news
that might interfere with his recovery was
concealed from him. His Secretary of
State, Robert Lansing, in an effort to hold
the administration together, called weekly
cabinet meetings, but when this procedure
came to the President's attention, he angrily
dismissed Lansing for his presumption, and
named a new Secretary of State, Bainbridge
Colby. The fact that the President was a
Democrat while both houses of Congress
were Republican also made for inefficiency.
Not only with reference to the Treaty of
Versailles, but in many other matters also,
the executive and legislative branches were
in continuous conflict.

Warren G. Harding

The selection of Harding as Wilson's
successor registered a conscious determination on the part of the Republican leaders

FARMERS *received little benefit from the soaring prosperity of the postwar years.*

in Congress to keep the Presidency weak. They had had their fill of presidential leadership from the time of Theodore Roosevelt, and they wanted a President who would not order them around. In Warren Gamaliel Harding (1865–1923) they found exactly what they were looking for. Harding had obtained most of his education as editor of the Marion, Ohio, *Daily Star*. He had drifted easily from journalism to politics, and had always associated himself with the most conservative wing of his party. It was Harding who had made the nominating speech for Taft against Roosevelt in the convention of 1912. He was defeated for the governorship of Ohio in 1910, but in 1914 won both nomination and election to the United States Senate. He was a genial good fellow, well liked by his neighbors, and thoroughly imbued with the common man's vanities and prejudices. He knew that he was no intellectual giant, but prided himself on his ability to get along with people, and took comfort in the thought that as President he could command the judgment of the "best minds" in the party. His most devoted political friend was Harry M. Daugherty, another Ohio machine politician, whose knowledge of the seamy side of politics was unexcelled. Daugherty's greatest ambition was realized when, as Harding's campaign manager, he piloted his candidate to victory at the Republican convention.

In his appointments Harding showed a curious inability to distinguish between good and bad. Such selections as Charles Evans Hughes as Secretary of State and Herbert Hoover as Secretary of Commerce were above reproach, but they were offset by the appointment of Albert B. Fall of New Mexico, a notorious anti-conservationist, as Secretary of the Interior, and Harry M. Daugherty, whose legal talents were mediocre or less, as Attorney-General. For Secretary of the Treasury Harding finally decided upon Andrew W. Mellon of Pittsburgh, one of the richest men in the United States, an understandable, but not wholly defensible, choice. Outside the Cabinet the President's lack of discrimination persisted. He made ex-President Taft Chief Justice of the Supreme Court when opportunity offered, a graceful and deserved compliment, but he turned over the newly organized Veterans' Bureau to a rogue named Charles R. Forbes who eventually landed in federal prison. In general, the new President regarded political offices as the lawful spoils of victory, and to members of the unsavory "Ohio gang" that followed him to Washington went many choice plums.

The Harding Scandals

There is no evidence that Harding had any other connection with the scandals that disgraced his administration than his bad judgment of men. One noisome set of scandals revolved about the name of Daugherty, whose position as chief law-enforcement officer of the United States opened up infinite possibilities for illegal actions. A friend of Daugherty, Colonel Thomas W. Miller, became Alien Property Custodian, with wide powers in restoring or retaining the possessions of aliens seized by the United States during the war. Miller's judgments were for sale; ultimately he was dismissed from office, and jailed on conviction of having taken a bribe. Daugherty's closest friend, next to Harding, was Jess Smith, who in a single case took $50,000 to arrange a settlement before Miller. Smith committed suicide. Daugherty's association with such characters naturally made him suspect, but when finally brought to trial for conspiracy to "defraud the United States," he was saved from conviction by a hung jury. Another focus of scandals, already noted, was the Veterans' Bureau. Forbes, its chief, was not of Daugherty's choosing, but only a chance acquaintance

THE TEAPOT DOME OIL FIELD, WYOMING.

DOHENY. Acquitted.

THE OIL SCANDALS. *A familiar campaign slogan was sometimes changed to read: "To the victors belong the oils." Three principals of the Harding oil scandals were Harding's Secretary of the Interior, Albert B. Fall, convicted of taking a bribe, and the two multimillionaires who tempted him, Edward L. Doheny and Harry F. Sinclair, both of whom were acquitted of criminal charges.*

FALL. Guilty.

SINCLAIR. Acquitted.

to whom Harding had taken a liking. Forbes was soon making deals with contractors in the building of hospitals and the purchase and sale of supplies at great gain to himself but at heavy loss to the government. His closest adviser, Charles F. Cramer, committed suicide; Forbes resigned, but was eventually convicted of defrauding the government.

Most sensational of the Harding scandals was that associated with the name of Albert B. Fall. As Secretary of the Interior, Fall professed to believe that certain oil lands, held as naval reserves by the Navy Department, should be in his custody, and he was able to persuade the President, and the Secretary of the Navy, Edwin Denby, to agree to the transfer, an action of dubious legality. Thereupon Fall, in return for a personal "loan" of $100,000, unsupported by a note or collateral, turned over the right to exploit the Teapot Dome reserve in Wyoming to the Sinclair oil interests, and for probably a much larger sum, the Elk Hills reserve in California to the Doheny group. Fall was ultimately exposed by a senatorial investigating committee headed by Senator Thomas W. Walsh of Montana, and in 1929 he was convicted of taking a bribe, and sent to jail for a year. But the two multi-millionaires to whom he had sold out, Harry F. Sinclair and Edward L. Doheny, won acquittals in the criminal cases lodged against them. In civil suits, however, their leases were annulled by the United States Supreme Court on the ground of "fraud," "collusion," and "conspiracy."

Harding never knew the whole truth about the scandals of his administration, but he knew enough by 1923 to make him sick at heart, and his acute distress at the misconduct of his friends may have had something to do with his collapse and death at San Francisco, August 2, 1923, on his way back from a trip to Alaska. Harding was not a bad man, but he was weak and incompetent. The scandals that disgraced his administration should be charged primarily against the politicians who brought about his nomination, despite their full knowledge of his shortcomings. As for the American people, they made a fine pageant of his funeral, but there was little real grief. He had failed completely during his brief term of office to capture the public imagination, and the yearnings for normalcy which he shared with the people had been only faintly realized. Even among those responsible for his nomination in 1920 there was a feeling that his death was perhaps a blessing, for shrewd prognosticators believed that the Republican Party, with Harding as its nominee, would have had little chance for success in the campaign of 1924.

Calvin Coolidge

Calvin Coolidge (1872–1933), who now succeeded to the Presidency, probably possessed somewhat greater native intelligence than Harding, and he had acquired from his New England background habits of honesty and frugality that now stood him in good stead. In his political and economic views, however, he was quite as conservative as his predecessor. Nominating conventions often choose their presidential candidate to represent one wing of the party, and the Vice-President another; this, indeed, was the intention of the manipulators who awarded the Republican nomination of 1920 to Harding. But the convention got out of hand and did as it pleased, with the result that the two candidates both represented the extreme conservative wing of the party. Throughout a long career of officeholding, Coolidge had done little to excite either opposition or approval. A Vermonter by birth, he attended Amherst College, studied law, and began to practice in 1897 at Northampton, Massachusetts. Always a dependable regular, he climbed aboard the political escalator in 1899 when he became a councilman; by 1901 he was city solicitor; by 1904 clerk

Calvin Coolidge. *Thirtieth President of the United States, Coolidge was the sixth Vice-President to succeed to the Presidency because of the death of his predecessor. He is shown here with Mrs. Coolidge and Senator Charles Curtis of Kansas (later Vice-President) on the way to the inauguration ceremonies, March 4, 1925.*

of courts; by 1907 a member of the legislature; by 1910 mayor of Northampton; by 1912 a member of the state senate; by 1916 lieutenant-governor; and by 1919 governor. He was conscientious in the discharge of his duties, abstemious of spoken words, utterly uninterested in trouble-making reforms. His most publicized act came in 1919 during the Boston police strike, when he somewhat belatedly called out the state militia to keep order. His telegram on this occasion to President Gompers of the American Federation of Labor well illustrated his gift for making commonplace statements sound significant: "There is no right to strike against the public safety by anybody, anytime, anywhere." Woodrow Wilson was one of the many to congratulate Coolidge upon his stand, thus contributing to the volume of publicity that was soon to transform him from an obscure governor of Massachusetts into the Republican nominee for the Vice-Presidency.

Coolidge as President accepted the Harding cabinet, making changes reluctantly and only under heavy pressure, and carried forward the work of the Harding administration without any perceptible change in direction. Fortunately he brought with him to his high office no faintest trace of corruption, and he had never been the kind of person who attracted to himself a "gang." Gradually the corruptionists who had saddled themselves upon Harding were eliminated, and the Republican leaders began to congratulate themselves on having escaped so successfully from the consequences of the Harding scandals. If Coolidge could be "built up" to presidential proportions, perhaps the defeat they had foreseen in 1924 could be avoided. Unimpressive in appearance and given to long lapses into silence, the new President was conspicuously lacking in glamour, but his unalloyed conservatism made him friends in influential circles, and before many months in spite of his handicaps he had become one of the most popular American Presidents.

Pressure for Pensions

With presidential leadership at low ebb, both during the later Wilson years and during the Harding-Coolidge era, the United States was at the mercy of the various pressure groups that knew best how to make their influence felt. One such group claimed to speak for the veterans, and argued earnestly that the men who had served in the armed forces had far more coming to them than the government had paid them. The end of hostilities had come suddenly, far sooner than anticipated, and as a result neither the government nor the people were prepared for peace. On the necessity of "bringing the boys home," however, there was complete agreement, and demobilization was pushed with the utmost speed, although the homesick American soldiers remained in Europe long enough to change the words incorrectly attributed to Pershing, "Lafayette, we are here," to "Lafayette, we are still here." Four and one-half million men were discharged within a year, and with no "G. I. Bill," as after the Second World War, to break the fall. The problem of getting civilian jobs again was not easy; moreover, the men who had stayed at home had got a two-year start on servicemen, many of whom had earned only a dollar a day. Why should not the government provide something by way of "adjusted compensation" to redress the balance? This plea the American Legion, which was founded in 1919 and soon emerged as the leading veterans' organization, pushed vigorously in Congress. Actually the government had sought in 1917 to forestall a repetition of the persistent pressure for pensions that had followed the Civil War. Through a Bureau of War Risk Insurance it had made generous provision for those who might sustain injuries, and when the war was over these provisions were further liberalized. In 1921 all problems pertaining to service-

men were turned over to a Veterans' Bureau, which built and administered hospitals, supervised rehabilitation activities, and ruled on claims for compensation. Its work cost the government on an average about $500 million a year. As for the uninjured veterans, the government had paid them a small discharge bonus, and to this many of the states had added small sums. But the veterans wanted more.

With congressmen keenly conscious of the veterans' vote, a bill finally passed both the House and the Senate in 1922 that would have granted $50 for each month of service to every veteran of the war. Enactment, however, was prevented by a presidential veto. Susceptible as he was to the veterans' pleas, Harding was even more susceptible to the pleas of his Secretary of the Treasury and other business leaders that the national budget must be balanced. But the American Legion continued its pressure, and in 1924 succeeded in marshaling a large enough majority in Congress to override the veto of Harding's like-minded successor, Calvin Coolidge. As passed the law took the form of a grant of paid-up insurance to fall due twenty years later. The amount owing each soldier was computed on the basis of $1.25 for each day overseas, and $1 for each day in service at home. On an average the policies ran to more than $1,000 each, and against his policy each veteran was permitted to borrow up to 22.5 per cent of its face value. Altogether this "bonus bill," as its opponents insisted on calling it, added about $3.5 billion to the cost of the war. It should not be forgotten, however, that many veterans really needed the bonus, nor that business, despite its eagerness to balance the budget, was very receptive toward tax reductions on high incomes, and other governmental favors.

Labor Unrest

Far less successful as a pressure group than the veterans was organized labor, despite the fact that it had been greatly strengthened by the war. The manpower shortage had raised wages to unprecedented heights, steadied employment, and added to the unions many new, if somewhat undisciplined, members. The restraints imposed upon labor by the patriotic desire of all classes to win the war were removed by the return of peace, and the mounting cost of living gave rise to the charge that wages, high as they were, had not risen correspondingly. Furthermore, the long period of prosperity had unfitted labor psychologically to accept such readjustments as sentiment in business circles demanded. Sensing that it was useless to try to achieve results through government, labor turned instead to strikes. The year 1919 proved to be one of the worst with respect to labor relations in the whole history of the United States. During this period the strikes that occurred were numbered in the thousands, and the number of workers affected in the millions. Sometimes labor won, as for example with the clothing workers of New York and the textile workers of New England, but in general public opinion tended to be against the strikes, and many of them failed. Among the most notable were a general strike in Seattle that was calmed down only by the intervention of outside labor leaders, a strike in the steel industry that lasted months before its failure was admitted, and a devastating coal strike that the government felt obliged to halt by an injunction.

Immigration Restriction

Another pressure group, somewhat composite in character, demanded the reversal of an old and once cherished national tradition — a hearty welcome to immigrants. Labor had long since begun to fear the competition of immigrants in the job market, and to demand a drastic limitation on the number of newcomers. Partly in response to this insistence Congress, in May, 1917, enacted over President Wilson's veto a literacy test that it hoped would limit immigration sharply in the postwar years. But what happened after the war seemed to confirm the workers' worst fears; in the year ending June 30, 1921, over 800,000 immigrants, eager to escape the poverty-striken conditions that the war had inflicted on Europe, crowded into the United States. This undesired influx particularly distressed the self-styled "one-hundred-percent Americans" — men and women, drawn from many social and economic groups, who had dedicated themselves to the preservation of old American ways, beliefs, and institutions. These nativists viewed all unassimilated immigrant minorities with great alarm, but regarded with particular concern the "hyphenated Americans," or "hyphenates," who during the war had revealed their double loyalties, both to their new country and to the country of their origin. The one-hundred-percenters also took deeply to heart the fact that nearly two-thirds of the postwar immigrants came from southern and eastern Europe instead of from the northern and western European countries which had furnished the majority of the old American stock. Moreover, the newcomers were mostly Roman Catholic, Greek Orthodox, or Jewish in religion, the same groups against which the intolerant American Protective Association movement of the 1890's had demonstrated; evidently the old intolerance had merely died down, and had not died out. In addition, the postwar years had witnessed a "Red Scare" of frightening proportions, and among the most turbulent of the radicals were many persons of immigrant origin.

Americans generally tended to associate the growth of violence and radicalism during this period with the Bolshevik revolution of November, 1917, in Russia, and the spread of Communism thereafter throughout eastern and central Europe. It was natural for them to assume that this new and foreign doctrine was reaching America through the immigrants. As if to justify such fears a few misguided individuals attempted during April, 1919, to send through the mails over thirty bombs addressed to prominent Americans who had expressed their opposition to Communism. Among them were Associate Justice Holmes, Postmaster-General Burleson, and Attorney-General Palmer, whose home was later wrecked by such a bomb. Then on September 16, 1920, a fearful explosion in front of the J. P. Morgan and Company offices on Wall Street killed thirty-eight people and injured hundreds. This outrage, together with the founding of the American Communist Party in the spring of 1920, convinced many people that action had to be taken against all foreign or foreign-inspired disturbers of the peace.

The "Red Scare"

Thus inspired, the Department of Justice, both under Attorney-General Palmer and his successor, Harry M. Daugherty, waged vigorous war against the radicals. With the assistance of the Department of Labor, which had authority to arrest and deport dangerous aliens, Palmer's agents raided radical meetings, sought out suspects in their residences, and accounted eventually for some 556 deportations, about half of whom sailed for Russia in the *Buford*, sometimes called the "Soviet Ark," in December, 1919. With the blood-lust of wartime not yet fully abated, state and local governments sometimes acted with even less restraint. Following a bloody fight on Armistice Day, 1919, at Centralia, Washington, between American Legion paraders and IWW members who defended their headquarters against attack, remnants of the IWW throughout the Northwest were arrested by the hundreds, brought to trial, convicted, and given long sentences. At least one of the alleged participants in the Centralia "outrage" was lynched. The two most notable victims of the red rage, however, had a legal trial. They were Nicola

Explosion on Wall Street. *As a kind of climax to the Red Scare, which so frightened many Americans during the two years that followed the war, came this explosion at the very heart of the New York financial district. The perpetrators of the outrage were never apprehended.*

Sacco and Vanzetti. *Many conservatives, both inside and outside the United States, shared the belief of most liberals that these men were executed, not because they were proved guilty of the crime with which they were charged, but because of their records as radicals.*

Sacco and Bartolomeo Vanzetti, two Italian workmen who were convicted of a double murder that occurred in South Braintree, Massachusetts, on April 15, 1920. Many competent investigators believed that these convictions were obtained less because of the evidence, which was wholly circumstantial, than because of the records of the two men as philosophical anarchists, but a prolonged nationwide effort failed to save them from execution. Unfortunately the "Red Scare" extended its hysteria from Communists to Socialists, pacifists, and every other variety of political dissenter. In New York, for example, the Assembly expelled its five Socialist members in 1920 merely because of their party affiliations.

The New Immigration Policy

With this background it was inevitable that the 1920's would produce some kind of legislation to restrict immigration. Since the literacy test had completely failed of its objective, Congress in 1921 passed an Emergency Immigration Act that assigned to each nation an immigrant quota consisting of not more than 3 per cent of the number of its nationals resident in the

United States according to the census of 1910. Immigrants from other American nations were exempted from the quota system, but in 1922 an amendment required that all aliens resident in an American country must have lived there not less than five years before being freed from the quota restrictions.

The law of 1921 was meant merely as a temporary stopgap while the details of the new immigration policy were being worked out, and in 1924 Congress passed another immigration act. This time the quota was set at 2 per cent of the nationals resident in the United States in 1890, thereby reducing still further the numbers eligible for admission, particularly from southern and eastern Europe. The law also provided that after July 1, 1927, the number of quota immigrants was to be limited to 150,000, while quotas were to be based upon "national origins," the same to be determined from a study of the census of 1920. The difficulty in determining the national origins of the American people completely baffled the committee of cabinet members (the Secretaries of State, Commerce, and Labor) charged with that duty, and not until 1929 were its half-hearted recommendations put into effect. Whatever their imperfections, the new quotas insured that an overwhelming proportion of the thin trickle of immigrants permitted to enter the United States originated in those countries that had first contributed to its settlement. Great Britain and northern Ireland, for example, were permitted to send 65,721 immigrants annually, while the Italian quota was only 5,802. A peculiarly unfortunate aspect of the Act of 1924 was the exclusion of all aliens ineligible to citizenship, a provision aimed specifically at the Japanese, who deeply resented the discrimination. The gentlemen's agreement of 1907 had worked well enough so that there was no good reason for its unilateral repeal; furthermore, since under the regular quota system the number of Japanese immigrants would have been insignificant anyway, the affront thus given a proud and sensitive people was as unnecessary as it was unwise. Undoubtedly it was one of the factors that led to the growing anti-American sentiment in Japan that culminated in Pearl Harbor.

The special favors shown to nations of the western hemisphere led at first to a heavy immigration from Mexico, but immigration officials tried to put a stop to this by refusing entrance to Mexican laborers on the ground that they were likely to become public charges. Ways of defeating the immigration regulations, however, were not hard to find, and whenever the demand for migratory agricultural workers was strong enough Mexican immigrants by the thousands crossed the border into California and the Southwest. These "wetbacks," as they were sometimes called, were frequently rounded up in large numbers and returned to Mexico, only to evade the immigration authorities again at the next convenient opportunity. During the depression years native American workers protested vigorously against such foreign competition, but with the coming of the Second World War the need for more manpower led to an agreement between the governments of Mexico and the United States (later confirmed by act of Congress) whereby Mexican laborers could be brought in under contract for specified periods, and then returned to Mexico. The use of these *braceros*, as they were called, was supposed not to undermine American wage levels, but employers sometimes worked contract laborers for nine-hour days and six-day weeks with take-home pay as low as $27 per week. From the first 40,000 in 1942 the flood grew to an annual half million by the 1960's, most of whom were used for "stoop-labor" tasks in the agriculture of California and the Southwest.

Nevertheless, the census of 1930 revealed that the proportion of aliens resident in the United States had at last begun to decline. The significance of this change did not go entirely unnoticed. Recent immigrants and their children, particularly those whose homelands lay in the areas discriminated against, could not but feel that they had been branded as unwanted, second-class citizens who were regarded as suspect solely because of their ancestry. They were ripe politically for protest, and ready to give their allegiance to whichever party might the more generously extend them the promise of equality. But the end of immigration had even more important connotations. It meant, no doubt, that northern European domination of American culture had been preserved; the infiltration of southern and eastern Europeans, with their different political, religious, and social concepts, was virtually brought to a close. But it meant also that American farms and factories, long dependent upon immigration for a steady supply of cheap labor and for a growing volume of domestic consumption, now had to do without both. The competition for labor would be stiffer; the demands of the immigrants for food-

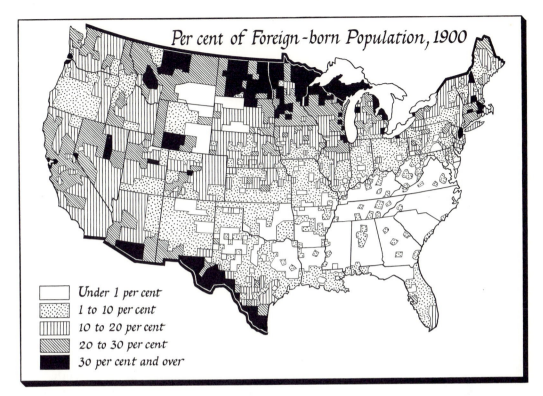

Per cent of Foreign-born Population, 1900

Under 1 per cent
1 to 10 per cent
10 to 20 per cent
20 to 30 per cent
30 per cent and over

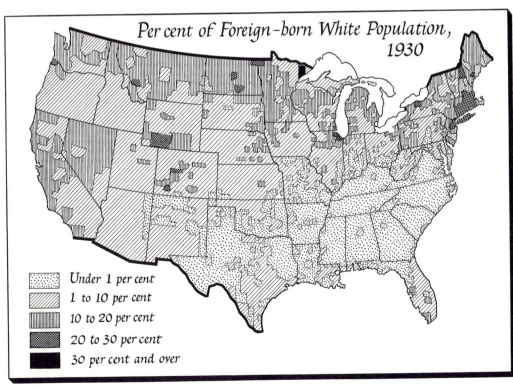

Per cent of Foreign-born White Population, 1930

Under 1 per cent
1 to 10 per cent
10 to 20 per cent
20 to 30 per cent
30 per cent and over

stuffs and manufactured articles would be missed. The embargo of the United States on immigration even had its international aspects. Where was the surplus population of Europe to go? Some of it was drained off to Latin America and to the overseas nations of the British Commonwealth. But there were plenty of would-be immigrants left at home to feed the fires of European discontent, and to encourage the ambitions of demagogues.

Anti-Negro Prejudice and the KKK

Lumped with the rising public insistence on immigration restriction was a spirit of intolerance turned against any group that the nativists disliked or feared: the radical, the Catholic, the Jew, and even one of the oldest American minority figures, the Negro. Enticed during the war by high wages, large numbers of Negroes had migrated from the South to the northern cities, only to find there much of the same discrimination they had left in the South. Friction between the races accounted for widespread riots and loss of life in Chicago, East St. Louis, and many other northern cities. The rate of lynchings, which had dropped to a low of thirty-five in 1917, shot up to seventy-six in 1919, and there were demands from both North and South that the Negro be "put in his place."

Growing out of this climate of fear and hatred was the Ku Klux Klan, a movement dedicated to organized intolerance, similar in many ways to European Fascism, but reminiscent also of the old Ku Klux Klan of the reconstruction period. This latter-day Klan was organized in November, 1915, near Atlanta, Georgia, by William J. Simmons. In the beginning, apparently, it had merely sentimental and mildly patriotic aims, and continued to be a small and harmless southern order until 1920–1921, when both its national officers and its purposes changed. Many people were undoubtedly attracted to the Klan by its theatrical and

mysterious ritual. The outlandish names of its many officers, such as "Kleagles" and "Goblins," the white nightshirts and masks disguising the identity of its members, its spectacular night marches and burning of fiery crosses, all attracted the unthinking. Others may have believed in the sincerity of its stated program, for it continued to pose as a patriotic organization stressing Americanism, Prohibition, and Christian morality. But its real purpose, as attested by its publications and actions, was to organize hatred against Catholics, Jews, Negroes, immigrants, and radicals. It spread palpably untrue stories about these groups and intimidated many individuals by burning fiery crosses before their homes or warning them out of the community. And although the national officers of the organization denied it, the Klan undoubtedly had a hand in many whippings, tar-and-featherings, and even killings. Invading politics, particularly in the South, the Middle West, and the Far West, the Klan sought to control public offices with the purpose of discharging Catholics who were teachers, or other public employees. In Oregon it put over a compulsory public education act aimed at parochial schools, a measure that the United States Supreme Court Court invalidated. At the crest of its strength in 1924–1925 the Klan had enrolled 4 or 5 million members, making its officers wealthy and its power for evil enormous. Fortunately its excesses and the return of sanity to many of its members sent it into a rapid decline. By 1927–1928 it was a mere shadow of its former membership and influence.

Postwar Business

Meantime the nation had had to work its way through one of those constantly recurring business cycles with which American history is dotted. For about six months after the signing of the armistice, business had experienced a "hesitation period," due in part to the ruthless manner in which the government had cancelled its war contracts. But by the middle of 1919 boom conditions almost equal to those of the war had set in, and the surge of prosperity continued unabated for another year. Business leaders were quick to ascribe this speedy recovery to the restoration of free enterprise, and to their success in providing the goods needed to overcome wartime shortages. But economists eventually assessed the situation far differently. Actually there was comparatively little pent-up demand for consumers' goods after the war; American participation had not lasted long enough, and governmental restraints had been too moderate. The stimulants that produced the postwar boom were in reality the same as those that had produced the war boom — government spending and deficit financing. After as well as during the war the government spent prodigally on shipbuilding and railroad maintenance. Also, it lent huge sums to its former war partners, and lesser sums to such newly created nations as Finland and Estonia. These loans were meant to stimulate European recovery, and they achieved good results. Further, they made possible the continuation of European purchases in the United States; American exports during the year 1919 were about a billion dollars higher than in any previous year. These goods were paid for with dollars that the United States itself had had to borrow — the Victory Loan of $4.5 billion was not floated until April, 1919. And the policy of low interest rates and easy credit that the government was obliged to foster in order to float the issues also tended to promote speculation. In business the speculative fever took the odd form of an over-accumulation of inventories. Dealers who believed in the war-shortage theory made excessive demands on manufacturers, and manufacturers, encouraged by the abnormal demand, provided more goods than the market could absorb. But before the inevitable crash came all parties concerned thought they were getting rich, prices skyrocketed phenomenally, and complaints about the high cost of living mounted even higher.

The Real Estate Boom

In agriculture the speculation took the form of a disastrous land boom. American farmers, to their ultimate undoing, were convinced that the market for American foodstuffs in Europe had become permanent, and that their prosperity was guaranteed for all time. Their optimism, whipped up systematically by the real estate men and the country bankers who stood to make heavy profits every time a farm changed hands, developed throughout most of the Middle West into a thoroughgoing speculative boom. The price of wheat, guaranteed by the government for an eighteen-

The Ku Klux Klan. *Klansmen did not always choose to conceal their identity, as this Washington parade of high-ranking Klan officials indicates.*

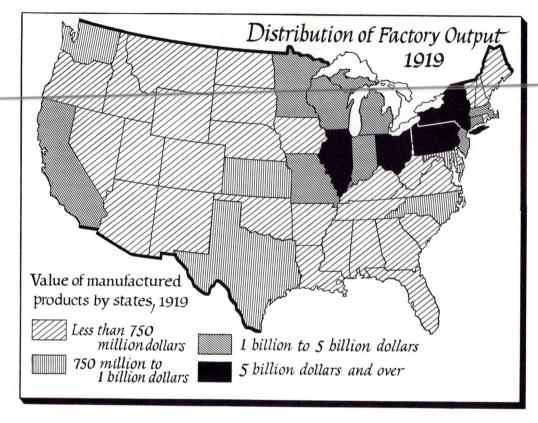

Distribution of Factory Output 1919

Value of manufactured products by states, 1919

Less than 750 million dollars

750 million to 1 billion dollars

1 billion to 5 billion dollars

5 billion dollars and over

month period after September 2, 1918, at $2.26 a bushel, rose by the spring of 1920 to more than $3. At the same time corn sold for over $2 a bushel, with other farm prices equally inflated. Naturally land prices went up, but sales were soon being made less because of the earning power of the land than because of the profits that were to be made by selling it at abnormally high figures. The land boom reached its climax in Iowa, where land worth from $80 to $100 an acre before the war sold during 1919 and early 1920 for from $200 to $400 an acre. During the year that ended in March, 1920, the sale price of Iowa farms increased on an average $63 per acre, or about 32 per cent. Most purchases were made possible only by heavy mortgages, but money for the purpose was available seemingly in an unending stream at the country banks, whose swollen deposits re-

flected the prosperity of their customers. Farm purchases included also electrical equipment, agricultural machinery, motor cars, and blooded livestock, all bought on the installment plan in the hope of future profits. Farmhouses were increasingly modernized, and for the first time in American history a large class of country dwellers lived under conditions that closely approximated the advantages of the city.

Business Recession

Most Americans assumed that the nation's postwar prosperity would be fairly permanent, although a premonition that economic conditions might take a turn for the worse appeared as early as October, 1919, when the stock market broke badly. By midsummer, 1920, postwar prices reached their highest peak, then turned sharply downward. What apparently triggered the decline was the decision of the federal authorities to discontinue after May 31, 1920, the $2.26 per bushel price support on wheat. But there were other important factors involved. Government spending was beginning to decline, and deficit financing had become a thing of the past. During the first six months of 1920 United States Treasury receipts exceeded expenditures by $831 million, in marked contrast with the huge deficits of preceding years. Thus the Treasury, instead of promoting the inflationary process, had begun to lay a heavy toll on income and purchasing power. One reason for the excess of receipts over expenditures was the rapid decline and final ending in 1920 of the loans from the United States upon which European purchasers of American products had so long depended. Confessing its inability to "assume the burdens of all the earth," the United States government refused to make new loans, thus precipitating a decline in foreign exchange that brought European currencies to unprecedentedly low levels. European purchasers found it practically impossible to pay the high prices demanded for American goods, the more so because of the high American tariff rates, raised still higher in 1921. The American public itself added to the general distress by indulging in a "buyers' strike" against the abnormally high retail prices that were still being charged. Aimed mainly at luxuries, the "strike" fell with particular force upon silk, which within a seven-month period fell from $18.40 a pound to $5.81. The resulting prostration of the silk industry in Japan lessened, in turn, the ability of the Japanese to buy American cotton.

The years 1920 and 1921 saw a general slackening in nearly every field of American business. Retailers and wholesalers who had bought at high prices found their shelves stocked with goods that no one could afford to buy. Manufacturers who had made heavy purchases of high-priced raw materials were confronted by wholesale cancellations of orders. Railroad earnings went down, and banks were forced to contract their loans. Stocks and bonds slumped disastrously, and speculators were particularly hard hit. A total of 8,881 business failures, with liabilities of $295 million, occurred in 1920, 19,652, involving $755 million, in 1921. With nearly 3.5 million men out of work, the country faced for the first time in many years a serious problem of unemployment.

Agricultural Conditions

The suffering in agriculture was even more acute than in industry. The European market upon which American farm prosperity had come to depend seemed irretrievably lost. Not only did European producers raise a greater percentage of the farm products their countries needed, but European purchasers turned also to other sources of supply. Meat from the Argentine, wheat from Canada, Australia, and Russia, cotton from Egypt and India tended increasingly to supplant imports from the United States. Even the American market failed the farmers, for the changed food habits of the people called for far less wheat and meat per capita than had been consumed earlier in the century. And yet the American farmer, equipped now with gasoline-driven tractors, could and did harvest larger crops than ever before. During the three years that followed the disastrous break of 1920, production of nine basic field crops equaled or surpassed that of the preceding three years. Naturally, the drop in farm prices was spectacular. With wheat at the lowest figure in twenty-five years, cotton at five cents a pound, and other farm commodities correspondingly deflated, statisticians could demonstrate at will that the cost of production for most farmers far exceeded the proceeds from sales. The dizzy boom in real-

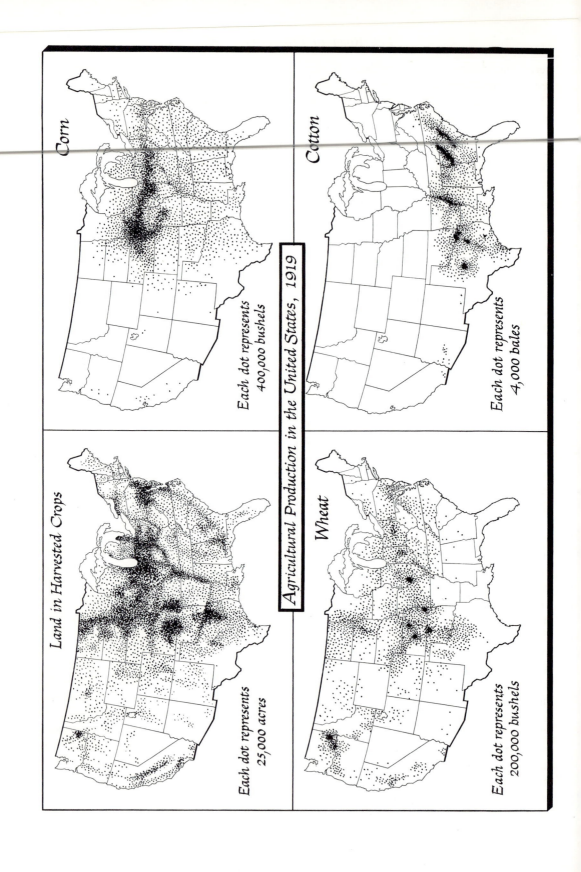

Land in Harvested Crops

Each dot represents
25,000 acres

Corn

Each dot represents
400,000 bushels

Agricultural Production in the United States, 1919

Wheat

Each dot represents
200,000 bushels

Cotton

Each dot represents
4,000 bales

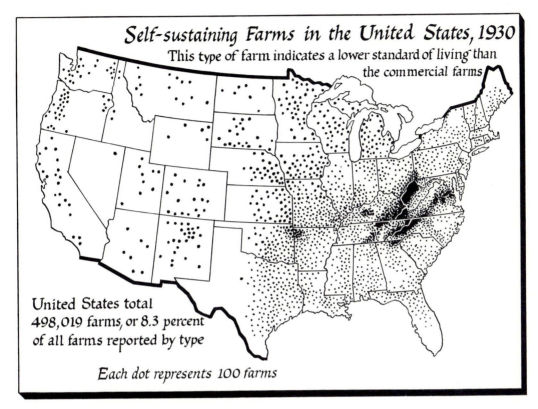

Self-sustaining Farms in the United States, 1930
This type of farm indicates a lower standard of living than the commercial farms

United States total
498,019 farms, or 8.3 percent
of all farms reported by type

Each dot represents 100 farms

estate values that had accompanied the war and the first months of peace collapsed with a frightening crash.

Low prices, unpaid mortgages, and constant foreclosures conspired inevitably to drive the farmers together. During and immediately after the war the National Non-Partisan League of North Dakota, an organization designed to bring the entire resources of the state to the aid of the farmer, scored remarkable, although only temporary, successes. More permanent were such orders as the American Farm Bureau Federation, the American Society of Equity, the Farmers' Union, and the old Grange, which in these troubled times took on new life. Largely as a result of their endeavors, a bipartisan "Farm Bloc" was formed in both houses of Congress to work together as a unit for whatever measures might benefit the farmers, and against anything that might injure them.

Business Pressure

It was against this economic background of hard times that the Harding-Coolidge administration took form. Nearly every item of legislation, nearly every administrative policy, was devised with this situation in mind. The depression had to be broken, and prosperity restored. Probably the most effective of all the pressure groups that operated on the national administration represented the business point of view, or in effect the big business point of view. The official voice of American business was the Chamber of Commerce of the United States, founded in 1912 at President Taft's suggestion "to reflect the views of American business." But the Chamber of Commerce was no mere reflector; it sought also to promote legislation, both state and national, that it deemed favorable to business, and to block measures that business opposed. Similar pressures came from the rapidly increasing number of trade associations, each of which spoke for some specialized group, such, for example, as the National Association of Manufacturers, one of the most powerful of these organizations. Built into the administration itself there was also a vast amount of business pressure. In domestic matters, the Republican regime was dominated by Secretary Mellon, whose name was synonymous with the aluminum industry, while the combined assets of the other members of the Harding-Coolidge cabinet probably ran into the hundreds of millions of dollars. The membership of Congress contained not a few individuals who were themselves businessmen, but many more who had gained office through the contributions and support of local business leaders, with whose views they were under some obligation to agree. In short, the Harding-Coolidge administration responded with alacrity to any pressures that the business world chose to apply. And, whatever the causal relationships, there can be no doubt that, with the exception of agriculture, the depression did wear itself out in minimum time, and that good times did return. The Republicans, as the party in power, took full credit for what had happened, and made every effort to convince the public that Republican rule and prosperity were synonymous.

Economy

The Harding-Coolidge formula for business recovery was never precisely stated in a political document, but it soon became fully apparent. First of all came economy in federal expenditures, a policy that under Harding was tolerated as a political necessity, but under Coolidge accurately reflected the presidential state of mind. In accordance with the terms of a Budget Act, passed in June, 1921, the President appointed a Director of the Budget, Charles Gates Dawes, whose business it was to scrutinize all requests for congressional appropriations, to eliminate duplications, and to pare down excesses. Estimates so obtained were then submitted to Congress, where in each house a single Committee on Appropriations determined the final recommendations. Dawes and the budget directors who succeeded him took their duties seriously, and the normal peacetime disbursements of the national government, if not actually reduced, were given little opportunity to expand. Considerable saving was accomplished by cutting down on the naval and military appropriations, but all such gains were seriously discounted by mounting bills for pensions and veterans' relief. Nevertheless, whereas expenditures due to war had absorbed 94 per cent of the national budget in 1920, they accounted for only 86 per cent in 1924. It is worth noting in this connection that throughout the early twenties state and local expenditures, due in considerable part to highway construction, mounted even more rapidly than federal spending declined. It is difficult to believe, therefore, that there was the direct relationship between "Coolidge economy" and the return of prosperity that Republican politicians were wont to claim. As a matter of fact, after passage of the Veterans' Bonus Bill of 1924, even federal expenditures began to mount again.

Reduction of Taxes

A second item in the recovery program was the reduction of taxes, particularly those that "penalized success" by robbing business of its "legitimate profits." Not content with the repeal of the excess-profits tax and the surtax reductions included in the Revenue Law of 1921, Mellon pressed Congress at every opportunity for further reductions:

High rates [he maintained] tended to destroy individual initiative and seriously impede the development of productive business. Taxpayers subject to the higher rates cannot afford for example to invest in American railroads or industries or embark on new enterprises in the face of taxes taking away 50 per cent or more of any return that may be realized. These taxpayers are withdrawing their capital from productive business and investing it instead in tax exempt securities and adopting other lawful methods of avoiding the realization of taxable income. The result is to stop business transactions that would normally go through and to discourage men of wealth from taking the risks incidental to developing and opening new businesses. Ways will always be found to avoid taxes so destructive in their nature and the only way to save the situation is to put taxes on a reasonable basis.

Mellon was unable to persuade Congress to reduce the maximum surtax as rapidly as he had hoped, but in the Revenue Act of 1924 the rate was brought down from 50 to 40 per cent, and two years later to 20 per cent. Other reductions did away with most of the wartime excise taxes, radically reduced the normal income-tax rates, modified the estate tax, and abolished the gift tax. In 1921 a man with a million-dollar income paid a federal tax of $663,000; by 1926, with the Mellon reductions in force, he paid less than $200,000. Unhappily a considerable proportion of the funds thus released for private use seems to have gone into highly speculative investments. Had the tax rates been permitted to remain at the wartime levels, it seems reasonable to suppose that the liquidation of the national debt might have proceeded even more rapidly than it did, and that the speculative craze of the later twenties might have been avoided. As it was, Mellon was able to lower the obligations of the United States during the decade of the twenties from about $24 billion to about $16 billion.

Government Withdrawal from Business

A third item in the Republican recovery program was the systematic elimination of

Andrew Mellon. *One wry comment on Mellon described him as "the only Secretary of the Treasury under whom three Presidents had served."*

the government from competition with private business. The Transportation Act of 1920, although passed before Wilson left office, was essentially a Republican measure, and in full accord with the policies adopted during the Harding-Coolidge regime. Under its terms the railroads of the country were handed back to their owners with generous indemnification for whatever damages they had suffered during the period of government operation. The Jones Merchant Marine Act of 1920 dealt in similar spirit with the shipping that the government had built or acquired for special wartime service. This measure created a Merchant Fleet Corporation with authority to operate the ships as long as necessary, to lay out new lanes for American overseas commerce, and to turn over the ships and the routes at minimum cost to private companies as fast as American purchasers could be found. When private purchasers failed to take over the ships rapidly enough, Congress by the Jones-White Act of 1928 offered new and still more generous inducements with somewhat better results. The intent, never fully realized, was to get the government out of the shipping business. Possibly the most striking case in point was the refusal of the administration to countenance any plan for the effective governmental operation of the Muscle Shoals power development in Alabama, begun during the First World War to aid in the production of nitrates. In a single stretch of thirty-seven miles the Tennessee River falls 134 feet. To make use of this power the government planned a series of dams and two nitrate plants. One of the nitrate plants was in operation by 1918, but the great Wilson Dam was not completed until 1925, when the wartime need for nitrates had long passed. To Senator Norris of Nebraska and others who were undismayed by the prospect of a government-owned business, the Muscle Shoals development seemed to offer an ideal opportunity for the production of cheap power, but Congress was persuaded to offer the whole property for sale. The only bid worth considering was made by Henry Ford, whose terms involved so heavy a loss to the government that they could not be accepted. A small trickle of power was sold to the Alabama Power Company for distribution in the surrounding territory, but for the most part the potentialities of this development remained unexploited until the time of the New Deal.

Restraints on Regulation

The distaste of the administration for governmental interference in business went much further, and called also for a drastic reduction in the amount of federal regulation. Legislation to accomplish this end would have been difficult to obtain, but the same purpose was achieved by indirect means. One by one the great regulatory bodies created by preceding administrations were packed with the friends of the very businesses they were supposed to regulate. The Interstate Commerce Commission was in effect handed over to the railroads, the Federal Trade Commission to the trusts, and the Federal Reserve Board to the bankers. For good measure the Tariff Commission was delivered into the custody of the protectionists. In criticism of a series of such Coolidge appointments, Senator Norris had this to say:

The effect of these appointments is to set the country back more than twenty-five years. It is an indirect but positive repeal of Congressional enactments, which no Administration, however powerful, would dare to bring about by any direct means. It is the nullification of federal law by a process of boring from within. If trusts, combinations, and big business are to run the government, why not permit them to do it directly rather than through this expensive machinery which was originally honestly established for the protection of the people of the country against monopoly and control?

Government Aids to Business

Not content merely with removing in so far as possible all discouraging checks to private enterprise, the administration in a great variety of ways gave business direct and substantial aid. The rationalization for such aid was sometimes called the percolator theory of national economics. This line of reasoning ran that if the top levels of business were kept prosperous then much of this prosperity would seep down to benefit the middle and working classes. The most traditional means of accomplishing this end was by protective tariffs, and these Congress promptly supplied through two

The Wilson Dam, *a part of the Muscle Shoals power development on the Tennessee River. Here, during World War I, the national government began construction of two nitrate plants and this large dam. Finally completed in 1925, after 1933 the Wilson Dam was taken over and operated by the Tennessee Valley Authority. It is 137 feet high and 4,860 feet long, with a reservoir area of about 16,100 acres.*

measures, the Emergency Tariff Act of 1921, and the Fordney-McCumber Act of 1922. The new laws raised tariff rates to the highest levels yet known, and insured American producers strongly against any significant foreign competition. But government assistance to business went much further than the tariff. For the shipping industry and the new aircraft corporations the government provided generous subsidies. For all businesses that might stand a chance to profit from tariff protection, it kept the tariffs high. For those with a taste for foreign investment, the State Department promised to lend a hand by denouncing bad foreign securities, and whether because of this, or in spite of it, American capital sped abroad in a seemingly endless stream. For the better promotion of foreign trade the Department of Commerce extensively and expensively reorganized its foreign service. For the benefit of domestic producers the Bureau of Standards offered elaborate facilities for testing, and recommended standard types in all sorts

of manufactured articles from building bricks to automobile tires. Secretary Hoover, as head of a commission to study waste in industry, brought in numerous suggestions bearing upon business efficiency. His work as head of the Department of Commerce was generally credited with having "elevated a relatively unimportant cabinet position to one of major rank." The *Detroit News* enthusiastically credited his activities with having ended the "threat to our prosperity."

Easy Credit

The government also aided business by encouraging the Federal Reserve System to provide easy credit, especially whenever an emergency threatened. Financial experts had noted that whenever the Federal Reserve Banks bought government securities, now on the market in far greater quantities than before the war, they made more credit available for member banks, while when they sold these securities the result was a tightening of credit. Always attentive to Wall Street advice, the national administration tended to favor the bond-buying alternative, and by encouraging the Federal Reserve Board to keep the rediscount rate low still further promoted the boom conditions that business in general seemed to want. European nations, eager to keep American investors interested in sending dollars abroad, also urged the United States to adopt an easy money policy, and according to Herbert Hoover greatly influenced the American decisions. But home pressure was by no means lacking, for easy credit meant a booming stock market, accelerated real estate expansion, vigorous construction activities, and generous installment terms. Small wonder that during the Coolidge era business achieved a degree of prosperity never known before.

The Disciplining of Labor

The return of the Republicans to power was accompanied, also, by a drastic change in the attitude of the national government toward labor. In business circles there was a great outcry in favor of the so-called "American plan," which in effect meant a complete return to the open shop, and an end to collective bargaining through independent unions. Some employers sought to forestall real unionism by "welfare capitalism," which in various ways gave the appearance of cutting the workers in on the profits of business, and by "company unions," which management could control. Toward all such efforts to keep labor in its place the national government showed a benevolent sympathy. Probably its most effective weapon for thwarting the ambitions of labor lay in the President's right to appoint the federal judges who must rule on the legality of the methods by which organized labor sought to operate. To Harding in his brief term of office fell the selection of four members of the United States Supreme Court, and the men he chose, Taft, Sutherland, Butler, and Sanford, were all conservatives. Less apparent, but hardly less important, was the careful attention given by Daugherty as Attorney-General to the records of all proposed appointees to the lower courts and to subordinate positions in the Department of Justice. Before he left office in 1924 he was thus able to make an indelible imprint upon the administration of justice in the United States. Characteristic of the stiffening attitude of the courts toward labor was the sweeping injunction Daugherty obtained when a strike of the railroad shopmen in 1922 seriously disrupted interstate commerce. From Federal Judge J. H. Wilkerson of Chicago, a Harding appointee, Daugherty obtained a temporary injunction that forbade every conceivable type of strike activity. "Not merely violence but picketing of all sorts, strike meetings, statements to the public, the use of union funds to carry on the strike, and the use of any means of communication by the leaders to direct it," all fell under the ban of the court. The fact that this injunction was sustained on appeal demonstrated the hollowness of the hope that the Clayton Antitrust Act had furnished an enduring "Magna Carta for Labor." Already the federal courts had legalized "yellow dog" contracts, which required workers to pledge themselves in advance not to join unions, and had further crippled union activities by limitations on boycotts and peaceful picketing.

Resistance to Farmer Pressure

Despite the alarming persistence of the depression in agriculture, the Harding-Coolidge administrations opposed most of the middle-western and southern demands for farm relief. The congressional Farm Bloc had little difficulty in obtaining as a part of the Emergency Tariff Act of 1921 increased duties on wheat to protect northwestern farmers against importation from

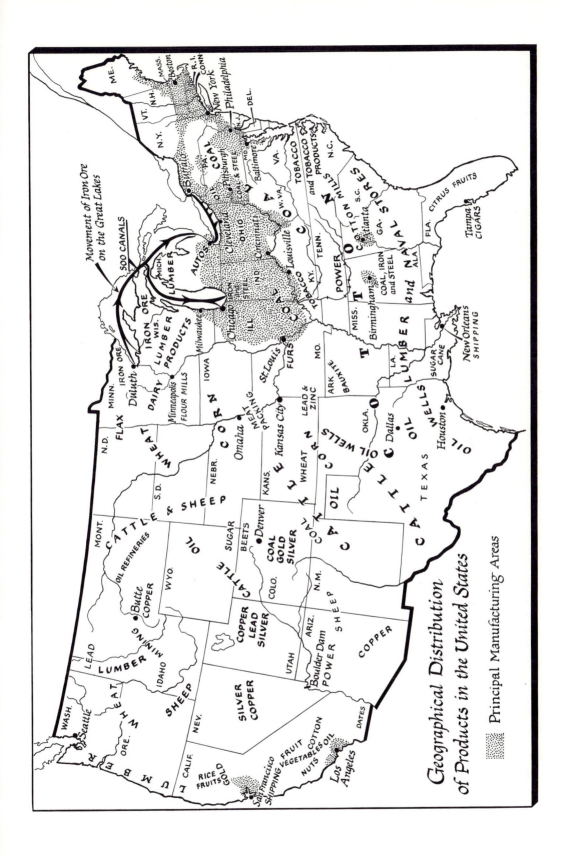

Geographical Distribution of Products in the United States

Principal Manufacturing Areas

Canada, and additional protection for such farm products as meat, wool, and sugar. But these duties, as every reputable economist knew, could not seriously affect the prices of commodities of which the United States had an "exportable surplus." The Farm Bloc was instrumental also in the passage of the Intermediate Credits Act of 1923, which created a system of banks designed to provide farmers with credits for not less than six months nor more than three years. But remedies more radical than tariff protection and easier credits were consistently opposed. The McNary-Haugen bill, an ingenious measure designed to raise the domestic price of certain farm crops by creating a governmental agency which could buy up and "dump" the surplus on foreign markets, was before Congress for several years, only to be vetoed by President Coolidge as "economically unsound." Another scheme for agricultural relief, the export debenture plan, proposed to place export bounties on specified agricultural commodities, to be paid by the United States in the form of debentures receivable for customs. On the presumption that these debentures would be purchased at a discount by importers, proponents of the plan argued that the bounty to the farmers would come directly out of the protective tariff. But this attempt, aimed no less than the McNary-Haugen bill "to get the farmer up on stilts" along with the tariff-protected manufacturer, failed even to pass Congress. With little assistance from the government, agricultural organizations did what they could to restore prosperity to the farms by promoting cooperative marketing, but in spite of their best efforts hard times for the nation's farmers continued.

Business Recovery

For business it was different. By the time Coolidge became President in 1923 the tide had turned strongly toward economic recovery, and in the campaign of 1924 the Republicans could count on prosperity as their best talking point. Steady gains were reported in iron and steel, in the automobile industry, in the building trades, and among wholesalers and retailers. Dividends that had vanished during the depression were resumed by a large number of corporations in 1923 and 1924, while occasional stock dividends demonstrated still more conclusively that times had changed. Even railroad earnings increased, and all signs pointed to still brighter economic skies. Naturally this abundant prosperity came to be closely associated with Republican policies, for the Republicans were in power when it arrived, and they cheerfully admitted their responsibility for bringing it to pass.

Farmer-Labor Discontent

Discontent with the blessings of Coolidge prosperity was nevertheless rife among two important elements of American society, the farmers and the urban workers. The farmers had plenty of hard work to do, but their efforts yielded only slender rewards, if any. The workers remained subject to their employers' "right to hire and fire" at will, and often lost their jobs because of technological improvements that enabled machines to do the work formerly done by men. Furthermore, the prosperity was spotty, even in business itself; throughout the twenties there were many ailing industries, such as coal, textiles, leather, shipbuilding, and railroad equipment. During the boom years unemployment estimates stood at an average of about 2.5 million. Since neither the Republicans nor the Democrats seemed much interested in the farmer-labor problem, why not, progressives asked, a new third party to represent the special interests concerned? With this end in view the railroad brotherhoods, whose members had not forgotten the advantages they had enjoyed under governmental operation during the war, sponsored in 1922 a Conference for Progressive Political Action that laid plans for independent voting in the congressional campaign of that year. Through a Committee of Fifteen it succeeded in helping to victory such party irregulars as LaFollette of Wisconsin, Shipstead of Minnesota, Wheeler of Montana, and LaGuardia of New York. Encouraged by this victory, the CPPA renewed its efforts in 1924, enlisting also the support of the American Federation of Labor, the more radical farm orders, the Socialist Party, and a Committee of Forty-Eight representing a self-selected group of liberal intellectuals. From this "united front," however, the Communists were rigorously excluded. Operating under the time-honored Progressive label, the coalition named a presidential ticket consisting of a Republican, LaFollette, for President, and a Democrat, Wheeler, for Vice-President. Its platform, written by LaFollette, proposed "to break the power of the monopoly system over the economic and political life of the American people," but clung too tenaciously to old reforms reminiscent of Populism, and emphasized too little the needs of the long-suffering city masses. Progressivism itself had failed to progress very far.

Election of 1924

With the all-powerful issue of prosperity working for them the Republicans entered the campaign of 1924 full of confidence. Their nomination for President went naturally to Coolidge, whom the public had come to regard as a kind of personification of prosperity. For Vice-President they chose Charles Gates Dawes, Harding's first Director of the Budget. The Democrats, seemingly determined to make certain of defeat, staged a long-drawn-out contest for the presidential nomination between William G. McAdoo, Wilson's Secretary of the Treasury, and Governor Al-

Fiorello H. LaGuardia. *New York City's "Little Flower" was one of the first of American progressives to sense the importance of reforms that would meet the needs of the city masses.*

fred E. Smith, a Tammany Irish Catholic of immigrant descent who had risen from the city streets to become one of the ablest governors the state of New York had ever had, and the idol of the eastern city democracies. Held in Madison Square Garden, New York, the Democratic convention served to emphasize the disparate character of the elements that composed the Democratic Party — on the one hand the agricultural South and West, and on the other the city machines that depended for their support mainly upon the votes of recent immigrants and their American-born offspring. Democrats of the South and West were overwhelmingly rural, Protestant, and native American; those of the great urban

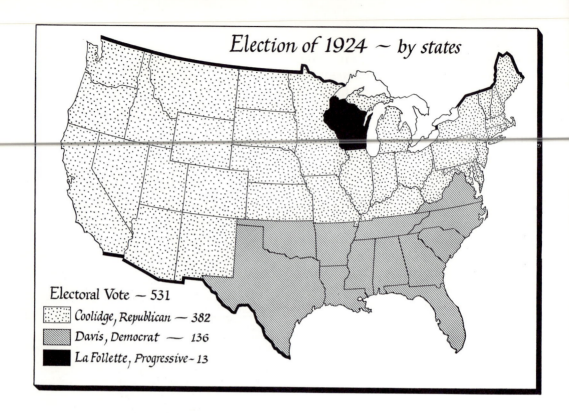

Election of 1924 ~ by states

Electoral Vote — 531

- Coolidge, Republican — 382
- Davis, Democrat — 136
- La Follette, Progressive – 13

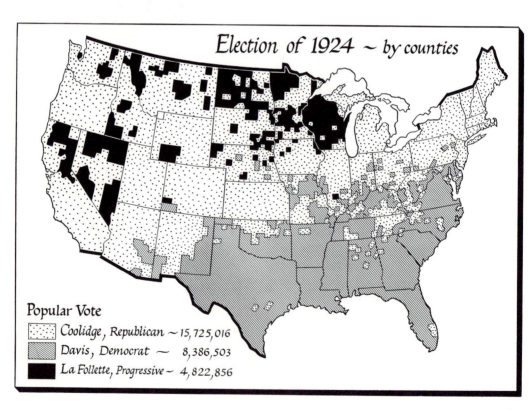

Election of 1924 ~ by counties

Popular Vote

- Coolidge, Republican ~ 15,725,016
- Davis, Democrat — 8,386,503
- La Follette, Progressive ~ 4,822,856

centers were city-minded, dominantly Catholic or Jewish in religion, and of assorted ethnic origins. The Ku Klux Klan had infected much of the South and West with its prejudice, and because Smith was a loyal Roman Catholic, Klan-conscious delegates refused to support him. Furthermore, Smith was an ardent "wet" on the prohibition issue, a source of great satisfaction to the city delegates, but a complete disqualification in the eyes of many from the South and West. It soon became apparent that neither Smith nor McAdoo could win the two-thirds majority then required for a Democratic nomination, but the convention took over one hundred ballots before it turned to John W. Davis of West Virginia and New York, a brilliant but conservative lawyer whose connection with the firm of J. P. Morgan and Company completely disqualified him in the eyes of labor and the western liberals. To compound this blunder the convention made another. For Vice-President it chose Governor Charles W. Bryan of Nebraska, brother of William Jennings Bryan, a man who had nothing but his name to recommend him for the post, but whose name alone was sufficient to alienate the eastern conservatives. With such a ticket, nominated after such a fight, the Democrats had not the slightest chance of winning.

The election was a Coolidge landslide. In the popular vote the Republican ticket won a plurality of more than 7 million, and a majority of about 2.5 million. The electoral college gave Coolidge 382 votes, Davis 136, and LaFollette 13. All of the Davis electoral vote came from the South and LaFollette carried only his own state, Wisconsin. Congress was safely Republican in both houses, and by much wider margins than after the elections of 1922. A warning, however, that all was not as well as it seemed was apparent from the fact that nearly 5 million voters had cast their ballots for LaFollette. The Wisconsin Senator did not long survive the election, but after his death in 1925 his son, Robert M. LaFollette, Jr., succeeded him in the Senate, and with other like-minded reformers continued to voice the protests of the underprivileged. Progressivism was by no means dead, even if conservatism was in the ascendancy; in the next decade the reformers would take over.

Election of 1928

In the midterm elections of 1926 prosperity was almost the only effective party issue, and the Republicans won again, but the election of 1928 was somewhat more complicated. There was much talk of another nomination for Coolidge, but the President announced in 1927 that he did not "choose to run." As a result, the Republican choice fell upon Herbert Hoover, Coolidge's Secretary of Commerce, whose name was almost as closely connected with the current wave of prosperity as that of the President himself. The nomination of Hoover was far from satisfactory to the still unprosperous farmers of the Middle West, and to appease them Senator Charles E. Curtis of Kansas, a former Farm Bloc leader, was named for Vice-President. The Democrats, with obvious southern and western reluctance, yielded to the pressure of the powerful Democratic city machines, and nominated Alfred E. Smith for President, taking what comfort they could from the nomination of Senator Joseph T. Robinson of Arkansas for Vice-President. Smith was a Catholic, a "wet," and a Tammany man. Robinson was a "dry" from a state that had few Catholics and no large cities. But no one was deceived. The ticket of Smith and Robinson, despite its "one-hundred-per-cent American" names, represented primarily the recent immigrants and their descendants who made up the bulk of the voting population in all the great cities of the East.

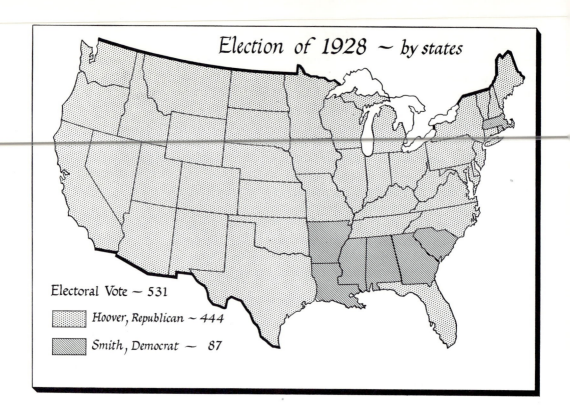

Election of 1928 ~ by states

Electoral Vote ~ 531

Hoover, Republican ~ 444

Smith, Democrat ~ 87

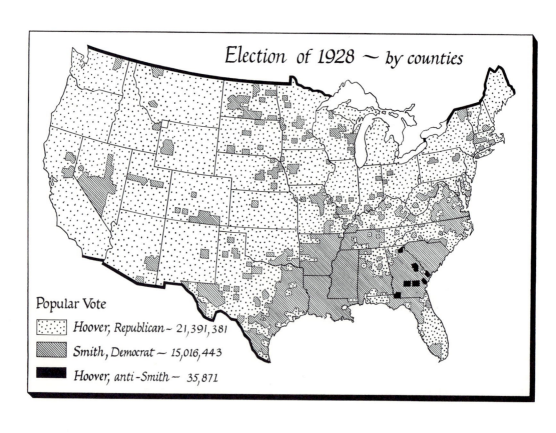

Election of 1928 ~ by counties

Popular Vote

Hoover, Republican ~ 21,391,381

Smith, Democrat ~ 15,016,443

Hoover, anti-Smith ~ 35,871

THE CAMPAIGN OF 1928. *Both Hoover and Smith campaigned vigorously during the weeks preceding the election. Hoover's better success in using the radio may have influenced some voters.*

HOOVER ON THE ROSTRUM. Hoover made fewer speeches than Smith, and depended more on the radio to reach the voters.

SMITH GREETING A WHISTLESTOP CROWD. Photograph of his train while it was passing through Chicago, September 18, 1928.

Hoover's Victory

Hoover's triumphant victory at the polls in November was due primarily to four factors: (1) the belief which he assiduously cultivated that the continuance of Republican rule meant the continuance of prosperity; (2) the prejudice of rural America against the Tammany background of a corrupt machine based on immigrant votes from which Smith had risen; (3) the deep-seated opposition of many American Protestants to the elevation of a Catholic to the Presidency; and (4) the determination of the evangelical churches to retain prohibition, which Smith denounced, but Hoover described as "a great social and economic experiment, noble in motive and far-reaching in purpose." "Hoover Democrats," voting the Republican ticket in large numbers, shattered the solid South; for the first time since reconstruction the Republicans carried Virginia, North Carolina, Tennessee, Florida, and Texas. Smith also lost his own state, New York, and every western and border state. The electoral vote stood 444 to 87, and the popular vote 21.4 million to 15 million. The Hoover landslide carried with it overwhelming Republican majorities in Congress and in some of the states.

The decisiveness of Hoover's victory tended to obscure some important results of the election. Far more significant than the temporary switch of some southern states into the Republican column was the shifting of the great urban centers toward the Democrats. In the two preceding presidential elections the twelve largest cities of the nation, taken together, had voted Republican by a decisive majority. But in 1928 they voted Democratic. This was the beginning of a trend that was to last far into the future. The non-Anglo-Saxon ethnic groups of the cities, dominantly Catholic or Jewish in religion, and definitely wet on the prohibition issue, were tired of being regarded as second-class citizens, and voted for Smith, not merely as pawns of some machine, but because they thought they had more to gain from a Democratic than from a Republican victory. Nor were they much interested in registering a futile protest vote. Norman Thomas, the Socialist candidate, received only about a quarter of a million votes, while the splinter party candidates got almost no votes at all. It was significant, also, that the reform vote of the Middle West that went for LaFollette in 1924 turned in large numbers to Smith in 1928. In Wisconsin, for example, the one state that LaFollette had carried, the Democratic ticket received only 68,000 votes in 1924, but over 450,000 in 1928. Thus the Republicans, despite their triumphant victory, had far more troubles ahead than they realized.

BIBLIOGRAPHY

For the transition to the 1920s, see J. D. Hicks, *Rehearsal for Disaster* (1961). The decade is surveyed in J. D. Hicks, *Republican Ascendancy, 1921–1933* (1960); and more briefly in Paul Carter, *The Twenties in America* (1968). Longer spans of time are covered by H. U. Faulkner, *From Versailles to the New Deal* (1950); G. E. Mowry, *The Urban Nation: 1920–1960* (1965); and D. A. Shannon, *Between the Wars: America, 1919–1941* (1965). Among the most lasting of the contemporary books are: Walter Lippmann, *Men of Destiny* (1927); André Siegfried, *America Comes of Age* (1927); J. C. Malin, *The United States after the World War* (1930); and F. L. Allen, *Only Yesterday* (1931), a lively work which long set the tone for interpretation of the era. Rich discussions of the interpretations of the period may be found in Henry May, "Shifting Perspectives on the 1920s," *Mississippi Valley Historical Review*, XLIII (1956), 405–427; and in Burl Noggle, "The Twenties: A New Historiographical Frontier," *Journal of American History*, LIII (1966), 299–314. Several stimulating essays are contained in *Change and Continuity in Twentieth-Century America: The 1920s* (1968), edited by John Braeman and others.

Now that his papers are available, Harding is at last coming in for serious scholarly attention. The most careful examination of his Presidency is R. K. Murray, *The Harding Era* (1969), but it is marred by the author's argumentative attitude. On Harding the man, Francis Russell, *The Shadow of Blooming Grove* (1968), is liveliest. On Harding the politician, Andrew Sinclair, *The Available Man* (1965), is provocative. S. H. Adams, *Incredible Era* (1939), is journalistic and undocumented, dwelling on the scandals. On the latter, see J. L. Bates, *The Origins of Teapot Dome* (1963); and Burl Noggle, **Teapot Dome* (1962). There are two outstanding monographs on conservation in the period: D. C. Swain, *Federal Conservation Policy, 1921–1933* (1963); and G. D. Nash, *United States Oil Policy, 1890–1964* (1968).

The best study of Coolidge is now D. R. McCoy, *Calvin Coolidge: The Quiet President* (1967). But see also the older work of W. A. White, *A Puritan in Babylon* (1938); and C. M. Fuess, *Calvin Coolidge* (1940). On the Supreme Court, see A. T. Mason, *William Howard Taft: Chief Justice* (1965); D. J. Danelski, **A Supreme Court Justice Is Appointed* (1965), a study of the selection of Pierce Butler; and W. F. Swindler, *Court and Constitution in the Twentieth Century* (1969). A. T. Mason, *Harlan Fiske Stone* (1956), is an admirable full life of the man Coolidge appointed to direct the clean-up in the Justice Department and later elevated to the Supreme Court. Interesting scholarly lives of extreme conservatives are J. F. Paschal, *Mr. Justice Sutherland* (1951); and Morton Keller, *In Defense of Yesterday: James M. Beck and the Politics of Conservatism* (1958). Good accounts of the 1928 campaign are E. A. Moore, *A Catholic Runs for President: The Campaign of 1928* (1956); R. V. Peel and T. C. Donnelly, *The 1928 Campaign: An Analysis* (1931); R. C. Silva, *Rum, Religion, and Votes* (1962); and V. D. Bornet, *Labor Politics in a Democratic Republic* (1964). A brief life of Governor Smith is Oscar Handlin, **Al Smith and His America* (1958); see also Matthew and Hannah Josephson, *Al Smith: Hero of the Cities* (1969). An exceptionally acute study of the Democratic Party from 1918 to 1932 is David Burner, *The Politics of Provincialism* (1967). Samuel Lubell, **The Future of American Politics* (2nd ed., 1956), contains a shrewd analysis of the implications of the 1928 campaign. A unique political study, which could serve as a model for other state monographs, is J. J. Huthmacher, *Massachusetts People and Politics, 1919–1933* (1959).

The standard survey of economic history is George Soule, **Prosperity Decade, 1917–1929* (1947). Immense detail is provided by the report of the Conference on Unemployment, *Recent Economic Changes in the United States* (2 vols., 1929). Interesting monographs include H. F. Williamson and others, *The American Petroleum Industry: The Age of Energy, 1899–1959* (1963); and G. G. Schroeder, *The Growth of Major Steel Companies, 1900–1950* (1953). A valuable synthesis is T. C. Cochran, **The American Business System: A Historical Perspective, 1900–1955* (1957). An acute analysis of the thinking of business leaders is J. W. Prothro, *The Dollar Decade: Business Ideas in the 1920s* (1954). On transportation, see especially K. A. Kerr, *American Railroad Politics, 1914–1920* (1968); and W. N. Leonard, *Railroad Consolidation under the Transportation Act of 1920* (1946). A basic study is H. G. Moulton and associates, *The American Transportation Problem* (1933). On the merchant marine and its problems, see P. M. Zeis, *American Shipping Policy* (1938).

On agriculture, see the excellent biographies of two political leaders deeply interested in the plight of the farmers: W. T. Hutchinson, *Lowden of Illinois* (2 vols., 1957); and H. E. Socolofsky, *Arthur Capper* (1962). A valuable survey of federal action is M. R. Benedict, *Farm Policies of the United States, 1790–1950* (1953). A major work on the beginning of the long farm depression is J. H. Shideler, *Farm Crisis, 1919–1923* (1957), by a leading agricultural historian. Theodore Saloutos and J. D. Hicks, **Agricultural Discontent in the Middle West, 1900–1939* (1951), which appears in paperback as *Twentieth-Century Populism*, traces the history of the principal farm orders from their formation, and shows their effect on the political life of states and nation. On the Farm Bureau, the laudatory official history by O. M. Kile, *The Farm Bureau Through Three Decades* (1948), should be contrasted with the highly critical treatment of Grant McConnell, **The Decline of Agrarian Democracy* (1953). On the farm relief, see J. D. Black, *Agricultural Reform in the United States* (1929); G. C. Fite, *George N. Peek and the Fight for Farm Parity* (1954); and Russell Lord, *The Wallaces of Iowa* (1947), which describes the work of all three Henry Wallaces.

Irving Bernstein, **The Lean Years: A History of the American Worker, 1920–1933* (1960), is an important study which takes some of the gloss off the vaunted prosperity decade. Philip Taft, *The A. F. of L. in the Time of Gompers*, previously cited, is continued with *The A. F. of L. from the Death of Gompers to the Merger* (1959); these works, however, do not supersede Selig Perlman and Philip Taft, *History of Labor in the United States, 1896–1932* (1935). Other important works in labor history include: David Brody, *Labor in Crisis: The Steel Strike of 1919* (1965); S. D. Alinsky, *John L. Lewis* (1949); Matthew Josephson, *Sidney Hillman* (1952); and Benjamin Stolberg, *Tailor's Progress* (1944), on the I.L.G.W.U. Conflicting interpretations and documentary evidence are gathered in *The Steel Strike of 1919* (1963), edited by C. E. Warne. A valuable new monograph is R. H. Zieger, *Republicans and Labor, 1919–1929* (1969).

R. K. Murray, *Red Scare: A Study in National Hysteria, 1919–1920* (1955), is a fine summary. But it can now be supplemented by Stanley Coben, *A. Mitchell Palmer* (1963); William Preston, Jr., *Aliens and Dissenters* (1963); and R. L. Friedheim, *The Seattle General Strike* (1964). Two older works of importance are D. J. Saposs, *Left Wing Unionism* (1926); and J. S. Gambs, *The Decline of the I.W.W.* (1932). Two scholarly works by Theodore Draper, *The Roots of American Communism* (1957), and *American Communism and Soviet Russia* (1960), treat the history of the movement to 1930 in brilliant fashion; see also Irving Howe and Lewis Coser, *The American Communist Party* (1957), a critical survey. Leading works on the decade's foremost radical cause are Felix Frankfurter, *The Case of Sacco and Vanzetti* (1927); G. L. Joughin and E. M. Morgan, *The Legacy of Sacco and Vanzetti* (1948); David Felix, *Protest* (1965); and H. B. Ehrmann, *The Case That Will Not Die* (1969).

On the progressive movement of the 1920s, the best books are F. E. Haynes, *Social Politics in the United States* (1924); and K. C. MacKay, *The Progressive Movement of 1924* (1947). See also the lives of LaFollette, Norris, and Gifford Pinchot, mentioned in the bibliographies for Chapters 13 and 14. On the Muscle Shoals controversy, symbol of agrarian radicalism in the 1920s, see P. J. Hubbard, *Origins of the TVA* (1961). Books about notable progressives of the period include: O. G. Villard, *Fighting Years* (1939); D. J. Humes, *Oswald Garrison Villard* (1960); Michael Wreszin, *Oswald Garrison Villard* (1965); Harry Barnard, *Independent Man: The Life of Senator James Couzens* (1958); H. L. Warner, *The Life of Mr. Justice Clarke* (1959); Howard Zinn, *La Guardia in Congress* (1959); Arthur Mann, *La Guardia: A Fighter Against His Times, 1882–1933* (1959); and B. K. Wheeler and P. F. Healy, *Yankee from the West* (1962). A. S. Link, "What Happened to the Progressive Movement in the 1920s?" *American Historical Review*, LXIV (1959), 833–851, is suggestive, if not completely convincing.

On the Negro, Gunnar Myrdal, *An American Dilemma: The Negro Problem and Modern Democracy* (2 vols., 2nd ed., 1964), is a work of unusual excellence; it is summarized by Arnold Rose, *The Negro in America* (1948). J. M. Mecklin, *The Ku Klux Klan* (1924), a good contemporary study, may now be supplemented by A. S. Rice, *The Ku Klux Klan in American Politics* (1962); D. M. Chalmers, *Hooded Americanism* (1965); C. C. Alexander, *The Ku Klux Klan in the Southwest* (1965); and K. T. Jackson, *The Ku Klux Klan in the City* (1967). Roger Daniels, *The Politics of Prejudice: The Anti-Japanese Movement in California and the Struggle for Japanese Exclusion* (1962), is a model monograph which illustrates the tie between progressivism and immigration "reform." Diplomatic aspects are examined by R. W. Paul, *The Abrogation of the Gentlemen's Agreement* (1936).

19

MASS CULTURE

*The consumer society · The automobile · Henry Ford · Mass con-
sumption · The movies · Censorship · Radio · Jazz · Journalism · Book publication · The new American woman · Prohibition · Gangsterism · The
Wickersham Commission · Educational changes · Religious trends · The
KKK · Foreign opinion of the U.S.A.*

The Consumer Society

The 1920's were not too old when
F. Scott Fitzgerald, the author who most
symbolized the new decade, commented
that whereas most generations were close
to those that preceded them, between his
and the past there was "an infinite and
unbridgeable gap." Most thinking people
agreed with his judgment. For in the great
social and political revolt of the twenties it
seemed that practically every ideal and
standard held by past generations was being
repudiated; most major social institutions
were changed, as well as ideas about art
and literature. During the previous twenty
years public energy had been expended in
one reform crusade after another, crusades
which were directed not only toward attaining more democratic institutions and
assuring the more equitable division of
goods among all classes, but also toward
the moral and cultural elevation of man.
The attempt to suppress prostitution and

the enactment of the prohibition law were
clear evidence of the latter. But the 1920's
witnessed an abrupt end to reform. In
the midst of the economic boom from 1922
to 1929 there seemed to be little need to
take political action to assure almost everyone of a high standard of living. In part,
it was the amazing prosperity of the time
that caused such a shift in public attitudes
and in the common way of life. The disillusionment with the result of the war as
compared with Woodrow Wilson's promises also had its weight. But probably of
even more importance was the impact of
the new consumer technology that produced such profound changes. At any
rate, most people during the 1920's were
preoccupied with acquiring the newest
model automobile; with cultivating and expressing their so-called personality; with
losing their inhibitions, and with enjoying

*THE FLAPPER, JAZZ AND PROHIBITION were all
phenomena of the gay and carefree 1920's.*

themselves irrespective of existing social conventions and, indeed, of the law. The United States, commented one critic, rushed from the great crusade for world government to the "hog trough of materialism." Looking back from the vantage point of the next decade Scott Fitzgerald called it a generation of miracles and excess, and one which "corrupted its elders and eventually overreached itself."

Two most important material facts help explain the great social changes during the 1920's. By 1920 more than one-half of the population was living in towns and cities, and during the next ten years that preponderance grew rapidly as 6 million more Americans left the countryside for the sidewalks. If Frederick Jackson Turner was right in assuming that the frontier and the availability of free land had profoundly changed American character and institu-

tions, then it was reasonable to suppose that the turn to the city as a way of life would produce changes equally great. The second powerful influence was the birth and incredibly rapid development of a new technology geared to the mass production of consumer articles. Hitherto much industrial production had been poured into so-called capital goods, into more railroads, bridges, and factories — a consumption pattern which in the main touched the masses only indirectly. But most of the new industries of the twenties produced for the masses. Out of the relationships and institutions built around this new activity came forces that were to make stupendous changes in society, changes dictated not only by the revolutionary character of the new production but also by the tastes and wants of mass consumers. Of these new industries perhaps the most potent was automobile manufacturing.

The Automobile

Founded largely on European ideas and inventions, the American automobile industry produced only four thousand cars in 1900, and growth remained modest until World War I. But during the war and after, production boomed, and by 1928 over 26 million automobiles and trucks were operating in the United States. By that time automobile production had become the key factor in the economy. The General Motors Corporation had surpassed the United States Steel Corporation in earning power, and the total automotive industry, together with its planetary industries, such as petroleum, rubber, glass, etc., employed more men and utilized more raw materials than any other single sector of the economy. Many men contributed to this imposing rise, especially to its more mechanical side, but the story of Henry Ford (1863–1947) will always be inseparable from this American saga of wheels and gasoline.

F. Scott Fitzgerald. *This brilliant writer, who perhaps better than any other embodied the spirit of disillusionment associated with the age, is shown here with his daughter, "Scotty."*

Henry Ford

Beginning at Detroit in 1893, Ford was making a fairly dependable car by the turn of the century, and by 1914 had produced a half million of his famous "Model T." Ford made no change in his general designs from 1909 to 1927. The car was ugly, it came in only one color, black, but it ran and it was cheap. Ford made his greatest contributions to industrial change not so much by his mechanical ideas as by his revolutionary concepts of production and distribution. In 1913 he established the production line and from then on he preached unrelentingly the gospel of standardized machine production, lower prices, and higher wages. It was only by continually lowering the price of his car and raising the wages of his workers, Ford stated, that he could sell to the millions.

Ford was an industrial autocrat with many strange ideas. In his early days he was anti-Semitic; he was suspicious of education and culture. He did not like books; he said, "they mess up my mind." And he preferred Napoleon to Christ because the former was a "hustler." But he did lower the price of his car from $950 in 1909 to $290 in 1924, meanwhile reducing the working hours of his men and raising wages substantially above those paid by other companies and other industries.

The fierce price competition of Ford and his most formidable competitor, the General Motors Corporation, founded in 1908 by William C. Durant, reduced the major motor companies from over two score in 1910 to essentially three by 1927. Low unit prices created the desperate necessity to produce and to sell in volume if a profit were to be made. This in turn laid a heavy stress on advertising, and eventually led to the sale of automobiles on long credit terms. During the 1920's 60 per cent of all automobiles were sold on credit. If the consumer could not be "educated" by advertising, the manufacturer had to adapt the product to his wants, fancied or otherwise. The salesman and the sales organization be-

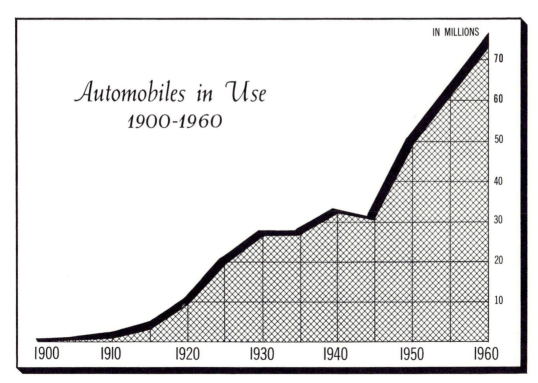

Automobiles in Use
1900-1960

IN MILLIONS

70
60
50
40
30
20
10

1900 1910 1920 1930 1940 1950 1960

came as important as the producer and the factory. And eventually the state of competition in the industry led it to the calculated promotion of obsolescence. By 1931 the industry was purchasing and destroying functioning cars in order to create a market. By that time also the necessity to promote more sales had led to the habit of introducing a "new model" every year. Henry Ford himself gave up a part of his original dream when in 1927 he was forced to introduce a new higher-priced model to meet the competition.

The automobile age brought many changes to society. Before 1920 no officially numbered highways existed, but public demand had spurred the rapid construction of paved inter-city roads, a development which destroyed the old isolation surrounding the farm, produced great effects on state governments, and was eventually to transform the transportation of both passengers and freight. The automobile also was to have profound effects upon the growth of cities. In a less obvious way it also affected such things as dress and public moral standards. Of equal importance to society was the automotive industry's introduction of new ways of doing business, techniques which other mass consumer industries soon made use of.

American Aviation

The amazing success of the automobile industry gave rise to the hope, not soon to be realized in full, of the early development of commercial aviation. American aviation began in 1903 when Orville and Wilbur Wright first made successful flights with power-driven planes at Kitty Hawk, North Carolina. In 1914 the industry was still in its infancy, but when the war ended in 1918 the United States had twenty-four aircraft plants capable of producing 21,000 aircraft a year. But cancellation of war contracts virtually wrecked the new industry, while both the Army and the Navy refused to concede to air power the significance it merited, even after General "Billy" Mitchell's bombers sank a surrendered German battleship, the *Ostfriesland*, and other target craft, in a test demonstration.

Meantime, "gypsy" fliers, who made a precarious living by taking passengers on "joy rides," kept the public air-conscious and prepared the way for commercial transportation; "stuntfliers" also revealed its possibilities, particularly for long-distance flights. The Atlantic was crossed by way of the Azores as early as May, 1919; from Newfoundland to Ireland in June of the same year; and from Great Britain to New York by a British dirigible the following July. But the achievement that most caught the country's fancy was the solo flight of youthful Charles A. Lindbergh, who took off from Roosevelt Field, Long Island, on May 20, 1927, and thirty-three hours later landed successfully near Paris. The fact that he was not the first to fly the Atlantic in no wise diminished Lindbergh's fame. By order of President Coolidge, he was brought home on a warship, and rose immediately to the status of the nation's greatest hero. Later in the month two army pilots reached Honolulu from California, while in June, 1931, another American aviator, Wiley Post, flew around the world in less than eight days' time

Air Mail Progress

The development of commercial aviation in the United States did not begin in earnest until several years after the signing of the armistice in 1918, although the government early gave its assistance by air-mail contracts. By 1924 a regular mail service had been established between New York and San Francisco, and four years later there were as many as forty-eight airways in the United States, covering 20,000 miles, and serving 355 cities. Most of these lines

SPIRIT OF ST. LOUIS, 1927. In this now primitive plane Charles A. Lindbergh crossed the Atlantic in a solo flight, May 20–21, 1927.

ASSEMBLY LINE METHODS. This picture, taken about 1914, shows the assembly of the magneto and flywheel unit on early Model T Fords. This was one of the first subassemblies to be integrated into the new assembly line techniques.

depended upon government mail contracts for their profits, and regarded the incidental carrying of passengers or freight as somewhat of a nuisance. When Hoover became President in 1929 his Postmaster-General, Walter Folger Brown, resolved to remedy this situation. The government subsidies were paid, he believed, not merely for carrying the mail, but also to encourage the development of a new and useful means of transportation which might incidentally serve the country well in time of war. Brown wrote new contracts, which, by abandoning the "per pound" basis for carrying the mail in favor of the "space-mile" principle, placed a premium on the building of larger planes. He also used his discretionary power in the awarding of contracts in such a way as to eliminate the small operators, whose ability to develop the industry was obviously less than that of the well-established and adequately financed lines.

As a result of Brown's policy American aviation was able to survive the blows it suffered from the depression. Many "little fellows" went under, but great systems developed which brought transportation by air into common use. Passenger comfort became a matter of first importance, and sufficient private business was obtained by the air lines to make possible the gradual reduction of governmental subsidies. It was inevitable, however, that the success of the large, government-aided operators should arouse the jealousy of their less favored competitors, and it was the complaints of the latter that had aroused Farley's wrath.

Steady improvements in airplane design and in safety and cheapness of service made the public more "air-minded" with each succeeding year. By the end of 1939 the nation's scheduled air lines reported that they had carried 1.9 million passengers during the year; but by 1952 this figure had grown to 27.8 million, and by 1960 to over 50.5 million. Meantime American air transport had become a multi-billion dollar industry.

Mass Consumption

The mass production and consumption process was accompanied by national advertising, the widespread development of the consumer credit system, and a great emphasis upon salesmanship and public relations. In 1902 the annual advertising revenue of the *Saturday Evening Post* amounted to about $300,000. Twenty years later it was over $28 million. Voicing this national call to consume was the salesman with his beguiling tongue. The sales organizations in many industries boomed and became as important as the producing sectors. To swell consumption, credit became easier, and the term of payment longer, for even the lowest priced articles.

Under this barrage of inducements to consume, the old habits of personal thrift began to crumble. National advertising witnessed the rise of a giant industry whose aim was to persuade people, often against their inclination, to buy. The process of selling became a national craze. One sold not only goods but ideas, religion, and especially oneself. All too often the new arts of persuasion borrowed heavily from ancient ways of deception and downright fraud. This mass-oriented consumer-conscious, and sales-stimulated capitalism also developed the very natural inclination to produce what the market wanted. Consumer likes and dislikes were studied and followed intensively. To a large degree, the standards of the masses thus became the standards of the nation.

The Movies

This dictation of national standards by the common man was most harmful when it invaded the cultural and educational institutions of the nation, in particular the new motion picture and radio industries.

The origin of the "movies" antedates the turn of the century. From the first "peep shows," which treated the viewer to only a brief episode, through the first picture with a "plot," "The Great Train Robbery" in 1903, and even up to the opening of World War I, progress was slow. In 1914 David W. Griffith made "The Birth of A Nation," an epic picture that centered on the Civil War and reconstruction. Griffith's budget of over $100,000 for the production, his use of crowd scenes and mass action, and his new camera techniques were revolutionary. The public responded with enthusiasm, and by 1918 the movie industry had become big business with headquarters in southern California. Soon its products were being distributed for the millions not only in the United States but throughout the world. By 1922 forty million tickets were being sold weekly, and such reigning stars as Charlie Chaplin, Harold Lloyd, Mary Pickford, and Douglas Fairbanks were better known than most politicians. The tales of their fabulous salaries and sumptuous lives were spread before the public by picture and word in the "movie magazines," which for a time threatened to crowd most other periodicals off the newsstands. The introduction of the "talking picture" in 1927 and the use of color further enhanced the popularity of films. By 1937 seventy-five million people were crowding into the nearly 90,000 movie palaces weekly; of this audience more than one-third were minors, and one-sixth were under fourteen years of age.

Censorship

As the motion picture industry assumed big business proportions it inevitably reflected big business attitudes. A few large Los Angeles companies accounted for most of the films made in this country, and competed with each other for the control of the market. Box office receipts became the chief criterion of excellence, and the pro-

ducers catered shamelessly to the public taste, good or bad. During the early 1920's some producers so insistently traded on sex and sex themes that a wave of protest swept the country. State legislatures enacted censorship laws of varying effectiveness, and the film industry appointed President Harding's Postmaster-General, Will H. Hays, to supervise the industry and to cultivate its public relations. Hays set up a production code regulating such things as the degree of dress and undress, the length of caresses, and the amount of profanity allowable. The Hays office, and the chief producers also, came to an understanding that evil could not go unpunished on the screen, and that good had to be rewarded. This synthetic censorship removed a certain element of realism from the films.

But the major reasons for the cinema's almost complete flight from reality related to the structure of its profits and the nature of its market. Production costs became so lavish, and the promise of massive profits in the making of "smash hit" pictures so alluring, that producers were constantly preoccupied with not insulting or alienating any significant part of the world market. Since the major part of a movie audience was adolescent in taste if not in years, pictures had to be patterned to the adolescent mind. One producer frankly admitted that he made his pictures so that they could be understood by a fourteen-year old. The majority of movie-goers were of the lower economic classes, and did not wish to be reminded of their own shabby surroundings. Therefore most movies were given luxurious settings. Because the masses, in their dreams of escape or attainment, wanted happy endings, tragedy was all but excluded. And since the treatment of any controversial subject was apt to reduce the potential market, or so the producers thought, the average movie did not touch upon such questions. The moving pictures of the 1920's and 1930's thus became almost

Radio City Music Hall. *This portion of the Rockefeller Center, in the heart of New York City, is the largest exclusively indoor theater in the world. Construction began on the Center in 1931.*

pure entertainment, removed equally from life and from art. Their value in lifting the cultural level of the nation was almost non-existent; the quality of their influence on public ethics and morality was certainly debatable. The novelist John Dos Passos commented that once the reading of the Bible had kept the American masses literate, but Hollywood had now usurped this important function, and its "great bargain sale of five and ten cent lusts and dreams" was creating "the new bottom level of our culture."

Radio

Another new influence upon American life was furnished by the radio. Wireless telegraphy and telephony were known before the outbreak of World War I, but during that struggle they proved to be of such tremendous military value that revolutionary improvements were made within a few years' time. After the war radio enthusiasts known as "hams," whose interest was primarily that of amateur scientists, bought millions of dollars' worth of equipment, and counted with joy the number of distant stations they could hear.

By 1920, the manufacturers of radio supplies were beginning to furnish programs as a means of promoting the use of what they had to sell, and from this practice the institution of radio broadcasting developed. The pioneer station in this endeavor was KDKA of Pittsburgh, which among other things successfully broadcast the returns of the election of 1920. Soon many broadcasting stations, generously supported by advertisers, were competing for control of the air, and to prevent complete chaos Secretary Herbert Hoover maintained an informal system of licensing in the Commerce Department. When in 1926 the Attorney-General ruled that the Secretary of Commerce was exceeding his legal authority, the resulting confusion led Congress to establish the following year a Federal Radio Commission of five members with the right to license broadcasting stations, and to determine the power, wave lengths, and hours of operation to be allotted to each. The radio act made the granting of a wave-length contingent upon the licensee conducting his station in the public interest, and gave the Commission power to revoke licenses. This standing threat served in practice to moderate the grosser abuses of an instrument which provided strong means of swaying public opinion and of improving or debasing public taste. In 1939 the industry formulated a much debated code which sought to exclude all broadcasts on controversial public issues except such as pertained to politics. By the Mayflower decision of 1941, however, the

Federal Communications Commission, created by an act of Congress in 1934, challenged the right to ban broadcasts on such issues and subsequently instituted proceedings against stations which censored labor news and suppressed other controversial discussion.

But radio, like the movies, became big business. By the 1940's there were radios in most homes. By that time, also, 730 of the 900 privately owned stations had been organized into four nationwide networks, the advertising receipts of which were enormous. In newscasting and in presenting political campaigns, the radio industry was at its best. Constrained to impartiality, it granted equal time to political candidates, and the entire nation was able to hear for the first time paramount public questions debated by aspiring office seekers. Radio also presented the news with less bias and distortion than did the nation's newspapers. And as the issues of the thirties began to divide the public along economic class lines, radio also helped to correct the disparity occasioned by the fact that the supporters of one party controlled most of the newspapers of the country. Occasionally, industries of national scope, like the United States Steel Corporation, which did not sell directly to the public, performed a significant service by subsidizing broadcasts of operas and symphony concerts. Radio was responsible for much of the astonishing rise in the appreciation of serious music. But the great majority of advertisers were interested in appealing to the mass market. National polls by telephone were used to determine the size of the listening audience, and a resulting "Hooper rating" was attached to each major program. Since advertisers naturally supported the programs which captured the largest audiences, the cultural level of radio, like that of the film, tended to reflect the level of the majority of its listeners. "Soap operas" and detective stories, both usually presented in interminable serials, and the ever-present jazz music, did little or nothing for the taste and education of the listeners. Instead such pro-

Radio Broadcasting. *Before television entered the competition, radio broadcasters attempted ambitious dramatizations. The actors at the microphone in this picture are presenting* Mr. District Attorney, *a serial.*

grams may have had the opposite effect of killing appreciation for anything better.

Jazz

With the advent of the automobile and the radio, man lost the quiet which was a part of nature and which had been preserved in a nontechnical rural society. This was particularly true when jazz music became the overwhelming favorite of radio. Jazz originated around the turn of the century among Negro musicians of New Orleans. From Basin Street in New Orleans it crept up the river to Beale Street in Memphis and then on to Chicago, where it rapidly became a favorite of both high society and low. From there it took the whole world by storm until there was scarcely a corner where its syncopated rhythms were not throbbing. Along with it came the popular dance, at least for the young in heart and muscle. The great popularity of jazz and the modern dance during the twenties threatened to extinguish even the memory of folk music and folk dancing. Such orchestra leaders as Duke Ellington, Louis Armstrong, and Paul Whiteman became household deities. To be at all a part of mass society one had to know the "hit" tunes, the accompanying maudlin and often meaningless words, and the latest dance, whether it be the fox trot, the Charleston, or the black bottom. Whether in this frenetic fusion of music and dance Americans, as one recent historian has claimed, came close to "mass exultation" and "religious feeling" is debatable. But certainly the combination of sound and movement provided the sexes with an opportunity for meeting and mingling at point-blank range hitherto unparalleled. The rapidity with which the hit songs and the dance of the moment were discarded for new favorites indicated a zest for quick change in fads and innovations which, if transferred to more serious institutions, might endanger society.

Louis Armstrong

Journalism

Just as films, radio, and music felt the great influence of the masses, so did the more traditional means of communication. After the introduction of the first true tabloid newspaper, the *New York Daily News*, in 1919, William Randolph Hearst followed suit with his *Daily Mirror;* and the fashion soon spread to other cities. Most of these new "picture papers" omitted all reference to serious cultural endeavors, played down important world news, and concentrated on sex, sin, and scandal. Their circulation grew enormously, and their success probably had much to do with the demise of such high quality newspapers as the *New York World*, sold in 1931 to the Scripps-Howard chain. Developments in magazines tended to follow those in newspapers. The decade saw a spectacular rise of "the pulps," a name derived from the cheap wood-pulp paper on which such magazines were printed. Their stock in trade was murder and detective stories, and most of all, the "true confession" stories in which the heroine, who had departed from the paths of virtue, repented and told all.

THE JAZZ AGE. *Paul White-man's concert at Aeolian Hall, New York, in 1924, presented George Gershwin's* Rhapsody in Blue, *and helped bring artistic respectability to jazz. The remarkable effectiveness of Negro musicians with this medium did much to promote the careers of such orchestra leaders as Louis Armstrong.*

PAUL WHITEMAN AND HIS ORCHESTRA.

Done up in gaudy colors and liberally sprinkled with pictures as shocking as the law permitted, such periodicals competed with the movie and the sport story magazines for public custom.

The death of many quality magazines and the "debasement" of reading habits is explained by one literary critic as due to the desire of the masses in a machine civilization to seek escape from the deadly pall of an enforced conformity by "vicariously living the life of divergence from the normal." Another critic, reflecting on the forced union of *Vanity Fair* with *Vogue*, commented that "no aristocratic magazine can be published in America." Since *Time, The Saturday Review of Literature, The American Mercury* (which advertised itself as the only magazine "that appeals to the civilized minority"), and the leftist *New Masses*, also originated and flourished in the decade, such gloom was not entirely justified. Still, the remark of a leading American author that he earned more money from one four-part "pulp serial" in a new mass circulation magazine than from all of the thirty books he had written,

indicated the threat of mass merchandising to quality in the arts.

Book Publication

Nor did book publishing escape the pull of the times. Sensational fiction was produced in quantity, the publisher of one such book announcing it as "intimate as a boudoir, as amusing as a peephole and as suggestive as a bill of fare." Even the old and decorous art of biography stooped to obtain mass approval. By stressing the defects and the unconventional actions of such national heroes as George Washington and Benjamin Franklin, a group of popular writers in the early twenties started the "debunking" tradition. From debunking, such authors later in the decade turned to the biography of the more scandalous characters of the past. Popular biography, one critic sourly observed, had turned from pulling down idols to "setting up criminals for inspection." But perhaps the most significant development in the popular book trade was the movement making book publishing into a big business. Although the selections of the Literary Guild and the

Book-of-the-Month Club, both organized in 1927, were far above the average book in quality, this application of mass merchandising techniques to the literary trade set a trend toward quantity as a substitute for quality. Soon most advertising and publicity skills were enlisted in the hope of making a novel into a "best seller." "Books," wrote Archibald MacLeish in 1928, "have become news to be merchandised to the masses."

The New American Woman

One of the most startling revolutions in twentieth-century American society was the change in the status and importance of women. The growing power of women as a class was foreshadowed well before the 1920's, particularly in their demands for political equality and for moral reform. During the twenties, however, women as a group seemed to lose their taste for reform, and apparently decided to enjoy the masculine world as it was. Throughout the decade one masculine sanctuary after another fell. Women invaded the business world en masse. As typists, secretaries, and even junior executives their numbers soon changed the entire nature of the office. Whereas in the early years of the century perhaps 2 million women were working, by 1913 ten million earned a weekly salary, and by 1955 that figure had jumped to 27 million, or over 30 per cent of the entire working force of the nation. Two women state governors were elected in the 1920's, "Ma" Ferguson in Texas and Nellie Tayloe Ross in Wyoming. The advent of the "shingle bob" not only witnessed the departure of most feminine long hair but also ended the male monopoly of the barber shop. But perhaps most revolutionary in what it symbolized was woman's invasion of the "speakeasy" — the 1920's equivalent of the pre-prohibition "saloon" — and later, of the post-prohibition "cocktail bar."

The typical "flapper," the name given to the new young woman of the twenties, tried to match men in almost every activity and accomplishment of life. She cut her hair in a boyish bob, discarded the corset, and shortened her skirt from ankle to knee. A flattened bosom, a lowered belt line, and a strict diet changed her appearance into something remotely resembling the adolescent male. She drank bootleg liquor, smoked cigarettes, appeared in "beauty contests," and discussed with her dates the latest theories of sex. Whether she had any more to do than men with the changing relations between the sexes is debatable, for signs of the rapidly changing morality were in the air of postwar America. The old standards no longer elicited reverence from either sex. As one of Hemingway's characters remarked in *The Sun Also Rises*, there were no standards; immorality was simply "the things that made you disgusted afterwards." Ellen Glasgow wrote four novels during the twenties. Among her four heroines, two had illegitimate children, one left her husband for another man, and the last scandalized Virginia society by her daring clothes and frank talk. The order of the new day was symbolized by the publication of Judge Ben Lindsey's book in 1927 urging the trial or "companionate" marriage. Two years later the first book on the techniques and principles of contraception was published in the United States, and the following year saw a book by Emily Hahn on the standard methods of seduction. Meanwhile in fifteen years the number of divorces had doubled, and a survey of marriages in 1929 indicated that over half were "unhappy" and that 15 per cent of husbands and wives queried felt that adultery need not be defended, as it was "normal" and presumably not harmful. Some social critics viewed this change in sexual morality as not at all disastrous for society. Others saw it as the portent of the collapse of civilization. But harmful or not, there was no gainsaying that women had achieved a status somewhat near to equality with men, and also that they had had a major hand in changing many of the old standards of middle-class morality and taste.

A character in John Steinbeck's *The Grapes of Wrath,* published in 1939, illustrates the continued erosion of old ethical and moral standards. "There ain't no sin and there ain't no virtue," he remarked, "There's just stuff people do. . . . Some of the things folks do is nice and some ain't nice; but that's as far as any man got a right to say."

Prohibition

Certainly many Americans seemed to feel this way about the bankruptcy of the "noble experiment" of prohibition and the resulting national crime wave. The rock on which prohibition foundered was enforcement. It was one thing to outlaw the existing liquor traffic, but quite another to prevent its replacement by illicit vendors of liquor who profited from breaking the law. The Eighteenth Amendment made no great change in the national appetite for strong drink, and a large minority of the population felt outraged that any such attack on personal liberty had been made. This was particularly true of the city populations in which the immigrant element constituted so important a part. Others who had never drunk before were impelled out of sheer defiance or perversity to do what the law forbade. Americans since colonial times had never felt obliged to obey a law that they did not like; indeed, many argued that the only way to defeat an obnoxious law was to prove that it could not be enforced. Thus a market for liquor still existed, and to supply it a whole new industry came into being. The ways of the "moonshiners," who since the days of the Whiskey Rebellion had hidden their stills in the mountains to avoid the payment of revenue, were extensively imitated; "rum-runners" brought a steady stream of cargoes

Nellie Tayloe Ross, *of Wyoming, was the first woman to be elected a state governor. Later she became Director of the United States Mint, the first woman ever to hold that office.*

from abroad to unpatrolled sections of the American coast; heavily laden smugglers crossed the border from Mexico and from Canada; chemical formulas, sometimes dependable and sometimes not, were used to "renovate" industrial alcohol by the removal of denaturants; private citizens set up toy stills, manufactured "home-brew" and "bathtub gin," turned the pure unfermented juice of the grape into more or less palatable wine.

The Volstead Act, by which Congress (over President Wilson's veto) defined intoxicating beverages as those containing as much as one half of one per cent alcohol, and created the machinery for enforcement, imposed upon federal officials an impossible task. "Bootleggers" had already gained valuable experience in the states where prohibition had preceded the Eighteenth Amendment. They knew how easily the problem of distribution could be solved by automobiles and trucks, and they were past masters at the arts of bribery and deception. Against these experts the Prohibi-

An Unsuccessful Attempt at Rum Running. *Here 500 cases of liquor, worth $40,000, are being removed from the* Anna Louise. *As a general rule, however, prohibition was ineffectively enforced, a situation which to many observers appeared intentional. Federal appropriations for the purpose were kept low, and state appropriations were often negligible.*

tion Bureau, which until 1927 was outside the civil service, mobilized a miscellaneous army of petty politicians and their friends. Furthermore, the entrance of the national government into the field of enforcement led the states to relax their efforts. Former wet states in many instances repealed the limitations they had once placed on liquor dealers, while dry states cheerfully resigned to federal agents the task of matching wits with the bootleggers. The United States Department of Justice found itself suddenly swamped with a type of business it had never known before, and prohibition cases clogged the federal courts. Thirty-five hundred civil cases and sixty-five thousand criminal cases were brought within a period of less than two years.

Gangsterism

Illicit liquor soon made possible one of the nation's biggest and most profitable businesses. Since it operated wholly outside the law, all restraints were eliminated, and competitors traded bloody blows. Backed by dependable gangs of thugs, the "big shots" fought furiously for the enormous profits of monopoly, and in each large city emerged a well-recognized king of the underworld, to whom, while his reign lasted, the whole business paid tribute. Deaths among the gangsters were numerous, but trials for these murders were rare and convictions still rarer. The gang leaders, successfully defended by highly paid criminal lawyers known as "mouthpieces," not only sneered openly at the prohibition agents, but systematically instituted one new "racket" after another. Gambling, prostitution, the trade in narcotics, and other illegal activities came naturally within the orbit of the "racketeers," but even the most legitimate of businesses were not immune. Restaurant keepers, cleaners and dyers, laundrymen, garage owners, anyone who took in cash might at a moment's notice be compelled to pay heavily for "protection" — against the protectors themselves! Failure to meet the racketeers' demands meant smashed windows, flattened tires, burned delivery trucks, bombed stores, and for the most obdurate, sudden death. Labor unions also were invaded for the splendid opportunity they offered to graft from membership dues. And in altogether too many instances city governments paid more attention to the demands of the racketeers than to the welfare of the citizens. Racketeering was at its worst in Chicago and New York, but few large cities escaped its ravages, and the whole nation paid tribute, directly or indirectly, to the power of gangland.

The Wickersham Commission

With conditions fast becoming unbearable, a Law Enforcement Commission of eleven members was appointed by President Hoover in 1929 to conduct an investigation. Headed by George W. Wickersham, who had been Attorney-General under President Taft, the Commission took its duties seriously, but when it reported in 1931 it was still undecided on what recommendations to make. Its findings of fact seemed to recognize the hopelessness of adequate enforcement, but a majority of its members recommended that the prohibition experiment be continued.[1] In the summer of 1932 President Hoover, in spite of the impending campaign, admitted that some changes in the existing system would have to be made, while the Democratic platform went the whole length of demanding repeal. Following the triumphant Democratic victory at the polls, Congress acted even before the new administration could take office. In February, 1933, the repeal amendment was submitted, and by the end of the year it was a part of the Constitution.

[1] Report of the National Commission on Law Observance and Enforcement, Seventy-first Congress, third session, *House Document* No. 722 (serial 9361).

J. Edgar Hoover. *As Director of the Federal Bureau of Investigation, Hoover's name became known throughout the nation. The FBI dates back to 1908, but its real effectiveness began only with legislation passed in 1934.*

The end of prohibition, however, did not mean the end of racketeering, for by this time the gangsters were deeply entrenched in all sorts of rackets. One of the most amazing of these was the "snatch racket," which in May, 1932, claimed its most famous victim when the infant son of Charles A. Lindbergh, the aviator who had flown the Atlantic in 1927, was kidnapped for ransom by a lone operator, and killed. As the profits from bootlegging disappeared, criminals turned instead to kidnapping, bank burglaries, and other bold crimes, and in an alarming number of instances easily made good their escape. Finally Congress, by a series of "crime control" acts passed in the spring of 1934, squarely faced the responsibility of the federal government in bringing the situation under control. By the terms of these laws criminals who crossed state lines during the course of their exploits were made liable to drastic penalties (for kidnappers,

Al Capone. *"The King of the Chicago Under-world" was convicted only of income tax evasion.*

death), and the Investigation Division of the Federal Department of Justice, headed by J. Edgar Hoover and known later as the Federal Bureau of Investigation, was given great freedom of action in enforcement. At the end of the year Hoover's agents had accounted by death for a dozen of the country's most notorious criminals, and had brought many others to justice. State officers, forced to compare results with the effective "G-men," also began to take their duties seriously. Early in 1935 the kidnapper of the Lindbergh baby was convicted and sentenced to death in New Jersey. That same year Thomas E. Dewey was made special prosecutor to conduct a drive against organized crime in New York City and achieved such conspicuous success that in 1937 he was given a popular mandate to continue the work as district-attorney of New York County. When other evidence failed, racketeers were sometimes convicted for federal income-tax evasion. This had happened to "Scarface Al" Capone, the underworld ruler of Chicago, as early as 1931, and his long imprisonment at

Alcatraz, the federal penitentiary located on an island in San Francisco Bay, served as a continual warning to would-be imitators. Toward the close of the decade there was reason to hope that at last the era of unrestrained lawlessness had approached its end.

Educational Changes

Faced with the materialism and lawlessness of the twenties, many reformers placed their hopes on education as a remedy. And certainly America responded with generous support. Compulsory school attendance up to sixteen or even eighteen years of age was required by law in most states. Thousands of new buildings were erected yearly and fitted out not only with comfortable classrooms but also with auditoriums, gymnasiums, and even swimming pools. By 1928 it was estimated that the United States gave as much to education in taxes and gifts as the rest of the world combined. In 1900 only one child in ten had entered high school, and only one in thirty-three had entered college. By 1931, 50 per cent went to high school, and one in seven continued to college, most of the increase coming in the postwar years. But even if the nation was not quite aware of it, quantity did not guarantee quality. The great numbers crowding into the high schools created a demand that the educational aims be radically changed to fit the needs, the intellectual capabilities, and the tastes of the majority. This condition and the emphasis placed upon John Dewey's theories of "education for life," urged chiefly by the graduates of Columbia University's Teachers College, radically shifted the emphasis away from cultural courses toward a more practical and vocational type of education. Moreover, the more zealous educational reformers demanded that the educational process be democratized so that every child, irrespective of his mental equipment, be promoted along with the rest. In 1927 the Chicago Federation of Labor joined the Chicago Teachers' Federation in condemning the use of intelligence tests in school because of their anti-democratic nature and results. By that time over seventy different subjects were being taught in the high schools, and the drift of the times was indicated by the announcement of a professor at Columbia University Teachers College that he had rendered the Declaration of Independence into "simplified English" and was rewriting "many deep tracts" in a language "adapted to the eighth grade level" so that all students would be on a more nearly equal footing in their understanding of the fruits of the past.

Colleges and universities attempted to stem this anti-intellectual trend, but all too often fell prey to the same forces that were victorious in the lower schools. There were, of course, many excellent additions to the lists of courses. Following Harvard's earlier lead, many colleges instituted new schools of business, a development which played a major part in changing the social attitudes of the coming generations of American businessmen. The institution in 1931 of a new curriculum at the State University of Iowa in which the imaginative and creative arts were emphasized was destined to enrich the typical campus, and eventually the cultural and artistic heritage of the nation. But along with these developments came more dubious additions — courses in "accident prevention," "mental hygiene," and "charm," together with such a bewildering proliferation of offerings in "physical culture" as to defy analysis. College athletics became big business during the twenties, with football receipts in 1929 amounting to over $20 million. And often it seemed that the major efforts of both students and faculties were being utilized in distinctly nonintellectual pursuits. Along with many other disturbed educators, Dean Christian Gauss of Princeton declared that the American colleges had become "a kind of glorified playground" and that most of the students then attending should be sacked. Ten years later, in 1938, the findings of a Carnegie Foundation study on "The Student and His Knowledge" seemed to bear out these gloomy sentiments. According to this report there was little relation between the time spent in college and either educational achievement or intelligence. More than half the students entering college, the report found, ranked in intelligence and in the ability to speak and write, well below the upper 25 per cent of those who did not go to college. Twenty-eight per cent of graduating college seniors did less well in intelligence and achievement tests than the average sophomore. Those seniors planning to teach ranked well below the average for their class, and some even below the average students of the better high schools.

Religious Trends

Besides education, the other great social institution which traditionally provided the ethical and moral cement that bound society together was the church. But during the twenties, on the surface at least, religion seemed to be either at a standstill or in retreat. Although immediately after the war the churches seemed suffused with vitality, the disillusionment over the peace, the materialism of the twenties, the growing spirit of extreme nationalism at home and abroad, and the disposition of the age to derogate ethics and things of the spirit, cast a pall over many religious activities. Whereas in 1919 contributions to missionary work had reached their highest level, by 1926 many churches admitted extreme difficulties in obtaining funds to support their foreign work. The fundamentalist revival, as shown in the anti-evolution laws in the South and the trial of John T. Scopes, lost the church much support from a generation increasingly interested in science. The

The Scopes Trial. *William Jennings Bryan, witness for the prosecution, and Clarence Darrow, counsel for the defense, are shown here at the famous "monkey trial" in Dayton, Tennessee.*

"monkey trial," as it was called, took place in the small town of Dayton, Tennessee, but through the press it quickly commanded a world-wide audience. Scopes, a high school science teacher, was arrested for violating the state Anti-Evolution Law. To his defense came Clarence Darrow, one of the nation's most brilliant trial lawyers. The star witness for the prosecution was William Jennings Bryan, whose World Fundamental Association had been influential in placing the law on the books of Tennessee and other southern states. Scopes was found guilty by the local jury, but the national consensus seemed to be that Bryan had been made to appear naive, and that such laws had no place on the statute books.

The continuing battle between the modernist or liberal Christians and the fundamentalists was also internally disruptive. For the first time in its history the Episcopal Church in 1925 deposed a bishop for heresy, and a few years later fundamentalists among the Presbyterians drove the nationally known minister Harry Emerson Fosdick from his pulpit in New York City

for being too liberal in his interpretation of the Scriptures. In the preceding twenty years, many churches had won the respect of a good many alienated working men by their emphasis upon the Social Gospel. Attacked during the twenties by both economic and religious conservatives, the Social Gospel movement lost a good deal of its vitality. Instead of answering the charge that the doctrines of the Social Gospel would lead to anarchy and revolution, their one-time supporters increasingly turned from day-to-day economic issues to the more congenial problems of prohibition and world peace. In light of the failure of prohibition, and the coming depression of 1929, this dominance of "the pew over the pulpit," as one minister described it, was perhaps unfortunate. It was significant that, save for Father Coughlin's radio organization of the Social Justice movement, the churches were remarkably silent during the great depression. Perhaps that silence supplied something of an answer to the 1939 query of a leading Protestant minister: why, he asked, had there not been anything resembling a religious revival during the depression days?

Despite the gloomy prediction that organized religion was in permanent eclipse, there were many indications that the church retained its essential vitality. Looking in one direction was the ecumenical movement, the subject of numerous conferences during the twenties and the thirties. Led by a group of minister-scholars in the Union Theological Seminary of New York — and supported by the powerful modernist *Christian Century* magazine, the campaign for a United Protestant church continued to attract support. Although the World Conference at Lausanne in 1937 was characterized by more wrangling than agreement, measurable progress was made within the United States. Not only did the Federal Council of the Churches of Christ established in 1908 continue active, but the even more inclusive organization of The National Conference of Jews and Christians was organized in 1931. The ability of Protestantism to sire new splinter groups was further evidence of an enduring vitality. The multiplication of cults and creeds continued, particularly in California, where Aimee Semple McPherson's Four Square Gospel Church drew national attention. Of more importance for the following decades was the organization founded by a North Dakota Lutheran minister and an ex-Y.M.C.A. secretary, Frank Buchman. The movement, variously known as Buchmanism, the Oxford Group, and later as Moral Rearmament, had as its aim the establishment of an international and interdenominational order of lay friars "always ready to be 'fools for Christ'." The order, which first blossomed at Oxford University in England, had no consecrated priests, but utilized the weekend houseparty where "group confession and the sharing of one's sin with the group" automatically guaranteed, according to its founder, "forgiveness and absolution." Because its appeal was mainly to the cultured and the wealthy, critics jibed that it was "the Salvation Army gone high hat," a movement of the up and out instead of the down and out. But Buchmanism seemed to have great appeal for educated youth, and perhaps its attack on Russia in the warlike thirties helped it spread throughout America.

Catholicism and Judaism

The steady growth of the Roman Catholic Church during the twenties and thirties, despite the fact that the stopping of immigration in the early twenties had cut off an incoming stream of believers, was also evidence of continuing strong religious life. The bigotry of the Ku Klux Klan and the defeat of Al Smith for the Presidency had caused, according to one Catholic writer, an abiding inferiority complex among many Catholics. Certainly this sense of not being accepted by the majority as quite Americans had undone some of Cardinal Gibbons' early work, and perhaps accounted for the increased activity of Catholics in

Aimee Semple McPherson. *As exponent of the Gospel Four Square, "Sister Aimee" drew great crowds of believers and onlookers to her Angelus Temple in Los Angeles.*

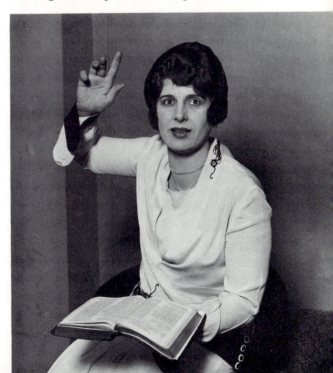

founding their own schools and cultural organizations. In 1928 Ludwig Lewisohn published *The Island Within*, in which the Jewish hero Arthur Levy, because of increased antagonism, gave up a lifelong attempt to identify with the gentile majority, concluded that the barriers to integration were insurmountable, and dedicated the rest of his life to his people and their separate characteristics. In the face of the rising anti-Semitism of the twenties, the Jewish Yeshiva University was founded in 1926. And separate institutions for the Jews, such as Libby's Hotel on Manhattan Island, and the Jewish Hotel and Restaurant near Harvard University, flourished.

The majority in America had themselves to blame during the twenties for much of the rising sense of separatism among minority religious groups. But with the depression and the rise of Fascism in Europe, the tide turned. The repeal of prohibition tended to identify large immigrant and "wet" Catholic groups with the majority in America. The New Deal's evident tolerance of all groups further cemented unity. The Fascist persecution in Europe not only created sympathy for the Jews, but also brought to America large groups of Jewish and Catholic intellectuals who enriched not only the cultural life of the nation but its religious tradition as well. American religion was far from moribund, but in 1929 it was difficult to be optimistic about its future. Two years before, the *Christian Century* reported that the evangelical churches had lost a half million members in the preceding year. And there was little in church statistics during the following eighteen months to increase the confidence of the faithful.

Foreign Opinion of the U.S.A.

By 1928–1929 many foreign intellectuals were aware that the vital industrial and economic power of the United States was rapidly making it a great cultural force among the world's nations. Consequently, they came in droves, surveyed the scene, and subsequently published their estimates of American culture. A few liked what they saw. André Siegfried, the Frenchman, saw much to criticize but also much to praise. The Irish poet George William Russell, known to the literary world as A.E., characterized the American people as youthful, competent and kindly, full of enormous energy, "evolving a beauty and elegance of their own." But most Europeans held a different opinion. They recognized that America had developed a new type of culture in which the taste of the masses, the desire for profits by businessmen, and the advertising cliché often set the norms. It was a culture that had little in common with the established and aristocratic societies of the European homelands, and one which by its enormous appeal to the common man everywhere, threatened to invade countries abroad. The title of a book by Lucien Romier, *Who will be Master — Europe or America?* predicted a cultural conflict. To such a threat the response of the European intellectual was predictable: America was a "Babbitt warren," dedicated to materialism, and the primitive tastes of the collective man were rapidly eradicating all traces of refinement, elegance, and artistic creativity. The United States, Count Keyserling wrote, had adjusted itself to its nomadic heritage; culturally it was "in the early stage of barbarism."

That there was much to be critical about, none could deny. But what most Europeans and many Americans overlooked was the promise held out by mass democratic education, and the fact that even then, above the culture of the masses, a large and vital segment of the population was devoted to the pursuit of artistic creation and to things of the mind and of the spirit. Since the educative process is slow and America's crusade for mass higher education had barely started before World War I, the full fruits of this radical experiment could not be harvested for generations. Even so, during the twenties art and music were rapidly gaining assurance and maturity, writers were creating a literature that was to stamp its character on all of western culture, and the intellectual student of society had never been less reluctant to lay angry hands upon a culture with a view to its reconstruction. If self-criticism is the mother of social transformation, then the American culture of the 1920's was in for some remarkable changes.

BIBLIOGRAPHY

Useful documentary collections on mass culture are *The Twenties: Fords, Flappers, and Fanatics* (1963), edited by G. E. Mowry; and *Culture of the Twenties* (1970), edited by Loren Baritz. An interesting study of changing views of American character in the twentieth century is T. L. Hartshorne, *The Distorted Image* (1968). In a lighter vein, Laurence Greene, *The Era of Wonderful Nonsense* (1939); Charles Merz, *The Great American Band Wagon* (1928); and Lloyd Morris, *Postscript to Yesterday: America: The Last Fifty Years* (1947), are useful works. R. S. and H. M. Lynd, *Middletown* (1929), is a brilliant sociological study of everyday life in Muncie, Indiana. *Recent Social Trends in the United States* (2 vols., 1933), by President Hoover's Research Committee on Social Trends, is indispensable.

On the automobile, the best brief survey is J. B. Rae, *The American Automobile* (1965); but see also the lively earlier work by D. L. Cohn, *Combustion on Wheels* (1944). An excellent collection of sources and readings is *Giant Enterprise: Ford, General Motors, and the Automobile Industry* (1964), edited by A. D. Chandler, Jr. Ford has excited the most scholarly interest. See Allan Nevins and F. E. Hill, *Ford* (3 vols., 1954–1963); Keith Sward, *The Legend of Henry Ford* (1948); and William Greenleaf, *Monopoly on Wheels* (1961). See also C. L. Dearing, *American Highway Policy* (1941), particularly good on the 1920s.

On the mass media, see *Mass Culture* (1957), edited by Bernard Rosenberg and D. M. White. On "public relations," see Otis Pease, *The Responsibilities of American Advertising, 1920–1940* (1958); and A. R. Raucher, *Public Relations and Business, 1900–1929* (1968). Gilbert Seldes, *Seven Lively Arts* (1924), *The Great Audience* (1950), and *The Public Arts* (1956), are essential to a discussion of mass media and culture. Among the welter of books on the movies perhaps Lewis Jacobs, *The Rise of the American Film* (1939), is the most historical and scholarly. But Leo Rosten, *Hollywood* (1941); Nathan Leites and Martha Wolfenstein, *Movies* (1950); and M. D. Huettig, *Economic Control of the Motion Picture Indusrty* (1944), should also be consulted. For radio see Erik Barnouw, *A History of Broadcasting in the United States* (2 vols., 1966–1968), a full-length narrative. Among the better works on jazz are Barry Ulanov, *A History of Jazz* (1952); and Rudi Blesh and Harriet Janis, *They All Played Ragtime* (1950). F. L. Mott, *American Journalism* (3rd ed., 1962), is the standard survey. Mott's *History of American Magazines* (5 vols., 1938–1968) extends to 1930.

For the great changes in American morals and the new status of women, see B. B. Lindsey and Wainwright Evans, *The Revolt of Modern Youth* (1925); and *Civilization in the United States: An Inquiry by Thirty Americans*, edited by H. E. Stearns (1922). On prohibition, a contemporary report is the Federal Council of the Churches of Christ in America, *The Prohibition Situation* (1925). But see also the impressionistic study by a British writer, Andrew Sinclair, *Prohibition: The Era of Excess* (1962), which appears in paperback under the subtitle. An excellent contemporary history is Charles Merz, *The Dry Decade* (1931). Herbert Asbury, *The Great Illusion* (1950), is popular and anecdotal. Virginius Dabney, *Dry Messiah: The Life of Bishop Cannon* (1949), is an eloquent attack upon this prominent dry leader. For the report of the Wickersham Committee, see Report of the National Commission on Law Observance and Enforcement, Seventy-first Congress, Third Session, *House Document No. 722* (serial 9361). On racketeering, R. B. Fosdick, *American Police Systems* (1920); and A. A. Bruce, *The Administration of Criminal Justice in Illinois* (1929), are dependable. Of particular interest because of its author's position is J. E. Hoover, *Persons in Hiding* (1938).

On education, the general works mentioned earlier continue useful here. Two books by John Dewey, *The School and Society* (1899), and *Democracy and Education* (1916), present the author's thesis that social utility should be the principal aim of education. See also E. H. Wilkins, *The Changing College* (1927); J. E. Kirkpatrick, *The American College and Its Rulers* (1926); and R. B. Fosdick, *The Story of the Rockefeller Foundation* (1952). Howard Beale, *A History of Freedom of Teaching in American Schools* (1941), and *Are American Teachers Free?* (1936), are pessimistic. Two important recent mongraphs are B. G. Rader, *The Academic Mind and Reform: The Influence of Richard T. Ely in American Life* (1966); and P. A. Graham, *Progressive Education: A History of the Progressive Education Association, 1919–1955* (1967).

For religious trends in the period, D. B. Meyer, *The Protestant Search for Political Realism* (1960), traces the decline of Social Christianity and the growth of pessimism in Protestantism. P. A. Carter, *The Decline and Revival of the Social Gospel, 1920–1940*

(1956); and R. M. Miller, *American Protestantism and Social Issues, 1919–1939* (1958), are written from other viewpoints. H. W. Schneider, *Religion in 20th Century America* (2nd ed., 1964), is a good general survey. N. F. Furniss, *The Fundamentalist Controversy, 1918–1931* (1954), concerns the clash between modernists and traditionalists. Gail Kennedy (ed.), *Evolution and Religion: The Conflict Between Science and Theology in Modern America* (1957), is one of the better cultural volumes in the Amherst Series. Richard Hofstadter, *Anti-Intellectualism in American Life* (1963), is important for this period. H. E. Fosdick, *The Living of These Days* (1956), is the work of a leading liberal Protestant churchman.

On the much described Scopes Case, see Ray Ginger, *Six Days or Forever?* (1958); and L. S. de Camp, *The Great Monkey Trial* (1968). On the principals involved, see especially: J. T. Scopes and James Presley, *Center of the Storm* (1967); Clarence Darrow, *The Story of My Life* (1932); Irving Stone, *Clarence Darrow for the Defense* (1941); and L. W. Levine, *Defender of the Faith* (1965), a study of Bryan's last decade. An excellent account of the controversy over evolution in North Carolina is W. B. Gatewood, Jr., *Preachers, Pedagogues, and Politicians* (1966).

G. H. Knoles, *The Jazz Age Revisited* (1955), is an interesting distillation of nearly one hundred British evaluations of America in the 1920s. One of the most interesting critiques was published by an American conservative, J. T. Adams, *Our Business Civilization* (1929). One of the areas in which reformers continued and expanded their work is discussed in an excellent monograph by C. A. Chambers, *Seedtime of Reform: American Social Service and Social Action, 1918–1933* (1963).

20

IDEAS AND THE FINE ARTS

IN THE MACHINE AGE

*Scientific indeterminism · Freud · European pessimism · H. L.
Mencken · Walter Lippmann · Reinhold Niebuhr · An intellectual class ·
Cultural alienation · Desire for an elite · The reform tradition · Flight to the
left · Cultural nationalism · A basic pessimism · Literature · F. Scott
Fitzgerald · Sinclair Lewis · Hemingway · Faulkner · Drama and poetry ·
Painting · Sculpture · Music*

As it had during the nineteenth and the early twentieth century, science continued throughout the twenties and the thirties to exert a profound influence upon men's minds. But around 1910 some basic assumptions about how the world was constructed and how it moved began to change. Most of the great eighteenth and nineteenth century scientists assumed that the physical world operated like a machine, with regularity, rhythm, and law in its predictable movements, and little or no place for chance. Darwin, in his evolutionary theories, saw similar law and regularity in the animal and plant worlds, which changed and evolved according to a law of the survival of the fittest with environment the controlling force. Both Herbert Spencer and Karl Marx, among others, applied such mechanic thinking to human society, and subsequently the most radical behaviorist

psychologists contended that individual man was simply a product of the forces that operated on him. In 1914, the father of American behaviorist psychology, John B. Watson, published his *Behaviorism*, in which he argued that man was almost completely a reactor to his environment. Give him a newborn baby, Watson declared, and he could make almost anything out of the child. Watson was still publishing books on behaviorism in the late twenties, and behaviorist doctrines were popular. But by that time a great change had occurred in the thinking of a major group of creative scientists.

Scientific Indeterminism

In 1905 Albert Einstein published his law of relativity. It was soon followed by Max

THE WASHINGTON SQUARE PLAYERS, in New York, presented plays by little-known promising dramatists.

Planck's quantum theory of the action of light waves, and Werner Heisenberg's discovery that atoms move in unpredictable patterns, a finding which led to his formulation of the principle of indeterminism. Meanwhile biologists had concluded that many new forms of plant and animal life resulted from mutations that were unpredictable. In his book *Creative Evolution* (1907), Henri Bergson, the influential French philosopher, insisted that the life of the species was not entirely governed by the physical environment, but was creative and unpredictable, and that life itself contained a force or spirit which accounted for much of the change. In sum, all these new hypotheses contradicted the mechanistic theory of the universe. Scientists still saw law in the universe, but many of the laws they now believed were mathematical, statistical, and probable rather than mechanistic and absolute. Instead of a well-oiled machine in which every part responded to every other in predictable and absolute sequence, the universe now looked more like a card game in which the laws of probability governed the ultimate outcome but each hand was highly uncertain. This new way of thinking threw doubt on cause and effect relationships, and introduced the possibility of the unpredictable, of chance, and of creation.

Other scientific findings made it apparent that a great part of the universe was out of the reach of man's five senses, that there were realms upon realms that he could neither see, feel, hear, taste, nor smell. As Erwin Schrödinger said in accepting the Nobel prize in 1933, "We can never say what reality *is* or what really *happens*, but only what is observable. . . ." Once again science had diminished man's stature compared to that of the universe around him. But although the new indeterminism forced man to admit his own vast limitations, it also opened the way for creative intelligence, intuitive and moral powers, and free will. For if the universe was no longer simply a mechanism, if the human personality was not merely the sum of the outside forces acting upon it (as the behaviorists believed), then man perhaps was not just a chip on an irresistible tide, powerless to change his direction or himself.

Sigmund Freud

At first only a few intellectuals felt the impact of the new science, but by the 1920's the results were more generally apparent. By the 1930's popular books, particularly those of the two great Cambridge scientists, Sir James Jeans and Sir Arthur Eddington, were disseminating the new thought to literate people everywhere. Along with the new scientific outlook the theories and writings of a group of European thinkers had profound influence upon the American mentality. Most important, as measured by their widespread reception, were the psychoanalytical theories of the Viennese physician, Dr. Sigmund Freud

Albert Einstein. *First an Old World then a New World scientist, Einstein was long associated with the theory of relativity. He also sought for a unified field theory, a mathematical system that would embrace electromagnetism and gravitation in one universal law. He was among the first to inform President Franklin D. Roosevelt that an atomic bomb was scientifically possible.*

Psychology and Psychoanalysis. *Six of the world's most distinguished investigators of the mind are shown in this photograph, taken in 1909 at Clark University. Seated: Sigmund Freud, G. Stanley Hall, Carl G. Jung. Standing: A. A. Brill, Ernest Jones, Sandor Ferenczi.*

(1856–1939). At the heart of Freudian doctrine was the concept that the human personality was largely motivated by the conflict between the subconscious mind and the super-ego, the first being the sum of the instinctual drives, particularly sex, and the second the sum of the moral and ethical conditioning of society. This continuing conflict often engendered strains in the human personality, inducing irrational dreams, and, in acute cases, violent and self-destructive action. Since the individual could seldom recognize or admit to himself the nature of the forces that set up strains within him, self-cure was seldom possible. But the properly trained psychoanalyst, by interpreting actions in the light of the individual's past, could make them understandable. This explanation, plus the therapy of "confession" on the physician's couch would, according to the theory, provide a catharsis after which the individual could

more rationally live both with himself and society.

Freud's repeated emphasis upon sex as the dominant instinctual drive was distasteful to many. But psychoanalysis worked in some cases, and Freud's theories rapidly gained acceptance, particularly by the postwar generation. Freud lectured at Clark University in 1909. Soon after, the new Bohemia of Greenwich Village in New York City ardently embraced his doctrines. In 1915 Walter Lippmann wrote an article in defense of Freud for the *New Republic*. During the postwar age of rebellion, the Viennese doctor became the darling of the intellectual and literary cults. The novels and short stories of Sherwood Anderson and the plays of Eugene O'Neill in particular leaned heavily upon his theories. Since popular and badly distorted accounts of Freudianism seemed to give excuse for indulgence, Freud became something

THEATER GUILD PRODUCTION. A scene from Eugene O'Neill's *Dynamo*, starring Katharine Calhoun.

EUGENE O'NEILL. Son of an actor, James O'Neill, and close student of psychology, O'Neill became the outstanding playwright of his age. He won two Pulitzer prizes in the early 1920's, and the Nobel prize for literature in 1936.

FREUDIANISM IN THE THEATER. *The remarkable influence that Freud exerted on American thought was shown with singular emphasis in the theater, particularly in the plays by Eugene O'Neill.*

of a demi-god for pleasure lovers. He was thus unfairly held accountable for much of the sensuality of the early twenties. But in the long run his approach made important contributions to mental therapy and helped clear away Victorian cant and hypocrisy. By the middle of the decade universities and churches were both making use of his ideas, and *Time* magazine in 1927 signalized his growing importance by putting his picture on its cover and devoting a long article to his theories. In general, Freud's doctrines were optimistic, since they held out hope of treatment and cure for the warped personality. But the people of the twenties, perhaps seeking intellectual justification for their own basic feelings, chose to emphasize the irrational, emotional, and abnormal characteristics which Freud attributed to human nature.

European Pessimism

During those same years Americans read and pondered the more genuinely pessimistic writings of other European intellectuals.

Early in the decade, Oswald Spengler's *Decline of the West* was translated and had a surprising sale in the United States. Attributing to society something like the cycle of the year, Spengler by a complicated historical analysis, proved to his own satisfaction that Western culture was at the end of its long summer and faced the blasts of winter. To him the days of western art, religion, and even democracy were numbered. Already, he wrote, there was ample evidence that the return of the Caesars was imminent. Since Mussolini had stormed Rome before Spengler's book was translated, and since Hitler's rise soon followed, many Americans looked upon Spengler as something of a major prophet. His vogue continued until 1934, when it seemed as if Spengler, then viciously attacking the democratic liberal virtues and enthusiastically supporting Hitler, had read his wishes for the future into his account of the past.

Of more enduring influence on Americans was the work of the Spanish aristocrat and philosopher, José Ortega y Gasset. His *Revolt of the Masses*, first made available in English in 1932, was a brilliant and trenchant attack on modern democracy and mass culture. Society was and always had been divided, he argued, between a creative, artistic, intelligent minority, and the unproductive multitudes. When the masses took over, then society, culture, art, freedom, and excellence were all doomed. The one characteristic of the mass mind was its "assurance to proclaim the rights of the commonplace and to impose them" on the rest of the population. "To be different" in such a state, Ortega y Gasset wrote, was "to be indecent." But the mass, he felt, could not govern itself, to say nothing of the state. Therefore dictatorship was inevitable.

A short time later (1935) the ideas of the Italian engineer, economist, and sociologist, Vilfredo Pareto, added further to the gloom. In four volumes of highly complicated social analysis, Pareto sought to prove that the majority of men were not logical, nor did they respond to rational appeals, but rather to emotions, sentiments, and myths.

H. L. Mencken

This deeply pessimistic European thought was paralleled by a similarly inclined home-grown variety. Whether H. L. Mencken (1880–1959) was a pessimist, a nihilist, or just a bad boy sticking a very sharp tongue out at American society is difficult to say. But Mencken was an able writer with a gift for the cutting phrase, and his lack of veneration for almost every American institution found a ready response among numerous intellectuals and sophisticates. Mencken's scorn was mainly turned against Puritanism and the prohibitionist mentality of the "Bible belt," the term he used to designate the South and the Middle West. Not far behind as objects of his attacks were the cultureless, money-grabbing businessmen. But Mencken spared few things from his irony and sarcasm. For him, man was a creature beneath contempt, an idiot, knave, and coward who had "not moved an inch in a thousand years." Reformers were worse and democratic government or mobocracy was "government by orgy." Theologians and professors he

Mencken and Nathan. *These two axe-wielding iconoclasts cut a wide swath through the petty pretenses of the American "booboisie." Through their green-covered* American Mercury *they spread their views relentlessly among the American elite.*

considered rather worse than politicians. The American people he characterized as "the most timorous, sniveling, poltroonish, ignoramus mob of serfs and goose-steppers ever gathered under one flag in Christendom since the end of the Middle Ages. . . ." Obviously Mencken was no worshipper of the doctrine of progress. To him much of truth was unascertainable, and most of society's problems insoluble. If he had positive beliefs they lay in the disciplines of art and letters, in the methods of science, and in the hope for a rule of the few rational supermen, or *Übermensch*.

In 1924, along with George Jean Nathan, Mencken established the *American Mercury*, a monthly magazine that practically became a Bible for many literate and cultured Americans and for a good many more who aspired to be. Mencken's attacks did much to maintain standards of taste and quality in the arts and letters when they were threatened by the rise of mass culture. His continuing ridicule of the fundamentalists helped blunt the attempt to impose their standards on religion, education, and morality. At the peak of his popularity the *New York Times* referred to him as "the most powerful private citizen in America." Despite such high praise, his influence failed to survive the decade. He had little to offer save savage criticism, and with the coming of the depression his negative attitude and lack of any constructive program quickly lost him his following.

Walter Lippmann

Much more influential on the American mind for the next forty years was Walter Lippmann (1889–   ). Born in New York City, and graduated from Harvard in 1909, Lippmann set out on an intellectual journey that was to take him to the top of American journalism and mark him as the one modern equivalent in power and influence to America's great editors of the past. Starting as a leftist in politics, Lippmann at the opening of the 1920's was an associate editor of the *New Republic*. He soon became the editor of the liberal and literate *New York World*, a position he held until 1931, when he became a special writer for the *New York Herald-Tribune*. As an editor and daily columnist Lippmann had measurable impact. But of even more significance, perhaps, was the series of books he wrote starting with *A Preface to Politics* in 1913. In pre-World War I years Lippmann was supremely confident that liberal and scientific man, by the use of his rational powers, could build a world society in which reason and the arts would flourish. He had been one of the young leaders of the rebellion against nineteenth-century politics, morals, and aesthetics. But after the peace of 1918 he steadily grew more pessimistic as he observed mass society in the twenties. Liberalism, he finally confessed, had been the "defender and the liberator" of the underdog, but had supplied no guide for the masses when they were free. It had "forged a weapon of release, but not a way of life." Once freed from the old morality and authorities, the mass majorities of the modern state, responding only to self-interest, had deified the "rule of the second best," and were threatening to obliterate the cultural and aesthetic heritage of the past. After the Scopes "monkey trial" in 1926, Lippmann wrote that the dogma of majority rule contained within it "some sort of deep and destructive confusion." As the decade progressed, he saw increasing anarchy in both international relations and domestic economic institutions. Casting about for remedies, he sought for means to balance the power of the masses and that of self-interested groups, and thus to blunt the conflict between them. During the thirties he talked of a "compensated economy" or a "free collectivism" in which the state would not dictate but would "balance, equalize, neutralize, offset and correct the private judgments of masses of individuals." Increasingly he looked to the past for institutional sanctions by which to mitigate the baser appetites of individuals. Lippmann was still an optimist about individual human nature; what was essentially wrong was that the civilizing and educating power of the past had been forgotten in mass man's twentieth-century rebellion against old authority, and there was little left to replace it. In *The Good Society* (1936) he urged his generation to develop once more a sense for the historic values of western civilization. Even before that he was speculating on a need for a new system of morals, which would include a new "high religion," a religion of the spirit, a religion of "disinterestedness."

Reinhold Niebuhr

Much of the same kind of change in attitudes took place in Reinhold Niebuhr, who as one of the leading speculative theologians of the time had a profound effect on Protestant thought. Born in Missouri in 1892, Niebuhr took a degree at Yale and occupied a Detroit pastorate from 1915 to 1928, when he joined the faculty of the Union Theological Seminary in New York city. Niebuhr at first was dedicated to the Social Gospel, and his theology was wholly optimistic in its estimate of man and his capabilities. During the twenties, however, he changed sharply, and though he remained a social radical, he eventually became the chief defender of an unorthodox but thoroughly conservative theology. In his book *Does Civilization Need Religion?* (1928), Niebuhr was still relatively hopeful for mankind, although he admitted that he had lost most of his earlier optimism. As Niebuhr watched society he was increasingly convinced that individual man was "essentially perverse," though not totally corrupt. But man in the mass was infinitely worse than the individual, since

Walter Lippmann. *From the time of the New Nationalism and the New Freedom to the time of the New Frontier, Lippmann was perhaps the most distinguished of American publicists, and one of the most widely read.*

the group or the state had no conscience. Moreover, Niebuhr was certain that the masses would triumph over the older individualistic society. From these "new barbarians" little improvement could be expected. Instead of progress, there would be simply change, which would have as much potential for frightfulness as for happiness. In his two books, *Beyond Tragedy* (1938) and *The Nature and Destiny of Man* (1941), Niebuhr took the final steps toward basic pessimism. Existing society was in a total process of decay, and the change "threatened the whole world with disaster." The one chance for reconstruction lay not in Lippmann's rationalistic and humanistic formulas, but in a return to faith. Human reason, he argued, was a servant of man's passions and a victim of the "caprices of nature." Hence it could not be trusted. What was needed was myth and the myth-maker. Only if men took "the leap of faith" into religious myth was there a chance of repairing what had been so severely damaged by rationalism. To the scientifically oriented twentieth century Niebuhr's demand for mysticism and irrationalism sounded like total heresy. Nevertheless, when the *Christian Century* in the late thirties polled Protestant ministers about their changing beliefs, a large number stated that they had turned from a preoccupation with present social needs to a more intense interest in the supernatural. And many of them indicated that the greatest cause for the shift had been the complex theological views of Reinhold Niebuhr.

John Dewey was one of the few Americans of outstanding intellectual stature in the period who fell prey to neither an embracing pessimism nor a retreat from the rationalistic approach. In his books and articles he contended that the only way to a good society was through human intelligence by the instrumental and scientific approach. But even Dewey was disheartened as he saw what happened when mass society embraced industrialism. In 1922 he wrote that the nation had reached "the point of reverence for mediocrity; for submergence of individuality in mass ideals and creeds." Five years later he admitted that the kind of knowledge and insight needed to organize a humane, collective democracy was still not yet in existence.

An Intellectual Class

Precisely at this time, when pessimism was darkest on both sides of the Atlantic, the United States produced its first large coherent group of self-conscious intellectuals. And perhaps the pessimistic temper of the age explains in part their continuing sense of nonidentity with, and at times hostility to, their own culture. Few national groups of intellectuals have been as consistently critical of their own society as American intellectuals from 1920 to the

present. Actually the origins of this group lay somewhere between 1910 and 1914. A few of its members came from Europe, but the overwhelming proportion were recruited from the prosperous native educated urban middle class. Attracted to the large cities, principally Chicago and New York, artists, novelists, dramatists, magazine editors, literary critics, and essayists formed colonies like that in Greenwich Village in New York City. There they established organizations such as the Liberal Club, where they debated and discussed their ideas; magazines like *The Masses* and the *Seven Arts*, in which they published their writings; and professional groups like the Washington Square Players, which produced their artistic works. Among the members of the Liberal Club were Walter Lippmann, Lincoln Steffens, John Reed, and Carl Van Vechten. Max Eastman was the editor of *The Masses*. The *Seven Arts* published the first writings of Eugene O'Neill, Sherwood Anderson, and Van Wyck Brooks. As these and scores of other bright young people came together more and more, they dissolved their old ties with the middle-class American culture they had been born in, and identified themselves with this new intellectual class. Like most such new classes of articulate people they rebelled against the past. "I am in revolt," said Hutchins Hapgood, a member of the Liberal Club. "I consider it my first duty to undermine subtly the foundations of the community." Specifically, most of these intellectuals were in revolt against conservative artistic codes and nineteenth-century morals. In the famous Armory Art Show of 1913 they shocked conservative aesthetic taste by introducing the country to the post-impressionist, Fauvist, and cubist movements in French art. In *The Masses* and the *Seven Arts* they depicted the squalid and erotic aspects of life in phrases which Frank Norris, Jack London, and even Theodore Dreiser had never dared to use. Meanwhile, at the Liberal Club discussions raged on such subjects as Freud and free love.

The Intellectual and Mass Culture

During the prewar years these rebels and bohemians were gay and confident, since they hoped to make society over to their own taste. America's entrance into the World War, which a minority of them opposed, introduced a sobering element. But it was not until the disillusioning peace, and until they saw the character of postwar society, that many of them became alienated from American culture, rebels not against the past but against the present and the future. A part of their new sense of alienation was unquestionably due to the indifference with which they were regarded by the new political leadership in Washington. Even though the Wilson administration had censored the anti-war activities of some of them, it had still largely identified with the intellectuals by using them in its war and peace effort. But the Harding, Coolidge, and Hoover administrations knew them not. Even more significant was what this new leadership symbolized. At the apex of postwar society the intellectuals saw the businessman, who had persuaded the country to accept materialist values which were not only indifferent but actually hostile to all that they stood for. "Advertising instead of truth," one of them angrily wrote, "cash instead of art, machines instead of men." The novelist F. Scott Fitzgerald ironically observed that most Americans travelling in luxury abroad in 1928 and 1929 "had the human value of Pekinese, bivalves, cretins, goats." The intellectuals looked with equal revulsion at the new mass culture as exemplified by the Hollywood movie, the radio, the tabloid, and the "true confession" pulp magazine. Even before the war Randolph Bourne, the New York essayist and critic, had sensed the advent of mass culture. He was glee-

Nude Descending a Staircase. *By Marcel Duchamp. This painting was one of the most controversial exhibits in the Armory Art Show of 1913. From the Philadelphia Museum of Art, Walter and Louise Arensberg Collection.*

ful, he wrote, at the demise of nineteenth-century standards, but he was not happy about the "low-brow snobbery" which was taking their place. When the full tide of the new mercantile culture burst upon the intellectuals, their scorn knew few if any limits. For this new "horde life," in which every artistic and superior human quality was "being submerged in the sea of the second-rate," they felt nothing but disgust. Measuring the new society against the one they had hoped for, they become despond-

SHERWOOD ANDERSON. In *Winesburg, Ohio*, published in 1919, Anderson gave a vivid, if unflattering, picture of small-town American life.

T. S. ELIOT. American born, but British by choice, Eliot compressed into 400 lines a devastating epic poem, *The Waste Land*, published in 1922.

ent and pessimistic. The attempt to civilize everyone had to be given up, *The Saturday Review of Literature* felt. Reading might make a full man, it speculated, but if the readers concentrated on the "gum-chewers' journals," it was pertinent to ask, "full of what?"

Cultural Alienation

As the intellectuals looked about them in the postwar world they were inclined to doubt the blessings of industrialism and urbanism. To this new age of smoke and steel, of dust and noise, of gaudy movie palaces and shrieking radios, most of them applied the word "sordid." "The old loveliness has almost gone," wrote Henry Seidel Canby, editor of *The Saturday Review of Literature*. In 1922 there appeared a volume edited by Harold E. Stearns, entitled *Civilization in the United States; An Inquiry by Thirty Americans*, among whom were many of the nation's leading commentators and critics. They covered most aspects of the culture, and almost to a man their reports were tracts of disappointment, indictment, and despair. The critic Malcolm Cowley described the book as "like an inquest over a man everyone disliked." Thus there arose in many of the creative

minds of the period a deep sense of alienation from their own culture, a sense which led some to foresake America and live permanently in Europe. Among the most eminent of these expatriates or self-exiles were two poets: T. S. Eliot, who went to England and eventually became a British citizen, and Ezra Pound, who made his home in Italy. But by far the largest group lived in Paris. Harold Stearns, Ernest Hemingway, Elliot Paul, Glenway Wescott, and Gertrude Stein were a few of the creative Americans who expressed their opinion of their native culture by preferring what they found along the banks of the Seine. For the stay-at-homes there were other ways of living apart. One was to turn one's back upon the majority, forget about causes, and live in a world of individual taste. "I am not without beliefs," wrote Heywood Broun, the newspaper columnist, "but they are vague and it is pleasanter that way." And Herbert Croly, who had so confidently written about *The Promise of American Life*, promised himself now that he would make "no more dashes into the political jungle" but content himself with the moral regeneration of individual man. Another escape from the dreary landscape of the present was to make art itself the

AMERICAN WRITERS. *Judged by any normal standards, the postwar decade was a great age in American literature. Writers of the period found little to approve in American society, but what they said about it had enduring vitality.*

GERTRUDE STEIN. The "Lost Generation" was the term that Gertrude Stein invented to characterize the disillusioned intellectuals of the period.

end and beginning of life. This extreme aestheticism exalted the artist and scorned or disregarded everyone else. Floyd Dell of Greenwich Village announced that for him "art was more important than the destinies of nations, and the artist a more exalted figure than the prophet." The most grasping and self-centered of businessmen displayed no more anti-social feelings than George Jean Nathan, who had helped found *American Mercury.* Declaring that he was not interested a whit in the world's social problems, he said his concern was for himself and a few close friends, and that for all he cared the rest of the world might "go to hell at today's sunset."

Desire for an Elite

This demand for "a new elite" was taken up by another group seeking something they could believe in. For years Harvard professors Paul Elmer More and Irving Babbitt had preached the doctrine of righteousness, restraint, taste, and order. Now joined by Norman Foerster of the State University of Iowa they published the credo of a "New Humanism," which deplored the materialist, scientific, and mechanical world of the twenties and sought one in which human ends and the things of

the spirit were emphasized. The appeal of the new doctrine was radically diminished when the philosopher George Santayana declared that what these new humanists proposed was not humanism at all, but a dogma for a new theocratic elite revolting against the three "R's," the Renaissance, the Reformation, and the French Revolution. Nevertheless, something of the same spirit, though with a sectional twist, was obvious in the Southern Agrarian movement of the 1930's. In the book entitled *I'll Take My Stand* (1930), Allen Tate, Robert Penn Warren, and John Crowe Ransom, among others, argued for a return to the old agrarian and feudal South in which a cultured elite presided over the great majority of farmers and artisans. The Old South, they argued, had been unique in American history because it had "founded and defended" a culture that was cognate with the high and aristocratic cultures of Europe before the French Revolution.

The Reform Tradition

The urge to form a cultural elite, profoundly conservative in its implications, was to grow stronger among certain intellectual groups, especially after World War II. But during the twenties and thirties most American intellectuals probably looked to the left rather than to the right. The general aim of the Greenwich Village group before World War I had been to overthrow the genteel culture and morality of the nineteenth century. The first issue of *The Masses* in 1913 proclaimed that it was "a Revolutionary and not a Reform Magazine." Some of this spirit of cultural rebellion was naturally directed toward political ends. *The Masses* closed down when it became involved in an anti-war program after 1917. But *The New Republic*, founded in 1914 by Herbert Croly, remained throughout the period a flourishing journal of reform and protest. On its staff were such figures as Walter Lippmann and Edmund Wilson, and its contributors covered the spectrum of creative, liberal, and radical thought. Many of John Dewey's articles on current issues appeared there. *The Nation*, which Oswald Garrison Villard changed from a nineteenth-century liberal magazine to one espousing progressive and radical democracy, also became a vehicle for the rebel spirit. Despite the efforts of these magazines and their contributors, however, the influence of Babbittry, Sinclair Lewis' word for the small town business outlook, and the business mentality in both politics and culture became more and more pervasive. As the twenties wore on, some intellectuals, disappointed with the increasing weakness of the reform tradition, began to search for more radical solutions.

Flight to the Left

The path to the extreme left had already been blazed by John Reed, the young Harvard graduate who left Greenwich Village to become a Communist and who died in Moscow in 1920, a Red hero, and was buried in the Kremlin. Few American-born intellectuals were connected with the origin and stormy early career of the Communist Party at the start of the decade. But

after the disillusionment of the Scopes trial and the Sacco-Vanzetti case, some of them began to look toward Moscow. After the economic crash of 1929, when it looked as if the whole world was moving toward a totalitarianism of either the left or the right, the leftward drift became even stronger. During most of the twenties, Lincoln Steffens, the old muckraker, had maintained an open mind about Communism. He was friendly to and interested in the radical Russian experiment, though still uncommitted. But by 1929 he wrote that he had had enough of "this rotten civilization." A good many others soon came to Steffens' conclusion that "democracy and a society caring about decent human ends could not be achieved by democratic means." About the same time Edmund Wilson called Russia "the moral top of the world where the light never really goes out." Among other celebrated literary figures, John Dos Passos and Theodore Dreiser had about as many kind words for the Russian system as they had sharp criticisms of their own. Though it was doubtful whether any of the highest creative and critical talents ever formally joined the Communist Party, the pull of the far left was strong. The pages of *The New Masses*, a frankly Marxist magazine, under the editorship of Joseph Freeman, were studded with well-known names. In 1931, V. F. Calverton published the first careful Marxian interpretation of American writing, *The Liberation of American Literature*. And during the thirties, the pronouncements of the American Writers Conferences became increasingly leftist. As late as 1939 the third Conference excoriated the Nazi persecution of intellectuals, but whitewashed and partially justified similar terror in the Soviet Union.

There is little doubt that during the twenties and thirties a substantial group of American intellectuals felt an extreme sense of alienation from their own society. Some of them had migrated to strange places;

others had looked for solace in strange doctrines. But for every intellectual who had flirted with Communism or who had followed a radical movement left or right, there were more who had remained personally committed to the patient, non-violent compromising ways of democracy and freedom. And by the late thirties many of the exiles began to return. The depression probably played its part in inspiring this movement. But perhaps the New Deal, with its positive policies of relief and reconstruction, did even more. The New Deal accomplished far more in the arts and literature than had all past administrations together. Its Federal Writers Project, and similar organizations for the drama, music, and the dance, not only gave jobs to scores of unemployed artists, but also cultivated in the population at large a taste for the arts which remained after the depression had run its course. Moreover, from the days of the "brain trust" on, the New Deal employed thousands of intellectuals in its planning and administrative agencies. Never before in the nation's history had the intellectual so much reason for identifying himself with the ruling political power. Perhaps that was one reason why the great depression produced few new utopias or radical schemes of social reconstruction.

Cultural Nationalism

Among the many intellectual exiles returning from Europe was Harold Stearns, who had edited the pessimistic analysis of American culture in the early twenties. "I have tried being homeless. . . ." he wrote, "it simply doesn't work." And in the volume *America Now*, he edited another evaluation of American culture. Published in 1938, the book contained little of the pessimism of his earlier volume. Some of its contributors, in fact, made claims for American supremacy over all other nations in culture and the arts. This note of a rising nationalism was also evident in the

disappearance of the historical debunkers and the rise of the interest in folk heroes like Paul Bunyan and Davy Crockett. And as the menace of Hitlerian Germany became more evident, patriotic sentiments multiplied. By 1940 many former critics of American society had become its ardent defenders. Dos Passos, Archibald MacLeish and Van Wyck Brooks, among others, were now attacking the literature of the twenties instead of the society which produced it. In particular they criticized the anti-war sentiment, the debunking, and the satirical novels as having brought American society into disrepute and as having destroyed the faith of the masses in the nation's cultural institutions. "We must never forget," Dos Passos now wrote, "that we are heirs to one of the grandest and most nearly realized world pictures in all history."

A Pessimistic Literature

Although many intellectuals were ready to return home before World War II, they were not going back to the same culture they had rebelled against. The break with the past in both life and literature was almost revolutionary, as attested by the novels written in these years. The pages of almost every volume of fiction bore testimony to the break with past conventions and beliefs. Perhaps the greatest innovation in this new writing was its acceptance of an abiding pessimism about man and his future. Hawthorne and Melville a century before had stressed the tragic element in life. But there was a great and essential difference between their strong heroes, who succumbed to the flaws in their own characters only after a courageous battle against them, and the heroes in the new mold. In the literature of the twenties the so-called hero was more often than not a victim and a passive figure. He was less a man who did things than one to whom nature and society did things. And most of the things were bad. Perhaps Lemuel

Pitkin, the hero of Nathanael West's *Cool Million*, set something of a record. In seeking his fortune Pitkin lost one thumb, one eye, one leg, all of his teeth, his scalp, and his money. He was imprisoned twice, kidnapped twice, and finally lost his life. Hero-victims of other novels were only a little behind him. What was worse was that little could be done about it. Men were "just another race of animals whose behavior," wrote Edmund Wilson in *I Thought of Daisy*, "was fixed by their environment and by the cells which they had had from their parents. . . ." For such pawns of biological fate there could be little censure but also little hope. "Madam," one of Hemingway's characters said, "there is no remedy for anything in life." Even worse was that no one in the universe cared. As a Dos Passos character in *The Big Money* dolefully exclaimed, life would end in blindness and death, but who cared? "Who on this bloody louse-infected globe gives one little, small, microscopic, vestigial hoot?" In the face of such questions and such answers it was obvious that the old faith in human nature and in progress had begun badly to erode.

Moreover, most American literature of the twenties was completely apolitical and almost asocial. Writers were not interested in economics, politics, or society. Instead they were preoccupied with individual character. Scott Fitzgerald carried this interest so far that in *Tender is the Night* he wrote a novel containing practically no description of locale or setting. This was also an age when creative literature was almost lacking in sentiment and even ethics. This new "hardboiled intelligentsia" would rather have been "accused of a crime than a sentiment." And as for noble actions, they were few indeed. Andrews, in Dos Passos' *Three Soldiers*, for example, deserted the army, and Mac in *42nd Parallel* deserted his pregnant girl friend. Male and female, many of the principal characters were like

John O'Hara's, of whom one critic wrote that since they had no values they had little pride and they could not be insulted.

Since the tension set up between man's desires and his ethics had been the stock in trade of older novelists, these new practitioners had to find other ways to interest readers. And usually they relied on conflict between people without ethics fighting for material or sensual gain. As Lieutenant Henry confessed in Hemingway's *A Farewell to Arms*, he was not made to think or to worry about his conscience, but to eat and drink and "sleep with Catherine." The frank treatment of sex, a trend before the war, now became general and often wearisome. The new woman was often depicted with the same sensual appetites as man, as in Faulkner's *Wild Palms*, Hemingway's *To Have and Have Not* and John O'Hara's *Butterfield 8*. Along with sex went perversion and often glorification of violence, until it seemed that writers were using Freud and his casebooks as their main sources of character. By the time they were through, the writers of the twenties and thirties had buried Victorian morality as deeply as the reforming progressives had interred Victorian economics.

The literary attack upon traditional morality also brought rural and village life under criticism. Beginning with Edgar Lee Masters' *Spoon River Anthology* and Sherwood Anderson's *Winesburg, Ohio*, both published before 1920, the "revolt from the village," as Sinclair Lewis phrased it, was at full gallop. Ignoring the fact that villages and small towns had produced a good many of their literary colleagues, these writers depicted the village as the abode of frustration and abnormality. The businessman also was sometimes an object of attack, as was the middle class in general. But many writers ignored bourgeois society, especially in its more normal aspects. They agreed in general with the sentiments of a Floyd Dell character that "Middle class life in America is dull enough in reality without having to endure it in books too." More and more the central figure of American fiction was a decadent aristocrat, an artist, a virile laborer, or a representative of the criminal class.

Literature and the Depression

The depression had a sharp but temporary influence on American letters. The cult of art for art's sake rapidly lost its vogue, "pure neutral intellectualism" was attacked, and demands were now made that art be used as "a social weapon." What this often meant in reality was description of the worst economic and social features of American society interspersed with demands for reform. Compared with the novels of the early twenties with their emphasis on the individual, those of the thirties tended to include numbers of undifferentiated characters who were less people than types. In Dos Passos' massive trilogy, *U.S.A.*, for example, capitalists, politicians, labor leaders and crooks abound, and there is a brilliant panorama of life in America, but there is no protagonist. The "social novel," as it was called, demanded less creative imagination of its authors than reportorial ability. The tendency was to substitute a mass of factual detail for the symbolic event or description. And all too often zeal for the social mission took the place of style. At their best, as in the works of John Dos Passos and James T. Farrell, the social and proletarian novels of the thirties had a good many commendable qualities. But the great majority of them were formless and uninspired political tracts, innocent of any real craftsmanship or creative ability. The tendency to substitute social aim for artistry became so pronounced that the third American Writers Conference in 1939 felt called upon to state that a political novel did not necessarily have any merit simply because of its theme. But by that time the gathering world crisis had turned public attention

away from domestic ills, and the so-called social novel tended to disappear.

Although American artists had vigorously attacked their own society during these years as one dominated by a materialist, business, and anti-cultural mentality, they ironically proved the contrary by their own artistic production. For at no time in the past had the nation produced so large a group of brilliant novelists, poets, dramatists, and painters. And at no time had American art been received with such acclaim. Before the war William Butler Yeats had sensed the coming cultural flowering. "The fiddles" he wrote, "are tuning as it were all over America." Looking back, W. H. Auden, the English poet, remarked, the American novelists "produced the only significant literature between the two great wars." And only by comparison with literature were the achievements in the other creative arts less spectacular.

F. Scott Fitzgerald

Perhaps the most representative writer of the postwar generation was F. Scott Fitzgerald (1896–1940). Minnesota born and Princeton educated, Fitzgerald served in the army and while in an officers training camp wrote *This Side of Paradise*. Published in 1920, the book brilliantly chronicled the lives and the spirit of the new generation of selfish, rebellious, cynical, and pleasure-loving youth. Fitzgerald went on to live the career of one of his jazz age heroes. For the next ten years his life was one great party carried on in Paris, in Italy, and on the Riviera. Needing money to pursue his Odyssey of pleasure, he wrote a great many indifferent and a few brilliant short stories for popular magazines. During the same period he produced what is probably his best work, *The Great Gatsby* (1925), a novel which revealed Fitzgerald's consciousness that his own way of life was dissipating his talent and splendid vitality. He returned home, finished *Tender Is the*

Sinclair Lewis. *A steady procession of novels by Lewis caricatured Americans and the American way of life with painstaking devotion to detail.*

Ernest Hemingway. *Leading spokesman of the "Lost Generation," Hemingway had a profound influence upon the writing of English wherever the English language was in use.*

Night (1934), and died at the age of 44 before he could complete his impressive *The Last Tycoon*, whose hero, the last of the great individualistic movie producers, died of a heart attack just as his position was threatened by New York bankers. Fitzgerald's ability at characterization, his insight into the motivations of his generation, and his real talent for memorable prose assure him a lasting place in American letters.

Sinclair Lewis

Like Fitzgerald, Sinclair Lewis (1885–1951) was also born in Minnesota and published his first successful novel, *Main Street*, in 1920. On the surface *Main Street* was an attack against the small-minded materialism of Gopher Prairie, the town's bleak ugliness, and its lack of culture. In *Babbitt* (1922), Lewis examined the life of the businessman of the Middle West in much the same satiric spirit and in the process coined a new word. His other more important works dealt with a hypocritical evangelist, *Elmer Gantry* (1927), an aspiring scientist, *Arrowsmith* (1925), and a likeable manufacturer of automobiles, *Dodsworth* (1929). Despite the fact that his books were enormously popular and that he won the first Nobel prize for literature given to an American, Lewis was scarcely a man of genius. Timely as they were, his characters today have a curiously flat, one-dimensional look, and his subjects are mostly dated. But whatever his literary future, his books will long remain a historian's source for small town life in the midlands.

Ernest Hemingway

A third middle-westerner, and by far the most talented, was Ernest Hemingway (1896–1961). Born in a Chicago suburb, Hemingway served in the ambulance corps of the Italian army during the war, after which he was a newspaper reporter and eventually drifted to Paris. His first novel,

The Sun Also Rises (1926), was an uncompromising picture of the hedonistic life of the expatriates. There followed *A Farewell to Arms* (1929), by far the best of the American war novels; a series of short stories, which include some of his finest and most memorable pieces; and books on big game hunting in Africa and on bullfighting. Hemingway's fiction deals mostly with tough, cynical activists whose approach to life, whether they be gangsters, bullfighters, or wealthy big game hunters, is to live dangerously and heroically. Basically the Hemingway hero is a pessimist who expects little from life and society, especially little justice. Thus Lieutenant Henry, the hero of *A Farewell to Arms*, speaks of time or fate as the killer "which attacks the very good and the very gentle and the very brave impartially. If you are none of these you can be sure it will kill you too, but there will be no special hurry." In the face of such a universe the aim of man should be to battle strenuously and to accept final defeat with stoic calm and dignity. Attracted by the Spanish character, Hemingway strongly sympathized with the Loyalists during the Civil War. And in 1940 he wrote *For Whom the Bell Tolls*, a statement of man's commitment to more than the heroic individual virtues stressed in his earlier works. His clean, spare prose, precise description, and his acute ear for dialogue have left a

heritage that the literary tradition will not soon exhaust.

William Faulkner

Of the many able writers the South has produced in the twentieth century, one of the most notable is William Faulkner (1897–1962). Born in New Albany, Mississippi, Faulkner returned to live at Oxford after

WILLIAM FAULKNER. This last studio portrait of Faulkner was taken in June, 1962.

THE COURTHOUSE IN OXFORD, MISSISSIPPI. Faulkner mentions the courthouse clock striking the hour.

WILLIAM FAULKNER AND MISSISSIPPI. *Faulkner's life and work were closely intertwined with Oxford, the Mississippi town in which he lived. The old courthouse with the Model T Fords in front is shown as it was in May, 1930, before the building was renovated. The cast-iron fence surrounding the yard was there before the Civil War.*

service in World War I. He first attracted attention with *Sanctuary* (1931), a sensational novel which he later said he had written to make money. But his literary fame was more rightfully won by a series of works dealing with the decaying aristocracy and the incredibly twisted and almost sub-human poor white classes of his mythical Yoknapatawpha County. *The Sound and the Fury* (1929) and *As I Lay Dying* (1930) won critical favor. His subsequent novels, among which were *Absalom, Absalom!* (1936), *The Unvanquished* (1939), and *The Hamlet* (1940) rapidly increased his reputation and won him a Nobel prize. Basically, Faulkner was interested in two themes. First, he was convinced that the South had been cursed with slavery and thus fell from primitive grace so that every one

Thomas Wolfe, *as a University of North Carolina undergraduate, both wrote and acted in plays. He was later a member of George Pierce Baker's student dramatic laboratory at Harvard, "The 47 Workshop." He is shown here as Buck Gavin in the play,* The Return of Buck Gavin.

in it was damned. Second, he believed that the South by forgetting its own heritage had cast itself adrift into a miasmal swamp from which there was no access unless it went back to its old virtues and strengths. Faulkner's prose is often extremely complex, and his search for the threads of guilt and expiation in the human mind makes his books difficult and obscure. But few have written about the modern South with such power and understanding.

Another Southerner of literary promise was Thomas Wolfe (1900–1938). Born in North Carolina, like his hero Eugene Gant, he roamed from New York to Oxford to Germany and beyond, spending his energies, searching for something he never found. Wolfe was a giant of a man and his prose came out in a torrent, especially in his four autobiographical novels, starting with *Look Homeward, Angel* (1929) and ending with *You Can't Go Home Again* (1940). In his short life Wolfe was never able to discipline either himself or his writing.

Drama and Poetry

For the first time in these years America also produced a Nobel prize winning dramatist. Eugene O'Neill (1888–1953) as a young man took leave of his warped paternal home to follow the sea. From there he came to Greenwich Village, where his first poetry and plays were written. But it was not until the 1920's that *The Emperor Jones* and a rapid succession of other plays caught the eye and favor of Broadway critics. Full of Freudian themes and often borrowing heavily from the great Greek tragedies, O'Neill's plays were grim and pessimistic accounts of man against nature, against the gods, and against himself. But despite the heavy prose and complex symbolism, his plays have a power which has been acknowledged on both sides of the Atlantic.

Close to O'Neill in theme, temper, and

tone was Robinson Jeffers (1887–1962), who wrote a series of long poems beginning with *Tamar* in 1924. Sometimes stressing the irrational and darkly compelling sexual forces in man, Jeffers more often celebrated the overwhelming amoral vitality of nature and natural forces. In the stellar galaxies he saw harmony and law; in society little but confusion, passion, and defeat.

Jeffers was little read. More popular were the middle-western poets Carl Sandburg and Vachel Lindsay. Both often took folk myths as their themes, but Sandburg was essentially a free-verse poet of the industrial city, while Lindsay more often looked back in his inventive melodious lyrics to the vanishing world of the village and the countryside. But perhaps the foremost poet of these years was Robert Frost (1875–   ). A landsman with a love and deep understanding of both nature and man, he was a superb craftsman, whose finely wrought and deceptively simple poems were in part a protest against the formlessness of much modern art and in part a warm testament to the old natural and human verities.

Robert Frost. *Writing mainly on characteristic features of New England country life, Frost four times won the Pulitzer prize for poetry.*

Painting

For the first time during these years American painting also came of age. Most of the rebellious and talented group which had participated in both the Ashcan exhibition and the Armory show of 1913 were still productive during the twenties and the thirties. They were joined after the war by the group of young painters and illustrators who had contributed to *The Masses* in Greenwich Village, and by a still younger group who attained maturity during the late twenties and the thirties. By that time American painting was fully abreast of post-impressionist developments in Europe and all the so-called French styles, ranging from cubism through expressionism to pure abstraction. The older realist tradition was carried on by a group of middle-western artists led by Grant Wood of Iowa, Thomas Hart Benton of Missouri, and John Steuart Curry of Kansas, who often painted the everyday scenes of the region with a precision of detail that rivalled the camera. Also close to the realist tradition were the works of Eugene Speicher, Charles Burchfield, Reginald Marsh, and Yasuo Kuniyoshi, who sought to make the real more convincing by intelligent selection and invention. Stuart Davis and Georgia O'Keeffe, among others, sought their effects (as the Polish painter Kandinsky had done) through the geometric organization of color and space. More and more painters became devotees of a highly personalized expressionism that tended toward the mystical, the irrational, and the subjective. Among the leading painters in this latter group were Max

Lincoln, *by George Gray Barnard. Among the many statues of Lincoln, this one by Barnard has probably been most criticized. But its rugged honesty has also won high praise.*

Weber, whose glowing colors were reminiscent of old stained glass, and Arthur Dove, whose vision led him into a magic world of his own, quite remote from that which most people were able to see.

As in literature, the creative and materialistic world of the middle classes was more

and more avoided as a subject for the canvas. The artist chose his models from the lower classes. And more often than not he chose to portray the warty, wrinkled, and distorted forms of humanity rather than those akin to classical modes. Freudian symbols appeared almost as much in painting as in writing. And the stream-of-consciousness in writing was perhaps paralleled in painting by a subjectivism which at times created a world of color and form mysteriously its own.

Although Reginald Marsh wrote that only three or four American artists could afford to live on the proceeds from their paintings, the artist could no longer complain that he was neglected. In 1928 an art patron paid over $40,000 for canvases by John Sloan, the president of the radical Society of Independent Artists. The following year witnessed the opening of the Museum of Modern Art in New York City. One year later the Whitney Museum was opened, solely dedicated to the purchase and acquisition of American art. Meanwhile American universities began to establish artists in residence, and during the depression the number of artists working on federal art projects was legion. By 1940 American painting was as vital as it was inventive, and a rapidly increasing public support augured well for a successful future.

Sculpture

American sculpture was also coming of age. Augustus Saint-Gaudens (1849–1907), famous for his *Adams Monument* in Washington, D.C., his equestrian *Sherman* in New York City, and his standing *Lincoln* in Chicago, had not only shown great originality in his own productions, but had also influenced deeply the development of his contemporaries and successors. Ablest of these, no doubt, was Daniel Chester French (1850–1931), who also won preeminence for monuments and memorials, most notably his *Minute Man* in Concord,

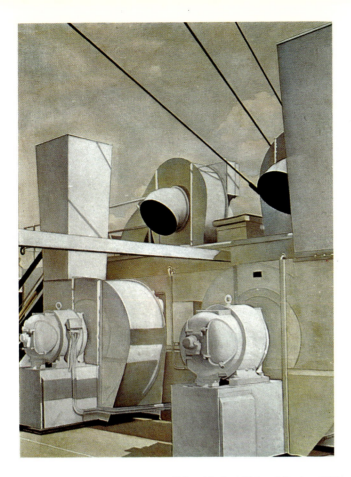

Charles Sheeler, *Upper Deck.* 1929.
Courtesy of the Fogg Art Museum,
Harvard University. Photographed
by Barney Burstein, Boston.

John Marin, *Maine Islands*. 1922.
The Phillips Collection, Washington, D.C.

Arthur G. Dove, *Fog Horns*. 1929. Collection, Colorado
Springs Fine Arts Center. Gift of Oliver B. James.

...cob Epstein, *Mother and Child*. 1913.
...ollection, The Museum of Modern Art,
...ew York. Gift of A. Conger Goodyear.

Joseph Albers, *Homage to the Square: Ascending*.
1953. Collection of the Whitney Museum
of American Art, New York.

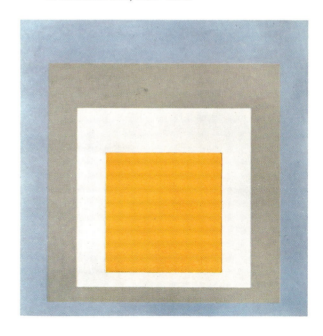

Georgia O'Keeffe, *Cow's Skull: Red, White, and Blue*. 1931.
The Metropolitan Museum of Art, Alfred Stieglitz Collection, 1949.

Charles H. Demuth, *Eggplant and Pears*.
Boston Museum of Fine Arts.

American art in the last thirty-five years or so has continued to reflect the variety of theories, styles, and preoccupations, the restless experimentation, and the deep concern with social and individual problems, which had become its dominant characteristic by the 1920's. Even the most faithfully representational painters, like Andrew Wyeth, were concerned less with externals than with some inward truth or essence, a characteristic in which they were true children of their time.

Andrew Wyeth, *Study No. 1 for Soaring.* (above) Courtesy of Mr. Maxim Karolik. Andrew Wyeth, *Soaring.* 1950. (below) Webb Gallery of American Art, Shelburne Museum, Shelburne, Vermont. Photographs by Barney Burstein, Boston.

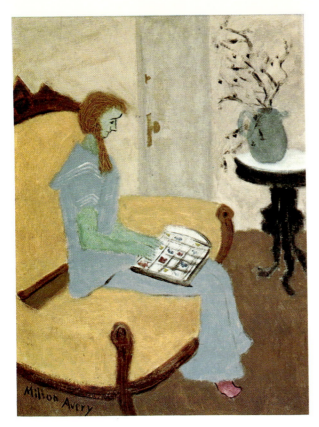

Milton Avery, *Girl At Play*.
The Joseph H. Hirshhorn Collection.
Photographed by Barney Burstein, Boston.

Raphael Soyer, *The Brown Screen.* 1956.
Courtesy of Forum Gallery.
Photographed by Barney Burstein, Boston.

Ben Shahn, *Builder*. c. 1947. The Collection
of Mr. and Mrs. Leonard B. Schlosser.
Courtesy of The Downtown Gallery.

Stuart Davis, *New York Waterfront*. 1938. Room of Contemporary
Art Collection, Albright-Knox Art Gallery, Buffalo, New York.

Lyonel Feininger, *The Glorious Victory of the Sloop Maria*. 1926. Collection,
City Art Museum of St. Louis. Photographed by Barney Burstein, Boston.

Yasuo Kuniyoshi, *Look, It Flies*. 1946.
The Hirshhorn Foundation Collection.
Photographed by Barney Burstein, Boston.

Max Weber, *Adoration of the Moon*. 1944.
Collection of the Whitney Museum
of American Art, New York.

Leonard Baskin, *Sorrowing Angel*. 1958.
Munson-William-Proctor Institute.
Photographed by Barney Burstein, Boston.

Jack Levine, *Street Scene No. 1*.
Boston Museum of Fine Arts.
Photographed by Barney
Burstein, Boston.

Massachusetts, a product of his earlier years, and his *Lincoln* in the Lincoln Memorial at Washington, completed in 1920. Lorado Taft (1860–1936) not only attained distinction as a sculptor, but in two books, *Modern Tendencies in Sculpture* (1920), and *The History of American Sculpture* (1924), did much to promote a better understanding by the public of the sculptor's contribution to society. George Gray Barnard (1863–1938) did many statues of heroic proportions, among them thirty-one figures for the state capitol at Harrisburg, Pennsylvania, and a bronze *Lincoln* for Lytle Park, Cincinnati, that won both warm praise and bitter criticism. Gutzon Borglum (1871–1941) was best known for his colossal figures, a head of Lincoln in Washington, and the gigantic heads of Washington, Lincoln, Jefferson, and Theodore Roosevelt, carved

out of "living rock" at Mount Rushmore, South Dakota. Later American sculptors, such as William Zorach, Gaston Lachaise, and Alexander Calder, broke with the academic tradition, which considered sculpture primarily in terms of public monuments and memorials, and, in line with the prevailing rejection of literalism, developed more personal and idiosyncratic styles.

Music

In Aaron Copland and Samuel Barber the nation produced its first notable composers. But of far more significance for the future was nationwide support for the reproduction of serious music. Throughout the twenties and the thirties America attracted for its many thriving symphony orchestras numerous renowned conductors from abroad. Arturo Toscanini's

Arturo Toscanini. *European born, Toscanini won his greatest fame as conductor of the New York Philharmonic from 1928 to 1936, and later as organizer and conductor of the National Broadcasting Company (NBC) Symphony Orchestra.*

engagement in 1927 by the New York Philharmonic was paralleled by Philadelphia's earlier acquisition of Leopold Stokowski, Boston's of Serge Koussevitsky, and Minneapolis' of Dimitri Mitropoulos. All these men were foreigners, but their coming indicated an American interest in good music and a willingness to support it that was as remarkable for the time as it was portentous for the future. Despite the lamentation of critics, especially those of the 1920's, America in 1940 was anything but a cultural wasteland. Instead it had become one of the cultural forces of the world, whose contributions to the realm of ideas and artistic creation were a matter of public record.

BIBLIOGRAPHY

The relationship of modern scientific thought with society is dealt with in two of A. N. Whitehead's more popular books: *Science and the Modern World* (1925), in which the philosopher includes a chapter on God along with one on relativity; and *Adventures of Ideas* (1933). Other useful works are Bernard Barber, *Science and the Social Order* (1952); Gail Kennedy (ed.), *Pragmatism and American Culture* (1950); and A. A. Roback, *History of American Psychology* (1952). But see also Wolfgang Köhler, *Gestalt Psychology* (2nd ed., 1947), which emphasizes the impact of behaviorism. Oscar Cargill, *Intellectual America: Ideas on the March* (1941), is suitable for the growth of Freud's influence in the United States. See also Benjamin Nelson (ed.), *Freud and the Twentieth Century* (1957). For Spengler and Ortega y Gasset the best introduction is their own works. Edgar Kemler, *The Irreverent Mr. Mencken* (1950), should be supplemented by the study found in Maxwell Geismar, *The Last of the Provincials* (2nd ed., 1949); William Manchester, *Disturber of the Peace* (1950); Alistair Cooke (ed.), *The Vintage Mencken* (1955); Sara Mayfield, *The Constant Circle* (1968); and Carl Bode, *Mencken* (1969). D. E. Weingast, *Walter Lippmann* (1949), is adequate, but the student should read two of the journalist's own books written during the twenties: *The Phantom Public* (1925) and *A Preface to Morals* (1929). An important work by the Protestant theologian Reinhold Niebuhr is *Leaves from the Notebook of a Tamed Cynic* (1929).

C. F. Ware, *Greenwich Village, 1920–1930* (1935); and Allen Churchill, *The Improper Bohemians* (1959), discuss the rise of a self-conscious intellectual class. The feeling of alienation of the intellectual from his native culture may be found in practically every book written on the arts and literary criticism during the twenties. Malcolm Cowley, *Exile's Return* (2nd ed., 1951); J. W. Krutch, *The Modern Temper* (1929); and Lionel Trilling, *The Liberal Imagination* (1950), all emphasize the air of gloom which characterized the creative mind in the decade. For the new humanism see Irving Babbitt, *Democracy and Leadership* (1924); and Norman Foerster (ed.), *Humanism and America* (1930). For the southern agrarian position, see Donald Davidson and others, *I'll Take My Stand* (2nd ed., 1962); and J. L. Stewart, *The Burden of Time: The Fugitives and Agrarians* (1965). Granville Hicks (ed.), *Proletarian Literature in the United States: An Anthology* (1935); and V. F. Calverton, *The Liberation of American Literature* (1932), a Marxist interpretation, illustrate the literary shift to the left. But perhaps the critical works of Edmund Wilson, particularly *Travels in Two Democracies* (1936), and the novels of John Dos Passos, will give the student a better appreciation of the rising radical temper. Indicative of the change in the literary mind during the thirties is the comparison to be made between the two volumes edited by Harold Stearns, *Civilization in the United States* (1922) and *America Now* (1938). John Dos Passos, *The Ground We Stand On* (1941), should also be contrasted with his earlier writings. A perennially fascinating topic is explored by Roderick Nash, *Wilderness and the American Mind* (1967).

For general recent literary history see: Malcolm Cowley (ed.), *After the Genteel Tradition* (1937), a collection of critical works on recent American novelists; F. J. Hoffman, *The Twenties* (1955); Edmund Wilson, *The Shores of Light* (1952); Van Wyck Brooks, *Days of the Phoenix: The Nineteen-Twenties I Remember* (1957); and W. B. Rideout, *The Radical Novel in the United States, 1900–1954* (1956). Edmund Wilson, *American Earthquake* (1958), contains many insights on the literature of the nineteen thirties. For the earlier period see *Echoes of Revolt: The Masses, 1911–1917* (1966), edited by W. L. O'Neill; and C. R. Dolmetsch, *The Smart Set: A History and Anthology* (1966).

Among the best biographical works on leading literary figures are Arthur Mizener, *The Far Side of Paradise* (1951); and Andrew Turnbull, *Scott Fitzgerald* (1962), excellent lives of Fitzgerald; Carlos Baker, *Ernest Hemingway* (1969); Hemingway's own *A Moveable Feast* (1964); and Philip Young, *Ernest Hemingway* (1952); Arthur and Barbara Gelb, *O'Neill* (1962); and Louis Sheaffer, *O'Neill, Son and Playwright* (1968), which covers his life until 1920; a second volume is promised. Harrison Smith (ed.), *From Main Street to Stockholm: Letters from Sinclair Lewis, 1919–1930* (1952); and Mark Schorer's fine biography, *Sinclair Lewis* (1961), contain the best insights into the thought of America's first Nobel prize winning writer. Faulkner is evaluated by Malcolm Cowley in his introduction to *The Portable Faulkner* (1946). An understanding of Thomas Wolfe as a person and a writer can be gleaned from Elizabeth Nowell, *Thomas Wolfe* (1960); and Andrew Turnbull, *Thomas Wolfe* (1968). On Edna St. Vincent Millay, see Jean Gould, *The Poet and Her Book* (1969).

J. I. H. Baur, *Revolution and Tradition in Modern American Art* (1951); R. L. Delevoy, *Dimensions of the 20th Century, 1900–1945* (1965); and Martha Cheney, *Modern Art in America* (1939), in addition to the previously cited Larkin, *Art and Life in America,* are good general works covering the developments in modern art. Jacques Schnier, *Sculpture in Modern America* (1948), is adequate for its subject. On music, J. T. Howard, *Our Contemporary Composers: American Music in the Twentieth Century* (3rd ed., 1946), is comprehensive. See also the more general survey by I. L. Sablosky, *American Music* (1969). But Aaron Copland, *New Music: 1900–1960* (2nd ed., 1969), by one of the nation's first really gifted composers, should be consulted. F. L. Wright, *When Democracy Builds* (1945) and *On Architecture* (1941), should be read as well as his previously cited *Autobiography.* G. C. Manson, *Frank Lloyd Wright* (1958), is a biographical study. *Built in USA, 1932–1944,* edited by Elizabeth Mock (1944), contains a good visual record of the nation's building achievements during the period. See also the major work by Paul Heyer, *Architects on Architecture: New Directions in America* (1966), superbly illustrated.

Grace Overmyer, *Government and Arts* (1939), is devoted to a study of the WPA cultural projects. J. A. Kouwenhoven, *Made in America: The Arts in Modern Civilization* (1948), contains material in the much neglected field of commercial design in which the United States has made major contributions.

Never Again — Until Next Time.

Section Five

DEPRESSION AND WAR

[1929–1945]

The depression that began during the first years of the Hoover administration lasted on in varying degrees of intensity until the outbreak of the Second World War. Hoover as President made a real effort to restore normal times, a radical departure from the behavior of most earlier Presidents, to whom a downward turn of the business cycle was a matter for business itself to handle, rather than the government. But Hoover soon realized that without governmental intervention the whole economic structure of the nation would collapse. For the banks, the railroads, the insurance companies, and a vast number of other great business corporations to be forced into bankruptcy was a greater calamity than the government could sit idly by and permit. Furthermore, as the needs of the unemployed outran the resources of state and local authorities, the national government had to assume an increasing responsibility for the problem of relief.

The measures taken by the Hoover administration thus served as a kind of springboard for the New Deal. Under Franklin D. Roosevelt the government went much further than Hoover had contemplated in its efforts to cure the depression, but the New Deal was not revolutionary. It sought to preserve, not to destroy, the capitalist system, but to achieve this end it was ready to make startling innovations. Roosevelt himself was less the theorist

534

All He Wants Is Elbow Room.

than the man of action, willing to try almost anything that seemed to give promise of help, and totally unembarrassed by contradictions and inconsistencies. He hoped by economic planning and the use of governmental authority to put an end to the business cycle, to maintain full employment, and to better the lot of the underprivileged, but it was principally reform that he had in mind, not revolution. By the end of his second administration, he had achieved much but at a cost in governmental indebtedness that then seemed colossal.

The New Deal took form amid the breakdown of world peace. While the United States had turned aside from the main currents of world affairs to enjoy the prosperity of the 1920's and to struggle against the adversity of the 1930's, the makers of national policy both in Europe and in Asia had pursued courses that could lead only to war. Russian Communism, Italian Fascism, German Naziism, and Japanese statism all had their predatory sides; each planned to expand its system and interests at the expense of its neighbors. Against these movements the League of Nations could make only futile gestures, while in the United States the number of those who were willing to risk anything by way of collective action against the potential aggressors was small indeed. The isolationists were dominant; the rest of the world could have its war if it wished, but the United States would keep out.

By 1937 it was apparent that Roosevelt leaned toward the side of collective security, but he was not able to secure a substantial following until war in Europe had actually broken out; then, as far as keeping the peace was concerned, it was too late. But it was not too late to show a united front toward the aggressors, and the danger to the United States involved in a complete Axis victory brought many belated conversions. With the defeat of France, Germany sought control of the Atlantic, while in Asia Japanese conquests at the expense of China, and the will for other conquests elsewhere, made Americans realize the danger to their Pacific outposts. No doubt Roosevelt saw well in advance of most Americans the inevitability of American participation in the war, and he did what he could to prepare his countrymen for it. With the attack on Pearl Harbor, "measures short of war" gave way to war measures on a more prodigious scale than the nation had ever known before.

The war was fought through to a complete victory, both in Europe and in Asia. In the Pacific theater, where the United States had the chief responsibility, it chose to fight a holding war until the defeat of the Axis powers in Europe. In Europe, the United States furnished the bulk of the troops and equipment required for the invasion of North Africa and Italy, and for the cross-channel attack from England that, together with the Soviet attack from the east, led to Germany's defeat. For all Allied participants, including the Soviets, American supplies were of fundamental importance. To carry on these vast undertakings, the American economy, lagging during the depression, went at last into full production.

During the war there was close cooperation between the Allied leaders. Whenever necessary this took the form of personal conferences, the last of which at Yalta, in 1945, laid plans for the postwar world. These plans were the results of compromise, and were based upon the necessities of the time. Looking backward, every participating nation could find fault with the decisions, and could wish that they had been different. But it seems clear that they represented the best current judgment of the men who made them.

21

THE GREAT DEPRESSION

Herbert Hoover · Background of the depression · The Panic of 1929 · Agriculture and the tariff · Hoover fights the depression · Reconstruction Finance Corporation · Hoover's Moratorium · Election of 1932 · The banking crisis · Significance of the depression

In spite of certain danger signs — the decline of the construction boom, the continued agricultural depression, and the collapse of the feverish Florida land speculations — most Americans had come to look upon "prosperity" as a normal condition by the end of Coolidge's term as President. This prosperity was at best uneven but probably most who did not share in it felt that they would be able to do so in the future. Therefore it was an optimistic United States which elected Herbert Hoover in 1928 on a platform which promised to continue the economic policies of the Harding-Coolidge period, a time which was often called "The New Era." Significantly, Hoover's campaign speeches were published under the title, *The New Day* (1929).

Hoover

Few Presidents have entered office with such a record of solid achievement in so many varied pursuits as Herbert Hoover (1874–1964). Born on an Iowa farm, the son of a Quaker blacksmith, he was orphaned at an early age and raised by relatives in Oregon. After graduating as a mining engineer from Stanford University, Hoover travelled widely. By 1914 he had a large fortune, the product of his skill as an engineer, promoter and administrator. Living in England at the outbreak of the First World War, he became interested in the plight of Americans stranded on the continent and then in the fate of other civilians behind the German lines. He served as chairman, first of the American Relief Commission, and later of the Commission for the Relief of Belgium. When the United States entered the war in 1917, Hoover returned from Europe to become Food Administrator, a position of immense responsibility which he handled with his usual forceful skill. Although he was an admirer of Woodrow Wilson and a supporter of the League of Nations, he spurned the offers of friends who wanted to see him as the Democratic nominee for President in 1920 by the simple announcement that he was a Republican, a previously well-kept secret.

It was inevitable that Harding should have found a place for Herbert Hoover in his administration. Hoover's willingness to

TICKER TAPE, wastebaskets full, told the story of the Wall Street crash, October, 1929.

Herbert Hoover. *Thirty-first President of the United States, Hoover, like Cleveland and Van Buren, was fated to become a "depression" President. By using the power of the national government in an effort to defeat the depression, he anticipated the New Deal, but he was unable to win re-election.*

accept the lowly cabinet post of Secretary of Commerce surprised many people but it was soon evident that Hoover was determined to make of his department one of the major elements of the executive branch. During the short depression of 1921 he proposed, if conditions became worse, a national program of public works to relieve public unemployment. He gave freely of his advice to Presidents Harding and Coolidge, to his fellow cabinet members (including even Secretary of the Treasury Mellon), to the business community, and to the public at large. Hoover's was a household name during the First World War and it remained one throughout the New Era. He was billed as "The Great Engineer" by Republican campaigners in 1928; in governmental and business circles he was known as a great administrator.

Hoover, however, lacked political skill. Never a candidate for office before he ran for President, he was an intensely shy person with a dislike of emotional display of any sort, either public or private. He had made his reputation as an executive in business and in appointive public offices. He had neither understanding of nor sympathy with career politicians of either party. It was not long before his own party leaders came to look upon him as a stranger and it became difficult for them to find what they were expected to do. Hoover lacked a flair for handling press conferences or for manipulating the public by his own oratory (which was barely adequate at best). Nor could he count on his cabinet for political assistance. The two leading members were Mellon, whose political skills were even less evident than Hoover's, and Henry L. Stimson, Secretary of State, who had served as Secretary of War and as Governor-General of the Philippines. Stimson had been the unsuccessful Republican candidate for Governor of New York in 1910 and had had his fill of running for office; his contacts were legal and business leaders rather than Republican organizational politicians. A politically inexperienced new President was operating, in his own shy way, with a generally undistinguished cabinet. Hoover was on his own as President, more remote from the people than any of his recent predecessors, except perhaps Woodrow Wilson.

Background of the Great Depression

Hoover was scarcely well seated in the presidential chair when the Great Depression began, and his administration, like Cleveland's second, became indelibly associated in the public mind with hard times. The Great Depression was preceded by a long period of speculation, this time mainly in stocks and bonds. The prosperity of the twenties was to a remarkable extent corporation prosperity. Few individuals owned great businesses; Henry Ford was an outstanding exception. Most "big businesses" were jointly owned by hundreds or thousands of stockholders, whose investments might vary from a $100 share to values running to many millions. Throughout the prosperous twenties stocks multiplied at an increasing tempo. The fact that business was actually owned by millions of investors was regarded with satisfaction by President Hoover and others as proof that it was essentially democratic, but any careful examination of corporation statistics showed that a comparatively small number of investors owned the greater part of the stock. Moreover, the direction of a given industry lay inevitably with the few insiders who represented the largest holdings. In a sense the control of business was less democratic than ever before. With investments so widely diffused, the individual with a 3 per cent holding might be as powerful as the majority stockholder of an earlier age. Thus, the ownership of property had been divorced from the power to control it, and the way was open for the few at the top of corporations to utilize the property of the many for their own purposes.

Stock Speculation

While many of those who purchased stocks were genuinely interested in obtaining sound investments, many others operated only as speculators, buying when prices were low, and selling when they rose. Some bought "on margin," depositing only enough money with their brokers to cover the probable range of fluctuation. They were sure to encounter difficulties if their guesses went wrong. This speculative demand for stocks was to a great extent responsible for the generally high price level of securities during the later twenties. Often the actual earning power of a given stock was far too low to justify the price at which it sold; valuations of twenty-five times the total earnings were by no means uncommon. Optimists refused to be alarmed at the situation and insisted that the high prices paid for securities were merely an

evidence of the healthy condition of American enterprise. Investors had faith in the soundness of business and were willing to back it with their dollars. Even the Federal Reserve Board, at least indirectly, supported speculation, for it kept the supply of credit plentiful even when much too much of the easy money was being used in outright stock speculations. Between September, 1927, and September, 1929, borrowings for speculation on the New York Stock Exchange rose from $3.3 billion to $8.5 billion. Prices of stocks, as one misguided observer noted, soared upward to "what looks like a permanently high plateau." One issue never known to pay a dividend climbed steadily from $40 to $450 a share.

In the midst of all this speculation a few pessimists warned that the business cycle might not be as obsolete as many seemed to believe, and that a crisis was probably close at hand. Too much of the country's credit was being diverted into stock-exchange notes, and industry, as a result of the easy money, was being tempted to overexpand. Who was to buy all the goods that producers could make? Already the building boom of the earlier twenties was on the decline, automobile sales were off, and oil production far exceeded the demand. But these wise protests were brushed aside by optimists in high places who assured investors that all was well. Two days before the market crashed, Charles E. Mitchell, president of the National City Bank of New York, asserted unequivocally: "I know of nothing fundamentally wrong with the stock market or with the underlying business and credit structures."

Panic of 1929

The stock market collapse came in October, 1929, when British interest rates were raised to 6.5 per cent in order to repatriate needed capital that had been attracted to the United States by the high speculative profits. As a result many European holdings were thrown on the market, and prices began to sag. Frightened at the prospect, and no longer able to borrow at will, American speculators also began to unload. On Thursday, October 24, 1929, 12.8 million shares changed hands, and until October 29, when the sales reached 16.4 million shares, the frantic selling continued. During the month of October the value of stocks listed on the New York Stock Exchange declined from $87 billion to $55 billion, or about 37 per cent. And this, it developed, was only the beginning. In spite of repeated assurances from high authorities, both in government and finance, that prosperity lay "just around the corner," no less than nine similar declines to "new low levels" were recorded within the next three years. By the first of March, 1933, the value of all stocks listed on the New York Stock Exchange was set at only $19 billion, less than one-fifth the inflated values of October 1, 1929.

In spite of optimistic efforts to maintain that the stock-market collapse was purely a paper loss which would not seriously undermine the fundamental soundness of American business, it was soon evident that a period of unparalleled depression had begun. The catastrophic fall in stock prices brought a sharp deflationary movement. Stock brokers called upon speculators to pay back the sums they had borrowed, banks made the same demands upon brokers and upon many businessmen who had used stocks as collateral for their loans. Since many were unable to pay, bankruptcies added to the credit stringency. Merchants refused credit to buyers of their wares and drastically reduced their inventories of goods. Prices dropped sharply; foreign trade fell off; factories curtailed production, and many closed their doors never to reopen them; real-estate values (but not payment rates on mortgages) declined; new construction, except on government works, practically

ceased; banks went under; worst of all, wages were cut drastically, and unemployment began to mount. By the end of 1930, 6 to 7 million workers were out of jobs; two years later the number had doubled. Nor was the United States alone in its distress. No longer able to secure American loans, foreign nations fell likewise into the abyss of depression; indeed, many of them, like Germany, had not far to fall. Once again the people of the United States were to learn by experience that whatever seriously affected one great nation was bound to affect all.

Causes of the Depression

Efforts to account for the plunge from prosperity to adversity soon demonstrated conclusively that no one factor, but a great number working together, produced such startling results. Economists were able to reach substantial agreement as to the principal causes of the depression, but they were by no means in harmony as to the importance of each cause. Among other disturbing influences they cited the following:

1. *Agricultural overexpansion*, both in the United States and elsewhere. American farmers produced more wheat, cotton, corn, livestock, and other commodities than they could sell at satisfactory prices, and to some extent the same condition existed in much of the rest of the world. Agricultural surpluses piled up at home and abroad with devastating effect on the price of each new crop. Farm purchases steadily declined, for farmers had less and less with which to buy. Payments on the heavy mortgage burden assumed in more prosperous times still further curtailed the farmers' buying power, and drove many of them to tenancy.

2. *Industrial overexpansion.* The American industrial plant had been overbuilt during the boom, and could not be operated at maximum capacity. There were too many factories and too much machinery. Industry was geared to produce far

Oh Yeah?

OCTOBER 16, 1929.

Stock prices have reached what looks like a permanently high plateau. I do not feel that there will soon, if ever, be a fifty or sixty point break below present levels, such as Mr. Babson has predicted.

I expect to see the stock market a good deal higher than it is today within a few months. — *Irving Fisher*

OCTOBER 22, 1929.

I believe the breaks of the last few days have driven stocks down to hard rock. I believe that we will have a ragged market for a few weeks and then the beginning of a mild bull movement that will gain momentum next year. . . . —*New York Herald Tribune*

OCTOBER 24, 1929.

If it is true that 15 billions in stock quotation losses have been suffered in the present break I have no hesitation in saying values are too low. —*New York Herald Tribune*

THE PERMANENTLY HIGH PLATEAU
THE NEW YORK TIMES 25 INDUSTRIALS BY CALENDAR WEEKS

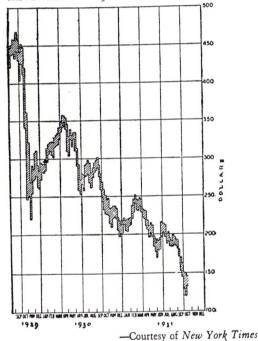

—Courtesy of *New York Times*

The Permanently High Plateau. *These pages from Angly's* Oh Yeah? *published during the Hoover years, feature the over-optimistic predictions that failed so completely to halt the depression.*

supply a new market. But now every American family that could afford an automobile (and many that could not) had one or sometimes more than one. With 26.5 million motor cars in operation by 1929, the market for automobiles was confined largely to replacements. The same condition existed in housing. Rapid building during the twenties had caused the lumber industry and others producing building materials to overexpand their markets.

3. *The increasing effectiveness of machines.* Ingenious labor-saving devices made possible greater production with comparatively less labor. Fewer men produced more goods. "Technological unemployment" might not be permanent, but the men who were thrown out of work by the new machines had to seek other jobs, and they sometimes failed to find them. Thus the buying power of labor was diminished. The new machines might make more goods, but whose wages were to pay for them? Introduction of labor-saving devices was rarely paralleled by increased wages, a shortening of the labor day and the labor week, and a diminishing use of women and children in industry.

4. *Capital surpluses were too high.* As a prominent banker, Frank A. Vanderlip, expressed it, "Capital kept too much and labor did not have enough to buy its share of things." This was more easily possible because of the monopolistic nature of much American business, which so greatly facilitated the control of prices. Throughout the boom years the tendency of business was to take too high profits, and to reinvest the capital thus accumulated in order to produce still more goods, which in return might produce still more profits. A wider distribution of earnings, particularly if paid out in the form of higher wages, might well have stimulated purchasing power and diminished the danger of ultimate collapse. The factor of under-consumption was probably as important as the overexpansion already noted.

more than it could sell. Automobiles, for example, had been turned out in steadily increasing numbers during the twenties to

5. *The overexpansion of credit*, both for productive and consumptive purposes. Money was plentiful and cheap throughout the twenties, and the policy of the Federal Reserve Board and the Coolidge administration was to keep it so. At the personal insistence of President Coolidge in 1927 the Federal Reserve Board eased credit restrictions. A year later when the New York Stock Exchange announced that brokers' loans amounted to $4 billion, the highest figure in history, both Secretary of Commerce Hoover and Governor Young of the Federal Reserve Board argued for the curtailment of easy money and credit. They were joined by a group of conservative bankers who thought even then that there was too much speculation in stocks. But it was not until after Hoover took office that the Board reversed itself and started to tighten credit. By that time it was too late to ward off disaster. It had been too easy to borrow, whether for business expansion, for speculation, or for the satisfaction of personal desires. There was

Sold Out. *This cartoon of October 25, 1929, caught well the mood of stockmarket speculators who had lost everything.*

too much installment buying, and too much of the national income was diverted into interest payments. In keeping with the speculative spirit of the times, purchasers cheerfully mortgaged their futures to obtain goods that would often be consumed before they could be paid for. The Coolidge policy had definitely encouraged both speculation and purchasing on credit.

6. *Banking and financial ethics.* After the Democratic victory of 1932, a Senate Committee began an investigation of the ethics and practices during the golden twenties of the great New York banks and investment companies. To a large extent such institutions controlled the American financial structure, and their ethics were bound to be reflected throughout the country. Among the officers of many such institutions the committee found a complete disregard for the welfare of depositors and the economic health of the country; in some they found outright fraud, chicanery, and theft. The officers of some great banks had used their depositors' money to operate enormous speculations in the stock market, and had divided the profits among themselves and a small group of powerful political figures. Heading the "Cut-in List," or the favored group of outsiders, of J. P. Morgan and Company, for example, were the names of Calvin Coolidge, General Pershing, Newton D. Baker, and Bernard M. Baruch. Other great bankers had sold worthless foreign bonds to their correspondent banks throughout the country, simply to collect the commission on the sales. These and other practices weakened the entire country's financial structure to such an extent that it was extremely vulnerable to the harsh demands of the depression.

7. *International trade was out of balance.* European nations, with their economies badly shattered by the war, had depended mainly on funds borrowed from American investors to pay for imports and to stabilize foreign exchange. The only way they might have repaid these obliga-

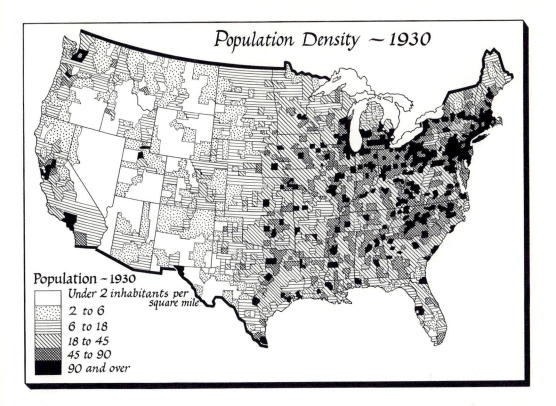

Population Density ~ 1930

Population ~ 1930

- Under 2 inhabitants per square mile
- 2 to 6
- 6 to 18
- 18 to 45
- 45 to 90
- 90 and over

tions was by shipping goods to the United States. But the Fordney-McCumber Tariff of 1922, followed by the Hawley-Smoot Tariff of 1930 (see below, p. 544), definitely lessened any such possibility. The debtor nations of Europe in self-defense were obliged to adopt high-tariff policies and by various other expedients to stimulate whatever industries were necessary to cut down their reliance on foreign goods. During the years 1922–1927 the production of British-made automobiles, for example, was increased from 49 per cent of the domestic supply to 86 per cent. Thus the United States, blindly committed to the protective principles of an earlier age, stood to lose both its export business and a good share of the money by which this business had been sustained. Many manufacturers understood the situation, and did their best to prevent the adoption of tariffs that in the long run were certain to bring disaster, but most citizens were slow to recognize that international trade was a mutual affair and were unprepared for the collapse that fol-

lowed the withdrawal of American credits.

Even more fundamental perhaps was the division of the world between rich nations, usually advanced industrially, and poor undeveloped nations trying to pay their way with agricultural and other primary products. Just as agricultural prices had fallen so drastically in the United States, so also had the world prices of primary commodities and metals. Thus a significant share of the market for manufactured goods was reduced at the same time the world's industrial capacity was rapidly increasing. In the world, as in the United States, most industrial producers were too rich and the buyers too poor to keep the international machinery of exchange operating.

8. *Political unrest throughout the world*, particularly in Europe, Asia, and South America, also added to the difficulties in sustaining prosperity. Intergovernmental debts, whether funded or not, constituted a continuing threat both to trade and to international good feelings. The reparations problem remained unsettled. Most

countries were overburdened with governmental debts, and few national budgets were in the balance. The War and the Peace of Paris bore a share of responsibility for the economic disarray. The break-up of the Austro-Hungarian Empire destroyed the economic unity of much of the Danube basin. The old patterns of trade and commercial intercourse were further obstructed by the nationalistic aspirations of the new states. With major cities like Vienna cut off from the hinterlands and farmers deprived of urban markets, economic confusion was the only possible result.

Finally, it can also be argued, a fortuitous element accentuated the depression. In most sharp downward movements of the economy during recent times, some activities failed to fall along with all the others. Thus while farm prices and factory production were going down, home construction and international trade might be stationary or were increasing in tempo, thus helping to cushion the total impact of the decline. But in 1929–1933 almost every line of economic activity seemed to be falling precipitately at the same time. Instead of a cushioning effect, one factor accentuated the other to produce in sum a frightening crisis.

Agriculture and the Tariff

During the campaign Hoover had promised an increase in agricultural duties as a way of helping the farmers. He hoped to escape a general tariff revision, but a more experienced politician could have foreseen that once tariff changing had begun there would be little chance of limiting its scope. The special session of Congress which the President called in the spring of 1929 was unable to agree on the provisions of a new tariff law but it did proceed to "do something about agriculture" in other ways.

Hoover's program for the relief of agriculture was enacted into law well before the panic days of October, 1929, but the depression in agriculture was of long standing. The Agricultural Marketing Act, signed June 15, 1929, was designed to help agriculture help itself by means of voluntary cooperation. Proponents of the measure believed that with appropriate federal encouragement the farmers could work together through cooperatives by applying the same principles of orderly production and distribution that governed the activities of prudent manufacturers. They could thus find means to curtail production when necessary, to shift to different crops as demand changed, and to eliminate wasteful and expensive methods of marketing. The act created a Federal Farm Board and provided it with a $500 million revolving fund from which it could lend to cooperatives, and to such stabilization corporations as it might set up for the purpose of buying, storing, and selling surpluses.

The Federal Farm Board succeeded in stimulating the formation of cooperatives but it failed dismally in its efforts to solve the problem of surpluses. Although it set up grain and cotton stabilization corporations which went into the market to make huge purchases, this action merely resulted in the governmental acquisition of vast amounts of wheat and cotton. When the Board eventually ran out of funds (it lost $184 million altogether), prices fell still further. In its final report the Board concluded that agricultural recovery would be impossible without production control.

Meantime, Congress had returned to the tariff. As a result of the usual log-rolling, the Hawley-Smoot Tariff raised the general level of protection by about 7 per cent. The measure was signed by President Hoover in June 1930, even though its rates were higher than he had asked for. More than a thousand economists had asked him to veto the tariff bill, pointing out that the measure was certain (1) to raise prices for the consumer; (2) to encourage wasteful and unnecessary concerns to remain in business; (3) to limit the exportation of products, both from farm and factory, by restricting

The Hawley-Smoot Tariff. *With the need for world trade a first necessity in the struggle for economic recovery, Congress nevertheless voted the highest tariff rates on record. For the next thirty years, with good reason, it never again trusted itself to make another general tariff revision.*

imports; (4) to yield no benefits to the farmers whose prices were fixed by what the exportable surplus would bring; and (5) to insure reprisals from foreign countries whose trade would be adversely affected. One of the first of the predicted reprisals came from Canada, which promptly increased the rates on most of its important imports from the United States, and others came thick and fast. In 1932 Great Britain, whose devotion to free trade had long been slipping, veered completely over to the protective-tariff policy. For the establishment of these higher trade barriers in the face of world-wide depression the United States bore a leading responsibility.

Hoover Fights the Depression

When the stock market broke in October 1929, President Hoover did not yet know how his farm recovery program would work in practice and he did not yet know how long it would take the Congress to deal with his tariff recommendations. Meanwhile, he had to deal with the immediate consequences of the crash, an ironic situation for the man who only the year before had promised "the final triumph over poverty" if only the country were "given a chance to go forward with the policies of the last eight years."

At first, the importance of the stock market crash was not widely appreciated. While thousands of individuals and firms suffered great losses as a direct result of their involvement in speculation in stocks and bonds, the economy itself declined slowly. Hoover announced, after the worst of the days on Wall Street in late October, that people should remain confident: "The fundamental business of the country, that is, the production and distribution of commodities, is on a sound and prosperous basis." In his memoirs, written a generation later, he admitted that he had been far more pessimistic than he felt he could indicate in public at the time without injuring the nation's confidence in the capitalist system. Hoover, a thrifty soul, had disapproved heartily of many of the speculative practices of the New Era. Unfortunately for his campaign to restore confidence, Hoover lacked the talent for inspiring it — he was not a very cheerful-looking person in the best of times. Indeed, the optimistic pronouncements of the administration came in time to become real liabilities, as the economy continued to decline. As late as March 1930, the President announced that his survey of the evidence had convinced him that "the worst effects of the crash upon unemployment will have been passed during the next sixty days." In time his enemies could taunt Hoover about his remarks, centering with bitter irony on the sentence: "Prosperity is just around the corner."

For a time Hoover directed his efforts mainly toward obtaining the voluntary co-operation of business and labor leaders in measures of self-help. At a series of conferences in Washington he talked against the curtailment of buying power that must inevitably follow the reduction of payrolls, and urged that "the first shock" of the depression "must fall on profits and not on wages." He insisted that wage scales ought not for the moment to be lowered at all, and succeeded in committing many industries to a policy of expansion in spite of the unsettled economic conditions. But "business as usual" soon proved to be a difficult formula for executives to maintain in the face of declining receipts and mounting inventories. In spite of good intentions, wages did go down and unemployment figures began to mount.

As the economy continued to fall, Hoover began to inaugurate more vigorous policies. Early in 1930 he asked and obtained from Congress huge sums to be used in the erection of public buildings, the improvement of rivers and harbors, and the building of federal roads. By these and similar expenditures, voted later, he sought to take up the slack of unemployment. Before he left office, more than $2.25 billion had been appropriated for such purposes. For a long time, however, the President opposed any more direct effort by the federal government to deal with the problem of unemployment. Direct relief, he maintained, was a function of the states, municipalities, and voluntary organizations. He argued that the granting of huge sums by the federal authorities would be too impersonal and would subject communities to the control of "a remote bureaucracy." It was not the function of the national government, he wrote, "to relieve individuals of their responsibilities to their neighbors." After the midterm elections of 1930, in which the Democrats won control of the House for the first time since 1918, Hoover faced an increasingly hostile Congress. Some Republican Senators advocated programs for spending and intervention in the economy far in advance of anything the President favored. Hoover had to deal with bitter opposition in Congress, something for which he was not temperamentally prepared.

As conditions steadily worsened, it became apparent that the combined resources of state, cities, and charities were completely inadequate. Some states were far harder hit than others. In the mining districts of West Virginia, the economies of many cities practically vanished. In the ordinarily productive states of the lower Mississippi Valley, a severe drought produced a near-famine. Eventually even the rich states were in deep trouble. The Pennsylvania Department of Public Welfare reported that one out of every three persons in the state was dependent upon charity and that all the public and private funds together could support

DESERT LANDS. To reclaim by irrigation such lands as these the Hoover Dam impounded in Lake Mead a huge volume of water.

the destitute at the barest minimum for two to five months of every year. Toledo was reduced to granting a relief allowance of 2.14 cents a meal, while Chicago, with 700,000 unemployed in May, 1932, had already spent all the relief funds that were supposed to last the year.

Reconstruction Finance Corporation

Eventually Hoover had to admit that only the federal government had the tax and credit resources necessary to meet the emergency. Even so, the President was still opposed to direct grants to citizens, whom he did not want to see become wards of the national government, and even to federal grants to the states, some of which were still solvent. Hoover did ask Congress for substantial appropriations from which loans could be made to states no longer able to finance relief. In spite of the mounting deficit in the federal budget, Congress made those appropriations. Indeed, the chief criticism of the Hoover program came from those who felt that it was not generous enough. Many of these critics were members of Hoover's own party — Senators Hiram Johnson of California, Robert M. LaFollette, Jr., of Wisconsin, George Norris of Nebraska, among others. Indeed, many of the senior Democratic members of Congress were as devoted to economy and "fiscal responsibility" as was President Hoover; frequently they provided the votes which blocked the aspirations of those who sought bigger spending programs.

To administer loans for state relief and other carefully restricted purposes, Congress in 1932 created a Reconstruction Finance Corporation, based on a First World War model. The first head of the RFC was Charles G. Dawes of Chicago, a banker-politician who had served as the first Director of the Budget under Harding and as Coolidge's Vice-President. The RFC lent freely not only to the states but also to banks, farm credit corporations, life-insur-

ance companies, and other financial organizations, and to the hard-pressed railroads. Those who favored more liberal spending for the relief of suffering people complained bitterly that the RFC was based on a "trickle-down" theory which assumed that money poured into institutions would somehow eventually trickle down to persons in need. The critics felt that this form of indirect relief to suffering individuals was no substitute for direct aid, even if conservatives felt that this "dole" would injure the moral fiber of the recipients. While Hoover himself lacked the political power to block a larger relief-spending program, he received the support of powerful conservative Democrats in Congress.

The RFC did forestall or delay many corporate bankruptcies with loans which reached almost $2 billion before Hoover left office. The President had not originated the concept of the RFC and he had signed the bill passed by Congress only after securing severe limitations on the lending authority of the new agency. Nevertheless, the RFC remains one of the major symbols of the increased power of the federal government over hitherto private sectors of American life.

Another innovation prepared the way for further direct involvement of the federal government with the private portion of the economy. For the benefit of homeowners who were about to lose their property, Hoover encouraged the passage of the Home Loan Bank Act of July 22, 1932. Under its terms a series of banks were established to discount home mortgages, and thus provide a service similar to that rendered by the Federal Reserve Banks in the commercial field. The large appropriations necessary to carry RFC and HLB into effect unbalanced the national budget by many billions of dollars. Hoover, in spite of his insistence upon strict limitations on government spending and upon the scope of relief and recovery programs, was thus open to charges of being a spendthrift.

Hoover's Moratorium

Not all the actions of the Hoover administration in its efforts to deal with the depression were concerned with internal affairs. When in March 1931, France refused to permit Germany and Austria to unite in a customs union, a series of events was set in motion which led to the almost complete collapse of European finances. Until that time the Great Depression was a primarily American affair. The finances of central Europe sank first, but eventually every European nation was affected, including Britain, which in September 1931 was forced to abandon the gold standard. American investors in foreign securities, particularly those of Germany, were hard hit, and American trade with Europe was drastically curtailed.

Hoover believed that the huge burden of intergovernmental debts — especially German reparations payments to France and Britain, and French and British war debt payments to the United States — constituted one of the chief impediments to world trade recovery. In June 1931, he advocated a moratorium for one year on both the principal and interest of all such obligations. This action was deeply resented by France, who wished to continue her collection from Germany, and it was far from popular in the United States; but eventually it was accepted by the fifteen governments involved, and went into effect. In 1932, the European powers attempted to solve the debt riddle for all time by granting Germany a three-year moratorium on reparations, and by establishing a new low figure, $714 million, as the amount to be paid. All this, however, was contingent upon the willingness of the United States to cancel its war debts, something which the American government refused. Reparation payments were never resumed by Germany. When the moratorium ended in 1932 only six governments met their obligations to the United States, but only Finland paid in full after the first year. In 1934 Congress passed the Johnson Act, which prohibited Americans from purchasing new securities of any nation in default on its debt to the United States. By this time the debts in fact, if not in law, had ceased to be, and their restraining influence upon the course of international trade could not have been great.

Politics and Social Conditions

The effect of the Great Depression upon the political fortunes of Herbert Hoover and the Republican party was disastrous. The Democratic National Committee, well-financed and skillfully managed, capitalized upon the growing tendency to hold the President personally responsible for the growing misery of the unemployed, as well as for the continued economic decline. Democratic publicists provided speech material for Hoover's political enemies and "editorials" for widespread distribution to the nation's hundreds of small newspapers. In these documents they identified Hoover as one of the architects of the economic policies of Harding and Coolidge which had, they insisted, led to the Great Crash. They cited Hoover's efforts to restrain the federal government from embarking upon a program of direct relief as proof that he cared little about the sufferings of the unemployed but much about the tax burden on those who still had the ability to pay. Shanty towns which were constructed by the unemployed who had lost their own homes were commonly dubbed "Hoovervilles," as the President's name was increasingly associated with full responsibility for the depression.

With social conditions steadily deteriorating, serious rumblings of discontent sounded throughout the country. At their annual convention, members of the usually cautious American Federation of Labor solemnly resolved: "We shall use our might to compel the plain remedies withheld by those whose misfeasance caused our woe."

The Bonus Army. *Bonus marchers from California, about 450 in number, paraded around the Capitol on July 12, 1932, then defied police orders by camping on the Capitol grounds.*

In the Middle West farmers were beginning to organize into militant groups for self-protection. Here and there armed men met and turned back sheriffs intent upon serving foreclosure writs, while others barricaded roads to stop the delivery of farm produce to the cities until agricultural prices rose.

The most publicized protest was the march of about 30,000 destitute war veterans on Washington, D.C. The demonstration lasted for several weeks in the late spring and summer of 1932; as many as 22,000 were present at different places around the capital city at one time. The "bonus marchers" (or Bonus Expeditionary Force as they liked to call themselves) demanded the immediate passage of the Patman Bonus Bill, a measure which provided for the prompt cash payment of the soldiers' bonus. The bonus to First World War veterans authorized by Congress in 1924 was not scheduled for full payment until the year 1945, but the protestors saw clearly enough that they would never need it more than they did in 1932. After the measure passed the House, President Hoover used the full force of his office to assist

in the defeat of the bill in the Senate. On the President's orders the remaining bonus marchers, about 2,000 bitter but still peaceful men, were driven out of their camp grounds by federal troops under the personal command of General Douglas MacArthur, Army Chief of Staff. Hoover's opposition to the bonus bill was defensible; indeed, many liberals who had no fondness for the President were also opposed, since they felt that Patman's measure was dangerously inflationary and would not aid those who most needed help. But the use of troops against unarmed and impoverished veterans roused great anger at Hoover throughout the country. The Battle of Anacostia Flats, as the action against the bonus marchers was derisively called, seemed to many people to be proof that the Hoover administration had little compassion for the poor and little real understanding of their plight.

Many Americans were in great distress by 1932. No accurate statistics were compiled at the time but at least 13,000,000 were unemployed, many millions had only part-time work, and something over a million people wandered about the country,

The Down-and-Outers. *A "White Angel" bread-line in San Francisco during the darkest days of the depression. Photograph by Dorothea Lange. The George Eastman House Collection.*

rootless, homeless, jobless. Newspapers reported cases of actual starvation in many areas, although few government officials were willing to admit that such things were happening. Of 39 governors replying to a query about this, only Gifford Pinchot of Pennsylvania, the veteran conservationist and progressive Republican, admitted that thousands of people in his state were in such distress that they were "practically starving." Coal mining areas, many of them already depressed before 1929, suffered intensely; the plight of those who lived in company towns, always difficult, was far worse when the companies themselves were barely operating or even shut down completely. In many parts of the country teachers went unpaid and students came to school weak from hunger. "Breadlines" and "souplines" were common sights in the cities of the nation. No one will ever know how many of those who suffered privation

and humiliation in the depths of the Great Depression were formerly prosperous members of middle-class America but the number must have been tens of thousands. Those who suffered most were those who had been at the bottom of the social and economic pyramid even during the New Era — the black, Indian, and Spanish-speaking minorities, rural laborers and share-croppers, and marginal unskilled industrial workers.

Election of 1932

Although the Republicans were faced with a serious defeat in 1932, the Republican Convention was controlled by strong administration supporters. Hoover was renominated, and his policies were accorded unstinted praise. President Hoover, in announcing that the government would assume responsibility for the nation's economic situation, promised greater loans to business and a much larger program of public works. But he was still stoutly opposed both to direct federal grants to the unemployed and to the federal control of agricultural production. Denouncing the federal bureaucracy which both measures would involve, he declared: "Not regimented mechanisms, but free men is our goal."

The Democrats, after a lively contest, emerged with Franklin D. Roosevelt, popular two-term governor of New York, as their candidate for President, and John Nance Garner, Speaker of the House, as their candidate for Vice-President. The Democratic platform blamed the Republicans for the depression, called for a drastic reduction in government expenses, a balanced federal budget, a sound currency, and the "removal of government from all fields of private enterprise." It promised federal aid to the states to care for the needy, a state system of unemployment and old-age insurance, an effective control of the farm crop surplus, an enlarged public-works program, and repeal of the national prohibition of liquor. During the campaign most of Roosevelt's speeches sounded as contradictory as the Democratic platform. He attacked Hoover for his spending programs, yet he proposed relief for the unemployed and a huge program of public works and reforestation. Without being specific he was for crop reduction, but he labeled as "a cruel joke" the Hoover farm board's advice to the farmers to allow 20 per cent of their wheat land to lie idle and to plow up every third row of their cotton. In only a few speeches did he do more than hint at what was to come. At Seattle he promised to modify the tariff by reciprocal trade agreements and at Portland, Oregon, he pledged the public development of power and water resources of the valleys of the Tennessee, Columbia, and Colorado rivers. Elsewhere his message was less specific. But his call for a New Deal in government, his promises to remember the "forgotten man," and his personal charm and

sense of confidence won the support of thousands of Republicans and independents.

When the returns were in, it was apparent that Hoover had been as badly defeated as Smith had been four years before. The electoral vote stood 472 to 59, and the popular vote, 22.8 million to 15.7 million. Hoover carried only six states: Maine, New Hampshire, Vermont, Connecticut, Delaware, and Pennsylvania. Both houses of Congress went overwhelmingly Democratic, and in the states the Democratic landslide carried into office many candidates who had regarded their names on the party ticket as either a courtesy or a joke. The vote for Norman Thomas, the Socialist candidate, was 884,791, smaller than his party's total in 1912. William Z. Foster, the Communist Party presidential nominee, received 102,991 votes. After three years of privation and misery, the American voters were still committed to the two-party system and to political democracy.

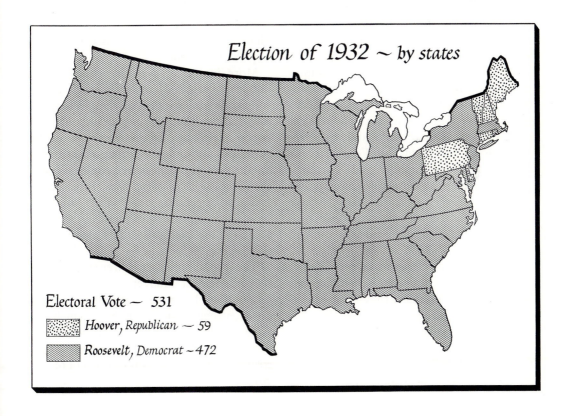

Election of 1932 ~ by states

Electoral Vote — 531

Hoover, Republican — 59

Roosevelt, Democrat — 472

The Banking Crisis

Before the adoption of the Twentieth Amendment, both a defeated President and the old Congress continued in power from the November elections until March 4 of the following year. This "lame duck" session was extremely embarrassing in the winter of 1932–1933 because of the enormity of the problems confronting the defeated President. Hoover tried to enlist the aid of the President-elect, but Roosevelt refused to commit himself on his future plans, particularly with regard to balancing the budget, a promise which Hoover felt might help restore confidence in the rapidly deteriorating financial situation. And since the harassed outgoing President received no support from either the financial community or the Democratic Congress, government practically came to a standstill in the interim before inauguration day.

Meanwhile the increasing public pessimism led to a banking crisis of unparalleled gravity. Unemployment was at its worst during the winter of 1932–1933, and was estimated at anywhere from 13 million to 17 million. Production in one great industry after another dropped to almost negligible proportions. Fear that the financial structure of the country was endangered showed in the mounting totals of gold exported and of gold and currency hoarded; by the middle of February, the disappearance of bullion and currency from the American economy amounted to about $30 million a day. In Detroit, where the drastic curtailment of automobile production had created a peculiarly difficult situation, the banks held on grimly. By mid-February, unable to make use of their frozen assets and drained of their deposits by frightened customers, they escaped collapse only when the governor of the state extended the holiday period by eight days, and then obtained from the legislature the right to prolong it if need be. With the Michigan banks suspended, the panic spread to one state after another, and nearly every state executive declared a long bank holiday. By inauguration day, bank deposits were temporarily unusable, bills remained unpaid, and credit was virtually unobtainable. The circulatory system of capitalism had stopped, and no one knew what the next day would bring.

Significance of the Depression

The Great Depression brought the New Era to an abrupt and decisive halt. Gone were the dreams of riches-for-all, of what later was to be called "the affluent society." The great leaders of business and finance, whose viewpoints had become national policies in the Harding-Coolidge period, suffered personal humiliation when their earlier optimistic remarks were thrown back at them by politicians and journalists and when they found themselves scorned where they had once been honored. Even where these leaders managed to survive the depression with their fortunes reasonably secure they were never again to enjoy the kind of idolatry that had once been their popular treatment.

More important was the effect on the public at large. Many went through the trauma of personal degradation, losing their jobs and their homes; they would not easily regain their faith in the workings of the American economy. Others, perhaps a majority of the American people, survived the depression in what was often called "reduced circumstances"; many of them would have difficulty in renewing their respect for the political leaders closely identified with the New Era.

The reputation that suffered most was that of Herbert Hoover, the shy engineer in politics. Later generations would discover a compassion for him which the American people refused to accord to him at the time. Although his successor was to struggle for years with the problem of "recovery," it was Hoover's name which remained identified with the Great Depression. The talents which made him the symbol of the New Era proved to be inadequate when he was faced with the need to communicate with the people. Many consider that the New Deal began under Hoover. Historians can find evidence to support this idea. But Hoover himself would have denied it — and it would have been news to his contemporaries, for he took care to hide many of his innovations from public view.

BIBLIOGRAPHY

The most useful syntheses of the Hoover administration are H. G. Warren, *Herbert Hoover and the Great Depression* (1959); and A. U. Romasco, *The Poverty of Abundance* (1965). Gene Smith, *The Shattered Dream* (1970), is vividly personal, suggesting better than anyone else the essential loneliness of Hoover. The second and third volumes of *The Memoirs of Herbert Hoover* (1952) reveal a great deal about the author's mind. Semiofficial works by friends of the administration, and valuable as sources are: W. S. Myers (ed.), *The State Papers and Other Public Writings of Herbert Hoover* (2 vols., 1934); W. S. Myers and W. H. Newton, *The Hoover Administration: A Documented Narrative* (1936); and R. L. Wilbur and A. M. Hyde, *The Hoover Policies* (1937). See also *The Memoirs of Ray Lyman Wilbur, 1875–1949*, edited by E. E. Robinson and P. C. Edwards (1960). D. C. Swain, *Wilderness Defender: Horace M. Albright and Conservation* (1970), is a study of an associate of Hoover and Wilbur.

Broadus Mitchell, *Depression Decade: From New Era to New Deal, 1929–1941* (1947), is a survey of economic history, critical in tone. Walter Johnson, *1600 Pennsylvania Avenue: Presidents and the People Since 1929* (2nd ed., 1963), is political history by a liberal who believes in a strong presidency and finds the Hoover record a dismal one. The first volume of A. M. Schlesinger, Jr., *The Age of Roosevelt*, which bears the subtitle, *The Crisis of the Old Order: 1919–1933* (1957), is a superbly written if somewhat distorted backdrop for the New Deal, of which the author is perhaps the leading scholarly partisan.

Dixon Wecter, *The Age of the Great Depression, 1929–1941* (1948), is a comprehensive and well-written survey of social history. F. L. Allen, *Since Yesterday: The Nineteen-Thirties in America, September 3, 1929–September 3, 1939* (1940), is a sprightly examination of social phenomena. A rich collection of documents gathered by D. A. Shannon, *The Great Depression* (1960), illustrates the impact of the depression upon the people. An exciting oral history of the depression is Studs Terkel, *Hard Times* (1970). Useful collections of readings are *The New Deal at Home and Abroad, 1929–1945* (1965), edited by C. A. Chambers; and *Depression, Recovery and War, 1929–1945* (1966), edited by A. B. Rollins, Jr. J. K. Galbraith, *The Great Crash, 1929* (1955), is a witty and beautifully written account of the stock market debacle. On monetary affairs, see Milton Friedman and Anna Jacobson, *The Great Contraction, 1929–33* (1965); and E. R. Wicker, *Federal Reserve Monetary Policy, 1917–33* (1966). Documents and varying interpretations are collected in *The Great Depression and American Capitalism* (1968), edited by R. F. Himmelberg. Aspects of the farm problem are covered in such varying works as *Agriculture Policy in the Twentieth Century* (1967), edited by George McGovern; F. W. Schruben, *Kansas in Turmoil, 1930–1936* (1969); and J. L. Shover, *Cornbelt Rebellion: The Farmers' Holiday Association* (1966). A sympathetic account of one of the chief casualties of the crash is Forrest McDonald, *Insull* (1962). There are two good studies of the Hawley-Smoot Tariff: E. E. Schattschneider, *Politics, Pressures and the Tariff* (1935), a valuable inside picture of the making of the tariff; and J. M. Jones, *Tariff Retaliation* (1934), an examination of its international implications. On Hoover's problems with the veterans, see W. W. Waters, *B.E.F.: The Whole Story of the Bonus Army* (1933). On a major public work project of the era, see P. L. Kleinsorge, *The Boulder Canyon Project* (1941).

In addition to the books on Secretary Stimson already cited, see the highly critical short study by R. N. Current, *Secretary Stimson: A Study in Statecraft* (1954). A fine scholarly work is R. H. Ferrell, **American Diplomacy in the Great Depression: Hoover-Stimson Foreign Policy, 1929–1933* (1957), based upon multiarchival research and objective in tone. W. S. Myers, *The Foreign Policies of Herbert Hoover, 1929–1933* (1940), is semiofficial and rather dull. A good survey of an area in which the administration had some success is Alexander DeConde, *Herbert Hoover's Latin-American Policy* (1951). On the Manchurian problem, see H. L. Stimson, *The Far Eastern Crisis: Recollections and Observations* (1936). Stimson's own book needs to be compared with two scholarly studies, S. R. Smith, *The Manchurian Crisis, 1931–1932* (1948); and Armin Rappaport, *Henry L. Stimson and Japan, 1931–1933* (1963). Excellent background material is to be found in Owen Lattimore, *Manchuria, Cradle of Conflict* (2nd ed., 1935). For the lasting importance of the Stimson Doctrine, see Robert Langer, *Seizure of Territory, The Stimson Doctrine and Related Principles in Legal Theory and Diplomatic Practice* (1947). Critical in tone is R. N. Stromberg, *Collective Security and American Foreign Policy* (1963). An excellent synthesis which brings out varying interpretations is J. E. Wiltz, **From Isolation to War, 1931–1941* (1968).

A superb account of the 1932 campaign is in Frank Freidel, *The Triumph* (1956), the third volume of his *Franklin D. Roosevelt*. Still useful is R. V. Peel and T. C. Donnelly, *The 1932 Campaign: An Analysis* (1935), by shrewd contemporary observers. While Freidel treats Roosevelt's governorship with insight, see also the topical study by Bernard Bellush, *Franklin D. Roosevelt as Governor of New York* (1955). An important analysis of urban politics of the period is contained in Alex Gottfried, *Boss Cermak of Chicago* (1962), a biography of a Democratic leader who was assassinated soon after leading his party to victory. On the tangled New York City politics of this period see Herbert Mitgang, *The Man Who Rode the Tiger* (1963), a life of Samuel Seabury.

22

THE NEW DEAL

Franklin D. Roosevelt · Direction of the New Deal · Relief · NRA ·
Labor · Farm program · Social security · Banking and securities reform ·
London Economic Conference · Reciprocal Trade Agreements · Tennessee
Valley Authority · Election of 1936 · Supreme Court struggle · Election
of 1938 · The New Deal Balance Sheet

Although the era of the Great Depression was to last until 1940, when defense spending finally brought the much sought "recovery," the period of Franklin Roosevelt's first two terms is almost invariably called the New Deal. This is a tribute to the ability of that colorful President to dramatize his program and, incidentally, to minimize the achievements of his predecessor. Hoover and Franklin Roosevelt were heirs of the progressive tradition in American politics, since they were influenced by Theodore Roosevelt's New Nationalism and Wilson's New Freedom. Both saw what the federal government could do with the economy from their important positions during the First World War. Both took part in the movement to bring about the formation of business trade associations in the 1920's. But the outgoing, convivial Roosevelt was as skillful in practical politics as Hoover was inept. The changeover from the Republican era to that of the Democrats was therefore as dramatic in appearance as it was in reality.

Franklin D. Roosevelt

Few Presidents have been met with as immediate and as terrifying a crisis as that confronting Roosevelt on March 4, 1933. The times called for dynamic leadership and enormous political skill, and Franklin Delano Roosevelt (1882–1945) soon proved that he had both. Born to a comfortable fortune, he was a graduate of Groton and Harvard and a lawyer; he had traveled frequently and spoke French fluently. In 1905 he had married his sixth cousin, Eleanor Roosevelt, a favorite niece of President Theodore Roosevelt. Like the other Roosevelts, they became the parents of a large family. Young Roosevelt, although a Democrat, cast his first vote for his Republican relative, for whom he had great admiration. In 1910 he was elected to the New York legislature, where he won the hatred of Tammany by his fight against its candidate for U.S. Senator. Partly because his

HOLLYWOOD BOWL, CALIFORNIA, a WPA project, gave employment and enjoyment to many Americans.

Franklin D. Roosevelt. *Thirty-second President of the United States, Roosevelt was the first President to break the no-third-term tradition. Few other Presidents have been so deeply loved or so roundly hated. A scion of wealth, he was spurned by his own class as a traitor to it, but was idolized by the underprivileged.*

name was Roosevelt and partly because he was an active pro-Wilson Democrat before the nominating convention, he became Assistant Secretary of the Navy under Woodrow Wilson, a post of major importance which he filled with distinction during the First World War. In 1920 he was the unsuccessful Democratic candidate for Vice-President. His political future was clouded in 1921, when an attack of infantile paralysis left him crippled in both legs. By an exhibition of will power he fought his way back to health and even learned to walk again, although not without firm support. Unconquered in spirit, he read widely, corresponded with political leaders and dedicated himself to the rebuilding of the Democratic Party along progressive lines. In 1928, despite the Republican landslide, he was elected governor of New York, and two years later he was re-elected by a huge

majority. As governor he inaugurated few important policies prior to the Great Crash, but with the coming of the depression he insisted that the state should provide for the hungry. He proposed a state unemployment insurance system and other reforms. His ability to deal adroitly with people, his infectious good humor, and his willingness to dabble with new ideas all enhanced his political standing, already powerful because he was governor of the nation's most populous state. His oratory, which proved to be one of his greatest assets as governor, gave him an additional advantage. He could command and hold the attention of great crowds with set speeches (often sprinkled with wit), but, more importantly, he quickly learned how to reach the public at large with radio talks of a remarkably intimate quality.

Presidential Leadership

Too deft a politician to accept responsibility without power when President Hoover asked for his cooperation in the "interregnum" between election and inauguration, Roosevelt acted quickly as soon as real power was his. He relied to a large extent upon a group of assistants and advisers, some of whom were given sub-cabinet positions, for the shaping of his policies. His cabinet included none of the great names of the Democratic Party, almost all of whom had opposed his nomination, and was chiefly built on personal friendships. Although it contained a few persons of independent mind and genuine ability, the cabinet was generally nondescript. During his campaign Roosevelt had come to appreciate the assistance of a group called "the brain trust," which included three Columbia professors, Raymond Moley, Rexford Guy Tugwell, and Adolf A. Berle, Jr. From these academic advisers, scorned as "theorists" by businessmen and politicians alike, he obtained many of the ideas he now prepared to enact into law.

THE ROOSEVELT BRAINTRUST. *As candidate for the Presidency, Roosevelt drew around himself a number of "bright young men" whose advice he sought and sometimes took. As President, he continued the same policy, but the turnover among his advisers was high. Some of them, like Moley, eventually came out openly against him.*

RAYMOND MOLEY. A professor of public law at Columbia University, Moley was for a time regarded as head of the braintrust. But he lost favor soon after Roosevelt became President, perhaps because he lacked that "passion for anonymity" that Roosevelt craved in his advisers.

The President proved his leadership during the banking crisis. The day after inauguration Roosevelt closed every bank in the country, and by the time he had assembled Congress in special session on March 9 he had ready for instant passage an Emergency Banking Act. Before the day was over, the law received the President's signature, breaking all known records. This measure authorized the Secretary of the Treasury to call in all gold, whether in the shape of coin, bullion, or gold certificates; it provided for the examination and reopening of all banks deemed sound, and for a system of "conservators" to take charge of all others; and it authorized an extensive issue of emergency currency to be used if necessary in halting runs. By March 13, banks which federal examiners found solvent began to reopen and the government's guaranty of their stability proved sufficient to restore public confidence. Only $15 million of the new emergency currency had to be used, and millions of dollars that the banks had paid to anxious depositors during the crisis be-

gan to flow back. Some 3,000 banks, scattered throughout the country, were either reopened under conservators or were not reopened at all, but there was no longer widespread fear about the essential soundness of the banking structure.

During the next few weeks the President had occasion again and again to demonstrate his capacity for effective leadership. Relying on the support of public opinion, he showed an unerring sense of the dramatic. Whether in a radio appeal to the nation or in a personally delivered message to Congress, he seldom failed to time his pronouncements exactly and irresistibly. He held frequent conferences with the representatives of the press, took them freely into his confidence, made them like him, and obtained through them a steady stream of favorable publicity. Like Theodore Roosevelt and Woodrow Wilson before him, he had no scruples about the constitutional right of the Executive to direct the course of legislation. His energetic "braintrusters," sometimes without much help from congressional committees, drafted the laws that Congress was called upon to pass. Although James A. Farley, as Postmaster-General and Democratic National Chairman, sought to manage patronage in such a manner as to aid the passage of legislation, he found it virtually impossible to deny jobs to members of Congress. Furthermore, the number of jobs at his disposal was limited, since several agency heads had no interest in building the power of the Democratic machine. The President knew that the best time to get his program through was while the country still regarded the steps taken as essential to meet an emergency, and while congressmen, with their hunger for patronage unappeased, were unwilling to interrupt the "honeymoon" period with which each new administration begins. To forestall long debates over bothersome details he frequently induced Congress to delegate much discretionary authority to the President himself, or to some executive officer. Thus many of the New Deal measures were passed in more or less skeleton form, with the details to be filled in later by the President and his advisers. Operating in this hasty fashion, the special session of Congress enacted into law within a hundred days many of the principal policies of the New Deal.

Direction of the New Deal

The Emergency Banking Act foretold at the very outset the direction in which the New Deal was to go. With the whole financial system in a state of collapse, the President had an opportunity to effect drastic change. Had he directed Congress to nationalize the banking system, a long step toward the state ownership and administration of all industry and finance would have been taken. He might also have turned to the right, to preserve the private-profit system at the expense, if need be, of democracy. But neither extreme position had any deep rooting in America, and one seemed as unlikely as the other to attract the democratically inclined Roosevelt.

There is no evidence that Roosevelt considered either way. In the 1932 campaign he had made few specific promises but he was clearly a part of the progressive-reform tradition. What he proposed was a middle course, more in line with American precedents. The business of the nation was to be left in private hands, but with controls set up by the government to prevent the ever-recurring booms and crises from which capitalism had suffered so long. Extreme individualism had already been limited by extensive governmental regulation; what Roosevelt had in mind was to extend regulation to the point where it would result in a planned economy. Underlying much of New Deal thought was the assumption that private capitalism had failed to provide a good national life and therefore the state had to assume the role of directing the nation's economic destiny. Since a favored few had been taking too much out of the national pot and the great majority not enough, it was the duty of the government to reapportion the national income by "soaking the rich" with high income and business taxes and using the proceeds for less fortunate groups. All of these ends, Roosevelt believed, might be accomplished by greatly increasing the regulatory powers of the government through the democratic method and without destroying the basic rights of the individual. Beyond this broad theory of a planned economy Roosevelt had few fixed ideas. By nature he was a politician and an experimenter. When his advisers made a proposal that seemed desirable on either political or social grounds, he would support them, even if many of their suggestions seemed to be working at cross purposes. Whatever final shape his program might take, the President was determined to provide relief for the unemployed, to help the farmer, to promote by every means at his disposal the restoration of prosperity, and so to reform the American system that another such depression would not occur.

Applying for Relief Jobs. *This photograph, taken in August, 1935, shows a typical line-up for work relief. Practically everyone preferred jobs to hand outs.*

The New Deal's direction was frequently unclear, for Roosevelt was fond of following several contradictory sets of advisers and policies at once. But the purposes of his programs were clear enough. It was soon apparent that the New Deal had set itself the triple task of relief, recovery, and reform. The legislation of the "hundred days," hastily conceived as it was, pointed toward one or more of these objectives. Inconsistencies were frequent; relief sometimes got in the way of recovery, and recovery in the way of reform. But occasionally, also, reform measures promoted recovery, and recovery almost always helped solve the problem of relief. Whatever their contradictions and interactions, the three goals remained constant, and they were never long forgotten. From time to time changes were based on experience, or even on political expediency, but they were invariably defended as merely a better way of accomplishing what the New Deal had set out to do. Most of the New Deal measures cost money, and the Economy Act, signed by the President on March 20, 1933, was soon recognized as an empty gesture. The savings made under its terms were only temporary, and were soon overbalanced by the extraordinary expenditures undertaken for relief, recovery, and reform.

Relief

In its attack on the relief problem the New Deal amplified what the Hoover administration had already begun. But the New Deal attitude toward relief was far more humanitarian and comprehensive than that of the preceding administration. From the first, Roosevelt insisted that no one should go hungry and that all considerations about social and political theory should be secondary to that objective. If local authorities could not provide food and shelter, then the national government would do it directly or indirectly without pausing to consider the costs and the long-term political or economic effects of such action. Secondly, the New Deal insisted that, if at all possible, jobs should be provided the needy and a direct dole paid only in cases of emergency. Roosevelt's consistent humanitarian spirit was exemplified by his declaration that no government could long afford to run a deficit "in the books of human fortitude." Through the Federal Emergency Relief Administration, created May 12, 1933, contributions instead of RFC loans were made available to the states for relief purposes. The law permitted local authorities to provide either work relief or an outright dole, but since in practice the dole was far more economical than "made work," it was used unsparingly. By the end of 1934 about one-sixth of the population of the country was on some kind of relief. At the head of the FERA was Harry Hopkins, a social work executive who had been in charge of relief activities in New York while Roosevelt was governor. Hopkins believed work relief preferable to the dole for psychological reasons, and under his urging the President established the Civil Works Administration in October, 1933, as a branch of the FERA. Through the CWA an effort was made to provide emergency jobs for workers who might otherwise have spent the winter on relief. The CWA actually gave millions of men the first employment they had had for years, but the per person cost was more expensive than the dole and its planning was still pretty meager. But it was a makeshift affair and, when critics pointed out its many administrative faults, its discontinuance in the spring of 1934 was inevitable.

WPA and CCC

It is clear that both Roosevelt and Hopkins at first underestimated the length of the emergency. During 1934, with recovery still far from evident, they watched relief rolls in vain for any sign of a lessening demand for help. They concluded that the situation would have to be dealt with on a semipermanent basis. At the same time, they wanted the federal program to be one of work relief, with responsibility for the "unemployables" shifted back to the states.

In harmony with these views, the new Relief Act of April 8, 1935, required the government to provide "work relief, and to increase employment by providing useful projects." For this purpose a total of nearly $5 billion was appropriated on the understanding that federal relief officials would help devise work projects, would prescribe rules for the selection of workers, and would regulate the conditions of labor. During the summer of 1935 the FERA handed over to a new Works Progress Administration, established in July under the direction of the energetic Hopkins, the task of providing work for all employables. The wage to be paid on all such projects was a "security wage," lower than that afforded by private employment but higher than the sums paid for direct relief. The WPA also undertook to provide the unemployed with the kind of work they were best fitted to do. By this time the many hastily planned projects of the FERA and the CWA had brought "made work" into ill-repute. Under WPA the nature of the work projects undertaken steadily improved although the derisive term "boondoggling" was applied to some of its projects. For the unskilled laborers, who con-

Hopkins and Unemployables. *These physically handicapped individuals are shown protesting to Harry L. Hopkins, Roosevelt's relief administrator, against being classified as "unemployables." Hopkins is to the right, and Harry Friedman, spokesman for the delegation, to the left.*

WORKS PROGRESS ADMINISTRATION. *The WPA undertook to provide as many as possible jobs for the unemployed, not merely at unskilled labor, but in the occupations to which the jobseekers had been accustomed when employed.*

SHARON WOODS PARK, SHARONVILLE, OHIO. This combination bridge and dam was built with WPA labor.

stituted the great majority of relief workers, jobs were found on such projects as the construction of country roads and city streets, the improvement of parks and playgrounds, and the building of flood-control or irrigation dams. Carpenters, plasterers, masons, plumbers, and other skilled laborers were used to erect or repair schoolhouses, libraries, city halls, courthouses, and other public buildings. Even the "white-collar" classes were not neglected, and projects were devised to aid artists, writers, actors, musicians, architects, and many others possessed of more or less professional abilities. At one time about 80 per cent of the nation's top-ranking artists were on the WPA rolls. Few aspects of American life were unaffected by the activities of the WPA. Supplementary to its program was the work of the National Youth Administration, through which needy high school and college students were enabled to earn small sums by assisting their teachers, while equally needy young people who were not in school were provided with useful part-time jobs.

Over a six-year span the WPA spent $11.3 billion, of which $4 billion were spent on roads and streets, $1 billion on public buildings, $1 billion on publicly owned utilities, and $2.5 billion on community projects, which included schools and recreation facilities. By 1941 the WPA had employed at one time or another 8 million different individuals, or about one-fifth of all workers in the country. The average number of WPA workers varied from 2 million in 1937 to well over 3 million in November, 1938, an election month. The WPA was terminated by the war in 1944, but as late as 1940, in the midst of the rearmament boom, it still had 2 million workers on its rolls. Although its appropriations passed by wide margins, the WPA was vigorously attacked partly because of its size and the extent of its operations. Labor leaders were critical because it paid lower wages than the "going rate," and conservatives because it was far more expensive than the dole. The Republicans charged, at times with good reason, that the relief rolls were being used by the administration for political purposes. The WPA had its vehement defenders, too. Scarcely a community had not benefited by repaired or newly constructed public buildings, improved streets and highways, new parks, playgrounds, and swimming pools, together with other more or less permanent contributions to the convenience and comfort of the public.

A relief project particularly cherished by the President was the Civilian Conservation Corps, created in 1933. The purpose of this

Civilian Conservation Corps. *CCC men are shown here moving a beam into place for the foundations of a bridge in a national park.*

organization was to establish conservation camps in every part of the country providing work for unmarried young men between the ages of eighteen and twenty-five. The CCC soon had more than 250,000 youths at work under army officers clearing forests, planting trees, improving roads, and preventing floods. Enlistments were for one year. The men received $1 a day each in addition to medical care and maintenance, but were required to allot $25 a month to dependents or relatives. Many of them were improved in health and morale as a result of their experience. The CCC lasted until well after the entrance of the United States into the Second World War.

Pump Priming and Recovery

The second broad objective of the New Deal was to get the economic wheels turning again so that jobs would be available for all those able to work, business would be profitable, and agricultural prices would rise. Government spending on a vast scale,

or, as it later came to be called, "pump priming," was to be a main instrument in the attempt at recovery. Consequently the RFC established during Hoover's administration was given greatly increased powers to lend huge sums to private industry, as well as to public agencies, at very low rates of interest. Starved for credit, the business world eagerly accepted billions in governmental loans, and eventually repaid most of them with interest. Supplementing this lending policy was a program of direct spending on public construction. The Public Works Administration, created in the opening days of the New Deal, was supplied by Congress with $3.3 billion to build post offices, harbors, and dams in the hope that such a large construction program would provide much new business for heavy industries and for the construction trades. Actually, the PWA developed slowly, partly because of the rigid honesty of its administrator, Secretary of Interior Harold L. Ickes, and partly because detailed plans for large projects took time to provide. Not until the business recession of 1937–1938 did the PWA become important. But by 1939 it had sponsored projects in all but three counties within the United States at an estimated cost of nearly $6 billion. And unquestionably the PWA helped the country recover from the 1937–1938 recession in much the same way that the other spending programs aided more general recovery.

A Managed Economy

A number of New Deal advisers were strongly influenced by the writings of the English economist John Maynard Keynes (1883–1946). Keynes considered budget-balancing to be a positive danger to economic recovery and argued in favor of government spending. It was his hope that the government could thus encourage private initiative by providing it with assistance; common American usage quickly dubbed this "pump priming." Keynes favored putting funds in the hands of those who would spend them for goods; he also thought that cheap credit and lower taxes would also aid the economy. His goal of recovery involved full employment and a greatly increased national product.

Keynes had also written extensively about the need for modern states to intervene radically in the economy for the purpose of directing the national output toward greater social utility. And though Roosevelt apparently was not directly influenced by the English economist, very early in the depression the President indicated his belief that a managed economy was necessary to achieve an equitable national life. In his speech of September 23, 1932, at the Commonwealth Club of San Francisco, the most philosophical of his campaign addresses, he stated that the main task before the country was not the further "discovery or exploitation of natural resources or necessarily producing more goods," but rather the job of "adjusting production to consumption, of distributing wealth and products more equitably." Although he then declared that the government should assume powers to direct the economy "only as a last resort," by 1933 he clearly felt that the time had come when it was necessary, if recovery were to be achieved, for the government to become a major partner in the shaping of the economy.

Recovery: The NRA

The most ambitious of the New Deal efforts to restore prosperity was the National Recovery Administration of 1933, under the terms of the National Industrial Recovery Act. The NRA, some of the ideas for which originated in the United States Chamber of Commerce, was the chief effort to devise a planned economy. As the depression deepened, many businesses sought to survive by slashing prices and by cutthroat selling. The purpose of the NRA was to permit industry and commerce to govern themselves in order to suppress "unfair competition," to apportion markets, limit production, and, to a degree, eliminate price competition. In return for such privileges, quite contrary to the antitrust laws, business had to agree to shorten working hours, raise wages, and attempt to increase employment. For all businesses not organized under their own individual "code" authority, the President issued a blanket code, which abolished child labor, fixed a thirty-five-hour week for ordinary labor with a minimum wage of forty cents an hour, and a forty-hour week for white-collar jobs with minimum wages of twelve to fifteen dollars a week. Labor had little voice in the making of the codes, and the interest of consumers was entirely ignored.

Under the energetic but erratic leadership of General Hugh S. Johnson, the NRA made a valiant effort to live up to the high hopes of those who sponsored it. But soon difficulties in the enforcement of the NRA codes appeared. "Chiselers" who ignored the rules put the honest dealer at a serious disadvantage. Wartime compulsion was lacking, and the hope that the code authorities set up by each business group could secure the obedience of all members proved illusive. Small business complained that the codes favored large industries, and a few important establishments, including the Ford Motor Company, refused entirely to cooperate. Business was extremely irritated at organized labor, which had regained much of its strength and used the strike persistently in trying to achieve its demands. Finally General Johnson, following a tempestuous outbreak against labor for its failure to do its part, as he saw it, resigned in September, 1934. By now the NRA was little more than a shambles. The following May the United States Supreme Court in a unanimous opinion found the law under which the NRA had been operating to be unconstitutional. The decision of the Court, that too much authority had been delegated by Congress to the President, and that the existing emergency gave Congress no authority that it would not have otherwise, angered the President. The already-feeble NRA organization was rapidly dismantled.

The Rise of Labor

Despite the New Deal's concern for workingmen, Roosevelt's initial plans for recovery from the depression paid scant attention to the trade unions, which had declined in strength in the 1920's. Thus his original proposals for the NRA had not included any labor provisions beyond those permitting him to set minimum wage and maximum hour provisions. To obtain the necessary votes in Congress, the historic Section 7(a) had to be added to the NRA bill. This section declared that labor had "the right to organize and bargain collectively through representatives of their own choosing." To implement the radical new labor policy, the President established a National Labor Board whose functions were taken over by the much more powerful National Labor Relations Board established by Congress in the summer of 1934. Under the stimulus of Section 7(a) and protected by a series of pro-labor decisions of the National Labor Relations Board, many unions which had been long dormant were reinvigorated in 1934–1935, with a consequent swelling of membership rolls and the outbreak of numerous strikes for union recognition, higher wages, and shorter hours. The renewed union activity drew bitter criticism from business interests and probably also helped persuade the President that a strong labor movement by its insistence on higher wages and shorter hours would aid recovery. After the NRA was declared unconstitutional, the administration actively supported the National Labor Relations Act, designed to soften the blow sustained by labor in the loss of Section 7(a).

The Wagner Labor Act

The Wagner Act, as the new labor bill was called after its sponsor, Senator Robert Wagner of New York, became with later modifications the basic federal statute controlling national labor relations. As such it was one of the New Deal's most important measures and one of the most controversial. Adding to the permissive grant of power to unions given by Section 7(a), the act placed the power of the government actively behind the organization of unions by enjoining all employers from certain types of anti-union activity. As well as declaring the refusal of an employer "to bargain collectively with representatives of his employees" as an unfair labor practice, it also denied the employer the right to "interfere with, restrain or coerce employees," to contribute financial or other support to so-called company unions, and to encourage or discourage membership in any union by hiring or firing practices. The act also provided for the creation of a National Labor Relations Board empowered to hold elections among workers for the purposes of collective bargaining, to hold investigations on an employee's charge of an unfair labor practice, and to issue cease and desist orders if in its judgment the charges were valid. The NLRB so zealously set about its function to implement the Wagner Act — one of its rulings denied to employers the right to criticize publicly any union activity and thus curtailed the basic right of free speech — that it excited widespread criticism and at times even incurred Roosevelt's displeasure. Its solicitous attitude, however, enabled the union movement to make almost revolutionary gains.

The C.I.O.

One result of the revitalized unionism was the division of organized labor into two competing organizations. Through the early days of the New Deal the American Federation of Labor adhered to the traditional Gompers policy of organizing most of its member unions on the basis of craft or skill. Even in the new mass production industries, where automatic machinery had made obsolete many individual skills and where most employees were simply production workers, the A.F. of L. insisted on dividing these new recruits among its old trade unions, which, on the whole, were governed by conservative-minded leaders preoccupied with problems of the skilled artisans. The mass production industries employed many Negroes and new immigrants, groups which the traditional A.F. of L. leaders had found it difficult to organize.

John L. Lewis, militant head of the United Mine Workers, one of the few industrially organized unions, took the lead in the formation of a Committee for Industrial Organization to promote the unionization of industries as units and not in ac-

cordance with specified trades or skills. Lewis was opposed by the A.F. of L. Executive Board, but, with the support of his own and several other powerful unions, he sent organizers into many of the great mass-production industries, such as automobiles, steel, textiles, rubber, aluminum, plate glass, and furniture. In most instances the C.I.O. plan of organization and fervent spirit met a long-felt need, old unions took on new life, and new unions were founded as needed. For cooperating with Lewis in his endeavors ten unions were expelled in 1936 from the A.F. of L., and as a result the C.I.O. assumed a separate identity. Claiming to represent a membership of nearly 4 million workers as against the 5 million A.F. of L., the C.I.O. changed its name in November, 1938, to the Congress of Industrial Organizations, and elected Lewis as its first president.

ORGANIZED LABOR. *Dissensions within labor led finally to an open split between the AFL and the CIO.*

THE AFL AND CIO LEADERS, Green and Lewis, are depicted as "Rival Builders" by Pease in the *Newark Evening News.*

The "Sit-down"

The methods by which the C.I.O. had risen to such great importance involved among other things the use of a weapon new to American labor history, the "sit-down" strike. Workers, instead of first leaving the factories and then picketing them to prevent the employment of "scabs," simply retained in idleness the posts they ordinarily held, and forcibly resisted removal. This technique was successfully employed in C.I.O. strikes against two leading automobile companies, the General Motors Corporation and the Chrysler Corporation. In both instances, with the assistance of Governor Frank Murphy of Michigan, agreements were finally reached to vacate the plants on condition that the C.I.O. union be recognized as the bargaining agent for its members, while later negotiations won other concessions. The United States Steel Corporation, long the despair of labor leaders, in March, 1937, quickly accorded the C.I.O. Steel Workers' Organizing Committee full bargaining authority for all its employees. Most of the other "Big Steel" companies also capitulated, but the "Little Steel" companies fought back. Strikes that began in May, 1937, spread rapidly through Pennsylvania, Ohio, and Illinois, and were accompanied by much disorder. Quick action of the employers prevented sit-down strikes, and without this weapon the unions lost the first round in the struggle. The steel companies, also, as the Senate Civil Liberties Committee's investigation of the strike revealed, had enrolled private armies equipped with modern arms and had liberally employed labor spies and strikebreakers. Shocked by these facts, public sentiment eventually supported the unions, and subsequent action by the NLRB ultimately brought a union victory in 1941.

Continued conflict between capital and labor after 1936 wearied the public and irritated the President. Many other Americans were alienated by the growing violence of C.I.O. activities and by certain strikes which they attributed to Communist agitators. The increasing disenchantment with organized labor, as well as a desire to protect non-union labor, prompted the search for other solutions to the wage problem and aided the passage of the Fair Labor Standards Act of 1938. By this act a national minimum wage and a maximum work week were set for restricted groups. The original minimum wage was set at twenty-five cents an hour and the maximum work week at forty-four hours, to be reduced to forty hours by 1940. Subsequent legislation after World War II raised the minimum wage and greatly extended the groups of workers covered. Few permanent acts of the New Deal were more revolutionary than the "Wages and Hours Act," which introduced government regulation into the very basis of the free market mechanism.

Agricultural Recovery

Parallel to the New Deal program for industry and labor was an equally comprehensive plan for the rehabilitation of agriculture. Striking out along what the President himself called "a new and untrod path," the Agricultural Adjustment Act of May 12, 1933, sought a remedy for the chronic overproduction that had for so long kept farm prices down. Frankly recognizing that the export market was too unreliable to be a factor in their planning, the framers of the act proposed to restrict the American output, if need be, to what the United States alone could consume. By careful supervision of production, the real income of farmers was to be brought back to the average levels of the five years preceding the First World War. An Agricultural Adjustment Administration was set up with authority to buy and hold surpluses of staple commodities, and to contract with the producers of specified basic commodities for whatever cooperation might be

Starving Livestock Win Relief. *Drought conditions in the western Middle West left Minnesota livestock in a desperate plight. A delegation of farmers, by displaying on the steps of the state Capitol a starving horse, a dying cow, and a lean hog, won a $500,000 appropriation for feed.*

needed to insure crop control. The cost involved in the crop-restriction program was to be met by a tax levied against the processors of farm produce, who in turn would pass the burden along to the consumers. The farmer would find himself at last on a parity with other economic groups.

Organized in the Department of Agriculture under Secretary Henry A. Wallace, the AAA experimented with crop-reduction programs, at first in cotton, wheat, corn, and hogs, then in numerous other farm products. As anticipated, benefit payments cut down production and brought up prices, although the prolonged drought of the western half of the Mississippi Valley probably affected the situation even more than the AAA. So devastating was the drought in some western states that many farmers had little to live on except the money they received from the government under their crop-reduction programs; furthermore, windstorms that swept through the western "dustbowl" threatened to render much land permanently useless. Caustic criticism of the AAA program was inevitable. Crop reduction, at a time when drought conditions threatened the country with shortages, was difficult to defend. Farmers whose lifelong habits had been based upon growing more on their lands found it hard to adjust to an economy of growing less. They signed the contracts and accepted the benefit payments because they needed the money, but they resented the system. The program had little for the marginal farmers and sharecroppers, since it was directed at the principal commercial crop producers. Processors complained bitterly at the heavy taxation forced upon them, and found themselves seriously handicapped in competing for foreign markets. Consumers paid steeply increased prices for nearly everything that came from the farm.

The AAA Invalidated

In spite of these criticisms the country was hardly prepared for the drastic action of the United States Supreme Court that announced January 6, 1936, in a six-to-three decision, that the AAA was unconstitutional. Justice Owen J. Roberts held that there was nothing in the Constitution to justify federal control of agricultural production; Congress had invaded a right reserved to the states. The implications of this decision disturbed the minority of the Court, which in a dissenting opinion of Justice Harlan F. Stone warned the majority that "courts are not the only agency of government that must be assumed to have capacity to govern."

In wrecking the AAA the Supreme Court did not destroy the entire New Deal structure for dealing with agriculture. A new Farm Credit Administration, established in March, 1933, had taken over every federal agency that had anything to do with agricultural credits. By 1934 it was lending on an average rate of $5 million a day. Much of this credit was used to refinance mortgages that might otherwise have been foreclosed, but loans for production and for marketing were also supplied. As a further aid in dealing with the mortgage problem, the Frazier-Lemke Moratorium Act of 1935 delayed foreclosure proceedings for a three-year period, provided a court of law would give its approval, both to the propriety of the delay and to the adequacy of the rental to be paid. For the benefit of farmers who were still keeping up the unequal struggle against marginal or sub-marginal lands the Resettlement Administration was formed in April, 1935. Its chief purpose was to buy up land from which farmers could not ordinarily make a living, and then to "resettle" the dispossessed owners in "healthy rural communities." The RA was less successful than its proponents had hoped, and eventually, renamed the Farm Security Administration, it turned its attention chiefly to helping tenant farmers become land owners.

The New AAA

The critical condition of agriculture required that some substitute be found immediately for the AAA. As a stopgap measure, Congress enacted in February, 1936, the Soil Conservation and Domestic Allotment Act. Direct payments to farmers were to be continued, but henceforth they were to be made in return for cooperation with the government in an elaborate program for the promotion of soil fertility, the prevention of erosion, and the more economic use of farm land. By placing restrictions on the planting of soil-depleting crops, some effort was made to control the production of such basic commodities as cotton, wheat, and corn, but surpluses continued to pile up.

Finally, in 1938 Congress enacted a new Agricultural Adjustment Act retaining the soil-conservation and benefit-payment features of the preceding program, and making provisions to limit the acreage allotments of wheat, cotton, corn, tobacco, and rice crops in accordance with probable needs. It also authorized the making of storage loans as a means of holding agricultural surpluses off the market; and it sanctioned resort to marketing quotas in emergencies, provided that two-thirds of the growers of the commodity concerned recorded their approval in a referendum vote. The sum of $212 million was appropriated in 1939 for "parity payments" to help bridge the gap between current prices and "parity prices" defined as those in the same ratio with other groups as existed in 1909–1914, a very good time for agriculture. For the benefit of wheat growers, a Federal Crop Insurance Corporation was established in the Department of Agriculture from which guaranties could be obtained to the amount of 50 or 75 per cent of normal yields.

Although participation in the AAA program was kept purely voluntary, the generous subsidies were hard for farmers to resist. About 5.25 million agricultural producers took part in the 1939 program, which involved nearly three-fourths of the crop land of the nation. An "ever normal granary" was promoted by loans on warehouse surpluses. By this device both producer and consumer hoped to be protected against shortages and price fluctuations. The marketing quota provisions of the act were also promptly invoked to protect the prices of cotton and of several types of tobacco, while nearly 170,000 wheat growers, some of them in drought-threatened

A TOWNSENDITE CONVENTION. Delegates to the first convention of the movement giving the Townsend pledge of allegiance, October 25, 1935.

DR. FRANCIS E. TOWNSEND. This sixty-eight year old resident of Long Beach, California, was the author of the plan and the leader of the movement.

OLD AGE PENSIONS. *A strong demand for government assistance to the aged was embodied in the Townsend Old Age Revolving Fund scheme.*

areas where there was little prospect of a crop, took out federal crop insurance. The cost of all this to the government exceeded $500 million annually in the prewar years and $2 billion to $3 billion after World War II.

Sinclair, Townsend, and Long

At times the Roosevelt administration slowed down the pace of reform while it studied matters at greater length than many persons felt was necessary. While his advisers studied proposals for unemployment insurance and old-age pensions, they worked in an atmosphere where other reformers were reaching a wide public. Upton Sinclair (1878–1968), novelist and perennial Socialist candidate for office, won the Democratic nomination for governor of California in 1934 with a complex plan to End Poverty in California (EPIC). Two features of the EPIC plan were a state pension of $50 per month for California residents over sixty who were "in need" and an elaborate scheme to put the unemployed to work producing goods for their own use. Sinclair, a tireless orator and pamphleteer, frightened conservatives and proved too radical even for the New Dealers, who did nothing to save him from defeat. One of the few Democrats to lose in 1934, Sinclair had prepared the way for future reforms. Another influential propagandist was Dr. Francis E. Townsend (1867–1960), a retired California physician. Tall, erect, dignified, he carried his gospel to the aged throughout the country. The Townsend Plan proposed to promote recovery by means of a $200 per month pension to all persons over sixty who were no longer gainfully employed and who agreed to spend the whole sum during that month. The "good doctor" proposed to finance the scheme by means of a 2 per cent tax on every transaction of business at every level. Most colorful of all the agitators was Huey P.

Huey P. Long. *This photograph of the controversial Senator from Louisiana was taken after a press interview in New York City, January 10, 1935.*

Long (1893–1935), who proposed a guaranteed annual income of $5,000 for every American family. As governor of Louisiana, Long had forced through his legislature a tax reform which financed impressive programs in public education, state institutions, and road-building. As United States Senator, he helped Roosevelt win the Democratic nomination in 1932 but soon became dissatisfied with Roosevelt's financial caution and with the administration's patronage policies. Long was a brilliant lawyer, something not always evident to the public which was either enchanted or horrified by his oafish, earthy mannerisms. By early 1935 Senator Long's vigorous "Share-Our-

Wealth" campaign, which he coupled with attacks on Roosevelt and the New Dealers, was beginning to have an impact in rural and small-town America. Long's assassination in the capitol building at Baton Rouge in September, 1935, removed from the scene the most colorful American demagogue of his time. Whether he was a power-mad dictator or a genuine friend of the poor was debated then and since. What is not in doubt is that Long did much to make Americans aware of the maldistribution of the national income and of the urgent need for drastic change.

Reform: Social Security

The third great objective of Roosevelt's New Deal was to reform existing institutions so that the possibility of another great depression would be minimized, and, in case another similar disaster was experienced, much of the personal distress of the thirties would be avoided. One of the most comprehensive New Deal reforms, and one which unquestionably touched more Americans than any other, was in social security. In an act of August 14, 1935, Congress established the Social Security Board, providing for old-age annuities, unemployment insurance, and more adequate care for the needy, the dependent, and the disabled. Until 1935 protection against these hazards had been a private matter, a not illogical situation as long as the country was largely agricultural. But now with a majority of the population living in cities and dependent upon a weekly pay check, the necessity for some such legislation was apparent.

The Social Security Act

The Social Security Act was called "the most complex measure ever considered by Congress." (1) By the familiar dollar-matching device it enabled the federal government to assist the states in the care of those physically unable to work. It particularly encouraged state provision for old-age pensions, for the care of dependent children, and for assistance to the needy blind. (2) It authorized grants to promote through state agencies the rehabilitation of the physically disabled, the care of mothers and children, and the improvement of the public health. Its most notable provisions, however, set up (3) an elaborate federal-state system of unemployment compensation, and (4) a strictly federal system of old-age insurance.

The plan for unemployment compensation required that each state desiring to cooperate with the federal government establish for the purpose an appropriate administrative agency. Because of the widely divergent conditions in different parts of the nation, the states were permitted considerable latitude in devising regulations to meet local requirements. Funds for the support of the program were provided by a payroll tax, paid by employers.

By the summer of 1937 all states and territories had complied with the requirements of the Social Security Act, and the next year the payment of benefits began. As the result of a series of political compromises the law excluded from its operation all government employees, farm laborers, domestic servants, casual workers, and the employees of charitable organizations. Yet probably half the working population of the country came under its protection. Anyone without work was required to register at his local employment office, which must try to help him find another job. If, after a specified waiting period, he remained unemployed, benefit payments were authorized. These payments continued until the worker had either exhausted all his wage credits, had reached the maximum period permitted by law, or had secured a job.

The Social Security Act provided for monthly payment benefits to eligible workers in industry and commerce who retired from employment at the age of sixty-five. The same groups were excepted from its operations as were denied the advantages of unemployment compensation. Payments were to begin on January 1, 1942, and were to continue until the time of death, with lump-sum settlements payable to the estates of those who died before reaching the age of sixty-five. Funds for carrying out the program were to be obtained by a tax on employees, deducted from their wages by employers, and an excise tax on payrolls. Equal sums were collected from employers and employees, at first amounting to a total of two per cent of the worker's income. All payments were made to a Trust Fund established by the Treasury, and it was expected that over a period of years the receipts and payments would be in approximate balance. By the time the promised payments began, some 25.5 million people were eligible for retirement benefits. Experience with the social security program led Congress to expand the original legislation repeatedly.

The Housing Problem

Another type of New Deal reform was that designed to eliminate city slums and provide better housing for the underprivileged. Coupled with this problem was the need of providing relief for large numbers of homeowners who would otherwise lose their property through mortgage foreclosures. To meet these needs government credit was for a time extended through the Home Owners' Loan Corporation, the purpose of which was to refinance home mortgages, and through locally established Federal Savings and Loan Associations, to provide funds for new building. When its lending ceased in 1936, the HOLC had acquired mortgages totaling $3 billion and had helped some million homeowners. The HOLC was probably the most effective relief measure for the middle class.

Federal Housing. *These modern apartments, built under the terms of the National Housing Act of 1937, replaced city slums.*

Another agency, the Federal Housing Administration, established in 1934, undertook to insure home mortgages of which it approved up to 80 (later 90) per cent of the appraised value of the property. This left private capital to provide the money, but the FHA took most of the risk. The most ambitious of the efforts to deal with housing came with the establishment of the United States Housing Authority in 1937. The purpose of this agency was to aid local communities to remedy their "shortage of decent, safe, and sanitary dwellings for families of low income." As a result of USHA activities, nineteen low-rent apartment houses had been constructed by the end of 1939 in thirteen different cities, and loans of more than $500 million for the use of 155 communities had been approved.

Financial Reforms

An important group of New Deal reforms was a series of financial regulatory measures aimed at correcting pre-1930 abuses and excesses. These and other measures made the government so potent in directing the nation's economy that the stock and commodity markets ever since have responded as much to the political news from Washington as they have to private economic stimuli. Kindred reform measures also directly affected the nation's prime interstate and oceanic carriers, the production and distribution of electric power, and the terms of international trade by alteration of the tariff rates.

Among the major financial measures was the Glass-Steagall Act of 1933 which, in addition to guaranteeing small depositors against bank failures, divorced commercial and investment banking; permitted national banks to establish branch banks; gave the Federal Reserve Board the right to place severe restrictions upon banks lending too freely for speculative purposes; forbade loans from their own banks to the executive officers of Federal Reserve Banks; and expanded the Federal Reserve System to include industrial and savings banks. Two years later, the old Federal Reserve Board was replaced by a Board of Governors of seven members appointed by the President, with widely expanded powers.

The President also seemed determined to experiment with a managed currency which would have the same buying power at all times. To the dismay of many conservatives, he promptly took the United States off the gold standard and secured from Congress a Gold Repeal Resolution which invalidated the gold clauses employed in many public and private contracts. Gold exports were forbidden; gold coin, gold bullion, and gold certificates were taken out of circulation; and a price fixed by the government was paid for all gold newly mined in the United States or offered for sale from abroad. A few months later, under the terms of a new Silver Purchasing Act, the Treasury began to buy silver, ostensibly to increase the supply of silver in the national monetary stocks. The effect of these measures upon the purchasing power of the dollar was far less marked than the President and his monetary advisers had anticipated, although the United States was soon in possession of most of the world's gold and silver. As long as this treasure remained impounded, there seemed to be no grave threat of currency inflation, except by congressional issues of paper money. Against this latter eventuality, however, the President took a firm and successful stand. Price levels of the mid-1930's remained below those of the 1920's.

Another Roosevelt reform was an attempt to deal with the problems of speculative investment. In 1934 an act established the Securities and Exchange Commission to take over from the Federal Trade Commission the administration of these regulations. While it was beyond the power of the SEC to guarantee the purchasers of securities against loss, it could and did compel the disclosure of such information as might enable investors to form intelligent opinions. The SEC was authorized also to restrict buying on margin or the purchase of stock on credit, to license stock exchanges, and to regulate their practices so as to stimulate legitimate trading and discourage mere gambling.

The London Economic Conference

Very early in his administration the President was called upon to decide whether he could achieve his domestic objectives and at the same time cooperate with other nations in an effort to conquer the world-wide depression. Apparently he at first thought that the two were not incompatible. He accepted, seemingly without reservation, the commitments of his predecessor with respect to American participation in the World Economic Conference to be held in London during the summer of 1933. He even considered permitting a discussion of war debts, although he finally held back. He appointed as head of the American delegation Secretary of State Hull, a strong supporter of the general lowering of trade barriers.

But a month after the Conference began and before the serious differences among the nations had become fully evident, Roosevelt abruptly announced that he would seek recovery in the United States through the establishment of a "sound internal economic system." His advisers had convinced him that he could not effectively intervene in the home free market to support and regulate prices and wages, and at the same time attempt to reestablish a free international market. In fact, the program of legislation which the President had pushed through Congress was based on the assumption that the United States would not tie its hands by international commitments. Since American assistance was fundamental in the development of any world program, there was nothing left for the Conference to do but wind up its affairs and go home.

It is highly doubtful if the Conference had had any real chance of success, for the differences between the British-led sterling group and the gold bloc (headed by France) were intense. Roosevelt's "torpedoing" of the gathering was much less significant than many thought. He felt that his main job was to achieve economic recovery in America. The community of interest necessary for world economic stabilization simply did not exist in 1933. The new President saw no hope for its early emergence and was unwilling to jeopardize his own domestic program for a lost cause.

Reciprocal Trade Agreements

On the old question of tariff reform, the New Deal made considerable headway. Wisely refraining from the customary effort at direct revision downward, it left the Hawley-Smoot Tariff in force, but proposed through a series of reciprocal trade agreements to bring duties on imports down to more reasonable levels. By this means, the customary "logrolling" by Congressmen representing constituents with special interests was avoided. A Trade Agreements Act, passed in June, 1934, authorized the President for a three-year period to negotiate agreements with other countries for the mutual lowering of tariff rates. Without referring the matter to Congress for consent, he might lower the existing duties by as much as 50 per cent, provided only that the free list not be disturbed. The exercise of this grant of authority, which was repeatedly renewed, fell at first to Secretary of State Cordell Hull, a lifelong devotee of the low-tariff principle. In five years Hull concluded more than twenty agreements, including two with Great Britain and Canada that were particularly comprehensive. Perhaps three-fourths of the exports and imports of the United States were affected, and as a result of the improved trade relations thus made possible, good will toward the United States mounted rapidly, especially among the nations of Latin America.

Electric Power and TVA

Although the electrical power industry had made great technical advances during the twenties, it had shown little sense of obligation to the public. Local distributing companies were ruthlessly combined into interstate giants which were promptly gathered up by holding companies which in turn were often controlled by top holding companies to the enormous profit of a few financial manipulators. Efforts of the New Deal to obtain a "death sentence" for all public utility holding companies failed, but Congress did give the Securities and Exchange Commission authority to limit their operations.

A dramatic approach to the problem of securing the maximum social benefits from electrical power was made through the creation of the Tennessee Valley Authority, a public corporation whose activities eventually extended far beyond the production of electric power. In this area the Roosevelt administration was ready to go much further than mere regulation and to experiment with actual government ownership and operation. Effectively guided by Senator George W. Norris of Nebraska, it singled out the Tennessee Valley for its first great project. This region, ramifying into seven states — Tennessee, Kentucky, Alabama, Mississippi, Virginia, North Carolina, and Georgia — and embracing some 40,000 square miles, seemed to offer an ideal testing ground for New Deal theories on social and economic planning. Here were a high proportion of the underprivileged, whom cheap power was expected to benefit; and here were vast natural resources, most of them inadequately exploited or being allowed to degenerate. Since the government had already spent huge sums upon the Muscle Shoals development, Norris believed that results might speedily be obtained in this region.

In May, 1933, Congress authorized the President to appoint a board of three directors, known as the Tennessee Valley Authority, to control the mighty project. The TVA was authorized to construct dams for the improvement of navigation and the control of floods; to develop new forms of fertilizer and to promote their use; to build and operate hydroelectric plants and to distribute the power they generated; and to take such other steps as it might see fit to promote the agricultural and industrial development of the region. The TVA was quickly organized, and with the Muscle Shoals plant as a starting point was soon supplying cheap electric power to a limited area. With the help of PWA funds it pushed rapidly the construction of six new dams, the largest of which, the Norris Dam, was completed in 1936. By 1940 TVA power was being generated at four dams, and was used both to carry forward new construction and to provide cheap power for residential and commercial consumers. By June, 1939, according to TVA estimates,

THE TENNESSEE VALLEY AUTHORITY. *This undertaking proved to be one of the outstanding achievements of the New Deal. TVA reservoirs eventually covered a total of 756,321 acres, and water releases from them kept the Tennessee River navigable from Knoxville to the Ohio, some 650 miles. TVA supplies current for the Atomic Energy Commission activities at Oak Ridge, Tennessee.*

FONTANA DAM. This 480-foot-high structure, on the Little Tennessee River in North Carolina, is TVA's highest dam.

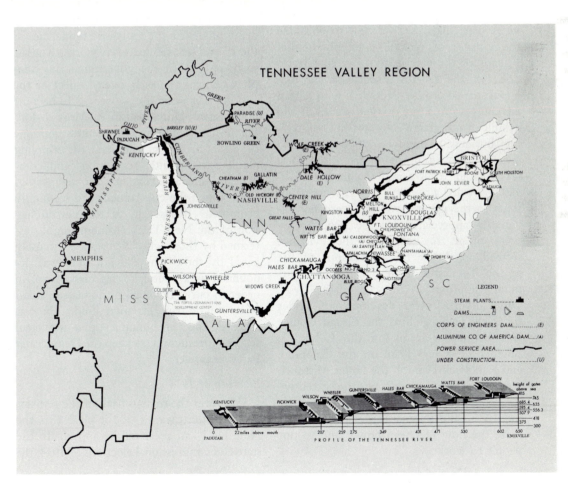

TENNESSEE VALLEY REGION

the Authority was serving about 180,000 customers, either directly or indirectly, and its acquisition later in the year of facilities belonging to the Tennessee Electric Power Company added perhaps 150,000 more.

Varieties of TVA Endeavor

The work of the TVA spread as time went on into many fields. It carried on an elaborate program for water control, and the consequent checking of erosion; it produced great quantities of fertilizer, and tested its effectiveness in most of the states of the Union; it experimented with low-cost housing for its employees; it promoted actively the use of the Tennessee River for commercial navigation; it extended the advantages of electricity to many farmers through a program of rural electrification; and it cooperated generously with local authorities in providing public-health services, particularly with a view to checking the ravages of malaria and tuberculosis. Friends of the competitive system bitterly criticized the TVA as a socialistic and monopolistic enterprise endowed with unfair advantages. As a tax exempt agency it had a built-in advantage over private tax-paying business. Moreover, as was pointed out, it removed property from the local tax rolls and thus raised the rates on privately owned property. TVA's contributions to the general welfare were not invariably appreciated by the people they were meant to help, but the evidence seemed conclusive that conditions of life in the Tennessee Valley had been enormously improved by the work of the TVA. Other hydroelectric developments under the New Deal, such as the Grand Coulee and Bonneville Dams on the Columbia, Boulder (Hoover) Dam on the Colorado, and Fort Peck Dam on the upper Missouri, were not accompanied by the extensive program of social betterment promoted by the TVA. But they were designed to promote the flow of cheap power and to put people to work.

Opposition to the New Deal

Naturally the extensive program of change under the New Deal aroused intense opposition. The policy of spending as freely to defeat the depression as the nation would spend to defeat an enemy in time of war provoked critics to the direst prophecies. When Hoover took office the national debt had stood at more than $17 billion; when he left office, at nearly $21 billion. But the New Deal expenditures by 1940 had doubled the debt of 1933, and the $45 billion limit set by Congress during the First World War soon had to be raised.

Moreover, the New Deal tax bill, frankly labeled by some of its proponents as one designed to "soak the rich," had raised income taxes to their highest peacetime levels. How long could the nation continue to "soak" the rich and to spend so lavishly without danger of bankruptcy? To many observers the socialistic tendencies of the New Deal seemed even worse than the spending. With the government in complete control of nearly every aspect of the nation's economic life, what was to become of "rugged individualism"? More baldly stated, how could private business continue to make profits in the face of crippling taxes, governmental regulation and competition, and an arrogance on the part of labor which the government had seemingly promoted? Roosevelt, as the personification of the New Deal, although highly esteemed by those who liked it, was intensely hated by those who did not. He was denounced as a traitor to his class, who, in order to curry favor with the masses, stood ready to destroy his own kind. He was accused, too, of building up a powerful federal bureaucracy to keep the Democratic Party in power.

Election of 1936

Whatever the reasons back of the returns, early elections soon made it clear that the New Deal had great public appeal. In the state and congressional elections of 1934, the

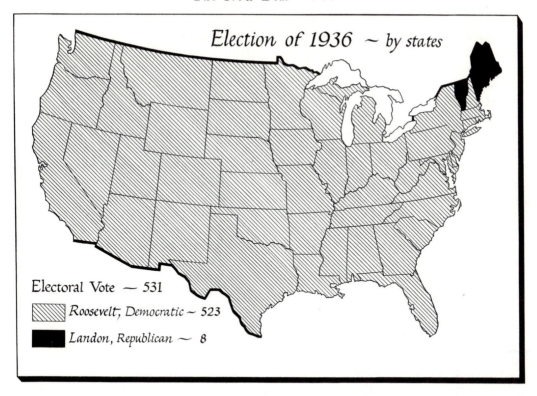

Election of 1936 ~ by states

Electoral Vote — 531

Roosevelt, Democratic ~ 523

Landon, Republican — 8

Democrats made unusual gains for a party in power. In the campaign of 1936 the Republicans were in a quandary to find a suitable presidential candidate, due to the shortage of talented officeholders. Their choice finally fell upon Governor Alfred M. Landon of Kansas, one of the few Republican governors to escape the Democratic sweeps. While surprisingly liberal, the Republican candidate and his platform were to the right of the Democrats. The Democrats, fully confident of victory, renominated their ticket of 1932, and elected it by a devastating landslide. Only two states, Maine and Vermont, voted for Landon. The electoral vote stood 523 for Roosevelt to 8 for Landon, and the popular vote 27.7 million to 16.6 million. Not since James Monroe was re-elected in 1820 with but a single opposing electoral vote had an election been so one-sided.

Among the many postelection observations of analysis, one stood out pre-eminently. It was apparent that the "vertical" lines of cleavage between the parties, so characteristic of nineteenth-century American politics, had given way to a "horizontal" division, which placed the more favored economic groups in the Republican column and the less favored elements in the Democratic. This was revealed with some clarity by the campaign contributions which for the Republicans amounted to about 9 million dollars, and for the Democrats to about 5.5 million dollars. A great majority of union labor, as well as the Catholic, Negro, and Jewish minorities, had voted for Roosevelt. As a consequence the New Deal carried every large city in the country, giving the Democratic party more of an urban tinge than it had ever had before.

Roosevelt and the Supreme Court

Roosevelt's overwhelming victory in 1936 no doubt furnished in part the explanation for his attempt to reform the Supreme Court, launched shortly after his second inauguration. Before the election he had not hesitated to express his irritation with decisions based upon precedents set in "horse-and-buggy days," but he had studiously refrained from attacking the Court during the campaign. Now, with 60 per cent of the nation's voters behind him, what might have been hazardous before seemed safe enough. That the Court majority was bitterly hostile to the New Deal seemed obvious. Out of nine important decisions involving New Deal measures, the Court upheld only two. Not a single member of the Court had been appointed by Roosevelt. Of the nine members of the Court, six were more than seventy years of age, and of these six, five were consistently conservative.

There were two ways in which reform of the Court could be effected: (1) by an amendment to the Constitution, which might either require retirement at a given age or set limits to the doctrine of judicial review; (2) by a law of Congress to provide for an increase in the number of justices, thus permitting the President to "pack" the Supreme Court with new appointees of less conservative views. Determined somehow to discipline the Court, the President chose the latter alternative. He coupled it with an ingenious provision for calling attention to the advanced age of some of the justices. The measure he urged on Congress would have set the age of seventy for the voluntary retirement of Supreme Court justices, and for each member of the Court who reached that age and failed to retire the President might appoint an additional justice until a maximum Court of fifteen members had been reached. The measure also provided for an extensive reorganization of the lower federal courts with a view to expediting business and increasing efficiency.

The President was quite unprepared for the furor that his "court-packing" bill evoked. Many Democrats professed to believe with the Republicans that a basic safeguard of American liberty was endangered, and that the President aspired to create a dictatorship. In the Senate, where the administration forces chose to stage the initial contest, Burton K. Wheeler of Montana, a left-wing Democrat, led the opposition with infinite resourcefulness. Wheeler claimed to hold no brief for the Court as constituted, but whatever change was to be made, he asserted, should be made by constitutional amendment. In the end the President for the first time on a matter of major importance failed to carry Congress with him. Astutely led by Chief Justice Hughes, the Court itself took a major part in the proceedings; by a series of decisions favorable to the New Deal, it materially weakened the President's case. Also, Justice Willis Van Devanter, senior member of the Court in point of service and a conservative, announced his determination to take speedy advantage of the act which Congress passed March 1, 1937, granting full pay to retiring justices over seventy years of age. Finally, the sudden death of Senator Joseph Robinson, administration floor leader in charge of the Court bill, put an end to the President's hopes. Congress passed a bill which instituted some of the reforms Roosevelt had called for in the lower courts, but it left the Supreme Court intact.

Nevertheless the President soon got what he wanted most, a court less conservative in character, which would no longer stand in the way of New Deal objectives. Had he been less impatient, he might have obtained the same result with far less bitterness and party dissension.

The Recession of 1937

The Supreme Court fight was barely ended when a downward trend in business, called by Democrats a recession and by Republicans a new depression, provided the administration with another major problem.

The unexpected slump was caused in no small part by the attempt of the national government to curtail expenditures, a fact which supported the argument of Roosevelt's opponents that there had been no real recovery, but only a continuous process of pump priming. New Dealers, on the other hand, charged that capital itself had gone on strike, and that business contraction in the interest of maintaining high price levels was a principal cause of the trouble. After initial hesitation, the administration moved to halt the decline. The Board of Governors of the Federal Reserve System promptly reversed the deflationary policy it had been pursuing since the summer of 1936, and a new reform program, at which Congress had balked while the Court battle went on, was instituted early in 1938. This included much additional pump priming, particularly through the WPA, the PWA, the RFC, and the USHA; the creation of a new AAA, already described, for the revival of agriculture; passage of the Fair Labor Standards Act, already discussed, and somewhat belatedly (1939) a wide grant of power to the President to reorganize the federal departments of government in the interest of greater efficiency. The conviction that methods of price control had been devised in monopolistic industries led also to an attempt to enforce the moribund antitrust laws. Since the days of the ill-starred NRA these regulations had been more or less in abeyance, but the President now chose Thurman W. Arnold of Yale to be Assistant Attorney-General, and charged him with the duty of reviving them.

Elections of 1938

The "Roosevelt Recession," even more than the unpopularity of the President's fight on the Supreme Court, left the New Deal vulnerable politically for the first time, and the elections of 1938 accurately recorded the shifting of public opinion. In spite of a demand from the President that four of his severest critics in Congress be defeated, three of them were renominated and re-elected. The election left both houses of Congress in Democratic hands, but Republican gains included 79 seats in the House and 8 in the Senate. Moreover, after the elections it was soon apparent that many southern Democrats were no longer willing to support further New Deal reforms. Instead they increasingly combined with middlewestern Republicans to form a conservative and antiurban coalition that was to persist for years. Many states now returned to their former Republican allegiance, electing Republican governors, or legislatures, or both. Noteworthy among these change-overs were Pennsylvania, Massachusetts, Connecticut, Michigan, Wisconsin, and Minnesota. Although 1938 marked still another Democratic victory, there was no denying that the political tide had turned. The future for conservatism and the Republican Party was much more promising.

The New Deal Balance Sheet

By 1938 the New Deal, which had been in power for six years, had made an indelible imprint upon American life. It had committed the federal government to provide for its citizens whenever economic adversity threatened the livelihood of any sizable number of them; it had attempted to manage production and prices of farm goods by subsidy and regulation; it had interfered in the financial and business life of the country by means of regulations and taxation, to an extent hitherto undreamed of in peacetime; it had intervened in the day-to-day relations of capital and labor; it had engaged in government construction, some of which competed outright with private capital and the quantity of which had never before been equaled in American history. In doing so much, it had greatly augmented the power of the federal government, particularly that of the executive branch, had minimized the power of the states, and had even invaded some of the rights which the Constitution seemed to reserve to private citizens. The sum of these activities meant in part a final farewell to *laissez faire*, a tremendous increase in the size and power of the federal bureaucracy, and the raising and spending of unprecedented sums in peacetime. Despite New Deal spending, taxation, and regulation, the various economic groups seemed to be getting about the same share of the national wealth in 1939 as they had in 1929. According to one study, the proportion of the national income represented by wages and salaries had risen during the period from 65.5 per cent to 68.2 per cent, and that of individual profits from 15.6 to 15.7 per cent, while interest and rents had declined from 11.5 per cent to 10.1 per cent, and corporation dividends from 7.4 per cent to 6 per cent. The farmer's real income in the period probably increased more than that of any other group, while people living on fixed incomes suffered most. At the beginning of 1939 there were still 8 million to 10 million unemployed in the United States, while millions of families continued to live below what the Department of Labor called a subsistence level. Unemployment in the United States did not disappear, and the per capita national income did not rise to its 1929 level, until the war spending of the forties began to affect the national economy. But in recreating confidence in the business and financial structure during these dreary years, the Roosevelt policies had

served an essential purpose. By providing jobs to the unemployed and feeding the destitute, the New Deal obviously prevented any great drift of public opinion to either the extreme left or right. Its contribution to American life through the construction of roads, streets, schools, parks, swimming pools, and playgrounds was incalculable. One art historian has recently written that no government since that of Periclean Athens had so stimulated architecture, painting, and music. But probably the greatest achievement of the New Deal was to recreate a feeling of confidence in the American people that the government at Washington was really their government, and that it could be used just as energetically to fight the enemies of the good life within the country as to fight an enemy attack from without.

After the elections of 1938 the New Deal program called for little additional reform, but looked rather toward defending the advances already made. Some of this growing caution unquestionably stemmed from the President's awareness that the country and Congress were in no mood for continued domestic innovations, and some of it from his growing preoccupation with foreign affairs. For by 1938 most well-informed statesmen recognized that civilization was faced with the imminent danger of a second world war.

BIBLIOGRAPHY

The finest survey of this period is provided by W. E. Leuchtenburg, *Franklin D. Roosevelt and the New Deal, 1932–1940* (1963). An excellent double-biography is A. B. Rollins, Jr., *Roosevelt and Howe* (1962). R. G. Tugwell, *The Democratic Roosevelt* (1957), is rich in insight. Dexter Perkins, *The New Age of Franklin Roosevelt, 1932–1945* (1957), is a brief overview, generally sympathetic and stressing foreign policy. D. W. Brogan, *The Era of Franklin D. Roosevelt* (1950), is lively and well-informed, the work of a Britisher who knows American politics. Basil Rauch, *The History of the New Deal, 1933–1938* (1944), is a pioneer effort at synthesis, highly sympathetic. P. K. Conkin, *The New Deal*

(1967), is a brief liberal critique. A hostile view of F.D.R. and his work is E. E. Robinson, *The Roosevelt Leadership, 1933–1945* (1955), a book by a conservative whose hero is Hoover. J. M. Burns, *Roosevelt: The Lion and the Fox* (1956), emphasizes domestic politics of the first two terms. An interesting study is O. L. Graham, Jr., *An Encore for Reform: The Old Progressives and the New Deal* (1967). Two scholarly studies of Roosevelt's thinking, both stressing his consistency, are D. R. Fusfeld, *The Economic Thought of Franklin D. Roosevelt and the Origins of the New Deal* (1956); and T. H. Greer, *What Roosevelt Thought* (1958).

A. M. Schlesinger, Jr., *The Coming of the New Deal* (1958), and *The Politics of Upheaval* (1960), cover domestic affairs in the first administration. Interesting collections which bring out some of the varying interpretations of the period are E. C. Rozwenc (ed.), *The New Deal* (2nd ed., 1959); and Morton Keller (ed.), *The New Deal* (1963). W. E. Leuchtenburg has edited two of the best books of readings on the New Deal, *Franklin D. Roosevelt* (1967), and *The New Deal* (1968). Other valuable collections include *The New Deal and the American People* (1964), edited by Frank Freidel; *The New Deal* (1969), edited by A. L. Hamby; *Franklin Delano Roosevelt* (1967), edited by G. D. Nash; *The New Deal* (1966), edited by Bernard Sternsher; and *New Deal Thought* (1966), edited by Howard Zinn. New Dealers have provided us with an abundance of memoirs. *The Secret Diary of Harold L. Ickes* (3 vols., 1953–1954), gives a running account, often gossipy and petty, of events from 1933 to Pearl Harbor. Fascinating details are given in *The Journals of David E. Lilienthal* (4 vols., 1964–1969). J. M. Blum, *From the Morgenthau Diaries* (3 vols., 1959–1967), is an able distillation of a great mass of data compiled by the Secretary of the Treasury; a summary volume is *Roosevelt and Morgenthau* (1970). Frances Perkins, *The Roosevelt I Knew* (1946), is the warm and friendly reminiscence of the Secretary of Labor. S. I. Rosenman, *Working with Roosevelt* (1952), tells a great deal about the preparation of the President's speeches. R. L.

Moley, *After Seven Years* (1939), the earliest important memoir, is harsh in its judgment, as is J. A. Farley, *Jim Farley's Story: The Roosevelt Years* (1948). Eleanor Roosevelt published a number of volumes of reminiscences, including *This Is My Story* (1937), and *This I Remember* (1949). A massive and illuminating volume is *Roosevelt and Frankfurter: Their Correspondence, 1928–1945* (1968), edited by Max Freedman. Other important memoirs include Herbert Feis, *1933: Characters in Crisis* (1966); Raymond Moley, *The First New Deal* (1966); R. G. Tugwell, *The Brains Trust* (1968); E. J. Flynn, *You're the Boss* (1947), by the famous "boss of the Bronx"; M. S. Eccles, *Beckoning Frontiers* (1951); and Francis Biddle, *In Brief Authority* (1962). R. E. Sherwood, *Roosevelt and Hopkins* (2nd ed., 1950), based upon the Hopkins Papers, is brilliantly written but thin on the prewar period.

On relief, the standard work is D. S. Howard, *The WPA and Federal Relief Policy* (1943), full and richly detailed. J. M. Keynes, *General Theory of Employment, Interest and Money* (1936), should be supplemented by a work of his leading American disciple, A. H. Hansen, *Fiscal Policy and Business Cycles* (1941). On the NRA see H. S. Johnson, *The Blue Eagle from Egg to Earth* (1935); and Sidney Fine, *The Automobile under the Blue Eagle* (1963). The social situation in one city is clearly presented in R. S. and H. M. Lynd, *Middletown in Transition* (1937).

On labor, the leading work is now Irving Bernstein, *Turbulent Years, 1933–1941* (1970), but it should be supplemented with *Labor and the New Deal* (1957), essays by various authorities, edited by Milton Derber and Edwin Young. Walter Galenson, *The CIO Challenge to the AFL: A History of the American Labor Movement, 1935–1941* (1960), is a massive work by a competent scholar. See also: Irving Howe and B. J. Widick, *The UAW and Walter Reuther* (1949); C. R. Walker, *American City* (1937), on the great Minneapolis strike of 1934; Sidney Fine, *Sit-Down: The General Motors Strike of 1936–1937* (1969); and J. S. Auerbach, *Labor and Liberty: The La Follette Committee and the New Deal* (1966). A provocative discussion of some notable labor and radical figures is Murray Kempton, *Part of Our Time* (1955). See also the scholarly analysis by F. A. Warren III, *Liberals and Communism: The "Red Decade" Revisited* (1966). The role of Roman Catholic leaders is traced in several important studies, including F. L. Broderick, *Right Reverend New Dealer, John A. Ryan* (1963); G. Q. Flynn, *American Catholics & the Roosevelt Presidency, 1932–1936* (1968); and D. J. O'Brien, *American Catholics and Social Reform* (1968).

On agriculture, see the useful survey by M. R. Benedict and O. C. Stine, *The Agricultural Commodity Programs: Two Decades of Experience* (1956). E. L. and F. H. Schapsmeier, *Henry A. Wallace of Iowa: The Agrarian Years, 1910–1940* (1968), gives a sympathetic view of the Secretary of Agriculture. Wallace's successor is treated in Dean Albertson, *Roosevelt's Farmer: Claude R. Wickard in the New Deal* (1961). Other useful scholarly studies on agriculture include C. M. Campbell, *The Farm Bureau and the New Deal* (1962); and Wilma Dykeman and James Stokely, *Seeds of Southern Change: The Life of Will Alexander* (1962). Important monographs are D. E. Conrad, *The Forgotten Farmers* (1965), on the New Deal's treatment of sharecroppers; Sidney Baldwin, *Poverty and Politics* (1968), a study of the Farm Security Administration; and T. A. Krueger, *And Promises to Keep: The Southern Conference for Human Welfare, 1938–1948* (1967). The best case study of one important agency is J. A. Salmond, *The Civilian Conservation Corps, 1933–1942* (1967). V. L. Perkins, *Crisis in Agriculture* (1969), is a close study of the early AAA. R. S. Kirkendall, *Social Scientists and Farm Politics in the Age of Roosevelt* (1966), is stimulating. Bernard Sternsher, *Rexford Tugwell and the New Deal* (1964), is a study of a leading agricultural reformer.

A rich, if depressing, study of Roosevelt's critics, including the more zany, is George Wolfskill and J. A. Hudson, *All But the People* (1969). A careful study of the anti-New Deal coalition is J. T. Patterson, *Congressional Conservatism and the New Deal* (1967). Conservative criticisms of the New Deal's alleged "regimentation" may be found in Herbert Hoover, *The Challenge to Liberty* (1934). The story of the leading right-wing group of the period is well told by George Wolfskill, *The Revolt of the Conservatives: A History of the American Liberty League, 1934–1940* (1962). D. R. McCoy, *Landon of Kansas* (1966), is a first-rate study of Roosevelt's 1936 opponent. On Coughlin, see C. J. Tull, *Father Coughlin and the New Deal* (1965); on Lemke, see E. C. Blackorby, *Prairie Rebel* (1963); and D. H. Bennett, *Demagogues in the Depression* (1969).

Financial matters are discussed in many works, notably G. G. Johnson, Jr., *The Treasury and Monetary Policy, 1933–1938* (1939); and J. A. Brennan, *Silver and the First New Deal* (1969), which deals with domestic pressures. On another important subject see J. M. Letiche, *Reciprocal Trade Agreements in the World Economy* (1948).

The literature on TVA is large; one of the most interesting studies is W. H. Droze, *High Dams and Slack Waters: TVA Rebuilds a River* (1965). Views of its administrator are set forth in D. E. Lilienthal, *TVA: Democracy on the March* (2nd ed., 1953). C. H. Pritchett, *The Tennessee Valley Authority: A Study in Public Administration* (1943), a favorable view, should be contrasted with the more critical Philip Selznick, *TVA and the Grass Roots* (1949). A rich study which examines efforts to establish a Connecticut Valley Authority is W. E. Leuchtenburg, *Flood Control Politics: The Connecticut River Valley Problem, 1927–1950* (1953). On rural electrification, see K. E. Trombley, *The Life and Times of a Happy Liberal: A Biography of Morris Llewellyn Cooke* (1954).

On social security, two valuable memoirs are available: E. E. Witte, *The Development of the Social Security Act* (1962); and A. J. Altmeyer, *The Formative Years of Social Security* (1966). Excellent for background is Roy Lubove, *The Struggle for Social Security, 1900–1935* (1968). A rich study in pension politics is Abraham Holtzman, *The Townsend Movement* (1963).

The controversy over the Supreme Court produced a vast amount of writing, which can be sampled in *Franklin D. Roosevelt and the Supreme Court* (2nd ed., 1969), edited by A. H. Cope and Fred Krinsky. Some of the background is found in R. H. Jackson, *The Struggle for Judicial Supremacy* (1941). There is no scholarly study of the "court fight," but two journalistic accounts are Joseph Alsop and Turner Catledge, *The 168 Days* (1938); and Leonard Baker, *Back to Back* (1967). For the aftermath see C. H. Pritchett, *The Roosevelt Court* (1948).

An attempt to assess the impact of the New Deal is A. A. Ekirch, Jr., *Ideologies and Utopias* (1969). One aspect of the ideology of the later New Deal is illustrated by the witty book of T. W. Arnold, *The Folklore of Capitalism* (1937). The best analysis of the Roosevelt recession is K. D. Roose, *The Economics of Recession and Revival* (1954). On the TNEC, see David Lynch, *The Concentration of Economic Power* (1946); a broader and more critical study is E. W. Hawley, *The New Deal and the Problem of Monopoly* (1966). On the early years of securities regulation see R. F. de Bedts, *The New Deal's SEC* (1964). There are two scholarly studies of governmental reorganization: B. D. Karl, *Executive Reorganization and Reform in the New Deal* (1963); and Richard Polenberg, *Reorganizing Roosevelt's Government* (1966). A careful work on one New Deal agency which was terminated is J. D. Mathews, *The Federal Theater, 1935–1939* (1967).

An important and neglected subject is discussed briefly in J. T. Patterson, *The New Deal and the States* (1969). On the New Deal South see the classic analysis by V. O. Key, *Southern Politics in State and Nation* (1949); Frank Freidel, *F. D. R. and the South* (1965); and W. D. Miller, *Mr. Crump of Memphis* (1964). On Huey Long the literature is vast but the beginning point for study is T. H. Williams, *Huey Long* (1969), a monumental biography. See also A. P. Sindler, *Huey Long's Louisiana* (1956); *Huey Long* (1970), a collection of readings edited by H. D. Graham; and *Huey P. Long* (1967), a "problems" volume edited by H. C. Dethloff. On California, see *I, Candidate for Governor and How I Got Licked* (1935), a colorful reminiscence of the EPIC campaign by Upton Sinclair; and R. E. Burke, *Olson's New Deal for California* (1953). On New York, see J. J. Huthmacher, *Senator Robert F. Wagner and the Rise of Urban Liberalism* (1968); and Arthur Mann, *La Guardia Comes to Power, 1933* (1965). The New Deal era in other states has scattered coverage, notably in J. W. Howard, *Mr. Justice Murphy* (1968), on Michigan; G. H. Mayer, *The Political Career of Floyd B. Olson* (1951), on Minnesota; and M. P. Malone, *C. Ben Ross and the New Deal in Idaho* (1970).

References on foreign policy are listed in the next bibliography. Note should be made here of J. B. Brebner, *The North Atlantic Triangle* (1945), a unique study of Anglo-American-Canadian relations; E. O. Guerrant, *Roosevelt's Good Neighbor Policy* (1950); and E. D. Cronon, *Josephus Daniels in Mexico* (1960).

Unfortunately there is no scholarly biography of the President's wife, since her papers are closed to scholars. The best efforts of scholars to write her life are represented by T. K. Hareven, *Eleanor Roosevelt* (1968), laudatory and covering her whole life; and J. R. Kearney, *Anna Eleanor Roosevelt* (1968), more critical and concentrating on the New Deal years.

23

WORLD CRISIS

Roosevelt's Foreign Policy · "The Good Neighbor" · Japanese Militarism · The Soviet Union · Fascism & Nazism · Neutrality Acts · Ethiopia & Spain · Appeasement · The Beginning of World War II · Continental Solidarity · The Fall of France · America Rearms · Election of 1940

Franklin D. Roosevelt, like his predecessor Herbert Hoover, had been an enthusiastic supporter of President Wilson's plans for a League of Nations. When the Senate refused to ratify the Treaty of Versailles, with its League membership agreement, Roosevelt fought for Wilsonian internationalism (or what was later to be called "collective security"), especially as the Democratic candidate for Vice-President in 1920. Hoover supported Harding and joined his cabinet but he, too, favored American entrance into the League. Both men, like all but the most devout Wilsonians, came to have serious reservations about the value of the League of Nations during the 1920's, when it seemed to become an appendage of the British and French foreign offices. Both men continued to believe that the peace of 1919 might have been lasting if the United States had joined the League at the outset but it is significant that neither Hoover nor Roosevelt, as President, sought American

entry into the now somewhat tarnished organization which met in the elegant halls of Geneva. Although two of the most notable nonmembers eventually joined (Germany in 1926, Soviet Russia in 1934), they exercised no more influence on the League than did the United States, which kept out. The League did little to eradicate most of the injustices and inequities written into the Peace of Paris. Its main role was that of a policeman to maintain the terms of the war settlement. Thus for the defeated and disappointed nations the League seemed to be an enemy. The reality of dictatorships and extreme nationalism in many parts of the world replaced Wilsonian dreams of universal democracy. Collective security, such as it was at the bottom of the Great Depression when Roosevelt became President, was already an empty slogan.

Roosevelt's Foreign Policy

By the time he ran for President in 1932, Roosevelt had a long record in foreign affairs but it was by no means a clear and consistent one. Early in his public life he

THE BURNING OF THE REICHSTAG, *on the night of February 27, 1933, was one steppingstone on the Nazi path to power.*

was a fervent nationalist, like his cousin Theodore, and as Assistant Secretary of the Navy he was something of a militarist, a favorite of the admirals. He became a convert to Wilsonian internationalism, however, and went down to defeat in 1920 carrying that banner. During the 1920's he maintained an active interest in world affairs but he showed many signs that he was somewhat disillusioned with the workings of the League, although he continued to say that American membership would have made a difference. He assailed the economic nationalism of the Harding-Coolidge-Hoover tariff policies.

As a candidate in 1932 Roosevelt was silent on foreign policy, as behooved a man who had the support of the internationalists Colonel E. M. House and Senator Cordell Hull as well as that of the fervent isolationists Senators Hiram Johnson and George W. Norris (to say nothing of the benevolent neutrality of Senator William E. Borah). In his inaugural address he said only this much:

In the field of world policy I would dedicate this Nation to the policy of the good neighbor — the neighbor who resolutely respects himself and, because he does so, respects the rights of others — the neighbor who respects his obligations and respects the sanctity of his agreements in and with a world of neighbors.

"The Good Neighbor"

The New Deal was at first a highly nationalistic program concerned with relief and recovery, for which Roosevelt had been willing to see the London Economic Conference end rather than tie his country to binding international monetary and trade agreements. But he had to concern himself with the affairs of Latin America, where he was soon able to demonstrate what he meant by "the good neighbor." He sought to achieve good will toward the United States, partly perhaps for its own sake, partly for the rebuilding of international trade in the western hemisphere, and partly for the development of mutual security in the event of European aggression in the New World.

He sent Secretary Hull to the Pan-American Conference in Montevideo, and cordially approved the doctrine on which the Conference agreed, that "no state has the right to intervene in the internal or external affairs of another." In 1936, he journeyed 7,000 miles by sea to Buenos Aires in order to open a special Inter-American Conference for the Maintenance of Peace, and told delegates that non-American states seeking "to commit acts of aggression against us will find a Hemisphere wholly prepared to consult together for our mutual safety and our mutual good."

A practical demonstration of how the Good Neighbor policy operated occurred in Cuba, which dared at last to attempt the overthrow by revolution of its current dictator, Gerardo Machado, who had long remained in power with the support of American investors and the State Department. When Roosevelt became President, he let it be known that Machado could expect no further backing from the American government. As a result the dictator was promptly driven from office. No American troops were landed, and American interests were watched over exclusively by recognized diplomatic agents. For the first time since the Spanish-American War a serious revolutionary outbreak in Cuba came to an end without military intervention by the United States. Furthermore, on May 29, 1934, a treaty between the United States and Cuba formally abrogated the Platt Amendment, which for a generation had rankled the Cubans. That same year a reciprocal trade treaty materially reduced the tariff on Cuban exports to the United States and checked the decline of Cuban-American trade.

Other evidence that the "big stick" policy was really at an end accumulated rapidly. By an agreement reached in August, 1934, the financial receivership which the United States maintained in Haiti was greatly liberalized, and the last detachment of American marines was ordered to leave the republic. About the same time negotiations were begun with Panama to abolish the special privileges that that nation had been forced to accord the United States, and after a long delay this, too, was accomplished. But the real test of the Good Neighbor policy came in Mexico, where many citizens of the United States still held major investments in oil and mining. The drastic Mexican law of 1938 expropriating all foreign-held oil properties was met with investor-inspired demands for stern action and, if necessary, the use of force. Roosevelt, however, refused to scuttle the Good Neighbor policy, and a potentially explosive situation was solved by mild if protracted diplomatic negotiations.

The early New Deal's anti-imperialist policy also affected American relations with the Philippines. In accordance with the Tydings-McDuffie Act of 1934, they became an autonomous Commonwealth with a President of their choosing and an elective National Assembly, with complete independence to come on July 4, 1946. Except for control over foreign relations and a few other specified restrictions, the Philippine nationalists had obtained practically all the political liberty they sought, but they were still far from happy. They knew full well that the economic prosperity of the islands had been built upon freedom of trade with the United States, a privilege that was now to be gradually withdrawn. They knew also that independence would carry with it the obligation of self-defense, and in Japan they recognized a dangerous enemy. At the request of the Philippine government, President Roosevelt authorized General Douglas MacArthur, retiring Army Chief of Staff, to train a strong local constabulary.

Japanese Militarism

The openly expressed expansionism of Japan threatened not only the Philippines but all of East Asia. Japan was a sort of theocracy, for the Emperor was worshiped as the Son of Heaven, and such privileges of government as were extended to the people were held to be merely gifts emanating from the divine will. In actual practice the Emperor was subject to the control of a small group of elder statesmen and privy councilors, often militarists whose advice he dared not reject. A parliament in the form of a two-house Diet existed, but the Cabinet was responsible only to the Emperor, and a peculiarly independent status was assigned to the ministers of War and Navy. Invariably these men were selected from among the highest-ranking active officers of the branches concerned. During the First World War, Japan had enjoyed an unusual prosperity. Her military contribution to the defeat of the Central Powers had been comparatively slight, but she had profited greatly from the sale of war goods to the Allies and from their use of her excellent fleet of merchantmen. After the war, American purchases of Japanese silk staved off economic disaster, but the Great Depression cut down American buying power and seriously imperiled Japanese prosperity. This situation played directly into the hands of the nation's powerful military leaders. War would bring plunder, and was thus an end in itself, but the military leaders had much civilian support for the theory that Japanese expansion was an economic necessity.

First on their list was Manchuria, still nominally part of China. Japanese bankers and industrialists were already entrenched there, but the militarists sought complete power over the region. Next might come the conquest of all of China, perhaps followed by Southeast Asia. Various terms were used to cloak the Japanese designs. Whether known as a "Monroe Doctrine for Asia," or the "New Order," or the "Co-Prosperity Sphere," what the Japanese leaders really wanted was a Far East exclusively dominated politically and economically by Japan.

The Manchurian "incident" of 1931 was the beginning of a procession of events that led directly toward the Second World War. On the faintest pretexts, Japanese troops occupied large sections of Manchuria, organized it into the satellite state of Manchukuo, and set a puppet Emperor on its throne. Because this act of aggression constituted a direct violation of the Kellogg-Briand Peace Pact, the United States refused to recognize Manchukuo. But since the Hoover administration refused to support Secretary Stimson's policy with economic or military pressure, even to the extent of promising to cooperate with proposed sanctions of the League of Nations, America's protests had no effect upon the Japanese expansionists. When the League of Nations voiced mild disapproval, Japan summarily gave notice of her intent to withdraw from the League. Hoover's Secretary of State had no difficulty in persuading President-elect Roosevelt to accept his Stimson Doctrine. The Democratic administration thereby committed itself to opposition in principle to Japanese expansion, a policy which was to have serious consequences for both countries.

The Soviet Union

The United States had steadfastly refused to recognize Communist Russia, even after the other major powers had done so. The Soviets had repudiated the Tsarist debt (to the injury of many foreign bond holders) and had continued to sponsor revolutionary activity in many countries through the Comintern or Third International. But after the death of Lenin in 1924 and the accession of Josef Stalin as his successor, Russian policy for a time veered away from world revolution and emphasized the building of socialism in Russia alone. Stalin promulgated three successive "five year plans" to make Russia industrially and agricultur-

V. I. Lenin, *a long-standing Bolshevik who had returned to Russia from exile the preceding April, and until the time of his death in 1924 headed the Bolshevik government.*

ally self-sustaining, and thus able to defend herself in case of war. This new Russian posture allayed somewhat the fears of most capitalist nations, and in 1934 Russia was invited to become a member of the League of Nations, where for the next four years she was a leader in arguing for collective security against potential aggression.

After the outbreak of the Great Depression, many Americans argued that there was more to be gained than lost by resuming diplomatic relations. And after the Roosevelt administration received assurances from the Soviet government that it would refrain from "agitation and propaganda within the United States," it did what Senator Borah and other liberals had long advocated and accorded recognition in November, 1933. Despite the growing acceptability of the Soviet government in international circles, mutual suspicion between the western democratic nations and the Communists remained, generated on the one side by Russia's continued support of Communist revolutionary parties throughout the world, and on the other by the Soviet fear that the capitalist countries were bent upon destroying Communism.

THE FÜHRER.

Fascism and Nazism

The year 1922 witnessed the rise of another European dictator, Benito Mussolini. Aided by economic distress, the chaotic condition of the existing democratic regime in Italy, and the possibility of a Communist revolution, Mussolini and his Black Shirt followers through the threat of force took over the government and rapidly proceeded to destroy democratic institutions. Since Fascism, as Mussolini called his movement, posed no immediate threat to capitalism — indeed, free unions and strikes were outlawed — and since he designated international Communism as the chief enemy of Fascism, he obtained a good deal of sympathy from the propertied classes in all countries. By instituting a relatively efficient government able to keep order, the Fascists also won considerable international support. But in the realm of foreign affairs, Mussolini's flamboyant nationalism, his encouragement of Italian militarists, and his expansionist claims on the Mediterranean, the Balkans, and Africa boded ill for the continued peace of southern Europe.

Because of the relatively backward state of Italian industrialism, and the poverty of both the land and its people, Fascist Italy by itself was scarcely a major threat to the peace of Europe. But the National Socialist or Nazi revolution in Germany was something far different. The continued weakness of the German Weimar democratic republic, the desire to revenge the defeat of 1918, the hope of recovering the lost German territories, the rising threat of Communism, and finally the withering effects of the Great Depression all played into the hands of Adolf Hitler, who, with a shrewd combination of force, rabble rousing, and politics, made himself chancellor of Germany in February, 1933. Soon, the last vestige of democracy was wiped out, and the nazification of the state was complete. Henceforth Hitler was Germany's only "Führer," and a powerful secret police suppressed the slightest show of criticism. Germany, like Russia and Italy, had become a totalitarian dictatorship; in every instance the individual existed for the state, not the state for the individual.

The Nazi ideology, like the Fascist, was less noted for common sense and consistency than for its appeal to the prejudices that Hitler found about him. The Nazis adopted in full the "stab-in-the-back" legend that Germany had been betrayed in 1918, not defeated, and demanded the complete overthrow of the Versailles settlement. This was held to be Germany's due, not merely because of injustices in the treaty, but because Germans, as members of the master race, had superior rights. Racism, more than anything else, was basic in the Nazi philosophy. The "Nordic," or "Aryan," race, of which the Germans were held to be the only really pure strain, was born to command; all other "races," Latin, Slav, Semite, Negro, Oriental, existed merely to take orders. Racial purity, in the Nazi scheme of things, was supremely important; mixtures with "impure" blood were an intolerable affront to the race. The Jewish "race" was the most reprehensible of all. It was both parasitic and unassimilable, the source of most of the woes of the world. Acting on these principles, the Nazis ordered the most fiendish persecutions of the Jews.

The Neutrality Acts

In view of the increasingly tense international situation, Americans debated foreign policy issues in a way they had not done since 1919. Many were convinced that American entry into World War I was a mistake that should never be repeated. They advocated strict neutrality for the United States, come what might. This sentiment was greatly strengthened by the rather sensational hearings of a Senate committee, headed by Senator Gerald P. Nye of North Dakota, which in 1934 began to examine the record of the munitions industries during and after the First World War. Extreme isolationists began to demand insistently that Congress enact neutrality laws so strict as to preclude all possibility of American involvement in case war again broke out in Europe.

Opposed to this point of view were the believers in collective security, who maintained that the world had become too small for any nation so large and influential as the United States to remain aloof from what was going on. If war came it might easily engulf the United States, but even if the United States failed to take part, it would still be intimately affected. Normal lines of trade would be broken up; the basis for a new world depression would be laid; and in a thousand other ways the United States would feel the impact of hostilities. The proper course, therefore, was to prevent war. Let the United States join with peace-loving nations to curb aggressors and to compel peace. Negative neutrality was not enough. War must be prevented.

The advocates of collective security were a small minority in the United States in the early New Deal years. They did not include either the President or the Secretary of State, since both were cautious men, respectful of public opinion and unsure of how best to maintain peace. A series of neutrality laws, passed by Congress and signed by Roosevelt, sought to eliminate all opportunities for the United States to be drawn into a non-American conflict. The first of these acts, passed in 1935 during the Italian attack on Ethiopia, required the President to impose an embargo upon the shipment of arms to belligerent nations, and authorized him to prohibit Americans from traveling upon the ships of belligerents. The second act, passed the following year, added a prohibition against the flotation of loans in the United States by any non-American belligerent. An even more comprehensive act became law in May, 1937. American merchant ships might not carry munitions to belligerents nor arm themselves against attack. Certain discretionary powers were also bestowed upon the President. He might forbid American ships to transport commodities of any kind to a belligerent nation; he might require all shipments to be made on a strictly "cash and carry" basis; and he might exclude enemy warships, submarines, and armed merchantmen from the use of American ports. These acts went far toward eliminating all the various causes of conflict that had led the United States into war in 1917. By them notice was also pointedly served upon European nations that the American people were no longer willing to defend the principles of neutrality for which they once had fought.

While the President found these laws increasingly bothersome, he managed to

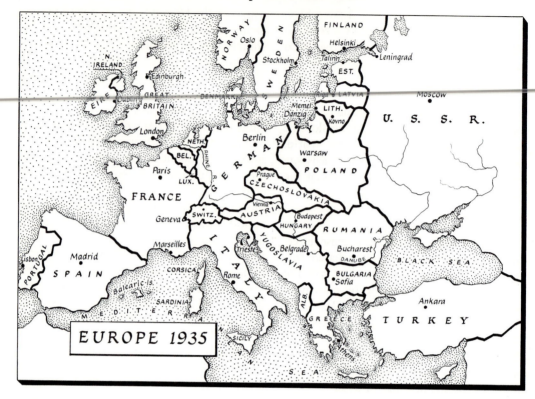

EUROPE 1935

adapt them to his own views on foreign policy. He recognized the existence of a state of war between Italy and Ethiopia, and declared the embargo on arms in force. This was advantageous to Ethiopia, which could not have purchased arms in America in any event, and an intended handicap to Italy, which might have done so. Secretary Hull also attempted to persuade American shippers to embargo voluntarily other products to Italy, especially scrap iron and oil. Pointing out that American shipments of goods to Italian Africa had increased twenty times, he stated bluntly that such shipments were "directly contrary to the policy of this government." Since Japan had not declared war against China, he refused to recognize the hostilities in the Orient as war, presumably to enable the Chinese to continue their purchases of American munitions. To Spain, where civil war existed, but with the Italians and Ger-

mans helping the insurgents and the Russians helping the Loyalists, he applied the embargo, much to the discomfiture of the Loyalists, who had the money with which to buy. The operations of the neutrality legislation actually aided the Fascists during the Spanish war, since American trade continued with Italy, who, although not officially at war, actively supported the Fascist leader, General Franco.

Ethiopia and the Spanish Civil War

In 1935, Mussolini began a war of conquest against Ethiopia, with the avowed intent of adding that African kingdom to his empire. This venture was so fraught with peril for the peace of Europe that for a time it seemed as if the League of Nations might employ effective economic sanctions to prevent it. If Italy could be kept from obtaining oil, it appeared that war could not go on. But the League finally backed down.

It applied sanctions, but not the oil sanctions that alone were well calculated to achieve results. The British navy, upon which the main brunt of enforcing the sanctions would have fallen, was inadequately prepared for war, and no state wanted to risk the disruption of world trade, which was just recovering from depression levels. Mussolini went ahead, practically unimpeded, with his plan of conquest, drove the Ethiopian monarch, Haile Selassie, into exile, and on May 9, 1936, announced that the Italian King had also assumed the title of Emperor.

Inflated with one victory, Mussolini soon sought another. When in 1936 a revolt broke out in Spain against the democratic government of the Spanish Republic, Mussolini sent his "legions" to the aid of the revolutionary leader, General Francisco Franco, whose Fascist tendencies were unmistakable. Aid for Franco came also from Germany, and some help for the "Loyalists," as the government forces were called, came from Russia. The civil war in Spain was widely recognized as a dress rehearsal for the coming world war, but the democratic nations were unwilling to do anything effective for the Loyalists, who, after two and a half years of bitter and bloody struggle, were defeated. In General Franco, the new dictator of Spain, both Hitler and Mussolini recognized a kindred spirit and a potential ally.

The China "Incident"

One result of Japanese aggression was to unite the faction-torn Chinese for self-defense. Even the deeply antagonistic Nationalists under Chiang Kai-shek and the Communists under Chang Hsueh-liang found ways of cooperating under Chiang Kai-shek as Generalissimo. Thus when the Japanese decided in 1937 to prosecute an undeclared war against China, their troops were confronted by organized opposition. But the Chinese were no match for the well-trained and well-supplied Japanese armies, who soon had under their control most of the Chinese seacoast and much of the adjacent interior. While the Japanese refused to admit that the China "incident" was a war, the League of Nations seemed to regard it as such, and after much delay recommended that the various member nations extend what aid they could to China. Over the Burma Road, which by 1938 American-trained engineers had completed with the use of Chinese labor, China was able to import some useful war materials, and eventually both the British and the American governments extended credits to China. An incident of the war was the destruction on December 12, 1937, by Japanese bombers, of an American gunboat, the *Panay*, on the Yangtze River. The act seemed deliberate, but the American public was apathetic and the apologies of the Japanese government were accepted.

Appeasement

Meanwhile, Nazi Germany under Hitler had abruptly embarked upon a program to secure Great Power status. It showed its contempt for the Peace of 1919 by giving notice of its withdrawal from the League of Nations. In 1935, following the required popular vote in the area, Germany took back the Saar Basin. In the next year Hitler sent troops into the Rhineland to reoccupy and remilitarize it; in spite of the Treaty of Versailles, the French did nothing to impede this drastic move. In 1938 the Nazis occupied Austria and incorporated that formerly independent state into Hitler's "Third Reich." The country next coveted by Hitler was Czechoslovakia, which Germany now almost completely surrounded, but the Führer chose at first to demand only the Sudetenland, a strip along the Czech-German border mainly inhabited by Germans. To retain this region, which was essential to her defense, Czechoslovakia was ready to fight. Russia had already

promised her aid in repelling a Nazi invasion, but in the end Czechoslovakia was
betrayed by nations she had thought were
her friends, France and England. Among
the peoples of the western democracies any
settlement seemed better than war. Accordingly, their governments were probably in accord with the weight of public
opinion when they proposed to keep Germany at peace by a policy of "appeasement." Prime Minister Chamberlain of
Great Britain and Premier Daladier of
France met with Hitler and Mussolini at
Munich in September, 1938, to find a solution short of war. They found it by demanding that Czechoslovakia yield to Hitler's requests in return for a solemn German
promise that this would be Hitler's last expansion in Europe. But in March, 1939, all
of Czechoslovakia was occupied by Hitler.
Not to be outdone, Mussolini the very next
month transported an army across the
Adriatic and took possession of Albania.

A Quarantine of Aggressors

Roosevelt demonstrated repeatedly that
he was aware of the dangers of Japanese,
German and Italian aggressions, but he seldom did more than signify his awareness to
the world. After the German occupation
of the Rhineland, Roosevelt denounced
those nations which had reverted "to the
old belief in the law of the sword" and
which had adopted the "fantastic conception" that they alone were chosen to be the
masters of human destiny. In a direct reference a year later to the German pogroms
against the Jews, he stated bluntly that he
could hardly believe "that such things could
occur in twentieth-century civilization."
Speaking before the Pan-American Union in
1939, he characterized the methods of Germany and Italy as those of the Huns and
Vandals. Roosevelt's rather cryptic utterance on collective security, prompted by
Japanese and Italian operations in China and
Ethiopia, came on October 5, 1937, during
an address delivered in Chicago:

It seems to be unfortunately true that the
epidemic of world lawlessness is spreading.
When an epidemic of physical disease starts
to spread, the community approves and joins
in a quarantine of the patients in order to protect the health of the community against the
spread of the disease. . . . War is a contagion,
whether it be declared or undeclared. It can
engulf states and peoples remote from the original scene of hostilities. We are determined
to keep out of war, yet we cannot insure ourselves against the disastrous effects of war and
the dangers of involvement. . . . There must be
positive endeavors to preserve peace. America
hates war. America hopes for peace. Therefore, America actively engages in the search
for peace.

It is notable that the American search for peace did not stand in the way of active naval expansion, particularly after the breakdown of all plans for disarmament. In January, 1938, the President asked Congress to appropriate a billion dollars for naval defense. A month later he asked for another huge increase in appropriations and that a start be made on a two-ocean navy. The following year he proposed doubling the military budget with a good part of the increase going to the air force. Except for the Presidential request to fortify the island of Guam, Congress agreed to the major parts of these military proposals. From the point of view of those who believed in collective security the navy was necessary if the United States was to have any influence in restraining "warmongers," while from the point of view of the isolationists it was necessary to defend American borders against a warmongering world.

Rome-Berlin Axis

By this time the alliance between Hitler and Mussolini, which began in 1935, was also extended to Japan. The objection of all three nations to the spread of Communism — a spread, incidentally, which is difficult to discover anywhere in this period — found expression in the Anti-Comintern Pact signed by Germany and Japan in 1936, and adhered to by Italy in 1937. Then in May, 1939, immediately following the Czechoslovakian and Albanian incidents, Germany and Italy concluded also a ten-year military alliance — the "Rome-Berlin Axis." The agreement pledged that if either power should become involved in war, the other would come to its aid "with all its military forces, on land, sea, and in the air."

End of Appeasement

The British and French governments, willing to overlook Mussolini's maneuvers in obscure Albania, were truly jarred by Hitler's absorption of the remnant of Czechoslovakia. His promise that the Sudetenland would be his final annexation had, incredibly, been believed by many important leaders in western Europe. The era of appeasement ended for nearly all British and French people in March, 1939, although the message seems not to have reached Adolf Hitler. That Hitler intended to press on with his program of expansion was at last clear to all. From Lithuania he demanded, and received, Memel. From Poland he demanded under threat of war consent to the restoration of the free city of Danzig to the Reich, and to the building of a German highway and railroad across the

The Munich Conference. *Representatives of four nations met at Munich, September 29, 1938, to buy peace at the expense of Czechoslovakia. From left to right: Neville Chamberlain, Edouard Daladier, Adolf Hitler, Benito Mussolini.*

Polish Corridor. With British and French opinion now running strongly against further appeasement, Prime Minister Chamberlain, with the full support of the French government, as well as his own, promised Poland all possible aid should her independence be threatened. Similar guarantees were soon given Greece and Rumania, and an Anglo-Turkish pact provided for mutual assistance "in the event of aggression leading to war in the Mediterranean area." France began to patch up her differences with Turkey over Syria, and the United States showed sudden concern. President Roosevelt, in a message of April 16, 1939, to the Axis dictators, asked them for assurance that they would not invade thirty named states. The recipients of the message treated it with a display of ridicule, which did little to reassure an anxious world.

The Russian-German Accord

Throughout these proceedings the great enigma had been Russia. That the signers of the Anti-Comintern Pact had anything but hatred for the Soviet system could hardly be doubted; they made it plain on every possible occasion that they intended to destroy it. But Britain and France, having sought to destroy the Communist regime in its infancy, were also uneasy about the Soviet Union, in spite of the fact that France had signed a treaty of alliance with it in 1935. Many people in the western democracies still feared the spread of Communism; many felt that it was far more dangerous than Fascism. During the negotiations that preceded Munich, Russia had been deliberately slighted. In that conference, which decided the fate of Czechoslovakia, one of Russia's near neighbors, no Russian had been permitted a voice. Many believed that Britain and France were building up Nazi Germany as a counterweight to Soviet Russia, and that a war to the death between Germany and Russia was their real objective. Great Britain and France seemed, by March, 1939, to be mildly interested in Russian collaboration, and a special British envoy was sent to Russia to negotiate an Anglo-Soviet pact. Throughout the summer of 1939, while Hitler voiced more and more threats against Poland, these negotiations continued, but without results. Then, to the amazement of most of the world, came the announcement that Russia and Germany had agreed late in August to a commercial pact for the exchange of German manufactured goods for Russian raw materials, and to a nonaggression pact by which each nation would respect the territory and sovereignty of the other. Thus reinforced, Hitler went ahead in a three

Rendezvous. *The British cartoonist, David Low, thus dramatically recorded the Russian-German agreement that paved the way for the Second World War.*

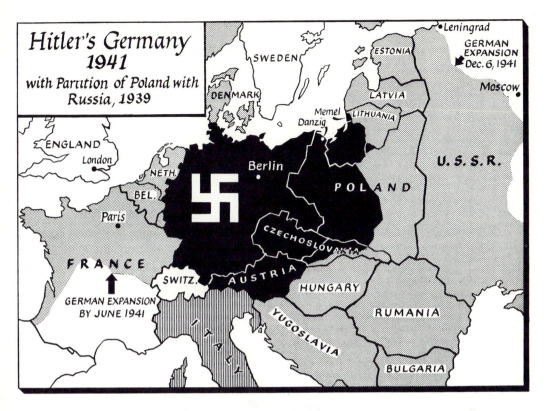

SWEDEN

DENMARK

ENGLAND
London

NETH.

BEL.

Paris

FRANCE

GERMAN EXPANSION
BY JUNE 1941

SWITZ.

ITALY

Berlin

Memel
Danzig

AUSTRIA

ESTONIA

LATVIA

LITHUANIA

POLAND

CZECHOSLOVAKIA

HUNGARY

YUGOSLAVIA

Leningrad

GERMAN
EXPANSION
Dec. 6, 1941

Moscow

U.S.S.R.

RUMANIA

BULGARIA

weeks' *Blitzkrieg* (lightning war) to conquer two-thirds of Poland, leaving the rest of that unhappy country to Russia.

The Second World War Begins

In response to the frantic demands of Poland, Great Britain and France on September 3, 1939, declared war on Germany, but they could not restrain the rapid Nazi drive. Both nations mobilized fully; the British re-established the blockade they had found so effective in the First World War, and the French manned their prodigious and much-publicized eastern defense, the Maginot Line. But for more than half a year there was little real fighting in the West, where some derisively called it a "phony war." Stalin, however, took advantage of the opportunity to overrun Russia's former Baltic provinces, Latvia, Lithuania, and Estonia. His efforts to invade Finland, however, met with stiff resistance. The tenacity with which the Finns defended their borders against the vastly

superior foe excited admiration in many parts of the world. But the odds against the Finns were too great, and in March, 1940, the Finnish government made peace. By the terms agreed upon, the Finnish boundaries were "rectified," but her independence was left intact.

Roosevelt Responds

Foreseeing clearly the trend of events in 1939, the President asked Congress to modify the Neutrality Act of 1937 by removing the mandatory feature of the embargo on arms to belligerents. It was the President's idea that the American government should be left free to follow traditional practice on this subject. No doubt he believed that the cause of peace would be served if the European dictators knew in advance that their opponents would be able to buy arms in the United States. But Congress was recalcitrant; the most the President could obtain was a promise from Congressional leaders that neutrality legislation would be the first order of business at the next session. Thus on September 1, 1939, when Hitler began his supreme effort to dominate Europe, the United States by its own actions found itself unable to aid embattled world democracy. Like the British before Munich, the American people wanted contradictory things: peace, a democratic world, and a world secure from aggression. Roosevelt made no plea for Americans to be "impartial in thought as well as in action," as Wilson had done in 1914. In 1939 the United States, while nominally neutral, was almost completely opposed to Nazi Germany.

Thus it came as no surprise that, following the German invasion of Poland, the President called a special session of Congress to revise the Neutrality Act. Meeting on September 21, 1939, it now agreed to permit the export of war goods on a "cash and carry" basis. But the prohibition of loans to participants was continued, American ships were barred from carrying passengers or war materials to belligerents, and travel by American citizens on the vessels of belligerents was forbidden. Neutral nations, thus bereft of a powerful champion of neutral rights, looked on helplessly while German submarines sank their ships.

"Continental Solidarity"

The rapid descent toward war in Europe led Roosevelt to renewed emphasis upon "continental solidarity" and "hemispheric defense." When the Pan-American Conference met in Lima, December 10, 1938, the United States was acutely conscious of the inroads being made by German and Italian propaganda in Latin-American states, and sought to unite the republics of the New World in a common defense against "aggressor nations." The agreement which Secretary Hull was able to obtain was not nearly as binding as the American government had hoped, but it affirmed that the peoples of America still had faith in "absolute adherence to the principles of international law," and that they would work together to defend the peace of the continent. When war actually broke out, delegates from the various American republics met at Panama, October 1, 1939, to consider a common policy of neutrality. After several days' deliberation they issued a declaration which asserted that the "waters adjacent to the American continent" must be "free from the commission of any hostile act by any non-American belligerent nation."

The occupation of the Dutch West Indies by the Allies after the defeat of the Netherlands brought no protest from the United States, but when France was compelled to sue for peace, notice was promptly served on Germany that the United States, under the terms of the Monroe Doctrine, could permit no transfer of American colonies from one European nation to another. The President also advocated that the Pan-American Conference, scheduled to meet in Havana on July 20, 1940, should adopt a new rule for territorial readjustments in the American hemisphere. On behalf of the United States he formally renounced all territorial aspirations, and he urged that the American republics should act together, each having equal voice, in determining what postwar rearrangements would be permitted in the New World. He suggested further that the system he favored for the Americas might well be applied in other continents also. Instead of Asia for the Japanese and Europe for the Germans, let each of the nations of Asia have an equal voice in Asiatic affairs, and each of the nations of Europe an equal voice in European affairs.

Act of Havana

At the Havana Conference the patient diplomacy of Secretary Hull helped to secure the Act of Havana. It forbade the transfer of any European colony to another non-American power, and stated that if any such transfer were attempted the colony in question would pass immediately under the joint control of the American states. To provide for the government of the colony a committee of twenty-one, to consist of one member for each American nation, might be summoned at will by any of the participating nations, and as an assurance against impotence this committee was to be considered fully constituted "from the date of the appointment of two-thirds of its members." Furthermore, actions might be taken with the approval of two-thirds of the members present, while a special emergency declaration gave the United States the support for the Monroe Doctrine from the other American nations that it long had craved:

If the necessity for emergency action be deemed so urgent as to make it impossible to await action of the committee, any of the American republics, individually or jointly with others, shall have the right to act in a manner required for its defense or the defense of the continent.

Canada

The Roosevelt administration also made a systematic effort to draw Canada more closely into the fraternity of American nations. Roosevelt, on a visit to Canada in 1938, reminded his hearers that the Monroe Doctrine applied as much to the territory north of the United States as to the territory south of it. "I give you assurance," he said, "that the people of the United States will not stand idly by if the domination of Canadian soil is threatened by any other empire." That Roosevelt meant what he said became evident two years later when he conferred on measures of joint defense with Prime Minister Mackenzie King of Canada at Ogdensburg, New York. By this time Canada was at war with Germany and Italy, while the United States, at least in theory, was a neutral. Nevertheless, the heads of the two governments agreed to set up a defense board, consisting of four or five members from each country, the business of which would be to "commence immediate studies relating to sea, land, and air . . . defense of the north half of the Western Hemisphere." On both sides of the border this declaration was hailed as the practical equivalent of a military alliance.

The Fall of France

In April, 1940, the phony war in the West came to a sudden end. Hitler's armies overran Denmark and Norway, the former without resistance, and the latter in spite of all the help that Allied ships and troops could give. In May the Nazi *Blitzkrieg* struck Belgium and Holland with devastating fury, and by the end of June it had brought them, as well as France, to surrender. Two weeks before France admitted defeat, Mussolini brought Italy into the war on Hitler's side, while the lesser nations of Europe that had not yet been conquered made every effort to curry favor with the victorious Germans. To most observers the invasion of England appeared imminent. The army that the British had landed on the Continent was able, almost miraculously, to withdraw at Dunkirk, but it had lost practically all its equipment. Only the royal air and naval forces blocked the way. Fully mindful of this fact, the British navy took prompt action to keep as many French warships as possible out of Hitler's hands. British naval forces attacked, and in large part destroyed, the French squadron at Oran in North Africa on July 3, 1940, and persuaded a similar squadron at Alexandria to remain immobilized.

In desperate but still defiant mood, the British prepared to carry on the war alone. "I have nothing to offer," said the new Prime Minister, Winston Churchill, "but blood, toil, tears, and sweat." The German air force began an aerial bombardment of Great Britain in August that destroyed large sections of London, as well as many other British cities, and lasted through the entire fall and winter. In fallen France, now ready to concede a German victory, a government subject to German dictation was set up at Vichy, with southeastern France and the overseas empire, theoretically at least, under its control. The Chief-of-State, aged Marshal Pétain, struggled with only slight success to maintain the fiction of French independence. Most of the other conquered countries established exile governments in London, where also a faction of "Free French," under the leadership of General Charles de Gaulle, claimed to represent France. Thus the British Isles remained one of the last bastions of freedom throughout once democratic Europe. Great Britain with her empire, in fact, now stood alone against the organized might of the dictators. Upon her hung the fate not only of Europe but also of Africa and Asia.

Most Americans probably believed during the "phony war" period that the European struggle might end in a stalemate. But after the fall of France they had to face the strong possibility of a Hitler victory. What then would happen to the New World? Some Americans seemed willing to take their chances. The first consideration, such persons believed, was that the United States must at any cost keep out of the war. Led by such adamant isolationists as Colonel Charles A. Lindbergh, and supported by the Hearst newspapers and the *Chicago Tribune*, they gave their sympathy and contributions to an America First Committee, which sought to discredit intervention. Opponents of the extreme isolationist view rallied similarly to the support of a Committee to Defend America by Aiding the Allies, headed for a time by the Kansas editor, William Allen White. Among those whose sympathies lay with this committee was the President of the United States. It was he who persuaded Congress to permit the shipment of American-made munitions to the enemies of Germany and Italy; furthermore, he had deliberately returned to the manufacturers as supposedly "outmoded" such military items as airplanes, knowing full well that they would promptly be shipped to the Allies.

America Rearms

Only a small minority of Americans, whatever their opinions on neutrality, opposed the further strengthening of American defenses. Obviously, with Japan determined to press her "new order" in Asia and Hitler on the loose in Europe, the United States needed a two-ocean navy. Even the Panama Canal was vulnerable if an enemy nation managed to obtain a nearby base for aircraft operation. Also, the revolutionary methods of land warfare used by the Germans had to be considered. Their attacks depended on the airplane, the tank, and other mechanized vehicles, equipment which the United States conspicuously lacked. It seemed clear to most Americans, whether isolationists, interventionists, or mere neutrals, that the least the nation should do was to perfect its armament with all possible speed, even if some insisted that preparedness was only a prelude to war. Congress gave unhesitating support to the defense program. By the end of September, total appropriations for defense had reached the gigantic sum of $13 billion. To facilitate further large-scale borrowing, the national debt limit was raised to $49 billion. Additional income and excise taxes were also voted, in defiance of the tradition that new taxes were not to be thought of in an election year. To furnish political supervision over the activities of army and navy, the President broke precedents right and left by making Henry L. Stimson, Secretary of State under Herbert Hoover, his Secretary of War, and Frank Knox, Republican vice-presidential candidate in 1936, his Secretary of the Navy. To put the industrial machine on a war basis, the President set up first a Defense Advisory Commission, then, when difficulties developed, an Office of Production Management. He showed some reluctance, however, to place the whole problem of production under one man's control, although William S. Knudsen, president of General Motors, headed both boards.

Unwilling to risk the delay involved in raising an army by volunteering, the President urged Congress to adopt a Selective Service Act. This plan met with the most determined opposition by the few isolationist Democrats and the great majority of the Republican members of both Houses. But by the middle of September, 1940, preparedness leaders in Congress were victorious. The new measure required all men between the ages of twenty-one and thirty-five inclusive to register for a year of military training. From this number the army planned to call into service during the first year about 800,000 men, and to replace them with a similar number each succeeding year. As the nation increased its cooperation with beleaguered Britain and the danger of war increased, the terms of the draft law were stiffened. The first class called had not yet completed its year of training when the President asked Congress to authorize the retention of all draftees in service for as much as eighteen months beyond the period for which they had originally been called. Congress complied on August 18, 1941, but only after a bitter legislative struggle, and then only by a majority of one vote in the House of Representatives. Meanwhile, units of the National Guard, the country's second line of defense, had been called into active service.

Measures "Short of War"

President Roosevelt, and a steadily increasing number of other Americans, believed the defense of the United States should be further promoted by effective measures "short of war" to help the British war effort. When it became known that the British navy was perilously short of destroyers, whereas the United States was not, pressure arose to sell "outmoded" American destroyers to the British, just as previously military airplanes had been sold to the Allies. Although specific legislation seemed to bar such action, the President was advised by Attorney-General Robert H. Jackson that his powers as Commander-in-Chief of the army and navy would permit him to exchange obsolete destroyers for such naval bases as he might deem essential to the defense of the United States. Accordingly, the President announced early in September that the United States had leased from the British government for a period of ninety-nine years eight bases, one each in Newfoundland, Bermuda, the Bahamas, Jamaica,

An Outmoded Destroyer.
This "four-stacker" was one of the fifty destroyers transferred to the British from the United States Navy.

St. Lucia, Trinidad, Antigua, and British Guiana. When these advanced positions were fully equipped, it was supposed that the Atlantic coastline of the United States, as well as the Panama Canal, would be completely safeguarded against attack from the east. In return for this "dismemberment of the British Empire," as the Axis Powers chose to term the deal, fifty American destroyers were turned over to British crews. It seemed evident that the hard pressed British, now fighting furiously against incessant attacks from the air as well as the constant threat of invasion by sea, could count on further aid from the United States when the need arose.

Election of 1940

With foreign relations so critical and with the necessity of hastening the national defense program so obvious, many observers regarded the necessity of holding a presidential election in 1940 as almost a calamity, but the Constitution was inexorable on this point. As events proved, this was no ordinary election. Shattering all precedents, the Democrats renominated Roosevelt for a third term, and chose Secretary of Agriculture Henry A. Wallace as his running mate. The Republicans, convinced that the leading contenders for their nomination lacked the popular appeal necessary to defeat the President, turned to an ex-Democrat and a businessman, Wendell L. Willkie of New York and Indiana. Both party platforms promised aid to Great Britain; both promised to keep the United States out of war. But platforms, as everybody knew, meant only what the candidates chose to make them mean. Charged with the intention of leading the United States into the war, Roosevelt replied: "I have said this before, but I shall say it again and again and again: Your boys are not going to be sent into any foreign war. . . . The purpose of our defense is defense." Willkie made a strenuous

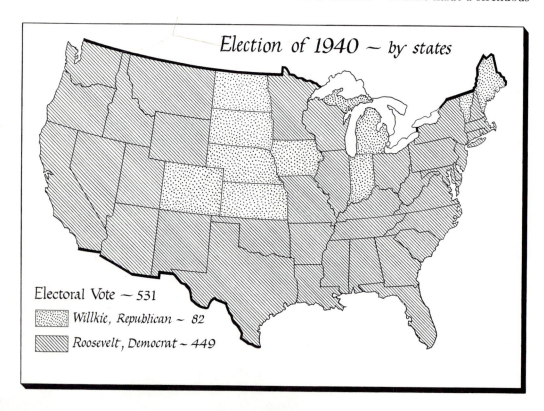

Election of 1940 – by states

Electoral Vote – 531

Willkie, Republican – 82

Roosevelt, Democrat – 449

but poorly paced campaign, stressing that in a democracy no one man should be considered indispensable, but the voters preferred in the crisis to stand by the President. About 50 million voters went to the polls, the largest number in American history up to that time. Of these nearly 55 per cent voted for Roosevelt, who carried 38 states with 449 electoral votes, while Willkie carried only 10 states with 82 electoral votes. Both houses of Congress and a majority of the state governments remained Democratic. Roosevelt was to have the opportunity to carry on in that time of world peril.

BIBLIOGRAPHY

One of the best ways to follow events in this chapter and the next is to read the fullest study of the President, J. M. Burns, *Roosevelt: The Soldier of Freedom, 1940–1945* (1970). A rich documentary collection is *Franklin D. Roosevelt and World Affairs* (3 vols., 1969), edited by E. B. Nixon and covering 1933–1937. R. A. Divine, *Roosevelt and World War II* (1969), is a series of stimulating lectures. For an overview of the war the best survey is Gordon Wright, *The Ordeal of Total War: 1939–1945* (1968).

Roosevelt's foreign policy is treated briefly and favorably by Allan Nevins, *The New Deal and World Affairs* (1950). Bitterly hostile are the principal revisionist treatments, C. A. Beard, *American Foreign Policy in the Making, 1932–1940* (1946); and C. C. Tansill, *Backdoor to War: The Roosevelt Foreign Policy, 1933–1941* (1952). A spirited reply to Beard is Basil Rauch, *Roosevelt: From Munich to Pearl Harbor* (1950). The fullest account of American foreign policy in the immediate prewar years may be found in two books by W. L. Langer and S. E. Gleason, *The Challenge to Isolation, 1937–1940* (1952), and *The Undeclared War, 1940–1941* (1953); the authors are friendly to the administration and have been dubbed "court historians" by the revisionists. A useful summary, a bit more critical in tone, is D. F. Drummond, *The Passing of American Neutrality, 1937–1941* (1955). An important source is Cordell Hull, *The Memoirs of Cordell Hull* (2 vols., 1948). See also the immensely detailed study by J. W. Pratt, *Cordell Hull* (2 vols., 1964).

The history of events in Europe leading up to the Second World War has produced a vast literature. G. A. Craig and Felix Gilbert (eds.), *The Diplomats, 1919–1939* (1953), is an interesting collection of essays by specialists. E. H. Carr, *The Twenty Years' Crisis, 1919–1939* (2nd ed., 1946), is an influential interpretation by a British liberal who is critical of his government's policies. F. L. Schuman, *Europe on the Eve* (1939), and *Night over Europe* (1941), give a vivid summary of diplomatic events from 1933 to 1940, from the viewpoint of a strong supporter of collective security. A. J. P. Taylor, *The Origins of the Second World War* (1961), is an attempt at revisionism which sees the war as a ghastly mistake brought about by blunderers on both sides.

Interesting interpretations by a leading American diplomat are in G. F. Kennan, *Russia and the West under Lenin and Stalin* (1961). On American policy toward the Soviet Union, see R. P. Browder, *The Origins of Soviet-American Diplomacy* (1953); and Beatrice Farnsworth, *William C. Bullitt and the Soviet Union* (1967). Fundamental for an understanding of Nazi Germany is Alan Bullock, *Hitler* (2nd ed., 1962), a brilliant biography. Differing interpretations of American policy toward Germany may be found in Robert Dallek, *Democrat and Diplomat: The Life of William E. Dodd* (1968); and Arnold Offner, *American Appeasement* (1969). The problem of Jewish refugees from Germany is treated by D. S. Wyman, *Paper Walls: America and the Refugee Crisis, 1938–1941* (1968), which concludes that the United States policies were quite ungenerous. Three works dealing with Nazi attitudes toward America are J. V. Compton, *The Swastika and the Eagle* (1967); Saul Friedländer, *Prelude to Downfall* (1967); and Alton Frye, *Nazi Germany and the American Hemisphere* (1967). Brice Harris, Jr., *The United States and the Italo-Ethiopian Crisis* (1964), is a brief scholarly study.

The literature on the Spanish Civil War is immense. The best general works are Gabriel Jackson, *The Spanish Republic and the Civil War, 1931–1939* (1965); and Hugh Thomas, *The Spanish Civil War* (1961). American policy is treated by F. J. Taylor, *The United States and the Spanish Civil War* (1956); and R. P. Traina, *American Diplomacy and the Spanish Civil War* (1968). Varying interpretations are found in *American Neutrality and the Spanish Civil War* (1963), edited by Allen Guttmann. The war's impact on American intellectuals is traced by Stanley Weintraub, *The Last Great Cause* (1968); and Allen Guttmann, *The Wound in the Heart* (1962). Varying interpretations of American participants on the Loyalist side are given by A. H. Landis, *The Abraham Lincoln Brigade* (1967); Cecil Eby, *Between the Bullet and the Lie* (1969); and R. Rosenstone, *Crusade on the Left* (1969).

J. W. Wheeler-Bennett, *Munich: Prologue to Tragedy* (1948), is scholarly and perspicacious. A collection of documents and varying interpretations is F. L. Loewenheim, *Peace or Appeasement?* (1965). On Anglo-American relations, see Forrest Davis, *The Atlantic System* (1941). Herbert Feis, *Seen from E. A.* (1947), relates some of the difficulties encountered by the State Department in operating under the neutrality laws. Another work of value, rather critical in tone, is L. C. Gardner, *Economic Aspects of New Deal Diplomacy* (1964). Robert Sobel, *The Origins of Interventionism: The United States and the Russo-Finnish War* (1960), is an interesting monograph which argues for the importance of its subject. See also J. A. DeNovo, *American Interests and Policies in the Middle East, 1900–1939* (1963).

On the Far East, see especially Dorothy Borg, *The United States and the Far Eastern Crisis of 1933–1938* (1964). J. K. Fairbank, *The United States and China* (2nd ed., 1958), is the standard general survey. Important testimony presented by the American Ambassador to Japan is J. C. Grew, *Turbulent Era* (1952). An excellent critical biography of Grew is W. H. Heinrichs, Jr., *American Ambassador* (1966).

R. A. Divine, *The Illusion of Neutrality* (1962), is a competent monograph dealing with the struggles over neutrality legislation. The best work on the Nye Committee is J. E. Wiltz, *In Search of Peace* (1963). But see also W. S. Cole, *Senator Gerald P. Nye and American Foreign Relations* (1962). Manfred Jonas, *Isolationism in America, 1935–1941* (1966), shows the variety in isolationism. *The Wartime Journals of Charles A. Lindbergh* (1970) documents the feeling of an influential opponent of war.

The battle between isolationists and interventionists may be followed in two monographs: Walter Johnson, *The Battle against Isolation* (1944), an account of the Committee to Defend America by Aiding the Allies; and W. S. Cole, *America First: The Battle against Intervention, 1940–1941* (1953). A frank study of the Chairman of the Senate Foreign Relations Committee is F. L. Israel, *Nevada's Key Pittman* (1963).

On Wendell Willkie and the 1940 campaign, the fullest account is Ellsworth Barnard, *Wendell Willkie* (1966). M. E. Dillon, *Wendell Willkie* (1952), emphasizes his pre-1940 years; Joseph Barnes, *Willkie* (1952), is chiefly concerned with foreign policy. D. B. Johnson, *The Republican Party and Wendell Willkie* (1960), assesses his impact on his newly chosen party. Some light on the still-elusive subject of Roosevelt's third nomination is given in Bernard Donahoe, *Private Plans and Public Dangers* (1965).

24

THE SECOND WORLD WAR

The Lend-Lease Act · Anglo-American alliance · Japanese-American relations · Pearl Harbor · "Europe First" · The home front · The North African and Italian campaigns · Conquest of Germany · The Pacific campaigns · The atom bomb · Costs of the war · The Yalta Conference · Death of Roosevelt

Roosevelt's election to an unprecedented third term in 1940 constituted an emphatic endorsement of his policy of "all-aid-short-of-war" to Britain. The American people, the majority of Congress, and the President himself were still opposed to committing the United States to "all-out-war," however, in spite of their willingness to aid Britain by every means short of direct participation. By early 1941 a number of civilian leaders, including Secretary of War Henry L. Stimson and Secretary of the Interior Harold L. Ickes, were advocates of war, and most high navy and army officials had concluded that American security demanded the defeat of Hitler (and, for some, Japan). It is probable that President Roosevelt shared this attitude, but he was too experienced a politician to lead a divided country into a struggle that would demand unity. He therefore minimized the talk of active war, while continuing to do everything in his power to aid the countries still resisting aggression.

The Lend-Lease Act

In order to facilitate the sending of aid to nations unable to pay cash for it, Roosevelt submitted an ingenious plan to Congress. Under it the United States government would have the authority to lend, lease, or otherwise transfer to the nations resisting aggressors such military equipment as American factories were able to produce and the American government to acquire. This measure, which amounted almost to a declaration of partial war, was fought for weeks by the isolationists in and out of Congress. Replying to the President's argument that lend-lease would not lead to war but rather would prevent it, Senator Wheeler of Montana charged that the Act would "plow under every fourth American boy" (a savage analogy to early New Deal agricultural policies), and give the President the dictatorial power "to conduct undeclared war anywhere in the world."

A MARINE RIFLEMAN in the mouth of a cave on Okinawa watches for enemy snipers.

Aiding the Montana Senator's attack were several of his Democratic colleagues together with the great majority of Republicans in both Houses. Willkie, however, and many who had voted for him, gave the lend-lease proposal their hearty support. Eventually the President's influence prevailed, and the Lend-Lease Act became law on March 11, 1941. Subsequently Congress appropriated $7 billion to finance the Act, and shipments to the embattled British were almost immediately on their way.

Anglo-American Alliance

Even after the passage of the Lend-Lease Act, which virtually ended American neutrality, most Americans were still opposed to committing the country to an all-out war. Many consoled themselves with Prime Minister Winston Churchill's famous and brilliantly timed remark in his radio address of February 9, 1941: "Give us the tools, and we will finish the job." But President Roosevelt, using his powers with skill, further implemented a policy which constituted an Anglo-American alliance.

In line with this policy, Axis, Danish, and French ships in American ports were seized. An executive agreement, reached April 10, 1941, between Secretary of State Hull and the Danish minister to Washington (who had refused to cooperate with his Nazi-dominated government), gave the United States permission to make military use of the island of Greenland. During the next few weeks of steadily mounting tension the President turned over fifty tankers to the British government, closed the Axis consulates in the United States, and, following the sinking in the South Atlantic of an American merchantman, proclaimed a state of "unlimited national emergency."

Meanwhile a virtual Anglo-American alliance had been consummated. During the debate on the Lend-Lease Act a full-dress meeting of the British and American general staffs had taken place in Washington.

Rapidly thereafter the two nations pooled their military intelligence and worked out elaborate plans for joint action. By September, 1941, American army transports were carrying thousands of British troops from Canada to Egypt where they were sorely needed in the critical battle for the Nile. Most of the above acts were performed by executive action and some were kept from the public. But whether the people realized it or not, the last pretense of American neutrality had evaporated.

Hitler on the Offensive

Meantime Hitler, after a winter of diplomatic preparation, made ready in the spring of 1941 to march his armies into the Balkans. Hungary, Rumania, and Bulgaria agreed to cooperate with his regime. The government of Yugoslavia was like-minded, but the Yugoslav army revolted and staged a brave but hopeless struggle against the invaders. Next the Greeks, whom Mussolini had been seeking in vain to conquer since the fall of 1940, were overwhelmed. The little British army sent to their aid from Egypt was driven out, and, after a short stand in Crete, was forced back to North Africa. There the British commander, General Sir Archibald Wavell, had recently pushed the Italians far to the west along the coast of Libya, but now the British hold on the eastern Mediterranean was tenuous indeed. Anticipating a German push to the oil fields of the Middle East, British and "Free French" forces, early in June, 1941, occupied Syria, but their chances of resisting a Nazi attack in force seemed slender.

Then on June 22, with Hungary, Rumania, and Finland as allies, Hitler attacked Russia. Washington and London were not unprepared for the turn of events; both, in fact, had warned Russia repeatedly that such an attack was a certainty. Despite all past differences, the United States and Great Britain received the U.S.S.R. to the anti-Nazi cause with cordiality. From

Churchill came the prompt announcement: "Any man or state who fights against Nazism will have our aid. Any man or state who marches with Hitler is our foe." And from Roosevelt came the assurance that supplies would soon be flowing from the United States to Russia under the terms of the Lend-Lease Act. To the surprise of most experts who recalled the Red Army's sorry showing against the Finns, the Russians offered sustained military resistance to the invading armies. Although the Germans and their allies took much territory and the Russians lost an enormous number of lives, the collapse they had confidently expected failed to occur. In the winter of 1941–1942, the Russian armies for several months even held the offensive and regained some of the ground they had lost.

With Russia, a Communist nation, fighting on the Allied side, the question of war aims was raised repeatedly. To answer this question, and also to give dramatic emphasis to the solidarity of Anglo-American opinion, President Roosevelt and Prime Minister Churchill met at Argentia Bay, Newfoundland, and on August 14, 1941, issued the Atlantic Charter. This document disclaimed for Great Britain and the United States any desire for territorial, or other, aggrandizement, or for any territorial changes not in accord with the wishes of the people concerned. It asserted the right of all peoples to choose the form of government under which they wished to live, and promised to promote equal access for all states, "great or small, victor or vanquished," to the raw materials of the world. Other named objectives included improved labor conditions; the unhindered use of the high seas; and the disarmament of aggressor nations as a step toward the abandonment of the use of force in international relations.

Battle of the Atlantic

By this time the increasing tempo of submarine attacks had brought the Battle of

THE SCORCHED EARTH. German soldiers advance through the burnt-out ruins of a Russian town.

the Atlantic to a crisis. Since a substantial number of freighters being sunk carried lend-lease materials, many Americans demanded that the United States join with Great Britain in convoying merchant fleets overseas. High officials of the navy also favored this policy as a prelude to actual hostilities. Admiral Stark considered "every day of delay in our getting into war as dangerous." But Roosevelt, leading a still undecided nation, ordered only that American ships and aircraft should "patrol" the western 2,000 miles of the Atlantic in order to advise the British as to the whereabouts of Axis craft. The President denied on May 27, 1941, that American ships were engaged in a "shooting war," but he promised that they would take whatever action was necessary to insure the delivery of war goods to Great Britain. He announced also, on July 7, 1941, that units of the United States navy had arrived in Iceland to supplement and ultimately replace the British forces already there; soon afterward he ordered the navy to keep open the sea lanes between Iceland (only 700 miles from the British coast) and the United States. The effectiveness of these actions brought speedy Axis retaliation. German submarines had already sunk eight American freighters

when, on September 4, 1941, an American destroyer was attacked while trailing a German submarine. Thereupon the President ordered destroyers to shoot submarines on sight. In mid-October another destroyer was hit, and eleven of her crew were killed. That same month, a second destroyer was torpedoed and sunk, with the loss of seventy-six of her crew. After these attacks, Congress, by a measure signed November 17, authorized the arming of American merchant ships and freed them from the remaining restrictions of the neutrality laws, which thus far had kept them outside "combat zones." The United States was by now engaged in a naval war, and complete participation seemed close at hand.

Japanese-American Relations

The attack on the United States, however, came from another quarter. In the Far East the irreconcilable differences between the Japanese "new order" and the American "open door" could not be resolved. Secretary Hull, on July 26, 1939, notified the Japanese government that the long-standing commercial treaty between Japan and the United States would be abrogated. This move was generally believed to anticipate an embargo on munitions shipments to Japan, but no such action was taken, and the conquest of China went on. In the summer of 1940, however, the United States forbade the export of essential war materials to any foreign country, without license, but by this time Japan was poised for action. From the Vichy French government, the Japanese extorted the right to occupy the northern part of French Indo-China, and in September, 1940, their troops took possession. The United States now countered with a complete embargo on the exportation of iron and steel scrap, except to Great Britain and the nations of the western hemisphere. The Japanese government quickly announced that a joint economic, political, and military alliance had been formed by Germany, Italy, and Japan.

The threat posed by the "Rome-Berlin-Tokyo Axis" was clear enough: Japan's next move would obviously be made with the support of the European members of the Axis. Hatred for British and American agents and diplomats in the Far East had long been freely exhibited; would the

Japanese, under Axis protection, now try to drive the West out of eastern Asia?

Interest in the Atlantic theater blinded many Americans to the perilous situation in the Far East, but when Japan, in July, 1941, obtained permission from Vichy-France to occupy the rest of Indo-China, the American State Department knew that trouble was at hand. Japanese troops pouring into this area posed a grave threat to the Philippine Islands, as well as to the British and Dutch possessions in the Far East, the main source of the world's tin and rubber supply. In protest, therefore, the American government on July 24 froze all Japanese assets in the United States, an action which the Dutch and British governments quickly paralleled. During the protracted discussions that followed, it was evident that neither nation would retreat from its respective position. The most the Japanese were willing to offer was a promise that they would not advance beyond Indo-China, provided the United States agreed to supply Japan with its needs for gasoline and oil, restore normal commercial relations between the two countries, guarantee the delivery to Japan of strategic supplies from the Netherlands Indies, and give no further aid to China. The American answer was presented by Secretary Hull on November 26, 1941. It included demands that Japan withdraw from both China and French Indo-China, recognize the government of Chiang Kai-shek, and abide by the principles of nonaggression and commercial equality. In return the United States promised to resume normal commercial relations with Japan and to release frozen Japanese assets in America.

Pearl Harbor

In October General Hideki Tojo had become head of a Japanese government controlled by the military, whose position was clearly indicated by its continued build-up of Japanese forces in Indo-China. Such actions, of course, discounted completely all hopes of a peaceful settlement, even though on November 15, 1941, a special Japanese envoy, Saburo Kurusu, arrived in Washington with what purported to be new Japanese proposals. Indeed, while the peace conversations were still in progress at Washington, early on the morning of December 7, a Japanese carrier-borne air force attacked the great American naval base at Pearl Harbor, in Hawaii. So complete was the surprise that most American aircraft were destroyed on the ground, leaving the

December 7, 1941, *"a date which will live in infamy,"* the Japanese attacked Pearl Harbor. The photograph shows a rescue crew beside the **USS West Virginia.**

American battle fleet at the mercy of the foe. Nineteen of the 86 American ships in the harbor were seriously hit, 5 capital ships were sunk or put out of action, and there were 4,575 killed, wounded, or missing. Had the Japanese been able to bring with them troops to effect a landing, they might well have taken Hawaii. Instead, they unified the American people by their sneak attack. Even their damage to the navy was less serious than it first seemed, since the carrier fleet was not caught at Pearl Harbor and since many vessels which were hit could be repaired quickly.

After the shock of Pearl Harbor had abated, and particularly after the war was over, critics of Roosevelt charged that he had cunningly placed the Japanese in such a position that their only alternative was to attack the United States. Only by this circuitous route, these critics argued, could the President achieve his chief goal of getting the United States into the European war. There is no evidence to support this "revisionist" view, although it is certain that Roosevelt underestimated the Japanese ability to damage the Pacific fleet, just as the Japanese leaders overestimated the importance of their attack on Pearl Harbor. The mistaken calculation of the Japanese militarists set off the train of events that led to direct American participation in both the Orient and Europe. It is hard to believe that Roosevelt could have seen any advantage in a two-front war, particularly when he was having to supply Britain and Russia while rearming his own country.

The day after Pearl Harbor, Congress, with only one dissenting vote, recognized the existence of a state of war between the United States and Japan, while Japan issued its overdue declaration of war against the United States and the British Empire. Within a few days, Germany and Italy, acting on their commitments to Japan, declared war against the United States, while Congress, by a unanimous vote in both houses, responded with similar declarations against the Axis powers in Europe. Thus the total war that most Americans had hoped to avoid at last became a fact.

"Europe First"

Even before Pearl Harbor, the United States government was secretly committed to what became known as the "Europe First" policy. General George C. Marshall, the Army Chief of Staff, and Admiral Harold R. Stark, Chief of Naval Operations, sent a memo dated November 5, 1941 to President Roosevelt, in which they delineated the policy, "If Japan be defeated and Germany remain undefeated, decision will still not have been reached. In any case, an unlimited offensive war should not be undertaken against Japan, since such a war would greatly weaken the combined effort in the Atlantic against Germany, the most dangerous enemy." This military decision had been reached in discussions with the British. Two weeks after Pearl Harbor, Churchill and his staff arrived in Washington for the Arcadia Conference. The prime minister was greatly relieved to discover that American policy had not been altered, in spite of the naval losses in the Pacific and of the clamor of many Americans for an immediate major offensive against Japan. On January 12, 1942, the British and American Chiefs of Staff agreed that "only the minimum of forces necessary for the safeguarding of vital interests in other theaters should be diverted from operations against Germany."

In the early months of 1942, Secretary Stimson, General Marshall, and other American leaders came to favor a cross-channel invasion of France from Britain in 1942, rather than the invasion of North Africa which Churchill had proposed at Arcadia. The Americans reached their decision more on the basis of what they considered was militarily expedient than as a result of the vigorous agitation of the Russians for a

"Second Front" in France to relieve German pressure on the East. At first Churchill seemed to agree but when he came to the United States for another conference in June he persuaded Roosevelt that a cross-channel invasion in 1942 was both risky and profitless. Roosevelt thereupon overruled his own military leaders and agreed to the North African invasion.

The Home Front

The solidarity of the "home front" during the years of American participation in the Second World War was virtually unbroken. The Japanese attack on Pearl Harbor, followed by declarations of war against the United States by both Germany and Italy, left little room for opposition to the war, even among isolationists. Few Americans of German or Italian descent were prepared to apologize for the behavior of Hitler or Mussolini, while not one Japanese on the Pacific Coast and in Hawaii, for all the suspicion with which they were regarded, was ever found guilty of sabotage or espionage. Communists in the United States were violently antiwar and isolationist during nearly two years of American neutrality, but after Hitler's attack on Russia, the "party line" reversed itself, and when the United States entered the war, American Communists gave their government consistent support. Some Socialists, led by Norman Thomas, a few clergymen, and a small number of conscientious objectors furnished about all the opposition there was to the war. Under the circumstances, there was little persecution of nonconformists.

Japanese Americans

The one notable blot on the American record of tolerance was the treatment of the Japanese in Hawaii and on the Pacific Coast. In the Hawaiian Islands between 30 and 40 per cent of the population were of Japanese ancestry; hence it was not possible to remove them to the mainland, as was actually suggested, without completely disrupting the economic life of the Islands. But the political rights of Hawaiians, regardless of race, color, or nationality, were almost totally abrogated during the war. Military law replaced civilian government, and army officers discharged the duties normally assigned to judges and police magistrates. Only with the greatest difficulty did the Hawaiians regain their normal rights, and to guard against any repetition of unpleasantnesses associated with army rule, they began immediately after the war a movement for statehood. On the Pacific Coast, even in California where they were most numerous, the Japanese constituted only a tiny fraction of the total population. By Executive Order of the President, later approved by Congress and upheld by the Supreme Court, they were herded into interior "relocation camps." Conditions in the camps were far from satisfactory, but in general the Japanese "evacuees" conducted themselves well. Despite the discrimination against their ancestry, many Americans of Japanese descent, both from Hawaii and from the mainland, served with distinction in the Army of the United States. After the war, the "relocation camps" were broken up, and their inmates were allowed to return to whatever remained of their normal life. Their enormous property losses were never repaid and many preferred to settle away from the unfriendly West Coast.

The Wartime Economy

Early in 1942 the War Production Board headed by Donald M. Nelson, together with numerous other boards and agencies created as events required, paved the way for a war government not unlike the one developed in the First World War. The Defense Plant Corporation spent over $16 billion in construction of government-owned factories to produce vitally needed materials and products, chief among which was synthetic rubber to replace the nation's Far Eastern natural rubber supply lost to the Japanese. To conserve existing rubber, low speed-limits for automobile traffic, as well as tire- and gasoline-rationing, were accepted as necessary evils. The chief means by which the WPB sought to accelerate war production were (1) by prohibiting the manufacture of a long list of civilian products containing iron and steel, (2) by a system of priorities directing essential materials and products to manufacturers and consumers, and (3) by a kind of national budgeting of steel, aluminum, and copper through what was called the Controlled Materials Plan. Just as the nation's basic metals were rationed among manufacturers according to war needs, so were many consumer products rationed among civilians. Since employers were competing fiercely for a dwindling labor supply, wages were set by the Office of Price Administration, as were rents and the prices of practically all basic commodities and services. Taxes rose astronomically, yet the people responded willingly to the plea that they invest at least 10 per cent of their incomes in war bonds.

By such means American energy was turned from peacetime pursuits to production for war. Hundreds of completely new war factories were built, and old plants were converted for the making of weapons. Shipyards increased their capacity enormously, and by the end of the war some of them were turning out a standardized merchant ship by almost production-line methods. Labor generally forgot its internal conflicts and carried on with only infrequent strikes. Farmers provided a steady flow of lend-lease foodstuffs abroad, while supplying adequately army and civilian needs both overseas and at home. By 1944 American industry accounted for over one-half the world's total war production, while at the same time maintaining the prewar civilian standard of living. By the end of 1942 a million American soldiers poured over-

seas, the spearhead of what was to become the most highly mechanized and the best equipped force in the world.

Wartime Society

Over fifteen million Americans served in the armed forces during World War II, in widely scattered parts of the world. While few of them had any apparent political objection to the war, the vast majority remained civilians in uniform, in spite of the best efforts of officers and "non-coms" to convert them into something else. Indeed, a large proportion of those officers and non-coms were themselves civilians in uniform, in spite of any impressions they tried to create at the time. The favorite cartoon character of most servicemen was undoubtedly Bill Mauldin's "G.I. Joe," a grimy, bedraggled, incorrigibly civilian soldier who found nothing glamorous in his tedious, dangerous duty. Those who went overseas frequently spent long periods away from "the States"; many who went to the Pacific in 1940 or 1941 spent the entire war abroad. Although penicillin and other new drugs helped to reduce the incidence of prolonged, serious disease and the development of blood plasma saved many lives, nothing could cure the boredom of most of those who served in subordinate roles in the armed services.

World War II was not a war of flags, parades, patriotic oratory and bombast. Perhaps the memory of World War I was too vivid for that. The naive, crusading qualities of earlier wars were replaced by grim determination, at least for many who saw duty. Internationalists emphasized that the United States, by refusing to participate in collective security arrangements after 1918, bore a major responsibility for the breakdown of world order; it is possible that their propaganda influenced some servicemen. But it is more probable that the popular attitude was more earthy: Japan had attacked the United States and Germany had come to Japan's aid; the only thing to do was to defeat Japan and Germany, as soon as possible. After that the civilians in uniform could go home again and pick up their private lives once more.

Life on the home front was drastically changed for millions of Americans. For most it was a time of unrelenting toil, shortages of housing and consumer goods, and (when people had time to think about it) irritation and boredom. The number of people gainfully employed rose from 45 million to as many as 70 million, a good many millions of whom were probably not fit for hard physical labor. Additionally, millions of people were shifted back and forth across the country, to new shipyards, aluminum plants, aircraft factories, construction jobs. Inevitably much social tension built up under these conditions, particularly for those families who had men away in the service.

The same rather glum spirit already noted among servicemen was also found on the home front. While there was almost no opposition to the war itself, there was much criticism of the management of the war, especially of the waste and of the emphasis on secrecy. Basic wage rates were kept down by a formula but abundant overtime work resulted in substantially larger incomes. Ironically, these larger incomes could not buy many of the things workers most wanted. Farm prices were controlled but not until prices had increased; farm income rose 90 per cent by 1943. Still farmers wanted more, in spite of the fact that they, too, could not buy many of the things they wanted during wartime. It was difficult for civilians to travel about during the war, unless they were being sent somewhere on defense orders. Gasoline was rationed, trains were crowded, automobiles were aging rapidly (and not being replaced "for the duration").

This rather unhappy, unlovely society produced the food and the equipment needed to win the war. It accumulated large earnings and placed them in bonds, savings stamps, and bank accounts. It worked and worked, waited and waited, grim, confident, and tired.

The War in 1942

For many months the war in the Pacific went badly for the United Nations, as the Allies now began to call themselves. The attack on Pearl Harbor was followed immediately by attacks on the Philippine Islands, Wake Island, Guam, Hong Kong, Malaya, and Thailand. The Thai government offered practically no resistance, Guam fell on December 11, Wake Island, December 24, and Hong Kong on Christmas Day, 1941. In the Philippines General MacArthur, whose forces during the last phases of the dispute with Japan had been somewhat augmented by troops from the United States, made a valiant stand on the Bataan peninsula and the island of Corregidor. But any further support from the United States armed forces was simply unavailable. Bataan capitulated on April 9, 1942, and Corregidor on May 6, 1942. Well before the end came, MacArthur, in response to an insistent demand from both the United States and Australia, left the Philippines by stealth to take command of the Allied forces in Australia. Meantime Japanese troops overran Malaya, captured Singapore, conquered Burma, and except for a few precarious footholds forced the United Nations completely out of the East Indies. With the Burma Road closed, aid to China decreased to almost nothing, and the Allies fell back upon India and Australia as bases of operation.

Elsewhere in the world the position of the United Nations was equally depressing. Operating off the Atlantic coast line and in the Caribbean, German submarines sank hundreds of American freighters during the first months of 1942 and produced an acute gasoline and oil shortage along the Atlantic seaboard. Far more important was the threatened collapse in the summer of 1942 of the United Nations' entire position in

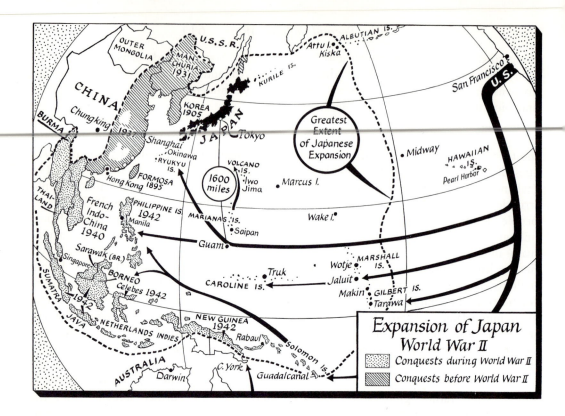

Expansion of Japan World War II

- Conquests during World War II
- Conquests before World War II

Russia and North Africa. By that time the German General Erwin Rommel was within seventy miles of Alexandria, threatening the British defense of the Suez Canal and the Middle East. By August German armies were fighting in the streets of Stalingrad on the Volga, thus threatening to cut off all of southern Russia and its vital oil supplies.

Stung to desperation by the unbroken procession of defeats, the people of the United States settled down with determination to create a war machine adequate to cope with their enemies. During 1942 Congress authorized increases in the size of the army and navy, and by 1945 America had over 12 million men under arms. The navy, which had only 4,500 ships in 1941, was by 1945 increased to 90,000 ships and landing craft. Included in this vast fleet were 23 battleships, 20 large carriers, 78 small carriers, and 72 cruisers. For the first time in the nation's history women were recruited in numbers for the fighting forces, some 100,000 volunteering for service in the Women's Army Corps (WAC) and over 80,000 in the naval counterpart, the WAVES. To house, equip, and supply this great force was in itself an enormous task. But in addition, the nation had to maintain and even increase the flow of lend-lease goods to its allies, and, of course, provide for the civilian population.

Invasion of North Africa

Well before the end of 1942 the tide of battle had begun to turn. While the Russians were grinding the German offensive to a stop at Stalingrad and the British were chasing the Afrika Korps westward, the United States had chalked up a series of costly but important naval victories in the Coral Sea, off Midway (the decisive battle of the naval war), and in the Solomon Islands. The initiative seemed definitely to have passed from the Japanese to the Allies on August 7, 1942, when the marines took Tulagi harbor and the airfield on Guadalcanal. Still disappointed in the progress made, the American people gave the Roosevelt administration a domestic setback on election day, November 3, by reducing substantially the Democratic majorities in both House and Senate, and by overthrowing Democratic control in many states.

Four days later, came the news that a huge Anglo-American armada had landed troops in French North Africa, with the avowed intention of occupying the entire North African seacoast of the French Empire, both Mediterranean and Atlantic. This daring operation had been planned at a meeting of Churchill and Roosevelt in Washington the preceding June, but the secret was well kept, and the Axis Powers were taken completely by surprise. Without serious loss 500 transports, supported by 350 warships, brought the invasion forces to their destination. General Dwight D. Eisenhower, in supreme command of operations on land, got his troops ashore with little serious fighting except at Casablanca and Oran. Although the Vichy-French government dared not condone the Allied invasion, some of its representatives in North Africa deliberately aided the invaders. The Allied invaders, with apparently no concern about the consent of the Al-

gerians themselves, planned to turn the area back to France. They had expected to make General Henri Giraud, a high-ranking French officer who had escaped from imprisonment in Germany, the chief French official in North Africa, but this plan did not meet the approval of the Free French leader in London, General Charles de Gaulle, who outmaneuvered both Giraud and the Allied leaders, and himself assumed control.

Tunisia

Obviously the Allied governments had hoped that their African conquests would extend to Tunisia before that colony could be occupied by the Axis, but in this they were disappointed. Early in 1943, German and Italian divisions under General Jurgen von Arnim were concentrated in Tunisia for a last-ditch fight, in which General Erwin Rommel's famous Afrika Korps, still retreating from Egypt, was expected to join. The final struggle came in May, 1943, when the British Eighth Army under General Sir Bernard Montgomery closed in from the east, and British, French, and American troops from the west. Von Arnim and Rommel were able to join forces, but were promptly defeated. All of

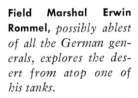

Field Marshal Erwin Rommel, *possibly ablest of all the German generals, explores the desert from atop one of his tanks.*

The Liberation of Paris. *American soldiers marching through Paris following its recapture, August 25, 1944.*

Tunisia, including the cities of Tunis and Bizerte, was occupied by the victorious Allied troops, who, during the final phases of the campaign, took well over 200,000 prisoners, among them von Arnim himself. Before the final collapse, Rommel had left Africa for Europe, but practically all the Axis troops which he and von Arnim had commanded were killed or captured.

Italy

The next great goal of Allied endeavor was Sicily, which Eisenhower's forces invaded on July 10, 1943, and conquered in less than six weeks. Before this task was completed, King Victor Emmanuel, assisted by elements in the Fascist Grand Council, forced Mussolini out of power, and set up a new government under Marshal Pietro Badoglio as premier. Although Badoglio surrendered to the Allies, the Nazis rescued Mussolini and carried on the battle. Stiff German resistance held the Allies back many months in Italy, but at length, on June 4, 1944, Rome was taken. The chief strategic purpose of the North African and Italian campaign was to clear the Mediterranean of enemy sea and air power, and this end was fully accomplished. By the fall of 1944, with Italy now recognized as a "co-belligerent," Allied arms had reached the valley of the Po.

The Second Front

Since 1942 a joint British-American staff had laid plans for an invasion of Germany through the heart of Europe, but the exact place of this "second front" had been a subject of long debate. Prime Minister Churchill and his military aides consistently argued for a thrust into the "soft underbelly" of Europe and up through the Balkans, freely admitting that one of their aims was to seal eastern Europe off from the advancing Communists. The American command, however, insisting that political arguments be subordinated to the fundamental military task of crushing Germany, held out for a direct cross channel attack against Hitler's "fortress Europa." On June 6, 1944, the long-awaited "second front" was launched from England across the Channel to the coast of Normandy. To conduct this campaign Eisenhower and Montgomery were transferred from Italy. Despite difficult weather and the lack of harbors, the invasion was completely successful, and the reconquest of France began.

On August 24–25, Paris was occupied by Allied troops amidst demonstrations of joy by its inhabitants. To reinforce the Channel invaders, another expedition landed August 15 on the Mediterranean coast of France, and worked its way northward with extraordinary rapidity. When winter set in, nearly all of France and Belgium had been freed, part of the Netherlands had been cleared of enemy troops, and Allied armies were fighting on German soil. Somewhat belatedly, the British and American governments recognized de Gaulle's "Free French" Committee as the provisional government of France. For Belgium and the Netherlands, governments-in-exile, long since functioning in England, had only to be transferred to the Continent.

On the Sea and in the Air

In the air and on the seas the German situation grew steadily more desperate. The attempt of the Nazis to bomb the British into submission had not only failed completely; it had brought devastating retaliation. While the Germans were able to make only "nuisance" raids over England, British and American bombers attacked German, German-held, and Italian cities by night and day. Harbor installations, airfields, war factories, railway yards, power plants, bridges, dams, and entire cities were subjected to almost continuous bombing. After the Allied landings on the French coast had been effected, a German secret weapon, the robot bomb, inflicted considerable casualties upon the civilian population of southern England, but it failed completely to halt the invasion. On the high seas, where German submarines had long taken a heavy toll, new devices for detecting and destroying them diminished drastically their effectiveness and all but eliminated them as a factor in the war. Lend-lease supplies flowed in a steady stream to Russia, while communications with the British Isles and the Mediterranean approached peacetime conditions.

Meantime on the eastern front the Germans, after losing at Stalingrad in 1942, retreated steadily before growing Russian strength. Not only were they forced to abandon all Russian territory, but they were also driven out of Bulgaria, Rumania, and Finland, each of which, like Italy, joined the Allies. By the end of 1944, Russian troops had invaded Poland, Hungary, Yugoslavia, Czechoslovakia, and East Prussia, while British forces were well along with the reconquest of Greece, and "partisans" under Marshal Tito were aiding in the liberation of Yugoslavia. The utter hopelessness of the German situation seemed plain to all except the Nazi leaders.

German V–2 Bomb. *During the war the Germans developed a flying bomb known as the* Vergeltungswaffe *(V–1, V–2), or retaliation weapon, and called by the British the "buzz bomb." The specimen shown here was captured intact by United States First Army soldiers.*

As fate seemed to be closing in on the Germans, their government proceeded rapidly with what it referred to as "the final solution" of the Jewish problem. The dreadful concentration camps at Belsen, Buchenwald, and Dachau were jammed with Jewish men, women, and children, thousands of whom were starved and tortured to death. Others were shipped east to the mass extermination camps in Poland. There, in the gas chambers of Majdanek, Treblinka, and Auschwitz, some six million persons, chiefly Jews and Poles, were methodically killed. The savagery of the Nazi leaders was nowhere better shown than in their all-too-successful attempt at "the final solution."

Many optimists, including General Eisenhower, had dreamed of victory in 1944, but as winter set in, the Allied campaigns, both eastern and western, slowed to a halt. To make matters worse, the Germans under Field Marshal Karl von Rundstedt launched an utterly unanticipated counterattack in the Belgium-Luxembourg sector that for a time seriously threatened the Allied position. But as the old year ended, the Allies, mainly through the efforts of General George S. Patton's Third American Army, brought the German drive to a standstill and regained the initiative.

Conquest of Germany

The time had now come for the careful synchronization of Allied activities on the eastern and the western fronts. In the eastern theater, the Russians delayed their customary winter offensive until January 12, 1945. Then they struck forcefully with five huge armies, and the German defenses were smashed from the Baltic to the Carpathians. By the end of February, Russian troops were on German soil only thirty-one miles from Berlin. In the west, Eisenhower was somewhat delayed by the von Rundstedt offensive, but by early March, Allied troops had penetrated into nearly every stronghold of the famed Siegfried Line, taking prisoners by the hundreds of thousands. Many Germans succeeded in withdrawing across the Rhine, but on March 7, owing to the failure of the retreating forces to destroy a bridge at Remagen, they were followed by American soldiers in considerable numbers. The bridge soon collapsed, but from newly established bridgeheads Allied forces in great strength pushed forward through the very heart of the Reich. The "scorched-

The Siegfried Line, *hailed by the Germans as impregnable, is shown here being easily penetrated near Roetgen, Germany, by American troops, some afoot and some riding a bulldozer tank.*

earth" policy that the Nazi leaders had ordered, together with the persistent bombing of German cities and the devastation incidental to military operations, left much of Germany in ruins.

No reliable evidence exists to indicate that Roosevelt had agreed to Russian troops occupying Berlin in advance of the troops of other nations. But the Anglo-American advance was halted when it might easily have reached Berlin ahead of the Russians. General Eisenhower took full responsibility for the decision, justifying it on the grounds that Berlin had no military value. For the same reason he also called back an American advance on Prague, thus enabling the Russians to occupy another capital city and dominate the reconstruction of another country. By the end of April, when the Russian and American forces met on the banks of the Elbe River, victorious Russian armies had occupied all of the various Nazi satellite nations in eastern Europe, the German armies in northern Italy had surrendered, and Mussolini had lost his life at the hands of a Milanese mob. The Russians fought their way street by street through the rubble of Berlin, and took possession of what was left of the stricken city. Hitler himself committed suicide and shortly afterward Admiral Karl Doenitz, to whom Hitler had transferred his authority, notified the Allies that Germany was ready to surrender. On May 8, 1945, the Allied victory in Europe was officially proclaimed.

The Pacific

By this time the Allies dominated the Pacific. In mid-November, 1942, the Japanese tried to oust the Americans from Guadalcanal, but failed, in large part because of naval defeats administered by American squadrons operating under the command of Admiral William F. Halsey. Japanese efforts to push across New Guinea in order to strike at Australia were also frustrated. After that, the bitter fighting

necessary to clear the way back to the Philippines could begin. By this time the American navy had recovered from its losses at Pearl Harbor, and with each succeeding month its strength increased. In the cold and fog of the Aleutians, where the Japanese had held two American islands, Kiska and Attu, since June, 1942, the Americans struck at Attu, May 11, 1943, and soon took the island. The Japanese then abandoned Kiska. The next great effort of the American navy was to drive the Japanese from the islands of the mid-Pacific. In November, 1943, marine and army forces successfully invaded several atolls in the Gilberts, among them Tarawa, where the fighting was particularly bloody. Kwajalein in the Marshalls was taken early in 1944.

It was now plain that the strategy of Admiral Chester W. Nimitz, commander-in-chief of the Pacific fleet, called for a direct advance across the Pacific to Asiatic waters. No effort was made to clear every island occupied by the Japanese, but important bases, with airfields that could dominate wide stretches of ocean, were taken and strongly held. By June, 1944, the advance had reached Saipan in the Marianas, 1,500 miles from Tokyo and 1,600 miles from Manila. Frightened by the approaching danger, the Japanese sent carrier-based planes to attack the American ships off Saipan, but the attackers suffered heavily, while American planes in turn inflicted severe damage upon the enemy fleet. The bloody but successful conquest of Saipan was followed in the next month by the occupation of nearby Guam and Tinian. Bomber attacks could now be made from these bases, as well as from China, upon Formosa and the Japanese homeland, and the exploit of the *Hornet*, which had sent its planes in April, 1942, to attack Tokyo, was repeated by land-based planes from Saipan. From this time on, the destruction of Japanese cities and industrial targets proceeded mercilessly.

Kwajalein Atoll. Following pre-invasion bombing, American infantrymen move in to mop up Japanese survivors.

"On the Sea and in the Air." Rabaul Harbor, New Britain. Burning in the foreground is a Japanese ship; to the left is a USAF North American B-25; fires along the shore are the work of U.S. bombers.

To shorten the bombing range to Japan, two more islands were taken by American land and naval forces early in 1945. The first, Iwo Jima, a tiny islet in the volcano group midway between Guam and Tokyo, provided the Japanese with three airfields and a radar station. Enemy intelligence was thus able to detect flights of Tokyo-bound American planes. So great was the nuisance value of this island that on February 19, 1945, two divisions of marines, supported by a prodigious show of naval force, undertook its conquest. The entrenched Japanese fought back furiously; the battle lasted a month, and American casualties reached 20,000, but the coveted terrain was won.

The last major amphibious operation in the advance on Japan began on Easter Sunday, April 1, when Okinawa, largest island in the Ryukyus, only 370 miles from Japan, was invaded. Fourteen hundred ships and upwards of 100,000 American soldiers and marines participated in the action. The Americans got ashore easily, but in southern Okinawa, toward which the Japanese retreated and reformed, the enemy staged a desperate and unexpectedly prolonged resistance. During this engagement Japanese *Kamikaze*, specially trained pilots who deliberately sought to smash their bomb-laden planes into the American ships, first made their appearance in large numbers. Enough of them succeeded in their suicidal missions to inflict serious losses upon the American fleet. But by the middle of June, the Americans were in complete control of the island. American bombers, operating from convenient airfields and from the decks of a host of task-force carriers, now burned and blasted the Japanese islands at will.

Meantime, the campaign of MacArthur to retake the Philippines had made notable progress. His forces bypassed the principal Japanese bases, and by "leapfrog" tactics landed at unexpected, and sometimes undefended, points along a predetermined route. By January, 1944, he had begun to advance in this fashion along the northern shores of New Guinea, and well before the end of the year he was ready to launch the actual invasion of the Philippines. On October 20, he landed with a large army on the island of Leyte, and began the reconquest he had promised earlier to the peoples of America and the Philippines. To protect MacArthur's movements, a heavy naval concentration under Admiral Halsey was obliged to fight one of the greatest sea-actions of history, for the Japanese at last decided that they must risk a major portion of their fleet. In the waters adjacent to Leyte, beginning on October 25, the Americans fought off the Japanese in a series of complicated and extensive actions so costly to the enemy as to reduce the Japanese navy to "fifth-rate" status.

After the battle of Leyte, organized resistance disintegrated slowly but surely. In January, 1945, MacArthur put ashore a formidable force at Lingayen Gulf, and began the fateful march to Manila. Japanese resistance was light at first, but the approaches to the capital were stubbornly defended, and not until February 3 could American troops enter it. After that, the Japanese staged within the city a last-ditch fight that lasted for weeks. Meantime Mindanao and certain lesser islands had been successfully invaded. Japanese hopes were waning fast, but stiff fighting continued on many of the islands until the end of the war.

The Asian Mainland

While the war in the Pacific was thus being planned and fought, Allied forces were attempting to block the Japanese from further conquests on the mainland of Asia. The task could hardly have been more difficult. With India as a base, some Allied aid to the Chinese was soon being flown in over the Himalayas, but it was never enough. Bad relations between the government of Chiang Kai-shek and the armed communist bands controlling much of North China added to the turmoil in that unhappy nation. Meager American air forces, operating under General Joseph W. Stilwell, aided Chiang's armies, but in spite of their best efforts Japanese troops were able to penetrate into Chinese territory almost at will.

Probably, Stilwell's principal achievement lay in clearing the Japanese from northern Burma so as to open a new supply route — the Ledo Road — from India to China. Using Chinese troops, he nearly completed this task when, in the fall of 1944, he was relieved of his command and recalled to the United States. This action was taken at the insistence of Chiang Kai-shek, with whom Stilwell had had numerous personal differences over the training and disposition of Chinese troops. American engineers went on with the road, however, and in January, 1945, the first motor caravan crossed it into China. Allied successes farther to the south in Burma, under the leadership of Lord Louis Mountbatten, were also heartening, but in spite of the achievements in Burma the war ended with the Japanese still in control of their principal gains on the mainland of Asia.

The Atom Bomb

Nevertheless, the Japanese ability to continue the war was waning fast. Far-ranging American submarines, joining their successes to those of American surface forces, helped to drive the Japanese navy and merchant marine almost completely from the seas. In consequence, connections between the home islands and the overexpanded Co-Prosperity Sphere broke down. In late May, 1945, Stalin informed the United States that certain Japanese officials had already talked to the Russians about terms for a possible peace. But it was also known that most Japanese militarists were intent upon avoiding unconditional surrender, even if that meant a last-ditch stand on the Japanese home islands. Consequently American plans for softening up the resistance to an invasion of the Japanese home island of Kyushu went on. With a view to shortening the war and saving hundreds of thousands of lives that a direct invasion of Japan might have cost, President Truman authorized the use of the secret and terrible weapon that Allied scientists had put at his disposal, the atomic bomb. The first atomic bomb was dropped on Hiroshima, August 6, 1945. Shortly thereafter, a similar bomb was dropped on Nagasaki. The results were cataclysmic — a single bomb proved more devastating than the concentrated action of a thousand ordinary bombers equipped with full loads of ordinary explosives. Nearly 130,000 people were killed, wounded, or missing at Hiroshima; seven-tenths of the city was leveled. At Nagasaki, a part of which was devastated, about 75,000 persons were killed or injured.

The development of the atomic bomb was the result of cooperative efforts by numerous American, British, Canadian, and European scientists, who, with the full backing of their governments, had pooled their resources in a successful effort to split the atom. Although the bomb may have shortened the war materially, many Americans regretted that their government had resorted to it before making greater efforts to induce Japan, who was already beaten, to surrender. A majority of the scientists contributing to the development of the bomb argued that its demonstration on some deserted spot should have preceded its actual use. In view of Japan's evident growing desire for peace, some military men felt that the unconditional surrender terms might have been modified. The fateful decision was made, however, to save American lives and to end the war quickly. The dropping of the bomb hurt American prestige throughout the world and continues to do so. The awesome destruction of Hiroshima and Nagasaki made clear how totally catastrophic another major war would be.

Japanese Surrender

For some months it was understood by the British and American chiefs of state that Russia intended eventually to enter the war against Japan. With the end so near, the Russian government found it inexpedient to delay longer, and on August 9, following a formal declaration of war, issued the day before, Russian troops began to advance against light opposition into Manchuria. Faced by this new threat, and assured by the President of the United States that only surrender could save Japanese civilization from total annihilation by the further use of atomic bombs, Japan gave up. The Allies agreed to the one Japanese condition — that they be allowed to retain their Emperor — on condition that he take orders from an Allied supreme commander,

Hiroshima. *The destruction wrought by an American atomic bomb on this Japanese city, followed by another bomb dropped on Nagasaki, concluded the war with Japan on the same note of violence with which it had begun at Pearl Harbor.*

to be resident in Japan. This offer the Japanese government accepted, and by August 14 the war was over. The documents of surrender were not actually signed until the formal surrender of September 1. Thereafter the occupation of Japan by American forces proceeded rapidly, and General MacArthur, acting through the Emperor, became the real ruler of Japan.

The Cost of the War

The cost in dollars, lives, and social dislocation was much heavier in the Second World War than it had been in the First. Expenditures for the Second World War reached about $300 billion, more than eight times as much as the nation spent on the First World War. Ironically, these defense expenditures brought full recovery from the Great Depression.

The cost in lives was about 393,000, at least three times as many as in 1917–1918, although far fewer in proportion to the amount of fighting done. The difference was due to better training before battle action and greater medical efficiency. Of the total 15.2 million people mobilized by the United States, over 1 million were reported as casualties. But even these figures were a small part of the total human costs of the war. Just how many soldiers and civilians on both sides of the line perished will probably never be known. Some 80 million men had been mobilized by all the powers, and of this number at least 15 million had been killed. In addition, countless civilians had died from the violence, disease, and hunger accompanying probably the greatest tragedy known to history.

The cost in dollars of the war was met in large part by borrowing, although heavy taxation made it possible to finance about 40 per cent of war expenditures from current income. Income taxes were made applicable to nearly everyone, and the public was encouraged to invest in bonds by regular payroll deductions if necessary. Eight special "drives," with a tremendous fanfare of advertising, sought to tap the nation's savings, particularly those of the small investor. Unlike the bonds of the First World War, which were all transferable and were frequently sold at a discount by hard pressed investors, the savings bonds of the Second World War were nontransferable, and were redeemable by the government on demand.

Allied Unity

The unity of effort that the Allies had attained during the war seemed to offer hope for the achievement of a successful world organization. There had been frequent conferences held by heads of states, their foreign ministers, and their military advisers. After the invasion of North Africa, Churchill and Roosevelt met at Casablanca, North Africa, in January, 1943, to lay further plans and to confer with de Gaulle and Giraud. Out of this conference came much undisclosed planning and an official announcement that only by "unconditional surrender" could the Axis nations obtain peace. Churchill, Roosevelt, and Chiang Kai-shek met in Cairo in November, 1943, and immediately thereafter for the first time both Churchill and Roosevelt conferred together with Stalin, at Teheran. So complete were the plans worked out at the Cairo and Teheran meetings that more than a year elapsed before the conferees got together again.

Yalta

Then, early in February, 1945, Churchill, Roosevelt, and Stalin met at Yalta in the Crimea. This conference not only agreed on the "timing, scope and coordination" of the last campaign against Germany, but also authorized the calling of the San Francisco Conference, where the United Nations was to be organized.

Of vast significance to the peace of the world was the attitude of the Russian leaders. President Roosevelt, knowing full well that Russian cooperation would be essential to world stability, had made every effort to win the confidence of the Russian leaders. He had accorded the most bountiful lend-lease aid to Russia; he had supported the early launching of a second front in France to relieve the pressure on the Russian armies to the East; and he had opposed a British-sponsored campaign in the Balkans to which Russia vehemently objected, and which, if successful, would have seen British and American troops rather than Russian in control of the Balkans and much of Central Europe at the end of the war.

The climax of Roosevelt's overtures to Russia came at Yalta. As part of the price necessary to win Stalin's cooperation, he acceded to the Russian demand that three of the Russian Soviet republics should be accorded membership in the United Nations. Also, as a gesture of conciliation, both to Russia and to American sentiment, he agreed to the principle of the great-power veto in all important acts of the Security Council. In European boundary settlements, Roosevelt conceded to Russia the right to annex all of eastern Poland, and to Poland the right to make compensatory annexations at the expense of Germany. These things, the President believed, he could not have prevented, even if he had tried. For in spite of frequent grave criticism leveled at the Yalta agreements it must be remembered that, at the time they were being made, Russia was in a far stronger position to exact concessions in Eastern Europe than were its western allies. Things might have been vastly different had Roosevelt prior to this time been willing to defy his military advisers, and to support Churchill's plan for the invasion of the Balkans and Central Europe simultaneously with, or even before, launching the attack on France. Things might also have been different if Roosevelt had not defied his military advisers who favored a Second Front in 1942 or 1943, something Churchill vigorously opposed. But this is all in the realm of speculation. The fact was that when the Yalta Conference convened, Russian troops were already far into Germany, and by February 20, 1945, they had advanced to within thirty miles of Berlin, whereas on the western front the ground lost by the German offensive under von Rundstedt had just been recovered and Allied troops were over 200 miles from Berlin. At this same time Russian occupation forces held all of Poland, eastern Czechoslovakia, and most of Hungary, and Tito's Communist Partisans were driving the Germans out of Yugoslavia, while the American invasion of Italy seemed hopelessly stalled in the Apennines. Moreover, Roosevelt secured from Russia in return for the Polish concessions a pledge that the then Russian-dominated Polish temporary government would be "reorganized on a broad democratic basis" and that "free elections" would be held in the immediate future under the supervision of the three governments. The Polish formula, in fact, was extended at Yalta to all the "liberated areas," with the three governments promising the rights of the Atlantic Charter to all liberated peoples and agreeing to assist the liberated states in the establishment through "free elections" of governments "broadly representative of all democratic elements in the population."

The Big Three at Yalta. *This photograph revealed to the American people, almost for the first time, the serious decline in their President's health, but witnesses at the Conference maintain that during its sessions his mind was fully alert.*

On the Far East, Roosevelt's attitude was determined by his military advisers, who urged him to pay almost any price in order to obtain assurance that Russia would join in the war against Japan. The atomic bomb had not yet been proved, and the prospect of direct invasion of the Japanese homeland seemed grim indeed. Roosevelt therefore agreed to conditions that would make Russia dominant in Manchuria at the end of the war, and in addition promised the Soviets the southern half of Sakhalin and the Kuril Islands. The concessions made to Russia in Manchuria were granted without the knowledge or consent of the Chinese government. In return, Stalin promised again — he had said the same thing to Cordell Hull in 1943 — that "in two or three months after Germany has surrendered the Soviet Union shall enter the war against Japan." He also promised to conclude a treaty of friendship with the nationalist government of China, which meant forsaking the Chinese Communists.

The Yalta Conference also ratified a plan — which had been in process of development ever since Teheran — for the eventual division of Germany into three zones of military occupation, one each for the British, American, and Russian forces. Later, at Potsdam, the French were awarded a zone. Berlin, the capital, although located deep in the Russian zone, was to be an international area under joint three- (later four-) power control. The seeds of future conflict were liberally strewn among the Yalta decisions, especially as they concerned Berlin and the divided rule of Germany. But on the whole, the Yalta decisions were not nearly as unfavorable to the West as many American critics have subsequently claimed. Had Russia lived up to the European agreements, the West would have won far more

than its military position in 1945 would have warranted.

Election of 1944

Nearly a year before the end of the war, the people of the United States were obliged to hold a presidential election. The war was going well, and its successful prosecution had in most minds a long priority over domestic policies. But the Constitution required an election. Except for the existence of war, there is little reason to suppose that Roosevelt would, or could, have run for a fourth term, but the need of his continued leadership during the crises was, for those who trusted him, a sufficient reason for renominating him. He had little opposition in the Democratic convention, but the Democratic city bosses joined forces with the southern conservatives to oust Henry A. Wallace as Vice-Presidential candidate in favor of Senator Harry S Truman, of Missouri, who had headed ef-

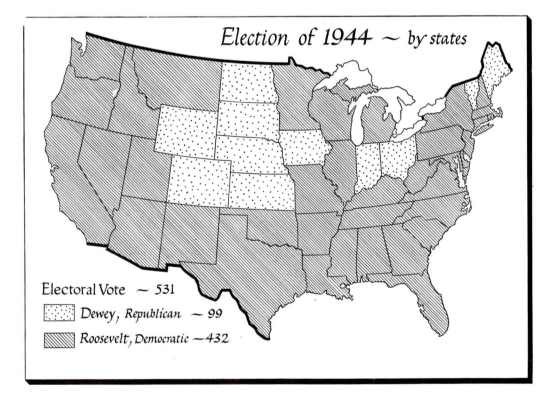

Election of 1944 ~ by states

Electoral Vote ~ 531
Dewey, Republican ~ 99
Roosevelt, Democratic ~ 432

fectively a Senate committee investigating the national defense program and had received much favorable public attention. The Republicans had expected a hard-fought campaign for the nomination between Governor Thomas E. Dewey, of New York, and Wendell Willkie, but when Willkie lost in the Wisconsin primary, he withdrew, and the nomination went to Dewey on the first ballot.

The campaign was notable for the wide range of agreement between the two candidates. But for the fourth time Roosevelt won a decisive victory. The President led in 36 states with 432 electoral votes, while Dewey led in 12 states with only 99 electoral votes. The Democrats also retained their majority in the Senate, greatly improved it in the House, and won a majority of the governorships. Aside from registering the confidence of the majority in Roosevelt's military leadership, the election demonstrated clearly that the American people were far more ready than they had been twenty-five years earlier to accept an important role in international affairs. The defeat of numerous outstanding isolationists and ex-isolationists made certain that the new Congress would be receptive to any plan of postwar cooperation that offered a reasonable hope of world peace.

Death of Roosevelt

During the campaign, the health of President Roosevelt had become a matter of considerable concern to the American public. The cares of office had obviously aged him. Lines on his face had deepened, he had lost weight, and he was noticeably less willing to exert himself to stand or walk. He suffered from colds and bronchial infections, and frequently took extended rests. But he had waged a vigorous campaign and had convinced the country that he was capable of carrying on, or so the election returns seemed to show. On April 12, 1945, however, he died suddenly at his winter home in Warm Springs, Georgia, of a massive cerebral hemorrhage. Like Woodrow Wilson, he was a casualty of the conflict in which he played so major a part. His death cast a gloom over America and the free world that even the imminence of victory could not completely erase.

BIBLIOGRAPHY

The best survey is A. R. Buchanan, *The United States and World War II* (2 vols., 1964); it contains a carefully selected bibliography. K. S. Davis, *Experience of War* (1965), is a popular account of American military activity. C. B. MacDonald, *The Mighty Endeavor* (1969), deals with American participation in the European war. On the war as a whole, Winston Churchill, *The Second World War* (6 vols., 1948–1953), is a brilliant interpretation. Two interesting critiques by military historians are H. W. Baldwin, *Great Mistakes of the War* (1950); and J. F. C. Fuller, *The Second World War* (1949). K. R. Greenfield (ed.), *Command Decisions* (1959), contains perceptive analyses by historians.

Among the memoirs of leading American participants the following are of particular importance: D. D. Eisenhower, *Crusade in Europe* (1948); O. N. Bradley, *A Soldier's Story* (1951); M. W. Clark, *Calculated Risk* (1950); E. J. King and W. M. Whitehill, *Fleet Admiral King: A Naval Record* (1952); J. W. Stilwell, *The Stilwell Papers*, edited by T. H. White (1948); and Douglas MacArthur, *Reminiscences* (1964). There is no memoir of General Marshall, but F. C. Pogue has published the first two volumes of his *George C. Marshall* (2 vols., 1963–8), which cover 1880–1942.

The outbreak of war with Japan has been the subject of many works, a number of which can be sampled in a convenient anthology, *Pearl Harbor: Roosevelt and the Coming of the War*, edited by G. M. Waller (2nd ed., 1965). See also R. A. Divine, *The Reluctant Belligerent* (1965). Herbert Feis, *The Road to Pearl Harbor: The Coming of the War between the United States and Japan* (1950), is scholarly and favorable to the administration; Walter Millis, *This Is Pearl!* (1947), is a more popular treatment from the same point of view. Bitterly critical of Roosevelt and Hull is the revisionist work by C. A. Beard, *President Roosevelt and the Coming of the War, 1941* (1948). A more temperate revisionist work which criticizes Roosevelt and Hull for their alleged inflexibility is P. W. Schroeder, *The Axis Alliance and Japanese-American Relations, 1941* (1958). A vivid reconstruction of events in Hawaii on December 7, 1941, is Walter Lord, *Day of Infamy* (1957). But see also the splendid work of Roberta Wohlstetter, *Pearl Harbor* (1962).

A brilliant treatment of naval warfare is S. E. Morison, *The Two-Ocean War* (1963), an abridgment of his *History of United States Naval Operations in World War II* (14 vols., 1947–1960). John Toland, *But Not in Shame* (1961), is a competent survey of the early months of the war. Other books of merit include E. B. Potter (ed.), *The Great Sea War* (1960); and Robert Leckie, *Strong Men Armed* (1962). Valuable works dealing with the navy include R. G. Albion and others, *Forrestal and the Navy* (1962); A. A. Rogow, *James Forrestal* (1964); and Armin Rappaport, *The Navy League of the United States* (1962), a study of the unofficial navy pressure group.

A brief survey of a tangled situation is Gaddis Smith, *American Diplomacy during the Second World War* (1964). An even broader treatment is John Snell, *Illusion and Necessity: The Diplomacy of Global War, 1939–1945* (1963). Herbert Feis, *Churchill—Roosevelt—Stalin: The War They Waged and the Peace They Sought* (1957), is a superb survey of wartime diplomacy by a former State Department officer who had access to archival materials. Feis continued his work with three shorter books: *Between War and Peace: The Potsdam Conference* (1960); *The Atomic Bomb and the End of World War II* (1966); and *Contest over Japan* (1967). W. F. Kimball, *The Most Unsordid Act* (1969), is a study of the passage of the Lend-Lease Act. T. A. Wilson, *The First Summit* (1969), is an account of the Argentia Conference. R. A. Divine, *Second Chance: The Triumph of Internationalism in America in World War II* (1967), shows how reluctant Roosevelt was to commit himself to a postwar world organization. See also W. H. McNeill, *America, Britain, and Russia: Their Cooperation and Conflict, 1941–1946* (1953). Willard Range, *Franklin D. Roosevelt's World Order* (1959), gathers together the President's expressed thinking about the international situation throughout his life. W. D. Leahy, *I Was There* (1950), is the memoir of a leading figure. Shrewd, objective analyses by careful scholars are in J. L. Snell (ed.), *The Meaning of Yalta: Big Three Diplomacy and the New Balance of Power* (1956). A collection which brings out divergent viewpoints is *The Yalta Conference*, edited by R. F. Fenno, Jr. (1955). Other important works on wartime diplomacy include W. L. Langer, *Our Vichy Gamble* (1947); and Herbert Feis, *The Spanish Story* (1948).

Eliot Janeway, *The Struggle for Survival: A Chronicle of Economic Mobilization in World War II* (2nd ed., 1968), is a lively overview, critical in tone. A substantial study of the key Congressional body is D. H. Riddle, *The Truman Committee* (1964). Records of some of the important wartime agencies are D. M. Nelson, *Arsenal of Democracy* (1946); and E. R. Stettinius, Jr., *Lend-Lease, Weapon for Victory* (1944). See also the general survey by D. L. Gordon and Royden Dangerfield, *The Hidden Weapon: The Story of Economic Warfare* (1947). W. W. Wilcox, *The Farmer in the Second World War* (1947), is illuminating. Other significant works include R. A. Young, *Congressional Politics in the Second World War* (1956); Laurence Wittner, *Rebels Against War* (1969), a study of the peace movement; and D. R. B. Ross, *Preparing for Ulysses* (1969), a monograph on the politics of demobilization.

Later phases of the European war are treated in a number of the works cited in the last bibliography. Charles de Gaulle, *War Memoirs*

(3 vols., 1955–1960), are of first importance. B. L. Montgomery, *Memoirs* (1958), is generally critical of the British field marshal's associates and superiors. Chester Wilmot, *The Struggle for Europe* (1952), by an Australian journalist, is pro-Montgomery, and critical of the American leadership. On American operations in France see Cornelius Ryan, *The Longest Day* (1959), the best on the invasion as a whole. Two excellent books on the Battle of the Bulge are R. E. Merriam, *The Battle of the Bulge (Dark December)* (1947); and John Toland, *Battle* (1959). The character and personality of General Patton have been evaluated in two books: Fred Ayer, Jr., *Before the Colors Fade* (1964); and Ladislas Farago, *Patton* (1964). John Toland, *The Last Hundred Days* (1966), describes the end of the European war. A special study of great interest is Walter Rundell, Jr., *Black Market Money* (1964). H. R. Trevor-Roper, *The Last Days of Hitler* (3rd ed., 1956), carefully sifts the evidence on what finally happened to Hitler.

Among the many books on later phases of the war in the Pacific are C. V. Woodward, *The Battle for Leyte Gulf* (1947); and R. F. Newcomb, *Iwo Jima* (1965). R. J. C. Butow, *Japan's Decision to Surrender* (1954), is a careful work based upon Japanese sources. Paul Kecskemeti, *Strategic Surrender: The Politics of Victory and Defeat* (1958), studies the surrender of the three Axis countries.

Among the many works treating the atomic bomb, the following are of particular interest here: J. P. Baxter, *Scientists Against Time* (1946); R. C. Batchelder, *The Irreversible Decision* (1961); and Lansing Lamont, *Day of Trinity* (1965). Both documents and conflicting interpretations are gathered in *The Atomic Bomb* (1968), edited by P. R. Baker.

Some scholars now find the origins of the Cold War in the last months of Roosevelt's life. Gabriel Kolko, *The Politics of War* (1969), is a massive work of a New Left historian, highly critical of Roosevelt. L. C. Gardiner, *Architects of Illusion* (1970), is insistent upon the continuity of policy from 1941 to 1949 and is also critical in tone. More conventional in approach is M. F. Herz, *Beginnings of the Cold War* (1966), which stresses American disillusionment with Soviet actions in early 1945.

"Gosh! I Didn't Jump That Hard!"

Section Six

THE POSTWAR WORLD

[1 9 4 5 - 1 9 7 0]

The people of the United States after the Second World War understood far better than after the First the need of American participation in world affairs. Most of the isolationists were silenced, if not wholly convinced. Those who believed in world cooperation as the only means of averting another world war hoped that Soviet Russia would abandon her interest in making all the world Communist, and would join with the United States and other free nations in a program of conciliation and peace. There seemed at first to be good reason for this hope. The Soviets helped create the United Nations, and ratified its charter. They drove hard bargains at Yalta and Potsdam, but for a time, even in the administration of occupied Germany, they seemed to be trying to get along with their former Allies.

The establishment of the Communist Information Bureau — the Cominform — in September, 1947, registered the long-foreshadowed abandonment by Russia and her satellites of whatever tendency they had previously shown to make terms with the rest of the world. Some time before this, many became convinced that, although Soviet policy still called for One World, what it had in mind was One Communist World, with every other form of government marked for destruction. Soviet assistance, most Americans believed, pushed the Communists on to victory in China, organized North

628

Korea for an assault on non-Communist South Korea, and maintained in every free nation a hard core of Communist agents whose ultimate objective was the overthrow of the local government. Only in the sphere of atomic weapons did the Americans maintain a clear military supremacy, and even in that the Russians had the bomb by 1949 and moved quickly to catch up with American power. The Soviet leaders, with their own conventional military strength held at near-wartime levels, had little to fear at first from the Americans, who had demobilized when the war ended.

The United States was obliged to act. In accordance with the Truman Doctrine, Greece and Turkey received sufficient aid to enable them to ward off the blows that the Soviets and their satellites had prepared against them. The European Recovery Plan, first announced by Secretary of State Marshall, made available to European countries the funds they needed to work their way back to economic health. If only they could recover their normal prosperity, American leaders reasoned, they would not so readily yield to Communist propaganda. By the North Atlantic Treaty, the free nations of the western world allied themselves, under American leadership, to resist aggression. And, when the Soviets tried to take over all Berlin, a British-American airlift defeated their plans. Similarly, their effort to take over

South Korea led to United Nations resistance, and a long-drawn-out war in which the Communist invaders failed to achieve their end. One result of this war was the rejuvenation of the American military forces. Another was the fateful precedent of United States intervention on the Asian mainland.

The death of Stalin early in 1953 led many people to hope that his successor would be willing to bring the cold war to an end. President Eisenhower stood willing to negotiate on any reasonable terms, but he failed completely to achieve a meeting of minds with the new Soviet leader, Nikita Khrushchev, who soon took over Stalin's authority. When Russian scientists, to the dismay of most Americans, demonstrated their superiority in rocketry and space exploration, Khrushchev brandished the missiles they had made for him and sought peace on his terms. But early in President Kennedy's administration, when Khrushchev failed in his attempts to station missiles on Cuban soil, he lost his leadership to two less flamboyant individuals, Leonid Brezhnev and Aleksei Kosygin. American scientists, spurred on by Kennedy's promise to put a man on the moon by 1970, actually did so in 1969.

The containment of Communism, long an American national policy, went to a new extreme when President Johnson dispatched large numbers of American troops to South Vietnam to protect that newly established nation from the domination of Communist North Vietnam. As evidence mounted that Americans could never win this war, student revolts and other anti-government outbreaks took place. Furthermore, the split that had developed between the Soviet Union and Red China convinced many Americans that there was now much less to fear than formerly from the spread of Communism. Popular disgust for the war he had escalated led Johnson to withdraw as a candidate for renomination, although his gesture failed to bring about a peace settlement. For his Republican successor, Nixon, American withdrawal from the war became a necessity.

Although wealth had accumulated as never before, those who shared in the mounting affluence began only slowly to realize how unevenly the nation's riches were spread. Many undereducated and underprivileged whites suffered from poverty in the midst of plenty, but chief attention focused on certain victimized ethnic groups, the Negroes and Americans of Mexican, Puerto Rican, or Asian descent. Similarly involved, but less militant, were the American Indians, many of whom were still left to stagnate on impoverished reservations. Rioting in numerous urban centers drew attention to the discontent of the blacks and stimulated many other non-whites to protest the inequalities from which they suffered.

In the spring of 1970 student protests against the continued American participation in the war in Southeast Asia, particularly its extension into Cambodia, led to more violence and, for a time, practically closed many American colleges and universities. The inflation which mounted steadily after 1965 proved difficult to curb by monetary measures, and Nixon began his second year in office facing increasing unemployment and economic recession in many parts of the country, as well as lawless minorities on the extreme right and left. It seemed certain that the strength of the American democratic system would be tested as it had not been since the Civil War.

25

THE TRUMAN ERA

*Harry S Truman · The United Nations · Demobilization · Infla-
tion and strikes · Internal politics · European settlement · Postwar Orient ·
The Truman Doctrine and the Cold War · The Marshall Plan · The Berlin
blockade · NATO · The Election of 1948 · A Balance of terror · The
Korean War*

Although there had been much more
planning for demobilization and reconver-
sion during the Second World War than
there had been during the First World
War, the period of transition to "peacetime" was still difficult. The second war
lasted much longer for the American participants, who were far more numerous
than those who took part in the first, and
the effect on the nation's economy was
much more drastic. Although there was
much less disillusionment in 1945–46 than
there had been in 1919, in part because
Americans had fewer illusions to lose, there
was some psychological let-down.

Political leadership during the Second
World War was necessarily focused upon
world affairs. President Roosevelt, to the
dismay of many Democrats, took relatively
little interest in domestic politics except
when his own position was at stake or when
very bitter enemies of his foreign policy
were up for election. He left the Democratic Party in disarray, a loose confederation of many elements — industrial workers, southern and western farmers, racial
minorities, and many middle-class people
who had become Democrats during the
New Deal and as yet saw no reason to
change parties.

Roosevelt left a somewhat less confused
situation in international affairs, although
toward the end of his life he had apparently concluded that the Grand Alliance of
the United States, the Soviet Union, and
Britain was in jeopardy. Whether he would
have been able to reaffirm the alliance can
never be known for certain, but it would
long be a matter of faith for the old New
Dealers that he could have succeeded where
his successors failed.

Truman

The death of Roosevelt threw the heavy
burden of reconverting the United States
to peace and reconstructing the war-torn
world upon Harry S Truman (1884–   ).
Unlike the flamboyant Roosevelt, Truman

INDEPENDENCE CEREMONY *in Burma, 1948.
Over fifty countries have gained independence
since World War II.*

Truman Takes Office. *Vice-President Truman being sworn in as President by Chief Justice Harlan Fiske Stone, in the presence of (left to right) Secretary of the Navy James V. Forrestal; Secretary of Agriculture Claude R. Wickard; behind Mr. Truman, Attorney General Francis Biddle and Secretary of the Treasury Henry Morgenthau, Jr.; Secretary of State Edward R. Stettinius, Jr.; Mrs. Truman; Chief Justice Stone; Speaker of the House of Representatives Sam Rayburn; and War Mobilization Director Fred Vinson.*

seemed to personify the typical ordinary American. He was from a small town in Missouri, and had served honorably as a National Guard officer in the First World War. He had gone into politics because he needed a job. As an organization Democrat, he won a county judgeship with the aid of "Boss" Thomas Pendergast, who controlled the Democratic Party in Kansas City and aspired to control the state. In Missouri a county judge is an administrative officer; Truman was neither a lawyer nor a "judge" in the usual sense. But he had under his control the expenditure of huge sums of money, particularly in the construction of highways and public buildings, and not the faintest suspicion of dishonesty was ever attached to any of his acts. At Pendergast's suggestion, he was nominated for the Senate in 1934, won as any other Democrat won that year, and was narrowly re-elected in 1940. His emergence as a senatorial investigator who was willing on occasion even to point out the shortcomings of the administration gave him much favorable publicity. When Henry Wallace was denied the Vice-Presidential renomination, Truman, partly because he was almost the only middlewesterner acceptable to all fac-

tions of his party, won the unsolicited post that a few months later was to make him President.

San Francisco Conference

The first great concern of the new President was to carry through to a successful conclusion the United Nations Conference on International Organization, already called by the United States, Great Britain, Russia, and China to meet in San Francisco, April 25, 1945.

To facilitate the creation of the new world organization, the same nations had held a meeting in the autumn of 1944 at Dumbarton Oaks in Washington and had agreed upon a set of tentative proposals. In many respects the new plan was similar to that of the League of Nations, but it contained nothing comparable to the historic Article X to which the United States Senate had so violently objected. It gave greater authority to the smaller Security Council (representing five great powers and six others elected for terms) and less to the larger Assembly. This eliminated a principal cause for delay and indecisiveness. It made more feasible the use of force against would-be aggressors, and put less trust in disarmament. An integral part of the plan was a Permanent Court of International Justice. The Charter, unlike the Covenant, would be entirely separate from any treaty of peace. Invited to the Conference at San Francisco were all of the nations, now more than fifty, that had joined in the hostilities against the Axis powers. At the Conference none of the fundamentals of the Dumbarton Oaks proposals was altered. Whatever the faults and virtues of the Charter, it was widely accepted, and in the United States Senate met negligible opposition.

Other Conferences

Exhibiting the general spirit of world cooperation of the Dumbarton Oaks and San Francisco conferences was a series of important international agreements already reached on a wide variety of subjects. At Bretton Woods in New Hampshire, a conference held in July, 1944, proposed an International Bank for Reconstruction and Development, with a parallel organization, the International Monetary Fund, to main-

tain stability in the exchange values of national currencies. Somewhat earlier a United Nations Relief and Rehabilitation Administration (UNRRA), a Food and Agriculture Organization of the United Nations, and a Provisional International Civil Aviation Organization had been set up. Within the Americas a conference at Chapultepec, Mexico, did much to cement intracontinental solidarity, although the United States soon became preoccupied with other areas and allowed much of its "good neighbor" prestige to dissipate.

The United Nations

The process of putting the San Francisco Charter into effect began at London on January 10, 1946, when the General Assembly opened its first session. A week later the Security Council also met there. On its recommendation, the Assembly chose Trygve Lie, a Norwegian, as the first Secretary-General of the United Nations. After much debate, New York City was chosen as the permanent headquarters of the new world organization.

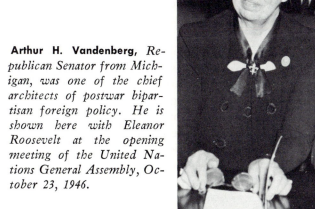

Arthur H. Vandenberg, *Republican Senator from Michigan, was one of the chief architects of postwar bipartisan foreign policy. He is shown here with Eleanor Roosevelt at the opening meeting of the United Nations General Assembly, October 23, 1946.*

The UN Headquarters. *In the foreground is the General Assembly Building, and behind it the 38-story Secretariat.*

It soon became apparent that the Security Council, under existing regulations, could never become the effective instrument that at least some of the framers of the United Nations Charter had hoped. The chief difficulty lay in the provision which permitted each great power to veto any important action that might be proposed. When Roosevelt and Churchill agreed to this provision they were merely carrying out the will of leading American Senators. They could hardly have foreseen the frequency with which one nation, Russia, would exercise the veto power. During the first seven years of the life of the United Nations the Russian veto was used fifty times, and by the early 1960's the number had exceeded one hundred.

In spite of the discouraging effect of the Russian vetoes, the United Nations was able to provide most of the machinery for world cooperation that had been contemplated by the San Francisco Charter. Most important were an Economic and Social Council; a Trusteeship Council with certain authority over mandates and over territory detached from a defeated nation; and an International Court of Justice to hear such cases in dispute between nations as might be referred to it.

Demobilization

The American public remained optimistic about the chances for world cooperation. Up to the end of the war Stalin's interest in cooperation had seemed genuine. He had abolished the Comintern, he had stopped the war on religion, and he had seemed willing to compromise on details at Yalta, even promising that the future of much of eastern Europe would be settled by democratic elections. In addition to these fair prospects the United States held a monopoly on the atomic bomb, the power of which seemed worth untold divisions of armed strength.

The rapid demobilization of American armed forces, taken in conjunction with the growing realization that the United States would not use the atomic bomb again except under the most critical conditions, may have been inevitable, although it later seemed mistaken. The existence of a well-trained army and a powerful navy might have given the nation much additional diplomatic strength during the impending sparring among the Allies for a peace settlement. But public insistence was too strong to be denied, and by December, 1945, the military forces were disintegrating at the rate of over 1.5 million a month, and by the next spring the Selective Service Law had to be extended for a year in order to keep military personnel even to the needed minimum. At the end of the year the army numbered only 670,000 men, the navy, 395,000, and the marine corps, 83,700.

Inflation and Strikes

Truman faced urgent domestic problems for which his experience in the Senate had given him little preparation. Although he was later to develop a reputation for making quick, decisive judgments, during his first eighteen months in office he seemed to be drifting much of the time. His somewhat ambivalent attitude on wage and price controls led to confusion. Unions which had held the line on wage rates during the war now demanded large raises to make up for the loss of overtime work. A wave of massive strikes hit the automobile industry, the coal mines, and the railroads, each leading to some success for the unions.

Higher wages, justifiably or not, resulted in higher prices, and pushed along the pronounced trend toward inflation that had set in immediately after the war came to an end. Price controls had been accepted as necessary evils as long as the war lasted; but with the fighting finished, the public echoed the impatience of businessmen for a return to the free market. Believers in price controls argued that if the great backlog of purchasing power built up during the war were turned loose, the resulting competition for the limited amount of goods available would produce a violent inflation of prices. But their opponents, led by the National Association of Manufacturers, held that, if controls were taken off, prices might rise temporarily, but would decline eventually as the volume of goods increased. The people were clearly tired of government restraints, and over the protest of President Truman Congress emasculated the act under which the Office of Price Administration had operated. Finally, yielding to irresistible pressure, the President announced on October 14, 1946, that all controls, except those on rents, would have to go. The effect was startling. By the end of the year the consumers' price index was 55.5 per cent higher than in August, 1939, and 31.7 per cent higher than in December, 1945. And prices had just begun to rise, for with each round of wage increases there came inevitably a wave of price increases.

Postwar Demobilization. *A junkpile of U.S. Army jeeps rusts away on Okinawa. The precipitate haste with which the United States demobilized its armed forces robbed the nation of its strongest diplomatic weapon in dealing with the Soviets.*

Elections of 1946

Upon entering office, Truman had promised to carry on the progressive policies of his predecessor. But that proved to be not entirely possible despite Democratic control of Congress through 1946. A definable drift toward conservatism, both in Congress and in the country at large, was already apparent under Roosevelt. When he died, the reform movement lost its great leader, and the revolt of conservatives against Presidential direction became more marked with each passing year. The Republicans, using the simple slogan "Had Enough?" won the Congressional elections of 1946 by a landslide, 241 to 188 in the House, and 51 to 45 in the Senate. State and local elections showed a similarly strong Republican trend. The Truman administration was suffering from strong resentment at its apparent willingness to let matters drift at home.

The Eightieth Congress

If a Democratic Congress and a Democratic President could not get along together, there was even less to hope for from a Democratic President and a Republican Congress. The Eightieth Congress was determined to make a record on economy and on tax reduction. The President could not restore appropriations that Congress had lopped off, however essential he might deem them, but he could, and did, veto a tax-reduction bill. The continued high tax rates were far from popular, but at the end of the year the President was able to point with pride at the achievement of a balanced budget for the first time in many years. Next year, however, he was unable to prevent substantial tax reductions, and the budget was unbalanced again. An even worse breach between the legislative and the executive branches came with the passage of the Taft-Hartley Labor-Management Relations Act, a clear reaction against the great strikes of 1946 which were popularly blamed for inflation.

The new labor law included many provisions most unpalatable to union leaders. It permitted employers to sue unions for breach of contract and for damages due to jurisdictional strikes; it prohibited the closed shop; it required a sixty day cooling-off period before strikes and lockouts that might disturb the national economy; it forbade unions to contribute to political campaign funds; and it required union officials to swear that they were not Communists, or else the organizations they represented would be ineligible for such assistance as they might otherwise receive from the National Labor Relations Board. Furthermore, it protected the states in their right to enact "right to work," or open shop, laws. This measure was vetoed by the President, but was repassed by overwhelming majorities and became law in June, 1947.

Atomic Energy Act

In this atmosphere of quarreling, one of the few positive measures that the Eightieth Congress was able to produce was legislation for the domestic control and development of atomic energy. A five-man commission was created, with exclusive authority over the development of this fateful new source of energy, and to head it the President chose David E. Lilienthal, for many years the vigorous head of TVA. Under the commission American scientists went ahead with basic research. But more than a few people, including many of the participating scientists, were uneasy over the implications for democracy of the need to keep ultra-secret the evolution of such a huge government corporation. Fortunately, a few members of Congress had easy access to the innermost developments of this portentous creation and in time some of the scientists' work was made available for peaceful purposes.

European Settlement

Meantime, American leaders had begun to feel that the wartime hope that the vic-

The Potsdam Conference. *President Truman sits left of center in the foreground with his back to the camera, Prime Minister Churchill is smoking the inevitable cigar, and Premier Stalin has a cigarette in hand.*

torious Allies could work together successfully in the pursuit of peace was an illusion. Just two weeks after her Yalta pledge to permit free, democratic elections in the liberated nations, Russia began the establishment of a Communist dictatorship in Rumania. Within another two weeks it was also clear that the Soviets would follow the same tactics in Poland. At the Potsdam Conference, during July and August, 1945, Russia's intentions toward eastern Europe became even more evident. Wherever the Russian army dominated, the U.S.S.R. established subsequent Communist regimes. As Churchill remarked at Potsdam, an "iron fence" was being built around them.

One of the Potsdam agreements stipulated that the peace treaties for Germany and Austria should not be undertaken until settlements had been reached on Italy, Finland, Hungary, Bulgaria, and Rumania. After much bickering, the task of drawing up these treaties was turned over to a council

of the foreign ministers of the appropriate great powers, while changes in the treaties so drafted might be suggested by a general peace conference representing all the Allies, to be held in Paris in May, 1946. It was during the course of these negotiations that President Truman and his new Secretary of State, James F. Byrnes, came to the conclusion that concessions to the Russians rarely, if ever, brought any concession in return. The American negotiators, with strong British and French backing, began to stand their ground against the Russians with such firmness that they were accused by some liberals in the United States of shifting to a "get-tough-with-Russia" attitude. Chief among these critics was Henry A. Wallace, who had become Secretary of Commerce in President Roosevelt's cabinet after the election of 1944, and had been retained by President Truman. In a speech delivered in New York on September 12, 1946, Wallace criticized American foreign policy as provocative of trouble, and urged that the United States recognize eastern Europe as a Russian sphere of influence. President Truman, after some hesitation, dismissed Wallace from his cabinet and gave the Byrnes policy his full support.

After lengthy negotiations, the five treaties were at last officially signed in Paris on February 10, 1947. The war-making potential of all five former German satellites was reduced to insignificance, heavy reparations were assessed against them, and all except Bulgaria were obliged to make extensive territorial readjustments. Italy, once Germany's closest associate, ceded land to France, Greece, Albania, and Yugoslavia, and turned over the administration of her colonies to the four principal Allies. Among the Allied powers the principal gainer from these treaties was Yugoslavia, a nation in which the Communists under Marshal Tito had already achieved complete control.

Germany and Austria

The restoration of peaceful relations with the minor enemy states had proved to be difficult, but with Germany and liberated Austria the task was to remain for years an impossibility. Germany was broken into four zones of military occupation, one for each of the "Big Four" powers, and the city of Berlin, although supposedly under joint four-power control, was similarly subdivided. The government of Germany as a whole was to be in the hands of an Allied Control Council composed of the four high commanding officers of the several zones. The conquered nation was to be administered as "a single economic unit," but all decisions of the Council had to be unanimous. Unfortunately, the western powers had no guarantee of uninterrupted access to Berlin, since the only way they could reach the city was through the Russian zone. A similar four-divisional plan was worked out for Austria and for Vienna, but there was one important difference; the existence of an independent Austrian government,

which eventually won the recognition of all four great powers. The Russians obtained formal consent from the other powers to their maintenance of "communication lines" with Austria through both Hungary and Rumania. This gave the Russian government the opportunity to keep military forces not only in Austria but in the two neighboring states also, even after peace treaties with them had been signed and ratified.

The occupation of Austria proceeded with relatively minor difficulties, but the occupation of Germany presented virtually insoluble problems. Germany in defeat was without a government, its cities and industries were in ruins, and it was overrun with displaced persons. The Allies worked out a plan for the trial of those Germans who were principally responsible for the war and were still alive. After ten months of hearings the international court at Nürnberg constituted for the purpose sentenced eleven "war criminals" to be hanged, and eight others to long prison terms. Three of the defendants were freed, and one of the condemned, Göring, escaped execution by suicide. Later, many less notable criminals were also brought to trial, and many convictions were obtained.

The Two Germanies

As time wore on, it became evident that Russian policy toward Germany had shifted. At the Potsdam Conference, all the great powers, Russia included, had wished to keep Germany decentralized, as the best available means of preventing the revival of the nation's military might, but eventually the Soviet leaders concluded that they might better profit from a highly industrialized Germany which they could dominate. For this program the western powers naturally showed scant sympathy. Working against odds to keep their sections together economically, the British and Americans first consolidated their zones for administrative purposes into a "Bizonia,"

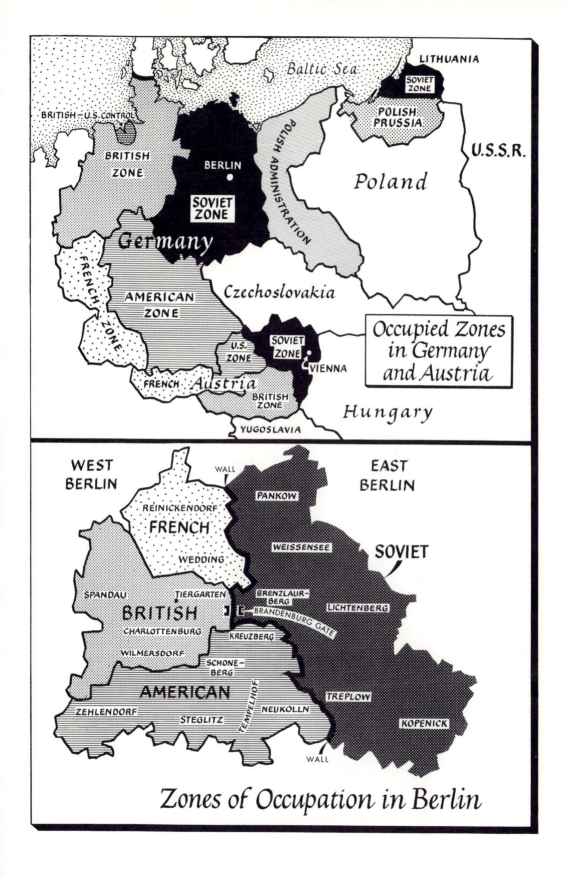

Occupied Zones in Germany and Austria

Baltic Sea

LITHUANIA

SOVIET ZONE

POLISH PRUSSIA

BRITISH – U.S. CONTROL

BRITISH ZONE

BERLIN

SOVIET ZONE

POLISH ADMINISTRATION

U.S.S.R.

Poland

Germany

FRENCH ZONE

AMERICAN ZONE

Czechoslovakia

U.S. ZONE

SOVIET ZONE

VIENNA

FRENCH

Austria

BRITISH ZONE

Hungary

YUGOSLAVIA

Zones of Occupation in Berlin

WEST BERLIN

EAST BERLIN

WALL

PANKOW

REINICKENDORF

FRENCH

WEISSENSEE

SOVIET

WEDDING

SPANDAU

TIERGARTEN

BRENZLAUR-BERG

BRITISH

BRANDENBURG GATE

LICHTENBERG

CHARLOTTENBURG

KREUZBERG

WILMERSDORF

SCHONE-BERG

AMERICAN

TEMPELHOF

ZEHLENDORF

STEGLITZ

NEUKOLLN

TREPLOW

KOPENICK

WALL

which the addition of the French zone presently made a "Trizonia." The break between East and West grew more marked with each succeeding month. Finally, in March, 1948, when the Russians refused all further participation in the Allied Control Council, almost the last vestige of governmental unity disappeared.

The net result was the creation of two Germanies, one to the west under the sponsorship of the western nations, and one to the east under Soviet control. Unhampered by Russian vetoes, the western powers in the next few years proceeded rapidly with the restoration of western Germany, while the Russians strove to build up a Communist-dominated industrial and military power in eastern Germany. Similarly, there evolved two Berlins, a western-occupied West Berlin, and a Russian-occupied East Berlin.

China

On the other side of the world, in eastern Asia, the road to peace was quite as long and tortuous as in Europe. In China the end of the war, instead of bringing peace, brought only conflict between the Nationalist government of Chiang Kai-shek and an increasingly powerful Communist regime which Russian backing had built up in Manchuria and northern China. In an effort to restore peace the government of the United States, in December, 1945, sent General George C. Marshall on a special mission to China to bring the warring factions together into one government. But the Marshall mission, in spite of the brief armistice it facilitated, failed utterly, and the war continued. On Marshall's recommendation, the United States reduced drastically its aid to Chiang's government and adopted a nearly neutral attitude. In the months that followed, the Communists went from one triumph to another until by the spring of 1949 the Nationalist armies were in full rout, and Chiang himself had fled to Formosa.

Korea

In Korea, as in China, the peace presented almost insuperable obstacles. At the Cairo Conference of 1943, Roosevelt, Churchill, and Chiang Kai-shek had pledged themselves to establish an independent Korea, but at the end of the war the United States and Russia divided the nation between them at the thirty-eighth

The Nürnberg Trials. *An international court decided the fate of the leading Nazi war criminals, but many legal experts challenged the resulting verdicts, not because the punishment was unwarranted, but on the ground that the court lacked legal authority for the actions it took.*

parallel for military occupation. The professed intent of the two powers was the establishment of an independent Korean government, but mutual distrust prevented any such development. Finally, during the summer of 1948, two Koreas appeared, a People's Republic in the northern zone, modeled on the Soviet pattern, and a Republic of Korea in the southern zone, with a nominally democratic constitution, under the dictatorial presidency of Syngman Rhee.

Japan

In Japan, American occupation had gone more smoothly than had at first been expected. The retention of the Emperor and the early creation of a Japanese government reduced to a minimum the problems of the American occupation forces. The Japanese people were cooperative; MacArthur gave the orders, and the Japanese government carried them out. Despite some efforts to give the Japanese occupation the appearance of joint Allied operation, it remained primarily an American affair. As in Germany, the war leaders were brought to trial, and eventually seven of them, including Tojo, the wartime premier, were executed. Efforts were made to break up large landed estates in the interest of a wider distribution of holdings, to dissolve the large corporations, to develop labor organizations after the western pattern, and to institute extensive educational reforms. But all these measures failed dismally to restore stable economic conditions in Japan, and the very survival of the nation seemed to depend upon the steady importation of unpaid-for supplies from the United States. After the outbreak of the Korean war in 1950, the Japanese economy prospered from the war purchases made by the United States.

After years of futile American efforts to bring it about, in September, 1951, a peace conference assembled at San Francisco where the occupation was declared at an end. In a treaty ratified by the Senate in March, 1952, Japan agreed to give up all claims to its former conquests. It further agreed to honor all its former debts, while the victors relinquished all reparations. A subsequent agreement between the Japanese government and the United States, made possible by the treaty, provided for American military bases within the Japanese home islands. To mollify the objections of New Zealand, Australia, and the Philippines, who feared to rearm Japan, the United States had previously concluded a defensive agreement with each of these countries. The American military bases so gained, together with those established on the former Japanese islands, now held as trust territories by the United States, gave this nation a great armed potential as well as widespread obligations throughout East Asia.

The Philippines

The United States gave the Philippine Islands their long-promised independence on July 4, 1946, although on terms that the Filipinos accepted with some reluctance. The American government provided for an effective Philippine army, and for the retention by the United States of important military and naval bases. In economic matters, a Philippine Trade Act paved the way for the gradual institution of American tariffs on goods imported from the Philippines, after an eight-year period of free trade on the quota basis. Congress also voted a total of $720 million to compensate the Philippine government and the owners of private property in the Islands for the war damage they had suffered. These acts, however, failed to solve the pressing internal problems of the Philippine Republic. The prewar sugar-coconut-to-bacco economy, which had profited the landlord-merchant class, but did little for the peasant, had been shattered by the war. Many of the peasants were loath to go back to it; and some of them, under the leadership of a left-wing organization known as the Hukbalahap, went into open revolt.

China,
Japan
and
Eastern
Asia

The success of Ramon Magsaysay, Secretary of Defense after 1950, in his campaign against the "Huks," coupled with his promises of reform, led to his election to the Philippine presidency in 1953. While the Filipinos made considerable economic progress, they suffered from the venality and inefficiency of their political leaders.

India, Burma, Malaya

Most of the colonial peoples in Asia had no intention of going back to the old system of subservience to foreign dominion. They had seen the white man defeated and humiliated, and they had lost their awe and fear of the Europeans. What they wanted when the Japanese were driven out was self-rule, such as the United States eventually granted to the Philippines. In recognizing this new spirit among colonial peoples, Great Britain was not far behind the United States. In India, the task was less one of getting the British out than of getting the Hindus and Moslems to agree on a plan of self-government. Finally, after a dreadful series of communal riots in which an enormous number of people were slaughtered, a divided country emerged. India, dominated by the Hindus, became a dominion in 1947 and a republic with membership in the British Commonwealth in 1949. Pakistan, dominated by the Moslems and divided into two parts, nearly 1,000 miles apart on the opposite sides of India, became a dominion in 1947 and a republic in 1956. In Burma, where there was less internal friction, immediate independence was granted. In Malaya, although British control continued for a time, two autonomous governmental units were organized, but in 1963 Britain welcomed the birth of the new state of Malaysia, which included not only the federated Malay states but parts of Borneo, and for a short time Singapore.

Indo-China, Indonesia

Unfortunately the willingness of the United States and Great Britain to grant home rule or independence to their empires was not fully shared by other nations who had possessions in the Orient. In the Dutch East Indies the returning European overlords met a determined Indonesian independence movement, and sharp fighting broke out. After mediation by the United Nations and protracted negotiations, the Dutch government unwillingly recognized the new Republic of Indonesia in December, 1949. The new state, comprising some 75 million people, eventually included all of the old Dutch East Indies possessions. Even more grudgingly the French ultimately retired from Indo-China. After almost continuous fighting against both local nationalists and Communists, who drew much of their strength from Red China, France in 1950 belatedly granted autonomy to the three states, Vietnam, Cambodia, and Laos. But by that time local Communists, under the leadership of Ho Chi Minh, had become powerful and their regime had won the recognition and support of the Soviet Union. What began as a jungle police action grew into a full-scale war between the Communist-dominated Vietminh and the forces supporting the French-recognized Vietnam government. By the end of 1952, 400,000 men, including over 200,000 French and French-colonial troops, were engaged in a desperate armed struggle to retain the former French colonies. The United States, in line with its general policy of the containment of Communism, gave $2 billion in aid to the French cause. Elsewhere in southern Asia there was little real peace; India and Pakistan were at odds over Kashmir; Indonesia coveted part of Malaysia; everywhere the agents of Moscow and Peking sought to turn dissension into conflict.

The Truman Doctrine and the "Cold War"

Meanwhile Soviet actions in Europe clearly indicated that the hope for "One World," inspired by wartime collaboration of Great Britain, Russia, and the United

States, and by the establishment of the United Nations, was for the indefinite future an illusion. Communist minorities took over in Poland, Yugoslavia, Bulgaria, Hungary, and finally even Czechoslovakia. The Russian zones in Germany and Austria were separated from other zones of occupation by heavy Red army patrols, and were stripped of their resources. From the Baltic to the Adriatic an "iron curtain" had descended, behind which the Soviet leaders could, many in the West feared, plan further expansion. In Italy and France they galvanized Communist minorities into action, apparently expecting to take over those governments. In Turkey they served notice that they must control the Dardanelles. In Greece they made every effort to promote a Communist revolution that would establish Russian influence on the shores of the Mediterranean. It seemed that the Russians were bent upon creating "One World," but that was to be a Communist world. And if democracy and freedom were to be saved, then the United States as the only western nation with adequate strength had to confront the Communist challenge.

It was the Greek situation which finally led the United States to take a positive stand against the Russians, and thus to begin the Cold War between the two great world powers. When the British government, in desperate economic straits, announced that it could no longer maintain a garrison in Greece, Truman and his advisers determined that the time had come to take a stand. The government of Greece had little to recommend it, except its anti-Communism, but it was at least subject to improvement. If the Communists came in, the liberties of one more "liberated" country would disappear. Faced by this situation, President Truman, on March 12, 1947, sent a message to Congress calling for immediate American aid for both Greece and Turkey. The United States, the President declared, "must

assist free peoples to work out their own destinies in their own way." To give strength to his words the President recommended that Congress vote $300 million for aid to Greece and $100 million for aid to Turkey. The Truman Doctrine, as this revolutionary demand came to be called, aroused much discussion in the United States. A small minority, headed by Henry A. Wallace on the left and Senator Robert A. Taft on the right, denounced it. Others regretted that the American nation had acted alone instead of through the United Nations. But the appropriations passed the Republican Congress substantially as the President requested, with Senator Arthur Vandenberg, Chairman of the Foreign Relations Committee, championing the President's cause. American policy toward Europe had by this time achieved a bipartisan status in its opposition to Russian expansion. Bipartisan cooperation in foreign policy contrasted with the bitter haggling then going on over domestic issues. As further evidence of the nonpartisan character of his policy, Truman in January, 1947, had replaced Secretary Byrnes as Secretary of State, with General George C. Marshall, a man who had never been in politics and had never expected to be.

The Marshall Plan

Marshall soon supplemented the Truman Doctrine with what was sometimes called the Marshall Plan, or European Recovery Plan. Governments struggled heroically to restore their war-torn economies, but the results generally were disheartening. Europe as a whole needed to be helped back to its normal economic life. If that could be done, the chief appeal of Communism would disappear. Secretary Marshall called upon European nations first to get together to see what they could do to help themselves, and then to state in concrete terms what additional aid they would need from the United States to accomplish the task.

The Marshall Plan, which proposed to supply the needed funds, was enthusiastically received throughout all western Europe. Russia and her satellites, to whom it was also open, pointedly refused to have anything to do with it and branded it an instrument of American imperialism.

Background of ERP

The European Recovery Plan (ERP) was by no means the first contribution of the United States toward the rehabilitation of the war-torn world. Lend-lease totals had recorded some $48.5 billion worth of American assistance in return for reverse lend-lease worth $7.8 billion. In the post-war settlements the sums due to the United States were reduced to millions rather than billions, although Russia steadfastly refused to negotiate a settlement of any sort. The Soviets still resented the tardiness of the Second Front and the abrupt manner in which Truman terminated lend-lease shipments in 1945. Further, to take the place of lend-lease funds, to which the British economy had been closely geared during the war, the United States Congress, late in 1945, voted to lend the British government a total of $4 billion with an interest charge of only 2 per cent, and with repayments in fifty equal installments, beginning in 1951.

THE RUSSIAN-TURKISH BORDER is patrolled ceaselessly by the Turkish army. In the photograph two soldiers walk by a village command post.

GREEK RESISTANCE ON THE ALBANIAN FRONTIER. The photograph shows Greek infantrymen storming a guerrilla outpost on a remote mountain top.

American aid to recovery had also included substantial contributions (about $11 billion) to the United Nations Relief and Rehabilitation Administration (UNRRA), which was created in 1943 and until 1947 distributed aid freely on both sides of the iron curtain. Thus in a sense the Marshall Plan grew out of American experience with postwar relief.

ECA Begins Work

As a result of the American overtures, sixteen nations of western Europe sent their representatives to Paris in July, 1947, and reported what they could do to help themselves and what they would need from the United States — $19 billion, to be spread over a four-year period. Scaled down to $17 billion, the program was accepted in principle by the United States. In April, 1948, Congress voted $5 billion as the first annual appropriation for ERP. To administer the program, an Economic Cooperation Administration (ECA) was set up, with Paul G. Hoffman, a Republican business executive, as chief. Soon ERP dollars were being invested in the restoration of railroads, in hydroelectric projects, new steel mills, cheap housing for the bombed-out masses, and agricultural machinery. By 1949 western Europe's agricultural and industrial production, due in large part to Marshall funds, had regained its 1939 figure. Evidence that ERP had also served, as was intended, to check the spread of Communism was not long in coming. The governments of France and Italy now eliminated all Communists from their cabinets, and despite the strikes and violence this entailed, stood their ground steadfastly. In Italy a free election showed 70 per cent of the electorate against the Communists, and only 30 per cent in favor of their Popular Front.

Communist Seizure of Czechoslovakia

In the face of this growing strength of free Europe the Russians, then rebuilding their own shattered economy, sought to defend their own interests. They established the Cominform in September, 1947, at least in part to offset the Truman Doctrine and the Marshall Plan. In February, 1948, with Russian support, the Communists seized power in Czechoslovakia, where until that time a multi-party government had been permitted to exist. Efforts were also made to discipline the Communist dictator of Yugoslavia, Marshal Tito, whom the Cominform in June, 1948, accused of deviation from the party line. But Tito, although fully cognizant of the hazards of his course, stood his ground and refused to be intimidated, a position he could maintain because his country was not occupied by the Soviet Union. During the next two years, while not renouncing his devotion to Communism, he moved ever closer to an understanding with the West.

The Berlin Blockade

But the outstanding action taken by Russia to show her displeasure with the western world occurred in Germany. In the summer of 1948, despairing of ever reaching any further agreements on German affairs with the Russian authorities, the western occupation powers announced their intention of establishing a government for West Germany, and issued a new currency. On the pretext that this currency reform would "place Berlin's economy and her working population in an untenable situation which only can be solved by Berlin's close connection with the eastern part of Germany," the Soviet authorities laid down a blockade against all movement of supplies from the West into Berlin. Since there were in the western-occupied section of the city some 2 million people whose lives depended on the continued importation of food from the West, it seemed clear that the Soviet intent was to force the western powers out of Berlin. With the western powers eliminated, nothing further would stand in the way of Russian control of the entire capital city — an important step toward a possible Russian domination of all Germany.

The "Air Lift"

Unwilling to risk provoking a new war, the United States and Britain decided not to try to force their way overland to Berlin. They avoided a direct confrontation with Russia by the use of aircraft. The western powers at once undertook to fly in the supplies necessary to feed the beleaguered Berliners. New airfields were opened up, and soon coal to keep the people warm and even to keep the factories going was reaching Berlin by air. Hundreds of airplanes were brought from the United States to participate in the operation. General Lucius D. Clay, the United States Military Governor in Germany, stated clearly the American position when he said, "They can't drive us out by any action short of war." The Russians did almost everything else. They withdrew their representative from the four-power Berlin city government, set up a separate police in their section of the city, excluded personnel of the lawful city government from the City Hall, which was within their area, and installed a German Communist as mayor. But in spite of all this, the air lift continued; furthermore, the western occupation authorities, not to be outdone by the Russians, clamped down a counter-blockade on trade between Trizonia and Soviet-dominated eastern Germany.

The air lift did much to make friends among the Germans for all who participated in it, particularly for the Americans who bore so large a proportion of the expense and furnished so many of the planes. With the assurance that they were not to be abandoned, the German leaders accepted the Allied invitation to work out a new constitution for the 45 million Germans living in the western occupational zones, with the result that a new Federal Repub-

The Berlin Airlift (Operation "Vittles"). *The photograph shows C–47s in the unloading line at Tempelhof Airport, Berlin. These planes carried a variety of cargoes, from engine crates to milk bottles. C–54s brought in the heavier loads.*

lic, with the little Rhine city of Bonn as its capital, came into existence.

Finally, in the spring of 1949, the Russian leaders revealed that they were now willing to lift their blockade, if at the same time the western powers would end their counter-blockade and agree to a meeting of the Council of Foreign Ministers to discuss the whole German question. Since the western powers had been willing to accept such an arrangement all along, the deal was quickly closed. All blockades were lifted May 12, 1949, and the Foreign Ministers began what proved to be a fruitless meeting on May 23. The West Germans, under their new constitution, however, achieved self-government with Konrad Adenauer, a Christian Democrat, as their first Chancellor, while the Russians set up in their zone the satellite German Democratic Republic.

North Atlantic Treaty Organization

Perhaps the most notable result of the Russian blockade and the air lift was its effect in influencing the United States to form a permanent military alliance with non-American powers. On March 15, 1949,

"Test Flight." A cartoon of the 1948 campaign by Barrow in the Rochester Democrat and Chronicle.

twelve nations — Belgium, Canada, Denmark, France, Great Britain, Iceland, Italy, Luxembourg, the Netherlands, Norway, Portugal, and the United States signed the North Atlantic Treaty. Two years later Greece and Turkey also joined. The North Atlantic Treaty Organization (NATO) provided for the mutual defense of all its members against armed attack over a period of twenty years. The members also agreed to develop a common general staff to work out plans for the armament and defense of the participating nations. The United States, it was generally understood, would make sizable financial contributions for equipping this North Atlantic army and would contribute military and naval forces.

Neither the North Atlantic Treaty nor the $1.5 billion called for in 1949 by the State Department to aid in equipping this international army was agreed to without protracted debate in Congress. A wing of the Republican Party led by Senator Taft insisted that the defense of Europe by troops against a possible Russian attack was at best a dubious gamble; he proposed to deter Russia from an attack by overwhelming air power. Opposition also arose throughout Europe to the expenditures of money for rearmament at the expense of recovery.

Despite such dissensions, the United States Senate approved the North Atlantic Treaty on July 21, 1949, by a vote of 82–13, and Congress subsequently appropriated $1.3 billion for its implementation. After General Dwight D. Eisenhower was appointed commander-in-chief of the new forces in December, 1950, with headquarters in France, the North Atlantic Army began to take shape. Along the Mediterranean area a combined British and American naval and air force stood guard, aided by Turkish and Greek land forces. With the United States thus committed to a mutual defense of western Europe, American land, air, and naval power dotted the map in a great arc from the Middle East to Norway. The purpose of this extensive deployment of American forces, an administration spokesman said, was to "contain" Communism and stop its penetration of Europe, the Middle East, and Africa. Although the Truman policy of containment, as it rapidly came to be called, met bitter criticism from ardent American nationalists as defeatist and resigned to the surrender of eastern Europe to the Communists, it was accepted by the majority of the public as the only alternative to another major war.

The Election of 1948

In the meantime, the American voters had again chosen their President. The Republicans, who renominated Governor Dewey, were supremely confident of victory. Their platform urged that greater responsibility be given to the states in such matters as housing, conservation, public health, and security for the aged. It favored also fewer governmental controls over business, and lauded the free-enterprise system as the "mainspring of material well-being and political freedom." It pledged the party to protect "both workers and employers against coercion and exploitation." The conservatism of these pronouncements reflected well the point of view of the Republican Eightieth Congress.

The Democrats entered the contest with little hope of victory. Despite Truman's advocacy of many liberal measures in the spring of 1948, many old New Dealers were disenchanted with the peppery, folksy little man from Missouri. Truman's spring speeches in support of civil rights and reform also served to widen the split between the conservative southern wing of the party and the more radical groups from the northern cities. In addition, Henry Wallace had announced the formation of a third party in opposition to Truman's foreign policy, which he claimed would lead the nation to war, and it was assumed that the new party would draw most of its support from former Democratic voters.

Despite considerable Democratic discontent with Truman's leadership, he was nominated without serious opposition. The chief excitement in the Democratic convention came from a successful effort, led by Mayor Hubert H. Humphrey of Minneapolis, to pledge the party to a program of full civil rights for Negroes. He moved to substitute for the rather vague civil-rights wording in the proposed platform a plank calling on Congress to support the President "in guaranteeing these basic and fundamental rights: (1) the right of full and equal political participation, (2) the right of equal opportunity of employment, (3) the right of security of person, and (4) the right of equal treatment in the services and defense of our nation." Although heatedly opposed by most southern delegates, the platform as finally adopted carried Humphrey's civil-rights plank. It also denounced unsparingly the record of the Eightieth Congress, called for the repeal of the Taft-Hartley Act, and advocated an extension of Social Security benefits, an increase in the minimum wage, more

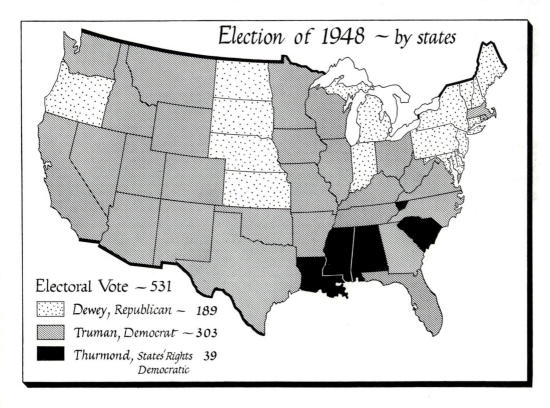

Election of 1948 ~ by states

Electoral Vote ~ 531

- Dewey, Republican ~ 189
- Truman, Democrat ~ 303
- Thurmond, States' Rights 39
  Democratic

adequate federal legislation on housing, and strong federal support of farm prices. On foreign policy the two platforms were in fundamental agreement.

Republican chances seemed improved by the defection of the extreme states'-rights faction of the Democratic Party. Offended by the civil-rights plank in their party platform, the "Dixiecrats" held a convention at Birmingham and nominated a separate States' Rights Democratic ticket, headed by Governor J. Strom Thurmond of South Carolina. It was apparent that Thurmond would carry at least four states in the Lower South. All the various public-opinion polls predicted confidently the election of Dewey, who campaigned with all the dignity of a sure winner.

The Democrats Win

Truman, on the other hand, conducted a vigorous campaign, almost unaided. He called a special session of the Republican-dominated Eightieth Congress to meet in July, right after the nominations, and asked it to put through legislation to halt rising prices, to meet the housing crisis, to protect civil rights, and to take various other steps called for by both platforms. When it adjourned without acting on his suggestions, he toured the country condemning it for its failure to deliver on promises in the Republican platform and branding it the worst Congress the nation had ever had. The election results were the greatest political upset in American history. The Republicans went down to a resounding defeat. Truman failed to capture a popular majority, but in the electoral college the vote stood Truman 303, Dewey 189, and Thurmond 39. In the congressional and state elections the Democratic victory was even more decisive. Both houses of Congress were overwhelmingly Democratic, and Democratic governors were chosen in most of the States.

The Fair Deal

Buoyed up by his triumph, which he considered to be a personal one, Truman presented the Eighty-first Congress in January, 1949, with a demand for an extensive program of reform. Promptly labeled the Fair Deal, this program called for the repeal of the Taft-Hartley Act, generous federal aid to education and public health, low-cost housing, an extension of the Social Security system, and a comprehensive federal law protecting civil rights throughout the nation. In the same month he described the nation's foreign policy as one based upon three points — resistance to Russian expansion, support of the United Nations, and continued large-scale aid to provide both military and internal economic strength to the nations resisting aggression. To these the President recommended the addition of a fourth point, a $45 million program of technical aid and investment by the government and private business for the undeveloped and colonial regions of the world. Through the development of sound economies and a rising living standard in these areas, Truman argued, the threat of internal Communist growth could be radically diminished.

Whatever hope the administration had for the passage of the program was dashed by a revival of the conservative trend in the country and a rapidly growing split in the Democratic Party between northern progressives and southern conservatives. Almost immediately a congressional coalition of southern Democrats and Republicans was formed to defeat the major parts of the Fair Deal. All the President could secure of his domestic program was a modest extension of the Social Security system, an increased program of federal housing, and an increase in the legal minimum wage.

While agreeing with the first three points of Truman's foreign policy, Congress virtually vetoed the Point Four program, as it became known, by appropriating only $10 million for the rehabilitation of backward areas. The mid-term congressional elections of 1950 brought defeat to many northern progressive Democrats. From that time on the conservative coalition made up of southern Democrats and Republicans became the real majority in Congress, and the administration was on the defensive. Only a presidential veto killed the so-called Tidelands Oil Bill, which would have given to the coastal states the control of the tidelands and the resources they contained. A similar veto, however, failed to stop the passage of the McCarran Immigration Act, which, though raising the total immigration quotas slightly, placed such a bewildering number of restrictions on immigrants and even visitors that many friendly countries protested.

A Balance of Terror

Simultaneously with the rejection of the Fair Deal the administration's foreign policy was being threatened by increasing pressures from Russia. Soon after the end of World War II both the United States and the United Nations had established bodies to make recommendations for the international control of atomic energy. As the July, 1946, American tests at the Bikini atoll demonstrated, a small number of such bombs could devastate an entire nation and possibly end civilization itself. Within a few months the American government presented a plan calling for the creation of an International Atomic Development Authority with wide powers to further the peaceful uses of the frightening new source of energy and to prevent its warlike employment anywhere in the world. The agency was to have unrestricted privileges of inspection in all nations, and its actions were not to be subjected to the usual veto power of the United Nations. Once a world authority was functioning, the United States promised to destroy all of its atomic weapons. Russia agreed to an international authority provided the United States at once destroyed its stockpile of weapons, the authority's inspection powers be radically limited, and each major nation retain its veto. Such conditions made agreement impossible, and the reason for the Russian position became amply clear on September 23, 1949. On that day President Truman announced that "within recent weeks an atomic explosion has occurred within the U.S.S.R." From that moment on the United States lost some of its power to influence world affairs, and a "balance of terror," as Churchill phrased it, began.

While by the spring of 1950 western Europe seemed secure against any Russian threat, East Asia was another matter. The Communist government of China had consolidated its power, while the Nationalist Chinese under Chiang Kai-shek held only the island of Formosa. At the same time, a new war in Korea threatened to bring the democratic world face to face with a second great war for survival.

The Korean War

After the division of Korea at the end of the Second World War, Americans sponsored the formation of a United Nations commission to supervise the selection of a constitutional convention for the entire peninsula. When Russian occupation authorities refused to permit the commission to enter North Korea, a Korean Republic organized in the American-controlled zone was recognized in 1948 by the United Nations as the official government for the entire country. The following year both Russia and the United States withdrew their troops from the divided peninsula, but not until both powers had established an armed native force in their respective zones. Thereafter both the Syngman Rhee government in the south and the Communist government in the north claimed to be the legal government of a unified Korea.

On June 25, 1950, Communist forces in large numbers crossed the thirty-eighth parallel on the pretext that the South Koreans had invaded their territory. It was immediately apparent that the South Koreans were no match for their well-armed adversaries. Before the Communist assault on South Korea, American policy in East Asia had been ill-defined, probably because of preoccupation with European problems. Confronted by the invasion, however, the President and Secretary of State Dean Acheson acted with dispatch. Within hours the Council of the United Nations had approved an American resolution ordering the North Koreans to retire, and on June 27, 1950, the Council authorized the use of armed force to stop aggression. Since the Russians were absent from the Security Council meetings, in protest against the refusal of the Council to seat a delegate of the Chinese Communist government, the Council escaped an interminable debate and the inevitable veto. The fact that the Russians were absent suggests that they were not in on the planning of the North Koreans' invasion.

On June 26, 1950, the day before the Council action, President Truman, without a formal resolution by Congress, which was not in session, authorized General Douglas MacArthur to support the South Koreans, and on the following day, after the Council action, MacArthur became the commander of a United Nations armed force. Most of the men making up the international army then and later were Americans, although units from Great Britain, Canada, Australia, and Turkey soon joined, as did small detachments from other nations. After some weeks of preparation, the United Nations forces stabilized the collapsing South Korean front and then began a counteroffensive, which by early October, 1950, had driven to the old border at the thirty-eighth parallel.

Chinese Intervention

Authorized by the United Nations General Assembly to proceed into North Korea, MacArthur within the following month had virtually defeated the enemy and was confidently predicting that American soldiers would be home by Christmas. In a few days, however, the entire character of the war changed. On November 25, 1950, Chinese Communist troops crossed the Yalu River in force and attacked the dispersed United Nations forces. After serious losses and a retreat far back into South Korea, the United Nations lines gradually were re-formed. Thereafter the weary struggle up the peninsula began again, but this time against a major foe capable of hurling vast numbers of men into battle and generously supplied with Russian arms.

With the entry of the Chinese into the war, a major policy debate took place in the United States, which at times threat-

ened to disrupt the administration's bi-partisan foreign policy, and even to break up the united front of the western European states struggling against Russian expansion. For some time many Republicans had bitterly criticized the Truman-Acheson policy for its alleged loss of China to the Communists. They became more insistent after China joined the war, and especially after a serious dispute between the administration and General MacArthur over the advisability of bombing Chinese airfields and cities and the use of the Chinese Nationalist troops on Formosa for an invasion of the mainland. MacArthur declared that both these measures were necessary to win the war and discounted the chance that Russia would intervene, thus converting the Korean conflict into a world war, with its threat of atomic destruction. The administration, on the other hand, steadfastly supported its own limited war concept. Moreover, since most of the European nations were adamant against an extension of the war, such a course would not have won the support of the United Nations. In the words of Chief-of-Staff General Omar Bradley, a full-scale Chinese war would have been "the wrong war, at the wrong place, at the wrong time and with the wrong enemy."

Irked at this decision, and at the administration's insistence upon civilian leadership in foreign policy, MacArthur several times made public his views, indiscretions that led finally to his dismissal by President Truman. Immediately the flamboyant MacArthur became the hero of a Republican group and was welcomed enthusiastically by a large public when he returned to the United States. Then followed a series of dramatic hearings before the Senate Military Affairs Committee, which underlined the growing Republican distrust of the administration's policy of containment of Communism rather than aggressive action, its preoccupation with the defense of Eu-

President Syngman Rhee and General Douglas MacArthur, *two principals of the Korean War.*

rope at the alleged expense of Asia, and of the United Nations, since that organization almost unanimously concurred in the decision to fight a limited war.

Peace Talks

The United Nations forces gradually recovered from their defeat in the early months of 1951, and by June had once again won back most of South Korea. Then, after a hint by Russia that a compromise truce might be arranged in Korea, formal peace negotiations began at Kaesong on July 10, 1951. Months were spent in haggling, and the talks were broken off only to be resumed at Panmunjom, where Chinese insistence that all prisoners of war be repatriated by force, if necessary, voided any hope of immediate peace.

By the time Eisenhower took office, the Korean negotiators had agreed upon most matters of importance except the vexing problem of what to do with prisoners of

Korean Armistice. *At Panmunjon, Colonel James C. Murray, USMC, as UN Liaison Officer (left), and Colonel Chang Chun San, Communist Liaison Officer, initial a map of the agreed-upon 145-mile demarcation line.*

war, in particular, the 46,000 Chinese and North Koreans taken by the United Nations forces who did not want to return to their own countries. Both sides finally agreed that the prisoners on either side would have the final right to return or stay. The truce, officially signed on July 27, 1953, divided Korea substantially as it had been divided before the war, at the same time expressing the pious hope that a united Korea might be created in the future by negotiation. Both sides promised to respect a demilitarized zone between the two halves of the country and not to augment armaments, conditions which were to be supervised by the representatives of five neutral powers.

War Mobilization

The Korean War turned out to be a far greater venture than anyone could have foreseen when it started in June, 1950. To provide the necessary manpower for the conflict and simultaneously expand America's armed forces, draft calls were increased, and Congress was forced to extend the Selective Service Act. The demands of the Korean War, added to the already booming rearmament program, also placed a strain upon the American economy. By

1952 America's defense budget had risen to $50 billion. As shortages of critical materials appeared, and as prices of goods in short supply mounted, the President again asked Congress for emergency powers. After much debate the Defense Production Act of September, 1950, was passed, granting to the President the power to impose price and wage controls and to ration strategic materials by a priority system. In January, 1952, Mobilization Director Charles E. Wilson ordered prices and wages frozen at the then current levels, but not before inflation had again raised the price level substantially. And as taxes again rose to pay the bills for the national effort, the country seemed to be reliving the days of the Second World War.

Results of the War

At the outset the United States furnished the bulk of the troops on the United Nations side, but as the war went on Republic of Korea forces, armed, trained, and equipped mainly by the Americans, came to exceed those of all other participants combined. South Korea lost 71,500 and the United States 25,000, killed in combat. Estimates of civilian South Koreans who had lost their lives in the war ran as high as

400,000, with far more than that number left homeless, and perhaps 100,000 orphans. The cost of the war to the United States alone reached $22 billion, but the losses of South Korea, where, for example, 75 per cent of the mines and textile mills had been destroyed, were almost incalculable. North Korean losses were even greater in proportion than those suffered by the South Koreans; the population of North Korea, some said, had declined from 8 million to 4 million. Chinese casualties may have exceeded a million.

In return for all this ghastly expenditure it was possible to count some possible gains. Much had been learned about air fighting, particularly with jet planes, although at heavy cost, for each side shot down nearly a thousand of its opponent's planes. The program of preparedness in the western world, languishing when the war began, had taken on a new life: now the United States alone had an army of 3.6 million men, and the NATO forces in Europe had been substantially increased. A major war, daily threatening to become a world war, had been limited, and neither side had used atomic weapons. An international army of sorts had fought in Korea under the aegis of the United Nations, perhaps pointing the way to the distant future when peace might be maintained by a world government supported by adequate police power. Communist aggression in this instance had been futile, since the battle lines came to rest in Korea about where they had started. But the Korean War was never a popular one in the United States. Many citizens questioned whether it was necessary. Many others deplored the fact that American entrance into the struggle had been achieved by the President without formal action by Congress. Many at the time regretted the stalemate at the end. These widespread doubts, and the sense of frustration with a peace that was not a peace, were to have a profound impact upon the American state of mind and upon internal policies.

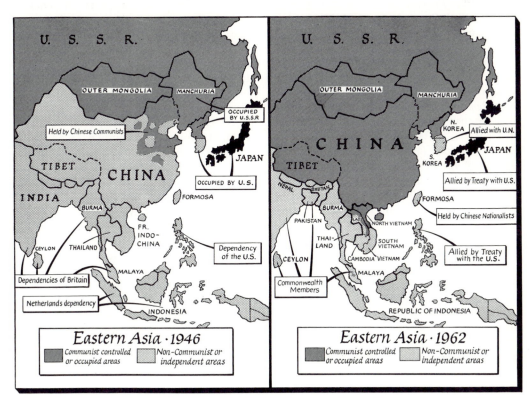

Eastern Asia · 1946

Communist controlled or occupied areas

Non-Communist or independent areas

Eastern Asia · 1962

Communist controlled or occupied areas

Non-Communist or independent areas

BIBLIOGRAPHY

E. F. Goldman, *The Crucial Decade — And After — America, 1945–1960* (1961), is a lively general survey, liberal in viewpoint. Herbert Agar, *The Price of Power: America since 1945* (1957), is particularly good on foreign policy. An excellent documentary collection is *The United States in the Contemporary World, 1945–1962*, edited by R. L. Watson, Jr. (1965). Interesting surveys of American foreign policy may be found in J. W. Spanier, *American Foreign Policy since World War II* (2nd ed., 1962); C. O. Lerche, Jr., *The Cold War . . . and After* (1965); and Walter LaFeber, *America, Russia, and the Cold War, 1945–1966* (1967). Other useful documentary collections include: *American Foreign Policy since 1945* (1969), edited by R. A. Divine; *America in the Cold War* (1969), edited by Walter LaFeber; and *Anxiety and Affluence, 1945–1965* (1966), edited by E. R. May.

The narrative account of Cabell Phillips, *The Truman Presidency* (1966), is friendly in tone. *The Truman Administration* (1966), edited by B. J. Bernstein and A. J. Matusow, is documentary.

H. S Truman, *The Memoirs of Harry S Truman* (2 vols., 1955–1956), is a peppery and revealing reminiscence, chiefly devoted to foreign policy. Jonathan Daniels, *Man of Independence* (1950), is a friendly biography by a Truman associate. Excellent background on Dewey is in Warren Moscow, *Politics in the Empire State* (1948). D. A. Shannon, *The Decline of American Communism* (1959), contains a critical account of the Wallace campaign, and is especially valuable for its description of Communist maneuvers. K. M. Schmidt, *Henry A. Wallace: Quixotic Crusade, 1948* (1960), is a full-length study, rather friendly to its subject. For contrast, see Dwight Macdonald, *Henry Wallace* (1948). C. D. MacDougall, *Gideon's Army* (3 vols., 1965), is a massive account of the Wallace campaign by a participant. Irwin Ross, *The Loneliest Campaign* (1968), focuses on Truman's victory.

J. F. Byrnes, *All in One Lifetime* (1958), is the memoir of Truman's first Secretary of State; it should be compared with his earlier reminiscence, *Speaking Frankly* (1947). Rich and exciting is the memoir of Robert Murphy, *Diplomat Among Warriors* (1964). A full-length study of Truman's second Secretary of State is R. H. Ferrell, *George C. Marshall* (1966). The waspish memoir of Truman's third Secretary of State is Dean Acheson, *Present at the Creation* (1969). A study of American public opinion on one major issue is W. J. Bosch, *Judgment on Nuremberg* (1970).

Two worthwhile monographs are J. F. Golay, *The Founding of the Federal Republic of Germany* (1958); and W. P. Davison, *The Berlin Blockade: A Study in Cold War Politics* (1958). An excellent and detailed study is J. E. Smith, *The Defense of Berlin* (1963), which covers 1945–1962.

Herbert Feis, *The China Tangle* (1953), is a rich, balanced account of events in China during and immediately after the Second World War. J. R. Beal, *Marshall in China* (1970), is a first-hand account. A scholarly work is Tang Tsou, *America's Failure in China, 1941–50* (1964). There are several helpful accounts of postwar Japan, among them: E. M. Martin, *The Allied Occupation of Japan* (1948); and R. A. Fearey, *The Occupation of Japan — Second Phase: 1948–1950* (1950). See also the broader works of E. O. Reischauer, *The United States and Japan* (2nd ed., 1965); and D. M. Brown, *Nationalism in Japan* (1955). A careful study is F. S. Dunn, *Peace-Making and the Settlement with Japan* (1963).

On Latin America, see Laurence Duggan, *The Americas: The Search for Hemisphere Security* (1949). R. J. Alexander, *Communism in Latin America* (1957), is full and rich. Edwin Lieuwen, *Arms and Politics in Latin America* (2nd ed., 1961), is an excellent critical appraisal of a perennial problem.

On the return to peacetime conditions in the United States there are a number of useful studies. Two stimulating works edited by S. E. Harris are *Economic Reconstruction* (1945), and *Saving American Capitalism* (1948). The diversity of viewpoints on the subject is well brought out in *Industry-wide Collective Bargaining: Promise or Menace?* (1950), a collection edited by C. E. Warne. A critical analysis of the position of the labor movement following the reunion, and the passage of "right to work" laws in several states, is Sidney Lens, *The Crisis of American Labor* (1959). Important studies of Truman domestic programs include R. A. Lee, *Truman and Taft-Hartley* (1966); R. O. Davies, *Housing Reform During the Truman Administration* (1966); and A. J. Matusow, *Farm Policies in the Truman Years* (1967).

On the United Nations and its efforts to keep the peace of the world, there is an ever-growing list of books. An interesting appraisal is H. G. Nicholas, *The United Nations as a Political Institution* (2nd ed., 1963). On postwar assistance to war-damaged nations, see *UNRRA: The History of the United Nations Relief and Rehabilitation Administration*, edited by George Woodbridge (3 vols., 1950), an official history. Special aspects of the work of the UN are treated in C. E. Toussaint, *The Trusteeship System of the United Nations* (1956); and Theodore Besterman, *UNESCO: Peace in the Minds of Men* (1951).

Much has also been written on the deterioration of American-Russian relations and the coming of the Cold War. Two early analyses are Sumner Welles, *Where Are We Heading?* (1946); and Walter Lippmann, *The Cold War* (1947). A New Left study which blames the labor movement for the perpetuation of the Cold War is Ronald Radosh, *American Labor and United States Foreign Policy* (1969). D. F. Fleming, *The Cold War and Its Origins, 1917–1960* (2 vols., 1961), puts much of the blame on the Truman administration. W. B. Smith, *My Three Years in Moscow* (1950), is an American Ambassador's memoir. Hugh Seton-Watson, *The East European Revolution* (3rd ed., 1956), is instructive.

The development of bipartisan foreign policy can be traced in A. H. Vandenberg, *The Private Papers of Senator Vandenberg*, edited by A. H. Vandenberg, Jr., and J. A. Morris (1952). H. B. Westerfield, *Foreign Policy and Party Politics: Pearl Harbor to Korea* (1955), traces the ups and downs of bipartisanship; in this connection see also R. A. Dahl, *Congress and Foreign Policy* (1949). Recent studies of the South and foreign policy are C. O. Lerche, Jr., *The Uncertain South* (1964); and A. O. Hero, Jr., *The Southerner and World Affairs* (1965). On the Marshall Plan see H. B. Price, *The Marshall Plan and Its Meaning* (1955).

L. M. Goodrich, *Korea: A Study of U.S. Policy in the United Nations* (1956), is a good introduction to the problem. The best general study of the war yet to appear is T. R. Fehrenbach, *This Kind of War* (1963). G. D. Paige, *The Korean Decision* (1968), is a close study of the Korean intervention. The activities of the marines are recounted in Andrew Geer, *The New Breed* (1952). The gifted military historian S. L. A. Marshall has published two vivid books on the Korean War: *The River and the Gauntlet* (1953), on the Yalu retreat; and *Pork Chop Hill* (1956). Eugene Kinkead, *In Every War but One* (1959), is a study of military morale in Korea; for a contrasting interpretation, see A. D. Biderman, *March to Calumny* (1963). The MacArthur dismissal is discussed at length in two recent scholarly works: J. W. Spanier, *The Truman-MacArthur Controversy and the Korean War* (2nd ed., 1965); and Trumbull Higgins, *Korea and the Fall of MacArthur* (1960). Richard Rovere and A. M. Schlesinger, Jr., *The MacArthur Controversy and American Foreign Policy* (1965), is a lively and readable defense of the administration. Louis Smith, *American Democracy and Military Power: A Study of Civil Control of the Military Power in the United States* (1951), deals with constitutional aspects of the problem. W. H. Vatcher, *Panmunjom* (1958), is a careful study of the armistice negotiations. Two collections of documents and conflicting interpretations are *Korea and the Theory of Limited War* (1967), edited by Allen Guttmann; and *The Debate over Thermonuclear Strategy* (1965), edited by A. I. Waskow. A. G. Theoharis, *The Yalta Myths: An Issue in U.S. Politics, 1945–1955* (1970), is an important monograph.

26

THE EISENHOWER YEARS

*"The Great Debate" · Election of 1952 · Dwight D. Eisenhower ·
Modern Republicanism · The loyalty issue · Foreign policy · Asia · The
Middle East · The Suez Crisis · Europe · Space and defense programs ·
The decline of colonialism · Eisenhower's farewell address*

The Korean War had not lasted many months before it became clear that the Truman administration had got itself into deep trouble. It was difficult to explain the concept of a "limited war" in which hundreds of Americans were losing their lives; it was hard to reply to General MacArthur's repeated pronouncement, "There is no substitute for victory." The decline of Truman's popularity was first apparent in the 1950 elections, when a large number of Democrats were defeated and Senator Taft won re-election in Ohio by a huge majority, in spite of the efforts of the labor movement to defeat him. The unpopular Korean War and the resulting high taxes and inflation, together with the charge that the administration had been "soft" on Communists (see p. 653), were major factors in 1950 and they promised to be important again in the 1952 election. By that time, too, the discovery of traces of corruption in certain federal departments gave the Republicans an important new issue. Truman

PRESIDENT DWIGHT D. EISENHOWER *pauses on his way to address the United Nations, September 22, 1960.*

announced in March, 1952, following the defeat of his ticket in the New Hampshire primary, that he would not be a candidate for re-election. By that time, however, it was clear that Truman's limited war-containment policy had been accepted by most Americans. Even if he could not himself bring about a truce in Korea, the result of a "great debate" about foreign policy in which the administration had won out made it possible for his successor to make peace.

"The Great Debate"

A long running argument about fundamentals of foreign policy, which was promptly called the "great debate," began on December 20, 1950. In a radio-television address, former President Herbert Hoover urged that the threat of Communism could best be met by strengthening the sea and air defenses of the Western Hemisphere. He cautioned the nation against sending its armies on vain missions to police the various threatened areas of the world. European nations, he asserted, were not doing enough to protect themselves. As for the Far East,

Japan should be encouraged to rearm in its own defense, and the non-Communist nations should not commit their "sparse ground forces" in a hopeless test of strength with Red China. Hoover's proposal was promptly attacked by Secretary Acheson, who likened it to "sitting quivering in a storm cellar waiting for whatever fate others may wish to prepare for us." Republican Senator John Foster Dulles, an international lawyer, was equally outspoken. He saw no need to "crawl back into our own hole in a vain hope of defending ourselves against the rest of the world," and pointed out that "solitary defense is never impregnable." Senator Taft, however, agreed with Hoover that sea- and air-power were the primary essentials for the protection of the United States, and doubted the constitutional right of the President to send troops to fight in Europe under the authority of the North Atlantic Treaty. In Congress the debate centered on the intention of the administration to send more troops from the United States to Europe. The appointment late in 1950 of General Eisenhower to head the NATO forces in western Europe, followed by the establishment of a Supreme Headquarters of the Allied Powers in Europe (SHAPE) near Paris, made it essential for the United States to reach a decision on this vital issue. However, when Eisenhower testified that four more American divisions were needed to insure the success of the NATO army, the Senate gave way. It adopted a qualifying resolution, however, that no additional ground troops should be sent to Europe without congressional approval.

Campaign of 1952

By this time the presidential campaign of 1952 was well under way. With a Republican victory once again generally conceded, the fight for the nomination of that party was a strenuous affair. Senator Taft, espe-

Robert A. Taft, *son of President Taft and Senator from Ohio, was the leading contender for the 1952 Republican nomination until General Eisenhower announced his candidacy.*

cially since his re-election, was the favorite of the conservative, nationalistic elements of the party. He entered the race early and appeared headed for victory, particularly when it became obvious that the more international-minded and liberal eastern wing of the Republican Party could scarcely expect to nominate Governor Dewey a third time. Taft was aging and ill, however, and

Adlai E. Stevenson, *grandson of a Vice-President by the same name, was the Democratic standard-bearer in 1952, and in 1956.*

some wondered if he had the strength to campaign. An alternative was General Eisenhower, who had turned down suggestions from leaders of both parties that he run in 1948. Eisenhower, who was alarmed at the possibility that isolationism might again sweep the country, also feared that those who wanted to engage in dangerous ventures on the Asian mainland might win power. The "great debate" apparently caused the general to issue a statement from Europe on January 7, 1952, that he was a Republican, and that he would accept the nomination provided he did not have to campaign for it. That the public in general wanted Eisenhower was hardly open to doubt, but the Taft forces did not yield readily. However, pro-Eisenhower forces controlled the convention machinery, enabling Eisenhower to win on the first ballot. Senator Richard M. Nixon of California, a strongly partisan Republican who had acquired some reputation as an investigator, was given the Vice-Presidential nomination.

President Truman's announcement on March 29, 1952, that he would not be a candidate for re-election, opened a battle for the Democratic nomination. Senator Estes Kefauver of Tennessee went to the convention with strong support because of the national reputation he had built up by televising the findings of his crime investigation committee. On the third ballot, however, the nomination went to Governor Adlai E. Stevenson of Illinois. Perhaps more than any other Democratic leader, Stevenson represented a compromise between the liberal Democrats of the North and the conservative Democrats in the South.

On foreign policy, the Republicans again stressed the great importance of Asia in American diplomacy, and denounced the Democrats for their failure to support Nationalist China more effectively. This failure to act, plus Acheson's alleged vacillating policy, the Republicans charged, had led directly to the Korean War. The Republicans also deplored the "negative, futile, and immoral policy of containment" and claimed that they would be much more positive in their struggle against Communism, both at home and abroad.

On domestic issues, the Democrats promised to preserve and extend the reforms of the past twenty years, to repeal the Taft-Hartley Act, and to extend public power projects. Their civil-rights plank promised to secure by federal legislation the rights of all citizens to equal employment, personal security, and equal voting privileges. The Republicans favored greater local and state control in such matters as hydroelectric power and the administration of federal lands. They promised also to "restore" to the states control over the tidelands and their resources, and to aid the states in securing civil rights by "supplemental" legislation. They charged, too, that the Democrats had countenanced corruption, wasted public funds, and had not taken firm enough measures against subversive civil servants.

In this campaign television for the first time played an important part in national politics. Millions of Americans watched both conventions on TV, and saw both Eisenhower and Stevenson in action as the campaign progressed. Stevenson found in television an important ally. His quickness of mind, his facility with words, and his dry humor won him many admirers.

The Eisenhower Victory

Eisenhower went out of his way to unite the warring Republican factions. He had been in substantial agreement with the Truman-Acheson foreign policy, but now he worked closely with Senator Taft, and gave isolationist Republicans who were candidates for office the same unreserved support that he gave to those who supported the administration's foreign policy. Accenting Democratic corruption, he promised to clean the "top to bottom mess" in Washington, and to "rout the pinks." He assailed the Truman foreign policy as being too timid in both Asia and Europe, and promised to secure freedom for the en-slaved peoples of Europe "by peaceful means." During the last week of the campaign he promised that, if elected, he would go to Korea, a statement interpreted by many voters to mean that he had a plan to end the Korean War, something the Democrats had not been able to do. To the observant only the size of the Eisenhower majority was surprising. His distinguished military record, attractive personality, and, above all, his expressed intention of uniting contending factions not only in the Republican Party, but in the country as a whole, appealed strongly to most Americans, and insured his election. Eisenhower won by 33.9 million to 27.3 million popular votes, and 442 to 89 electoral votes. Along with the Presidency the Republicans won a majority in the House of 221 to 213, and by the slenderest possible margin, a majority in the Senate. Thus for the first time in twenty years the party found itself in full power in Washington.

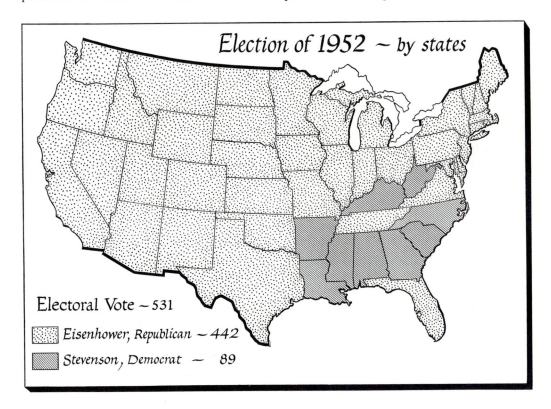

Election of 1952 ~ by states

Electoral Vote ~ 531

Eisenhower, Republican ~ 442

Stevenson, Democrat ~ 89

Dwight D. Eisenhower

Dwight D. Eisenhower (1890–1969) was born in Denison, Texas, but his parents moved to Abilene, Kansas, when he was only a year old. He was graduated from West Point in 1915. For several years he served as special assistant to General Douglas MacArthur, went with him to Manila, and helped work out plans for defense of the Philippines. During the Louisiana war maneuvers of 1941, the excellence of his staff work marked him for promotion, and immediately after Pearl Harbor General Marshall called him to Washington, where he became head of the War Plans Division, then chief of the Operations Division. When finally it was decided that Marshall should stay in Washington, Eisenhower was Marshall's choice for commander of the United States forces in Europe, and in December, 1943, he became Supreme Allied Commander. His military successes, coupled with his skill in dealing with the great variety of nationalities placed under his command, made him a leading world figure. After the war, President Truman appointed him Chief of Staff to succeed Marshall, a position he surrendered in 1948 to become president of Columbia University. But he was still subject to call for military duty, and in December, 1950, the President sent him on a second mission to Europe, this time as head of the NATO defense forces. Again he was successful and again he had a major voice in making the Truman foreign policy, despite the later strictures he was to cast upon it.

Eisenhower, in spite of a full-length career spent in the regular army, had a most unmilitary personality. A gregarious middlewesterner, with a warm smile and a modest manner, Eisenhower was accustomed to the exercise of authority even if he was new to civilian practical politics. Although his spoken sentences often did not scan when they were transcribed and published, he seldom had trouble in making himself understood. He enjoyed poker and golf, played with other successful men, but seemed to care little for ceremonial functions. Richard H. Rovere has well characterized the wartime manner of the general:

While MacArthur in the Orient moved around under a heavy load of braid and medals, or else walked truculently through palaces in a limp open-collared shirt, achieving great conspicuousness in either dress, and while Patton's tank helmet of lacquered plastic, his pearl-handled pistols, and his boots of burnished leather glistened so brightly in the sun that they could light up half-tone engravings on wartime newsprint, Eisenhower, with nothing to glisten but his smile, made a neat and unpretentious appearance before the high and mighty of Europe in the kind of jacket worn here at home by fastidious gas-station attendants.

Modern Republicanism

After the election Eisenhower paid his promised visit to Korea where his influence may have helped to lead to the truce finally signed in July, 1953. On his return he settled down to the task of selecting the personnel of his administration. In forming his cabinet he continued his campaign policy of seeking to heal the breach in the Republican Party between the conservative nationalists on the one hand, and the moderate internationalists on the other.

In office Eisenhower proved to be somewhat less conservative than he had seemed as a candidate. What he apparently had in mind was the modernization of Republican ideology by a strong infusion of the New Deal-Fair Deal interest in social welfare and equal opportunity for all. At the same time he sought to emphasize the advantages of private over public enterprise, and called for the elimination as far as possible of government competition with private business, and the reduction of government controls over the nation's economic life. In dealing with Congress, however, he was unwilling to use effectively his tremendous personal popularity to put through his program of "modern Republicanism."

Management of the Congressional Republicans was complicated by the sudden death of Senator Taft in July, 1953. Fortunately many Democrats, despite their irritation with Eisenhower's strongly partisan 1952 campaign record, agreed with him on important legislative matters, and supported him when their help was needed. What developed was a kind of bipartisan "government of the middle," in which the moderates of both parties maintained control, to the despair of both the conservative Republicans and the liberal Democrats. A bipartisan working arrangement between the administration and the Democratic leaders facilitated much of Eisenhower's program. House Speaker Sam Rayburn and Senate Majority Leader Lyndon B. Johnson, both of Texas, played powerful roles when the Democrats regained control of Congress after the 1954 elections. With some nudging from Rayburn and Johnson, the first Republican administration in twenty years ratified the New Deal-Fair Deal's social legislation.

Dwight D. Eisenhower, *thirty-fourth President of the United States, was the first regular army officer since Ulysses S. Grant to be chosen to the Presidency. His election emphasized anew the hold of the "great man tradition" on the American people in their choice of a President.*

Congressional Conservatism

In general, however, the President did better with the conservative aspects of his program than with those involving liberal ideas. Congress promptly enabled him to redeem his pledge to return Pacific and Gulf Coast offshore oil lands to the adjacent states, an action generally favored by the oil interests. The Reconstruction Finance Corporation, to the satisfaction of private bankers, was allowed to die, and the price and wage controls instituted during the Korean War were eliminated. Federal power projects suffered from the President's preference for a "partnership" policy with local and usually private authorities. He supported Secretary of Agriculture Benson's proposal to reduce agricultural price supports, but despite both lowered price supports and sharp acreage reductions, the surplus in basic crops continued throughout the Eisenhower years as an unsolved problem.

Portions of the presidential program that carried a New Deal flavor met a decidedly mixed reaction from Congress. The President failed to obtain the revision of the Taft-Hartley Act that he had promised during the campaign, and his recommendations for federal aid to schools and for a national prepaid health insurance plan were unavailing. The housing appropriations made by Congress were much below his requests. He did persuade Congress, however, to continue the tariff-reduction authority granted him under the Reciprocal Trade Act. He also won congressional assent to American participation in the completion of the Great

Lakes — St. Lawrence Seaway, a project for which Hoover, Roosevelt, and Truman had sought in vain to win favorable action. The changed attitude of Congress resulted in large measure from the decision of the Canadian government to construct the Seaway alone, along an all-Canadian route, if the United States continued its refusal to share in the work.

Budget-Balancing

In theory the Republicans were also adamant for a reduction in both federal expenditures and taxes, for achieving a balanced budget, and for stopping inflation. The Treasury, therefore, set about funding the federal debt on a long-term basis at higher interest rates, and the President recommended substantial cuts in the $79 billion budget inherited from the Truman administration. Since almost two-thirds of the total budget went for defense purposes, severe reductions had to be made in the military appropriations. Opponents argued that there had been no corresponding lessening in the need for national defense, and that the primary purpose of the President and his Secretary of Defense, Charles E. Wilson, former head of General Motors, was only to keep taxes down and balance the budget. The presidential decision to cut the air force drastically, despite the persistence of the cold war, aroused particularly vigorous criticism. Many Republicans had high hopes that foreign aid could also be substantially reduced, and some reductions in this item were made, although increases in allotments to Asiatic countries wiped away some of the savings made by awarding lower sums to Europe. A 10 per cent cut in income taxes was made and there were reductions also in excise taxes. A full-dress tax revision measure that became law in August, 1954, afforded some relief to individuals, but did more to help corporations. The Eisenhower administration achieved its first balanced budgets in 1956 and 1957, but a severe recession during the latter year put it back in the red again. Meantime the national debt continued to grow, reaching a total of nearly $285 billion by 1959, and inflation continued, although at a reduced rate.

The Loyalty Issue

One of the major issues of the era was loyalty or "internal security" and the Eisenhower administration was forced to deal with it repeatedly, especially in its early years. In this period disloyalty was almost invariably equated with pro-Communism, and Communism was seen as essentially a monolith directed from Moscow, occupied with the promotion of World Revolution (which included, of course, the destruction of all capitalist governments).

That Communist Party leadership was conspiring to overthrow the government of the United States by force and violence was the verdict of a federal jury in New York, which in the fall of 1949 convicted eleven outstanding Communists on this charge. Critics of labor maintained that Communists had won actual control of many unions, and were deliberately fomenting labor unrest. Deeply concerned by these accusations, leading labor figures, such as Philip Murray, President of the CIO, made every effort to root out Communist officeholders and eliminate left-wing unions. Similar charges against college and university faculties led to some dismissals and the imposition of special loyalty oaths. There were charges, too, that Communists had worked their way into the federal government, particularly into the State Department. The outstanding case in this connection was that of Alger Hiss, who had held a position in the State Department from 1936 to 1947, had attended the Yalta meeting of the Big Three, and had been secretary-general of the San Francisco Conference which had drawn up the United Nations Charter. Hiss, on the basis of revelations made by Whittaker

THE SPY SCARE. *Discovery in 1949 that the Soviets had exploded an atomic bomb, coupled with the Communist sneak attack in Korea the following year, inspired some politicians to make a frantic search for disloyal Americans on whom to blame these and other misfortunes.*

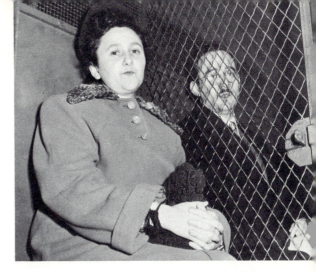

Ethel and Julius Rosenberg. Convicted in Federal Court on espionage charges, these two atomic spies were executed for treason, a most unusual peacetime penalty.

Alger Hiss at Yalta. The young man carrying the brief case is Alger Hiss. His role at Yalta was of great unimportance.

Whittaker Chambers and Wife. Testimony by Chambers, himself a confessed ex-Communist and perjurer, helped convict Alger Hiss, a former State Department employee, on a perjury charge. Hiss had sworn that he had never been a Communist.

Chambers, a confessed ex-Communist, was convicted of perjury in January, 1950, and was sentenced to five years in prison for having sworn that he was not a Communist. The very next month Dr. Klaus Fuchs, a naturalized British citizen who had worked with both the British and the American teams on atomic research, confessed to British authorities that he had turned over to Russian agents vitally important secrets relating to the atomic bomb. He was promptly tried, convicted, and sentenced. Others accused of helping reveal atomic secrets to Russia included Julius Rosenberg, an engineer, and his wife Ethel, who were convicted of treason, and after a long delay were executed in June, 1953.

Joseph R. McCarthy

Inevitably the anti-Communist issue found its way into politics. Senator Joseph R. McCarthy, a Republican from Wisconsin, achieved prominence when he charged that there were large numbers of Communist sympathizers and bad security risks in the State Department, and demanded that Secretary of State Acheson be made to resign. The erratic McCarthy's loose charges were without evidence, but were nevertheless echoed by those anxious to discredit the Truman administration. Further responding to the anti-Communist feeling, Congress in September, 1950, passed the Internal Security Act, which required all Communist and Communist-front organizations to register with the Attorney-General, forbade aliens who had ever been Communists to enter the country, discriminated in naturalization proceedings against Communists who had already entered, and empowered the government to hold Communists and Communist-sympathizers in detention camps during time of war. The loosely drawn bill was vetoed by the President as an unreasonable attack on civil rights and liberties, but Congress promptly passed it over his veto.

The vitriolic McCarthy proved to be a formidable campaigner for his party in the elections of 1950 and 1952. Even Eisenhower felt obliged to endorse him in spite of McCarthy's repeated allegations about the incompetence or even disloyalty of Eisenhower's old chief, General George C. Marshall. The Republicans in the 1952 campaign promised to rid the federal service of what McCarthy liked to call "security risks." Under the Truman administration employees had been dismissed only if the government had reasonable grounds for considering them disloyal. The new regulations under Eisenhower were much more comprehensive; an employee might be dismissed as a security risk because he drank too much or talked too much, because he was related to or had associated with a Communist, or because he had expressed opinions in the past that happened to coincide with the Communist position. Under the new regulations some 2,600 employees were dismissed by October, 1954. Since only a handful of the total number dismissed were even accused of subversion, the administration was charged with destroying the morale of the federal service and the very essence of the civil-service principle in order to justify unwarranted calumnies made during the preceding election campaign.

Meanwhile, various committees of Congress were continuing their own un-American activities investigations. Of these the most conspicuous was the Senate Governmental Operations Committee headed by McCarthy. This committee, and others like it set up by the several states, investigated all sorts of people, and while publicly exposing some Communists, at times they also violated the basic civil liberties of many individuals. As the zeal to investigate mounted, and as people were branded as disloyal often on ridiculously flimsy evidence, a reaction occurred. Some of McCarthy's charges on television — particularly those which intimated that Presidents Truman and Eisenhower were guilty of laxity toward Communism — strained credulity to the breaking point; others brought him into conflict with the army authorities, and led to an undignified television hearing that further reduced his public stature. Finally, in December, 1954, the Senate voted 67 to 22 to sustain a charge against him of conduct unbecoming a senator. When McCarthy died suddenly in 1957, the worst aspects of McCarthyism were already over, although innocent victims of his terrorism were to suffer for years to come.

Elections of 1954, 1956, and 1958

Although Eisenhower retained his phenomenal personal popularity, his administration was never able to command a controlling majority of Congress after the 1954 elections. Despite the vigorous and in-

tensely partisan 1954 campaign by Vice-President Nixon, keyed largely to the charge that the Democrats were "soft on Communism," the Republicans lost control of Congress. After recovering from two serious illnesses, Eisenhower did manage to win a second victory over Stevenson in 1956. But his re-election to the Presidency by an even greater number of votes than he had won in 1952 was a very personal one. For while the President was winning re-election, his party suffered further losses in the House, in the Senate, and in the governorship races among the states. This trend was further emphasized in the Congressional elections of 1958, when the Democrats again increased their margins of control in both houses of Congress and among the state governments. Obviously, the increasing amount of independent voting loosened a sense of party responsibility and

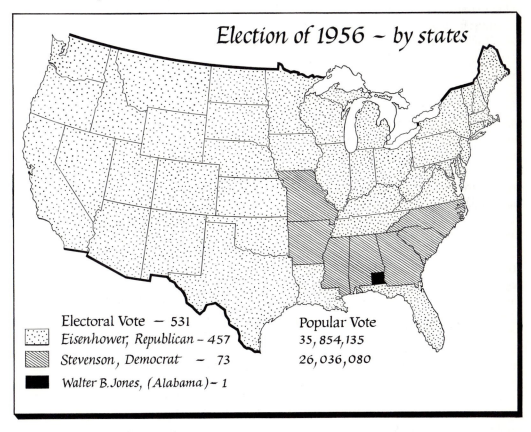

Election of 1956 ~ by states

Electoral Vote — 531

Eisenhower, Republican – 457

Stevenson, Democrat — 73

Walter B. Jones, (Alabama) ~ 1

Popular Vote

35,854,135

26,036,080

made it difficult for the President to obtain congressional assent to his legislative program without aid from Rayburn and Johnson. It also testified to a growing conviction by many voters that the national parties no longer afforded a clear alternative and that the only real choice was between individual candidates. The belief was nurtured by the close similarity between the programs of the national parties; perhaps, too, it was due to the continued control of Congress by the alliance between southern Democrats and conservative Republicans, mostly from the Middle West, that seemed triumphant no matter which party won the formal elections.

The Eisenhower administration was by no means barren in the field of domestic legislation after the Democrats took control of Congress in 1955. Especially notable was the Federal Aid Highway Act of 1956, which appropriated funds for a vast system of interstate highway building, "the biggest peacetime construction project of any description ever undertaken by the United States or any other country," in the words of President Eisenhower. The funding of this was to come from increased taxes on gasoline, diesel oil, tires, buses and trailers, and was to be matched by the states. Admission to the union was granted to Alaska (1958) and Hawaii (1959), the first new states since 1912. Finally, Eisenhower signed a measure to protect the voting rights of minorities, the Civil Rights Act of 1957, a weakened version of what Attorney-General Herbert Brownell had asked but still the first successful piece of civil rights legislation to pass Congress in eighty-two years.

Foreign Affairs: Asia

During the campaign of 1952, John Foster Dulles, who was to become Eisenhower's Secretary of State, had bitterly criticized the Truman-Acheson policy of containment and had promised if the Republicans were successful, a more positive foreign policy. In line with this promise the President soon "deneutralized" Formosa, "unleashing" Chiang Kai-shek from Truman's restrictions which barred him from attacking the Chinese mainland. But since Chiang had not nearly the strength required for such an attack, this unleashing resulted in exactly nothing. For a time it also seemed as if the United States under the urging of Dulles might directly intervene in the French struggle against the Communists and nationalists in Indo-China, where, despite enormous American aid, the French had suffered one reverse after another, culminating in their disastrous defeat at Dienbienphu in May, 1954. Convinced at last that Eisenhower, whatever Dulles might wish, would never come to their aid with American troops, the French agreed to attend a conference at Geneva the following July, at which Red China was represented, but not the United States. The French had hoped to retain Laos, Cambodia, and Vietnam as autonomous governments within the French Union, but the settlement gave both Laos and Cambodia their independence, and divided Vietnam at the seventeenth parallel, with the Communists under Ho Chi Minh in control of North Vietnam and the former Vietnamese government in control of South Vietnam. A plan for all-Vietnamese elections later to decide on reunification was never implemented because of opposition from the United States and South Vietnam, although the United States had tacitly agreed to abide by the Geneva agreement.

SEATO

To shore up crumbling East Asia, Secretary of State Dulles hastily organized a pact to contain Communism there. The resulting South East Asia Treaty Organization (SEATO), officially subscribed to at Bangkok in February, 1955, by Pakistan, the Philippines, Thailand, Australia, New Zealand, France, Great Britain, and the United States, was designed to do for East Asia

John Foster Dulles as Secretary of State enjoyed far greater freedom in the making of American foreign policy than most American Presidents had permitted any of their subordinates to exercise. A believer in personal diplomacy, he flew for interviews to nearly every part of the world. Here, Dulles and Eisenhower confer out-of-doors during the Geneva Conference of 1955.

what NATO was doing for western Europe. But SEATO never did create an organized defense force, and its members, in case of Communist aggression, were bound only to consult. Furthermore, such important Asian nations as India, Burma, Indonesia, and Ceylon not only refused to join, but regarded the new organization with disfavor as an undue interference by the West in Asiatic affairs. In April, 1955, the Conference of Asiatic and African nations held at Bandung, Indonesia, further emphasized a growing antiwestern spirit. This conference, in which Red China's premier Chou En-lai played a major role, adopted a strongly worded resolution against the "neo-colonialism" of the West.

During Eisenhower's second administration American-Chinese relations again approached the boiling point when, late in August, 1958, Red China opened a bombardment of the supply lines that bound two small offshore islands, Quemoy and Matsu, to Formosa. These islands, regarded by Chiang Kai-shek as stepping-stones for his return to the continent, were now garrisoned by almost one-third of Chiang's troops. Their protection, Eisenhower asserted, was increasingly important to the defense of Formosa, and Secretary Dulles warned the Peking government not to seek their recovery. With the American Seventh Fleet under orders to keep supply lines open from Formosa to within three miles of the beleaguered shores, the risk of open warfare between Red China and the United States seemed great. Dulles finally induced Chiang to announce that he would not use force in his attempt to regain the mainland. The United States, in return, reassured Chiang that Red China would never be permitted to reconquer Formosa. This diplomatic exchange amounted in effect to a recognition of the fact that there were two Chinas, one on the mainland and one on Formosa. However, the United States still officially refused to recognize Communist China and insisted that Chiang's government must represent China in the United Nations. The offshore islands remained in Chiang's possession.

The Middle East

Secretary Dulles' plans for a positive policy against Communist encroachment were as ineffective in the Middle East as they had been in East Asia. In the Middle East the sources of conflict were many and complex. Local potentates bargained with oil companies for profits, and the various companies, supported by their home governments, competed vigorously among themselves. Heated antagonisms existed between the East and the West, an inevitable legacy of the colonialism which World War II had practically wiped away in the region. Compounding the tension was Arab nationalism, which was accentuated by the birth of the state of Israel and the way it had come into being.

Hitler's hideous persecution of the Jews had given great impetus to the Zionist movement for the creation of a Jewish homeland in Palestine. The British government, which since 1922 had held a mandate over the area, had pledged itself by the Balfour Declaration of 1917 to promote this end. Jewish refugees fled Hitler's terror by every possible means toward Palestine, and continued the migration even after the war ended. The influx of so many Jews angered the local Arabs, who could count on the support of such neighboring Arab states as Trans-Jordan, Egypt, Iraq, Saudi Arabia, Syria, and Lebanon. Both Great Britain and the United States, because of their need for Arabian oil, were reluctant to offend the Arab rulers. British policy was pro-Arab, even to the setting of drastic limitations on the number of Jews to be admitted to Palestine, limitations that the ingenuity of the refugees found many ways to circumvent. At length, with violence between Arabs and Jews on the increase, the British government requested the Assembly of the United Nations to study the problem. The resulting report failed to bring the contending factions any closer to peace.

State of Israel

British action finally brought the situation to a head. Despairing of its ability to maintain peace, and unwilling to bear the continued expense involved, the British govern-ment announced early in 1948 that it was withdrawing from Palestine. When in May the British High Commissioner actually left, the Jews proclaimed the independent state of Israel. The new state received immediate recognition from the United States and the Soviet Union, but its Arab neighbors promptly attacked it with what military might they could muster. In the fighting that followed, the outnumbered Jews outfought the Arabs, and made clear their determination to preserve Israel. The United Nations, trying to do something to stop the fighting, at length decided through the General Assembly to authorize the five great powers to send a mediator to Palestine. For this task the powers chose Count Folke Bernadotte of Sweden, who in June, 1948, achieved a truce, only to be assassinated by Jewish extremists who wished the war to continue until the new nation should dominate all Palestine. Bernadotte's successor, the American Ralph Bunche, worked out a provisional settlement involving the establishment of a Jewish state. Early in 1949 even the British government capitulated to the inevitable, and recognized Israel. The Arab states, however, persistently refused to acquiesce and united in a boycott against their new neighbor. This economic war, together with the presence in the neighboring Arab states of about 800,000 Arab refugees from the new Israel, and almost daily marauding by small groups on both sides of the border, dimmed the hope of any real peace.

The rise of Israel added just one more conflicting interest for American policy to resolve in the Middle East. In domestic politics the numerous Jewish votes inclined American sentiment toward Israel. But the great American oil companies held important oil concessions in Saudi Arabia, Kuwait, and Iran, which, together with large British and Dutch companies, produced most of the oil consumed by America's European allies. Moreover, Arab nationalism had to be pacified lest it look to Russia. Consequently, the American policy in the Middle East since Truman's presidency had been one of forestalling any Communist intercession in the region while attempting to work out an agreement between Israel and the Arab states. Although agreement proved impossible, development loans were made to both the Jews and the Arabs, and the Communist threat was countered by yet another Dulles-inspired international pact, the Middle East Treaty Organization (METO) with Great Britain, Pakistan, Iran, Iraq (who withdrew in 1959), and Turkey as adherents, and the United States as an unofficial benefactor.

The Suez Crisis

This precarious Middle Eastern balance, always in danger of disruption, was destroyed by the precipitate action of Egypt. After the British had finally withdrawn early in the 1950's, Colonel Gamal Abdel Nasser emerged as the strong man of the new Egyptian republic. Claiming that the Israeli government was arming against him, and that the West would not give him arms enough to meet the challenge, he made a bargain with Czechoslovakia to exchange Egyptian cotton for Russian-type arms. Apparently Nasser had in mind not only the extinction of Israel, but also the creation of an all-Arab federation with himself at its head. He supported the nationalist movements in French North Africa, and in his propaganda developed a strongly anti-western line. One of Nasser's favorite projects was the Aswan High Dam on the upper Nile River, from the building of which he expected to expand the Egyptian economy. Toward the financing of this $1.3 billion undertaking, the United States had agreed to supply $56 million, Great Britain $14 million, and the International Bank for Reconstruction and Development $200 million. But Nasser, hoping to play the East against the West in his search for additional

Dr. Ralph Bunche, *a high-ranking United Nations official, won the Nobel peace prize in 1950 for his part in bringing about an Arab-Israeli truce. Ten years later he served as special representative of the United Nations in the Congo crisis.*

funds, let it be known that he was considering a Soviet proposal to finance the project. In consequence, Secretary Dulles precipitately withdrew the American offer, after which both Great Britain and the International Bank also backed out. Thereupon Nasser, in angry retaliation, announced on July 26, 1956, the nationalization of the Suez Canal, the income from which would be used for building the High Dam.

Most outraged by Nasser's coup were Great Britain and France. The British government owned 44 per cent and private French shareholders over 43 per cent of the Canal stock, so profits were involved, although the company's concession was due to expire in 1968. The graver dangers were that Nasser, under Soviet influence, might not only stop the flow of vital oil through the Canal to western Europe, but also by his all-Arab, anti-Israel crusade bring on a third world war. For a time American restraint kept the British and the French from military intervention, but early in November, 1956, a Franco-British force took Port Said and began to occupy all Egyptian territory adjacent to the Canal. At the same time, the Israelis launched a successful attack on Egyptian troops in retaliation, they claimed, for constant border outrages.

Knowing that the course of action they had chosen would be regarded with disfavor by the United States, the anti-Egyptian allies had not consulted the American government in advance, assuming, apparently, that it would accept a *fait accompli*. But instead the Eisenhower administration, working mainly through the United Nations where the Soviet and neutralist blocs gave it enthusiastic support, demanded and obtained an immediate end to hostilities, together with the speedy withdrawal of all the attacking forces. Meantime Nasser, whose forces had shown up badly in the fighting, vented his rage by blocking the Canal with sunken ships, while at the same time Arab sabotage, particularly in Syria, ended the westward flow of oil through three out of four of the Middle East's great pipelines. After several months the Canal was reopened, the pipelines were in part repaired, and oil began to flow westward again.

The Eisenhower Doctrine

Neither the British nor the French governments would accept further responsibility for the Middle East, and the United States had little choice but to fill the vacuum of power it had helped to create. In recognition of this development, Congress, at the President's insistence, gave its approval to what was generally called the Eisenhower Doctrine. By it, the United States agreed to support against external Communist aggression any Middle Eastern power that asked for American help. Congress also granted the President, at his request, a special fund of $200 million to use against Communist expansion in the Middle East. The most significant application of the Eisenhower Doctrine came in July, 1958, when Lebanon, following an anti-western takeover in neighboring Iraq, appealed to Eisenhower for help. Thereupon the President ordered 9,000 American marines and paratroopers to the vicinity of Beirut, with appropriate air and naval protection. Two days later the British landed troops in Jordan. Despite a series of threats from Khrushchev and anguished outcries from Nasser, the American troops remained in Lebanon until October, when the crisis seemed to have ended. After 1958, the peace in the Middle East remained in precarious balance. METO never really matured into a full-fledged alliance, and the enmity between Arab and Jew did not abate. Moreover, Russian aid and military equipment was welcomed not only in Egypt but in various other Arab states. The Eisenhower Doctrine thus did not accomplish its purpose.

European Defense

The process of achieving western unity in the cause of mutual defense proved to be long and arduous. The United States had demanded that the nations of Europe furnish their fair share of NATO manpower. But the American government also insisted that West Germany be permitted to rearm, a frightening thought to the nations, particularly France, which had so recently suffered from German militarism. Furthermore, many West Germans had had their fill of war, and were opposed to rearmament. A French counter-proposal for a unified European Defense Community (EDC) went unratified, in spite of American encouragement. Nevertheless, at American insistence, plans for German rearmament and participation in NATO were drawn up.

On the economic front progress toward European unity was more encouraging. A hopeful indication of future cooperation came with the formation on August 1, 1952, at Luxembourg, of the European Coal and Steel Community (ECSC). This French-inspired organization created a single market for coal and steel throughout Italy, France, West Germany, and the Benelux countries. It acted as a powerful stimulant to economic prosperity in the nations concerned, and led eventually to two other important steps toward European union, the Common Market, designed to break down customs barriers among the ECSC powers, and Euratom, a unified organization to promote the industrial use of atomic energy. By treaties signed at Rome, March 25, 1957, the new European Community, with ECSC, the Common Market, and Euratom were all closely intertwined.

Germany and NATO

Many people throughout western Europe had become increasingly anxious about Secretary Dulles' aggressive language. The Secretary of State's declaration that the United States would no longer fight Communism in local wars, but would rely on "massive retaliatory power" was generally interpreted as a threat of an atomic attack on Russia in case Russian aggression continued. The support of some Republicans for a policy of "liberation" of states already overrun by the Communists also added to the tension. Distrust of American diplomatic leadership cost the United States much support throughout Europe, and there was much discussion, originating particularly in France, of the possibility of constituting western Europe as a "third force" to be used as an intermediary between Russia and the United States. The re-election of the pro-American government of Konrad Adenauer in West Ger-

many proved to be a counterweight to the third force proponents. By cooperating fully with the American insistence on German rearmament, Adenauer succeeded in winning not only practically full sovereignty for his Federal Republic but also membership in NATO, for which he agreed to supply eventually twelve divisions of troops.

Hungarian Revolt

Any remaining illusion that the way to a real peace with Russia was to be relatively easy was shattered by the events in Hungary during the autumn of 1956. There, as in Poland, Khrushchev's speeches denouncing Stalin's crimes of self-glorification, wholesale murder, and mass repression had ignited anti-Russian movements. In Poland the new Soviet rulers made terms with the revolt, permitting a Communist government somewhat independent of Moscow to take over.

But in Hungary, where a sudden revolution won widespread support within the Hungarian army, there was bitter fighting and ruthless suppression. Death totals, estimated as high as 50,000, and not all Hungarian, occurred before Russian troops and tanks were able to win an uneasy peace. More than 150,000 refugees fled to the West by way of neighboring Austria. By a decisive vote in which many neutralist nations joined the western bloc, the United Nations Assembly voiced in vigorous resolutions its censure of Russian behavior. But the Soviet government, unlike the invaders of Egypt, persisted in its course, blamed American propaganda for all the trouble in Hungary, and through its puppet government in Budapest refused even to grant United Nations investigators permission to enter the stricken nation. President Eisenhower publicly expressed his sympathy with the heroic fight of the Hungarians for freedom, but denied that the American government had in any way sought to promote a

The Hungarian Revolt *began on October 23, 1956, in Budapest with a student demonstration in favor of full independence. Early in the day this giant statue of Stalin, hated symbol of Soviet domination, was toppled by the crowd. The revolt had seemingly succeeded by the end of the month, but early in November new Soviet units from outside Hungary moved in to crush all resistance.*

revolt that was foredoomed to failure. One result of the ruthless Russian policy in Hungary was that the NATO alliance, which had shown signs of falling apart, began to draw together again.

Space Exploration

The suppression of the Hungarian people ended for a time further discussion by American leaders of liberating eastern European nations. But Europe's fear of atomic devastation, in case of another world war, preserved its desire to obtain a greater voice in the determination of western policy. This was especially true after the development of space rockets, which made the whole continent vulnerable to attack.

The "space race" was inaugurated in October, 1957, when the Soviets announced that their scientists had put a 184-pound artificial satellite, Sputnik I, into circulation around the earth. A month later Sputnik II appeared, about six times as large, and carrying a live dog. Soviet propagandists found in this triumph conclusive evidence that their scientists had far outstripped those of the United States, or any other country, while many Americans, long given to assuming their nation's pre-eminence in scientific achievement, were deeply humili-

ated. Actually American progress in space exploration was not as laggard as the public at first seemed to think, for on January 31, 1958, the United States sent up its first small satellite, Explorer I, weighing only 30.8 pounds, but containing instruments that, among other things, discovered the Van Allen radiation belt, a find of great significance. Other American satellites soon followed, but in the race to penetrate space the Soviets long continued their lead. They were first to orbit the moon and the sun, and to hit the moon.

U.S. Defenses

American anxiety over Soviet successes in space reflected real concern for the national defense. In order to cut down on military expenditures, the Eisenhower administration had subordinated reliance on expensive conventional methods of warfare to dependence on atomic weapons, from which the nation could get "more bang for a buck." Secretary of Defense Wilson had his doubts about basic research, which to him meant "when you don't know what you are doing," and saw little virtue in heavy expenditures on a missile program when air power of proved capacity stood ready to carry American nuclear weapons anywhere in the world. From air bases that ringed the Communist nations American bombers could more cheaply provide the massive retaliation that would hold Red aggression in leash. On the other hand, the Russians, from the end of the Second World War on, had seemingly been more perceptive than the Americans about the importance of research in rocketry and missiles. The Soviet government had made every effort to "capture," or recruit, German scientists engaged in this work, and had probably absorbed far more such talent than came to the United States. But American "missilemen," despite discouragement and shortage of funds, continued their efforts, even if in rival programs.

If a nation had the rocketry to lift a satellite into space, a reasonable deduction was that it could also land missiles at will almost anywhere on the planet. The U.S.S.R., with its intermediate range ballistic missile (IRBM) program already well along, claimed as early as August 26, 1957, to have tested successfully an intercontinental ballistic missile (ICBM), and by January, 1959, Khrushchev declared publicly that he had these weapons in mass production. However, the United States IRBM program soon yielded the air force Thor, the army Jupiter, and the navy Polaris, the latter designed for use by submerged submarines. By 1960 these weapons were paralleled by the Minuteman, the Titan, and the Atlas, all in the ICBM class. Supplemented as they were by air-borne nuclear bombs, they successfully maintained the balance of terror.

The effectiveness of the new atomic weapons, whether bombs or warheads for rockets and lesser projectiles, could be determined only by actual tests, which until 1958 the atomic powers carried out in remote and unpopulated regions. But the results of these explosions could not be localized, for the radioactive debris they produced drifted far and wide in the stratosphere, and if sufficiently multiplied would

eventually descend as "fall-out" to endanger life anywhere on the planet. Conscious of world opinion on the subject, and possibly convinced also of Russian leadership in the atomic race, the U.S.S.R. announced March 30, 1958, that it would suspend further testing if the other atomic powers would do likewise. Not until 1963 did the U.S. and U.S.S.R. agree to a ban on above ground testing of the bombs. Even so France and China, both of whom were feverishly attempting to develop their own atomic weapons, were not parties to the agreement.

Eisenhower's Personal Diplomacy

In April, 1959, Secretary Dulles, to whom the President had delegated principal authority over foreign policy, resigned in ill-health, and died the following month. From that date Eisenhower embarked upon a course of personal diplomacy in an effort to achieve something near world peace before his administration ended. During the

Atlas Production Line. *U.S. Air Force Atlas intercontinental ballistic missiles are assembled and checked out in this section of the San Diego, California, Convair plant, February, 1959.*

spring of 1959 the tensions were great. The previous autumn Russia had served an ultimatum on the West declaring that if Berlin were not made a demilitarized free city within six months, she would sign a separate peace treaty with East Germany. After the West absolutely refused to negotiate on the basis of an ultimatum, there subsequently occurred many feverish high level negotiations. Eisenhower himself visited Great Britain, France, and Germany, and Vice President Nixon journeyed to Russia. Then, on August 3, 1959, President Eisenhower announced that Khrushchev had accepted his invitation to confer with him in the United States.

Khrushchev's visit to the United States the following month went off without incident. He spent a weekend with Eisenhower at Camp David in the Maryland mountains, and while the conferees reached no agreement on disputed issues, they parted amicably enough. Khrushchev got his way about the summit conference, for which official preparations began the following December, but he had long since given up his insistence on a specific time limit for the Berlin settlement he demanded.

Few observers had expected the summit conference to end world tensions, but the manner of its collapse was totally unforeseen. Two weeks before the date set for it to open the Soviets shot down over central Russia a United States U-2 reconnaissance plane, and captured its pilot, who confessed that he was on a spy mission. Although some Americans tried to cover matters up, Eisenhower took full responsibility for the flight. Despite the super-charged international atmosphere both President Eisenhower and Premier Khrushchev showed up in Paris, May 16, 1960, for the summit conference. Thereupon Khrushchev, who might understandably have refused to ap-

Vice-President Richard Milhous Nixon, *on his 1959 visit to the U.S.S.R. is shown here with Khrushchev at the Moscow Fair.*

pear, used the conference instead for a vituperative denunciation of both the United States and President Eisenhower, and then scuttled the conference by refusing to deal further with the President unless he offered impossible apologies.

Decline of Colonialism

During the waning months of Eisenhower's administration another important issue served to aggravate tensions between the Communist nations and the West. In September, 1960, at a spectacular meeting of the United Nations, Khrushchev angrily demanded that the "imperialist nations" free all their colonies without delay. Actually the western powers were far along with this task, especially in Africa, the last of the colonial continents. France had granted independence to Tunisia and Morocco in 1956, and two years later had called General de Gaulle to the presidency of a Fifth Republic, clothed with virtually dictatorial powers to deal with the explosive Algerian situation. De Gaulle gave the various French colonies the right to remain French, to secede completely from the French Community, or to become self-governing states within it comparable to the nations of the British Commonwealth. All of them chose one of the last two alternatives, and were soon well on the way toward some degree of independence. Great Britain, likewise, continued with the liquidation of its empire.

Only Portugal remained obdurate. Belgium, which had long ruled the Belgian Congo with severity, pulled out prematurely, leaving its former colony in near anarchy. Here the United Nations, in an effort to restore some semblance of order, followed its post-Suez precedent, and sent in a police force recruited in the main, this time, from other African powers. The UN action greatly irritated Khrushchev, who was working for a Communist regime in the Congo, and it explained in part his hostility to the new United Nations Secre-tary-General, Dag Hammarskjöld. As in the case of the Israeli border defenders, the Communist bloc refused to pay anything toward the upkeep of the new military force that Hammarskjöld had called into being.

The Rise of Neutralism

Meantime, additional admissions to the United Nations, mostly from Africa, had brought its membership by the end of 1960 to ninety-nine (soon to be larger), nearly twice the original number, and had shifted the balance of power in the Assembly from the West to "uncommitted" Asian and African nations that refused to follow the lead of either Washington or Moscow.

Since 1953 Dulles had strongly contended against such "neutralism," as it came to be called, implying that those countries who were not positively for the West were against it. But following the lead of India, most of the new nations of Asia and Africa preferred to remain neutral and seek favors from both sides. Thus the Dulles-Eisenhower foreign policy had not only failed to achieve anything more positive than the Truman-Acheson "containment" formula; it had actually witnessed the loss of ground to the Communists in Asia and the growth of neutralism there and elsewhere. Moreover, Eisenhower, instead of ending his administration with the long step toward peace that he had envisioned, left office with world tensions still high.

Eisenhower's Farewell Address

The Eisenhower years seemed to many people to be a period of negativism in government, in spite of several notable legislative accomplishments and in spite of the President's efforts to cut down waste in government spending, especially in the military field he knew so well. Ironically, Eisenhower, the professional military man, came in time to be seen as the most peaceful of the postwar presidents. His refusal to commit American air and ground forces to help France put down the Indo-China revolution, in the face of strong contrary recommendations of Dulles, Nixon, and Radford, is perhaps the most striking evidence of his suspicion of military adventurism. On January 17, 1961, he delivered a farewell address, drawing attention to the development of "a permanent armaments industry of vast proportions" and to the fact that three and a half million people were "directly engaged in the defense establishment." His last words were a warning:

This conjunction of an immense military establishment and a large arms industry is new in the American experience. The total influence — economic, political, even spiritual — is felt in every city, every state house, every office of the federal government. We recognize the imperative need for this development. Yet we must not fail to comprehend its grave implications. Our toil, resources, and livelihood are all involved; so is the very structure of our society.

In the councils of government we must guard against the acquisition of unwarranted influence, whether sought or unsought, by the military-industrial complex. The potential for the disastrous rise of misplaced power exists and will persist.

We must never let the weight of this combination endanger our liberties or democratic processes. We should take nothing for granted. Only an alert and knowledgeable citizenry can compel the proper meshing of the huge industrial and military machinery of defense with our peaceful methods and goals, so that security and liberty may prosper together.

BIBLIOGRAPHY

One of the best approaches to the Eisenhower period is by way of the numerous memoirs which have already appeared. The President's own reminiscences, *The White House Years* (2 vols., 1963–1965), are a convenient starting point, for they reveal much of the character of their author. Richard Nixon, *Six Crises* (1962), contains some revealing memories of the Vice-President, although it is not a full-scale autobiography. Sherman Adams, *Firsthand Report* (1961), is the reminiscence of the controversial Secretary to the President. L. L. Strauss, *Men and Decisions* (1962), is the memoir of the Chairman of the Atomic Energy Commission, whose nomination for a cabinet post was rejected by the Senate. J. W. Martin and R. J. Donovan, *My First Fifty Years in Politics* (1960), is the autobiography of the former Speaker of the House, who was deposed from the minority leadership during Eisenhower's second term. E. J. Hughes, *The Ordeal of Power* (1963), is an "inside" account by an able journalist who sought to make the administration more liberal.

An interesting collection of evaluations is *Eisenhower as President*, edited by Dean Albertson (1963). Divergent journalistic sketches are M. J. Pusey, *Eisenhower, the President* (1956), by a warm admirer; and Marquis Childs, *Eisenhower: Captive Hero* (1958), by a liberal critic. A valuable behind-the-scenes report on the first term is R. J. Donovan, *Eisenhower: The Inside Story* (1956). R. H. Rovere, *Affairs of State: The Eisenhower Years* (1956), is a collection of witty running critiques by a liberal journalist.

Serious scholarly works on Eisenhower's domestic policies are already beginning to appear. The passage of the Landrum-Griffin Act is studied by A. K. McAdams, *Power and Politics in Labor Legislation* (1964). A critical account of the urban renewal program is Martin Anderson, *The Federal Bulldozer* (1964). Substantial monographs on two major issues are E. R. Bartley, *The Tidelands Oil Controversy* (1953); and Aaron Wildavsky, *Dixon-Yates: A Study in Power Politics* (1962). Of related interest is D. A. Frier, *Conflict of Interest in the Eisenhower Administration* (1969). Two studies of Eisenhower's civil rights program are J. W. Anderson, *Eisenhower, Brownell and the Congress* (1964); and F. R. Dulles, *The Civil Rights Commission: 1957–1965* (1968). W. R. Willoughby, *The St. Lawrence Waterway: A Study in Politics and Diplomacy* (1961), is based upon documentation from both sides of the border. A valuable study of an issue which took twenty years to resolve is W. J. Block, *The Separation of the Farm Bureau and the Extension Service* (1960).

A. T. Mason, *The Supreme Court from Taft to Warren* (1958), is a running commentary on the trend of decision-making. Scholarly studies of the Supreme Court under Warren include C. H. Pritchett, *Congress versus the Supreme Court, 1957–1960* (1961); and W. F. Murphy, *Congress and the Court* (1962).

The loyalty issue is debated in a collection of contemporary writings brought together in *Loyalty in a Democratic State*, edited by J. C. Wahlke (1952). A careful scholarly work is R. S. Brown, Jr., *Loyalty and Security: Employment Tests in the United States* (1958). C. H. Pritchett, *Civil Liberties and the Vinson Court* (1954), brings out the division within the Supreme Court. An interesting collection of materials is Allen Guttmann and B. M. Ziegler (eds.), *Communism, the Courts and the Constitution* (1964). Highly critical of the work of investigating committees are R. K. Carr, *The House Committee on Un-American Activities* (1952); and Walter Goodman, *The Committee* (1968). An excellent synthesis is Earl Latham, *The Communist Controversy in Washington* (1966). On "McCarthyism" see R. H. Rovere, *Senator Joe McCarthy* (1959); Richard Hofstadter, *The Paranoid Style in American Politics and Other Essays* (1965); M. P. Rogin, *The Intellectuals and McCarthy* (1967); and *The Meaning of McCarthyism* (1965), a collection of documents and conflicting interpretations edited by Earl Latham. The best work on one celebrated security incident is P. M. Stern, *The Oppen-heimer Case* (1969). The Hiss trial and the issues it raised are discussed temperately in Alistair Cooke, *A Generation on Trial: U.S.A. v. Alger Hiss* (2nd ed., 1952). A fascinating memoir is Whittaker Chambers, *Witness* (1952). Highly critical is the study by H. L. Packer, *Ex-Communist Witnesses* (1962).

The best general study of the Eisenhower foreign policy is L. L. Gerson, *John Foster Dulles* (1967). See also his semi-official biography by J. R. Beal, *John Foster Dulles* (1957). Diplomatic problems of one important area are covered by R. H. Fifield, *The Diplomacy of Southeast Asia, 1945–1958* (1958). An excellent general survey is Crane Brinton, *The Americans and the French* (1968). N. A. Graebner, *The New Isolationism* (1956), devotes much attention to domestic forces promoting foreign commitments which the author considers unrealistic. Among the many volumes appraising administration foreign policies, the following are samples: C. B. Marshall, *The Limits of Foreign Policy* (1954); and H. L. Roberts, *Russia and America: Dangers and Prospects* (1956). The views of an experienced "realist" are set forth in G. F. Kennan, *The Realities of American Foreign Policy* (1954), and *Russia, the Atom and the West* (1958), the latter being particularly critical of Dulles. G. A. Almond, *The American People and Foreign Policy* (2nd ed., 1960), is a useful survey. J. C. Campbell, *Defense of the Middle East: Problems of American Policy* (2nd ed., 1960), summarizes events after 1945. A lengthy and valuable synthesis is Kenneth Love, *Suez: The Twice-Fought War* (1969). Hugh Seton-Watson, *Neither War Nor Peace: The Struggle for Power in the Postwar World* (2nd ed., 1962), is a convenient summary of events near the close of the Eisenhower period.

The establishment of Israel has been treated in many works. A good introduction is Joseph Dunner, *The Republic of Israel: Its History and Its Promise* (1950). Gerald De Gaury, *The New State of Israel* (1952), is a discussion of pressing problems. An important scholarly work is Samuel Halperin, *The Political World of American Zionism* (1961).

H. A. Kissinger, *Nuclear Weapons and Foreign Policy* (1957), is by an influential military theoretician; it explores the possibilities dispassionately. T. K. Finletter, *Power* and Policy: *U.S. Foreign Policy and Military Power in the Hydrogen Age* (1954), is the analysis of a former Democratic Secretary of the Air Force. M. D. Taylor, *Uncertain Trumpet* (1960), is a critique of what its author, a former Army Chief of Staff, considered excessive reliance upon nuclear weapons. Herman Kahn, *On Thermonuclear War* (2nd ed., 1960), is a controversial study of what is possible after the bombs start to fall. See also the dispassionate study by Robert Gilpin, *American Scientists and Nuclear Weapons Policy* (1962).

The best study of the Democrat twice defeated by Eisenhower is Bert Cochran, *Adlai Stevenson: Patrician Among the Politicians* (1969). Rather uncritical are the other important Stevenson studies: K. S. Davis, *A Prophet in His Own Country* (1957); and S. G. Brown, *Conscience in Politics* (1961).

27

KENNEDY'S NEW FRONTIER

Election of 1960 · John F. Kennedy · The Bay of Pigs · Defense and Space · The Missile Crisis · Test-Ban Treaty · Kennedy's domestic program · The assassination · Lyndon B. Johnson · Election of 1964 · Johnson's foreign troubles

Dwight Eisenhower was seventy years old by the time of the 1960 election. Barred by his own inclinations (and the Twenty-Second Amendment to the Constitution) from seeking a third term, the President watched, and occasionally participated in, a tense battle between candidates aged 43 and 47. A new generation was now in the political ascendancy. However this election might turn out, a post-New Deal President would be faced with the serious economic recession, increasingly severe urban problems, a mounting unwillingness of racial minorities to accept inferior status, and (above all) potentially deadly international crises.

Election of 1960

Against this setting the American people decided the succession to Eisenhower. The President's heir-apparent was Vice-President Richard M. Nixon, who had lined up the country's Republican leaders behind his candidacy by years of vigorous campaigning throughout the nation.

In the first half of 1960 the Democrats provided most of the political excitement, as they went through the complicated process of deciding their nomination. The principal candidates were three prominent United States Senators, Hubert Humphrey of Minnesota, John F. Kennedy of Massachusetts, and Lyndon B. Johnson of Texas. Two well-financed and brilliantly managed primary campaigns, in Wisconsin and West Virginia, showed that Kennedy had powerful support in the Middle West and border areas; after a humiliating defeat in West Virginia, Humphrey withdrew from the race. In July the Democratic convention met in Los Angeles and nominated Kennedy on the first ballot, with only a few votes to spare. Kennedy offered the vice-presidential nomination to Johnson, the powerful majority leader of the Senate, in an apparent effort to strengthen the ticket in the Protestant South, where Kennedy's Catholicism might turn out to be a liability. Johnson, to the surprise of many, accepted the second position on the ticket. The platform emphasized the negativism the Democrats claimed had characterized the Republican administration, although they were careful not to attack President Eisenhower.

ASTRONAUT ALAN SHEPARD *walks toward the rocket which carried him into space.*

They demanded greater government action to stimulate the economy, with an annual 5 per cent increase in the gross national product (GNP) as the goal; more generous welfare measures and a minimum wage of $1.25 per hour; "not less than 90 per cent of parity" for agricultural income; a vigorous campaign for racial equality; generous foreign aid to underdeveloped nations; and a strengthening of the "conventional" or non-atomic national defenses.

The Republican convention, held two weeks later in Chicago, was in comparison a somewhat tame affair. Nixon was nominated for President without incident, and at his suggestion the delegates chose Henry Cabot Lodge, United States Ambassador to the United Nations, for Vice-President. Due to the intervention of Governor Nelson A. Rockefeller of New York, the platform contained a more aggressive stand on civil rights than the original platform makers had intended, and specific advocacy of

an intensified missile program. It also called for "a crash research program" to develop new uses for farm products, the extension of "business-like methods" to government operations, and promises on foreign aid and economic growth not very different from those of the Democrats.

As usual, the campaign turned more on personalities than on issues, although Kennedy hammered hard on the need for greater economic growth to outdistance the rising power of the U.S.S.R., and to forge ahead along what he called "the new frontier." A series of four Nixon-Kennedy television debates, or more accurately "confrontations," furnished the chief excitement of the campaign. Probably from 65 to 75 million Americans watched and listened while the Senator and the Vice-President replied to questions asked by a panel of news reporters, and commented also on the views expressed by each other. Kennedy handled himself well enough to render ri-

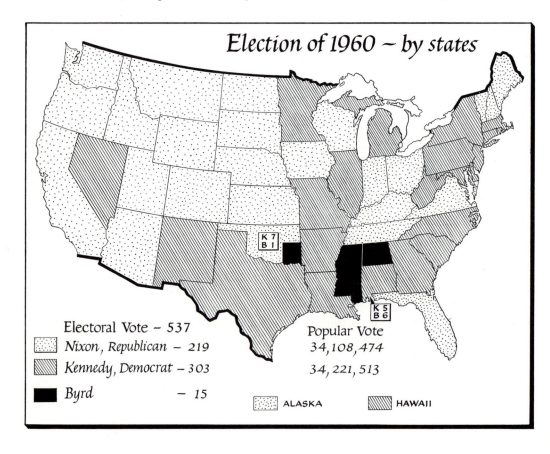

Election of 1960 – by states

K 7
B 1

K 5
B 6

Electoral Vote – 537

Nixon, Republican – 219

Kennedy, Democrat – 303

Byrd – 15

Popular Vote
34,108,474
34,221,513

ALASKA   HAWAII

Democratic Nominees, *John F. Kennedy and Lyndon Johnson, after their acceptance speeches in the Los Angeles Coliseum, August 15, 1960. To the right of Johnson are Sam Rayburn, James Roosevelt, and three unsuccessful aspirants, Adlai Stevenson, Hubert Humphrey and Stuart Symington.*

diculous the aspersions Republicans had cast on his maturity, and the debates undoubtedly won him many votes. Kennedy's Roman Catholic religion was a factor in the campaign, and undoubtedly cost the Democratic candidate millions of votes in the predominantly Protestant and rural sections of the South and West. But in the urban industrial areas, where Catholics were most numerous, the religious issue certainly helped him.

Election results were surprisingly close. In a total popular vote of nearly 69 million, Kennedy outdistanced Nixon by only 113,000 votes, while in the electoral college he received 303 votes to Nixon's 219. The Democrats, aided by strong Negro and Jewish as well as Catholic backing, won relatively narrow victories in the eastern seaboard states, in the Deep South, and in Illinois, but lost most of the Middle West, including Ohio, the border states, and the Far West, including California. Both houses of Congress remained Democratic by reduced but still substantial margins, but the conservative southern delegations held the balance of power in each. The narrowness of the Democratic victory was regarded with some misgivings by both foreign and domestic observers, and served somewhat to undermine the mandate with which Kennedy took office.

John F. Kennedy

John Fitzgerald Kennedy (1917–1963), the son of Joseph P. Kennedy, a Boston multimillionaire who had held high office during the New Deal, attended Harvard University, from which he graduated in 1940. At the outbreak of World War II, he entered the armed forces and served with distinction as a naval officer in the South Pacific where he was severely injured in combat. In 1946 he won election for the first of three terms to the national House of Representatives, and in 1952, despite the overwhelming Eisenhower landslide, he was elected to the United States Senate. Four years later at the Democratic Convention in Philadelphia he came within a few votes of winning his party's nomination for Vice-President. Re-elected to the Senate in 1958, he immediately opened an aggressive campaign for the 1960 Democratic nomination for the Presidency.

Kennedy's keen wit and youthful vigor helped him to overcome many difficulties. He had three apparent liabilities — his alleged immaturity, his religion, and his father — and he overcame all of them during the course of the campaign. He demonstrated that he could discuss national problems on a basis of equality with his opponent during the television debates; he campaigned with

President John F. Kennedy *answering a reporter's question during a news conference in Washington in 1961.*

such energy that he could scarcely be typed as either a playboy or a dilettante; he surrounded himself with men of serious purpose. His Catholicism was something else, however. He could not turn his back on his faith (even supposing he had been willing to do so) without offending fellow Catholics, many of whom had been raised on the bitter legend that Al Smith had lost the Presidency in 1928 only because he had been a Catholic. Kennedy waited for the attacks of those who felt that a Catholic could not possibly discharge his oath of office as President because of his loyalty to Rome. He then defended his integrity and independence, notably before a group of Baptist clergymen in Houston. A leader of a pro-Nixon Protestant group, the National Conference of Citizens for Religious Freedom, warned his colleagues of the dangers of Kennedy's election: "Our American culture is at stake. I don't say it won't survive, but it won't be what it was." Kennedy's

reaction was typical: "I would like to think he was complimenting me, but I'm not sure he was."* Anti-Catholicism remained a factor in the campaign but Kennedy managed to convert it into an asset in some regions. The problem of the father was Joseph P. Kennedy's record as an isolationist who had become defeatist while serving as Ambassador to Britain (1937–1940) and who had become the friend and patron of the notorious red-baiting Senator Joseph R. McCarthy. John Kennedy was close to his father, who was ambitious for his sons and who aided them in many ways. During the campaign, Kennedy set forth his own program in such a way as to make it clear that, while he was fond of his father, he did his own political thinking.

The New Frontier

Kennedy's inaugural address, delivered on a bitterly cold day while Washington lay under a deep blanket of snow, recalled the spirit of the "new frontier" to which he had drawn attention in his acceptance speech in Los Angeles. In foreign affairs he promised a more vigorous policy: "Let every nation know, whether it wishes us well or ill, that we shall pay any price, bear any burden, meet any hardship, support any friend, oppose any foe to assure the survival and the success of liberty." Although he was quite general about domestic programs he did, in the most quoted part of his inaugural speech, stress the need for personal sacrifice: "And so, my fellow Americans, ask not what your country can do for you; ask what you can do for your country."

From the opening days of his administration, Kennedy raised the hopes of those who advocated a fresh approach in both foreign and domestic affairs. During the campaign he had proposed a Peace Corps through which individual Americans might

* Theodore C. Sorensen, *Kennedy* (Harper & Row, 1965) p. 188.

volunteer to serve their nation abroad in nonmilitary missions, chiefly in underdeveloped countries. Launched by executive order, March 1, 1961, and placed on a statutory basis by Congress the following September, the Peace Corps achieved far greater success than its critics had anticipated. By the end of its first sixteen months 3,642 volunteers had been sent abroad, and only 77 had failed to serve out their full terms of enlistment. The acceptance of Peace Corps men and women by the great variety of peoples to whom they were sent grew as they demonstrated their effectiveness in such fields as education, sanitation, agriculture, and home economics.

Kennedy's appointments in general did not follow the traditional pattern of rewards for political service; in this respect he was even less traditional than Franklin D. Roosevelt had been in 1933. For key positions in his administration he chose some Republicans, such as Allen W. Dulles, brother of Eisenhower's late Secretary of State, whom he continued as Director of the Central Intelligence Agency, and C. Douglas Dillon, Eisenhower's Undersecretary of State, whom he made Secretary of the Treasury. Other appointees, like Robert S. McNamara, the youthful president of the Ford Motor Company, who became Secretary of Defense, were from industry and without experience in politics. For Secretary of State he passed over several more prominent candidates (including Adlai Stevenson, whom he made Ambassador to the United Nations) to select Dean Rusk, president of the Rockefeller Foundation. As his Attorney-General he named his own younger brother, Robert, despite the outcries of nepotism that arose from both parties. Most of Kennedy's other appointees were relatively youthful liberals who had already demonstrated their abilities in business, education, or government.

The Kennedy style was apparent in the new President's relations with the public.

In his speeches and news conferences he relied less upon histrionics and emotion than upon informed, tightly reasoned, vigorous prose. Despite frequent flashes of humor, he sometimes displayed a solemn earnestness of purpose. He made no attempt to disguise his interest in men of intellectual and cultural attainments, as for example in assigning a prominent part in the inaugural ceremonies to Robert Frost, the poet, or in giving a dinner for Nobel Prize winners, or in recommending to Congress the creation of a medal of honor for outstanding contributors to American life and culture. In foreign policy his willingness to take risks that he deemed necessary won general approval. Liberals who had once doubted his dedication to progressive principles responded cordially to his domestic program. By the autumn of 1963 his standing with the people was such that his re-election in 1964 was generally conceded.

The Bay of Pigs

One of Kennedy's first diplomatic problems emerged in Cuba, where in 1959 a successful revolution against the dictator, Fulgencio Batista, had brought Fidel Castro to power. To the great distress of the many Americans who had backed him, Castro's regime soon displayed a definite trend toward Communism. His oppressive rule drove thousands of Cubans into exile, most of them to the United States, particularly to nearby Florida. Under Eisenhower the American government was unwilling to intervene in Cuba directly, but sought with little success to isolate the island both diplomatically and economically. When Kennedy took office, however, he found that the American Central Intelligence Agency had planned and promoted the training in Guatemala of a counter-revolutionary refugee expedition, which was ready to land on Cuban shores. With some misgivings, Kennedy allowed the invasion to proceed, although with the reservation that the United

Khrushchev and Castro *greet each other during the 1960 meeting of the United Nations Assembly in New York.*

States must not provide planes for air cover. This decision probably helped to assure the failure of the expedition, which on April 17, 1961, landed 1,500 men at the Bay of Cochinos (Pigs), only to meet disastrous defeat. The unwillingness or inability of the Cuban population to rise up against Castro, as the exiles and their backers expected, was the fundamental reason for the failure of this operation. Kennedy was deeply humiliated by the fiasco, but unhesitatingly assumed complete responsibility for permitting it to happen.

Because of the much graver situations in Europe and Asia, the United States had paid relatively little attention to the Latin part of its own hemisphere. Although billions of dollars in United States funds had provided economic assistance for other parts of the world, Latin America had received little American aid. While the region had not suffered from war damage, its archaic and usually corrupt governments, often controlled by a small clique of ruling families, had served effectively to keep most of their people in squalor. A relatively static economic structure, combined with one of the world's highest birth rates, tended to intensify the already existing massive poverty.

The presence of a Russian-backed Communist regime in Cuba had some effect upon all the governments of Latin America, many of which feared that their very existence was imperiled. Faith in the United States was at low ebb, particularly after the abortive Cuban invasion. To meet this new emergency, the American government proposed an Alliance for Progress, reminiscent of the European Recovery Plan that had worked so well. At an Inter-American Economic and Social Council meeting, held in Punta del Este, Uruguay, in August, 1961, the United States urged the Latin-American nations to promote such essentials as land reform; better taxation systems; adequate housing, health, and sanitation facilities; and sensible labor-management relations. In what came to be called the Declaration of Punta del Este, to which the United States and all the Latin-American republics except Cuba subscribed, the United States promised to supply a major part of the $20 billion in outside capital needed to institute the program. The Latin-American nations agreed in return to devote to it a rapidly increasing share of their resources. But it was easier to plan the Alliance for Progress than to make it work.

National Defense

In order to cope with a rapidly shifting world, the Kennedy administration made important changes in the nation's defense policy. Convinced by conversations with Khrushchev in Vienna in June, 1961, that the Soviet leader was determined to carry out his promised support for "uprisings" against existing non-Communist governments, President Kennedy reversed the Eisenhower policy of dependence on the atomic bomb as a deterrent. In line with Secretary McNamara's views, Congress increased substantially the strength of the army and navy and retained many air force contingents previously scheduled for deactivation. To dampen further Russian interest in "bush wars," Kennedy let it be known that the United States itself would resort to guerrilla warfare, if that should be necessary to prevent Communist takeovers; also that he would not hesitate to use atomic weapons should the defense of the free world require it.

During the campaign of 1960 there had been much talk of the "missile gap" that was supposed to exist between the United States and the Soviet Union. The Kennedy administration immediately raised the budget figures both for long-range missiles and for the so-called "space race." In July, 1961, the United States scored a spectacular achievement by launching an Atlas E missile and dropping it in a designated target area 9,050 miles away in the Indian Ocean. But the following September the Soviets also launched long-range missiles and guided them for 7,500 miles into the central Pacific area.

Space Exploration

The race between the United States and the Soviet Union in space exploration accented sharply the military and political rivalry of the two nations. President Ken-

nedy had been in office only a few months when he announced that the American government should commit itself to the project of "landing a man on the moon and returning him safely to earth." Experts held that the ultimate cost of this undertaking might be as high as $40 billion, but Congress approved it and voted initial funds for the project. In this area of competition, however, the Soviets had a substantial lead. During 1961 their cosmonauts had repeatedly circled the earth and landed their craft successfully; the United States matched this in 1962. American space flights, however, unlike those of the Soviets took place amidst a maximum of publicity. Millions of television viewers witnessed both the launching of the rocket and the recovery of the astronaut.

The Berlin Wall

Meanwhile, tension between East and West over Berlin had caused great anxiety. Angered by the steady stream of refugees that flowed at the rate of about 20,000 a month from East Germany through Berlin to the West, the Communist authorities on August 13, 1961, closed off East Berlin from the rest of the city and erected a concrete and barbed-wire wall along the border to keep would-be escapees at home. Although the Allied powers vigorously protested the

The Brandenburg Gate. *The Communist rulers of East Germany, in order to stop the flight of so many of their supposedly "happy" people through Berlin to West Germany, erected barbedwire and concrete barriers to shut off their section of the divided city. The Berlin Wall thus became a monument to the discontent of East Germans with Communist rule.*

action of the Communists in so dividing Berlin, they studiously avoided an armed clash and confined their efforts to the protection of the territory they held. Kennedy rejected Khrushchev's demands that West Berlin be turned into a free city, that Allied troops be withdrawn, and that East Germany be recognized by the western powers. He called into service enough National Guard and Reserve units to enable him to send 45,000 more men to Europe and to ready more troops for combat service. The Berlin wall still stood, but to some westerners its creation seemed to be a major Communist blunder, an admission to the world that Communism could not stand competition with a free society. President Kennedy emphasized further the intent of the United States to stand firm in the defense of West Berlin by visiting the city himself in July, 1963, and electrified a vast audience by the assertion, *"Ich bin ein Berliner."*

The Congo

Another major difficulty was brought about by the chaotic conditions that continued in the Congo. There, after the Belgian withdrawal, the contest finally settled down to a test of endurance between what passed for a central government at Leopoldville, and the Katanga provincial government at Elisabethville, headed by Moise Tshombe. In an effort to restore order, the United Nations intervened with military force, but the factional fighting continued. To add to the confusion the Soviets attempted to support incipient governments, the first under Patrice Lumumba, who was murdered, and the second under Antoine Gizenga, a local leader in the eastern part of the country. Since the Soviet Union, its satellites, and France steadfastly refused to pay their assessments for maintaining United Nations forces in the Congo, the steady drain on the world organization's budget threatened it with bankruptcy. This condition was eventually relieved by an American loan of $100 million to the UN, and the evacuation in 1963 of all UN forces in the Congo.

Southeast Asia

By supporting the United Nations in its attempt at pacification, the United States was able to avoid direct intervention in the Congo, but matters were far different in Southeast Asia. There civil war continued as the accord arrived at by the Geneva Conference broke down. Kennedy's first crisis in this area occurred in Laos, a tiny underdeveloped kingdom in the northwest part of Indo-China. After 1954 neither the Soviet Union nor the United States was willing to permit Laos to be the neutralist country it was supposed to be; each superpower poured in military aid in an attempt to see its favorite faction win out. The Communist-led Pathet Lao forces seemed close to victory when Kennedy was inaugurated. Although he was urged by his military advisers to increase American aid, even to the extent of committing land forces to the anti-Communist side in Laos, Kennedy refused to do so. Instead he rejected the "domino theory" then much in vogue — the idea that the nations were like dominoes and if one "fell" to Communism its neighbors would be sure to fall — and promoted a cease-fire, another Geneva conference, and the re-establishment of the neutralist government of Prince Souvanna Phouma. The second Geneva accord was signed in July, 1962, by fourteen governments, including Red China and North Vietnam.

In Vietnam, Kennedy's policies were less clear-cut. The Eisenhower administration had given military aid and economic support to the government of South Vietnam, the "democratic" half of the divided country. Included in this aid were some 900 American "advisers" on duty when Kennedy took office. The Communist-led gov-

The War in Vietnam. *American "advisers," equipped with helicopters and a variety of military vehicles, participated much more actively in the fighting than their designation implied.*

ernment of North Vietnam sought to take over the whole country; the weak and corrupt government of South Vietnam did not constitute much of a barrier. Although the Joint Chiefs of Staff recommended in the spring of 1961 that the United States commit American combat troops in Vietnam, Kennedy was skeptical, understandably so since the same body had recommended the Bay of Pigs adventure to him. However, Kennedy did not move to neutralize Vietnam, as he had Laos; instead, he sought to bolster the South Vietnam regime, while encouraging it to reform. By the end of 1961 the military assistance mission numbered 2,000 men; by the end of 1963 the total reached 15,500. A sizable increase took place after the Berlin wall went up, an obvious "show of force" designed to impress the Russians with his determination to resist the aggression of one side against another in a civil war in Southeast Asia. Kennedy's escalation of American forces in Vietnam, while much less spectacular than that which his chief military advisers

sought, was in large part a reaction to Soviet actions in other parts of the world.

The Missile Crisis

After the Bay of Pigs episode, Castro admitted openly that Cuba had become a Communist state, the first, but he vowed not the last, in the western hemisphere. Soon he was receiving substantial assistance, both civilian and military, from the Soviet Union. Many Americans counseled some form of United States intervention, perhaps a blockade that would prevent Soviet shipments and personnel from reaching Cuba, but the President refused to be stampeded into any action that might result in war. In the fall of 1962, however, he learned that the Cuban government was receiving from the Soviets missiles and bombers capable of destroying most United States and Caribbean cities and the Panama Canal. As a result he announced, October 22, 1962, a "quarantine" against the delivery to Cuba of any such weapons and ordered the navy and the air force to make it effective. He further warned that an attack by Cuban-based missiles on American targets would be construed as an attack coming from the Soviet Union itself, and that retaliation by the United States would follow immediately. Kennedy insisted that the missile sites already being built in Cuba must be dismantled.

Khrushchev, faced by the tough American stand, gave in. Soviet ships on the way to Cuba with military equipment turned back rather than face the American blockade. Khrushchev also promised to remove all offensive weapons and to permit inspection to prove that they were gone. In return he asked only that the United States lift its blockade and agree not to invade Cuba, a concession that the President was willing to make, but only on evidence that the Soviets had converted their words into deeds. When Castro refused to permit the inspection that Khrushchev had promised, the United States deployed air flights over Cuba, from which it learned that all missiles designed for offensive use were being dismantled and returned to Russia, and that Soviet forces in Cuba were being evacuated. With this assurance, the quarantine was lifted.

The Test-Ban Treaty

After the Cuban confrontation, which had brought the United States and the Soviet Union so frighteningly near to war, the two nations showed an unmistakable interest in the prevention of similar incidents for the future. In order to reduce the danger of accidental war, they agreed on April 5, 1963, to establish a "hot line" between Moscow and Washington, by means of which the responsible leaders of the two nations could communicate with each other directly and at a moment's notice. Also, they joined with Great Britain in subscribing, on July 25, 1963, to a "test-ban" treaty signed at Geneva, which forbade atomic testing in the air, in space, and under water. The test-ban agreement was ratified not only by the three principal atomic powers but by many other nations. However, France and Red China refused to agree to it.

Following the test-ban agreement, Khrushchev showed a greater degree of willingness to cooperate with the West on scientific and cultural matters; he made no new demands concerning Berlin and the German problem; he showed little interest in promoting Red China's bid for supremacy in Southeast Asia. The hopes of the western nations for a *détente*, during which a war-weary world might seek further to resolve its differences, were dimmed perceptibly when the Soviet Presidium suddenly ousted Khrushchev, October 14, 1964, and replaced him with Leonid L. Brezhnev as First Secretary of the Communist Party, and Aleksei N. Kosygin as Premier. Many observers felt that Khrushchev had by then achieved a reputation for bungling and that the Presidium felt the need for more effective leadership. For the time being it was unclear to the world what the change-over would signify.

The Communist Schism

Perhaps the most significant foreign development of the Kennedy years was the growing rift between the Soviet Union and China. The cause of this split, the Chinese declared, was Khrushchev's departure from the Marxist-Leninist doctrine that capitalism could be overthrown only by violence. Two weeks before Kennedy took office the Soviet leader had outlined in a major address a new approach to East-West relations. Since an atomic war might well wipe out both the Communist and the free nations, such a conflict, Khrushchev declared, must not occur. Instead, the Communists should seek their ultimate goal of world socialism by the steady subversion of existing "imperialist" nations, by promoting national uprisings, by waging guerrilla wars for the liberation of subject peoples, and above all by demonstrating the superiority of their social and economic system. This Russian policy of "peaceful co-existence," as Khrushchev sometimes termed it, seemed to Chou En-lai and his adherents a complete betrayal of the Communist cause. The split ran deeper than mere differences in ideology, for the two nations were historic enemies. They had conflicting claims along the Siberian-Chinese border, and both sought exclusive domination of the Communist parties in the new nations of Asia and Africa. By 1958, the Soviets ordered the withdrawal of all aid to China. A by-product of the Soviet absorption in the dispute with China was the effort made by various satellite states of eastern Europe to seek greater independence from their Russian overlords.

Domestic Affairs

During the campaign of 1960, Kennedy had promised that under a Democratic administration the economic growth of the United States would surge forward at a far more rapid rate than during the Eisenhower years. But before he could concern himself with growth the new President had to face the problems of a business recession which reached a disheartening low just as he took office. With the number of jobless standing at 6.9 per cent of the working population, Congress agreed to a temporary thirteen week extension of unemployment benefits, approved an area development program that Eisenhower had twice vetoed, liberalized social security payments, extended the minimum wage protection to an additional 3.6 million workers, and provided for an increase in the minimum wage. These measures, together with substantial federal expenditures on highways, aided materially in promoting recovery.

With the end of the recession in sight, the President set about exploring the New Frontier that he had described in his campaign. During his first two years his efforts were virtually blocked in this endeavor, in part by the long-standing congressional coalition of southern Democrats and conservative Republicans, and in part by the critical position of the country in international finance. For the time being the President himself was unwilling to promote the kind of deficit spending that some of his supporters had expected, not only because he was eager to prevent inflation, but also because of the unfavorable balance of payments that had developed in the country's foreign accounts. The United States no longer sold more abroad than the combined totals of what it bought and what it sent abroad for military purposes, economic aid, tourist expenditures, and investment. Instead of the relatively even balance of payments that before 1958 had long kept about $22 billion worth of gold in the United States Treasury, the balance had turned strongly in favor of Europe. American losses by 1962 had brought the Treasury's gold resources down to less than $17 billion. Since about two-thirds of this gold was needed to back federal reserve notes, the United States actually had available less than $6 billion for use in international settlements. The Kennedy administration could not, therefore, run the risk of an inflationary spiral that might further reduce the nation's gold supply and lower the value of the dollar. The most conspicuous success that the President won from his refractory Congress was the passage in 1962 of a foreign free trade bill that gave him unprecedented freedom in adjusting American tariffs to competitive needs.

Reform Programs

The Kennedy administration was able to take a few other steps toward reform. The Federal Power Commission undertook with some success to bring natural gas producers under more effective control. The Food and Drug Administration, as a result of investigations begun by Senator Kefauver, scored several successes, including legislation that greatly strengthened the safeguards surrounding the production, testing, and sale of medicines. Meanwhile, Attorney-General Robert Kennedy launched antitrust suits against corporations deemed guilty of price-fixing and illegal mergers.

The Kennedy administration also intervened in a threatened national steel strike to obtain an agreement maintaining the existing wage scale with some additional fringe benefits, together with what it regarded as an understanding that the companies would not raise the price of steel products. The agreement was designed to stop the inflationary pay-raise, price-rise cycle that had so long prevailed in major industries. But as soon as the wage contract was safely signed, the United States Steel Corporation, in what seemed to the President, the workers, and most of the public an act of bad faith, raised the price of steel. When most of the other steel companies followed suit, Kennedy in a televised press conference angrily denounced those who had instigated the price increases for their "irresponsible defiance" and "ruthless disregard" of the nation's welfare. The increase, he said, was not only inflationary, but would add a billion dollars to the nation's defense costs and would impair the ability of American firms to compete in the world market. United States Steel defended its action and announced that the higher prices would stand. But the President let it be known that military contractors would thereafter shift as much as possible of their steel purchases to firms maintaining the old price. After two steel companies announced that they would not raise their prices and a third reversed its action, United States Steel and the others capitulated. The incident revealed not only the power of the federal government as a prime purchaser, but also the extent to which it had moved into the market mechanism establishing the level of wages and prices.

The 1962 mid-term elections indicated popular approval of the new administration. In Congress, the Democrats won four additional seats in the House and held their own in the Senate, the first time since 1934 that any party in power had not suffered a mid-term reverse. Possibly because of this vote of confidence, the President, in January, 1963, called upon Congress to enact an extensive program of domestic legislation, including a $10 billion tax cut to encourage business and diminish unemployment, the extension of social security and public health benefits, and the establishment of a Community Corps, comparable to the Peace Corps, to enroll and train young Americans "out of school and out of work."

The new Congress, despite its overwhelmingly Democratic majorities, seemed little disposed to give the President what he wanted, largely because conservative southern Democrats held most of the important committee assignments in both houses. Attention tended to focus on foreign aid, the tax cut, and civil rights. The continuance of the foreign aid program, which had cost the United States $100 billion since 1945, was denounced as wasteful, inefficient, and mismanaged, serving mainly to ensure a balance-of-payments deficit for the United States. The tax cut, which normally should have pleased the business community, was less welcome because it proposed to close certain valued loopholes and was not to be accompanied by a corresponding cut in expenditures. It was intended to stimulate business and prevent another of the periodic recessions that had so regularly marked the preceding decade. The civil rights program, to the anger of most southern Democrats, proposed that the national government should interfere with the rights of the states to deal as they chose with Negroes.

The Assassination

President Kennedy took a trip to Texas in the fall of 1963, in an effort to bolster his position following his advocacy of strong civil rights legislation and, incidentally, to improve relations among the factions of Texas Democrats. After speaking in Fort Worth on the morning of November 22, he went on to Dallas to deliver another address. As he rode in an open limousine with Mrs. Kennedy from the airport to the center of the city, rifle shots rang out. The President was mortally wounded. The assassin, Lee Harvey Oswald, a neurotic with leftwing sympathies who had a job in the building from which he fired the rifle, was apparently acting on his own for no evidence of conspiracy was ever discovered. Oswald was quickly arrested. Two days later, while still under arrest, Oswald was himself killed by an overwrought Dallas nightclub operator.

As soon as Kennedy's death was announced to a stunned country, Vice-President Johnson took the oath of office as President. He had been riding in a car behind Kennedy in the Dallas motorcade. The plane which carried John Kennedy's body back to Washington also contained the new President. For four intense days, until the late President's body was buried at Arlington National Cemetery, the nation watched scenes of melancholy and grandeur. Many who could neither understand nor appreciate John Kennedy in life for a time, at least, felt very close to him.

Lyndon B. Johnson

Fortunately for the peace of the country, the new President showed a welcome and quite unexpected dignity during the period of transition. He was little known outside his home state and the halls of Congress, although he had traveled widely during his years as Vice-President. Ten years older than his predecessor and with over twice as much service in national government, Johnson was a master of congressional politics. He had never run in a two-party contest until 1960, nor had he ever really cultivated Democratic leaders outside his own area.

Johnson had shared in most important decisions of the Kennedy administration and could assure the nation and the world that an informed and experienced hand was at the helm. He retained every member of the Kennedy cabinet and all other administrative heads and emphasized repeatedly that he would work for the goals that Kennedy had sought, both at home and abroad. Foremost among these aims was the strong civil rights measure to which Kennedy had

The Kennedy Funeral. *The elaborate ceremonies that preceded the President's interment were viewed on television by countless numbers, both within and without the United States. The flag-draped casket containing the President's body is shown here in the Capitol Rotunda in Washington.*

Lyndon Baines Johnson. *The remarkable facility shown by Kennedy's successor in obtaining from Congress legislation that a large majority of the people wanted assured his nomination and election to the Presidency "in his own right" (1964). But some who voted for him then condemned the stern measures he ordered later in Vietnam.*

gram and two years later was elected to Congress, where he remained for five additional terms. During World War II he saw service for several months in the South Pacific as a member of the Naval Reserve, but returned to his seat in the House at the request of President Roosevelt, who had summoned all Congressmen back to Washington. In 1948, after a bitterly fought campaign, he won the Democratic nomination for United States Senator, tantamount to election in one-party Texas. His margin was a humiliating 87 votes, which gave his enemies a chance to taunt him as "Landslide Lyndon." Before his first term was over he had become leader of the Democratic minority. After his overwhelming re-election to the Senate in 1954, he became majority leader in the new Democratic Senate.

In many ways the new President differed markedly from his predecessor. A typical southwesterner, he was in his personal relations hospitable and informal. Although not as impressive as Kennedy in public speaking, he was exceptionally effective in direct dealings with politicians. Regarded generally as a moderate conservative before the election of 1960, he nevertheless cherished a deep concern for the welfare of the ordinary farmer, the city worker, and the various minority groups. Although a man of principle, he was a realist and was not afraid to compromise; to him domestic politics was the art of the possible. Johnson was a complex person, earthy and reverent, hard-boiled and sentimental, an almost elemental personal force. He was aware, too, much so, perhaps, that the country looked upon him as an accident, that he would have to prove himself worthy of his position. Fortunately for him, he was at his best in congressional matters and it was there where his predecessor had been weak.

Johnson and Congress

On taking over the Presidency, Johnson found the main features of the Kennedy

committed his administration. Johnson's forthright support of civil rights legislation reassured, and was meant to reassure, those who had feared that the new President's Texas background and his close friendships with many southern politicians might make a difference.

Lyndon Baines Johnson (1908–   ) was born near Stonewall, Texas, the descendant of frontiersmen. After graduation from Southwest State Teachers College at San Marcos, Texas, in 1930, he taught for a time in the Texas public school system. In 1932 he became secretary to a Congressman. Thus introduced to Washington, Johnson was not long in finding his true vocation. Under Franklin D. Roosevelt he became director in 1935 of his state's NYA pro-legislation hopelessly stalled in Congress, but he knew better than most politicians how to prod that body into action. He kept it in session, despite its desire to adjourn for the holidays, until it had passed the long-delayed foreign aid bill. He also used his influence to pry the Kennedy tax reduction bill out of the committees that were blocking it and to push it through Congress. He achieved this goal in part by cutting the proposed Kennedy budget from over $100 billion to just under that sum, thus satisfying some critics who demanded tax cuts should be accompanied by reduced spending. Although crippling amendments had eliminated most of the reforms from the original bill, Congress passed an $11.5 billion tax cut bill.

The President's next major effort was to expedite passage of the civil rights measure, long held up in the House of Representatives. Proud of the fact that Congress, while he was Senate majority leader, had passed the first civil rights legislation since Reconstruction, he pushed hard for action on the pending bill. The proposed measure sought (1) to promote the freer registration of voters, (2) to forbid discrimination in such public facilities as hotels, restaurants, and stores, (3) to authorize action by the Attorney-General against school segregation and other discriminatory practices, and (4) to create a federal agency for the enforcement of equality in job opportunity. Early in 1964 the House passed the measure, substantially as Kennedy had wanted it. In the Senate, however, it met a determined southern filibuster, the longest in that body's history. But after eighty-seven days of wearisome talk, the necessary two-thirds majority for cloture was made possible by the adoption of a series of Republican-sponsored amendments, designed to increase moderately the power of local governments in the administration of the measure. On June 10, 1964, for the first time in its history, the Senate voted 71 to 29 for cloture on a civil rights measure, thus assuring the passage of the bill.

The administration scored similar successes with other measures it sponsored. By the time Congress adjourned for the autumn campaign, it had passed measures to increase the pay of Congressmen, federal judges, and civil servants, to give financial aid to state and local governments attempting to provide adequate mass transportation for the burgeoning cities, and to create within government-owned lands wilderness sanctuaries that eventually might include as many as 60 million acres. Altogether, the congressional record for significant legislation was one of the most impressive since New Deal days. Since in good part this record was due to Johnson's remarkable legislative ability, he faced with confidence the campaign of 1964, in which it was obvious that he would be the Democratic candidate to succeed himself.

The Election of 1964

After the defeat of Nixon in 1960, Governor Nelson A. Rockefeller of New York seemed to be the leading candidate for the 1964 Republican presidential nomination. Rockefeller, a liberal on domestic issues and a firm supporter of the bipartisan collective-security foreign policy, won re-election by a wide margin in 1962, the same election in which his rival Nixon was humiliated in an effort to become governor of California. Rockefeller's chances were injured by his second marriage in May, 1963, to a woman who had given up custody of her children to win her own divorce. Rockefeller won the Oregon primary but lost in California by a narrow margin to Senator Barry M. Goldwater of Arizona, the idol of the party's right wing. Goldwater's supporters, who opposed every liberal measure of the Kennedy-Johnson administration and demanded "a choice not an echo," blocked every effort of the liberal-moderate wing to develop an alternate candidate. The San

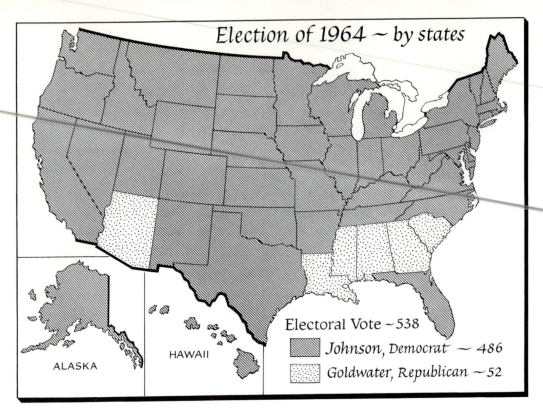

Election of 1964 ~ by states

Electoral Vote ~ 538

Johnson, Democrat — 486

Goldwater, Republican ~ 52

ALASKA

HAWAII

Francisco convention approved the rigorous curtailment of federal activities that Goldwater advocated, thus leaving the protection of civil rights and much else to the states, as so many white southerners demanded. After nominating Goldwater on the first ballot, the convention listened to him deliver a rousing, uncompromising speech. His conclusion, which was to be quoted often during the campaign, offered no comfort to the Republican moderates: "Extremism in the defense of liberty is no vice! Moderation in the pursuit of justice is no virtue!" The many faithful right-wing Republicans, forced by what they considered "expediency" to support so many Republicans of different views through the years, now had an opportunity to fight for one of their own for President.

In contrast to the drama at San Francisco, where hatreds fairly crackled, the Democratic convention at Atlantic City in August was a dull affair. It nominated Johnson without opposition and approved his hand-picked candidate for Vice-President, Senator Hubert Humphrey, long a leader of the party's liberals.

The choice was clear enough: a Democratic victory meant a continuation of the Kennedy-Johnson policies, while a Republican victory meant full retreat. Democratic campaigners quoted Goldwater's now-famous criticisms of social security and the TVA, and they described him as an extremist in foreign policy. They used as evidence his opposition to the Test-Ban Treaty, his advocacy of truculence in dealing with the Soviet Union, and his apparent willingness to employ nuclear weapons in Vietnam. Many businessmen who usually had favored the Republican Party turned to Johnson, whose prudence in economic matters and leadership in foreign affairs they had come to trust. Only a handful of important newspapers supported Goldwater. The result was an enormous landslide, with 486 electoral votes for Johnson and 52 for Goldwater. Only six states — Arizona, Louisiana, Mississippi, Alabama, Georgia, and South Carolina — voted for the Republican candidate, who got 27 million popular votes to Johnson's 43 million. The Democrats also increased their majorities in both houses of Congress. Among the newly elected members was former Attorney-General Robert F. Kennedy, who had resigned from the cabinet to run for Senator in New York. In the Senate he became a colleague of the late President's other brother, Edward M. Kennedy of Massachusetts. Lyndon Johnson was now President in his own right, and by acclamation, but the Kennedy family remained a major force in the Democratic Party.

Johnson's Foreign Troubles

No matter how bright things seemed to appear on the domestic scene for Johnson, he faced serious difficulties abroad, notably in Vietnam and in the Caribbean. He further escalated the American commitment in Southeast Asia and reversed the historic American disavowal of the use of marines in Latin America. In doing these things President Johnson soon found that his supporters began to slip away from him.

Johnson, more attentive to military advice than his predecessor had been, sent great quantities of military equipment, including helicopters, to aid the South Vietnamese government in counter-guerrilla warfare. Along with this material, he sent a steadily increasing stream of military "advisers," including technicians, pilots, and even ground troops, numbering altogether over 45,000 by mid-1965. Political instability in South Vietnam hampered American efforts to reform the economy and to train the Vietnamese army. Still the Johnson administration pressed on. In August, 1964, when it was reported that North Vietnamese boats had attacked American destroyers in the Gulf of Tonkin, the President ordered a retaliatory attack on coastal installations, and obtained from Congress a resolution authorizing him to "take all necessary steps, including the use of armed force" to protect nations in the area asking for help. In February, 1965, he ordered continued air attacks on military installations,

transportation routes, and bridges in North Vietnam. This further escalation of the war aroused heated protests within the United States. Johnson avowed his willingness to open "unconditional discussions" with any other power or powers interested in ending hostilities and to invest huge sums in economic development of Southeast Asia if stability could be restored. His supporters argued that his military actions were based on a desire to get a negotiated peace, but the logic of this position was hard for many to grasp.

Also difficult to understand was the militancy of Johnson's reaction (or over-reaction in the view of many) to events in the Dominican Republic. There the democratic government set up under Juan Bosch after the fall of the dreaded dictator Trujillo gave way seven months later to a military junta. When, in April, 1965, rebellion broke out in turn against this regime, Johnson took the long-renounced step of "sending in the marines," the first such action against a neighboring republic in over thirty years. Early detachments were dispatched ostensibly to protect the lives of Americans and other foreigners caught in the fighting zone, but the heavy reinforcements that followed were admittedly sent to prevent a Communist takeover, such as had happened in Cuba. The reaction of Latin America to unilateral intervention by the "Colossus of the North" was understandably one of intense hostility. An election in mid-1966 gave the presidency to a moderate, Joaquin Balaguer. The United States withdrew its troops but the memory of their presence would long remain in Latin America.

Thus in two widely separated parts of the world Lyndon Johnson encountered complicated and bitter troubles. Many of those who had, in such vast numbers, supported him with their votes in November, 1964, were beginning to have doubts about his leadership in foreign policy by the middle of the following year.

BIBLIOGRAPHY

There is no scholarly full-length study of John Kennedy, but J. M. Burns, *John F. Kennedy: A Political Profile* (2nd ed., 1961), is excellent on the pre-presidential years. A convenient anthology of writings about him is *John F. Kennedy and the New Frontier* (1966), edited by A. DiP. Donald. J. T. Crown, *The Kennedy Literature* (1968), is an annotated bibliography of published materials. Popular, friendly journalistic accounts are William Manchester, *Portrait of a President* (1962); and Hugh Sidey, *John F. Kennedy, President* (1964). A rather acid biography of Joseph P. Kennedy is R. J. Whalen, *The Founding Father* (1964). Among the President's own works are *Profiles in Courage* (1956), sketches of Senators whose fighting spirit captivated the young Senator; and collections of speeches entitled *To Turn the Tide* (1962) and *The Burden and the Glory* (1964); and *A Nation of Immigrants* (1964).

T. H. White, *The Making of the President, 1960* (1961), is a superb dramatic account of the campaign of 1960; the author's partiality for Kennedy does not mar the work's value. Of the many books on the Republican candidate, the most substantial is Earl Mazo, *Richard Nixon* (1959), by a rather admiring journalist. An elaborate collection of studies of the Nixon-Kennedy confrontations is *The Great Debates* (1962), edited by Sidney Kraus.

The most important memoirs of the Kennedy era published so far are T. C. Sorensen, *Kennedy* (1965), heavily factual and remarkably detached; and A. M. Schlesinger, Jr., *A Thousand Days* (1965), the brilliant work of a historian on the fringes of power. More personal are Pierre Salinger, *With Kennedy* (1966); Evelyn Lincoln, *My Twelve Years with John F. Kennedy* (1965); and P. B. Fay, Jr., *The Pleasure of His Company* (1966). Two accounts of policy-making are J. L. Sundquist, *Politics and Policy* (1968), a large work covering Eisenhower and Johnson as well as Kennedy; and T. C. Sorensen, *Decision-Making in the White House* (1963), by Kennedy's chief aide. Douglass Cater, *Power in Washington* (1964), is a well-informed political analysis by a journalist who was to join the staff of President Johnson.

Scholarly studies of the Kennedy administration are rare. The best to date is Jim F. Heath, *John F. Kennedy and the Business Community* (1969), which emphasizes the President's basic caution; the same point is brought out by Richard Harris, *The Real Voice* (1964), an able journalist's account of the Kefauver drug industry investigation. S. E. Harris, *Economics of the Kennedy Years and a Look Ahead* (1964), stresses the President's conversion to Keynesian ideas; the author, a Harvard economist, was a friend and adviser to Kennedy. Critical in tone are B. D. Nossiter, *The Mythmakers* (1964), by a liberal; and Milton Friedman, *Capitalism and Freedom* (1964), by a conservative. J. K. Galbraith, *The New Industrial State* (1967), is a witty analysis with recommendations by the country's leading liberal economist; it is perhaps significant that he served the administration as a diplomat.

The Kennedy assassination has been the subject of a large number of books, most of them of little value. The basic source is *The Assassination of President Kennedy* (1964), the official report of the Warren Commission. A valuable collection is *The Weight of the Evidence: The Warren Report and Its Critics* (1968), edited by Jay David. The most celebrated of the critiques of the Warren Commission is Mark Lane, *Rush to Judgment* (1966). William Manchester, *The Death of a President* (1967), is a huge, detailed account; originally commissioned by the Kennedy family, it was repudiated by them and its publication created a sensation.

On the 1964 campaign, the best journalistic study is T. H. White, *The Making of the President, 1964* (1965). A well-informed columnist's account of the way the Goldwater forces took over the Republican Party is R. D. Novak, *The Agony of the G. O. P., 1964* (1965). J. H. Kessel, *The Goldwater Coalition: Republican Strategies in 1964* (1965), is a study by a political scientist.

On foreign policy under Kennedy, a memoir of importance is Roger Hilsman, *To Move a Nation: The Politics of Foreign Policy in the Administration of John F. Kennedy* (1967). Two general narratives of post-1945 foreign policy are C. O. Lerche, Jr., *The Cold War . . . and After* (1965); and P. Y. Hammond, *The Cold War Years* (1969). Conflicting interpretations are gathered together in *Recent American Foreign Policy* (1968), edited by L. S. Kaplan. Seyom Brown, *The Faces of Power* (1968), is a discussion of the international balance of power since 1945; the author is a frank exponent of the use of power. Very different in tone is Norman Cousins, *In Place of Folly* (2nd ed., 1962), a plea for disarmament in the nuclear age. Two critiques by an eminent political scientist, R. E. Osgood, are *NATO: The Entangling Alliance* (1962) and *Alliances and American Foreign Policy* (1968). A. P. Whitaker, *Spain and Defense of the West: Ally and Liability* (1961), is critical. Two dispassionate studies of value are F. R. Willis, *France, Germany and the New Europe, 1945–1967* (2nd ed., 1968); and H. S. Hughes, *The United States and Italy* (2nd ed., 1965). Brief and illuminating is Herbert Feis, *Foreign Aid and Foreign Policy* (1964). R. J. Walton, *The Remnants of Power: The Tragic Last Years of Adlai Stevenson* (1968), tells of Stevenson's troubles with the "realists"; it makes melancholy reading no matter what one thinks of its hero.

A handy introduction to once-remote areas of the world is G. A. Lensen, *The World beyond Europe* (2nd ed., 1966). Robert Blum, *The United States and China in World Affairs* (1966), is a valuable study of the period since 1949; R. P. Newman, *Recognition of Communist China? A Study in Argument* (1961), is the best introduction to a much-debated subject. An enormous work on Red China is Edgar Snow, *The Other Side of the River* (1962), by a veteran left-wing journalist. E. O. Reischauer, *The United States and Japan* (3rd ed., 1965), is by a Harvard scholar who served as Kennedy's ambassador. Competent surveys in the same series are J. W. Gould, *The United States and Malaysia* (1969); W. N. Brown, *The United States and India and Pakistan* (2nd ed., 1963); and C. F. Galla-gher, *The United States and North Africa: Morocco, Algeria and Tunisia* (1963). An amusing and enlightening diary of Kennedy's emissary to India is J. K. Galbraith, *Ambassador's Journal* (1969). On relations with Africa see Arnold Rivkin, *Africa and the West* (1962); and *The United States and Africa* (2nd ed., 1963), edited by Walter Goldschmidt.

On American involvement in Vietnam the literature is vast, uneven, and mostly critical. An excellent collection of documents and varying interpretations is *Vietnam and American Foreign Policy* (1968), edited by J. R. Boettiger. An important study by American academic specialists is G. McT. Kahin and J. W. Lewis, *The United States in Vietnam* (2nd ed., 1969). The views of a French expert are presented in Jean Lacouture, *Vietnam: Between Two Truces* (1966), who argues that the war began in the south and should be settled there. David Halberstam, *The Making of a Quagmire* (1965), is a vivid critique by an able American journalist.

Two important discussions of Latin American policies are A. A. Berle, Jr., *Clear and Present Danger* (1962); and W. D. Rogers, *The Twilight Struggle* (1967), a study of the Alliance for Progress. On the Cuban situation varying interpretations may be found in Theodore Draper, *Castro's Revolution* (1962); and H. L. Matthews, *Fidel Castro* (1969). The Bay of Pigs affair is described by two able journalists, K. E. Meyer and Tad Szulc, *The Cuban Invasion* (1962). On the Missile Crisis, see D. L. Larson, *The "Cuban Crisis" of 1962* (1963), a collection of documents; Elie Abel, *The Missile Crisis* (1966), well-informed journalism; and R. F. Kennedy, *Thirteen Days* (1969), the posthumous memoir of the President's brother. *The United States, Cuba and the Cold War: American Failure or Communist Conspiracy?* (1970), edited by L. D. Langley, is a useful collection of documents and conflicting interpretations.

28

THE AFFLUENT SOCIETY

The new American · Population movements · The postwar economy · A new business attitude · The middle-class worker · The upper economic classes · "The Lonely Crowd" · Educational changes · Rising religious interests · A renewed pessimism · The new conservatism · A changed liberalism · Postwar literature

The New American

When André Siegfried, the French historian, visited the United States during the 1950's he was obviously perplexed. Thirty years before, after a similar visit, he had written a critical but friendly account of the nature of American society. In attempting the same task in 1955 he appeared at a loss for descriptive terms. The "old Americans" had disappeared, and the new ones he could not quite place. The existing society was neither British nor Germanic; instead it was something new, "not only in dimension but in quality," and the American was "a new type," who was in a sense a "stranger to western Europeans." What Siegfried sensed was partially explained by population statistics. In the 1920's population experts had predicted that the recent immigration restrictions plus the then steadily lowering birth rate would cause the total population to level off

BUY NOW, PAY LATER. *One of many ways of beguiling dollars from prosperous Americans.*

sometime around 1965–1970, after which no great changes would be experienced. Instead, the birth rate after 1940 had rocketed upward, a fact which, taken with steadily increasing longevity, was responsible for a spectacular jump in population. Whereas the birth rate had been 17 or 18 per thousand in the 1930's, during the fifteen years after the Second World War it varied from 19.5 to 24.6 per thousand. After 1960 the rate fell off again, dropping to 19.4 in 1965 and 17.4 in 1968; the experts of the 1920's turned out to be right after all. Meanwhile life expectancy, which had gone up from 47.3 years in 1900 to 70.2 years in 1968, was still extending. By the 1969 estimates population numbered 203 million people compared with 179 million in 1960.

The postwar gains were startling because immigration had contributed little to the totals. The proportion of foreign born in the country dropped from 13.6 per cent in 1900 to less than 6 per cent in 1955, with the result that unless the nation changed its immigration policy, people of foreign birth were due almost to disappear. Except for the Negro and the smaller racial minorities (see ch. 29), the population that André Siegfried looked at in 1955 was almost a homogeneous one, from which the large immigrant groups of fifty years before had practically disappeared. By 1970 the melting pot had done most of its work. Through acculturation and assimilation the hyphenated American of the First World War, whose sentiments had been divided between the Old World and the New, had practically disappeared. And even, for example, the attachments of a former Italian for Americans of like ancestry were rapidly dissolving. American surnames might represent a medley of European nations, but increasingly American citizens thought of themselves only as Americans. Intermarriage among the descendants of different immigrant groups, and with the older American stock, had played an important part in this change of sentiment. Many an American citizen who on one side of his family stemmed only recently from Europe, was eligible on the other side for membership in the Sons or Daughters of the American Revolution, or even in the Society of Mayflower Descendants. But for whatever reason the average American who went to Europe in 1970, no matter what his family origins had been, felt he was a foreigner and that his real home lay thousands of miles to the West.

Population Movements

If the population had changed both quantitatively and qualitatively, many old American traits and customs nonetheless remained. Both the geographical and the social mobility of the population had struck foreign commentators very early in the nation's history. People moved about even more than they had before. The war, the accompanying prosperity, the almost universal ownership of automobiles, the beckoning of opportunities in new industries

such as aero-space and in relocated businesses of all sorts were among the causes of this folk-wandering that resulted in changes in the character of the country and its people. One of these movements, that from the farm to the city, was a continuation of an old drift. In 1900, 60 per cent of the population was classed as rural; in 1950, only 38 per cent; and fifteen years later the figure had dropped to under 30 per cent. The country was becoming increasingly urban, less and less rural.

Curiously, however, the rapid growth of the city did not result in a commensurable amount of urban political influence. Many of the middlewestern and southern farm states remained without great cities. Yet despite the smallness of their populations, the vote of their two United States Senators had the same weight as the votes of the Senators from New York and California. In nearly every state, whether urban or rural, redistricting lagged far behind the changes in population, and in both state legislatures and in Congress, the power of the rural voters at election time was much greater than their numbers justified. In 1962, however, the Supreme Court handed down its momentous decision in *Baker* v. *Carr*, which ruled that the failure of the state of Tennessee to reapportion its state legislature in accordance with recent population changes violated the equal protection clause of the Fourteenth Amendment. While not demanding absolute equality in voting districts, this and subsequent cases did ensure a substantial equality that pointed to rapidly growing urban power throughout the nation.

Although the farmer and the villager were going to the city, a part of the city populace was also moving to the country — or at least to the suburbs. The steady increase in city ground rents, taxes, crime, dirt, air pollution, and noise caused many urban dwellers to look to the countryside for quiet, fresh air, cheap living, and a

The Suburban Revolution. *A striking phenomenon of American life, which first appeared in the twenties but came into full fruition following World War II, was the growth of suburban America.*

healthier environment in which to bring up children. Suburban centers mushroomed, and by 1955 it was estimated that one-sixth of the total population lived in these new social units which were of the city but often not officially a part of it. Suburban life came in time to have important effects upon those who lived it. The hours which the average worker spent in commuting meant that he had far less time to devote to his family. The cleavage between the place he lived in and the place he worked in meant at best divided loyalties. The result of grouping together numbers of like-minded people, often in rows of almost identical houses, is still unclear. More detectable, however, is the effect of the suburban movement upon the city itself. While the population of the metropolitan area surrounding a city increased rapidly, that of the city itself as a political unit often went down. According to the 1960 census, seven of the ten largest cities in the country

had either lost population or had failed to gain. Moreover, the city's loss to its satellite suburbs appeared to be mainly people from the higher economic levels and from the younger and more vigorous groups. What that meant in the loss of urban leadership was still undetermined, but the loss in business and taxes was painfully apparent. By 1970 the hearts of a good many cities seemed to be dying of slow rot, and the ability of municipalities to maintain essential services was at best questionable. While urban renewal was widely discussed and there were evidences of it in a good many cities, the predicted flow of population back to urban centers was as yet but a trickle.

One other persistent characteristic of the postwar population movement was the widespread urge to settle in more moderate or sub-tropical climates. The census of 1960 indicated that the postwar rush to Florida, and to California, Texas and the other Southwest and Pacific Coast states, was continuing and even accelerating. California, with an increase of over 5 million people in the ten-year span, led the movement. By 1969 its total population of approximately 19 million now exceeded that of New York (18 million). Following at an appreciable distance in total growth were Florida, New York, Texas, Ohio, Michigan, and Illinois. Something of the shift in political power occasioned by the shift in population can be seen in the redistribution of seats in the national House of Representatives. After the 1960 census, the Far West, together with Hawaii and Alaska, gained twelve seats while the East was losing six, and the Middle West and the South three each.

The rapid increase in the population, together with greater longevity, caused many problems. After the decade of the thirties, when the birth rate had been low, the new increase meant that a far greater proportion of the population was concentrated at both ends of life, among the young and the old. Increasing births put vast demands on an already burdened school system, and the lengthened life span meant more pressure by the aged for better medical care and social institutions. In 1900 only 4 per cent of the population had been over sixty-five years of age. In 1955 this percentage had more than doubled, and estimates for 1975 indicated that 21 million people, or fully 10 per cent of the population, would be over the retirement age of sixty-five. For the twenty years following 1960 the burden thus placed upon the producing element of the population in their middle years was to be increasingly heavy. The fall-off in the birth-rate after 1960 may have alleviated this situation to some extent.

The Postwar Economy

The economists of the 1930's made some miscalculations about the future shape of the economy. Recalling the twenties, many economists had predicted a sharp primary depression immediately after the war and the possibility of an even greater one sometime thereafter. By the early 1960's nothing of that order had occurred. Instead, the economic machine had poured out an unequalled volume of goods. After the doldrums of the thirties the record of production during the Second World War was amazing; by 1945 the nation's production was about two-thirds greater than it had been in 1939. The country had achieved the remarkable feat of producing most of the world's munitions and improving the standard of living at the same time. By 1945–1946 a huge war-born backlog of purchasing power, estimated at $150 billion, stimulated a boom that lasted for a quarter-

Peaceful Uses of Atomic Energy *are legion. It is widely used in scientific research, medicine, and the production of electric power. Below, the first atomic powered ship, the Savannah.*

century with only a few short and minor setbacks. By 1955 it was estimated that the American productive machine, with only 6 per cent of the world's population at its disposal, was yielding almost 50 per cent of the world's goods. Since only 5 to 6 per cent of this total product was exported, the result was untold riches for the American consumer. After 1955, however, the economy's rate of growth lessened as compared with the major increases attained by Japan and some countries of Western Europe.

This huge outpouring of goods had not come about without striking changes in the structure, control, and character of the nation's industrial institutions, including greatly increased concentration of corporate power and production in the hands of a relatively few giant organizations. In 1950 the Federal Trade Commission reported that the historic evolution of industry toward larger and fewer units of control had accelerated even beyond the prewar rate. In thirteen of the twenty-six most important industrial groups the concentration, said the Commission, was "extreme." Three or fewer companies accounted for 60 per cent or more of the total production in each of those thirteen areas. The same kind of evolution was taking place in banking, in merchandising, and in the service industries. Although small business still flourished in some areas, more and more the corporation which hired thousands of employees became the standard unit of business from the extractive industries to the merchandising outlets. The increasing dominance of a few large companies in many industrial areas, such as the manufacture of automobiles or electrical equipment, stimulated the organization of trade associations which often became important organs of self-government. Over 12,000 such associations were issuing regulations barring cutthroat competition and fixing fair standards of business conduct. Under such a regime price competition in the classical sense tended to disappear. Administered prices arrived at by tacit agreement among two or three of the larger companies often set a pattern for the whole industry.

A New Business Attitude

However gigantic, the postwar corporation seldom used its strength openly in an antisocial way. Instead of the public-be-damned attitude of the business leaders of the nineteenth century, the new slogan was that the consuming public should at all costs be pleased. As industrial units grew larger, the whims and tastes of the

TECHNOLOGICAL REVOLUTION *on the farm proceeded rapidly after World War II. Powered machines did away with heavy labor in the fields and electricity brought most of the urban amenities to the house.*

A MECHANICAL COTTON PICKER at work near Athens, Georgia.

masses were increasingly studied and catered to. Market research bureaus and public relations experts attempted to keep corporation executives informed as to public preferences. The fundamental gospel of postwar business was mass production, and in order to ensure the requisite mass consumption, business — though with some exceptions — attempted to hold unit prices down. Most big companies preferred making pennies on millions of units rather than dollars on a few thousand. Wages rose steadily during the period, and the constantly increasing cost of labor spurred industry to adopt labor-saving devices wherever possible. "Automation" went so far that some factories and offices were run by a handful of skilled operators and a bewildering number of sophisticated machines. Increased labor costs and the huge capital charges for the new automatic machines were partially responsible for a steady rise in prices, but in spite of the higher prices the margin of profit declined throughout the period, and by 1960 or soon after some industries were in trouble because of the "profit squeeze."

The Managerial Society

In part the change in the attitude of business toward the public was caused by the chastening effects of the Great Depression of the 1930's, but it was probably more markedly the effect of the new kind of businessman who ran the modern corporation. Large industries steadily recruited college and university-trained men from the business schools. Much more knowledgeable in economics and related subjects, some of these men also had a heightened sense of social responsibility. The members of this new managerial class were often freer to respond to the public good than the old corporate managers had been. They were no longer so largely dependent upon Wall Street bankers. The postwar corporation financed many of its operations out of its own earnings, and with that development finance capitalism or the direction of industry by Wall Street bankers tended to weaken. Simultaneously, the traditional pressure of the stockholders for large dividends was softened. In the American Telephone and Telegraph Company, for example, over a million individuals held shares, and the maximum holding did not exceed 0.1 per cent of the total. With ownership so widely diffused, the control of such companies lay not so much with a few leading stockholders as in former days, or with Wall Street, as with management itself. The organization of many kinds of businesses into highly mixed "conglomerates," against which the provisions of the anti-trust laws seemed virtually impotent, added another dimension to the concentration in ownership and management control.

The new spirit of this "managerial revolution" was well expressed by the officials of the American Telephone and Telegraph Company, who stated publicly in the mid-fifties that they no longer represented the stockholders but were "trustees" for four important groups, the suppliers, the workers, the stockholders, and the public. Their function as trustees was to see that each of the four groups obtained a fair return for their goods, their money, or their work. Looking at their functions and their claims, A. A. Berle, in a book entitled *The Fictions of Modern Capitalism: Power Without Property* (1959), described these new managers as civil servants without government status. If this were true, and it appeared to be, this new class had enormous power. To the interesting question of who would manage the managers, Mr. Berle replied that "public consensus" would provide a proper check on their use of arbitrary power. But much more real as a check upon business activities was the increasing role of government in the total economic life of the country. To an extent unimaginable in the 1920's, government regulated corporations through a maze of complex devices. It set minimum wage rates below which they might not pay; it limited corporation advertising claims; it partially controlled their supply of credit; it bulked ever larger in wage negotiations; and through a multiplicity of taxes it not only helped determine the rate of profit but also gained a knowledge of corporation activities that ensured even more precise regulation whenever it was deemed necessary. Pointing out the extent of this control, Frederick Lewis Allen observed: "The limitations are so numerous and severe that to speak of [corporation managers] as engaged in 'free enterprise' is more picturesque than accurate. They are managing private institutions operating under a series of severe disciplines, and committed to doing so with an eye to the general welfare."[1]

Welfare Unionism

The labor union was another check upon selfish use of power by big business. Resuscitated by the New Deal, unions grew rapidly in the postwar years, and by 1955, 25 per cent of the nation's workers, or about 17 million, belonged to labor organizations. Except in the more rural regions, the openshop had practically disappeared by 1960, and the power of the unions was indicated by the increasing number of "fringe benefits" which they had secured in addition to higher wage scales. Although Walter Reuther, the president of the United Automobile Workers, had failed to secure his demands for a "look at the books" of the automobile industry and for a profit-sharing plan, labor made many other gains. Collective medical plans, numerous insurance schemes, and liberal retirement provisions beyond those provided by the social security agency were features of the new "welfare unions." Dave Beck, long a leader of the International Brotherhood of Team-

sters and briefly its president, and his long-time rival Harry Bridges, President of the International Longshoremen's and Warehousemen's Union, vied with one another to secure benefits for their members. They were so successful that teamsters and longshoremen (on the West Coast, where the ILWU was dominant) achieved a remarkable amount of security and slipped into the middle class from a status far below. Unions often fought for political power and sometimes partially succeeded, especially in Michigan and Minnesota. But in the political arena the record was not all one way. The Taft-Hartley Act and the right-to-work provisions, passed mostly in agricultural states, were followed by the effective end to the expansion of unionism among the unorganized. Unions fought back and succeeded in blocking the passage of right to work acts in such states as California and Washington. They had, however, lost their organizing momentum in many areas and in many crafts and industries. The congressional investigations of 1958–1959 indicated a singular lack of democratic procedures in many unions, and extensive graft and corruption in the handling of some union insurance funds.

During the late 1960's anti-union sentiment continued to grow, in part because of the impact of high wage demands upon inflation, and in part because of the obvious bias in some unions against recruitment from minority groups. Despite such setbacks the long-term record of postwar unionism was on balance a favorable one. There had been no mass violence during a strike since the Little Steel Strike of 1937. Although some major work stoppages had hurt national production severely, and others had appeared futile even to labor, the phenomenal increase in production during these years plus the remarkable rise in workers' real incomes was evidence that the labor union played an important and valuable part in the national economy.

[1] *The Big Change* (1952), p. 240.

The Labor Agreement *between General Motors and the United Automobile Workers in 1950 guaranteed peace in the industry for five years. Exuberant at the signing, a smiling Walter Reuther, UAW president, grasps the hand of Harry Anderson, a vice president of GM.*

The Middle-Class Worker

Whatever the causes, the working class, or more precisely the top three-quarters of its members, fared far better than ever before. In the year 1900 the American worker made on the average only $300 or $400 a year, and recurring unemployment, especially for the unskilled, was likely to be chronic. Working time ran normally to sixty hours a week, often more; and the number of those who were "underfed, underclothed, and poorly housed" was estimated at not less than 10 million. Literally hundreds of thousands of children were wage earners, many of them at the expense of schooling. By midcentury the changes that had occurred in the position of labor were little short of revolutionary. The diminished value of the dollar makes statistical comparison difficult, but according to the United States Department of Commerce the national average family income in 1955 was $5,600 a year and that of non-farm families $6,300 a year. Only 15 per cent were below the assumed subsistence level of $2,000, and 20 per cent of families had incomes of less than $3,000. Over 30 per cent of families had incomes of $5,000. These averages went steadily up as the decade progressed. By 1960, 41 per cent of families were earning more than $5,000 a year. By that time also the forty-hour week was standard in industry.

The ordinary worker, far from harboring proletarian sentiments, thought of himself as middle class. Although the quantity of available housing never seemed quite to catch up with the demands of a steadily increasing population, he was frequently well housed. Housing projects in the cities, both publicly and privately financed, had eliminated most of the pestilential tenements of a half century earlier. During the decade of the forties the net gain in housing units for the nation as a whole reached 8,550,000, and the housing boom continued into the fifties with new construction at the rate of about a million units a year. The

Federal Housing Administration, established in 1934 and merged in 1965 with the new Department of Housing and Urban Development, continued to underwrite mortgages, and much additional assistance came through such agencies as the Veterans Administration. The proportion of working-class families who lived in respectable houses or apartments, equipped with good kitchens, central heating, adequate plumbing, electrical refrigerators, telephones, and comfortable furniture, was far greater than it had ever been before; even farm houses, except in the more primitive areas, were acquiring "all modern conveniences." No longer was the high standard of living restricted to the favored upper classes. Large numbers of working-class families could afford to wear good clothes, own an automobile and a television set, attend the movies, buy a house on the installment plan, take out insurance, enjoy vacations. In spite of all this, recent statistics show that the lowest quarter of the nation's working population has not made economic gains comparable to those of the majority, wage rates for unskilled labor have not increased as rapidly as those for skilled labor, and a large number of the significantly numerous unemployed have been among the unskilled.

On the farm, thanks largely to rural electrification and the gasoline engine, the backbreaking duties of an earlier generation had considerably diminished. At the same time work opportunities on farms also decreased; more and more both farmers and farm laborers found themselves moving to towns and cities. In 1935, 90 per cent of the farms in the United States had no electricity; in 1954, 90 per cent of them had it. In 1935 a farmer had to pay from ten to seventeen cents per kilowatt hour for the electric current he bought; in 1954 it cost him on the average only a little over three cents. The variety of tools which had come into use included such innovations as corn- and cotton-picking machines, milking machines,

combines that harvested and threshed the grain in one operation, tractors to supply power for every variety of machine used in the fields. "Stoop-labor," as in the production of sugar beets and vegetables, still existed, much of it now furnished in the West and Southwest by Mexicans, either legal entrants known as *braceros*, or "wetbacks," but in a constantly reducing ratio. In fact, the nation counted only 1.5 million farm laborers in 1968 in comparison with 9.5 million in 1940, although agricultural production had risen steadily.

The Upper Economic Classes

The United States had certainly not achieved the "classless society" which some revolutionists set as their goal, but except for the "big rich," many of whom somehow contrived to retain their supremacy, the disparity of incomes between those in the upper brackets and those in the lower brackets was showing a diminution. High taxes accounted in large part for this state of affairs. Even after the ablest lawyers had taken full advantage of every loophole in the law, a really large earned income, if honestly reported, tended to drop to modest proportions after taxes. For example, under the 1968 tax levies a married couple with no dependents had to pay a $20,672 income tax on a $50,000 income; a $51,796 tax on a $100,000 income; a $153,263 tax on a $250,000 income; and a $322,575 tax on a $500,000 income. The rates on incomes over $100,000 had been lowered in the previous decade. By 1969 only seven states had neither personal nor corporate income tax. In most, estate taxes on inheritances, property taxes, sales taxes, and a host of "nuisance" taxes took additional tolls. There were still many loopholes through which the "big rich" could escape, such as the low tax on capital gains (25 per cent), which were often purely speculative, tax-exempt state and municipal bonds, and the generous allowance for depletion of resources that made many oilmen rich. Whereas the depletion tax assumed that an oil field would be exhausted in less than four years, the actual figure was closer to fifteen. High salaries, too, could be made much higher by ultra-liberal expense accounts, especially when they provided free automobiles, long vacations, and lavish entertainment, in addition to a sizable surplus often untaxed. During the Kennedy administration Treasury officials, arguing that a large amount of income was not being reported for taxes, attempted to tighten up the regulations on expense accounts as well as to institute withholding taxes on returns from saving accounts and securities. From the Treasury figures it was evident that many wealthy people were escaping from the high tax rates while the salaried man or the wage earner paid his full quota. A study in 1962 of the ownership pattern concluded that during the fifties the share of the national wealth owned by a few of the "big rich" had increased significantly. Subsequent reports at the end of the sixties indicated that a substantial number of the wealthy with incomes over a million dollars a year were able to avoid all income taxes. This, together with the mountainous federal budgets, led to a formidable demand for a complete revision of the tax structure. But since so many powerful people, including some members of Congress, benefited from tax loopholes, it was doubtful if truly fundamental changes could be expected in the immediate future.

A Countervailing Society?

The abundance produced by industry and agriculture and its widespread distribution among most classes brought forth much praise and admiration. The new business system was described as a people's capitalism and a democratic capitalism, and was claimed to be much more effective in raising the entire economic level of the nation than any other system, past or present.

"They've Been Going Together For Quite A While." Herblock in *The Washington Post.*

André Siegfried felt that business, in tapping "democratic purchasing power" by keeping prices low, had uncovered a new mode of operation which would impart vitality to the economy for years to come. Despite all this jubilation, other authorities raised serious questions and criticisms. They were not sure that the "countervailing power" of business, labor, and government would check each other to the extent that the Harvard economist, John K. Galbraith, seemed to think. What would happen, they asked, if business and labor got together? How could government then assure the unorganized part of the population relative economic justice? They further pointed out that the great prosperity of the fifteen postwar years had been buttressed by enormous military expenditures by government, amounting to over $80 billion per year by 1968. What would happen in the event of a genuine peace, so that the government stopped such spending during a period of relative depression? Other critics saw the massive emphasis of the system on distribution and salesmanship as an encouragement of false materialistic values. The "hucksters," or advertising men, these critics asserted, cared only to sell their wares at any costs, and were invading the whole field of public relations, including politics. One textbook on advertising frankly stated that the duty of a salesman was to "exploit the irrational and, at all times, to avoid the pitfalls of rational sales resistance. . . ." In view of such advice, and the development of techniques of subliminal suggestion whereby a customer is persuaded to act without being aware of persuasion, what was to become of the rational, thinking individual? A still more serious question concerned the nation's ability to survive in face of the long-term competition of Soviet Russia. In *The Affluent Society* (1958), Galbraith argued that the nation was spending far too much of its energies on the private and not nearly enough on the public sector of the economy — too much on consumers' goods and not enough on schools, universities, and the basic scientific research upon which national existence depended. Whether an economic system so thoroughly committed to mass production and consumption could change its emphasis without a major crisis remained to be seen.

Development of Mass Culture

During the postwar economic boom the development of mass culture continued. As the wage level went up and the hours of work went down, public demand converted the leisure-time industries into big business. More and more the national heroes of the masses were drawn from the entertainment industries. The typical folk hero was no longer the hero of work or achievement, but the "hero of leisure" — the baseball star, the television "personality," the football player, the movie star. As the national image of such traditional great men as Washington, Lincoln, and Edison dimmed, a variety of ever-changing, rather improbable, and soon forgotten characters became the idols of the crowd. Reacting to the same forces which impelled other businesses, the agencies devoted to public information and amusement tended to combine into monolithic organizations. A cause for real concern was the drift of the daily newspaper toward monopoly. Whereas in 1909 2,600 papers had been published in the nation's 1,300 largest cities, by 1969 only 1,752 remained. In only one out of twelve cities were there competing papers, and in ten entire states not one city had a rival daily newspaper. That this growing monopoly of the press was not as serious as it might have been a few decades earlier was due to the development of radio and television. Barred from general use before 1947 because of technical and financial difficulties, television developed rapidly after that date. Television programs were on the whole neither much worse nor much better than those offered by radio in a comparable stage of development. At its best, in the presentation of current affairs or of drama, television could be superb. But its dependence on advertisers, who naturally wished to appeal to the largest possible market, usually meant that the programs were tailored to the great mass, and that the intellectual and cultural interests of minority groups were largely ignored. In the late fifties, after public investigation had established manipulation and "rigging" in many television and radio shows, particularly quiz shows and "disk jockey" programs devoted to the playing of popular records, there were insistent demands for reform and it was even seriously proposed that a national nonprofit trust, divorced from government, should be formed to offer quality programs. One positive result of this criticism was the organization of educational TV stations, a development speeded up by a congressional act offering federal funds to such projects on a matching basis. Educational TV had a generally small proportion of the viewing audience but its importance was growing steadily in many parts of the nation by 1970.

Fragmentation of the Cultural Market

To a degree the success of television led to improvement in the quality of both movies and radio. Because of the strong appeal of television to the mass market, these other media were hard hit financially. Seeking a way out of their difficulties, both radio and movies began to produce programs of superior merit for much smaller, specialized audiences. Some radio stations offered day-long programs of serious music, for example, and the movies produced adult and experimental pictures often on extremely low budgets which would have been unheard of in the industry's heyday.

A similar fragmentation of the national mass market was producing like results in the publishing industry. With costs increasing, the publisher no longer depended after 1950 solely upon the hard-backed national best seller to produce a profitable year. Paperback books, sold in large quantities in every kind of outlet, including drugstores and supermarkets, increased the sale of trashy works full of sensationalism and violence. But paperbacks also made available for mass sale numbers of classics, both new and old, and of serious nonfiction. Simultaneously, the birth of many specialized book clubs in such subjects as art, history, medicine, Asian studies, and fine literature indicated that there was a profitable market in cultivating the tastes of the minority.

"The Lonely Crowd"

No society, perhaps, had ever been probed and analyzed more thoroughly than that of America since the Second World War. Among a host of serious studies of what was wrong with it, one of the most

David Riesman, *author of* The Lonely Crowd, *is representative of the new academician influential in molding public opinion and public policy.*

widely read was David Riesman's *The Lonely Crowd* (1950). Riesman's thesis was that the intensely individualistic American had become so much a creature of conformity that he was no longer an independent individual. The once "inner directed personality" had become "other directed," bent by the standards of the mass media, society's stereotypes, and the state. The eminent psychiatrist, Erich Fromm, contended in his *Escape from Freedom* (1941) that the average citizen could no longer endure the solitary agony of making a free choice. And Walter Lippmann in *The Public Philosophy* (1955) wrote of the "inner barbarians" who were in but not of the culture to which they belonged, and who threatened the very existence of the rational and cultured state. Since they had no criteria of true and false, save that of immediate self-interest, they were prone to accept the cheap, the irrational, and the popular. Most foreign commentators agreed that the American overconformed. Undeniably, the American over the years had become more and more a conformist in actions, dress, amusements, and many other things. Given the degree of centralization which existed in the culture, this was understandable and in part even desirable. In the mechanistic and highly technical society of the mid-twentieth century the anarchistic individual of the frontier would probably have been a menace. But whether the American mind was conformist to such a degree as was sometimes charged is debatable. The very existence of such eloquent critics as Riesman, Fromm, and Lippmann seemed to argue that it was not, as did also the national debate over the purposes and ends of the educational system.

Educational Changes

After the Second World War the American faith in education was, if anything, stronger than ever. In 1940 the average citizen left school after 9.3 years of training; by 1968 the comparable figure was 12.1 years. By 1968 nearly one-third of persons 25 years old or older had completed high school and 10.5 per cent had finished four years or more of college. Increasingly, success in almost any line of work seemed to call for a higher education. Of the 6,500 men under 40 years of age cited for extraordinary achievement in 1940, only 214 were without a college education. But as the numbers thronging the schools increased, so did the criticism directed at the elementary and secondary schools for their failure in teaching the basic techniques of reading, writing, and arithmetic, and for their unwillingness to segregate the superior students from the mass so that abler minds would be stimulated instead of stultified. Books such as *Why Johnny Can't Read* were widely read, and, especially after the first Sputnik challenged American scientific accomplishments; the whole education system became a subject for national discussion

and concern. Such criticism, and the growing competition for places in colleges and universities, had some good results in elementary and secondary schools. A higher standard of work was demanded from the abler students, who were more and more frequently taught separately from their slower colleagues, not always to the advantage of either group. Advanced subjects such as science and foreign languages were introduced at an earlier age than formerly, and some non-intellectual activities such as driver education, which had been dumped on the schools by society, were in some communities stripped from the curriculum. Colleges and universities also reacted to criticism, but for them the problem seemed for a time to be easier because increased enrollments enabled many of them to establish more highly selective entrance requirements. The federal government extended indirect aid to education and research through the National Science Foundation and the more recently established foundation for the arts and humanities. During Johnson's administration federal aid to education was greatly increased at all levels by many devices. The Federal School Aid Act of 1967 provided over $9 billion for aid to elementary and secondary education alone. So much aid to education was granted that federal funds became major budget items of the public schools as well as those of the universities, both public and private. The threat to cancel many grants to common and secondary schools became a potent weapon through which the federal government sought southern compliance with the civil rights acts. Federal funds were also granted to individuals, ranging from free lunches to scholarships and to the underwriting of bank loans made on liberal terms to students seeking to continue their education.

That there was much that needed changing in the educational system was undeniable. But that the system was as bad as some critics made out was questionable. During 1949–1968, United States citizens won 55 Nobel prizes for achievements in science as compared with the next highest national group, the British, who won eighteen. Even considering the difference in population and the relative amounts of money devoted to education in the two countries, these results did not entirely condemn the American school system.

Rising Religious Interests

The period following the Second World War, unlike the 1920's, was one of rising interest in religion and church-going. By 1969 the largest number of Americans in history, 130 million, or 63 per cent of the total population, claimed membership among some 250 varieties of churches. But even though 75 million were not church members, religion itself was no longer a center of debate, for few of this number were actually antagonistic to churches and their work. André Siegfried noted that among the most prominent developments in American Protestantism was an emphasis upon ritual and elegance, a de-emphasis on practical Christianity, and a growing interest in doctrine. This was certainly true among the Protestant clergy, among whom the movement toward neo-orthodoxy, or the stressing of certain classical Christian dogmas, was gaining popularity. The return of many Jews to the orthodox synagogues and the growth of a Jewish cultural movement also indicated a conservative trend.

On the other hand, by far the most popular evangelist of the period, Billy Graham, who had started life as a strict fundamentalist, became less and less literal in his interpretation of the Scriptures and more of a modernist as his following increased. It was perhaps his manner rather than his words alone which gave this impression. Part of the period, when the power of Roman Catholicism seemed to be flourishing, Protestantism for a short time grew sensitive. President Truman's 1951 proposal to appoint an ambassador to the Vatican was met with such a storm of criticism that the plan was shelved. At about the same time *The Christian Century* ran a long series of articles appraising the rising power of the Catholic Church. The questions of whether the state should advocate birth control and subsidize the non-public parochial schools continued to divide some Protestants from some Catholics. On the other hand, the ecumenical movement among the Protestant sects was stronger during the 1950's than it had been before the war. The growing number of union churches, and the estimated 300,000 marriages a year which crossed Protestant, Catholic, and Jewish religious barriers, were also counter-evidence. Finally, although the tendency to vote along religious lines was certainly apparent in some areas during the 1960 presidential election, the fact remained that a professed Catholic had been elected President in a country dominated by a large Protestant majority.

Renewed Pessimism

The world-shattering events between 1939 and 1970 had a profound effect upon American thought. The collapse of western Europe before the dictatorships, the use by the police states of torture and genocide as studied policy, the chaotic condition of the world after the war, the balance of atomic terror during the period of the cold war, and the dreadful loss of life in the many wars (declared or not), all left indelible marks upon the nation's intelligentsia. Gone almost entirely from their thought was the nineteenth century faith in ordered progress. We were, wrote Walter Lippmann, facing a future so chaotic that there were no reliable maps. Gone also was the once fervently held belief in the essential goodness of man. Even some of his stoutest defenders from the humanist and rationalist traditions were now willing to concede that he was an ambivalent creature whose capacity for good was equalled by his capacity for evil — an animal, said Max Lerner, "with bestial impulses that can be multiplied by the multiple cunning of his brain." Also a thing of the past was the one-time complete confidence that man could control the future. "Of all the sorrows which afflict mankind," Reinhold Niebuhr wrote, quoting Herodotus, "the bitterest is this, that one should have consciousness of much but control over nothing." In such an atmosphere of pessimism, the hopefulness that had inspired the optimistic political credos of the nineteenth and early twentieth century disappeared from the thought of many intellectuals. Their energies were now turned away from the future reform toward formulas which would preserve the gains of the past. Many held that the root cause of much of the social disorder in the past fifteen years had been the rise of the mass man. Such thinkers held that the creation of an educated elite based upon merit and ability might help to redress the balance. A good many former leftists, including Max Lerner and Edmund Wilson, talked in such terms. So did former moderates like Reinhold Niebuhr, Walter Lippmann, and Raymond Moley, the old New Deal brain-truster. Elton Mayo put the case rather strongly in his *Human Problems of an Industrial Civilization*. Such a creative minority, he believed, was necessary to compel the masses to accept the "rational" solutions required for survival. Many of the same people and others of more conservative tastes believed that a reconstruction of natural law, as a check on the passions of the mob, was a necessary condition for the perpetuation of western civilization. But these men had no answer to the question how either the elite or the natural law could excite in the masses the necessary reverence and obedience without recourse to the violent methods of the police states.

The New Conservatism

The same gloomy atmosphere, plus the realization that so many of the old goals of equality and abundance had been reached, gave birth to a political movement mostly made up of intellectuals who called themselves the New Conservatives. The very name reflected a precipitate change in the political climate. For years conservatism had been in such ill repute that few intellectuals, and fewer politicians, dared assume a conservative label. As in many such movements the new conservatism was made up of various kinds of people and many shades of doctrine. At its extreme right were a number of former radicals including Max Eastman, the former editor of the *Masses*, the novelist John Dos Passos, John Chamberlain, who had once predicted that some sort of a socialist world organization was a historical necessity, and Whittaker Chambers, the former Communist who had figured prominently in the Alger Hiss affair. Most such people were grouped around the *National Review*, an ultra-conservative magazine with a subscription list larger than those of the *New Republic* or the *Nation*. William Buckley, the editor of the *National Review*, stood at the extreme right in the new movement. In one of his books, *Up From Liberalism*, he commented that "all that is finally important in human experience is behind us . . . the crucial explorations have been undertaken. . . ." Buckley did not seem to act on this premise, however, for he continued to edit his magazine, to publish books, to debate with liberals and even tried his hand at political campaigning, running for Mayor of New York on the Conservative Party ticket. Whatever his philosophy, Buckley was quite interested in here and now. Most of the intellectual and academic supporters of the new movement were more moderate in their views than those connected with the *National Review*. But in general the attitude of the New Conservative toward human nature was at best ambivalent. He was friendly toward traditional religion, hostile to the more outspoken claims of rationalism, and insistent that man as an individual was a creature of free will and thus bore a major responsibility for his actions, good and bad. In political terms he was a foe of class action, of social planning, and of the belief that all men were potentially good. He viewed the traditional individual freedoms of the press, of speech, and of worship as interconnected, but more often than not he stressed the primacy of economic freedom as the one without which the others could not long exist. No strong admirer of security, because he was sure it led to a levelling process in society, he was a defender of the creative individual in the arts, literature, and thought, as well as in economic activity. And to that extent he was an elitist, but his hoped-for elite was one based upon ability rather than upon simple inheritance of either name or money.

A Changed Liberalism

Not all intellectuals by any means were ready to join the New Conservative movement away from rationalism and experiment toward reliance upon more ancient approaches and institutions. Walter Lippmann, for one, still believed that the major troubles of the past fifty years had not been occasioned by the rationalistic approach to problems but rather by the irrational answers which governments had given to the problems confronting them. "We live," he wrote in the mid-fifties, "in a rational order in which by sincere inquiry and rational debate we can distinguish the true and the false, the right and the wrong." Others were suggesting that what was needed was a reinvigoration of the democratic revolutionary tradition. And still others had no regrets about the individual losing himself in the economic or social class. In fact, they saw the class as the only efficient instrument of bargaining

in a mass society and believed that the conflict between classes was the only way in which freedom might be preserved. In much the same way that John K. Galbraith hoped that a rough economic justice might issue from the countervailing power and conflict between the major economic groups in the country, Arthur M. Schlesinger, Jr., historian and leader of Americans for Democratic Action, believed that the competition between classes for leverage on the government was the only insurance left for the preservation of freedom and a substantial amount of justice. "Class conflict," he wrote in *The Vital Center*, "is essential if freedom is to be preserved. . . ."

The New Left

Much further in the direction of radicalism stood the New Left, mostly led by nonprofessional youthful agitators. Many of these radicals scorned bureaucracy so much so that they counted the Communists among their enemies as representatives of the old establishments. Although their program was nebulous, it partook of some anarchistic doctrines. Their advocacy of the overthrow of most existing institutions and of the outmoded values of the past, together with their insistence on direct action and decisions in the streets, posed a major threat to the future of democratic institutions. Certainly the manifestations of the New Left, the student activist groups, and the more volunteeristic activities of the "Hippies" constituted a major indictment of society as they found it.

Postwar Literature

American literature after the Second World War was marked by no such burst of originality as that which had characterized the rebellious and experimental writers of the nineteen twenties. Indeed, several of the great innovators of the earlier times were still the major figures of the later. Scott Fitzgerald's and Sinclair Lewis' popularity had died in the nineteen thirties, but Hemingway remained a best-seller until his death in 1961 and even after, as his posthumous works were published. Faulkner produced four books between 1945 and his death in 1962 in which the old sense of overwhelming tragedy was only gradually mellowed and diluted. Moreover, there were few authentic new voices to speak for their time as Fitzgerald had done for the Jazz Age, Hemingway for the "lost generation," or Lewis and Faulkner in their different ways for the Midwest and the South. American literature after the Second World War was dispiritingly similar to what had gone before. Most writers exhibited the same desire to escape from existing society and its problems, but there was little of the high indignation or bitter disillusionment of the twenties. The novels about the Second World War contained few pacifist pronouncements against war; rather they expressed a sense of the helplessness of the individual or even the group caught by an all-powerful force. The most successful and influential of these novels were *The Naked and the Dead* (1948), by Norman Mailer (1923–   ); and *From Here to Eternity* (1951) by James Jones (1921–   ). Powerful as they were in these books, neither Mailer nor Jones achieved the impact on their generation which Dos Passos and Hemingway had had on their time. The average writer told of a peculiar world of his own creation, a world of the mind and the imagination where the individual was free from most social restraints. In this private arena, often rather nebulous, the characters were sometimes little more than social symbols, like Truman Capote's buyer of human dreams. When the characters were more realistic, they were seldom concerned with the important, or even the day-to-day, issues of society. Few were social rebels, and when they did revolt they did so in curious ways, like Nelson Algren's Rhino Gross — ex-abortionist, ex-con-man, who wrapped his daily garbage in a neat package and left it on a street car for the well dressed and the greedy to carry home. This pungent but ineffectual act of rebellion illustrates the postwar writer's overwhelming estimate of the powerlessness of man in modern society. James Gould Cozzens said he had no thesis in his novels, except that man was caught by "relentless inexorable forces" and that he got "a very raw deal from life." In Cozzens' writings the precept that freedom was the knowledge of necessity is repeated again and again. The standard hero in much postwar writing was not a protagonist but a victim of circumstances, depicted in such a way that he compelled sympathy.

Another persistent theme was the loneliness of the individual and his inability to communicate with his fellows. In the writings of Carson McCullers, Truman Capote, and Tennessee Williams the thesis of David Riesman's *The Lonely Crowd* is illustrated again and again. The creative mind seems to have felt that as the masses of men became increasingly literate, and more and more like each other, they were ever more mute and incapable of sympathetically identifying with their fellows. "We're all of us sentenced to solitary confinement inside our own skins for life," one of Tennessee Williams' characters says in *Orpheus Descending*. The lonely hero of modern fiction lived in an irrational, amoral universe, where cause and effect had lost their once intimate and logical relationship, and where chance or caprice seemed often to be the prime mover. The mutation process seemed to operate fortuitously in literature as it was thought to operate in biology. There was no comprehending society, one of John O'Hara's characters declared in *Ten North Frederick*. Any small thing, good or bad, might set its implacable hostility toward an individual into motion, and once in motion it was impossible to stop. This growing belief in irrationalism

Tennessee Williams, *one of America's most able playwrights, has delved deeper into the human psyche than any other dramatist since Eugene O'Neill.*

may have contributed to the lack of structure in both the modern novel and the play.

In *The Literary Situation* Malcolm Cowley noted that American literature in the period was something like that produced after the time of the Antonines in the still glorious but declining days of Rome. There was in both a reluctance to experiment, since everything seemed to have been tried; there was an inclination to stay away from political values and present issues; and there was an increasing concern with writing about the great works of the past rather than in creating new ones. Whether the de-emphasis upon the truly creative was an indication of a growing conservative spirit is debatable, but the values of the new critics, as Cowley pointed out, certainly tended in that direction. The new critics were also more or less opposed to the scientific and technologically-minded world that surrounded them. Their chief targets were science, sociology, naturalism, and liberalism. They emphasized instead tradition, moral values, symbols, and myths.

The New Writers

The weight of criticism was to some extent responsible for the paucity of creative writers comparable in talent and numbers to those of the twenties and thirties. But while there were few literary giants in the postwar years, there were some highly skilled craftsmen. Among the most interesting was Truman Capote (1924–   ), whose haunting and imaginative works were peopled with sensitive and ill-adjusted individuals like those in *The Grass Harp* (1953), searching for human values in a disinterested world. In *Other Voices: Other Rooms* (1948), one of Capote's characters utters the poignant lament of a society eternally on the move without either a spiritual or a geographical base: ". . . we go screaming round the world, dying in our rented rooms, nightmare hotels, eternal homes of the transient heart." Carson McCullers (1917–1967), another gifted southern writer, in *The Heart Is a Lonely Hunter* (1940), *The Member of the Wedding* (1946), and *The Ballad of the Sad Café* (1951) examined the spiritual isolation of both young and old, and even the crippled, in contemporary society. The theme of suicide and death as possible escapes is often present in her fiction and her verse. Nelson Algren (1909–   ) recruited as his central characters worthless, nameless derelicts from the lowest depths of the Chicago and New Orleans slums. Like Frankie Machine in *The Man with the Golden Arm* (1949), a dealer in a gambling den and a dope addict, they carry their loneliness and guilt with them to the grave. "For me," wrote Tennessee Williams (1914–   ), one of the country's most important dramatists, "the dominating premise had been the need for understanding and tenderness and

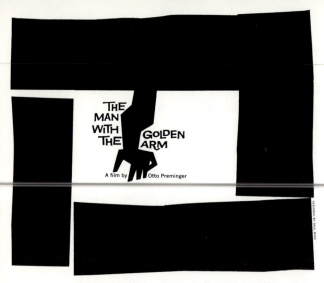

A film by Otto Preminger

Nelson Algren *reached into the depths of the social strata for his characters. His "man with the golden arm" was a professional gambler and a dope addict.*

fortitude among individuals trapped by circumstances." Williams' people, often from the contemporary South, are usually trapped by their compulsive sex urges, which they can neither understand nor control. His estimate of things is fairly stated by one of his characters: "A crazy man, deaf, dumb, and blind could have put together a better kind of world than this is."

Thoroughly exceptional in modern American fiction are the characters of James Gould Cozzens (1903–   ), who are consistently drawn from the professional classes. Whether officers of the air corps as in *Guard of Honor* (1948), or lawyers or doctors as in other novels, they are on the whole logical and able, with a sense of responsibility to their fellows and to their profession. In Cozzens' irrational world, where the strongest of men are frail in the face of their passions and of circumstances, and where present good often sires the evil of the future, the principal virtues are fortitude and stoicism. In *By Love Possessed* (1957), the real hero is Julius Penrose, a cripple with an unfaithful wife, who meets every disaster and triumph with imperturbability or jest. Exceptional also to the norms of modern fiction were the

outlook and the characters of J. D. Salinger (1919–   ) and of Saul Bellow (1915–   ). After the publication of *The Catcher in the Rye* (1951), a popular and even critical cult grew up around Salinger, who seemed to capture the spirit of restless, rootless youth by means of its own jargon. In *The Adventures of Augie March* (1953), *Herzog* (1964) and *Mr. Sammler's Planet* (1970), Bellow's heroes are buffeted by the impersonal world and by fellow human beings. But they are not simply victims of circumstance. In *The Victim* (1947), Bellow expresses the idea that men are not limited in stature but can grow in any direction and to any dimension. Moreover, they are accountable for their actions, many of which are significant. A man's character, according to Augie March, is his fate — "or what he settled for. . . ." In the end the last laugh is on nature and eternity because "it thinks it can win over us and the power of hope."

State of American Culture

Most of the nation's creative writers, like the majority of the ablest essayists, theologians, and social commentators, were deeply pessimistic about man and his future, and indeed the cultural future of the country. But such an opinion was scarcely reflected by the great mass of the people. As far as general culture was concerned, the pessimism of the intellectuals did not wholly square with the facts. For in the midst of many banal books, and even worse movies, radio, and television programs, there were some indications by 1970 that the general cultural and artistic upswing that had been so marked in the twenties and the thirties was still in motion. At almost every important state and private educational institution, artists and musicians had been added to the faculty. Many universities had respectable art museums, and university presses were turning out hundreds of scholarly publications every year. Creative writing, the dance, the theater, the moving picture, and television had been made legitimate subjects of study, and it is possible that the rapid growth in popularity of both the ballet and the little theater was directly related to the earlier activities of institutions of higher education. Before 1920 the string quartet was practically unknown in the United States. By 1970 scores of chamber music groups, some with worldwide reputations, flourished in all parts of the country. By the same date thirty major professional symphony orchestras, several of them comparable in quality to the best in Europe, were playing regular schedules in the major cities.

The Performing Arts

One of the most impressive postwar artistic developments was the amount of money and energy poured into both the performing arts and into the cultivation of American painting. Perhaps central to this activity was the construction of performing art centers in both Washington, D.C., and New York. But the development of the National Museum of Art in Washington into one of the world's great depositories of paintings, the opening of the Guggenheim Museum in New York and of art centers in as widely separated places as Los Angeles, and Atlanta, as well as the establishment of the State Art Museum of North Carolina, the latter supported by public taxes, indicated the intensity and breadth of the movement.

The increasing American interest in painting had been foreshadowed by the native painters of the twenties. Thereafter the depression and the Second World War gave a strong impetus to American painting. The Federal Arts Projects during the depression made the federal government for the first time in the nation's history a substantial patron of the fine arts. And the wholesale flight of many leading European artists to America during the war so stimulated an interest in painting that New York was well on the way to displacing Paris as the art capital of the world. Certainly the most influential art movement in the postwar world, abstract impressionism, was dominated by American artists. In Jackson Pollock, Willem de Kooning, Robert Motherwell, and Robert Rauschenberg, America had a major group of artists whose influence was to be seen around the world. In art, as in science, industry, and politics, the nation had become a leader of western civilization.

The American Achievement

A good many things in the country could justly be criticized during the nineteen sixties. But in looking at both sides of the ledger the American people had little reason to despair about their society. In the course of the years they had constructed a decent democratic political system whose strength and stability was attested by the intense loyalty of its peoples. They had also built a sound economic system, one which had gone far toward removing the masses from poverty. No advanced state, including those of the "classless" variety, had progressed further toward an equitable division of goods among its citizens. It was still relatively easy to move up the social and economic scale. Extensive educational and cultural facilities were among the best and most accessible. Despite the portrayal of social misfits by novelists, the average American had no reason to regard his fellow citizen as anything remotely approaching a monster. Measured by the size and extent of its charities, no country was more benevolent to its own unfortunates or to those of the rest of the world. For a nation of heterogeneous and strangely assorted people, many of whose forefathers had landed on American shores with little or nothing, and who had been recruited mostly from Europe's underprivileged and unwanted folk, this was not a bad record.

BIBLIOGRAPHY

Among the more general works on recent American society which can be read with profit are: F. L. Allen, *The Big Change (1952), an optimistic survey of the new America; J. K. Galbraith, *The Affluent Society (2nd ed., 1969), much more critical; D. W. Brogan, *The American Character (2nd ed., 1956), an informed British estimate; W. L. Warner, *American Life: Dream and Reality (1953), by a sociologist; an interesting compilation edited by James Burnham is What Europe Thinks of America (1953); and Max Lerner, *America as a Civilization: Life and Thought in the United States Today (1957), a large collection of both complacent and critical essays. Notable documentary collections are *American Society Since 1945 (1969), edited by W. L. O'Neill; and *The 1940s: Profile of a Nation in Crisis (1969), edited by C. E. Eisinger.

Among the best appraisals of American economic institutions is J. K. Galbraith, *American Capitalism (2nd ed., 1956), an optimistic scholarly study. A. A. Berle, *Power Without Property (1959), contains a study of the changing interior relationships in America's large corporations, as does also the earlier Peter F. Drucker, *The New Society: The Anatomy of the Industrial Order (1950). A. A. Berle, *The Twentieth Century Capitalist Revolution (1954), can also be read with profit. C. W. Mills *The Power Elite (1956), contains a trenchant but perhaps overdrawn analysis of the power relationships among big wealth, big business, and big government. Another work by Mills, *White Collar (1951), is a biting account of the new middle classes.

On labor, a major new survey and analysis is D. C. Bok and J. T. Dunlop, *Labor and the American Community (1970). An interesting short work is W. H. Miernyk, *Trade Unions in the Age of Affluence (1962). Ralph and Estelle James, *Hoffa and the Teamsters (1965), is a lively study of the largest union and its controversial leader. C. W. Mills, The New Men of Power (1948), argued that labor leaders were themselves becoming part of the power elite. Michael Harrington, *The Other America: Poverty in the United States (1962), is a valuable corrective to more optimistic accounts of the economy. Sidney Lens, Poverty: America's Enduring Paradox (1969), is a popularly written historical survey. A study of the Area Redevelopment Administration is S. A. Levitan, Federal Aid to Depressed Areas (1964).

Among the many recent books on the South and its problems, see especially T. D. Clark, *The Emerging South (2nd ed., 1968), the shrewd assessment of one of the country's leading historians. Brooks Hays, A Southern Moderate Speaks (1959), expresses the views of a Congressman from Arkansas who lost his seat to a white racist. Important works emphasizing religious aspects of recent southern developments are J. McB. Dabbs, *Who Speaks for the South? (1965); and K. K. Bailey, Southern White Protestantism in the 20th Century (1964). Impassioned indictments of segments of the white South are J. W. Silver, *Mississippi: The Closed Society (2nd ed., 1966); and Howard Zinn, The Southern Mystique (1964). Other works dealing with the blacks and integration are listed in the next bibliography.

One of the nation's more perceptive students of mass culture, Dwight Macdonald, sees some hope for the future in the fragmentation of the cultural market; see his essay, "Masscult and Midcult," in his Against the American Grain (1962). For treatments of various cultural media see Hortense Powdermaker, *Hollywood: The Dream Factory (1950); and Russell Lynes, *The Tastemakers (1954). More perceptive and more general criticism of recent American society can be obtained from David Riesman and others, *The Lonely Crowd (1950), which argues that the American personality has changed greatly in the past fifty years; Walter Lippmann, *The Public Philosophy (1955), that the nation must regain a sense of its past and must renew its devotion to its common ideals; Erich Fromm, *Escape from Freedom (1941), that modern society has found freedom too much of a burden; and W. H. Whyte, Jr.,

The Organization Man (1956), which discusses the effects of modern business organization upon the individual personality of the businessman.

Recent educational changes are discussed in Paul Woodring, *A Fourth of a Nation* (1957); Jacques Barzun, *The House of Intellect* (1959); and Arthur Bestor, *Educational Wastelands* (1953), and *The Restoration of Learning* (1955). Will Herberg, *Protestant, Catholic, Jew* (1955), stresses the withering in America of theological differences among the creeds; Paul Blanshard, *American Freedom and Catholic Power* (1949), is an attack upon the Catholic Church. John Cogley (ed.), *Religion in America* (1958), contains a good many thoughtful essays by representatives of various creeds. An intriguing sociological study is E. D. Baltzell, *The Protestant Establishment* (1964).

The tenets of the new conservatism are sharply if somewhat arbitrarily defined in W. F. Buckley, Jr., *Up From Liberalism* (1959); and in more political terms by Barry Goldwater, *The Conscience of a Conservative* (1960). M. M. Auerbach, *The Conservative Illusion* (1959), is a well-reasoned critique. M. S. Evans, *The Future of Conservatism* (2nd ed., 1969), is the cheerful view of a highly conservative journalist. The gloomy analysis of a conservative political scientist is in Andrew Hacker, *The End of the American Era* (1970). Interesting critiques of American political and social values are found in Daniel Bell, *The End of Ideology* (1960); and Renata Adler, *Toward a Radical Middle* (1969). The changing views of a leading liberal, A. M. Schlesinger, Jr., can be traced in his *The Vital Center* (1949); *The Politics of Hope* (1962); and *The Crisis of Confidence* (1969). Jane Jacobs has argued persuasively in favor of urban life and against efforts to homogenize it in *Death and Life of Great American Cities* (1961); and *The Economy of Cities* (1969). See also the stimulating commentary of Scott Donaldson, *The Suburban Myth* (1969).

On literature, see especially Malcolm Cowley, *The Literary Situation* (1954), a perceptive discussion of the postwar decade. J. B. Gilbert, *Writers and Partisans* (1968), is a history of literary radicalism, with special attention to the *Partisan Review*. A valuable collection of essays is *The Intellectual Migration: Europe and America, 1930–1960* (1969), edited by Donald Fleming and Bernard Bailyn. A discussion of trends in drama is C. W. E. Bigsby, *Confrontation and Commitment* (1967).

29

MINORITY GROUPS

*Race and Progressivism · Rise of racism · The American Negro ·
Spanish Americans · The American Indian · Oriental Americans*

Protests from minority groups were by no means new to American history, but during the 1960's they rose to unprecedented heights. Except for African slaves, earlier minorities had consisted for the most part of non-English but white immigrants from Europe who in due time managed to achieve some degree of assimilation into the native American stock. But the minority groups that made themselves heard in the 1960's differed from the majority mainly in race and color and they posed a far more serious problem. The new protests came mainly from the blacks, the Spanish-Americans of mixed Indian or Negro ancestry, the native American Indians, and the Orientals.

As the twentieth century opened, the chief challenge to the old American stock still came from the hordes of immigrants from southern and eastern Europe. To them were added a comparatively small number of Asians. Although official agreements and anti-Oriental campaigns greatly reduced the number of most Asians entering the country, as many as 30,000 Japanese alone had

A YOUNG PROTESTOR makes her point in a peaceful parade.

reached the relatively thinly populated states of the Pacific Coast in a single year.

Race and Progressivism

During the twentieth century a steady improvement in the relations between majority and minority groups might reasonably have been expected. Until 1929 the period was generally prosperous with only a few sharp, short reverses marring the general economic climate. Though the level of real wages rose very little until 1915, and the farmer suffered during the twenties, jobs were fairly plentiful, and thus intolerance was not fueled by sustained economic adversity. The first twenty years of the century were dominated by the reforming impulses of the progressive movement. Though the progressive mentality was shot through with assumptions of racial supremacy, it also contained benevolent attitudes toward the poor and the distressed, and particularly toward the newcomers pouring into the large eastern cities from Europe. It can be argued, of course, that the interest of the urban progressive in housing, public health, fire and police reforms contained large elements of self-interest for the dominant majority. But regulations limiting the hours of work for women and children, those for protection from industrial hazards, and the widespread establishment of settlement houses in the big city slums were mainly altruistic.

Much of the reform spirit at the opening of the century was also based upon the rationalistic spirit of the new social sciences and humanitarian zeal stemming from both the social gospel movement and the crusade for women's rights. Predicated on the assumptions that mankind, whatever his race and nationality, was alike in basic aptitudes, that his significant differences arose not from his genes but from his past social environment and that by changing his environment one could alter both his existing condition and his attitudes, the new studies in anthropology, sociology, and economics argued for a new tolerance toward minorities. The social gospel movement in religion, dedicated to infusing everyday life with the ethics of Christ, underlined a more compassionate attitude toward the disadvantaged. Thus the fact that race and minority relations in all sections of the country deteriorated badly during the progressive period needs explanation. A part of the answer lies in the widely held opinion that the period came at the crest of north-western European supremacy throughout the world. Seemingly the future belonged to the peoples of Great Britain, France, Germany, and the United States. By the Spanish-American War and the acquisition of empire, the United States had obviously joined the exclusive circle of "superior" nations. The belief that the Teutons or the Anglo-Saxons had been responsible for the advance of mankind was heralded in most of the nation's newspapers and magazines, and even in academic halls. The pseudo-scientific doctrine of eugenics held that the world's various people could be categorized by their widely varying accomplishments and that any admixture of the races usually resulted in the deterioration of the more advanced ones.

The Immigrants

The ready acceptance of such doctrines in an otherwise enlightened age can be explained in the satisfaction of self-esteem that it gave to the majority. But perhaps a more likely reason lay in the feelings of uncertainty and even fear for the future from the human tide of strange immigrants pouring into the eastern cities and, to a lesser degree, into Pacific ports. In no other short period had the old American stock been threatened with more radical change

New York in 1898. *Immigrants of many nationalities market in New York's Lower East Side.*

Ellis Island. *These immigrants have been inspected and found admissible to the United States. They are waiting for a train for the trip to points outside New York City.*

than during the opening years of the twentieth century.

The new immigrant's clothing, manners, speech, and on the West Coast his color and size, set him distinctly apart. The Catholic, Jewish, and Greek Orthodox faiths of the newcomers from Europe also rubbed the native's sensitivities. As Catholic schools and Jewish synagogues proliferated, it was even argued by some of the more irrational nativists that the Italian immigration was sponsored by the Vatican to make up for the falling rate of incoming Irish. The ironic note that at the height of American missionary efforts abroad, Protestant dominance at home was being threatened, was not lost on the leaders of traditional churches.

Rise of Racism

This sensitivity to the flood of immigrants produced some of the most racist writings in American history. Emphasizing the "yellow peril," a phrase given international currency by the German Emperor, a California writer, Homer Lea, predicted in his *Valor of Ignorance* (1909) a Japanese military occupation of the whole Pacific Coast. In the East the two most influential racist authors were Madison Grant and Lothrop Stoddard. Grant, a New York lawyer, published in 1916 his pessimistic *Passing of the Great Race*. Stoddard, a Harvard graduate, followed four years later with *The Rising Tide of Color Against White World Supremacy*. Although both of these books were pointed specifically against the colored races, southern members of Congress had repeatedly made the point that one of the reasons for "inferiority" of the southern and eastern Europeans was their admixture of African and Asiatic blood.

Native Americans felt threatened in business and politics by the new immigrants. Since the 1890's some labor union leaders had demanded the same protection against cheap foreign labor that the industrialists had enjoyed from cheap foreign goods. The A.F.of L. in 1903 officially joined hands with the "Anglo-Saxon elitists" to support immigration restriction. The "block voting" of the new immigrants, organized by big city machines, was also the subject of much condemnation, particularly since the ballots were usually cast for the Democratic Party in sections of the country where the upper economic classes were normally Republican. Among the newcomers from southern, central, and eastern Europe the presence of a small but highly articulate group of radicals devoted to anarchism, socialism, and Marxism further excited the political passions of the majority.

As already noted, the prejudice of native Americans against immigrants was heightened by the experiences of World War I, which tended to cast doubt on the loyalty of "hyphenated Americans." After the war came the Red Scare, which blamed numerous acts of violence on the influx of Old World radicals. These years also produced a general demand for the limitation of immigration to end the unprecedented postwar rush of immigrants to American shores. The result was the quota system of the temporary Immigration Act of 1921, which limited immigration to a trickle, followed by the Act of 1924, which made the new policy permanent and for good measure excluded all aliens ineligible for citizenship, a discrimination deeply resented by the Japanese government.

The American Negro

Of all the twentieth-century campaigns against minorities the most persistent and comprehensive was the one launched in the South against one of the oldest and one of the most disadvantaged groups in the country — the American Negro. Deprived of equal educational opportunities in a section noted for its poverty-stricken public schools, confined mostly to laboring on land belonging to whites, and usually relegated in the few southern cities to the most menial positions, the plight of the freedman was incomparably more dismal than that of any other American group, save possibly the American Indian. Despite the Civil War-inspired Amendments to the Constitution and the Civil Rights Act of 1875, which guaranteed the "full and equal enjoyment" of all public institutions including accommodations at "inns, public conveyances . . .

theatres and other places of public amusements," Negroes never remotely approached the status of legal equality with even the poorest and the most ignorant whites. In direct defiance of the federal law southerners were determined to maintain the pre-Civil War social order. By the 1890's most southern schools, churches, and other public institutions were virtually segregated. Although the Negro was no longer a slave he belonged to a desperately underprivileged caste.

Nevertheless until the 1890's, despite almost insurmountable handicaps, the Negro had made some gains. Not a few had become landholders, some had gone to the northern cities where, even though forced to live in the slums, they were able to obtain a better education than was possible in the South. Even in the South a black leadership was slowly evolving from "self-made" individuals and from the graduates of the struggling Negro colleges supported largely by northern philanthropy. Moreover, until 1900 a surprising number of Negroes voted in the South and by agreements with white conservatives held a number of minor offices. During the early Populist period in not a few southern states white and black farmers combined in political action against the section's upper economic classes.

New Discrimination

It had seemed for a time that the blacks might eventually be accepted as an integral part of the southern community. But in the 1890's a massive reactionary wave of discrimination began that left the black a virtually untouchable caste, living in the white southern community but no longer a part of it. With the amendment to the Mississippi Constitution in 1896 a campaign was started to eliminate the black from political life. Section five of that amendment read that to be registered all voters had to be able to read any section of the state constitution "or be able to understand the same when

"Jim Crowism." *A drinking fountain for blacks in a streetcar terminal in Oklahoma City, 1939.*

read to him or give a reasonable interpretation thereof." Variations of this "understanding clause," plus the additions of such devices as the poll tax, requirements for "good character," and the "white primary," were quickly adopted by other southern states. The effectiveness of the devices, which incidentally were often used to disfranchise poor whites, was demonstrated by the election statistics of Louisiana. In 1896, over 130,000 blacks had voted in the state, but by 1904 that number had dropped to 1,342.

As early as 1883 the Supreme Court had destroyed much of the force of the Civil Rights Act of 1875 by deciding that the equal protection of the laws clause of the Fourteenth Amendment did not apply to privately owned establishments or individual acts. The Court's decision of 1896, in *Plessy* vs. *Ferguson*, broadened the possibility of discrimination by legalizing the concept of "separate but equal" facilities in public institutions such as schools. As a consequence, the southern crusade for better public schools, beginning about 1900, had little effect upon the blacks; in fact the disparity of educational opportunities between the races probably increased rather

than decreased. Booker T. Washington, in his famous 1895 speech, asked for an emphasis on technical education for Negroes to insure them a basic means of livelihood. Applauded at the time by many whites throughout the South, Washington's proposals were largely ignored, since such education was expensive. Without technical training and excluded from unions, the blacks were kept out of jobs in rising southern industries. Through state licensing laws they were even forced out of some of their traditional occupations, such as the barbering trade.

Although segregation had been practiced informally in the nineteenth century, much intermingling between the races had regularly occurred, especially in the small towns and country. But after the turn of the century the phenomenal rise of southern racist demagogues, such as Tom Watson of Georgia and James K. Vardaman of Mississippi, was paralleled by the widespread adoption of "Jim Crow" laws, which virtually separated the races. The movement started in 1905 when Georgia created separate parks for the two races. During the following year Montgomery, Alabama, provided for separate street cars, a rule that was rapidly expanded to include taxis, waiting rooms, and hospitals. In 1910 Baltimore required that city blocks be inhabited by either all whites or all blacks; and three years later the editor of the North Carolina *Progressive Farmer* seriously proposed segregation in the country districts.

World War I and After

During World War I the position of the black, like that of many recently arrived immigrants, was simultaneously bettered and threatened. Scarcity of labor and a rise in wages improved the economic standing of both groups, and the need for labor in the North rapidly accelerated the hitherto slow migration of blacks to the northern cities. From 1910 to 1930 over three million blacks went north, with the result that sizable Negro communities grew up in practically every large city. Moreover, 360,000 Negroes served in the armed forces during World War I and, though mainly utilized in segregated labor battalions, a good number were introduced for the first time to non-southern and less discriminatory practices.

On the other hand, the war worked to the disadvantage of both the recently arrived immigrant and the black. The emphasis on Americanism, patriotism, and unity and the attack upon foreign-born Americans accentuated the rising tide of intolerance already in evidence before the war. During the postwar period of hysteria against radicalism, which was thought to be mainly imported from abroad, and with the emphasis upon isolation and conformity, minority groups were looked upon with suspicion in almost every community in the nation. The black confronted especial difficulties both in the South and in the North. Southern whites for the most part noted with concern that the uniform had given the Negro

a degree of "protection and consideration" that he would not have when he returned home, while the high wages had made him "shiftless and irresponsible." Congressman James F. Byrnes of South Carolina emphasized that, if the two races were to live together in peace, it should be understood "that the war has in no way changed the attitude of the white man toward social and political equality. . . ."

After the armistice the blacks and the returning white veterans were often in competition for jobs. As race prejudice flared up there were shocking numbers of race riots in at least twenty-five northern and southern cities. Among the most destructive and bloody were those of Chicago, East St. Louis, and Oklahoma City. The subsequent rise of a new Ku Klux Klan was thus the organized result of passions common to both the North and South.

During the 1920's nativism remained a major force in the country. In 1922 an attempt to pass a federal anti-lynching law, labeled by Congressman John Rankin of Mississippi as a "bill to encourage rape,"

Negro Troops. *A contingent of Negro troops arrives home from Europe at the end of the First World War.*

Ku Klux Klan. *The Imperial Wizard kissing the flag at a meeting in Atlanta, Georgia of the Ku Klux Klan in 1921.*

was easily defeated. The results of the 1928 election, in which the southern states containing the most blacks remained loyal to the Democratic Party, indicated that the deep South at least was far more interested in the racial question (and thus clung to the traditional party of the white South) than it was in economic matters where New Era prosperity might have tempted it to become Republican. When the wife of Oscar De Priest, the first Negro elected to Congress since 1901, was invited to tea at the White House by Mrs. Hoover, cries of outrage resounded throughout the South. Southern cities continued to extend and broaden their "Jim Crow" legislation, and the rapid growth of the Ku Klux Klan in the rural Middle West, where the black was conspicuous by his absence, the history of the Sacco-Vanzetti trial in Massachusetts, and the anti-Catholicism involved in the defeat of Alfred Smith in 1928 testified to the persistence of what later became known as WASP (White, Anglo-Saxon Protestant) prejudices.

On the other hand, the twenties provided ample evidence that the most violent elements of American nativism were subsiding. In part this was unquestionably a result of strict immigration restriction. No longer could super-racists and patriots point to the impending danger of the older stocks being overwhelmed. In part the rapid Americanization and the economic advance of the white immigrants and their children made them far less conspicuous. The anthropological studies of Franz Boas, together with those of his later disciples Ruth Benedict and Margaret Mead, helped to destroy the existing myths about race. By the end of the decade, the theories on race superiority and Anglo-Saxon supremacy had been discarded by most educated people. The rapidly rising proportion of Americans going to college, the increasing urbanization of the country, and especially the race excesses of Nazi Germany, all tended toward a more tolerant viewpoint. By the end of the Second World War, although prejudice against the Catholic, the

Jew, and the citizens of southern and eastern Europe still existed, the public expressions of such sentiments had become distinctly unpopular. After the decade of the twenties the minority problem had become one mostly concerned with color and not culture or religion.

The New Negro

Despite the continued disparity in the quality of the black and white schools in the South and the sizable obstacles to his cultural rise in the North, the black made some remarkable advances in the twenties and thirties. In 1870 less than ten per cent of the blacks between ages five and twenty were in school; by 1930 more than sixty per cent were so enrolled. By 1930 an increasingly competent Negro leadership was emerging in both the North and the South, a leadership reflected in the growth and success of nationwide organizations dedicated to the welfare of the race.

The earliest and most important of such organizations was the National Association for the Advancement of Colored People. As early as 1905 at the all-black Niagara Falls conference the idea for the organization was advanced by W. E. B. DuBois. After receiving a Ph.D. degree from Harvard, DuBois, a Massachusetts-born Negro, taught for many years at Atlanta University and in 1910 became editor of the organ of the NAACP, *The Crisis*. In 1903 he had published *The Souls of Black Folk*, a rational critique of Booker T. Washington's policy of accommodation to the prevailing southern racial attitudes. Much more vigorous than Washington in demanding Negro rights, DuBois rapidly became the outstanding national Negro political and cultural leader. In 1909 a group of white liberal leaders together with a few blacks founded the NAACP. This organization plus the National Urban League, organized two years later, and both financed in good part by white philanthropists, were especially effective in attempting to protect the Negro's civil rights as well as maintaining a lobby in his interest at Washington.

The rising temper of the black race, especially in the northern cities, was well illustrated by the first significant black nationalist movement, centered around the dynamic figure of Marcus Garvey. Coming from the West Indies in 1916, Garvey had a magnetic personality with a compelling style of public speaking. He soon enrolled a half million northern blacks in his Universal Negro Improvement Association, dedicated to inspiring self-respect among the members of his race. Garvey encouraged Negroes to support black businesses, extolled the history of black culture, and eventually promoted a movement to transport American Negroes back to Africa. Among other leaders of the race during the twenties was A. Phillip Randolph who organized and edited *The Messenger*, a black socialist magazine that argued for a combination of black and white workingmen, and for the use of violence to attain Negro equality. In 1925, Randolph organized the Brotherhood of Sleeping Car Porters, and thus became the first important black labor leader.

Led by white southern liberals, the Commission on Inter-racial Cooperation was organized in 1919, dedicated to black educational progress, anti-lynching, and anti-discrimination. Its successors, the Southern Regional Conference and the more radical Southern Conference for Human Welfare established in 1939, included in their programs the demand for an end to race segregation. The importance of black political power in the northern cities made itself felt for the first time on a national issue. One of the chief pressure groups against President Hoover's nomination of the southern conservative John J. Parker for the Supreme Court was the NAACP. According to one historian, Parker was "the first important victim of the Negro's newly won power."

During his first administration Franklin Roosevelt was confronted by a southern-dominated Congress. In the 73rd Congress

A Negro Slum. *A backyard in a typical Negro slum. This photograph was taken in Cincinnati, Ohio in the 1920's.*

(1933–1935) nine of the fourteen major Senate Committees and twelve of seventeen in the House were headed by southerners. Consequently until 1941 the New Deal did little or nothing to help the Negro directly. It could be argued that the blacks as one of the poorer sections of the nation's population were helped by the New Deal's generous relief and recovery programs. But since many programs were administered by local politicians, economic discrimination in the South reduced the benefits to the race. In the northern cities where the rate of black unemployment was staggering, the relief programs became the major element in a massive political reversal. In the election of 1936 the Negro wards of the great cities changed their traditional allegiance from the Republican Party to the Democratic Party, a radical shift that reshaped the nature of the Democratic Party and made it far more liberal.

Negro Culture

The northern migration and urbanization of the black provided him with educational and economic opportunities that he had never before experienced, this despite the fact that he was everywhere the last to be hired and the first to be fired. As a result, beginning about 1920, a new educated and cultured Negro elite began to appear. James Weldon Johnson (1871–1938), secretary of the NAACP during the 1920's, was a leader of this group. He participated as a poet, essayist, and anthologist; his books, *Black Manhattan* (1930) and *Along This Way* (1933), provide a chronicle of Negro cultural achievement. In 1925 Alain Locke, a Howard University professor educated at Harvard and Oxford, edited *The New Negro,* an anthology of contemporary black writers. This volume called attention to a "Harlem Renaissance" and the wealth of talent that was developing among the black race. Although writers and poets such as Arna Bontemps, Claude McKay, and Jean Toomer may not have been of the first rank, certainly Langston Hughes (1902–1967) was. Hughes, the most prolific of all American black writers, was to be followed during the next twenty years by some major literary figures such as Richard Wright (1908–1960), whose bitterly realistic *Native Son* (1940) won critical acclaim and a wide readership; Ralph Ellison (1914–), winner of the National Book award with his sensitive and polished novel *The Invisible Man* (1956); and James Baldwin (1924–), whose novels, short stories, plays, and essays have made him one of the leading figures in American intellectual and public life.

The emergence of concert artists such as Marian Anderson and Paul Robeson and, on the more popular level, of jazz musicians such as Louis Armstrong was less surprising since the musical talent of the blacks had already been well demonstrated. Perhaps the fields of college and professional sports best revealed the black advance. The 1936 Olympic Games triumphs of Jesse Owens were most appropriately set on a world stage before the master racist Adolf Hitler. But Owens' career at Ohio State University and the careers of many other black college stars during the thirties set a pattern that rapidly became commonplace in northern colleges. Until the thirties, organized professional sports, like most other lucrative professions, had barred the blacks from participation. The signing in 1946 of Jackie Robinson by the Brooklyn Dodgers, for whom he rapidly became a star, was thus a landmark. Within twenty years black professional stars often outnumbered whites in football, basketball, and baseball.

Such achievements by blacks in fields once regarded as white monopolies accelerated still further the demands for recognition of racial equality. Largely through the work of James Farmer, the Congress of Racial Equality was organized in 1942. Two years later Walter White, the Executive Secretary of the NAACP, called a national conference of twenty black organizations to frame "A Declaration by Negro Voters," in which the demands for equality of political, educational, and economic opportunity were clearly formulated.

World War II

Then came the Second World War, in which the blacks, although segregated in the armed forces, contributed very significantly to victory. At home the war industries hastened the move to the cities and to the North. Consequently the black vote in many cities and in some states became important. The emphasis on freedom during the war, the postwar growth of independent African states, and most importantly the broadening of the American black's own aspirations led to a new militancy, especially in the northern cities, to which the Negro migration from the South had taken on mass proportions.

Not only the blacks, but many egalitarian-minded whites also, joined in the demand for equal civil rights for the ever more impressive Negro minority. In 1950 there were about 15 million Negroes in the United States, of whom 9 million lived in the South, with the rest concentrated in the larger cities of the North and West. To varying degrees, social discrimination still existed in all sections of the country. But almost everywhere substantial progress had been made toward equal treatment. The number of Negroes lynched each year dropped from a humiliating total of 106 in 1900 to none in 1952. The civil and political disabilities from which the Negroes had suffered were also on the decline. In 1948 the Supreme Court ruled that the "white covenants," by which property owners in the North had excluded Negroes

Jackie Robinson *of the Brooklyn* Dodgers *making a double play with his customary finesse.*

from residential districts, could not be judicially enforced. And although fierce resistance against black admission to white districts persisted in most northern cities, at least the legal pattern had been established that discrimination in housing could not be maintained by legal action. The increasing black voting power in the North had much to do with breaking down the restrictions on black suffrage in the South. By 1958, well over a million blacks, representing one quarter of those of voting age, were registered to vote in eleven southern states. Throughout the rural districts of the deep South, however, the great majority of the blacks, as late as 1960, was still denied the ballot, and despite federal legislation there was every indication that local opposition to black voting remained adamant. Discrimination against blacks in the use of theaters, hotels, hospitals, and restaurant facilities was, especially in the North, beginning to give way. Segregation of blacks in the armed forces was officially abandoned after 1951; thereafter the number of blacks winning commissions and promotions in all branches of the service steadily increased.

Brown vs. Board of Education

Probably most important of all, discrimination against blacks in education had received a serious blow. Following a trend already well established, the Supreme Court ruled, May 17, 1954, in *Brown* vs. *Board of Education* that the old judicial doctrine of "separate but equal" facilities for the races would no longer satisfy the requirements of the Constitution, and that Negroes must everywhere be permitted to attend the same public schools as whites. This unanimous opinion was delivered by the new Chief Justice, Earl Warren, whom President Eisenhower had appointed in 1953. Accordingly, the Court ordered the integration of schools to take place everywhere "with all deliberate speed." In the District of Columbia segregation was immediately abolished by order of the school board, and in a few states officials moved voluntarily toward compliance with the Court decision. But most southern governors and legislatures sought by various means to circumvent this radical step. By 1960 only 765 of the 2,838 schools in the seventeen southern and border states were desegregated.

In some cases southern opposition went to extreme lengths. Civil disorder manifested itself particularly in Little Rock, Arkansas, in September, 1957, when Governor Orval Faubus challenged the federal authority, and again in 1960 in New Orleans when Governor James Davis sought to obstruct the orders of the local school board and those of a federal judge. After much hesitation, President Eisenhower ordered federal troops to Little Rock with instructions to enforce integration, and in New

"If You Both Would Stop Pushing So Hard —."
A plea for moderation in the integration issue. Hesse, in the St. Louis Globe Democrat.

Orleans both local police and federal marshals were needed to prevent possible serious rioting. In 1959 Virginia slowly started to desegregate in a few districts, but only after much delay and an attempt to close all the public schools in the state and convert them into segregated private institutions. After Virginia's tardy action it seemed certain that the upper South would eventually follow, although in many rural districts throughout the deep South the struggle for school integration was bitterly resisted by the white population. Had it not been for an important group of southern moderates, these years of transition might have been far more turbulent than they were. But a large number of southern clergymen and educators, supported by many of the section's most influential newspapers, urged compliance with the law. Their courageous action turned a possible large-scale tragedy into a relatively peaceful, if painfully "deliberate," movement.

Political and Economic Equality

Meanwhile, in 1957, the Eisenhower administration had asked for a sweeping civil rights law. After much negotiation and debate Congress, under the leadership of Senator Lyndon B. Johnson of Texas, finally passed a compromise measure which did, however, include some federal protection for Negro voting rights in the South. In 1960 the national platforms of both parties contained strong civil rights planks, and during the campaign all four top candidates, including Senator Johnson, strongly supported the stand of their parties. Although there was considerable disagreement in the South over these developments, it seemed reasonably clear in 1960 that the blacks in both the South and the North had at least made a start toward achieving substantial legal equality. The final test as to whether America could solve its race problems without much disorder and bloodshed was yet to come.

In spite of these reform measures, the economic status of the blacks remained far less satisfactory than that of the whites. Whatever security the need of their labor had once given them in the South was undermined by the increasing use of farm machinery. For thousands there was no alternative but flight to the industrial centers. During the depression of the 1930's the relief measures of the New Deal had proved to be a boon to the blacks, and resulted, incidentally, in a wholesale drift to the Democratic Party. Fortunately the rising tide of prosperity of the 1940's lifted the Negroes along with the rest of the population. Their incomes tended to be substantially lower than those of the whites, their living conditions less satisfactory, and their jobs less secure, but in comparison with their earlier economic status, they had made progress. Many had lifted themselves from the bottom fifth of the "spending units" to the fourth, third, and even second fifths. The rise in their economic status was reflected in a variety of other ways. Illiteracy among them had declined from 44.5 per cent in 1900 to 11 per cent in 1950. More and more of them attended colleges and universities — a total of 74,526 in 1950, according to United States Office of Education statistics, although this figure was probably too low, since many institutions kept no records that distinguished between white and black students. Also, they were increasingly well organized and more eager to secure and safeguard their rights, although usually with such restraint and decorum as to elicit widespread admiration even in the South.

The Negro Revolution

What was often called "the Negro revolution" was an outstanding phenomenon of the year 1963 — the 100th anniversary of the freeing of the slaves. Undoubtedly the grim persistence of economic hardship for so large a proportion of the race was the chief motivating force behind the movement. The blacks had come a long way since slavery, but the great majority of them remained in the lowest income bracket or among the unemployed. This condition was the more keenly felt because of the social and political discriminations from which they suffered, particularly in the states of the old Confederacy, where many of them were still denied even the right to vote. In the North, although they were granted full political rights, they usually had to live in segregated areas and to send their children to schools that were segregated in fact, if not in law. They were at a disadvantage, too, in the competition for employment; some labor unions even denied them the privilege of membership.

During the first two years of his administration President Kennedy had not requested any significant civil rights legislation. Early in March, 1961, however, he created a Committee on Equal Employment Opportunity, with Vice-President Johnson at its head, which solicited and obtained antidiscrimination pledges from leading defense contractors. The Department of Labor also won from the Interstate Commerce Commission a ruling against segregation in southern bus terminals. The responsibility for this decision was shared in some degree by the Congress of Racial Equality (CORE), which had promoted "freedom rides" by representatives of both races into the deep South and had precipitated incidents at Birmingham, Alabama, and Jackson, Mississippi, which won sympathy for the Negro cause throughout most of the nation.

Except in Mississippi and South Carolina school desegregation made slow but steady gains, although the percentage of blacks attending schools with whites remained extremely low. Negroes were encouraged, however, by Kennedy's willingness to name members of their race to high office. He appointed two Negroes to federal judgeships, another to be Ambassador to Norway, and he made Dr. Robert C. Weaver Administrator of the Housing and Home Insurance Agency. But when, early in 1962, the President sought to create a Department of Urban Affairs, with a seat in the Cabinet, to which he intended to appoint Weaver as its first Secretary, the conservative coalition in Congress promptly turned the measure down. The President's hope of easing racial tension in the South received a rude jolt when Governor Ross R. Barnett of Mississippi personally intervened to prevent registration at the University of Mississippi of a black student, James H. Meredith, whose admission had been ordered by a federal court. To obtain compliance with the court order, the President sent in scores of federal marshals and, shortly thereafter, army units. In the rioting that accompanied Meredith's appear-

Protesters *prepare to set out on a march from the steps of a Negro church in Birmingham, Alabama in 1963.*

ance on campus, two persons were killed and many others injured, but Meredith was duly registered and began to attend classes.

Martin Luther King, Jr.

Encouraged by such resolute action on the part of the federal government, black leaders now stepped up their campaign for equality in both the North and the South. Outstanding among them was Martin Luther King, Jr., a well-educated Baptist minister who preached peaceful resistance, somewhat after the Gandhi pattern that had helped free India. He won his first victory at Montgomery, Alabama, where he led a yearlong boycott, beginning in December, 1955, against a local bus company for its discrimination against blacks in the seating of passengers. The company, to save itself from bankruptcy, eventually gave in. During the next few years racial demonstrations of one kind or another erupted in all parts of the nation; most notable was the epidemic of "sit-ins" and "freedom rides" in the deep South. Participants in these activities scrupulously avoided violence and cheerfully incurred arrest for their refusal to abide by local rules and customs; King himself went to jail at Albany, Georgia, in December, 1961, and twice more the following year. Early in 1963 he recruited thousands of blacks to parade peacefully in favor of equal rights at Birmingham. The dispersal of these marchers by the Birmingham police, who made free use of police dogs and fire hoses, aroused massive sentiment in favor of the black cause throughout the nation and the world. For his success in obtaining greater rights for Negroes by nonviolent means, Martin Luther King was awarded the 1964 Nobel Peace Prize.

The Washington March

Increasingly black protest began to insist on drastic economic readjustments. Organizations such as CORE and NAACP every-where demanded that more and better jobs be made available to blacks. The climax of the Negro revolt came with the Washington march, August 28, 1963, in which some 200,000 black and white sympathizers from all over the nation participated, walking in orderly fashion from the Washington Monument to the Lincoln Memorial. Not a single deed of violence marred the demonstration. Meanwhile, southern extremists continued to fight nonviolence with violence. Black homes and churches were bombed, and several black leaders and white civil rights workers were murdered in cold blood.

Revulsion against these wild deeds undoubtedly aided the Negro cause, both in the North and in most of the South. Previously indifferent individuals and corporations made a sincere effort to add blacks to their payrolls. One of the difficulties they encountered was that so few blacks had the skills needed for the positions to which they aspired; some employers met this problem with on-the-job training, a requirement also for many of the whites they hired. The need for better educational opportunities for blacks was apparent, and more and more school boards recognized the necessity for desegregation and for new types of vocational education. Measures designed to end or ameliorate racial discriminations in housing also won increasing attention and occasional adoption.

No unprejudiced observer could argue, however, that the blacks had achieved anything approximating equality of opportunity with the whites. In both the North and the South many of them lived in slums, where every cultural institution from parks to schools was decidedly inferior. Whereas less than 5 per cent of the whites lived in housing that was considered substandard, 40 per cent of the blacks were so domiciled. Black unemployment was regularly higher than white; in 1966 the rate for whites was 3.3 per cent, and for blacks 7.3 per cent.

Discriminations in promotions were rife everywhere; always the blacks found greater difficulties than the whites in escaping from the lower-paid and more menial jobs. Even in the armed forces, where desegregation was rigorously enforced, the blacks in 1960 constituted 9 per cent of the enlisted men, 10 per cent of the noncommissioned officers, but only 2 per cent of the commissioned officers. Under these circumstances it is not surprising that the nonviolent methods preached by King soon gave way to more direct action.

Spanish Americans

Aside from the blacks, the second largest colored minority consisted of citizens of Spanish-American descent. Totaling well over 5 million in 1970, they were mostly clustered in three different geographical areas of the nation, Florida, New York City, and the Southwest. On the whole the three groups had little in common with each other. The quarter million or so refugees from Castro's Cuba, most of whom lived in Miami, Florida, were not underprivileged and offered few social problems to the nation. Although they arrived impoverished, they were mostly from Cuba's upper and middle classes, and through their own efforts they soon established an enterprising enclave within the resort city. Their unemployment rate was low, with fewer of their members on relief than in any other comparable group.

In addition there were another million Spanish-speaking people of Puerto Rican descent, about seventy per cent of whom had created a Spanish-speaking Harlem and other racial centers in New York, usually in close proximity to the resident blacks. Puerto Rican immigration went back to 1919 when a small group, assisted by the island government, came to New York to fill low-paid jobs. Attracted by labor contractors for the garment trades, their numbers slowly increased until the Second World War. The advent of the postwar industrial expansion, cheap air transportation, and the sizable unemployment in Puerto Rico accelerated their movement. The Puerto Ricans arrived in New York with several marked handicaps. They were desperately poor, most of them were uneducated, and many of them were taken for Negroes. Many of them thus encountered the same social and economic barriers that limited the opportunities of the American Negro. Since the Puerto Ricans often competed with English-speaking peoples, tensions and open hostilities between them were not infrequent.

Since they were the last of the sizable immigrant groups to arrive, Puerto Ricans, not surprisingly, suffered from many of the same social problems with which earlier groups had struggled. Unemployment was rife among them, especially the young, the incidence of disease and crime was high, family incomes were low, and the family itself tended to disintegrate. By 1969 40 per cent of the total funds paid out by New York City for relief of dependent children, involving 185,000 needy and apparently husbandless mothers, went to Puerto Ricans. By comparison only 47 per cent of such funds was paid to female members of the much larger black population.

By the end of the sixties, however, there were indications that the second generation group of Puerto Ricans were already outstripping the blacks in taking advantage of educational opportunities and in the rise of their income levels. The birth rate was considerably below that for the blacks, as was also the involvement in violent or serious crime. It seemed altogether probable that given time, the average Puerto Rican, provided he was not too dark of skin, might dissolve into the general American community and thus escape the deprivations of his immigrant past.

Mexican Americans

Over 4.6 million Americans of Spanish-Mexican descent live in an area stretching

Mexican-Americans. *These migrant workers are picking lettuce in Southern California.*

through California, Arizona, New Mexico to Texas, and reaching up into Colorado. Although over 2 million of these people lived in California and 1.5 million in Texas, they were in the majority only in a few localities, mainly along the southeastern Rio Grande valley and in North Central New Mexico. In New Mexico as a whole they amounted to a quarter of the total population. Although many of these Chicanos, to give them their own adopted name, were originally agricultural workers, the majority by the end of the 1960's had moved to the city, almost 900,000 of them living in Los Angeles alone.

In the past the fluidity of the Mexican-American population was due to the lack of border controls, the varying economic conditions in the United States, and the intense recruitment of Mexicans as agricultural workers in times of acute labor shortages. Although many of the "wet backs" who crossed the border illegally were returned home, and although the flow of Mexican agricultural laborers has been increasingly regulated by both governments, the chil-

dren of Mexican parents, if born in the United States, were automatically citizens. For the most part these first generation Mexican Americans were impoverished and illiterate agricultural laborers. But they and their children have increasingly drifted to the cities where they compete for jobs with the underskilled whites and blacks. Of California's estimated 2.25 million Mexican Americans, approximately 80 to 85 per cent now live in the state's cities.

Often referred to as "the forgotten minority," the Mexican-American community became militant only in the last few years of the sixties. Unquestionably their recent demands for equal rights have been prompted by the successes of the blacks. The growing numbers of Mexican Americans, their concentration in the cities, and their dim but increasing awareness that they are descended from one of the most advanced of ancient societies have helped to fan their indignation. Living in some of the worst slums or *barrios* in the country, with an unemployment rate below that of the blacks and with their difficulties with the language and their sensitivity to the fact that the dominant Americans held them in varying degrees of contempt, the Mexican Americans of the Southwest have increasingly demanded equal rights and protection under the law. As one of their foremost leaders bluntly stated: "We are free men and we demand justice."

Cesar Chavez

Although more or less organized discontent sporadically marked the Chicano communities, the most significant protest occurred in 1965–66 when Cesar Chavez launched his strike and national boycott against the grape growers of California's interior valleys. Rising out of the San Jose slums, this son of impoverished Mexican immigrants first organized the National Farm Worker's Union in 1962. Despite lack of protection from the National Labor Relations Board, which had no jurisdiction over farm workers, and the determined opposition of the "Anglo" landholders, together with most of the local and state government officials, Chavez persisted until "La Raza," his term for the strike and boycott, became a rallying cry of every Mexican-American community of the Southwest. It provided the spark that ignited a region-wide determination of the Mexican Americans to claim their rights as free and equal citizens.

The Mexican-American protest followed along lines similar to those developed by the black. In the *barrios* militant organizations like the Brown Berets of Los Angeles arose. Legal defense and educational opportunity funds were organized, the most significant financed by the Ford Foundation. Mexican-American college students demanded the introduction of Chicano studies, a demand first recognized by the University of California in its course on "La Raza" introduced in the autumn of 1969. And the special federal job opportunity programs were rapidly extended to include the Chicano as well as the black. By 1970 it was apparent that the once neglected minority was on the move, and that another important racial leaven had been added to the already bubbling cultural pluralism of the Southwest.

The American Indian

Since a Bureau of Indian Affairs had existed in Washington for more than a century, the Indians were hardly a "forgotten minority." The first Americans and the only minority group who did not immigrate into the country, they had unquestionably been the object of massive discrimination. Under the Dawes Act of 1887, hailed at the time as the "Emancipation Proclamation of the red men," Indians were granted individual homesteads (see page 94). The stated philosophy behind the act was to make them self-reliant and equal citizens of the Republic. The actual results were far different. By 1933 the Indian had lost most of his homesteads, either by legal or fraudulent transactions, as well as over 60 million acres of his original reservation lands labeled under the 1887 act as surplus. Of the 52 million acres of land left to the Indian, over half was desert or near desert. The de-reservation policy was also accompanied by an effort at "detribalization" which meant training the youth in the American language and culture, Christianization, and instruction in vocational subjects. But instead of disappearing into the white population as was hoped, most of the young Indians went back to the tribe. Since this educational process had also stressed the suppression of their own languages, traditional crafts, and culture, they came back bereft of their original means of livelihood. It is small wonder that 600,000 to 800,000 Indians inhabiting the country in the time of Columbus had shrunk by 1930 to 225,000.

A better day for the Indian momentarily appeared with the election of Franklin D. Roosevelt and his appointment of John Collier as the Commissioner of Indian Affairs. Instead of trying to make the Indian into second-rate whites, Collier worked to restore their traditional culture and ways of making a livelihood. Although this paternalistic policy was again reversed after World War II, the American Indian population rose by 1970 to about the figure estimated for pre-Columbian days. This population rise has not meant prosperity, however, since most Indians still live on or out of reservations in the direst poverty. Of all American minorities the condition of the Indian is the most abject and hopeless. One recent study of a California tribe indicated that their life expectancy was 44 years as compared to the average for the United States of 70, and their suicide rate 15 per cent above the country's norm.

The recent surge of other minorities toward more equitable treatment has infused the campaign for a square deal for the Indian with new vigor. In numerous conferences held during the sixties the Indian made it clear that he wanted to remain an Indian and pursue his traditional ways on the lands of his fathers, but whether much can be done is still debatable. The Indian's small numbers, his lack of educated leaders, and his scattered places of residence all contribute to his impotence. Many feel that affluent America owes more than talk to its most historic and, at the same time, most indigent minority group.

Oriental Americans

The census of 1960 counted over 464,000 citizens of Japanese descent, 237,000 Chinese, and 176,000 Filipinos. Clustered mainly in Hawaii and on the Pacific Coast, all three groups were by that time highly urban people, although before World War II many Japanese had owned or operated truck farms.

The Chinese are a clannish people, living in limited areas and tending either to be independent wholesalers or retailers or to

Navaho Indian workers *laying a pipeline to carry gas across their reservation in northern New Mexico.*

Japanese-Americans, *many of them native-born, entering a World War II relocation camp at Tule Lake, California.*

work for others of their race. The Japanese are far more adventurous, branching out into business and the professions, while the Filipinos tend to look for work in personal service and general manufacturing. Educational achievement sharply differentiated the Orientals, with the Filipinos at the bottom and the Japanese and Chinese at the top of a list of all the minority groups. In percentage of students enrolled in colleges the Japanese-Americans by 1970 topped even the Jewish group, which hitherto had led all racial or religious elements in the country. The Japanese also led all colored groups in per-capita income. A California study of 1960 indicated that the annual median income for males over 14 years of age in the state placed the whites first with $5,109, the Japanese next with $4,389, those with Spanish surnames next with $3,849, the Chinese next with $3,803, and the blacks last with $3,553.

All three of the Oriental groups met with discrimination before the Second World War, and the Japanese and Chinese had suf-fered from the Oriental exclusion policy of the Immigration Act of 1924, which separated them from their families. But the Japanese alone were struck with the massive prejudice arising from World War II, in a discriminatory policy that caused a total disruption of their lives (see page 609). By President Roosevelt's Executive Order 9066, for the first time a large group of American citizens was forced to leave their homes and livelihoods for "relocation centers." The spirit behind the incredible order was well stated by General DeWitt: "A Jap is a Jap. . . . They are a dangerous element whether loyal or not." The policy rudely violated the Bill of Rights and the Constitution and resulted in major financial losses for the evacuated. Many of them lost their jobs and, if they owned property, had to sell it for less than it was worth.

The shamefulness of this episode was illuminated after the war when it was officially declared that the Japanese-Americans had been overwhelmingly patriotic. Since even the Japanese born in the United States, the

Nisei, were at first officially declared "enemy aliens," American citizens were thus denied the right to volunteer for the armed forces. When, after persistent effort, the Japanese-American Citizen's League succeeded in correcting this classification, a volunteer Japanese unit, the 442nd Infantry Combat Team, was trained and sent to Italy where it became one of the most heroic and most decorated units of the war. A Hawaiian outfit composed of the many island races, but mostly Orientals, adopted the reckless motto, "Go for Broke," and won similar distinction in combat.

When the Japanese returned from the war, they had virtually to start again carving out their place in American society. By almost any index imaginable — education, family cohesion, the lack of juvenile delinquency and adult crime, and achievement in the professions and business — Japanese-Americans by the decade of the seventies had proved that a non-Caucasian group can make signal contributions to American society.

A Nation of Colors

By 1970 about 30 million American citizens, almost 15 per cent of the total population, were peoples of black, brown, red, or yellow complexion. Save for the Indian and the Negro, they had come to the United States voluntarily seeking the same goals that most other immigrants had sought. They came with the assurances of the Declaration of Independence and the Consituation that all men would be treated equally before the law. During most of the nation's history that had probably not been so. In the fifties, by the fiat of the Supreme Court, equal protection of the laws was demanded of all governmental agencies, federal, state, and local. Subsequent court decisions and congressional legislation sought to impart the same dictum for many areas of private activities. Particularly under the Johnson administration vast sums were appropriated to help the underprivileged groups overcome their liabilities. By 1970 the nation to a great extent had triumphed over the bigotries arising from a multiplicity of religions and nationalities. Catholics, Jews, and the still dominant Protestant majority were at peace with each other. The Italian, the Greek, the Slav, and a multitude of other nationalities had been accepted and were rapidly disappearing into the American amalgam. But, for the foreseeable future, Americans faced the far greater challenge of triumphing over the discredited but still world-wide prejudice among whites against peoples with colored skins.

BIBLIOGRAPHY

Understanding Minority Groups (1956), edited by J. B. Gittler, contains perceptive essays by leading authorities on the main non-white minorities. A superb work on nativism is John Higham, *Strangers in the Land* (1955). A lively general survey of the 20th-century civil rights movement is J. P. Roche, *The Quest for the Dream* (1963). A perceptive study of several minority groups in New York City is Nathan Glazer and D. P. Moynihan, *Beyond the Melting Pot* (1963).

J. H. Franklin, *From Slavery to Freedom* (3rd ed., 1967), is the beginning point for the study of black Americans, both because of its comprehensive text and its extensive bibliography. Documentary and historiographical collections include: *The Negro American* (1967), edited by L. H. Fishel, Jr., and Benjamin Quarles; *The Negro in Twentieth Century America* (1967), edited by J. H. Franklin and Isidore Starr; *Negro Protest Thought in the Twentieth Century* (1965), edited by F. L. Broderick and August Meier; *Understanding Negro History* (1968), edited by D. W. Hoover; and *The Black Experience in America* (1970), edited by J. C. Curtis and L. L. Gould.

Special studies in black history are at last becoming numerous and of generally high quality. C. McL. Green, *The Secret City* (1967), is an account of race relations in Washington, D.C. Two major works are Gilbert Osofsky, *Harlem: The Making of a Ghetto, 1890–1930* (1966); and A. H. Spear, *Black Chicago: The Making of a Negro Ghetto, 1890–1920* (1967). The belief that nothing except time and education could solve the "Negro Problem" runs through the only book on the subject written by a muckraker, R. S. Baker, *Following the Color Line* (1908). Why Baker felt this way is partially explained in I. A. Newby, *Jim Crow's Defense: Anti-Negro Thought in America, 1900–1930* (1965). On DuBois, see his *Autobiography* (1968); and the biographies by F. L. Broderick (1959), and E. M. Rudwick (2nd ed., 1968), both in paperback. The official history of one influential organization is C. F. Kellogg, *NAACP* (vol. I, 1967, covers 1909–1920). See also A. E. Strickland, *History of the Chicago Urban League* (1966). E. M. Rudwick, *Race Riot at East St. Louis, July 2, 1917* (1964), is full and horrifying. The best work on Garvey is E. D. Cronon, *Black Moses* (1955). Walter White, *A Man Called White* (1948), is the memoir of the head of the NAACP in the New Deal era. Particularly useful for black history of a rather neglected period is *The Negro in Depression and War: Prelude to Revolution, 1930–1945* (1969), a collection of historical writings edited by Bernard Sternsher. One dreadful case is fully studied by D. T. Carter, *Scottsboro* (1969); see also Wilson Record, *The Negro and the Communist Party* (1951). Robert Shogan and Tom Craig, *The Detroit Race Riot* (1964), is a vivid account of the worst racial incident of the Second World War. A fresh monograph is R. M. Dalfiume, *Desegregation of the U.S. Armed Forces, 1939–1953* (1969).

On the desegregation decision, see the collection of documents edited by B. M. Ziegler, *Desegregation and the Supreme Court* (1958).

Efforts of southern whites to find social science arguments against desegregation are described by I. A. Newby, *Challenge to the Court, 1954–1966* (1967). The first decade following the Supreme Court's decision is described by Benjamin Muse, *Ten Years of Prelude* (1964). Manifestations of changed black attitudes are described in many books, but note especially Dan Wakefield, *Revolt in the South* (1960); L. E. Lomax, *The Negro Revolt* (1962); and C. E. Lincoln, *Black Muslims in America* (1961). On Martin Luther King, Jr., the best study is D. L. Lewis, *King: A Critical Biography* (1970). Howard Zinn, *SNCC: The New Abolitionists* (1964), treats the early period of one militant civil rights group. Russell Barrett, *Integration at Ole Miss* (1965), is the best work on one important subject. The growing impatience of black students is shown in *The Middle-Class Negro in the White Man's World* (2nd ed., 1969), by Eli Ginzberg and others. See also Ray Marshall, *The Negro and Organized Labor* (1965); and *The Negro and the American Labor Movement* (1968), edited by Julius Jacobson. James Baldwin, *Nobody Knows My Name* (1961), is an eloquent statement by a major black writer. See also R. A. Bone, *The Negro Novel in America* (2nd ed., 1969); and Edward Margolies, *Native Sons* (1968), a study of 20th century black American authors, beginning with DuBois.

Background on Puerto Rico is found in R. G. Tugwell, *The Stricken Land* (1947), by the World War II governor; and Thomas Mathews, *Puerto Rican Politics and the New Deal* (1960). *Puerto Rican Journey: New York's Newest Immigrants* (1950), by C. W. Mills and others, is an early account of the big postwar migration. Excellent journalistic works are Christopher Rand, *The Puerto Ricans* (1958), which compares life in Puerto Rico with New York; and Dan Wakefield, *Island in the City* (1959), a description of East Harlem. C. O. Senior, *The Puerto Ricans* (1965), is a brief but moving description. Sociological studies of poverty in this group are P. C. Sexton, *Spanish Harlem* (1965); and two works by Oscar Lewis, *La Vida* (1966), and *A Study of Slum Culture: Backgrounds for La Vida* (1968). An interesting comparative work is Oscar Handlin, *The New-comers: Negroes and Puerto Ricans in a Changing Metropolis* (1959).

A moving study of the Spanish-speaking people of 19th-century California is Leonard Pitt, *The Decline of the Californios* (1966). Carey McWilliams, *North from Mexico* (2nd ed., 1961), is an excellent survey; it may now be supplemented by Stan Steiner, *La Raza: The Mexican Americans* (1970). An earlier work of continuing interest is Manuel Gamio, *Mexican Immigration to the United States* (1930). Ernesto Galarza, *Merchants of Labor: The Mexican Bracero Story* (1964), is focused on California. *La Raza: Forgotten Americans* (1966), edited by Julian Samora, is a collection of scholarly essays. The best work on Cesar Chavez is Peter Matthiessen, *Sal Si Puedes* (1969). Studies of Mexican Americans in Texas include P. S. Taylor, *An American-Mexican Frontier* (1934); P. R. Kibbe, *Latin Americans in Texas* (1946); and William Madsen, *Mexican-Americans of South Texas* (1964). Essential for an understanding of the Mexican "culture of poverty" is Oscar Lewis, *Children of Sanchez* (1961).

On American Indians, the chief general works are H. E. Driver, *Indians of North America* (2nd ed., 1969); W. T. Hagan, *American Indians* (1961); and A. M. Josephy, Jr., *The Indian Heritage of America* (1968). *The Indian in America's Past* (1964), edited by J. D. Forbes, is a handy documentary collection. Both narrative and documents are in E. H. Spicer, *A Short History of the Indians of the United States* (1969). Among the many studies of the plight of the modern-day Indian note especially W. H. Blumenthal, *American Indians Dispossessed* (1955); L. C. Kelly, *The Navajo Indians and Federal Indian Policy, 1900–1935* (1968); and Edmund Wilson, *Apologies to the Iroquois* (1960), by a distinguished literary critic. *Our Brother's Keeper: The Indian in White America* (1969), edited by E. S. Cahn, is an important collection of writings. On the new mood of militancy, see especially Stan Steiner, *The New Indians* (1967); and Vine Deloria, Jr., *Custer Died for Your Sins: An Indian Manifesto* (1969).

On the Japanese exclusion movement, the basic monograph is Roger Daniels, *The Politics of Prejudice* (1962). On Japanese-Americans in general, see Carey McWilliams, *Prejudice* (1944); and Bill Hosokawa, *Nisei: The Quiet Americans* (1969). A. W. Lind, *Hawaii's Japanese* (1946), is a sociological study. Standard on the evacuation is a three-volume set edited by D. S. Thomas: D. S. Thomas and Richard Nishimoto, *The Spoilage* (1946); D. S. Thomas and others, *The Salvage* (1952); and Jacobus ten Broek and others, *Prejudice, War, and the Constitution* (1954). Other books on the evacuation include Morton Grodzins, *Americans Betrayed* (1949); A. R. Bosworth, *America's Concentration Camps* (1967); and Audrie Girdner and Anne Loftis, *The Great Betrayal* (1969). Of the many books on Japanese-American participation in the army, one of the most moving is T. D. Murphy, *Ambassadors in Arms: The Story of Hawaii's 100th Battalion* (1954).

30

THE GREAT SOCIETY

AND THE

NEW FEDERALISM

Civil Rights · Urban Riots · Death of King · Student Revolts ·
Escalation in Vietnam · Peace Efforts · The Arab-Israeli War · Elections
of 1966 and 1968 · Nixon · The Menace of Inflation · Minority Groups ·
Law and Order · Men on the Moon · A New Foreign Policy?

Although renamed "the great society," the legislative objectives of the Johnson administration after the election of 1964 continued with little alteration the program of "the new frontier." Backed by a commanding majority in both houses of Congress and a strong consensus on the part of the people, the President was able to push through a series of broad measures in the fields of social welfare and education, many of them designed to promote what he called a "war on poverty." On March 9, 1965, he signed the Appalachia Aid Act, which appropriated $1.1 billion to fight poverty in the backward mountain areas from southern Pennsylvania into the deep South. On July 30 following, he signed into law a health insurance plan, usually called Medi-

care, for persons sixty-five years of age or older. One part of this program, financed by a payroll tax, covered hospital and convalescence costs; another, effective a year later, provided, in return for a $3 a month voluntary payment, many other health services, including 80 per cent of the fees charged by physicians. Meantime an Elementary and Secondary Education Act had appropriated $1.3 billion in aid for schools where the children of low-income families were concentrated, with incidental benefits to parochial as well as public schools. Later in the year the President approved a college-aid bill that made possible substantial scholarships for needy undergraduates.

Other anti-poverty measures brought retirement protection to 94 per cent of all persons aged sixty-five or over, increased social security benefits by 7 per cent, and,

SYMBOLS OF PROTEST. *Two demonstrators make the peace and strike symbols.*

with state cooperation, provided unemployment insurance to about 80 per cent of the nation's salary and wage earners. Congress also established a Job Corps, analogous to the CCC of the New Deal but under civilian control, for the vocational education of unemployed youths; a Neighborhood Youth Corps for special work-training in impoverished localities; a Domestic Peace Corps to support volunteer workers in depressed areas; and a Project Head Start to bring pre-school training to children of the culturally deprived.

Nor was that all. Congress created a new Department of Housing and Urban Development, with a seat in the Cabinet; authorized $3.3 billion to be used over a period of five years for the renovation of depressed areas and regions; instituted federal rent subsidies for low-income tenants of new housing projects; provided assistance to low-income owners who wished to improve their dwellings; and expanded its Food Stamp program of 1964 for aid to needy families. The administration of these programs, which to some extent overlapped, Congress assigned to various existing departments and to a new Office of Economic Opportunity.

Civil Rights

Among the poorest of the poor were the southern black people, whose ability to help themselves was greatly lessened by state restrictions on their right to vote. To deal with this situation, Congress in August, 1965, passed a Voting Rights Act, which put an end to the literacy test, so commonly used to deprive Negroes of their franchise, and authorized federal officials to register voters in states and localities where less than half the population of voting age was registered or had voted in the November, 1964, election. A protest march from Selma, Alabama, to the state capital, Montgomery, held in March, 1965, dramatized the situation. Organized and led by the

Reverend Martin Luther King, Jr., the Selma demonstration attracted civil rights workers, both black and white, from all over the nation. Night riders, probably members of the Ku Klux Klan, murdered one of the participants, Mrs. Viola Liuzzo of Detroit, Michigan; twice all-white juries refused to convict her alleged murderer. Next year, when James Meredith undertook a civil rights walk by himself through Mississippi, he was shot, but not killed. A march undertaken in his name the following June showed the growing antipathy of the Negroes for the southern whites, and the little reliance some now placed upon non-violence. It seemed evident, as once before during Reconstruction, that only the power of the federal government could enforce Negro voting rights in the South.

Urban Riots

While northern Negroes usually could vote, they suffered from other types of discrimination, particularly in employment, in housing, and in schooling. This condition

Martin Luther King, Jr., *leading the protest march from Selma to Montgomery, Alabama in 1965.*

The Newark Riot. *A black boy lies wounded after being shot in the riot of 1967.*

was by no means new, but it had worsened radically since World War II. Many of the blacks involved were recent emigrés from the South, where labor-saving devices such as cotton-picking machines had robbed them of the only kind of work they knew how to do. They had come to the northern cities seeking jobs or, if they failed in that, welfare payments. With the Negroes jammed together in the poorest sections of the cities, their chronic discontent led to serious explosions, the first of which occurred in the Watts area of Los Angeles, during August, 1965. Before the rioting ended, thirty-four persons had lost their lives, over a thousand others had suffered injury, and nearly 4,000 were in jail. Property losses ran to an estimated $40 million. Only by the use of units of the California National Guard was order restored. That same summer similar outbreaks occurred in many other cities, including Chicago, San Diego, Hartford, and Springfield, Massachusetts.

Summer rioting in the Negro sections of American cities became frighteningly common. Almost invariably the trouble began with some incident on a hot night — the shooting of a car-thief suspect as in Atlanta, or police efforts to remove demonstrators from a municipal building as in Boston, or a rumor that the police had beaten up a Negro cab-driver as in Newark, New Jersey. The Newark riot (July, 1967) was on a scale comparable to the Watts disorder and required 3,000 national guardsmen to suppress. That same month in Detroit both state and federal troops were called in to end the rioting. In Cleveland, Ohio, on the night of July 23–24, 1968, the cause of the disorder was ominously different — a premeditated rifle attack by some Black Nationalists on a police detachment that led to the death of four Negroes and three policemen. The incident touched off an explosion of racial tension in which burning and looting caused $1.5 million property loss. Fortunately, the skillful handling of the situation by Mayor Carl B. Stokes, a Negro, promoted the rapid restoration of order.

Dozens of American cities had similar experiences; every urban area with a large black population could only wonder when its turn would come. Invariably the rioters blamed police brutality as the immediate cause for the Negro outbreaks, and white prejudice and white bigotry for the underlying conditions that made rioting inevitable.

Death of King

In Memphis, Tennessee, a prolonged strike, mainly by Negro garbage workers, took on a strongly racist tinge. Martin Luther King, Jr., still preaching and practicing the doctrine of nonviolence, came to lead a demonstration on behalf of the strikers. But extremists turned what he had intended to be a peaceful march into a rock-throwing, burning, looting orgy that resulted in one death and many injuries and arrests, and brought both the police and the national guard into action. While pondering his next move, King was killed by a rifle shot, April 4, 1968, as he stood on the balcony of a local motel. His death shocked the nation hardly less than the assassination of President Kennedy four and one-half years earlier. The death of King precipitated outbreaks of violence in at least 125 American cities. The worst rioting occurred in Baltimore, Chicago, Kansas City, and Washington, which, according to one observer, took on the appearance of "the besieged capital of a banana republic."

At the time of his death King had already made plans for a Poor People's March on Washington, and his successor, the Reverend Ralph D. Abernathy, undertook to carry forward the program. With the permission of capital officials, Abernathy erected a camp in West Potomac Park to accommodate the hundreds of marchers who began to arrive in mid-May. Heavy rains turned the camp grounds into a quag-

mire and made "Resurrection City" into a miserable place for the blacks, whites, Mexican Americans, Indians, and Puerto Ricans who tried to live there. On June 19 some 55,000 persons marched from the Washington Monument to the Lincoln Memorial, where they listened to impassioned protests against the existence of poverty and discrimination in affluent America. Abernathy then led some of his followers to Capitol Hill, where, like the leaders of Coxey's Army three-quarters of a century before, they were arrested for trespass and briefly jailed.

In general the city disturbances of the 1960's were the result of spontaneous combustion rather than organized planning. The NAACP remained, despite much provocation, studiously nonviolent, as did also the Southern Christian Leadership Conference (SCLC), of which Martin Luther King, Jr., had been president. But the advocates of "black power," as defined by

Coretta King. *Martin Luther King's widow at her husband's funeral in Atlanta, Georgia, April 10, 1968.*

Stokely Carmichael and H. Rap Brown of the Student Nonviolent Coordinating Committee (SNCC), urged Negroes to abandon nonviolence and use arms, if necessary, to obtain equal rights. With this point of view CORE also seemed to agree when it joined SNCC in the rejection of white members. So also did such other Negro orders as the Black Muslims and the Black Panthers. To these militants, the summer riots were but "dress rehearsals for revolution," but to Negro moderates black power could be best interpreted as black influence or black pride. Whatever the methods, most blacks agreed that members of their race should no longer accept an inferior status, but should combine forces to better their lot. It was a great misfortune that the death of Martin Luther King, Jr., had robbed the moderates of their most potent voice.

The Kerner Report

The racial violence that occurred during the summer of 1967 led President Johnson to appoint (July 27, 1967) a National Advisory Commission headed by Governor Otto Kerner of Illinois to "investigate the origins of the recent disorders in our cities" and to recommend ways "to prevent or contain such disorders in the future." In its first report the following month the Commission urged an increase of the number of Negroes in the National Guard and the special training of guardsmen for riot duty. Its final report in 1968 was the work of a staff of 150 full-time investigators and ran to 240,000 words. The verdict of the bipartisan Commission was that white racism was mainly responsible for the fact that the nation was moving rapidly toward two mutually hostile societies, "one black, one white, separate but unequal." Thanks to persistent white indifference toward Negro needs, the Negro ghettos suffered from poor educational and recreational opportunities, from inferior housing, from unemployment due to job discrimination,

from discontent brought on by the persistent advertising of unattainable luxury goods, and the like. Furthermore, few Negroes put much faith in the impartiality of the police or in white justice, or for that matter in the awareness of white businessmen of Negroes' needs. Even moderate Negroes believed that the rioting had served a useful purpose in making the whites aware of the intolerable conditions in the ghettos. Most Negroes, the report said, still accepted the idea of integration, but for a vocal minority the appeal of black nationalism — black power — was irresistible. The commission subsidized other studies of violence in America whose conclusions shocked many Americans into an acute awareness of growing dangers to the social fabric.

Student Revolts

The minority ethnic groups were not alone in voicing protests against "The Establishment" and its dominant institutions in American life. The generation gap — youth against maturity — seemed also to be widening. College students, a few of whom had left their campuses to participate in civil rights demonstrations in the South, began to challenge academic authority. At the University of California, Berkeley, a Free Speech Movement, sparked in the fall of 1964 by regulations that forbade on-campus political fund-raising, kept the campus in a turmoil for the remainder of the academic year. On one occasion sit-in demonstrators blocked an administration building until about 700 of them were arrested and hauled off to jail. The ferment spread quickly to other institutions, with every aspect of the educational process coming under attack. Students and their collaborators complained that classes were too large, access to teachers too difficult, courses irrelevant to problems of the modern world, rules too puerile for young adults to tolerate. At some universities the

Riot at Berkeley. *A student is carried off by the police in the University of California, Berkeley, riots of 1969.*

fact that the authorities gave out student grades for draft boards to use in deciding on student deferments aroused student wrath. Organized protests against the war in Vietnam became frequent and occasionally violent. On many campuses armed-forces recruiting officers endured much harassment, while the personnel representatives of corporations that engaged in the production of war materials fared even worse. In the spring of 1968 student and non-student violence all but shut down Columbia University and forced the resignation of President Grayson Kirk.

Those who sought to understand such behavior pointed to the undemocratic character of many university administrations. Columbia, for example, denied even the faculty the right of participation in the making of university policy. Disorders at Harvard and Cornell in the spring of 1969 were touched off by the demands of black students and their supporters for special autonomous programs in black studies. At Cambridge police action against students brought about serious division among administration, faculty, and students and, for a time, threatened to disrupt Harvard. At Ithaca blacks emerged fully armed from a building they had seized; news photographs of the scene seemed to confirm the worst fears of those who felt that law and order had broken down. The unresponsiveness to social change of bureaucracies in general, whether in education, or in business, or in government (particularly law enforcement), unquestionably had much to do with fomenting student unrest.

"Hippies"

If anything, the off-campus revolt of youth was even more pronounced than that of college students. Many young people chose to dramatize their opposition to the middle-class standards of their elders in a variety of ways. Crowds of them clustered around every sizable campus to join in the student demonstrations and to voice their disapproval of "the square world." Many of the dissidents (or "hippies" as they were usually called) were the children of affluent parents, but they questioned the goals that their predecessors had set for themselves, wealth in particular. Why, they asked, should a man work his life away in the service of some money-mad corporation? Or become a fifth-wheel bureaucrat? Or a time-serving politician? Was not the whole establishment that ran society shot through with corruption and hypocrisy? Why should young people consider themselves bound by its antiquated moral codes? Or its conventions of dress, hygiene, and behavior?

The revolt of the students and the hippies rubbed off on many of the more conventional youth of the nation. The use of narcotics, particularly marijuana, became widespread. The old moralities declined, particularly with the increasing ease of birth control. Traditional religion, despite such bizarre innovations as "rock-and-roll" masses, lost ground. A few young men of draft age burned their draft cards, or fled to Canada, or went to jail rather than to fight for what they regarded as an unjust cause in Vietnam. Even so, there were optimists among the older generation, some of whom found reason for hope in youth's challenge of tradition, its condemnation of adult hypocrisy, its emphasis on the rights of the individual, its search for new values. Out of this ferment, they claimed, might come substantial rewards.

Escalation in Vietnam

The changes in attitude of American youth came against a background of steady escalation of the war in Vietnam. To many

Americans the President appeared to have abandoned the policy of limited involvement that he had advocated during the campaign of 1964 in favor of using unrestrained military power. While American ground troops did not in fact invade North Vietnam and American air forces tried not to bomb civilian targets, American troops increasingly took over from South Vietnam the main responsibility for the fighting in the south, and American bombers, operating from aircraft carriers and from land bases as far away as Guam, stepped up their activities on both sides of the Seventeenth Parallel. Guerrilla fighting, as conducted by the Viet Cong and their North Vietnamese allies, depended mainly on hit-and-run tactics. There were no general engagements and few operations involving more than small detachments of troops.

In an effort to counterbalance the continuous infiltration of North Vietnamese troops and to bolster up the fighting spirit of the South Vietnamese, the United States increased its fighting forces in the Vietnam area to 381,000 by the end of 1966 and to 525,000 by the spring of 1968. Besides these troops, South Korea committed 45,000 effective fighting men, and Australia, the Philippines, Thailand, and New Zealand small detachments each. The South Vietnamese soldiers numbered an additional 700,000, but the South Vietnamese were rarely as effective fighters as their North Vietnamese adversaries. This was in part because of the rampant corruption, both in the South Vietnamese army itself and in the unstable South Vietnamese government, but corruption was but a single element in the basic weakness of leadership.

"Hawks" vs. "Doves"

Americans grew steadily more critical of President Johnson's leadership of the war. At one extreme were the "hawks" who demanded an even greater military effort. To them, the loss of South Vietnam to the

Communists would mean the inevitable loss of the other nations of Southeast Asia. Most of the military supplies used by the Viet Cong and the North Vietnamese came either from Red China or from the Soviet Union. While American bombers did not hesitate to raid the railroads leading from Red China, they carefully kept away from the great harbor of Haiphong lest the destruction of Soviet ships might bring the Soviet Union into the war. American airmen took care also to hit only the edges of the North Vietnamese capital, Hanoi, despite the enemy's practice of storing quantities of war materials in civilian areas. Some hawkish Americans favored the abolition of all bombing restrictions, the invasion of North Vietnam by ground troops, and even the employment of atomic weapons, if necessary to win the war.

At the other extreme were the "doves," who charged that American involvement in Vietnam was immoral and unjustified, or at best a mistake, for the combined resources of North Vietnam, Red China, and the Soviet Union would forever prevent an American victory. The distance from the United States, they argued, presented insoluble logistic problems; furthermore, the importance to the United States of keeping Southeast Asia out of the hands of the Communists was not great enough to warrant the expenditure of thousands of American lives, hundreds of American airplanes, and billions of American dollars. The most pacific of the doves favored the immediate withdrawal of all United States troops; the more moderate urged the American government to negotiate its way out of the dilemma on the best terms it could get. Opponents of the war also tended to believe that, with an end to the bombing, the North Vietnamese leader, Ho Chi Minh, would become independent of both Red China and the Soviet Union, somewhat after the pattern set by Marshal Tito in Yugoslavia.

The Tet Offensive

The comfortable assumption by most Americans that even if the United States could not win the war in Vietnam, at least it could not lose it, was rudely shaken by an unexpected enemy offensive launched January 30, 1968. Both sides had agreed to a thirty-six hour truce in celebration of "Tet," the lunar New Year, but the American command canceled it for the five northern provinces when intelligence reports told of a massive Communist build-up around Khesanh, an exposed northern outpost. The object of the Tet offensive, however, proved to be the principal South Vietnamese cities, all of which the Americans had up to this time believed to be relatively

The War in Vietnam. *A paratrooper of the 173rd Airborne Brigade gets a helping hand.*

safe from direct attack. To their surprise, no less than thirty provincial capitals, a number of district towns, and all the principal United States and South Vietnamese air bases experienced heavy rocket and mortar fire and the infiltration in large numbers of enemy troops. The bloodiest fighting occurred in Hué, the old imperial capital, which was almost destroyed, leaving more than 70 per cent of its inhabitants homeless. The damage to Saigon was also considerable, and produced nearly 40,000 refugees. It took weeks of hard fighting for the allied forces to redeem the attacked cities and installations, and even longer to regain the offensive. Total fatalities for the period ran to about 2,000 for the Americans and twice that number for the South Vietnamese. Estimates of enemy casualties ran as high as 50,000. By this time the United States had suffered as many casualties in Vietnam as it had in Korea during the 1950's. It was now clear that as long as the Viet Cong and the North Vietnamese would fight, the Soviet Union and Red China would supply them with the materials they needed. Most Americans were ready to concede that the only way out of the impasse would be through negotiation.

Peace Efforts

While the doves regularly denounced President Johnson and Secretary Rusk as hawks, President Johnson had from the beginning accompanied his escalation of the war with offers of peace negotiations "without pre-conditions." As a means to this end he suspended the bombing of North Vietnam for five days in mid-May, 1965, and for thirty-seven days in December, 1965–January, 1966. But President Ho Chi Minh rejected all such offers. As he viewed it, the United States was an aggressor against the Vietnamese people, and unconditional American withdrawal was the only road to peace. Efforts of U Thant, Secretary General of the United Nations, and of Pope Paul VI to get the warring sides together likewise came to naught. The North Vietnamese government would not even acknowledge that it had troops in South Vietnam.

Finally, on March 31, 1968, after Johnson had unconditionally ended the bombing of all North Vietnam above the Twentieth Parallel, Ho agreed to discussions. Representatives of the two governments met in Paris the following month, with Averell Harriman the chief negotiator for the United States and Xuan Thuy (who insisted that the purpose of the talks was the "unconditional cessation of U.S. bombing raids and other acts of war") for North Vietnam. For months the talks consisted of little more than mutual recriminations. The United States demanded that North Vietnam, in return for the complete cessation of all bombing north of the Seventeenth Parallel, should offer some *quid pro quo*, but President Ho's emissaries refused to make any concessions until after the bombing ceased. On October 31, 1968, Johnson gave in to this demand.

Unlike the earlier defense of South Korea, which won United Nations approval, the involvement of the United States in Vietnam had little world support. Some NATO members, France in particular, were hostile to American action in Vietnam. While many Britons opposed American intervention, their government stood steadfastly by its ally in policy, even if sending no troops to help.

The position of the United States in Europe also deteriorated. President de Gaulle of France, in his determination to promote French leadership in continental Europe, not only used his power to keep Great Britain out of the Common Market, but in 1966 withdrew all French troops from NATO control and ordered NATO to remove its headquarters from French soil. The Allies speedily transferred SHAPE to Belgium and revised their plans for the defense of Europe. De Gaulle also courted the USSR openly, visiting Moscow in the summer of 1966, Poland in 1967, and Rumania in 1968. In a deliberate affront to what he called the "Anglo-Saxon powers," he visited French Canada in July, 1967, and in a Montreal speech echoed the battlecry of the French Canadian separatists for "*Quebec Libre.*" In France his policies were admired by some and at least condoned by the majority. Following his suppression of a widespread revolt of French students and workers in May, 1968, he called a Parliamentary election and won an overwhelming victory. The following year, however, he staked his office on a plebiscite, and lost. His former premier, Georges Pompidou, succeeded him.

The Arab-Israeli War

Meantime a six days' war between Israel and its Arab neighbors in June, 1967, added to the world's tensions. President Nasser of Egypt brought on the hostilities, perhaps unintentionally, by demanding the withdrawal of the United Nations peace-keeping forces that for ten years had guarded the UAR-Israeli border. Nasser may have been bluffing, but when the UN acceded to his demand, the Israeli government on the morning of June 5 used its military planes to destroy all nineteen of Egypt's airfields and most of its aircraft. In the ground fighting that followed the Egyptian troops were helpless against the superior morale and training of the Israelis, who overran and held the entire Sinai peninsula. Similarly one-sided fighting pushed the Jordanian forces eastward across the Jordan River and routed the Syrians out of the high terrain from which they had long harassed their Israeli neighbors. Only after the Israeli troops had won a complete victory did their government heed the demands of the UN to cease fire.

Throughout the discussions that followed in the UN Security Council, it was ap-

The Arab-Israeli War. *An Israeli tank entering Syria during the Arab-Israeli war in June, 1962.*

parent that the Soviet Union and its allies regarded the Arab defeat as a blow to their prestige, as indeed it was, for they had deliberately armed and backed Nasser. They demanded that the Israeli forces retreat to their prewar frontiers, but despite UN pressure towards this goal, the victors stood their ground. Again, as in 1956, the cessation of fighting brought no formal peace, while this time the Suez Canal remained closed to all commerce. The humiliation of the Arab nations left the Soviet leaders very resentful toward the United States and Great Britain, whom they blamed for the Israeli victory.

American-Soviet Relations

Nevertheless, there were increasing signs that the desire of the United States to live in peace with the USSR was being reciprocated. The growing rift between Red China and the Soviet Union showed itself in the tendency of each to blame the other for not adequately supporting North Vietnam and by a series of border skirmishes between small units of their armed forces in remote areas. Quite possibly, Soviet leaders may have decided to be more conciliatory toward the rest of the world in view of their troubles with China. The Soviets agreed in December, 1967, on a treaty to prevent the use of nuclear weapons in outer space. Next year they signed a treaty that would obligate non-nuclear powers not to produce or receive nuclear weapons, the nuclear powers promising in return to make available to other nations the full peaceful benefits of atomic energy and to seek effective limitations on armament.

Some of the ground thus gained was lost in August, 1968, when armed forces of the Soviet Union, East Germany, Poland, Hungary, and Bulgaria suddenly invaded Czechoslovakia. The experiment in "liberal" communism which the Czechs had launched in January, 1968, was crushed by military force. Significantly, the United States government did not react in the traditional cold war manner; it protested, as did the governments of Yugoslavia and Rumania and the Communist parties of many countries of the world, but it made no significant changes in its defense or foreign policies as a result of the Czech invasion.

Elections of 1966

The involvement of the Johnson administration in so many serious problems both at home and abroad cost it heavily in popularity. The anti-poverty program revealed many flaws and failed to achieve all its intended goals; the Negroes, despite their civil rights gains, still found themselves the victims of social and economic discrimination; southern whites who resented the civil rights efforts of the federal government joined northern whites who blamed the blacks for "crime in the streets" to produce an anti-Negro "backlash" that seriously undermined the party in power. Above all, discontent with the war in Vietnam mounted steadily; hawks demanded stronger measures that would win the war in a hurry, while doves demanded every degree of retreat.

Not surprisingly, the Republicans made substantial gains in the mid-term elections of 1966. When the results were in, the Democrats still maintained control of both houses of Congress, but the Republicans had gained four seats in the Senate and forty-seven in the House, thus making possible the revival of the old conservative coalition of southern Democrats and northern Republicans, through which progressive legislation could be blocked at will. In the states the Republicans also did well; the total number of Democratic governors declined from thirty-three to twenty-four.

Johnson and Congress

The Johnson administration found the new Congress far less cooperative than its predecessor and during its last two years made little headway toward "the great society." Also, the heavy expenditures required for the anti-poverty measures and the Vietnam war, working together with a tax cut in 1964, unbalanced the national budget more seriously with each passing year. In consequence the country had begun to experience great inflation; wages were up, sometimes in response to strikes, and prices rose higher and higher. Furthermore, the balance of payments problem was beginning to get out of hand; by the summer of 1968 the amount of gold remaining in the national treasury had dropped to under $11 billion. Congress, therefore, although approving the requested defense expenditures, severely cut foreign aid, balked at many of the President's requests for other new appropriations, and delayed the 10 per cent surtax on incomes by which he proposed to finance them and to cool off the economy. When finally at its second session it agreed to the additional tax, it did so only on condition that the President must cut his annual budget by $6 billion. Bitter criticism of Lyndon Johnson for his over-optimistic pronouncements about the progress of the war in Vietnam and for the "weaknesses" many detected in his domestic program indicated how swiftly the political atmosphere had changed.

The failure of the United States to secure the release of eighty-two officers and crew of one of its spy ships, the *Pueblo*, captured by the North Koreans far from their shores, January 23, 1968, was deemed by many critics as typical of the administration's impotence. Not until late in December, after the fall elections, did the American government secure the release of the captives. The ship and all its secret equipment were never returned.

Johnson suddenly announced on March 31, 1968, that he would not be a candidate

to succeed himself. He did this at the same time that he ordered the restriction of American bombing in North Vietnam to the area south of the Twentieth Parallel, and deliberately linked the two together, thus emphasizing that by freeing himself from political obligations he would be able to pursue more intently the cause of peace.

Election of 1968

This important decision resulted in a wild scramble for the Democratic nomination. Already two candidates had made known their intention to wrest the nomination away from Johnson. As far back as November, 1967, Senator Eugene McCarthy of Minnesota, a vigorous opponent of American involvement in Vietnam, had declared his candidacy. Following McCarthy's victory over the President in the New Hampshire primary, Senator Robert F. Kennedy, another Vietnam critic, announced his own

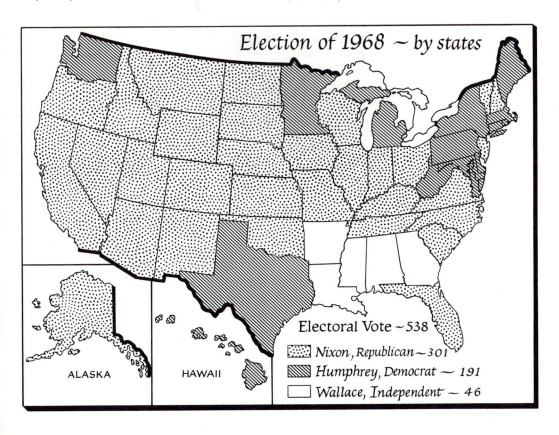

Election of 1968 ~ by states

ALASKA   HAWAII

Electoral Vote ~ 538

Nixon, Republican ~ 301
Humphrey, Democrat ~ 191
Wallace, Independent ~ 46

candidacy. After the President's renunciation, Vice-President Humphrey threw his hat into the ring, but by this time it was too late for him to file in any of the presidential primaries. Following the California primary (June 4, 1968), in which Kennedy narrowly defeated McCarthy, came the assassination of Kennedy by an Arab nationalist who deplored the Senator's sympathetic attitude toward the Israeli government. This monstrous deed left the contest for the nomination to McCarthy and Humphrey.

The growing dissatisfaction with the Vietnam war and with President Johnson gave the Republicans good reason to believe that they could win in 1968. From the disaster of 1964 they had learned that they must broaden their appeal to include all factions of the party, not the ultra conservatives alone. Former Vice-President Richard M. Nixon early emerged as the leading contender for the nomination. When the Republicans held their convention in Miami, August 5–9, Nixon won easily on the first ballot. For second place on the ticket he recommended the relatively unknown Governor Spiro T. Agnew of Maryland, passing over such liberal celebrities as Governor George Romney of Michigan, for whom 178 delegates actually voted in protest against Nixon's choice. But the convention ended in a high degree of harmony, with all contenders pledging support to the Nixon-Agnew ticket.

After Kennedy's death McCarthy continued his active campaign for the nomination and drew to his standard a remarkable collection of college students and intellectuals who opposed the "establishment" and the Vietnam war. But he failed to win over the entire Kennedy faction, part of which went to Humphrey and part to Senator George McGovern of South Dakota, a dove. At their convention, held in Chicago, August 26–30, the Democrats nominated Humphrey on the first ballot and chose as

his running-mate Senator Edmund S. Muskie of Maine, who had been little known outside his own state. The Democratic convention was marred by scenes of wild disorder in several parts of the city, as protestors clashed with Chicago police and Illinois National Guard. No one was killed, but many youths were badly beaten up and the image of "police brutality" was indelibly impressed on the TV audience.

The campaign aroused far less enthusiasm than most of its predecessors; a poll taken after it was well along found 56 per cent of the voters wishing that they had someone else to vote for. Some excitement was provided by the candidacy of former Governor George C. Wallace of Alabama. Wallace was an unabashed demagogue who denounced in colorful language the federal usurpation of states' rights, the desegregationist stand of the Warren Supreme Court, the untrustworthiness of all "pointy-headed" intellectuals, and the failure of the administration to use strong enough measures to win the war in Vietnam. To the surprise of most party regulars, he won enough national support to get his third party ticket on the ballot in every state, usually as the American Independent Party. Before election day there seemed to be a real danger that the Wallace vote might deny both Nixon and Humphrey a victory in the electoral college, but in the end the Alabama fire-eater carried only five southern states, Georgia, Alabama, Mississippi, Louisiana, and Arkansas, with a total of 45 electors. Nixon won thirty-two states (some by very narrow pluralities) with 302 electoral votes, while Humphrey carried thirteen states and the District of Columbia, with a total of 191 votes. One North Carolina elector, however, although instructed for Nixon, voted for Wallace, making the vote as cast 301 for Nixon, 191 for Humphrey, and 46 for Wallace. In the popular vote of about 72 million the difference between the totals amassed by the two leading candidates was just under 500,000 votes. Some 43.4 per cent of the voters had cast their ballots for Nixon to 42.7 per cent for Humphrey and 13.5 for Wallace. Nixon's winning vote in 1968 was about 3 million less than his losing vote in 1960 and he failed to carry a single large city.

The full impact of the election was more decisive than the split vote might seem to indicate. The fact that an overwhelming majority, both in the electoral college and in the popular vote, had cast their ballots against the Democratic candidate made it evident that the Johnson policies, for which Humphrey stood, had lost their appeal. The people were tired of the war in Vietnam, and at home they seemed to prefer "law and order" in the cities to further steps in the direction of the "great society."

Nixon

Richard Milhous Nixon (1913–   ), 37th President of the United States, took office with a somewhat obscure mandate. Most Americans hoped that he would somehow bring to an end the involvement of the United States in the Vietnam War, although there was no unanimity about how he was expected to achieve this. The voters apparently relied on him to re-establish law and order in troubled parts of the country, although it was not clear what part the nation's President could play in this situation. At least some of the voters hoped that the Nixon administration would solve a number of acute domestic problems — racial discrimination, inflation, poverty, and social instability. Again, there was no general agreement about how these pressing matters could be settled; indeed, extremely conservative elements in his own party seemed to prefer that he not even try to deal with them. The Republican Party, while still basically conservative under the Congressional leadership of Senator Everett McKinley Dirksen of Illinois and Representative Gerald Ford of Michigan, contained an

increasingly vocal liberal minority of urban-oriented spokesmen, including about a dozen Senators and nearly that many Governors. It is significant that when Dirksen died on September 7, 1969, the Republican Senators voted to replace him with a moderate, Hugh Scott of Pennsylvania.

The Nixon Cabinet

Nixon's cabinet appointments all went to Republicans but they illustrated the wide variety of viewpoints present in the party. Secretary of State William P. Rogers was a firm supporter of the Paris peace negotiations with the North Vietnamese, although the new chief American negotiator was the veteran hawk and former ambassador to South Vietnam, Henry Cabot Lodge. Secretary of Defense Melvin R. Laird had been an outspoken supporter of the war and friend of the military establishment while serving as a Congressman from Wisconsin. Attorney-General John Mitchell, a member of Nixon's New York law firm, and Secretary of the Treasury David Kennedy, a Chicago banker, were considered conservative on domestic issues, especially where public spending was concerned. But the cabinet included a number of people who were concerned with the solution of urgent social problems, notably Secretary of Health, Education, and Welfare Robert Finch; Secretary of Housing and Urban Development George Romney; and Secretary of Transportation John A. Volpe; significantly, all three were former state officials new to the national political scene. James Farmer, Assistant Secretary of Health, Education, and Welfare, was the highest-ranking Negro appointee in the Nixon Administration.

Nixon made three other major appointments of special advisers, since he was determined to have coordination in his policies through powerful individuals working within the office of the President. Professor Arthur H. Burns of Columbia, head of the

Council of Economic Advisors under Eisenhower, was named as Counselor to the President (a new post holding cabinet status) and was subsequently named to head the Federal Reserve Board. Professor Henry Kissinger of Harvard was appointed special adviser on national security affairs. Just how important a role he was to play was publicly demonstrated when the President took him, as well as Secretary of State Rogers, along on Nixon's first presidential trip to Europe, an eight-day journey which featured stops in Brussels, London, Bonn, Berlin, Rome, and Paris. The third appointee was the most unusual of all, Daniel Patrick Moynihan, a liberal Democrat, as special adviser on urban affairs. Moynihan, Director of the Joint Center for Urban Studies of the Massachusetts Institute of Technology and Harvard University, was a colorful and controversial student of social problems. To him would fall the job of coordinating the several urban affairs programs of the various parts of the federal government.

The End of the Warren Court

To Nixon fell the task of replacing Chief Justice Earl Warren, who had resigned effective June 30, 1969. As Warren's successor President Nixon picked Judge Warren Burger, member of the United States Court of Appeals for the District of Columbia circuit since 1956. Burger, 61 years old, was known as a critic of some of the Supreme Court's recent decisions upholding the rights of defendants in criminal cases, and thus his appointment was welcomed by those who felt that the Supreme Court was making the task of law enforcement officers too difficult. However, Burger was also known as a vigorous supporter of civil rights and thus his appointment did not upset those who feared that the newly acquired rights of Negroes would be endangered.

Warren had originally resigned in June, 1968, in a letter to President Johnson, giving as his reason his advanced age (77). Many people believed that he took this action less because of his age than because he wished Johnson to appoint his successor. In choosing Warren to be Chief Justice of the United States, President Eisenhower had hoped that the California governor's calm temperament and his proven administrative ability would enable him to unite a badly torn Supreme Court. This task Warren accomplished with skill, but to Eisenhower's surprise and displeasure the new Chief Justice influenced the Court in a decidedly liberal direction. Not content merely to point the way toward desegregation in the schools, in public accommodations, and in housing, the Warren Court undertook also to eliminate the "third degree" methods commonly attributed to the police in dealing with suspected criminals and to insure the right of all defendants to a fair trial. This attitude on the part of the Court was not without certain social and ethnic overtones. The great majority of those who were accused of crime were without financial means and a disproportionate share of them were either blacks or members of some other minority group.

Another series of Warren Court decisions decreed that legislative districts, including those for the election of members to the national House of Representatives, to both houses of bicameral state legislatures, and even to city councils, must be apportioned according to population on the principle of "one man, one vote" to ensure equal representation. The most important effect of these decisions was to reduce the over-representation of rural areas, both in state and nation, and to give the great urban centers the voting power that their numbers merited. Only the United States Senate was beyond the reach of the Court, since the Constitution provides "that no state, without its consent, shall be deprived of equal representation in the Senate."

Warren's decisions were anathema to extreme conservatives of all sections and parties. The Court was denounced for its evident intention to promote equality before the law for the poor and the rich of all races, for catering to thugs who used their new-found freedoms to multiply their crimes, and for its interference with the rights of states to determine for themselves the basis of representation. The John Birch Society, an extreme right-wing organization which saw in every liberal trend a communist conspiracy, used roadside billboards and other advertising to call for Warren's impeachment. When President Johnson nominated Associate Justice Abe Fortas to succeed Warren, the ultraconservatives in the Senate made every effort to block his confirmation. Johnson was a lame-duck President, Fortas' opponents argued, who had no moral right to make such appointments but should leave that task to his successor. Their real objection, of course, was that Fortas' views coincided with those of Warren, and their hope was that a Republican victory would result in a conservative appointment. A Senate filibuster, which administration forces were unable to break, brought out charges of unethical (or at least injudicious) practices on the part of Fortas. Fortas asked that his nomination be withdrawn and soon after Johnson's term ended he resigned from the court, following the publication of evidence indicating that Fortas had accepted (and later returned) a fee from a foundation the founder of which had been convicted of fraudulent stock manipulation. To succeed Fortas, President Nixon first nominated Clement F. Haynsworth of South Carolina, then G. Harrold Carswell of Florida, both of whom the Senate rejected. Haynsworth, as a federal circuit judge, it developed, had shown less regard for ethical principles than the Senate thought essential, while Carswell, in a similar post, had shown little distinction. Publicly professing to believe that the Senate would not confirm any southerner, Nixon then named Harry A. Blackmun of Minnesota, another federal circuit judge

and "strict constructionist," whom the Senate quickly confirmed by a vote of 94 to 0.

The New Federalism

President Nixon spent much of his first six months in office studying defense and foreign policies and selecting the members of his administrative staff. When the North Koreans shot down an American spy plane in international waters, April 15, 1969, with loss of life to all its crew, Nixon, like Johnson before him in the *Pueblo* incident, found it inexpedient to attempt retaliation. Critics deplored his lack of accomplishment and of any sense of urgency about the many national problems he had stressed during the campaign.

Thus the President surprised the country when he suddenly proposed an elaborate series of welfare reforms in a televised broadcast early in August, 1969. Although some scoffers promptly dubbed his program "Nixon's New Deal," he himself preferred the title "The New Federalism," a term he repeated three times during the address. There were five basic elements in the Nixon program: (1) a "family assistance system" which would guarantee a minimum income to all families in all states; (2) administration of all welfare by the Social Security system; (3) requirement that each household head (except mothers with pre-school children) would have to take a job or enter a suitable job-training program, if one were available; (4) job-training programs, while still financed by the federal government, would gradually be turned over to the states for administration; and (5) the return of some federal tax dollars to the states, generally free of restrictions. The powerful influence of Finch and Moynihan was clearly evident in this ambitious program, which at first failed to win widespread support in Congress.

Despite some misgivings, the first stage of the plan seemed by the spring of 1970 to be moving toward victory in Congress. The proposed legislation would put a floor of at least $1,600 a year under family incomes everywhere in the nation. Further, welfare recipients might also take paying jobs and lose only fifty cents from their welfare checks for each dollar of income earned until they had reached the so-called "poverty level" of $3,920 for a family of four. Benefits for the aged, the disabled, and the blind would rise from $90 a month to $110. The new measure, designed to go into effect July 1, 1971, would, if enacted, increase the number of persons on relief from about 10 million to about 25 million, at an estimated cost to the federal government for the first year of $4.4 billion.

The Menace of Inflation

The readiness of the Nixon administration to embark on so expensive a program was the more remarkable in view of its otherwise insistent efforts to curb inflation. Two related methods of achieving this end were (1) the reduction of government expenditures and (2) a balanced budget. With the latter goal in mind, the President persuaded Congress to extend temporarily the 10 per cent income tax surcharge, enacted during the Johnson administration (see p. 755). But he won this concession from the Democratic Congress only on condition that he consent to a long overdue revision of the whole tax structure. The new law that resulted early in 1970, while less comprehensive than some reformers had hoped for, won bipartisan approval. It closed some of the "loopholes" by which favored interests had previously avoided taxes; for example, it reduced the oil depletion allowance from 27.5 per cent to 22 per cent. This and other changes, it was estimated, would bring an additional $9 billion into the Treasury; but Congress, well aware of the problems faced by low-income tax-payers, used up perhaps $7 billion of this gain by lowering rates and increasing exemptions. Nixon signed the bill with some misgivings, for he feared that the increased revenue would be eaten away by overly generous appropriations. An inflationary deficit, he said, would be "irresponsible and intolerable."

Presidential budgets are submitted in January of each year for the twelve-month period beginning the following July 1. During his last days in office Johnson asked Congress for a total of $195.3 billion for the fiscal year 1969–1970. This figure Nixon promptly reduced by about $5.8 billion. Congressional leaders claimed that their total appropriations for the year were less by $7.7 billion than the President had asked for, but of this saving some $5.6 billion came out of expenditures for defense that, with the Vietnam War still unresolved, might have to be restored. For the fiscal year 1970–1971, the President asked for $200.8 billion, the largest such figure in history, but less by $1.3 billion than predicted expenditures. It seemed certain that the battle of the budget would long continue.

Meantime the Federal Reserve Board, also with a view to halting inflation, instituted a tight money policy that eventually raised the prime interest rate to 8.5 per cent, the highest on record. Strikes and the threat of strikes brought labor costs up and the ultimate consumer had to pay the bill. The Federal Reserve policy was intended to "cool down" the economy, if possible without producing a recession of the kind that had occurred three times during the Eisenhower administration. Hardest hit was the housing industry, which almost came to a standstill. On the stock market the trend was steadily downward, with bonds issued by companies of the highest credit rating bringing at least 8.5 to 9 per cent, when they sold at all. Business expansion as a whole failed to slow down correspondingly, although in the early months of 1970 the aerospace and automobile industries appeared to be in trouble and unemployment began to rise. Even so, consumer prices kept on going up. It began to seem that the administration's reduced domestic spending and tight money policies had unintentionally produced both higher prices and a recession.

Minority Groups

What the new administration's attitude would be toward minority groups aroused much speculation both during and after the campaign of 1968. Since comparatively few of the minority voters had supported the Republican ticket, expediency seemed to indicate that the party in power should either seek to win them over by conciliation or write them off as a loss and conciliate their opponents. There were many indications that the President and his advisers had chosen the latter alternative. Some observers believed that he had given his approval to a "southern strategy," designed to win over to the Republican Party many Democrats as well as the white extremists who had voted for Wallace. Nixon's nominations to the Supreme Court could be so construed. So also could the attitude of Attorney-General Mitchell toward the Voting Rights Act of 1965 (see p. 745), due to expire in 1970. The Act of 1965 had been directed specifically against those southern states which by literacy tests and similar devices deliberately sought to restrict non-white voting. Late in 1969 Mitchell recommended that the ban on voting discriminations be made nationwide and that the required changes in voting procedures should no longer come automatically under the scrutiny of the Department of Justice and the federal courts, a policy that civil rights advocates claimed would result in the wholesale disenfranchisement of blacks. Mitchell's measure passed the House, but stalled in the Senate. It revealed the willingness of the Nixon administration to work less vigorously for black voting rights in the South.

The new administration was also less insistent upon school integration in the South. The dual system of education that the Supreme Court had outlawed in 1954, with its compulsory separation of blacks from whites, existed by law only in the South, and it was only in that area that federal enforcement was undertaken. Early in the Nixon administration the Department of Justice joined in the request of some southern districts for further delay in complying with the integration orders of federal judges, but the United States Supreme Court, with Chief Justice Burger concurring, sustained the lower courts and ruled that fifteen years of "all deliberate speed" was enough. Despite this decision, it was obvious that the Nixon administration had taken another stand in line with its "southern strategy."

Further support for this point of view came from an unexpected source early in 1970 when Senator Ribicoff of Connecticut, a liberal Democrat, charged that the North was guilty of "monumental hypocrisy" and "rampant racism" in forcing desegregation on the South while condoning it in most northern cities. In the North, to be sure, there were no school laws specifically separating the races, but segregation in housing often accomplished the same end. Many cities had made a start at desegregation by revising district boundaries and even busing children considerable distances to achieve balanced integration. Even so, *de facto* segregation was about as common in the northern central cities as *de jure* segregation in the South. When a Los Angeles superior court judge ruled early in 1970 that the city school board must somehow balance the races in 583 schools, President Nixon openly defended the right of children to attend the schools closest to their homes and deplored busing them elsewhere as a means of achieving integration. Nixon's attitude may have stemmed in part from a private communication from Moynihan, leaked to the press, advising the President that on the racial question the time might have come for "benign neglect." Most whites in the South and many in the North tended to approve Nixon's stand, but civil rights leaders of both races were outraged.

Law and Order

Linked with the racial question by the fact that so many of the impoverished blacks were involved in crime was the demand for law and order that Nixon emphasized constantly during the campaign of 1968. But there was little to indicate that the return of the Republicans to power in the nation and in a majority of the states had done much to discourage law-breakers. The first six months of 1969 showed an increase of 9 per cent in crime over the first six months of 1968, with crimes of violence such as robbery, rape, assault, and murder up by 13 per cent. In the city of Washington, where Nixon had promised an all-out war on crime, serious offenses increased during the first ten months of 1969 by 29 per cent. Organized crime, such as the Mafia or Cosa Nostra, continued to flourish. Criminologists had held for years that the causes of crime were closely related to poverty, but politicians found it easier to blame these troubles on inadequate laws and indifferent law enforcement. Yet new legislation, whether state or national, had little effect. States and cities drew on their already strained financial resources to strengthen their police departments and asked in vain for federal aid, while their problems compounded. Law enforcement officers blamed the courts for failure to convict offenders, for light sentences, and for easy paroles, but throughout the country jails and prisons were overcrowded and widely regarded as schools for criminals.

The rising volume of "crime in the streets" was accompanied by even more serious acts of violence, the objectives of which could only be described as revolutionary. In retrospect, campus revolts of the preceding few years seemed less de-signed to promote educational goals than to bring down an extremely vulnerable pillar of the "establishment." Incidents of the early 1970's tended to confirm this view. The accidental explosion of a cache of bombs that destroyed a Greenwich Village house was traced to a group of revolutionaries who had intended to use the weapons they were making for the destruction of buildings on the Columbia University campus. Business districts adjacent to troubled campuses sometimes suffered more than the universities themselves; during one riot a mob deliberately destroyed by fire a bank near the Santa Barbara campus of the University of California. Similar incidents occurred in other cities.

Along with these attacks on business and education came comparable efforts to discredit the nation's courts. One such among many was the trial of the "Chicago Seven," indicted for inciting the rioting that accompanied the Democratic National Convention of 1968. Throughout the proceedings the defendants and their lawyers took every opportunity to make a laughing-stock of the judicial process. In Washington the Department of Justice argued that the various incidents were unconnected, and in no sense parts of a conspirational plan, but for the public at large the sheer quantity and general distribution of the disorderly acts was unsettling, to say the least.

Men on the Moon

The successful efforts of the National Aeronautics and Space Administration to put a man on the moon provided welcome relief from the dismal course of events on the earth below. The space exploration program, launched by President Kennedy in 1961 (see p. 687), and enthusiastically supported by Presidents Johnson and Nixon, had by this time cost approximately $24 billion. Many Americans questioned both the morality and the wisdom of spending so much money on outer space when so

President Richard M. Nixon *and the Apollo 11 astronauts. From left to right: Edwin A. Aldrin, Michael Collins, President Nixon, Neil A. Armstrong.*

many urgent social problems needed attention, but the nation and the world watched with unmeasured excitement the launching of Apollo 11, and the feats of Neil A. Armstrong and Colonel Edwin A. Aldrin as they guided their small Eagle craft to a safe moon landing and then ventured out for the first moon walks, July 20, 1969. They then linked up with the space ship Columbia, operated by their colleague, Michael Collins, and climbed aboard for the 240,000 mile trip back to earth.

By this time the technological skills of approximately 300,000 people had been employed in the space exploration program. Its complexities far surpassed the imaginations of most Americans, but scientists were deeply interested in the many pictures taken by the astronauts and in the samples of moon rocks they had brought back with them. Four months later another team, Charles Conrad, Jr., Alan L. Bean, and Richard F. Gordon, Jr., piloted Apollo 12 on a similarly successful mission, with another moon landing on November 19, 1969. Apollo 13, however, which blasted off in mid-April, 1970, with Astronauts James A.

Lovell, Jr., Fred W. Haise, Jr., and John L. Swigert, Jr., met with serious trouble far out in space, but after circling the moon almost miraculously returned to earth. It seemed unlikely that the Nixon administration would be willing to seek the enormous funding to "send a man to Mars," as Vice-President Agnew suggested.

A New Foreign Policy?

Well aware that the fate of his administration might depend on his ability to terminate direct military involvement in the Vietnam War, Nixon at first took great pains not to offend the "doves," led by Senator J. William Fulbright of Arkansas, who in turn treated the President with great consideration. The doves were pleased when Nixon announced that he would begin the phased withdrawal of troops from Vietnam, although they grew skeptical when he failed to add quickly to the first 25,000 returnees. Nixon began a tour of the world by meeting the "moon men" where they touched down in the South Pacific, and at Guam proclaimed that the United States would never again intervene in

Southeast Asia unless in response to a clear threat by a nuclear power. His obvious intent was to indicate a "lowered profile" for the American nation in foreign affairs, and a greater insistence that countries endangered by Communist aggressors should make every effort to defend themselves. At Bangkok, however, he promised to "stand proudly with Thailand against those who might threaten it from abroad or from within," while in Vietnam he predicted that the war there might yet be considered "one of America's finest hours." After quick stops in India and Pakistan, the President visited Bucharest, where he received a tumultuous welcome from the citizens of "independent" Communist Rumania.

Nixon attempted also in a well-publicized TV address, November 3, 1969, to clarify and elaborate his statements on Southeast Asia. He promised to continue the withdrawal of American ground forces on a timetable geared to the ability of the South Vietnamese army to take over the fighting, the willingness of North Vietnam to diminish its war efforts, and the progress of the Paris peace talks. The response to the President's address was remarkably cordial.

The reasons for this attitude were not hard to explain. In the first place, Nixon was actually bringing some of the troops home; after the return of the first 25,000 he announced other similarly small but steady withdrawals. On April 20, 1970, when the number left in Vietnam was already less than 430,000, the President announced that he would bring 150,000 more men home during the next twelve months. Few Americans believed that he planned to take all American troops out of the war-torn area, but the general expectation was that he would reduce the numbers involved to about 200,000 men. Their duty would be primarily to back up the South Vietnamese, who eventually would take over all the ground fighting. To the "great silent majority" to whom Nixon's proposals appealed, the presence of American soldiers in South Vietnam seemed less reprehensible because the North Vietnamese government showed no willingness to follow the American example in reducing the number of its troops in South Vietnam. The behavior of the North Vietnamese delegation in Paris also played into Nixon's hands. Even after the death of Ho Chi Minh, September 5, 1969, they remained as intransigent as ever. Neither Henry Cabot Lodge, who succeeded Harriman as the chief American negotiator, nor David Bruce, who succeeded Lodge, had any more success than Harriman in working out an agreement. It was apparent that the only thing the North Vietnamese government would consider was an American surrender, a solution which many people in the United State considered impossible.

If a majority of Americans stood ready to accept Nixon's "Vietnamization" policy, a vocal and apparently growing minority did not. On October 15, 1969, and again on November 15 following, hundreds of thousands of those who opposed the war marched in the streets of every great American city. Many of the President's critics, including prominent members of both political parties, called for a more accelerated program of troop withdrawal from Vietnam, and a timetable that would remove all American forces by a given date, regardless of the consequences to the existing government of South Vietnam. That government, many contended, was not worth saving anyway and should be replaced by a coalition that would include representation of all elements in South Vietnam. The character of the fighting into which the war had degenerated was also unsettling. An alleged massacre by American soldiers of the inhabitants of the village of My Lai, March 16, 1968, apparently matched, if it did not exceed, the worst soldiers had done to the Indians during the wars on the plains (see p. 89). Furthermore, high ranking offi-

Peace Rally in Washington. *On November 15, 1969 one of the largest crowds in American history demand an end to the war in Vietnam.*

cers had sought to cover up the evidence. These incidents added materially to the unpopularity of the war, which was by now almost universally deplored. Support for Nixon merely registered the fact that many people trusted him to close out the conflict on reasonable terms.

Even this limited acquiescence in the Nixon policy suffered a severe jolt when the news broke that the war was being expanded beyond the borders of South Vietnam. When reports began to circulate that American military advisers in Laos had lost their lives in conflict, there was a great outcry against the prospect of "another Vietnam." This was as nothing, however, compared to the turmoil produced a little later over Cambodia. There a rightist coup overthrew the neutralist government of Prince Sihanouk, and began hostilities against the Viet Cong and North Vietnamese who had long made use of Cambodian territory as

"sanctuaries." President Nixon, ten days after promising the withdrawal of 150,000 American troops from South Vietnam, announced the use in force of American as well as South Vietnamese troops to eliminate the enemy "sanctuaries" in Cambodia, from which the allies in South Vietnam had suffered so much. Perhaps the President meant to serve warning to all concerned that there could be an end to American patience; perhaps, also, he believed that eliminating the sanctuaries would enable him to accomplish more easily the removal of American troops from South Vietnam. At the same time he also authorized the bombing of anti-aircraft installations on North Vietnamese territory, directly north of the demilitarized zone.

A host of administration critics argued that the real effect of these measures would be the deepening of the American involvement and the prolongation of the war. All over the United States, hundreds of campuses that had been quiet erupted in dissent, while anti-administration politicians fairly exploded in anguished rhetoric at the escalation of the war. Police and national guard struggled in vain to keep the mobs of students and other protesters under control; many universities simply closed down, some for the remainder of the academic year. At Kent State University, Ohio, guardsmen fired directly into a crowd, killing four students and wounding many others. At Jackson State College, Mississippi, white policemen shot two protesting black students to death, and injured many others.

Faced by all this protest, the administration made haste to insist that its invasion of Cambodia was purely temporary and would be completed by the end of June; also, that it had no intention of further bombings in North Vietnam. But its credibility had suffered a disastrous blow. The demand for immediate withdrawal of all American troops from Southeast Asia and for immediate peace showed greater vigor than ever before.

The Draft

Resentment against the draft was chronic among young Americans. Campus protests regularly made an issue of it, conscientious objectors multiplied, and many prospective draftees went into exile. Nixon held out hope of abolishing the draft altogether, and as a gesture of conciliation removed General Lewis B. Hershey, who for twenty-eight years had gathered unpopularity as its director. The President succeeded also in instituting a lottery system, designed to let young men know well in advance the order in which they might expect to be called into service. The regulations still permitted draft boards to defer students to attend college until graduation, but no longer showed special favors to graduate students. All nineteen year olds were required to register.

Relations with the Soviets

Nixon, like his predecessors, hoped confidently for a *detente* with the Soviet Union, one that would enable the two superpowers to live side by side in peace and without fear. On one issue of importance they were able to agree. After protracted negotiations they proclaimed in force (March, 1970) a Nuclear Nonproliferation Treaty that forbade nuclear powers to transmit atomic weapons to non-nuclear powers, who in turn promised not to develop nuclear arsenals themselves. Forty-five other nations, besides the United States and the Soviet Union, also signed the treaty, but neither France nor China would go along. It was significant, nevertheless, that the two greatest powers could act together on anything so important.

Meantime, during the final weeks of 1969, the United States and the Soviet Union also sent representatives to Helsinki, Finland, to lay plans for strategic-arms limitations talks (SALT). The cost of nuclear weaponry, which each power already had in sufficient abundance to destroy the other, had become unbearable. The only possible purpose for additional expenditures was to enable one power to make a "first strike" sufficiently devastating that the other could not reply. In an effort, no doubt, to enable the United States to "negotiate from strength" Nixon in 1969 added the full power of his administration to that of the military establishment to secure Congressional approval of a modified Safeguard Anti-Ballistic Missile (ABM), designed to destroy enemy missiles before they could reach their targets. To many Americans such an "overkill" system seemed unnecessary; while the House of Representatives complied readily with the President's recommendation, the Senate concurred by a vote of 51 to 49.

The Middle East

Tension between the two superpowers remained at its highest in the Middle East.

The six days' war of 1967 was followed by a long series of reprisals and counter-reprisals, culminating in what almost amounted to guerrilla warfare. The Soviets soon replaced the arms that the Egyptians had lost during the war and at the same time strengthened greatly Soviet naval power in the eastern Mediterranean. But the Israelis, who also depended on imported weaponry, ran into trouble when President de Gaulle, for reasons best known to himself, refused to permit Israel to take possession of the French-made warplanes it had already bought and paid for. Furthermore, de Gaulle's successor, Pompidou, permitted a generous sale of planes to Libya, Egypt's nearest neighbor to the west and close ally. When the Israeli government sought to buy in the United States the extra planes it needed, it ran into Nixon's policy of "even-handedness" in dealing with the Arabs and the Israelis. The Israelis sought in vain to buy during the next five years an additional $1 billion worth of war planes. Some pro-Israeli Americans feared that Nixon might try to buy peace with the Soviets and security for American oil interests in the Middle East at the expense of Israel's safety. Secretary Rogers, however, in announcing Nixon's decision, asserted that the United States would not permit the balance of power to shift too decisively in favor of the Arabs.

Surprisingly, in the summer of 1970, the United States persuaded Israel and Egypt to agree on a three months' cease fire, during which they would seek a permanent peace through the mediation of Gunnar Jarring, a Swedish representative of the United Nations. Each side, it was decided, should make no military moves and should police its own borders. From the very first day, however, the Israelis alleged that the Egyptians, with Soviet assistance, were bringing in new missiles on the Egyptian side of the Suez Canal, a breach of faith that was soon confirmed by United States observers. The Israelis, therefore, while continuing to observe the truce, refused to go ahead with the negotiations until the illegally placed missiles were removed.

The prospect of peace in the Middle East was still further imperiled by the activities of Palestinian commandos, or guerrillas, in Jordan, Syria, and Lebanon, where their presence was tolerated in varying degrees by the governments concerned. In September, 1970, one faction of commandos, which had long made the hijacking of planes carrying Israelis a specialty, forced a Pan-American 747 to land in Cairo, where, after evacuating the passengers, they blew up the plane. Three other flights, a TWA, a Swissair, and a BOAC, were landed in the Jordanian desert north of Amman. In due time these planes, too, were blown up, and their passengers held as hostages for the release of captured commandos. Finally King Hussein of Jordan, frightened by the growing power of the commandos within his borders, opened up an all-out war against them that all but destroyed the city of Amman, and brought Syrian tanks across the border to help the guerrillas. The threat of Israeli, and perhaps American, intervention led the Syrians to withdraw and temporarily gave the King the upper hand, but he had to settle for a truce that left the Palestinian guerrillas strong. In due time all the airplane passengers were freed, on the understanding that Switzerland, West Germany, and Great Britain would release seven captured Arab terrorists. To further complicate the Middle Eastern problem, a massive heart attack, suffered by President Nasser of Egypt in late September, removed from the scene the only really outstanding leader in the Arab world.

Party Politics

With the midterm elections of 1970 in prospect, the Democrats seemed at great disadvantage. They were plagued by an unpaid debt of $8.3 million, left over from the campaign of 1968, and by inadequate leadership. Senator Edward Kennedy lost political strength after an unfortunate automobile accident late at night, which resulted in the drowning of his young woman companion. The Senator's failure to report this incident promptly cast grave doubts on the quality of his judgment. Humphrey had suffered defeat, Muskie was still not well known, and McCarthy had seemingly withdrawn from politics. The party also lacked a cause to rally around. Despite the noisy dissent, Nixon's Vietnamization policy satisfied many voters, his southern strategy beckoned warmly to the once solid South, and his welfare proposals might, if enacted, take from the Democrats one of their strongest issues. Furthermore, the country, except for the very noisy and highly visible extremists, seemed in a conservative mood. When Vice-President Agnew attacked the liberal-oriented New York-Washington news media for slanting their interpretations, the reaction of the public was unexpectedly favorable; thereafter he won recognition as the principal spokesman for conservatives against the "effete snobs" of the liberal-intellectual world.

The Republicans even anticipated the Democrats in an attack on the pollution of the American environment, a problem that suddenly seemed to take precedence over all others in the American mind. President Nixon, in his 1970 state of the union message to Congress, brought this situation into sharp political focus. He and his party would make its remedy their first consideration. There was no doubt that the air in most American cities was no longer fit to breathe; the water of the nation's lakes, rivers, and seashores so poisoned by filth as to endanger all underwater life; the land robbed of too many forests and too much agricultural potential; the cities increasingly choked with people; the very survival of the human race endangered. The President was not very specific as to what he could do about all this, but at least he knew how to make political capital of the situation.

Quo Vadis?

Looking to the future, perplexed Americans seemed to be of two minds. Pessimists could see no reasonable ground for hope. Abroad, the war in Vietnam had bogged down, the Middle East was in a state of acute tension, and the armament race, if not halted, might lead to another world war. At home, the relations between the races grew worse rather than better, law and order had broken down, urban life was becoming intolerable. Optimists, however, despite many misgivings about the present, looked forward with confidence to the distant future. The nation had known serious problems before and had always survived. It had come a long way; why should it now falter and fail? Most encouraging of all was the fact that it was facing up to the problems that beset it. There is an element of hope in the recognition of an existing evil. If Americans could really identify the causes of the troubles that confronted them, surely they could find the means to correct them.

BIBLIOGRAPHY

No scholarly biography of Johnson has yet been published, although his memoirs are scheduled to appear shortly. The best account of his early life is W. C. Pool and others, *Lyndon Baines Johnson: The Formative Years* (1965). A full-length book on the first part of his Presidency is Rowland Evans and Robert Novak, *Lyndon B. Johnson: The Exercise of Power* (1966); another journalistic account, briefer and more sympathetic, is Hugh Sidey, *A Very Personal Presidency* (1968). Undocumented, verbose and savagely critical is Alfred Steinberg, *Sam Johnson's Boy* (1968). Revealing of both subject and author is E. F. Goldman, *The Tragedy of Lyndon Johnson* (1969), the memoir of a Princeton historian who was the President's part-time emissary to the intellectuals. P. L. Geyelin, *Lyndon B. Johnson and the World* (1966), is both informative and critical. Important works on the War on Poverty are S. A. Levitan, *The Great Society's Poor* (1969); J. L. Sundquist, *On Fighting Poverty* (1969), the reminiscence of a participant; and Kenneth Clark and Jeannette Hopkins, *A Relevant War Against Poverty* (1969). A collection of critiques is *The Great Society Reader: The Failure of American Liberalism* (1967), edited by M. E. Gettleman and David Mermelstein.

The literature concerning student unrest is proliferating. Conflict between generations is nowhere better documented than in G. F. Kennan, *Democracy and the Student Left* (1968), which contains a critical periodical article by Kennan, a large number of responses (mostly hostile) and Kennan's reply. An attempt at comparative analysis of student movements, with Freudian overtones, is L. S. Feuer, *The Conflict of Generations* (1969). A vivid account of the Columbia University crisis is *Up Against the Ivy Wall* (1968), by J. L. Avorn and others. A muckraking account of the operations of higher education, stressing the government and business subsidies for research (a frequent target of student protest), is James Ridgeway, *The Closed Corporation: American Universities in Crisis* (1968). Critical essays by radical intellectuals may be found in Christopher Lasch, *The Agony of the American Left* (1969); and Noam Chomsky, *American Power and the New Mandarins* (1969). Theodore Roszak, *The Making of a Counter Culture* (1969), typifies the attitude of one segment of youthful rebels against established mores.

On the urban riots a basic source is *The Report of the National Advisory Commission on Civil Disorders* (1968); one of the several studies developed for the commission is J. H. Skolnick, *Politics of Protest* (1969). Books on individual riots are numerous; the best are Jerry Cohen and W. S. Murphy, *Burn, Baby, Burn* (1966), on Watts; Tom Hayden, *Rebellion in Newark* (1967), by a New Left Leader; H. G. Locke, *The Detroit Riot of 1967* (1969), by a Negro who was a police official; and B. W. Gilbert and others, *Ten Blocks from the White House* (1968), on Washington, D.C.

The Black Power Revolt (1968), edited by F. B. Barbour, is an excellent collection of documents and current writings. Articles are collected in *Black Protest in the Sixties* (1970), edited by August Meier and Elliott Rudwick; and in a volume edited by P. W. Romero, *In Black America: 1968: The Year of Awakening* (1969). Accounts of changing attitudes are given in Lerone Bennett, Jr., *Confrontation: Black and White* (1965); and Benjamin Muse, *The American Negro Revolution* (1968). The position of a moderate black leader is put in W. M. J. Young, *Beyond Racism* (1969). Documentation for the militant viewpoints may be found in Stokely Carmichael and C. V. Hamilton, *Black Power* (1967); L. M. Killian, *The Impossible Revolution* (1968); Floyd McKissick, *Three-Fifths of a Man* (1969); H. Rap Brown, *Die Nigger Die!* (1969); and Bobby Seale, *Seize the Time: The Story of the Black Panther Party and Huey P. Newton* (1970).

Useful on foreign affairs is R. E. Osgood and others, *America and the World: From the Truman Doctrine to Vietnam* (1970). An important memoir of a Defense Department official who opposed further escalation of the Vietnam War in early 1968 is Townsend Hoopes, *The Limits of Intervention* (1969). A scholarly work of great importance is J. T. McAlister, Jr., *Viet Nam: The Origins of Revolution* (1969). Three harsh critiques of American policy in Vietnam are J. W. Fulbright, *The Arrogance of Power* (1967); R. N. Goodwin, *Triumph or Tragedy* (1966); and A. M. Schlesinger, Jr., *The Bitter Heritage* (1967). One of the ablest correspondents in Vietnam is Robert Shaplen; his *The Lost Revolution* (2nd ed., 1966) and *Time Out of Hand* (1969) document his own disillusionment. B. B. Fall, *Viet-Nam Witness, 1953–66* (1966), is a posthumous collection of 26 articles of generally high quality; Harrison Salisbury, *Behind the Lines — Hanoi, December 23–January 7* (1967), is by the veteran *New York Times* correspondent. E. O. Reischauer, *Beyond Vietnam: The United States and Asia* (1967), is a moderate reassessment by the well-known scholar-diplomat. Don Luce and John Sommer, *Vietnam: The Unheard Voices* (1969), is an account by two civilians of their gradual disillusionment with their work in the "pacification" program.

On the Six-Days' War and its broad implications two books are of particular importance: Theodore Draper, *Israel and World Politics: Roots of the Third Arab-Israeli War* (1968); and F. J. Khouri, *The Arab-Israeli Dilemma* (1968), a comprehensive and lucid account of a complex situation. W. R. Polk, *The United States and the Arab World* (2nd ed., 1969), is an excellent and dispassionate survey.

Two full-length journalistic accounts of the 1968 election are available: T. H. White, *The Making of the President, 1968* (1969), third in a series; and Chester Lewis and others, *An American Melodrama* (1969), a book put together by correspondents of the *Sunday Times* of London. On the ill-fated campaign of Robert F. Kennedy, see *To Seek a Newer World* (1967), a collection of his speeches; W. V. Shannon, *The Heir Apparent* (1967), a liberal journalist's pre-campaign analysis; and Jack Newfield, *Robert Kennedy: A Memoir* (1969), a revealing reminiscence. Memoirs of the Eugene McCarthy campaign are numerous; the most important are probably E. J. McCarthy, *The Year of the People* (1969); Jeremy Larner, *Nobody Knows* (1970); Arthur Herzog, *McCarthy for President* (1969); and Ben Stavis, *We Were the Campaign* (1969).

An interesting description of the two majority party conventions is *Miami and the Siege of Chicago* (1968) by Norman Mailer, novelist turned journalist turned politician. Daniel Walker, *Rights in Conflict* (1968), is a report to the Kerner Commission on the disorders at the Democratic convention; it is critical of the Chicago police. Nothing new of importance on Nixon has appeared except for the memoir of one of his public relations aides, Joe Mc-

Ginnis, *The Selling of the President 1968* (1969). On the Democratic candidate the best biography is still Winthrop Griffith, *Humphrey* (1965). Some of the demands for a "new politics" are put forth in Michael Harrington, *Toward a Democratic Left* (1968), the program of the leader of the Socialist Party. The most comprehensive life of George Wallace is Marshall Frady, *Wallace* (1968); it is critical but it brings its subject to life. On the Far Right, valuable works are *The Radical Right* (1963), edited by Daniel Bell; *Protest from the Right* (1968), edited by R. A. Rosenstone; and George Thayer, *The Farther Shores of Politics* (2nd ed., 1968), which also treats left-wing movements.

An excellent collection of essays dealing with crucial issues, both foreign and domestic, is *Agenda for the Nation* (1968), edited by Kermit Gordon for the Brookings Institution. An inkling of Nixon administration policies can perhaps be found in the works of several of the men who accepted appointments from him. Among these are D. P. Moynihan, *On Understanding Poverty* (1969), and *Toward a National Urban Policy* (1970), edited by Moynihan; Herbert Stein, *The Fiscal Revolution in America* (1969); and H. A. Kissinger, *The Troubled Partnership* (1965) and *American Foreign Policy: Three Essays* (1969). A critique of one of the administration's defense policies is Abram Chayes and J. B. Wiesner, *ABM* (1969). On the Warren Court the following are especially valuable: J. D. Weaver, *Warren* (1967), the best biography; Archibald Cox, *The Warren Court* (1968), a brief analysis by a former Solicitor General; *The Warren Court: A Critical Analysis* (1969), edited by R. H. Sayler and others; and Anthony Lewis, *Gideon's Trumpet* (1964), a superb account of one of the Warren Court's greatest cases. The literature on the space program is vast but tends to be either over-technical or juvenile; the best general survey is probably R. S. Lewis, *Appointment on the Moon: The Inside Story of America's Space Venture* (1968).

The politics of the Nixon era are portrayed rather acidly by the liberal cartoonist-journalist John Osborne, *The Nixon Watch* (1970). K. P. Phillips, *The Emerging Republican Ma-*

jority (1969), prescribes a strategy for attaining full conservative Republican control. G. E. Reedy, a former assistant to President Johnson, describes the fearful position of the chief executive in *The Twilight of the Presidency* (1970). A critique of the "old politics" and a plan for political realignment is presented in the witty if somewhat naive short book by J. K. Galbraith, *Who Needs the Democrats and What It Takes to Be Needed* (1970). The literature on the new ecology issue is already huge; note should be taken of an extremely convenient and useful collection, *The Environmental Handbook* (1970), edited by Garrett De Bell.

APPENDIX

The Declaration of Independence

IN CONGRESS, JULY 4, 1776.

THE UNANIMOUS DECLARATION OF THE THIRTEEN UNITED STATES OF AMERICA

WHEN, in the course of human events, it becomes necessary for one people to dissolve the political bands which have connected them with another, and to assume, among the powers of the earth, the separate and equal station to which the laws of nature and of nature's God entitle them, a decent respect to the opinions of mankind requires that they should declare the causes which impel them to the separation.

We hold these truths to be self-evident, that all men are created equal; that they are endowed by their Creator with certain unalienable rights; that among these, are life, liberty, and the pursuit of happiness. That, to secure these rights, governments are instituted among men, deriving their just powers from the consent of the governed; that, whenever any form of government becomes destructive of these ends, it is the right of the people to alter or to abolish it, and to institute a new government, laying its foundation on such principles, and organizing its powers in such form, as to them shall seem most likely to effect their safety and happiness. Prudence, indeed, will dictate that governments long established, should not be changed for light and transient causes; and, accordingly, all experience hath shown, that mankind are more disposed to suffer, while evils are sufferable, than to right themselves by abolishing the forms to which they are accustomed. But, when a long train of abuses and usurpations, pursuing invariably the same object, evinces a design to reduce them under absolute despotism, it is their right, it is their duty, to throw off such government and to provide new guards for their future security. Such has been the patient sufferance of these colonies, and such is now the necessity which constrains them to alter their former systems of government. The history of the present King of Great Britain is a history of repeated injuries and usurpations, all having, in direct object, the establishment of an absolute tyranny over these States. To prove this, let facts be submitted to a candid world: —

He has refused his assent to laws the most wholesome and necessary for the public good.

He has forbidden his governors to pass laws of immediate and pressing importance, unless suspended in their operation till his assent should be obtained; and, when so suspended, he has utterly neglected to attend to them.

He has refused to pass other laws for the accommodation of large districts of people, unless those people would relinquish the right of representation in the legislature; a right inestimable to them, and formidable to tyrants only.

He has called together legislative bodies at places unusual, uncomfortable, and distant from the depository of their public records, for the sole purpose of fatiguing them into compliance with his measures.

He has dissolved representative houses repeatedly for opposing, with manly firmness, his invasions on the rights of the people.

He has refused, for a long time after such dissolutions, to cause others to be elected; whereby the legislative powers, incapable of annihilation, have returned to the people at large for their exercise; the state remaining, in the meantime, exposed to all the danger of invasion from without, and convulsions within.

He has endeavored to prevent the population of these States; for that purpose, obstructing the laws for naturalization of foreigners, refusing to pass others to encourage their migration hither, and raising the conditions of new appropriations of lands.

He has obstructed the administration of justice, by refusing his assent to laws for establishing judiciary powers.

He has made judges dependent on his will alone, for the tenure of their offices, and the amount and payment of their salaries.

He has erected a multitude of new offices, and sent hither swarms of officers to harass our people, and eat out their substance.

He has kept among us, in time of peace, standing armies, without the consent of our legislatures.

He has affected to render the military independent of, and superior to, the civil power.

He has combined, with others, to subject us to a jurisdiction foreign to our Constitution, and unacknowledged by our laws; giving his assent to their acts of pretended legislation:

For quartering large bodies of armed troops among us:

For protecting them by a mock trial, from punishment, for any murders which they should commit on the inhabitants of these States:

For cutting off our trade with all parts of the world:

For imposing taxes on us without our consent:

For depriving us, in many cases, of the benefit of trial by jury:

For transporting us beyond seas to be tried for pretended offences:

For abolishing the free system of English laws in a neighboring province, establishing therein an arbitrary government, and enlarging its boundaries, so as to render it at once an example and fit instrument for introducing the same absolute rule into these colonies:

For taking away our charters, abolishing our most valuable laws, and altering, fundamentally, the powers of our governments:

For suspending our own legislatures, and declaring themselves invested with power to legislate for us in all cases whatsoever.

He has abdicated government here, by declaring us out of his protection, and waging war against us.

He has plundered our seas, ravaged our coasts, burnt our towns, and destroyed the lives of our people.

He is, at this time, transporting large armies of foreign mercenaries to complete the works of death, desolation, and tyranny, already begun, with circumstances of cruelty and perfidy scarcely paralleled in the most barbarous ages, and totally unworthy the head of a civilized nation.

He has constrained our fellow citizens, taken captive on the high seas, to bear arms against their country, to become the executioners of their friends, and brethren, or to fall themselves by their hands.

He has excited domestic insurrections amongst us, and has endeavored to bring on the inhabitants of our frontiers, the merciless Indian savages, whose known rule of warfare is an undistinguished destruction of all ages, sexes, and conditions.

In every stage of these oppressions, we have petitioned for redress, in the most humble terms; our repeated petitions have been answered only by repeated injury. A prince, whose character is thus marked by every act which may define a tyrant, is unfit to be the ruler of a free people.

Nor have we been wanting in attention to our British brethren. We have warned them, from time to time, of attempts made by their legislature to extend an unwarrantable jurisdiction over us. We have reminded them of the circumstances of our emigration and settlement here. We have appealed to their native justice and magnanimity, and we have conjured them, by the ties of our common kindred, to disavow these usurpations, which would inevitably interrupt our connections and correspondence. They, too, have been deaf to the voice of justice and consanguinity. We must, therefore, acquiesce in the necessity which denounces our separation, and hold them, as we hold the rest of mankind, enemies in war, in peace, friends.

We, therefore, the representatives of the United States of America, in general Congress assembled, appealing to the Supreme Judge of the world for the rectitude of our intentions, do, in the name, and by the authority of the good people of these colonies, solemnly publish and declare, that these united colonies are, and of right ought to be, free and independent states: that they are absolved from all allegiance to the British Crown, and that all political connection between them and the state of Great Britain is, and ought to be, totally dissolved; and that, as free and independent states, they have full power to levy war, conclude peace, contract alliances, establish commerce, and to do all other acts and things which independent states may of right do. And, for the support of this declaration, with a firm reliance on the protection of Divine Providence, we mutually pledge to each other our lives, our fortunes, and our sacred honor.

The Constitution of the
United States

WE the people of the United States, in order to form a more perfect union, establish justice, insure domestic tranquillity, provide for the common defense, promote the general welfare, and secure the blessings of liberty to ourselves and our posterity, do ordain and establish this Constitution for the United States of America.

ARTICLE I
SECTION 1

All legislative powers herein granted shall be vested in a Congress of the United States, which shall consist of a Senate and House of Representatives.

SECTION 2

1. The House of Representatives shall be composed of members chosen every second year by the people of the several States, and the electors in each State shall have the qualifications requisite for electors of the most numerous branch of the State legislature.

2. No person shall be a representative who shall not have attained to the age of twenty-five years, and been seven years a citizen of the United States, and who shall not, when elected, be an inhabitant of that State in which he shall be chosen.

3. Representatives and direct taxes[1] shall be apportioned among the several States which may be included within this Union, according to their respective numbers, which shall be determined by adding to the whole number of free persons, including those bound to service for a term of years, and excluding Indians not taxed, three fifths of all other persons.[2] The actual enumeration shall be made within three years after the first meeting of the Congress of the United States, and within every subsequent term of ten years, in such manner as they shall by law direct. The number of representatives shall not exceed one for every thirty thousand, but each State shall have at least one representative; and until such enumeration shall be made, the State of New Hampshire shall be entitled to chose three, Massachusetts eight, Rhode Island and Providence Plantations one, Connecticut five, New York six, New Jersey four, Pennsylvania eight, Delaware one, Maryland six, Virginia ten, North Carolina five, South Carolina five, and Georgia three.

4. When vacancies happen in the representation from any State, the executive authority thereof shall issue writs of election to fill such vacancies.

5. The House of Representatives shall choose their speaker and other officers; and shall have the sole power of impeachment.

SECTION 3

1. The Senate of the United States shall be composed of two senators from each State, chosen by the legislature thereof,[1] for six years; and each senator shall have one vote.

2. Immediately after they shall be assembled in consequence of the first election, they shall be divided as equally as may be into three classes. The seats of the senators of the first class shall be vacated at the expiration of the second year, of the second class at the expiration of the fourth year, and of the third class at the expiration of the sixth year, so that one third may be chosen every second year; and if vacancies happen by resignation, or otherwise, during the recess of the legislature of any State, the executive thereof may make temporary appointments until the next meeting of the legislature, which shall then fill such vacancies.[1]

3. No person shall be a senator who shall not have attained to the age of thirty years, and been nine years a citizen of the United States, and who shall not, when elected, be an inhabitant of that State for which he shall be chosen.

4. The Vice President of the United States shall be President of the Senate, but shall have no vote, unless they be equally divided.

5. The Senate shall choose their other officers and also a president pro tempore, in the absence of the Vice President, or when he shall exercise the office of the President of the United States.

6. The Senate shall have the sole power to try all impeachments. When sitting for that purpose, they shall be on oath or affirmation. When the President of the United States is tried, the chief justice shall preside: and no

[1] Revised by the 16th Amendment.
[2] Revised by the 14th Amendment.

[1] Revised by the 17th Amendment.

iv

person shall be convicted without the concurrence of two thirds of the members present.

7. Judgment in cases of impeachment shall not extend further than to removal from office, and disqualifications to hold and enjoy any office of honor, trust or profit under the United States: but the party convicted shall nevertheless be liable and subject to indictment, trial, judgment and punishment, according to law.

SECTION 4

1. The times, places, and manner of holding elections for senators and representatives, shall be prescribed in each State by the legislature thereof; but the Congress may at any time by law make or alter such regulations, except as to the places of choosing senators.

2. The Congress shall assemble at least once in every year, and such meeting shall be on the first Monday in December, unless they shall by law appoint a different day.

SECTION 5

1. Each House shall be the judge of the elections, returns and qualifications of its own members, and a majority of each shall constitute a quorum to do business; but a smaller number may adjourn from day to day, and may be authorized to compel the attendance of absent members, in such manner, and under such penalties as each House may provide.

2. Each House may determine the rules of its proceedings, punish its members for disorderly behavior, and, with the concurrence of two thirds, expel a member.

3. Each House shall keep a journal of its proceedings, and from time to time publish the same, excepting such parts as may in their judgment require secrecy; and the yeas and nays of the members of either House on any question shall, at the desire of one fifth of those present, be entered on the journal.

4. Neither House, during the session of Congress, shall, without the consent of the other, adjourn for more than three days, nor to any other place than that in which the two Houses shall be sitting.

SECTION 6

1. The senators and representatives shall receive a compensation for their services, to be ascertained by law, and paid out of the Treasury of the United States. They shall in all cases, except treason, felony, and breach of the peace, be privileged from arrest during their attendance at the session of their respective Houses, and in going to and returning from the same; and for any speech or debate in either House, they shall not be questioned in any other place.

2. No senator or representative shall, during the time for which he was elected, be appointed to any civil office under the authority of the United States, which shall have been created, or the emoluments whereof shall have been increased during such time; and no person holding any office under the United States shall be a member of either House during his continuance in office.

SECTION 7

1. All bills for raising revenue shall originate in the House of Representatives; but the Senate may propose or concur with amendments as on other bills.

2. Every bill which shall have passed the House of Representatives and the Senate, shall, before it becomes a law, be presented to the President of the United States; if he approves he shall sign it, but if not he shall return it, with his objections to that House in which it shall have originated, who shall enter the objections at large on their journal, and proceed to reconsider it. If after such reconsideration two thirds of that House shall agree to pass the bill, it shall be sent, together with the objections, to the other House, by which it shall likewise be reconsidered, and if approved by two thirds of that House, it shall become a law. But in all such cases the votes of both Houses shall be determined by yeas and nays, and the names of the persons voting for and against the bill shall be entered on the journal of each House respectively. If any bill shall not be returned by the President within ten days (Sundays excepted) after it shall have been presented to him, the same shall be a law, in like manner as if he had signed it, unless Congress by their adjournment prevent its return, in which case it shall not be a law.

3. Every order, resolution, or vote to which the concurrence of the Senate and the House of Representatives may be necessary (except on a question of adjournment) shall be presented to the President of the United States; and before the same shall take effect, shall be approved by him, or being disapproved by him, shall be passed by two thirds of the Senate and House of Representatives, according to the rules and limitations prescribed in the case of a bill.

SECTION 8

The Congress shall have the power

1. To lay and collect taxes, duties, imposts, and excises, to pay the debts and provide for the common defense and general welfare of the United States; but all duties, imposts, and excises shall be uniform throughout the United States;

2. To borrow money on the credit of the United States;

3. To regulate commerce with foreign nations, and among the several States, and with the Indian tribes;

4. To establish a uniform rule of naturalization, and uniform laws on the subject of bankruptcies throughout the United States;

5. To coin money, regulate the value thereof, and of foreign coin, and fix the standard of weights and measures;

6. To provide for the punishment of counterfeiting the securities and current coin of the United States;

7. To establish post offices and post roads;

8. To promote the progress of science and useful arts, by securing for limited times to authors and inventors the exclusive right to their respective writings and discoveries;

9. To constitute tribunals inferior to the Supreme Court;

10. To define and punish piracies and felonies committed on the high seas, and offenses against the law of nations;

11. To declare war, grant letters of marque and reprisal, and make rules concerning captures on land and water;

12. To raise and support armies, but no appropriation of money to that use shall be for a longer term than two years;

13. To provide and maintain a navy;

14. To make rules for the government and regulation of the land and naval forces;

15. To provide for calling forth the militia to execute the laws of the Union, suppress insurrections and repel invasions;

16. To provide for organizing, arming, and disciplining the militia, and for governing such part of them as may be employed in the service of the United States, reserving to the States respectively, the appointment of the officers, and the authority of training the militia according to the discipline prescribed by Congress;

17. To exercise exclusive legislation in all cases whatsoever, over such district (not exceeding ten miles square) as may, by cession of particular States, and the acceptance of Congress, become the seat of the government of the United States, and to exercise like authority over all places purchased by the consent of the legislature of the State in which the same shall be, for the erection of forts, magazines, arsenals, dockyards, and other needful buildings; and

18. To make all laws which shall be necessary and proper for carrying into execution the foregoing powers, and all other powers vested by this Constitution in the government of the United States, or in any department or officer thereof.

SECTION 9

1. The migration or importation of such persons as any of the States now existing shall think proper to admit, shall not be prohibited by the Congress prior to the year one thousand eight hundred and eight, but a tax or duty may be imposed on such importation, not exceeding ten dollars for each person.

2. The privilege of the writ of habeas corpus shall not be suspended, unless when in cases of rebellion or invasion the public safety may require it.

3. No bill of attainder or ex post facto law shall be passed.

4. No capitation, or other direct, tax shall be laid, unless in proportion to the census or enumeration hereinbefore directed to be taken.[1]

5. No tax or duty shall be laid on articles exported from any State.

6. No preference shall be given by any regulation of commerce or revenue to the ports of one State over those of another: nor shall vessels bound to, or from, one State be obliged to enter, clear, or pay duties in another.

7. No money shall be drawn from the treasury, but in consequence of appropriations made by law; and a regular statement and account of the receipts and expenditures of all public money shall be published from time to time.

8. No title of nobility shall be granted by the United States: and no person holding any office of profit or trust under them, shall, without the consent of the Congress, accept of any present, emolument, office, or title, of any kind whatever, from any king, prince, or foreign State.

SECTION 10

1. No State shall enter into any treaty, alliance, or confederation; grant letters of marque and reprisal; coin money; emit bills of credit; make anything but gold and silver coin a tender in payment of debts; pass any bill of attainder, ex post facto law, or law impairing the obligation of contracts, or grant any title of nobility.

2. No State shall, without the consent of the Congress, lay any imposts or duties on imports or exports, except what may be absolutely necessary for executing its inspection laws: and the net produce of all duties and imposts laid by any State on imports or exports, shall be for the use of the treasury of the United States; and all such laws shall be subject to the revision and control of the Congress.

[1] Revised by the 16th Amendment.

3. No State shall, without the consent of the Congress, lay any duty of tonnage, keep troops, or ships of war in time of peace, enter into any agreement or compact with another State, or with a foreign power, or engage in war, unless actually invaded, or in such imminent danger as will not admit of delay.

ARTICLE II

SECTION 1

1. The executive power shall be vested in a President of the United States of America. He shall hold his office during the term of four years, and, together with the Vice President, chosen for the same term, be elected as follows:

2. Each State shall appoint, in such manner as the legislature thereof may direct, a number of electors, equal to the whole number of senators and representatives to which the State may be entitled in the Congress: but no senator or representative, or person holding an office of trust or profit under the United States, shall be appointed an elector.

The electors shall meet in their respective States, and vote by ballot for two persons, of whom one at least shall not be an inhabitant of the same State with themselves. And they shall make a list of all the persons voted for, and of the number of votes for each; which list they shall sign and certify, and transmit sealed to the seat of the government of the United States, directed to the president of the Senate. The president of the Senate shall, in the presence of the Senate and House of Representatives, open all the certificates, and the votes shall then be counted. The person having the greatest number of votes shall be the President, if such number be a majority of the whole number of electors appointed; and if there be more than one who have such majority, and have an equal number of votes, then the House of Representatives shall immediately choose by ballot one of them for President; and if no person have a majority, then from the five highest on the list the said House shall in like manner choose the President. But in choosing the President, the votes shall be taken by States, the representation from each State having one vote; a quorum for this purpose shall consist of a member or members from two thirds of the States, and a majority of all the States shall be necessary to a choice. In every case, after the choice of the President, the person having the greatest number of votes of the electors shall be the Vice President. But if there should remain two or more who have equal votes, the Senate shall choose from them by ballot the Vice President.[1]

[1] Voided by the 12th Amendment.

3. The Congress may determine the time of choosing the electors, and the day on which they shall give their votes; which day shall be the same throughout the United States.

4. No person except a natural born citizen, or a citizen of the United States, at the time of the adoption of this Constitution, shall be eligible to the office of President; neither shall any person be eligible to that office who shall not have attained to the age of thirty-five years, and been fourteen years a resident within the United States.

5. In case of the removal of the President from office, or of his death, resignation, or inability to discharge the powers and duties of the said office, the same shall devolve on the Vice President, and the Congress may by law provide for the case of removal, death, resignation, or inability, both of the President and Vice President, declaring what officer shall then act as President, and such officer shall act accordingly, until the disability be removed, or a President shall be elected.

6. The President shall, at stated times, receive for his services a compensation, which shall neither be increased nor diminished during the period for which he shall have been elected, and he shall not receive within that period any other emolument from the United States, or any of them.

7. Before he enter on the execution of his office, he shall take the following oath or affirmation: — "I do solemnly swear (or affirm) that I will faithfully execute the office of President of the United States, and will to the best of my ability, preserve, protect and defend the Constitution of the United States."

SECTION 2

1. The President shall be the commander in chief of the army and navy of the United States, and of the militia of the several States, when called into the actual service of the United States; he may require the opinion, in writing, of the principal officer in each of the executive departments, upon any subject relating to the duties of their respective offices, and he shall have power to grant reprieves and pardons for offenses against the United States, except in cases of impeachment.

2. He shall have power, by and with the advice and consent of the Senate, to make treaties, provided two thirds of the senators present concur; and he shall nominate, and by and with the advice and consent of the Senate, shall appoint ambassadors, other public ministers and consuls, judges of the Supreme Court, and all other officers of the United States, whose appointments are not herein otherwise provided for, and which shall be established by law: but the Congress may by law vest the

appointment of such inferior officers, as they think proper, in the President alone, in the courts of law, or in the heads of departments.

3. The President shall have power to fill up all vacancies that may happen during the recess of the Senate, by granting commissions which shall expire at the end of their next session.

SECTION 3

He shall from time to time give to the Congress information of the state of the Union, and recommend to their consideration such measures as he shall judge necessary and expedient; he may, on extraordinary occasions, convene both Houses, or either of them, and in case of disagreement between them with respect to the time of adjournment, he may adjourn them to such time as he shall think proper; he shall receive ambassadors and other public ministers; he shall take care that the laws be faithfully executed, and shall commission all the officers of the United States.

SECTION 4

The President, Vice President, and all civil officers of the United States, shall be removed from office on impeachment for, and conviction of, treason, bribery, or other high crimes and misdemeanors.

ARTICLE III

SECTION 1

The judicial power of the United States shall be vested in one Supreme Court, and in such inferior courts as the Congress may from time to time ordain and establish. The judges, both of the Supreme and inferior courts, shall hold their offices during good behavior, and shall, at stated times, receive for their services, a compensation, which shall not be diminished during their continuance in office.

SECTION 2

1. The judicial power shall extend to all cases, in law and equity, arising under this Constitution, the laws of the United States, and treaties made, or which shall be made, under their authority; — to all cases affecting ambassadors, other public ministers and consuls; — to all cases of admiralty and maritime jurisdiction; — to controversies to which the United States shall be a party;[1] — to controversies between two or more States; — between citizens of different States; — between citizens of the same State claiming lands under grants of different States, and between a State, or the citizens thereof, and foreign States, citizens or subjects.

[1] Revised by the 11th Amendment.

2. In all cases affecting ambassadors, other public ministers and consuls, and those in which a State shall be party, the Supreme Court shall have original jurisdiction. In all the other cases before mentioned, the Supreme Court shall have appellate jurisdiction, both as to law and to fact, with such exceptions, and under such regulations as the Congress shall make.

3. The trial of all crimes, except in cases of impeachment, shall be by jury; and such trial shall be held in the State where the said crimes shall have been committed; but when not committed within any State, the trial shall be at such place or places as the Congress may by law have directed.

SECTION 3

1. Treason against the United States shall consist only in levying war against them, or in adhering to their enemies, giving them aid and comfort. No person shall be convicted of treason unless on the testimony of two witnesses to the same overt act, or in confession in open court.

2. The Congress shall have power to declare the punishment of treason, but no attainder of treason shall work corruption of blood, or forfeiture except during the life of the person attainted.

ARTICLE IV

SECTION 1

Full faith and credit shall be given in each State to the public acts, records, and judicial proceedings of every other State. And the Congress may by general laws prescribe the manner in which such acts, records and proceedings shall be proved, and the effect thereof.

SECTION 2

1. The citizens of each State shall be entitled to all privileges and immunities of citizens in the several States.[1]

2. A person charged in any State with treason, felony, or other crime, who shall flee from justice, and be found in another State, shall on demand of the executive authority of the State from which he fled, be delivered up to be removed to the State having jurisdiction of the crime.

3. No person held to service or labor in one State under the laws thereof, escaping into another, shall, in consequence of any law or regulation therein, be discharged from such service or labor, but shall be delivered up on claim of the party to whom such service or labor may be due.[2]

[1] Elaborated by the 14th Amendment, Sec. 1.
[2] See the 13th Amendment, abolishing slavery.

SECTION 3

1. New States may be admitted by the Congress into this Union; but no new State shall be formed or erected within the jurisdiction of any other State; nor any State be formed by the junction of two or more States, or parts of States, without the consent of the legislatures of the States concerned as well as of the Congress.

2. The Congress shall have power to dispose of and make all needful rules and regulations respecting the territory or other property belonging to the United States; and nothing in this Constitution shall be so construed as to prejudice any claims of the United States, or of any particular State.

SECTION 4

The United States shall guarantee to every State in this Union a republican form of government, and shall protect each of them against invasion; and on application of the legislature, or of the executive (when the legislature cannot be convened) against domestic violence.

ARTICLE V

The Congress, whenever two thirds of both Houses shall deem it necessary, shall propose amendments to this Constitution, or, on the application of the legislatures of two thirds of the several States, shall call a convention for proposing amendments, which in either case, shall be valid to all intents and purposes, as part of this Constitution when ratified by the legislatures of three fourths of the several States, or by conventions in three fourths thereof, as the one or the other mode of ratification may be proposed by the Congress; Provided that no amendment which may be made prior to the year one thousand eight hundred and eight shall in any manner affect the first and fourth clauses in the ninth section of the first article; and that no State, without its consent, shall be deprived of its equal suffrage in the Senate.

ARTICLE VI

1. All debts contracted and engagements entered into, before the adoption of this Constitution, shall be as valid against the United States under this Constitution, as under the Confederation.[1]

2. This Constitution, and the laws of the United States which shall be made in pursuance thereof; and all treaties made, or which shall be made, under the authority of the United States, shall be the supreme law of the land; and the Judges in every State shall be bound thereby, anything in the Constitution

[1] See the 14th Amendment, Sec. 4, for additional provisions.

or laws of any State to the contrary notwithstanding.

3. The senators and representatives before mentioned, and the members of the several State legislatures, and all executive and judicial officers, both of the United States and of the several States, shall be bound by oath or affirmation to support this Constitution; but no religious test shall ever be required as a qualification to any office or public trust under the United States.

ARTICLE VII

The ratification of the conventions of nine States shall be sufficient for the establishment of this Constitution between the States so ratifying the same.

Done in Convention by the unanimous consent of the States present the seventeenth day of September in the year of our Lord one thousand seven hundred and eighty-seven, and of the independence of the United States of America the twelfth. In witness whereof we have hereunto subscribed our names.

AMENDMENTS

First Ten Amendments submitted by Congress September 25, 1789. Ratified by three-fourths of the States December 15, 1791.

ARTICLE I

Congress shall make no law respecting an establishment of religion, or prohibiting the free exercise thereof; or abridging the freedom of speech, or of the press; or the right of the people peaceably to assemble, and to petition the government for a redress of grievances.

ARTICLE II

A well regulated militia, being necessary to the security of a free State, the right of the people to keep and bear arms, shall not be infringed.

ARTICLE III

No soldier shall, in time of peace be quartered in any house, without the consent of the owner, nor in time of war, but in a manner to be prescribed by law.

ARTICLE IV

The right of the people to be secure in their persons, houses, papers, and effects, against unreasonable searches and seizures, shall not be violated, and no warrants shall issue, but upon probable cause, supported by oath or affirmation, and particularly describing the place to be searched, and the persons or things to be seized.

ARTICLE V

No person shall be held to answer for a capital, or otherwise infamous crime, unless on a presentment or indictment of a grand jury, except in cases arising in the land or naval forces, or in the militia, when in actual service in time of war or public danger; nor shall any person be subject for the same offense to be twice put in jeopardy of life or limb; nor shall be compelled in any criminal case to be a witness against himself, nor be deprived of life, liberty, or property, without due process of law; nor shall private property be taken for public use without just compensation.

ARTICLE VI

In all criminal prosecutions, the accused shall enjoy the right to a speedy and public trial, by an impartial jury of the State and district wherein the crime shall have been committed, which district shall have been previously ascertained by law, and to be informed of the nature and cause of the accusation; to be confronted with the witnesses against him; to have compulsory process for obtaining witnesses in his favor, and to have the assistance of counsel for his defense.

ARTICLE VII

In suits at common law, where the value in controversy shall exceed twenty dollars, the right of trial by jury shall be preserved, and no fact tried by a jury shall be otherwise reëxamined in any court of the United States, than according to the rules of the common law.

ARTICLE VIII

Excessive bail shall not be required, nor excessive fines imposed, nor cruel and unusual punishments inflicted.

ARTICLE IX

The enumeration in the Constitution of certain rights shall not be construed to deny or disparage others retained by the people.

ARTICLE X

The powers not delegated to the United States by the Constitution, nor prohibited by it to the States, are reserved to the States respectively, or to the people.

ARTICLE XI

Submitted by Congress March 5, 1794. Ratified January 8, 1798.

The judicial power of the United States shall not be construed to extend to any suit in law or equity, commenced or prosecuted against one of the United States by citizens of another State, or by citizens or subjects of any foreign State.

ARTICLE XII

Submitted by Congress December 12, 1803. Ratified September 25, 1804.

The electors shall meet in their respective States, and vote by ballot for President and Vice President, one of whom, at least, shall not be an inhabitant of the same State with themselves; they shall name in their ballots the person voted for as President, and in distinct ballots, the person voted for as Vice President, and they shall make distinct lists of all persons voted for as President and of all persons voted for as Vice President, and of the number of votes for each, which lists they shall sign and certify, and transmit sealed to the seat of the government of the United States, directed to the President of the Senate; — The President of the Senate shall, in the presence of the Senate and House of Representatives, open all the certificates and the votes shall then be counted; — The person having the greatest number of votes for President, shall be the President, if such number be a majority of the whole number of electors appointed; and if no person have such majority, then from the persons having the highest numbers not exceeding three on the list of those voted for as President, the House of Representatives shall choose immediately, by ballot the President. But in choosing the President, the votes shall be taken by States, the representation from each State having one vote; a quorum for this purpose shall consist of a member or members from two thirds of the States, and a majority of all the States shall be necessary to a choice. And if the House of Representatives shall not choose a President whenever the right of choice shall devolve upon them, before the fourth day of March next following, then the Vice President shall act as President, as in the case of the death or other constitutional disability of the President. The person having the greatest number of votes as Vice President shall be the Vice President, if such number be a majority of the whole number of electors appointed, and if no person have a majority, then from the two highest numbers on the list, the Senate shall choose the Vice President; a quorum for the purpose shall consist of two thirds of the whole number of Senators, and a majority of the whole number shall be necessary to a choice. But no person constitutionally ineligible to the office of President shall be eligible to that of Vice President of the United States.

ARTICLE XIII

Submitted by Congress February 1, 1864. Ratified December 18, 1865.

SECTION 1

Neither slavery nor involuntary servitude, except as punishment for crime whereof the party shall have been duly convicted, shall exist within the United States, or any place subject to their jurisdiction.

SECTION 2

Congress shall have power to enforce this article by appropriate legislation.

ARTICLE XIV

Submitted by Congress June 16, 1866. Ratified July 28, 1868.

SECTION 1

All persons born or naturalized in the United States, and subject to the jurisdiction thereof, are citizens of the United States and of the State wherein they reside. No State shall make or enforce any law which shall abridge the privileges or immunities of citizens of the United States; nor shall any State deprive any person of life, liberty, or property, without due process of law; nor deny to any person within its jurisdiction the equal protection of the laws.

SECTION 2

Representatives shall be apportioned among the several States according to their respective numbers, counting the whole number of persons in each State, excluding Indians not taxed. But when the right to vote at any election for the choice of electors for President and Vice President of the United States, representatives in Congress, the executive and judicial officers of a State, or the members of the legislature thereof, is denied to any of the male inhabitants of such State, being twenty-one years of age, and citizens of the United States, or in any way abridged, except for participation in rebellion, or other crime, the basis of representation therein shall be reduced in the proportion which the number of such male citizens shall bear to the whole number of male citizens twenty-one years of age in such State.

SECTION 3

No person shall be a senator or representative in Congress, or elector of President and Vice President, or hold any office, civil or military, under the United States, or under any State, who having previously taken an oath, as a member of Congress, or as an officer of the United States, or as a member of any State legislature, or as an executive or judicial officer of any State, to support the Constitution of the United States, shall have engaged in insurrection or rebellion against the same, or given aid or comfort to the enemies thereof. But Congress may by a vote of two thirds of each House, remove such disability.

SECTION 4

The validity of the public debt of the United States, authorized by law, including debts incurred for payment of pensions and bounties for services in suppressing insurrection or rebellion, shall not be questioned. But neither the United States nor any State shall assume or pay any debt or obligation incurred in aid of insurrection or rebellion against the United States, or any claim for the loss or emancipation of any slave; but all such debts, obligations, and claims shall be held illegal and void.

SECTION 5

The Congress shall have power to enforce, by appropriate legislation, the provisions of this article.

ARTICLE XV

Submitted by Congress February 27, 1869. Ratified March 30, 1870.

SECTION 1

The right of citizens of the United States to vote shall not be denied or abridged by the United States or by any State on account of race, color, or previous condition of servitude.

SECTION 2

The Congress shall have power to enforce this article by appropriate legislation.

ARTICLE XVI

Submitted by Congress July 12, 1909. Ratified February 25, 1913.

The Congress shall have power to lay and collect taxes on incomes, from whatever source derived, without apportionment among the several States, and without regard to any census or enumeration.

ARTICLE XVII

Submitted by Congress May 16, 1912. Ratified May 31, 1913.

The Senate of the United States shall be composed of two senators from each state, elected by the people thereof, for six years; and each senator shall have one vote. The electors in each State shall have the qualifications requisite for electors of the most numerous branch of the State legislature.

When vacancies happen in the representation of any State in the Senate, the executive authority of such State shall issue writs of election to fill such vacancies: *Provided,* That the legislature of any State may empower the executive thereof to make temporary appointments until the people fill the vacancies by election as the legislature may direct.

This amendment shall not be so construed as to affect the election or term of any senator chosen before it becomes valid as part of the Constitution.

ARTICLE XVIII[1]

Submitted by Congress December 17, 1917. Ratified January 29, 1919.

After one year from the ratification of this

[1] Repealed by the 21st Amendment.

article, the manufacture, sale, or transportation of intoxicating liquors within, the importation thereof into, or the exportation thereof from the United States and all territory subject to the jurisdiction thereof for beverage purposes is hereby prohibited.

The Congress and the several States shall have concurrent power to enforce this article by appropriate legislation.

This article shall be inoperative unless it shall have been ratified as an amendment to the Constitution by the legislatures of the several States, as provided in the Constitution, within seven years from the date of the submission hereof to the states by Congress.

ARTICLE XIX

Submitted by Congress June 5, 1919. Ratified August 26, 1920.

The right of citizens of the United States to vote shall not be denied or abridged by the United States or by any State on account of sex.

The Congress shall have power by appropriate legislation to enforce the provisions of this article.

ARTICLE XX

Submitted by Congress March 3, 1932. Ratified January 23, 1933.

SECTION 1

The terms of the President and Vice President shall end at noon on the 20th day of January, and the terms of Senators and Representatives at noon on the 3d day of January, of the years in which such terms would have ended if this article had not been ratified; and the terms of their successors shall then begin.

SECTION 2

The Congress shall assemble at least once in every year, and such meeting shall begin at noon on the 3d day of January, unless they shall by law appoint a different day.

SECTION 3

If, at the time fixed for the beginning of the term of the President, the President-elect shall have died, the Vice President-elect shall become President. If a President shall not have been chosen before the time fixed for the beginning of his term, or if the President-elect shall have failed to qualify, then the Vice President-elect shall act as President until a President shall have qualified; and the Congress may by law provide for the case wherein neither a President-elect nor a Vice President-elect shall have qualified, declaring who shall then act as President, or the manner in which one who is to act shall be selected, and such person shall act accordingly until a President or Vice President shall have qualified.

SECTION 4

The Congress may by law provide for the case of the death of any of the persons from whom the House of Representatives may choose a President whenever the right of choice shall have devolved upon them, and for the case of the death of any of the persons from whom the Senate may choose a Vice President whenever the right of choice shall have devolved upon them.

SECTION 5

Sections 1 and 2 shall take effect on the 15th day of October following the ratification of this article.

SECTION 6

This article shall be inoperative unless it shall have been ratified as an amendment to the Constitution by the legislatures of three-fourths of the several States within seven years from the date of its submission.

ARTICLE XXI

Submitted by Congress February 20, 1933. Ratified December 5, 1933.

SECTION 1

The Eighteenth Article of amendment to the Constitution of the United States is hereby repealed.

SECTION 2

The transportation or importation into any State, Territory, or possession of the United States for delivery or use therein of intoxicating liquors in violation of the laws thereof, is hereby prohibited.

SECTION 3

This article shall be inoperative unless it shall have been ratified as an amendment to the Constitution by conventions in the several States, as provided in the Constitution, within seven years from the date of the submission thereof to the States by the Congress.

ARTICLE XXII

Submitted by Congress March 12, 1947. Ratified March 1, 1951.

No person shall be elected to the office of the President more than twice, and no person who has held the office of President, or acted as President, for more than two years of a term to which some other person was elected President shall be elected to the office of the President more than once.

But this article shall not apply to any person holding the office of President when this article was proposed by the Congress, and shall not prevent any person who may be holding the office of President, or acting as President, during the term within which this article becomes operative from holding the office of

President or acting as President during the remainder of such term.

This article shall be inoperative unless it shall have been ratified as an amendment to the Constitution by the legislatures of three-fourths of the several states within seven years from the date of its submission to the states by the Congress.

ARTICLE XXIII

Submitted by Congress June 16, 1960. Ratified April 3, 1961.

SECTION 1

The District constituting the seat of Government of the United States shall appoint in such manner as the Congress may direct:

A number of electors of President and Vice-President equal to the whole number of Senators and Representatives in Congress to which the District would be entitled if it were a State, but in no event more than the least populous State; they shall be in addition to those appointed by the States, but they shall be considered, for the purpose of the election of President and Vice-President, to be electors appointed by a State; and they shall meet in the District and perform such duties as provided by the twelfth article of amendment.

SECTION 2

The Congress shall have power to enforce this article by appropriate legislation.

ARTICLE XXIV

Submitted by Congress August 27, 1962. Ratified January 23, 1964.

SECTION 1

The right of citizens of the United States to vote in any primary or other election for President or Vice President, or for Senator or Representatives in Congress, shall not be denied or abridged by the United States or any State by reason of failure to pay any poll tax or other tax.

SECTION 2

The Congress shall have power to enforce this article by appropriate legislation.

The Fourteen Points

GIVEN TO CONGRESS BY PRESIDENT WILSON, JAN. 8, 1918

I. Open covenants of peace, openly arrived at, after which there shall be no private international understandings of any kind but diplomacy shall proceed always frankly and in the public view.

II. Absolute freedom of navigation upon the seas, outside territorial waters, alike in peace and in war, except as the seas may be closed in whole or in part by international action for the enforcement of international covenants.

III. The removal, so far as possible, of all economic barriers and the establishment of an equality of trade conditions among all the nations consenting to the peace and associating themselves for its maintenance.

IV. Adequate guarantees given and taken that national armaments will be reduced to the lowest point consistent with domestic safety.

V. A free, open-minded, and absolutely impartial adjustment of all colonial claims, based upon a strict observance of the principle that in determining all such questions of sovereignty the interests of the populations concerned must have equal weight with the equitable claims of the government whose title is to be determined.

VI. The evacuation of all Russian territory and such a settlement of all questions affecting Russia as will secure the best and freest cooperation of the other nations of the world in obtaining for her an unhampered and unembarrassed opportunity for the independent determination of her own political development and national policy and assure her of a sincere welcome into the society of free nations under institutions of her own choosing; and, more than a welcome, assistance also of every kind that she may need and may herself desire. The treatment accorded Russia by her sister nations in the months to come will be the acid test of their good will, of their comprehension of her needs as distinguished from their own interests, and of their intelligent and unselfish sympathy.

VII. Belgium, the whole world will agree, must be evacuated and restored, without any attempt to limit the sovereignty which she enjoys in common with all other free nations. No other single act will serve as this will serve to restore confidence among the nations in the laws which they have themselves set and determined for the government of their relations with one another. Without this healing act the whole structure and validity of international law is forever impaired.

VIII. All French territory should be freed and the invaded portions restored, and the wrong done to France by Prussia in 1871 in the matter of Alsace-Lorraine, which has unsettled the peace of the world for nearly fifty years, should be righted, in order that peace may once more be made secure in the interest of all.

IX. A readjustment of the frontiers of Italy should be effected along clearly recognizable lines of nationality.

X. The peoples of Austria-Hungary, whose place among the nations we wish to see safeguarded and assured, should be accorded the freest opportunity of autonomous development.

XI. Rumania, Serbia, and Montenegro should be evacuated; occupied territories restored; Serbia accorded free and secure access to the sea; and the relations of the several Balkan states to one another determined by friendly counsel along historically established lines of allegiance and nationality; and international guarantees of the political and economic independence and territorial integrity of the several Balkan states should be entered into.

XII. The Turkish portions of the present Ottoman Empire should be assured a secure sovereignty, but the other nationalities which are now under Turkish rule should be assured an undoubted security of life and an absolutely unmolested opportunity of autonomous development, and the Dardanelles should be permanently opened as a free passage to the ships and commerce of all nations under international guarantees.

XIII. An independent Polish state should be erected which should include the territories inhabited by indisputably Polish populations, which should be assured a free and secure access to the sea, and whose political and economic independence and territorial integrity should be guaranteed by international covenant.

XIV. A general association of nations must be formed under specific covenants for the purpose of affording mutual guarantees of political independence and territorial integrity to great and small states alike.

The Four Freedoms

FROM PRESIDENT ROOSEVELT'S ANNUAL MESSAGE TO CONGRESS, JAN. 6, 1941

In the future days, which we seek to make secure, we look forward to a world founded upon four essential human freedoms.

The first is freedom of speech and expression — everywhere in the world.

The second is freedom of every person to worship God in his own way — everywhere in the world.

The third is freedom from want — which, translated into world terms, means economic understandings which will secure to every nation a healthy peacetime life for its inhabitants — everywhere in the world.

The fourth is freedom from fear — which, translated into world terms, means a world-wide reduction of armaments to such a point and in such a thorough fashion that no nation will be in a position to commit an act of physical aggression against any neighbor — anywhere in the world.

That is no vision of a distant millennium. It is a definite basis for a kind of world attainable in our own time and generation. That kind of world is the very antithesis of the so-called new order of tyranny which the dictators seek to create with the crash of a bomb.

To that new order we oppose the greater conception — the moral order. A good society is able to face schemes of world domination and foreign revolutions alike without fear.

Since the beginning of our American history we have been engaged in change — in a perpetual peaceful revolution — a revolution which goes on steadily, quietly adjusting itself to changing conditions — without the concentration camp or the quick-lime in the ditch. The world order which we seek is the cooperation of free countries, working together in a friendly, civilized society.

This nation has placed its destiny in the hands and heads and hearts of its millions of free men and women; and its faith in freedom under the guidance of God. Freedom means the supremacy of human rights everywhere. Our support goes to those who struggle to gain those rights or keep them. Our strength is in our unity of purpose.

To that high concept there can be no end save victory.

The Atlantic Charter

ISSUED AUGUST 14, 1941

The President of the United States of America and the Prime Minister, Mr. Churchill, representing His Majesty's Government in the United Kingdom, being met together, deem it right to make known certain common principles in the national policies of their respective countries on which they base their hopes for a better future for the world.

First, their countries seek no aggrandizement, territorial or other;

Second, they desire to see no territorial changes that do not accord with the freely expressed wishes of the peoples concerned;

Third, they respect the right of all peoples to choose the form of government under which they will live; and they wish to see sovereign rights and self government restored to those who have been forcibly deprived of them;

Fourth, they will endeavor, with due respect for their existing obligations, to further the enjoyment of all States, great or small, victor or vanquished, of access, on equal terms, to the trade and to the raw materials of the world which are needed for their economic prosperity;

Fifth, they desire to bring about the fullest collaboration between all nations in the economic field with the object of securing, for all, improved labor standards, economic advancement and social security;

Sixth, after the final destruction of Nazi tyranny, they hope to see established a peace which will afford to all nations the means of dwelling in safety within their own boundaries, and which will afford assurance that all men in all lands may live out their lives in freedom from fear and want;

Seventh, such a peace should enable all men to traverse the high seas and oceans without hindrance;

Eighth, they believe that all the nations of the world, for realistic, as well as spiritual reasons, must come to the abandonment of the use of force. Since no future peace can be maintained if land, sea or air armaments continue to be employed by nations which threaten, or may threaten aggression outside of their frontiers, they believe, pending the establishment of a wider and permanent system of general security, that the disarmament of such nations is essential. They will likewise aid and encourage all other practicable measures which will lighten for peace-loving peoples the crushing burden of armaments.

Charter of the United Nations

WE, the peoples of the United Nations determined to save succeeding generations from the scourge of war, which twice in our lifetime has brought untold sorrow to mankind, and

To reaffirm faith in fundamental human rights, in the dignity and worth of the human person, in the equal rights of men and women and of nations large and small, and

To establish conditions under which justice and respect for the obligations arising from treaties and other sources of international law can be maintained, and

To promote social progress and better standards of life in larger freedom, and for these ends

To practice tolerance and live together in peace with one another as good neighbors, and

To unite our strength to maintain international peace and security, and

To insure, by the acceptance of principles and the institution of methods, that armed force shall not be used, save in the common interest, and

To employ international machinery for the promotion of the economic and social advancement of all peoples, have resolved to combine our efforts to accomplish these aims.

Accordingly, our respective governments, through representatives assembled in the city of San Francisco, who have exhibited their full powers found to be in good and due form, have agreed to the present Charter of the United Nations and do hereby establish an international organization to be known as the United Nations.

CHAPTER I

Purposes and Principles

ARTICLE 1

The purposes of the United Nations are:

1. To maintain international peace and security, and to that end: to take effective collective measures for the prevention and removal of threats to the peace, and for the suppression of acts of aggression or other breaches of the peace, and to bring about by peaceful means, and in conformity with the principles of justice and international law, adjustment or settlement of international disputes or situations which might lead to a breach of peace;

2. To develop friendly relations among nations based on respect for the principle of equal rights and self-determination of peoples, and to take other appropriate measures to strengthen universal peace;

3. To achieve international co-operation in solving international problems of an economic, social, cultural or humanitarian character, and

in promoting and encouraging respect for human rights and for fundamental freedoms for all without distinction as to race, sex, language or religion; and

4. To be a center for harmonizing the actions of nations in the attainment of these common ends.

ARTICLE 2

The organization and its members, in pursuit of the purposes stated in Article 1, shall act in accordance with the following principles:

1. The organization is based on the principle of the sovereign equality of all its members.

2. All members, in order to ensure to all of them the rights and benefits resulting from membership, shall fulfill in good faith the obligations assumed by them in accordance with the present Charter.

3. All members shall settle their international disputes by peaceful means in such a manner that international peace and security, and justice, are not endangered.

4. All members shall refrain in their international relations from the threat or use of force against the territorial integrity or political independence of any state, or in any other manner inconsistent with the purposes of the United Nations.

5. All members shall give the United Nations every assistance in any action it takes in accordance with the present Charter, and shall refrain from giving assistance to any state against which the United Nations is taking preventive or enforcement action.

6. The organization shall ensure that states not members of the United Nations act in accordance with these principles so far as may be necessary for the maintenance of international peace and security.

7. Nothing contained in the present Charter shall authorize the United Nations to intervene in matters which are essentially within the domestic jurisdiction of any state or shall require the members to submit such matters to settlement under the present Charter; but this principle shall not prejudice the application of enforcement measures under Chapter VII.

CHAPTER II

Membership

ARTICLE 3

The original members of the United Nations shall be the states which, having participated in the United Nations Conference on International Organization at San Francisco, or have previously signed the Declaration by United Nations of Jan. 1, 1942, sign the present Charter and ratify it in accordance with Article 110.

North Atlantic Treaty

SIGNED AT WASHINGTON, D.C., APRIL 4, 1949

The Parties to this Treaty reaffirm their faith in the purposes and principles of the Charter of the United Nations and their desire to live in peace with all peoples and all governments.

They are determined to safeguard the freedom, common heritage and civilization of their peoples, founded on the principles of democracy, individual liberty and the rule of law.

They seek to promote stability and well-being in the North Atlantic area.

They are resolved to unite their efforts for collective defense and for the preservation of peace and security.

They therefore agree to this North Atlantic Treaty:

ARTICLE 1

The Parties undertake, as set forth in the Charter of the United Nations, to settle any international disputes in which they may be involved by peaceful means in such a manner that international peace and security, and justice, are not endangered, and to refrain in their international relations from the threat or use of force in any manner inconsistent with the purposes of the United Nations.

ARTICLE 2

The Parties will contribute toward the further development of peaceful and friendly international relations by strengthening their free institutions, by bringing about a better understanding of the principles upon which these institutions are founded, and by promoting conditions of stability and well-being. They will seek to eliminate conflict in their international economic policies and will encourage economic collaboration between any or all of them.

ARTICLE 3

In order more effectively to achieve the objectives of this Treaty, the Parties, separately and jointly, by means of continuous and effective self-help and mutual aid, will maintain and develop their individual and collective capacity to resist armed attack.

ARTICLE 4

The Parties will consult together whenever, in the opinion of any of them, the territorial integrity, political independence or security of any of the Parties is threatened.

ARTICLE 5

The Parties agree that an armed attack against one or more of them in Europe or North America shall be considered an attack against them all; and consequently they agree that, if such an armed attack occurs, each of them, in exercise of the right of individual or collective self-defense recognized by Article 51 of the Charter of the United Nations, will assist the Party or Parties so attacked by taking forthwith, individually and in concert with the other Parties, such action as it deems necessary, including the use of armed force, to restore and maintain the security of the North Atlantic area.

Any such armed attack and all measures taken as a result thereof shall immediately be reported to the Security Council. Such measures shall be terminated when the Security Council has taken the measures necessary to restore and maintain international peace and security.

ARTICLE 6

For the purpose of Article 5 an armed attack on one or more of the Parties is deemed to include an armed attack on the territory of any of the Parties in Europe or North America, on the Algerian departments of France, on the occupation forces of any Party in Europe, on the islands under the jurisdiction of any Party in the North Atlantic area north of the Tropic of Cancer or on the vessels or aircraft in this area of any of the Parties.

ARTICLE 7

This Treaty does not affect, and shall not be interpreted as affecting, in any way the rights and obligations under the Charter of the Parties which are members of the United Nations, or the primary responsibility of the Security Council for the maintenance of international peace and security.

ARTICLE 8

Each Party declares that none of the international engagements now in force between it and any other of the Parties or any third state is in conflict with the provisions of this Treaty, and undertakes not to enter into any international engagement in conflict with this Treaty.

ARTICLE 9

The Parties hereby establish a council, on which each of them shall be represented, to consider matters concerning the implementation of this Treaty. The council shall be so organized as to be able to meet promptly at any time. The council shall set up such subsidiary bodies as may be necessary; in particular it shall establish immediately a defense committee which shall recommend measures for the implementation of Articles 3 and 5.

ARTICLE 10

The Parties may, by unanimous agreement, invite any other European state in a position to further the principles of this Treaty and to contribute to the security of the North Atlantic area to accede to this Treaty. Any state so invited may become a party to the Treaty by depositing its instrument of accession with the Government of the United States of America. The Government of the United States of America will inform each of the Parties of the deposit of each such instrument of accession.

ARTICLE 11

This Treaty shall be ratified and its provisions carried out by the Parties in accordance with their respective constitutional processes. The instruments of ratification shall be deposited as soon as possible with the Government of the United States of America, which will notify all the other signatories of each deposit. The Treaty shall enter into force between the states which have ratified it as soon as the ratifications of the majority of the signatories, including the ratifications of Belgium, Canada, France, Luxemburg, the Netherlands, the United Kingdom and the United States, have been deposited and shall come into effect with respect to other states on the date of the deposit of their ratifications.

ARTICLE 12

After the Treaty has been in force for ten years, or at any time thereafter, the Parties shall, if any of them so requests, consult together for the purpose of reviewing the Treaty, having regard for the factors then affecting peace and security in the North Atlantic area, including the development of universal as well as regional arrangements under the Charter of the United Nations for the maintenance of international peace and security.

ARTICLE 13

After the Treaty has been in force for twenty years, any Party may cease to be a party one year after its notice of denunciation has been given to the Government of the United States of America, which will inform the Governments of the other Parties of the deposit of each notice of denunciation.

ARTICLE 14

This Treaty, of which the English and French texts are equally authentic, shall be deposited in the archives of the Government of the United States of America. Duly certified copies thereof will be transmitted by that Government to the Governments of the other signatories.

The States of the Union

(with dates of ratification of the Constitution or admission to the Union)

1. Delaware	Dec. 7, 1787	26. Michigan	Jan. 26, 1837
2. Pennsylvania	Dec. 12, 1787	27. Florida	Mar. 3, 1845
3. New Jersey	Dec. 18, 1787	28. Texas	Dec. 29, 1845
4. Georgia	Jan. 2, 1788	29. Iowa	Dec. 28, 1846
5. Connecticut	Jan. 9, 1788	30. Wisconsin	May 29, 1848
6. Massachusetts	Feb. 6, 1788	31. California	Sept. 9, 1850
7. Maryland	Apr. 28, 1788	32. Minnesota	May 11, 1858
8. South Carolina	May 23, 1788	33. Oregon	Feb. 14, 1859
9. New Hampshire	June 21, 1788	34. Kansas	Jan. 29, 1861
10. Virginia	June 25, 1788	35. West Virginia	June 19, 1863
11. New York	July 26, 1788	36. Nevada	Oct. 31, 1864
12. North Carolina	Nov. 21, 1789	37. Nebraska	Mar. 1, 1867
13. Rhode Island	May 29, 1790	38. Colorado	Aug. 1, 1876
14. Vermont	Mar. 4, 1791	39. North Dakota	Nov. 2, 1889
15. Kentucky	June 1, 1792	40. South Dakota	Nov. 2, 1889
16. Tennessee	June 1, 1796	41. Montana	Nov. 8, 1889
17. Ohio	Mar. 1, 1803	42. Washington	Nov. 11, 1889
18. Louisiana	Apr. 30, 1812	43. Idaho	July 3, 1890
19. Indiana	Dec. 11, 1816	44. Wyoming	July 10, 1890
20. Mississippi	Dec. 10, 1817	45. Utah	Jan. 4, 1896
21. Illinois	Dec. 3, 1818	46. Oklahoma	Nov. 16, 1907
22. Alabama	Dec. 14, 1819	47. New Mexico	Jan. 6, 1912
23. Maine	Mar. 15, 1820	48. Arizona	Feb. 14, 1912
24. Missouri	Aug. 10, 1821	49. Alaska	Jan. 3, 1959
25. Arkansas	June 15, 1836	50. Hawaii	Aug. 21, 1959

Other Governmental Units

(with appropriate dates)

District of Columbia	Created, July 16, 1790; governmental status fixed, June 11, 1878
Guam	Acquired by treaty, Dec. 10, 1898; became unincorporated territory, Aug. 1, 1950
Puerto Rico	Acquired by treaty, Dec. 10, 1898; achieved commonwealth status, July 3, 1952
American Samoa	Acquired by treaty, Dec. 2, 1899; transferred from Navy to Interior, July 1, 1951
Panama Canal Zone	Acquired by treaty, Nov. 8, 1903; government defined, Aug. 24, 1912
Virgin Islands	Acquired by treaty, Aug. 4, 1916; U.S. took possession, March 31, 1917

Presidents, Vice-Presidents, and Cabinet Members

President	Vice-President	Secretary of State	Secretary of Treasury	Secretary of War
17. Andrew Johnson......1865 Unionist Tennessee		W. H. Seward......1865	Hugh McCulloch......1865	E. M. Stanton......1865 U. S. Grant......1867 L. Thomas......1868 J. M. Schofield......1868
18. Ulysses S. Grant......1869 Republican Illinois	Schuyler Colfax......1869 Republican Indiana Henry Wilson......1873 Republican Massachusetts	E. B. Washburne......1869 Hamilton Fish......1869	Geo. S. Boutwell......1869 W. A. Richardson......1873 Benj. H. Bristow......1874 Lot M. Morrill......1876	J. A. Rawlins......1869 W. T. Sherman......1869 W. W. Belknap......1869 Alphonso Taft......1876 J. D. Cameron......1876
19. Rutherford B. Hayes......1877 Republican Ohio	William A. Wheeler......1877 Republican New York	W. M. Evarts......1877	John Sherman......1877	G. W. McCrary......1877 Alex. Ramsey......1879
20. James A. Garfield......1881 Republican Ohio	Chester A. Arthur......1881 Republican New York	James G. Blaine......1881	Wm. Windom......1881	R. T. Lincoln......1881
21. Chester A. Arthur......1881 Republican New York		F. T. Frelinghuysen......1881	Chas. J. Folger......1881 W. Q. Gresham......1884 Hugh McCulloch......1884	R. T. Lincoln......1881
22. Grover Cleveland......1885 Democratic New York	T. A. Hendricks......1885 Democratic Indiana	Thos. F. Bayard......1885	Daniel Manning......1885 Chas. S. Fairchild......1887	W. C. Endicott......1885
23. Benjamin Harrison......1889 Republican Indiana	Levi P. Morton......1889 Republican New York	James G. Blaine......1889 John W. Foster......1892	Wm. Windom......1889 Charles Foster......1891	R. Proctor......1889 S. B. Elkins......1891
24. Grover Cleveland......1893 Democratic New York	Adlai E. Stevenson......1893 Democratic Illinois	W. Q. Gresham......1893 Richard Olney......1895	John G. Carlisle......1893	D. S. Lamont......1893
25. William McKinley......1897 Republican Ohio	Garret A. Hobart......1897 Republican New Jersey Theodore Roosevelt......1901 Republican New York	John Sherman......1897 Wm. R. Day......1897 John Hay......1898	Lyman J. Gage......1897	R. A. Alger......1897 Elihu Root......1899
26. Theodore Roosevelt......1901 Republican New York	Chas. W. Fairbanks......1905 Republican Indiana	John Hay......1901 Elihu Root......1905 Robert Bacon......1909	Lyman J. Gage......1901 Leslie M. Shaw......1902 G. B. Cortelyou......1907	Elihu Root......1901 Wm. H. Taft......1904 Luke E. Wright......1908

President	Vice President	Secretary of State	Secretary of Treasury	Secretary of War
27. William H. Taft.........1909 Republican Ohio	James S. Sherman......1909 Republican New York	P. C. Knox.........1909	F. MacVeagh.........1909	J. M. Dickinson.........1909 H. L. Stimson.........1911
28. Woodrow Wilson.........1913 Democratic New Jersey	Thomas R. Marshall....1913 Democratic Indiana	Wm. J. Bryan.........1913 Robert Lansing.........1915 Bainbridge Colby......1920	W. G. McAdoo.........1913 Carter Glass.........1918 D. F. Houston.........1920	L. M. Garrison.........1913 N. D. Baker.........1916
29. Warren G. Harding.........1921 Republican Ohio	Calvin Coolidge.......1921 Republican Massachusetts	Chas. E. Hughes.......1921	Andrew W. Mellon.....1921	John W. Weeks.........1921
30. Calvin Coolidge.........1923 Republican Massachusetts	Charles G. Dawes.........1925 Republican Illinois	Chas. E. Hughes......1923 Frank B. Kellogg.......1925	Andrew W. Mellon.....1923	John W. Weeks.........1923 Dwight F. Davis.......1925
31. Herbert Hoover.........1929 Republican California	Charles Curtis.........1929 Republican Kansas	Henry L. Stimson......1929	Andrew W. Mellon.....1929 Ogden L. Mills.........1932	James W. Good.........1929 Pat. J. Hurley.........1929
32. Franklin D. Roosevelt.........1933 Democratic New York	John Nance Garner......1933 Democratic Texas Henry A. Wallace.......1941 Democratic Iowa Harry S. Truman.......1945 Democratic Missouri	Cordell Hull.........1933 E. R. Stettinius, Jr...1944	Wm. H. Woodin.........1933 Henry Morgenthau, Jr...1934	Geo. H. Dern.........1933 H. A. Woodring.........1936 H. L. Stimson.........1940
33. Harry S. Truman.........1945 Democratic Missouri	Alben W. Barkley.........1949 Democratic Kentucky	James F. Byrnes.........1945 Geo. C. Marshall.........1947 Dean G. Acheson.........1949	Fred M. Vinson.........1945 John W. Snyder.........1946	Robt. H. Patterson.......1945 K. C. Royall.........1947 *
34. Dwight D. Eisenhower.........1953 Republican Kansas	Richard M. Nixon.........1953 Republican California	John Foster Dulles.....1953 Christian A. Herter.....1959	George M. Humphrey....1953 Robert B. Anderson....1957	
35. John F. Kennedy.........1961 Democratic Massachusetts	Lyndon B. Johnson.........1961 Democratic Texas	Dean Rusk.........1961	C. Douglas Dillon.......1961	
36. Lyndon B. Johnson.........1963 Democratic Texas	Hubert H. Humphrey.....1965 Democratic Minnesota	Dean Rusk.........1963	C. Douglas Dillon.......1963 Henry H. Fowler.......1965 Joseph W. Barr.........1968	
37. Richard M. Nixon.........1969 Republican	Spiro T. Agnew.........1969 Republican Maryland	William P. Rogers......1969	David M. Kennedy.........1969	

*Lost cabinet status in 1947

Cabinet Members (continued)

Attorney-General	Postmaster-General	Secretary of Navy	Secretary of Interior	Secretary of Agriculture
17. James Speed.....1865 Henry Stanbery...1866 Wm. M. Evarts...1868	Wm. Dennison...1865 A. W. Randall...1866	Gideon Welles.....1865	John P. Usher....1865 James Harlan....1865 O. H. Browning..1866	
18. E. R. Hoar......1869 A. T. Ackerman...1870 Geo. H. Williams..1871 Edw. Pierrepont...1875 Alphonso Taft....1876	J. A. J. Creswell..1869 Jas. W. Marshall.1874 Marshall Jewell..1874 James N. Tyner...1876	Adolph E. Borie...1869 Geo. M. Robeson...1869	Jacob D. Cox....1869 C. Delano....1870 Zach. Chandler...1875	Cabinet status since 1889.
19. Chas. Devens.....1877	David M. Key...1877 Horace Maynard.1880	R. W. Thompson...1877 Nathan Goff, Jr...1881	Carl Schurz.....1877	
20. W. MacVeagh....1881	T. L. James.....1881	W. H. Hunt......1881	S. J. Kirkwood...1881	
21. B. H. Brewster...1881	T. O. Howe.....1881 W. Q. Gresham...1883 Frank Hatton...1884	W. E. Chandler...1881	Henry M. Teller..1881	
22. A. H. Garland....1885	Wm. F. Vilas....1885 D. M. Dickinson..1888	W. C. Whitney....1885	L. Q. C. Lamar...1885 Wm. F. Vilas....1888	N. J. Colman....1889
23. W. H. H. Miller...1889	J. Wanamaker....1889	Benj. F. Tracy.....1889	John W. Noble...1889	J. M. Rusk......1889
24. R. Olney........1893 J. Harmon........1895	W. S. Bissell....1893 W. L. Wilson....1895	Hilary A. Herbert..1893	Hoke Smith......1893 D. R. Francis....1896	J. S. Morton.....1893
25. J. McKenna.......1897 J. W. Griggs......1897 P. C. Knox......1901	James A. Gary...1897 Chas. E. Smith...1898	John D. Long.....1897	C. N. Bliss......1897 E. A. Hitchcock..1899	James Wilson....1897
26. P. C. Knox......1901 W. H. Moody.....1904 C. J. Bonaparte...1907	Chas. E. Smith...1901 Henry C. Payne..1902 Robt. J. Wynne..1904 G. B. Cortelyou...1905 G. von L. Meyer.1907	John D. Long.....1901 Wm. H. Moody...1902 Paul Morton....1904 C. J. Bonaparte...1905 Victor H. Metcalf..1907 T. H. Newberry...1908	E. A. Hitchcock..1901 J. R. Garfield....1907	James Wilson...1901

Other Members

Secretary of Commerce and Labor
Established Feb. 14, 1903

Georg B. Cortelyou.........1903
Victor H. Metcalf......1904
O. S. Straus........1907
Chas. Nagel........1909
(Department divided, 1913.)

Secretary of Commerce

W. C. Redfield....1913
Joshua W. Alexander....1919
H. C. Hoover....1921
H. C. Hoover....1925
W. F. Whiting....1928
R. P. Lamont....1929
R. D. Chapin....1932
D. C. Roper....1933
H. L. Hopkins....1939
Jesse Jones....1940
Henry A. Wallace..1945
W. Averell Harriman....1946
Charles W. Sawyer....1948
Sinclair Weeks....1953
Lewis L. Strauss..1958
Frederick H. Mueller....1959
Luther H. Hodges........1961
John T. Connor....1964
A. B. Trowbridge..1967
C. R. Smith....1968
Maurice H. Stans....1969

Secretary of Defense
Established July 26, 1947.

James V. Forrestal.1947
Louis A. Johnson..1949
George C. Marshall......1950
Robert A. Lovett..1951
Charles E. Wilson.1953
Neil H. McElroy..1957
Thomas S. Gates, Jr.......1959
Robert S. McNamara....1961
Clark M. Clifford..1968
Melvin R. Laird..1969

Secretary of Health Education, and Welfare
Established April 1, 1953.

Oveta Culp Hobby.1953
Marion B. Folsom.1955
Arthur S. Flemming........1958
Abraham A. Ribicoff......1961
Anthony J. Celebrezze....1962
John W. Gardner.....1965
Wilbur J. Cohen..1968
Robert H. Finch..1969
Elliott Richardson.1970

#						Secretary of Labor Established March 4, 1913	Secretary of Housing and Urban Development Established Sept. 9, 1965. Secretary of Transportation Established Oct. 15, 1966
27. G. W. Wickersham.1909	F. H. Hitchcock..1909	G. von L. Meyer..1909	R. A. Ballinger...1909 W. L. Fisher....1911	James Wilson....1909		
28. J.C. McReynolds...1913 Thos. W. Gregory..1914 A. M. Palmer....1919	A. S. Burleson....1913	Josephus Daniels...1913	F. K. Lane......1913 J. B. Payne.....1920	D. F. Houston...1913 E. T. Meredith..1920	W. B. Wilson.....1913 J. J. Davis.......1921	
29. H. M. Daugherty..1921	Will H. Hays...1921 Hubert Work....1922 Harry S. New...1923	Edwin Denby.....1921	Albert B. Fall...1921 Hubert Work....1923	H. C. Wallace....1921	W. N. Doak...1930	
30. H. M. Daugherty..1923 Harlan F. Stone..1924 John G. Sargent..1925	Harry S. New....1923	Edwin Denby.....1923 Curtis D. Wilber..1924	Hubert Work....1923 Roy O. West....1928	H. M. Gore.....1924 W. M. Jardine...1925	Frances Perkins..1933	
31. Wm. D. Mitchell..1929	Walter F. Brown.1929	Chas. F. Adams...1929	Ray L. Wilbur..1929	Arthur M. Hyde..1929		
32. H. S. Cummings..1933 Frank Murphy....1939 Robt. H. Jackson..1940 Francis Biddle....1941	James A. Farley..1933 Frank C. Walker..1940	Claude A. Swanson.1933 Chas. Edison......1940 Frank Knox......1940 James V. Forrestal..1944	Harold L. Ickes..1933	H. A. Wallace....1933 C. R. Wickard..1940	L. B. Schwellenbach....1945	
33. Tom C. Clark....1945 J. H. McGrath..1949 James P. McGranery....1952	Robt. E. Hannegan......1945 Jesse L. Donaldson....1947	James V. Forrestal..1945 *	Harold L. Ickes..1945 Julius A. Krug..1946 O. L. Chapman...1951	C. P. Anderson...1945 C. F. Brannan....1948	M. J. Tobin.....1948	
34. Herbert Brownell, Jr.....1953 Wm. P. Rogers...1957	Arthur E. Summerfield...1953		Douglas McKay..1953 Fred A. Seaton..1956	Ezra T. Benson..1953	M. P. Durkin...1953 James P. Mitchell.1953	
35. Robt. F. Kennedy 1961	J. Edward Day...1961 J. A. Gronouski..1963		Stewart L. Udall..1961	Orville L. Freeman.......1961	Arthur J. Goldberg......1961	
36. Robt. F. Kennedy 1963 Nicholas Katzenbach....1964 Ramsey Clark...1967	J. A. Gronouski..1963 Lawrence F. O'Brien........1965 W. Marvin Watson........1968		Stewart L. Udall 1963	Orville L. Freeman......1963	W. Willard Wirtz..1962	Robert C. Weaver..1966 Robert C. Wood...1969 George Romney....1969 Alan S. Boyd.....1966
37. John N. Mitchell..1969	Winton M. Blount........1969		Walter J. Hickel..1969	Clifford M. Hardin........1969	George P. Shultz.........1969	John A. Volpe....1969

*Lost cabinet status in 1947

Justices of the United States Supreme Court

John Jay, N.Y.*	1789–1795	Lucius Q. C. Lamar, Miss.	1888–1893
John Rutledge, S.C.	1789–1791	**Melville W. Fuller,** Ill.	1888–1910
William Cushing, Mass.	1789–1810	David J. Brewer, Kan.	1889–1910
James Wilson, Pa.	1789–1798	Henry B. Brown, Mich.	1890–1906
John Blair, Va.	1789–1796	George Shiras, Jr., Pa.	1892–1903
Robert H. Harrison, Md.	1789–1790	Howell E. Jackson, Tenn.	1893–1895
James Iredell, N.C.	1790–1799	Edward D. White, La.	1894–1910
Thomas Johnson, Md.	1791–1793	Rufus W. Peckham, N.Y.	1895–1910
William Paterson, N.J.	1793–1806	Joseph McKenna, Calif.	1898–1925
John Rutledge, S.C.	1795–1795	Oliver W. Holmes, Mass.	1902–1932
Samuel Chase, Md.	1796–1811	William R. Day, Ohio	1903–1922
Oliver Ellsworth, Conn.	1796–1799	William H. Moody, Mass.	1906–1910
Bushrod Washington, Va.	1798–1829	Horace H. Lurton, Tenn.	1910–1914
Alfred Moore, N.C.	1799–1804	Charles E. Hughes, N.Y.	1910–1916
John Marshall, Va.	1801–1835	Willis Van Devanter, Wyo.	1911–1937
William Johnson, S.C.	1804–1834	Joseph R. Lamar, Ga.	1911–1916
Brockholst Livingston, N.Y.	1806–1823	**Edward D. White,** La.	1910–1921
Thomas Todd, Ky.	1807–1826	Mahlon Pitney, N.J.	1912–1922
Joseph Story, Mass.	1811–1845	James C. McReynolds, Tenn.	1914–1941
Gabriel Duval, Md.	1811–1836	Louis D. Brandeis, Mass.	1916–1939
Smith Thompson, N.Y.	1823–1843	John H. Clarke, Ohio	1916–1922
Robert Trimble, Ky.	1826–1828	**William H. Taft,** Conn.	1921–1930
John McLean, Ohio	1829–1861	George Sutherland, Utah	1922–1938
Henry Baldwin, Pa.	1830–1844	Pierce Butler, Minn.	1922–1939
James M. Wayne, Ga.	1835–1867	Edward T. Sanford, Tenn.	1923–1930
Roger B. Taney, Md.	1836–1864	Harlan F. Stone, N.Y.	1925–1941
Philip P. Barbour, Va.	1836–1841	**Charles E. Hughes,** N.Y.	1930–1941
John Catron, Tenn.	1837–1865	Owen J. Roberts, Pa.	1930–1945
John McKinley, Ala.	1837–1852	Benjamin N. Cardozo, N.Y.	1932–1938
Peter V. Daniel, Va.	1841–1860	Hugo Black, Ala.	1937–
Samuel Nelson, N.Y.	1845–1872	Stanley Reed, Ky.	1938–1957
Levi Woodbury, N.H.	1845–1851	Felix Frankfurter, Mass.	1939–1962
Robert C. Grier, Pa.	1846–1870	William O. Douglas, Conn.	1939–
Benj. R. Curtis, Mass.	1851–1857	Frank Murphy, Mich.	1940–1949
John A. Campbell, Ala.	1853–1861	**Harlan F. Stone,** N.Y.	1941–1946
Nathan Clifford, Me.	1858–1881	James F. Byrnes, S.C.	1941–1942
Noah H. Swayne, Ohio	1862–1881	Robert H. Jackson, N.Y.	1941–1954
Samuel F. Miller, Iowa	1862–1890	Wiley B. Rutledge, Iowa	1943–1949
David Davis, Ill.	1862–1877	Harold H. Burton, Ohio	1945–1958
Stephen J. Field, Calif.	1863–1897	**Fred M. Vinson,** Ky.	1946–1953
Salmon P. Chase, Ohio	1864–1873	Thomas C. Clark, Texas	1949–
William Strong, Pa.	1870–1880	Sherman Minton, Ind.	1949–1956
Joseph P. Bradley, N.J.	1870–1892	**Earl Warren,** Calif.	1953–
Ward Hunt, N.Y.	1872–1882	John M. Harlan, N.Y.	1955–
Morrison R. Waite, Ohio	1874–1888	William J. Brennan, Jr., N.J.	1956–
John M. Harlan, Ky.	1877–1911	Charles E. Whittaker, Mo.	1957–1962
William B. Woods, Ga.	1880–1887	Potter Stewart, Ohio	1958–
Stanley Matthews, Ohio	1881–1889	Byron R. White, Colo.	1962–
Horace Gray, Mass.	1881–1902	Arthur J. Goldberg, Ill.	1962–
Samuel Blatchford, N.Y.	1882–1893	Abe Fortas, Tenn.	1965–1969
		Thurgood Marshall, Md.	1967–
*Chief Justices in boldface type.		**Warren E. Burger,** Minn.	1969–
		Harry A. Blackmun, Minn.	1970–

Speakers of the House of Representatives, 1863–1962

Schuyler Colfax, Indiana	1863–1869	Frederick H. Gillett, Massachusetts	1919–1925
James G. Blaine, Maine	1869–1875	Nicholas Longworth, Ohio	1925–1931
Michael C. Kerr, Indiana	1875–1876	John Nance Garner, Texas	1931–1933
Samuel J. Randall, Pennsylvania	1876–1881	Henry T. Rainey, Illinois	1933–1934
Joseph W. Keifer, Ohio	1881–1883	Joseph W. Byrns, Tennessee	1935–1936
John G. Carlisle, Kentucky	1883–1889	William B. Bankhead, Alabama	1936–1940
Thomas B. Reed, Maine	1889–1891	Sam Rayburn, Texas	1940–1947
Charles F. Crisp, Georgia	1891–1895	Joseph W. Martin, Jr., Massachusetts	1947–1949
Thomas B. Reed, Maine	1895–1899	Sam Rayburn, Texas	1949–1953
David B. Henderson, Iowa	1899–1903	Joseph W. Martin, Jr., Massachusetts	1953–1955
Joseph G. Cannon, Illinois	1903–1910	Sam Rayburn, Texas	1955–1961
Champ Clark, Missouri	1911–1919	John W. McCormack, Massachusetts	1962–1970

INDEXES

Index of Place Names On Maps

General Index